ANGLO-SAXON MANUSCRIPTS

A Bibliographical Handlist of Manuscripts and Manuscript Fragments Written or Owned in England up to 1100

Anglo-Saxon Manuscripts is the first publication to list every surviving manuscript or manuscript fragment written in Anglo-Saxon England between the seventh and the eleventh centuries or imported into the country during that time. Each of the 1,291 entries in Helmut Gneuss and Michael Lapidge's *Bibliographical Handlist* not only details the origins and provenance, dates, and current location of the manuscript, but also provides bibliographic entries that list facsimiles, descriptions, studies of script, codicology, binding, illumination, editions, linguistic analyses, and general studies relevant to that manuscript. A general bibliography, designed to provide full details of author-date references cited in the individual entries, includes more than 4,000 items.

Compiled by two of the field's greatest living scholars, the Gneuss-Lapidge *Bibliographical Handlist* stands to become the most important single-volume research tool to appear in the field since Greenfield and Robinson's *Bibliography of Publications on Old English Literature*. Their achievement in the present book will endure for many decades and serve as a catalyst for new research across several disciplines.

(Toronto Anglo-Saxon Series)

HELMUT GNEUSS is emeritus professor of English at the University of Munich.

MICHAEL LAPIDGE is emeritus professor of Anglo-Saxon at the University of Cambridge.

HELMUT GNEUSS AND MICHAEL LAPIDGE

ANGLO-SAXON MANUSCRIPTS

A BIBLIOGRAPHICAL HANDLIST
OF MANUSCRIPTS AND MANUSCRIPT
FRAGMENTS WRITTEN OR OWNED
IN ENGLAND UP TO 1100

UNIVERSITY OF TORONTO PRESS
Toronto Buffalo London

© University of Toronto Press 2014
Toronto Buffalo London
www.utppublishing.com

Reprinted in paperback 2015

ISBN 978-1-4426-4823-4 (cloth)
ISBN 978-1-4426-2927-1 (paper)

Library and Archives Canada Cataloguing in Publication

Gneuss, Helmut, compiler
Anglo-Saxon manuscripts : a bibliographical handlist of manuscripts and manuscript
fragments written or owned in England up to 1100/[compiled by] Helmut Gneuss
and Michael Lapidge.

(Toronto Anglo-Saxon series ; 15)
Includes bibliographical references and indexes.
ISBN 978-1-4426-4823-4 (bound). – ISBN 978-1-4426-2927-1 (paperback)

1. Manuscripts, English (Old) – Union lists.   2. Manuscripts, English (Old) – England –
Union lists.   3. Manuscripts, Medieval – Union lists.   4. Manuscripts, Medieval – England –
Union lists.   5. Anglo-Saxons – Sources – Bibliography – Union lists.   6. Union catalogs.
I. Lapidge, Michael, 1942–, compiler   II. Title.   III. Series: Toronto Anglo-Saxon series ; 15

Z6605.A56G64 2014   015.42'031   C2013-908550-5

University of Toronto Press gratefully acknowledges the financial assistance of the
Centre for Medieval Studies, University of Toronto in the publication of this book.

University of Toronto Press acknowledges the financial assistance to its publishing
program of the Canada Council for the Arts and the Ontario Arts Council, an agency
of the Government of Ontario.

Canada Council
for the Arts

Conseil des Arts
du Canada

ONTARIO ARTS COUNCIL
CONSEIL DES ARTS DE L'ONTARIO
an Ontario government agency
un organisme du gouvernement de l'Ontario

Funded by the   Financé par le
Government   gouvernement
of Canada   du Canada

in memoriam
Mechthild Gretsch
(1945—2013)

Contents

Preface

The aims, history and development of this *Bibliographical Handlist* and its predecessors have been treated in some detail elsewhere,[1] so only a brief outline in this preface is needed. Plans were laid for the eventual handlist when HG was a research student and British Council scholar at St John's College, Cambridge, from 1953 to 1955, and HG wishes to express his gratitude for the opportunities which this period in Cambridge provided. Work on the project began in earnest in 1970, when HG spent part of a year as visiting professorial fellow at Emmanuel College, Cambridge; it then continued during the 1970s, when under the planning and direction of HG, student assistants and *Assistenten* in the Department of English at the University of Munich began recording bibliographical references to manuscripts written or owned in England up to 1100. The result was originally intended as a research tool for graduate students and PhD candidates in the Munich Department, and as such proved its usefulness, although it was clear at this early stage that completeness and perfection with regard to the manuscripts to be listed, or the bibliographical references to be recorded, could not easily and quickly be achieved. At the suggestion and invitation of Peter Clemoes, the founder and chief editor of *Anglo-Saxon England*, a list of all the Anglo-Saxon manuscripts thus far

---

1 See H. Gneuss, 'A Handlist of Anglo-Saxon Manuscripts', *Latin Culture in the Eleventh Century. Proceedings of the Third International Conference on Medieval Latin Studies*, ed. M.W. Herren, C.J. McDonough and R.G. Arthur, Publications of the Journal of Medieval Latin, 2 vols. (Turnhout, 2005) I, 345–52; and '*A Handlist of Anglo-Saxon Manuscripts*: Origins, Facts, Problems', in *Anglo-Saxon Books and their Readers: Essays in Celebration of Helmut Gneuss's Handlist of Anglo-Saxon Manuscripts*', ed. T.N. Hall and D. Scragg (Kalamazoo, MI, 2008), pp. 1–21; and see also the introductions to the 'Preliminary List' (cited below, n. 2), to the *Handlist* (cited below, n. 3), pp. 1–3, and the two sets of 'Addenda and Corrigenda' (below, n. 4).

identified was published as a 'Preliminary List' in 1981.[2] It was meant as an interim inventory and, in particular, as a search list, helping scholars to find manuscript books and fragments that had been hitherto overlooked. As such, the 'Preliminary List' was successful: a great deal of relevant, valuable information was received by HG from the scholarly community at large, much of it based on recent discoveries.

As a result of this information, a much fuller version of the list was planned and published in 2001 with the title *Handlist of Anglo-Saxon Manuscripts*,[3] this time with the aim of providing more detailed (if not comprehensive) listings of the contents of each manuscript or fragment, an amount of detail which could not have been accommodated in the 'Preliminary List', given the format of that work; the *Handlist* was also provided with various indexes, including in particular one of texts and authors.

In the years following the publication of the *Handlist*, the study of Anglo-Saxon manuscripts continued to expand, and as new information and insights became available, it seemed appropriate periodically to supplement the *Handlist*; two issues of 'Addenda and Corrigenda' were published in 2003 and 2012.[4]

After HG had retired from his Chair in Munich, further bibliographical work for the *Handlist* was continued, from 2002 onwards, under the direction of Mechthild Gretsch (†), in the Department of English at the University of Göttingen, where the materials so far collected (particularly as concerned the manuscripts containing Old English which had been treated by N.R. Ker [1957]) were brought up to date, verified and revised, again mainly by student assistants. By this time the handwritten predecessor of the eventual *Bibliographical Handlist* had come to occupy twenty large box-files in HG's Eichenau residence; the materials in these box-files, when reduced to some sort of order, would ultimately result in the 1,291 individual entries of the present work.

By this stage, a third version of the *Handlist*, this time with bibliographies for each manuscript, appeared to be feasible;[5] that it actually took

---

2 H. Gneuss, 'A Preliminary List of Manuscripts written or owned in England up to 1100', *ASE* 9 (1981), 1–60.

3 H. Gneuss, *Handlist of Anglo-Saxon Manuscripts. A List of Manuscripts and Manuscript Fragments written or owned in England up to 1100*, MRTS 241 (Tempe, AZ, 2001).

4 H. Gneuss, 'Addenda and Corrigenda to the *Handlist of Anglo-Saxon Manuscripts*', *ASE* 32 (2003), 293–305; *idem*, 'Second Addenda and Corrigenda to the *Handlist of Anglo-Saxon Manuscripts*', *ASE* 40 (2012), 293–306.

5 HG had adverted to this possibility in the preface to the *Handlist* (2001), p. 15: 'My main effort will now be devoted to the preparation of a "Bibliographical Handlist of

shape is owed to the fact that in 2005 ML joined HG as author and editor. ML had, ever since the 1970s, taken a keen interest in and contributed extensively to work on the eventual *Handlist*. ML and HG now jointly revised, supplemented and organized the entries, especially the individual bibliographies as well as the comprehensive bibliography pertaining to the volume, while ML entered in the computer the developing version of the *Bibliographical Handlist* as it was to be printed and, in doing so, created and determined the arrangement, layout and typography of the entries. ML also thoroughly revised and expanded the index of authors and texts.

We are especially and deeply grateful for the strong and continuous support of a number of distinguished scholars who contributed information, references and expert advice over many years; in the early stages of the project especially Bernhard Bischoff (†), Neil Ker (†), T.A.M. Bishop (†), David Dumville and Simon Keynes; and, at a subsequent stage, Richard Gameson and Drew Hartzell. Since the late 1990s, Michael Gullick has unselfishly shared with us the results of his extensive manuscript research. Rebecca Rushforth, too, contributed substantially to our work. Birgit Ebersperger also assisted in many ways, and over very many years, beginning with her work as a member of the research team in the Department of English in Munich, and continuing in more recent times, when she has been preparing and completing the edition of Bernhard Bischoff's catalogue of ninth-century continental manuscripts.

The *Handlist* in its present form is unthinkable without the active support and encouragement of these and numerous other colleagues in various fields of Anglo-Saxon studies, all of whom generously shared knowledge of their discoveries with HG and ML. In addition to those scholars named in the previous paragraph, the following helped us in various ways (it is hoped that there are no serious omissions from the following alphabetical list): Bruce Barker-Benfield, Carl Berkhout, Walter Berschin, Mary Catherine Bodden, Michelle P. Brown, Julian Brown (†), Mildred Budny, Donald Bullough (†), James P. Carley, Peter Clemoes (†), Jimmy Cross (†), Maria Amalia D'Aronco, Ian Doyle, Elaine M. Drage, Alan Frantzen, David Ganz, Lilli Gjerløw (†), Malcolm Godden, Timothy Graham, Christopher Hohler (†), Peter Jackson, Colette Jeudy, Sarah L. Keefer, Matti Kilpiö, Gabriele Knappe, Patrizia Lendinara, Tristan Major, Rosamond McKitterick, Raymond Page (†), Malcolm Parkes (†), Susan Rankin, Frank A. Rella, Fred C. Robinson, Pamela Robinson, Donald

Anglo-Saxon Manuscripts", recording all essential publications (palaeographical and codicological work, editions, facsimiles, reproductions etc.) on each of the manuscripts in the *Handlist*.'

Scragg, Richard Sharpe, William Stoneman, Rodney Thomson, Jennifer Morrish Tunberg, Jean Vezin, Linda Voigts, Teresa Webber, Gernot Wieland and Joseph Wittig.

The role and initiative of the teams of young bibliographers in Munich and Göttingen should not be forgotten: among those in Munich mention must be made especially of Karl Toth (†), Birgit Ebersperger, Carolin Schreiber, and above all Ursula Lenker, who researched and recorded gospel books, gospel lists and much else besides; and in Göttingen especially Andreas Lemke, Andre Mertens, Janna Riedinger and Friederike Szamborzki. And when the book was in page proof, Ursula Lenker and two of her Hilfskräfte, Carolin Harthan and Laura Herbig, provided invaluable assistance with proofreading, particularly of the Index of Authors and Texts.

When the book was on the verge of being submitted for publication, various scholars helped us to fill bibliographical lacunae involving items and information not otherwise available to us: A.S.G. Edwards, Nigel Morgan, Susan Rankin, Michael Reeve and Paul Szarmach. Also at this final stage, Drew Jones and Charlie Wright read carefully through large portions of the typescript and made many helpful comments on the layout and presentation, and supplied many bibliographical references which had escaped us. And — just before the book was about to be submitted to the University of Toronto Press — Ian Doyle drew our attention to a newly found fragment of Ælfric's *Grammar*, which we were able to incorporate at the very last minute.

Our thanks are also due to Suzanne Rancourt and the editorial team of the University of Toronto Press, especially Barb Porter for overseeing production and Catherine Plear for her exemplary and meticulous copy-editing, and above all to Andy Orchard, whose infectious enthusiasm for the project has ensured that it would find a place in his Toronto Anglo-Saxon Series, and that funds would be forthcoming to ensure its publication in a convenient and accessible format.

Finally, the dedication records our lasting debt to a beloved wife and beloved friend. On 14 March 2013, on the very eve of the submission of the typescript, Mechthild Gretsch passed away peacefully after a long struggle with cancer. Mechthild had championed and supported the project in many ways over many years, not least by organizing the assistance of her doctoral students during the tenure of her chair in English Philology in Göttingen (2000–6). Through her involvement the resulting book has been enriched in ways too numerous to count, and its two authors at least will never forget this debt.

HG and ML (31 March 2013)

Abbreviations

AB	*Analecta Bollandiana*
ABR	*American Benedictine Review*
AH	*Analecta Hymnica Medii Aevi*, ed. G.M. Dreves and C. Blume, 55 vols. (Leipzig, 1886–1922)
AHDLMA	*Archives d'histoire doctrinale et littéraire du moyen âge*
AnM	*Annuale mediaevale*
ANQ	*American Notes & Queries*
ANS	*Anglo-Norman Studies*
AntJ	*The Antiquaries' Journal*
art(s)	article(s) as listed in entries in N.R. Ker (1957)
ASE	*Anglo-Saxon England*
ASMMF	*Anglo-Saxon Manuscripts in Microfiche Facsimile*, ed. A.N. Doane et al. (Binghamton, NY and Tempe, AZ, 1994–)
ASNSL	*Archiv für das Studium der neueren Sprachen und Literaturen*
ASPR	The Anglo-Saxon Poetic Records, ed. G.P. Krapp and E.V.K. Dobbie, 6 vols. (New York, 1932–53)
AST	Anglo-Saxon Texts (Woodbridge)
BAR	British Archaeological Reports
BBCS	*Bulletin of the Board of Celtic Studies*

BCLL	M. Lapidge and R. Sharpe, *A Bibliography of Celtic-Latin Literature, 400–1200* (Dublin, 1985)
BCS	W. de G. Birch, *Cartularium Saxonicum*, 3 vols. and index (London, 1885–93)
BGDSL	*Beiträge zur Geschichte der deutschen Sprache und Literatur* [for volumes from 1955–80 specified as printed in Halle or Tübingen]
BHL	[Bollandists], *Bibliotheca Hagiographica Latina*, 2 vols. (Brussels, 1899–1901, with supplements, 1911, 1986]
BJRL	*Bulletin of the John Rylands [University] Library [of Manchester]* (Manchester)
BLJ	*British Library Journal*
BLR	*Bodleian Library Record*
CALMA	*Compendium Auctorum Latinorum Medii Aevi (C.A.L.M.A.)*, ed. M. Lapidge, C. Leonardi and F. Santi (Florence, 2000–)
Cat. Add. B.M.	*Catalogue of Additions to the Manuscripts in the British Museum* (London, 1843–) [cited by date of acquisition and year of publication]
Cat. gén. Dép. (Octavo)	*Catalogue général des manuscrits des bibliothèques publiques de France. Départements* (Octavo Series), 65 vols. (Paris, 1886–1990).
Cat. gén. Dép. (Quarto)	*Catalogue général des manuscrits des bibliothèques publiques des Départments* (Quarto Series), 7 vols. (Paris, 1849–85).
CC	Christ Church (Canterbury)
CCCM	Corpus Christianorum, Continuatio Mediaevalis (Turnhout, 1966–)
CCM	Corpus consuetudinum monasticarum, ed. P. Engelbert and K. Hallinger (Siegburg, 1963–)
CCSL	Corpus Christianorum, Series Latina (Turnhout, 1953–)
ChLA	*Chartae Latinae Antiquiores*, ed. A. Bruckner, R. Marichal et al. (Olten, Lausanne and Zurich, 1954–)

CLA	E.A. Lowe, *Codices Latini Antiquiores*, 11 vols. and Supplement (Oxford, 1934–71; 2nd ed. of vol. II, 1972)
CMCS	*Cambridge* [later *Cambrian*] *Medieval Celtic Studies*
Colophons	[Benedictines of Bouveret], *Colophons de manuscrits occidentaux des origines au XVIe siècle*, 6 vols., Spicilegii Friburgensis Subsidia (Fribourg, 1965–82)
Councils & Synods	Whitelock, D., M. Brett and C.N.L. Brooke, ed. (1981), *Councils and Synods with Other Documents Relating to the English Church*. I. *A.D. 871–1204*, 2 vols. (Oxford)
CPG	*Clavis Patrum Graecorum*, ed. M. Geerards, 5 vols. and Supplement (Turnhout, 1983–98)
CPL	*Clavis Patrum Latinorum*, ed. E. Dekkers and A. Gaar, 3rd ed. (Steenbrugge, 1995)
CPPM I, II	*Clavis Patristica Pseudepigraphorum Medii Aevi*, I. *Opera homiletica*, ed. J. Machielsen, 2 vols. (Turnhout, 1990) [*CPPM* I]; *Clavis Patristica Pseudepigraphorum Medii Aevi*, II. *Theologica, Exegetica, Ascetica, Monastica*, ed. J. Machielsen, 2 vols. (Turnhout, 1994) [*CPPM* II]
CSASE	Cambridge Studies in Anglo-Saxon England
CSEL	Corpus Scriptorum Ecclesiasticorum Latinorum (Vienna, 1866–)
CSLMA	*Clavis Scriptorum Latinorum Medii Aevi: Auctores Galliae, 735–987*, ed. M.-H. Jullien and F. Perelman (Turnhout, 1994–)
DACL	*Dictionnaire d'archéologie chrétienne et de liturgie*, ed. F. Cabrol, H. Leclercq et al., 15 vols. in 30 (Paris, 1907–53)
DAEM	*Deutsches Archiv für Erforschung des Mittelalters*
DUJ	*Durham University Journal*
EEMF	Early English Manuscripts in Facsimile, 28 vols. (Copenhagen, 1951–2001)

EETS	Early English Text Society
— o.s.	original series
— s.s.	supplementary series
EGS	*English and Germanic Studies*
EHR	*English Historical Review*
ELN	*English Language Notes*
EME	*Early Medieval Europe*
ES	*English Studies*
EStn	*Englische Studien*
FMS	*Frühmittelalterliche Studien*
HBS	Henry Bradshaw Society Publications
HZ	*Historische Zeitschrift*
ill(s)	illustration(s)
JEGP	*Journal of English and Germanic Philology*
JMLat	*The Journal of Medieval Latin*
JTS	*Journal of Theological Studies*
JWCI	*Journal of the Warburg and Courtauld Institutes*
KCD	J.M. Kemble, *Codex Diplomaticus Aevi Saxonici*, 6 vols. (London, 1839–48)
KCLMS	King's College London Medieval Studies
Kenney	J.F. Kenney, *The Sources for the Early History of Ireland* (New York, 1929)
Keil, *GL*	H. Keil, *Grammatici Latini*, 8 vols. (Leipzig, 1857–80)
LMA	*Lexikon des Mittelalters*, 9 vols. (Munich and Zurich, 1980–99)
LSE	*Leeds Studies in English*
MÆ	*Medium Ævum*
MBKDS	Mittelalterliche Bibliothekskataloge Deutschlands und der Schweiz, 4 vols. in 9 parts (Munich, 1918–)
MGH	Monumenta Germaniae Historica

— AA	– Auctores Antiquissimi
— Epist.	– Epistulae
— PLAC	– Poetae Latini Aevi Carolini
— SS rer. Meroving.	– Scriptores rerum Merovingicarum
MLJ	*Mittellateinisches Jahrbuch*
MLN	*Modern Language Notes*
MLQ	*Modern Language Quarterly*
MLR	*Modern Language Review*
MP	*Modern Philology*
MRTS	Medieval and Renaissance Texts and Studies (Tempe, AZ)
MS	*Mediaeval Studies*
NLWJ	*National Library of Wales Journal*
NM	New Minster (Winchester)
NM	*Neuphilologische Mitteilungen*
NPS I, II	*The New Palaeographical Society*, 1st ser. (London, 1903–12) [I]; 2nd ser. (London, 1913–30) [II]
N&Q	*Notes & Queries*
Nun	Nunnaminster (Winchester)
ODNB	*The Oxford Dictionary of National Biography*, ed. H.C.G. Matthew and B. Harrison, 60 vols. (Oxford, 2004)
OEN	*Old English Newsletter*
OM	Old Minster (Winchester)
PBA	*Proceedings of the British Academy*
PL	Patrologia Latina, ed. J.-P. Migne, 221 vols. (Paris, 1844–64)
pl(s)	plate(s)
PMLA	*Publications of the Modern Language Association of America*
PQ	*Philological Quarterly*
PRIA	*Proceedings of the Royal Irish Academy*

prov.	provenance
RB	*Revue Bénédictine*
RES	*Review of English Studies*
RS	Rolls Series (London, 1858–96)
Schenkl	H. Schenkl, *Bibliotheca Patrum Latinorum Britannica*, 3 vols. in 1 (Vienna, 1891–1908; repr. Hildesheim, 1969) [cited by item number]
SChr	Sources Chrétiennes (Paris, 1941–)
SEP	*Studies in English Philology*
Settimane	*Settimane di studio del Centro italiano di studi sull'alto medioevo* (Spoleto)
SK	D. Schaller and E. Könsgen, *Initia Carminum Latinorum saeculo undecimo Antiquiorum* (Göttingen, 1977)
SK Suppl.	D. Schaller and E. Könsgen, *Initia Carminum Latinorum saeculo undecimo Antiquiorum* fortgeführt von Thomas Klein. *Supplementband* (Göttingen, 2005)
SM	*Studi medievali*
SN	*Studia Neophilologica*
StA	St Augustine's (Canterbury)
Stegmüller	F. Stegmüller, *Repertorium biblicum Medii Aevi*, 7 vols. and Supplement (Madrid, 1950–61)
TCBS	*Transactions of the Cambridge Bibliographical Society*
Thorndike–Kibre	L. Thorndike and P. Kibre, *A Catalogue of Incipits of Medieval Scientific Writings in Latin*, 2nd ed. (Cambridge, MA, 1963)
TRHS	*Transactions of the Royal Historical Society*
TUEPh	Texte und Untersuchungen zur Englischen Philologie (Munich and Frankfurt am Main)
Walther, *Proverbia*	H. Walther, *Proverbia sententiaeque latinitatis medii aevi: Lateinische Sprichwörter und Sentenzen des Mittelalters in alphabetischer Ordnung*, 6 vols. (Göttingen, 1963–9).

WIC	H. Walther, *Initia carminum ac versuum medii aevi posterioris Latinorum: Alphabetisches Verzeichnis der Versanfänge mittellateinischer Dichtungen*, 2nd ed. (Göttingen, 1969)
ZfdA	*Zeitschrift für deutsches Altertum*

ANGLO-SAXON MANUSCRIPTS

A Bibliographical Handlist of Manuscripts
and Manuscript Fragments Written
or Owned in England up to 1100

Introduction

In the work which follows, the serial numbers from the 'Preliminary List' (1981) and the *Handlist of Anglo-Saxon Manuscripts* (2001) have been retained. Inevitably many new manuscript fragments have come to light since 2001, and these have been intercalated where appropriate (using decimal points) into the alphabetical sequence of libraries in the two original numbered series (Libraries in the British Isles = I, Libraries outside the British Isles = II). In cases in which cities have been renamed (such as Leningrad, renamed St Petersburg in 1991), the manuscripts have retained their original position in the sequence in order to avoid the confusion which renumbering would occasion. *Membra disiecta* of an originally single manuscript are not separately numbered but are treated together as one item. The 'group item' is normally placed in the list where the main component belongs, if there is one, or, if there is no main one, where the first component occurs. The other component(s) are specified in the group in the order which they have in the list, and a cross-reference to the main group item is supplied at the point(s) in the list at which the other component(s) occur. In the very few cases in which items have been assigned new serial numbers, cross-references are inserted at the appropriate location in the original sequence in order to guide readers to the new entry.

The following have been included in the Handlist:

(1) Manuscripts certainly written in England up to 1100. For the problem of late eleventh-century manuscripts, see below.
(2) Manuscripts written in Scotland, Wales and Cornwall if they certainly or very probably reached England by 1100. A few manuscripts from those parts of Britain, written before 1100, have been included, although it is unlikely that they had an English provenance, temporary

or permanent, before the end of the eleventh century. This has been clearly stated in every case.

(3) Manuscripts written in Ireland or on the European continent (including Brittany) if they certainly or very probably found their way to England by 1100. Doubtful cases are clearly marked as such.

A manuscript falling into any of these three categories is included, whether or not it was exported or re-exported from England and, if it was, irrespective of whether this occurred during the Anglo-Saxon period or later.

The following have been excluded:

1.   Single-leaf documents. For such manuscripts, covering the period up to 1066, see Sawyer (1968), revised and augmented (and fully searchable) as the *Electronic Sawyer*: www.esawyer.org.uk.
2.   Manuscripts that were written, or annotated, or decorated, by Anglo-Saxon scribes and artists on the Continent but that are not known to have been in England at any time before 1100. Doubtful cases are clearly marked as such.
3.   Manuscripts in Anglo-Saxon scripts written by English or by continental scribes, (trained and) working at Anglo-Saxon centres on the Continent.
4.   Continental manuscripts presumably lent for copying in Anglo-Saxon England and afterwards returned, where there is no certain evidence for the sojourn of such a book in England.[1]

Two doubtful areas need to be mentioned. The first concerns eighth-century manuscripts, mainly in Insular script, written, according to expert opinion (e.g., that of E.A. Lowe in *CLA*), 'presumably' in England, or either in England or an Anglo-Saxon centre on the Continent. We have included some thirty of these manuscripts which are now thought to have possibly or probably originated in an English scriptorium.[2] Here HG was able over many years to consult Bernhard Bischoff — whose important

---

1   For an example, see Dumville (1993g) 54–5 n. 240.
2   One problematical area is the surviving liturgical fragments in libraries in Oslo and Stockholm (see below, nos. **870.2–871.5, 872.5, 873, 874.3, 875.1.1, 936, 936.1–9,** and **937.1**), which palaeographical opinion is beginning to regard as probably having been written in Scandinavia, whereas they were earlier thought to have been written in England and subsequently exported to Scandinavia. The matter is complex, and still very much *sub iudice*; for that reason we normally describe the origin of such manuscripts as 'England? Scandinavia?'.

contribution to *CLA* is well known — who considered more than twenty books in this category as certainly or probably English.[3]

A related problem is posed by early continental or Irish manuscripts that may have reached the Anglo-Saxon missionaries in Germany, either via England or more directly from Italy or Ireland; of these we have included nos. **799, 827.6,** and **827.7.** A further group of early manuscripts that could not be ignored are those that are thought to have been written either in Ireland or in England (probably Northumbria). They are represented by nos. **213, 214, 218, 664.5, 773.3, 893** and **929.**

Lost, destroyed and untraced manuscripts and fragments have been recorded under their former owners; it is to be hoped that at least some of them may turn up again one day. See nos. **643, 830.5, 831.4, 842.5** (formerly no. 943), **855.5** and the *membra disiecta* listed under nos. **176** and **441.1.** For lost copies of manuscripts containing Old English texts or glosses, see also N.R. Ker (1957) nos. 403–12.

THE LAYOUT OF THE *BIBLIOGRAPHICAL HANDLIST*

Following the serial number and the shelf-mark of each item, the date, origin and provenance (where known) are given on a separate line, followed (beginning on a new line) by the contents of the manuscript or fragment.

Numbering of Items

The serial numbers of the 'Preliminary List' and of the *Handlist* have been retained so as to avoid the confusion which any re-numbering would entail. New entries are indicated by a decimal point and figure (and occasionally by two figures). Newly identified *membra disiecta* have been recorded, but, in accordance with previous practice, have not been given a serial number of their own. Separate serial numbers for parts of manuscripts now bound as one volume have been allocated only when it seemed unlikely that these parts had been together before 1100, but absolute consistency in such cases may not have been attained. Serial numbers of items deleted from either the 'Preliminary List' or the *Handlist* have in no case been re-used.

---

3 These are nos. **281.5, 791.3, 791.6, 799.5, 804.5, 808.3, 808.5, 818.5, 830.5, 831.6, 831.7, 836.5, 840.5, 840.6, 848.6, 848.7, 855.5, 933.5, 943.4, 944.5** and **946.5.**

Dates

All dates given at the beginning of each entry refer to the main items; where texts have been added later, their date is usually indicated in parentheses immediately following the respective title. The opinion of expert palaeographers in their most recent publications have always been followed. The accuracy and specificity of dating a book or fragment depend on various kinds of evidence in each individual case: what is known about the history of a manuscript, about the scriptorium in which it was written, its contents and, above all, its handwriting. Dates given may therefore be more or less specific and narrow, sometimes even uncertain. As a consequence, the form of dates given in the following work does not follow a consistent system, the aim being simply to provide a date as precise as is at present possible for each item. Where the opinion of experts differs, this difference has been accommodated by listing the two (or sometimes three) suggested dates, always linked by 'or'.

Origin and Provenance

Care has been taken to distinguish clearly between origin (where the manuscript was written) and provenance (where it was owned), as far as these are known. Dates for pre-1100 provenance have been given if possible. The following conventions have been used:

place-name (unmarked):	place of origin
'prov.' + place-name:	provenance before 1100
('prov.' + place-name):	provenance after 1100

Where the place of origin and/or provenance of a manuscript is probable or uncertain, this has been indicated by 'prob.' or by a question mark. The places of provenance, if more than one is known, are listed in chronological order. Where no place or region of origin is given, it is to be assumed that the manuscript in question originated in England.

The known places of origin or provenance in Anglo-Saxon England are almost exclusively cathedrals, cathedral priories and Benedictine abbeys and nunneries. For the houses in Canterbury and Winchester various abbreviations are used (CC, StA, NM, Nun, OM) which are explained in the abbreviations, above, pp. xiii–xix.

Contents

The lists of contents of manuscripts in the present work are fuller than those in the 'Preliminary List' of 1981 and the *Handlist* of 2001; short of producing thorough-going catalogue entries (by giving, for example, the folios occupied by each item in a manuscript, changes of scribe, etc.), we have attempted to provide complete records of the contents of each manuscript, listed in the order in which they occur in the manuscript. (Note, however, that it has not been possible to list individual homilies in Latin homiliaries, or individual saints' Lives in Latin legendaries, or individual hymns in Latin hymnals, or individual prayers in liturgical manuscripts, etc.) Several considerations need to be borne in mind.

First, concerning Latin contents: In the case of patristic works, we employ the title assigned to the work in *CPL* (regardless of what title the work bears in the manuscript itself), and also the number of the work in *CPL*, so as to facilitate identification.[4] Hagiographical texts are identified by means of *BHL* numbers. Short, mainly anonymous Latin poems are identified by reference to the repertory of Schaller and Könsgen (SK) and its recent supplement by Thomas Klein (SK Suppl.), or, occasionally, to Walther's *Initia* (WIC). In cases where a poem is not listed in either SK or WIC, we usually supply its incipit. But we have not attempted to list every item in large poetic collections (such as the *Carmina Cantabrigiensia* or 'Cambridge Songs' in no. **12**, or the huge collection of Latin verse in no. **493**); such information can usually be found by consulting one of the editions listed under 'ED' in a particular entry. With regard to anonymous Latin prose texts, especially individual homilies, there is (alas) no standard *incipitarium*, and such works are identified only if they happen to be listed in *CPL* or *CPPM*. By the same token, in the case of *computistica*, we have not attempted to identify the (frequently numerous) tables and short texts which make up a computistical collection, save to indicate the broad class to which the computus in question belongs (e.g., 'Winchester computus', 'Leofric-Tiberius computus', etc.). And, as mentioned above, it obviously would not be possible, let alone convenient, to list every item or prayer in

---

4 But there are a few exceptions to this principle, notably concerning works by Aldhelm: the *Carmen de uirginitate* (described by *CPL* as *De uirginitate (metrice)*: *CPL* 1333), *De uirginitate* (prose) (described by *CPL* as *De laudibus uirginitatis*: *CPL* 1332), and *Enigmata* and *Epistola ad Acircium*, lumped together under *CPL* 1335; and Boethius, where we use *De consolatione Philosophiae* for *Philosophiae consolatio* (*CPL* 878).

liturgical manuscripts and prayer books.[5] By the same token, the individual texts which, together with the canticles, constitute *cantica* in psalter manuscripts (e.g., the *Te Deum*, *Gloria*, *Pater noster*, Apostles' Creed [*Credo*]) are not listed separately.

In the case of manuscripts with Old English contents, the symbols which were first devised for the 'Preliminary List' are retained, as follows:

(no symbol)	text in Latin
*	text in Old English prose
**	text in Old English alliterative verse
(*)	text partly in Old English
+*	text in Latin, accompanied by a prose version in Old English; or a Latin—Old English glossary
°	Latin text with continuous Old English interlinear gloss, or having substantial sections, or a fairly large number of words, glossed in Old English
(f)	only minor fragments of a text are preserved

For texts in languages other than Latin or Old English, the language is specified in the entries. In the case of translations into Old English, the translator's name, if known, follows in round brackets the name of the author, as for example: Gregory (Werferth), *Dialogi*; in the case of translations into Latin from Greek, the name of the Greek author is given first, followed by the title of the work, and then the Latin translator, in the form: Eusebius, *Historia ecclesiastica*, trans. Rufinus. In the case of translations from Greek into Latin, the translation is identified by reference to *CPG*.

The following details have not normally been recorded:

minor additions and alterations
scattered glosses in Latin or Old English
supply leaves[6]
additions of any kind, and glosses (English, French or Latin) entered
    after 1100
introductory texts to biblical books
canon tables and lists of *capitula*[7]
illustrations and decoration (which are treated by art historians in bibli-

---

5 With certain exceptions involving items which have been edited separately by modern scholars, such as coronation *ordines* (in pontificals), liturgical calendars, litanies, etc.
6 An important contribution to this problem is Parkes (1997b).
7 An exception is made in the case of gospel pericopes; on their importance, see Lenker (1997).

ography listed under DEC for each relevant entry)
musical notation[8]

Presentation of Bibliography Relevant to Each Manuscript

In order to facilitate consultation, the bibliography relevant to each manuscript is classified under several headings, as follows:

MS: The bibliographical items listed here treat the manuscript as a physical object: its construction, script, binding, as well as lists and/or discussions of its contents.

DEC: Includes discussions of the decoration or art-work contained in the particular manuscript.

FACS: Here are listed facsimiles or illustrations, either of the entire manuscript (complete facsimiles are usually given pride of place in these entries) or of individual folios or pages. When the source indicates what folio or page is in question, we give this information in square brackets following the plate or illustration number; when a source fails to indicate the folio we state '[folio not specified]'.

ED: Here we attempt to list all editions of texts which are either based on this manuscript or for which this manuscript was collated. Note that in the case of Latin texts, we cite an edition only when the manuscript itself has been collated (where possible we give the siglum used by the editor to identify readings from this manuscript); editions which do not record readings from the manuscript are not listed (as is frequently the case with classical and patristic Latin texts, where editors tend to base their editions on manuscripts earlier than the surviving Anglo-Saxon witnesses).[9] In the case of manuscripts of Old English homilies and homiletic materials, and of several other complex miscellaneous manuscripts such as no. **363**, we

---

8 Now catalogued exhaustively by Hartzell (2006).
9 Scholars seeking reliable editions of patristic texts which happen not to be listed here (because the manuscript in question happened not to be collated) may consult *CPL* under the number cited for the relevant text. For editions of Classical Latin texts, reference may be made to *Tusculum Lexikon*, ed. W. Buchwald, A. Hohlweg and O. Prinz (Munich, 1982); the *Oxford Latin Dictionary*, ed. P.W. Glare (Oxford, 1968–82), pp. ix–xxi; and *The Oxford Classical Dictionary*, ed. S. Hornblower and A. Spawforth, 3rd ed. (Oxford, 1996). For editions of Medieval Latin authors (500–1500), see *CALMA* (currently extending as far as the name Gregorius) and *Tusculum Lexikon*.

have attempted to list for each individual item in the manuscript (as given in the numbered sequence of articles by N.R. Ker (1957), here specified as 'art(s)') the most recent edition available.

LANG: Discussions of distinctive features of the language of the manuscript: principally, in the case of manuscripts containing Old English, of dialectal features which may help to localize the manuscript. Only on rare occasions have scholars treated the linguistic features of Latin manuscripts, but we have attempted to cite such treatments wherever relevant.

ST: A broadly conceived category, which may include studies (including bibliographies) of one or more of the texts preserved in a particular manuscript; that is to say, of information which may be relevant in situating the manuscript in a cultural context, or evaluating its position in a textual transmission. For the most part, studies listed under this heading will contain mention of the manuscript itself; it would not be feasible to include, for example, general discussions of Latin texts which happen to be preserved in Anglo-Saxon manuscripts, or of the authors who composed them. But note that we do not normally list interpretations, translations, source studies, studies of metre and style, etc.

Finally, users of the present work will be aware that there are digitized images (including complete reproductions) of many of the manuscripts listed here. We have not thought it possible (or necessary) to list, under FACS, every image which may be consulted on the Internet; several of the most important sites may be conveniently listed here:

1. All manuscripts in Cambridge, Corpus Christi College (including our nos. **36–117**), are available in full digitized facsimile and provided with helpful introductions at Parker on the Web (Version 1.0): www.harrassowitz.de/Parker_on_the_Web.html (accessible by subscription only).

2. Selected images of the illuminated and decorated Anglo-Saxon manuscripts in the British Library are available in the *Catalogue of Illuminated Manuscripts*, at www.bl.uk/catalogues/illuminatedmanuscripts/searchMS-No.asp. The images include Anglo-Saxon manuscripts from the following collections: Arundel (our nos. **303, 304, 305.5, 306, 306.5**), Burney (no. **307**), Egerton (nos. **409, 410, 410.5** and **411**), Harley (nos. **413, 415, 417, 421, 422, 423, 424, 426, 427, 428.4, 428.5, 429, 430, 431, 433, 434.5, 435, 438, 439, 440** and **443**), Royal (nos. **444, 445, 446, 447, 448, 449, 450, 451, 452, 453.2, 453.4, 453.6, 453.8, 455, 456.4, 456.8, 457, 457.4, 457.8, 458, 459, 462, 464, 465, 466,**

467, 469, 469.3, 469.5, 470, 472, 473, 475, 478, 479, 481, 483, 485, 486, 487.5, 489, 491–3, 494, 496, 497, 497.2 and 498), Sloane (no. 498.1) and Stowe (nos. 499 and 500). Images from Anglo-Saxon manuscripts in the Additional and Cottonian collections have not been uploaded as of 30/6/2012.

3. Complete digitized facsimiles of a small number of decorated Anglo-Saxon manuscripts in the Bodleian Library, Oxford, are accessible through the Bodleian's site, www.digital.bodleian.ox.ac.uk/medieval_home, in the categories 'Celtic Manuscripts', 'Western Manuscripts' and 'Medieval and Renaissance Manuscripts'; these manuscripts include our nos. 530, 531, 538, 583, 583.3, 585 and 640.

4. Selected images (with transcriptions and descriptions) of several manuscripts containing penitential texts (including our nos. 59.5, 65.5, 73, 363, 644, 656 and 808) are available at www.anglo-saxon.net/penance/.

During preparation of the present *Bibliographical Handlist*, our working *terminus* for publications has been 2010; for works published by that date or earlier, we have tried to offer systematic coverage. (For works published in the nineteenth century, particularly on manuscript illumination, our coverage is not systematic, for the reason that nineteenth-century writings are usually mentioned by the more recent bibliographies to which we refer.) Works published *after* 2010 are treated less systematically, but we have endeavoured to include all those works which, in our opinion, are of unquestionable importance for Anglo-Saxon manuscript studies; for works such as these, the absolute *terminus* is the end of December 2012.

I

Libraries in the British Isles
(nos. 1—774.1)

1. Aberdeen, University Library, 216

s. xi ex., Salisbury

Contents: Bede, *Expositio Apocalypseos* [*CPL* 1363]; pseudo-Jerome (pseudo-Victorinus?), *Comm. in Apocalypsin* [*CPL* 1221]

MS: Schenkl no. 3256; M.R. James (1932) 61–2; N.R. Ker (1976b) 41, 45, 49 [repr. N.R. Ker (1985) 163, 169, 173]; Webber (1992) 143; R. Gameson (1999a) no. 4; Gryson (2001) 15–16

FACS: N.R. Ker (1976b) pl. VI (a) [fol. 36r]

ED: Gryson (2001) [Bede, *Expositio Apocalypseos*, coll. as U]

ST: Lambert (1969–72) no. 490; N.R. Ker (1976b) 24 [repr. N.R. Ker (1985) 144]; Webber (1992) 12, 15, 143

1. 5. Aberystwyth, National Library of Wales, 735 C

[fols. 1–26]: s. xi¹, France (Limoges?), prov. England or Wales, s. xi

[fols. 27–47]: s. xi, France? in England or Wales before 1100?

Contents [fols. 1–26]: Boniface, *Aenigmata* [*CPL* 1564a]; Ausonius, *Eclogae* xiv [SK 4582]; astronomical drawings; pseudo-Sallust and pseudo-Cicero, *Inuectiuae*; Cicero, *Somnium Scipionis*; Macrobius, *Comm. in Somnium Scipionis* (f); Germanicus, *Aratea*; [fols. 27–47]: Hyginus, *Astronomica*

MS: McGurk (1973) 197, 205–7; Munk Olsen (1982–) I.525; Le Boeuffle (1983) lii; Reeve (1983b) 21; Bischoff (1989b) 32, 34 nn. 7, 21; Gneuss (2003b) 294; Wieland (2009) 150, 154

DEC: McGurk (1973) 198–204, 207–10

FACS: McGurk (1973), pls. I–VI [fols. 3v, 4r, 4v, 10v, 12r, 13v, 14r, 14v, 15r, 16r, 17r, 17v, 18v, 19r, 19v, 20r, 20v, 21r, 21v]

ED: Le Boeuffle (1983) [Hyginus, *Astronomica*, coll. as W]

Badminton, Gloucestershire, Duke of Beaufort Muniments, 704.1.16: see no. **262. 5**

Brockenhurst (Hants.), Parish Church, Parish Register, s.n. [former owner]: see now no. **759. 3**

2. 5. Cambridge, University Library, Dd. 2. 7

s. xi ex., Canterbury CC

Contents: Jerome *Epistulae* [*CPL* 620] and pseudo-Jerome, *Epistulae suppositiae* [*CPL* 633]

MS: Hardwick—Luard (1856–67) I.40-1; R. Gameson (1999a) no. 18; Binski—Zutshi (2011) 12 [no. 8]

DEC: Binski—Zutshi (2011) 12

FACS: Binski—Zutshi (2011) 8 [fol. 1v]

2. 8. Cambridge, University Library, Ee. 1. 23, fols. 1–69

s. xi/xii

Contents: Paschasius Radbertus, *De assumptione B.V.M.* [cf. *CPL* 633]; Ephraem Syrus, six *sermones* (in Latin translation) [*CPL* 1143]

MS: Hardwick—Luard (1856–67) II.19–20; R. Gameson (1999a) no. 20

FACS: Binski—Zutshi (2011) fig. 290 [fol. 13r]

ST: C.D. Wright (2002) 217

3. Cambridge, University Library, Ee. 2. 4 (with Oxford, Bodleian Library, lat. theol. c. 3 (S.C. 31382), ff. 1, 1*, 2)

s. x med., W or SW England? (Glastonbury?)

Contents: Smaragdus of Saint-Mihiel, *Expositio in Regulam S. Benedicti*

MS: Hardwick—Luard (1856–67) II.26; N.R. Ker (1956) 15; T.A.M. Bishop (1964–8d) 396–7; T.A.M. Bishop (1971) 2 [no. 3]; Gretsch (1973) 44–5; Spannagel—Engelbert (1974) xvi, lii, liii; Gretsch (1974) 127, 130; Rella (1977) 75, 96 n. 7, 161 [no. 4]; Clemoes (1985) no. 23; O'Brien O'Keeffe (1985) 67; Carley (1987) 199 n. 10; Voigts (1988) 85, 91–2; Lapidge (1991c) 977 [repr. Lapidge (1993a) 27]; Budny (1992) 137; Dumville (1993g) 8, 97–8; R. Sharpe et al. (1996) 185 [no. 150]; Gretsch (1999a) 255 and n. 91; R.M. Butler (2004) 202–3; Wieland (2009) 140; R. Gameson (2012a) 39 and n. 99, 59 and n. 198; Rushforth (2012) 201 and n. 24

FACS: T.A.M. Bishop (1964–8d) pl. XXIX (a) [fol. 141r]; T.A.M. Bishop (1971) pl. II.3 [fol. 161v]; Budny (1992) pl. 8 (a) [fol. 147v]; Dumville (1993g) pl. II [fol. 121r]

ED: Spannagel—Engelbert (1974) [collated as C, as part of a group π which also includes no. **883** below]

LANG: T.A.M. Bishop (1964–8d) 398

ST: Rella (1980) 75–6, 96 n. 7; R. McKitterick (2012) 329

4. Cambridge, University Library, Ff. 1. 23

s. x/xi or xi in. or xi$^{2/4}$ or xi med., Ramsey? Canterbury?

Contents: prayers (add. s. xi med. or xi^2); Psalterium Romanum°; canticles°; litany; prayers and benedictions

MS: Hardwick—Luard (1856–67) II.312–13; M.R. James (1903) 527; Mearns (1914) 52, 79; C.E. Wright (1949–53) 225; Weber (1953) xiv; N.R. Ker (1957) no. 13; Backhouse et al. (1984b) no. 64; Clemoes (1985) no. 8; P.R. Robinson (1988) I, no. 29; Muir (1988) xxxii; Dumville (1991–5) 40–1; Lapidge (1991a) 62–3; Dumville (1992a) 53; Lapidge (1992a) 100–3, 126–9 [repr. Lapidge (1993a) 388–91, 414–17]; Vaciago (1993) 4 [no. 8]; Dumville (1993g) 59–63, 79-80, 83–4, 155; M.P. Brown (1996) 139–40; Corrêa (1996) 294 n. 39, 295 n. 42; Gneuss (1998) 276; Treharne (1998) 242; Gretsch (1999a) 283–5; Gretsch (2000) 86; Liuzza (2000) 149; Binski—Panayotova (2005) no. 17 [T. Webber]; Hartzell (2006) no. 11; Biggs (2007a) 16; Karkov (2007a) 145; Barker-Benfield (2008) III.1738–9, 1825; Graham (2009) 161–2; Wieland (2009) 116; Binski—Zutshi (2011) 8–9 [no. 5]; R. Gameson (2012a) 46, 73, 76; Rushforth (2012) 203 and n. 43; Scragg (2012a) nos. 227–9; Toswell (2012) 471, 478–9

DEC: F. Wormald (1945) 125–6, 133 [repr. F. Wormald (1984) 48–9, 58, 63]; Rice (1952) 129, 220; F. Wormald (1952) 59 [no. 2]; Dodwell (1954) 10–13, 20, 26, 31; F. Wormald (1957b) 31 [repr. F. Wormald (1984) 145]; Alexander (1970a) 61, 63–4, 70, 73, 148, 171, 189; E. Temple (1976) no. 80; Brownrigg (1978) 263; Ohlgren (1986) no. 185; Raw (1990) 199–200; R. Gameson (1991) 73–4; R. Gameson (1995b) 90–1, 100–1 *et passim*; Deshman (1997) 110 n. 5; Karkov (2006b) 102; Karkov (2007a) 145; Binski—Zutshi (2011) 8–9; O'Reilly (2011) 217; R. Gameson (2012c) 289 n. 139

FACS: Steger (1961) pl. 12 [fol. 1v (4v)]; F. Wormald (1984) ills. 51, 64–5, 78 [fols. 5r, 13v, 37v, 208v]; R. Gameson (1991) figs. 9, 11 [fols. 29v, 208v]; Budny (1992) pls. 33–4 [fols. 88r, 171r]; Binski—Panayotova (2005) 71 [fol. 88r]; M.P. Brown (2007a) pl. 102 [fol. 5r]; Binski—Zutshi (2011) 9 [fol. 4r], colour pls. V.5 [fol. 5r], VI.5 [fol. 88r], VII.5 [fol. 171r]; Owen-Crocker (2009) fig. 6.2 [fol. 5r]; R. Gameson (2012) pl. 21.3 [fol. 249v]

ED: Hardwick (1854) 267–70 [litany]; Wildhagen (1910) 1–537 [base MS (= C) for Psalterium Romanum and canticles and OE gloss]; Weber

(1953) [Psalterium Romanum coll. as C]; Lapidge (1991a) 93–7 [litany]; Pulsiano (2001a) [Latin and OE gloss to Pss. I-L coll. as C]

LANG: A. Campbell (1967a) 81–92; Bierbaumer (1977a); Hofstetter (1982) 460–1; Dance (2004) 35–6 n. 29

ST: Wildhagen (1913) 466–71; Gjerløw (1961) 144; Pulsiano (1998b) 105 n. 1; Boynton (1999) 237 n. 162 [collation with Paris, BNF, fr. 103]; Pulsiano (2000) 167; Rosenthal (2007) 24 n. 24

5. Cambridge, University Library, Ff. 2. 33, fols. i, ii, vi and vii

s. xi ex., Bury St Edmunds

Contents: *Concilium Africanum* [A.D. 424–5] [*CPL* 1765g] (f)

MS: T.A.M. Bishop (1949–53) 434; R.M. Thomson (1972) 625–6; Clemoes (1985) no. 28; Laing (1993) 43–4; R. Gameson (1999a) no. 21

LANG: Laing (1993) 44

6. Cambridge, University Library, Ff. 3. 9

s. xi ex., Canterbury CC

Contents: Hiezechiel (excerpt); Gregory, *Homiliae in Hiezechielem* [*CPL* 1710]

MS: Hardwick—Luard (1856–67) II.414; Dodwell (1954) 17, 120; N.R. Ker (1960) 14–15; Clemoes (1985) no. 12; R. Gameson (1995a) 117–18 nn. 77, 79, 134 n. 150, 142; R. Gameson (1999a) no. 22; T.N. Hall (2001) 132 [no. 5]; Binski—Zutshi (2011) 12–13 [no. 9]

DEC: Dodwell (1954) 17; R. Gameson (1995a) 117 n. 44; Binski—Zutshi (2011) 12

FACS: Dodwell (1954) pl. 11 (b) [fol. 56r]; Binski—Zutshi (2011) 13 [fol. 2r], colour pl. VIII.9 [fol. 56r]

7. Cambridge, University Library, Ff. 4. 42

s. ix^2 and x, Wales, prov. s. x/xi W. England

Contents: three brief prose texts; hymn [SK 10920], s. x; Iuvencus, *Euangelia* [*CPL* 1385], s. ix^2, with Welsh, Irish and Latin glosses, s. x^1, and Latin glosses, s. x/xi [*BCLL* 89]; Welsh verses, s. x^1; grammatical notes [*BCLL* 84]; sequence [*BCLL* 120]; poems [*BCLL* 81] (partly illegible), s. ix^2

MS: Hardwick—Luard (1856–67) II.473; W. Stokes (1860) 204; Bradshaw (1889) 455; Lindsay (1912a) 16–18 [no. 4]; T.A.M. Bishop (1964–8c) 258; Bischoff (1966–81) II.258; T.A.M. Bishop (1971) no. 21; Korhammer (1980) 30; Rella (1980) 72; Lapidge (1982a) 108, 111–13 [repr. Lapidge (1996b) 471, 475–8]; Oates (1982) 81–7; R.M. Thomson (1982b) 4–5; Clemoes (1985) no. 34; DeBrún—Herbert (1986) xii, 108–9; Dumville (1987) 160 n. 63; Harvey (1991) 181, 190–1, 193; Milfull (1996) 66; Huws (2000) 9, 67; McKee (2000a); R. Gameson (2012a) 43 n. 112, 66 and n. 228; McKee (2012a) 169 and n. 8

FACS: McKee (2000c) [complete facsimile]; Lindsay (1912a) pls. VI–VII [fols. 1r, 7v]; Lapidge (1982a) pl. I [fo. 2v] [repr. Lapidge (1996b) 476]; M. Irvine (1994) 373 [fol. 6r]

ED: W. Stokes (1860) [base text for Latin and Old Welsh glosses]; McKee (2000b); Haddan—Stubbs (1869–71) I.198 [Latin biblical glosses], 622–3 [sequence]; Bayless—Lapidge (1998) 260 [prose note on the evangelists, fol. 1r]; Dronke (2005) 25–6 [sequence]

LANG: Lindsay (1912a) 16–18 [on spelling and syntax marks]

ST: W. Stokes (1860) 204–49; W. Stokes (1873); Dronke (1981) 225–7 [sequence]; *BCLL* (1985) nos. 81, 84, 89, 120; Lapidge (1986c) 97–101; Lapidge (1988–9) 444 n. 4; Harvey (1991) 181–97; Wieland (1998) 16 n. 23; McKee (2000a); Dronke (2005) 14–24 [sequence]; Howlett (2007); Charles-Edwards (2012) 400 and n. 59; McKee (2012b) 342 and n. 15

8. Cambridge, University Library, Ff. 4. 43

s. x⁴/⁴, Canterbury CC

Contents: Smaragdus of Saint-Mihiel, *Diadema monachorum*

MS: Hardwick—Luard (1856-67) II.473–4; Rochais (1953) 252–3 n. 3; T.A.M. Bishop (1959–63a) 94; T.A.M. Bishop (1959–63b) 414, 421; N.R. Ker (1964) 29–30; T.A.M. Bishop (1971) xxv, 6; Clemoes (1985) no. 24; O'Brien O'Keeffe (1985) 65; Dumville (1992a) 47; Dumville (1993g) 18 n. 53, 99, 101–3; Graham (1998a) 25; Wieland (2009) 140; R. Gameson (2012b) 109 and n. 55, 111 n. 65; Rushforth (2012) 204 and n. 48

FACS: T.A.M. Bishop (1959–63b) pls. XIII (a) [fol. 28r], XIV (a) [fol. 26v]

ST: Rädle (1974) 52 n. 112 [erroneously records this MS as a copy of Smaragdus, *Comm. in Donatum*]

9. Cambridge, University Library, Ff. 5. 27, fol. 1

s. vii/viii, Monkwearmouth-Jarrow

Contents: Psalterium Romanum (f; Ps. XC.7–XCII.5)

MS: T.A.M. Bishop (1949–53) 433; T.A.M. Bishop (1954); Lowe (1960) 19; Bischoff (1966-81) II.330; *CLA* Supplement (1971) no. 1682; G. Henderson (1982) 1–2; Parkes (1982) 4, 5, 17, 22 [repr. Parkes (1991a) 96, 97, 112, 118]; Clemoes (1985) no. 7; Dumville (1999) 69; Wieland (2009) 117

DEC: G. Henderson (1982) 4–5, 46 n. 4

FACS: T.A.M. Bishop (1954) pl. 1; Lowe (1960) pl. XIV; G. Henderson (1982) pl. 1

ST: D.H. Wright (1961a) 445; Pulsiano (1998b) 105 n. 3; Pulsiano (2001a) xxvii

11. Cambridge, University Library, Gg. 3. 28

s. x/xi, Cerne? (prov. Durham)

Contents: Ælfric, *Catholic Homilies* (First and Second Series)*, *De temporibus anni**; *Pater noster**; Apostles' Creed*; Niceno-Constantinopolitan Creed*; prayers*; Ælfric, *De paenitentia**, Pastoral Letter I* (incomplete); *Admonitions in Lent*

MS: Hardwick—Luard (1856–67) III.71–82; Fehr (1914/1966) xvi, cxxxii; Mynors (1939) no. 19; K. Sisam (1953a) 165–70; N.R. Ker (1957) no. 15; N.R. Ker (1964) 61; Pope (1967) I.34–5; Godden (1979) xliii; Clemoes (1985) no. 45; Doyle (1988) 217 n. 57; Dumville (1988) 54, 59, 62–3; Dumville (1992a) 107–8; Clemoes (1994a) 347; Clemoes (1997) 24–5, 68–9; Swan (2000b) 62, 64; Acker (2004) 127–8; Dance (2004) 34 n. 24; Godden (2004) 366 n. 52; *ASMMF* XVII (2008) 1–20 [no. 95; Wilcox]; M. Blake (2009) 15–18; Graham (2009) 201; Scragg (2009b) 80; R. Gameson (2012b) 115 n. 83; Raw (2012) 460 and n. 5; Scragg (2012a) nos. 230–6

FACS: *ASMMF* XVII (2008) no. 95 [complete facsimile]; Godden (1979) frontispiece [fol. 225v]; M. Blake (2009) pls. 1–2 [fols. 255r, 259r]

LANG: Godden (1979) lxxviii–lxxxii; Hofstetter (1987) 38–66; Scragg (2006)

ED [the order of the following items is that of the manuscript, listed according to Ker's numbering of individual articles (see N.R. Ker (1957) 13–20); only the most recent editions are cited]:

(Catholic Homilies, First Series)

arts. 1–2: Clemoes (1997) 173–7 [base MS (= K) for Ælfric's prefaces (Latin and English)]

art. 3: Clemoes (1997) 178–89 [Hom. I (*De initio creaturae*) coll. as K]

art. 4: Clemoes (1997) 190–7 [Hom. II (Christmas) coll. as K]

art. 5: Clemoes (1997) 198–205 [Hom. III (St Stephen) coll. as K]

art. 6: Clemoes (1997) 206–16 [Hom. IV (Assumption of St John the Evangelist) coll. as K]

art. 7: Clemoes (1997) 217–23 [Hom. V (Holy Innocents) coll. as K]

art. 8: Clemoes (1997) 224–31 [Hom. VI (Circumcision of the Lord) coll. as K]

art. 9: Clemoes (1997) 232–40 [Hom. VII (Epiphany) coll. as K]

art. 10: Clemoes (1997) 241–8 [Hom. VIII (Third Sunday after Epiphany) coll. as K]

art. 11: Clemoes (1997) 249–57 [Hom. IX (Purification of B.V.M.) coll. as K]

art. 12: Clemoes (1997) 258–65 [Hom. X (Quinquagesima Sunday) coll. as K]

art. 13: Clemoes (1997) 266–74 [Hom. XI (First Sunday in Lent) coll. as K]

art. 14: Clemoes (1997) 275–80 [Hom. XII (Sunday in Mid-Lent) coll. as K]

art. 15: Clemoes (1997) 281–9 [Hom. XIII (Annunciation of B.V.M.) coll. as K]

art. 16: Clemoes (1997) 290–8 [Hom. XIV (Palm Sunday) coll. as K]

art. 17: Clemoes (1997) 299–306 [Hom. XV (Easter Sunday) coll. as K]

art. 18: Clemoes (1997) 307–12 [Hom. XVI (First Sunday after Easter) coll. as K]

art. 19: Clemoes (1997) 313–16 [Hom. XVII (Second Sunday after Easter) coll. as K]

art. 20: Clemoes (1997) 317–24 [Hom. XVIII (*In letania maiore*) coll. as K]

art. 21: Clemoes (1997) 325–34 [Hom. XIX (*Feria .III. De dominica oratione*) coll. as K]

art. 22: Clemoes (1997) 335–44 [Hom. XX (*Feria .IIII. De fide catholica*) coll. as K]

art. 23: Clemoes (1997) 345–53 [Hom. XXI (Ascension Day) coll. as K]

art. 24: Clemoes (1997) 354–64 [Hom. XXII (Pentecost) coll. as K]

art. 25: Clemoes (1997) 365–70 [Hom. XXIII (Second Sunday after Pentecost) coll. as K] art. 26: Clemoes (1997) 371–8 [Hom. XXIV (Third Sunday after Pentecost) coll. as K]

art. 27: Clemoes (1997) 379–87 [Hom. XXV (St John the Baptist) coll. as K]

art. 28: Clemoes (1997) 388–99 [Hom. XXVI (SS. Peter and Paul) coll. as K]

art. 29: Clemoes (1997) 400–9 [Hom. XXVII (St Paul) coll. as K]

art. 30: Clemoes (1997) 410–17 [Hom. XXVIII (Eleventh Sunday after Pentecost) coll. as K]

art. 31: Clemoes (1997) 418–28 [Hom. XXIX (St Laurence) coll. as K]

art. 32: Clemoes (1997) 429–38 [Hom. XXX (Assumption of B.V.M.), lines 151–273, coll. as K (lines 1–150 are lacking in this MS)]

art. 33: Clemoes (1997) 439–50 [Hom. XXXI (St Bartholomew) coll. as K]

art. 34: Clemoes (1997) 451–8 [Hom. XXXII (Decollation of John the Baptist) coll. as K]

art. 35: Clemoes (1997) 459–64 [Hom. XXXIII (Seventeenth Sunday after Pentecost) coll. as K]

art. 36: Clemoes (1997) 465–75 [Hom. XXXIV (Dedication of the Church of St Michael) coll. as K]

art. 37: Clemoes (1997) 476–85 [Hom. XXXV (Twenty-first Sunday after Pentecost) coll. as K]

art. 38: Clemoes (1997) 486–96 [Hom. XXXVI (All Saints) coll. as K]

art. 39: Clemoes (1997) 497–506 [Hom. XXXVII (St Clement) coll. as K]

art. 40: Clemoes (1997) 507–19 [Hom. XXXVIII (St Andrew) coll. as K]

art. 41: Clemoes (1997) 520–3 [Hom. XXXIX (First Sunday in Advent) coll. as K]

art. 42: Clemoes (1997) 524–30 [Hom. XL (Second Sunday in Advent) coll. as K]

(Catholic Homilies, Second Series)

art. 43: Godden (1979) 1–2 [base MS (= K) for Ælfric's prefaces (Latin and English)]

art. 44: Godden (1979) 3–11 [base MS (= K) for Hom. I (Christmas)]

art. 45: Godden (1979) 12–18 [base MS (= K) for Hom. II (St Stephen)]

art. 46: Godden (1979) 19–28 [base MS (= K) for Hom. III (Epiphany)]

art. 47: Godden (1979) 29–40 [base MS (= K) for Hom. IV (Second Sunday after Epiphany)]

art. 48: Godden (1979) 41–51 [base MS (= K) for Hom. V (Septuagesima Sunday)] art. 49: Godden (1979) 52–9 [base MS (= K) for Hom. VI (Sexagesima Sunday)]

art. 50: Godden (1979) 60–6 [base MS (= K) for Hom. VII (First Sunday in Lent)]

art. 51: Godden (1979) 67–71 [base MS (= K) for Hom. VIII (Second Sunday in Lent)]

art. 52: Godden (1979) 72–80 [base MS (= K) for Hom. IX (St Gregory)]

art. 53: Godden (1979) 81–91 [base MS (= K) for Hom. X (St Cuthbert)]

art. 54: Godden (1979) 92–109 [base MS (= K) for Hom. XI (St Benedict), except for lines 24–110]

art. 55: Godden (1979) 110–26 [base MS (= K) for Hom. XII (Sunday in Mid-Lent)]

art. 56: Godden (1979) 127–36 [base MS (= K) for Hom. XIII (Fifth Sunday in Lent)]

art. 57: Godden (1979) 137–49 [base MS (= K) for Hom. XIV (Palm Sunday)]

art. 58: Godden (1979) 150–60 [base MS (= K) for Hom. XV (Easter Sunday)]

arts. 59–60: Godden (1979) 161–8 [base MS (= K) for Hom. XVI (Another Sermon for Easter Sunday)]

arts. 61–2: Godden (1979) 169–73 [base MS (= K) for Hom. XVII (SS. Philip and James)]

art. 63: Godden (1979) 174–6 [base MS (= K) for Hom. XVIII (Discovery of the Holy Cross), lines 1–61]

art. 64: Godden (1979) 176–9 [base MS (= K) for Hom. XVIII (SS. Alexander, Eventius and Theodolus), lines 62–156]

art. 65: Godden (1979) 180–9 [base MS (= K) for Hom. XIX (*Feria. .II. in Letania maiore*)]

art. 66: Godden (1979) 190–8 [base MS (= K) for Hom. XX (*Feria .III. in Letania maiore*)]

art. 67: Godden (1979) 199–203 [base MS (= K) for Hom. XXI (Vision of Dryhthelm from Bede, *HE* V.xii), lines 1–137]

art. 68: Godden (1979) 204–5 [base MS (= K) for Hom. XXI (*Hortatorius sermo*), lines 138–80]

art. 69: Godden (1979) 206–12 [base MS (= K) for Hom. XXII (*Feria .IIII. in Letania maiore*)]

art. 70: Godden (1979) 213–17 [base MS (= K) for Hom. XXIII (Third Sunday after Pentecost), lines 1–125]

art. 71: Godden (1979) 217–20 [base MS (= K) for Hom. XXIII (*Alia narratio*), lines 126–20] art. 72: Godden (1979) 221–9 [base MS (= K) for Hom. XXIV (St Peter)]

art. 73: Godden (1979) 230–4 [base MS (= K) for Hom. XXV (Eighth Sunday after Pentecost)]

art. 74: Godden (1979) 235–40 [base MS (= K) for Hom. XXVI (Ninth Sunday after Pentecost)]

art. 75: Godden (1979) 241–7 [base MS (= K) for Hom. XXVII, lines 1–181 (St James)]

art. 76: Godden (1979) 247–8 [base MS (= K) for Hom. XXVII, lines 182–231 (The Seven Sleepers of Ephesus)]

art. 77: Godden (1979) 249–54 [base MS (= K) for Hom. XXVIII (Twelfth Sunday after Pentecost)]

art. 78: Godden (1979) 255–9 [base MS (= K) for Hom. XXIX (Assumption of B.V.M.)]

art. 79: Godden (1979) 260–7 [base MS (= K) for Hom. XXX (First Sunday in September)]

art. 80: Godden (1979) 268–71 [base MS (= K) for Hom. XXXI (Sixteenth Sunday after Pentecost), lines 1–107]

art. 81: Godden (1979) 271, lines 1–10 [base MS (= K) for second part of Hom. XXXI (St Mary)]

art. 82: Godden (1979) 272–9 [base MS (= K) for Hom. XXXII (St Matthew)]

art. 83: Godden (1979) 280–7 [base MS (= K) for Hom. XXXIII (SS. Simon and Jude)]

art. 84: Godden (1979) 288–97 [base MS (= K) for Hom. XXXIV, lines 1–332 (St Martin)]

art. 85: Godden (1979) 297–8 [base MS (= K) for *Excusatio dictantis*]

art. 86: Godden (1979) 299–303 [base MS (= K) for Hom. XXXV (Feast of an Apostle)]

art. 87: Godden (1979) 304–9 [base MS (= K) for Hom. XXXVI (Feast of Several Apostles)]

art. 88: Godden (1979) 310–17 [base MS (= K) for Hom. XXXVII (Feast of Holy Martyrs)]

art. 89: Godden (1979) 318–26 [base MS (= K) for Hom. XXXVIII (Feast of a Confessor)]

art. 90: Godden (1979) 327–34 [base MS (= K) for Hom. XXXIX (Feast of Holy Virgins)]

art. 91: Godden (1979) 335–45 [base MS (= K) for Hom. XL (Dedication of a Church)]

art. 92: Godden (1979) 345 [base MS (= K) for *Oratio*]

(other Ælfrician works)

art. 93: Henel (1942a) 2–82, even pages [base MS (= G) for *De temporibus anni*]; M. Blake (2009) 76–96 [base text (= G) for *De temporibus anni*]

art. 94: Thorpe (1844–6) II.596–600 [base text for OE *Pater noster*, Creeds, etc.]

art. 95: Thorpe (1844–6) II.602–8 [base text for *De paenitentia*]

art. 96: Thorpe (1844–6) II.608 [base text for *Admonitions in Lent*]

art. 97: Fehr (1914/1966) 1–34 [base text (= Gg) for Pastoral Letter I]

ST: Pope (1931); Willard (1950); Harlow (1959); Collins—Clemoes (1974) 319–21; Korhammer (1976) 151; Bzdyl (1977) 98–102; Dumville (1992a) 107–8 n. 71; Clemoes (1994a) 350–1; J. Hill (1996) 244; S. Irvine (2000) 54–5; Proud (2000) 120–1, 126; Scragg (2012b) 558

11. 5. Cambridge, University Library, Gg. 4. 15, fols. 1–108

s. xi/xii (prov. Eynsham)

Contents: Bede, *Super Epistulas catholicas expositio* [*CPL* 1362]

MS: Hardwick—Luard (1856–67) III.160; R. Gameson (1999a) no. 27

11. 8. Cambridge, University Library, Gg. 4. 28

s. xi/xii

Contents: Jerome, *Comm. in Prophetas minores* (Osee, Amos, Ionas, Abdias, Micha, Naum) [*CPL* 589]; account of a *libellus* by Athanasius

MS: Hardwick—Luard (1856–67) III.174–5; R. Gameson (1999a) no. 28; R. Gameson (2012a) 46 n. 144

ST: Lambert (1969–72) no. 216

12. Cambridge, University Library, Gg. 5. 35

s. xi med., Canterbury StA?, (prov. ibid.)

Contents: Iuvencus, *Euangelia* [*CPL* 1385], with glosses; Sedulius, *Carmen paschale* [*CPL* 1447], with glosses from commentary by Remigius; Sedulius, *Hymni* [*CPL* 1449]; poems on Sedulius [SK 15784, 14842, 14841]; Arator, *Historia apostolica* [*CPL* 1504], with glosses; poems on Arator [SK 17136, 177]; Prosper of Aquitaine, *Epigrammata ex sententiis S. Augustini* [*CPL* 526], preceded by prefatory poem [SK 5836]; Prosper, *Versus ad coniugem* [*CPL* 531; SK 458]; Prudentius, *Psychomachia* [*CPL* 1441], with glosses; Prudentius, *Dittochaeon* [*CPL* 1444]; Lactantius, *De aue Phoenice* [*CPL* 90; SK 4500];

Boethius, *De consolatione Philosophiae* [*CPL* 878], with commentary by Remigius; Hrabanus Maurus, *De laudibus S. Crucis*; Hucbald of Saint-Amand, *De harmonica institutione*; Aldhelm, *Carmen de uirginitate* [*CPL* 1333]; Milo, *Carmen de sobrietate* [SK 12570]; Fredegaud/Frithegod of Canterbury and Brioude, 'Ciues celestis patrie' (lapidary poem) [SK 2326]; Latin hymns and poems [SK 1409a (by Wulfstan Cantor?), 10856 (from Prudentius, *Hamartigenia* 931–66), 11339, 17765, 12551 (Eugenius of Toledo (?) *Heptametron de primordio mundi*), 14640 (*Sancte sator*), 6687, 10204, 2086a, 16284, 14633, 10905, 2593, 16044]; Abbo of Saint-Germain-des-Prés, *Bella Parisiacae urbis*, bk. III; Hucbald of Saint-Amand, *Ecloga de caluis* [SK 1949]; Eusebius, *Aenigmata* [*CPL* 1342]; Tatwine, *Aenigmata* [*CPL* 1564]; Boniface, *Aenigmata* [*CPL* 1564a]; Symposius, *Aenigmata* [*CPL* 1518]; Aldhelm, *Enigmata* [*CPL* 1335], with glosses; pseudo-Smaragdus (pseudo-Alcuin), two monitory poems for a prince [SK 7810, 10988]; *Versus (cuiusdam Scotti) de alphabeto* [SK 12594]; *Disticha Catonis*; pseudo-Columbanus (pseudo-Alcuin), *Praecepta uiuendi* [SK 5960]; Bede, *Versus de die iudicii* [*CPL* 1370]; Bede, *Aenigmata* [SK 11204]; Oswald of Ramsey, Latin poem 'On composing verse' [SK 2086a]; Hisperic poems: *Rubisca* [SK 11608; *BCLL* 314]; *Adelphus adelphe* [SK 251; *BCLL* 897]; Greek alphabet and prayers; *Versus in Symbolum* [SK 2593]; medical verses [SK 3618, 11969] and excerpts, mainly from pseudo-Soranus (*Quaestiones medicinales*) and 'Petrocellus' (*Practica Petrocelli*); *Bibliotheca magnifica de sapientia* [SK 9505]; the 'Cambridge Songs' [fifty Latin poems – including five extracts from Statius, Vergil, and Horace – and two macaronic poems in mixed Latin and Old High German], also including twenty-seven extracts from the metres of Boethius, *De consolatione Philosophiae*, and seven Latin religious poems]; poem by pseudo-Vergil [SK 16845]

MS: Hardwick—Luard (1856–67) III.201–5; Ehwald (1919) 50–2, 220–1, 334–5; Weinberger (1934) xvi; McKinlay (1942) 39–41 [no. 66]; Beccaria (1956) no. 70; Lapidge (1975a) 75–6, 84–5, 100 n. 2 [repr. Lapidge (1993a) 113–14, 122–3, 138 n. 2]; Rigg—Wieland (1975) [full list of contents: pp. 120–9]; Bolton (1977a) 54–5; Munk Olsen (1980) no. 83; Fenlon (1982) no. 6; Lapidge (1982a) 99, 103, 105, 108, 113–15, 127 [repr. Lapidge (1996b) 455, 462, 466, 472, 479, 485, 498]; Gibson et al. (1983) 143–7; Clemoes (1985) no. 40; Bischoff (1986) 125; Oates (1986) 413–15; Lapidge (1988a) 49 [repr. Lapidge (1993a) 161]; P.R. Robinson (1988) I, no. 44; Lapidge (1992b) 104, 106–7 [repr. Lapidge (1993a) 94, 96–7]; Vaciago (1993) 4 [no. 9]; Gibson et al. (1995–2001)

I.40–1 [no. 5]; Springer (1995) 43–5; Bergmann (1996) 565 and n. 31;
Gwara (1996a) 93 n. 41; Lendinara (1996) 618 n. 7, 623, 625, 638;
Wieland (1997a) 170; Knappe (1998) 15 n. 44; Lapidge (1998) 32;
Gretsch (1999a) 186; Gneuss (2000–3) 156–9; *ASMMF* IX (2001) 1–31
[no. 96; Doane]; Karkov (2001a) 115 n. 3; R.I. Page (2001) 239–40; J.
Schneider (2003) 297–9; Lapidge (2004a) 141 and n. 21, 142; Lapidge
(2004b) 441 n. 6, 445–6; Dronke (2005b) 402–4; R. Gameson (2005a)
65, 68, 69, 71 n. 2, 73 nn. 27 and 32; Hartzell (2006) no. 13;
Chardonnens (2007b) 545–6; Toswell (2007) 211; Barker-Benfield
(2008) I.50, 53, 54–5, 229–30, 235, 255, 262, 279, 366, 367, 559–60, 595,
610, 614, II.890, 928, 982–3, 1013–14, 1111, 1356–7, 1373, 1374–5,
1376, 1377, 1378, 1379, 1381, 1389, 1392, 1394, 1395, 1396, 1402,
1404–5, 1498, III.1675, 1676, 1680, 1701, 1709–14, 1716, 1752, 1754,
1758, 1764, 1766, 1785, 1817; Petruccione (2008) 232 and n. 9; Graham
(2009) 178; Wieland (2009) 143, 148, 149, 150–1, 156; Banham (2011)
342–3; Binski—Zutshi (2011) 9–11 [no. 6]; R. Gameson (2012a) 83
n. 298; R. Gameson (2012d) 362 and n. 75; Lapidge (2012b) 23, 32;
Rankin (2012) 505 n. 113, 506 n. 117; Scragg (2012a) no. 237

DEC: Ohlgren (1986) no. 224; R. Gameson (1991) 71 n. 68; R. Gameson
(1995b) 11–12; R. Gameson (2005a) 71 n. 2, 73 n. 31; Binski—Zutshi
(2011) 10

FACS: Breul (1915) twenty plates [fols. 432r–441v]; Rigg—Wieland
(1975) pl. I [fol. 53r]; Gibson et al. (1983) pls. IV [fol. 441r], V [*olim*
fol. 442r], VI [*olim* fol. 442v]; Ohlgren (1986) pls. 48–50 [fols. 211r,
218v, 225r]; M. Irvine (1994) 359 [fol. 86r]; Huglo (1987) pls. XXIV–
XXV [fols. 264r, 266v]; *ASMMF* IX (2001) no. 96; Binski—Zutshi
(2011) 10 [fols. 1r, 211r]

ED: Giles (1851) 49 [*Versus in Symbolum* (SK 2593) from this MS], 50–3
[*Bibliotheca magnifica de sapientia* (SK 9509) from this MS]; Von
Winterfeld (1899) 116–21 [Abbo of Saint-Germain, *Bella Parisiacae
urbis*, bk. III, coll. as C]; Tupper (1904–5) [Bede, *Aenigmata*, from this
MS]; Ehwald (1919) 97–149 [Aldhelm, *Enigmata*, coll. as C], 350–471
[Aldhelm, *Carmen de uirginitate*, coll. as C]; Strecker (1926)
['Cambridge Songs' from this MS, fols. 432r–441v]; McKinlay (1951)
[Arator, *Historia apostolica*, coll. as C]; Lapidge (1975a) 103–5 [base
text for glossarial poems of medical terminology from Canterbury,
fols. 422v–423r], 106–7 [base text for Oswald of Ramsey, 'On composing verse', fol. 419r] [repr. Lapidge (1993a) 141–3, 144–5]; Lapidge
(1982a) 104 [base text for *Disticha Catonis* I.1–3], 107 [base text for

Prosper, *Epigrammata*, fol. 127r], 110–11 [base text for Iuvencus, *Euangelia* i.1–12, fol. 1v], 115 [base text for *Commentum super Sedulium*, i.1–5, from fol. 53v; all with glosses] [repr. Lapidge (1996b) 463, 469, 474–5, 481]; Dronke et al. (1982) 59–65 [Wulfstan, 'Aula superna poli', fols. 362v–363r], 66–8 ['Terrigenae bene nunc laudent'], 68–74 ['Turgens in terra'], 79–84 [Sapphic stanzas 'Alme facture'], 84–8 ['Dauid regis inclita proles'], 88–92 ['Dauid uates Dei'], 92–4 ['Virgo Dei genitrix']; M.L. Cameron (1983) 154 [incipits for medical items, fols. 423r, 425–31, 445v–446r]; Kitson (1983) 115–20 ['Ciues celestis patrie' coll. as C]; Herren (1987) 94–103 [*Rubisca* coll. as Ca], 104–11 [*Adelphus adelphe* coll. as Ca]; Ziolkowski (1994) [the 'Cambridge Songs' from this MS, fols. 432r–441v]; Bergamin (2005) [Symposius, *Aenigmata*, coll. as g]; Dronke (2005b) 403 ['Cambridge Songs' no. 40], 404 ['Cambridge Songs' no. 27]; Gretsch—Gneuss (2005) 10–14 [*Sancte sator* coll. as G]

ST: Rigg—Wieland (1975); Korhammer (1980) 36; Dronke et al. (1982); Gibson et al. (1983); Kitson (1983) 109–23 [on 'Ciues celestis patrie']; Wieland (1983) [glosses to Arator and Prudentius]; Bradley (1984); Bradley (1985); R.I. Page (1992a); *CPPM* II, no. 3216b [*Praecepta uiuendi*]; M. Irvine (1994) 358–64; M.P. Brown (1996) 138; Knappe (1996) 197–201 [on *Bibliotheca magnifica*]; Wieland (1998) 4–6, 17 n. 27, 19 n. 48, 20 n. 50; *CSLMA* II (1999) 76, 357; Gretsch (1999a) 186; Lapidge (2004a) 140–3 [on 'Ciues celestis patrie']; Hartzell (2006) no. 13 [neumes]; Alcamesi (2007) 154–6, 166–8 [on glosses to *Disticha Catonis*]; Lendinara (2007a) 80; Maion (2007) 505–6, 511–12 [medical texts]; Wittig (2007) 188 [glosses on Boethius]; Ziolkowski (2007) 43 n. 13, 101–2 *et passim*; Petruccione (2008) 232–3, 234–6; Lendinara (2010) 120–1; D'Aronco (2011) 232–3; Godden (2011) 92; Jayatilaka (2011) 105, 106, 107–8, 117; Lendinara (2011a) 487 and n. 42; Gwara (2012) 519–20; Lapidge (2012b) 23–6, 31–5

13. Cambridge, University Library, Hh. 1. 10

s. xi³/⁴, Exeter

Contents: Ælfric, *Grammar*⁺* and *Glossary*⁺*

MS: Hardwick—Luard (1856–67) III.261–4; T.A.M. Bishop (1954–8a) 192, 194; N.R. Ker (1957) no. 17; T.A.M. Bishop (1971) no. 28; Drage (1978) 337–9; Sauer (1978) 36, 93; Clemoes (1985) no. 42; P.R. Robinson (1988) I, no. 48; Conner (1993) 3; R.I. Page (1993a) 10; R. Gameson (1996b) 144 n. 28; Treharne (2003) 161; *ASMMF* XVI

(2008) 61–4 [no. 97; Lucas]; Menzer (2004) 104–7; Treharne (2007b) 17; Graham (2009) 187, 200–1, 202; Scragg (2012a) nos. 239–44

FACS: *ASMMF* XVI (2008) no. 97

LANG: T. Hunt (1991) I.100, 111–18 [French glosses]

ED: Zupitza (1880/2001) [Ælfric, *Grammar* and *Glossary*, coll. as U]; Menzer (2004) 106 [glosses on fol. 67r], 108 [part of fol. 72r]

ST: Buckalew (1978) 153–64

13. 5. Cambridge, University Library, Ii. 2. 1

s. xi/xii or xii in., Canterbury CC

Contents: Priscian *Institutiones grammaticae* (bks. I–XVIII, incomplete) [*CPL* 1546] with gloss; Priscian (?), *De accentibus* [*CPL* 1552] (f)

MS: Hardwick—Luard (1856–67) III.371; N.R. Ker (1964) 30; Gibson (1972) 108; Passalacqua (1978) no. 92; Bursill-Hall (1981) 47 [no. 44.16]; Clemoes (1985) no. 41; Gibson (1993b) 125 and n. 12, 245 and nn. 49, 50; R. Gameson (1999a) no. 30; Barker-Benfield (2008) I.xcv n. 91, II.1335, 1377, III.1820–1; R. Gameson (2008) 69–70; Binski—Zutshi (2011) 15–16 [no. 13]

DEC: Binski—Zutshi (2011) 15–16

FACS: Binski—Zutshi (2011) 16 [fol. 3r]

14. Cambridge, University Library, Ii. 2. 4

s. xi³ᐟ⁴, Exeter

Contents: Gregory (Alfred), *Regula pastoralis*⃰

MS: Hardwick—Luard (1856–67) III.372–3; T.A.M. Bishop (1954–8a) 198; N.R. Ker (1957) no. 19; Horgan (1973); A.F. Cameron (1974) 222; Drage (1978) 340–1; Sauer (1978) 93; Horgan (1981); Clemoes (1985) no. 44; Horgan (1986) 119–24; P.R. Robinson (1988) I, no. 54; Robinson—Stanley (1991) 21; Conner (1993) 3–4; Graham (1991–5b); R. Gameson (1996b) 144 with n. 29; Schreiber (2003) 62–4 *et passim*; Treharne (2003) 161; Treharne (2007b) 17; R. Gameson (2012b) 114 n. 82; Gullick (2012) 298 and n. 24, 299 n. 30; Scragg (2012a) no. 245

DEC: Graham (1991–5b) 636

FACS: P.R. Robinson (1988) II, pl. 21 [fol. 70r]; Robinson—Stanley (1991) pls. 6.1.1.1–2 [fols. 6v–7r]

ED: Carlson (1975) [*Pastoral Care* coll. as I.2]; Carlson (1978) [*Pastoral Care* coll. as I.2]; Schreiber (2003) 191–453 [parts of *Pastoral Care* coll. as U]

ST: R.I. Page (1993a) 103–4; R. Gameson (1998) 242 n. 45

15. Cambridge, University Library, Ii. 2. 11 (with Exeter, Cathedral Library, 3501 (the 'Exeter Book'), fols. 0–7)

s. xi³/⁴, Exeter

Contents: records⁺* (s. xi/xii and later); inventory of Leofric's donations to Exeter*; donation inscription⁺*; gospels with pericope rubrics*; Gospel of Nicodemus*; *Vindicta Saluatoris**

MS: Hardwick—Luard (1856-67) III.384; Bosworth—Waring (1865) xiii–xiv [gospels]; Skeat (1871) vi–vii [gospels]; Bright (1904–6) I.xix–xx [gospels]; Förster (1933a); Förster (1933b); T.A.M. Bishop (1954–8a) 193, 196; N.R. Ker (1957) no. 20; N.R. Ker (1964) 82; N.R. Ker (1962–92) II.807; Morrell (1965) 183–4 [gospels]; Grünberg (1967) 20–8; Gibson (1972) 108; Metzger (1977) 449 [gospels]; Drage (1978) 342–6; Sauer (1978) 93; Scragg (1979) 259; Clemoes (1985) no. 6; P.R. Robinson (1988) I, no. 55; Liuzza (1988) 75–80; Pelteret (1990) nos. 91–134 [list of records]; Dumville (1992a) 120; Conner (1993) 3, 13, 239, 241, 243–4, 249; R.I. Page (1993a) 105; Graham (1991–5a) [donation inscription]; Lapidge (1994b) 133–5, 137; Liuzza (1994–2000) I. xvii–xx; Pelteret (1995) xv–xvi [manumissions]; R. Gameson (1996b) 144; Lenker (1997) 17–18; Parkes (1997b) 124 and n. 105; Rushforth (2001) 142; Treharne (2003) 161; R.M. Butler (2004) 174; N.M. Thompson (2004) 61; J. Hill (2005a) 85–6; Biggs (2007a) 30 [Biggs, Morey]; Treharne (2007b) 17; R. Gameson (2012a) 46 n. 142, 73 and n. 249; Scragg (2012a) nos. 246–64

FACS: P.R. Robinson (1988) II, pl. 22 [fol. 2r]; Brantley (1999) pl. III [fols. 31v–32r]

ED: Thorpe (1842) [base MS (= A) for gospels]; Skeat (1871–87) [gospels coll. as A]; Tupper (1895) [rubrics to gospels coll. as A]; Hulme (1903–4) 591–610 [Gospel of Nicodemus coll. as A]; Bright (1904–6) [gospels coll. as A]; Grünberg (1967) [base MS for gospels]; T.P. Allen (1968) [base MS for Gospel of Nicodemus]; Liuzza (1994–2000) vol. I [gospels coll. as A]; Cross (1996b) [base MS for Gospel of Nicodemus and *Vindicta Saluatoris*]

LANG: Korhammer (1976) 164, 166

ST: K. Sisam (1953a) 145, 202; H.C. Kim (1973); Gneuss (1985) 106–7; Rosenthal (1992) 147; Lapidge (1994b) 133 [booklist]; Cross (1996c) [Gospel of Nicodemus and *Vindicta Saluatoris*]; T.N. Hall (1996) [Gospel of Nicodemus and *Vindicta Saluatoris*]; Lenker (1999) 141–78; N.M. Thompson (2004) 63; J. Hill (2005a) 85; Okasha (2006) 68 [inscriptions]; Thornbury (2011) 299 and n., 301 and n.

16. Cambridge, University Library, Ii. 2. 19, fols. 1–216

s. xi/xii, (prov. Norwich)

Contents: Paulus Diaconus, *Homiliarium* (Easter vigil to fourth Sunday after Epiphany) [companion vol. to no. **24**]

MS: Hardwick–Luard (1856–67) III.388–93; N.R. Ker (1949–53) 12–13 [dated to s. xii in.]; N.R. Ker (1964) 136; Römer (1972b) 34; Clayton (1985) 218; Clemoes (1985) no. 21; M.P. Richards (1988) 104–8 [full list of contents]; R. Gameson (1999a) no. 31; T.N. Hall (2001) 124, 127 [no. 13]; T.N. Hall (2004b) 87, 90, 92, 100–5; T.N. Hall (2007) 236–7; J. Hill (2007a) 86–7, 91–2; Binski–Zutshi (2011) 15 [no. 12]

DEC: Binski–Zutshi (2011) 15

FACS: R. Gameson (1999a) pl. 11 [fol. 1r]; Binski–Zutshi (2011) 15 [fol. 1r]

17. Cambridge, University Library, Ii. 3. 33, fols. 1–194

s. xi/xii, Canterbury CC

Contents: *De natiuitate S. Mariae*; Gregory (?), *Symbolum fidei* [*CPL* 1714 (p. 558)]; Gregory, *Registrum epistularum* (enlarged version) [*CPL* 1714]; *Conuersio Berengarii* [from Gregory VII, *Registrum* VI.17a]

MS: Hardwick–Luard (1856–67) III.435–6; Dodwell (1954) 120; N.R. Ker (1960) 15; N.R. Ker (1964) 29–30; Clemoes (1985) no. 31; P.R. Robinson (1988) I, no. 58; Petzold (1990) 18–19, 22; R. Gameson (1995a) 117 n. 72, 121 n. 94, 142; Binski–Zutshi (2011) 11 [no. 7]

DEC: R. Gameson (1991) 84 n. 120, 93 n. 172; R. Gameson (1995a) 117 n. 72, 142; Binski–Zutshi (2011) 11

FACS: P.R. Robinson (1988) II, pl. 32 [fol. 57r]; Petzold (1990) fig. 5 [fol. 120v]; Binski–Zutshi (2011) 11 [fol. 5r]

ST: Ker (1960) 15; Petzold (1990) 19, 22–3

18. Cambridge, University Library, Ii. 4. 6

s. xi med., Winchester NM, (prov. Tavistock)

Contents: thirty-six Homilies* (mostly by Ælfric)

MS: Hardwick—Luard (1856–67) III.442–6; N.R. Ker (1957) no. 21; N.R. Ker (1964) 188; Pope (1967) I.39–48; T.A.M. Bishop (1971) xv n. 2; Callison (1973); Collins—Clemoes (1974) 319–20; Godden (1979) xlv–xlvii; Hanley (1979); Clemoes (1985) no. 46; Conner (1993) 36; Clemoes (1997) 28–30, 69–82, 109, 112–13; Kleist (2007b) 451; Teresi (2007a) 290–3, 296–7, 299–301; R. Gameson (2012a) 70 and n. 241; Scragg (2012a) nos. 265–8

FACS: Willard (1950)

ED [the order of the following items is that of the manuscript, listed according to the numbering of individual articles in N.R. Ker (1957) 32–4; only the most recent editions are cited]:

art. 1: Godden (1979) 39–40 [Ælfric, CH II, Hom. IV (Second Sunday after Epiphany), lines 289–325, coll. as M; lines 1–288 are missing from M]

art. 2: Clemoes (1997) 241–8 [Ælfric, CH I, Hom. VIII (Third Sunday after Epiphany), coll. as M]

art. 3: Godden (1979) 217–20 [Ælfric, CH II, Hom. XXIII, lines 127–98 (*Alia narratio de euangelii textu*), coll. as M]

art. 4: Godden (1979) 41–51 [Ælfric, CH II, Hom. V (Septuagesima Sunday), coll. as M]

art. 5: Godden (1979) 52–9 [Ælfric, CH II, Hom. VI (Sexagesima Sunday), coll. as M]

art. 6: Clemoes (1997) 258–65 [Ælfric, CH I, Hom. X (Quinquagesima Sunday), coll. as M]

art. 7: Skeat (1881–1900) I.260–82 [Ælfric, *Lives of Saints*, no. XII (Ash Wednesday), coll. as W]

art. 8: Clemoes (1997) 266–74 [Ælfric, CH I, Hom. XI (First Sunday in Lent), coll. as M]

art. 9: Godden (1979) 60–6 [Ælfric, CH II, Hom. VII (First Sunday in Lent), coll. as M]

art. 10: Godden (1979) 67–71 [Ælfric, CH II, Hom. VIII (Second Sunday in Lent), coll. as M]

art. 11: Pope (1967–8) I.264–80 [Ælfric, Supp. Hom. IV (Third Sunday in Lent), coll. as M] art. 12: Clemoes (1997) 275–80 [Ælfric, CH I, Hom. XII (Sunday in Mid–Lent), coll. as M]

art. 13: Godden (1979) 110–20 [Ælfric, CH II, Hom. XII (Sunday in Mid–Lent), lines 1–373 (with distinctive ending), coll. as M]

art. 14: Godden (1979) 121–6 [Ælfric, CH II, Hom. XII (*Secunda sententia de hoc ipso*), lines 374–582, coll. as M]

art. 15: Skeat (1881–1900) I.282–306 [Ælfric, *Lives of Saints*, no. XIII (*De oratione Moysi* in Mid–Lent), coll. as W]

art. 16: Godden (1979) 127–36 [Ælfric, CH II, Hom. XIII (Fifth Sunday in Lent), coll. as M]

art. 17: Godden (1979) 137–49 [Ælfric, CH II, Hom. XIV (Palm Sunday), coll. as M]

art. 18: Clemoes (1997) 290–8 [Ælfric, CH I, Hom. XIV (Palm Sunday), coll. as M]

art. 19: Clemoes (1997) 299–306 [Ælfric, CH I, Hom. XV (Easter Sunday), coll. as M]

art. 20: Godden (1979) 150–60 [Ælfric, CH II, Hom. XV (Easter Sunday), coll. as M]

arts. 21–2: Godden (1979) 161–8 [Ælfric, CH II, Hom. XVI (another sermon for Easter Sunday), coll. as M]

art. 23: Clemoes (1997) 307–12 [Ælfric, CH I, Hom. XVI (First Sunday after Easter), coll. as M]

art. 24: Clemoes (1997) 313–16 [Ælfric, CH I, Hom. XVII (Second Sunday after Easter), coll. as M]

art. 25: Pope (1967–8) I.340–50 [base MS (= M) for Ælfric, Supp. Hom. VII (Fourth Sunday after Easter)]

art. 26: Pope (1967–8) I.357–68 [base MS (= M) for Ælfric, Supp. Hom. VIII (Fifth Sunday after Easter)]

art. 27: Cross—Bazire (1982) 83–9 [base MS (= M) for Hom. 6 (*Feria .II. in Letania maiore*)]

art. 28: Cross—Bazire (1982) 95–9 [base MS (= M) for Hom. 7 (*Feria .III. in Letania maiore*)]

art. 29: Clemoes (1997) 317–24 [Ælfric, CH I, Hom. XVIII (*In Letania maiore*), coll. as M]

art. 30: Godden (1979) 206–12 [Ælfric, CH II, Hom. XXII (*Feria .IIII. in Letania maiore*), coll. as M]

art. 31: Clemoes (1997) 345–53 [Ælfric, CH I, Hom. XXI (Ascension Day), coll. as M]

art. 32: Pope (1967–8) I.378–89 [base MS (= M) for Ælfric, Supp. Hom. IX (Sunday after Ascension Day)] art. 33: Clemoes (1997) 354–64 [Ælfric, CH I, Hom. XXII (Pentecost), coll. as M]

art. 34: Pope (1967–8) I.396–405 [base MS (= M) for Ælfric, Supp. Hom. X (Pentecost)]

art. 35: Pope (1967–8) I.479–89 [base MS (= M) for Ælfric, Supp. Hom. XII (First Sunday after Pentecost)]

art. 36: Clemoes (1997) 317–24 [Ælfric, CH I, Hom. XVIII (*In letania maiore*), lines 14–213, coll. as M]

art. 37: Clemoes (1997) 325–34 [Ælfric, CH I, Hom. XIX (*Feria .III. De dominica oratione*), coll. as M]

LANG: Callison (1973)

ST: Callison (1973); A.F. Cameron (1974) 222; Horsley—Waterhouse (1984) 223; R.I. Page (1993a) 97; J. Hill (1996) 244; Scragg (1998) 79–80, 83 n. 24; Treharne (1998) 235; Proud (2000) 123; Treharne (2000b) 23; Teresi (2007a)

19. Cambridge, University Library, Ii. 6. 32 (the 'Book of Deer')

s. ix or more prob. s. x, prob. Scotland (or Ireland?), (prov: Cistercian abbey of Deer, Aberdeenshire)

Contents: gospels (only parts of Matthew, Mark, Luke; John complete)

MS: Hardwick—Luard (1856–67) III.530–2; Kenney (1929) no. 502; McRoberts (1953) 3 [no. 2]; N.R. Ker (1964) 57; Gamber (1968–88) no. 149; T.J. Brown (1972) 241 n. 5 [repr. T.J. Brown (1993a) 275 n. 146]; K. Hughes (1980) 15, 22–4, 24–5, 36–7; Clemoes (1985) no. 3; Netzer (1994) 111, 242 n. 31; Werner (1997a) 30 n. 38; Geddes (1998) 537–8, 547; Dumville (2007a) 183–212; Dumville (2007c) 185–208; Dumville (2007d) 83–6; Binski—Zutshi (2011) 4–6 [no. 2]; M.P. Brown (2012) 135; R. Gameson (2012a) 42 and n. 116; McKee (2012a) 172

DEC: T.J. Brown (1972) 241 n. 5 [repr. T.J. Brown (1993a) 275 n. 146]; Alexander (1978a) no. 72; K. Hughes (1980) 22–33; Clemoes (1985) no. 3; Ohlgren (1986) no. 72; M.P. Brown (1996) 99; Geddes (1998) 537–49; M.P. Brown (2003c) 236–8; O'Loughlin (2007) 152; I. Henderson (2008); Binski—Zutshi (2011) 4–5

FACS: Stuart (1869) pls. I–XX [fols. 1v, 2r, 3r, 3v, 4r, 4v, 5r, 16v, 17r, 28v, 29r, 29v, 30r, 40r, 41v, 42r, 84v, 85r, 85v, 86r], XXI [details of fols. 44r, 45v, 51v, 66v, 75v, 54v, 76r], XXII [details of fols. 67r, 70v, 71v, 72v, 77r, 83v, 78r, 78v]; K. Hughes (1980) pls. I–III [fols. 4v, 29v–30v, 41v, 51v, 54v]; Ohlgren (1986) no. 2 [fol. 4v]; Geddes (1998) 539–40, 542, 544 [fols. 1v, 4v, 16v, 29v, 41v, 85v, 86r]; M.P. Brown (2007a) pl. 61 [fol. 86r]; Rushforth (2007) 74 [fol. 1v]; Forsyth (2008) colour pls. 1–22 [fols. 1v, 2r, 3r, 3v, 4r, 4v, 5r, 16v, 17r, 28v, 29r, 29v, 30r, 40r, 41v, 42r, 84v, 85r, 85v, 86r, 54v (detail), 71v (detail)]; Binski—Zutshi (2011) 5 [fols. 1v, 29v], 6 [fol. 30r], colour pl. III.2 [fol. 16v]

ED: B. Fischer (1988–91) [gospel excerpts coll. as Hc]

LANG: K. Hughes (1980) 25; Dumville (2007c) 209–10

ST: McBain (1884–5); K.H. Jackson (1972) 7–16; K. Hughes (1980) 15, 22–5, 33–5; *BCLL* (1985) no. 1032; McGurk (1987) 174 [repr. McGurk (1998) no. II]; Ellis—Ellsworth (1994); McGurk—Rosenthal (1995b) 270; M.P. Brown (1996) 148; Saenger (1997) 333 n. 11; Geddes (1998) 545–7; Dumville (2007c) 190–201, 207–8; Dumville (2007d) 86; O'Loughlin (2007) 156–64; Forsyth (2008); O'Loughlin (2009)

20. Cambridge, University Library, Kk. 1. 23, fols. 1–66

s. xi/xii, Canterbury CC

Contents: Ambrose, *Exameron* [*CPL* 123]

MS: Hardwick—Luard (1856–67) III.592–3; Bishop (1949–53) 435–6; N.R. Ker (1960) 15, 29; N.R. Ker (1964) 30; Römer (1972b) 38; Clemoes (1985) no. 10; P.R. Robinson (1988) I, no. 63; Webber (1995) 149 n. 150, 157; Bankert et al. (1997) 14, 18; Gullick (1998c) 179–80 and n. 17; R. Gameson (1999a) no. 39; Binski—Zutshi (2011) 13–14 [no. 10]

DEC: Dodwell (1954) 17; Lawrence (1982) 108; R. Gameson (1995a) 121, 142; Binski—Zutshi (2011) 13–14

FACS: N.R. Ker (1960) pl. 7 [fol. 46r]; Webber (1995) pl. 15 (a) [fol. 45]; Binski—Zutshi (2011) 13 [fol. 3r]

20. 1. Cambridge, University Library, Kk. 1. 23, fols. 67–135

s. xi ex., Canterbury CC

Contents: Ambrose, *De paenitentia* [*CPL* 156]; Augustine (?), *De utilitate agendae paenitentiae* [*Sermo* cccli: *CPL*, p. 121]; Augustine, *De utilitate credendi* [*CPL* 316], *De fide et symbolo* [*CPL* 293], *Ad inquisitiones Ianuarii* [*Epist.* liv, lv], preceded by excerpts from Augustine, *Retractationes* [*CPL* 250]; Augustine, *Epistula* cxxvii; pseudo-Augustine, *Sermo* clxxx; Augustine, *De excidio urbis Romae* [*CPL* 312]; pseudo-Augustine, *Sermo de fide* (*Sermo* ccclxxxix); Augustine, *Sermones* cccl, cccxlvi–cccxlviii, cclix

MS: Hardwick—Luard (1856–67) III.592–3; Bishop (1949–53) 435–6; N.R. Ker (1964) 30; Römer (1972b) 38; Clemoes (1985) no. 10; P.R. Robinson (1988) I, no. 63; Webber (1995) 149 n. 150, 157; Gullick (1998c) 179–80 and n. 17; R. Gameson (1999a) no. 40; Webber (2012) 213 and n. 9

DEC: Dodwell (1954) 17; Lawrence (1982) 108; R. Gameson (1995a) 121, 142

FACS: Webber (1995) pl. 15 (b) [fol. 76r]

21. Cambridge, University Library, Kk. 1. 24 (with London, British Library, Cotton Tiberius B. v, fols. 74, 76 + London, British Library, Sloane 1044, fol. 2)

s. viii, prob. Northumbria, prov. Ely s. x; s. x^2, x/xi [records*]

Contents: gospels (Luke, John); records*

MS: Hardwick—Luard (1856–67) III.594–5; J. Wordsworth et al. (1889–1954) I. xxvii; Frere (1934) 224 no. 2; *CLA* II (1935) no. 138; Bischoff—Hofmann (1952) 8 n. [on Tiberius B. v, fol. 76]; N.R. Ker (1957) no. 22; McGurk (1961a) no. 5; McGurk (1962) 28 [repr. McGurk (1998) no. VII]; N.R. Ker (1964) 78; G. Henderson (1982) 29–30; Clemoes (1985) no. 1; A.G. Watson (1987a) 35 and n. 2; Dumville (1992a) 102–4, 120, 122; Marsden (1995) 266; Sole (1998) 132–3; P. Wormald (1999) 191 n. 117; *ASMMF* IX (2001) 32–6, 65–79, 80–1 [nos. 102, 229, 305; Doane]; Keynes (2003) 5 [no. 14]; Hartzell (2006) no. 14; M.P. Brown (2012) 152 and n. 151; R. Gameson (2012a) 42 n. 117 [wrongly cited as Kk. 1. 14]; Scragg (2012a) nos. 269–71

DEC: G. Henderson (1982) 29–31; R. Gameson (1995b) 204; R. Gameson (2012c) 289 n. 141

FACS: G. Henderson (1982) pls. 8–11 [fols. 186r, 190r (detail), 192r (detail)]; *ASMMF* IX (2001) nos. 102, 229, 305

ED: B. Fischer (1988–91) [gospel excerpts coll. as Eh]

ST: Lenker (1997) 404–6

22. Cambridge, University Library, Kk. 3. 18 (with London, British Library, Cotton Domitian ix, fol. 10?)

s. xi^2, Worcester

Contents: Bede, *Historia ecclesiastica**

MS: Hardwick—Luard (1856–67) III.628; N.R. Ker (1948) 41; N.R. Ker (1949) 29; N.R. Ker (1957) no. 23; N.R. Ker (1964) 206; Clemoes (1985) no. 43; Dumville (1986) 11–12; Robinson—Stanley (1991) 18; Laing (1993) 46; R.I. Page (1993a) 9–10; Graham (1994b) 6–7; O'Brien O'Keeffe (1994) 241; R. Gameson (1999a) no. 41; Bredehoft (2004) 145–6, 151, 169; Rowley (2004) 13–14, 20, 26, 31; R. Gameson (2005a) 94, 101–4; Roberts (2005) 100–2 [no. 22]; Treharne (2007b) 17; Graham (2009) 200, 202–3; Rowley (2011) 24–5; Crick (2012) 184 n. 47; R. Gameson (2012a) 70 and n. 241; Scragg (2012a) nos. 87, 172, 272–4

FACS: Robinson—Stanley (1991) pl. 2.5 [fol. 72v]; Roberts (2005) colour pl. 3 [fol. 8v], pl. 22 [fol. 8v]; Owen-Crocker (2009) fig. 6.21 [fol. 41r]; Rowley (2011) pl. 6 [fol. 8v]

ED: T. Miller (1890–8) [OE Bede coll. as Ca]; J.M. Schipper (1897–9) [OE Bede coll. as Ca, with Latin text based on C. Plummer (1896)]; Whitelock (1974) [chapter-headings to OE Bede]; Dumville (1986) 21–5 [base text (= V) for genealogy, fols. 3v–4r]

LANG: Hofstetter (1987) 316–18; Rowley (2004) 15

ST: N.R. Ker (1937) 28–9; R. Derolez (1954) 6 [Scandinavian runic alphabet on fol. 10r]; Whitelock (1962); R.I. Page (1972–6) 76–9; A.F. Cameron (1974) 221–2; Grant (1974) 113; Buckalew (1978) 164; Greenfield—Robinson (1980) 319–21 [bibliography]; Franzen (1991) 63, 103–4 [glosses in tremulous Worcester hand]; O'Brien O'Keeffe (1994) 247–8; R. Gameson (1996a) 219, 232 n. 118, 237; R. Gameson (1998) 242 n. 46; Collier (2000) 125, 202–3 [tremulous Worcester hand]; Waite (2000) 42–5, 321–53 [annotated bibliography]; Bredehoft (2001) 27; Bredehoft (2004) 145; Rowley (2004) 21–2; Rowley (2011)

23. Cambridge, University Library, Kk. 3. 21

s. xi¹ or xi med., prob. Abingdon

Contents: Boethius, *De consolatione Philosophiae* [*CPL* 878], with commentary [?by Remigius] (redaction K); two rota poems on the Assumption of the Virgin [SK Suppl. 9424a, 17347a]; names of the winds⁺*

MS: Hardwick—Luard (1856–67) III.630; Weinberger (1934) xvi; N.R. Ker (1957) no. 24; N.R. Ker (1964) 2; T.A.M. Bishop (1971) 13 [no. 15]; Bolton (1977a) 40, 55; Wittig (1983) 187; Clemoes (1985) no. 35; Vaciago (1993) 4 [no. 10]; Gibson et al. (1995–2001) I. 44–5; Lapidge (1998) 32–3, 42 n. 46; Wieland (1998) 17 n. 23; R.I. Page (2001) 219–20; Godden (2005) 331, 337–40; Hartzell (2006) no. 15; Wittig

(2010) 250; Binski—Zutshi (2011) 6–7 [no. 3]; Teresi (2011) 415 and n. 4; R. Gameson (2012a) 61 and n. 213, 67–8 and n. 236; Scragg (2012a) nos. 275–6

DEC: R. Gameson (1995b) 203 n. 69; Binski—Zutshi (2011) 6–7

FACS: M. Irvine (1994) 18 [fol. 85r]; Binski—Zutshi (2011) 6 [fol. 1r], 7 [fols. 15v, 103v]

ED: Bolton (1977a) 60–78 [mythological glosses to Boethius coll. as K]; Troncarelli (1981) 38–45 [rhetorical glosses to Boethius coll. as H]; Clayton (1986) 424–5 [poems on the Assumption of the Virgin]

ST: Bolton (1977a) 55; Bolton (1977b); Troncarelli (1981) 3, 36, 49, 156; R.I. Page (1981) 109–11; Graham (1998a) 32; R.I. Page (2001) 222–8; Wittig (2007) 188; Godden (2011) 72–85, 92; Jayatilaka (2011) 117; Teresi (2011) 426–35 [names of the winds]

24. Cambridge, University Library, Kk. 4. 13

s. xi/xii, (prov. Norwich)

Contents: Paulus Diaconus, *Homiliarium* (Septuagesima to Easter vigil, Sanctorale) [companion vol. to no. **16**]

MS: Hardwick—Luard (1856–67) III.658–63; N.R. Ker (1949–53) 13; N.R. Ker (1964) 137; Römer (1972b) 42; Clayton (1985) 218; M.P. Richards (1988) 97–103 [full list of contents]; R. Gameson (1999a) no. 42; T.N. Hall (2001) 124, 127, 129 [no. 14], 134 [no. 15]; T.N. Hall (2004b) 87, 90; T.N. Hall (2007) 234 n. 20, 236–7, 245, 257 n. 101; J. Hill (2007a) 91–2; Binski—Zutshi (2011) 14 [no. 11]; R. Gameson (2012a) 80 n. 281

DEC: Binski—Zutshi (2011) 14

FACS: Binski—Zutshi (2011) 14 [fol. 1r]

ST: Lambert (1969–72) nos. 217a, 309, 911; Römer (1972b) 42; *CPPM* I, nos. 857, 1279, 1475

25. Cambridge, University Library, Kk. 5. 16 (the 'Moore Bede')

c. or after 737, Northumbria, prov. Aachen s. viii ex.

Contents: Bede, *Historia ecclesiastica* [*CPL* 1375]

MS: Hardwick—Luard (1856–67) III.688–9; C. Plummer (1896) I.lxxxix–xci; Lindsay (1912b) 59; *CLA* II (1935) no. 139; M.R. James (1935) 231; Bischoff—Hofmann (1952) 144–5; Lowe (1960) 24 [no. XXXIX];

McGurk (1961b) 6, 8, 10–11 [no. 20] [repr. McGurk (1998) no. V]; D.H. Wright (1964); Bischoff (1966–81) III.160–1; Colgrave—Mynors (1969) xliii–xliv; Bischoff (1976a) 692; T.J. Brown (1982) 115 [repr. T.J. Brown (1993a) 216]; Parkes (1982) [repr. Parkes (1991) 93–120]; Clemoes (1985) no. 30; Bischoff (1986) 124; D.J. McKitterick (1986) 135–7; O'Brien O'Keeffe (1987) 140–2; Bischoff et al. (1988a) 15 n.; P.R. Robinson (1988) I, no. 68; R. McKitterick (1989a) 313; Kiernan (1990) 49–53; Robinson—Stanley (1991) 18; Webster—Backhouse (1991) 19; Parkes (1992) 125 n. 64; Saenger (1997) 334 n. 21; Bischoff (1998—) I, no. 845a; Dumville (1999) 65, 107; Lapidge (2000a) 28; Szarmach (2001) 263–4; W. Schipper (2003) 153; Binski—Panayotova (2005) no. 3 [R. McKitterick]; Lapidge (2006) 41; Rumble (2006b) 4 n. 18; Dumville (2007f) 56, 59–60, 65–6; Lapidge (2008–10) I.xc–xcii, xciv–cxv; M.P. Brown (2012) 158 and n. 173; R. Gameson (2012a) 25 and n. 45, 37, 42 n. 117, 51, 53 n. 182; R. Gameson (2012b) 113 and n. 77; Garrison (2012) 648 and nn. 85, 87

DEC: O'Brien O'Keeffe (1987) 140–2

FACS: Hunter Blair (1959) [complete facsimile]; Lowe (1960) pl. XXXIX (a) [fol. 25r]; Bischoff (1966-81) III, pl. VIII [fol. 128v]; Robinson—Stanley (1991) pl. 2.1 [fol. 128v]; T.J. Brown (1993a) ill. 55 [fol. 70v (details)]; Lapidge (2000a) 28 [fol. 70v (details)]; Binski—Panayotova (2005) 50 [fol. 63r]; M.P. Brown (2007a) pl. 24 [fol. 43v]; Dumville (2007f) 61 [fol. 128v]; Owen-Crocker (2009) fig. 2.3 [fol. 89v]

ED: C. Plummer (1896) [base MS (= M) for Bede, *Historia ecclesiastica*]; Lapidge (2008–10) [Bede, *Historia ecclesiastica*, coll. as M]

LANG: Bullough (1998a) 111, 113 n. 28, 121 n. 60

ST: K. Sisam (1953a) 275–6; Bischoff (1966–81) III.246–7 n. 20; T.J. Brown (1972) 226, 230 [repr. T.J. Brown (1993a) 104, 107]; T.J. Brown (1975) 261, 265 [repr. T.J. Brown (1993a) 155, 170]; R. McKitterick (1986–90) 313; T.J. Brown (1993b) 199; O'Brien O'Keeffe (1994) 222, 227–8, 230–1, 234–7, 245–9; Dumville (2007f); Lapidge (2008b); R. McKitterick (2012) 333

26. Cambridge, University Library, Kk. 5. 32, fols. 49–76

fols. 49–60: 1012×1030, perh. 1021×1022, Canterbury StA?, prov. SW England s. xi^2 (Glastonbury?); fols. 61–72 + 76: s. xi/xii, W England

Contents: fols. 49–60: liturgical calendar; computus material; excerpts from Byrhtferth, *Enchiridion** (s. xi ex.); fols. 61–72 + 76: Dionysius Exiguus, *Cyclus paschalis magnus* [*CPL* 2284], with added annals and obits

MS: Hardwick–Luard (1856–67) III.701–2; J.A. Robinson (1927); F. Wormald (1934) vi; N.R. Ker (1957) no. 26; N.R. Ker (1964) 90; T.A.M. Bishop (1971) xxiii n. 1; Kotzor (1981) I. 302*–304*; Clemoes (1985) no. 25; Gerchow (1988) 221–2, 330–1 [no. 8]; P.R. Robinson (1988) I, no. 69; Dumville (1992a) 51–65; Dumville (1993g) 79–85, 108 n. 128; Baker–Lapidge (1995) xlvi, xvliii, lii, cxxi–cxxii; N. Orchard (1995b) 88 n. 10; McKee (1997); R. Gameson (1999a) no. 44; Liuzza (2001); Chardonnens (2007b) 508, 550; Rushforth (2008a) 33–4 [no. 13]; Binski–Zutshi (2011) 7–8 [no. 4]; Scragg (2012a) no. 277

DEC: R. Gameson (1991) 75; Binski–Zutshi (2011) 7–8

FACS: Binski–Zutshi (2011) 8 [fol. 58r], colour pl. IV.4 [fol. 13v]

ED: F. Wormald (1934) 71–83 [liturgical calendar (no. 6)]; Henel (1937) 122–5 [excerpts from Byrhtferth]; Baker–Lapidge (1995) 180–4 [part of Byrhtferth, *Enchiridion* iii. 3, coll. as K]; Rushforth (2008a) no. 13 [liturgical calendar]

ST: F. Wormald (1971a); Kotzor (1981) I.302*–311*; Lapidge (1988b) 259 n. 30 [repr. Lapidge (1993a) 217 n. 30]; Dumville (1992a) 21, 25, 27, 51–65; Borst (2001) I.292

27. Cambridge, University Library, Kk. 5. 34

s. x ex., prob. Winchester OM or NM, (prov. Glastonbury)

Contents: Augustine, *Quaestiones Euangeliorum* [*CPL* 275] [excerpt, text altered]; Ausonius, *Ephemeris* iii [SK 11338], *Technopaegnion* vi–xiv; three Anglo-Latin poems from Winchester [SK 15226, 5533, 3197]; Remigius Favius (?), *Carmen de ponderibus et mensuris* [SK 12104]; pseudo-Vergil, *Culex, Aetna*

MS: Hardwick–Luard (1856-67) III.703–6; Lapidge (1972) 94–5 [repr. Lapidge (1993a) 234–5]; Römer (1972b) 43; Carley (1987) 204–12; A.G. Watson (1987a) 38 n. 2; Dumville (1993g) 145 n. 26; R. Gameson (2012d) 356 n. 45

ED: R. Ellis (1907) [*Culex* coll. as C]; Goodyear (1965) [*Aetna* coll. as C]; R.P.H. Green (1991) 8–10, 175–83 [Ausonius coll. as D]; Lapidge (1972) 108–37 [repr. Lapidge (1993a) 248–76] [base text for three Winchester poems]

ST: Lapidge (1972) 85–107 [repr. Lapidge (1993a) 225–47] [Winchester poems]; Raios (1983) 85–6 [*Carmen de ponderibus*]; L.D. Reynolds (1983) 437–40

28. Cambridge, University Library, Ll. 1. 10 (the 'Book of Cerne')

c. 820×840, Mercia, prov. Worcester?, (prov. Cerne?)

Contents: prayerbook: Exhortation to prayer* (f); gospel extracts; acrostic poem [SK 412]; 74 prayers and poems, including *Lorica* of Laidcenn mac Baith° [*CPL* 1323; *BCLL* 294; SK 15745] and hymn by (pseudo?-)Hilarius [SK 7445]; breviate psalter; Harrowing of Hell (liturgical drama?)

MS: Hardwick—Luard (1856–67) IV.5–6; Kuypers (1902) ix–xxx; N.R. Ker (1957) no. 27; McGurk (1962) 29 n. 37, 31 [repr. McGurk (1998) no. VII]; N.R. Ker (1964) 49; Gamber (1968–88) no. 175; T.J. Brown (1972) 245–6 n. 2; Dumville (1972); T.J. Brown (1975) 265–6 [repr. T.J. Brown (1993a) 157]; Alexander (1978a) no. 66; T.J. Brown (1980) 13; Bestul (1981b) 4; T.J. Brown (1982a) 115 n. 18 [repr. T.J. Brown (1993a) 216, 286 n. 18]; Bischoff (1983b) 293; Clemoes (1985) no. 2; Lapidge (1986b) 47 [repr. Lapidge (1996b) 143]; Morrish (1988) 517, 522–4; Muir (1988) xxvii–xxviii; P.R. Robinson (1988) I, no. 73; M.P. Brown (1991) 40; Webster—Backhouse (1991) 211 [no. 165]; Dumville (1992a) 101–2; Conner (1993) 61, 131, 160; Vaciago (1993) 4 [no. 11]; M.P. Brown (1996) 28–44, 45–67; M.P. Brown (1997) p. A 34; Deshman (1997) 124; Webster—Brown (1997) 241–2 [no. 124]; Muir (1998) 12–14; Brantley (1999) 55; Dumville (1999) 119; C.A. Jones (1999) 115; Crowley (2000) 123, 144; Franzen (2001b); M.P. Brown (2001b); M.P. Brown (2001c) 51–8; *ASMMF* VII (2000) 4–27 [no. 107; Doane]; Binski—Panayotova (2005) no. 4 [R. McKitterick]; Roberts (2005) 32; M.P. Brown (2007a) 91; Binski—Zutshi (2011) 3–4 [no. 1]; M.P. Brown (2012) 127–8, 138 and n. 76, 158, 162–3; R. Gameson (2012a) 38 and n. 93, 43 n. 123, 51, 53, 90 n. 329; Raw (2012) 460 and n. 1, 461 and nn. 14 and 17, 462–4

DEC: Kendrick (1938) 165–8; Rice (1952) 176; McGurk (1956) 260 n. 1 [repr. McGurk (1998) no. I]; Wheeler (1977); Alexander (1978a) no. 66; Brownrigg (1978) 257; G. Henderson (1982) 54–5 n. 46 [on evangelist miniatures]; D.M. Wilson (1984) 91; F. Wormald (1984c) 21–2; Ohlgren (1986) no. 66; Raw (1990) 200; M.P. Brown (1996) 68–128 [detailed analysis of decoration]; Budny (1999) 266 [fol. 21v]; M.P.

Brown (2007a) 108, 111, 115; M.P. Brown (2007d); Karkov (2009) 211–12; Binski—Zutshi (2011) 3–4; M.P. Brown (2011b) 37, 39–40; Rosenthal (2011) 238–40; N. Edwards (2012) 246 n. 14

FACS: D.M. Wilson (1984) pl. 100 [fol. 31v]; F. Wormald (1984) ills. 29–31 [fols. 21v, 12v, 31v]; Morrish (1988) pls. 1 [fol. 48v], 3 [fol. 3v]; M.P. Brown (1996) pls. I–VI [fols. 21v–22r, 2v, 3r, 12v, 13r, 31v, 32r, 91v], figs. 1–7 [fols. 66v, 56r, 94v, 2r, 21r, 40r, 50v]; Budny (1999) 266 [fol. 21v (detail)]; *ASMMF* VII (2000) no. 107; Binski—Panayotova (2005) 52 [fols. 12v–13r]; Roberts (2005) pl. 4 [fol. 2r]; M.P. Brown (2007a) pls. 50–1 [fols. 21v, 43r]; Owen-Crocker (2009) figs. 7.5 [fol. 31v], 7.6 [fol. 32r], 7.7 [fol. 56r]; Binski—Zutshi (2011) 4 [fols. 2v, 3r], 5 [fol. 12v], colour pls. I.1 [fol. 21v], II.1 [fol. 31v]; R. Gameson (2012) pl. 4.5 [fol. 43r]

ED: Kuypers (1902) 3–198 [diplomatic edition of entire MS]; W. Meyer (1917) [Latin poems and hymns]; Dumville (1972) 376–7 [Harrowing of Hell], 388–9 [acrostic poem], 400–5 [collations of breviate psalter]; Herren (1987) 76–89 [*Lorica* of Laidcenn coll. as C]; B. Fischer (1988–91) [gospel excerpts coll. as Hc]; Gretsch—Gneuss (2005) 11–13 [base MS for *Sancte sator*]

ST: E. Bishop (1918) 142–7, 165–70, 173–4; Kenney (1929) no. 578; Wilmart (1932) 571–7 [*Oratio S. Gregorii*]; Levison (1946) 295–302; Lambert (1969–72) no. 950; F. Wormald (1971b) [repr. F. Wormald (1984) 76–84]; Dumville (1972) 374–406; Dumville (1973) 320–4; McNamara (1973) 219–20; McNamara (1975) 72–4 [no. 60], 98–9 [no. 84], 101–2 [no. 86B]; Contantinescu (1974) 21–3 [psalter extracts and link with Alcuin]; Salmon (1976) 225; M.P. Brown (1986) 127–9; Bestul (1979) 3–4; *BCLL* (1985) nos. 294, 1281, 1286, 1289–99; Muir (1988) xxvii–xxviii; Sims-Williams (1990) 436; C.D. Wright (1993) 46 n. 186, 112; *CPL* (1995) no. 2019; M.P. Brown (1996) 19, 129–61; Corrêa (1996) 290 nn. 15–18; Raw (1997) 145–53; Frantzen (2001b)

29. Cambridge, University Library, Ll. 1. 14, fols. 70–108

s. xi^2 or xi ex.

Contents: *Regula S. Benedicti* [*CPL* 1852]; *Memoriale qualiter*; *Indicium regulae* [on use of hymns]; *Capitulare monasticum*; *Ad clericum faciendum* (pontifical *ordo*)

MS: Hardwick—Luard (1856–67) IV.8–9; Bateson (1894b) 694–5; Morgand (1963) 181–2; Semmler (1963) 507; Gretsch (1973) 384–6; Clemoes

(1985) no. 22; Graham (1998a) 25, 55 n. 9, 60 n. 58; R. Gameson (1999a) no. 45; R. Gameson (2012a) 52

ED: Morgand (1963) 229–61 [*Memoriale qualiter* coll. as S]; Semmler (1963) 515–35 [*Capitulare monasticum* coll. as G7]

ST: Traube (1910) 61, 86; Gneuss (1968) 45–6 n. 14; Gretsch (1974); Mordek (1995) 97–8 [on text-type of *Capitulare monasticum*]; Gneuss (2000) 240–1, 246–7 [on *Indicium regulae*]

30. Cambridge, University Library, Add. 3206

s. xi^2

Contents: Handbook for a confessor* (f); Wulfstan, *Institutes of Polity** (f), '*Canons of Edgar*'* (f)

MS: N.R. Ker (1957) no. 11; Jost (1959) 12; Fowler (1965) 3; Fowler (1972) xv; Clemoes (1985) no. 29; R. Gameson (1999a) no. 14; Rushforth (2004–7) 115; Treharne (2007b) 18 n. 16; Ringrose (2009) 81; Scragg (2012a) no. 224

ED: Jost (1959) 104, 173, 178 [Wulfstan, *Institutes of Polity*, chs. xvii–xviii and xx, coll. as Uc], 178–209 ['*Canons of Edgar*' coll. as Uc]; Fowler (1972) 20 [base MS (- Cu) for '*Canons of Edgar*' 1, 2, 5–8]

ST: Whitelock et al. (1981a) I.313

Cambridge, University Library, Add. 3330: see no. **857**

30. 3. Cambridge, University Library, Add. 4166 no. 2 (tracing)

s. xi ex. or xii^1

Contents: prayer*

MS: Rushforth (2004–7); Gneuss (2008a) 412

30. 4. Cambridge, University Library, Add. 4406 no. 74

s. xi med. – xi$^{3/4}$

Contents: Priscian, *Institutiones grammaticae* [*CPL* 1546] (f)

MS: Gneuss (2003b) 294 [information from M. Gullick]

30. 5. Cambridge, University Library, Add. 4543

s. x^1 (prob. before 930) or x med. or later, Wales, prov. England s. x? (or in Wales throughout the Middle Ages?)

Contents: (Welsh) computus (f), calendar (f)

MS: Quiggin (1911); Lindsay (1912a) 18–19 [no. 5]; Dumville (1987) 160 n. 67; Dumville (1992a) 118; Huws (2000) 9; Ringrose (2009) 204

FACS: Huws (2000) pl. 4

ST: I. Williams (1926–7); Charles-Edwards (2012) 399 and n. 57

30. 7. Cambridge, University Library, Add. 6220 no. 14

s. xi^1

Contents: Augustine, *De Trinitate* [*CPL* 329] (f)

MS: Gneuss (2003b) 294 [information from M. Gullick]

30. 7. 2. Cambridge, University Library, Add. 6220, no. 69

s. xi/xii

Contents: missal (f)

MS: Gneuss (2012) 288 [information from M. Gullick]

30. 8. Cambridge, University Library, Inc. 5. B. 3. 97 [also recorded as Add. 6000], binding slips

s. xi/xii, Canterbury CC?

Contents: gradual (f)

MS: Hartzell (2006) no. 18

Cambridge, University Library, Syn. 6. 54. 7 (7095) (ptd bk): see no. **35**

31. Cambridge, Clare College 17 (N. 1. 2. 2)

s. xi ex. or xii in., England or France, (prov. s. xii$^{2/4}$ England)

Contents: Smaragdus of Saint-Mihiel, *Diadema monachorum*

MS: M.R. James (1905a) 35; Rochais (1953) 252–3; P.R. Robinson (1997b) 78 and n. 21; Graham (1998a) 56 n. 22; R. Gameson (1999a) no. 48; Binski—Panayotova (2005) no. 67 [T. Webber]

32. Cambridge, Clare College 18 (N. 1. 9)

s. xi/xii or xii in., prob. St Albans

Contents: Orosius, *Historiae aduersum paganos* [*CPL* 571]; Iustinus, *Epitome* of Pompeius Trogus, *Historiae Philippicae* [part]

MS: M.R. James (1905a) 36–7; T.A.M. Bishop (1949–53) 439–40; T.A.M. Bishop (1954–8a) 197–8; Gullick (1990) 63, 78 n. 18; R. Gameson (1996b) 154 and n. 77; Gullick (1998d) 7 and nn. 40–4; R. Gameson (1999a) no. 49

DEC: R.M. Thomson (1986a) 36 and n. 47

FACS: Gullick (1998d) pls. 1–2 [fols. 54r (detail), 13r]

34. Cambridge, Clare College 30 pt. i (N. 1. 1. 8)

s. xi^2 or xi$^{3/4}$, Worcester

Contents: Gregory, *Dialogi* [*CPL* 1713]

MS: M.R. James (1905a) 47–50; T.A.M. Bishop (1971) 20 n. 1; Gullick (1996–9a) 90 n. 3; R. Gameson (1999a) no. 50; Binski—Panayotova (2005) no. 22 [T. Webber]; R. Gameson (2005a) 94, 101–4

DEC: C.M. Kauffmann (1975) no. 4; Ohlgren (1986) no. 215; R. Gameson (2005a) 75–6, 78; R. Gameson (2012c) 274 n. 75

FACS: R. Gameson (1996a) pl. 10 [fol. 2r]; Binski—Panayotova (2005) 87 [fol. 2r]; R. Gameson (2005a) fig. 5 [fol. 68r, erroneously labelled 'part II' of MS]

ST: N.R. Ker (1960) 8 n. 2, 20 n. 4; Yerkes (1976a); Yerkes (1977–80) 245 [glosses copied into no. **92**]; Yerkes (1979) xviii; Franzen (1991) 71–2, 75, 81, 123 [tremulous Worcester hand]; R. Gameson (1996a) 218 n., 223–4, 226, 237; Collier (2000) 195, 199

34. 1. Cambridge, Clare College 30 pt. ii (N. 1. 1. 8)

s. xi^2 or xi$^{3/4}$, Worcester

Contents: Defensor of Ligugé, *Liber scintillarum* [*CPL* 1302]; Iulianus Toletanus, *Prognosticum futuri saeculi* [*CPL* 1258]; Alcuin, *De fide sanctae et indiuiduae Trinitatis* (incomplete)

MS: M.R. James (1905a) 47–50; T.A.M. Bishop (1971) 20 n. 1; Hillgarth (1976) xxvi; R. Gameson (1999a) no. 51; Binski—Panayotova (2005) no. 22 [T. Webber]

ST: *CSLMA* II (1999) 134–9 [Alcuin]; Bremmer (2008)

35. Cambridge, Clare College, s.n. (pastedowns) (with Cambridge, University Library, Syn. 6. 54. 7 (7095) [ptd bk])

s. xi ex. or xii in., Bury St Edmunds

Contents: Solinus, *Collectanea* (f)

MS: Guy (1972–6); L.D. Reynolds (1983) xxxv and n. 168; Dumville (1993g) 78–9 n. 360; R. Gameson (1999a) no. 52; Gneuss (2003b) 295

FACS: Guy (1972–6) pl. facing p. 67 [fols. 3r, 4v, 5v, 7r]

36. Cambridge, Corpus Christi College, 9

xi$^{3/4}$, Worcester

Contents: pp. 1–60: liturgical calendar, *computistica* and Easter tables: s. xi^2; four additional Vitae (s. xi ex. and xii in., Worcester); pp. 61–458 (with London, BL, Cotton Nero E. i, vol. ii, fols. 166-180): Office legendary (October–December) [companion vol. to no. **344**]: s. xi$^{3/4}$

MS: M.R. James (1912) I.21–30; Levison (1919–20) 545, 573; N.R. Ker (1939–40); N.R. Ker (1940) 82; Colgrave (1956) 21–3; N.R. Ker (1957) no. 29; N.R. Ker (1960) 53; T.A.M. Bishop (1971) 20; McIntyre (1978); Kotzor (1981) I. 277*–278*, 302*–311*; Dumville (1992a); Budny (1993) 27; Jackson—Lapidge (1996) 141–3 [complete list of contents]; Budny (1997) I.609–22 [no. 41]; R. Gameson (1999a) no. 54; R. Gameson (2005a) 92, 101–4; Chardonnens (2007b) 503, 549; T.N. Hall (2007) 247–50; Upchurch (2007) 29–32, 111; Rushforth (2008a) 43–4; R. Gameson (2012a) 87 n. 316; Rushforth (2012) 209 n. 74; Scragg (2012a) nos. 21–2

DEC: Budny (1997) I.618–22 [inventory of decoration and illustration]

FACS: Budny (1993) pl. 4 [fol. 13r]; Budny (1997) II, pls. 560–87 [fols. 1r, 1v, 9r, 10r, 11r, 12r, 13r, 19r, 64r, 64v, 70v, 96r, 115v, 131r, 134v, 136v, 149v, 162r, 166r, 181r, 181v, 182v, 185r, 189r, 202r, 217v]

ED: F. Wormald (1934) 225–37 [liturgical calendar (no. 18)]; Gerchow (1988) 226–7 [no. 12] [obits]; Love (1996) [*Vita S. Rumwoldi* coll. as C]; Upchurch (2007) 172–248 [*Passio S. Caeciliae* coll. as C]; Rushforth (2008a) no. 20 [liturgical calendar]

ST: Zettel (1982); Baker—Lapidge (1995) lii [*computistica*]; Love (1996) xviii–xxiii, clxxiv–clxxv; Biggs et al. (2001) 123–5, 407–8 *et passim*; Borst (2001) I.292

37. Cambridge, Corpus Christi College, 12

s. x^2, Worcester?, (prov. ibid.)

Contents: Gregory (Alfred), *Regula pastoralis**

MS: M.R. James (1912) I.32–3; K. Sisam (1953a) 145–7, 228; N.R. Ker (1957) no. 30; Horgan (1973) 153–4; Horgan (1986) 114–16; Robinson—Stanley (1991) 21; Budny (1993) 24–5, 28–9; R.I. Page (1993a) 103–4; Budny (1997) I.187–93 [no. 13]; Collier (2000) 202; W. Schipper (2003) 159–61; Schreiber (2003) 55–7; Karkov (2004) 101; Graham (2009) 183–4, 191; R. Gameson (2012a) 23, 24 and n. 40; D. Ganz (2012) 195 and n. 43; Scragg (2012a) nos. 21–2

DEC: Budny (1993) 28–9; Budny (1997) I.193 [inventory of decoration]

FACS: Horgan (1986) 108 [fol. 1r]; Robinson—Stanley (1991) pls. 6.1.2.1–2 [fols. 3v–4r], 6.2.1.1–2 [fols. 224v–225r]; O'Brien O'Keeffe (1985a) pl. VI (a) [fol. 3r (detail)]; Budny (1993) pl. 3 [fol. 3r]; Budny (1997) II, pl. 153 [fol. 4r]; Owen-Crocker (2009) figs. 2.8 [fol. 4r], 6.13 [fol. 3r]

ED: Carlson (1975–8) [OE *Pastoral Care* coll. as C12]; Schreiber (2003) 191–453 [base text (= C) for edition of parts of the OE *Pastoral Care* (prose preface, metrical preface, chs. i–iv, xix–xxvi, xxxvi–xxxvii, xlvii–lvi, lxv, metrical epilogue)]

LANG: Horgan (1981) 221; Budny (1997) I.188

ST: Horgan (1973) 153–69; A.F. Cameron (1974); Horgan (1986); Franzen (1991) 60–3 [glosses]; Laing (1993) 21; Budny (1993) [glosses]; R.I. Page (1993a) 103–4; Lucas (1995) [metrical epilogue]; R. Gameson (1996a) 237; M. Ellis (1998); R. Gameson (1998) 242 n. 45; Collier (2000) 195, 198–200, 202–6 [glossing of tremulous Worcester hand]; Waite (2000) 23–7, 199–226 [bibliography]

38. Cambridge, Corpus Christi College, 23, fols. 1-104

s. x² or x ex. or xi in., S England (Canterbury? SW England?), prov. Malmesbury prob. by s. xi¹

Contents: Gennadius, on Prudentius (*De uiris inlustribus* [CPL 957], ch. xiii); Prudentius, *Psychomachia* [CPL 1441], *Peristephanon* [CPL 1443]; epigrams for the basilica of St Agnes by Constantia [SK 2659] and Damasus [SK 4939]; Prudentius, *Contra Symmachum* [CPL 1442] (f); (works by Prudentius with glosses; *Psychomachia* illustrations with OE titles added s. x/xi—xi/xii)

MS: M.R. James (1912) I.44–6; Bergman (1926) xlv–xlvi; Lavarenne (1943–51) I.xxx; T.A.M. Bishop (1949–53) 434–5; N.R. Ker (1957) no. 31; N.R. Ker (1964) 128; R.M. Thomson (1982b) 16; Dumville (1992a) 83; Lapidge (1992d) 146–7 [repr. Lapidge (1996b) 46–7];

Dumville (1993g) 105–6; Vaciago (1993) 5 [no. 13]; Clemoes (1994b) 371–2; Budny (1997) I.275–437 [no. 24]; Wieland (1998) 1, 4, 6–9, 11; Binski—Panayotova (2005) no. 11 [R. McKitterick]; Withers (2007) 72, 74, 287; Graham (2009) 174–5; Scragg (2012a) nos. 24–7

DEC: Stettiner (1905) 17; Rice (1952) 213; F. Wormald (1945) 134 [repr. F. Wormald (1984) 74]; F. Wormald (1952) 60 [no. 4]; E. Temple (1976) no. 48; Ohlgren (1986) no. 153; Raw (1990) 196; R. Gameson (1995b) 8, 10, 37, 93, 186 n. 168, 194; Budny (1997) I.290–437 [inventory of decoration and illustration]; Wieland (1997a) 169 n. 3, 170–1, 175–84; Dodwell (2000) 115; C.M. Kauffmann (2003) 39, 41; Rosenthal (2011) 235

FACS: Stettiner (1905) pls. 31–2 [fol. 7v], 33–4 [fol. 33r], 49–50 [fols. 3v, 4r, 4v, 5r, 5v, 6r, 6v], 51–2 [fols. 8r, 8v, 9r, 10r, 10v, 11r, 11v], 53–4 [fols. 12r, 12v, 13r, 13v, 14r, 14v], 55–6 [fols. 15r, 16v, 17r, 17v, 18r, 18v, 19v], 57–8 [fols. 20r, 20v, 21r, 21v, 23r, 23v], 59–60 [fols. 24r, 24v, 25r, 25v, 26r, 26v, 27r], 61–2 [fols. 27v, 29v, 30r, 30v, 31r, 31v], 63–4 [fols. 32r, 32v, 33v, 34r, 35r, 35v], 65–6 [fols. 36r, 36v, 37r, 37v, 38r, 39v, 40r, 40v, 41v, 42r]; F. Wormald (1945) pls. VII (b) [fol. 13v], VII (c) [fol. 208v]; F. Wormald (1952) pl. 6 (b) [folio not specified]; E. Temple (1976) ills. 155–8 [fols. 2r, 37v, 17v]; R.I. Page (1992a) pl. 2 [fol. 2r]; Dumville (1993g) pls. VIII–IX [fols. 64r, 56v]; Budny (1997) II, pls. 222–95 and V–IX [fols. ii v, 1r, 3v–4r, 5v–13r, 14v–16r, 17v–20r, 21r–25r, 27v–32r, 33r–36r, 37v–39r, 41r, 45r, 63r, 76v, 91r, 95r, 100r, 103v–104r]; Karkov (2001a) pls. III–VIII [fols. 4v, 10v, 11r, 29v, 35r, 7r]; Binski—Panayotova (2005) 63 [fols. 17v–18r]; Withers (2007) 72 [fol. 29v]; Owen-Crocker (2009) figs. 5.6 [fol. 7r], 6.8 [fol. 8v]

ED: Zupitza (1876) [OE titles]; Bergman (1926) [Prudentius *carmina* coll. as K]; Lavarenne (1943–51) [Prudentius, *Psychomachia*, coll. as K]; Meritt (1945) [OE glosses]

LANG: Budny (1997) I.279–80

ST: R.I. Page (1973a); R.M. Thomson (1978) 121; Brownrigg (1978) 246 n. 2; Bately (1980) xlix; R.M. Thomson (1982b) 17; Wieland (1985); Wieland (1987); Raw (1990) 196; T. Hunt (1991) I.20; Lapidge (1992d) 146–7 [repr. Lapidge (1996b) 46–7]; R.I. Page (1992a) 79–95; Wieland (1998) 13; Karkov (2001a); Wieland (2001) 181; Menzer (2004) 97 n. 4; Petruccione (2008) 232, 236–8, 247–51

39. Cambridge, Corpus Christi College, 41

s. xi^1; with additions of s. xi^1 – xi med.; prob. S England, prov. Exeter by s. xi$^{3/4}$

Contents: Bede, *Historia ecclesiastica**: s. xi¹; additions (s. xi¹–xi med.):
mass sets (from a sacramentary); Office chants; Old English
Martyrology* (f); charms⁽*⁾; *Solomon and Saturn*** (f); medical recipe*;
six homilies*; Apocalypse of Thomas*; Gospel of Nicodemus*;
prayers; donation inscription⁺* (s. xi³/⁴)

MS: M.R. James (1912) I.81–5; R. Derolez (1954) 401, 420; N.R. Ker
(1957) no. 32; Drage (1978), 310–12; Kotzor (1981) I.89*–108*;
Robinson—Stanley (1991) 18, 22, 24 [arts. 1, 5, 6, 16]; Dumville
(1992a) 67, 70, 90, 130; Conner (1993) 3, 13; Dumville (1993g) 77
n. 350; R.I. Page (1993a) 9–10; Scragg (1996) 211 [arts. 11, 17]; Budny
(1997) I.501–24 [no. 32]; P.P. O'Neill (1997) 139 n. 2, 153 n. 56;
Brantley (1999) 53; P. Wormald (1999) 186 n. 100; Teresi (2000) 109–10;
Frantzen (2001a); *ASMMF* XI (2003) 1–27 [no. 25; Grant]; R.M. Butler
(2004) 213–15; Rowley (2004) 13–14, 20–2, 26, 29–33; N.M. Thompson
(2004) 62–3; Bredehoft (2006) 722–32; Hartzell (2006) no. 20 [margina-
lia]; Jolly (2007) 135, 137–9, 141–6, 154–9; W. Schipper (2007b) 41–2;
Anlezark (2009) 5–6; Graham (2009) 200, 202–3; Scragg (2009b) 71–2;
Wieland (2009) 121; Rowley (2011) 23–4; R. Gameson (2012a) 23, 34
n. 80, 41 and n. 106; R. Gameson (2012b) 108 and n. 53; Scragg (2012a)
nos. 28–32

DEC: F. Wormald (1945) 133 [repr. F. Wormald (1984) 72]; F. Wormald
(1952) 60 [no. 5]; E. Temple (1976) no. 81; Ohlgren (1986) no. 186;
R. Gameson (1991) 71 n. 69; R. Gameson (1995b) 225–6, 228 n. 214,
230; Budny (1997) I.513–24 [inventory of decoration and illustration];
R. Gameson (2012c) 285, 287 n. 133

FACS: F.C. Robinson (1980) three unnumbered plates [pp. 482, 483, 484];
Robinson—Stanley (1991) pls. 2.6 [p. 322], 8.1–3 [pp. 482–4], 12.1.1–3
[pp. 196–8], 19.1 [p. 182], 19.2.1–2 [p. 206], 19.3.1–4 [pp. 350–3]; R.I.
Page (1993a) pl. 8 [fol. 1r]; Budny (1997) II, pls. 396–444 [pp. 1, 61,
124, 131, 161, 175, 206, 212, 224, 229, 230, 233, 246, 248, 251, 252, 253,
254, 256, 259, 261, 264, 266, 268, 272, 273, 276, 282, 285, 289, 292,
298–9, 300, 301, 307, 327, 340, 352, 357, 368, 394, 400, 410, 433, 440,
474, 484, 485, 488]; *ASMMF* XI (2003) no. 25; Jolly (2007), 181–3
[pp. 182, 206–7, 329]; Owen—Crocker (2009) figs. 3.5 [p. 300], 3.6
[p. 272]; Rowley (2011) pls. 4–5 [pp. 422, 324]

ED: T. Miller (1890–8) [OE Bede coll. as B]; J.M. Schipper (1897–9) [OE
Bede coll. as B]; Hulme (1903–4) [base text for Gospel of Nicodemus];
Menner (1941) [*Solomon and Saturn* coll. as B]; Tristram (1970) [base
MS for Homilies for the Assumption and for St Michael (arts. 11, 17)];

Schaefer (1972) [base MS for Homily for Palm Sunday (art. 18)]; Grant (1979) 206–8, 272, 329 [base MS for charms and Latin *liturgica*]; Kotzor (1981) [OE Martyrology coll. as D]; Grant (1982) [base MS for Homilies for the Assumption, St Michael, Palm Sunday (arts. 11, 17, 18)]; Scragg (1992) 87 [Vercelli Hom. IV (art. 9) coll. as D]; Anlezark (2009) 60–4 [base MS for *Solomon and Saturn*]

LANG: Grant (1989); Rowley (2004) 14–17, 27; Anlezark (2009) 6–12

ST: K. Sisam (1953a) 32–3; H.C. Kim (1973); Hohler (1980); F.C. Robinson (1980) 12–25 [Metrical Epilogue to OE Bede]; Hollis—Wright (1992) 234–6, 239–40 [recipe, charms]; C.D. Wright (1993) 219; O'Brien O'Keeffe (1994) 234, 241, 248; Corrêa (1996) 306; Keefer (1996); Graham (1997a) [Abraham Wheelock]; Franzen (2001b); R.M. Butler (2004) 213–15; Rowley (2004) 11–12, 13, 14, 18, 21–2; Jolly (2007); Anlezark (2009) 12–57 [*Solomon and Saturn*]; Pfaff (2009) 66; Rowley (2011); Scragg (2012b) 559

40. Cambridge, Corpus Christi College, 44

s. xi$^{2/4}$ or xi med. or xi$^{3/4}$, Canterbury (StA or CC?), (prov. Ely)

Contents: excerpt from Amalarius, *Liber officialis* III.i*; pontifical (including litanies and second English coronation *ordo*)

MS: M.R. James (1912) I.88–90; N.R. Ker (1957) no. 33; T.A.M. Bishop (1959–63a) 93–5; N.R. Ker (1964) 40, 78; Brückmann (1973) 403–4; Lapidge (1991a) 63; Dumville (1993g) 122 n. 57; R.I. Page (1993a) 46–7; Vaciago (1993) 5 [no. 14]; Budny (1997) I.675–85 [no. 46]; Parkes (1997b) 102 and n. 8; O'Brien O'Keeffe (1998b) 224 n. 50; Bjorklund (2004) 222; O'Brien O'Keeffe (2006) 265; Barker-Benfield (2008) I.lviii–lix, III.1811; Wieland (2009) 124; R. Gameson (2012a) 87 n. 316; Rankin (2012) 492; Rushforth (2012) 209 and nn. 72–3; Scragg (2012a) nos. 33–4

DEC: Lawrence (1982) 102; R. Gameson (1991) 68 n. 39; Budny (1997) I.684–5 [inventory of decoration]

FACS: R.I. Page (1993a) pl. 28 [fol. 1r]; Budny (1997) II, pls. 616–20 [pp. 82, 209, 210, 331, 358]

ED: Legg (1900) [coronation *ordo*]; Liebermann (1903-16) I.416 [*Iudicium Dei* IX, coll. as Ch]; Trahern (1973) 475–8 [prefatory texts on fols. 1r–v, p. 1]; Lapidge (1991a) 98–102 [litanies]; Graham (1995a) 12–13 [prefatory texts on pp. 12–13]

ST: D.H. Turner (1971) xxx–xxxix [pontifical]; Dumville (1992a) 68, 71–2, 78, 91–4; R. Gameson (1995a) 102 n., 123; Heslop (1995) 64 n.; Nelson — Pfaff (1995) 92; Corrêa (1996) 301 n.; N. Orchard (2002) I.76–7, 104, 106, 108, 141, 204 n. 226; N. Orchard (2005) cxlv, clxxvi, cxciii, 444

41. Cambridge, Corpus Christi College, 57

s. x/xi, Abingdon or Canterbury?, prov. Abingdon

Contents: *Regula S. Benedicti* [*CPL* 1852] with interpolations (and glosses s. xi); Ambrosius Autpertus (pseudo-Fulgentius), *Admonitio* (excerpt from *De conflictu uitiorum et uirtutum*); *Memoriale qualiter*; 'De festiuitatibus anni' (Ansegisus, *Capitularium collectio*, II. 33); *Capitulare monasticum*; Usuard of Saint-Germain-des-Prés, *Martyrologium* (with additions and necrology s. xi med. and later); two formula-letters announcing the death of a monastic priest or deacon [add. in the 1040s]; Smaragdus of Saint-Mihiel, *Diadema monachorum* (incomplete)

MS: Bateson (1894b) 692, 694; M.R. James (1912) I.114–18; N.R. Ker (1957) no. 34; Morgand (1963) 179–80; Semmler (1963) 506; N.R. Ker (1964) 2; Gretsch (1973) 28–9; R.I. Page (1979) 29–32; Thacker (1988) 55, 62–3; Lapidge — Winterbottom (1991b) lxi n. 92; Dumville (1992a) 123; Dumville (1993b) 243–4; Dumville (1993g) 8, 76, 136, 153–4; R.I. Page (1993b) 19 [Norse runes]; Vaciago (1993) 5 [no. 15]; Blockley (1994); Mordek (1995) 94–5; Budny (1997) I.439–53 [no. 25]; Graham (1998a) 21–31; Gretsch (1999a) 251–4; *ASMMF* XI (2003) 28–38 [no. 27; Graham]; Gretsch (2003a) 111–13; R.M. Butler (2004) 207–8; N.M. Thompson (2007) 117–18; Wieland (2009) 127; R. Gameson (2012a) 67 n. 232; R. Gameson (2012d) 372 n. 109; D. Ganz (2012) 196 n. 45; Scragg (2012a) nos. 35–9

DEC: F. Wormald (1945) 134 [repr. F. Wormald (1984) 74]; E. Temple (1976) no. 30(x); Ohlgren (1986) no. 127; Budny (1997) I.449–53 [inventory of decoration]

FACS: Dumville (1993g) pl. XV [fols. 85r, 101v]; Graham (1996) 16 [runes on fol. 30v]; Budny (1997) II, pls. 296–320 [fols. 1v, 11v, 12r, 12v, 22r, 37r, 38r, 41r, 49r, 57r, 76v, 85v, 90r, 91v, 92v, 94v, 97v, 108v, 112v, 120v, 144v, 146v, 147r, 160r]; Graham (1998a) pls. 1–10 [fols. 124v, 76v, 97v, 8r, 85r, 102r, 121v, 94v, 5r, 58v]; *ASMMF* XI (2003) no. 27; Owen-Crocker (2009) figs. 2.14 [fol. 120v], 6.10 [fol. 58v]

ED: Morgand (1963) 229–61 [*Memoriale qualiter* coll. as E]; Semmler (1963) 515–35 [*Capitulare monasticum* coll. as G4]; Hanslik (1977) [*Regula S. Benedicti* coll. as g]; Chamberlin (1982) [base MS for *Regula S. Benedicti*]; Gerchow (1988) 252 [formula letters], 335–8 [obits in martyrology]

ST: Traube (1910) 120–1; Morgand (1955) 765–74; Meyvaert (1963) 98, 100, 102, 110; Gretsch (1974) 126–8; Rella (1977) 56; Keynes (1980) 239 n. 22; Gerchow (1988) 245–52 [no. 18]; Cross (1992b); Dumville (1992a) 123 and n. 207; R. Gameson (1996b) 168 n. 160, 175–6; Graham (1996) 17–19; Jayatilaka (1996); Keynes (1996a) 59–60; Graham (1998a) 21–69; Gretsch (2003a); Crick (2011) 7 n. 24; R. McKitterick (2012) 329

42. Cambridge, Corpus Christi College, 69

s. viii ex./ix in. or ix[1], S England

Contents: Gregory, *Homiliae .xl. in Euangelia* [*CPL* 1711], bk. II [*Hom. xxi–xl*]

MS: Schenkl no. 4874; M.R. James (1912) I.148; Lindsay (1915) 450; *CLA* II (1935) no. 121; McGurk (1961b) 10 [repr. McGurk (1998) no. V]; Clayton (1985) 218; Dumville (1987) 150 n. 13; Parkes (1992) 125 n. 64; M.P. Brown (1996) 171–2; Budny (1997) I.89–94 [no. 5]; T.N. Hall (2001) 119, 121 [no. 1]; Étaix (1996) nos. 42, 242, 566; Lapidge (2006) 305; Wieland (2009) 126; M.P. Brown (2012) 165; R. Gameson (2012a) 42 n. 117

DEC: Budny (1997) I.92–4 [inventory of decoration and illustration]

FACS: Budny (1997), II, pls. 25–53 [fols. 1r, 2v, 4r, 4v, 9r, 10r, 11r, 14v, 20r, 20v, 25r, 25v, 29v, 31r, 31v, 32r, 35v, 40v, 41r, 44r, 47v, 48r, 52r, 59r, 62v, 67v, 68r, 72r, 78v]

ED: Etaix (1999) [Gregory, *Homiliae in Euangelia*, coll. as A]

ST: Bischoff (1954a) 138; M.P. Brown (2001b) 282

43. Cambridge, Corpus Christi College, 130

s. xi/xii or xii in., SW England

Contents: *Collectio Lanfranci* [*Concilia, Decreta pontificum*]; Lanfranc, *Epist.* xlix; lists of popes and Roman emperors (added s. xii[1])

MS: M.R. James (1912) I.301–4; Z.N. Brooke (1952) 78, 231–5; S. Williams (1971) 80; Clover — Gibson (1979) 17; Webber (1992) 48; R. Gameson

(1999a) no. 57; Kéry (1999) 116, 239–43 [contents, with full bibliography]; Gullick (2001) 105–7; Barker-Benfield (2008) III.1728, 1822

FACS: Gullick (2001) pl. 35 [fol. 7v]

ED: Clover—Gibson (1979) 154–60 [*Ep.* xlix coll. as Cc]

44. Cambridge, Corpus Christi College, 140 (with Cambridge, Corpus Christi College 111, pp. 7–8, 55–6)

s. xi¹, xi², s. xi/xii, Bath [all parts]

Contents: gospels* (s. xi¹); manumissions*; homily*; lists of popes and English bishops (s. xi/xii); list of relics*; agreement of confraternity* (s. xi²)

MS: Bosworth (1865) xiii; Skeat (1871) v–vi [colophon]; Bright (1904–6) I.xv–xvi; M.R. James (1912) I.236–48, 323–6; N.R. Ker (1957) no. 35; Abel (1962) 324–54; Morrell (1965) 183; Metzger (1977) 448–9; P.R. Robinson (1978) 234 [repr. P.R. Robinson (1994) 29]; Scragg (1979) 257; Dumville (1988) 61; Pelteret (1990) 90–5 [nos. 70–86]; Dumville (1992a) 120; R.L. Harris (1992) 307; Dumville (1993g) 136 n. 106; R.I. Page (1993a) 5; Liuzza (1994–2000) I.xxv–xxxiii; Keynes (1996a) 56 n. 60 [art. 9]; Budny (1997) I.577–92 [no. 38]; Lenker (1997) 15–16, 34–41; Treharne (1998) 241; Scragg (2009b) 71; R. Gameson (2012a) 44, 87 n. 316; R. Gameson (2012b) 108 and n. 52; Scragg (2012a) nos. 40–55

DEC: Budny (1997) I.583–92 [inventory of decoration]

FACS: Liuzza (1994–2000) I, frontispiece [fol. 45r]; Budny (1997) II, pls. 486–533 [fols. 3v, 4v, 5r, 5v, 6v, 7r, 7v, 9r, 10v, 11v, 12v, 13r, 13v, 14r, 23v, 25r, 26v, 27v, 29v, 35v, 36v, 45r, 50v, 51v, 57v, 58r, 62r, 62v, 63r, 64v, 65r, 70r, 76r, 76v, 78v, 79v, 88v, 90v, 92v, 94r, 102r, 105r, 112v, 116r, 118r, 129r, 131r, 135v]; Owen-Crocker (2009) fig. 3.4 [fol. 1v]

ED: Skeat (1871, 1874, 1878, 1887) [OE gospels coll. as I]; Bright (1904–6) [base MS (= Corp.) for OE gospels]; R.I. Page (1966) 17–21 [art. 5: English bishops list]; Grünberg (1967) [OE gospels coll. as Cp]; Liuzza (1994–2000) I.xxvi–xxx [manumissions; confraternity agreement], I.3–202 [base MS (= Cp) for OE gospels]

LANG: Korhammer (1976) 163–5, 168; Liuzza (1994–2000) II.121–54

ST: R.I. Page (1965a); Keynes (1986b) 210; Pelteret (1990) 79–85 [manumissions (Ker art. 2)], 86 [agreement (Ker art. 3)], 70–2 [lists of relics (Ker art. 7)], 73–7 [manumissions (Ker art. 8)], 78 [confraternity agreement (Ker art. 9)]; Graham (1991–5a) 453–5; Liuzza (1994–2000) vol. II

45. Cambridge, Corpus Christi College, 144

s. ix[1], S. England, prob. SW England, (prov. Canterbury StA)

Contents: two glossaries[+*]

MS: M.R. James (1912) I.330–1; *CLA* II (1935) no. 122; N.R. Ker (1957) no. 36; Pheifer (1974) xxviii–xxxi; Lapidge (1986b) 58 [repr. Lapidge (1996b) 154]; Bischoff et al. (1988a) 22–5; Morrish (1988) 520, 522, 525–6, 528, 537; Webster–Backhouse (1991) 78–9 [no. 63]; R.I. Page (1993a) 99; Gneuss (1994) 66, 71; M.P. Brown (1996) 171–2; Dionisotti (1996) 218, 228, 238, 249; Lapidge (1996c) 415, 441; Lendinara (1996) 627–31; Budny (1997) I.95–108 [no. 6]; Dumville (1999) 116–17; R. Gameson (1999c) 362; Lapidge (2000a) 22; Meaney (2004) 495; C.D. Wright (2006) 199; Dumville (2007d) 83–6; Hines (2007) 73; Barker-Benfield (2008) I.5 n. b, 50, 52, 95, II.1334, III.1759, 1770–1, 1781, 1814; Graham (2009) 180–1; Wieland (2009) 146; Alcamesi (2011) 508 and n. 1; M.P. Brown (2012) 165; R. Gameson (2012a) 38 and n. 93, 43 n. 123

DEC: Brownrigg (1978) 257–8; Budny (1997) I.106–8 [inventory of decoration]

FACS: Bischoff et al. (1988a) [full facsimile of both glossaries]; Webster–Backhouse (1991) 78 [fol. 52r]; R.I. Page (1993a) pl. 58 (a) [fol. 14v (detail)]; Budny (1997) II, pls. 54–79 [fols. 4r, 8r, 8v, 11v, 13v, 16v, 17r, 21r, 28r, 30r, 30v, 31r, 32r, 33v, 37r, 39v, 40r, 43v, 45v, 47r, 48v, 49r, 52r, 52v, 54v]; Lapidge (2000a) 22 [fol. 13v (details)]; Owen-Crocker (2009) figs. 2.6 [fol. 31r], 6.12 [fol. 13v]; Lendinara et al. (2011) pl. XVI [fol. 1r]

ED: Wright–Wülker (1884) 1–54 [Latin-OE glosses only, in both glossaries]; Sweet (1885) 35–107 [Latin-OE glosses in both glossaries]; Hessels (1890) [complete edition of both glossaries]; Lindsay (1921a) [complete ed. of Glossary II only]; Wynn (1962) [Latin-OE glosses in both glossaries]; Sweet–Hoad (1978) 1–101 [Latin-OE glosses in both glossaries]; Gneuss (1994) 74–86 [grammatical terms in Glossary I, coll. as C]

LANG: Kuhn (1939); A. Campbell (1959) [phonology and morphology of OE glosses extensively recorded as Cp]; Karl Brunner (1965) [recorded as Cp or Corp]; Hogg (1992) [recorded as CorpGl]

ST: Sweet (1885) 5–7; Gruber (1904); Schlutter (1908) 432–48; Lindsay (1921b); Pheifer (1974) xxviii–xxx; Kotzor (1981) I.250* n. 314; Milani (1984); Pheifer (1987); Bischoff et al. (1988a) 56–60, 62–3; A.K. Brown (1992) 103–4, 109 [nos. 1, 14]; Pheifer (1992); R.I. Page (1993a) 99; Pheifer (1994) 271, 286–7, 290–5; Dionisotti (1996) 241; Herren (1998) 98–101; R. Gameson (1999c) 362; Gretsch (1999a) 154–6, 197; M.P. Brown (2001b) 282; Dietz (2001) 148; Dekker (2010) 160–2; Alcamesi (2011); Rusche (2011) 402–14

46. Cambridge, Corpus Christi College, 146

s. xi in., Winchester OM (or Canterbury CC?); xi² - xii in. [supplement], Worcester

Contents: pontifical (including litanies and second English coronation *ordo*) and benedictional; supplement [pp. 1–60, 319–30]

MS: Liebermann (1903–16) I.xxi; M.R. James (1912) I.332–5; Hohler (1956) 161; N.R. Ker (1957) no. 37; Brückmann (1973) 405–6; Hohler (1975) 73 and 224 n. 54; Rella (1977) 57; Fenlon (1982) 17–20; Lapidge (1986a) 268; Prescott (1987) 130, 132; P.R. Robinson (1988) I, no. 134; Hartzell (1989) 78 n. 80, 84; Lapidge (1991a) 63; Dumville (1992a) 68, 72–3, 77, 89–94, 151; Dumville (1993g) 72–3; Graham (1995a) 7–8 n. 16; Budny (1997) I.495–9 [no. 31]; Sole (1998) 132; R. Gameson (1999a) no. 58; P. Wormald (1999) 194 n. 133; N. Orchard (2002) I.75; R. Gameson (2005a) 96, 101–4; C.A. Jones (2005a) 111, 122–5, 129; C.A. Jones (2005b) 236–7 n. 50; N. Orchard (2005) ci, cxxix; Foys (2006) 279–80; Hartzell (2006) no. 24; O'Brien O'Keeffe (2006) 265–6; Swan (2007b) 39; Pfaff (2012) 458 and n. 34; Scragg (2012a) no. 56

DEC: R. Gameson (1991) 68 n. 39; Budny (1997) I.499 [inventory of decoration]; C.A. Jones (2005a) 111 [rubrics]

FACS: Huglo (1987) pl. XX [p. 18]; Rankin (1996) pl. 12 [pp. 18, 86, 341]; Budny (1997) II, pls. 388–95 [pp. 63, 159, 165, 204, 19, 20, 54, 322]

ED: Liebermann (1903–16) I.401–9 [*Iudicium Dei*], 435–6 [*Excommunicatio*]; Lapidge (1991a) 103–5 [litanies]

ST: Fenlon (1982) 19 [neumes]; Prescott (1987) 132, 148–55; Rankin (1987) 136 [neumes]; Corrêa (1996) 301 n.; R. Gameson (1996a) 233, 237; Rankin (1996) 338–9, 341, 343, 345–6; Rasmussen (1998) 177, 404; C.A. Jones (2005a) 113, 121 n. 58, 124, 128; C.A. Jones (2005b) 243–5

48. Cambridge, Corpus Christi College, 153

fols. 1–68: s. ix ex. or x$^{1/3}$, Wales [Martianus Capella], supplemented in
England s. x^1; fols. 69–96: s. x^1 or x med. or x$^{3/4}$, S England, perh.
Canterbury [distich and 'Dunchad' commentary]

Contents: Martianus Capella, *De nuptiis Philologiae et Mercurii* with
Welsh glosses, supplemented in England; Latin distich [SK 15723];
'Dunchad' (Martin of Laon?), Commentary on Martianus Capella

MS: M.R. James (1912) I.344–6; Lindsay (1912a) 19–22 [no. 6]; Leonardi
(1959) 464 and n. 113; Leonardi (1960) 20–1 [no. 28]; T.A.M. Bishop
(1964–8c); Rella (1977) 72; Parkes (1983) 139; Dumville (1987) 160
n. 63; Dumville (1992a) 116–17 and n. 150; Dumville (1994a) 137 and
n. 24, 139 and n. 34, 141 and n. 44; Budny (1997) I.109–18 [no. 7];
Wieland (2009) 149; R. Gameson (2012a) 43 n. 122; McKee (2012a) 169
and n. 7; Rushforth (2012) 202 and n. 36

DEC: F. Wormald (1952) 60 [no. 6]; Budny (1997) I.113–18 [inventory of
decoration and illustration]; N. Edwards (2012) 246 and n. 12

FACS: Lindsay (1912a) pls. IX–X [fols. 17r, 67r]; Bishop (1964–8c) pls.
XXI (a) [fol. 18r], XXI (b) [fol. 25v], XXII (b) [fol. 75r]; Budny (1997)
II, pls. 80–101 [fols. 1r, 7r, 14r, 29r, 29v, 30r, 33v, 34r, 35r, 35v, 36r, 36v,
37r, 39v, 45v, 57v, 67v, 69v, 75r, 79r, 82r, 83r]

ST: W. Stokes (1872); W. Stokes (1873); Bradshaw (1889) 281–3; Glauche
(1970) 45–6; C.E. Lutz (1971) 371–2; *BCLL* (1985) no. 1182 [on the
'Dunchad' commentary]; *CSLMA* I (1994) 310–12; McKee (2012b) 340
and n. 7; *CALMA* III. 154 ('Dunchad')

50. Cambridge, Corpus Christi College, 162, pp. 1–138, 161–564

s. x ex. or xi in., SE England

Contents: Homilies* (mostly by Ælfric)

MS: M.R. James (1912) I.363–8; N.R. Ker (1957) no. 38; Pope (1967)
I.22–4; Tristram (1970) 78–87 [esp. for art. 38]; F.C. Robinson (1973)
449; Godden (1979) xxxi–xxxiii; Scragg (1979) 242–3; Clayton (1985)
226; Dumville (1988) 59–61; R.I. Page (1993a) 50–1, 54–5; Scragg (1996)
213 [on art. 55]; Budny (1997) I.463–73 [no. 28]; Clemoes (1997) 13–16;
Parkes (1997b) 139 n. 109; Scragg (1998); Treharne (1998) 235, 242; W.
Schipper (2003) 159; N.M. Thompson (2004) 60, 62 n. 84; Anlezark
(2006) 62 n. 5; Biggs (2007a) 31 [Biggs, Morey], 78 [C.D. Wright], 80

[Lees]; K. Powell (2008); Graham (2009) 202; Scragg (2009b) 61–2, 81; Crick (2012) 181; M. Fox (2012) 60; R. Gameson (2012a) 67 n. 232; R. Gameson (2012b) 107 and n. 48; Scragg (2012a) nos. 57–69

DEC: F. Wormald (1952) 60–1 [no. 7]; Budny (1997) I.470–3 [inventory of decoration and illustration]

FACS: Willard (1950); Pope (1967) I. 312 [p. 275]; R.I. Page (1993a) pls. 39, 56 [pp. 160 (detail), 387]; Budny (1997) II, pls. 332–81 [pp. 1, 30, 44, 52, 66, 79, 97, 109, 125, 161, 174, 184, 206, 207, 237, 243, 252, 257, 274, 284, 298, 301, 305, 322, 333, 335, 341, 343, 347, 351, 365, 382, 391, 398, 403, 422, 432, 441, 472, 483, 490, 491, 508, 516, 524, 530, 547, 553, 563, 564]; Owen-Crocker (2009) fig. 6.19 [p. 531]

ED [the order of the following items is that of the manuscript, listed according to the numbering of individual articles in N.R. Ker (1957) 51–6; only the most recent editions are cited]:

art. 1: Clemoes (1997) 178–89 [Ælfric, CH I, Hom. I (*De initio creaturae*), coll. as F]

art. 2: Clemoes (1997) 325–34 [Ælfric, CH I, Hom. XIX (*Feria .III. De dominica oratione*), coll. as F]

art. 3: Clemoes (1997) 335–44 [Ælfric, CH I, Hom. XX (*Feria .IIII. De fide catholica*), coll. as F]

art. 4: Napier (1901) [base MS for anonymous Homily on the Observance of Sunday]; Lees (1986) 117–23 [base MS for anonymous Homily on the Observance of Sunday]; D. Haines (2010) 126–44 [base MS for 'Letter D']

art. 5: Godden (1979) 180–9 [Ælfric, CH II, Hom. XIX (*Feria .II. in Letania maiore*), coll. as F]

art. 6: Skeat (1881–1900) I.282–306 [Ælfric, *Lives of Saints* no. XIII (*De oratione Moysi* in Mid–Lent), coll. as F]

arts. 7–8: Godden (1979) 110–26 [Ælfric, CH II, Hom. XII (Sunday in Mid–Lent), coll. as F]

art. 9: Godden (1979) 29–40 [Ælfric, CH II, Hom. IV (Second Sunday after Epiphany), coll. as F]

art. 10: Clemoes (1997) 241–8 [Ælfric, CH I, Hom. VIII (Third Sunday after Epiphany), coll. as F]

art. 11: Godden (1979) 41–51 [Ælfric, CH II, Hom. V (Septuagesima Sunday), coll. as F]

art. 12: Godden (1979) 52–9 [Ælfric, CH II, Hom. VI (Sexagesima Sunday), coll. as F] art. 13: Clemoes (1997) 258–65 [Ælfric, CH I, Hom. X (Quinquagesima Sunday), coll. as F]

art. 14: as Skeat (1881–1900) I.260–82, with distinctive introduction [Ælfric, *Lives of Saints*, no. XII (Ash Wednesday), not collated]

art. 15: Clemoes (1997) 266–74 [Ælfric, CH I, Hom. XI (First Sunday in Lent), coll. as F]

art. 16: Godden (1979) 60–6 [Ælfric, CH II, Hom. VII (First Sunday in Lent), coll. as F; the passage at the end of the homily, found only in this MS and marked for deletion, is ptd Godden (1979) 353]

art. 17: Pope (1967–8) I.230–42 [Ælfric, Suppl. Hom. II (*Feria .VI. in prima ebdomada Quadragesimae*), coll. as F]

art. 18: Godden (1979) 67–72 [Ælfric, CH II, Hom. VIII (Second Sunday in Lent), coll. as F]

art. 19: Förster (1932) 53–72 [Vercelli Hom. III coll. as T]; Scragg (1992) 73–82 [Vercelli Hom. III coll. as F]

art. 20: Pope (1967–8) I.248–56 [base MS (= F) for Ælfric, Suppl. Hom. III (*Feria .VI. in secunda ebdomada Quadragesimae*)]

art. 21: Pope (1967–8) I.264 [only the first four words of Ælfric, Suppl. Hom. IV (Third Sunday in Lent) are preserved in this MS]

art. 22: Pope (1967–8) I.288–300 [base MS (= F) for Ælfric, Suppl. Hom. V (*Feria .VI. in tertia ebdomada Quadragesimae*)]

art. 23: Clemoes (1997) 275–80 [Ælfric, CH I, Hom. XII (Sunday in Mid–Lent), coll. as F]

art. 24: Pope (1967–8) I.311–29 [base MS (= F) for Ælfric, Suppl. Hom. VI (*Feria .VI. in quarta ebdomada Quadragesimae*)]

art. 25: Godden (1979) 127–36 [Ælfric, CH II, Hom. XIII (Fifth Sunday in Lent), coll. as F]

art. 26: Assmann (1889/1964) 65–72 [base text (= S^1) for Ælfric, Homily for Friday after the Fifth Sunday in Lent]

art. 27: Godden (1979) 137–49 [Ælfric, CH II, Hom. XIV (Palm Sunday), coll. as F]

art. 28: Schaefer (1972) 18–33 [anonymous homily for Palm Sunday coll. as B]

art. 29: as Assmann (1889/1964) 151–63 [anonymous homily *In cena Domini*; not collated]

art. 30: Förster (1932) 1–42 [Vercelli Hom. I coll. as T]; Scragg (1992) 7–43, odd pages [Vercelli Hom. *De parasceue* coll. as G]

art. 31: Schaefer (1972) 83–114 [anonymous homily for Holy Saturday coll. as B] art. 32: Schaefer (1972) 174–84 [base MS for anonymous homily for Easter Sunday]

art. 33: Clemoes (1997) 307–12 [Ælfric, CH I, Hom. XVI (First Sunday after Easter), coll. as F]

art. 34: Clemoes (1997) 313–16 [Ælfric, CH I, Hom. XVII (Second Sunday after Easter), coll. as F]

art. 35: Luiselli Fadda (1977) 71–99 [Hom. IV (*In Letania maiore*) coll. as C]; Szarmach (1981a) 69–72 [Vercelli Hom. XIX coll. as G]; Bazire—Cross (1982) 16–23 [base MS for Rogationtide Hom. 1 (*Feria .II. in Letania maiore*)]; Scragg (1992) 315–26 [Vercelli Hom. XIX coll. as G]

art. 36: Szarmach (1981a) 77–80 [Vercelli Hom. XX coll. as G]; Bazire—Cross (1982) 31–8 [base text for Rogationtide Hom. 2 (*Feria .III. in Letania maiore*)]; Scragg (1992) 332–43 [Vercelli Hom. XX coll. as G]

art. 37: Bazire—Cross (1982) 47–54 [base MS (= F) for Rogationtide Hom. 3 (*Feria .IIII. in Letania maiore*)]

art. 38: Tristram (1970) 162–72 [base MS for anonymous Ascension Day homily)

art. 39: Clemoes (1997) 354–64 [Ælfric, CH I, Hom. XXII (Pentecost), coll. as F]

art. 40: Clemoes (1997) 365–70 [Ælfric, CH I, Hom. XXIII (Second Sunday after Pentecost), coll. as F]

arts. 41–2: Godden (1979) 213–20 [Ælfric, CH II, Hom. XXIII (Third Sunday after Pentecost), coll. as F]

art. 43: Clemoes (1997) 371–8 [Ælfric, CH I, Hom. XXIV (Fourth Sunday after Pentecost), coll. as F]

art. 44: Godden (1979) 230–4 [Ælfric, CH II, Hom. XXV (Eighth Sunday after Pentecost), coll. as F]

art. 45: Godden (1979) 235–40 [Ælfric, CH II, Hom. XXVI (Ninth Sunday after Pentecost), coll. as F]

art. 46: Clemoes (1997) 410–17 [Ælfric, CH I, Hom. XXVIII (Eleventh Sunday after Pentecost), coll. as F]

art. 47: Godden (1979) 249–54 [Ælfric, CH II, Hom. XXVIII (Twelfth Sunday after Pentecost), coll. as F]

art. 48: Godden (1979) 268–71 [Ælfric, CH II, Hom. XXXI (Sixteenth Sunday after Pentecost), coll. as F]

art. 49: Godden (1979) 271 [Ælfric, *De sancta Maria*, coll. as F]

art. 50: Clemoes (1997) 459–64 [Ælfric, CH I, Hom. XXXIII (Seventeenth Sunday after Pentecost), coll. as F]

art. 51: Clemoes (1997) 476–85 [Ælfric, CH I, Hom. XXXV (Twenty-First Sunday after Pentecost), coll. as F] art. 52: Wenisch (1992) 50–2 [base text for anonymous homily *Nu bidde we eow for Godes lufon*]

art. 53: Clemoes (1997) 520–3 [Ælfric, CH I, Hom. XXXIX (First Sunday in Advent), coll. as F]

art. 54: Clemoes (1997) 524–30 [Ælfric, CH I, Hom. XL (First Sunday in Advent), coll. as F]

art. 55: Tristram (1970) 428–9 [base MS for homily *In die depositionis beati Augustini Anglorum doctoris*]

LANG: Pope (1967) I.23–4; Tristram (1970) 87–98 [art. 38]; Scragg (1994a) 333 n. 30, 342 [south-eastern dialect forms]

ST: Horsley—Waterhouse (1984) 223; Lees (1986) 123–42; M.P. Richards (1988) 88–90; Bately (1993); Budny (1993) 28; S. Irvine (1993) 48–9, 51, 55–6; R.I. Page (1993a) 97–8; J. Hill (1996) 244; Collier (2000) 195; Szarmach (2002) 304; Acker (2004) 122 n. 3, 126, 127 n. 21, 130–1, 135–6; Bjorklund (2004) 229 n. 31; M.P. Richards (2006) 292–3; Treharne (2007a) 260; Healey (2007) 14–15; Scragg (2012b) 558

51. Cambridge, Corpus Christi College, 163

s. xi², prob. xi$^{4/4}$, prob. Worcester (Winchester OM? at or for Nunnaminster?)

Contents: pontifical (*Pontificale Romano-Germanicum*, including litanies); blessings; benediction; hymn [SK 5629]; sermon; parts of Office of the Dead

MS: M.R. James (1912) I.368–9; Andrieu (1931–61) I.96–9; Brückmann (1973) 406–7; Lapidge (1981–5) 20–1, 24–6 [full list of contents]; Lapidge (1991a) 64; Dumville (1992a) 68, 73, 91; R.I. Page (1993a) 51; Nelson—Pfaff (1995) 96; Gullick (1996–9a); Budny (1997) I.593–8 [no. 39]; R. Gameson (1999a) no. 61; Pfaff (2001) 184–6; N. Orchard (2002) I.228–9; R. Gameson (2005a) 94, 101–4; Hartzell (2006) no. 25; O'Brien O'Keeffe (2006) 266

DEC: R. Gameson (1991) 68 n. 39; Gullick (1996–9a) 90–1; Budny (1997) I.597–8 [inventory of decoration]

FACS: Huglo (1987) pl. XIX [p. 43]; Budny (1997) II, pls. 534–49 [pp. 24, 36, 39, 40, 46, 50, 52, 53, 54, 122, 158, 159, 189, 190, 226]

ED: Lapidge (1991a) 106–9 [litanies]; Lapidge (2003a) 137–8 [blessing for St Swithun]; Sansterre (2006) 290 [blessing for St Peter]

ST: Lapidge (1983) 21–2 [comparison with no. **406. 5**]; Rankin (1987) no. 14; Hamilton (2001) 129; C.A. Jones (2005a) 114

52. Cambridge, Corpus Christi College, 173, fols. 1–56

s. ix/x, Wessex, perh. Winchester, prov. Winchester by s. x med., prov. Canterbury CC s. xi ex. or xii in.

Contents: West Saxon royal genealogy* [s. ix/x]; *Anglo-Saxon Chronicle* A* [s. ix/x — xi²]; *Acta Lanfranci* [s. xi ex.]; laws*: *Alfred* and *Ine* [s. x²/⁴]; lists of popes and English bishops [s. x² or x ex. — xii in.]

MS: C. Plummer (1892–9) I.x; II.xxiii–xxvii; M.R. James (1912) I.395–9; Dickins (1952) 6; N.R. Ker (1957) no. 39; T.A.M. Bishop (1964–8b) 247; N.R. Ker (1964) 30, 199; Parkes (1976b) [repr. Parkes (1991) 143–69]; Bately (1980) xxiii; A. Lutz (1981) xxx–xxxi; Dumville (1986) 5; Dumville (1987) 163–4; Morrish (1988) 532–4, 537; P.R. Robinson (1988) I, nos. 135–6; Webster — Backhouse (1991) 258–9 [no. 233]; M.P. Brown (1991) 45; Robinson — Stanley (1991) 22–3; Dumville (1992b) 55–139; Lapidge (1992d) 156 [repr. Lapidge (1996b) 56]; Conner (1993) 54–5, 57–9, 62–77, 79–80; R.I. Page (1993a) 6–7, 60; Dumville (1994a) 144, 147–8, 153; M.P. Brown (1996) 40, 180; Budny (1997) I.151–60 [no. 11]; Sato (1997b); R. Gameson (1999a) no. 62 [additions and revision]; P. Wormald (1999) 163–72; Bredehoft (2001) 221–2; Brown — Farr (2001a) 59; Bredehoft (2004) 150, 151 n. 30, 157–9, 167, 169; Roberts (2005) 48–50; Hough (2006) 114, 115 and n. 8, 116, 132; Rumble (2006a) viii; Biggs (2007a) 17; C. Bishop (2007b) 101–3, 105, 118; Grimmer (2007) 103 n. 5; Graham (2009) 176, 192–4; Scragg (2009b) 75; D. Ganz (2012) 189 and n. 9; Keynes (2012) 542, 552; Scragg (2012a) nos. 70–81; P. Wormald (2012) 533 [no. 1]

DEC: Budny (1997) I.159–60 [inventory of decoration]

FACS: Flower — Smith (1941) [full facsimile of arts. 1–5]; Robinson — Stanley (1991) pls. 14.1.1.1–3 [fols. 26v–27r], 14.2.1–4 [fol. 27r], 14.3.1 [fol. 28v], 14.3.1.1–2 [fols. 28v–29r]; R.I. Page (1993a) pl. 6 [fol. 1r (detail)]; Budny (1997) II, pls. 106–9 [fols. 1v, 13r, 40v, 47r]; Bredehoft (2001) pls. II–III [fols. 1r, 10r], V [fol. 13r]; Roberts (2005) pl. 8 [fol. 15r], p. 51 [fol. 21r]; Hough (2006) pl. 15 [fol. 47r]; M.P. Brown (2007a) pl. 66 [fol. 13v]; Owen-Crocker (2009) figs. 2.7 [fol. 12r], 3.7 [fol. 29v], 4.2 [fol. 28v]

ED: C. Plummer (1892–9) [base MS for A-text of *Anglo-Saxon Chronicle*]; A.H. Smith (1935) [annals for 832–900 from A-text of *Anglo-Saxon Chronicle*]; Dickins (1952) [base MS (= A) for West Saxon royal genealogy]; R.I. Page (1966) 22–4 [lists of English bishops]; A. Lutz (1981) [A-text of *Anglo-Saxon Chronicle* used to supplement G-text]; Bately (1986) [base MS (= A) for A-text of *Anglo-Saxon Chronicle* and lists of popes and English bishops]; Dumville (1986) 21–5 [West Saxon royal genealogy coll. as P]

LANG: A.H. Smith (1935) 13–15; Shannon (1964); Sprockel (1965); Bately (1980) xxxix–xlix; Hofstetter (1987) 396–7; Gretsch (1999a) 319; Gretsch (2000) 98–102, 105; Gretsch (2001) 172; C. Bishop (2007b) 104

ST: C. Plummer (1892–9) II.xxiii–xxvii; R.I. Page (1965a); Dumville (1976) 27–9; Torkar (1976) 320, 326; Greenfield—Robinson (1980) 346–53 [bibliography]; Keynes—Lapidge (1983) 75–81; Keynes (1986b) 210; Kennedy (1989) 2605, 2744–80 [bibliography]; Dumville (1992b) 55–139; Keynes (1999a) [episcopal lists]; M.P. Brown (2001b) 282 [Canterbury School decoration]; Hough (2006) 121, 123–4, 127–32; Treharne (2007a) 262; Tristram (2007) 203 n. 57; Keynes (2012) 542, 552 *et passim*

53. Cambridge, Corpus Christi College, 173, fols. 57-83

s. viii^2, S England, prob. Kent, prov. Winchester from s. ix ex. or x in.?, prov. Canterbury CC

Contents: Sedulius, Letters I and II to Macedonius (s. ix), *Carmen paschale*° [*CPL* 1447], two hymns° [*CPL* 1449]; epigram by Damasus on St Paul [SK 7486]; excerpts from Augustine, *De ciuitate Dei* [*CPL* 313], XVIII. 23, with three versions of Sibylline prophecies

MS: M.R. James (1912) I.399–401; *CLA* II (1935) no. 123; N.R. Ker (1957) no. 40; N.R. Ker (1964) 199; T.A.M. Bishop (1964–8b) 246; Parkes (1976b) [repr. Parkes (1991) 143–69]; Rella (1977) 40 [no. 108]; Lapidge (1982a) 113 [repr. Lapidge (1996b) 477–8]; Sims-Williams (1982) 34; Bischoff (1986) 125 n.; Dumville (1987) 164; Dumville (1992b) 85–139; R.I. Page (1993a) 6–7, 126; Vaciago (1993) 5–6 [no. 16]; Blockley (1994) 80; O'Brien O'Keeffe (1994) 226; M.P. Brown (1996) 40, 171–2; Lapidge (1996c) 415, 441; Budny (1997) I.75–87 [no. 4]; Wieland (1998) 16 n. 23; R. Gameson (1999c) 359; Graham (2009) 171, 175–7; M.P. Brown (2012) 165; R. Gameson (2012a) 28 n. 59, 42 n. 117; Scragg (2012a) no. 82

DEC: Budny (1997) I.84-7 [inventory of decoration and illustration]

FACS: R.I. Page (1982) 155 [fol. 59r]; Budny (1997) II, pls. 10-24 [fols. 1r/57r, 3r/59r, 3v/59v, 12r/68r, 12v/68v, 13v/69v, 14v/70v, 16r/72r, 16v/72v, 17v/73v, 18r/74r, 20v/76v, 24r/80r, 25r/81r, 27r/83r]; Owen-Crocker (2009) fig. 6.9 [fol. 61v]

ST: Bischoff (1954a) 138; Gneuss (1968) 103, 117, 122–3; F.C. Robinson (1973) 449; Parkes (1976a) 166 n. 17 [repr. Parkes (1991) 126 n. 17]; R.I. Page (1979) 43–5; R.I. Page (1982) 154, 156–9; Wieland (1985) 171–2; O'Brien O'Keeffe (1987) 144; Graham (2000a); M.P. Brown (2001b) 282; Lendinara (2003) 96

54. Cambridge, Corpus Christi College, 178, pp. 1–270 + 162, pp. 139–60

s. xi¹, prob. Worcester, (prov. ibid.)

Contents: Ælfric, *Hexameron**, (version of Alcuin's) *Interrogationes Sigewulfi in Genesin**, homilies and homiletic pieces*, *De duodecim abusiuis saeculi**; Ælfric (?), Letter to Brother Edward*; *De infantibus non baptizandis**

MS: M.R. James (1912) I.414–17; N.R. Ker (1949); N.R. Ker (1957) no. 41A; N.R. Ker (1964) 206; Pope (1967–8) I.62–7; Godden (1979) lxviii–lxx; Clayton (1985) 229; Stoneman (1987); Franzen (1991) 49–50; Laing (1993) 22; R. Gameson (1996a) 237; Budny (1997) I.846; Clemoes (1997) 37–40; R.I. Page (1999) 86–7; S. Irvine (2000) 44; Clayton (2002) 265–6; Acker (2004) 122–31; Meaney (2004) 366–8, 370; N.M. Thompson (2004) 62; Clayton (2005) 376–9; Clayton (2007) 32–8; Swan (2007b) 33; Scragg (2009b) 82; Johnson—Rudolf (2010) 3–5; M. Fox (2012) 60–1; Scragg (2012a) nos. 83–8

DEC: Acker (2004) 126–7

FACS: Willard (1950); Pope (1967) II, frontispiece [p. 156]; Stoneman (1987) 79 [p. 142]; R.I. Page (1993a) pls. 57, 60 [pp. 31, 291]; Johnson— Rudolf (2010) fig. 3 [p. 119]

ED [the order of the following items is that of the manuscript, listed according to the numbering of individual articles in N.R. Ker (1957) 60–3; only the most recent editions are cited]:

art. 1: Clemoes (1997) 178–89 [Ælfric, CH I, Hom. I (*De initio creaturae*), coll. as R]

art. 2: Crawford (1921) 33–74 [Ælfric, *Hexameron*, coll. as B]

art. 3 [**CCCC 162, pp. 139–60**]: MacLean (1884) 2–59 [base MS (= C) for Ælfric, *Interrogationes Sigewulfi*]; Stoneman (1983) [Ælfric, *Interrogationes Sigewulfi*, coll. as R]

art. 4 [beginning with CCCC 162, p. 160]: Clemoes (1997) 371–8 [Ælfric, CH I, Hom. XXIV (Fourth Sunday after Pentecost), coll. as R]

art. 5: Clemoes (1997) 325–34 [Ælfric, CH I, Hom. XIX (*Feria .III. De dominica oratione*), coll. as R] art. 6: Pope (1967–8) I.415–47 [Ælfric, Suppl. Hom. XI (Octave of Pentecost), coll. as R]

art. 7: Morris (1867–8) 296–304 [a composite homily *De duodecim abusiuis saeculi*, drawn variously from Ælfric, *Lives of Saints*]

art. 8: Skeat (1881–1900) I.364–83 [Ælfric, *Lives of Saints* XVII (*De auguriis*), lines 1–267, not collated] augmented by Pope (1967–8) II.790–6 [base MS (= R) for Ælfric, Suppl. Hom. XXIX ('Saul and the Witch of Endor')]

art. 9: Pope (1967–8) II.590–609 [base MS (= R) for Ælfric, Suppl. Hom. XVIII (*Sermo de die iudicii*)]

art. 10: Godden (1979) 249–54 [Ælfric, CH II, Hom. XXVIII (Twelfth Sunday after Pentecost), coll. as R]

art. 11: Assmann (1889/1964) 49–64 [Ælfric, Homily for the Common of a Confessor (= Hom. IV), coll. as S¹]

art. 12: Clemoes (1997) 520–3 [Ælfric, CH I, Hom. XXXIX (First Sunday in Advent), augmented with a passage from CH I OE Preface, lines 57–119 (Clemoes (1997) 174–6), both coll. as R]

art. 13: Clayton (2002) 280–2 [Ælfric (?), *Letter to Brother Edward*, coll. as R]; Clayton (2007) [Ælfric (?), *Letter to Brother Edward*, coll. as R]

art. 14: Skeat (1881–1900) II.120–4 [an excerpt, entitled *Qui sunt oratores, laboratores, bellatores*, from Ælfric, *Lives of Saints* XXV, coll. as H]

art. 15: Napier (1888) 154–5 [base MS for anonymous homily *De inphantibus non baptizandis*]

art. 16: Godden (1979) 333 [an extract from Ælfric, CH II, Hom. XXXIX (Feast of Holy Virgins), lines 184–98, coll. as R]

art. 17: Godden (1979) 238–9 [an extract from Ælfric, CH II, Hom. XXVI (Ninth Sunday after Pentecost), lines 108–33, coll. as R]

art. 18: Pope (1967–8) II.676–712 [base MS (= R) for Ælfric, Suppl. Hom. XXI (*De falsis diis*)]

art. 19 (colophon): N.R. Ker (1957) 62; Acker (2004) 122–3

art. 20: Clemoes (1997) 281–9 [Ælfric, CH I, Hom. XIII (Annunciation of B.V.M.), coll. as R]

art. 21: Clemoes (1997) 190–7 [Ælfric, CH I, Hom. II (Christmas), coll. as R]

art. 22: Clemoes (1997) 224–31 [Ælfric, CH I, Hom. VI (Circumcision of the Lord), coll. as R]

art. 23: Godden (1979) 19–28 [Ælfric, CH II, Hom. III (Epiphany), coll. as R]

art. 24: Clemoes (1997) 249–57 [Ælfric, CH I, Hom. IX (Purification of the Virgin), coll. as R] art. 25: Godden (1979) 60–6 [Ælfric, CH II, Hom. VII (First Sunday in Lent), coll. as R]

art. 26: Godden (1979) 137–49 [Ælfric, CH II, Hom. XIV (Palm Sunday), coll. as R]

art. 27: Clemoes (1997) 296–7 [an extract from Ælfric, CH I, Hom. XIV (Palm Sunday), lines 167–93, coll. as R]

art. 28: Clemoes (1997) 299–306 [Ælfric, CH I, Hom. XV (Easter Sunday), coll. as R]

art. 29: Clemoes (1997) 307–12 [Ælfric, CH I, Hom. XVI (First Sunday after Easter), coll. as R]

art. 30: Godden (1979) 206–12 [Ælfric, CH II, Hom. XXII (*Feria .IIII. in Letania maiore*), coll. as R, augmented by Ælfric, Suppl. Hom. XXVa–c (Pope (1967–8) II.755–7), base text (= R)]

art. 31: Clemoes (1997) 345–53 [Ælfric, CH I, Hom. XXI (Ascension Day), coll. as R]

art. 32: Clemoes (1997) 354–60 [Ælfric, CH I, Hom. XXII (Pentecost), lines 1–169, coll. as R]

ST: R.I. Page (1973) 67; A.F. Cameron (1974) 221, 223; J. Hill (1996); *CSLMA* II (1999) 486; Acker (2004) 128–33; Clayton (2005); Alcamesi (2010) 189–91, 200–2

55. Cambridge, Corpus Christi College, 178, pp. 287–457

s. xi¹, prob. Worcester, (prov. ibid.)

Contents: *Regula S. Benedicti*⁺* [*CPL* 1852]; Seven Ages of the World (encyclopedic note)*

MS: Schröer (1885–8) xix–xxi; M.R. James (1912) I.417; N.R. Ker (1957) no. 41B [pp. 63–4]; N.R. Ker (1964) 206; T.A.M. Bishop (1971) 20 [no. 22]; Fowler (1973) xiv; Gretsch (1973) 30–2; W. Schipper (1987); Franzen (1991) 49–51, 124–7; Laing (1993) 22; R. Gameson (1996a) 237; Budny (1997) I.545–56 [no. 35]; Gretsch (1999a) 227; Jayatilaka (2003) 154–7, 182–6; Rumble (2006b) 11 and n. 59, 14 and n. 75; Álvarez López (2007a); Swan (2007b) 33; Teresi (2007a) 308; Wieland (2009) 138; Scragg (2012a) nos. 89–91

DEC: Budny (1997) I.552–6 [inventory of decoration]

FACS: T.A.M. Bishop (1971) pl. XX [p. 302]; R.I. Page (1993a) pls. 38, 40, 57, 60 [p. 291]; Budny (1997) II, pls. 461–3 [pp. 362, 364, 458]; Bjorklund (2004) 225 [p. 291]

ED: Schröer (1885–8/1964) xxi [Seven Ages of the World], 1–133 [base MS for OE Rule of St Benedict]; Schröer (1888/1978) [Latin text of *Regula S. Benedicti* coll. as A]

LANG: Schröer (1885–8) xli–xliv; Rohr (1912); Gretsch (1973) 307–77; Hofstetter (1987) 30–6; Gretsch (1999a) 89–131, 185–225

ST: Gretsch (1974); Tristram (1985) 82 n. 63 [Seven Ages of the World]; Gretsch (1999a) 226–60; Collier (2000) 195, 198 [tremulous Worcester hand]; Jayatilaka (2003) 154–7; Bjorklund (2004) 224

56. Cambridge, Corpus Christi College, 183

934×939, S England, (Wessex? Winchester? Glastonbury?), prov. Chester-le-Street, prov. Durham

Contents: Bede, *Vita S. Cudbercti* (prose) [*CPL* 1379; *BHL* 2019]; excerpts from *Historia ecclesiastica* concerning St Cuthbert (IV. xxix–xxx); lists of popes, of the seventy Disciples of Christ, of English bishops and kings; encyclopedic notes (as in nos. **90** and **451**): on Christ's Incarnation, the Ages of the World, the Ages of Man, the numbers of bones, veins and teeth in humans, the Dimensions of the World, the Temple of Solomon, the Tabernacle, St Peter's in Rome, Noah's Ark, the numbers of books in the Old and New Testament, the number of verses in the Psalms, units for measuring distances, the order of events in the Seven Days of Creation, the site of Jerusalem; glossary[(+*)]; Bede, *Vita S. Cudbercti* (verse) [*CPL* 1380; *BHL* 2020]; Mass and rhymed Office of St Cuthbert, with hymn and (add. s. x) sequence [SK 9224, 7173]; list of ecclesiastical vessels* (s. x); record* (s. xi[2])

MS: M.R. James (1912) I.426–41; Mynors (1939) no. 16; N.R. Ker (1957) no. 42; T.A.M. Bishop (1964–8b) 247; T.A.M. Bishop (1971) 14 no. (b); Dumville (1976) 25–6; Parkes (1976b) 163 [repr. Parkes (1991) 160]; Rella (1977) 50; Piper (1978) 214; Fenlon (1982) 2–6; Backhouse et al. (1984b) no. 6; Keynes (1985a) 180–5; Dumville (1987) 174–5, 177–8; P.R. Robinson (1988) I, no. 137; Raw (1990) 196; Lapidge (1991c) 972–3 [repr. Lapidge (1993a) 22–3]; Dumville (1992a) 18, 75, 106–9, 123, 144; Lapidge (1992d) 157 [repr. Lapidge (1996b) 57]; Conner (1993) 56, 63, 65, 69; R.I. Page (1993a) 99–100; Dumville (1994a) 158; Lapidge (1994b) 113; Gwara (1996a) 97; Lendinara (1996) 626–7; Budny (1997) I.152–8 [no. 12]; Bullough (1998a) 120; Sole (1998) 110–20; Gretsch (1999a) 203, 352–9, 366–8; Puhle (2001) II.123–5 [R. Kahsnitz]; R.M. Butler

(2004) 204–5; Karkov (2004) 63–8; Binski—Panayotova (2005) no. 111
[T. Webber]; Gretsch (2005) 83–95; Hartzell (2006) no. 26; Roberts
(2006) 39; Graham (2009) 179; R. Gameson (2012a) 51 n. 169;
R. Gameson (2012b) 97 and n. 11; D. Ganz (2012) 189–90 and n. 13;
Rankin (2012) 486 and n. 15, 504; Scragg (2012a) no. 92

DEC: Rice (1952) 182–3; Dodwell (1971b) 81, 221 n. 47; F. Wormald
(1971b) 309–10 [repr. F. Wormald (1984) 80]; E. Temple (1976) no. 6;
M. Baker (1978); D.M. Wilson (1984) 156; Ohlgren (1986) no. 84; R.
Gameson (1991) 79 n. 110; Lapidge (1992d) 157 [repr. Lapidge (1996b)
57]; Deshman (1995) 226–7, 233, 244; R. Gameson (1995b) 20, 25,
58–9, 119, 152–3, 180, 183–4, 200, 251, 255–6; Budny (1997) I.167–85
[inventory of decoration]; Gretsch (1999a) 203, 366–7; Karkov (2004)
4, 55–63, 87, 103, 174–5; Karkov (2009) 208, 214; R. Gameson (2012c)
250 and nn. 4, 6 and 9, 251 n. 9, 274, 286

FACS: D.M. Wilson (1984) pls. 192–3 [fols. 6r, 42v (details)], 203 [fol. 1v];
Keynes (1985a) pl. X [fol. 62v]; R.I. Page (1993a) pl. 58 (b) [fol. 70v
(detail)]; Deshman (1995) fig. 142 [fol. 1v]; Budny (1997) II, pls. IV
[fol. 1v], 110–52 [fols. 1v–2r, 5v–6r, 7v–8r, 9v–10r, 11v, 12v, 14r, 15v,
17v, 18v, 19v–20r, 21r, 24v, 26r, 27r, 28r, 28v, 29v, 30v, 31v, 33v, 34v, 36v,
37v, 38v–39r, 39v–40r, 42r, 42v, 44r, 47r, 48r, 49r, 50r, 51r, 52v, 53r, 53v,
54v, 56r, 57r, 70r, 71r, 72r]; Puhle (2001) II.124 [fol. 1v]; M.P. Brown
(2003c) fig. 49 [fol. 1v]; Nees (2003) fig. 3 [fols. 1v–2r]; Karkov (2004)
fig. 4 [fol. 1v]; Binski—Panayotova (2005) 246–7 [fols. 1v, 53r (detail)];
Owen-Crocker (2009) fig. 6.11 [fol. 70r]; R. Gameson (2012) pl. 22.1
[fol. 94r]

ED: Jaager (1935) [Bede, *Vita metrica S. Cudbercti*, coll. as C]; Colgrave
(1940) [Bede, prose *Vita S. Cudbercti*, coll. as C$_1$]; Hohler (1956)
169–75, 181–2, 188–9 [Office and sequence coll. as A]; R.I. Page (1966)
8–12 [episcopal lists]; Dumville (1976) [royal genealogies]; N. Orchard
(1995a) 96–7 [base MS for Mass of St Cuthbert]; Milfull (1996) 253–5
[hymn for St Cuthbert coll. as Cu]; Sole (1998) 140–4 [Office for
St Cuthbert coll. as A]; Dekker (2007) 281–4 [base MS for miscellaneous notes]

LANG: Budny (1997) I.152

ST: J.A. Robinson (1918) 9–14; J.A. Robinson (1923) 53; Colgrave (1940)
20–1; Hohler (1956); R.I. Page (1965b); Gneuss (1968) 113; Hohler
(1975) 221–2 n. 30; Parkes (1976b) 163 n. 4 [repr. Parkes (1991) 160
n. 4]; Keynes (1986b) 210; Bonner (1989b) 393–4; Rollason (1989);
Raw (1990) 196; Sims-Williams (1990) [Six Ages of Man]; R.I. Page

(1993a) 99–100; Corrêa (1996) 300 n. 60; Milfull (1996) 63, 69; Gretsch (1999a) 362–4; Keynes (1999a) [episcopal lists]; Lendinara (2001a) 190 [glosses to Bede]; Bredehoft (2001) 10, 34–5, 178 n. 43 [genealogies]; Hiley (2003) 179 n. 14 [Office of St Cuthbert]; Nees (2003) 355–61; R.M. Butler (2004) 205, 207; Dekker (2007) [miscellaneous notes]; C. Bishop (2007b) 118; Dekker (2010) 164 n. 82

57. Cambridge, Corpus Christi College, 187

s. xi/xii, prob. Canterbury CC, (prov. ibid.)

Contents: Eusebius, *Historia ecclesiastica*, trans. Rufinus [*CPG* 3495]

MS: Siegmund (1949) 78; Dodwell (1954) 120; R. Gameson (1995a) 121 n. 88, 142; Webber (1995) 158; R. Gameson (1998) 243 n. 48; R. Gameson (1999a) no. 63; R. Gameson (2012a) 68

FACS: Rushforth (2007) 56 [fol. 1r]

58. Cambridge, Corpus Christi College, 188

s. xi[1], perh. xi[2/4], (prov. Hereford Cathedral?)

Contents: Ælfric, *Hexameron** (incomplete); *Catholic Homilies* (First Series, expanded)*

MS: M.R. James (1912) I.445–8; N.R. Ker (1957) no. 43; Pope (1967) I.59–62; A.F. Cameron (1974) 228 n. 21; Needham (1976) 12 n. 2; Laing (1993) 22; R.I. Page (1993a) 47–8; Clemoes (1994a) 345; Budny (1997) I.571–5 [no. 37]; Clemoes (1997) 36–7; Parkes (1997b) 138 n. 103; Acker (2004) 128–9; Meaney (2004) 370; Graham (2009) 202; R. Gameson (2012b) 107 and n. 48; Scragg (2012a) nos. 93–4

DEC: Budny (1997) I.575 [inventory of decoration]

FACS: Pope (1967) frontispiece [p. 123]; Budny (1997) II, pls. 484–5 [pp. 32, 394]

ED [the order of the following items is that of the manuscript, listed according to the numbering of individual articles in N.R. Ker (1957) 66–9; only the most recent editions are cited]:

art. 1: Crawford (1921) [Ælfric, *Hexameron*, coll. as C (lacks lines 1–22)]

art. 2: Clemoes (1997) 191–7 [Ælfric, CH I, Hom. II (Christmas), coll. as Q]

art. 3: Clemoes (1997) 198–205 [Ælfric, CH I, Hom. III (St Stephen), coll. as Q] art. 4: Clemoes (1997) 206–16 [Ælfric, CH I, Hom. IV (Assumption of St John the Evangelist), coll. as Q]

art. 5: Clemoes (1997) 217–23 [Ælfric, CH I, Hom. V (Holy Innocents), coll. as Q]

art. 6: Clemoes (1997) 224–31 [Ælfric, CH I, Hom. VI (Circumcision of the Lord), coll. as Q]

art. 7: Clemoes (1997) 232–40 [Ælfric, CH I, Hom. VII (Epiphany), coll. as Q]

art. 8: Clemoes (1997) 241–8 [Ælfric, CH I, Hom. VIII (Third Sunday after Epiphany), coll. as Q]

art. 9: Clemoes (1997) 249–57 [Ælfric, CH I, Hom. IX (Purification of the Virgin), coll. as Q]

art. 10: Clemoes (1997) 258–65 [Ælfric, CH I, Hom. X (Quinquagesima Sunday), coll. as Q]

art. 11: Clemoes (1997) 266–74 [Ælfric, CH I, Hom. XI (First Sunday in Lent), coll. as Q]

art. 12: Pope (1967–8) I.264–80 [base MS (= Q) for Ælfric, Suppl. Hom. IV (Third Sunday in Lent)]

art. 13: Clemoes (1997) 275–80 [Ælfric, CH I, Hom. XII (Sunday in Mid–Lent), coll. as Q]

art. 14: Clemoes (1997) 281–9 [Ælfric, CH I, Hom. XIII (Annunciation of B.V.M.), coll. as Q]

art. 15: Clemoes (1997) 290–8 [Ælfric, CH I, Hom. XIV (Palm Sunday), coll. as Q]

art. 16: Clemoes (1997) 299–306 [Ælfric, CH I, Hom. XV (Easter Sunday), coll. as Q]

art. 17: Clemoes (1997) 307–12 [Ælfric, CH I, Hom. XVI (First Sunday after Easter), coll. as Q]

art. 18: Clemoes (1997) 313–16 [Ælfric, CH I, Hom. XVII (Second Sunday after Easter), coll. as Q]

art. 19: Clemoes (1997) 317–24 [Ælfric, CH I, Hom. XVIII (*In Letania maiore*), coll. as Q]

art. 20: Clemoes (1997) 325–34 [Ælfric, CH I, Hom. XIX (*Feria .III. De dominica oratione*), coll. as Q]

art. 21: Clemoes (1997) 335–44 [Ælfric, CH I, Hom. XX (*Feria .IIII. De fide catholica*) coll. as Q]

art. 22: Clemoes (1997) 360–4 [Ælfric, CH I, Hom. XXII (Pentecost), lines 166–256, coll. as Q]

art. 23: Pope (1967–8) I.415–47 [base MS (= Q) for Ælfric, Suppl. Hom. XI (Octave of Pentecost)] art. 24: Clemoes (1997) 365–70 [Ælfric, CH I, Hom. XXIII (Second Sunday after Pentecost), coll. as Q]

art. 25: Clemoes (1997) 371–8 [Ælfric, CH I, Hom. XXIV (Fourth Sunday after Pentecost), coll. as Q]

art. 26: Clemoes (1997) 379–87 [Ælfric, CH I, Hom. XXV (St John the Baptist), coll. as Q]

arts. 27–8: Clemoes (1997) 388–99 [Ælfric, CH I, Hom. XXVI (SS. Peter and Paul), coll. as Q]

art. 29: Clemoes (1997) 400–9 [Ælfric, CH I, Hom. XXVII (St Paul), coll. as Q]

art. 30: Clemoes (1997) 410–17 [Ælfric, CH I, Hom. XXVIII (Eleventh Sunday after Pentecost), coll. as Q]

art. 31: Clemoes (1997) 418–28 [Ælfric, CH I, Hom. XXIX (St Laurence), lines 1–269, coll. as Q; the remainder is lost]

art. 32: Clemoes (1997) 429–33 [Ælfric, CH I, Hom. XXX (Assumption of B.V.M.), lines 113–273, coll. as Q; lines 1–112 are lost]

art. 33: Clemoes (1997) 434–50 [Ælfric, CH I, Hom. XXXI (St Bartholomew), coll. as Q]

art. 34: Clemoes (1997) 451–8 [Ælfric, CH I, Hom. XXXII (Decollation of St John the Baptist), coll. as Q]

art. 35: Assmann (1889/1964) 24–48 [Ælfric, Homily on the Nativity of the Virgin (= Hom. III), coll. as S[1]]

art. 36: Clemoes (1997) 459–64 [Ælfric, CH I, Hom. XXXIII (Seventeenth Sunday after Pentecost), coll. as Q]

art. 37: Clemoes (1997) 465–75 [Ælfric, CH I, Hom. XXXIV (Dedication of the Church of St Michael), coll. as Q]

art. 38: Clemoes (1997) 476–85 [Ælfric, CH I, Hom. XXXV (Twenty-First Sunday after Pentecost), coll. as Q]

arts. 39–40: Clemoes (1997) 486–96 [Ælfric, CH I, Hom. XXXVI (All Saints), coll. as Q]

art. 41: Clemoes (1997) 497–506 [Ælfric, CH I, Hom. XXXVII (St Clement), coll. as Q]

art. 42: Clemoes (1997) 507–19 [Ælfric, CH I, Hom. XXXVIII (St Andrew), coll. as Q]

art. 43: Clemoes (1997) 520–3 [Ælfric, CH I, Hom. XXXIX (First Sunday in Advent), coll. as Q]

art. 44: Clemoes (1997) 524–30 [Ælfric, CH I, Hom. XL (Second Sunday in Advent), coll. as Q]

art. 45: Assmann (1889/1964) 49–64 [Ælfric, Homily for the Feast of a Confessor (= Hom. IV), coll. as S[1]] art. 46: only two lines of a homily *De die iudicii* remain, which was possibly that ptd Pope (1967–8) II.590–609 [Ælfric, Suppl. Hom. XVIII]

ST: Pope (1931); C.E. Wright (1949–53); K. Sisam (1953a) 175–83; Clemoes (1959b) 234; Harlow (1959); Collins—Clemoes (1974) 319, 325 n. 12; Clemoes (1994a) 351; Graham (2000c) 114 n. 64; Lee (2000) [use of MS by L'Isle]

59. Cambridge, Corpus Christi College, 190, pp. iii–xii, 1–294

s. xi[1], Worcester?, prov. Exeter by xi med.; Exeter additions s. xi med. – xi[2]

Contents [a version of Wulfstan's 'Handbook']: *Poenitentiale pseudo-Theodori*; *Ubi sunt* sermon; Wulfstan's Canon Law Collection (*Excerptiones pseudo-Egberti* (recension B), partial text); texts and excerpts concerned with ecclesiastical law and the liturgy; *Ecclesia sponsa* (excerpts from Atto of Vercelli); *De tribulationibus*; 'Expositio officii sacrae missae'; Ælfric, Latin Pastoral Letters I and II; Wulfstan, Homily VIIIa; benedictions; *Admonitio episcoporum*; Alcuin, *Epist.* xvi (f), xvii, cxiv; *De ecclesiasticis gradibus*; Hrabanus Maurus, *De institutione clericorum* II.1–10; *Ordo Romanus* XIII A; *De ecclesiastica consuetudine* (including excerpts from Amalarius, *Liber officialis* and *Regularis concordia*); *Institutio beati Amalarii* (excerpts from *Liber officialis*); Abbo of Saint-Germain-des-Prés, *Serm.* x, xii, xiii (all abbreviated); chrism service; excerpts from Defensor of Ligugé, *Liber scintillarum* [*CPL* 1302]; Adso, *De Antichristo*; Exeter additions (s. xi med. - xi[2]): hymn [SK 11017]; excerpts from Decreta and Councils, and from *Collectio canonum Hibernensis* [*CPL* 1794]; charm*; Capitula of canons of Councils of Winchester (1070) and Windsor (1070); penitential articles issued after the Battle of Hastings

MS: Bateson (1895); M.R. James (1912) I.452–60; Lindsay (1912a) 32–40 [no. 9(i)]; Fehr (1914/1966) xvii–xix [Fehr], cxxx–cxxxi [Clemoes]; Pope (1931); T.A.M. Bishop (1954–8a) 193–7; Bethurum (1957) 8; N.R. Ker (1957) no. 45A; Aronstam (1974) 14–16; Drage (1978) 156–7, 170–2, 313–16; Dumville (1992a) 40, 134; Conner (1993) 3, 39; Dumville (1993g) 52 n. 228, 55 n. 245; Vaciago (1993) 6 [no. 17]; Lapidge (1994b) 137; Budny (1997) I.535–44 [no. 34]; C.A. Jones (1998a) 235, 237–9, 241–3, 251 n. 72; Cross—Hamer (1999) 55–61; P. Wormald (1999) 214–15, 220–1; Sauer (2000); Bredehoft (2004) 155 n. 41; T.N. Hall (2004a) 94, 97, 108, 110; J. Hill (2004) 321; C.A. Jones (2004) 330–2, 337, 343, 347 n. 89, 351–2; G. Mann (2004) 246 n. 29,

260–1, 264 n. 92; A. Orchard (2004) 66 n. 15; C.A. Jones (2005a) 115–18; C.A. Jones (2005b) 235–9, 246–75, 279–81, 283; Hartzell (2006) no. 27; Frantzen (2007) 40–1, 43–4, 53–6, 61–7; Treharne (2007b) 17; Van Rhijn (2009) ix–xi, xlvi–l, lv–lvi; Wieland (2009) 127, 140; A. Orchard (2012) 696 [no. 2]; Scragg (2012a) nos. 95–8; P. Wormald (2012) 534 [no. 10]

DEC: Budny (1997) I.543–4 [inventory of decoration]

FACS: Dumville (1993g) pl. III [p. iii]; Budny (1997) II, pls. 456–60 [pp. x, 1, 25, 77, 132–3]; Puhle (2001) II.452 [p. 281]; Keynes (2007) pl. I [p. 142]

ED: Thorpe (1840) 277–306 [base MS for *Poenitentiale pseudo-Theodori*]; Napier (1883/1967) 29–32 [Latin homily *De baptisma* coll. as W]; Fehr (1914/1966) 35–57 [Ælfric, Latin Pastoral Letter I to Wulfstan, coll. as O], 58–67 [Ælfric, Latin Pastoral Letter II to Wulfstan, coll. as O]; Bethurum (1957) 169–71 [Wulfstan, *Homily* VIIIa coll. as W], 367–73, odd pages [anonymous Latin *Sermo in Cena Domini ad penitentes* coll. as W]; Whitelock et al. (1981a) II.575–6, 580–1, 583–4 [base MS (= A) for Councils of Winchester, Windsor, Penitential articles issued after the Battle of Hastings]; Cross (1993d) [excerpt from Atto, *Ecclesia sponsa*]; C.A. Jones (1998a) 257–70 [base MS (= O) for *De ecclesiastica consuetudine* and *Institutio beati Amalarii*]; Cross—Hamer (1999) 114–70 [Wulfstan's 'Canon Law Collection' coll. as X]; C.A. Jones (1999) 128–39 [base MS for *Expositio officii*]; T.N. Hall (2004a) 110–13 [base MS for *Admonitio episcoporum*]; Di Sciacca (2007a) [*Ubi sunt* sermon]; Keynes (2007) 174–5 [*De tribulationibus*]; Van Rhijn (2009) 1–133 [*Poenitentiale pseudo-Theodori* coll. as C]

Various of the Latin texts listed above contain occasional OE notes and glosses, listed as follows by N.R. Ker (1957) 70–1:

art. *a*: Thorpe (1840) II.6 [OE gloss to the word *parricidio* in *Poenitentiale pseudo-Theodori*]

art. *b*: Storms (1948) 202–4 (no. 11A) [base MS for OE charm, *Gyf feoh sy underfangen*]

art. *c*: Fehr (1914/1966) 247 [OE gloss to the antiphon *In sudore uultus tui*]

art. *d*: Rhodes (1889) 22, 61 [OE glosses to Defensor of Ligugé, *Liber scintillarum*]

LANG: G.K. Anderson (1941) 5–13

ST: Bateson (1895); Bethurum (1942); Rochais (1950) 294–305; Rochais
(1957b) 207; Clemoes (1960) [on the compilation of this MS and
no. **73**]; Fowler (1963); Frantzen (1983b) 142 nn. 73, 75; *BCLL* (1985)
no. 1183; Cross (1992); Cross (1993d); C.A. Jones (1998a); Cross—
Hamer (1999); *CSLMA* II (1999) 150, 184, 239; C.A. Jones (1999)
[*Expositio officii*]; Sauer (2000) 340; Biggs et al. (2001) 18–19 [Cross,
A. Brown]; Gneuss (2003b) 295 [Abbo]; T.N. Hall (2004a); C.A. Jones
(2004); G. Mann (2004); C.A. Jones (2005a); C.A. Jones (2005b); N.
Orchard (2005) cl–clvi; Valtorta (2006) 48 [Atto of Vercelli]; Di Sciacca
(2007a); Keynes (2007) 172–7, 205–6; Bremmer (2008)

59. 5. Cambridge, Corpus Christi College, 190, pp. 295–420

s. xi med. and xi$^{3/4}$, Exeter; whole MS prov. Exeter

Contents [pp. 319–50, 365–420] (s. xi med.): Ælfric, Pastoral Letters II*
and III*; Ordines for Easter vigil and Whitsun vigil*; penitential
(*Confessionale pseudo–Egberti*)*; excerpt from Chrodegang, *Regula
canonicorum* (enlarged version, ch. 83)*; penitential (*Poenitentiale
pseudo-Egberti*)*; excerpts concerned with confession and penitence*;
Old English Canons of Theodore [Text B]*; laws*: *Mirce, Að, Hadbot*
[pp. 295–318, 351–64] (s. xi$^{3/4}$): Ælfric, Pastoral Letter I*, *Catholic
Homilies* II. xxxvi; *De ecclesiasticis gradibus* [Wulfstan, *Institutes of
Polity* xxiv. 1–52]; two anonymous homilies* [Cameron (1973) nos. B.
3. 2. 9, B. 3. 2. 23]

MS: Liebermann (1903–16) I.xxxv; M.R. James (1912) I.460–3; Fehr
(1914/1966) xiii–xix [Fehr], cxxx [Clemoes]; Spindler (1934) 1–4;
T.A.M. Bishop (1954–8a) 193; Bethurum (1957) 8; N.R. Ker (1957)
no. 45B; Raith (1964) x–xiii; Drage (1978) 317–21; Godden (1979)
lxxii–lxxiii; P.R. Robinson (1988) I, no. 138; Budny (1997) I.535–44;
P. Wormald (1999) 186 n. 100, 203 n. 164, 221–3, 250 (table 4. 9);
Fulk—Jurasinski (2012) xix–xxi; R. Gameson (2012a) 72 n. 246; Scragg
(2012a) nos. 99–105

FACS: Fulk—Jurasinski (2012) pl. 2 [p. 417]

ED [the order of the following items is that of the manuscript, listed
according to the numbering of individual articles in N.R. Ker (1957)
71–3; only the most recent editions are cited]:

art. 1: Fehr (1914/1966) 68 [base MS (= O) for Ælfric, Latin preface to
Pastoral Letter I to Wulfstan]

art. 2: Fehr (1914/1966) 68–144 [Ælfric, OE Pastoral Letter I to Wulfstan, coll. as O]

art. 3: Fehr (1914/1966) 146–220 [Ælfric, OE Pastoral Letter II to Wulfstan, coll. as O]

art. 4: Fehr (1914/1966) 228–31 [base MS for Ælfric, *De officio Missae in Vigilia Pascae*]

art. 5: Fehr (1914/1966) 232–3 [base MS for Ælfric, *De officio Missae in Vigilia Pentecosten*]; followed by a Latin formula of excommunication, ed. Liebermann (1903–16) I.434 (base MS (= O)]

art. 6: Spindler (1934) 170–94 [*Confessionale pseudo-Egberti* coll. as O]

art. 7: Langefeld (2003) 335 [OE version of the Enlarged Rule of Chrodegang, ch. 83, coll. as F]

art. 8: Spindler (1934) 172 (*o–x*) [repetition of a chapter from the *Confessionale pseudo-Egbercti*]

art. 9: Raith (1933/1964) 1–69 [OE *Poenitentiale pseudo-Egbercti* coll. as O]

art. 10: Thorpe (1840) II.222–4 [coll. Spindler (1934) 174 (*z*)]

art. 11: Fulk—Jurasinski (2012) 77–8 [base MS for OE formulas and directions for the use of confessors]

art. 12: Fulk—Jurasinski (2012) 15–16 [base MS for *OE Canons of Theodore*, Text B]

art. 13: Förster (1942a) 14–18 [base MS for OE form of confession and absolution]

art. 14: Liebermann (1903–16) I.462, central column [*Be Mercena lage* coll. as O]

art. 15: Liebermann (1903–16) I.464, central column [*Be Mercena lage* (2) coll. as O]

art. 16: Liebermann (1903–16) I.464–8, central column [*Be gehadendra aðe* and *Hadbot* coll. as O]

art. 17: Fehr (1914/1966) 1–34 [Ælfric, OE Pastoral Letter to Wulfsige, coll. as O]

art. 18: Godden (1979) 304–9 [Ælfric, CH II, Hom. XXXVI (Feast of Several Apostles), coll. as X^a]

art. 19: Raith (1933/1964) 17–19 [*De ecclesiasticis gradibus* coll. as C_1]; Jost (1959) 223–41 [*De ecclesiasticis gradibus* coll. as O]

art. 20: OE *Sermo in capite ieiunii ad populum*: unprinted?

art. 21: Bethurum (1957) 366–72, even pages [base MS (= W) for anonymous OE *Sermo in Cena Domini ad penitentes*]

LANG: Fulk—Jurasinski (2012) xxviii–xxxv

ST: Fehr (1914/1966); Whitelock (1942); Hohler (1975) 223 n. 46; Scragg (1979) 259; Frantzen (1983a) 40–5; Frantzen (1983b) 132–4, 138 n. 57, 142 nn. 73, 75, 164 n. 41, 171 n. 57; Frantzen (1985); R. Gameson (1996b) 149; P. Wormald (1999) 164, 186 n. 100, 203 n. 164, 211 n. 196, 212 n. 199, 214, 219–23, 250, 452 and n. 129, 463 n. 177; Langefeld (2003) 47–50, 62 n. 103; Fulk—Jurasinski (2012) xxxvi–lx

60. Cambridge, Corpus Christi College, 191

s. xi$^{3/4}$, Exeter

Contents: Chrodegang, *Regula canonicorum* (enlarged version)$^{+*}$ (originally or later bound with nos. **62** and **65. 5**)

MS: M.R. James (1912) I.463–4; T.A.M. Bishop (1954–8a) 193–8; N.R. Ker (1957) no. 46; N.R. Ker (1964) 82; T.A.M. Bishop (1971) 24 [no. 28]; Drage (1978) 322–4; P.R. Robinson (1988) I, no. 139; Voigts (1988) 84; R.I. Page (1993a) 92; Lapidge (1994b) 137; Gwara (1998) 145; P. Wormald (1999) 206 n. 167; *ASMMF* XI (2003) 39–47 [no. 39; Graham]; Langefeld (2003) 44–6; Treharne (2003) 161; Bertram (2005) 175–6; Treharne (2007b) 17; Graham (2009) 191, 201; R. Gameson (2012a) 17 and n. 17, 45 and n. 133, 73 and n. 249; Scragg (2012a) nos. 106–8

FACS: Napier (1916) frontispiece [p. 29], opp. p. 70 [p. 114]; T.A.M. Bishop (1971) pl. XXIV [p. 100]; P.R. Robinson (1988) II, pl. 24 [p. 40]; R.I. Page (1993a) pl. 52 [fol. 127r]; *ASMMF* XI (2003) no. 39; Owen-Crocker (2009) fig. 6.20 [p. 95]

ED: Napier (1916) 1–99 [base MS for Rule of Chrodegang, Latin and Old English], 129–31 [scribal alterations in Latin text]; Langefeld (2003) [base MS (= C) for Rule of Chrodegang, Latin and Old English]

LANG: Hofstetter (1987) 94–100; Langefeld (2003) 97–142

ST: Napier (1916); Förster (1933c); Sauer (1978) 33–6, 42, 93, 188; Cocchiarelli (1986); Langefeld (1986) 197–204; Conner (1993) 3; R.I. Page (1993a) 92; R. Gameson (1996b) 144; Budny (1997) I.847; Graham (1998a); Langefeld (2003) 44–5; Bjorklund (2004) 222

61. Cambridge, Corpus Christi College, 192

s. x med. (prob. 952), Landévennec, prov. England (Canterbury StA?) s. x^2, (prov. prob. Canterbury CC)

Contents: Amalarius, *Liber officialis* (Retractatio prima); excerpts from Eusebius, *Historia ecclesiastica*, trans. Rufinus [*CPG* 3495] and works of Jerome; *Ordo Romanus* XXXII (added)

MS: M.R. James (1912) I.465–6; Rella (1980) 110; Deuffic (1986) 296–7 [no. 19]; A.G. Watson (1986) 141, 147 [repr. A.G. Watson (2004) no. IV]; Dumville (1992a) 115 and n. 142, 135; Dumville (1992b) 182 n. 68; Lapidge (1992b) 100 n. 24 [repr. Lapidge (1993a) 90 n. 24]; Dumville (1994b); Budny (1997) I.195–203 [with full list of contents at I.202]; C.A. Jones (2001) 27–32, 296; Barker-Benfield (2008) III.1811, 1813

DEC: Budny (1997) I.202–3 [inventory of decoration]

FACS: *NPS* I, pl. 109 [fol. 49r]; Budny (1997) II, pls. 154–9 [fols. 3r, 85v, 88v, 93r, 95r, 96v]

ST: Bradshaw (1889) 474; Hanssens (1934) 70–3; Hanssens (1948–50); Dumville (1993d); C.A. Jones (2001); R. McKitterick (2012) 330 and n. 105

61. 5. Cambridge, Corpus Christi College, 193

s. ix$^{2-3/3}$, prob. N France, perh. Soissons, prov. England by s. xi?

Contents: Ambrose, *Exameron* [*CPL* 123]

MS: M.R. James (1912) I.466–7; *CLA* II (1935) no. 124; McGurk (1961b) 9 [no. 7] [repr. McGurk (1998) no. V]; Gasparri (1966); T.A.M. Bishop (1990) 535–6; D. Ganz (1990) 50–3, 143; Budny (1997) I.119–31 [no. 8]; Bischoff (1998—) I, no. 814; Lapidge (2006) 167; R. Gameson (2012d) 346

DEC: Budny (1997) I.130–1 [inventory of added decoration and illumination]

FACS: Budny (1997) II, pl. 747 [fol. "ii" r]

ED: Schenkl (1897) [Ambrose, *Exameron*, coll. as C]

ST: Bullough (2003a) 353 n. 56

62. Cambridge, Corpus Christi College, 196

s. xi^2, Exeter

Contents: Old English Martyrology*; *Vindicta Saluatoris**

MS: M.R. James (1912) I.471–2; T.A.M. Bishop (1954–8a) 193; N.R. Ker (1957) no. 47; N.R. Ker (1964) 82; T.A.M. Bishop (1971) 24; Kotzor

(1974); Drage (1978) 325–6; Sauer (1978) 33–6, 93; Kotzor (1981) I.75*–88*; P.R. Robinson (1988) I, no. 141; Conner (1993) 3; R.I. Page (1993a) 48–9; Lapidge (1994b) 137; Budny (1997) I.xxxvi, 479, 528, 538; Treharne (2003) 161; Treharne (2007b) 17; R. Gameson (2012a) 17 and n. 17, 87 and n. 316; Scragg (2012a) no. 109–10

FACS: Kotzor (1981) I, pl. 6 [p. 10]

ED: Kotzor (1981) [Old English Martyrology coll. as C]; Cross (1996b) [OE *Vindicta Saluatoris* coll. as D]

LANG: Kotzor (1981) I.315*–440*; Hofstetter (1987) 409–10

ST: Kotzor (1974); Kotzor (1981) I.118*–171*; R. Gameson (1996b) 144 and n. 32

63. Cambridge, Corpus Christi College, 197B (with London, BL, Cotton Otho C. v + Royal 7. C. xii, fols. 2, 3) [64 mounted fragments of originally 109 or 110 folios]

s. vii/viii or viii in., Northumbria (prob. Lindisfarne), prov. S England (Canterbury StA?) s. viii²/ix in.

Contents: gospels (f)

MS: M.R. James (1912) I.472–5; *CLA* II (1935) no. *125 [and II (1935) no. 217 for Royal 7. C. xii, fols. 2, 3]; McGurk (1961a) nos. 2, 29; T.J. Brown (1972) 226, 227, 229, 235, 246 [repr. T.J. Brown (1984) 104, 105, 107, 112, 273 n. 95]; M.P. Brown (1989a) 158; Webster—Backhouse (1991) no. 83 (a)–(b) [Backhouse]; M.P. Brown (1991) 66; Dumville (1992a) 104; R.I. Page (1993a) 7–8, 49, 52; R. Gameson (1994b) 28, 34; M.P. Brown (1996) 167; Budny (1997) I.55–73 [no. 3]; Prescott (1997) 393 n. 22; Prescott (1998) 258; Budny (1999) 252–4; Dumville (1999) 43–4, 45–6; Marsden (1999) 297; M.P. Brown (2003b) 134–7; Dance (2004) 34 n. 24; Binski—Panayotova (2005) no. 2 [R. McKitterick]; Emms (2006) 19; Barker-Benfield (2008) I.530, III.1646, 1664, 1733–4, 1792, 1797, 1910–11; M.P. Brown (2012) 135, 151, 153; R. Gameson (2012a) 28 n. 59, 42 n. 117; R. Gameson (2012b) 111 n. 67; Gullick (2012) 297 n. 14

DEC: Kendrick et al. (1956–60) I.92, 190–1; Henry (1965) 162, 174–6, 178, 184, 192; Henry (1974) 180, 226; Köhler—Mütherich (1971–99) VII.45 n. 50; Köhler (1972) 36–41; Nordenfalk (1977) 48–9; Alexander (1978a) no. 12; G. Henderson (1982) 8–9, 53 n. 44; Ohlgren (1986) no. 12; G. Henderson (1987) 68–71, 90–2, 95–6; Backhouse (1989) 169–72; R.I. Page (1993a) 7–8; R. Gameson (1994b) 38–9; M.P. Brown

(1996) 78, 90, 167, 178; Budny (1997) I.64–73 [inventory of decoration]; M.P. Brown (2003a) 47–50, 81 n. 94; Tilghman (2011) 96; Netzer (2012) 235 and n. 60

FACS: G. Henderson (1982) pl. 2 [unspecified folio of the Otho MS]; M.P. Brown (1991) pls. 66 (a)–(b) [fols. 1r; Otho fol. 27r]; R.I. Page (1993a), pls. 7, 33, 34 [fols. 1r, 2r, 8r]; Budny (1997), pls. II–III [fols. 1r, 2r], 8–9 [fols. 5r, 6r]; G. Henderson (1987) pls. 91–2 [both fol. 2r (details)]; Budny (1999) 253–4 [fol. 1r (detail)]; M.P. Brown (2003a) 27 [fol. 1v]; M.P. Brown (2003b) figs. 4 [fol. 3r], 5 [Otho, fol. 45r]; M.P. Brown (2003c) figs. 22 (a) [fols. 1v–2r], 22 (b) [Otho, fol. 27r]; M.P. Brown (2007a) pl. 33 [fol. 1r]

ED: B. Fischer (1988–91) [gospel excerpts coll. as Eg]; McGurk (1994a) 110–13 [repr. McGurk (1998) no. IX] [Hebrew names in gospels coll. as Eg]

ST: McGurk (1955) [repr. McGurk (1998) no. IV]; McGurk (1961a) no. 2; Page—Bushnell (1975) no. 2; Rella (1977) 21; Verey (1989) 143–4; McGurk (1994a) [repr. McGurk (1998) no. IX]; Netzer (1994) 8, 22, 49, 106–7, 112, 114, 213 n. 68, 216 n. 63, 224 n. 21, 240 n. 29; O'Sullivan (1994) 80–94; Pickwoad (1994); M.P. Brown (1996) 131; Keynes (1996b) 116, 129, 145 n. 23, 154 n. 116; R.I. Page (1998) 289–90; Budny (1999) 252–4; Marsden (1999) 297; Verey (1999) 330–4

64. Cambridge, Corpus Christi College, 198

s. xi¹, Worcester? additions s. xi² W England, (prov. Worcester)

Contents: Homilies* (mostly by Ælfric); a version of the Phoenix story*; Office of St Guthlac (part; s. xi ex.)

MS: M.R. James (1912) I.475–81; N.R. Ker (1957) no. 48; Pope (1967) I.20–2; T.A.M. Bishop (1971) 22; Godden (1979) xxviii–xxxi; Scragg (1979) 241; Clayton (1985) 222, 226; Scragg (1985) 304 n. 23, 309–15; Franzen (1991) 51–3; Scragg (1992) xxviii; R.I. Page (1993a) 52–3, 95–7; Scragg (1994a) 320, 342; Scragg (1996) 212; Budny (1997) I.557–69 [no. 36]; Clemoes (1997) 10–13; Godden (2004) 369; N.M. Thompson (2004) 41, 51, 60–1; R. Gameson (2005a) 92; Hartzell (2006) no. 28; Biggs (2007a) 41; Toswell (2007) 212; Treharne (2007b) 18 n. 16; Wieland (2009) 191; Scragg (2012a) nos. 111–24

DEC: F. Wormald (1952) 61 [no. 8]; E. Temple (1976) no. 88; Ohlgren (1986) no. 193; R. Gameson (1991) 74 n. 79; Deshman (1995) 147; Budny (1997) I. 566–9 [inventory of decoration and illustration]; Biggs (2008)

FACS: Willard (1950); E. Temple (1976) fig. 58 [p. 1]; Budny (1992) pl. 39 [p. 1]; R.I. Page (1993a) pls. 55 [fol. 218r], 61 [fol. 220r]; Deshman (1995) fig. 121 [p. 1]; Budny (1997) II, pls. 464–83 [fols. 1*r, 1r, 7r, 34v, 44r, 57v, 64v, 73r, 81r, 90r, 104r, 132v, 153r, 196v, 202r, 218r, 228v, 298v, 321v, 360r]; Biggs (2008) figs. 12.1–12.3 [all of fol. iir]

ED [the order of the following items is that of the manuscript, listed according to the numbering of individual articles in N.R. Ker (1957) 77–81; only the most recent editions are cited]:

art. 1: Förster (1932) 107–31 [Vercelli Hom. V (Christmas) coll. as S]; Scragg (1992) 111–21 [Vercelli Hom. V coll. as F]

art. 2: Clemoes (1997) 198–205 [Ælfric, CH I, Hom. III (St Stephen), coll. as E]

art. 3: Clemoes (1997) 206–16 [Ælfric, CH I, Hom. IV (Assumption of St John the Evangelist), coll. as E]

art. 4: Clemoes (1997) 217–23 [Ælfric, CH I, Hom. V (Holy Innocents), coll. as E]

art. 5: Clemoes (1997) 224–31 [Ælfric, CH I, Hom. VI (Circumcision of the Lord), coll. as E]

art. 6: Clemoes (1997) 232–40 [Ælfric, CH I, Hom. VII (Epiphany), coll. as E]

art. 7: Förster (1932) 149–59 [Vercelli Hom. VIII (First Sunday after Epiphany) coll. as S]; Scragg (1992) 143–8 [Vercelli Hom. VIII coll. as F]

art. 8: Godden (1979) 29–40 [Ælfric, CH II, Hom. IV (Second Sunday after Epiphany), coll. as E]

art. 9: Clemoes (1997) 241–8 [Ælfric, CH I, Hom. VIII (Third Sunday after Epiphany), coll. as E]

art. 10: Clemoes (1997) 249–57 [Ælfric, CH I, Hom. IX (Purification of the Virgin), coll. as E]

art. 11: Godden (1979) 72–80 [Ælfric, CH II, Hom. IX (St Gregory), coll. as E]

art. 12: Godden (1979) 81–91 [Ælfric, CH II, Hom. X (St Cuthbert), coll. as E]

art. 13: Godden (1979) 92–109 [Ælfric, CH II, Hom. XI (St Benedict), coll. as E]

art. 14: Clemoes (1997) 281–9 [Ælfric, CH I, Hom. XIII (Annunciation of B.V.M.), coll. as E]

art. 15: Godden (1979) 41–51 [Ælfric, CH II, Hom. V (Septuagesima Sunday), coll. as E] art. 16: Godden (1979) 52–9 [Ælfric, CH II, Hom. VI (Sexagesima Sunday), coll. as E]

art. 17: Clemoes (1997) 258–65 [Ælfric, CH I, Hom. X (Quinquagesima Sunday), coll. as E]

art. 18: Godden (1979) 60–6 [Ælfric, CH II, Hom. VII (First Sunday in Lent), coll. as E]

art. 19: Förster (1932) 53–71 [Vercelli Hom. III (Second Sunday in Lent) coll. as S]; Scragg (1992) 73–83 [Vercelli Hom. III coll. as F]

art. 20: as Assmann (1889/1964) 138–43 [anonymous Hom. XI (Third Sunday in Lent), not collated]

art. 21: as Belfour (1909) 50–8 [Hom. VI (Fourth Sunday in Lent)], not collated

art. 22: Assmann (1889/1964) 144–50 [anonymous Hom. XII (Fifth Sunday in Lent) coll. as S]

art. 23: Schaefer (1972) 18–33 [base MS (= A) for anonymous Hom. for Palm Sunday]

art. 24: Assmann (1889/1964) 151–63 [anonymous Hom. XIII (*In cena Domini*) coll. as S¹]

art. 25: Förster (1932) 1–42 [Vercelli Hom. I (Parasceue) coll. as S]; Scragg (1992) 7–43, odd pages [Vercelli Hom. I (E) coll. as F]

art. 26: Schaefer (1972) 83–114 [base MS (= A) for anonymous Hom. for Holy Saturday]

art. 27: Clemoes (1997) 299–306 [Ælfric, CH I, Hom. XV (Easter Sunday), coll. as E]

art. 28: Clemoes (1997) 307–12 [Ælfric, CH I, Hom. XVI (First Sunday after Easter), coll. as E]

art. 29: Clemoes (1997) 313–16 [Ælfric, CH I, Hom. XVII (Second Sunday after Easter), coll. as E]

art. 30: Godden (1979) 169–73 [Ælfric, CH II, Hom. XVII (SS. Philip and James), coll. as E]

art. 31: Godden (1979) 174–6 [Ælfric, CH II, Hom. XVIII, lines 1–61 (Discovery of the Holy Cross), coll. as E]

art. 32: Godden (1979) 176–9 [Ælfric, CH II, Hom. XVIII, lines 62–156 (SS. Alexander, Eventius and Theodolus), coll. as E]

art. 33: Clemoes (1997) 345–53 [Ælfric, CH I, Hom. XXI (Ascension Day), coll. as E]

art. 34: Clemoes (1997) 354–64 [Ælfric, CH I, Hom. XXII (Pentecost), coll. as E]

art. 35: Clemoes (1997) 365–70 [Ælfric, CH I, Hom. XXIII (Second Sunday after Pentecost), coll. as E] art. 36: Godden (1979) 213-17 [Ælfric, CH II, Hom. XXIII, lines 1–125 (Third Sunday after Pentecost), coll. as E]

art. 37: Godden (1979) 217–20 [Ælfric, CH II, Hom. XXIII, lines 126–98 (*Alia narratio de evangelii textu*), coll. as E]

art. 38: Clemoes (1997) 379–87 [Ælfric, CH I, Hom. XXV (St John the Baptist), coll. as E]

arts. 39–40: Godden (1979) 221–9 [Ælfric, CH II, Hom. XXIV (St Peter), coll. as E]

arts. 41–2: Clemoes (1997) 388–99 [Ælfric, CH I, Hom. XXVI (SS. Peter and Paul), coll. as E]

art. 43: Clemoes (1997) 400–9 [Ælfric, CH I, Hom. XXVII (St Paul), coll. as E]

art. 44: Godden (1979) 67–71 [Ælfric, CH II, Hom. VIII (Second Sunday in Lent), coll. as E]

art. 45: Godden (1979) 127–36 [Ælfric, CH II, Hom. XIII (Fifth Sunday in Lent), coll. as E]

art. 46: Godden (1979) 150–60 [Ælfric, CH II, Hom. XV (Easter Day), coll. as E]

arts. 47–8: Godden (1979) 161–8 [Ælfric, CH II, Hom. XVI (Another Sermon for Easter Day), coll. as E]

art. 49: Godden (1979) 310–17 [Ælfric, CH II, Hom. XXXVII (Feast of Holy Martyrs), coll. as E]

art. 50: Godden (1979) 318–26 [Ælfric, CH II, Hom. XXXVIII (Feast of a Confessor), coll. as E]

art. 51: Godden (1979) 327–34 [Ælfric, CH II, Hom. XXXIX (Feast of Holy Virgins), coll. as E]

art. 52: Skeat (1881–1900) II.66–124 [Ælfric, *Lives of Saints* no. XXV (Maccabees), coll. as C]

art. 53: Clemoes (1997) 418–28 [Ælfric, CH I, Hom. XXIX (St Laurence), coll. as E]

art. 54: as Morris (1880) 137–59 [Blickling Hom. XIII (Assumption of the Virgin), not collated]

art. 55: Clemoes (1997) 465–75 [Ælfric, CH I, Hom. XXXIV (Dedication of the Church of St Michael), coll. as E]

art. 56: Godden (1979) 288–97 [Ælfric, CH II, Hom. XXXIV, lines 1–332 (St Martin), coll. as E]

art. 57: Godden (1979) 297–8 [Ælfric, CH II, Hom. XXXIV (*Excusatio dictantis*), coll. as E]

art. 58: Godden (1979) 241–7 [Ælfric, CH II, Hom. XXVII (St James), coll. as E] art. 59: Skeat (1881–1900) I.320–36 [Ælfric, *Lives of Saints*, no. XV (St Mark), coll. as C]

art. 60: Skeat (1881–1900) I.116–46 [Ælfric, *Lives of Saints*, no. V (St Sebastian), coll. as C]

art. 61: Clemoes (1997) 266–74 [Ælfric, CH I, Hom. XI (First Sunday in Lent), coll. as E]

art. 62: a composite Lenten homily, combining an Ælfrician piece on penitence (Thorpe (1844–6) II.602–8) with part of Blickling Hom. X (Morris (1880) 111–15)

art. 63: Pope (1967–8) I.264–80 [Ælfric, Suppl. Hom. IV (Third Sunday in Lent), coll. as E]

art. 64: as Blickling Hom. XIX [Morris (1880) 229–49, not collated]

art. 65: Clemoes (1997) 439–47 [Ælfric, CH I, Hom. XXXI (St Bartholomew), omitting lines 244–334, coll. as E]

art. 66: Clemoes (1997) 178–89 [Ælfric, CH I, Hom. I (*De initio creaturae*), coll. as E]

art. 67: F. Kluge (1885c) 477–9; N.F. Blake (1990) 95–6 [text based on Cotton Vespasian D. xiv with variants from the present MS]

ST: Willard (1936); Willard (1950); K. Sisam (1953a) 154–6; Harlow (1959); Horsley—Waterhouse (1984) 223; R.I. Page (1993a) 95–7, 101; R. Gameson (1996a) 214–15, 222, 237; J. Hill (1996) 244; Rankin (1996) 338; Scragg (1998) 72–3, 77–8 [relation between this MS and no. **50**]; Treharne (1998) 235 [similarity to no. **100**]; Collier (2000) 195 [tremulous Worcester hand]; S. Irvine (2000) 45, 49, 54–7; Proud (2000) 126, 128; N.M. Thompson (2004) 51; Scragg (2012b) 558, 560–1

65. Cambridge, Corpus Christi College, 201, pp. 1–7, 161–7

s. xi in.

Contents: *Regularis concordia** (f); *Judgement Day II*** [OE version of Bede, *Versus de die iudicii (CPL* 1370)]; *Exhortation to Christian Living***; *Summons to Prayer**

MS: M.R. James (1912) I.485–91; N.R. Ker (1957) no. 49A; Robinson—Stanley (1991) 25–6; Budny (1997) I.476, 483, 485; Caie (2000) 1–21; Cowen (2004) 397 n. 2; Godden (2004) 361–2; T.N. Hall (2004a) 94–5; C.A. Jones (2004) 329 n. 18, 332 n. 33, 351; Lionarons (2004b) 74, 80; Lionarons (2004c) 418, 424; Meaney (2004) 467 n. 18, 474 n. 49, 476, 483; A. Orchard (2004) 71; Wilcox (2004b) 376–7, 388–93; P. Wormald (2004) 14, 17; M. Heyworth (2007) 218–22; Treharne (2009b) 108–11; J. Hill (2011) 249 and n. 3; Scragg (2012a) nos. 125–6, 126a

FACS: Robinson—Stanley (1991) pls. 23.1–5 [pp. 161–5], 23.5–24 [pp. 166–7]; Owen-Crocker (2009) figs. 4.6 [p. 166] 4.7 [p. 167]

ED: Zupitza (1890) [*Regularis concordia*]; Dobbie (1942) 58–67 [*Judgement Day II*], 67–70 [*Exhortation to Christian Living, Summons to Prayer*]; Caie (2000) 84–103 [base MS for *Judgement Day II*]

LANG: Hofstetter (1987) 89–93; Caie (2000) 45–51; Dance (2004) 35 n. 26; A. Orchard (2004) 69 n. 24, 70 n. 28; Wilcox (2004b) 382–7

ST: F.C. Robinson (1989) [argues that *Exhortation* and *Summons to Prayer* are one poem]; J. Hill (1991b); Kornexl (1993) cxlix–clii; Dance (2004) 30; N.M. Thompson (2004) 63; P. Wormald (2004) 10; J. Hill (2006a); J. Hill (2011) *passim*

65. 5. Cambridge, Corpus Christi College, 201, pp. 8–160, 167–76

s. xi¹ or xi med., Winchester NM?

Contents: On the Seven Ages of the World+*; Homilies⁽*⁾ (twenty by Wulfstan); Ælfric, Pastoral Letter II (revised version)*; a collection of Anglo-Saxon laws*; Wulfstan, *Institutes of Polity*, 'Canons of Edgar'*; De ecclesiasticis gradibus*; 'Benedictine Office'+* (with excerpts from Hrabanus Maurus, *De clericorum institutione* II.1–10); Handbook for a confessor*; *Apollonius of Tyre*; Kentish royal saints*, Resting-places of English saints*; Genesis* (part, from OE Hexateuch); *Lords Prayer II** and *Gloria I**; forms of absolution and confession

MS: Liebermann (1903–16) I.xxii–xxiii; M.R. James (1912) I.485–91; Fehr (1914/1966) xiv–xvi; Bethurum (1957) 2–3; N.R. Ker (1957) no. 49B; Ure (1957) 9–14; Goolden (1958) xxxii–xxxiv; Jost (1959) 8–9; Fowler (1972) xi–xiii; Dumville (1992a) 134; Dumville (1993g) 55 n. 245; Lapidge (1994b) 144; Budny (1997) I.475–86 [no. 29]; Withers (1999) 112–18; P. Wormald (1999) 164, 204–5, 206–10, 211 n. 194, 248 n. 332, 250, 292, 309, 332 n. 315, 382 n. 535, 391, 395 n. 600, 397 nn. 612–13, 458 n. 154; Karkov (2004) 138; A. Orchard (2004) 76–7; Ambrose (2005) 114–15; Anlezark (2006) 64–71, 76–81; Hough (2006) 114, 133; Rumble (2006a) viii; M. Heyworth (2007) 218; Withers (2007) 229–30, 233, 261–3; Marsden (2008) xxxvi–xxxviii, liv–lvi; R. Gameson (2012a) 52; Raw (2012) 460; Scragg (2012a) nos. 127–37; P. Wormald (2012) 534 [no. 8]

DEC: Budny (1997) I.485–6 [inventory of decoration]; Marsden (2000) 48

FACS: Ångstrøm (1937) pls. III–V [pp. 121, 147, 167]; Fowler (1972) frontispiece [p. 99]; Robinson—Stanley (1991) pls. 25–26.1–2 [pp. 167–9], 26.2–27 [pp. 169–70]; Budny (1997) II, pls. 382–5 [pp. 8, 9, 52–3, 62–3]

ED [the order of the following items is that of the manuscript, listed according to the numbering of individual articles in N.R. Ker (1957) 83–90; only the most recent editions are cited]:

art. 1: Napier (1883/1967) 1–5 [Hom. I coll. as C]

art. 2: Napier (1883/1967) 311–13 [Hom. LXII (*De aetatibus mundi*) coll. as C]

art. 3: Napier (1883/1967) 6–20 [Wulfstan, Hom. II (*Sermo Lupi episcopi*), coll. as C]; Bethurum (1957) 142–56 [Hom. VI (*Sermo Lupi episcopi*) coll. as C]

art. 4: Napier (1883/1967) 20–1 [Wulfstan, Hom. III, part 1 (*De fide catholica*), coll. as C]; Bethurum (1957) 157–65 [Wulfstan, Hom. VII (*De fide catholica*), coll. as C]

art. 5: Napier (1883/1967) 21–9 [Wulfstan, Hom. III, part 2, coll. as C]

art. 6: Napier (1883/1967) 108–10 [Wulfstan, Hom. XIX (*Sermo ad populum*), coll. as C]; Bethurum (1957) 225–32 [Wulfstan, Hom. XIII (*Sermo ad populum*), coll. as C]

art. 7: Napier (1883/1967) 110–11 [Hom. XX coll as C]

art. 8: Napier (1883/1967) 111 [Hom. XXI coll. as C]

art. 9: Napier (1883/1967) 112–15 [Hom. XXII coll. as C]

art. 10: Napier (1883/1967) 122–7 [Hom. XXV (*To folce*) and XXVI paras. 2–3, coll. as C]

art. 11: Napier (1883/1967) 116–19 [Hom. XXIII coll. as C]

art. 12: Napier (1883/1967) 128–30 [Hom. XXVII (*To eallum folce*) coll. as C]

art. 13: Napier (1883/1967) 167–9, 130–4 [Hom. XXXIV (*Sermo Lupi*) and XXVIII (*Be godcundre warnunge*) coll. as C]; Bethurum (1957) 250–4 [Hom. XIX (*Be godcundre warnunge*) coll. as C]

art. 14: Napier (1883/1967) 169–72 [Hom. XXXV (*Be mistlican gelimpan*) coll. as C]

art. 15: Napier (1883/1967) 180 [base MS (= C) for Hom. XXXVIII ('Her is git oþer god eaca')]

art. 16: Napier (1883/1967) 180–1 [base MS (= C) for Hom. XXXIX ('Ðis man gerædde, ða se micela here com to lande')]; Liebermann (1903–16) I.262, left-hand column [*VIIa Atr* coll. as D] art. 17: Fehr (1914/1966) 68–140, right-hand column [Ælfric, OE Pastoral Letter I to Wulfstan, coll. as D]

art. 18: Jost (1959) 109–14 [Wulfstan, *II Institutes of Polity*, cc. 145–53 (*Be gehadedum mannum*), coll. as D$_1$]

art. 19: Jost (1959) 131–5 [base MS (= D$_1$) for Wulfstan, *II Institutes of Polity*, cc. 187–97 (*To gehadedum and læwedum*)]

art. 20: Jost (1959) 139–50 [base MS (= D$_1$) for Wulfstan, *II Institutes of Polity*, cc. 1–11 (*Be eallum cristenum mannum*)]

art. 21: Liebermann (1903–16) I.380–5, left–hand column [*Northu.* coll. as D]

art. 22: Liebermann (1903–16) I.194–8, even pages, right-hand column [*II Eg.* coll. as D]

art. 23: Liebermann (1903–16) I.200–6, even pages, right-hand column [*III Eg.* coll. as D]

art. 24: Liebermann (1903–16) I.237–47, odd pages, left-hand column [*V Atr.* coll. as D]

art. 25: Napier (1883/1967) 66–7 [Hom. X, second para., coll. as C]

art. 26: Napier (1883/1967) 188 n. + 66 [part of Hom. XL + part of Hom. X, coll. as C]

art. 27: Napier (1883/1967) 189 n. + 68 [part of Hom. XL + part of Hom. X, coll. as C]

art. 28: Liebermann (1903–16) I.146–8, left-hand column [*I As.* coll. as D]

art. 29: Napier (1883/1967) 60, 65 [part of Hom. IX (*De cristianitate*) + part of Hom. X (*Her ongynð be cristendome*), coll. as C]; Bethurum (1957) 194–210 [Hom. Xb (*De cristianitate*) + Xc (*Her ongynð be cristendome*) coll. as C]; A. Orchard (2004) 72–3, 75–7, 81–2, 85, 87–9

art. 30: Napier (1883/1967) 41–9 [Hom. VI (*De uisione Isaie prophete*) coll. as C]; Bethurum (1957) 211–20 [Hom. XI (*De uisione Isaie prophete*) coll. as C]

art. 31: Napier (1883/1967) 52–6 [Wulfstan, Hom. VII (*De septiformi spiritu*), coll. as C, omitting the beginning (pp. 50–2, line 23)]; Bethurum (1957) 185–91 [Wulfstan, Hom. IX (*De septiformi spiritu*), coll. as C]

art. 32: Napier (1883/1967) 76–80 [Wulfstan, Hom. XI + XII (*De Antichristo*), coll. as C]; Bethurum (1957) 113–18 [Wulfstan, Hom. Ia + Ib (*De Antichristo*), coll. as C]

art. 33: Napier (1883/1967) 80–7 [Wulfstan, Hom. XIII (*Secundum Marcum*), coll. as C]; Bethurum (1957) 134–41 [Wulfstan, Hom. V (*Secundum Marcum*), coll. as C] art. 34: Napier (1883/1967) 87–90 [Wulfstan, Hom. XIV (*Lectio sancti euangelii secundum Matheum*), coll. as C]; Bethurum (1957) 119–22 [Wulfstan, Hom. II (*Lectio sancti euangelii secundum Matheum*), coll. as C]

art. 35: Napier (1883/1967) 90–4 [Wulfstan, Hom. XV (*Secundum Lucam*), coll. as C]; Bethurum (1957) 123–7 [Wulfstan Hom. III (*Secundum Lucam*) coll. as C]

art. 36: Napier (1883/1967) 94–102 [Wulfstan, Hom. XVI (*De temporibus Antichristi*), coll. as C]; Bethurum (1957) 128–33 [Hom. IV (*De temporibus Antichristi*) coll. as C]

art. 37: Napier (1883/1967) 182–90 [Hom. XL (*In die iudicii*) coll. as C]

art. 38: Napier (1883/1967) 190–1 [Wulfstan, Hom. XLI (*Verba Ezechiel prophete*), coll. as C]; Bethurum (1957) 240–1 [Wulfstan, Hom. XVIb (*Verba Ezechiel prophete*), coll. as C]

art. 39: Napier (1883/1967) 191 [Hom. XLI (end) coll. as C]

art. 40: Napier (1883/1967) 156–67 [Wulfstan, Hom. XXXIII (*Sermo Lupi ad Anglos*), coll. as C]; Bethurum (1957) 261–6 [Wulfstan, Hom. XX (*Sermo Lupi ad Anglos*), coll. as C]; Whitelock (1976) [*Sermo Lupi* coll. as C]

art. 41: Napier (1883/1967) 167–9 [Hom. XXXIV (*Sermo Lupi*) coll. as C]; Bethurum (1957) 276–7 [Hom. XXI ('Her is gyt rihtlic warnung') coll. as C]

art. 42: Jost (1959) 40–2 [base MS (= D_2) for Wulfstan, *I Institutes of Polity*, cc. 1–5 (*Be cinincge*)], 52–4 [base MS (= D_2) for Wulfstan, *I Institutes of Polity*, cc. 16–23 (*Be cinedome*)], 55–8 [base MS (= D_2) for Wulfstan, *I Institutes of Polity*, cc. 24–34 (*Ælc cynestol*)], 59–61 [base MS (= D_2) for Wulfstan, *I Institutes of Polity*, cc. 35–40 (*De episcopis*)], 67–73 [base MS (= D_2) for Wulfstan, *I Institutes of Polity*, cc. 41–56 (*Item: Byscopas sculon bocum*)], 78–80 [base MS (= D_2) for Wulfstan, *I Institutes of Polity*, cc. 57–65 (*Be eorlum*)], 84 [base MS (= D_2) for Wulfstan, *I Institutes of Polity*, cc. 66–7 (*Be sacerdum*)], 109–14 [base MS (= D_2) for Wulfstan, *I Institutes of Polity*, cc. 68–77 (*Be gehadedum mannum*)], 122 [base MS (= D_2) for Wulfstan, *I Institutes of Polity*, cc. 78–80 (*Be abbodum*)], 123–4 [base MS (= D_2) for Wulfstan, *I Institutes of Polity*, cc. 81–3 (*Be munecum*)], 128 [base MS (= D_2) for Wulfstan, *I Institutes of Polity*, c. 84 (*Be minecenan*)], 129 [base MS (= D_2) for Wulfstan, *I Institutes of Polity*, cc. 85–6 (*Be preostum and be nunnan*)], 130–4 [base MS (= D_2) for Wulfstan, *I Institutes of Polity*, cc. 87–92 (*Be læwedum mannum*)], 136–7 [base MS (= D_2) for Wulfstan, *I Institutes of Polity*, cc. 93–7 (*Be wudewan*)], 138–52 [base MS (= D_2) for

Wulfstan, *I Institutes of Polity*, cc. 98–116 (*Be circan*)], 154–64 [base MS (= D₂) for Wulfstan, *I Institutes of Polity*, cc. 117–28 (*Be eallum cristenum mannum*)]

art. 43: Liebermann (1903–16) I.263–8, left-hand column [*VIII Atr.* coll. as D]

art 44: Liebermann (1903–16) I.184–6, even pages, left-hand column [*I Em.* coll. as D]

art. 45: Fowler (1972) 2–18 [Wulfstan, *Canons of Edgar*, coll. as D]

art. 46: Liebermann (1903–16) I.456 [*Geþyncðo* coll. as D], 458 [*Norðleod* coll. as D], 464–8 [*Mirce, Að I, Had* all coll. as D]

art. 47: Napier (1883/1967) 29–41 [Hom. IV–V (*Sermo de baptismate* in Latin and OE) coll. as C]; Bethurum (1957) 169–71 + 175–84 [Hom. VIIIa (Latin *Sermo de baptismate*) + Hom. VIIIc (OE version) coll. as C]

art. 48: Raith (1933/1964) 17–19 [base MS for *De ecclesiasticis gradibus*]; Jost (1959) 223–41 [*De ecclesiasticis gradibus* coll. as O]

art. 49: Ure (1957) 81–102 [OE 'Benedictine Office' coll. as C, omitting metrical portions; for which see below, art. 57]

art. 50 [confessional and penitential texts] Raith (1933/1964) 76–81 [extracts from OE version of Halitgar's Penitential coll. as C]; Fowler (1965) 16 [confessional text coll. as D], 17–34 [base MS for penitential texts]

art. 51: Liebermann (1903–16) I.278–80 [*I Cn. Inscr.* coll. as D], I.308–12 [*II Cn.* coll. as D], 252–6 [*VI Atr.* coll. as D]

art. 52: Jost (1959) 104–5 [base MS (= D₃) for Wulfstan, *II Institutes of Polity*, cc. 130–4 (*Be sacerdan*)] + Liebermann (1903–16) I.284 [*I Cn.* 4]

art. 53: Goolden (1958) 2–42, even pages [base MS for OE *Apollonius of Tyre*]

art. 54: Liebermann (1889) 1–8 [base MS for brief treatise on Kentish Royal Saints]

art. 55: Liebermann (1889) 9–18 [base MS for OE 'Lists of Saints' Resting–Places']

art. 56: Marsden (2008) 63–70, 73–84 [parts of OE Genesis coll. as Co]

art. 57 [metrical paraphrases of *Pater noster* and *Gloria*]: Dobbie (1942) 70–4 [base MS for OE *Lords Prayer II*], 74–7 [OE *Gloria I* coll. as C]

art. 58: Latin formulas of absolution, confession: unprinted?

LANG: Ure (1957) 67–70; Goolden (1958) xxvii–xxxii; Fowler (1972) xx–xxvi; Dance (2004)

ST: Burchfield (1953); K. Sisam (1953a) 279; Morrell (1965); Torkar (1981) 33–5 [Ker arts. 25–7]; Tristram (1985) 82 n. 63 [Ages of the

World]; M.P. Richards (1986) [laws]; Withers (1999) 128–9 [OE Genesis]; M.P. Richards (2000) [Genesis]; Wilcox (2000) 92–3 [version of *Sermo Lupi*]; Godden (2004) 361–2; C.A. Jones (2004) 352; A. Orchard (2004) 71–90; Wilcox (2004b) [version of *Sermo Lupi*]; Hough (2006) 120–1; Scragg (2012b) 559

66. Cambridge, Corpus Christi College, 201, pp. 179-272

s. xi³/⁴; Exeter [orig. joined with no. 60?]

Contents: Theodulf of Orléans, *Capitula*⁺*; Homily*; Usuard of Saint-Germain-des-Prés, *Martyrologium* (f, s. xi ex.)

MS: M.R. James (1912) I.491; T.A.M. Bishop (1954–8a) 193–9; N.R. Ker (1957) no. 50; T.A.M. Bishop (1971) 24; Drage (1978) 327–8; Sauer (1978) 30–7; Scragg (1979) 256; P.R. Robinson (1988) I, no. 144; Scragg (1992) xxxv; Conner (1993) 4; R. Gameson (1996b) 145 and n. 33; Budny (1997) I.479, 527, 603; Frantzen (2007) 40–1; Treharne (2007a) 263–4; Treharne (2007b) 17; Scragg (2012a) no. 106

FACS: Sauer (1978) 514 [p. 179], 515 [p. 231], 516 [p. 246]; P.R. Robinson (1988) II, pl. 2 [p. 270]

ED: Sauer (1978) [base MS (= A) for Latin and OE versions of *Capitula* of Theodulf, and OE Homily]; Scragg (1992) 90–104 [Vercelli Hom. IV coll. as R]

ST: Fowler (1972) xxxvi–xxxix; Sauer (1978); Brommer (1984); Sauer (1996)

67. Cambridge, Corpus Christi College, 206

s. x¹, England (perh. Canterbury) rather than NE France, prov. England (Canterbury, or St Albans, or Bury St Edmunds?) s. xi/xii

Contents: Martianus Capella, *De nuptiis Philologiae et Mercurii*, bk. IV; Alcuin, *Carm.* lxxiii (part); pseudo-Augustine, *Categoriae decem ex Aristotele decerptae* [*CPL* 362], with glosses; pseudo-Apuleius, *Peri hermeneias* (incomplete); Porphyrius, *Isagoge*, trans. Boethius; glosses on Boethius's second commentary on the *Isagoge* [*CPL* 881]; extracts from Augustine, *De Trinitate* [*CPL* 329]; questions and answers on theological matters; notes on logical matters; Boethius, theological tractates, with gloss: *Quomodo Trinitas* [*CPL* 890], *Utrum Pater et Filius* [*CPL* 891], *Quomodo substantiae* [*CPL* 892], *Contra Eutychen et Nestorium* [*CPL* 894]; Alcuin, *De dialectica* with prologue (*Carm.* lxxvii.1); Augustine (?), *De dialectica*

MS: Schenkl no. 4899; M.R. James (1912) I.495–8; Leonardi (1959) 467
n. 126; Leonardi (1960) 21–2 [no. 29]; Minio-Paluello (1961) 70
[no. 2036]; Bishop (1971) xii n. 2; Römer (1972b) 51; B.D. Jackson
(1975) 9, 12; Marenbon (1981) 181–3; R.M. Thomson (1982b) 10; Munk
Olsen (1982–) I.21; Dumville (1992b) 181 n. 60; Gibson et al. (1995–
2001) I.52–3 [no. 19]; Knappe (1996) 129 n. 1, 186 and n. 2; Budny
(1997) I.211–18 [no. 16]; Dumville (1999) 127; R. Gameson (1999a)
p. 61 [addition (s. xii¹) on fol. 1]; Teresi (2007b) 131–2; Barker-Benfield
(2008) III.1823; Wieland (2009) 150; R. Gameson (2012b) 109 n. 56

DEC: Gibson et al. (1995–2001) I.53; Budny (1997) I.216–18

FACS: Budny (1997) II, pls. XIII [fol. 1r], 162–70 [fols. 17v, 38r, 43r, 45v,
57r, 58v, 72r, 78v, 80r, 101r]; Teresi (2007b) pl. 1 [fol. 38r]

ED: Marenbon (1981) 185–93 [glosses to *Categoriae decem* coll. as C]

ST: Minio-Paluello (1971) *passim* [*Categoriae decem*]; B.D. Jackson (1975)
78; Marenbon (1981) 12–29, 116–38 *et passim* [*Categoriae decem*];
Gibson (1982) 56; Gibson (1993a) I.125 n. 13; *CSLMA* II (1999) 92–3
[Alcuin, *Carm.* lxxiii], 130–3 [Alcuin, *De dialectica*]; Teresi (2007b);
CALMA II.241; R. McKitterick (2012) 328

68. Cambridge, Corpus Christi College, 214

s. x ex. or xi in., Canterbury?

Contents: Boethius, *De consolatione Philosophiae*° [*CPL* 878]

MS: M.R. James (1912) I.511–12; Weinberger (1934) xvi; T.A.M. Bishop (1954–
8a) 187; N.R. Ker (1957) no. 51; N.R. Ker (1964) 39; Bolton (1977a) 58;
Hale (1978); Vaciago (1993) p. 6 [no. 18]; Gibson et al. (1995–2001) I.53–4
[no. 20]; Budny (1997) I.xxxv; Wieland (1998) 17 n. 23; R.I. Page (2001)
228–32; Wittig (2007) 188; Graham (2009) 170; Scragg (2012a) nos. 138–9

FACS: Owen-Crocker (2009) fig. 6.6 [fol. 107r]

ED: Hale (1978) [base MS]

ST: Rosier (1964a); F.C. Robinson (1973) 444–6; Bolton (1977a) 58; Sauer
(1978) 449; Korhammer (1980) 34–6, 38–9, 49; Troncarelli (1981) 3, 49;
Graham (1998a) 68 n. 149; R.I. Page (2001) 233; Godden (2011) 92

69. Cambridge, Corpus Christi College, 221, fols. 1–24

s. x¹ or x med. or x², perh. Canterbury StA (or Brittany?)

Contents: Alcuin, *De orthographia* (incomplete); Bede, *De orthographia*
[*CPL* 1566]

MS: M.R. James (1912) I.519–20; T.A.M. Bishop (1954–8a) 188–9; C.W. Jones (1975) 3–5; Dionisotti (1982) 137; Codoñer (1996) 74–5; Bruni (1997) xxxiii; Budny (1997) I.205–9 [no. 15]; Bischoff (1998 —) I, no. 180; Hartzell (2006) no. 29; Barker-Benfield (2008) II.1396, III.1811; Wieland (2009) 145

DEC: Budny (1997) I.209 [inventory of decoration]

FACS: Budny (1997) II, pls. 160–1 [fols. 1r, 14v]

ED: C.W. Jones (1975) [Bede, *De orthographia*, coll. as C]; Bruni (1997) [Alcuin, *De orthographia*, coll. as C]

ST: R.M. Thomson (1975) 382; R.M. Thomson (1987) 61 n. 151; Saenger (1997) 86, 334 n. 19; *CSLMA* II (1999) 143; McKee (2012b) 340 and nn. 5–6

69. 5. Cambridge, Corpus Christi College, 221, fols. 25–64

s. x, England (? or s. ix Continent, prov. England s. x or xi)

Contents: Cassiodorus, *De orthographia* [*CPL* 907], Caper, *De orthographia*; Agroecius, *Ars de orthographia* [*CPL* 1545]

MS: M.R. James (1912) I.519–20; Budny (1997) I.207–9; Hartzell (2006) no. 30; Wieland (2009) 145

ST: R.M. Thomson (1975) 382; R.M. Thomson (1987) 61 n. 151

70. Cambridge, Corpus Christi College, 223

s. ix$^{3/4}$, Arras, Saint-Vaast, prov. s. ix ex. Saint-Bertin, prov. England s. x^1

Contents: French regnal list (with additions); four recipes, three medical (s. x); Gennadius, on Prudentius (*De uiris inlustribus* [*CPL* 957], ch. xiii); Prudentius, *Cathemerinon* [*CPL* 1438], *Apotheosis* [*CPL* 1439], *Hamartigenia* [*CPL* 1440], (computus note added s. x/xi, England), *Psychomachia* [*CPL* 1441], *Peristephanon* [*CPL* 1443], *Contra Symmachum* [*CPL* 1442], *Dittochaeon* [*CPL* 1444], *Epilogus* [*CPL* 1445]; Iohannes Scottus Eriugena, *Carm.* ix [SK 1417]

Additions in England: pontifical prayer; benedictions; Gregory, *Registrum epistularum* XI. 4 (f); two alphabets: s. x/xi, Latin and OE glosses, s. x and xi

MS: M.R. James (1912) I.521–5; Bergman (1926) xxiii, xxvii–xxviii; Lavarenne (1943–51) I.xxv–xxvi; Wallace–Hadrill (1950) 213; N.R. Ker (1957) no. 52; M.P. Cunningham (1966) xix–xx; Lapidge (1977a) 449 n. 8; Rella (1980) 110; P.R. Robinson (1988) I, no. 146; Herren (1993)

21; Vaciago (1993) 6–7 [no. 19]; Blockley (1994); Budny (1997) I.137–49 [no. 10]; Wieland (1997a) 171 and n. 7, 181; Bischoff (1998 —) I, no. 816; Wieland (1998) 3–5; Karkov (2001a) 115 n. 3, 116 nn. 4, 6, 119 n. 22; Hartzell (2006) no. 31; Morgan — Panayotova (2009) I.22 [no. 2]; Wieland (2009) 148, 156; D. Ganz (2012) 189 n. 7; R. Gameson (2012d) 348 and n. 13; Rankin (2012) 505 n. 112; Scragg (2012a) nos. 140–1

DEC: Budny (1997) I.147–9 [inventory of decoration]; Morgan — Panayotova (2009) I.22

FACS: Budny (1997) II, pls. 104–5 [pp. 347, 348]; Morgan — Panayotova (2009) I.22 [p. 92]

ED: Traube (1886–96) 550–2 [base MS for Iohannes Scottus Eriugena, *Carm.* ix]; Bergman (1926) [Prudentius, *Carmina*, coll. as C]; Lavarenne (1943–51) [Prudentius, *Carmina*, coll. as C]; Meritt (1945) nos. 28, 66 [OE glosses]; M.P. Cunningham (1966) [Prudentius, *Carmina*, coll. as C]; Herren (1993) 116–21 [base MS for Iohannes Scottus Eriugena, *Carm.* ix (= no. 25 in Herren's edition)]

ST: Grierson (1940c) 553; Lapidge (1977a); R.I. Page (1979) 32–43; Wieland (1987) 213–31; Wieland (1997b); Wieland (1998) 17 nn. 24 and 27, 19 nn. 46, 48 and 49, 20 n. 50; Ziolkowski (2007) 263; R. McKitterick (2012) 328

72. Cambridge, Corpus Christi College, 260

s. x² or x ex., Canterbury CC

Contents: Boethius, *De institutione musica* [CPL 880] V.16–18, serving as introduction to *Musica Enchiriadis*; *Scholica Enchiriadis de musica*; *Commemoratio breuis de tonis*

MS: M.R. James (1912) II.10; T.A.M. Bishop (1959–63b) 415; Fenlon (1982) 6–10; Bower (1988) 214 [no. 15]; Biggs et al. (1990) 76–7 [Wittig]; C. Meyer et al. (1992) 3; Gerchow (1999) 389–90 [Torkewitz]; C. Meyer (2003) 377; Wieland (2009) 155; Rankin (2012) 506

FACS: Fenlon (1982) i [fols. 30v–31r]; Gerchow (1999) 390 [fol. 1r]

ED: H. Schmid (1981) 1–59 [*Musica Enchiriadis* coll. as Q], 60–156 [*Scholica Enchiriadis de musica* coll. as Q]

ST: R. McKitterick (2012) 328 [MS erroneously cited as CCCC 209]

73. Cambridge, Corpus Christi College, 265

s. xi med. - xi³/⁴, Worcester [pp. 1-268]; s. xi², Worcester [pp. 269–367]; s. xi ex. or xii in., Worcester [pp. 368–442]

Contents: pp. 1–268 (a version of Wulfstan's 'Handbook'): Alcuin, *Epist.* xvii, cxiv; First Capitulary of Gerbald of Liège; *Poenitentiale Egberti* [*CPL* 1887], Prologue and chs. i–xiii; Wulfstan's Canon Law Collection ('*Excerptiones Pseudo-Egberti*', recension A); excerpts mainly from *Poenitentiale Theodori* and other penitentials, and from Theodulf, *Capitula*; Handbook for a confessor*; excerpts from: Ansegisus, *Capitularium collectio* and other capitularies, from *Admonitio generalis* (789) and *Institutio canonicorum* (Aachen Council of 816), from collection of canons; Abbo of Saint-Germain-des-Prés, *Sermo* xiii; Ælfric, Pastoral Letters 2 and 3; Wulfstan, Homily VIIIa; 'De officio missae'; *De ecclesiasticis gradibus*; Hrabanus Maurus, *De institutione clericorum* II.1–7; forms of excommunication; laws: *Eadgar IV*$^{+*}$; Chrism mass *ordo*; Ælfric, Letter to the Monks of Eynsham

pp. 269–367: excerpts from Amalarius, *Liber officialis* (complete version); excerpts from *Pontificale Romano-Germanicum*; Amalarius (?), *Eclogae de ordine Romano*

pp. 368–442: Bernold of Constance, *Micrologus de ecclesiasticis obseruationibus*; *De ordine missae, De antiphonis*

MS: Bateson (1895) 721–31; Liebermann (1903–16) I.xx; M.R. James (1912) II.14–21; Fehr (1914/1966) xiv [Fehr], cxxviii [Clemoes]; Andrieu (1931–61) I.99–101; Bethurum (1957) 8; N.R. Ker (1957) no. 53; Bishop (1971) 22 n. 1; Aronstam (1974) 20–2; Hohler (1975) 223; Lapidge (1983) 463 n. 52; Haggenmüller (1991) 55–7, 160–2; Dumville (1993g) 136–7; Vaciago (1993) 7 [no. 20]; Budny (1997) I.605–7 [full list of contents]; C.A. Jones (1998a) 238 n. 24; C.A. Jones (1998b) 71–7; C.A. Jones (1998c) 696–701; Cross—Hamer (1999) 41–8 [list of contents]; R. Gameson (1999a) nos. 65–6; C.A. Jones (1999) 123 n. 79; P. Wormald (1999) 210–24 and nn. 193–223, 233 and 240, 317 n. 248, 458 n. 156; Sauer (2000) 377; Hamilton (2001) 218–19; T.N. Hall (2004a) 94, 100, 108; J. Hill (2004) 321; C.A. Jones (2004) 327–8, 351–2; R. Gameson (2005a) 92, 94, 101–4; C.A. Jones (2005a) 121 n. 58, 122–5; C.A. Jones (2005b) 241; Foys (2006) 271–4, 277–80, 283–4; Hough (2006) 115, 122, 136; Rumble (2006a) viii; Biggs (2007a) 63–4 [C.D. Wright]; Frantzen (2007) 40–1; M. Heyworth (2007) 218; Treharne (2007b) 17; Wieland (2009) 127; Crick (2012) 184 and n. 47; R. Gameson (2012a) 82 n. 293, 87 n. 316; A. Orchard (2012) 696 [no. 3]; Scragg (2012a) nos. 87, 142–52; P. Wormald (2012) 534 [no. 9]

DEC: Budny (1997) I.607–8 [inventory of decoration]; C.A. Jones (2005b) 242 [rubrics]

FACS: Sauer (1998) pl. 7 [p. 122]; Budny (1997) II, pls. 550–9 [pp. 3, 160, 197, 210, 211, 269, 292, 298, 303, 325]; R. Gameson (1999a) pl. 2 [p. 222]; R. Gameson (2005a) fig. 3 [p. 298]

ED: Napier (1883/1967) [Wulfstan, Hom. IV, coll. as X]; Liebermann (1903–16) I.206–15 [base MS (= C) for *Eg IV*]; Fehr (1914/1966) 35–57 [Ælfric, OE Pastoral Letter 2, coll. as C], 58–67 [Ælfric, OE Pastoral Letter 3, coll. as C]; Bethurum (1957) 169–71 [Wulfstan, Hom. VIIIa, coll. as X]; Fowler (1965) 16–32 [Handbook for a Confessor coll. as C]; Sauer (1978) [*Capitula Theodulfi* (pp. 121–42) coll. as C]; Cross— Hamer (1997) [base MS (= Z) for Wulfstan's Canon Law Collection, Recension A (pp. 66–113) and Recension B (pp. 114–72)]; C.A. Jones (1998b) 110–48 [base MS for Ælfric, Letter to the Monks of Eynsham]; T.N. Hall (2004a) 110–13 [*Admonitio episcoporum utilis* coll. as X]

ST: Selborne (1888); Bethurum (1942); Whitelock (1942); Clemoes (1960); Fowler (1963); Lambert (1969–72) no. 960; Fowler (1972) liv–lvi; Brückmann (1973) 407; J.R. Hall (1975); Frantzen (1983b) 133 n. 40 [Penitential attrib. to Bede]; *BCLL* (1985) no. 1183; N.R. Ker (1985b) [study of Coleman's notes]; Cross (1992b); Dumville (1992a) 68, 73–4, 91, 134–8; Mordek (1995) 95–7; J. Barrow (1996) 92; R. Gameson (1996a) 238; Schmitz (1996) 362–3; Cross—Hamer (1997); C.A. Jones (1998b) 71–91; C.A. Jones (1998c) 697–701; O'Brien O'Keeffe (1998b) 211, 217 n. 29, 221, 229; *CSLMA* II (1999) 10, 185, 239; P. Wormald (1999) 211–19, 221 n., 317 n., 392 n., 459 n.; Sauer (2000) 341, 354–75; Bjorklund (2004) 222; Godden (2004) 371; G. Mann (2004) 246 n. 26, 258, 276 n. 117; P. Wormald (2004) 10; C.A. Jones (2005a) 124; C.A. Jones (2005b) 241, 282; Hough (2006) 122–3; M. Heyworth (2007) 218–22 ['Late Old English Handbook for the Use of a Confessor']

74. Cambridge, Corpus Christi College, 267

s. xi/xii, Canterbury, StA

Contents: chants for the Office of St Mellitus; Freculf of Lisieux, *Historiae*; Peter Damian, *De quindecim signis diem iudicii praecedentibus* [*CPPM* II, no. 411]

MS: M.R. James (1912) II.22–3; Dodwell (1954) 122; T.A.M. Bishop (1955) 2–3; N.R. Ker (1964) 40; N.R. Ker (1976b) 30 [repr. N.R. Ker (1985) 150]; R. Gameson (1995a) 102 n. 28, 126 n. 115, 132, 143; N. Orchard (1995b) 92; Budny (1997) I. 687–92 [no. 47]; R. Gameson (1999a) no. 67; M.I. Allen (2002) I.120*–122*; Hartzell (2006) no. 33; Rankin (2012) 492 and n. 44; Rushforth (2012) 209 n. 74

DEC: Lawrence (1982) 103, 104; Budny (1997) I.691–2 [initials]

ED: M.I. Allen (2002) [Freculf, *Historiae*, coll. as C]; Hartzell (2006) 49 [Office of St Mellitus]

ST: Lambert (1969–72) no. 654; *CSLMA* III (2010) 37–42 [Freculf]; *CALMA* III. 568 [Freculf]

75. Cambridge, Corpus Christi College, 270, fols. 1 and 197

s. xi ex. or xi/xii, prob. Canterbury StA

Contents: Bede, *Historia ecclesiastica* (f)

MS: M.R. James (1912) II.26; Colgrave—Mynors (1969) lvii–lviii; Budny (1997) I.693, 695–6; R. Gameson (1999a) no. 68; Barker-Benfield (2008) I.607, III.1736–7; Wieland (2009) 142

ST: R. Gameson (1998) 242 n. 46

76. Cambridge, Corpus Christi College, 270, fols. 2–173

1091×1100, Canterbury StA

Contents: sacramentary

MS: Rule (1896) xi–xvi; M.R. James (1912) II.25–6; T.A.M. Bishop (1949–53) 438; T.A.M. Bishop (1955) 2; N.R. Ker (1957) p. 267; T.A.M. Bishop (1959–63a) 94; N.R. Ker (1964) 40; N.R. Ker (1960) 29 and n. 2, 30, 42 and n. 1; Anselm Hughes (1963) xi–xiii; Lawrence (1977); Lawrence (1982) 102; Dumville (1992a) 67; R. Gameson (1995a) 102 n. 28, 114 n. 64, 123 and n. 100, 144; Budny (1997) I.693–704 [no. 48]; R. Gameson (1999a) no. 69; C.A. Jones (1999) 114–15; Barker-Benfield (2008) I.530, II.1445, III.1655 n. 43, 1733, 1736–7; Pfaff (2012) 456 and n. 23; Rankin (2012) 501; Webber (2012) 222 n. 56

DEC: Dodwell (1954) 27; Alexander (1978c) 102 and n. 39; Lawrence (1982) 102; R. Gameson (1995a) 124 n. 102; Budny (1997) I.697–704 [inventory of decoration]

FACS: Rule (1896), frontispiece [fol. 70r], cxiii [fol. 9v]; Dodwell (1954) pl. 16 (d) [fol. 46r (detail)]; Lawrence (1982) pl. XXXII (C) [fol. 46r (detail)]; Budny (1997) II, pls. XIV [fol. 12r], 642–75 [fols. 10v, 12r, 12v, 13r, 16r, 33v, 34r, 35r, 41r, 46r, 48v, 51v, 53r, 54r, 64r, 65v, 71v, 78r, 82v, 86r, 90v, 92v, 96v, 98r, 98v, 101v, 109r, 111r, 114v, 116v, 118v, 129r, 135v, 138r]

ED: Rule (1896) [base MS for sacramentary]

ST: Warren (1883) 294–302; Rule (1896) ix–clxxxiv; Förster (1943) 52–3; Heslop (1995) 62–4, 67 n. 37, 83; N. Orchard (1995b) [relationship to no. 291]; Thacker (1999) 385 and n. 68; Pfaff (2001) 186–7; N. Orchard (2002) I.59, 169–70, 172–3, 175, 196, 230; Pfaff (2009) 113–17

77. Cambridge, Corpus Christi College, 272 (the 'Achadeus Psalter')

883×884, Rheims, prov. England s. xi, (prov. Canterbury CC)

Contents: Psalterium Gallicanum with psalter collects (and with commentary mainly from Cassiodorus: England s. xi med. or xi²); litany; Ps. CLI; canticles; prayers and responsories

MS: Frere (1894–1932) no. 886; M.R. James (1912) II.27–32; Mearns (1914) 63; Köhler—Mütherich (1971–99) VI/ii.48–51, 200–6; Keynes—Lapidge (1983) 214 n. 26; P.R. Robinson (1988) I, no. 149; Lapidge (1991a) 64–5; Dumville (1993g) 131 and n. 91; Budny (1997) I.xxxiv; P.P. O'Neill (1997) 162; Bischoff (1998—) I, no. 817; Gretsch (1999a) 31 and n. 72, 249 and n. 68, 273–7; Pratt (2001) 48; Pulsiano (2001a) xxvii; Binski—Panayotova (2005) no. 15 [R. McKitterick]; Hartzell (2006) no. 34; Biggs (2007a) 16–17; Rushforth (2008–); Morgan—Panayotova (2009) I.19–21 [no. 1]; Wieland (2009) 116, 117; Rushforth (2011) 43–5; R. Gameson (2012d) 351 and n. 29; Stoppacci (2012—) I.134; Toswell (2012) 472

DEC: Boutemy (1954–5); Köhler—Mütherich (1971-99) VI/ii.204–6; Morgan—Panayotova (2009) I.19–21

FACS: Köhler—Mütherich (1971–99) *Tafeln* VI, pls. 174 [fols. 150r, 151r], 175 [fols. 151v, 152r], 176 [fols. 152v, 153r], 177 [fols. 153v, 154r], 178 [fols. 98r, 1r, 51r, 163r (all details)]; P.R. Robinson (1988) II, pl. 7 [fol. 154r]; Binski—Panayotova (2006) 68 [fols. 153v–154r], 69 [fol. 98r (detail)]; Rushforth (2008–) pls. 1 [fol. 58r], 2 (a)–(e) [fols. 40v, 51v, 69r, 133v, 108r (all details)]; Morgan—Panayotova (2009) I.19 [fols. 151v–152r], I.20 [fol. 98r], I.21 [fols. 150r (detail), 1r (detail)]; R. Gameson (2012) pl. 14.2 [fol. 47r]

ED: Lapidge (1991a) 110–14 [litany]; Pulsiano (2001a) [Pss. I–L coll. as δ]

ST: Lambert (1969–72) nos. 157, 959; Römer (1972b) 51; Muir (1988) xxxii; Corrêa (1996) 294 n.; Pulsiano (1998b) 105 n. 2; Krüger (2007) 270, 337

79. Cambridge, Corpus Christi College, 276, fols. 1–54

s. xi ex., Canterbury, StA

Contents: Paulus Diaconus, *Historia Romana* [incorporating Eutropius, *Breuiarium historiae Romanae*] [*CPL* 1181]; list of Roman and Byzantine emperors; spurious charter by Pope Leo VIII [Jaffé, *Regesta* 3704]

MS: M.R. James (1912) II.38–9; T.A.M. Bishop (1955) 2; T.A.M. Bishop (1959–63a) 95; R. Gameson (1995a) 106 n. 40, 143; Budny (1997) I.711–16 [no. 50]; R. Gameson (1999a) no. 71; Mortensen (1999–2000) 169 [no. 23]; Barker-Benfield (2008) II.924–6, 943, 946, III.1795

DEC: Lawrence (1982) 102, 103; Budny (1997) I.715 [inventory of decoration]

FACS: Budny (1997) II, pls. 688–92 [fols. 1v–2r, 5v, 18v, 22v, 48v]

ED: Crivellucci (1914) [coll. as A3]; Santini (1979) [Eutropius excerpts coll. as Y]

ST: A.G. Watson (1965) 138; Chiesa—Stella (2005) 486–91

80. Cambridge, Corpus Christi College, 276, fols. 55–134

s. xi/xii, Canterbury StA

Contents: Dudo of Saint-Quentin, *Historia Normannorum* (incomplete)

MS: M.R. James (1912) II.276; Alexander (1970a) 28 n. 2, 40, 212; R. Gameson (1995a) 114 n. 64, 144; R. Gameson (1999a) no. 72; Budny (1997) I.711–16 [no. 50]; Barker-Benfield (2008) II.924–6, 943, 946, III.1795

DEC: R. Gameson (1995a) 124 and n. 104; Budny (1997) I.715–16 [inventory of decoration]

FACS: Budny (1997) II, pls. 693–5 [fols. 55r, 115v, 122r]

ED: Lair (1865) [Dudo coll. as C]

ST: Manitius (1911–31) II.264; Huisman (1984)

81. Cambridge, Corpus Christi College, 279

s. ix/x or x in., NW France, perh. in or near Tours, prov. England by c. 1000, (prov. Worcester)

Contents: *Sinodus episcoporum* ('First Synod of St Patrick') [*CPL* 1102]; collection of canons ('Excerpts from the Fathers') [*BCLL* 610]; *Liber ex lege Moysi* [*CPL* 1793; *BCLL* 611] with Latin, Irish and Breton glosses; canons concerning baptism (*De baptismo*) and bishops (*De episcopo*); excerpts from *Collectio canonum Hibernensis* [*CPL* 1794; *BCLL* 612]; selection of canons

MS: M.R. James (1912) II.42–4; Kenney (1929) nos. 30, 83; Bieler (1963)
15, 23; N.R. Ker (1964) 206; Mordek (1975) 258; Rella (1977) 164
[no. 5]; DeBrún—Herbert (1986) 109 [no. 52]; Deuffic (1986) 297
[no. 20]; Kottje (1987) 62; Dumville (1992a) 148–9; Dumville (1993g) 48
and n. 211; Simpson (1994); Bischoff (1998—) I, no. 818; Kéry (1999)
75, 78; P. Wormald (1999) 419 nn. 10 and 13, 421 nn. 20 and 22; Lapidge
(2006) 167–8; Meeder (2009) 183–5; Morgan—Panayotova (2009) I.24

DEC: Morgan—Panayotova (2009) I.24

FACS: Morgan—Panayotova (2009) I.24 [p. 72]

ED: Bradshaw (1893) 30 [*De baptismo*; *De episcopo*]; Bieler (1963) 54–8
[base MS for *Sinodus episcoporum*]; Faris (1976) 1–8 [base MS for
Sinodus episcoporum]; McHugh (1983) [excerpts from this MS];
Simpson (1994) 118–19 [selection of canons]; Meeder (2009) 191–218
[*Liber ex lege Moysi* and Latin glosses coll. as W]

ST: Bradshaw (1893); Stokes—Strachan (1901–3) II.xii; Bieler (1963) 15,
23, 160–75, 240, 251–3; McHugh (1983) [study (with partial edition)
of this MS]; R. Sharpe (1984); *BCLL* (1985) nos. 599, 610–11; Kottje
(1987) 61–4 [*Liber ex lege Moysi*]; Dumville (1993h); C.D. Wright
(1993) 258; Simpson (1994); Kéry (1999) 73–80; Meeder (2009) [*Liber
ex lege Moysi*]

82. Cambridge, Corpus Christi College, 285, fols. 75–131

s. xi in.

Contents: Aldhelm, *Carmen de uirginitate* [*CPL* 1333]

MS: M.R. James (1912) II.51; Ehwald (1919) 346; N.R. Ker (1957) no. 54;
Bishop (1971) xxv, 18 [no. 20]; Vaciago (1993) 7 [no. 21]; Budny (1997)
I.459–62 [no. 27]; R. Gameson (2012a) 45, 50 and n. 160; Lapidge
(2012b) 32; Scragg (2012a) nos. 153–4

DEC: Budny (1997) I.462 [inventory of decoration]

FACS: Budny (1997) II, pls. 327–31 [fols. 112r, 119v, 121v, 122v, 125r]

ED: Napier (1900) no. 22 [OE glosses]; Ehwald (1919) 350–471
[Aldhelm, *Carmen de uirginitate*, coll. as C¹]

ST: Lendinara (2001a) 213; Lapidge (2012b) 31–5

83. Cambridge, Corpus Christi College, 286 (the 'St Augustine Gospels')

s. vi² or vi/vii, Italy (Rome?), prov. S. England (Minster-in-Thanet?), s.
vii/viii, perh. Canterbury s. viii/ix, prov. Canterbury StA s. x (or ix?)

Contents: gospels; documents* (s. x)

MS: M.R. James (1912) II.52–6; *CLA* II (1935) no. 126; Bischoff (1952) 93 n.; Bischoff (1962) 329, 331, 337; N.R. Ker (1957) no. 55; Lowe (1960) 17 [no. II(a)]; McGurk (1961a) no. 3 and pp. 8 n. 3, 10, 16; McGurk (1961b) 8–9 [repr. McGurk (1998) no. V]; N.R. Ker (1964) 41; Gamber (1968–88) no. 404; Sawyer (1968) 45 [documents]; Petrucci (1971) 108, 110–11; T.J. Brown (1975) 252 [repr. T.J. Brown (1993a) 149]; T.J. Brown (1980) 13; Dodwell (1982) 96; G. Henderson (1982) 15, 41–5; Bischoff (1986) 108 n., 246, 248 n.; Dumville (1987) 171 and n. 4 [no. 4]; Bischoff (1988b) 321; Webster–Backhouse (1991) 17–19 [no. 1]; Dumville (1992a) 99, 120, 122; Dumville (1992b) 94–5; T.J. Brown (1993b) 195, 198; R. Gameson (1994b) 44 n. 88; McGurk (1994b) 11, 19 [repr. McGurk (1998) no. XII]; Netzer (1994) 13, 71, 82, 89–90, 96–7, 99, 208 n. 6, 213 n. 2, 229 n. 132, 236 n. 45; Springer (1995) 123–4; Lapidge (1996c) 414, 440; Budny (1997) I.1–50 [no. 1]; Webster–Brown (1997) 234 [no. 92]; Budny (1999) 252; Dumville (1999) 95; R. Gameson (1999c) 317–22; Marsden (1999) 285; Binski–Panayotova (2005) no. 1 [R. McKitterick]; Rushforth (2007) 54; W. Schipper (2007b) 34; Barker-Benfield (2008) I.442, 530, III.1655, 1660, 1695–6, 1730–1, 1732, 1735, 1782; Wieland (2009) 117; M.P. Brown (2012) 125, 145; R. Gameson (2012a) 34 and n. 82, 53; Gullick (2012) 308 and n. 87; Marsden (2012) 412–13; Scragg (2012a) nos. 155–6

DEC: Köhler (1930–60) I.80, 82; F. Wormald (1952) 61 [no. 9]; McGurk (1961a) 10, 16 [repr. McGurk (1998) no. VI]; McGurk (1962) 23, 31 [repr. McGurk (1998) no. VII]; Nordenfalk (1977) 95; Weitzmann (1977) 112–15; G. Henderson (1982) 15–23, 26, 28–9, 61 n. 86; F. Wormald (1984c); Raw (1990) 197; McGurk (1994b) 16 [repr. McGurk (1998) no. XII]; R. Gameson (1995b) 71–2, 110, 178 n. 135, 183, 197; Lapidge (1996c) 413–14; Budny (1997) I.15–50 [inventory of decoration and illustration]; C.M. Kauffmann (2003) 51, 77, 225; M.P. Brown (2011b) 34, 40; Netzer (2012) 226 and n. 5, 236–7 and n. 73

FACS: D.H. Wright (1967) pls. V (m)–(n) [fols. 40r, 61v]; Weitzmann (1977) pls. 41–2 [fols. 125r, 129v]; G. Henderson (1982) pls. 4, 5 (a)–(b) [fols. 125r, 129r]; F. Wormald (1984) pls. 1 [fol. 125r], 2 [fol. 129v], ills. 7–24 [details from fols. 125r, 129v]; G. Henderson (1987) pl. 173 [fol. 129v]; M.P. Brown (1991) pl. 5 [fol. 129v]; Webster–Backhouse (1991) 18 [fol. 129v]; Dumville (1992b) 104 [fol. 74v]; Netzer (1994) pl. 80 [fol. 129v]; Budny (1997) II, pls. 1–6 [fols. 125r, 129v, 78v, 75r, 265r, 1*v]; Emms (1999a) 417 [fol. 74v]; R. Gameson (1999c) 317 [details of fols. 125r, 129v, 130r, 18r]; Marsden (1999) 286–7 [fols. 39r, 55r (details)]; Cichon (2002) pl. 2 [fol. 129v]; Binski—Panayotova (2005) 46 [fol. 125r]; M.P. Brown (2007a) pl. 4 [fol. 129v]; Rushforth (2007) 54 [fol. 125r]; W. Schipper (2007b) 46–7 [fols. 45v, 194v], 49 [fol. 18v]

ED: J. Wordsworth et al. (1889–1954) [gospels coll. as X]; B. Fischer (1988–91) [gospel excerpts coll. as Jx]

LANG: G. Henderson (1982) 33–40

ST: Glunz (1933) 15, 17, 19–21, 294–6; McGurk (1956) 259, 262 [repr. McGurk (1998) no. I]; F. Wormald (1971b) 309 [repr. F. Wormald (1984) 79]; Verey et al. (1980) 68–74, 106–8; McGurk (1995a) 256, 259 [repr. McGurk (1998) no. XIII]; M.P. Brown (1996); Lenker (1997) 398; Emms (1999a) 417; R. Gameson (1999c); Marsden (1999) 285–312; Verey (1999) 330; Emms (2006) 20; R. McKitterick (2012) 315

85. Cambridge, Corpus Christi College, 291

s. xi/xii, Canterbury StA

Contents: Bede, *De temporum ratione* [*CPL* 2320]; computistical texts and tables; Isidore, *De positione .vii. stellarum errantium* [= *De natura rerum*, ch. xxiii] [*CPL* 1188]; list of the names of the winds; Bede, *Epistola ad Wicthedum de paschae celebratione* [*CPL* 2321]; more *computistica*; Paschal tables (for the years 1064–1595)

MS: Schenkl no. 4916; M.R. James (1912) II.66–7; C.W. Jones (1939) 114; Laistner—King (1943) 120, 148; N.R. Ker (1964) 41; C.W. Jones (1977) 241, 244; C.W. Jones (1980) 633; R. Gameson (1995a) 102 n. 28, 143; Budny (1997) I.705–10 [no. 49]; R. Gameson (1999a) no. 74; Barker-Benfield (2008) I.447, 516

DEC: Lawrence (1982) 102; R. Gameson (1995a) 126 n. 116; Budny (1997) I.708–10 [inventory of decoration and illustration]

FACS: Budny (1997) II, pls. XVI (a) [fol. 3r], 676–87 [fols. 1r, 3r, 5r, 30r, 68r, 84r, 87v, 88r, 92r, 94r, 107r, 122r]

86. Cambridge, Corpus Christi College, 302

s. xi/xii, SE England?

Contents: Ælfric, *Hexameron* (incomplete)*; Homilies* (mostly by Ælfric)

MS: C.L. White (1898) 116–17; M.R. James (1912) II.92–4; Crawford (1921) 7, 15–17; Bethurum (1957) 4; N.R. Ker (1957) no. 56; Pope (1967) I.51–3; Tristram (1970) 99–121; Callison (1973);

Collins—Clemoes (1974) 319; Scragg (1979) 247; Scragg (1992) xxx–xxxi; Laing (1993) 23; Budny (1997) I.850; Parkes (1997b) 139 n. 107; Scragg (1998) 82 n. 9; R. Gameson (1999a) no. 75; Proud (2000) 123–4; Swan (2000b) 67; Treharne (2000a) 1; Treharne (2000b) 13–20, 23–5, 37–9; Wilcox (2000) 84–5; Teresi (2002) 211–17; *ASMMF* XI (2003) 48–54 [no. 48; Treharne]; W. Schipper (2003) 159; Biggs (2007a) 80 [C.D. Wright]; J. Hill (2007a) 88 n. 54; Swan (2007b) 33 n. 12; Teresi (2007a) 285–93, 296–7; Treharne (2007a) 261; Scragg (2012a) nos. 157–8

FACS: Treharne (2000b) pl. 1 [p. 29]; *ASMMF* XI (2003) no. 48

ED [the order of the following items is that of the manuscript, listed according to the numbering of individual articles in N.R. Ker (1957) 96–8; only the most recent editions are cited]:

art. 1: Crawford (1921) 35–74 [Ælfric, *Hexameron*, coll. as D (lines 1–31 are lacking in this MS)]

art. 2: Clemoes (1997) 520–3 [Ælfric, CH I, Hom. XXXIX (First Sunday in Advent), coll. as O]

art. 3: Clemoes (1997) 524–30 [Ælfric, CH I, Hom. XL (Second Sunday in Advent), coll. as O]

art. 4: Skeat (1881–1900) I.364–83 [Ælfric, *Lives of Saints*, no. XVII (*De auguriis*), coll. as E]

art. 5: Bethurum (1957) 172–4 [base MS for Wulfstan, Hom. VIIIb (*Dominica .IIII. uel quando uolueris*)]

art. 6: Clemoes (1997) 190–7 [Ælfric, CH I, Hom. II (Christmas), coll. as O]

art. 7: Clemoes (1997) 198–205 [Ælfric, CH I, Hom. III (St Stephen), coll. as O]

art. 8: Clemoes (1997) 206–16 [Ælfric, CH I, Hom. IV (Assumption of St John the Evangelist), coll. as O]

art. 9: Assmann (1889/1964) 13–23 [Hom. II (a homiletic version of Ælfric's *Letter to Sigefyrð*) coll. as S]

art. 10: Teresi (2002) 226–9 [an anonymous homily for the Third Sunday in Lent coll. as K]

art. 11: Assmann (1889/1964) 164–9 [base MS (= S) for an anonymous homily on the Last Judgement]

art. 12: Napier (1883/1967) 257, line 9—265 [the second part of Hom. XLIX (*Larspell*) coll. as D]; Szarmach (1981a) 11–16 [Vercelli Hom. X coll. as K^2]; Scragg (1992) 203–13 [Vercelli Hom. X, lines 122–275 coll. as k] arts. 13–14: Godden (1979) 41–51 [Ælfric, CH II, Hom. V (Septuagesima Sunday), coll. as O]

art. 15: Godden (1979) 52–9 [Ælfric, CH II, Hom. VI (Sexagesima Sunday), coll. as O]

art. 16: Clemoes (1997) 258–65 [Ælfric, CH I, Hom. X (Quinquagesima Sunday), coll. as O]

art. 17: Skeat (1881–1900) I.260–82 [Ælfric, *Lives of Saints*, no. XII (Ash Wednesday), coll. as E]

art. 18: Clemoes (1997) 266–74 [Ælfric, CH I, Hom. XI (First Sunday in Lent), coll. as O]

art. 19: Godden (1979) 60–6 [Ælfric, CH II, Hom. VII (First Sunday in Lent), coll. as O]

art. 20: Godden (1979) 67–71 [Ælfric, CH II, Hom. VIII (Second Sunday in Lent), coll. as O]

art. 21: Pope (1967–8) I.264–80 [Ælfric, Suppl. Hom. IV (Third Sunday in Lent), coll. as O]

art. 22: Clemoes (1997) 275–80 [Ælfric, CH I, Hom. XII (Sunday in Mid–Lent), coll. as O]

art. 23: Godden (1979) 127–36 [Ælfric, CH II, Hom. XIII (Fifth Sunday in Lent), coll. as O]

art. 24: Assmann (1889/1964) 65–72 [Ælfric, Hom. for Friday after the Fifth Sunday in Lent (= Hom. V), coll. as S²]

art. 25: Clemoes (1997) 290–8 [Ælfric, CH I, Hom. XIV (Palm Sunday), coll. as O]

art. 26: Godden (1979) 137–9 [Ælfric, CH II, Hom. XIV (Palm Sunday), coll. as O]

art. 27: Assmann (1889/1964) 151–63 [anonymous homily *In Cena Domini* (= Hom. XIII) coll. as S²]

art. 28: Godden (1979) 150–60 [Ælfric, CH II, Hom. XV (Easter Sunday), coll. as O]

art. 29: Clemoes (1997) 314–16 [Ælfric, CH I, Hom. XVII (Second Sunday after Easter), coll. as O (lacks lines 1–45)]

art. 30: Clemoes (1997) 317–24 [Ælfric, CH I, Hom. XVIII (*In Letania maiore*), coll. as O]

art. 31: Tristram (1970) 173–85 [base MS for anonymous Rogationtide homily]; Hanley (1979) 102–34 [base MS for anonymous Rogationtide homily]; Bazire—Cross (1982) 70–4 [base MS for anonymous Rogationtide Hom. 5]

art. 32: Clemoes (1997) 325–34 [Ælfric, CH I, Hom. XIX (*Feria .III. De dominica oratione*), coll. as O] art. 33: Napier (1883/1967) 250–65 [Hom. XLIX (*Larspell*) coll. as D]; Szarmach (1981a) 12–16 [Vercelli Hom. X coll. as K¹]; Scragg (1992) 196–213 [Vercelli Hom. X coll. as K]

art. 34: Clemoes (1997) 335–44 [Ælfric, CH I, Hom. XX (*Feria .IIII. De fide catholica*), coll. as O]

LANG: Crawford (1921) 13–15; Callison (1973); Teresi (2002) 217–21

ST: Napier (1883/1967) 355–7 [Ostheeren]; Callison (1973); A.F. Cameron (1974) 220; Scragg (1979) 247; R.I. Page (1993a) 97; C.D. Wright (1993) 215; J. Hill (1996) 244; Scragg (1998) 83 n. 24; S. Irvine (2000) 41–3, 55; Teresi (2000) 99–116; Acker (2004) 129; Teresi (2007a) 285–90, 294–5, 299, 308; Zacher (2007) 185

87. Cambridge, Corpus Christi College, 304

s. viii¹, Italy, prov. s. ix ex. or x in. England (Canterbury CC? Malmesbury?)

Contents: Isidore, *Versus in bibliotheca* [*CPL* 1212; SK 15860: excerpts]; Iuvencus, *Euangelia* [*CPL* 1385]

MS: M.R. James (1912) II.100–2; Beeson (1913) 133–66; *CLA* II (1935) no. 127; Brownrigg (1978) 241 n. 1; Rella (1980) 110; Lapidge (1982a) 108–9 [repr. Lapidge (1996b) 470–4]; Lapidge (1996c) 414–15; Budny (1997) I.51–4 [no. 2]; R. Gameson (1999c) 366 n. 43; Martín Sánchez (2000) 128–30; Hartzell (2006) no. 35

DEC: Lapidge (1996c) 414–15; Budny (1997) I.54 [decoration added in England]

FACS: Budny (1997) II, pl. 7 [fol. 74v]

ED: Huemer (1891) [Iuvencus, *Euangelia*, coll. as C]; Lapidge (1982a) 109–10 [base text for Iuvencus, *Euangelia* I.1–12 (fols. 5v–6r)] [repr. Lapidge (1996b) 473–4]; Martín Sánchez (2000) 210–35 [Isidore, *Versus in bibliotheca*, coll. as C]

ST: Manitius (1911–31) I.69; Schanz et al. (1914–20) IV/i.212; Lapidge (1982a) 108–9 [repr. Lapidge (1996b) 470–8]; R.M. Thomson (1982b) 3–4: R.M. Thomson (1987) 100

88. Cambridge, Corpus Christi College, 307, pt. 1 (fols. 1–52)

s. x in., Worcester?

Contents: Felix, *Vita S. Guthlaci* [*BHL* 3723; *CPL* 2150]; two acrostic poems [SK 4297, 2361: s. x med.]

MS: M.R. James (1912) II.105–7; Colgrave (1956) 26–7; Morrish (1986) 94 n. 15, 105 n. 55; Dumville (1987) 166–7 and nn. 97–9; Morrish (1988) 536; Lapidge (1991c) 963–5 [repr. Lapidge (1993a) 13–15]; Dumville (1992a) 108 n. 75; Wieland (2009) 130

FACS: Morrish (1988) pl. 9 [fol. 6v]

ED: M.R. James (1912) II.105–6 [acrostics]; Colgrave (1956) [*Vita S. Guthlaci* coll. as C$_1$]

ST: Colgrave (1956) 46–52

88. 5. Cambridge, Corpus Christi College, 309, flyleaves

s. xi ex. or xi/xii, England or more prob. Continent. In England by 1100?

Contents: Sallust, *Bellum Iugurthinum* (f)

MS: M.R. James (1912) II.109

90. Cambridge, Corpus Christi College, 320, pt. ii (fols. 117–70)

s. x^2 or x ex., Canterbury StA

Contents: formulas and directions for the use of confessors* (s. x/xi); *Poenitentiale Theodori* (incomplete) [*CPL* 1885]; Gregory and Augustine of Canterbury, *Libellus responsionum* [cf. *CPL* 1714]; poem by Archbishop Theodore [SK 16100]; Order of confession; *Poenitentiale Sangermanense* [rectius *Cantabrigiense*]; encyclopedic notes (as in nos. **56** and **451**): on Christ's Incarnation, the Ages of the World, the Ages of Man, the numbers of bones, veins and teeth in humans, the Dimensions of the World, the Temple of Solomon, the Tabernacle, St Peter's in Rome, Noah's Ark, the numbers of books in the Old and New Testament, the number of verses in the psalms, units for measuring distances, the order of events in the Seven Days of Creation, the site of Jerusalem; fragment of the *Scriftboc**

MS: M.R. James (1912) II.132–7; T.A.M. Bishop (1954–8b) 326, 330; N.R. Ker (1957) no. 58; T.A.M. Bishop (1971) no. 7; Frantzen (1983a) 38; Sauer (1991) 22–3; Webster—Backhouse (1991) 74–5 [no. 58; M.P. Brown]; Dumville (1992a) 134; Lapidge (1992a) 123 n. 111 [repr. Lapidge (1993a) 411 n. 111]; Budny (1997) I. 225–30 [no. 18]; Delen (2002); Barker-Benfield (2008) I.754, II.1480, III.1811–12; Scragg (2012a) no. 159

DEC: Budny (1997) I.230 [inventory of decoration]

FACS: Budny (1997) II, pls. 172–3 [pp. 83, 95]; R. Gameson (2012) pl.
7b.3 [fol. 149r]

ED: Haddan—Stubbs (1869–71) III.176–203 [base MS (= C) for
Poenitentiale Theodori]; Finsterwalder (1929) 285–7 [*Poenitentiale
Theodori*]; Sauer (1993) [base MS for exhortations (pp. 42–3, 48, 50)];
Lapidge (1995b) 275 [repr. Lapidge (1996b) 240] [poem by Archbishop
Theodore]; Delen et al. (2002) [*Poenitentiale Sangermanense* rectius
Cantabrigiense]; Dekker (2007) 281–4 [chronological and other notes];
Fulk—Jurasinski (2012) 79–80 [base MS for formulas and directions
for the use of confessors], 81 [base MS for fragment of the *Scriftboc*]

ST: Lapidge (1975b) 817; Scragg (1979) 260; Frantzen (1983b) 131 nn.
30–1, 164 n. 40; Frantzen (1985) 26–7; Lapidge (1986b) 46–7 [repr.
Lapidge (1996b) 142–3]; Bischoff—Lapidge (1994) 71, 186, 210; A.
Orchard (1994) 30; Lapidge (1995b) 260, 275 [repr. Lapidge (1996b)
225, 240]; Dekker (2007)

91. Cambridge, Corpus Christi College, 321, fol. 139*

s. xi[1] or xi med.

Contents: dialogue on Alleluia*

MS: M.R. James (1912) II.138 [transcription of OE text]; N.R. Ker (1957)
no. 59; Budny (1997) I.xxxvi; Scragg (2012a) no. 160

92. Cambridge, Corpus Christi College, 322

s. xi[1], Worcester? (prov. Worcester?)

Contents: Gregory (Werferth), *Dialogi**

MS: Hecht (1900–7) I.vii; M.R. James (1912) II.138–9; N.R. Ker (1957)
no. 60 and p. lxiv; Yerkes (1986a) 335–7; Franzen (1991) 75, 77, 109,
124; R.I. Page (1993a) 53–5, 100; Budny (1997) I.623–8 [no. 42];
R. Gameson (1999a) no. 77; R. Gameson (2005a) 94, 101–4; Treharne
(2007b) 17; Crick (2012) 184 and n. 47; R. Gameson (2012a) 87 n. 316;
Scragg (2012a) no. 161

DEC: Budny (1997) I.628 [inventory of decoration]

FACS: Budny (1997) II, pls. 588–95 [fols. 6v, 34r, 40v, 41v, 48r, 58r, 67v,
110v]

ED: Hecht (1900–7) vol. I [base MS (= C) for OE translation of the
Dialogi]; Yerkes (1977a) [base MS (= C) for corrections to Hecht's
edition of the *Dialogi*]

LANG: Hecht (1900–7) II.134–83; Yerkes (1982a); Hofstetter (1987) 312–15

ST: Hecht (1900–7) vol. II; A.F. Cameron (1974) 224; Yerkes (1977b); Yerkes (1977c); Yerkes (1977–80); Yerkes (1978a) 245 [glosses on fol. 20]; Yerkes (1978b); Yerkes (1979); P.S. Baker (1980) 25–6; O'Brien O'Keeffe (1985) 72; Langefeld (1986) 199–202; Yerkes (1986a); R.I. Page (1993a) 98–100; Godden (1997); Waite (2000) 46–8, 354–68

93. Cambridge, Corpus Christi College, 326

s. x/xi, Canterbury CC

Contents: *Aldhelm*** (OE poem); Aldhelm, *De uirginitate* (prose)° [*CPL* 1332]; Abbo of Saint-Germain-des-Prés, *Bella Parisiacae urbis* III.1-17, with Latin gloss; glosses; *sententiae*; On Adam's creation; Latin poem (by Alcuin?) [SK 10046]; *De ebrietate* [extract from a florilegium]; three Latin notes, one on grammar; rota poem [SK 11297]; runic colophon (?)

MS: M.R. James (1912) II.143–6; Ehwald (1919) 219–20; N.R. Ker (1957) no. 61; Goossens (1974) 19; Lapidge (1975a) 76, 83 n. 2 [repr. Lapidge (1993a) 114, 121 n. 2]; Silagi (1979) 665 n.; Robinson—Stanley (1991) 22; Dumville (1992a) 20; Vaciago (1993) 7 [no. 22]; Gwara (1996a) 93; Lendinara (1996) 617 n. 7; Budny (1997) I.245–52 [no. 21]; Gwara (1997a) 568; Gwara (1998) 140 n. 7; Gwara (2001) I.109*–113*; R. Gameson (2001d) 41; Meaney (2004) 498; Hartzell (2006) no. 37; Biggs (2007a) 4; Wieland (2009) 143; Lendinara (2010) 113–17; Lapidge (2012b) 27; Scragg (2012a) nos. 162–5

DEC: F. Wormald (1945) 134 [repr. F. Wormald (1984) 73]; E. Temple (1976) no. 19 (iv); Ohlgren (1986) no. 100; R. Gameson (1995b) 221 nn. 169 and 172, 222 nn. 179 and 181; Budny (1997) I.251–2 [inventory of decoration and illustration]

FACS: Robinson—Stanley (1991) pls. 9.1–2 [pp. 5–6]; Budny (1997) II, pls. 192–202 [pp. 5, 6, 7, 11, 36, 54, 57, 66, 71b, 77, 202]

ED: Napier (1900) no. 4 [OE glosses to Aldhelm, prose *De uirginitate*]; Förster (1908b) 479–81 [On Adam's creation]; M.R. James (1912) II.144–5 [Abbo; Latin poem (by Alcuin?)]; Ehwald (1919) 229–323 [Aldhelm, prose *De uirginitate*, coll. as C¹]; Dobbie (1942) 97–8 [OE poem *Aldhelm*]; Meritt (1945) 1 [OE scratched glosses to Aldhelm]; R.I. Page (1975) [OE glosses]; Gwara (1997b) [OE scratched glosses to Aldhelm]; Gwara (2001) vol. II [Aldhelm, prose *De uirginitate*, with OE and Latin glosses, coll. as C1]

ST: Förster (1907–8) 479–81; R. Derolez (1954) 421; T.A.M. Bishop (1954–8a) 187; T.A.M. Bishop (1959–63b) 414–15; R.I. Page (1973a); R.I. Page (1975); Lendinara (1986) 84; F.C. Robinson (1989); Biggs et al. (1990) 115 [*De ebrietate*; C.D. Wright]; Lendinara (1990) 140–2; *CSLMA* I (1994) 3–5 [Abbo of Saint–Germain]; Gwara (1997a); Gwara (1997b); Gretsch (1999a) 144; *CSLMA* II (1999) 82–3 [Latin poem (by Alcuin?)]; Biggs et al. (2001) 15–18 [Abbo, *Bella Parisiacae urbis*; Lendinara]; Gwara (2001) vol. I; Biggs (2007a) 4–5 [Adam's creation]; Lendinara (2011a) 487 and n. 42; Lapidge (2012b) 26–31

94. Cambridge, Corpus Christi College, 328, pp. 1–80

s. xi/xii or xii in., Canterbury CC?, (prov. Winchester OM)

Contents: Osbern, *Vita S. Dunstani* [*BHL* 2344–5]; mass and sequence (*AH* LIII.237) for St Dunstan [both probably composed by Osbern]; excerpts from Eadmer, *Vita S. Dunstani* [*BHL* 2346], chs. lvii, xlvi

MS: Stubbs (1874) xlvi–xlvii; M.R. James (1912) II.148–9; Budny (1997) I.731–5 [no. 53]; R. Gameson (1999a) no. 78; Turner—Muir (2006) xcii–xciii; Hartzell (2006) no. 38; Winterbottom—Lapidge (2012) clix

DEC: Budny—Graham (1993) [scribal portrait of Dunstan on p. 1]; R. Gameson (1995a) 117 n. 77; Budny (1997) I.735 [inventory of decoration]

FACS: Budny (1997) II, pl. 712 [p. 1]

ED: Stubbs (1874) 69–161 [base MS (= CC) for Osbern, *Vita S. Dunstani*], 442–3 [base MS for mass and sequence]; Turner—Muir (2006) [excerpts from Eadmer, *Vita S. Dunstani*, coll. as Win]

ST: Legg (1891–7) 1549 [sequence]; Budny—Graham (1993) 83–96 [portrait of Dunstan]; N. Orchard (1995a) 91 n. 25 [mass]; Winterbottom—Lapidge (2012)

95. Cambridge, Corpus Christi College, 330 pt. i

s. xi/xii or xii in., Normandy? Malmesbury?, (prov. Malmesbury)

Contents: Martianus Capella, *De nuptiis Philologiae et Mercurii*; list of the Muses; verses on the Muses [SK 2425]

MS: M.R. James (1912) II.153–4; Leonardi (1960) 22–3 [no. 30]; N.R. Ker (1964) 128 and n. 9; T.A.M. Bishop (1964–8c) 267; R.M. Thomson (1978) 124–5; A.G. Watson (1987a) 48; Budny (1997) I.737–41 [no. 54]; R. Gameson (1999a) no. 80

DEC: Budny (1997) I.740–1 [inventory of decoration]

FACS: Budny (1997) II, pls. 713–22 [fols. 1r, 9r, 27v, 35v, 50r, 62v, 70r, 73v, 77v, 79r]

ST: R.M. Thomson (1975) 392–4; R.M. Thomson (1982b) 15–16; Bodden (1988) 230–1; R. McKitterick (2012) 328

96. Cambridge, Corpus Christi College, 330 pt. ii

s. ix ex., France, prov. England s. x, (prov. Malmesbury)

Contents: 'Dunchad' (Martin of Laon?), Commentary on Martianus Capella; *glossae collectae*

MS: M.R. James (1912) II.154; Leonardi (1960) 22–3 [no. 30]; T.A.M. Bishop (1964–8c) 267; R.M. Thomson (1978) 124–5; R. Gameson (1999a) no. 80

FACS: T.A.M. Bishop (1964–8c) pl. XXII (a) [fol. 15r]

ST: T.A.M. Bishop (1964–8c) 257, 267–71 [on relationship to no. 48]; C.E. Lutz (1971) 371–2; *BCLL* (1985) no. 1182; R.M. Thomson (1987) 81–2, 111; *CALMA* III.154 ['Dunchad']

97. Cambridge, Corpus Christi College, 352

s. x med. or x^2, prob. Canterbury StA, (prov. ibid.)

Contents: Boethius, *De institutione arithmetica* [*CPL* 879], with scholia s. x and xi/xii

MS: M.R. James (1912) II.185–6; T.A.M. Bishop (1964–8c) 259–62; N.R. Ker (1964) 41; T.A.M. Bishop (1971) no. 4; Rella (1977) 72; Dumville (1987) 150 n. 12; Gibson et al. (1995–2001) I.54–5 [no. 21]; Gwara (1996a) 94 n. 47; Budny (1997) I.237–43 [no. 20]; Oosthout—Schillling (1999) v–vi; Treharne (2007a) 255; Graham (2009) 170

DEC: Gibson et al. (1995–2001) I.55; Budny (1997) I.240–3 [inventory of decoration and illustration]

FACS: Budny (1997) II, pls. 179–91 [fols. 1r, 2r, 4r, 4v, 5r, 9r, 14r, 30r, 33r, 42r, 43v, 44v, 77r]; Owen-Crocker (2009) fig. 6.5 [fol. 4v]

ED: Oosthout—Schilling (1999) [Boethius, *De institutione arithmetica*, coll. as F]

ST: Biggs et al. (1990) 75–6 [Wittig]

98. Cambridge, Corpus Christi College, 356, pt. iii

s. x^2 or $x^{4/4}$, prob. Canterbury StA

Contents: 'Abba' glossary; Hebrew alphabet; medical recipe (s. xi)

MS: M.R. James (1912) II.189–90; T.A.M. Bishop (1954–8a) 188; T.A.M. Bishop (1954–8b) 334–6; Lendinara (1990a) 134 n. 8; Lendinara (1996) 631–2; Budny (1997) I.231–5 [no. 19]; Barker-Benfield (2008) I.595, III.1812; Wieland (2009) 156

DEC: Budny (1997) I.234–5 [inventory of decoration]

FACS: Budny (1997) II, pls. 174–8 [fols. 1r, 15r, 16v–17r, 21v, 22v]

ST: Lindsay (1917) ['Abba' glossary]; T.A.M. Bishop (1966) App. 3; Bodden (1988) 230 n. 49; Gneuss (1994) 66–7

99. Cambridge, Corpus Christi College, 361

s. xi med. or xi², England? Malmesbury?, (prov. Malmesbury)

Contents: Gregory, *Regula pastoralis* [*CPL* 1712]; *Passio S. Mauritii* (f; s. xi/xii; a version of *BHL* 5746)

MS: M.R. James (1912) II.193–4; N.R. Ker (1964) 128; Clement (1984a) 41; Budny (1997) I.667–73 [no. 45]; R.M. Thomson (1987) 78–9, 112

DEC: Budny (1997) I.670–3 [inventory of decoration and illustration]

FACS: Budny (1997) II, pls. 609–15 [fols. 1r, 5v, 54r, 58v, 63r, 68v, 95v]

ST: R.M. Thomson (1978) 121; Lucas (1980) 5; R.M. Thomson (1982b) 16; Clement (1985a); Clement (1986) 150 n. 25; R. Gameson (1998) 242 n. 45; Biggs et al. (2001) 335–7 [*Passio S. Mauritii*]; Schreiber (2003) 24–6, 31–3

100. Cambridge, Corpus Christi College, 367, pt. ii (fols. 45–52)

s. xi med., prob. Worcester

Contents: Goscelin (?), *Vita breuior S. Kenelmi* [lections ii (part), iii–viii]; booklist*; Vision of Leofric* (s. xi²); two sequences for Epiphany [SK 5530, 8630: s. xi²]

MS: M.R. James (1912) II.202–4; N.R. Ker (1957) no. 64; N.R. Ker (1964) 205; McIntyre (1978) 202; Dumville (1992a) 124; Gatch (1992) 160; Lapidge (1992a) 118–19 n. 85 [repr. Lapidge (1993a) 406–7 n. 85]; Love (1996) cxxi–cxxii, cxxiv; McDougall—McDougall (1997) 216 n. 41; R. Gameson (1999a) no. 83; *ASMMF* XI (2003) 67–73 [no. 54; Treharne]; R. Gameson (2005a) 92; Hartzell (2006) no. 40; Swan (2007b) 37–8; Treharne (2007b) 17; Scragg (2012a) nos. 166–7

DEC: Budny (1997) I.851

FACS: *ASMMF* XI (2003) no. 54

ED: Napier (1907–10) 180–8 [Vision of Leofric]; Lapidge (1994b) 130–2 [booklist]; Love (1996) 126–9 [base MS for *Vita brevior S. Kenelmi*]

LANG: A.F. Cameron (1974) 222; Yerkes (1979) xvi n. 2; Laing (1993) 23

ST: Antropoff (1965); Pulsiano (1985b) [Vision of Leofric]; Gatch (1992) [Vision of Leofric]; R. Gameson (1996a) 217 n. 72, 238; Rankin (1996) 338; R. Sharpe et al. (1996) 653–4 [no. B.114]; Thacker (1996) 260 n. 106; N.M. Thompson (2004) 60

101. Cambridge, Corpus Christi College, 368

s. x/xi (or xi²?), England

Contents: *Regula S. Benedicti* [*CPL* 1852] (incomplete; text to ch. lxi. 7)

MS: M.R. James (1912) II.204–5; Farmer (1968) 27; Gretsch (1973) 29–30; Rella (1977) 56; Dumville (1993g) 8 n. 4; Budny (1997) I.455–8 [no. 26]

DEC: Budny (1997) I.457–8 [inventory of decoration and illustration]

FACS: Budny (1997) II, pls. 321–6 [fols. 8r, 11v, 13r, 18r, 20r, 22v]

ED: Gretsch (1973) 68–87 [chs. v, xxvii, xxviii, xxix, xxx, lviii coll. as *q*]

ST: Gretsch (1973) 111–13; Gretsch (1974) 126–37 [discussion of variant readings (*q*)]

102. Cambridge, Corpus Christi College, 383

s. xi/xii, prob. London, St Paul's

Contents: a collection of Anglo-Saxon laws*; charm*; and additions of s. xii¹: record*; West-Saxon royal genealogy* (incomplete)

MS: M.R. James (1912) II.230–1; Dickins (1952) 8; N.R. Ker (1957) no. 65; Torkar (1981) 105–7; Dumville (1986) 12; M.P. Richards (1986) 181–4; Webster—Backhouse (1991) no. 242; R.I. Page (1993a) 48; R. Gameson (1999a) no. 85; P. Wormald (1999) 165, 185 n. 97, 228–30, 235, 250, 257 n. 359, 265, 292; S. Irvine (2000) 42–3; Treharne (2000a) 1; Baxter (2004) 165 n. 17; *ASMMF* XI (2003) 74–80 [no. 55; Lucas]; Hough (2006) 115, 121, 122, 134; Rumble (2006a) viii; Grimmer (2007) 103 n. 5; Scragg (2012a) nos. 168–9; P. Wormald (2012) 534 [no. 12]

FACS: R.I. Page (1993a) pl. 32 [opening]; *ASMMF* XI (2003) no. 55; Hough (2006) pl. 16 [p. 27]; Owen-Crocker (2009) fig. 6.14 [fol. 57r]

ED [the order of the following items is that of the manuscript, listed according to Ker's numbering of individual articles (see N.R. Ker (1957) 111–13; only the most recent editions are cited]:

art. 1: Liebermann (1903–16) I.51–123 [base MS (= B) for *Ælf.–Ine*]

art. 2: Liebermann (1903–16) I.388–90 [base MS (= B) for *Blas., Forf. 1*]

art. 3: Liebermann (1903–16) I.390 [base MS (= B) for *Forf. 2*]

art. 4: Liebermann (1903–16) I.192–4 [base MS (= B) for *Hundredgemot*]

art. 5: Liebermann (1903–16) I.216–20 [base MS (= B) for *I Atr.*]

art. 6: Liebermann (1903–16) I.126–8, col. 2 [base MS (= B) for *A. Gu*]

art. 7: Liebermann (1903–16) I.128–34 [base MS (= B) for *E. Gu*]

art. 8: Liebermann (1903–16) I.150–2 [base MS (= B) for *II As.*]

art. 9: Liebermann (1903–16) I.294–306 [base MS (= B) for *I Cnut*]

art. 10: Liebermann (1903–16) I.308–70 [base MS (= B) for *II Cnut*]

art. 11: Liebermann (1903–16) I.138–40 [base MS (= B) for *I Ew.*]

art. 12: Liebermann (1903–16) I.140–4 [base MS (= B) for *II Ew. 1–7*]

art. 13: Liebermann (1903–16) I.144 [base MS (= B) for *II Ew. 8*]

art. 14: Liebermann (1903–16) I.184 [base MS (= B) for *I Em.*]

art. 15: Liebermann (1903–16) I.186–90 [base MS (= B) for *II Em.*]

art. 16: Liebermann (1903–16) I.396–8 [base MS (= B) for *Swerian*]

art. 17: Liebermann (1903–16) I.126–8, col. 1 [base MS (= B) for *A. Gu*]

art. 18: Liebermann (1903–16) I.442–4 [base MS (= B) for *Wif*]

art. 19: Liebermann (1903–16) I.392–4 [base MS (= B) for *Wer*]

art. 20: Storms (1948) 204 [OE charm (no. 11B); this MS not collated]

art. 21: Liebermann (1903–16) I.400 [base MS (= B) for *Becwæð*]

art. 22: Liebermann (1903–16) I.220–6 [base MS (= B) for *II Atr.*]

art. 23: Liebermann (1903–16) I.374–8 [base MS (= B) for *Dunsæte*]

art. 24: Liebermann (1903–16) I.444–53 [base MS (= B) for *Rect.*]

art. 25: Liebermann (1903–16) I.453–5 [base MS (= B) for *Gerefa*]

art. 26: A.J. Robertson (1939) 144 [no. LXXII] [base MS for List of the Contributions of Men required for Manning a Ship]

art. 27: Dickins (1952) 2–4 [base MS (= S) for West Saxon genealogy]; Dumville (1986) 21–5 [West Saxon genealogy coll. as W]

ST: Liebermann (1900) [art. 26]; M.P. Richards (1988) 47, 49, 51; P. Wormald (1999) 234; Bredehoft (2001) 27; Hough (2006) 116, 121, 122, 124, 128, 134; Gneuss (2012) 288

103. Cambridge, Corpus Christi College, 389

s. x² or x³/⁴ or x ex., Canterbury StA; frontispiece added ibid. s. xi med.

Contents: Jerome, *Vita S. Pauli primi eremitae* [*CPL* 617; *BHL* 6596]; Felix, *Vita S. Guthlaci* [*CPL* 2150; *BHL* 3723]

MS: M.R. James (1912) II.239–40; Dodwell (1954) 27–8, 122; Colgrave (1956) 27–8; N.R. Ker (1957) no. 66; T.A.M. Bishop (1971) 3 [relationship of script to no. **684**]; Rella (1977) 158; Dumville (1992a) 139;

Vaciago (1993) 7 [no. 23]; Dumville (1994a) 138; Budny (1997) I.265–74 [no. 23]; Binski—Panayotova (2005) no. 112 [Webber]; Lapidge (2006) 316; Barker-Benfield (2008) I.606, III.1683, 1747, 1748, 1779, 1782–3, 1816; Wieland (2009) 130; D. Ganz (2012) 193 and n. 35; Scragg (2012a) no. 170

DEC: F. Wormald (1952) 61 [no. 10]; E. Temple (1976) no. 36; Lawrence (1982) 102; Ohlgren (1986) no. 141; R. Gameson (1991) 74–5; R. Gameson (1995a) 122; R. Gameson (1995b) 185; Budny (1997) I.269–74 [inventory of decoration and illustration]

FACS: Lambert (1969–72) IVA, pl. III [fol. 1v]; Budny (1997) II, pls. X [fol. 1v], 209–21 [fols. 2r, 3v, 4r, 6r, 9v, 11r, 11v, 17v, 18r, 22v, 27r, 33v, 56r]; R. Gameson (2000b) pl. 2 [fol. 22v]; Binski—Panayotova (2005) 248 [fol. 22v]; Rushforth (2007) 43 [fol. 1v]; Withers (2007) 80 [fol. 17v]

ED: Oldfather (1943) [*Vita S. Pauli* coll. as MS. 26]; Meritt (1945) no. 15 [five OE glosses]; Colgrave (1956) [*Vita S. Guthlaci* coll. as C₂]

ST: Lambert (1969–72) nos. 261, 995; Boynton (1999) 237 [comparison with Paris, BNF, lat. 103]; Biggs et al. (2001) 244–7 [St Guthlac], 378–81 [St Paul the Hermit]; Withers (2007) 76–8

104. Cambridge, Corpus Christi College, 391

s. xi³/⁴, Worcester

Contents: *portiforium*: liturgical calendar; *computistica*; Psalterium Gallicanum; Ps. CLI; canticles; litany; hymnal; Monastic canticles; collectar with Office chants; exorcisms, blessings, ordeals; prayers⁺*; Mass prayers; Offices; votive offices; prognostics* (including *lunaria*)

MS: M.R. James (1912) II.241–8; Dewick—Frere (1914–21) II.xvii–xix; Mearns (1914) 63, 83; N.R. Ker (1957) no. 67; Gjerløw (1961) 25, 132–4; N.R. Ker (1964) 206; Gamber (1968–88) no. 1693; Gneuss (1968) 8 n. 12, 55, 78, 103, 106–8, 113, 120, 122; T.A.M. Bishop (1971) 20 n. 1 [no. 22]; Korhammer (1976); Rella (1977) 79–80; Gneuss (1985) 112–13 [nos. F.1, G.1]; Lapidge (1986a) 269; Gerchow (1988) 266–8, 340; P.R. Robinson (1988) I, no. 157; Hartzell (1989) 77, 84; Lapidge (1991a) 65; Dumville (1992a) 25; Budny (1993) 27–8; Dumville (1993g) 4 n. 15; Günzel (1993) 203, 205; Laing (1993) 23; Vaciago (1993) 7 [no. 24]; Corrêa (1995) 57–8; Springer (1995) 124; Keynes (1996a) 59 n. 86; Milfull (1996) 43–7; Budny (1997) I.629–44 [no. 43]; Bullough (1998a) 129 n. 83; C.A. Jones (1998a) 241 n. 35; Muir (1998) 15; Teviotdale (1998) 224; R. Gameson (1999a) no. 86; P. Wormald (1999)

186–7 nn. 100–1; Liuzza (2001) 206, 208, 210, 213–14; J. Barrow (2004) 156; R. Gameson (2005a) 95, 101–4; Foys (2006) 279–80; Hartzell (2006) 53–66 [no. 42]; Biggs (2007a) 16–17; Chardonnens (2007b) 51–3, 503–5, 549; Heslop (2007) 67–8; Treharne (2007b) 17; Rushforth (2008a) 44–6 [no. 21]; Wieland (2009) 134; Liuzza (2011) 8–9; R. Gameson (2012a) 22 and n. 33; R. Gameson (2012b) 100 and n. 25; Pfaff (2012) 457–8 and n. 27; Rankin (2012) 503 and n. 101; Raw (2012) 460, 461 and n. 9; Scragg (2012a) nos. 171–3; Toswell (2012) 472

DEC: F. Wormald (1952) 61–2 [no. 11]; Dodwell (1971b) 222 n. 121; C.M. Kauffmann (1975) no. 3; Ohlgren (1986) no. 214; Raw (1990) 197; R. Gameson (1991) 68–70; Dumville (1992a) 52, 54 [parallels with no. **26**]; R. Gameson (1995b) 122 n. 24; Budny (1997) I.634–44 [inventory of decoration and illustration]; Rosenthal (2011) 234; R. Gameson (2012c) 280

FACS: Huglo (1987) pl. XXI [p. 662]; Budny (1993) pl. 1 [pp. 24–5]; Corrêa (1996) pl. 11 [p. 536]; Milfull (1996) pl. II(b) [p. 245]; Rankin (1996) pl. 12 [pp. 295, 635, 670 (details)]; Budny (1997) II, pls. XI [p. 24], 596–603 [pp. 2–3, 24–5, 46, 122, 192, 295, 422, 443]; R. Gameson (2005a) fig. 2 [pp. 24–5]

ED: Dewick—Frere (1914–21) II.295–495 [base MS for abstract of the 'Wulfstan Collectar' (pp. 503–85), for liturgical calendar with local obits (pp. 589–602), for litany (pp. 602–5), for hymnal (pp. 605–8), for various offices (pp. 608–10)]; F. Wormald (1934) 3–14 [liturgical calendar (no. 17)]; Förster (1929) 718 [base MS (= W) for the marvellous properties of three days (p. 260) and blood-letting days (p. 273)]; Hurst—Fraipont (1955) 419–23 [Bede, Ascension Hymn, coll. as *Cant*]; Anselm Hughes (1958–60) [base MS for collectar; a collection of blessings, ordeals, prayers, Offices (pp. 295–704 of MS)]; Korhammer (1976) 254–351 [Monastic canticles coll. as C]; Gerchow (1988) 340 [obits in liturgical calendar]; Lapidge (1991a) 115–19 [litany]; Davril (1995) [Mass prayers coll. as Wu]; Milfull (1996) 109–467 [hymnal coll. as C; base MS for hymns nos. 157–9]; Pulsiano (2001a) [Pss. I–L coll. as ε]; Chardonnens (2007b) *passim* [prognostics]; Rushforth (2008a) no. 21 [liturgical calendar]

ST: McLachlan (1929); Knowles (1963) 553; Korhammer (1973) 181; A.F. Cameron (1974) 221; Hohler (1975) 74; Kotzor (1981) I.303*–305*; Bestul (1984) 355–64; Clayton (1984) 225 [Marian feasts]; Lapidge (1988b) 259 n. 30 [repr. Lapidge (1993a) 217 n. 30]; Muir (1988) xxix [analogues with seventeen prayers in no. **333**]; Franzen (1991) 69–70 [glosses]; Corrêa (1992) 245–83 [comparison of liturgical formulae with no. **223**]; Ortenberg (1992); Günzel (1993) 198–201, 206–7 [private prayers]; Baker—Lapidge (1995) lii; Heslop (1995) 64 n. 32 [litany]; J. Barrow (1996) 88 [community of Worcester]; M.P. Brown (1996) 140–3, 157–8, 160; Corrêa (1996) 286, 288 n. 5, 292 n. 25; R. Gameson (1996a) 219–22, 238; Mason (1996a) 208–9; Mason (1996b) 282; Milfull (1996) 93–103; Rankin (1996) 326–7, 338–40, 343, 345; Lenker (1997) 492; Pulsiano (1998b) 85–6, 88, 105 nn. 4–5, 109 n. 22 [comparison with no. **407**]; Pfaff (1999b) 82–4; Collier (2000) 195; Borst (2001) I.290 [liturgical calendar]; Liuzza (2001) 213–14 [bibliography]; Pfaff (2001) 191–2; R. Gameson (2005a); Rankin (2005a) 220–2; Chardonnens (2007a) 336 [prognostics]; Chardonnens (2010) 246–9; Liuzza (2011) 1–77 [prognostics]

105. Cambridge, Corpus Christi College, 399

s. ix¹ or ix med., N. France (W France?), prov. England by s. x¹

Contents: Iulianus Toletanus, *Prognosticum futuri saeculi* [*CPL* 1258]

MS: M.R. James (1912) II.262–3; Hillgarth (1957) 24 [no. 13]; Hillgarth (1976) liv; Budny (1997) I.133–6 [no. 9]; Bischoff (1998—) I, no. 819; Lapidge (2006) 168, 318; R. Gameson (2012a) 63 and n. 223

DEC: Budny (1997) I.136 [inventory of added decoration and illustration]

FACS: Budny (1997) II, pls. 102–3 [fols. "ii"v–1r, 71r]

ED: Hillgarth (1976) [Iulianus Toletanus, *Prognosticum*, coll. as C]

106. Cambridge, Corpus Christi College, 411

s. x², Canterbury (CC?), or s. x¹, W France (Loire valley: Tours?)?, prov. Abingdon?, (prov. Canterbury)

Contents: Mass chants (s. xi/xii or xii); Psalterium Gallicanum, with scholia; canticles; two litanies (one added s. x/xi); prayers; seven gospel pericopes (add. s. xii)

MS: M.R. James (1912) II.296–8; T.A.M. Bishop (1954–8a) 187; Gneuss (1985) 115 [no. H.4]; Bischoff (1986) 167 n.; Lapidge (1988b) 260 [repr. Lapidge (1993a) 218]; Lapidge (1991a) 65–6; Dumville (1992a) 74–5, 151; Dumville (1993g) 108 n. 127, 155 n. 90; Budny (1997) I.253–63 [no. 22]; Gretsch (1999a) 275–7; Pulsiano (2001a) xxvii; Binski—Panayotova (2005) no. 18 [Webber]; Hartzell (2006) no. 43 [Mass chants]; Biggs (2007a) 16–17; Shepard (2007) 201; Barker-Benfield (2008) III.1742, 1823; Rushforth (2011) 45–50

DEC: F. Wormald (1952) 62 [no. 12]; E. Temple (1976) no. 40; F. Wormald (1984) 103, 106; Ohlgren (1986) no. 145; R. Gameson (1995b) 198; Budny (1997) I.260–3 [inventory of decoration and illustration]

FACS: Dumville (1993g) pls. X, XVI [fols. 15r, 140v]; Budny (1997) II, pls. I [fol. 1v], 203–8 [fols. 24r, 26r, 30r, 40r, 81v, 138r]; Binski—Panayotova (2005) 73 [fol. 40r]; Lendinara et al. (2011) pl. I [fol. 4v; MS wrongly described as CCCC 441]

ED: Lapidge (1991a) 120–4 [litanies]; Pulsiano (2001a) [Pss. I–L coll. as ζ]

ST: Römer (1972a) 54; Rosenthal (1992) 159; Corrêa (1996) 294 n.; Pulsiano (1998b) 105 n. 2; R. McKitterick (2012) 329

107. Cambridge, Corpus Christi College, 415

s. xi/xii or xii in., Normandy or England?

Contents: 'Norman Anonymous', tracts

MS: M.R. James (1912) II.303–8; Pellens (1966) xii–xiii; P.R. Robinson (1988) I, no. 162; Budny (1997) I.xxxv; R. Gameson (1999a) no. 87; C.D. Wright (2006) 195, 199–200 and n. 27

FACS: Pellens (1977) [complete facsimile]; Pellens (1964–8) pls. XIV–XVI [pp. 190, parts of pp. 204, 225, 292, 298]; P.R. Robinson (1988) II, pl. 35 (a)–(b) [pp. 1, 265]

ED: Pellens (1966) 5–31 [arts. 1-30 as listed in M.R. James (1912) II.296–8]; C.D. Wright (2006) 205–10 [*Prouerbia Grecorum* (as part of 'Norman Anonymous') coll. as N]

ST: Pellens (1964–8); Pellens (1966) xiv–xxxviii; Nineham (1967); Pellens (1973); *LMA* I.673–4; C.D. Wright (2006), 195, 199–200, 206–11 [app. crit.]

108. Cambridge, Corpus Christi College, 419 [with 421, pp. 1–2]

s. xi¹, prob. SE England (Canterbury?), prov. Exeter

Contents: fifteen homilies* (six by Wulfstan); prayer*

[no. **108** is a companion vol. to no. **109**, below]

MS: M.R. James (1912) II.311–12; Bethurum (1957) 1–2; N.R. Ker (1957) no. 68; N.R. Ker (1964) 82; Pope (1967) I.80–3; Drage (1978) 329–30;

Godden (1979) lxxi–lxxii; Scragg (1979) 249–51; Torkar (1981) 33–4; P.R. Robinson (1988) I, no. 164; Scragg (1992) xxxii; Conner (1993) 4, 15; R.I. Page (1993a) 51–2; Budny (1997) I.525–33 [no. 33]; Clemoes (1997) 46–8; Parkes (1997b) 139 n. 108; P. Wormald (1999) 345 n. 380; Proud (2000) 127; Wilcox (2000) 84; *ASMMF* VIII (2000) 1–6 [no. 58; Wilcox]; Cowen (2004) 397 n. 2, 423–4; Lionarons (2004b) 72, 75 n. 26; Meaney (2004) 483; A. Orchard (2004) 71; Wilcox (2004b) 376–7, 391–2; Treharne (2007b) 20; Graham (2009) 202; Crick (2012) 181; Scragg (2012a) nos. 174–176d

DEC: E. Temple (1976) no. 82; Ohlgren (1986) no. 187; R. Gameson (1995b) 91 n. 110; Budny (1997) I.531–3 [inventory of decoration and illustration]

FACS: Scragg (1992), pl. III [p. 195]; Budny (1997) II, pls. 445–52 [pp. 1, 38, 73, 161, 204, 235, 329, 347]; *ASMMF* VIII (2000) no. 58

ED [the order of the following items is that of the manuscript, listed according to the numbering of individual articles in N.R. Ker (1957) 115–16; only the most recent editions are cited]:

art. 1: Napier (1883/1967) 191–205 [base MS (= B) for Hom. XLII (*De temporibus Antichristi*)]

art. 2: Napier (1883/1967) 205–15 [base MS (= B) for Hom. XLIII (*Sunnandæges spell*)]

art. 3: Napier (1883/1967) 226–32 [base MS (= B) for Hom. XLV (*Sermo angelorum nomina*)]

art. 4: Napier (1883/1967) 156–67 [Hom. XXXIII (*Sermo Lupi ad Anglos*) coll. as B]; Bethurum (1957) 255–60 [base MS (= B) for Hom. XX (*Sermo Lupi ad Anglos*)]; Whitelock (1976) [coll. as B for *Sermo Lupi*]

art. 5: Napier (1883/1967) 32–41 [Hom. V (*Sermo de baptismate*) coll. as B]; Bethurum (1957) 175–84 [Hom. VIIIc (*Sermo de baptismate*) coll. as B]

art. 6: Napier (1883/1967) 6–20 [Hom. II (*Sermo Lupi episcopi*) coll. as B]; Bethurum (1957) 142–56 [Hom. VI (*Sermo Lupi episcopi*) coll. as B]

art. 7: Napier (1883/1967) 20–9 [Hom. III (*De fide catholica*) coll. as B]; Bethurum (1957) 157–65 [Hom. VII (*De fide catholica*) coll. as B]

art. 8: Napier (1883/1967) 182–8, 54–6 [Hom. XL (*In die iudicii*) + VII (end) coll. as B]; Bethurum (1957) 189–91 [Hom. IX (end) coll. as B]; Scragg (1992) 53–64, odd pages [base MS (= N) for Vercelli Hom. II (version N)] art. 9: Napier (1883/1967) 65–76, 108–11 [Hom. X ('Her ongynð be cristendome') + XIX–XX (*Sermo ad populum*) coll. as B]; Bethurum (1957) 200–10 + 225–32 [Hom. Xc ('Her ongynð be cristendome') + XIII (*Sermo ad populum*) coll. as B]

art. 10: Napier (1883/1967) 111–22 [Hom. XXI–XXIV coll. as B]

art. 11: Napier (1883/1967) 232–42 [base MS (= B) for Hom. XLVI (*Larspell*)]; Jost (1959) 242–7 [coll. as Wulf XLVI]

art. 12: as Skeat (1881–1900) I.364–82 [Hom. *De auguriis*, not collated]

art. 13: as Belfour (1909) 50–8 [Hom. for Fourth Sunday in Lent, not collated]

art. 14: Assmann (1889/1964) 138–43 [Hom. (no. XI) for the Third Sunday in Lent coll. as S]

art. 15: Pope (1967–8) II.623–5, 804–6 [base MS (= V) for homily *De uirginitate*]

art. 16: Förster (1942a) 49 [base MS for OE prayer]

LANG: Fowler (1972) xxi–xxii; A. Orchard (2004) 69 n. 24, 70 n. 28, 77 n. 57, 90 n. 85; Wilcox (2004b) 382-9

ST: J. Hill (1996) 244; R. Gameson (1996b) 149; Dance (2004) 30 n. 4; Scragg (2012b) 559

109. Cambridge, Corpus Christi College, 421

pp. 3–98, 209–224 (arts. 1–5, 10, 11): s. xi$^{3/4}$, Exeter; pp. 99–208 and 225–354: s. xi^{1}, prob. Canterbury; prov. all parts Exeter.

Contents: fifteen homilies* (ten by Ælfric): pp. 99–208, 225–354

[no. **109** is a companion vol. to no. **108**, above]

MS: M.R. James (1912) II.313–15; F. Wormald (1952) 62 [no. 13]; T.A.M. Bishop (1954–8a) 192–9; Bethurum (1957) 1; N.R. Ker (1957) no. 69; Pope (1967) I.80–3; Callison (1973); Drage (1978) 331–3; P.R. Robinson (1978) 236 [repr. P.R. Robinson (1994) 31–2]; Godden (1979) lxxi–lxxii; Scragg (1979) 249–53 [extensive description]; P.R. Robinson (1988) I, no. 164; R.I. Page (1993a) 51–2; R. Gameson (1996b) 145 and n. 34; Budny (1997) I.525–33 [no. 33]; Clemoes (1997) 46–8; McDougall—McDougall (1997) 220 n. 52; *ASMMF* VIII (2000) 7–14 [no. 59; Wilcox]; Lionarons (2004c) 417–22, 426, 428; Wilcox (2004b) 393–4; Binski—Panayotova (2005) no. 14 [R. McKitterick]; Toswell (2007) 212; Treharne (2007b) 20; Crick (2012) 181; Scragg (2012a) nos. 106, 174–8

DEC: E. Temple (1976) no. 82; Ohlgren (1986) 187; Raw (1990) 197; R. Gameson (1991) 71–3; R. Gameson (1995b) 91, 174

FACS: E. Temple (1976) ill. 254 [p. 1]; P.R. Robinson (1988) II, pl. 27 [p. 209]; Budny (1997) II, pls. 453–5 [pp. 133, 170, 287]; *ASMMF* VIII (2000) no. 59; Binski—Panayotova (2005) 67 [p. 1]

ED [the order of the following items is that of the manuscript, listed according to the numbering of individual articles in N.R. Ker (1957) 117–18; only the most recent editions are cited]:

art. 1: Clemoes (1997) 354–64 [Ælfric, CH I, Hom. XXII (Pentecost), coll. as V]

art. 2: Godden (1979) 299–303 [Ælfric, CH II, Hom. XXXV (Feast for an Apostle), coll. as V]

art. 3: Godden (1979) 310–17 [Ælfric, CH II, Hom. XXXVII (Feast for Holy Martyrs), coll. as V]

art. 4: Godden (1979) 318–26 [Ælfric, CH II, Hom. XXXVIII (Feast for a Confessor), coll. as V]

art. 5: Godden (1979) 327–34 [Ælfric, CH II, Hom. XXXIX (Feast for Holy Virgins), coll. as V]

art. 6: Pope (1967–8) I.415–47 [Ælfric, Suppl. Hom. XI (Octave of Pentecost), coll. as V]

art. 7: Napier (1883/1967) 243, line 22—245 [Hom. XLVII coll. as A (omitting the opening paragraph]; Baker—Lapidge (1995) 236–40 [Byrhtferth, *Enchiridion* IV.2.77–125, coll. as C]

art. 8: Napier (1883/1967) 246–50 [Hom. XLVIII (*Ammonitio amici*) coll. as A]; Baker—Lapidge (1995) 242–8 [Byrhtferth, *Enchiridion*, 'Postscript', coll. as C]

art. 9: Napier (1883/1967) 250–65 [Hom. XLIX (*Larspell*) coll. as A]; Szarmach (1981a) 11–16 [Vercelli Hom. X coll. as N]; Scragg (1992) 196–213 [Vercelli Hom. X coll. as N]

art. 10: Napier (1883/1967) 266–74 [base MS (= A) for Hom. L (*Larspell*)]

art. 11: Napier (1883/1967) 90–4 [Hom. XV (*Secundum Lucam*) coll. as A]; Bethurum (1957) 123–7 [Hom. III (*Secundum Lucam*) coll. as A]

art. 12: Clemoes (1997) 317–24 [Ælfric, CH I, Hom. XVIII (*In Letania maiore*), coll. as V]

art. 13: Clemoes (1997) 325–34 [Ælfric, CH I, Hom. XIX (*Feria .III. De dominica oratione*), coll. as V]

art. 14: Clemoes (1997) 335–44 [Ælfric, CH I, Hom. XX (*Feria .IIII. De fide catholica*), coll. as V]

art. 15: Clemoes (1997) 345–53 [Ælfric, CH I, Hom. XXI (Ascension Day), coll. as V]

LANG: Callison (1973)

ST: Callison (1973); Wilcox (1988); P.R. Robinson (1978) 236 [repr. P.R. Robinson (1994) 31–2]; Baker—Lapidge (1995) cxxii–cxxiv; Zacher (2007) 185; Scragg (2012b) 559

110. Cambridge, Corpus Christi College, 422, pp. 1–26

s. x¹ or x²/⁴ or x med.

Contents: *Solomon and Saturn**; *Solomon and Saturn***

MS: M.R. James (1912) II.315–16; Dobbie (1942) l–lii; N.R. Ker (1957) no. 70A; Robinson—Stanley (1991) 22; Dumville (1994a) 144; Bredehoft (2004) 156, 167; Biggs (2007a) 12; Karkov (2007a) 135; Anlezark (2009) 1–4; Scragg (2012a) no. 179

FACS: Robinson—Stanley (1991) pls. 12.2.1–25 [pp. 1–22]; Dumville (1994a) pl. III [p. 13]

ED: Menner (1941) 83–104 [verse], 168–71 [prose]; Dobbie (1942) 31–48 [verse coll. as A for lines 1–30; base MS for verse, lines 31–506]; Cilluffe (1981) [base MS for prose]; Anlezark (2009) 64–95 [base MS for both prose and verse]

LANG: Anlezark (2009) 6–12

ST: Anlezark (2009) 12–57

111. Cambridge, Corpus Christi College, 422, pp. 27–570 (the 'Red Book of Darley')

s. xi med. (1060/1?), prob. Winchester (NM?), prov. Sherborne?, (prov. prob. Darley Dale, Derbyshire, church of St Helen)

Contents: *lunarium*⁺*; masses; benedictions, prayers, exorcisms; liturgical calendar; *computistica*⁽*⁾; prognostics*; masses; manual services (including two litanies); Office of the Dead; Offices

MS: M.R. James (1912) II.316–22; N.R. Ker (1957) no. 70B; van Dijk—Walker (1960) 639 [no. 101]; D.H. Turner (1962) vii–viii; N.R. Ker (1964) 179; T.A.M. Bishop (1971) xv n. 2; Rella (1977) 57, 82; Gerchow (1988) 227–8 [no. 13], 331; P.R. Robinson (1988) I, no. 165; Lapidge (1991a) 66; Vaciago (1993) 8 [no. 25]; Baker—Lapidge (1995) xlviii [computus]; Budny (1997) I.645–66 [no. 44]; P.P. O'Neill (1997) 139–40, 153 n. 56, 161, 164, 168; C.A. Jones (1998a) 239 n. 26; C.A. Jones (1999) 119 nn. 63, 67; Liuzza (2001) 198, 214–15; N. Orchard (2002) I.122; *ASMMF* XI (2003) 81–97 [no. 60; Graham]; Binski—Panayotova (2005) no. 44 [Webber]; Hartzell (2006) no. 44; Chardonnens (2007b) 48,

506–7, 549; Karkov (2007a) 136, 137 n. 9, 139–41; Rushforth (2008a) 41–3 [no. 19]; Pfaff (2009) 94–6; R. Gameson (2012a) 22 and n. 34; Pfaff (2012) 456 and n. 21; Rankin (2012) 503 and n. 102

DEC: Rice (1952) 191–2; F. Wormald (1952) 62–3 [no. 14]; E. Temple (1976) no. 104; Ohlgren (1986) no. 209; Raw (1990) 197; R. Gameson (1991) 70 n. 49; R. Gameson (1995b) 33 n. 120, 232–3, 243; Budny (1997) I.652–66 [inventory of decoration and illustration]; Karkov (2007a); Karkov (2009) 216–17

FACS: E. Temple (1976) ills. 300–1 [pp. 51, 52]; P.R. Robinson (1988) II, pl. 30 [p. 53]; Budny (1997) II, pls. XII [pp. 52–3], 604–8 [pp. 28–9, 41, 50–1, 360, 520]; *ASMMF* XI (2003) no. 60; Binski—Panayotova (2005) 125 [p. 53]; Karkov (2007a) 138 [p. 51]; Minnis—Roberts (2007) pl. 3 [pp. 52–3]; Rushforth (2007) 53 [p. 53]; Owen-Crocker (2009) fig. 7.9 [p. 52]; R. Gameson (2012) pl. 7b.5 [p. 86]

ED: Warren (1883) 273–5 [masses]; Liebermann (1903–16) I.435–7 [base MS (= Ca) for formulas of excommunication (pp. 310, 319)]; Fehr (1921) 48–63 [Visitation of the sick]; Henel (1934) [*computistica*]; F. Wormald (1934) 183–95 [liturgical calendar (no. 14)]; R.I. Page (1978) 148–58 [liturgical rubrics]; Lapidge (1991a) 125–31 [litanies]; Graham (1993) 439–46 [liturgical directions]; Lapidge (2003a) 80–2 [mass for St Swithun]; Rushforth (2008a) no. 19 [liturgical calendar]

ST: Kemble (1839–48) II.367–70; Warren (1883) 271–5; K. Sisam (1944); K. Sisam (1953a) 32–3; R.I. Page (1965b); Hohler (1972) 39–47; R.I. Page (1973b) 4–5; Hohler (1975) 72, 82, 223; Korhammer (1976) 239; Grant (1979) 108–12; Kotzor (1981) I.302*–304*; Lapidge (1988b) 259 n. 30 [repr. Lapidge (1993a) 217 n. 30]; Dumville (1992a) 25, 27, 36, 50–1, 53–5, 57, 60, 67, 74–5, 110, 129, 131; C.D. Wright (1993) 234; Pfaff (1995a) 56–7 [Corrêa], 100–8 [Keefer]; Pfaff (1995b) 21–4; Lenker (1997) 488; Pulsiano (1998b) 87–8, 108 n. 15, 109 n. 19 [comparison with no. 407]; Borst (2001) I.292; Gittos (2005b); Keynes (2005a) 75–6; N. Orchard (2005) clxxix, clxxxi; Chardonnens (2007a) 336; Chardonnens (2010) 249

112. Cambridge, Corpus Christi College, 430

s. ix ex. or ix/x, Saint-Amand, prov. s. x England (prob. Canterbury StA), (prov. Glastonbury)

Contents: Martin of Braga, *Formula uitae honestae* [*CPL* 1080]; Ferrandus of Carthage, *Ep.* vii (*ad Reginum comitem*) [*CPL* 848]; Ambrosius Autpertus, *Sermo de cupiditate*

MS: M.R. James (1912) II.337–8; C.W. Barlow (1950) 211–12; T.A.M.
Bishop (1954–8b) 329 [supply leaf]; Carley (1986) 114; Carley (1994)
265–8; Budny (1997) lvii [binding]; R. Sharpe et al. (1996) 207 [B.39.319],
234 [B.44.11]; Bischoff (1998—) I, no. 820; Lapidge (2006) 168, 321;
Barker-Benfield (2008) III.1812; R. Gameson (2012d) 352 and n. 31

ED: C.W. Barlow (1950) 236–50 [Martin of Braga, *Formula uitae honestae*, coll. as C]

ST: Valtorta (2006) [Ambrosius Autpertus]

114. Cambridge, Corpus Christi College, 448

fols. 1-86: s. x¹ or s. x med., S. England (or Worcester?)

fols. 87–103: s. xi/xii, S England (or Worcester?), (prov. whole MS
Winchester)

Contents [fols. 1–86]: Prosper of Aquitaine, *Epigrammata ex sententiis
S. Augustini* [*CPL* 526] and *Versus ad coniugem* [*CPL* 531; SK 458];
Isidore, *Synonyma de lamentatione animae peccatricis* [*CPL* 1203]

Contents [fols. 87–103]: Sibylline prophecies [SK 8495]; *Physiologus*
(lion, unicorn, panther only); Latin poems (including SK 10279 by
pseudo-Vergil); note on the languages of the world; Prosper, *Sententiae
ex operibus S. Augustini* [*CPL* 525], no. 390; Prudentius, *Peristephanon*
[*CPL* 1443] (Prologue only), Prudentius, *Dittochaeon* [*CPL* 1444];
Seven Wonders of the World

MS: M.R. James (1912) II.360–3; T.A.M. Bishop (1971) 20 n. 1 [on scribe
of fols. 87–103]; Lapidge (1982a) 105 [repr. Lapidge (1996b) 467];
Dumville (1987) 175–6; Faraci (1990) 14; Dumville (1993g) 56 n. 245;
R.I. Page (1993a) 93; Budny (1997) II.219–33 [no. 17]; Lapidge (2006)
312, 327–30, 341; Biggs (2007a) 17; Di Sciacca (2011) 300–1 and nn.
6–12; R. Gameson (2012b) 114 n. 78

FACS: Dumville (1993g) pl. IV [fol. 41r]; Budny (1997) II, pl. 171 [fol. 1r];
Di Sciacca (2007b) 123 [fol. 42v]; Lendinara et al. (2011) pl. IX [fol. 1r]

ED: Lapidge (1982a) 106 [base MS for one of Prosper's *Epigrammata* with
accompanying glosses] [repr. Lapidge (1996b) 468]

ST: Römer (1972b) 54; Lapidge (1982a) 133 n. 52 [repr. Lapidge (1996b)
469 n. 52]; R.I. Page (1983); Sauer (1983) 30, 40–1, 48; Toth (1984); Sauer
(1989) 61; R.I. Page (1993a) 93; Szarmach (1999) 173–5; Lendinara
(2003) 97; Alcamesi (2007b) 169–73; Di Sciacca (2007b); Di Sciacca
(2008) 68–71, 168–9; Di Sciacca (2011) 302–26

115. Cambridge, Corpus Christi College, 449, fols. 42-96

s. xi¹

Contents: Ælfric, *Grammar*⁺* (incomplete; fols. 1–41 supplied s. xvi) and *Glossary*⁺*

MS: M.R. James (1912) II.363; N.R. Ker (1957) no. 71; Buckalew (1978) 153–9, 163; R.I. Page (1993a) 10, 48, 100; Parkes (1997b) 138 n. 102; Scragg (2012a) nos. 180–1

FACS: R.I. Page (1993a), pls. 31, 59 [defective opening and fol. 89r]

ED: Zupitza (1880/2001) [Ælfric, *Grammar* and *Glossary*, coll. as C]

116. Cambridge, Corpus Christi College, 473 (the 'Winchester Troper')

s. x/xi or xi²ᐟ⁴, with additions s. xi¹ and later, Winchester OM

Contents: troper (*cantatorium*)

MS: Frere (1894a) xxvii–xxix; M.R. James (1912) II.411–12; P. Wagner (1912) 86–7; Handschin (1936); N.R. Ker (1957) no. 72; Husmann (1964) 150; Gneuss (1968) 116; Holschneider (1968) 14–20; Planchart (1977) I.17–33; Fenlon (1982) 13–17 [no. 4]; Gneuss (1985) 105 [no. C.1]; P.R. Robinson (1988) I, no. 171; Hartzell (1989) 82; Lapidge — Winterbottom (1991b) xxxi, xxxvi, xxxviii, lxxxiv, cxxv, cxxvi n. 50, clv; Dumville (1993g) 136; Lapidge (1994a) 134–5; Budny (1997) I.487–93 [no. 30]; Gretsch (1999a) 199, 301; Lapidge (2004b) 446–7; Hartzell (2006) 88–109 [no. 46]; Rankin (2007) 3–15, 19–46; Wieland (2009) 122; R. Gameson (2012a) 70 n. 240; Pfaff (2012) 455 and n. 18; Rankin (2012) 488 and n. 20, 501; Scragg (2012a) no. 182

DEC: Budny (1997) I.491–3 [inventory of decoration]; R. Gameson (2012c) 288 n. 137

FACS: Rankin (2007) [complete facsimile]; see also Frere (1894a) pls. 4–17 [sequences, fols. 82r–88v], 18–21 [organa, fols. 153r–154v], 22 ['Fulgens preclara', fol. 96r–v], 23 [Alleluias, fol. 2v], 24 [organa for Alleluia, fol. 163r], 25 [tract for organa, fols. 146v, 195r]; Wooldridge (1897) pls. II–VI; Fenlon (1982) 14, 16 [fols. 163v–164r, 3r]; M. Berry (1988) pls. I–III [fols. 27r, 96r, 164v–165r]; Lapidge (1994a) pl. VIII [fol. 147r]; Budny (1997) II, pls. 386–7 [fols. 76v–77r, 182v–183r]; Lapidge (2003a) pls. XII–XIV [fols. 39v, 87v, 186v]

ED: *AH* XXXVII.40, 53 [coll. under various sigla for sequences]; Frere (1894b) 3–98 [base MS (= CC) for Latin texts of tropes, sequences, proses]; Planchart (1977) II.1–10 [inventory, with Latin texts, of the tropes; coll. *passim* as CC]

ST: Planchart (1973) I.61–6 [notation], I.67–327 [trope repertory], II.31–342 [catalogue of tropes]; M. Berry (1988) 155–7; Lapidge (1994a) 134–5 [on script of Wulfstan Cantor]; Pfaff (1995a) 40–2 [Teviotdale]; Rankin (1996) 331, 339, 342 [on liturgical music]; Hiley (1998); Rankin in Lapidge (2003a) 191–202 [music of the troper (= C), esp. that for St Swithun]; Huglo (2005) 34–6 [musical notation]; Rankin (2007) 49–74 [composition and compilation of the repertories]

117. Cambridge, Corpus Christi College, 557 (with Lawrence, University of Kansas, Kenneth Spencer Research Library, Pryce C2: 1)

s. xi med., Worcester?, (prov. Worcester)

Contents: Homily (for *Inuentio S. Crucis*)* (f)

MS: N.R. Ker (1957) no. 73; Vaughan—Fines (1959–63) 117; Colgrave—Hyde (1962); N.R. Ker (1964) 206; R.L. Collins (1976); N.R. Ker (1976a) 122; Laing (1993) 25; Budny (1993) 23; R.I. Page (1993a) 49–50; R.I. Page (1995) 502–29; Scragg (1996) 220; Budny (1997) I.xxxv; Stoneman (1997) 117; *ASMMF* VII (2000) 1–3, 28–30 [nos. 63, 153; Doane]; R. Gameson (2005a) 92; Scragg (2012a) no. 183

FACS: Budny (1993) 32 [fols. 1r, 2r]; R.I. Page (1993a) pl. 35 [two binding strips]; R.I. Page (1995) figs. 1–2 [rectos and versos of fragments]; *ASMMF* VII (2000) nos. 63, 153

LANG: A.F. Cameron (1974) 221

ST: Robb (1975); Scragg (1979) 262; Franzen (1991) 54, 79 [glosses]; R. Gameson (1996a) 238; Collier (2000) 195

Cambridge, Corpus Christi College, EP-0-6 (ptd bk.): see no. **648**

118. Cambridge, Fitzwilliam Museum, 88–1972, fols. 2–43

s. xi/xii or xii in., Canterbury?, (prov. Shrewsbury)

Contents: gospel lectionary with collects, and some homilies on Temporale gospels

MS: N.R. Ker (1964) 179 [MS. owned by F. Wormald until 1972]; Giles (1972–6b) 248 [no. 218]; Wormald—Giles (1982) 568–70; Lenker (1997) 473–6; R. Gameson (1999a) no. 96; Sheppard (2005) 177–8 [binding]; Barker-Benfield (2008) III.1823–4

118. 5. Cambridge, Fitzwilliam Museum, 88–1972, fols. 44–56

s. xi/xii or xii in., prob. Canterbury StA, (prov. Shrewsbury)

Contents: gospel lectionary with collects (incomplete)

MS: N.R. Ker (1964) 179 [MS. owned by F. Wormald until 1972]; Giles
  (1972–6b) 248 [no. 218]; Wormald—Giles (1982) 568–70; R. Gameson
  (1999a) no. 97

119. Cambridge, Fitzwilliam Museum 45-1980

s. ix ex., W France (Brittany, Dol region?), or Loire valley?, prov.
  England by s. x med.

Contents: gospels (incomplete), gospel list

MS: N.R. Ker (1957) no. 7*; Giles (1972–6a) 87 [no. BL. 1]; N.R. Ker
  (1976a) 121; Wormald—Alexander (1977) 1–12, 25–8; Woudhuysen
  et al. (1982) 31 [no. 27]; Deuffic (1986) 296 [no. 18]; Vaciago (1993) 8
  [no. 26]; O'Reilly (1994) 217–22; Bischoff (1998—) I, no. 821; A.S.G.
  Edwards (2004); Scrase (2005) no. 27; Lapidge (2006) 168; Scragg
  (2012a) nos. 184–5

DEC: Nordenfalk (1978)

FACS: Wormald—Alexander (1977), pls. A–H [colour plates: fols. 14v,
  21v, 22r, 63v, 83v, 87r, 125r, 128r], i–xxvii [fols. 1r, 15r, 15v, 16r, 16v, 17r,
  17v, 18r, 18v, 19r, 19v, 20r, 20v, 21r, 22v, 23v, 24v, 62v, 64r, 87v, 89v, 129r,
  130r, 41r, 46r, 49r, 50v]; Woudhuysen et al. (1982) 30 [fol. 63v]

ED: Napier (1900) nos. 17, 20–1, 25, 27–8, 61 and xxxiii n. 2 [OE gloss-
  es]; Meritt (1961) 443 [OE glosses]; B. Fischer (1988–91) [gospel
  excerpts coll. as Bz]

ST: *BCLL* (1985) no. 964; Dumville (1992a) 114; Lenker (1997) 418–19

120. Cambridge, Gonville and Caius College 144/194

s. x¹, England?, prov. Canterbury StA

Contents: Remigius of Auxerre, Commentaries on Sedulius (*Carmen
  paschale* and Hymns) and on *Disticha Catonis* (part); sermon (f);
  fols. 79–86: a collection of verse excerpts (added s. xi), incl. Prudentius,
  Hamartigenia [*CPL* 1440] lines 931–66 [SK 10856]; Hibernicus Exul,
  Carm. viii ('Verba philosophiae') [SK 13757]; *Monosticha Catonis* lines
  1–32 [SK 16936]; Venantius Fortunatus, *Carmina* [*CPL* 1033] IX. ii,
  lines 1–70, 73–82, 87–90, 99–104, 109–10, 117–22 [SK 1112], III. xxx

[SK 5349], VIII. ii [SK 4384]; pseudo-Columbanus (pseudo-Alcuin), *Praecepta uiuendi* [SK 5960]; Prudentius, *Dittochaeon* [*CPL* 1444], nos. xlv–xlix, xl–xlii

MS: Schenkl no. 2745; M.R. James (1907–8) I.161–3; Sanford (1924) 205; N.R. Ker (1964) 41; T.A.M. Bishop (1954–8a) 187–9; Glauche (1970) 52, 56; T.A.M. Bishop (1971) 19; R.S. Cox (1972) 3; Rella (1977) 118, 164; R.W. Hunt (1979) 282–4; Rella (1980) 110; Lapidge (1982a) 104, 114, 131–2 n. 36 [repr. Lapidge (1996b) 434 and n. 36, 481]; Munk Olsen (1982–) I.67; Jeudy (1991) 496; Springer (1995) 124–5; Lapidge (2006) 329, 335; Alcamesi (2007a) 152–3; Barker-Benfield (2008) I.lii n. 11, lxi n. 28, II.1374, III.1713, 1811; Wieland (2009) 151

ED: Lapidge (1982a) 115 [base text for Remigius, *Comm. super Sedulium*, fol. 9r, coll. with no. **735**] [repr. Lapidge (1996b) 482]; Alcamesi (2007a) 171–8 [Remigius on *Disticha Catonis*]

ST: Boas (1952) lxiii; R.W. Hunt (1979) 282–4 [Venantius Fortunatus excerpts]; *CPPM* II, no. 3216b [*Praecepta uiuendi*]; Alcamesi (2007a) 157–8; McKee (2012b) 340 and nn. 5–6; *CSLMA* III (2010) 466 [Hibernicus Exul]; R. McKitterick (2012) 328, 329

120. 3. Cambridge, Gonville and Caius College, 466/573, two endleaves

s. xi med.

Contents: missal (f)

MS: M.R. James (1907-8) II.540–1; Wieland (2009) 123

120. 6. Cambridge, Gonville and Caius College, 734/782a

s. xi[1], Canterbury CC

Contents: mass lectionary (f)

MS: T.A.M. Bishop (1971) 22 [with shelfmark mistakenly given as 732/754], 25; Dumville (1993g) 131 n. 90, 139; Rushforth (2001) 137, 141–4; Wieland (2009) 121; Rushforth (2012) 207 n. 64

FACS: Rushforth (2001), pls. IX–X [recto and verso]

121. Cambridge, Gonville and Caius College, 820 (h)

s. viii ex.

Contents: biblical text [Prophetae minores] (f)

MS: *CLA* II (1935) no. 129; M.P. Brown (1989b) 41–2; R. McKitterick (1989a) 315; Marsden (1995) 32, 41, 43, 55, 236–7, 305; Wieland (2009) 115; Marsden (2012) 420 and n. 67

ST: Marsden (1995) 249–53

121. 5. Cambridge, Jesus College, 5 (Q. A. 5), flyleaves

s. xi[1]

Contents: missal (f)

MS: M.R. James (1895) 4; Hartzell (2006) no. 46; Wieland (2009) 123

122. Cambridge, Jesus College, 15 (Q. A. 15), fols. i–x and 1–10 (binding leaves)

s. xi[1], SE England (prov. Durham)

Contents: Ælfric, *Homilies** (f)

MS: M.R. James (1895) 13–14; N.R. Ker (1957) no. 74; Pope (1967) I.88–91; Godden (1979) lxxiii–lxxiv; Dumville (1992a) 107–8; Clemoes (1997) 53–4; *ASMMF* XVI (2008) 5–13 [no. 65; Wilcox]; Scragg (2012a) no. 186

FACS: *ASMMF* XVI (2008) no. 65

ED [the order of the following items is that of the manuscript, listed according to the numbering of individual articles in N.R. Ker (1957) 123; only the most recent editions are cited]:

art. 1: Pope (1967–8) I.444–7 [Ælfric, Suppl. Hom. XI (Octave of Pentecost), lines 526–74, coll. as f[b]]

art. 2: Godden (1979) 180–9 [Ælfric, CH II, Hom. XIX (*Feria .II. in Letania maiore*), amplified by the incorporation of Suppl. Hom. XXIV (Pope (1967–8) II.752), coll. as f[b]]

art. 3: Godden (1979) 249–50 [Ælfric, CH II, Hom. XXVIII (Twelfth Sunday after Pentecost), lines 1–22, coll. as f[b]]

art. 4: Clemoes (1997) 317–24 [Ælfric, CH I, Hom. XVIII (*In Letania maiore*, part), coll. as f[b]]

art. 5: Clemoes (1997) 325–6 [Ælfric, CH I, Hom. XIX (*Feria .III. De dominica oratione*), lines 1–15, 31–4, coll. as f[b]]

LANG: Clemoes (1997) 53

123. Cambridge, Jesus College, 28 (Q. B. 11)

s. xi ex., France, (prov. Durham)

Contents: Greek alphabet; Priscian, *Institutiones grammaticae* [*CPL* 1546]; Priscian, *De accentibus* (?) [*CPL* 1552] (incomplete)

MS: M.R. James (1895) 36–7; Mynors (1939) 30; N.R. Ker (1964) 61; Gibson (1972) 108; Passalacqua (1978) no. 79; A.G. Watson (1987a) 17; Gneuss (1990) 11 n. 35 [repr. Scragg (2003) 83 n. 35]; Law (1997) 217 n. 4; Lapidge (2006) 326; Lendinara (2007a) 85 n. 105, 109

124. Cambridge, Magdalene College, Pepys 2981 (2) (with London, BL, Sloane 1086, fol. 119)

s. viii^2

Contents: gospels (f)

MS: M.R. James (1923) 116–17; *CLA* II (1935) no. 132; McGurk (1961a) no. 4; McKitterick—Whalley (1989) 4

125. Cambridge, Magdalene College, Pepys 2981 (3)

s. ix/x

Contents: Psalterium Romanum (f)

MS: M.R. James (1923) 117; McKitterick—Whalley (1989) 4; Pulsiano (2001a) xxvii

ED: Pulsiano (2001a) [this fragment coll. as η]

126. Cambridge, Magdalene College, Pepys 2981 (4)

s. ix^1, prob. Northumbria

Contents: biblical text [Danihel] (f)

MS: M.R. James (1923) 117; M.P. Brown (1989b) 41–2; McKitterick—Whalley (1989) 5; Marsden (1995) 43, 236, 253–6, 305; Wieland (2009) 115; Marsden (2012) 420 and n. 67

127. Cambridge, Magdalene College, Pepys 2981 (5)

s. ix/x or x^1, Winchester

Contents: Remigius, Scholia on Martianus Capella (f)

MS: M.R. James (1923) 117; Parkes (1983) 129–40; R. McKitterick
(1986-90) 314–15; Dumville (1987) 164; McKitterick—Whalley (1989)
5; Lapidge (1991c) 963 [repr. Lapidge (1993a) 13]; Lapidge (2006) 136

FACS: Parkes (1983) pl. II

127. 3. Cambridge, Magdalene College, Pepys 2981 (7)

s. xi², England?

Contents: Priscian, *Institutiones grammaticae* [*CPL* 1546] (f)

MS: M.R. James (1923) 117–18; Gibson (1972) 108; Passalacqua (1978)
no. 81; McKitterick—Whalley (1989) 6; R. Gameson (1999a) no. 109;
Gneuss (2003c) 83 n. 35; Lapidge (2006) 326

Cambridge, Magdalene College, Pepys 2981 (16): see no. **442**

Cambridge, Magdalene College, Pepys 2981 (18): see no. **219**

Cambridge, Magdalene College, Pepys 2981 (19): see no. **220**

127. 6. Cambridge, Magdalene College, Pepys 2981 (52)

s. xi¹, England

Contents: missal (f)

MS: McKitterick—Whalley (1989) 11, 15; Hartzell (2006) no. 47

128. Cambridge, Pembroke College, 17

s. ix¹ or ix med., Tours area, prov. England s. xi, (prov. Bury St Edmunds)

Contents: Jerome, *Comm. in Esaiam* [*CPL* 584], bks. VIII–XVIII

MS: Schenkl no. 2579; M.R. James (1905) 18; R.M. Thomson (1972)
622–3 and nn. 23, 27; Clemoes (1985) no. 11; R. Sharpe et al. (1996) 53
[B.13.3]; Bischoff (1998—) I, no. 828; Rushforth (2002) 99–104;
Lapidge (2006) 168

ST: Lambert (1969–72) no. 207; R. McKitterick (2012) 329

129. Cambridge, Pembroke College, 23

s. xi², France (Saint-Denis?), prov. by s. xi/xii England, (prov. Bury
St Edmunds)

Contents: Paulus Diaconus, *Homiliarium* (Easter to Advent)
[Companion vol. to no. **130**]

MS: Schenkl no. 2561; M.R. James (1905) 20–2; R.M. Thomson (1972)
626–7 nn. 50, 56; Rella (1977) 117; Smetana (1978) 87; Clayton (1985)
218; M.P. Richards (1988) 109–10; Dumville (1991–5) 41; R. Sharpe et
al. (1996) 70 [B.13.115]; Gransden (1998b) 254; Webber (1998) 188;
R. Gameson (1999a) no. 110; T.N. Hall (2001) 122–3, 126, 127 [no. 8];
Rushforth (2002) 66–8, 100–3; T.N. Hall (2007) 237; J. Hill (2007a) 75,
86–7, 91; T.N. Hall (2008a) 38, 49–50 nn. 51–2; R. Gameson (2012a) 79
n. 279

DEC: R. Gameson (1991) 68, 106 n. 33

FACS: Szarmach (2006) 82–3 [fol. 289r, 289v]

ST: Lambert (1969–72) nos. 217a, 708.3; Römer (1972b) 74; Szarmach
(2006) 78–81; T.N. Hall (2008a) 32–59

130. Cambridge, Pembroke College, 24

s. xi², France (Saint-Denis?), prov. by s. xi/xii England, (prov. Bury
St Edmunds)

Contents: Paulus Diaconus, *Homiliarium* (Sanctorale, Commune SS.)
[Companion vol. to no. **129**]

MS: M.R. James (1905) 23–5; R.M. Thomson (1972) 626–7 nn. 50, 56;
Rella (1977) 117; Smetana (1978) 87; Clayton (1985) 218; M.P. Richards
(1988) 109–10; Dumville (1991–5) 41; Gransden (1998b) 254; Webber
(1998) 188; T.N. Hall (2001) 123, 126, 127 [no. 9]; R. Gameson (1999a)
no. 111; Rushforth (2002) 66–8, 100–3; Biggs (2007a) 53–4; T.N. Hall
(2007) 237–9; J. Hill (2007a) 75, 86–7, 91; T.N. Hall (2008a) 38, 49–50
nn. 51–2; R. Gameson (2012d) 368 n. 101

DEC: R. Gameson (1991) 68, 106 n. 33

FACS: Gransden (1998b) pl. LXVII (b) [fol. 361r (detail)]; Webber (1998)
pl. XLV (a) [fol. 374v]

ED: T.N. Hall (2008a) 64–7 [lesson for All Saints]

ST: Lambert (1969–72) nos. 26, 62, 74; Römer (1972b) 74–5; T.N. Hall
(2002b) 118–20

131. Cambridge, Pembroke College, 25

s. xi ex. or xi², (prov. Bury St Edmunds)

Contents: *Homiliarium* of Saint-Père (Chartres); Hrabanus Maurus, *De
institutione clericorum*, II.1–10; sequence [SK 575]

MS: Schenkl no. 2527; M.R. James (1905) 25–9; T.A.M. Bishop (1949–53) 434; R.M. Thomson (1972) 626–7 and n. 55; R. McKitterick (1977) 107–9; Clayton (1985) 213, 218; Clemoes (1985) no. 20; Cross (1987) [monograph-length description of MS and contents]; Dumville (1991–5) 41; C.A. Jones (1999) 123 n. 79; *CSLMA* II (1999) 154, 499 [Cross (1987) items 65, 93]; R. Gameson (1999a) no. 112; T.N. Hall (2001) 123, 127 [no. 10]; Szarmach (2002); Rittmueller (2004) 131*– 133*, 203*–207*, 217*; Biggs (2007a) 23 [T.N. Hall], 35 [Clayton], 39, 47, 79 [Lees]; T.N. Hall (2007) 249

DEC: R. Gameson (1991) 105 n. 10

FACS: Szarmach (2002) 306–7 [fols. 173r, 175v]

ED: Biggs (1996) 303–6 [Alcuin, *Vita S. Martini* (*BHL* 5625) expanded]; Cross (1987) [item 65; items 11 and 26 are partially coll. Rittmueller (2004) as Pe]; Szarmach (2002) 308–25 [base MS for homilies, fols. 173r–180r]

ST: Barré (1962); Lambert (1969–72) no. 720; Römer (1972b) 75; Dolbeau (1988); Dumville (1992a) 124; Biggs (1996) 290, 296; Godden (1996) 263, 267; T.N. Hall (2002) 117–18, 120; McNamara (2002) 240, 270–1; C.A. Jones (2004) 352; N.M. Thompson (2004) 53–5; Abram (2007) 430–5; Conti (2007) 383; T.N. Hall (2007) 249; N.M. Thompson (2007) 100; C.D. Wright (2007) 32, 34, 42 n. 85; T.N. Hall (2008a) 44–5, 47, 59; C.D. Wright (2008)

132. Cambridge, Pembroke College, 41

s. xi in. or xi$^{1/4}$, Canterbury CC?, (prov. Bury St Edmunds)

Contents: Augustine, *Enchiridion* [*CPL* 295]

MS: Schenkl no. 2498; M.R. James (1905) 41; T.A.M. Bishop (1954–8b) 187; T.A.M. Bishop (1959–63b) 414, 419, 421, 423; N.R. Ker (1960) 8 n. 2; N.R. Ker (1964) 18; M. Evans (1969) x; Römer (1972b) 75; R.M. Thomson (1972) 622 and n. 24; Rella (1977); Clemoes (1985) no. 13; Dumville (1992a) 20; Dumville (1993g) 78 n. 360; R. Sharpe et al. (1996) 79 [B.13.186]; Gransden (1998b) 253–4; Lapidge (2006) 288

DEC: R. Gameson (1991) 105 n. 10

FACS: Gransden (1998b) pl. LXVII (A) [fol. 13r (detail)]

132. 3. Cambridge, Pembroke College, 46, fols. A and B

s. x$^{2/4}$ or x med., (prov. Bury St Edmunds)

Contents: gradual (f)

MS: M.R. James (1905) 45; Rushforth (2002) 190–1; Hartzell (2006) no. 48; Wieland (2009) 122; Rankin (2012) 487 and n. 17

132. 4. Cambridge, Pembroke College, 46, fols. 82 and 83

s. ix/x or x in., N. France? (Brittany?), (prov. Bury St Edmunds)

Contents: sacramentary (f)

MS: M.R. James (1905) 45; R.M. Thomson (1984) 190 n. 9; Bischoff (1998–) I, no. 829; Rushforth (2002) 99–104; Hartzell (2006) 112; Rankin (2012) 497

ST: R. McKitterick (2012) 329

133. Cambridge, Pembroke College, 81

s. ix$^{2/3}$, S France?, (prov. Bury St Edmunds)

Contents: Bede, *De templo Salomonis* [*CPL* 1348]; *In libros Regum quaestiones .xxx.* [*CPL* 1347]; *Super Canticum Abacuc allegorica expositio* [*CPL* 1354]

MS: M.R. James (1905) 69–70; Laistner—King (1943) 43, 62, 75; N.R. Ker (1964) 18; R.M. Thomson (1972) 622–3; R.M. Thomson (1982b) 5; Hurst—Hudson (1983a) 379–80; Clemoes (1985) no. 15; Dumville (1993g) 78 n. 360; Lapidge (1996c) 424; R. Sharpe et al. (1996) 75 [B.13.151]; Gransden (1998b) 229, 252–3; Bischoff (1998–) I, no. 830; Rushforth (2002) 99–104; Lapidge (2006) 168

FACS: Gransden (1998b) pl. LXV (A) [fol. 4r (detail)]

ED: Hurst (1962) 293–322 [Bede, *In libros Regum*, coll. as R]; Hurst (1969) 144–234 [Bede, *De templo Salomonis*, coll. as R]; Hurst—Hudson (1983a) 381–409 [Bede, *Super Canticum Abacuc*, coll. as C^1]

134. Cambridge, Pembroke College, 83

s. ix^1 or ix med., Saint-Denis, prov. Bury St Edmunds s. xi^2

Contents: record* (s. xi/xii); Bede, *In Lucae euangelium expositio* [*CPL* 1356]

MS: Schenkl no. 2508; M.R. James (1905) 73–4; Laistner—King (1943) 45; N.R. Ker (1957) no. 76; R.M. Thomson (1972) 622 n. 23; Vezin (1982) 134; Clemoes (1985) no. 16; Vezin (1986) 38–9; Dumville (1992a) 124; Dumville (1993g) 78 n. 360; Lapidge (1996c) 424 n. 75;

R. Sharpe et al. (1996) 82 [B.13.209]; Bischoff (1998—) I, no. 831; Gransden (1998b) 253; Rushforth (2002) 99–104; Lapidge (2006) 168; R. Gameson (2012d) 369 and n. 102; Scragg (2012a) no. 187

FACS: Gransden (1998b) pl. LXV (B) [fol. 18r (detail)]

ED: Förster (1913) [base MS for OE record]; A.J. Robertson (1939) 252, 501–2 [base MS for OE record]

ST: R.M. Thomson (1972) 22; Vezin (1982) 134 n. 25; Atsma—Vezin (1988); Knowles et al. (2001) 32 [Abbot Baldwin]

135. Cambridge, Pembroke College, 88

s. x^1, France (Saint-Denis?) (or England?), prov. Canterbury StA by s.x^2, (prov. Bury St Edmunds)

Contents: record* (s. xi); Laidcenn mac Baith, *Ecloga de Moralibus in Iob* [*CPL* 1716; *BCLL* 293]

MS: Schenkl no. 2505; M.R. James (1905) 81; Bischoff (1954b) 237; N.R. Ker (1957) no. 77; N.R. Ker (1960) 8 and n. 1; N.R. Ker (1964) 19; T.A.M. Bishop (1971) xii, xxv; N.R. Ker (1972b) 77–8 and n. 4; R.M. Thomson (1972) 622, 623 n. 27; Rella (1977) 165; Rella (1980) 111; Clemoes (1985) no. 17; Dumville (1992a) 124; Dumville (1993g) 78 n. 360; Budny (1997) I.460; Bischoff (1998—) I, p. 183 [unnumbered entry]; Gransden (1998b) 253; Rushforth (2002) 99–104; Barker-Benfield (2008) III.1824; Castaldi (2010) 400; Scragg (2012a) nos. 188–93

FACS: Gransden (1998b) pl. LXVI (B) [fol. 87r (detail)]

ED: Förster (1913) 158 [OE record]; A.J. Robertson (1939) 248, 497 [OE record]; Adriaen (1969) [*Ecloga de Moralibus in Iob* coll. as C]

ST: Manitius (1911–31) I.99–100; *BCLL* (1985) no. 293; Castaldi (2010) 395–401

136. Cambridge, Pembroke College, 91

s. $ix^{1/3}$, N France, (prov. Bury St Edmunds)

Contents: Jerome, *Tractatus .lix. in Psalmos* [*CPL* 592]; verse epilogue [SK 9575]; Macedonian names of the months; anonymous letter; *Translatio S. Bartholomaei* (f)

MS: Schenkl no. 2509; M.R. James (1905) 83–4; N.R. Ker (1964) 19; R.M. Thomson (1972) 622 n. 23; Clemoes (1985) no. 18; Dumville (1993g)

78 n. 360; Sharpe et al. (1996) 53; McDougall—McDougall (1997) 210; Bischoff (1998—) I, no. 832; Gransden (1998b) 253; Rushforth (2002) 99-104; Tibbetts (2003) 28; Lapidge (2006) 168, 316, 340; Rushforth (2011) 58; R. Gameson (2012d) 368 n. 102

FACS: Gransden (1998b) pl. LXVI (A) [fol. 18v]; Tibbetts (2003) pl. 8 [fol. 13v]

ED: M.R. James (1905) 84 [verse epilogue]; Morin (1897a/1958) xi [the anonymous letter], 1–447 [Jerome, *Tractatus in Psalmos*, coll. as A]

ST: *DACL* XI.1629 [Leclercq]; Lambert (1969–72) no. 220; Biggs et al. (1990) 98–9 [C.D. Wright]; R. McKitterick (2012) 329

136. 5. Cambridge, Pembroke College, 103*

s. xi[1]

Contents: service-book (f)

MS: Hartzell (2006) no. 50

ST: Lapidge (1991a) 4–6 ['Prayer of the Faithful']

137. Cambridge, Pembroke College, 108

s. ix[2/3], E France, (prov. Bury St Edmunds)

Contents: Iustinianus, *Edictum de fide (Confessio fidei)* [*CPG* 6885] in Latin translation; pseudo-Jerome, *Epist. supp.* xvi [*Libellus fidei: CPL* 633 (p. 220) = *CPL* 731]; Augustine (?), *Oratio in librum de Trinitate* [*CPL* 328]; pseudo-Prosper, *De fide, de spe et de caritate* [excerpt from Halitgar's *Penitential* II. iv–vi]; pseudo-Vigilius of Thapsus, *Disputatio fidei inter Arium et Athanasium* [*CPPM* II, no. 1692; cf. *CPL* 812], with anon. preface to Vigilius of Thapsus, *Contra Arianos, Sabellianos, Photinianos dialogus* [*CPL* 807]; Eusebius, *Historia ecclesiastica*, trans. Rufinus [*CPG* 3495], excerpt [X.1–14]

MS: Schenkl no. 2491; M.R. James (1905) 103–4; N.R. Ker (1964) 19; Schieffer (1971) 293; Schieffer (1972) 268; R.M. Thomson (1972) 622 n. 23; Clemoes (1985) no. 14; R. Sharpe et al. (1996) 76 [B.13.163]; Bischoff (1998—) I, no. 833; Rushforth (2002) 99–104; Meeder (2004–7) 137–42

ED: Schieffer (1971) 295–7 [Iustinianus, *Edictum de fide*, coll. as P]; Schieffer (1972) 273–7 [Iustinianus, *Edictum de fide*, coll. as P]

ST: Siegmund (1949) 156; Lambert (1969–72) no. 316; Römer (1972b) 75; Meeder (2004–7); Lapidge (2006) 168, 302, 337; R. McKitterick (2012) 329

138. Cambridge, Pembroke College, 301

s. xi in. or xi^1, Peterborough?

Contents: gospels

MS: M.R. James (1905) 263–6; T.A.M. Bishop (1949–53) 441; T.A.M. Bishop (1967a) 41; T.A.M. Bishop (1971) 21 [no. 23]; Clemoes (1985) no. 4; McGurk (1986b) 46–9, 51, 53, 54, 56–63 [repr. McGurk (1998) no. XIV]; Heslop (1990) 173–4, 181; Backhouse—Webster (1991) no. 53 [D.H. Turner]; Dumville (1991–5) 41–2; Ohlgren (1992) 6; Dumville (1993g) 139–40; McGurk—Rosenthal (1995b) 286 [repr. McGurk (1998) no. XV]; Binski—Panayotova (2005) no. 9 [T. Webber]; R. Gameson (2012a) 70 n. 240, 80 n. 286; McGurk (2012) 439 and n. 11, 440–1, 446 [no. 3]

DEC: E. Temple (1976) no. 73; Brownrigg (1978) 264–5; Ohlgren (1986) no. 178; Raw (1990) 198; R. Gameson (1991) 79 n. 106; McGurk (1993) 255 [repr. McGurk (1998) no. XI]; R. Gameson (1995b) 119 n. 2, 122 n. 25, 195, 197, 209, 218 *et passim*; Karkov (2007c) 58; Pulliam (2011) 71; R. Gameson (2012c) 283 and n. 118, 284 and n. 124

FACS: M.R. James (1905) pls. between pp. 264–5 [fols. 10v, 11r]; T.A.M. Bishop (1971) pl. XXI [fols. 67r, 68r]; Ohlgren (1992) pls. 9.1–9.23 [fols. 1v, 2r, 2v, 3r, 3v, 4r, 4v, 5r, 5v, 6r, 6v, 7r, 7v, 8r, 8v, 10r, 11r, 44v, 45r, 70v, 71r, 108v, 109r]; Binski—Panayotova (2005) 60 [fol. 10v]; Karkov (2007c) fig. 7 [fol. 44v]; Rushforth (2007) 42 [fol. 10v]

ST: Glunz (1933) 133–48; Lenker (1997) 33, 448 n. 111, 449 n. 115, 453 n. 129, 467

139. Cambridge, Pembroke College, 302

s. xi med., Canterbury?, prov. Hereford Cathedral

Contents: gospel lectionary; Hereford diocesan bounds* (added s. xi^2)

MS: M.R. James (1905) 266–9; N.R. Ker (1957) no. 78 [OE bounds]; Sawyer (1968) 45 and no. 1561 [OE bounds]; Backhouse et al. (1984b) no. 70; Clemoes (1985) no. 5; McGurk (1986b) 45 [repr. McGurk (1998) no. XIV]; Dumville (1992a) 120, 123; Ohlgren (1992) 8–9; Mynors—Thomson (1993) xv n. 4, xvii; McGurk—Rosenthal (1995b)

270 [repr. McGurk (1998) no. XV]; Lenker (1997) 461–2; R. Gameson
(2002c); Binski—Panayotova (2005) no. 43 [Webber]; R. Gameson
(2005a) 92; Karkov (2006a) 50 n. 13; Heslop (2007); Rushforth (2007)
75; Teviotdale (2010); R. Gameson (2012a) 29 and nn. 65, 66, 70 and
n. 242, 91 n. 331; R. Gameson (2012b) 95 and n. 4; Scragg (2012a)
no. 194

DEC: Rice (1952) 211–12; E. Temple (1976) no. 96; Ohlgren (1986)
no. 201; R. Gameson (1991) 104 nn. 9–11; R. Gameson (1995b) 153
n. 7, 178–9, 182 n. 148, 194, 218; Heslop (2007) 65–70; Karkov (2007c)
55–7; Rushforth (2007) 31, 39; Broderick (2011) 279–80; R. Gameson
(2012c) 272 and n. 71, 290 n. 145; McGurk (2012) 440 and n. 21

FACS: *NPS* I, pl. 238 (a)–(f) [fols. 5v, 6v, 60v, 61r, 88v, 89r]; M.R. James
(1905) pls. between pp. 268–9 [fols. 60v, 61r]; Ohlgren (1992) pls.
14.1–14.15 [fols. 1r–6v, 9r, 9v, 38r, 38v, 60v, 61r, 88v, 89r]; Keynes
(2000) 18 [fol. 8r]; Binski—Panayotova (2005) 124 [fols. 60v, 61r];
Heslop (2007) figs. 3 (a) [fol. 9r (detail)], 3 (c) [fol. 60v (detail)], 3 (f)
[fol. 88v (detail)], 4 (a) [fol. 61r (detail)], 4 (c) [fol. 61r (detail)];
Karkov (2007c) figs. 1 [fols. 5v–6r], 2 [fol. 6v], 3 [fol. 9r], 4 [fol. 60v];
Panayotova (2007) pl. IV [fol. 38r]; Rushforth (2007) 31 [fol. 38r],
39 [fol. 60v]; Teviotdale (2010) figs. 3.1–2 [fols. 27r, 51v]

ED: Förster (1941) 769 [OE diocesan bounds]

ST: Glunz (1933) 67, 154–5; Förster (1941) 767–76; Finberg (1961) 225–7;
Sims-Williams (1990) 43–6; R. Gameson (1996a) 223 n.; Keynes (2000)
18 and n. 59; N.P. Brooks (2008) 31 n. 7

140. Cambridge, Pembroke College, 308

s. ix², Rheims, prov. England s. ix ex.?, (prov. Ely)

Contents: Hrabanus Maurus, *Comm. in Epistulas Pauli*, bks. IX–XIX

MS: M.R. James (1905) 275–6; Carey (1938) 57; Vezin (1973) 218–23;
Keynes—Lapidge (1983) 214 n. 26; Clemoes (1985) no. 19; Bischoff
(1986) 25 n. 17; P.R. Robinson (1988) I, no. 277; Bischoff (1990) 10
n. 17; Bischoff (1998—) I, no. 834; R. McKitterick (2004b) 223–4, 237
[erroneously described as 'commentary on Genesis']; Lapidge (2006)
49 n. 87, 168; R. Gameson (2012d) 348 and n. 13

FACS: Vezin (1973) pl. 1 [fols. 1r, 74v, 72r, 229r (details)]; Binski—
Panayotova (2005) 54 [fols. 71v–72r]

ST: R. McKitterick (2012) 328, 330 and n. 110

141. Cambridge, Pembroke College, 312C, nos. 1 and 2 (with Haarlem, Stadsbibliotheek, 188 F 53 and Sondershausen, Schlossmuseum, Lat. liturg. IX. 1) (binding strips)

s. xi med., prov. Flanders by 1069, Bruges from 1087?

Contents: Psalterium Gallicanum° (f)

MS: N.R. Ker (1957) no. 79; R. Derolez (1972); N.R. Ker (1976a) 122; Clemoes (1985) no. 9; Gneuss (1998) 273–5, 277, 278; Pulsiano (2001a) xxvi; Huber-Rebenich—Hirschler (2004) 119; Hartzell (2006) no. 53; Gneuss (2008a) 417 [the Sondershausen leaf]; Scragg (2012a) no. 195

DEC: R. Gameson (1995b) 220 n. 164

FACS: Gneuss (1998) pls. III–IV [Sondershausen fols. 1r, 1v]; Huber-Rebenich—Hirschler (2004), front cover and pl. 13 [Sondershausen fol. 1r]

ED: Dietz (1968) [Pembroke]; R. Derolez (1972) [Haarlem]; Gneuss (1998) 283–5 [Sondershausen as base text for fragment of Anglo-Saxon psalter]

LANG: Gneuss (1998) 281–2

ST: Sisam—Sisam (1959) 67 n. 1; Gneuss (1998) 279–81 [glosses]; Gneuss (2008a) 417

142. Cambridge, Pembroke College, 312C, no. 5

s. x/xi

Contents: Venantius Fortunatus, *Carmina* [*CPL* 1033] I. v–vii (f)

MS: M.R. James (1905) xl; R.W. Hunt (1979) 282; Clemoes (1985) no. 36

143. Cambridge, Pembroke College, 313 / 20

s. xi² or xi/xii, Bury St Edmunds?

Contents: pontifical (f)

MS: N.R. Ker (1962–92) II.246; R.M. Thomson (1972) 623 n. 25; Clemoes (1985) no. 26; R. Gameson (1999a) no. 115

DEC: R. Gameson (1991) 105 n. 10

ST: Dumville (1992a) 67 [wrongly listed as a fragmentary 'missal']; Gneuss (2003b) 295

143. 5. Cambridge, Pembroke College, C. 8 [ptd bk.], pastedowns

s. xi

Contents: missal (f)

MS: Hartzell (2006) no. 54; Wieland (2009) 122

ST: Dumville (1992a) 67

144. Cambridge, Peterhouse, 74

1081×1088, and later additions, prov. Durham s. xi ex.

Contents: *Collectio Lanfranci* [*Concilia, Decreta pontificum*]

MS: M.R. James (1899) 90–3; Z.N. Brooke (1931) 231–5; Mynors (1939)
   no. 50; R. Powell (1962) 4; N.R. Ker (1964) 62; S. Williams (1971) 79–80;
   P.R. Robinson (1988) I, no. 280; Gullick (1994) 106–8; Williman
   (1996–9) 440; Gullick (1998a) 30 n. 38; R. Gameson (1999a) no. 116;
   Kéry (1999) 116, 240 [*Collectio Lanfranci*]; Gullick (2000) 208 n.;
   Gullick (2001) 102–3, 117

FACS: P.R. Robinson (1988) II, pl. 36 [fol. 115r]

ST: Z.N. Brooke (1931) 63, 162; Sheerin (1975b); Webber (1992) 47–8;
   Philpott (1994) 131; R. Gameson (1998) 236 n. 25; Gullick (2008)

145. Cambridge, Peterhouse, 251, fols. 106–91

s. xi ex. or xi/xii, Canterbury StA

Contents: Galen, *Ad Glauconem de medendi methodo*, and *Liber tertius*;
   Liber Aurelii de acutis passionibus; *Liber Esculapii de chronicis passionibus*; Galen (?), *De podagra*

MS: M.R. James (1899) 307–10; T.A.M. Bishop (1954–8a) 189; T.A.M.
   Bishop (1959–63a) 95; M.L. Cameron (1984) 162–3 and nn. 38–42;
   M.L. Cameron (1993) 71 and n. 21; R. Gameson (1995a) 102 n. 28;
   R. Gameson (1999a) no. 117; Barker-Benfield (2008) I.516, II.1230,
   1261, III.1820; R. Gameson (2008) 192, 203–4

DEC: Lawrence (1982) 102

146. Cambridge, Queens' College, (Horne) 75 (with Oxford, Bodleian Library, Eng. th. c. 74 + Bloomington, Indiana University, Lilly Library, Poole 40 + New Haven, Yale University, Beinecke Library, Osborn fa 26)

s. xi in.

Contents: Ælfric, Homilies* (f) and Lives of Saints* (f)

MS: N.R. Ker (1957) no. 81; N.R. Ker (1976a) 123; Dumville (1988) 60–1; Clemoes (1997) 54–5 [M.R. Godden]; Stoneman (1997) 103, 119, 122; Wilcox (2006a) 239, 256; Scragg (2012a) no. 200

FACS: Collins – Clemoes (1974) 74 [Yale and Bloomington fragments]

ED: Clemoes (1997) 291–4 [Ælfric, CH I, Hom. XIV (Palm Sunday), lines 34–113 coll. as f^c], 316 [Ælfric, CH I, Hom. XVII (Second Sunday after Easter), lines 79–89, coll. as f^c], 335–6 [Ælfric, CH I, Hom. XX *Feria .IIII. De fide catholica*), lines 1–39, coll. as f^c]

ST: R.L. Collins (1960) [discovery of Indiana University, Lilly Library, Poole 10]; Collins – Clemoes (1974) [on the origin of the fragments]; R.L. Collins (1976) 38–42 [Yale University Beinecke Library, Osborn Collection and Bloomington, Indiana, Indiana University Lilly Library Poole 10 are identified as a fragments of this MS]; J. Hill (1996) 243, 245

146. 5. Cambridge, St John's College 5 (A. 5), part i

s. xi/xii, Canterbury CC

Contents: Gratianus Augustus, *Epistula ad Ambrosium* [cf. *CPL* 160]; Ambrose, *De fide* [*CPL* 150], *De Spiritu Sancto* [*CPL* 151], *De incarnationis dominicae sacramento* [*CPL* 152]

MS: M.R. James (1913) 5–6; Gullick (2010) 8 n. 10

ST: Webber (1992) 53–4; Gneuss (2012) 288–9

147. Cambridge, St John's College, 35 (B. 13)

s. xi ex., (prov. Bury St Edmunds)

Contents: Gregory, *Homiliae in Hiezechielem* [*CPL* 1710]; *Trinubium Annae* (s. xi/xii)

MS: Schenkl no. 2600; M.R. James (1913) 47; N.R. Ker (1960) 8 n. 2; N.R. Ker (1964) 19; R.M. Thomson (1972) 625 n. 39, 626; Rella (1977) 160; R. Sharpe et al. (1996) 81 [B.13.201]; Gransden (1998b) 265–6; R. Gameson (1999a) no. 119; T.N. Hall (2001) 131, 133 [no. 3]; Biggs (2007a) 83 [Biggs, T.N. Hall]

DEC: R. Gameson (1991) 65–75

FACS: R. Gameson (1991) fig. 12 [fol. 110v]; Gransden (1998b) pl. LXXX (A) [fol. 105r (detail)]

ED: T.N. Hall (2002) 115 [*Trinubium Annae*]

ST: T.N. Hall (2002)

148. Cambridge, St John's College 59 (C. 9) (the 'Southampton Psalter')

s. x/xi, Ireland, (prov. Dover), in England before 1100?

Contents: Psalterium Gallicanum with glosses (Latin and Irish); three rhyming prayers [not in SK]; canticles

MS: M.R. James (1913) 76–8; Mearns (1914) 68; Kenney (1929) no. 476; N.R. Ker (1964) 58; de Brún—Herbert (1986) 110 [no. 53]; P.L. Heyworth (1989) 207; Biggs et al. (1990) 97 [C.D. Wright]; Dumville (1992a) 112; Pulsiano (2001a) xxvii; Duncan (2004); Binski—Panayotova (2005) no. 16 [R. McKitterick]; Dumville (2007d) 83–6; M.P. Brown (2012) 135; R. Gameson (2012a) 42 and n. 115; Toswell (2012) 473

DEC: Henry (1960) 23–40; Henry (1965) 58–9, 106–8; Köhler—Mütherich (1971–99) VII.44 n. 47; Alexander (1978a) no. 74; Ohlgren (1986) no. 74; Huws (2000) 113–14; Harbison (2011) 147–8

FACS: Alexander (1978a) ills. 350–3 [fols. 4v, 38v, 71v, 72r]; Binski—Panayotova (2005) 70 [fols. 68v–69r]; P.P. O'Neill (2012) pls. 1, 2 (a)—(c) [fols. 6r and 6v, 55r, 90r (details)]

ED: Stokes—Strachan (1901-3) I.xiv, 4–6 [Irish glosses]; Pulsiano (2001a) [Pss. I–L coll. as θ]; P.P. O'Neill (2012) 4–359 [complete MS]

ST: H.M. Bannister (1910–11a); R.L. Ramsay (1912) 471–3 [Latin glosses]; McNamara (1973) 241–2 [psalter text]; *BCLL* (1985) no. 509; Pulsiano (1998b) 105 n. 2; P.P. O'Neill (2002); Duncan (2004)

149. Cambridge, St John's College, 73 (C. 23)

s. xi/xii, Bury St Edmunds

Contents: gospels, gospel list

MS: M.R. James (1913) 96–8; T.A.M. Bishop (1954–8a) 185–7; T.A.M. Bishop (1971) xix, xxiii; R.M. Thomson (1972) 618 n. 3, 625–7; A.G. Watson (1987a) 5; P.R. Robinson (1988) I.110; Lenker (1997) 454; Gransden (1998b) 266; R. Gameson (1999a) no. 120; Rushforth (2012) 209 n. 73

DEC: R. Gameson (1991) 104 n. 9, 105 n. 10, 106 n. 32; R. Gameson (2012c) 285 and n. 126

FACS: T.A.M. Bishop (1954–8a) pls. X (a), XI (a), XI (b) [fols. 1v (detail), 91v (detail), 44v (detail)]; Gransden (1998b) pl. LXXX (B) [fol. 117r (detail)]

ST: McGurk (1986b) 51, 55 [repr. McGurk (1998) no. XIV]; Lenker (1997) 442–50

150. Cambridge, St John's College 82 (D. 7), fols. 89–92

s. x med.

Contents: creed (*Quicumque uult*), canticle [*Canticum Moysi*] (f)

MS: M.R. James (1913) 111; Pulsiano (1995) 81; Wieland (2009) 136

151. Cambridge, St John's College, 87 (D. 12), fols. 1–50

s. xi^2, France, (prov. Dover), in England before 1100?

Contents: Statius, *Thebais*

MS: Schenkl no. 2616; M.R. James (1903) 523 [no. 391]; M.R. James (1913) 115–17; A.G. Watson (1981) 44 n. 5 [repr. A.G. Watson (2004) no. XI]; R. Gameson (1999a) no. 121

ED: Klotz—Klinnert (1902/1973) [Statius, *Thebais*, coll. as D; but see M.D. Reeve in L.D. Reynolds (1983) 395 n. 13]; Garrod (1906) [Statius, *Thebais*, coll. as D]

ST: Garrod (1904); L.D. Reynolds (1983) xxxiv n. 159

152. Cambridge, St John's College, 101 (D. 26), fols. 1–14

s. x^2, Canterbury StA (Glastonbury?)

Contents: Cassian, *De institutis coenobiorum* [*CPL* 513], bk. XII (f)

MS: Schenkl no. 2625; M.R. James (1913) 134 [text erroneously identified as Cassian, *Conlatio* XII]; T.A.M. Bishop (1954–8b) 324, 330; T.A.M. Bishop (1971) 5 n. 2; Barker-Benfield (2008) II.772, III.1812, 1815; Wieland (2009) 141

ST: Lake (2003) 41 n. 56; Lapidge (2006) 295–6

152. 7. Cambridge, St John's College, 147 (F. 10), flyleaves i–iii, 57–9

s. x^2

Contents: Alcuin, *Expositio in Euangelium Iohannis* (f)

MS: M.R. James (1913) 181; Rushforth (2009) 73–5

FACS: Rushforth (2009) pl. 3 [fol. i (recto)]

ST: *CSLMA* II (1999) 371–5

152. 9. Cambridge, St John's College, 164 (F. 27), flyleaves i–ii

s. xi med., prob. Canterbury StA

Contents: commentary (the 'Einsiedeln Commentary') on the *Artes* of
  Donatus (f)

MS: M.R. James (1913) 198; Rushforth (2009) 75–7

FACS: Rushforth (2009) pl. 4 [fols. i (verso)–ii (recto)]

ST: Gneuss (2012) 289

153. Cambridge, St John's College, 164 (F. 27)

s. x, prob. England, (prov. Canterbury StA)

Contents: Adrevald of Fleury, *Historia translationis S. Benedicti* [*BHL*
  1117]; parts of rhymed offices for St Augustine of Canterbury and
  Abbot Hadrian (s. xi); Adrevald of Fleury, *Miracula S. Benedicti* [*BHL*
  1123] with prefatory verses [SK 11436]; Odo of Cluny, Sermon for the
  feast of St Benedict

MS: Schenkl no. 2640; M.R. James (1913) 197–9; N.R. Ker (1964) 41;
  Biggs et al. (2001) 109–12; Hartzell (2006) no. 56; T.N. Hall (2007) 253,
  261–2; Barker-Benfield (2008) III.1745, 1784

ST: Gneuss (1968) 114–15; *CSLMA* I (1994) 36–42; *CALMA* I.47 [R.
  Love]; Lapidge (2012a) 690; R. McKitterick (2012) 328

153. 5. Cambridge, St John's College, 236 (L. 9)

c. 1075, Canterbury CC

Contents: Acts of the Council of London (1074×1075)

MS: M.R. James (1913) 275; Clover — Gibson (1979) 20; Whitelock et al.
  (1981) II.609–10

ED: Whitelock et al. (1981) II.612–16

ST: Whitelock et al. (1981) II.607–11

154. Cambridge, St John's College, Aa. 5. 1, fol. 67

s. viii¹, Northumbria, or s. viii or ix¹, S England?, (prov. Ramsey)

Contents: Cassiodorus, *Expositio psalmorum* [*CPL* 900] (f)

MS: Schenkl no. 2648; M.R. James (1913) 242; *CLA* Supplement (1971) no. 1679; Lapidge (1988–9) 454; Dumville (1992a) 104–5; Knappe (1996) 217 and n. 3; Lapidge (1996c) 432; Crick (1997) 70 and n. 36; Lapidge (1998) 39 n. 12; Lapidge (2000a) 19, 23; Rushforth (2011) 60–1; Stoppacci (2012–) I.22

FACS: Lapidge (2000a) 19, 23 [illustrations of single words]

ST: Bailey (1983) 189; Bailey–Handley (1983) 54–5; Halporn (1985); Lapidge (2006) 296

154. 5. Cambridge, St John's College, Ii. 12. 29 [ptd bk], flyleaves

s. ix¹ or ix med., France

Contents: Isidore, *Etymologiae* [*CPL* 1186], bks. XVIII–XIX (f)

MS: N.R. Ker (1954) 112 [no. 1207]; Bischoff (1998–) I, no. 836

155. Cambridge, Sidney Sussex College, Δ. 5. 15 (100), pt. ii

s. x³/³, prob. Winchester OM (Ramsey?); additions s. xi¹ and xi/xii, Durham; prov. whole MS, Durham

Contents: pontifical services (s. x³/³); mass of St Cuthbert (s. xi¹); antiphons for the Office of St Nicholas (s. xi/xii)

MS: C. Wordsworth (1885) 54–72; M.R. James (1897) 120–2; Mynors (1939) no. 29; N.R. Ker (1957) no. 82; N.R. Ker (1964) 62; T.A.M. Bishop (1971) 14 [no. 16]; Brückmann (1973) 410; Rella (1977) 57, 80; Banting (1989) xxxix–li [full description]; Gneuss (1985) 132 [no. R.4]; Lapidge–Winterbottom (1991b) lxxviii–lxxix; Rollason (1989) 422–3; Dumville (1992a) 68, 75–6, 79, 89–91, 94, 104, 107, 221 n. 30; Lapidge (1992a) 111 [repr. Lapidge (1993a) 399]; Dumville (1993g) 65; Lapidge (1996c) 432 n. 113; Bullough (1998a) 125, 127; Hartzell (2006) no. 57; Scragg (2012a) no. 201

DEC: R. Gameson (1995b) 238 n. 18

FACS: T.A.M. Bishop (1971) pls. XIV (a)–(b) [fols. 3r, 14v]; Banting (1989) pl. 2 [fol. 6r]

ED: Banting (1989) 155–70 [base MS for the 'Sidney Sussex Pontifical']

ST: Hohler (1975); N. Orchard (1995a) 90–1, 95; Bullough (1996) 21 n. 71; Corrêa (1996) 288, 299–306; R. Gameson (1996a) 201 n.; Thacker (1996) 250 n.; Pfaff (2001) 181; N. Orchard (2002) I.218; C.A. Jones (2004) 328, 338–9, 342; N. Orchard (2005) xxxii, cii, cxxxvii–cxxxviii, 446

155. 5. Cambridge, Trinity College, B. 1. 16 (15)

s. xi/xii, Canterbury, CC (?), (prov. ibid.?)

Contents: hymn [SK 1545] (first stanza only); sequence [WIC 5464]; Berengaudus, *Comm. in Apocalypsin*; Haimo of Auxerre, *Expositio in Canticum canticorum* (incomplete)

MS: M.R. James (1900–4) I.17–19; N.R. Ker (1964) 39; Fenlon (1982) 24–9 [Rankin]; R. Gameson (1999a) no. 124; Hartzell (2006) no. 58

FACS: Fenlon (1982) 25, 28 [fols. 4r, 2r]

ST: *CSLMA* III (2010) 288–97, 357–8 [Haimo, *Expositio in Canticum canticorum*]

155. 6. Cambridge, Trinity College, B. 1. 17 (16)

s. xi ex. or xi/xii, Canterbury CC

Contents: Jerome, *Comm. in Euangelium Matthaei* [*CPL* 590]; *Physiologus* (excerpt on the hyena)

MS: M.R. James (1900–4) I.19–20; M.R. James (1903) 508, 514; N.R. Ker (1964) 31; Webber (1995) 154, 157; R. Gameson (1999a) no. 125; Gullick—Pfaff (2001) 285 and n. 3; Gneuss (2003b) 296; Bouet—Dosdat (2005) 97

FACS: Bouet—Dosdat (2005) fig. 1 [fol. 3r]

ST: Lambert (1969–72) no. 217

156. Cambridge, Trinity College, B. 1. 29 (27), fols. 1-47

s. xi/xii, France, (prov. Buildwas, Cistercian abbey), in England before 1100?

Contents: pseudo-Jerome, *Expositio in Canticum canticorum* [cf. *CPL* 194a]

MS: Schenkl no. 2179; M.R. James (1900–4) I.33–6; N.R. Ker (1964) 14; R. Gameson (1999a) no. 126

ST: Lambert (1969–72) no. 450; *CPPM* II, no. 2391

157. Cambridge, Trinity College, B. 1. 30A (28) (with New Haven, Yale University, Beinecke Library 320)

s. x$^{2/4}$ or x med.

Contents: pontifical (f)

MS: M.R. James (1900–4) I.42; Shailor (1984–2004) II.126–8; Dumville (1991–5) 42–3; Dumville (1992a) 68, 76, 95; Keynes (1992) 11 [no. 3]; Dumville (1994a) 144 and n. 60; Stoneman (1997) 121; Gneuss (2003b) 296

FACS: Keynes (1992) pl. III [verso of Cambridge fragment]; Dumville (1994a) pl. IV [recto of Cambridge fragment]

ED: M.R. James (1900–4) I.42 [Cambridge fragment]

ST: *CPL* 1900f [listed among *Documenta ad Gelasianum uetus proxime accedentia*, with James's erroneous dating]

157. 7. Cambridge, Trinity College, B. 1. 37 (35), fols. 46–97

s. xi ex. and/or s. xii in., Salisbury

Contents: Anselm, *Proslogion, Repetitio of Proslogion, Cur Deus magis assumpserit*, fifteen letters (and six letters inserted after 1100 on fols. 67–8), Prosper, *Pro Augustino responsiones ad capitula obiectionum Vincentianarum* [*CPL* 521]: 1090 × 1093; Anselm, *Monologion* (incomplete): s. xi ex. or xii in.

MS: M.R. James (1900–4) I.46–8; R. Gameson (1999a) nos. 128–31; Sharpe–Webber (2009)

158. Cambridge, Trinity College, B. 1. 40 (38)

s. xi ex., Canterbury StA

Contents: Augustine, *De diuersis quaestionibus .lxxxiii.* [*CPL* 289]

MS: M.R. James (1900–4) I.53; T.A.M. Bishop (1949–53) 438; T.A.M. Bishop (1955) 2; T.A.M. Bishop (1959–63a) 94; N.R. Ker (1964) 41; Römer (1972b) 91; Mutzenbecher (1975) li, lxi; R. Gameson (1995a) 102 n. 28, 144; R. Gameson (1999a) no. 132; T.N. Hall (2004b) 97 n. 18; Barker-Benfield (2008) I.423, 510, 528, II.919, 924, 1499, III.1732, 1736, 1795, 1821, 1882

DEC: Dodwell (1954) 122; Lawrence (1982) 102; R. Gameson (1995a) 105 n. 35, 137 n. 161

FACS: Lawrence (1982) pl. XXXII (B) [fol. 1r]

ED: Mutzenbecher (1975) 1–249 [Augustine, *De diuersis quaestionibus*, coll. as C]

159. Cambridge, Trinity College, B. 1. 42 (40)

s. x², Canterbury StA

Contents: Cyprianus Gallus, *Pentateuchos* [*CPL* 1423]

MS: Peiper (1891) ix–x; M.R. James (1900–4) I.54–5; N.R. Ker (1964) 41; Strongman (1977–80) 24; Keynes (1992) 19–20 [no. 9]; Barker-Benfield (2008) I.406, II.1380, III.1706, 1814; R. Gameson (2012a) 49 n. 148

FACS: Keynes (1992) pl. IX [fol. 1r]

ED: Peiper (1891) [Cyprianus Gallus coll. as C]

161. Cambridge, Trinity College, B. 3. 5 (84)

s. xi ex., Canterbury CC

Contents: Jerome, *Comm. in Prophetas minores* [*CPL* 589], *Comm. in Danielem* [*CPL* 588]

MS: M.R. James (1900–4) I.103–4; T.A.M. Bishop (1949–53) 435–6; N.R. Ker (1964) 31; Bodden (1988) 231; Webber (1995) 149 n. 18, 154, 157; Gullick (1998c) 179–80; R. Gameson (1999a) no. 140; Barker-Benfield (2008) I.505

DEC: Dodwell (1954) 17, 120; Lawrence (1982) 107, 108; R. Gameson (1995a) 116 n. 71, 142

FACS: Dodwell (1954) pl. 45 (c) [fol. 3r (detail)]; Lawrence (1982) pl. XXXIII (B) [folio not specified]

ST: Lambert (1969–72) nos. 215, 216

162. Cambridge, Trinity College, B. 3. 9 (88)

s. xi/xii, Canterbury CC

Contents: Ambrose, *Expositio euangelii secundum Lucam* [*CPL* 143]

MS: M.R. James (1900–4) I.109–10; N.R. Ker (1964) 32; Webber (1995) 157; Bankert et al. (1997) 32; R. Gameson (1999a) no. 141

DEC: Dodwell (1954) 20, 37, 72, 120; R. Gameson (1995a) 106 n., 117 n., 118 n., 121 n., 143

FACS: Dodwell (1954) pls. 5 (h) [fol. 130r (detail)], 44 (a) [fol. 15r (detail)];
Webber (1995) pls. 2, 3 (b) [fols. 4r, 15r]

ST: Webber (1995) 157

162. 1. Cambridge, Trinity College, B. 3. 10 (89)

s. xi/xii, Canterbury CC

Contents: Ambrose, *Epistulae* [*CPL* 160], *Contra Auxentium de basilicis
tradendis* [= *Epist.* lxxviii], *De traditione basilicae* [= *Epist.* lxxix], *De
obitu Theodosii* [*CPL* 159], *De Nabuthae* [*CPL* 138]; pseudo-Ambrose, *De SS. Geruasio et Protasio* [= *Epist.* ii: *CPL* 2195; *BHL* 3514]

MS: M.R. James (1900–4) I.110–11; R. Gameson (1999a) no. 142

ST: Bankert et al. (1997) 52

162. 6. Cambridge, Trinity College, B. 3. 14 (93)

s. xi/xii, Préaux, (prov. Canterbury CC)

Contents: Richard of Préaux, *Comm. in Genesim*, pt. ii [companion vol.
to no. **504. 8**]

MS: M.R. James (1900–4) I.114–15; R. Gameson (1995a) 108 n. 45;
Webber (1995) 158; R. Gameson (1999a) no. 143

163. Cambridge, Trinity College, B. 3. 25 (104)

s. xi ex. (1080s), Canterbury CC

Contents: Augustine, *Confessiones* [*CPL* 251], *Retractationes* [*CPL* 250]
II.vi, *De haeresibus* [*CPL* 314]

MS: M.R. James (1900–4) I.123; M.R. James (1903) 18 [no. 33], 156
[no. 96]; Southern (1963) 243; N.R. Ker (1964) 32; Römer (1972b) 93;
Rella (1977) 159; N.P. Brooks (1984) 269 [no. 39]; Keynes (1992) 33–4
[no. 21]; Webber (1995) 158; R. Gameson (1999a) no. 144; R. Gameson
(2012a) 19 n. 24; Webber (2012) 215 n. 15

FACS: Keynes (1992) pl. XXI [fol. 63v]

163. 5. Cambridge, Trinity College, B. 3. 31 (110)

s. xi/xii, Canterbury CC

Contents: Augustine, *Retractationes* [*CPL* 250] II. xv; *Epistula ad
Aurelium* [*Epist.* clxxiv] [*CPL* 262]; *De Trinitate* [*CPL* 329]

MS: M.R. James (1900–4) I.131–2; N.R. Ker (1964) 32; Römer (1972b) 93–4; R. Gameson (1999a) no. 145; Gullick—Pfaff (2001) 285; Gneuss (2003b) 296

164. Cambridge, Trinity College, B. 3. 33 (112)

s. xi/xii, Canterbury CC

Contents: Augustine, *De adulterinis coniugiis* [*CPL* 302], *De mendacio* [*CPL* 303], *Contra mendacium* [*CPL* 304], *De cura pro mortuis gerenda* [*CPL* 307], *De uera religione* [*CPL* 264], *De natura et origine animae* [*CPL* 345]; pseudo-Augustine, *Sermo Ariani cuiusdam* [*CPL* 701], *Contra sermonem Arianorum* (from Syagrius, *Regulae definitionum contra haereticos prolatae* [*CPL* 560]); Augustine, *Contra aduersarium legis et prophetarum* [*CPL* 326]

MS: Schenkl no. 2245; M.R. James (1900–4) I.135–6; N.R. Ker (1964) 32; Römer (1972b) 94; Gullick (1998c); R. Gameson (1999a) no. 147

DEC: Dodwell (1954) 120; R. Gameson (1995a) 117 n., 121 n., 142

ST: Webber (1992) 51 n. 26; Webber (1995) 158; Gullick (1998c) 178, 189

165. Cambridge, Trinity College, B. 4. 2 (116)

s. xi ex., Canterbury CC

Contents; gospel of John; Augustine, *Tractatus in Euangelium Ioannis* [*CPL* 278]

MS: M.R. James (1900–4) I.140; Dodwell (1954) 120; N.R. Ker (1964) 32; Römer (1972b) 94; C.E. Wright (1972) 64, 71, 114; Webber (1995) 158; R. Gameson (1999a) no. 148; Barker-Benfield (2008) I.517

DEC: R. Gameson (1995a) 132 n., 143

165. 5. Cambridge, Trinity College, B. 4. 5 (119)

s. xi/xii, Préaux, (prov. Canterbury CC)

Contents: Florus of Lyon, *Comm. in Epistolas Pauli* (ad Romanos — ad Corinthios I)

Companion vol. to no. **567. 5**

MS: M.R. James (1900–4) I.142–3; Webber (1995) 158; R. Gameson (1999a) no. 149

DEC: R. Gameson (1995a) 131 n. 37

166. Cambridge, Trinity College, B. 4. 9 (123)

s. xi/xii, Canterbury CC

Contents: Gregory, *Moralia in Iob* [*CPL* 1708], bks. XVII–XXXV

MS: M.R. James (1900-4) I.146–7; N.R. Ker (1964) 32; Webber (1995) 154, 158; R. Gameson (1999a) no. 150

DEC: Dodwell (1954) 17; R. Gameson (1995a) 117 n., 121 n., 132 n., 143

FACS: Webber (1995) pl. 5 (a) [fol. 108v]

167. Cambridge, Trinity College, B. 4. 26 (140)

s. xi ex., Canterbury CC

Contents: Augustine, *Epistulae* [*CPL* 262]

MS: M.R. James (1900–4) I.163–6 [incl. full list of the *Epistulae* in this MS]; N.R. Ker (1964) 32; Römer (1972b) 95 [full list of the *Epistulae* in this MS]; R. Gameson (1999a) no. 152; Webber (2012) 215 n. 15

DEC: Dodwell (1954) 120; Lawrence (1982) 108; R. Gameson (1995a) 117 n. 78, 143

FACS: Lawrence (1982) pl. XXXIII (D) [folio not specified]; Webber (1995) pl. 3 (a) [fol. 2r]

ST: R. Gameson (1995a) 106 n.; Webber (1995) 158

168. Cambridge, Trinity College, B. 4. 27 (141)

s. x ex., Canterbury CC

Contents: Isidore, *Mysticorum expositiones sacramentorum seu Quaestiones in Vetus Testamentum* [*CPL* 1195]; Adalbert of Metz, *Speculum Gregorii* (epitome of *Moralia*); Augustine, *In Ioannis epistulam ad Parthos tractatus .x.* [*CPL* 279]

MS: M.R. James (1900–4) I.166–7; T.A.M. Bishop (1959–63a) 94; T.A.M. Bishop (1959–63b) 413–14, 416–17, 419–20; N.R. Ker (1964) 32; T.A.M. Bishop (1971) xxv, 6; N.R. Ker (1972b) 77–8; Römer (1972b) 95; N.P. Brooks (1984) 267 [no. 3]; Dumville (1992a) 47; Keynes (1992) 25–6 [no. 14]; Wieland (2009) 133; R. Gameson (2012a) 23 and n. 36, 40 and n. 102; R. Gameson (2012d) 351 and n. 24; Rushforth (2012) 204 and n. 46

FACS: T.A.M. Bishop (1959–63b) pls. XIV (b)–(c) [fols. 108v, 153r]; Keynes (1992) pl. XIV [fol. 126v]

ST: N.R. Ker (1960) 8 n. 2; C. Brett (1991) 53; R. McKitterick (2012) 328, 329 and n. 104

Cambridge, Trinity College, B. 5. 2 (148): see no. **270**

169. 5. Cambridge, Trinity College, B. 5. 24 (170)

s. xi/xii, Canterbury CC

Contents: Jerome, *Comm. in Esaiam* [*CPL* 584], bks. XI–XVIII

MS: M.R. James (1900–4) I.223; Webber (1995) 154, 158; R. Gameson (1999a) no. 157

170. Cambridge, Trinity College, B. 5. 26 (172)

s. xi ex., Canterbury CC

Contents: Augustine, *Enarrationes in psalmos* [*CPL* 283], pss. I–L [companion vol. to nos. **171** and **937. 5**]

MS: M.R. James (1900–4) I.224–5; N.R. Ker (1964) 33; Römer (1972b) 97; Webber (1995) 158; R. Gameson (1999a) no. 158

DEC: Dodwell (1954) 17–18, 76, 120; C.M. Kauffmann (1975) 55–6 [no. 6]; Ohlgren (1986) no. 217; R. Gameson (1991) 74 n. 77; R. Gameson (1995a) 117 n. 78, 136 n. 159, 143

FACS: Dodwell (1954) pl. 10 (b) [fol. 1r]

ST: Webber (1995) 158; Gullick (1998c)

171. Cambridge, Trinity College, B. 5. 28 (174)

s. xi ex., Canterbury CC

Contents: Augustine, *Enarrationes in psalmos* [*CPL* 283], pss. CI–CL [companion vol. to nos. **170** and **937. 5**]

MS: M.R. James (1900–4) I.226; N.R. Ker (1964) 33; T.A.M. Bishop (1949–53) 435–6; Römer (1972b) 97; R. Gameson (1999a) no. 159

DEC: Dodwell (1954) 17; R. Gameson (1995a) 117n., 118 n., 143

FACS: Webber (1995) pls. 4 (b)–(c) [fols. 87v, 60v (details)]; Gullick (1998c) 182 [fol. 1r]

ST: Webber (1995) 158; Gullick (1998c) 181–2

172. Cambridge, Trinity College, B. 10. 4 (215)

s. xi$^{1/4}$, Canterbury CC? Peterborough?

Contents: gospels, gospel list

MS: M.R. James (1900–4) I.287–92; N.R. Ker (1957) lvii; N.R. Ker (1964) 103; T.A.M. Bishop (1967a) 39; T.A.M. Bishop (1971) xv, xxiii, 22; Brownrigg (1978) 248, 260 n. 3, 264–6; Backhouse et al. (1984b) no. 49 [D.H. Turner]; N.P. Brooks (1984) 269; McGurk (1986b) 43–4, 46, 48–55 [repr. McGurk (1998) no. XIV]; Heslop (1990) 154 n. 10, 166, 168, 171, 182; Dumville (1992a) 85, 87; Keynes (1992) 32–3 [no. 20]; Dumville (1993g) 116 n. 29, 139; McGurk–Rosenthal (1995) 258–62; Lenker (1997) 450–1; Binski–Panayotova (2005) no. 10 [Webber]; Coatsworth (2006) 88 n. 45; McGurk–Rosenthal (2006) 194 n. 46, 196; R. Gameson (2012a) 41 n. 107, 70 n. 240, 80 n. 286; McGurk (2012) 438 and n. 7, 446 [no. 4]

DEC: Dodwell (1954) 10, 12, 13, 18, 19, 23, 27; E. Temple (1976) no. 65; G. Henderson (1982) 61 n. 85; Ohlgren (1986) no. 170; Clayton (1990) 171–2; Raw (1990) 198–9; Ohlgren (1992) 5, 59–62; McGurk (1993) 255 [repr. McGurk (1998) no. XI]; R. Gameson (1995b) 13, 28, 119–22, 130, 155, 180, 197, 206, 210 n. 121, 218, 230; C.M. Kauffmann (2003) 57; R. Gameson (2012c) 283 and n. 118, 290 and n. 144

FACS: Dodwell (1954) pls. 7 (b), 7 (c), 11 (a), 14 (a) [fols. 60r, 133r, 90r, 16v (details)]; Dodwell (1982) 52–3, 184 [fols. 21r, 12r]; Backhouse et al. (1984b) pl. XIII [fol. 16v]; Keynes (1992) pl. XX [fol. 25r]; Ohlgren (1992) pls. 7.1–7.24 [fols. 9r–16v, 17v, 18r, 59v, 60r, 89v, 90r, 132v, 133r]; Brantley (1999) pl. IV [fol. 164v]; Binski–Panayotova (2005) 61 [fol. 15v]; McGurk–Rosenthal (2006) figs. 16–17 [fols. 12r, 59v]; R. Gameson (2012) pl. 18.3 [fol. 17v]

ST: Glunz (1933) 140–8; McGurk–Rosenthal (1995b) 258–60 [repr. McGurk (1998) no. XV] [on relation to other Judith gospels]; Lenker (1997) 107–14, 191–5, 237–42, 442–50

173. Cambridge, Trinity College, B. 10. 5 (216) (with London, British Library, Cotton Vitellius C. viii, fols. 85–90)

s. viii^{1}, prob. Northumbria, (prov. Durham)

Contents: Epistulae Pauli with gloss (derived partly from Pelagius, *Expositiones .xiii. epistularum Pauli* [*CPL* 728]); Damasus, Epigram on St Paul [SK 7486]; Jerome, *Epist.* lxxiii; excerpts from works of Jerome, from Cassian, *Conlationes*, from Isidore, *Etymologiae*, and from biblical Genesis and Abacuc

MS: M.R. James (1900–4) I.293–6; *CLA* II (1935) no. 133; Mynors (1939) no. 8; N.R. Ker (1957) no. 83; McGurk (1961b) 10 [repr. McGurk (1998) no. V]; N.R. Ker (1964) 62; T.A.M. Bishop (1964–8a); T.J. Brown (1972) 226 [repr. T.J. Brown (1993a) 104]; T.J. Brown (1975) 268 [repr. T.J. Brown (1993a) 159]; T.J. Brown (1982a) 116–17 [repr. T.J. Brown (1993a) 218]; P.L. Heyworth (1989) 197; Keynes (1992) 8–9 [no. 1]; Vaciago (1993) 8 [no. 28]; McGurk (1994b) 18 [repr. McGurk (1998) no. XII]; Lapidge (2000a) 28; Ó Cróinín (2001) 34; *ASMMF* XII (2004) 1–9, 84–95 [nos. 78, 255; Wright—Hollis]; Hartzell (2006) no. 59; R. Gameson (2012a) 28 n. 59; Marsden (2012) 420 and n. 69

FACS: Keynes (1992) pl. I [fol. 20r]; T.J. Brown (1993a) ill. 49 [fol. 20r (details)]; Lapidge (2000a) 28 [fol. 20r (details)]; *ASMMF* XII (2004) nos. 78, 255

ED: J. Wordsworth et al. (1889–1954) [Pauline epistles coll. as S]; Napier (1900) no. 62 [OE glosses]

ST: Lindsay (1915) 450; Frede (1961) 77; T.A.M. Bishop (1964–8a); Frede (1964) 142; Lambert (1969–72) nos. 219, 354, 990; *BCLL* (1985) no. 2; Ní Chatháin (1987b) 192–5; Dumville (1997) 21 n. 28; Ó Cróinín (2001) 34

174. Cambridge, Trinity College, B. 11. 2 (241)

s. $x^{2/4}$ (930s) or x med., Canterbury StA; additions, s. $xi^{3/4}$, Exeter; whole MS prov. Exeter

Contents: Amalarius, *Liber officialis* (Retractatio prima; with glosses s. x^2 - xi^1): s. $x^{2/4}$ or x med.; additions: antiphon (s. xi^1); further additions (s. $xi^{3/4}$): *Dies Aegyptiaci*; excerpts from Amalarius, *Liber officialis* (Good Friday, interpolated text); donation inscription[+*]

MS: M.R. James (1900–4) I.327–8; F. Wormald (1945) 134 [repr. F. Wormald (1984) 60–1]; Hanssens (1948–50) I.129, 162–9, 198; N.R. Ker (1957) no. 84; T.A.M. Bishop (1954–8a) 193–7; N.R. Ker (1964) 82; E. Temple (1976) no. 21; Rella (1977) 85, 88; Drage (1978) 150–1, 157–8, 334–6; P.R. Robinson (1988) I, no. 334; Dumville (1991) 43; Dumville (1992a) 90, 116, 135; Keynes (1992) 16–17 [no. 6]; Dumville (1993e) 7–9; Vaciago (1993) 8 [no. 29]; Dumville (1994a) 137, 139, 141–2, 151; Lapidge (1994b) 139; R. Gameson (1996b) 149; Dodwell (2000) 152 n. 206; Lapidge (2000a) 13; C.A. Jones (2001) 17; Ambrose

(2005) 108; Hartzell (2006) no. 60 [antiphon]; Chardonnens (2007b) 545; Treharne (2007a) 256–7; Barker-Benfield (2008) I.lviii, II.1381, 1488, III.1811, 1812–13; R. Gameson (2012a) 39 and n. 97; D. Ganz (2012) 192–3 and n. 28; Scragg (2012a) no. 202

DEC: F. Wormald (1945) 122–4 [repr. F. Wormald (1984) 58–61]; Rice (1952) 178; E. Temple (1976) no. 21; Ohlgren (1986) no. 109; R. Gameson (1992a) 191; Keynes (1992) 16; R. Gameson (1995b) 3 n. 10, 217, 244 n. 60

FACS: F. Wormald (1984) ill. 61 [initial **H**]; Budny (1992) pl. 42 (a) [fol. 67r (detail)]; R. Gameson (1992a) pl. 42 (a) [fol. 67r]; Keynes (1992) pl. VI [fol. 53v]; R. Gameson (2000b) pl. 1 [fol. 44r]; Lapidge (2000a) 13 [fol. 53v (details)]; Lockett (2002) pl. II (a) [fol. 53v (details)]

ED: Hanssens (1948-50) II [*Liber officialis*, Retractatio I, coll. as T (CanT₁)]; C.A. Jones (2001) 200–10 [excerpts coll. as T², but text ptd from this MS on 201, 204–5]

ST: Chaplais (1966) no. XV; N.R. Ker (1976b) 30 [repr. N.R. Ker (1985) 150]; Rankin (1984) 112; *CSLMA* I (1994) 131–5; Dumville (1994b); P. Wormald (1999) 170 n. 34; C.A. Jones (2001) 27–32, 121–2, 175, 182, 278–9; Crick (2011) 7; R. McKitterick (2012) 328, 330 and n. 105

175. Cambridge, Trinity College, B. 14. 3 (289)

s. x/xi, Canterbury CC

Contents: Arator, *Historia apostolica* [*CPL* 1504] with scholia (by 'Anonymus X'); Dunstan, (part of) acrostic poem [SK 10972]

MS: M.R. James (1900–4) I.404–6; M.R. James (1903) 4, 9, 25; McKinlay (1942) 41–2 [no. 67]; N.R. Ker (1957) no. 85; T.A.M. Bishop (1959–63a) 94; T.A.M. Bishop (1959–63b) 414–15, 418, 421–2; N.R. Ker (1964) 33; T.A.M. Bishop (1971) 7; Lapidge (1975a) 96 n. 2 [repr. Lapidge (1993a) 134 n. 2]; Lapidge (1982a) 116, 138 n. 101 [repr. Lapidge (1996b) 484 and n. 101]; N.P. Brooks (1984) 267 [no. 4]; Keynes (1992) 27–8 [no. 16]; Vaciago (1993) 8–9 [no. 30]; Gwara (1996a) 92–3; Wieland (1998) 15 n. 11, 16 n. 23; *ASMMF* XII (2004) 10–14 [no. 78; Wright—Hollis]; Binski—Panayotova (2005) no. 12 [R. McKitterick]; Orbán (2006) I.24–5; Petruccione (2008) 234 n. 15; Scragg (2012a) no. 203

DEC: F. Wormald (1945) 135 [repr. F. Wormald (1984) 74]; E. Temple (1976) no. 34; Brownrigg (1978) 260 n. 3; Ohlgren (1986) no. 139; R. Gameson (1992a) 99 and n. 48

FACS: McKinlay (1942) pl. XXIV [fol. 5r]; Lapidge (1982a) 119 [fol. 5r] [repr. Lapidge (1996b) 488]; Ramsay et al. (1992) pls. 43 (b), 44 (a), 44 (b) [fols. 5r, 3r, 34v]; Keynes (1992) pl. XVI [fol. 5r]; *ASMMF* XII (2004) no. 78; Binski—Panayotova (2005) 64 [fols. 2v–3r]

ED: McKinlay (1951) [Arator coll. as C]; Lapidge (1982a) 118 [base MS for *Epistula ad Florianum* (lines 1–12), fol. 5r] [repr. Lapidge (1996b) 487]; Orbán (2006) [Arator coll. as C]

ST: Kristeller et al. (1960—) I.241-3 [scholia by 'Anonymus X']; Lapidge (1982a) 117–21, 138 n. 103 [repr. Lapidge (1996b) 485–93 with n. 103]; Wieland (1985) 158–9; Clayton (1990) 104–5

175. 1. Cambridge, Trinity College, B. 14. 3 (289), flyleaves 1–4

s. ix[1] or ix med., Nonantola, prov. England s. xi, (prov. prob. Canterbury CC)

Contents: Ambrose, *Expositio de Psalmo CXVIII* [*CPL* 141] (f)

MS: M.R. James (1900–4) I.405; Bischoff (1983a) 114–16; Bankert et al. (1997) 31–2; Keynes (1997a) 117 n. 75; Bischoff (1998—) I, no. 837; *ASMMF* XII (2004) 12 [no. 78; Wright—Hollis]; D. Ganz (2004) 500; Gneuss (2008b) 135; Rushforth (2011) 58; R. Gameson (2012d) 363–4 and n. 80

FACS: *ASMMF* XII (2004) no. 78

ST: R. McKitterick (2012) 329

175. 5. Cambridge, Trinity College, B. 14. 30 (315)

fols. 1–57: s. xi ex.; fols. 58–129: s. xi ex. (both parts prov. Exeter, prov. Leicester, Augustinian canons)

Contents [fols. 1–57]: nine sermons (four erroneously attrib. to Augustine); Odilo of Cluny, *Sermo* xiv; Paschasius Radbertus, *De assumptione B.V.M.* [cf. *CPL* 633]; lections on the Life of the Virgin; Fulbert of Chartres, *Sermo* iv

Contents [fols. 58–129]: Ambrose, *De uirginibus* [*CPL* 145], *De uiduis* [*CPL* 146], *De uirginitate* [*CPL* 147], *Exhortatio uirginitatis* [*CPL* 149]; Nicetas of Remesiana (?), *De lapsu uirginis consecratae* [*CPL* 651]

MS: M.R. James (1900–4) I.427–8; T.A.M. Bishop (1954–8a) 198–9; Römer (1972b) 97; R. Gameson (1996b) 154 and n. 79, 159; Bankert et al. (1997) 16; Gwara (1998) 145; Webber—Watson (1998) 151 [nine sermons itemized a–i]; R. Gameson (1999a) nos. 160–1; Webber (2006) 138

176. Cambridge, Trinity College, B. 15. 33 (368) (with fragment formerly Weinheim, Sammlung E. Fischer, s.n., lost)

s. x in., S England (Winchester?)

Contents: Isidore, *Etymologiae* [*CPL* 1186] V.xxxiii–IX.vii

MS: M.R. James (1900–4) I.498–500; Lindsay (1911) I.ix; Lindsay (1915) 213, 450; T.A.M. Bishop (1964–8b); T.A.M. Bishop (1964–8d) 396; T.A.M. Bishop (1971) 4; Parkes (1976b) 156–62 [repr. Parkes (1991) 150–9]; Rella (1977) 78 and nn. 71–2, 161; Parkes (1983) 131 and n. 8; Roper (1983) 127; Bately (1986) xxiv; Dumville (1987) 165–6, 169–73; Lapidge (1991c) 963–4 [repr. Lapidge (1993a) 13–14]; Dumville (1992b) 85–6, 95; Keynes (1992) no. 2; Conner (1993) 52, 61, 64, 70; Budny (1997) I.80–1, 153; Bischoff (1998 –) I, p. 184; Dumville (2005) 311; R. Gameson (2012a) 49, 59 n. 195

FACS: T.A.M. Bishop (1964–8b) pls. XVIII (a), XVIII (b), XIX (b) [fols. 3r, 9r, 110v (details)]; Parkes (1976b) pl. VI [fol. 54r] [repr. Parkes (1991) pl. 26 (fol. 54r)]; Dumville (1987) pl. VII [fol. 127r (detail)]; Dumville (1992b) pl. III [fol. 127r (detail)]

ED: Lindsay (1911) [Isidore, *Etymologiae* V.xxxiii–IX.vii coll. as *Trin.*]

ST: Ebersperger (1999) 80; P. Wormald (1999) 168 n. 16, 170 n. 34

NOTE: A fragment once in the collection of Ernst Fischer at Weinheim (near Heidelberg) and containing *Etym.* I. iii–ix, may have been part of this manuscript, but cannot now be traced. See Beeson (1915) 17; Lindsay (1916) 492; T.A.M. Bishop (1964–8b) 252; and Dumville (1987) 169 n. 115.

177. Cambridge, Trinity College, B. 15. 34 (369)

s. xi med., prob. Canterbury CC

Contents: Ælfric, Homilies*

MS: M.R. James (1900–4) I.500–2; N.R. Ker (1957) no. 86; Pope (1967) I.77–80; Collins–Clemoes (1974) 319; Strongman (1977–80) 16; Godden (1979) lxx–lxxi; N.P. Brooks (1984) 269 [no. 55]; Keynes (1992) 34–5 [no. 22]; Dumville (1993g) 139–40; Clemoes (1997) 45–6; Binski–Panayotova (2005) no. 13 [R. McKitterick]; Kleist (2007b) 462, 465; *ASMMF* XVI (2008) 17–26 [no. 80; Wilcox]; R. Gameson (2012b) 115 and n. 83; Rushforth (2012) 207 n. 64; Scragg (2012a) nos. 204–8

DEC: Rice (1952) 200; F. Wormald (1952) 63 [no. 15]; Dodwell (1954) 34, 246; E. Temple (1976) no. 74; Brownrigg (1978) 263; Backhouse et al. (1984b) no. 63; Ohlgren (1986) no. 179; Raw (1990) 199; Deshman (1995) 96, 119; R. Gameson (1991) 70 nn. 54–6; R. Gameson (1995b) 24, 87, 90, 193 n. 4; Heslop (2004) 292 n. 19

FACS: M.R. James (1900–4) IV, pl. XI [fol. 1r]; Rice (1952) pl. 61 (b) [fol. 1r]; Dodwell (1954) pl. 24 (b) [fol. 1r]; Pope (1967) II.358 [fol. 1r]; E. Temple (1976) ill. 241 [fol. 1r]; Keynes (1992) pl. XXII (b) [p. 356]; Deshman (1995) fig. 90 [fol. 1r]; Binski—Panayotova (2005) 66 [fols. 232v–233r]; *ASMMF* XVI (2008) no. 80

ED [the order of the following items is that of the manuscript, listed according to the numbering of individual articles in N.R. Ker (1957) 130-2; only the most recent editions are cited]:

art. 1: Clemoes (1997) 299–306 [Ælfric, CH I, Hom. XV (Easter Sunday), coll. as U]

arts. 2–3: Godden (1979) 161–8 [Ælfric, CH II, Hom. XVI (Another Sermon for Easter Sunday), coll. as U]

art. 4: Clemoes (1997) 307–12 [Ælfric, CH I, Hom. XVI (First Sunday after Easter), coll. as U]

art. 5: Clemoes (1997) 313–16 [Ælfric, CH I, Hom. XVII (Second Sunday after Easter), coll. as U]

art. 6: Assmann (1889/1964) 73–80 [base MS for Ælfric, Hom. for the Third Sunday after Easter (= Hom. VI)]

art. 7: Pope (1967–8) I.340–50 [Ælfric, Suppl. Hom. VII (Fourth Sunday after Easter), coll. as U]

art. 8: Pope (1967–8) I.357–68 [Ælfric, Suppl. Hom. VIII (Fifth Sunday after Easter), coll. as U]

art. 9: Clemoes (1997) 317–24 [Ælfric, CH I, Hom. XVIII (*In Letania maiore*), coll. as U]

art. 10: Clemoes (1997) 325–34 [Ælfric, CH I, Hom. XIX (*Feria .III. De dominica oratione*), coll. as U]

art. 11: Clemoes (1997) 335–44 [Ælfric, CH I, Hom. XX (*Feria .IIII. De fide catholica*), coll. as U]

art. 12: Clemoes (1997) 345–53 [Ælfric, CH I, Hom. XXI (Ascension Day), coll. as U]

art. 13: Pope (1967–8) I.378–89 [Ælfric, Suppl. Hom. IX (Sunday after Ascension Day), coll. as U]

art. 14: Clemoes (1997) 354–64 [Ælfric, CH I, Hom. XXII (Pentecost), coll. as U] art. 15: Pope (1967–8) I.396–405 [Ælfric, Suppl. Hom. X (Pentecost), coll. as U]

art. 16: Napier (1883/1967) 50–60 [Hom. VII–VIII (*De septiformi spiritu*) coll. as T; not collated by Bethurum (1957) 184–91 (Hom. IX = Napier Hom. VII)]

art. 17: Pope (1967–8) I.415–47 [Ælfric, Suppl. Hom. XI (Octave of Pentecost), coll. as U]

art. 18: Pope (1967–8) I.479–89 [Ælfric, Suppl. Hom. XII (First Sunday after Pentecost), coll. as U]

art. 19: Clemoes (1997) 365–70 [Ælfric, CH I, Hom. XXIII (Second Sunday after Pentecost), coll. as U]

art. 20: Godden (1979) 213–17 [Ælfric, CH II, Hom. XXIII (Third Sunday after Pentecost), lines 1–125, coll. as U]

art. 21: Clemoes (1997) 371–8 [Ælfric, CH I, Hom. XXIV (Fourth Sunday after Pentecost), coll. as U]

art. 22: Pope (1967–8) II.497–507 [base MS (= U) for Ælfric, Suppl. Hom. XIII (Fifth Sunday after Pentecost)]

art. 23: Pope (1967–8) II.515–25 [base MS (= U) for Ælfric, Suppl. Hom. XIV (Sixth Sunday after Pentecost)]

art. 24: Pope (1967–8) II.531–41 [base MS (= U) for Ælfric, Suppl. Hom. XV (Seventh Sunday after Pentecost)]

art. 25: Godden (1979) 230–4 [Ælfric, CH II, Hom. XXV (Eighth Sunday after Pentecost), coll. as U]

art. 26: Godden (1979) 235–40 [Ælfric, CH II, Hom. XXVI (Ninth Sunday after Pentecost), coll. as U]

art. 27: Pope (1967–8) II.547–59 [base MS (= U) for Ælfric, Suppl. Hom. XVI (Tenth Sunday after Pentecost)]

art. 28: Clemoes (1997) 410–17 [Ælfric, CH I, Hom. XXVIII (Twelfth Sunday after Pentecost), coll. as U, lacking lines 221–6]

ST: Gatch (1977) 55; Clemoes (1980) 230–3; Acker (2004) 134; Wilcox (2006b)

178. Cambridge, Trinity College, B. 16. 3 (379)

s. $x^{2/4}$ or x med., S or W England

Contents: cryptogram (fol. *1r); Hrabanus Maurus, *De laudibus S. Crucis*

MS: M.R. James (1900–4) I.516–17; Rella (1977) 80, 161; Gneuss (1978) 142–4; Dumville (1987) 175–6; Dumville (1992a) 144; R. Gameson (1992c) 157 and n. 196; Keynes (1992) 11–14 [no. 4]; P. Wormald

(1999) 169; Binski—Panayotova (2005) no. 6 [R. McKitterick]; W. Schipper (2007a); W. Schipper (2009) 286 and n. 13; Wieland (2009) 151; R. Gameson (2012a) 77 n. 273; D. Ganz (2012) 192 and n. 25

DEC: F. Wormald (1971b) 309 [repr. F. Wormald (1984) 80]; Deshman (1974) 183, 190, 197, 199; E. Temple (1976) no. 14; Deshman (1977); F. Wormald (1984b); Ohlgren (1986) no. 92; R. Gameson (1995b) 11–12, 20, 89 n. 104, 147, 152–3, 180, 185; R. Gameson (2012c) 250 and nn. 7–8

FACS: F. Wormald (1984) ill. 91 [fol. 1v]; E. Temple (1976) ills. 45–6, 48 [fols. 3r, 30v, 1v]; Keynes (1992) pls. IV (a)–(b) [fols. 30v, 34r]; Binski—Panayotova (2005) 55 [fol. 6v]; Panayotova (2007) pl. III [fol. 3v]; W. Schipper (2007a) figs. 1 (c) [fol. 26r (detail)], 2 (a) [fol. 25v (detail)], 3 (a) [fol. 1v], 3 (b) [fol. 28r (detail)], 4 (a) [fol. 5v], 4 (b) [fol. 4r (detail)]; W. Schipper (2009) figs. 7–10 [fols. 4v, 27v, 3v, 24v–25r]

ED: Keynes (1992) 13 [cryptogram]

ST: Brownrigg (1977) 257; Gneuss (1978) 142–4; Bischoff (1998–) I, no. 37 [on Amiens B.M. 223, from Fulda (not Corbie), related to Anglo-Saxon copies]; W. Schipper (2007a); W. Schipper (2009); R. McKitterick (2012) 328, 330 and n. 112

179. Cambridge, Trinity College, B. 16. 44 (405)

s. xi² (1059×1079), Normandy (Bec?), prov. Canterbury CC; s. xi ex. – xii in., Canterbury CC

Contents: *Collectio Lanfranci* [*Concilia, Decreta pontificum*]: s. xi²; papal letters to Lanfranc and *Conuersio Berengarii* [from Gregory VII, *Registrum* VI.17a]: s. xi ex. – xii in.

MS: M.R. James (1900–4) I.540–1; Z.N. Brooke (1931) 231–5; T.A.M. Bishop (1949–53) 436; T.A.M. Bishop (1959–63b) 414; Dodwell (1954) 7; N.R. Ker (1960) 25, 28 n. 7, 42 n. 5; Southern (1963) 19 n. 3; C.N.L. Brooke (1967) 56–8; S. Williams (1971) 78–9; N.R. Ker (1976b) 30 n. 5 [repr. N.R. Ker (1985) 150 n. 5]; Gibson (1978) 179–81, 205; N.R. Ker (1985) 75–6, 84–5; P.R. Robinson (1988) I, no. 342; M. Brett (1992) 161 n. 11; Webber (1995) 148 and nn. 15, 18; Saenger (1997) 212 and n. 71; Gullick (1998c) 175 and nn. 7, 8; R. Gameson (1999a) no. 162; Kéry (1999) 116, 240; Gullick (2001) 100–2 and n. 5; Cowdrey (2003) 138–43; Gullick (2008); Webber (2012) 213 and n. 4

DEC: Lawrence (1982) 107; R. Gameson (1995a) 109 n. 47

FACS: Dodwell (1954) pls. 4 (c)–(d) [pp. 396, 405 (details)]; N.R. Ker

(1960) pls. 4–5 [pp. 404–5]; P.R. Robinson (1988) II, pl. 29 [p. 211]; Gullick (2008) pls. 5.1–4 [details of pp. 2, 147, 181 and enlargement], 5.7 [slip between pp. 82 and 83]

ED: Liebermann (1901) [papal letters]

ST: Z.N. Brooke (1931); S. Williams (1971); Kéry (1999) 239–43 [discussion and bibliography for *Collectio Lanfranci*]

179. 4. Cambridge, Trinity College, R. 3. 33 (613), flyleaves

s. xi ex.

Contents: Jerome, *Epistulae* [*CPL* 620] (f)

MS: M.R. James (1900–4) II.110; Gneuss (2003b) 296–7

179. 5. Cambridge, Trinity College, R. 3. 57 (629)

s. xi/xii, Canterbury CC?

Contents: Horace, *Carmina* (with argumenta and scholia), *Epodon liber*, *Carmen saeculare*, *Ars poetica*, *Sermones*

MS: M.R. James (1900–4) II.125–6; N.R. Ker (1964) 39; Gneuss (2003b) 297

180. Cambridge, Trinity College, R. 5. 22 (717), fols. 72–158

s. x/xi, prov. Sherborne?, (prov. prob. Salisbury)

Contents: Gregory (Alfred), *Regula pastoralis**; Iuvenalis, *Sat.* III. 48–9; excerpt from a pseudo-Augustinian sermon on the Immaculate Conception (*Expositio de secreto gloriosae incarnationis Domini nostri Iesu Christi*) [*CPPM* II, no. 195]

MS: M.R. James (1900–4) II.191–2; K. Sisam (1953a) 145; N.R. Ker (1957) no. 87; N.R. Ker (1964) 171; Carlson (1975–8) I.14; Robinson—Stanley (1991) 21; Keynes (1992) 29 [no. 17]; Gneuss (2003b) 297; Schreiber (2003) 57–60; *ASMMF* XII (2004) 15–24 [no. 81; Wright—Hollis]; Scragg (2012a) nos. 217–20

FACS: Robinson—Stanley (1991) pl. 6.1.3 [fol. 72r]; Keynes (1992) pl. XVII [fol. 72r]; *ASMMF* XII (2004) no. 81

ED: Carlson (1975, 1978) [*Pastoral Care* coll. as R5]; Schreiber (2003) 191–453 [*Pastoral Care*, Prefaces and chs. i–iv, xix–xxvi, xxxvi–xxxvii, xlvii–lvi, lxv, and Epilogue, all coll. as T], 455 [excerpt from the pseudo-Augustinian sermon]

LANG: Ångstrom (1937) 39; Carlson (1975) 14; Horgan (1973) 163; Horgan (1981) 213–21

ST: Magoun (1949) 119; Römer (1972b) 97–8 [pseudo-Augustinian sermon]; Horgan (1973) 166; Horgan (1986) 120–2; *CPPM* I, no. 1237 [pseudo-Augustinian sermon]; O'Brien O'Keeffe (1990) 88–94; *CPPM* II, no. 195 [pseudo-Augustinian sermon]; R. Gameson (1998) 242 n. 45; Schreiber (2003) 59

181. Cambridge, Trinity College, R. 7. 5 (743)

s. xi in. – xi², (prov. prob. N England)

Contents: Bede, *Historia ecclesiastica* [*CPL* 1375] (with addenda and alterations, s. xii)

MS: Mayor—Lumby (1881) 414; M.R. James (1900–4) II.219–22; Colgrave—Mynors (1969) xlvii–xlviii; Rella (1977) 69 ['probably a direct copy of MS Tiberius C. ii']; Robinson—Stanley (1991) 20; Keynes (1992) 30 [no. 18]; R. Gameson (1999a) no. 176

FACS: Keynes (1992) pl. XVIII [fol. 57v]

ED: Mayor—Lumby (1881) [Bede, *Historia ecclesiastica*, bks. III–IV coll. as C³]

ST: O'Brien O'Keeffe (1990) 30–1 and n. 25, 35, 42; O'Brien O'Keeffe (1994) 231–2, 237, 246

182. Cambridge, Trinity College, R. 9. 17 (819), fols. 1–48

s. xi/xii

Contents: Ælfric, *Grammar*⁺* (abbrev.); grammatical note⁺*; *Disticha Catonis**; apophthegms*

MS: Zupitza (1880/2001) viii; M.R. James (1900–4) II.256–8; Westlake (1907) 119; N.R. Ker (1957) no. 89; Karl Brunner (1965) 41–4; R.S. Cox (1972) 4–6, 29–31; Strongman (1977–80) 16; Lapidge (1982a) 103, 130 n. 28 [repr. Lapidge (1996b) 461 and n. 28]; Keynes (1992) 36 [no. 24]; R.I. Page (1993a) 10; R. Gameson (1999a) no. 178; Treharne (2000a) 1; Treharne (2000b) 19, 37; Menzer (2004) 95, 102–4; *ASMMF* XVI (2008) 35–41 [no. 82; Lucas]; Scragg (2012a) no. 221

FACS: Keynes (1992) pl. XXIV [fol. 45r]; *ASMMF* XVI (2008) no. 82

ED: Zupitza (1880/2001) [Ælfric, *Grammar*, coll. as T]; I.A. Brunner (1965) [OE *Disticha Catonis* coll. as T]; R.S. Cox (1965) [base MS for

OE *Disticha Catonis*]; R.S. Cox (1972) [base MS (= T) for OE *Disticha Catonis*, and base MS (= SA) for OE apophthegms]

ST: T. Hunt (1991) I.26; Hollis—Wright (1992) 15–33; Menzer (2004) 104, 119

184. Cambridge, Trinity College, R. 14. 50 (920)

s. xi med.

Contents: Galen, *Liber tertius*

MS: M.R. James (1900–4) II.336; Beccaria (1956) 407; Thorndike—Kibre (1963) col. 200; Keynes (1992) 35–6 [no. 23]; R. Gameson (1999a) no. 181; Banham (2011) 343

FACS: Keynes (1992) pl. XXIII [fol. 35r]

ST: M.L. Cameron (1983) 143; M.L. Cameron (1984) 163

185. Cambridge, Trinity College, R. 15. 14 (939), pt. i

s. x¹, France, Loire region? (prov. Canterbury StA) [cf. no. **185. 1**]

Contents: pseudo-Boethius, *De geometria* [*CPL* 895] bk. I; texts and excerpts on geometry and metrology (including excerpts from: Isidore, *Etymologiae* [*CPL* 1186], Hyginus Gromaticus, *De limitibus*, Frontinus ('De agrorum qualitate'), pseudo-Censorinus, *De geometria*, Cassiodorus, *Institutiones* [*CPL* 906] bk. II, *Excerpta Euclidis*); Epaphroditus and Vitruvius Rufus, *Excerpta geometrica*; Balbus, *Ad Celsum expositio et ratio omnium mensurarum*; Remigius Favius (?), *Carmen de ponderibus et mensuris* [SK 12104] (incomplete); *Libellus de mensuris, de ponderi- bus, de mensuris in liquidis*

MS: Schenkl no. 2360; M.R. James (1900–4) II.349–53; Thulin (1911) 13–14; N.R. Ker (1964) 41; Folkerts (1970) 39, 95, 175; Fenlon (1982) 10–11 [Rankin]; Raios (1983) 84–5; Reeve (1983a) 5; Keynes (1992) 23–4 [no. 12]; Toneatto (1994) 278–88; Barker-Benfield (2008) III.1879, 1880, 1881

FACS: Keynes (1992) pl. XII [fols. 91v–92r]

ED: Folkerts (1970) 173–217 [*Excerpta Euclidis* coll. as T]

ST: Folkerts (1982); Folkerts (1989) 21; Biggs et al. (1990) 79–80 [Wittig]

185. 1. Cambridge, Trinity College, R. 15. 14 (939), pt. ii

s. xi¹, Saint-Vaast, Arras, (prov. England by s. xiii), both **185** and **185. 1** in England before 1100?

Contents: tonary

MS: M.R. James (1900–4) II.353–4; Huglo (1971) 321–2; Fenlon (1982) 10–13 [Rankin]; Escudier (1987); Keynes (1992) 23

FACS: Fenlon (1982) pl. II [fols. 6v–7r]

ST: N. Orchard (2005) xli

186. Cambridge, Trinity College, R. 15. 32 (945)

s. xi in. [pp. i–ii, 1–12, 37–218]; s. xi^1 (1035/6) [pp. 13–36]; whole MS Winchester NM, prov. by s. xi ex. Canterbury StA

Contents [pp. i–ii, 1–12, 37–218]: *Inuolutio sphaerae* (excerpt from Aratus, *Phainomena*, in Latin translation); Abbo of Fleury, *De differentia circuli et sphaerae* and *De duplici signorum ortu uel occasu*; *Dies Aegyptiaci*; Hyginus, *Astronomica*; Martianus Capella, *De nuptiis Philologiae et Mercurii*, bk. VIII (part with gloss); Helperic, *De computo*; Abbo of Fleury, *De figuratione signorum* (based on Hyginus); prayers; tract on the stars; Cicero, *Aratea* (incomplete)

Contents [pp. 13–36]: liturgical calendar; *computistica* ['Winchester Computus']

MS: M.R. James (1900–4) II.363–6, 428; Van de Vyver (1935) 140–1, 150; T.A.M. Bishop (1954–8a) 189–92; N.R. Ker (1957) no. 90; Leonardi (1959) 467 [no. 128]; N.R. Ker (1964) 41, 103; T.A.M. Bishop (1971) xviii n. 4, 23; Munk Olsen (1982–) I.331, 526–7; Gneuss (1985) 140 [no. X.16]; P.R. Robinson (1988) I, no. 357; Keynes (1992) 30–2 [no. 19]; Viré (1992) xvi; Dumville (1993g) 136; Baker–Lapidge (1995) xliv, xlix–lii; Liuzza (2001) 215; *ASMMF* XII (2004) 31–9 [no. 84; Wright–Hollis]; Chardonnens (2007b) 507–8, 550; Barker-Benfield (2008) II.1188, III.1836, 1917; Wieland (2009) 150, 152, 154; Scragg (2012a) nos. 222-3

DEC: F. Wormald (1952) 64 [no. 19]

FACS: P.R. Robinson (1988) II, pl. 18 [p. 15]; Keynes (1992) pl. XIX [p. 21]; *ASMMF* XII (2004) no. 84

ED: F. Wormald (1934) 127–39 [liturgical calendar (no. 10)]; R.B. Thomson (1985) [base MS (= B) for Abbo, *De differentia circuli et sphaerae* and *De duplici signorum ortu*]; Rushforth (2008a) no. 15 [liturgical calendar]

ST: Sanford (1924) 216; Henel (1934); Van de Vyver (1935) 140–50; C.W. Jones (1939) 115; C.E. Lutz (1971) 381; McGurk (1974) 1; Stroud (1979) 230; Kotzor (1981) I.302*–311*; McGurk (1983) 67–70, 108;

Lapidge (1988b) 259 n. 30 [repr. Lapidge (1993a) 217 n. 30]; Ridyard (1988) 117–18; Keynes (1996a) 68–9; Pulsiano (1998b) 99; Biggs et al. (2001) 8–10 [Lendinara]; Borst (2001) I.92–3; Chardonnens (2007a) 320 n. 8; *CSLMA* III (2010) 421–9 [Helperic]

188. Cambridge, Trinity College, O. 1. 18 (1042)

s. x/xi (or x^2?), Canterbury StA, or Glastonbury?

Contents: *Voces animantium*; four Latin poems (SK 16461, 3448, 1872 [lines 4–8], 2652); Augustine, *Enchiridion* [*CPL* 295], glossed; Dunstan, acrostic poem [SK 10972]

MS: M.R. James (1900–4) III.19–22; M.R. James (1903) 506; T.A.M. Bishop (1954–8b) 323–4, 329–30, 334; N.R. Ker (1957) no. 92; T.A.M. Bishop (1959–63b) 412–13; N.R. Ker (1964) 39, 91; Römer (1972b) 98; F.C. Robinson (1973) 455; Lapidge (1975a) 96 n. 2 [repr. Lapidge (1993a) 134 n. 2]; Rella (1977) 158 n. 6; Lendinara (1990) 134 n. 8; Keynes (1992) 20–1 [no. 10]; Vaciago (1993) 9 [no. 32]; *ASMMF* XII (2004) 40–4 [no. 86; Wright—Hollis]; T.N. Hall (2004b) 97 n. 18; Hartzell (2006) no. 63; Barker-Benfield (2008) I.527, III.1813, 1818; Scragg (2012a) nos. 209–11

DEC: E. Temple (1976) no. 30(i); Ohlgren (1986) no. 118

FACS: Keynes (1992) pls. X (a)–(b) [fols. 12r, 112v]; *ASMMF* XII (2004) no. 86

ED: Napier (1900) no. 27 [OE glosses]; Lapidge (1975a) 108–11 [repr. Lapidge (1993a) 146–9] [base MS for acrostic poem by Dunstan]; Lendinara (2005) 117–18 [*uoces animantium*]; Winterbottom—Lapidge (2012) 166–72 [base MS for acrostic poem by Dunstan]

ST: Clayton (1990) 104–5

188. 8. Cambridge, Trinity College, O. 2. 30 (1134), fols. 1–72

s. xi/xii, (prov. Southwark, Augustinian priory of St Mary Overy)

Contents: pseudo-Augustine, *De unitate S. Trinitatis* [*CPL* 378]; excerpts (in dialogue form) from Isidore, *De differentiis uerborum* [*CPL* 1187], *Etymologiae* [*CPL* 1186], Gregory, *Moralia in Iob* [*CPL* 1708], and Augustine, *Enarrationes in Psalmos* [*CPL* 283]; Isidore, *De fide catholica contra Iudaeos* [*CPL* 1198]

MS: M.R. James (1900–4) III.126–7; Römer (1972b) 98; R. Gameson (1999a) no. 164; *ASMMF* XII (2004) 59–62 [no. 88; Wright—Hollis]

FACS: *ASMMF* XII (2004) no. 88

189. Cambridge, Trinity College, O. 2. 30 (1134), fols. 129–72

s. x med., Canterbury StA

Contents: list of sins; introductory poem to Benedictine Rule (doubtfully attrib. to Simplicius, abbot of Montecassino) [SK 13285]; *Regula S. Benedicti* [*CPL* 1852], with gloss; four sermons (s. x/xi)

MS: M.R. James (1900–4) III.127–9; T.A.M. Bishop (1954–8b) 324–6; N.R. Ker (1957) no. 94; T.A.M. Bishop (1959–63a) 93; N.R. Ker (1964) 180; Gretsch (1973) 22–4; Hanslik (1977) xviii–xix; Rella (1977) 56; R.I. Page (1981) 106–7; Keynes (1992) 17–18 [no. 7]; Dumville (1993g) 98 n. 78; Vaciago (1993) 9 [no. 33]; Dodwell (2000) 152 n. 206; T.N. Hall (2006) 133–5, 142–7; Treharne (2007a) 256–7; Barker-Benfield (2008) II.1381, III.1705, 1813; Graham (2009) 179; Wieland (2009) 125; D. Ganz (2012) 193 and n. 29; Scragg (2012a) nos. 212–13

DEC: F. Wormald (1952) 63 [no. 16]

FACS: Keynes (1992) pl. VII [fol. 130r]; Lockett (2002) pl. II (d) [fol. 130r]

ED: Napier (1900) no. 58 [OE glosses]; Rusche (2002) [list of sins]; T.N. Hall (2006) 137–9, 156–70 [Latin sermon on fols. 168v–172v]

ST: Traube (1910) 85; Brechter (1938); Meyvaert (1963); Gretsch (1973) *passim*; Gretsch (1974) 126–37; Brunhölzl (1975) 514; *CPPM* II, no. 3606a [introductory poem to Benedictine Rule]; Graham (1998a) 33, 41, 63 n. 83; Rusche (2002) 172–83 [list of sins]; T.N. Hall (2006) 139–41, 146–51

190. Cambridge, Trinity College, O. 2. 31 (1135)

s. x/xi, Canterbury CC

Contents: Prosper, *Epigrammata ex sententiis S. Augustini* [*CPL* 526] and *Versus ad coniugem* [*CPL* 531; SK 458] with gloss; *Disticha Catonis*, with gloss; Bede, *Versus de die iudicii* [*CPL* 1370]; Prudentius, *Dittochaeon* [*CPL* 1444] (all except Prosper incomplete); responsory from Office for St Æthelthryth (f; s. xi²)

MS: M.R. James (1900–4) III.129–31; Sanford (1924) 212 [no. 82]; N.R. Ker (1957) no. 95; T.A.M. Bishop (1959–63b) 413–14, 419–21; N.R. Ker (1964) 39; Rella (1977) 96 n. 9; Lapidge (1982a) 105–7 [repr. Lapidge (1996b) 466–8]; N.P. Brooks (1984) 267 [no. 5]; A.G. Watson (1987a) 10; Keynes (1992) 26–7 [no. 15]; Vaciago (1993) 9–10 [no. 34]; *ASMMF* XII (2004) 66–71 [no. 89; Wright—Hollis]; Menzer (2004) 97 n. 4; Hartzell (2006) no. 64; Lendinara (2007b) 206; Wieland (2009) 151; R. Gameson (2012b) 108 and n. 53; Scragg (2012a) nos. 214–15

DEC: Rice (1952) 197; E. Temple (1976) no. 30(vi); Ohlgren (1986) no. 123; R. Gameson (1995b) 223–4

FACS: Keynes (1992) pl. XV [fol. 34r]; *ASMMF* XII (2004) no. 89

ED: Meritt (1945) nos. 13, 24 [OE glosses]; Lapidge (1982a) 103–4 [base MS for *Disticha Catonis* I.i.1–3], 106 [base MS for Prosper, *Epigr.* praef.] [repr. Lapidge (1996b) 463–4, 467]

ST: Boas (1952) lx; R.S. Cox (1972) 3; R.I. Page (1981) 107–9; Toth (1984); Wieland (1985) 163–4; Biggs et al. (1990) 156 [Wieland]; T. Hunt (1991) I.19–20 [French and Latin glosses]; Lendinara (2007b) 177, 181, 183

191. Cambridge, Trinity College, O. 2. 51 (1155), pt. i

s. x^2

Contents: Prudentius, *Psychomachia* [*CPL* 1441]

MS: M.R. James (1900–4) III.166–7; N.R. Ker (1964) 33, 41; Biggs et al. (1990) 153 [Wieland]; Keynes (1992) 18–19 [no. 8]; Wieland (1997a) 170; Karkov (2001a) 115 n. 3, 116 n. 7; Barker-Benfield (2008) I.92 n. 67, III.1809, 1824–5

FACS: Keynes (1992) pl. VIII [fol. 1r]

ST: Wieland (1987) 216; Wieland (1998)

192. Cambridge, Trinity College, O. 2. 51 (1155), pt. ii

s. xi/xii, Canterbury (CC?), (prov. Canterbury CC?)

Contents: Priscian, *Institutiones grammaticae* [*CPL* 1546], bks. I–XVIII; Priscian (?), *De accentibus* [*CPL* 1552] (incomplete)

MS: M.R. James (1900–4) III.167–8; N.R. Ker (1960) 30; N.R. Ker (1964) 41; Gibson (1972) 108; Passalacqua (1978) no. 84; Yerkes (1983a) 130; Keynes (1992) 18–19 [no. 8]; R. Gameson (1999a) no. 165; Barker-Benfield (2008) I.92 n. 67, II.1279, 1335, III.1809, 1820; R. Gameson (2008) 70–1

DEC: Dodwell (1954) 17, 19, 26, 122; C.M. Kauffmann (1975) no. 8; Ohlgren (1986) no. 219; R. Gameson (1991) 65–75

FACS: Dodwell (1954) pls. 11 (c), 15 (b), 15 (d) [fols. 91r, 81v, 34r (details)]; C.M. Kauffmann (1975) ills. 13–16 [fols. 46r, 58r, 91r, 100r (details)]; Lawrence (1982) pl. XXXIII (A) [folio not specified]; R. Gameson (1991) fig. 2 [fol. 105r]

ST: Bursill-Hall (1981) 54 [no. 53.7]; Bodden (1988) 231

193. Cambridge, Trinity College, O. 3. 7 (1179)

s. x² or x ex., Canterbury StA?, (prov. ibid.)

Contents: Boethius, *De consolatione Philosophiae* [*CPL* 878], with commentary by Remigius (redaction T); Lupus of Ferrières, *De metris Boethii*; *Epitaphium Helpis* (wife of Boethius) [SK 6193]

MS: M.R. James (1900–4) III.188–9; M.R. James (1903) 302 [no. 993]; Weinberger (1934) xvi; N.R. Ker (1957) no. 95* [pp. lxiii and 38]; N.R. Ker (1964) 42; Bolton (1977a) 40, 51; Rella (1977) 77, 162; Backhouse et al. (1984b) no. 33 [D.H. Turner]; Keynes (1992) 22 [no. 11]; Vaciago (1993) 10 [no. 35]; Gibson et al. (1995–2001) I.81–2 [no. 51]; Lapidge (1998) 32, 33, 42 n. 46; Wieland (1998) 15 n. 14, 17 n. 23; R.I. Page (2001) 239–40; *ASMMF* XII (2004) 72–7 [no. 90; Wright—Hollis]; Hartzell (2006) no. 66; Barker-Benfield (2008) I.69 n. c; Wittig (2010) 250; R. Gameson (2012a) 29 and n. 62; Rankin (2012) 505 n. 111; Scragg (2012a) no. 216

DEC: F. Wormald (1945) 134 [repr. Wormald (1984) 73]; Rice (1952) 196; F. Wormald (1952) 63–4 [no. 17]; E. Temple (1976) no. 20; Brownrigg (1978) 247 n. 6; Ohlgren (1986) no. 108; R. Gameson (1992c) 145 n. 136; R. Gameson (1995b) 23, 193 n. 3; R. Gameson (2012c) 252 n. 11

FACS: F. Wormald (1952) pl. 3 [fol. 1r]; G. Henderson (1987) 119 [fol. 129v]; R. Gameson (1992a) pl. III [fol. 1r]; Keynes (1992) pl. XI [fol. 31r]; *ASMMF* XII (2004) no. 90

ED: Stewart (1917) [Remigius commentary partially coll. as C]; Meritt (1945) no. 12 [OE glosses]; Bolton (1977a) [mythological glosses to Boethius coll. as T]

ST: Courcelle (1939); Courcelle (1967) 405; Bolton (1977a) 51, 60; Wittig (1983); O'Brien O'Keeffe (1985a) 3; Troncarelli (1987) 210–11 [no. 70]; Bodden (1988) 227 n. 40; Biggs et al. (1990) 77 [Wittig]; Rosenthal (1992) 159; Wittig (2007) 188; Godden (2011) 92; Jayatilaka (2011) 112, 117; R. McKitterick (2012) 328

194. Cambridge, Trinity College, O. 3. 35 (1207)

s. xi/xii, (prov. Chichester Cathedral)

Contents: Ambrose, *Exameron* [*CPL* 123]

MS: M.R. James (1900–4) III.217–18; N.R. Ker (1964) 50; Bankert et al. (1997) 18; R. Gameson (1999a) no. 166; Lapidge (2006) 280

195. Cambridge, Trinity College, O. 4. 10 (1241)

s. x²ᐟ⁴, Canterbury StA, (prov. ibid.)

Contents: Iuvenalis, *Satirae*, with gloss; 'Cornutus', Commentary on Persius; Persius, *Satirae* (partly glossed); Martial, Epigram I.xix

MS: M.R. James (1900–4) III.258–9; M.R. James (1903) 365 [no. 1439]; Sanford (1924) 212; T.A.M. Bishop (1954–8b) 324–6; T.A.M. Bishop (1959–63a) 93–5; N.R. Ker (1964) 42; Bodden (1979) 259; Munk Olsen (1982–) I.563–4; L.D. Reynolds (1983) 202, 295; Keynes (1992) 14–16 [no. 5]; Dumville (1994a) 139; Dodwell (2000) 152 n. 206; Barker-Benfield (2008) II.1188, 1391, III.1812, 1813; Wieland (2009) 148; R. Gameson (2012a) 29 and n. 62

FACS: Keynes (1992) pls. V (a)–(b) [fols. 94v, 110v]; Lockett (2002) pl. II (b) [fol. 53v]

ED: Clausen (1959) [Iuvenalis, *Satirae*, coll. as T (Persius not collated)]

ST: Kristeller et al. (1960–) III.212–15 ['Cornutus' commentary]; Pulsiano (2001b)

196. Cambridge, Trinity College, O. 4. 11 (1242)

s. x², N France or Flanders, in England before 1100?, (prov. Canterbury StA)

Contents: Hucbald of Saint-Amand, *Ecloga de caluis* [SK 1949]; Iuvenalis, *Satirae*, with gloss; four Latin poems [including SK 638, 2425, 1701]; hymn [SK 14230; s. xi]

MS: M.R. James (1900–4) III.260–1; M.R. James (1903) 365 [no. 1440]; Sanford (1924) 212; N.R. Ker (1964) 42; Munk Olsen (1982–) I.564; Keynes (1992) 24–5 [no. 13]; Barker-Benfield (2008) I.91 n. a, II.890, III.1712–13; R. Gameson (2012a) 29 and n. 62

FACS: James (1900–4) IV, pl. VIII (1); Keynes (1992) pl. XIII [fol. 3r]

196. 5. Cambridge, Trinity College, O. 4. 34 (1264)

s. xi/xii, Canterbury CC

Contents: Orosius, *Historiae aduersum paganos* [*CPL* 571]; Iulius Honorius, *Cosmographia* (f; remainder in O. 4. 36, destroyed)

MS: M.R. James (1900–4) III.282–3; M.R. James (1903) 508; T.A.M. Bishop (1949–53) 432; Bately—Ross (1961) no. 24; N.R. Ker (1964) 34 and nn. 8–9; Webber (1995) 153, 158; R. Gameson (1999a) no. 168; Mortensen (2000) 123 [no. 27]

DEC: R. Gameson (1995a) 117 n. 74, 120–1 and n. 87, 142

ST: Bately (1980) lviii

NOTE: Trinity College MSS. O. 4. 34 and O. 4. 36 originally formed one volume. The second of these, O. 4. 36, which contained the remainder of Iulius Honorius, Iordanes, *De origine actibusque Getarum* [*CPL* 913] and the *Itinerarium Antonini Augusti,* was destroyed on 12 July 1880 in a fire at the home of Theodor Mommsen at Charlottenburg.

198. 5. Cambridge, Trinity College, O. 10. 23 (1475)

s. xi ex., (prov. Exeter)

Contents: Gregory of Tours, *Miraculorum libri* [*CPL* 1024], bks. I–VII

MS: M.R. James (1900–4) III.515–16; Gwara (1998) 145; R. Gameson (1999a) no. 171

FACS: R. Gameson (1999a) pl. 5 [fol. 1r]

ST: R. Gameson (1996b) 154 n. 80, 159–60

199. Cambridge, Trinity College, O. 10. 28 (1480)

s. xi/xii, Canterbury CC

Contents: Paulus Diaconus, *Historia Romana* (incorporating Eutropius, *Breuiarium historiae Romanae*) [*CPL* 1181]

MS: Schenkl no. 2465; M.R. James (1900–4) III.517–18; T.A.M. Bishop (1949–53) 432; N.R. Ker (1964) 34 n. 9; Webber (1995) 153, 158; R. Gameson (1999a) no. 172; Mortensen (2000) 169 [no. 24]

DEC: Lawrence (1982) 108; R. Gameson (1995a) 117 n. 74, 120–1 and n. 87, 142

ST: Bodden (1988) 218

200. Cambridge, Trinity College, O. 10. 31 (1483)

s. xi/xii, Canterbury CC

Contents: *Inuentio S. Crucis* [*BHL* 4169]; Victor of Vita, *Historia persecutionis Africanae prouinciae* [*CPL* 798]

MS: M.R. James (1900–4) III.519–20; T.A.M. Bishop (1949–53) 432; N.R. Ker (1964) 34 n. 9; Webber (1995) 153–4, 158; R. Gameson (1999a) no. 173

DEC: R. Gameson (1995a) 117 n. 74, 120–1 and n. 87, 142

ST: Biggs et al. (2001) 264–5 [Biggs, Whatley], 401–2

200. 5. Cambridge, Trinity College, O. 11a. 5[12]

s. ix/x, NE France, in England before 1100?

Contents: Aristotle, *Categoriae* (in Latin translation by Boethius) (f); pseudo-Augustine, *Categoriae decem ex Aristotele decerptae* [*CPL* 362] (f)

MS: Schenkl no. 2469; Gibson et al. (1995–2001) I.85–6 [no. 55]

ST: Minio-Paluello (1971) *passim* [*Categoriae decem*]; Marenbon (1981) 12–29, 116–38 *et passim* [*Categoriae decem*]

202. Cambridge, Trinity Hall, 24, fols. 78–83

s. viii?

Contents: benedictional (f)? sacramentary (f)? [palimpsest, lower script]

MS: M.R. James (1907) 40; Lowe (1960) no. 12; Gamber (1968–88) 237; *CLA* Supplement (1971) no. 1680; Rushforth (2007) 38–9 n. 10; Wieland (2009) 120

204. Canterbury, Cathedral Library and Archives, Lit. A. 8 (68)

s. xi/xii, Canterbury StA

Contents: Augustine and pseudo-Augustine, ninety-one sermons (eighty-nine from the collection 'De uerbis Domini et apostoli')

MS: T.A.M. Bishop (1954–8a) 189; T.A.M. Bishop (1959–63a) 95; N.R. Ker (1962–92) II.267; Römer (1972b) 100; R. Gameson (1995a) 102 n. 28, 144; R. Gameson (1999a) no. 190; T.N. Hall (2004b) 97 n. 18; Barker-Benfield (2008) I.385, 516, 539, III.1819; R. Gameson (2008) 183–98 [no. 17]; R. Gameson (2012a) 72 n. 244

DEC: Dodwell (1954) 122; Lawrence (1982) 102, 104; R. Gameson (1995a) 126 n. 115

FACS: Lawrence (1982) pl. XXXII (D) [folio not specified]; R. Gameson (1995a) pl. 8 (b) [fol. 41v (detail)]; R. Gameson (2008) 184–7 [fols. 1v, 3r, 3v, 27r, 41v]

205. 5. Canterbury, Cathedral Library and Archives, Lit. E. 28, fols. 1–7

s. xi/xii (after 1089), Canterbury CC

Contents: Domesday monachorum

MS: R. Gameson (1999a) no. 193

ED: Douglas (1944)

ST: Galbraith (1974) 76, 78–84

Canterbury, Cathedral Library and Archives, Add. 16: see no. **448**

205. 8. Canterbury, Cathedral Library and Archives, Lit. E. 42 and E. 42A, pt. i

s. xi/xii or xii[1], Canterbury CC

Contents: legendary (f)

MS: N.R. Ker (1962–92) II.289–97; Love (1996) xxiv, clxxvi–clxxvii; Parkes (1997b) 110–11, 122–3; R. Gameson (1999a) no. 194; Gullick — Pfaff (2001) 291 n. 17; R. Gameson (2008) 227–47 [no. 22]

DEC: Dodwell (1954) 66, 70, 78; R. Gameson (1995a) 119 and n. 83, 136, 140, 143, 157

FACS: Dodwell (1954) pl. 42 (d) [fol. 36v]; R. Gameson (1995a) pls. 4 (c), 5 (b), 6 (a) [fols. 19r, 9r, 52r (all details)]; Parkes (1997b) pl. 8 [fol. 74v]; R. Gameson (2008) 226, 228–33 [fols. 9r, 16v, 29v, 35v, 69r, 76r]

ST: Southern (1990) 420 and n. 13; Gneuss (2012) 290 [information from M. Gullick]

NOTE: for other surviving parts of this legendary, originally in seven volumes, see R. Gameson (2008) no. 22

206. Canterbury, Cathedral Library and Archives, Add. 20 [*olim* Box CCC no. xix*a*]

s. xi[3/4], Canterbury CC?, (prov. prob. ibid.)

Contents: Chrodegang, *Regula canonicorum* (enlarged version)[+*] (f)

MS: N.R. Ker (1957) no. 97; T.A.M. Bishop (1959–63a) 94–5; N.R. Ker (1962–92) II.315; N.R. Ker (1964) 34; A.G. Watson (1987a) 11; Dumville (1992a) 71; *ASMMF* V (1997) 1–2 [no. 109; Doane]; R. Gameson (1999a) no. 187; Langefeld (2003) 46–7; Treharne (2007b) 18 n. 16; R. Gameson (2008) 127–31 [no. 12]; Scragg (2012a) no. 278

FACS: *ASMMF* V (1997) no. 109; R. Gameson (1999a) pl. 1 [recto]; R. Gameson (2008) 126 [verso]

ED: Langefeld (2003) [Latin and OE *Regula canonicorum* coll. as D]

207. Canterbury, Cathedral Library and Archives, Add. 25

s. x ex., (prov. prob. Canterbury CC)

Contents: Gregory (Werferth), *Dialogi** (f)

MS: N.R. Ker (1957) no. 96; N.R. Ker (1962–92) II.315; N.R. Ker (1964) 34; *ASMMF* V (1997) 3–5 [no. 110; Doane]; R. Gameson (2008) 85–7 [no. 5]; Scragg (2012a) no. 279

FACS: *ASMMF* V (1997) no. 110; R. Gameson (2008) 84 [fol. 4r]

ED: Yerkes (1977b) 121–35 [base MS (= A) for Werferth's translation of Gregory, *Dialogi*]

LANG: Yerkes (1979)

ST: M.R. James (1903) no. 306 [on probable source of fragment]; Yerkes (1986a) 335–8

208. Canterbury, Cathedral Library and Archives, Add. 32

s. xi in.

Contents: Gregory, *Dialogi* [*CPL* 1713] (f)

MS: N.R. Ker (1957) lxiii [no. 97*]; R. Gameson (2008) 89–93 [no. 6]; R. Gameson (2012b) 113 and n. 75; Scragg (2012a) no. 280

FACS: R. Gameson (2008) 88 [recto of leaf]

208. 8. Canterbury, Cathedral Library and Archives, Add. 122

s. xi[1]

Contents: homiletic fragment (unidentified)

MS: R. Gameson (2008) 117–19 [no. 10]

FACS: R. Gameson (2008) 116 [one side]

ED: R. Gameson (2008) 117–18

209. Canterbury, Cathedral Library and Archives, Add. 127/1

s. xi[1]

Contents: Paulus Diaconus, *Homiliarium* (f)

MS: N.R. Ker (1962–92) II.315–16; Clayton (1985) 218; Cross—Hall (1993a); T.N. Hall (2007) 234, 245; J. Hill (2007a) 93; R. Gameson (2008) 107–15 [no. 9]; Wieland (2009) 126

FACS: R. Gameson (2008) 106, 108–9 [fols. 4v, 5v, 7r]

210. Canterbury, Cathedral Library and Archives, Add. 127/12

s. x$^{3/3}$

Contents: *Homiliarium* of Saint-Père, Chartres (f)

MS: N.R. Ker (1962–92) II.316–17; Clayton (1985) 218; Cross (1987) 1, 49; Cross (1991) 205; R. Gameson (2008) 79–83 [no. 4]

FACS: R. Gameson (2008) 80 [fol. 1r]

211. Canterbury, Cathedral Library and Archives, Add. 127/19 and PRC 49/1/1–2

s. ix/x or x^1, prob. N France, prov. prob. Canterbury StA

Contents: Priscian, *Institutiones grammaticae* [*CPL* 1546], glossed (f)

MS: N.R. Ker (1962–92) II.317–18; Gibson (1972) 108, 115; Passalacqua (1978) nos. 97, 344; Bischoff (1998–) I, no. 853; R. Gameson (2002d) 182; Barker-Benfield (2008) II.1335, 1336, III.1826; R. Gameson (2008) 63–71 [no. 2]; Wieland (2009) 145

FACS: R. Gameson (2008) 64 [fol. 1r]

ST: D. Ganz (2001a) 105

212. Canterbury, Cathedral Library and Archives, Add. 128/52

s. xi$^{1/4}$

Contents: missal (f)

MS: N.R. Ker (1962–92) II.321; Dumville (1992a) 67; Hartzell (2006) no. 70; R. Gameson (2008) 99–105 [no. 8]; Wieland (2009) 123; Rankin (2012) 492 and n. 42, 501 and n. 87

FACS: R. Gameson (2008) 100 [fol. 3v]

212. 2. Canterbury, Cathedral Library and Archives, Add. 172

[formerly listed as no. **695**]

s. xi ex., Canterbury StA

Contents: Canticum canticorum; Epistulae Pauli, with gloss, partly by Lanfranc; Apocalypsis Iohannis

MS: M.R. James (1903) 209; N.R. Ker (1964) 47; R. Gameson (1995a) 100 and n. 21, 102 n. 28, 124 n. 103, 144; R. Gameson (1999a) no. 189; Barker-Benfield (2008) I.xxxii, lx, 504, 527, 531, II.924, 926, 1372, III.1739; R. Gameson (2008) 147–68 [no. 15]; Wieland (2009) 136;

R. Gameson (2012a) 27, 34 n. 79, 50; R. Gameson (2012b) 101 and n. 26; R. Gameson (2012d) 367 and n. 98; Gullick (2012) 299 and nn. 27 and 30, 301 and n. 43

FACS: R. Gameson (2008) 149–53 [fols. 1v, 9v, 116r, 147r, 170r]

ST: Gibson (1971) 88–9 *et passim* [repr. Gibson (1993a) no. XII]

212. 3. Canterbury, Cathedral Library and Archives, Add. 172, fol. 189 [endleaf]

s. xi³/⁴, prov. Canterbury StA

Contents: collectar (f [reject leaf?])

MS: R. Gameson (1999a) no. 189; R. Gameson (2008) 121–5 [no. 11]

FACS: R. Gameson (2008) 120 [fol. 189r]

ED: R. Gameson (2008) 121–3

212. 4. 1. Canterbury, Cathedral Library and Archives, PRC 49/2

[formerly listed as no. **524. 6**]

s. xi in.

Contents: Haimo of Auxerre, *Homiliarium* (f)

MS: N.R. Ker (1962–92) II.315–16; Cross—Hall (1993a); R. Gameson (2008) 95–8 [no. 7]

FACS: R. Gameson (2008) 94 [fol. 1v]

ST: *CSLMA* III (2010) 350–5

212. 4. 2. Canterbury, Cathedral Library and Archives, PRC 49/24/1–7

s. x (²/³?), France, prov. Canterbury StA (in England before s. xii?)

Contents: Cassiodorus, *Expositio psalmorum* [*CPL* 900] (f)

MS: R. Gameson (2008) 73–8 [no. 3]

FACS: R. Gameson (2008) 72 [PRC 49/24, fol. 2r]

212. 5. Canterbury, Cathedral Library and Archives, U3/162/28/1

s. xi/xii, Canterbury StA

Contents: Augustine, *Enarrationes in psalmos* [*CPL* 283] (f)

MS: N.R. Ker (1960) 30; N.R. Ker (1964) 42; A.G. Watson (1987a) 13
n. 2; R. Gameson (1995a) 102 n. 28, 144; R. Gameson (1999a) no. 195;
Barker-Benfield (2008) I.91 n. b, 92 n. 6, 510, 517, 520, 539, 606,
III.1819, 1820; R. Gameson (2008) 199–207 [no. 18]; R. Gameson
(2012a) 72 n. 244

FACS: R. Gameson (2008) 200 [fol. 1r]

212. 6. Canterbury, Cathedral Library and Archives, U4/20/2

s. xi$^{3/4}$, S England (? Canterbury)

Contents: Paulus Diaconus, *Homiliarium* (f)

MS: T.N. Hall (2004b) 97 n. 18; R. Gameson (2008) 133–7 [no. 13]

FACS: R. Gameson (2008) 132 [fol. 2v]

212. 7. Chichester, Diocesan Record Office, Ep. I/17/20

s. xi

Contents: canticles (f) [presumably from a psalter MS]

MS: N.R. Ker (1962–92) II.399

212. 8. Chichester, West Sussex Record Office, Cap. I/17/2

s. viii^2 [before 780], S England (Selsey?)

Contents: Psalterium Romanum (f [or reject leaf?]); charter of Oslac

MS: Keynes (1991) 3 [no. 2]; Dumville (1992a) 127 n. 232; S.E. Kelly
(1998) no. 11

FACS: Keynes (1991) pls. 2 (a)–(b) [face and dorse]

ED: S.E. Kelly (1998) 46–8 [Oslac charter]

ST: Stenton (1955) 37–8; Bruckner—Marichal (1967) no. 236; Chaplais
(1968) 333–5; Sawyer (1968) no. 1184; Whitelock (1979) no. 76; H.L.
Rogers (1981); Scharer (1982) 260–1 and nn. 4, 5; Welch (1983) 323–31;
Webster—Backhouse (1991) 202–3 [no. 157; Prescott]

Deene Park Library (near Kettering, Northamptonshire), Trustees of the
late Mr G. Brudenell, I. 2. 21: see no. **648**

213. Dublin, Trinity College, 57 (A. 4. 5) (the 'Book of Durrow')

s. vii^2, Northumbria or Iona or Ireland?

Contents: gospels

MS: Kenney (1929) no. 455; *CLA* II (1935) no. 273; R. Powell (1956);
McGurk (1961a) no. 86; McGurk (1961b) 8, 13 [no. 39] [repr. McGurk
(1998) no. V]; Gamber (1968–88) no. 142; T.J. Brown (1972) 221–35,
245–6 n. 2 [repr. T.J. Brown (1993a) 99–111, 273 n. 95]; T.J. Brown
(1974) 128 [repr. T.J. Brown (1993a) 134]; T.J. Brown (1982a) 105–6,
113 [repr. T.J. Brown (1993a) 205–8, 214]; G. Henderson (1982) 29; T.J.
Brown (1984) 326 [repr. T.J. Brown (1993a) 239]; T. O'Neill (1984)
no. II and 97 n. 61; Bischoff (1986) 122–3, 262; G. Henderson (1987)
19–55, 141–6, 179–80, 183–94; McGurk (1987) 171 [repr. McGurk
(1998) no. II]; Bischoff (1988a) 14; P.L. Heyworth (1989) 143; Colker
(1991) I.104–6; R. Gameson (1994b) 28, 30; Netzer (1994); Meehan
(1996); Dumville (1999) 28, 43, 45, 99–100; M.P. Brown (2003a) 452;
M.P. Brown (2004) 292; Nees (2006) 91; Dumville (2007d) 83–7;
Wieland (2009) 118; M.P. Brown (2012) 125, 136, 149; R. Gameson
(2012a) 41 n. 108, 80, 86; McKee (2012a) 172

DEC: Nordenfalk (1947); Elbern (1955); McGurk (1956) 260 [repr.
McGurk (1998) no. I]; McGurk (1961a) 11–13 [repr. McGurk (1998)
no. VI]; McGurk (1962) 20 [repr. McGurk (1998) no. VII]; Werner
(1969); Köhler—Mütherich (1971–99) VII.45 n. 50, 73 n. 14; Nordenfalk
(1977) 35–47 and pls. 2–8; Alexander (1978a) no. 6; G. Henderson
(1982) 22, 29, 53 n. 44; D.M. Wilson (1984) 33–6; Ohlgren (1986) no. 6;
G. Henderson (1987) 19–55; R. Gameson (1991) 85 n. 129; R. Gameson
(1994b) 39 n. 71; Werner (1997a) 23–4; M.P. Brown (2011b) 32, 33, 34,
36; Nees (2011) 14, 16, 19–21, 26–7, 30; Netzer (2011) 3–5, 6–8, 9–13;
O'Reilly (2011) 191–2, 204; Tilghman (2011) 96–7; Werner (2011) 295–6,
297–8, 300, 310; Netzer (2012) 230 and n. 34, 231

FACS: Luce et al. (1960) [complete facsimile]; D.M. Wilson (1984) pls.
22–5 [fols. 21v (several details), 191v]; G. Henderson (1987) pls. 2–3
[fols. 1v, 3v], 6–7 [fols. 4r, 10r], 8–12 [fols. 11r, 22r, 86r, 85v, 125v],
14–15 [fols. 248r, 17r], 26 [fol. 125v (detail)], 32 [fol. 193r], 41–2 [fols.
192v, 2r], 53 [fol. 21v], 61 [fol. 84v], 63–4 [fols. 124v, 191v]; T.J. Brown
(1993a) ills. 19–21 [fols. 11r, 17r, 86r]; Netzer (1994) pl. 93 [fol. 191v];
Netzer (1999) figs. 25.1, 25.2, 25.4, 25.6 [fols. 1v, 3v, 125v, 192v]; M.P.
Brown (2003c) fig. 23 [fol. 21v]

ED: J. Wordsworth et al. (1889–1954) [gospels coll. occasionally as
durmach.]; Weber—Gryson (1994) [gospels coll. as D]

LANG: G. Henderson (1982) 34, 38

ST: Best (1926–8); McGurk (1955b) 105 [repr. McGurk (1998) no. IV];
McGurk (1962) 25 [repr. McGurk (1998) no. VII]; McGurk (1963) 170

[repr. McGurk (1998) no. VIII]; Verey et al. (1980) 70, 106; *BCLL* (1985) no. 516; McGurk (1993) 244 [repr. McGurk (1998) no. XI]; McGurk (1994a) [repr. McGurk (1998) no. IX]; McNamara (1995) 71, 74; *CSLMA* II (1999) 370; Micheli (1999) 357; Netzer (1999)

214. Dublin, Trinity College, 58 (A. 1. 6) (the 'Book of Kells')

s. viii² or viii/ix, Northumbria? Pictland? Iona? Kells?

Contents: gospels

MS: Kenney (1929) no. 471; *CLA* II (1935) no. 274; Gwynn (1954); R. Powell (1956); T.J. Brown (1959) 250, 254 [repr. T.J. Brown (1993a) 245, 250]; McGurk (1961a) no. 87; McGurk (1962) 30 [repr. McGurk (1998) no. VII]; Gamber (1968–88) no. 143; T.J. Brown (1972) 219–46 [repr. T.J. Brown (1993a) 97–122]; T.J. Brown (1982a) 109 [repr. T.J. Brown (1993a) 209]; G. Henderson (1982) 6; T. O'Neill (1982) no. V and 65, 97–8; T.J. Brown (1984) 326 [repr. T.J. Brown (1993a) 239]; Bischoff (1986) 119, 262; G. Henderson (1987) 131–98; P.L. Heyworth (1989) 144; Colker (1991) I.106–8; R. Gameson (1994b) 28, 30; McGurk (1994a) [repr. McGurk (1998) no. IX]; McGurk (1994b) 12, 14 [repr. McGurk (1998) no. XII]; Meehan (1994a); Netzer (1994); O'Mahoney (1994); McNamara (1995) 85–6, 89, 104; Farr (1997); Dumville (1999) 62, 79, 81, 98; Netzer (1999) 319, 320, 325; Marsden (1999) 303, 310 n. 65; Webster—Brown (1997) 241–2 [nos. 123, 125]; M.P. Brown (2003c) 452; M.P. Brown (2004) 292; Dumville (2007d) 83–7; Farr (2007) 133; Wieland (2009) 118; M.P. Brown (2012) 131, 135, 138–9, 155; R. Gameson (2012a) 18, 88; McKee (2012a) 172

DEC: Westwood (1868) 25–33; Köhler (1930–60) I.326–8, 331, 333; McGurk (1956) 262 [repr. McGurk (1998) no. I]; McGurk (1961a) 11–13 [repr. McGurk (1998) no. VI]; McGurk (1962) 20, 22 [repr. McGurk (1998) no. VII]; Werner (1972); Henry (1974); Nordenfalk (1977) 108–24 and pls. 39–47; Alexander (1978a) no. 52; Alexander (1978b) no. 2; S. Lewis (1980); G. Henderson (1982) 28, 48 n. 20, 51 n. 31; D.M. Wilson (1984) 129; Ohlgren (1986) no. 52; G. Henderson (1987) 131–78; Deshman (1995) 244; R. Gameson (1995b) 218 n. 154; M.P. Brown (1996) 100–3; Farr (1997); Werner (1997a) 23–4; Farr (1999) 336, 340, 342–4; MacLean (1999); Meehan (2000); Pochat (2005) 147; M.P. Brown (2007a) 106, 108, 114–15; Dooley (2007); Farr (2007) 118, 120–2, 124–7, 131, 133; Karkov (2009) 205, 223; M.P. Brown (2011b) 31, 36; Farr (2011b) 226–7, 228; Nees (2011) 14, 25; Netzer (2011) 3–4, 11; O'Reilly (2011) 192–7, 194–5, 198, 202, 204; Pulliam

(2011) 60, 61–71, 74–6, 77–8; Rosenthal (2011) 226–7, 232–3; Tilghman (2011) 94, 96, 101–3, 106–8; Werner (2011) 297–8, 299, 300, 301, 302–3, 304; N. Edwards (2012) 245; Netzer (2012) 230, 240–2

FACS: Alton—Meyer (1951) [complete facsimile]; P. Fox (1990) [complete facsimile]; D.M. Wilson (1984) pls. 147–8 [fols. 29r, 32v]; G. Henderson (1987) pls. 188 [fol. 1r], 190–5 [fols. 1v, 2r, 2v, 3r, 3v, 4r], 200 [fol. 4v], 202–3 [fols. 5r, 5v], 206–8 [fols. 12r, 16v, 8r], 211–15 [fols. 33r, 114v, 124r, 129v, 130r], 216–19 [fols. 187v, 203r, 290v, 5r], 221 [fol. 7v], 223–4 [fols. 28v, 32v], 227–8 [fols. 29r, 34r], 231 [fol. 114r], 234 [fol. 124r], 236 [fol. 130r], 238 [fol. 188r], 240 [fol. 188r], 242 [fol. 202v], 252 [fol. 291v], 254–5 [fols. 201v, 292r]; T.J. Brown (1993a) ills. 34–7 [fols. 67r, 92v, 76v, 19r]; Deshman (1995) fig. 202 [fol. 114r]; Farr (1999) fig. 27.4 [fol. 114r]; Meehan (2000) pls. 1 [fol. 191v], 4 [fol. 152v], 6 [fol. 53v], 8 [fol. 252v], 9–10 [fol. 188r], 12–13 [fol. 124r]; M.P. Brown (2003c) pls. 32 (a)–(d) [fols. 29r, 33r, 34r, 29v]; Farr (2007) 119 [fol. 7v], 132 [fol. 191v]

ED: J. Wordsworth et al. (1889–1954) [gospels coll. as Q]; B. Fischer (1988–91) [gospel excerpts coll. as Hq]

LANG: G. Henderson (1982) 33, 35, 38; Horsley—Waterhouse (1984) 217

ST: Friend (1939) [canon tables]; McGurk (1955b) [repr. McGurk (1998) no. IV]; O'Sullivan (1958–9) [on donor of MS]; McGurk (1963) [repr. McGurk (1998) no. VIII] [chapter-lists]; Verey et al. (1980) 70–5; *BCLL* (1985) no. 520; G. Henderson (1987) 179–98 [on MS as relic]; Meyvaert (1989); McGurk (1993) 244 [repr. McGurk (1998) no. XI] [canon tables]; McGurk (1994a) [Hebrew names] [repr. McGurk (1998) no. IX]; McGurk (1994b) 19, 21 [repr. McGurk (1998) no. XII]; O'Mahoney (1994); McGurk (1995a) 256, 259 [repr. McGurk (1998) no. XIII]; McNamara (1995) 71, 77–85, 88, 92, 96, 99, 100; Werner (1997b); Meehan (1998a); Marsden (1999) 290–1 [manuscript affiliation]; Netzer (1999) 321, 325; McGurk (2001); Beall (2005) 192; Vitz (2006) 447 [liturgy]

214. 3. Dublin, Trinity College, 98 (B. 3. 6)

s. xi ex., Canterbury CC

Contents: pontifical (including third English Coronation *ordo*), benedictional

MS: Brückmann (1973) 394; Colker (1991) I.195–7 [full list of contents]; R. Gameson (1995a) 102 n. 27, 119 n. 83, 120 n. 86, 142; Webber (1995)

155, 158; R. Gameson (1999a) nos. 200, 201; Gullick — Pfaff (2001); C.A. Jones (2005a) 121 n. 58; C.A. Jones (2005b) 244, 284; Hartzell (2006) no. 82; Rankin (2012) 494 and n. 53

FACS: H.A. Wilson (1910) pl. III [fol. 23r]; Colker (1991) II, pl. 2 [fol. 25r]; Gullick — Pfaff (2001) pls. 58–60 [fols. 11v, 52r, 70r, 82r, 98r, 153r (details)]

ST: H.A. Wilson (1910) xiii, xvi–xxii; D.H. Turner (1971) xl; Moeller (1971–9) III.44; C.A. Jones (2005b) 243

214. 6. Dublin, Trinity College, 158 (D. 4. 15), fol. 94

s. x^2

Contents: unidentified text (f)

MS: Colker (1991) I.273

215. Dublin, Trinity College, 174 (B. 4. 3), fols. 1–44, 52–6, 96–103

s. xi ex., Salisbury (supplemented ibid. s. xii in.)

Contents: twenty-five *passiones et uitae sanctorum* [*BHL* 429–30, 4973, 7854, 2708, 8072, 4980c, 2970, 8020a, 108–9, 2718, 8559–61, 1989, 8096, 6477, 93, 619, 4546d, 7614, 4862–3, 4529, 905, 3723, 323, 2041, 7374 respectively]; five homilies for saints' days (Augustine, *Serm.* cclxxvi, cccxvi, ccclxxxii, *Sermo app.* ccxvii; Caesarius, *Serm.* ccxx); Gaudentius, *Tractatus de Maccabeis* [*CPL* 215]

[Companion vol. to nos. **754. 5** and **754. 6**?]

MS: Schenkl no. 3312; N.R. Ker (1949–50) 154 n. 1, 161, 180–1, 186 [repr. N.R. Ker (1985) 176 n. 1, 183, 202–3, 208]; Colgrave (1956) 42–3; N.R. Ker (1957) no. 103; N.R. Ker (1964) 24; Römer (1972b) 331; N.R. Ker (1976b) 24 [repr. N.R. Ker (1985) 144]; Colker (1991) I.320–8 [full list of contents]; Dumville (1992a) 140; Webber (1992) 12–13, 23–4, 40, 70, 143, 158; Lapidge (1993a) 481; R. Gameson (1995a) 106 n. 40; R. Gameson (1999a) no. 202; Biggs et al. (2001) 31–2; *ASMMF* V (1997) 11–21 [no. 116; Lucas]; Lapidge (2004a) 138; Love (2005) 219–22; T.N. Hall (2007) 250–1; Upchurch (2007) xii, 110; Scragg (2012a) no. 315

FACS: *ASMMF* V (1997) no. 116

ED: Upchurch (2007) 114–71 [*Passio SS. Iuliani et Basilissae* coll. as D]

ST: N.R. Ker (1985c) 195; Biggs et al. (2001) 22–486 *passim*

216. Dublin, Trinity College, 176 (E. 5. 28), fols. 1–26

s. xi/xii, Barking?

Contents: Goscelin, *Vita S. Æthelburgae* [*BHL* 2630b], *Vita S. Wulfhildae* [*BHL* 8736b]

MS: Schenkl no. 3387; Esposito (1910–11); Esposito (1913a) 11; Colker (1965) 393–4; Gneuss (1976a) 310, 312 [repr. Gneuss (1996a) no. IX]; Meehan (1986) 102; Colker (1991) I.337–9; Dumville (1992a) 140; Tite (1997a) 270; R. Gameson (1999a) no. 203

ED: Esposito (1913a) 12–33 [base MS for Goscelin, *Vita S. Wulfhildae*]; Colker (1965) 398–431 [Goscelin, *Vita S. Æthelburgae*, coll. as D]

ST: Gneuss (1976a) 308–14 [repr. Gneuss (1996a) no. IX]; Love (1996) xliv; R. Sharpe (2001) 151–4

216. 3. Dublin, Trinity College, 370a (D. 1. 25^A)

s. xi^2, Crowland?

Contents: antiphoner (f)

MS: N.R. Ker (1964) 56; Roberts (1970) 216–17; Colker (1991) I.792–3; R. Gameson (1999a) no. 205; Hartzell (2006) no. 83; Rankin (2012) 502 and n. 96

216. 4. Dublin, Trinity College, 371 (D. 1. 26), pp. i–ii, 149–50

s. xi^2, StA?

Contents: gradual (f)

MS: Colker (1991) I.794–5; R. Gameson (1999a) no. 207; Hartzell (2006) no. 84

217. Durham, Cathedral Library, A. II. 4

s. xi ex. (before 1096), Normandy, prov. Durham

Contents: booklist (s. xi/xii); Bible (vol. ii: Prophets — Apocalypse); Remigius of Auxerre (Haimo of Auxerre?), *Expositio in Apocalypsin* (abbrev., incomplete)

MS: Mynors (1939) no. 30; T.A.M. Bishop (1954–8a) 198; Bischoff (1986) 172 n.; A.G. Watson (1987a) 19; Gullick (1990) 62–4; Gullick (1994) 102, 106; Gullick (1998a) 25 [nos. 9–10]; R. Gameson (1999a) no. 210; Lawrence-Mathers (2003) 32–5, 45, 49, 80, 228 n. 62; Shepard (2007) 273; R. Gameson (2012d) 366 and n. 94; Marsden (2012) 426 and n. 94

DEC: Rice (1952) 122–3; F. Wormald (1945) 129 [repr. F. Wormald (1984) 67]; Dodwell (1954) 116–17; R. Gameson (1995b) 120; R. Gameson (1998) 247–9; R. Gameson (2012c) 281 and n. 108

FACS: *NPS* I, pl. 17 [fol. 1r]; Rice (1952) pl. 86 (c) [fol. 87r]; F. Wormald (1984) ills. 71, 80 [fols. 36v, 65r (details)]; Browne (1988) pl. 15 [front flyleaf]; Gullick (1990) 62, 64 [fols. 1r, 146v]; Gullick (1994) pl. 4 [fol. 170v (detail)]; R. Gameson (1998) 247–9 [fol. 87v]; Lawrence-Mathers (2003) pl. I [fol. 1r]

ED: Raine (1838) 117–18 [repr. Becker (1885) 172–3] (booklist)]; C.H. Turner (1917–18) [booklist]; Browne (1988) 154–5 [booklist]

ST: C.H. Turner (1917–18); Glunz (1933) 191–4; Browne (1988) 154 *et passim*; R. Gameson (1998) 231 n. 6; R. Gameson (2003) 147 and n. 70; *CSLMA* III (2010) 279–88 [*Expositio in Apocalypsin*]

218. Durham, Cathedral Library, A. II. 10, fols. 2–5, 338–9 (with Durham, Cathedral Library, C. III. 13, fols. 192–5 + C. III. 20, fols. 1–2)

s. vii med., Northumbria (or Ireland?), prov. prob. Chester-le-Street, prov. Durham.

Contents: gospels (or New Testament?) (f)

MS: *CLA* II (1935) no. 147; Mynors (1939) no. 6; Nordenfalk (1947) 141–74; McGurk (1956) 256 [repr. McGurk (1998) no. I]; McGurk (1961a) no. 9; T.J. Brown (1972) 232, 233, 246 n. [repr. T.J. Brown (1993a) 110, 111, 273 n. 95]; T.J. Brown (1982a) 105, 106, 113 [repr. T.J. Brown (1993a) 205, 206, 207, 212, 214]; T.J. Brown (1984) 313–15, 321 [repr. T.J. Brown (1993a) 224–7, 234]; Bischoff (1986) 114, 116 n., 262; B. Fischer (1988–91) I.15*; Bonner (1989b) 391; Webster—Backhouse (1991) no. 79; Werner (1997a) 24–5, 27, 30; Dumville (1999) 30–1, 43, 45, 98, 99; Netzer (1999) 321; Piper (2007) 94; Wieland (2009) 118; M.P. Brown (2012) 125, 149; R. Gameson (2012a) 19 and n. 23, 51; Marsden (2012) 415 and n. 36

DEC: McGurk (1955b) 106 [repr. McGurk (1998) no. IV]; Nordenfalk (1977) 16, 32; Alexander (1978a) no. 5; Ohlgren (1986) no. 5; G. Henderson (1987) 27–9; Werner (1997a) 24–5; Karkov (2009) 216, 223; Netzer (2012) 229–30 and n. 30

FACS: Mynors (1939) pl. 4 [fol. 2r]; Nordenfalk (1977) fig. IV [fol. 2r], pl. 1 [fol. 3v]; G. Henderson (1987) pls. 20–1 [fols. 2r, 3v]; Bonner et al. (1989a) pl. 31 [fol. 2r]; Webster—Backhouse (1991) 112 [fol. 3v]; T.J. Brown (1993a) ill. 18 [fol. 2r]; M.P. Brown (2003a) 6 [fol. 2r]

ED: B. Fischer (1988–91) [gospel excerpts coll. as Ee]

LANG: Horsley — Waterhouse (1984) 217

ST: Bischoff (1951a) 262; Verey (1969); T.J. Brown (1975) 253 [repr. T.J. Brown (1993a) 150]; Ryan (1987); Verey (1989) 145–6; McGurk (1994b) 2, 9, 22 [repr. McGurk (1998) no. XII]; McKee (2012b) 342 and n. 12

219. Durham, Cathedral Library A. II. 16 (with Cambridge, Magdalene College, Pepys 2981 (18))

s. viii¹, Northumbria, prov. prob. Chester-le-Street, prov. Durham

Contents: gospels

MS: Rud (1825) 18–19; *CLA* II (1935) no. 148(a)–(c); Mynors (1939) no. 7; Lowe (1960) 20 [no. XVII]; McGurk (1961a) no. 10; Bischoff (1966–81) II.330; A.G. Watson (1987a) 19; Bonner (1989b) 391–2; Parkes (1992) 125 n. 64; Story (1993); R. Gameson (1994b) 45 n. 91; Netzer (1994) 106, 240 n. 30; O'Sullivan (1994) 81–2; Parkes (1997b) 102 and n. 16; Dumville (1999) 44, 71; M.P. Brown (2003b) 139; Gerchow (2004) 52; M.P. Brown (2012) 134 n. 54, 136, 151; R. Gameson (2012a) 51 n. 171

DEC: McGurk (1961a) 14 [repr. McGurk (1998) no. VI]; Alexander (1978a) no. 16; Ohlgren (1986) no. 16; M.P. Brown (1996) 128; M.P. Brown (2003b) 139

FACS: Lowe (1960) pl. XVII [fol. 34v]; M.P. Brown (2003b) figs. 6–8 [fols. 37r, 91r, 122v–123r]; Owen-Crocker (2009) fig. 2.2 [fol. 91r]

LANG: M.P. Brown (1996) 130–1

ED: J. Wordsworth et al. (1889–1954) [gospels coll. as Δ (John only)]; C.H. Turner (1931) 217 [liturgical notes]; B. Fischer (1988–91) [gospel excerpts coll. as Nd, Ne, Nf]

ST: McGurk (1961a) 13–14 [repr. McGurk (1998) no. VI]; Verey (1969); Verey et al. (1980) 65, 68–73; Verey (1989) 148; McGurk (1994b) 9, 22 [repr. McGurk (1998) no. XII]; McNamara (1995) 105; Lenker (1997) 102–6, 396–7; Marsden (1999) 297; Verey (1999) 328

220. Durham, Cathedral Library, A. II. 17, fols. 2–102 (with Cambridge, Magdalene College, Pepys 2981 (19)) **(the 'Durham Gospels')**

s. vii ex. or viii in., Northumbria, prob. Lindisfarne, prov. Chester-le-Street, prov. Durham

Contents: gospels (incomplete), with pericope notes; addition, s. x/xi: poem on King Æthelstan [SK 2143]

MS: Westwood (1868) 48–9; *CLA* II (1935) no. 149; Mynors (1939) no. 3; Nordenfalk (1947) 156; Kendrick et al. (1956–60) I.89–90, 100–6, 245–9; N.R. Ker (1957) no. 105; McGurk (1961a) no. 13; McGurk (1962) 29–30 [repr. McGurk (1998) no. VII]; Henry (1963); N.R. Ker (1964) 63; T.J. Brown (1972) 225–45 [repr. T.J. Brown (1993a) 103–22]; T.J. Brown (1974) 128, 131, 133 [repr. T.J. Brown (1993a) 126, 130, 134]; Piper (1978) 215 n. 4; Verey et al. (1980) 15–31, 36–49, 63–7; T.J. Brown (1982a) 108 [repr. T.J. Brown (1993a) 208]; G. Henderson (1982) 8; Ó Cróinín (1982) [review of Verey et al. (1980)]; T.J. Brown (1984) 323, 326 [repr. T.J. Brown (1993a) 235, 239]; Bischoff (1986) 123, 262; M.P. Brown (1986) 133; A.G. Watson (1987a) 19; Bonner (1989b) 391–2; M.P. Brown (1989a) 157, 159; Bruce-Mitford (1989); P.L. Heyworth (1989) 186, 198; M.P. Brown (1991) 63; Webster— Backhouse (1991) no. 81; R. Gameson (1994b) 28, 30–1, 47; McGurk (1994b) 5 n. 15 [repr. McGurk (1998) no. XII]; Netzer (1994) 35–7 *et passim*; O'Sullivan (1994) 80; *CPL* (1995) no. 1956; McNamara (1995) 89–90; Werner (1997a) 24; Dumville (1999) 44–5, 62, 65, 69, 93–5, 98–9, 115; Marsden (1999) 296–7; Lawrence-Mathers (2003) 20–1; M.P. Brown (2004) 291; Hartzell (2006) no. 85; *ASMMF* XIV (2007) 1–2 [no. 67 (Pepys 2981 (19)); Doane], 3–14 [no. 118 (Durham A.II.17); Keefer]; Keefer (2007b) 86, 91–2, 106; M.P. Brown (2012) 136, 144, 149, 151; R. Gameson (2012a) 26 and n. 50, 28 n. 59, 51; R. Gameson (2012b) 114; Gullick (2012) 299 n. 28; Marsden (2012) 418 and n. 58

DEC: McGurk (1955b) 106 [repr. McGurk (1998) no. IV]; McGurk (1956) 259 [repr. McGurk (1998) no. I]; Nordenfalk (1977) 56–7; Köhler—Mütherich (1971–99) VII.44 n. 47; Alexander (1978a) no. 10; Verey et al. (1980) 53–63 [E. Coatsworth]; G. Henderson (1982) 28; D.M. Wilson (1984) 36–8; Ohlgren (1986) no. 10; G. Henderson (1987) 57–72, 78–84, 90–1; Bruce-Mitford (1989) 175–6, 179–85; Coatsworth (1989) 296; Cramp (1989) 220; R. Gameson (1994b) 32, 38; M.P. Brown (1996) 83, 115, 167; Deshman (1997) 114; Keefer (2007b) 104–7; O'Loughlin (2007) 152; Karkov (2011) 136, 141, 143; Werner (2011) 305–6, 307, 310; Netzer (2012) 230, 235

FACS: Verey et al. (1980) [complete facsimile]; Mynors (1939) frontispiece [fol. 39r]; T.J. Brown (1972) pls. II (a)–(b) [fols. 8r, 39v], IV (a)–(b) [fols. 4v, 7r], VI (c)–(e) [fols. 21r, 67r, 75v]; Nordenfalk (1977) pls. 13–14 [fols. 1r, 38v]; D.M. Wilson (1984) pls. 26–7 [fols. 69r (detail), 38v]; G. Henderson (1987) 69 [fol. 79v], 70 [fol. 38r], 75 [fol. 39r], 76–7 [fols. 74r, 2v (details)], 78 [fol. 2r], 79 [fol. 2r (detail)], 83 [fol. 2r (detail)], 85–7 [all fol. 2r (details)], 89–90 [fols. 38r, 69r (details)]; T.J. Brown (1993a) ills. 31–2 [fols. 2r, 66r]; Fuchs (2002) fig. 82 [fol. 74v (detail)]; M.P. Brown (2003b) fig. 1 [fol. 71v]; M.P. Brown (2003c) pls. 26–7 [fols. 2r, 38v]; *ASMMF* XIV (2007) nos. 67, 118; Keefer (2007b) 113 [fol. 104r], 114 [fol. 106r], 115 [fol. 34r]

ED: Lapidge (1981a) 87–90 [Æthelstan poem (fol. 31v) coll. as D] [repr. Lapidge (1993a) 75–8]; B. Fischer (1988-91) [gospel excerpts coll. as Ef]

ST: Glunz (1933) 18, 32; Kunze (1947) 60–1; McGurk (1961b) 11 [repr. McGurk (1998) no. V]; Verey (1969); Klauser (1972) xxxi [no. 7]; T.J. Brown (1975) 253 [repr. T.J. Brown (1993a) 150]; Verey et al. (1980) 68–108 [reconstruction of the Durham Gospels; collation of biblical text]; Lapidge (1981a) 83–4, 88–93 [Æthelstan poem] [repr. Lapidge (1993a) 71–2, 76–81]; Verey (1989) 143, 146 [gospel text]; Raw (1990) 203; Lapidge (1993a) 471; McGurk (1994a) [Hebrew names] [repr. McGurk (1998) no. IX]; McGurk (1994b) 22 [repr. McGurk (1998) no. XII]; O'Sullivan (1994) 80; Szerwiniack (1994) 193–258 [Hebrew names]; McNamara (1995) 77–9, 83 [textual parallels with no. **214**]; Keefer (1997); Lenker (1997) 102–6, 135–46, 398–9 [pericope notes in the MS (cited as Mf)]; Marsden (1999) 296–7; Fuchs (2002) 225–6

221. Durham, Cathedral Library, A. II. 17, fols. 103–11

s. vii/viii, Monkwearmouth-Jarrow, prov. Chester-le-Street, prov. Durham

Contents: gospel of Luke (f)

MS: *CLA* II (1935) no. 150; Mynors (1939) no. 3; N.R. Ker (1957) no. 105; Lowe (1960) 19 [no. XIII]; T.J. Brown (1972) 231 [repr. T.J. Brown (1993a) 109]; Verey et al. (1980) 31–4 [Verey], 49–51 [T.J. Brown]; B. Fischer (1988–91) I.15*; O'Sullivan (1994) 80; Lawrence–Mathers (2003) 20–1; M.P. Brown (2004) 291; Gerchow (2004) 52; *ASMMF* XIV (2007) 3–14 [no. 118; Keefer]; R. Gameson (2012a) 19 n. 25, 37 n. 86, 67; R. Gameson (2012b) 114

DEC: Netzer (2012) 232 and n. 46

FACS: Verey et al. (1980) [complete facsimile]; Mynors (1939) pl. 2 [fol. 106r]; Lowe (1960) pl. XIII [fol. 106r]; M.P. Brown (2003c) fig. 46 [fol. 106r]; *ASMMF* XIV (2007) no. 118

ED: C.H. Turner (1931) 199–216 [text of Luke XXI.33 — XXIII.44]; B. Fischer (1988–91) I.15*-16* [gospel excerpts (Luke) coll. as Nz]

ST: Keefer (1997) [on the scribe Boge]

222. Durham, Cathedral Library, A. III. 29

s. xi ex. (before 1096), Durham

Contents: Paulus Diaconus, *Homiliarium* (Temporale: Easter to 25th Sunday after Whitsun; Sanctorale: May to Dec.)

[Companion vol. to no. **226**; and cf. no. **249. 3**]

MS: Rud (1825) 45–56 [full list of contents]; Schenkl no. 4380; Mynors (1939) no. 49; N.R. Ker (1962–92) II.315; Rella (1977) 117; Smetana (1978) 87–8; Clayton (1985) 219; R.M. Thomson (1986a) 36 and n. 45; A.G. Watson (1987a) 19; M.P. Richards (1988) 96 and n. 48, 103, 110; Dumville (1994d), 200, 208; R. Gameson (1999a) no. 211; T.N. Hall (2001) 124, 127 [no. 15]; Lawrence-Mathers (2003) 47; Gerchow (2004) 52; T.N. Hall (2004b) 87, 92, 100–5; Biggs (2007a) 25–6 [Clayton]; T.N. Hall (2007) 237 n. 30, 239–41; J. Hill (2007a) 75, 90–1

ST: Lambert (1969–72) nos. 0, 206, 217, 217a, 309, 350, 350 bis, 671, 708.3; Römer (1972b) 103; Browne (1988) 154 *et passim*

222. 3. Durham, Cathedral Library, A. III. 31, fols. 1–4, 288–91

s. x ex.

Contents: medical text (unidentified)

222. 8. Durham, Cathedral Library, A. IV. 16, fols. 66–109

s. xi/xii, Durham

Contents: Augustine, *De Genesi ad litteram* [*CPL* 266] (incomplete)

MS: Schenkl no. 4382; Mynors (1939) no. 100; Römer (1972b) 103; A.G. Watson (1987a) 21; Gullick (1994) 104; Gullick (1998a) 19, 26 n. 15; R. Gameson (1999a) no. 213; Lawrence-Mathers (2003) 165–6

223. Durham, Cathedral Library, A. IV. 19

s. ix/x or x in., S England, prov. Chester-le-Street; s. x^2 (c. 970), Chester-le-Street; prov. whole MS Durham

Contents:

s. ix/x or x in.: collectar°, liturgical texts° (benedictions, exorcisms, prayers, two Masses);

s. x^2: a collection of texts for Mass and Office°; educational memoranda°:
list of *notae iuris*; various notes (On the materials from which Adam
was made; On the nature of the winds; On Roman imperial dignitaries;
On the titles of kings [in six languages]; *De ecclesiae gradibus*; On the
burial-places of the Apostles; alphabet of names and words with
religious interpretations); OE gloss to all texts

MS: Mynors (1939) no. 14; R. Derolez (1954) 401–2; Kendrick et al.
(1956–60) II.25–32; N.R. Ker (1957) no. 106; Gamber (1968–88)
no. 1517; Gneuss (1968) 101–3; Squires (1973); T.J. Brown (1975) 291
[repr. T.J. Brown (1993a) 173]; Backhouse et al. (1984b) no. 7; Bischoff
(1986) 118 n. 66, 193 n. 5 [*notae iuris*]; Dumville (1987) 168–9; P.L.
Heyworth (1989) 186; Corrêa (1992) 76–84; Dumville (1992a) 106–7,
129–30, 145; Conner (1993) 58, 67, 70, 84, 212; Vaciago (1993) 10–11;
M.P. Brown (1996) 142, 180; P.P. O'Neill (1997) 162; Stanley –
Robinson (2001) 242; Dumville (2005) 309; Hartzell (2006) no. 87;
O'Brien O'Keeffe (2006) 266; Roberts (2006) 29; *ASMMF* XIV (2007)
15–51 [no. 119; Keefer]; Biggs (2007a) 4, 77; Keefer (2007b) 86, 93,
105–6; Graham (2009) 165; Wieland (2009) 121, 137–8; R. Gameson
(2012b) 102 and n. 35; Jolly (2012); Pfaff (2012) 452 and n. 7; Scragg
(2012a) nos. 316–17

DEC: F. Wormald (1945) 114 [repr. F. Wormald (1984) 53 and fig. 48];
Rice (1952) 177; E. Temple (1976) no. 3; Ohlgren (1986) no. 81; Raw
(1990) 204; R. Gameson (1991) 67, 105 n. 16 [on fol. 84r]; R. Gameson
(1995b) 238; M.P. Brown (1996) 177–8; Keefer (2007b) 96–8

FACS: T.J. Brown (1969a) [complete facsimile]; Corrêa (1992) pls. I–II
[fols. 6r, 35v]; M.P. Brown (2003c) fig. 45 (b) [fol. 46v]; *ASMMF* XIV
(2007) no. 119; Keefer (2007b) 111 [fol. 59r], 112 [fol. 59v]; Owen-
Crocker (2009) fig. 5.3 [fol. 27v]

ED: Liebermann (1903–16) I.403 [benediction on p. 109 = *Iudicium Dei*
no. 15]; Thompson – Lindelöf (1927) [complete transcription of MS];
Squires (1971) [OE gloss to the Collectar]; Corrêa (1992) 141–235
[base MS for Collectar]; Milfull (1996) [hymns coll. as E]; Muir (1988)
113–16 [Celtic *capitella* coll. as D]; Roberts (2006) 29 n. 11 [four lines
of a note by Aldred]

LANG: Lindelöf (1890); Lindelöf (1901a)

ST: N.R. Ker (1943) [glosses by the scribe Aldred]; Hohler (1975) 62, 72,
223–4; Korhammer (1976) 45; Piper (1978) 214; Bonner (1989b) 393–4;
N. Orchard (2005) cxxxvi, clxvii, 444; Jolly (2012)

224. Durham, Cathedral Library, A. IV. 19, fol. 89

s. viii, Northumbria

Contents: mass lectionary (f)

MS: *CLA* II (1935) no. 151; Mynors (1939) no. 12; T.J. Brown (1969a) 37; Lenker (1997) 115, 457; Rushforth (2001) 143; *ASMMF* XIV (2007) 49 [no. 119; Keefer]

FACS: T.J. Brown (1969a) [complete facsimile: fol. 89r–v]; *ASMMF* XIV (2007) no. 119

225. Durham, Cathedral Library, A. IV. 28

s. xi/xii or xii in., (prov. Durham)

Contents: Bede, *Expositio Apocalypseos* [*CPL* 1363]

MS: Mynors (1939) no. 26; A.G. Watson (1987a) 21; Gryson (2001) 31–2 [no. 23]; Lawrence-Mathers (2003) 223; Piper (2007) 88

ED: Gryson (2001) [Bede, *Expositio Apocalypseos*, coll. as D]

ST: Sparks (1954) [text-type of biblical quotations]; *CPPM* II, no. 2012

225. 5. Durham, Cathedral Library, B. II. 1

s. xi/xii, (prov. Durham)

Contents: Iosephus, *Antiquitates Iudaicae* (anonymous Latin version), *De bello Iudaico*, trans. Hegesippus

MS: Mynors (1939) no. 85; A.G. Watson (1987a) 22; Gullick (1996–9b) 254–5 and nn. 34, 36; R. Gameson (1999a) no. 215; Lawrence-Mathers (2003) 76–8, 81–2, 87–8

226. Durham, Cathedral Library, B. II. 2

s. xi ex. (before 1096), Durham

Contents: Paulus Diaconus, *Homiliarium*, original version (from Advent to Easter)

[Companion vol. to no. **222**; and cf. no. **249. 3**]

MS: Rud (1825) 93–7 [list of contents]; Mynors (1939) no. 48; Römer (1972b) 104; Smetana (1978) 96 n. 57; Clayton (1985) 219; A.G. Watson (1987a) 22; Browne (1988) 154 *et passim*; M.P. Richards (1988) 96 n. 48; Dumville (1994d) 202, 208; R. Gameson (1999a) no. 216; T.N. Hall

(2001) 124, 127 [no. 16]; Lawrence-Mathers (2003) 47 and fig. 3; T.N. Hall (2004b) 87; T.N. Hall (2007) 249 n. 67; J. Hill (2007a) 89

227. Durham, Cathedral Library, B. II. 6

s. xi ex. (before 1096), (prov. Durham)

Contents: Ambrose, *De Ioseph patriarcha* [*CPL* 131], *De patriarchis* [*CPL* 132], *De paenitentia* [*CPL* 156], *De excessu fratris* [*CPL* 157], *De bono mortis* [*CPL* 129], *De obitu Valentiniani* [*CPL* 158], *De paradiso* [*CPL* 124] (incomplete), *De Abraham patriarcha* [*CPL* 127] (bk. I only), *De Nabuthae* [*CPL* 138]; Augustine, *De decem chordis* (= *Serm.* ix: added s. xi/xii)

MS: Mynors (1939) no. 46; N.R. Ker (1964) 66; Römer (1972b) 104; A.G. Watson (1987a) 22; Gullick (1990) 63, 68–9; Gullick (1994) 104; Bankert et al. (1997) 14, 22, 25, 26, 28, 29, 30, 49, 51; Gullick (1998a) 15, 30 n. 39; R. Gameson (1999a) no. 217; Lawrence-Mathers (2003) 41, 46, 50, 71

DEC: R. Gameson (1998) 248 n. 63

FACS: Gullick (1994) pl. 3 (b) [fol. 79r (detail)]

ST: Browne (1988) 155 *et passim*; R. Sharpe (1998) 286; Anlezark (2006) 63 n. 6

228. Durham, Cathedral Library, B. II. 9

s. xi ex. (before 1096), prov. Durham

Contents: Jerome, *Comm. in Prophetas minores* [*CPL* 589]

MS: Rud (1825) 104; Schenkl no. 4393; Mynors (1939) no. 37; N.R. Ker (1964) 66; A.G. Watson (1987a) 22; Browne (1988) 149–53; Gullick (1990); R. Gameson (1999a) no. 220; Lawrence-Mathers (2003) 46, 54; Gullick (2005b)

ST: Lambert (1969–72) no. 216; Browne (1988) 154 *et passim*; R. Sharpe (1998) 299

229. Durham, Cathedral Library, B. II. 10, fols. 1–183

s. xi ex. (before 1096), Canterbury CC, prov. Durham

Contents: Jerome, *Epistulae* [*CPL* 620] (includes pseudonymous letters and letters to Jerome); Origen, *Homiliae .ii. in Canticum canticorum*, trans. Jerome [*CPG* 1432]; Jerome, *Aduersus Heluidium* [*CPL* 609], *Contra Vigilantium* [*CPL* 611]

MS: Rud (1825) 104–6 [full list of the Jerome Letters]; Schenkl no. 4394; Mynors (1939) no. 38; Dodwell (1954) 116 n. 2, 120; N.R. Ker (1960) 128; A.G. Watson (1987a) 22; Webber (1995) 151n., 152; R. Gameson (1999a) no. 221; Lawrence-Mathers (2003) 38, 44, 226

DEC: F. Wormald (1945) 130 n. 75 [repr. F. Wormald (1984) 68 n. 75]; Lawrence (1982) 108; R. Gameson (1995a) 118 n., 143

FACS: Mynors (1939) pl. 26 [fol. 1v]; Lawrence (1982) pl. XXXIII (C) [fol. 1v]

ST: Lambert (1969–72) no. 900; Römer (1972b) 104; Browne (1988) 154 *et passim*; R. Sharpe (1998) 297–8, 300

230. Durham, Cathedral Library, B. II. 11

fols. 1–108: s. xi ex. (before 1096), Normandy, prov. Durham; fols. 109–37: s. xi ex. (before 1096), Normandy, prov. Durham

Contents: fols. 1–108: Jerome, *Liber quaestionum hebraicarum in Genesin* [*CPL* 580]; Eusebius, *Onomasticon*, trans. Jerome as *De situ et nominibus locorum Hebraicorum* [*CPG* 3466]; Jerome, *Liber interpretationis hebraicorum nominum* [*CPL* 581]; *Epist.* cxxv (*ad Rusticum*) [*CPL* 620]; pseudo-Jerome, *Interpretatio alphabeti Hebraeorum* (and explanation of Greek alphabet) [*CPL* 623a], *Hebraicae quaestiones in libros Regum*, *Hebraicae quaestiones in Paralipomena*, *Decem temptationes populi Israel*, *De sex ciuitatibus ad quas homicida fugit*, *Expositio in Canticum Deborae*, *Expositio in Lamentationes Hieremiae* [*CPL* 630], *Super aedificium Prudentii*, *Epist. supp.* [*CPL* 633] xxiii, xliv–xlv, *De sphaera caeli*; Jerome (?), *Notae diuinae legis necessariae* [*CPPM* II, no. 976]; texts, excerpts and short verse compositions (including WIC 12589, 14969, 11179) dealing with the etymology of Hebrew names, with science (computus, geometry, metals, stones) and with music, including excerpt from Guido of Arezzo, *Micrologus*; excerpt from *Liber pontificalis* [*CPL* 1568]

Contents: fols. 109–37: Fulbert of Chartres, *Epistolae, tractatus, Sermones* i and vii–viii, *Carmina*; Robert II, king of France and Gauzlin, *Epistolae*

MS: Rud (1825) 106–9; Mynors (1939) no. 39; Behrends (1976) xlvii; Clayton (1985) 219; A.G. Watson (1987a) 22; Meehan (1994b) 439; Toneatto (1994) 324–33; Gullick (1998a) 30 [no. 40]; R. Gameson (1999a) nos. 222–3; Lawrence-Mathers (2003) 45–6, 50; Hartzell (2006) no. 88; Giliberto (2007b) 275–6; T.N. Hall (2007) 257; Barker-Benfield (2008) I.506, 507; Rankin (2012) 506

FACS: Rollason (1998) pl. 6 (c) [fol. 94v (detail)]

ED: Behrends (1976) 2–238 [letters of Fulbert of Chartres coll. as D], 242–70 [poems of Fulbert of Chartres coll. as D]; Giliberto (2007b) 259–60 [*De lapidibus* coll. as D]

ST: Manitius (1911–31) II.242 and n. 1 [Robert II and Gauzlin]; Lambert (1969–72) nos. 200–2, 323, 344–5, 400, 404, 408–9, 411–12, 460, 468, 531, 625; Browne (1988) 154 *et passim*

231. Durham, Cathedral Library, B. II. 13, fols. 7–226

s. xi ex. (before 1096), Normandy, prov. Durham

Contents: Augustine, *Enarrationes in psalmos* [*CPL* 283] (Pss. LI–C); Latin poem [ten hexameters; not in SK, SK Suppl. or WIC] around portrait of William of Saint-Carilef [fol. 102r], inc. 'Optime presul aue dum seruas tempora uite'

[companion vol. to no. **232**]

MS: Rud (1825) 110–11; Mynors (1939) no. 31; T.A.M. Bishop (1954–8a) 198; N.R. Ker (1964) 66; Römer (1972b) 105; A.G. Watson (1987a) 22; Gullick (1990) 67, 79 nn. 31, 32, 80 n. 39; Gullick (1998a) 17 n. 9; R. Gameson (1999a) no. 224; Lawrence-Mathers (2003) 44–6, 50, 81; R. Gameson (2012a) 61 n. 209

DEC: F. Wormald (1945) 130 [repr. F. Wormald (1984) 68]; Rice (1952) 222; R. Gameson (1991) 84 n. 117; R. Gameson (2003) 143 n. 49; R. Gameson (2012c) 281 and n. 107

FACS: H.D. Hughes (1925) pl. opp. p. 14 [fol. 102r (detail)]; F. Wormald (1945) pls. VIII (a), IX (a)–(b) [fols. 28v, 68r, 215v]; Browne (1988) pl. 16 [fol. 102r]; Alexander (1992) pl. 14 [fol. 102r]; Aird (1994) pl. 79 [fol. 102r]; Rollason (1998) pl. 48 [fol. 49r]; R. Gameson (2003) pl. 7 [fol. 49r (detail)]; Lawrence-Mathers (2003) pl. 10 [fol. 181v]

ST: F. Wormald (1945) 129–31 [repr. F. Wormald (1984) 67–8]; Browne (1988) 154 *et passim*; Aird (1994) 293; R. Gameson (1998) 249

232. Durham, Cathedral Library, B. II. 14, fols. 7–200

s. xi ex., Normandy, prov. Durham

Contents: Augustine, *Enarrationes in psalmos* [*CPL* 283] (Pss. CI–CL); verse colophon [inc. 'Hoc exegit opus Guillelmus episcopus illo'; not in SK, SK Suppl. or WIC]

[companion vol. to no. **231**]

MS: Rud (1825) 111–12; Mynors (1939) no. 32; N.R. Ker (1964) 66; *Colophons* no. 5709; Römer (1972b) 105; A.G. Watson (1987a) 22; Gullick (1998a) 17 n. 9; R. Gameson (1999a) no. 225; Lawrence-Mathers (2003) 34, 40–1, 45, 51; Piper (2007) 92; R. Gameson (2012d) 366 and n. 95, 371; Webber (2012) 216 and n. 21

DEC: Dodwell (1954) 116; R. Gameson (1991) 74 *et passim*; R. Gameson (2012c) 281 and n. 107

FACS: Gullick (1990) 68 [fol. 168r]; Lawrence-Mathers (2003) pl. 4 [fol. 7r]

ED: Rud (1825) 111 [verse colophon]

ST: Browne (1988) 154 *et passim*; R. Gameson (1998) 249

233. Durham, Cathedral Library, B. II. 16

s. xi ex., Canterbury StA, prov. Durham before 1100?, (prov. Durham)

Contents: Augustine, *Tractatus in Euangelium Ioannis* [*CPL* 278]

MS: Rud (1825) 112; Mynors (1939) no. 35; T.A.M. Bishop (1955) 1–2; N.R. Ker (1960) 30; Piper (1978) 220 and n. 20; A.G. Watson (1987a) 23; R. Gameson (1995a) 102 n. 28; R. Gameson (1999a) no. 226; Lawrence-Mathers (2003) 38; T.N. Hall (2004b) 97 n. 18; Barker-Benfield (2008) I.lix, 517, 530, III.1821

DEC: Dodwell (1954) 116 n. 2; Lawrence (1982) 102, 103; R. Gameson (1995a) 126 n. 112, 137 n. 161, 139 n. 169; R. Gameson (1998) 248 n. 63 *et passim*; Lawrence-Mathers (2003) 55, 81

FACS: Mynors (1939) pls. 24 (a)–(b) [fols. 76v, 110v]; R. Gameson (1991) fig. 25 [fol. 108v]; R. Gameson (1995a) pl. 12 [fol. 62v]

ST: Römer (1972b) 105; R. Gameson (1998) 250 and n. 75; Pfaff (2009) 65–6

234. Durham, Cathedral Library, B. II. 17

s. xi ex. (before 1096), Normandy, prov. Durham

Contents: Augustine, *Tractatus in Euangelium Ioannis* [*CPL* 278]

MS: Rud (1825) 113; Mynors (1939) no. 36; N.R. Ker (1964) 66; Römer (1972b) 105; A.G. Watson (1987a) 23; Gullick (1990) 69–72; R. Gameson (1998a) 247; Gullick (1998a) 17 n. 9; R. Gameson (1999a) no. 227

DEC: R. Gameson (1995a) 131 n. 138; R. Gameson (1998) 247

FACS: Gullick (1990) 69, 70, 71 [fols. 4v, 5r, 180v]

ST: Browne (1988) 154 *et passim*; R. Gameson (1998) 250 n. 75

235. Durham, Cathedral Library, B. II. 21, fols. 9–158

s. xi ex. (before 1096), Durham

Contents: Augustine, *Epistulae* [*CPL* 262]

MS: Rud (1825) 119–20 [full list of Augustine, *Epistulae*]; Mynors (1939) no. 34; Römer (1972b) 106–7; A.G. Watson (1987a) 23; Gullick (1994) 104, 106; Gullick (1998a) 15 and n. 5, 25; R. Gameson (1999a) no. 229; Lawrence-Mathers (2003) 43–4, 52–3, 61, 71

FACS: Lawrence-Mathers (2003) pl. 5 [fol. 12r]

ST: Browne (1988) 154 *et passim*; R. Sharpe (1998) 299

236. Durham, Cathedral Library, B. II. 22, fols. 27–231

s. xi ex. (before 1096), Durham (or N France?), or Canterbury StA, prov. Durham

Contents: Augustine, *De ciuitate Dei* [*CPL* 313] with *Retractatio* [*CPL* 250] II. xliii; Lanfranc's notes on *De ciuitate Dei* and (add. s. xi/xii) on the Latin translation of Plato's *Timaeus*; grammatical notes (s. xi/xii)

MS: Rud (1825) 121; Mynors (1939) no. 33; Rella (1977) 28; Parkes (1992) 255; Gullick (1994) 101; Gullick (1998a) 25 n. 6; R. Gameson (1999a) 230; Lawrence-Mathers (2003) 22, 38, 43, 54, 56, 81–2, 86; Barker-Benfield (2008) III.1827, 1833

FACS: Parkes (1992) pl. 53 [fol. 181r]; Gullick (1994) pl. 2 (c) [fol. 181r (detail)]; Rollason (1998) pl. 45 [fol. 133v]; Lawrence-Mathers (2003) pl. 3 [fol. 27v]

ST: Römer (1972b) 107; Browne (1988) 154 *et passim*; R. Sharpe (1998) 298

237. Durham, Cathedral Library, B. II. 30 (the 'Durham Cassiodorus')

s. viii$^{2/4}$, Northumbria (York?), (prov. Durham); fols. 3–4 and 265 supply leaves s. xi/xii

Contents: Cassiodorus, *Expositio psalmorum* [*CPL* 900] (breviate version)

MS: Rud (1825) 128–9; *CLA* II (1935) no. 152; Mynors (1939) no. 9; Adriaen (1958) xv–xvi; Lowe (1960) 24; McGurk (1961b) 22 [no. 22]

[repr. McGurk (1998) no. V]; Bischoff (1962) 332; Bailey (1978); T.J. Brown (1982) 110 [repr. T.J. Brown (1993a) 210]; G. Henderson (1982) 29, 42; Webster—Backhouse (1991) no. 89 [Backhouse]; R. Gameson (1994b) 46 n. 103; Netzer (1994) 92, 99, 219–20 n. 25, 235 n. 12; O'Sullivan (1994) 82; M.P. Brown (1996) 172; Parkes (1997b) 102 and n. 7; Webster—Brown (1997) 226 [no. 65]; Gullick (1998a) 27 n. 34; Dumville (1999) 75; Gerchow (1999) 377–8; Gretsch (1999a) 29; Gerchow (2004) 52; Gullick (2004) 32 n. 51; Piper (2007) 88; J.A. Haines (2008) 219–20; Rushforth (2011) 59–60; M.P. Brown (2012) 134 n. 54, 145 and n. 113, 151; R. Gameson (2012a) 25, 37, 42 n. 117, 49, 51, 75; Garrison (2012) 648–9 and n. 90

DEC: Dodwell (1971b) 108–9; T.J. Brown (1972) 230 [repr. T.J. Brown (1993a) 108]; Nordenfalk (1977) 10, 85, 87; Alexander (1978a) no. 17; Bailey (1978) 7-20; D.M. Wilson (1984) 61; Ohlgren (1986) no. 17; Cramp (1989) 225 and n. 42; R. Gameson (1991) 85 n. 129; McGurk (1994b) 17 [repr. McGurk (1998) no. XII]; R. Gameson (1995b) 31 n. 115; M.P. Brown (1996) 76; Gretsch (1999a) 103; Cochrane (2007); Farr (2011b) 219–20

FACS: Westwood (1868) pls. 17–18 [fols. 81v, 172v]; Mynors (1939) pls. 8-10 [fols. 83v, 81v, 172v]; Lowe (1960) pl. XXXVIII (c) [fol. 202v]; Nordenfalk (1977) pls. 27–8 [fols. 81v, 172v]; D.M. Wilson (1984) pls. 31 [fol. 81v], 53 [fol. 172v]; M.P. Brown (1991) pl. 58 [fol. 172v]; T.J. Brown (1993a) ill. 39 [fol. 202v]; M.P. Brown (2007a) pl. 37 [fol. 172v]; J.A. Haines (2008) 221 [fol. 24r], 222 [fol. 172v], 223 [fol. 24r (detail)]

ED: Adriaen (1958) [*Expositiones* on Pss. I, II, III, XX, XXI, CVI, coll. as D]

ST: Lehmann (1917) 361; Mynors (1939) 21–2; T.J. Brown (1972) 245–6 [repr. T.J. Brown (1993a) 272–3 n. 95]; Halporn (1974); Halporn (1981); Bailey (1983); Bailey—Handley (1983); Bullough (1983) 18–22 [links of MS with Alcuin]; Halporn (1985); Halporn (1987); Bonner (1989b) 392; M.P. Brown (1989a) 153 n. 9; Bullough (1991) 54–5, 86 n. 69; *CPPM* II, no. 2121; McGurk (1994b) 10 [repr. McGurk (1998) no. XII]; Knappe (1996) 217–18; Lapidge (1996c) 414; Bullough (2004) 256–8; J.A. Haines (2008); Love (2012) 614–15 and nn. 44–6

238. Durham, Cathedral Library, B. II. 35, fols. 38–118

s. xi ex. (before 1096), Normandy or England, (prov. Durham)

Contents: Bede, *Historia ecclesiastica* [*CPL* 1375]

MS: Rud (1825) 141–4; C. Plummer (1896) I.cv–cvi; Mynors (1939) no. 47; Colgrave–Mynors (1969) xlix; Rella (1977) 29–30; A.G. Watson (1987a) 23; Gullick et al. (1993) 16–17; O'Brien O'Keeffe (1994) 237; Gullick (1998a) 17, 31; Norton (1998) 84 n. 52; R. Gameson (1999a) no. 232; Lawrence-Mathers (2003) 32, 41, 53, 214, 223–5, 231, 256–8

FACS: Rollason (1998) pl. 50 [fol. 77v]; R. Gameson (1999a) pl. 8 [fol. 77v]; Lawrence-Mathers (2003) pl. 6 [p. 72]

ED: C. Plummer (1896) [Bede, *Historia ecclesiastica*, coll. as D]

LANG: O'Brien O'Keeffe (1994) 232

ST: Browne (1988) 155 *et passim*; Meehan (1994b) 440–2, 446; R. Gameson (1998) 242 n. 46; Meehan (1998b) 134–6; Norton (1998) 79–87, 89, 100; Piper (1998b); Story (1998) 212 n. 30; Bullough (2004) 216 n. 261; Westgard (2010)

239. Durham, Cathedral Library, B. III. 1

s. xi ex. (before 1096), Normandy, prov. Durham

Contents: Origen, *Homiliae in Vetus Testamentum: Hom. in Genesin*, trans. Rufinus [*CPG* 1411]; *Hom. in Exodum*, trans. Rufinus [*CPG* 1414]; *Hom. in Leuiticum*, trans. Rufinus [*CPG* 1416]; *Hom. in Iesu Naue*, trans. Rufinus [*CPG* 1420]; *Hom. in librum Iudicum*, trans. Rufinus [*CPG* 1421]; *Hom. in I Reg.*, trans. Rufinus [*CPG* 1423]; *Hom. in Canticum canticorum*, trans. Jerome [*CPG* 1432]; *Hom. in Isaiam*, trans. Jerome [*CPG* 1437]; *Hom. in Hieremiam*, trans. Jerome [*CPG* 1438]; *Hom. in Ezechielem*, trans. Jerome [*CPG* 1441]; Rufinus, *De benedictionibus patriarcharum* [*CPL* 195] (excerpt)

MS: Rud (1825) 145; Mynors (1939) no. 45; T.A.M. Bishop (1949–53) 439; T.A.M. Bishop (1954–8a) 198; Piper (1978) 226 n. 32; A.G. Watson (1987a) 23; Gullick (1990) 63–4; R. Gameson (1999a) no. 233; R. Gameson (2003) 150 and n. 81; Lawrence-Mathers (2003) 45, 52–4

DEC: R. Gameson (1998) 247

FACS: Mynors (1939) pl. 31 [fol. 106v]; Rollason (1998) pl. 46 [fol. 1r]; R. Gameson (2003) pl. 13 [fol. 1r (detail)]

ST: Lambert (1969–72) nos. 206, 209, 212, 214; Browne (1988) 154 *et passim*; R. Sharpe (1998) 298; Piper (2007) 98

240. Durham, Cathedral Library, B. III. 9

s. xi ex., (prov. Durham)

Contents: Gregory (?), *Symbolum fidei* [cf. *CPL* 1714 (p. 558)]; Gregory, *Registrum epistularum* [*CPL* 1714]

MS: Rud (1825) 155; Mynors (1939) no. 41; A.G. Watson (1987a) 23; Lawrence (1994) 459; Gullick (1998a) 15, 24 n. 3; Gullick (1998b) 112 n. 16; R. Gameson (1999a) no. 235; Lawrence-Mathers (2003) 43–4, 56, 63, 71

FACS: Mynors (1939) pl. 39 [fol. 65v]; Rollason (1998) pl. 44 [fol. 1v]; Lawrence-Mathers (2003) pl. 8 [fol. 1v]

ST: Browne (1988) 154 *et passim*

241. Durham, Cathedral Library, B. III. 10

s. xi ex. (before 1096), Normandy, prov. Durham

Contents: Gregory, *Moralia in Iob* [*CPL* 1708], bks. I–XVI

MS: Rud (1825) 156; Mynors (1939) no. 40; T.A.M. Bishop (1949–53) 439; T.A.M. Bishop (1954–8a) 198; N.R. Ker (1972b) 77–8; N.R. Ker (1976b) 27 and n. 1 [repr. N.R Ker (1985) 147 and n. 1]; A.G. Watson (1987a) 23; Browne (1988) 147; Gullick (1998a) 17 n. 9; R. Gameson (1999a) no. 236; Lawrence-Mathers (2003) 45, 53–4, 81

FACS: Rollason (1998) pl. 47 [fol. 3r]

ST: R. Sharpe (1998) 299

241. 3. Durham, Cathedral Library, B. III. 10, fol. ii

s. xi/xii

Contents: unidentified sermon (f)

MS: R. Gameson (1999a) no. 238

241. 5. Durham, Cathedral Library, B. III. 10, fols. 1*bis* and 241

s. xi ex. or xii in., prob. Normandy, prov. Durham

Contents: breviary (f)

MS: Browne (1988) 147–8; R. Gameson (1999a) no. 237

ST: R. Gameson (1998) 237, 250 n. 74

Durham, Cathedral Library, B. III. 10, fols. 239 and 242: see no. **243. 5**

242. Durham, Cathedral Library, B. III. 11, fols. 1–135

s. xi ex., Continent (Liège?), prov. Durham

Contents: Gregory, *Homiliae .xl. in Euangelia* [*CPL* 1711]; homilies (mostly as in Haimo of Auxerre, *Homiliarium*)

MS: Rud (1825) 156–8 [full list of homilies]; Schenkl no. 4429; Mynors (1939) no. 42; A.G. Watson (1987a) 23; R. Gameson (1999a) no. 239; T.N. Hall (2001) 120, 121, 125, 127 [no. 4]; Lawrence-Mathers (2003) 47

ST: Browne (1988) 154 *et passim*; Gneuss (2003b) 297; *CSLMA* III (2010) 350–5 [Haimo]

242. 5. Durham, Cathedral Library, B. III. 11, fols. 136–59

s. xi ex., Liège, (prov. Durham)

Contents: antiphoner

MS: Mynors (1939) no. 42; Hesbert (1963–79) V.8, VI.297, 395 [full list of contents]; Gneuss (1985) 118 and n.; Rankin (1985) 338–9; Browne (1988) 147–8; R. Gameson (1999a) no. 240; Hartzell (2006) no. 90; Steiner (2007)

FACS: Frere (1923) [complete facsimile]; Frere (1894–1932) I, pl. 3 [folio not specified]

ED: Hesbert (1963–79) V.36, 63, 87, 109 *et passim* [coll. as no. 229]

ST: R. Gameson (1998) 250 n. 74

243. Durham, Cathedral Library, B. III. 16

s. xi ex. (before 1096), Normandy, prov. Durham

Contents: Hrabanus Maurus, *Comm. in Matthaeum*, with introductory poem [SK 9447]

MS: Rud (1825) 160; Mynors (1939) no. 44; Dodwell (1954) 115; A.G. Watson (1987a) 23; Gullick (1990) 63, 67; R. Gameson (1999a) no. 245; Lawrence-Mathers (2003) 45–6, 60

FACS: Gullick (1990) 63, 67 [fols. 130v, 131r]

ST: Browne (1988) 154 *et passim*; R. Gameson (1998) 249

243. 5. Durham, Cathedral Library, B. III. 16, fols. 159–60 (with Durham, Cathedral Library, B. II. 10, fols. 239, 242)

s. xi ex., Normandy, prov. Durham

Contents: Augustine, *Sermones* [*CPL* 284] (f)

MS: Rud (1825) 160; Römer (1972b) 111; R. Gameson (1999a) no. 246

244. Durham, Cathedral Library, B. III. 32

s. xi¹ – xi med.; Canterbury, prob. CC (StA?)

Contents: Hymnal°, Monastic canticles°: s. xi²/⁴ ; proverbs⁺*: s. xi med.; Ælfric, *Grammar*⁺*: s. xi¹ or xi med.

MS: Rud (1825) 174 [list of contents]; Joseph Stevenson (1851) x, 171; Mearns (1914) 83; Mynors (1939) no. 22; N.R. Ker (1957) no. 107; Gneuss (1968) 85–90; Korhammer (1976) 75; Dumville (1992a) 20, 107; Hollis – Wright (1992) 34; Vaciago (1993) 11 [no. 40]; Milfull (1996) 27–41; Gneuss (1997) 26–7; Treharne (1998) 242; W. Schipper (2003) 157; Karkov (2004) 93 n. 43; Hartzell (2006) no. 91; *ASMMF* XIV (2007) 59–81 [no. 120; Keefer]; Keefer (2007b) 86, 89–90, 99–100, 109; Barker-Benfield (2008) II.1372, III.1786; Graham (2009) 165; Wieland (2009) 135; R. Gameson (2012a) 16 and n. 10, 60 and n. 204; R. Gameson (2012b) 108 and n. 50; Scragg (2012a) nos. 318–24

DEC: F. Wormald (1935) [comparison with no. **363**]; F. Wormald (1952) 64 [no. 20]; Dodwell (1954) 5, 120; E. Temple (1976) no. 101; Lawrence (1982) 105; Ohlgren (1986) no. 206; R. Gameson (1991) 74 n. 79; R. Gameson (1995b) 114, 193 n. 4, 228, 231–2; Wieland (1998) 3; Keefer (2007b) 99–100

FACS: Mynors (1939) pl. 15 (a) [fol. 2r]; F. Wormald (1952) pl. 29 [fol. 56v]; Korhammer (1976) 246 [fol. 46r]; E. Temple (1976) ill. 315 [fol. 56v]; Milfull (1996) 30–1 [fols. 1v, 2r]; *ASMMF* XIV (2007) no. 120; Keefer (2007b) 110 [fol. 2r]

ED: Zupitza (1880/2001) [Ælfric, *Grammar*, coll. as D]; Hurst – Fraipont (1955) 419–23 [Bede's Ascension Day hymn coll. as *Durh.*]; Arngart (1956) [base MS for OE proverbs on fols. 43v–45v]; Gneuss (1968) 241–2 [base MS for Dunstan hymn]; Korhammer (1976) 254–350 [base MS for Monastic canticles and OE gloss]; Arngart (1981) [base MS for OE proverbs on fols. 43v–45v]; Milfull (1996) [base MS (= D) for Latin hymnal, OE gloss, and trans. of Latin]

LANG: Gneuss (1968) 157–93; Korhammer (1976) 151–235; Hofstetter (1987) 106–16; Milfull (1996) 70–91; Crowley (2000) 142–3, 146–8

ST: Zupitza (1880/2001) v; Gneuss (1968) 85–90, 122, 198, 241, 246, 248 *et passim*; Korhammer (1973) 180–1; F.C. Robinson (1973) 453–5; Hohler (1975) 220 n. 10; Korhammer (1976) 115–21 *et passim*; Arngart (1977) 101–4; Korhammer (1980) 37; Arngart (1981) 188–300; Gneuss (1990) 6 n. 11 [repr. Scragg (2003) 77 n. 11 (text on declinations)];

Blockley (1994) 80; R. Gameson (1995a) 102 n. 28, 111–12 n. 55, 131 n. 135; Springer (1995) 129; Gneuss (1997) 26–7

245. Durham, Cathedral Library, B. IV. 6, fol. 169*

s. vi, Italy, prov. Northumbria

Contents: biblical text (1 Macchabeorum) (f)

MS: Rud (1825) 178–9; *CLA* II (1935) no. 153; Mynors (1939) no. 1; Lowe (1960) 7–8, 17; Bischoff (1966–81) II.329, 331; Piper (1978) 226 n. 32; A.G. Watson (1987a) 24; Marsden (1995) 83–5; R. Gameson (1999a) nos. 252–4; Marsden (1999) 308 n. 97; Lawrence-Mathers (2003) 20; Emms (2006) 20 and n. 18; Wieland (2009) 115; M.P. Brown (2012) 144 and n. 105; Marsden (2012) 415 and n. 39

FACS: Mynors (1939) pl. 1 [recto]; Lowe (1960) pl. II (b) [recto]

ED: C.H. Turner (1909) 541 [complete text]

ST: Lowe (1972b) II.475–6; Marsden (1995) 83–5 *et passim*; R. Sharpe (1998) 298; Love (2012) 612–13 and n. 34

246. Durham, Cathedral Library, B. IV. 9

s. x med., (prov. Durham)

Contents: Gennadius, on Prudentius (*De uiris inlustribus* [*CPL* 957], ch. xiii); Prudentius, *Praefatio operum* [*CPL* 1437], *Cathemerinon* [*CPL* 1438], *Apotheosis* [*CPL* 1439], *Hamartigenia* [*CPL* 1440], *Psychomachia* [*CPL* 1441], *Peristephanon* [*CPL* 1443], *Contra Symmachum* [*CPL* 1442], *Dittochaeon* [*CPL* 1444], *Epilogus* [*CPL* 1445], all glossed; Optatianus Porphyrius, *Carm.* xv [SK 605]

MS: Rud (1825) 181; Bergman (1926) xxxviii–xxxix; Mynors (1939) no. 18; Lavarenne (1943–51) I.xxvi; N.R. Ker (1957) no. 108; M.P. Cunningham (1966) xix; Rella (1977) 161 n. 5; Piper (1978) 226 n. 32; A.G. Watson (1987a) 24; D. Ganz (1993) 173 and n. 28; Dumville (1994a) 150 n. 100; R. Gameson (1996b) 167 n. 150; Hartzell (2006) no. 92; *ASMMF* XIV (2007) 83–97 [no. 121; Keefer]; Wieland (2009) 148; Rankin (2012) 505 n. 112; Scragg (2012a) nos. 325–6

FACS: Mynors (1939) pls. 14 (a)–(b) [fols. 14r, 111r]; *ASMMF* XIV (2007) no. 121

ED: Napier (1900) no. 47 [OE glosses]; Bergman (1926) [Prudentius, *carmina*, coll. as D]; Lavarenne (1943–51) [Prudentius, *carmina*, coll. as D]; M.P. Cunningham (1966) [Prudentius, *carmina*, coll. as D]

ST: Wieland (1985) 168–9 and n. 25, 171; Wieland (1987) 216, 218–21, 225–6; Biggs et al. (1990) 150–6 [Wieland]; Karkov (2001a) 119 n. 22; Petruccione (2008) 250–1

246. 8. Durham, Cathedral Library, B. IV. 12, fols. 1–120

s. xi/xii or xii in., both parts Durham

Contents (fols. 1–38): Fulgentius of Ruspe, *Epist.* viii [*CPL* 817], *De fide ad Petrum* [*CPL* 826]; Gennadius, *Liber siue diffinitio ecclesiasticorum dogmatum* [*CPL* 958]; Augustine, *Serm.* cccli ('De utilitate agendae paenitentiae'), cccxciii ('De paenitentibus') [*CPL* 284 (p. 121), 285 (p. 123)]

Contents (fols. 39–120): Prosper of Aquitaine, *De gratia Dei et libero arbitrio* [*CPL* 523], *Pro Augustino responsiones ad capitula obiectionum Gallorum calumniantium* [*CPL* 520], *Pro Augustino responsiones ad capitula obiectionum Vincentianarum* [*CPL* 521], *Pro Augustino responsiones ad excerpta Genuensium* [*CPL* 522]; Augustine, *De octo Dulcitii quaestionibus* [*CPL* 291], *Serm.* cc [*CPL* 284]; pseudo-Augustine, *Hypomnesticon*, bk. VI [*CPL* 381]; *Sermones app.* cxxi, cxxxviii, cxxxviii; Ambrose, *De mysteriis* [*CPL* 155], *De Spiritu Sancto* [*CPL* 151] (prologue only); *De apologia prophetae Dauid* [*CPL* 135]; pseudo-Jerome, *De essentia diuinitatis* [*Epist. supp.* xiv: see *CPL* 633]

MS: Rud (1825) 183–5; Schenkl no. 4449; Mynors (1939) no. 59; Römer (1972b) 111–12; Gullick (1994) 103–4 and n. 33; Gullick (1998a) 15 n. 5, 17, 19 n. 16, 26 and n. 32 [no. 11]; R. Gameson (1999a) nos. 258–9

FACS: Gullick (1994) pls. 3 (c)–(d) [fols. 121v, 39v (details)]

ST: Lawrence-Mathers (2003) 156–7

247. Durham, Cathedral Library, B. IV. 13

s. xi ex. (before 1096), prov. Durham

Contents: Gregory, *Homiliae in Hiezechielem* [*CPL* 1710]

MS: Rud (1825) 186; Mynors (1939) no. 43; N.R. Ker (1964) 68; A.G. Watson (1987a) 24; Browne (1988) 144, 148, 150, 152, 154; Gullick (1994) 104, 106; Gullick (1998a) 25 n. 7; R. Gameson (1999a) no. 262; T.N. Hall (2001) 132 [no. 6]; Lawrence–Mathers (2003) 43–4, 56, 71

FACS: Gullick (2000) 206 [fols. 1v, 7v]

248. Durham, Cathedral Library, B. IV. 24, fols. 5–127

all parts prov. Durham s. xi/xii (by 1096); numerous later additions, esp. obits

Contents (fol. 5): confraternity conventions (s. xi ex., Durham)

Contents (fols. 6–11): liturgical calendar, with obits but no saints' feasts (s. xi ex)

Contents (fols. 12–45): Usuard of Saint-Germain-des-Prés, *Martyrologium*, with obits; gospel lectionary for use in the Chapter Office (with gospels abbreviated?) (s. xi ex.)

Contents (fols. 47–71): Lanfranc, *Constitutiones* (s. xi ex. [1091×1096], Canterbury CC)

Contents (fol. 74r): William of Saint-Carilef, *Epistola* (s. xi/xii)

Contents (fols. 74v–123): *Regula S. Benedicti*[+*] [*CPL* 1852] (s. xi² or xi/xii)

Contents (fols. 124–7): liturgical and other notes (s. xi/xii)

MS: Rud (1825) 204–18; Glunz (1933) 191; Mynors (1939) no. 51; Knowles (1951) xxiii; N.R. Ker (1957) no. 109; N.R. Ker (1964) 68; Gretsch (1974) 126; Piper (1978) 215–16; A.G. Watson (1987a) 25; Gullick (1994); Piper (1994); Webber (1995) 155; Gullick (1998c) 183–4; R. Gameson (1999a) no. 269; Gretsch (1999a) 227, 245; Knowles—Brooke (2002) xliv; Lawrence-Mathers (2003) 24, 26, 35–6, 42, 56, 58–9, 71, 78, 147; Moore (2004) 101; *ASMMF* XIV (2007) 99–109 [no. 122; Keefer]; Álvarez-López (2007b) 209–23; Scragg (2012a) no. 327; Webber (2012) 216 and nn. 22–4, 217 n. 26

DEC: R. Gameson (1995a) 97, 142

FACS: Mynors (1939) pls. 33 (a)–(b) [fols. 5v, 116r]; Gullick (1998c) 184 [fol. 67v]; Rollason (1998) pls. 6 (d), 42–3 [fols. 33v (detail), 90v, 98v]; Lawrence-Mathers (2003) pl. 2 [fol. 74v]; *ASMMF* XIV (2007) no. 122

ED: Caro (1898) [collates OE 'Rule of St Benedict' with Schröer (1885–8)]; Knowles (1951) 1–149 [base MS for Lanfranc, *Constitutiones*]; Piper (1998a) 187–201 [base MS for obits in calendar and martyrology]; Knowles—Brooke (2002) [Lanfranc, *Constitutiones*, coll. as D]; Rollason (2000) 238–40 [collation of William, *Epistola*]

LANG: Gretsch (1999a) 116, 213

ST: Bischoff (1938) 81, 83; Gretsch (1973) 37–40; Gretsch (1974) 128–37; Wieland (1985) 167; Browne (1988) 155 *et passim*; Piper (1994); R. Gameson (1998) 238; Graham (1998a) 55 n. 15; Gullick (1998a); Piper (1998a); Jayatilaka (2003) 166–73; G. Barrow (2004) 111–13; M.P. Richards (2006) 291; Pfaff (2009) 109, 182

Durham, Cathedral Library, C. III. 13, fols. 192–5: see no. **218**

Durham, Cathedral Library, C. III. 20, fols. 1–2: see no. **218**

249. Durham, Cathedral Library, C. IV. 7, flyleaves

s. viii, prob. Northumbria

Contents: biblical text (Leuiticus XIV, XV, XXVI)

MS: Rud (1825) 297; Schenkl no. 4471; *CLA* II (1935) no. 154; Mynors
(1939) no. 10; Munk Olsen (1982 —) I.322–3 [main MS]; Marsden
(1995) 17 n. 86, 43, 237–40; R. Gameson (1999a) nos. 272–3; Marsden
(2012) 420 and n. 66

FACS: Mynors (1939) pl. 11 [verso of front flyleaf]

249. 3. Durham, Cathedral Library, C. IV. 12, binding strips

s. xi ex., Durham

Contents: Paulus Diaconus, *Homiliarium* (f) [from companion vol. to
nos. **222** and **226**?]

MS: R. Gameson (1999a) no. 275; T.N. Hall (2004b) 87

250. Durham, Dean and Chapter Muniments, Misc. Charter 5670

s. xi[1]

Contents: Psalterium Gallicanum (f)

MS: Mynors (1939) no. 23; Pulsiano (2001a) xxviii

ED: Pulsiano (2001a) 320–35 [fragment coll. as κ]

251. Durham, University Library, Cosin V. v. 6

s. xi[4/4] or xi ex., Canterbury CC, prov. Durham

Contents: gradual with *Kyriale*; *Laudes regiae*; added sequences (s. xi/xii)

MS: Mynors (1939) 47; Anselm Hughes (1972) 4–5; Hartzell (1975);
Gneuss (1985) 104 [no. B.1]; A.G. Watson (1987a) 29; R. Gameson
(1999a) no. 284; Lawrence-Mathers (2003) 37; Hartzell (2006) no. 95;
R. Gameson (2007) 35 [no. 2]; Pfaff (2009) 180–3; R. Gameson (2012a)
70 and n. 242; Pfaff (2012) 347 and n. 24; Rankin (2012) 493 and n. 49,
497 and n. 68

DEC: R. Gameson (1991) 93 n. 173; R. Gameson (1995a) 117 n. 77, 120
n. 86, 143

FACS: Hartzell (1975) pl. III (a) [fol. 40r]; R. Gameson (2007) 34 [fols. 29v–30r, 78v–79r]; R. Gameson (2012) pl. 22.4 [fol. 31v]

ST: Browne (1988) 147; Rankin (1996) 336; R. Gameson (1998) 250 n. 74, 251 n. 77

251. 5. Edinburgh, National Library of Scotland, Advocates 18. 4. 3, fols. 1–122

s. xi ex., (prov. Durham)

Contents: Palladius of Helenopolis, *Historia Lausiaca*, trans. as *Paradisus* by 'Heraclides' [*CPG* 6036; *BHL* 6532, 6534]; Victor of Vita, *Historia persecutionis Africanae prouinciae* [*CPL* 798]; Paschasius Radbertus, *De corpore et sanguine Domini*; Augustine, *Sermo* lii ('De sacramentis altaris') [*CPL* 284 (p. 111)]

MS: Raine (1838) 67, 118; Mynors (1939) no. 60; Römer (1972b) 115; A.G. Watson (1987a) 29; Gullick (1998a) 15, 24 n. 1; Piper (1998b) 311, 316 n. 80; R. Gameson (1999a) nos. 287–8; Gullick (2000) 208 n.; Webber (2012) 216 and n. 19

252. Edinburgh, National Library of Scotland, Advocates 18. 6. 12

s. xi ex. or xii in., (prov. Thorney)

Contents: Persius, *Satirae*; Latin epigram [SK 14414]; Avianus, *Fabulae*; *Cato nouus* (incomplete); Latin poetic fragment [SK 9929]; *Gesta Ludouici imperatoris* [SK 3866] (incomplete); excerpts from Horace, *Epistulae*; three Latin poems [WIC 11654, 13383, 14284 (Marbod of Rennes)]; three Latin epigrams and three riddles; Abbo of Saint-Germain-des-Prés, *Bella Parisiacae urbis*, bk. III; Symposius, *Aenigmata* (incomplete)

MS: Schenkl no. 3030; N.R. Ker (1948–55); A. Vernet (1948) 39–40; N.R. Ker (1964) 189 and n. 5; Lowe (1964) no. 47; A.G. Watson (1969) 18 [repr. A.G. Watson (2004) no. IX]; *CLA* Supplement (1971) no. 1690; I.C. Cunningham (1973) 84–5; Munk Olsen (1982 —) I.446; T. Hunt (1991) I.64–5; R. Gameson (1999a) no. 290; Lendinara (2010) 121–2

FACS: A.G. Watson (1969) pl. V (a) [fol. 1r] [repr. A.G. Watson (2004) no. IX, pl. IX]

ST: Gamber (1968-88) no. 278e; Lapidge (1975a) 75 n. 3 [repr. Lapidge (1993a) 113 n. 3]; Lapidge (1977a) 449; Reeve (1983c) 31 n. 19; Lendinara (1986) 83 nn. 57–8; R. Gameson (1998) 243 n. 50; Biggs et al. (2001) 16 [Lendinara]; Pulsiano (2001b); Lendinara (2011a) 487 and n. 42

253. Edinburgh, National Library of Scotland, Advocates 18. 7. 7

s. x ex., OE glosses partly s. xi, (prov. Thorney)

Contents: Sedulius, Letter I to Macedonius, *Carmen paschale*° [*CPL* 1447], *Hymni* [*CPL* 1449]; four poems on Sedulius [SK 15784, 14842, 14841, 12954]; poem by pseudo-Vergil [SK 16845]

MS: Schenkl no. 3033; N.R. Ker (1948–55); A. Vernet (1948) 38, 50–1; N.R. Ker (1957) no. 111; N.R. Ker (1964) 189; A.G. Watson (1969) 18 [repr. A.G. Watson (2004) no. IX]; I.C. Cunningham (1973) 87–8; Lapidge (1982a) 114 [repr. Lapidge (1996b) 479–80]; Vaciago (1993) 11 [no. 42]; Springer (1995) 48–9; *ASMMF* V (1997) 28–34 [no. 125; I.C. Cunningham]; Wieland (1998) 16 n. 34; Hartzell (2006) no. 96; Scragg (2012a) 329–30

FACS: *ASMMF* V (1997) no. 125

ED: Meritt (1945) no. 30 [OE glosses]

ST: Glauche (1970) 100 n. 89; F.C. Robinson (1973) 458–61, 466 n. 76; Korhammer (1980) 55; Lapidge (1982a) 137 n. 93 [repr. Lapidge (1996b) 483 n. 93]; R.I. Page (1982) 159

254. Edinburgh, National Library of Scotland, Advocates 18. 7. 8
[palimpsest, upper script]

s. xi ex., (prov. Thorney)

Contents: Cicero, *In Catilinam* I–IV; pseudo-Sallust and pseudo-Cicero, *Inuectiuae*; Atticus of Constantinople (?), *Epistula formata*; explanation of Greek letters

MS: Schenkl no. 3034; N.R. Ker (1948–55); A. Vernet (1948) 48–50; A.G. Watson (1969) 18 [repr. A.G. Watson (2004) no. IX]; I.C. Cunningham (1973) 88–9; Munk Olsen (1982—) I.167; L.D. Reynolds (1983a) 350–2; R. Gameson (1999a) no. 291; R. Gameson (2012a) 19 and n. 27

FACS: N.R. Ker (1948–55) pls. III–IV

ED: L.D. Reynolds (1991) 225–37 [Sallust and Cicero, *Inuectiuae*, coll. as S]

ST: Lambert (1969–72) no. 628

255. Edinburgh, National Library of Scotland, Advocates 18. 7. 8
[palimpsest, lower script; fragments]

fols. 1?, 4, 5, 8?, 9, 16, 28, 31: Augustine, *De Trinitate* [*CPL* 329]: s. viii

fols. 12, 13, 23, 30: service-book, prob. sacramentary: s. xi in.

fols. 19, 22: *Passio S. Laurentii* [*CPL* 2219; *BHL* 4754]: s. viii[1]

fols. 26, 33: Gregory, *Homiliae .xl. in Euangelia* [*CPL* 1711]: s. viii ex.

fols. 27, 32 and fols. in 18. 6. 12: unidentified text

MS: N.R. Ker (1948–55); Lowe (1964) no. 47; Gamber (1968–88) no. 278e; *CLA* Supplement (1971) nos. 1689–91; Römer (1972b) 115–16; Clayton (1985) 219 [fols. 26, 33]; T.N. Hall (2001) 122, 126, 128 [no. 6] [fols. 26, 33]; Wieland (2009) 126; and see the references cited for no. **254**, above

255. 5. Edinburgh, University Library, 56 (D. b. III. 8)

s. xi[1], Ireland or Scotland, in Scotland or England by s. xi[2]

Contents: Psalterium Hebraicum

MS: Borland (1916) 100–2, 327 [W.M. Lindsay]; McRoberts (1953) 3 [no. 4]; Finlayson (1962); Gjerløw (1980) I.169; Dumville (1992a) 112 n. 111; Dumville (2007d) 83–6, 88; Rushforth (2007) 76

DEC: N. Edwards (2012) 248

FACS: Finlayson (1962) [complete facsimile]; Borland (1916) pl. XV [fol. 50v]; Rushforth (2007) 77 [fol. 50r]

ST: McNamara (1973) 243–4; *BCLL* (1985) nos. 511, 1031

Eton College 220, no. 1: see no. **669**

256. Exeter, Cathedral Library, 3500

c. 1086, prob. Salisbury, (prov. Exeter)

Contents: Exon Domesday

MS: N.R. Ker (1962–92) II.800–7; Galbraith (1974) 184–8; N.R. Ker (1976b) 35 [repr. N.R. Ker (1985) 156]; Rumble (1985); Webber (1989); Webber (1992) 13–17; Conner (1993) 4; Pfaff (1994) 74; R. Gameson (1999a) no. 294; Webber (2012) 220

FACS: N.R. Ker (1976b) pl. III [fol. 9r] [repr. N.R. Ker (1985) pl. 20 (a)]

ST: Galbraith (1974) 64–72 *et passim*; Keynes (2006) R 231

Exeter, Cathedral Library, 3501, fols. 0–7: see no. **15**

257. Exeter, Cathedral Library, 3501, fols. 8–130 (the 'Exeter Book')

s. x[2], prob. SW England (or Canterbury CC??), prov. Exeter by s. xi[3/4]

Contents (OE poetry): *Christ I-III***; *Guthlac* (A and B)**; *Azarias***; *Phoenix***; *Juliana***; *Wanderer***; *Seafarer***; *Widsith***; *Maxims I***; *Riming Poem***; *Physiologus*** (*Panther***, *Whale*** and *Partridge***); *Soul and Body II***; *Deor***; *Wulf and Eadwacer***; Riddles**; *Wife's Lament***; *Judgement Day I***; *Husband's Message***; *Ruin***; other shorter poems**

MS: Chambers et al. (1933) 55–67 [Förster]; Krapp–Dobbie (1936) ix-xxv; N.R. Ker (1957) no. 116; N.R. Ker (1964) 82; Parkes (1976b) 163 [repr. Parkes (1991) 160]; Drage (1978) 347–8; Pope (1978); McGovern (1983); Backhouse et al. (1984b) no. 153; J. Hill (1986); J. Hill (1988) 4–9; Muir (1991b); Dumville (1992a) 83; Conner (1993); Conner (1994); Pfaff (1994) 61; R. Gameson (1996b); Brantley (1999) 50 n. 22, 61–2; Lapidge (2000a) 13; Muir (2000) I.1–44; Orton (2001) 213, 222; W. Schipper (2003) 161; R.M. Butler (2004) 175, 178–9, 181, 183, 195–6, 199–204, 205–7; Roberts (2005) 60–2 [no. 11]; C. Bishop (2007b) 97–9; Rambaran–Olm (2007) 207; Cucina (2008) [bibliography]; Graham (2009) 189; Treharne (2009b) 99–101; Crick (2012) 181; R. Gameson (2012a) 24, 58–9 and n. 199; Raw (2012) 460; Scragg (2012a) no. 341

DEC: R. Gameson (1995b) 223 n. 183

FACS: Chambers et al. (1933) [complete facsimile]; Muir (2006) [complete electronic facsimile]; [facsimiles of individual leaves are too numerous to list, but note *inter alia permulta*]: Conner (1993) pls. I–VII [fols. 20v, 53r, 98r, 100r, 125r, 125v (details)]; R. Gameson (1996b) pls. III–IV [fols. 45v, 1v]; Lapidge (2000a) 13 [fol. 45v (details)]; Roberts (2005) pl. 11 [fol. 32v]; Owen-Crocker (2009) figs. 4.1 [fol. 8r], 6.15 [fol. 9r]

ED [note that early editions and partial editions are not recorded]: **complete manuscript:** Krapp–Dobbie (1936), Muir (1994) [2nd ed. 2000]; **individual poems: Juliana:** Woolf (1955; rev. 1978); **Christ I:** J.J. Campbell (1959); **Seafarer:** Gordon (1960), Pope (1981), Klinck (1992), Cucina (2008); **Widsith:** Chambers (1912), Malone (1962); **Wanderer:** Leslie (1966; rev. 1985), Dunning–Bliss (1969), Pope (1981), Klinck (1992); **Azarias:** Farrell (1974); **Maxims:** Shippey (1976); **Deor:** Malone (1977), Pope (1981); **Riddles:** Williamson (1977); **Resignation:** Malmberg (1979; rev. 1982); **Guthlac:** Roberts (1979); **Wife's Lament, Husband's Message, Ruin:** Leslie (1988); **Phoenix:** N.F. Blake (1990)

LANG: Govern (1983) 90–9

ST: Chambers et al. (1933); K. Sisam (1953a) 31–2, 97–108, 291–2; Pope (1969) [study of missing leaf]; Pope (1974) [study of lacuna]; Bliss — Frantzen (1976) 385–402 [reconstruction and dislocation]; Pope (1978) 25–65; Greenfield — Robinson (1980) 20–1 [bibliography]; Pope (1981) [damage and reconstruction]; O'Brien O'Keeffe (1985) [Riddle 40]; Muir (1989); Muir (1991a); Muir (1991b); Kiernan (1994a) 42, 44–6; Frank (1998) 207–21; Brantley (1999) [*Descent into Hell*]; R.M. Butler (2004); J. Hill (2005a) 85; Rambaran-Olm (2007) 207–8 [*Descent into Hell*]; Treharne (2007a) 262; Cucina (2008); Scragg (2012b) 553–4

258. Exeter, Cathedral Library, 3507

s. x², S England (Canterbury CC or Sherborne?), prov. Exeter s. xi²

Contents: Hrabanus Maurus, *De computo*; Latin verses [SK 7632 (= Vergil, *Georg.* I.231-9), 6489, 12559 (Ausonius), 3727, 12524, 1716, 8931, 12491]; prose notes on computus; Greek, Hebrew and three runic alphabets; Isidore, *De natura rerum* [*CPL* 1188]

MS: Schenkl no. 3787; R. Derolez (1954) 219–37; N.R. Ker (1957) no. 116*; N.R. Ker (1962–92) II.813–14; N.R. Ker (1964) 82; N.R. Ker (1976b) 24, 35 [repr. N.R. Ker (1985) 144, 156]; Drage (1978) 349–50; Conner (1993) 4, 86–9 *et passim*; Dumville (1992a) 64, 82 and n. 88; Dumville (1993g) 100 n. 89; R. Gameson (1996b) 162–4 and n. 128; Chardonnens (2007b) 546; Wieland (2009) 153; R. Gameson (2012a) 67 n. 232; D. Ganz (2012) 194 and n. 39; Scragg (2012a) no. 342

DEC: R. Gameson (2012c) 262 n. 38

FACS: Conner (1993) pls. XII–XIII [fols. 12v, 68r]

ST: Thiel (1969) 125 [Hebrew alphabet]; Bullough (1977) 50 n. 61b; Munk Olsen (1982 —) II.336; Muir (1991b); Gneuss (1992) 124 n. 66 [Hebrew alphabet]; R. McKitterick (2012) 328

258. 3. Exeter, Cathedral Library, 3512

s. xi ex., Exeter?, (prov. ibid.)

Contents: *Collectio Lanfranci* [*Decreta pontificum* only]

[companion vol. to no. **601. 5**]

MS: N.R. Ker (1962–92) II.819–21; N.R. Ker (1964) 82; R. Gameson (1996b) 154; R. Gameson (1999a) no. 295; Kéry (1999) 240–1; Gullick (2001b) 110–11

258. 8. Exeter, Cathedral Library, 3548A

s. x^1, N France or Brittany, prov. Exeter possibly s. xi^2

Contents: missal (f)

MS: Lega–Weekes (1916–17); Förster (1933a) 25 n. 77; N.R. Ker (1962–92) II.839–40 [erroneously classed as 'Sacramentarium']; Drage (1978) 351–2; Hartzell (1989) 86 n. 108; Dumville (1992a) 67, 76, 89, 155; Conner (1993) 5, 14, 17, 20

259. Exeter, Cathedral Library, 3548C

s. x^2 or x ex., Winchester?, prov. s. xi prob. Exeter

Contents: benedictional (f)

MS: S.F.H. Robertson (1905); Förster (1933a) 26 n. 87; N.R. Ker (1962–92) II.840–1; Brückmann (1973) 419; Drage (1978) 353–4; Dumville (1992a) 69, 77, 84–5, 89; Conner (1993) 5, 18, 20, 28, 42–3; Dumville (1993g) 145 n. 23; R. Gameson (1996b) 152 and n. 67

FACS: S.F.H. Robertson (1905) [fol. 1r]

259. 5. Exeter, Cathedral Library, FMS/1, 2, 2a

s. x^1, N France?

Contents: Orosius, *Historiae aduersum paganos* [*CPL* 571] (f)

MS: N.R. Ker (1962–92) II.845; Drage (1978) 355; Conner (1993) 5, 14, 17, 20, 28; R. Gameson (1996b) 152 and n. 68; Wieland (2009) 142

260. Exeter Cathedral, FMS/3

s. x in. or x^1, England, (prov. Exeter)

Contents: *Vita S. Basilii* [*BHL* 1023] (f)

MS: N.R. Ker (1962–92) II.845; Drage (1978) 356; Dumville (1987) 171; Conner (1993) 5, 14, 20, 28–9; R. Gameson (1996b) 152; Corona (2002); Corona (2006) 39–40, 139–40, 193, 198

261. Glasgow, University Library, Hunterian 431 (V. 5. 1), fols. 1–102

s. x/xi or xi in., (prov. Worcester) [fols. 103–58 supplied s. xii in.]

Contents: Gregory, *Regula pastoralis* [*CPL* 1712]

MS: Young—Aitken (1908) 354–5; N.R. Ker (1960) 8, 52; N.R. Ker
(1964) 206; Rella (1977) 84, 159; Clement (1984a) 41; Clement (1985a)
13; Franzen (1991) 29, 71–2, 128; Dumville (1993g) 55 n. 245;
R. Gameson (1996a) 238; R. Gameson (1999a) no. 303 [fols. 103–58];
Schreiber (2003) 24 and n. 11; R. Gameson (2005a) 97

ST: R. Gameson (1996a) 238; R. Gameson (1998) 242 n. 45; Collier (2000)
195 n. 1, 199–205

262. Gloucester Cathedral, 35

s. xi¹, xi med., xi², (prov. Gloucester, all fragments)

Contents: Ælfric, Homilies* (f), Lives of Saints* (f) [s. xi¹]; Life of
St Mary of Egypt* (f) [s. xi med.]; *Regula S. Benedicti*, ch. iv* (f) [s. xi²]

MS: N.R. Ker (1957) no. 117; N.R. Ker (1972a) 5; Gretsch (1973) 43–4;
Gretsch (1974) 126–37; Godden (1979) lvii; Scragg (1979) 263; Scragg
(1996) 220 [art. 2]; Clemoes (1997) 55–6; Gretsch (1999a) 227; Magennis
(2002) 16 nn. 47–9; Lapidge (2003a) 580; Scragg (2012a) nos. 346–9

FACS: Earle (1861) [collotype facsimiles of the leaves containing Ælfric's
'Life of St Swithun' and the anonymous 'Life of St Mary of Egypt']

ED: Earle (1861) 112 [base MS for OE Rule of St Benedict, ch. iv];
Needham (1976) [Ælfric, 'Life of St Swithun', coll. as G]; Godden
(1979) 221–2 [Ælfric, CH II, Hom. XXIV, coll. as fᵈ]; Clemoes (1997)
398–9 [Ælfric, CH I, Hom. XXVI, coll. as fᵈ]; Lapidge (2003a) 590–
608 [Ælfric, 'Life of St Swithun', coll. as G]

ST: J. Hill (1996) 244; Biggs et al. (2001) 322; Lapidge (2003a) 582–5

262. 5. Gloucester, Gloucestershire Record Office, D 2700 (single leaf)

[the shelfmark refers to a collection of fragments of which the single leaf
containing Venantius is but one; the collection, which formerly was
part of the Duke of Beaufort Muniments, is on (temporary) deposit
in the Gloucestershire Record Office]

s. x³/⁴, Canterbury?

Contents: Venantius Fortunatus, *Carmina* [*CPL* 1033], bk. V, Praefatio (f)

MS: N. Davis (1969) 447–8; R.W. Hunt (1979) 280

ED: R.W. Hunt (1979) 281 [Venantius Fortunatus coll. as Y]

ST: N. Davis (1969) 448, 450–1; R.W. Hunt (1979) 281

263. Hereford, Cathedral Library, O. III. 2

s. ix², France, prov. England (Salisbury?) s. xi ex., (prov. Hereford by
s. xii med.)

Contents: Jerome, *De uiris inlustribus* [*CPL* 616]; *Decretum Gelasianum de
libris recipiendis et non recipiendis* [*CPL* 1676]; Gennadius, *De uiris
inlustribus* [*CPL* 957]; Augustine, *Retractationes* [*CPL* 250]; Cassiodorus,
Institutiones [*CPL* 906], bk. I; Isidore, *In libros ueteris et noui Testamenti
prooemia* [*CPL* 1192], *De ecclesiasticis officiis* [*CPL* 1207] (excerpts), *De
ortu et obitu patrum* [*CPL* 1191], *Allegoriae quaedam S. Scripturae* [*CPL*
1190]; excerpt from a grammarian 'Terrentius'

MS: Schenkl no. 4090; A.T. Bannister (1927) 28–9; Mynors (1937) xv–xvi,
xlvii–xlix; N.R. Ker (1960) 11; N.R. Ker (1964) 97; Mutzenbecher
(1974) xl; Rella (1977) 22–3; N.R. Ker (1976b) 30 [repr. N.R. Ker
(1985) 150]; Webber (1992) 35–6, 46, 57; Mynors—Thomson (1993)
17–18; Bischoff (1998—) I, no. 1523; Barker-Benfield (2008) I.508, 510;
R. Gameson (2012d) 368 and n. 103, 364 n. 105

ED: Mynors (1937) [Cassiodorus, *Institutiones* bk. I, coll. as H; and p. xv
n. (the excerpt from 'Terrentius')]

ST: Lambert (1969–72) no. 260; Römer (1972b) 126; Löfstedt (1981)
161–2 ['Terrentius']; R. McKitterick (1989a) 206–7; R. Gameson (1998)
232 n. 7; D. Ganz (2004) 502; R. McKitterick (2012) 329 [MS erroneously cited as O. II. 2]

263. 5. Hereford, Cathedral Library, O. III. 6, fol. 1

s. x ex., (prov. Hereford, Franciscans)

Contents: sacramentary (f)

MS: Schenkl no. 4094; A.T. Bannister (1927) 31-2; Mynors—Thomson
(1993) 20

264. Hereford, Cathedral Library, O. VI. 11

s. xi ex., (prov. Hereford, St Guthlac's Priory)

Contents: Paschasius Radbertus, *De assumptione B.V.M.* [cf. *CPL* 633];
Jerome, *Epist.* xxxix, xxxi, liv, xxii; 'Martinellus': Sulpicius Severus,
Vita S. Martini [*CPL* 475], *Epist.* I and III [*CPL* 476]; Gregory of
Tours, excerpts from *De uirtutibus S. Martini* [*CPL* 1024; cf. *BHL*
5618d] and *Historia Francorum* [*CPL* 1023], *Vita S. Bricii* [*BHL* 1452,

from *Historia Francorum*, II.1]; Sulpicius Severus, *Dialogi* II, III, I [*CPL* 477]; Guitmund of Aversa, *Confessio de S. Trinitate*; Odo of Glanfeuil (pseudo-Faustus), *Vita S. Mauri* [*BHL* 5772]; two responsories for St Peter (additions, including WIC 12877a)

MS: Schenkl no. 4144; A.T. Bannister (1927) 69–70; N.R. Ker (1964) 99; Mynors–Thomson (1993) 44; R. Gameson (1999a) no. 309; Hartzell (2006) no. 108

FACS: Owen-Crocker (2009) fig. 1.8 [fol. 48v]

ST: Lambert (1969–72) no. 309; Biggs et al. (2001) 330–2, 338–9

265. Hereford, Cathedral Library, O. VIII. 8

s. xi ex., prov. Hereford

Contents: *Collectio Lanfranci* [*Concilia, Decreta pontificum*]

MS: Schenkl no. 4165; A.T. Bannister (1927) 87; Z.N. Brooke (1931) 97, 231–5; S. Williams (1971) 80 ['Excerpta 5']; Mynors–Thomson (1993) 57; R. Gameson (1999a) no. 310; Kéry (1999) 116, 240; Gullick (2000) 208 n.; Gullick (2001) 103–5, 117; Gullick (2012) 303 and n. 52; Webber (2012) 222 and n. 57

FACS: Gullick (2001) pl. 34 [fol. 45r (detail)]

265. 5. Hereford, Cathedral Library, O. IX. 2

s. xi ex.

Contents: Old Testament (Samuhel, Regum, Isaias, Hieremias, Hiezechiel, Danihel, Prophetae minores)

MS: Schenkl no. 4171; A.T. Bannister (1927) 91; Mynors–Thomson (1993) 60; R. Gameson (1999a) no. 311; R. Gameson (2012a) 45 n. 132

266. Hereford, Cathedral Library, P. I. 2 (the 'Hereford Gospels')

s. viii med., W Midlands or Wales, prov. Hereford s. xi[1]

Contents: gospels (incomplete); records* (added s. xi med.)

MS: Schenkl no. 4181; Lindsay (1912a) 41–3; A.T. Bannister (1927) 98–9; Glunz (1933) 66; Hopkin-James (1934); *CLA* II (1935) no. 157; McGurk (1956) 266 [repr. McGurk (1998) no. I]; N.R. Ker (1957) no. 119; McGurk (1961a) no. 15; Sawyer (1968) nos. 1462, 1469 [OE records]; Bischoff (1986) 121; McGurk (1987) 174 [repr. McGurk

(1998) no. II]; Sims-Williams (1990) 181; Webster—Backhouse (1991) 127–8 [no. 91]; Dumville (1992a) 118 and n. 120; Mynors—Thomson (1993) 65–6; R. Gameson (1994b) 40–3, 48; Dumville (1999) 123; R. Gameson (2000a); Huws (2000) 5; R. Gameson (2002c); Karkov (2006a) 58 and n. 39; M.P. Brown (2012) 135; R. Gameson (2012a) 19 and n. 27, 37 and n. 90, 43, 49 and n. 149, 53 n. 182, 67 n. 234, 74 n. 254; R. Gameson (2012b) 115 and n. 86; Marsden (2012) 419 and nn. 63–4; McKee (2012a) 168; Scragg (2012a) nos. 350, 350a, 351

DEC: Glunz (1933) 66; McGurk (1955b) 106–7 [repr. McGurk (1998) no. IV]; Alexander (1978a) no. 38; Ohlgren (1986) no. 38; Webster—Backhouse (1991) 127–8; R. Gameson (1994b) 40–2; N. Edwards (2012) 245–6; R. Gameson (2012c) 289 n. 141

FACS: *NPS* I, pls. 233 [fols. 102r, 106r], 234 [fols. 134v, 135r]; Alexander (1978a) ills. 197–9 [fols. 1r, 36r, 102r]; Webster—Backhouse (1991) 127 [fol. 102r]; R. Gameson (2012) pl. 9.1 [fol. 102r]

ED: A.J. Robertson (1939) nos. 78, 99 [records]; B. Fischer (1988–91) [gospel excerpts coll. as Hh]

ST: McGurk (1956) 263 [repr. McGurk (1998) no. I]; T.J. Brown (1984) 326 [repr. T.J. Brown (1993a) 239]; P. Wormald (1988a) 264 [no. 80 = Sawyer (1968) no. 1462]; McGurk (1994b) 22 [repr. McGurk (1998) no. XII]; Keynes (2000) 16–18 [records]

266. 5. Hereford, Cathedral Library, P. I. 10

s. xi/xii, W England

Contents: Didymus of Alexandria, *De Spiritu Sancto* trans. Jerome [*CPG* 2544]; pseudo-Augustine and pseudo-Orosius, *Dialogus quaestionum .lxv.* [*CPL* 373a]; Vigilius of Thapsus (?), *Contra Felicianum Arianum* [*CPL* 808]; Augustine, *Epist.* cxxx ('De orando Deo') [*CPL* 262], *Sermo* xxxvii [*CPL* 284 (p. 111)], *De octo Dulcitii quaestionibus* [*CPL* 291]; two anonymous short patristic texts (pseudo-Gregory, *De iuramentis episcoporum*; *Multis modis dimittitur peccatum*)

MS: Schenkl no. 4189; A.T. Bannister (1927) 106–7; Chaplais (1987) *passim*; Mynors—Thomson (1993) 69–70; R. Gameson (1999a) no. 314; P.R. Robinson (2003) I, no. 127

ST: Siegmund (1949) 66 [Didymus]; Lambert (1969–72) no. 258; Römer (1972b) 128

267. Hereford, Cathedral Library, P. II. 5, fols. 1–145

s. xi²

Contents: Palladius of Helenopolis, *Historia Lausiaca*, trans. in Latin as *Paradisus* by 'Heraclides' [*CPG* 6036; *BHL* 6532, 6534]; Leontius of Cyprus, *Vita S. Iohannis Eleemosynarii* trans. Anastasius Bibliothecarius [*BHL* 4388]; Iohannes Diaconus, *Vita S. Nicholai* [*BHL* 6104–5]

MS: Schenkl no. 4201; A.T. Bannister (1927) 119–20; Dumville (1992a) 140; Mynors—Thomson (1993) 76; R. Gameson (1999a) no. 315

ST: Judge (1934) 92–3; Siegmund (1949) 126 [Palladius]; Biggs et al. (2001) 269–70 [*Vita Iohannis Eleemosynarii*], 356–60 [*Vita S. Nicholai*]; Wellhausen (2003) v [Palladius]

268. Hereford, Cathedral Library, P. II. 10, fols. i and 61

s. viii, prob. Northumbria

Contents: pseudo-Alcuin, *Liber quaestionum in euangeliis* [*CPL* 1168; *BCLL* 1267] (f, from Matthew)

MS: Schenkl no. 4025a; A.T. Bannister (1927) 124; Glunz (1933) 18; *CLA* II (1935) no. 158; Lowe (1960) 19; McGurk (1961b) 11 [no. 24] [repr. McGurk (1998) no. V]; Bischoff (1966–81) I.245, II.330, 338; Biggs et al. (1990) 102–4 [C.D. Wright]; Sims-Williams (1990) 183 and n. 32; Dumville (1992a) 105; Mynors—Thomson (1993) 78; Rittmueller (2004) 63*–67*, 140*–142*, 215*

FACS: Lowe (1960) pl. XV (a)–(b)

ED: Rittmueller (2004) [*Liber quaestionum in euangeliis* coll. as He]

ST: *BCLL* (1985) no. 1267; *CSLMA* II (1999) 471–3

268. 2. Hereford, Cathedral Library, P. V. 1, fols. 1–28

s. xi/xii or xii in., prob. CaCC (prov. Battle)

Contents: Lanfranc, *Constitutiones*; Vigilius of Thapsus (?), *Contra Felicianum Arianum* [*CPL* 808]

MS: Schenkl no. 4237; Knowles (1951) xxiii–xxiv; Römer (1972b) 129; Mynors—Thomson (1993) 95–6; R. Gameson (1999a) no. 319; Knowles—Brooke (2002) xliv–xlv

ED: Knowles—Brooke (2002) 2–220 [Lanfranc, *Constitutiones*, coll. as H]

268. 4. Hereford, Cathedral Library, P. VI. 1, fol. 177

s. x^2

Contents: missal or sacramentary (?) (f)

MS: Schenkl no. 4252; A.T. Bannister (1927) 160–1; Dumville (1992a) 68; Mynors—Thomson (1993) 103

ED: L.E.G. Brown (1904) 207–8

268. 6. Hertford, Hertfordshire Record Office, Gorhambury X. D. 4. B and X. D. 4. C

s. xi^2, prov. St Albans?

Contents: Office lectionary (f)

MS: R.M. Thomson (1982a) I.77; A.G. Watson (1987a) 59; R. Gameson (1999a) no. 324

Kingston Lacy, Dorset, National Trust: see no. **501. 3**

Langley Marish, Buckinghamshire, Parish church: see no. **501**

Leeds, University Library: see no. **696**

269. Lichfield, Cathedral Library, 1 (the 'St Chad Gospels')

s. viii$^{2/4}$ or viii med., W Midlands or Northumbria?, prov. Wales (prob. Llandeilo Fawr, Carmarthenshire) s. ix, prov. Lichfield prob. s. x^1; Welsh, Latin and Old English marginalia s. viii/ix – xi^1 [no Welsh additions before s. ix (?); the OE record is s. xi^1]

Contents: gospels (incomplete); record*

MS: Westwood (1868) 56–8; Scrivener (1887) v–vi; Lindsay (1912a) 1–7, 46–7; Savage (1915) 5–21; Kenney (1929) no. 468; *CLA* II (1935) no. 159; N.R. Ker (1942–3) 4; McGurk (1956) 266 [repr. McGurk (1998) no. I]; N.R. Ker (1957) no. 123; McGurk (1961a) no. 16; McGurk (1962) 22, 30 [repr. McGurk (1998) no. VII]; N.R. Ker (1962–92) III.113–14; N.R. Ker (1964) 115, 119; R. Powell (1965); Stein (1981); McGurk (1987) 174 [repr. McGurk (1998) no. II]; M.P. Brown (1989a) 156, 160; Bruce-Mitford (1989) 176, 185, 187; P.L. Heyworth (1989) 10, 126, 142, 165, 180, 182, 188, 209; R.I. Page (1989) 258; Webster—Backhouse (1991) no. 90; Dumville (1992a) 104 n. 45, 117–18, 120; T.J. Brown (1993a) 109, 273 n. 95; McGurk (1994b) 19, 21 [repr. McGurk (1998) no. XII]; Webster—Brown (1997) 232 [no. 82]; Huws (2000) 5, 7, 9; M.P. Brown (2003a) 255, 257–8, 265, 380–3 *et passim*; Rumble (2006b) 12 and n. 66; M.P. Brown (2012) 134 n. 55, 135, 150, 151, 153–4 and n. 158; R. Gameson (2012a) 28 n. 59, 43, 52, 67, 80; McKee (2012a) 168; McKee (2012b) 338–9; Scragg (2012a) no. 353

DEC: Kendrick (1938) 137–9; McGurk (1961a) no. 16; Nordenfalk (1977) 76–83; Alexander (1978a) no. 21; D.M. Wilson (1984) 87; Ohlgren (1986) no. 21; G. Henderson (1987) 122–9; M.P. Brown (2007d); M.P. Brown (2008); M.P. Brown (2011b) 34–7; Tilghman (2011) 93–4; R. Gameson (2012c) 289 n. 141; Netzer (2012) 230; N. Edwards (2012) 244–5

FACS: Scrivener (1887) frontispiece, vii, 3 [pp. 5, 43, 217]; Lindsay (1912a) pls. I–II [pp. 141, 218]; Nordenfalk (1977) pls. 23–6 [pp. 5, 142, 218, 220]; Alexander (1978a) ills. 76–82 [pp. 4, 5, 142, 218, 219, 220, 221]; D.M. Wilson (1984) pls. 32 [p. 218], 98–9 [pp. 5 (detail), 221]; G. Henderson (1987) pls. 180–2 [pp. 218, 5, 220], 184–6 [pp. 220, 142, 221]; Webster—Backhouse (1991) pl. 90 [pp. 220–1]; Huws (2000) pl. 1 [pp. 2, 141]; M.P. Brown (2007a) pls. 31–2 [pp. 5, 218]; Charles-Edwards—McKee (2008) pl. I [p. 141]; R. Gameson (2012) pl. 5.1 [p. 141]

ED: Scrivener (1887) [coll. with gospel text of no. **825**]; J. Wordsworth et al. (1889–1954) [gospels coll. as L]; Hopkin-James (1934) [base MS for gospels]; N.R. Ker (1957) 158 [OE record]; B. Fischer (1988–91) [gospel excerpts coll. as Hl]

LANG: Scrivener (1887) vii–xvi [orthography of biblical text]

ST: Scrivener (1887); Bradshaw (1889) 458; McGurk (1956) 263 [repr. McGurk (1998) no. I]; McGurk (1961a) 11 [repr. McGurk (1998) no. VI]; M. Richards (1973); Jenkins—Owen (1983); Jenkins—Owen (1984); D. Brown (1982); *BCLL* (1985) no. 156; Dumville (1987) 160 and nn. 66, 68; P. Wormald (1988a) 264 [no. 78] [OE record]; R. Gameson (1994b) 38; P. James (1996); Keynes (1996a) 55 [English names; OE record]; Eberlein (2003) 388, 391 [medieval price of MS]; Charles-Edwards—McKee (2008); Charles-Edwards (2012) 390 and nn. 6–7

269. 1. Lichfield, Cathedral Library, 1a

s. x², France?

Contents: Boethius, *In categorias Aristotelis* [*CPL* 882] (f); Aristotle, *De interpretatione*, trans. Boethius [*CPL* 883] (f)

MS: N.R. Ker (1962–92) III.113–14; Gibson et al. (1995–2001) I.107–8 [no. 78]

270. Lincoln, Cathedral Library, 1 (A. 1. 2) (with Cambridge, Trinity College, B. 5. 2)

both vols. s. xi ex. or xi/xii, E England (Lincoln?), prov. Lincoln

Contents: two-volume Bible: Genesis — Iob, Psalterium Gallicanum [Lincoln MS], Prouerbia Salomonis — Macchabeorum, New Testament (lacking some Epistulae) [Trinity MS]

MS: Schenkl no. 3831; M.R. James (1900–4) I.182–6; Woolley (1927) 1–2; N.R. Ker (1964) 116; R.M. Thomson (1989) 3; R. Gameson (1999a) nos. 154 [Trinity], 328 [Lincoln]; Biggs (2007a) 58; Shepard (2007) 270; Marsden (2012) 426 and nn. 95–6

DEC: C.M. Kauffmann (1975) no. 13

FACS: C.M. Kauffmann (1975) ills. 30–1 [fols. 71v, 86v]; R. Gameson (1999a) pl. 12 [Trinity B. 5. 2, fol. 129v]

ST: Glunz (1933) 230

271. Lincoln, Cathedral Library, 13 (A. 1. 26)

s. xi ex. or xi/xii, (prov. Lincoln)

Contents: Augustine, *De Genesi ad litteram* [*CPL* 266] with *Retractationes* [*CPL* 250] I. xviii, *De Genesi contra Manichaeos* [*CPL* 265]; pseudo-Augustine and pseudo-Orosius, *Dialogus quaestionum .lxv.* [*CPL* 373a]

MS: Schenkl no. 3850; Woolley (1927) 6–7; N.R. Ker (1964) 116; Römer (1972b) 135; A.G. Watson (1987a) 44; R.M. Thomson (1989) 12; R. Gameson (1999a) no. 331

272. Lincoln, Cathedral Library, 106 (A. 4. 14)

s. xi ex. or xi/xii, Normandy or England?

Contents: *Collectio Lanfranci* [*Concilia* (excerpts)]; *Canones Apostolorum*; Gregory, *Epist.* I.24 [*CPL* 1714]; first four Ecumenical Councils (Nicaea, Constantinople, Ephesus, Chalcedon); Atticus of Constantinople (?) *Epistola formata*; Greek alphabet

MS: Woolley (1927) 69–70; Z.N. Brooke (1931) 80, 232, 237; S. Williams (1971) 83 ['Excerpta 17']; R.M. Thomson (1989) 79–80; Kéry (1999) 241

273. Lincoln, Cathedral Library, 158 (C. 2. 2)

s. xi ex., Normandy or England

Contents: Paulus Diaconus, *Homiliarium* (beginning of Lent to Easter vigil, Sanctorale 25 Jan.– 30 Nov., Commune sanctorum)

MS: Schenkl no. 4022; Woolley (1927) 119–34; Smetana (1978) 86 [unreliable]; Clayton (1985) 219; A.G. Watson (1987a) 45 and n. 2; M.P. Richards (1988) 119–23; R.M. Thomson (1989) 124–7; R. Gameson (1999a) no. 340; T.N. Hall (2001) nos. 16 [134], 18 [125, 127]; Hartzell (2006) no. 116; T.N. Hall (2007) 234 n. 20, 242–3 and n. 53; J. Hill (2007a) 93

ST: Lambert (1969–72) nos. 51, 59, 217a; Römer (1972b) 136

274. Lincoln, Cathedral Library, 182 (C. 2. 8) [with 184, fol. 1]

s. x/xi, Abingdon, (prov. Lincoln)

Contents: Bede, *Homiliae in Euangelia* [*CPL* 1367]

MS: Schenkl no. 4027; Woolley (1927) 132–3; Laistner—King (1943) 117; Hurst (1955) xviii; N.R. Ker (1957) no. 124; T.A.M. Bishop (1971) xii, 13 [no. 15]; T.A.M. Bishop (1967b); Rella (1977) 78, 88, 162 n. 15; Clayton (1985) 219; R.M. Thomson (1989) 146; Dumville (1993g) 102 and n. 101; T.N. Hall (2007) 258–9; Wieland (2009) 127; Rushforth (2012) 205 and n. 50; Scragg (2012a) no. 354

FACS: T.A.M. Bishop (1971) pl. XIII [fol. 34v]

ED: Hurst (1955) [Bede, *Homiliae*, coll. as L]

ST: T.A.M. Bishop (1967b); Lapidge (1975a) 75 n. 5 [repr. Lapidge (1993a) 113 n. 5]

Lincoln, Cathedral Library, 184 (C. 1. 13) fol. 1: see no. **274**

275. Lincoln, Cathedral Library, 298A

s. viii^2, Northumbria

Contents: gospels (f)

MS: Woolley (1927) 183; *CLA* II (1935) no. 160; McGurk (1961a) no. 17; R.M. Thomson (1989) 205

276. Lincoln, Cathedral Library, 298B

s. xi^2

Contents: Hexateuch* (f; from Numeri)

MS: Crawford (1922) 6; Woolley (1927) 183; N.R. Ker (1957) no. 125; Morrell (1965); R.M. Thomson (1989) 205; R. Gameson (1999a) no. 347; Treharne (2007b) 18 n. 16; Marsden (2008) lxiii–lxv; Scragg (2012a) no. 355

DEC: Morrell (1965) 10–11

ED: Crawford (1922) [OE Hexateuch coll. as Ln]; Marsden (2008) [OE Hexateuch coll. as Ln]

ST: Morrell (1965); Clemoes (1994b) 370; Marsden (2008) lxxi–lxxii, clvii–clx

277. Lincoln, Cathedral Library, 298C (with London, British Library, Harley 3405, fol. 4)

s. xi med., Winchester?

Contents: antiphoner (f)

MS: Woolley (1927) 183; A.G. Watson (1987a) 70 n. 1; R.M. Thomson (1989) 205; Hartzell (2006) no. 117; Rankin (2012) 502 and n. 93

Lincoln, Cathedral Library, V. 5. 11 (ptd. bk.): see no. **524**

277. 3. Lincoln, Dean and Chapter Muniments, A/2/20/2

s. xi med.

Contents: lectionary (f)

278. London, British Library, Add. 7138

s. x²; Canterbury StA? or Crediton or Exeter

Contents: record (account of the division of the West Saxon dioceses)

MS: Keynes (1991) 5 [no. 9]; Conner (1993) 215 n. 1

FACS: Keynes (1991) pl. 9 [face and dorse]

ED: Whitelock et al. (1981) I.167–9 [base MS]; Conner (1993) 221–3 [coll. as A]

ST: J.A. Robinson (1918) 20–3; Whitelock (1979) 892–3; N.P. Brooks (1984) 211–12 and n. 7; Keynes (1991) 5 [no. 9]; Conner (1993) 215–20; N. Orchard (2002) I.209

279. London, British Library, Add. 9381 (the 'Bodmin Gospels')

s. ix/x, Brittany; s. x med.—xi/xii, prov. whole MS s. x, St Petroc's, Padstow, then Bodmin

Contents: gospels, gospel list (s. ix/x), records[*] (s. x med.—xi/xii)

MS: Jenner (1923); Jenner (1924); Förster (1930) 77–82; Frere (1934) 79; N.R. Ker (1957) no. 126; N.R. Ker (1964) 10; Klauser (1972) xlix; Pollard (1975) 158; Deuffic (1986) 300; McGurk (1986b) 48 n. 27 [repr. McGurk (1998) no. XIV]; Dumville (1988) 53; Olson (1989) 71–2; Dumville (1992a) 114, 116–17, 120; Bischoff (1998—) II, no. 2357; Cohen (1999) 67–9; Dumville (1999) 125; Ambrose (2005) 113; Lemoine (2005) 184, 187–8; Hartzell (2006) no. 118; Gullick (2012) 295 n. 5; McKee (2012a) 170; Rushforth (2012) 202–3 and n. 38; Scragg (2012a) nos. 356–61

DEC: McGurk (1986b) 45 n. 3 [repr. McGurk (1998) no. XIV]

ED: Haddan—Stubbs (1869–71) I.676–83 [base MS for manumissions]; Förster (1930) 83–99 [base MS for manumissions]; Pelteret (1990) nos. 87–9 [three manumission records]; B. Fischer (1988–91) [gospel excerpts coll. as Hx]

ST: Haddan—Stubbs (1869–71) I.698; Jenner (1923); Jenner (1924); Förster (1930); Glunz (1933) 69, 112–13, 119; *BCLL* (1985) nos. 121, 168; McGurk (1987) 165 n. 2 [repr. McGurk (1998) no. II]; McGurk (1993) 254 [repr. McGurk (1998) no. XI]; Pelteret (1995) xiv–xv; McGurk (1996) 121 [repr. McGurk (1998) no. X]; Lenker (1997) 416–18; Lemoine (2005) 187–8, 190

280. London, British Library, Add. 11034

s. x?, prob. England

Contents: Bede, *Versus de die iudicii*, part (lines 128–55 only) [*CPL* 1370; SK 10633]; pseudo-Priscian, *Carmen de sideribus* [SK 151]; Arator, *Historia apostolica* [*CPL* 1504] (incomplete, with scholia by 'Anonymus X'); Modoin of Autun, *Ecloga* (for Charlemagne) [SK 1825]

MS: *Cat. Add. B.M. 1836–1840* (1843) 26; Dümmler (1881) 382; McKinlay (1942) 43–4 [no. 70]; Lapidge (1982a) 117 n. 100 [repr. Lapidge (1996b) 484 n. 100, 485]; Orbán (2006) 36–8; Hartzell (2006) no. 119; Lendinara (2007b) 203–4; Wieland (2009) 151, 155

FACS: McKinlay (1942) pl. XXVI [fol. 8r]

ED: Dümmler (1881) 384–91 [base MS for Modoin, *Ecloga*]; McKinlay
(1951) [Arator, *Historia apostolica*, coll. as V]; Hurst—Fraipont (1955)
439–44 [Bede, *Versus de die iudicii*, coll. as γ]; Lapidge (1982a) 121 [repr.
Lapidge (1996b) 490] [base MS for Arator, *Epist. ad Florianum* (fol. 3r),
with glosses]; Orbán (2006) [Arator, *Historia apostolica*, coll. as La]

ST: Manitius (1911–31) I.550–1 [citing Dümmler's ed. of this MS]; Jaager
(1935) 54; Laistner—King (1943) 127; Kristeller et al. (1960—) I.242–3;
Wieland (1985) 157–8; Wieland (1998) 16 n. 23; Lendinara (2007b) 177,
180

281. London, British Library, Add. 15350, fols. 1 and 121

s. vii–viii, prob. Italy, (prov. Winchester OM)

Contents: *Verba seniorum* [*CPG* 5570; *BHL* 6527] (= *Vitas patrum*, bk.
V) XIII. 9—XIV. 1, 10–17

MS: *Cat. Add. B.M. 1841–1845* (1850) 1; Thompson—Warner (1881–4)
II.62; Wilmart (1922) 190; *CLA* II (1935) no. 164; Siegmund (1949)
137; A.G. Watson (1963) 209, 211 [repr. A.G. Watson (2004) no. III];
P. Jackson (1992) 123; Emms (2006) 20 and n. 15; T.N. Hall (2007)
255–7

ST: Traube (1909–20) I.195; Lindsay (1915) 460; G.R.C. Davis (1958)
no. 1042 [on the Winchester cartulary with which the two leaves were
bound]; Lambert (1969–72) no. 570; Laing (1993) 61–2

281. 3. London, British Library, Add. 19835

s. xi/xii, Normandy or England

Contents: Heiric of Auxerre, *Collectanea* (from Suetonius, Orosius,
Valerius Maximus); theological treatises; treatise on Greek alphabet;
Fulbert of Chartres, fourteen *Epistolae* and two sermons; liturgical
directions and expositions; excerpts from Jerome and Augustine on the
psalms; interpretations of biblical names (f)

MS: *Cat. Add. B.M. 1854–1875* (1875–80) I.9; Schullian (1935) 156–7;
Behrends (1976) lx; Schullian (1981) 708; R. Gameson (1999a) no. 348

ED: Quadri (1966) 77–161 [Heiric, *Collectanea*, coll. as A]

ST: Schullian (1935); Quadri (1966); *CSLMA* III (2010) 382–4 [Heiric,
Collectanea]

281. 5. London, British Library, Add. 21213, fols. 2–25

[palimpsest, lower script]

s. viii ex., prob. England

Contents: gospels (f)

MS: *Cat. Add. B.M. 1854–1875* (1875–80) I.340–1; *CLA* II (1935) no. 169; Lowe (1964) 89 [no. 64] [repr. Lowe (1972b) II.499–500 (no. 64)]; McGurk (1961a) no. 19; B. Fischer (1965) 196

282. London, British Library, Add. 23211

c. 871×899, Wessex

Contents: computistical verses and note; genealogies of West Saxon and East Saxon kings*; Old English Martyrology* (f)

MS: *Cat. Add. B.M. 1854–1875* (1875–80) I.848; N.R. Ker (1957) no. 127; Kotzor (1981) I.43*–55*; Dumville (1986) 2–4; Dumville (1987) 156 n. 49; Morrish (1988) 531 n. 62; Webster—Backhouse (1991) 46–7; Dumville (1992b) 92 n. 182; Webster—Brown (1997) 218–19 [no. 36]; Dumville (1999) 120; Dumville (2005) 310; Roberts (2005) 45; Rauer (2007) 145

FACS: Dumville (1986) 3 [fol. 1v]; Dumville (1992b) pls. IV–V [fols. 1r, 2v]; Roberts (2005) p. 45 [fol. 1r]

ED: Kotzor (1981) vol. II [Martyrology fragment coll. as A]; Dumville (1986) 21–5 [genealogies coll. as N]

ST: Kotzor (1974); R.I. Page (1974); Rauer (2000); Bredehoft (2001) 20, 23, 26–7, 35, 177 n. 27, 179 n. 47, 183 n. 72 [West Saxon regnal table]; Rauer (2007)

283. London, British Library, Add. 23944

s. ix$^{3/4}$, prob. Paris-Beauvais region, prov. England s. xi ex., (prov. Burton-on-Trent)

Contents: Augustine, *De nuptiis et concupiscentia* [*CPL* 350], *Contra Iulianum* [*CPL* 351]

MS: *Cat. Add. B.M. 1854–1875* (1875–80) I.921–2; N.R. Ker (1960) 12–13, 54–7; N.R. Ker (1964) 15; Römer (1972b) 154; N.R. Ker (1976b) 30 [repr. N.R. Ker (1985) 150]; Rella (1977) 25–6; Webber (1992) 46–7; R. Sharpe et al. (1996) 33–4 [on Burton library catalogue, s. xii]; Bischoff (1998—) II, no. 2390; R. Gameson (2012d) 368 and n. 103

FACS: N.R. Ker (1960) pl. 28 (a) [fol. 107r]

ST: R. McKitterick (2012) 329

284. London, British Library, Add. 24193

s. ix[1], France (Orléans area?), prov. England s. x[3/4]; fols. 1–16 and 159 replacement leaves, England s. x[3/4]

Contents: Venantius Fortunatus, *Carmina* [*CPL* 1033]; prose exposition of the Lord's Prayer and Creed

MS: *Cat. Add. B.M. 1854–1875* (1875–80) II.19; Manitius (1911–31) I.181 [anonymous poem on Poitiers (SK 4992)]; R.W. Hunt (1979) 279–80; Voigts (1988) 83, 85 [on nos. **809. 8** and **809. 9**, both removed from this MS]; Bischoff (1998–) II, no. 2392; R. Gameson (2012a) 64 and n. 224; R. Gameson (2012d) 348 and n. 14, 350, 352–3 and n. 34

ED: R.W. Hunt (1979) 281–2 [Venantius, *Carmina*, variants coll. as X]

ST: R.W. Hunt (1979) 286–7; Voigts (1988) 83

285. London, British Library, Add. 24199, fols. 2–38

s. x ex.; some drawings s. xi[2], xi/xii, (prov. Bury St Edmunds)

Contents: Prudentius, *Psychomachia* [*CPL* 1441], glossed

MS: *Cat. Add. B.M. 1854–1875* (1875–80) II.21; Boutemy (1938); N.R. Ker (1964) 20; T.A.M. Bishop (1971) xxii; R.M. Thomson (1972) 622–3 and n. 23; Backhouse et al. (1984b) no. 46; Wieland (1985) 161, 168–71; Wieland (1987); Biggs et al. (1990) 153–4 [Wieland]; Dumville (1993g) 78 n. 360, 145 n. 25; Wieland (1997a) 170–1; Wieland (1998) 4; Karkov (2001a) 115 n. 3, 116 n. 7, 124; Hartzell (2006) no. 120

DEC: F. Wormald (1945) 128 n. 4 [repr. Wormald (1984) 66 n. 70]; F. Wormald (1952) 66 [no. 24]; F. Wormald (1957b) 31, 32 [repr. F. Wormald (1984) 146, 147]; E. Temple (1976) no. 51; Brownrigg (1978) 248 n. 2; Ohlgren (1986) no. 156; R. Gameson (1991) 76; R. Gameson (1995b) 8, 15, 157 n. 33; Wieland (1997a) 171–81, 183; Wieland (1998) 6–9, 11, 14–15, 17 n. 27, 18 n. 37, 19 n. 42, 45–6; Scott (2009) 25; R. Gameson (2012c) 284 and n. 123

FACS: Westwood (1868) pl. 44; Stettiner (1905) pls. 37 [fol. 2v], 38 [fol. 3v], 39 [fol. 24v], 40 [fol. 24r], 41 [fol. 28r], 42 [fol. 29v], 49–50 [fols. 2r, 3r, 4r, 4v, 5r], 51–2 [fols. 6r, 6v, 7v, 8r, 8v, 9r], 53–4 [fols. 9v, 10r, 10v, 11r, 11v, 12r], 55–6 [fols. 12v, 14r, 14v, 15r, 15v, 16r], 57–8 [fols. 16v, 17r, 17v, 18r, 18v, 19v], 59–60 [fols. 20r, 20v, 21r, 21v, 22r, 22v, 23r, 23v],

61–2 [fols. 15v, 26r, 26v, 27r, 27v, 28v], 63–4 [fols. 29r, 30r, 30v, 31r, 31v], 65–6 [fols. 32r, 32v, 33r, 33v, 34v, 36r, 37r, 37v]; E. Temple (1976) ills. 163, 166 [fols. 16v, 17r]; F. Wormald (1984) ill. 119 [fol. 18r]; M.P. Brown (2007a) pls. 108–9 [fols. 11r, 18r]; Scott (2009) 25 [fol. 21v (detail)]

ST: R.I. Page (1992a); Wieland (1998) 6–8, 11, 14 n. 3, 19 n. 49; Wieland (2001) 181

286. London, British Library, Add. 28188

s. xi$^{3/4}$, Exeter

Contents: pontifical (including litanies) [incomplete], benedictional [incomplete]

MS: *Cat. Add. B.M. 1854–75* (1875–80) II.440–1; E. Bishop (1918) 239–40; Dewick—Frere (1918–21) II.614–18; T.A.M. Bishop (1954–8a) 193–7; N.R. Ker (1964) 82; Brückmann (1973) 426; Hohler (1975) 74, 224 n. 56; Rella (1977) 88; Drage (1978) 357–8; A.G. Watson (1979) I, no. 322; Prescott (1987) 130; Lapidge (1988b) 260 [repr. Lapidge (1993a) 218]; Lapidge (1991a) 67; Conner (1993) 5, 43; Dumville (1993g) 63; Lapidge (1994b) 136; R. Gameson (1996b) 145 and n. 35; Treharne (2003) 161; Wieland (2009) 124; Pfaff (2012) 453–4 and nn. 12–14

DEC: R. Gameson (1991) 68 n. 39

FACS: A.G. Watson (1979) II, pl. 40 [fol. 99v]; Prescott (1987) pl. 4 [fol. 123r]

ED: Lapidge (1991a) 132–7 [litanies]

ST: Clayton (1984) 227 [Marian feasts]; Dumville (1992a) 68, 79, 90–1, 94; N. Orchard (2002) I.76 n. 160, 207, 218, 220, 227, 230; N. Orchard (2005) cii n. 180 *et passim*

London, British Library, Add. 32246: see no. **775**

287. London, British Library, Add. 33241

s. xi med., Flanders (Saint-Omer?) or Normandy, (prov. Canterbury StA)

Contents: *Encomium Emmae Reginae*

MS: *Cat. Add. B.M. 1882–1887* (1889) 281; Campbell—Keynes (1998) xli–xlv, xciii–xcv; Wieland (2009) 143

DEC: Backhouse et al. (1984) 144 [no. 148]; M.P. Brown (1991) 18; Neuman de Vegvar (1992); Karkov (2004) 4–5; R. Gameson (2012c) 277 and n. 91; R. Gameson (2012d) 355 and n. 44

FACS: Gransden (1974) pl. III [fols. 1v, 2r]; Roesdahl et al. (1981) 156 [fol. 1v]; Campbell–Keynes (1998) ills. 2–5 [fols. 1v, 2r, 8r, 56r]; Karkov (2004) fig. 21 [fol. 1v]; M.P. Brown (2007a) pl. 131 [fol. 1v]

ED: Campbell–Keynes (1998) [base MS (= L) for *Encomium Emmae*]

ST: Karkov (2004) 146–55, 161–2, 174–5; Keynes (2006) B 85, K 60–74

London, British Library, Add. 34652, fol. 2: see no. **357**

288. London, British Library, Add. 34652, fol. 3

s. xi²

Contents: Chrodegang, *Regula canonicorum* (enlarged version)* (f)

MS: *Cat. Add. B.M. 1894–1899* (1901) 28; Napier (1903); N.R. Ker (1957) no. 128; R. Gameson (1999a) no. 350; Langefeld (2003) 47; Treharne (2007b) 18 n. 16; Scragg (2012a) no. 362

ED: Langefeld (2003) [Chrodegang, *Regula canonicorum*, coll. as E]

289. London, British Library, Add. 34652, fol. 6

s. xi/xii

Contents: biblical text (Canticum canticorum [f]; capitula to Sapientia)

MS: *Cat. Add. B.M. 1894–1899* (1901) 28; Marsden (1995) 386–90, 473 *et passim*; R. Gameson (1999a) no. 351

290. London, British Library, Add. 34890 (the 'Grimbald Gospels')

s. xi¹ᐟ⁴, Canterbury CC, prov. Winchester NM; s. xi ex., Winchester NM

Contents: gospels and gospel list (s. xi¹ᐟ⁴); Letter by Fulk of Rheims to King Alfred (s. xi ex., Winchester NM)

MS: *Cat. Add. B.M. 1894–1899* (1901) 110–12; T.A.M. Bishop (1954–8a) 191; R. Powell (1962) 5; N.R. Ker (1964) 103; T.A.M. Bishop (1971) xv, 22 [no. 24]; Pollard (1975) 150–2; Keynes–Lapidge (1983) 331; Backhouse et al. (1984b) no. 55; McGurk (1986b) 44, 46–8, 51–63 [repr. McGurk (1998) no. XIV]; Heslop (1990) 166, 182; Dumville (1991–5) 44–5; Dumville (1992a) 120; Pfaff (1992a) 270; Dumville (1993g) 127, 139; Raw (1994) 266 n. 17; Lenker (1997) 420–4; Dodwell (2000) 122 n. 96; Rushforth (2001) 139 n. 15, 140, 142; Farr (2003) 122; K.L. Brown (2004b) 181, 186; R. Gameson (2004b); Karkov (2006a) 44; Withers (2007) 64; R. Gameson (2012a) 27 and n. 57, 40 n. 105, 80, 87 nn. 311, 316, 88, 92; Gullick (2012) 299 and nn. 25, 26; Marsden (2012) 423 and n. 78; McGurk (2012) 438 and n. 7, 446 [no. 8]

DEC: Dodwell (1971b) 145; Alexander (1975a) 149; E. Temple (1976) no. 68; Brownrigg (1978) 246 n. 2; D.M. Wilson (1984) 174, 176; F. Wormald (1984) 107, 119; Ohlgren (1986) no. 173; Raw (1990) 212; R. Gameson (1991) 105 n. 14; R. Gameson (1992a) 211 and n. 102; Deshman (1995) 98–9, 104, 113, 148, 157, 250; R. Gameson (1995b) 17, 42, 69, 103, 127, 187, 206, 218, 230 *et passim*; McGurk—Rosenthal (1995b) 286 n. 89 [repr. McGurk (1998) no. XV]; Farr (2003) 122–5; K.L. Brown (2004b) 186; Karkov (2004) 140; O'Reilly (2011) 206–8; Rosenthal (2011) 241–3; Withers (2011) 260–1; R. Gameson (2012c) 268–9 and n. 54, 282 and n. 116, 284 and n. 124, 289 n. 142, 290 n. 145, 291–2

FACS: D.M. Wilson (1984) pl. 264 [fol. 114v]; F. Wormald (1984) ill. 112 [fol. 10v]; Budny (1992) 115 [fol. 114v]; R. Gameson (1992a) pls. 51–2 [fols. 114v, 115r (detail)]; Deshman (1995) figs. 92–3 [fols. 114v, 115r]; R. Gameson (1995b) pls. 18 (a)–(b) [fols. 114v, 115r]; R. Gameson (2000b) pl. 12 [fol. 11r]; Farr (2003), figs. 3–4 [fols. 12r, 115r]; K.L. Brown (2004b) pls. 3 [fol. 1r], 4 [fols. 10v, 73v, 114v]; M.P. Brown (2007a) pls. 122–3 [fols. 114v, 115r]; Withers (2007) 66 [fol. 73v]; R. Gameson (2012) pl. 10.8 [fol. 74r]

ED: Whitelock et al. (1981a) I.8–11 [Letter by Fulk]

ST: Glunz (1933) 144–5; O'Reilly (1992); Dodwell (2000) 150 [connections between Rheims and England]; K.L. Brown (2004b) 186–7; Keynes (2006) K 59

291. London, British Library, Add. 37517 (the 'Bosworth Psalter')

s. x$^{3/4}$, x/xi, and xi in.; whole MS Canterbury (CC?)

Contents: liturgical calendar: s. x/xi; Psalterium Romanum° with extensive Latin commentary, Ps. CLI; canticles°: s. x$^{3/4}$; litany: s. x/xi or xi in.; prayers, hymnal, Monastic canticles: s. x$^{3/4}$; OE glosses: s. xi in.; Ordinary and canon of the Mass, Mass of the Holy Trinity, part of the Office for the Dead: s. x/xi

MS: *Cat. Add. B.M. 1906–1910* (1912) 65–7; Gasquet—Bishop (1908); Wildhagen (1913) 453–60; Mearns (1914) 52, 79, 82, 94; Weber (1953) xiv; N.R. Ker (1957) no. 129; N.R. Ker (1964) 35, 42; Korhammer (1973); Pollard (1975) 149–50; Korhammer (1976) 74 *et passim*; Pollard (1976) 55; Rella (1977) 82; A.G. Watson (1979) I, no. 381; Backhouse et al. (1984b) no. 36; McGurk (1986b) 53 n. 51; M.P. Brown (1990) 62; Dumville (1991) 45; Lapidge (1991a) 67; R. Gameson (1992a) 188; Vaciago (1993) 12–13 [no. 50]; *ASMMF* II (1994) 1–12 [no. 166; Pulsiano]; Raw (1994) 266; N. Orchard (1995b); Springer (1995) 144;

R. Gameson (1996b) 175, 182; Gneuss (1998) 276 n. 9, 277, 282; Gretsch (1999a) 40, 282–3; Gretsch (2000) 86; Biggs (2007a) 16; Chardonnens (2007b) 508–9, 550; Shepard (2007) 201; Wieland (2009) 116, 134, 138; R. Gameson (2012a) 39 and n. 100, 67 n. 233, 80 n. 283; R. Gameson (2012b) 114; D. Ganz (2012) 194 and n. 37; Gullick (2012) 299 and n. 26; Rushforth (2012) 203 and n. 42; Scragg (2012a) nos. 363–4

DEC: Rice (1952) 196; E. Temple (1976) no. 22; Alexander (1978c) 97–8; Brownrigg (1978) 240 n. 6, 246 n. 2, 261; Lawrence (1982) 102; Ohlgren (1986) no. 110; Raw (1990) 212; R. Gameson (1992a) 188–9, 209–11; R. Gameson (1995b) 145, 219 n. 159, 223 n. 183; R. Gameson (2012c) 262 and n. 36

FACS: Gasquet—Bishop (1908) pls. I–IV [fols. 33r, 105r, 2r]; E. Temple (1976) ills. 81–3 [fols. 74r, 94v, 4r]; A.G. Watson (1979) II, pl. 23 [fol. 2v]; M.P. Brown (1990) pl. 21 [fol. 47v]; R. Gameson (1992a) pl. 24 [fol. 33r]; *ASMMF* II (1994) no. 166; R. Gameson (2000b) pl. 4 [fol. 33r]; M.P. Brown (2007a) pl. 83 [fol. 33r]; Owen-Crocker (2009) figs. 2.13 [fol. 81r], 5.4 [fol. 2r]

ED: Lindelöf (1909) [OE glosses]; F. Wormald (1934) 57–69 [liturgical calendar (no. 5)]; Weber (1953) [Psalterium Romanum coll. as B]; Hurst—Fraipont (1955) 419–23 [Ascension hymn by Bede coll. as L^f]; Makothakat (1972) [base MS for Latin psalms, OE gloss, and Latin commentary]; Korhammer (1976) [Monastic canticles coll. as B]; Wieland (1982) [base MS (= B) for hymnal]; Lapidge (1991a) 138–9 [litany]; Milfull (1996) [hymns coll. as B]; Pulsiano (2001a) [Pss. I–L, Latin and OE gloss coll. as L]; Rushforth (2008a) no. 9 [liturgical calendar]

LANG: Crowley (2000) 130

ST: Sisam—Sisam (1959) 56; Gamber (1968–88) no. 1614; Gneuss (1968) 55, 60–8, 104–5 *et passim*; F. Wormald (1971a); Hohler (1975) 75; Kotzor (1981) I.302*–311* [no. 5]; Gerchow (1988) 226; Dumville (1992a) 25, 27, 36–8, 45, 48–65; Lapidge (1992d) 142 [repr. Lapidge (1996b) 42]; Rosenthal (1992) 145, 153–4, 160; Thacker (1992) 223, 237; Conner (1993) 53, 59, 63, 73–4; Dumville (1993g) 100, 148 n. 42; R. Gameson (1996a) 201 n.; Pulsiano (1998b) 105 n. 1; Gretsch (1999a) 26–7; Gneuss (2000) 238 n. 44; Borst (2001) I.166; N. Orchard (2002) I.8, 54, 158–84; Milfull (2004)

292. London, British Library, Add. 37518, fols. 116–17

s. viii[1]

Contents: sacramentary and gospel lectionary (f)

MS: *Cat. Add. B.M. 1906–1910* (1912) 67; Kenney (1929) 630; *CLA* II
(1935) no. 176; Bourque (1949–52) I.182–3, II.223 n. 4; H. Frank
(1954) 75; Gamber (1958) 63; Lowe (1960) 21 [no. 24]; Gamber
(1968–88) no. 411; Bullough (1983) 11 n. 26; Sims-Williams (1990) 285
and n. 54; *CPL* (1995) no. 1900b; Webster–Brown (1997) 243
[no. 132]; R. Gameson (1999c) 346; Bullough (2004) 206; Pfaff (2009)
41–2; Marsden (2012) 414 and n. 33

FACS: Lowe (1960) pls. XXIV (a)–(b) [fols. 116r, 117r]; R. Gameson
(1999c) 346–7 [fols. 116r, 117r]

ED: Baumstark (1927); Mohlberg (1960) 266–7

ST: Bischoff (1998–) II, no. 2404 [flyleaves (fols. 116–17) in this vol.
containing Tironian notes]; Gneuss (2012) 291

293. British Library, Add. 37777 (with London, British Library, Add.
45025 + Loan 81)

s. vii ex. or viii in., Monkwearmouth-Jarrow, prov. Worcester?

Contents: Bible (f, from Regum, Ecclesiasticus)

[cf. no. **501. 3**]

MS: *Cat. Add. B.M. 1906–1910* (1912) 136–7; *CLA* II (1935) no. 177;
Cat. Add. B.M. 1936–1945 (1970) 69–70; Lowe (1960) 19; Bischoff
(1962) 330; McGurk (1962) 18 [repr. McGurk (1998) no. VII]; N.R.
Ker (1964) 105 and n. 7, 207 and n. 9; A.G. Watson (1979) I, no. 383;
Parkes (1982) 3; Bischoff (1985) 351–2; Sims-Williams (1990) 182 and
nn.; Webster–Backhouse (1991) no. 87 (a)–(c); Dumville (1992a)
99–100, 104, 117, 120; Gibson (1993b) 4 n. 21; McGurk (1994b) 2, 3
[repr. McGurk (1998) no. XII]; Marsden (1995) xiv, 40, 43–4, 55, 90–2,
123–9; M.P. Brown (1996) 166; R. Gameson (1996a) 230 and nn. 111,
112; Meyvaert (1996) 879–80; Budny (1997) I.614–15; Webster–
Brown (1997) 247 [no. 152]; Budny (1999) 249; Dumville (1999) 69;
M.P. Brown (2001b) 284; Beall (2005) 188; Wieland (2009) 115;
Hanna–Turville-Petre (2010) 122; M.P. Brown (2012) 125 and n. 18,
141 n. 93, 146 n. 125; Marsden (2012) 417 and n. 53

DEC: Netzer (2012) 232 and n. 44

FACS: Lowe (1960) pl. X [Add. 37777, verso]; A.G. Watson (1979) II,
pl. 2 [Add. 45025, fol. 2r]; M.P. Brown (1991) pl. 57 [Add. 45025,
fol. 2v]; Marsden (1995) pl. II [Loan 81, verso]; M.P. Brown (2003b)
fig. 9 [Add. 45025, fol. 11v]; M.P. Brown (2003c) fig. 30 [Add. 45025,

fol. 2v]; M.P. Brown (2007a) pl. 21 [Add. 45025, fol. 2v]; Hanna—Turville-Petre (2010) pl. 23 [Add. 45025, fol. 2v]

ST: A.G. Watson (1979) I.80; Marsden (1998) 66, 72, 77, 79, 84 [Bede's contribution to the biblical text]; Beall (2005) 191–4

293. 5. British Library, Add. 38130

s. xi/xii, possibly s. xi ex. (after 1081/2), prob. St Neot's

Contents: *Vita I S. Neoti* [*BHL* 6054]; *Translatio S. Neoti* [*BHL* 6055], with two homilies on St Neot; Abbo of Fleury, dedicatory epistle to the *Passio S. Eadmundi* [*BHL* 2392] (added; incomplete); Bede, *Historia ecclesiastica* [*CPL* 1375]

MS: *Cat. Add. B.M. 1911–1915* (1925) 30–1; Colgrave—Mynors (1969) xlviii; Dumville—Lapidge (1984) lxxviii–lxxix; R. Gameson (1999a) no. 353; Gneuss (2012) 291

ED: Dumville—Lapidge (1984) 111–42 [*Vita I* and *Translatio S. Neoti* coll. as A]

294. London, British Library, Add. 38651, fols. 57–8

s. xi in., before 1023, Worcester or York

Contents: sermon notes*

MS: *Cat. Add. B.M. 1911-1915* (1925) 179 no. G(2); N.R. Ker (1957) no. 130; N.R. Ker (1971) 321 [repr. N.R. Ker (1985) 15] [Wulfstan's hand]; A.G. Watson (1979) I, no. 391; Dance (2004) 31 n. 6; A. Orchard (2004) 66 n. 15; A. Orchard (2012) 696 [no. 5]; Scragg (2012a) no. 307

FACS: Loyn (1971) [complete facsimile, including fols. 57v, 58r]

ST: R. Gameson (1996a) 238

295. London, British Library, Add. 40000

s. x in., France, prob. Brittany, or SW France?, with additions s. x/xi, xi/xii, and later, Thorney, prov. Thorney by 1100

Contents: gospels (s. x in.), pericope notes (s. x/xi), confraternity lists (s. xi/xii and later)

MS: *Cat. Add. B.M. 1916–1920* (1933) 276–9; Jørgensen (1933); N.R. Ker (1964) 189; Klauser (1972) xxxvi; A.G. Watson (1979) I, no. 400; C. Clark (1984); Deuffic (1985) 300; McGurk (1986b) 45 n. 4 [repr.

McGurk (1998) no. XIV]; C. Clark (1987); McGurk (1987) 165 n. 2 [repr. McGurk (1998) no. II]; Gerchow (1988) 186–9; Dumville (1992a) 114, 121; Laing (1993) 64; Vaciago (1993) 13 [no. 51]; Blockley (1994); Lenker (1997) 400–3; Rushforth (2001) 143; Insley (2004) 92–6; Moore (2004) 98 n. 8, 101; Lemoine (2005) 184; R. Gameson (2012d) 348–9 and n. 16; Gullick (2012) 305 and n. 67; Scragg (2012a) nos. 365–6, 366.5

ED: B. Fischer (1988–91) [gospel excerpts coll. as Ob]; Gerchow (1988) 326–8 [early confraternity book]

ST: Glunz (1933) xiv, 137–40; Whitelock (1940); B. Fischer (1988–91) I.24*; Gerchow (1988) 186–97; McGurk—Rosenthal (1995b) 286 n. 91 [repr. McGurk (1998) no. XV]; Keynes (1996a) 61; Insley (2004) 92–6; Moore (2004) 98, 101; Lemoine (2005) 189–90

296. London, British Library, Add. 40074

s. x/xi, Canterbury (CC or StA?)

Contents: 'Martinellus': Sulpicius Severus, *Vita S. Martini* [*CPL* 475], *Epistulae* [*CPL* 476], *Dialogi* [*CPL* 477]; pseudo-Sulpicius, *Tituli metrici de S. Martino* [*CPL* 478; SK 17053]; note on the basilica at Tours; *Symbolum 'Clemens trinitas'* (the 'Confessio S. Martini') [*CPL* 1748a]

MS: *Cat. Add. B.M. 1921–1925* (1950) 20–1; Dumville (1993g) 98 n. 79; Barker-Benfield (2008) III.1813

297. London, British Library, Add. 40165 A.1

s. iv ex., Africa?

Contents: Cyprian, *Epistulae* lv, lxxiv, lxix [*CPL* 50] (f)

MS: *Cat. Add. B.M. 1921–1925* (1950) 64; *CLA* II (1935) no. 178; Bévenot (1961) 9–15, 52–3, 62; McGurk (1961b) no. 3; Rella (1977) 165; Bévenot (1980); Parkes (1992) 139 n. 105; Webber (1992) 45–6; W. Schipper (2003) 153–4; W. Schipper (2004); Emms (2006) 20; W. Schipper (2007b) 34–5

FACS: *NPS* II, pl. 101 [fragments A–C]; W. Schipper (2004) figs. 8.1 [fol. 2v], 8.2 [fol. 3r], 8.3 [fol. 2v], 8.4 [fol. 2v (details)], 8.5 [fol. 2v], 8.6 [fol. 2v (ultraviolet light)], 8.7 [fol. 2v (detail)], 8.8 [fol. 2r (detail)], 8.9 [fol. 2v (detail)], 8.10 [fol. 2v (detail)]; W. Schipper (2007b) 45 [fol. 2v], 48 [fol. 5v]

298. London, British Library, Add. 40165 A.2

s. ix ex. or ix/x

Contents: Old English Martyrology* (f)

MS: *Cat. Add. B.M. 1921–1925* (1950) 64–5; C. Sisam (1953) 209–10; N.R. Ker (1957) no. 132; Kotzor (1981) I.109*–117*; Morrish (1988) 535, 537; Dumville (1999) 120; Rauer (2007) 146

FACS: *NPS* II, pl. 102 [front fly-leaf, verso; back fly-leaf, recto]

ED: Kotzor (1981) vol. II [Old English Martyrology coll. as E]

ST: C. Sisam (1953)

299. London, British Library, Add. 40618

s. viii², Ireland, prov. s. x med. S England (Canterbury StA?)

Contents: gospels

MS: *CLA* II (1935) no. 179; *Cat. Add. B.M. 1921–1925* (1950) 95–7; McGurk (1956) 250 [repr. McGurk (1998) no. I]; McGurk (1961a) no. 20; Finlayson (1962) xxviii–xxix; T.J. Brown (1982a) 114 [repr. T.J. Brown (1993a) 215]; Backhouse et al. (1984b) no. 8; Dumville (1987) 161, 168; McGurk (1987) 173–4 [repr. McGurk (1998) no. II]; Dumville (1992a) 111; Dumville (1992b) 95 n. 197, 131 n. 348; R. Gameson (1994b) 47 n. 107; McGurk (1994b) 14 [repr. McGurk (1998) no. XII]; Netzer (1994) 235 n. 14; Lapidge (1996c) 410–11; Webster—Brown (1997) 243–4 [no. 133]; W. Schipper (2003) 153; K.L. Brown (2004a) 10–11; M.P. Brown (2007a) 17–18, 87; Wieland (2009) 118; R. Gameson (2012a) 22 n. 32, 26 n. 51, 41 n. 110

DEC: McGurk (1956) 261 [repr. McGurk (1998) no. I]; F. Wormald (1971b) 309 [repr. F. Wormald (1984) 80]; Alexander (1978a) no. 46; Ohlgren (1986) nos. 46, 93; R. Gameson (1991) 95 n. 181; Deshman (1995) 109–10; R. Gameson (1995b) 200; M.P. Brown (1996) 97; Farr (2003) 120–2; K.L. Brown (2004a) 10; Barker-Benfield (2008) III.1735, 1813

FACS: *NPS* II, pls. 140–1 [fols. 22v, 29v]; F. Wormald (1984) ills. 89, 92–9 [fols. 22v, 49v, 50r]; Dumville (1987) pl. III [fol. 66r]; M.P. Brown (1991) pl. 69 [fols. 22v–23r]; Dumville (1992a) pl. VII [fol. 66r]; Deshman (1995) fig. 101 [fol. 22v]; Backhouse (1997) pl. 3 [fol. 21v]; Farr (2003) fig. 2 [fols. 22v–23r]; K.L. Brown (2004a) pls. 2 [fol. 21v], 3 [fols. 22v, 23r, 49v, 50r (details)]; M.P. Brown (2007a) pls. 75–7 [fols. 21v, 49v, 50r]; Roberts—Webster (2011), pls. II–IV [fols. 22v, 49v, 50r]

ED: B. Fischer (1988–91) [gospel excerpts coll. as Ha]

ST: *BCLL* (1985) no. 525; McGurk (1986b) 45 [repr. McGurk (1998) no. XIV]; McGurk (1987) 165–6 [repr. McGurk (1998) no. II]; Farr (2011a) *passim*; McKee (2012b) 342 and n. 14

299. 5. London, British Library, Add. 43405, fols. i and v

s. xi[1], (prov. Muchelney?)

MS: *Cat. Add. B.M. 1931–1935* (1967) 133

Contents: missal (f)

London, British Library, Add. 45025: see no. **293**

London, British Library, Add. 46204: see no. **344. 5**

300. London, British Library, Add. 47967 (the 'Tollemache Orosius')

s. x[1] or x[2/4], Winchester?

Contents: Orosius, *Historiae aduersum paganos* [*CPL* 571] in OE translation*; note* on Adam, Noah, and Old Testament figures (s. xi)

MS: T.A.M. Bishop (1954–8b) 324–6; N.R. Ker (1957) no. 133; T.A.M. Bishop (1959–63a) 93; T.A.M. Bishop (1964–8b) 247; N.R. Ker (1964) 200 and n. 7; Parkes (1976b) 156–7 [repr. Parkes (1991) 150–4]; Bately (1980) xxiii–xxv; *Cat. Add. B.M. 1951–1955* (1982) 121–3; Parkes (1983) 130, 135 n. 45; Backhouse et al. (1984b) no. 2; Carley (1986) 117; Dumville (1987) 170–1 n. 128; Webster–Backhouse (1991) 262–3; Dumville (1992b) 67–8, 72; Lapidge (1992d) 156 [repr. Lapidge (1996b) 46]; Conner (1993) 53; M.P. Brown (1996) 180; O'Brien O'Keeffe (1998a) 158 n. 40; Edwards–Griffiths (2000); Roberts (2005) 52–5 [no. 9]; Bately (2006) 40; C. Bishop (2007b) 118; D. Ganz (2012) 188 n. 4, 189 and n. 11; R. Gameson (2012a) 39 and n. 95, 59 n. 195; Scragg (2012a) nos. 21–2, 368

DEC: F. Wormald (1945) 118 [repr. F. Wormald (1984) 57]; F. Wormald (1952) 65 [no. 22]; F. Wormald (1971b) 305 [repr. F. Wormald (1984) 76]; E. Temple (1976) no. 8; Brownrigg (1978) 253 n. 1; Ohlgren (1986) no. 86; M.P. Brown (1991) 50; R. Gameson (2012c) 287 and n. 133

FACS: A. Campbell (1953) [complete facsimile]; F. Wormald (1984) pl. 58 ['p. 128' (detail)]; Bately (1980) frontispiece [fol. 5v]; M.P. Brown (1991) pl. 52 [fol. 1r]; M.P. Brown (2005) pl. 71 [fol. 5v]; Roberts (2005) pl. 9 [fol. 48v], p. 55 [fol. 1r]

LANG: Bately (1980) xxxix–xlix; Hofstetter (1987) 307–8; Gretsch (1999a) 320; Gretsch (2000) 98–102, 105; Gretsch (2001) 172

ED: N.R. Ker (1957) 165 [note on Adam]; Cyrus (1968) [base MS]; Bately (1980) [OE Orosius coll. as L]

ST: F. Wormald (1971b) [repr. F. Wormald (1984) 76–84]; Saenger (1997) 41–2; Gretsch (1999a) 320

301. London, British Library, Add. 49598 (the 'Benedictional of St Æthelwold')

s. x² (971×984), Winchester, prob. OM

Contents: benedictional, with prefatory poem by Godeman [SK 12366]

MS: Warner – Wilson (1910) ix–lx; Tolhurst (1933); K. Sisam (1953a) 270; T.A.M. Bishop (1954–8b) 333; N.R. Ker (1964) 103, 200; Vezin (1968) 285 and n. 13; T.A.M. Bishop (1971) xx–xxii, 10 [no. 12]; Brückmann (1973) 431; Korhammer (1976) 244; A.G. Watson (1979) I, no. 421; Backhouse et al. (1984b) no. 37; Bischoff (1986) 168, 289; Conner (1993) 18, 42–3; Dumville (1993g) 53, 145; Lapidge (1994a) 131–2; W. Schipper (1994); Deshman (1995) 257–61; Bullough (1998a) 125 n. 72; Muir (1998) 10; Gretsch (1999a) 296–304; *Cat. Add. B.M. 1956–1965* (2000) I.120–6; Prescott (2001) 20–6; C.A. Jones (2004) 337; Karkov (2004) 85; Biggs (2007a) 33 [Clayton]; Gatti (2007) 98, 118 n. 81; Withers (2007) 165–6; D. Ganz (2008) 16–17; Pfaff (2009) 81–3; R. Gameson (2012a) 39 and n. 98, 59, 65, 87 n. 311; R. Gameson (2012b) 107, 114; Gullick (2012) 308 and n. 92; Pfaff (2012) 458 and n. 30; Rushforth (2012) 200 and n. 13, 203 and n. 42

DEC: Rice (1952) 185–9; F. Wormald (1959); Dodwell (1971b) 55, 145; F. Wormald (1971b) 309–10 [repr. F. Wormald (1984) 80]; Lester (1973); Alexander (1975a) 148; Alexander (1975b) 169, 171, 172, 176–83; E. Temple (1976) no. 23; Deshman (1977) 154–73; Brownrigg (1978) 245–6, 266; Dodwell (1982) 52–3, 157; D.M. Wilson (1984) 160, 169; Ohlgren (1986) no. 111; Heslop (1990) 163–5; Raw (1990) 212–13; R. Gameson (1991) 106 n. 38; Deshman (1995) [comprehensive study of decoration in the MS]; R. Gameson (1995b) 9, 15–16, 29–32, 34, 45–8, 58, 59–60, 62, 98, 114, 116, 121, 125, 127–8, 137–8, 143–6, 148, 153, 155, 158, 163–4, 199–203, *et passim*; Dodwell (2000) 107; Karkov (2004) 85–8, 106 nn. 112, 113–14, 119, 128, 130, 133–4 [portraits]; Gatti (2007) 98, 118–19 [on fol. 118v]; Withers (2007) 165–7, 349 n. 24, 350 n. 25; Karkov (2009) 213–14, 225–9; O'Reilly (2011) 203–4; Pulliam (2011) 71, 77; R. Gameson (2012c) 252 and n. 12, 253–4 and n. 14, 255–8, 282–3, 291

FACS: Warner—Wilson (1910) [complete facsimile]; Prescott (2001) [complete facsimile]; E.M. Thompson (1895) pl. 5 [fol. not specified]; A.G. Watson (1979) II, pls. 19 (a)–(b) [fols. 5r, 36r]; D.M. Wilson (1984) pls. 216 [fol. 90v], 217 [fol. 21v], 218 [fol. 4r], 219 [fol. 118v]; F. Wormald (1984) ills. 99–107 [fols. 1v, 4r, 9v, 34v, 70r, 90v, 91r, 118v, 51v][pls. originally ptd in F. Wormald (1959)]; Heslop (1990) pls. I (c) [fol. 7v (detail)], II [fol. 68r]; M.P. Brown (1991) 72–3 [fols. 51v, 52r]; Deshman (1995) pls. 1–35 [fols. 1r, 1v, 2r, 2v, 3r, 3v, 4r, 5v, 6r, 9v, 10r, 15v, 16r, 17v, 19v, 22v, 23r, 24v, 25r, 34v, 45v, 51v, 52r, 56v, 64v, 67v, 70r, 90v, 91r, 92v, 95v, 97v, 99v, 102v, 118v]; R. Gameson (1995b) pls. 10 [fol. 5v], 11 (a) [fol. 102r], 13 (a) [fol. 118v], 23 (a)–(b) [fols. 90v, 91r], 30 [fol. 99r]; Backhouse (1997) pl. 10 [fol. 45v]; M.P. Brown (2007a) pls. 86–7 [fols. 51v, 52r]; Gatti (2007) 97 [fol. 118v]; Withers (2007) 116 [fol. 118v]; Owen-Crocker (2009) figs. 7.19–21 [fols. 97v, 118v, 102v]; R. Gameson (2012) pls. 7b.2 [fol. 8v], 10.4 [fol. 102v]

ED: Moeller (1971–9) [benedictional coll. as AE]; Lapidge (1975a) 104–5 [repr. Lapidge (1993a) 143–4] [Godeman poem]; Lapidge—Winterbottom (1991b) lxxix–lxxxiii [benedictions for St Swithun]

LANG: Gretsch (1999a) 296–304

ST: Warner—Wilson (1910) xii–xiii [translation of the Godeman poem]; F. Wormald (1959) 7–8 [translation of the Godeman poem; repr. Deshman (1995) 148]; F. Wormald (1971b) [repr. F. Wormald (1984) 76–84]; Prescott (1987) 120; Prescott (1988); *Colophons* no. 549; Lapidge—Winterbottom (1991b) lxxix–lxxxiii; Dumville (1992a) 69, 77, 84–5, 90, 94; Lapidge (1992d) 174 [repr. Lapidge (1996b) 74]; Deshman (1995); Corrêa (1996) 292 n.; R. Gameson (1996a) 205 n., 231 n.; Deshman (1997) 136; Rasmussen (1998) 225–9, 231–54; R. Gameson (2001d) no. 17; Knowles et al. (2001) 74, 256; Heslop (2004) 281; Karkov (2004) 100; N. Orchard (2005) xxviii, xxxii, clxxxiii–cxci; Pfaff (2009) 81–3; Farr (2011a) 95–6

London, British Library, Add. 50483 K: see no. **857**

301. 5. London, British Library, Add. 56488, fols. i–iii, 1–5

s. xi¹, (prov. Muchelney?)

Contents: breviary (f)

MS: *BL Cat. Add. n.s. 1971-1975* (2001) 5–6; Hartzell (2006) no. 124; Wieland (2009) 134; Rankin (2012) 487 and n. 19, 503 and n. 98

ST: G.R.C. Davis (1958) no. 685; Sawyer (1968) p. 47; Pfaff (2009) 96

302. London, British Library, Add. 57337 (the 'Anderson Pontifical')

s. x/xi (or 1020s?), Canterbury CC (or Winchester OM?)

Contents: pontifical (including litany and second English Coronation *ordo*); benedictional (incomplete)

MS: Brückmann (1973) 431–2; N.R. Ker (1976a) 127 [no. 416]; D.H. Turner et al. (1980) no. 46; Lapidge (1986a) 270; Prescott (1987) 134–8 [full list of contents]; A.G. Watson (1987a) 11; Heslop (1990) 169–70; Dumville (1991–5) 45–6; Lapidge (1991a) 67–8; Dumville (1992a) 77; Dumville (1993g) 60–1, 106–7 nn. 117–18; Vaciago (1993) 13 [no. 52]; Nelson—Pfaff (1995) 91; Stoneman (1997) 125; Rasmussen (1998) 167–257; *BL Cat. Add. n.s. 1971–1975* (2001) 72–5; C.A. Jones (2004) 343 n. 73, 344 nn. 77–80; C.A. Jones (2005a) 113, 128, 130; C.A. Jones (2005b) 236–7 n. 50, 245–6; N. Orchard (2005) cii–ciii *et passim*; Hartzell (2006) no. 125; O'Brien O'Keeffe (2006) 266–7; R. Gameson (2012a) 34 n. 78; Rushforth (2012) 205 and n. 51; Scragg (2012a) no. 369

FACS: *Sotheby's Sale Catalogue 11 July 1971*, lot 35, frontispiece [fol. 103r], 14 [fol. 18r]; Prescott (1987) pl. 1 [fol. 103r]; Rasmussen (1998) pls. 7–8 [fols. 18r, 103r]

ED: Gough (1974) [OE glosses; but see corrigenda by Bierbaumer (1977b)]; Lapidge (1991a) 140–1 [litany]; Conn (1993)

ST: Prescott (1987) 121–3, 134–8 [relationship of benedictional to no. **301**]; Corrêa (1996) 301 n.; Keefer (1998); N. Orchard (2002) I.75–6; C.A. Jones (2005a) 113, 128; C.A. Jones (2005b) 244

302. 2. London, British Library, Add. 61735

1007×1025, Ely

Contents: farming memoranda

MS: Skeat (1902) 831–2; N.R. Ker (1957) no. 80; Verey et al. (1980) 52 and n. 154; Backhouse et al. (1984b) no. 150; Dumville (1992a) 127; *BL Cat. Add. n.s. 1976–80* (1995) 266–7; P. Wormald (1999) 187 n. 103; Scragg (2012a) nos. 370–3

FACS: *Sotheby's Sale Catalogue 11 Dec. 1979*, lot 25

ED: A.J. Robertson (1939) 252–9 [App. II no. 9], 502–5

LANG: Skeat (1902) 831–2; Napier (1906) 38–9

ST: Förster (1921b) 132 and n. 2; Hart (1966) 32, 47; Stoneman (1997) 128; Keynes (2003) 6 and n. 18

London, British Library, Add. 62104: see no. **524**

302. 3. London, British Library, Add. 63143

s. x/xi

Contents: gospels (f)

MS: B. Quaritch *Bookhands of the Middle Ages, Part I, Catalogue 1036* (London, 1984) no. 56; *Cat. Add. B.L. 1981–5* (1994) 231; McGurk (2012) 446 [no. 9]

ST: Stoneman (1997) 129

302. 4. London, British Library, Add. 63651

s. xi in.

Contents: prayers (f; from a service-book?)

MS: B. Quaritch *Bookhands of the Middle Ages, Part II, Catalogue 1056* (London, 1985) no. 46; *Cat. Add. B.L. 1986–90* (1993) 4

FACS: Quaritch *Bookhands* no. 46

ST: Stoneman (1997) 130

London, British Library, Add. 71687: see no. **857**

302. 5. London, British Library, Add. 79528 [formerly Handlist no. 756. 5]

s. xi^2, Bury St Edmunds?

Contents: missal (f)

MS: Gneuss (2003b) 303; B. Quaritch *Bookhands of the Middle Ages, Part VII, Catalogue 1315* (London, 2004) no. 56; Hartzell (2006) no. 358; Gneuss (2012) 291

FACS: B. Quaritch *Bookhands of the Middle Ages, Part VII, Catalogue 1315* (London, 2004) no. 56

303. London, British Library, Arundel 16

s. xi/xii, Canterbury CC, (prov. Dover)

Contents: Osbern, *Vita et miracula S. Dunstani* [*BHL* 2344–5]

MS: Stubbs (1874) xliii–xliv; R. Gameson (1995a) 142; Graham—Watson (1998b) 11, 56–7, 69; R. Gameson (1999a) no. 355

DEC: Boase (1953) 42; Dodwell (1954) 48 n. 1, 120; C.M. Kauffmann (1975) no. 7; Ohlgren (1986) no. 218; R. Gameson (1991) 74 n. 77; Budny—Graham (1993); R. Gameson (1995a) 118 n., 136 n.; Tite (1997a) 272

FACS: Boase (1953) pl. 10 (a) [fol. not specified]

ED: Stubbs (1874) 69–128 [Osbern, *Vita S. Dunstani*, coll. as F], 129–61 [base MS (= F) for Osbern, *Miracula S. Dunstani*]

ST: Winterbottom—Lapidge (2012) cli–cliv

304. London, British Library, Arundel 60

s. xi², prob. 1073; added prayers s. xi ex.; whole MS Winchester NM

Contents: *lunarium* for blood-letting; liturgical calendar; computus material ('Winchester Computus'); Psalterium Gallicanum°; Ps. CLI; canticles°; litany; prayers; added prayers (s. xi ex.); Six Ages of the World⁺*; list of bishops of Winchester: c. 1099

MS: Mearns (1914) 63, 79; Wildhagen (1920); Wilmart (1932) 211, 572; F. Wormald (1944) 131–2 [repr. F. Wormald (1984) 156–7]; F. Wormald (1945) 126, 129 [repr. F. Wormald (1984) 64, 67]; Dodwell (1954) 118–19; N.R. Ker (1957) no. 134; Gjerløw (1961) 116, 134–5, 137, 142; N.R. Ker (1964) 103; A.G. Watson (1969) 36 [repr. A.G. Watson (2004) no. IX]; F. Wormald (1973) 122; A.G. Watson (1979) I, no. 436; Lapidge (1983) 16 n. 22, 17 [repr. Lapidge (1993a) 458 n. 22, 459]; Backhouse et al. (1984b) no. 67 [D.H. Turner]; Lapidge (1991a) 68; Dumville (1992a) 25; Laing (1993) 66; *ASMMF* II (1994) 13–18 [no. 174; Pulsiano]; Keynes (1996a) 102, 115 n. 47; Pulsiano (1998b) 85, 103, 105 n. 1; R. Gameson (1999a) no. 356; Gretsch (1999a) 268; Dodwell (2000) 110 n. 38; Gretsch (2000) 86; Borst (2001) I.278–80; Liuzza (2001) 198, 215; Kidd (2002); Biggs (2007a) 16; Chardonnens (2007b) 509, 550; Rosenthal (2007) 22 n. 10; Treharne (2007b) 19 n. 16; Rushforth (2008a) 49–50; Crick (2012) 185 and n. 49; R. Gameson (2012a) 43–4, 46 and n. 142; Rushforth (2012) 209 n. 74; Scragg (2012a) nos. 387–8; Webber (2012) 221 and n. 48

DEC: F. Wormald (1944) 131–2 [repr. F. Wormald (1984) 156–7]; Rice (1952) 210, 216–17; F. Wormald (1952) 66 [no. 25]; C.M. Kauffmann (1975) no. 1; E. Temple (1976) no. 103; Ohlgren (1986) nos. 208, 212; Raw (1990) 213; R. Gameson (1991) 74–5, 81, 103; R. Gameson (1995b) 82, 90, 98, 120, 129, 208, *et passim*; Kidd (2000); Karkov (2007c) 56; Rosenthal (2007) 22–4; R. Gameson (2012c) 272 and n. 71, 273 and n. 72

FACS: E.M. Thompson (1895) pl. 7 [fol. not specified]; A.G. Watson (1979) II, pl. 55 [fol. 149r]; F. Wormald (1984) ills. 79, 118, 185 [fols. 13r, 12v, 52v]; R. Gameson (1991) figs. 19, 30 [fols. 13r, 52v]; *ASMMF*

II (1994) no. 174; Backhouse (1997) pl. 19 [fols. 52v–53r]; Kidd (2000) pls. 1–3 [fols. 12v, 52v, 11v]; Rosenthal (2007) 34 [fol. 12v]

ED: Logeman (1889) 106 [bishops of Winchester]; Oess (1910) [Psalter and canticles, Latin and OE gloss]; Förster (1925a) 192–3 [base MS for Six Ages of the World]; F. Wormald (1934) 141–53 [liturgical calendar (no. 11)]; Lapidge (1991a) 142–7 [litany]; Pulsiano (2001a) [Pss. I–L, Latin and OE gloss, both coll. as J]; Chardonnens (2007b) 288, 386–7, 443 [*lunarium*; dog days and Egyptian days in calendar]; Rushforth (2008a) no. 24 [liturgical calendar]

LANG: Oess (1910) 15–17; Bierbaumer (1977a); Crowley (2000) 130

ST: Lindelöf (1904); Gasquet—Bishop (1908) 76–118; Wildhagen (1921); Wilmart (1932) 211, 572; C.W. Jones (1939) 120; F. Wormald (1946) 75–6, 84–6; Sisam—Sisam (1959); Gjerløw (1961) 134; Raw (1961) 37–42; Korhammer (1976) 239–40; Bestul (1981a) 271–5; Kotzor (1981) I.302*–303*; Tristram (1985) 32 *et passim*; Lapidge (1988b) 259 n. 30 [repr. Lapidge (1993a) 217 n. 30]; Dumville (1993g) 59–64 and nn.; Baker—Lapidge (1995) xlviii–lii [Winchester computus]; Corrêa (1996) 293 n.; Pulsiano (1998b) 86–7 [parallels to no. 407]; Gretsch (1999a) 26–7, 90, 97; Chardonnens (2007b)

305. 5. London, British Library, Arundel 125

s. ix[1], NE France (prob. Saint-Bertin), prov. England by s. x/xi

Contents: Iob [with Hieronymian preface and capitula], Ezras [with Hieronymian preface]

MS: Rand (1929) 175; Bischoff (1980) 107; Bischoff (1998—) II, no. 2411; R. Gameson (2012a) 79 n. 279; R. Gameson (2012d) 353 and n. 34

FACS: Forshall (1834–40) pl. 1 (b) [fol. 95r (detail)]; Rand (1929) pl. CLIX (2) [fol. 52r]

306. London, British Library, Arundel 155, fols. 1–135 and 171–91

1012×1023, Canterbury CC, with additions ibid. s. xi[2] (OE gloss, *Gloria*, Creeds, *Pater noster*); further insertions ibid. s. xii[1]

Contents: liturgical calendar; computus material; Psalterium Romanum (extensively corrected to Gallicanum, s. xi[2]); canticles; [insertions of s. xii[1]: canticles (continued), litany, Mass prayers, hymnal, Monastic canticles, Office of the Dead]; and prayers°; add. s. xi[2]: *Gloria*, creeds, *Pater noster*

MS: Mearns (1914) 63, 83; N.R. Ker (1957) no. 135; T.A.M. Bishop (1959–63a) 94; N.R. Ker (1964) 35; T.A.M. Bishop (1971) 22 [no. 24]; A.G. Watson (1979) I, no. 447; D.H. Turner et al. (1980) 104; Backhouse et al. (1984b) no. 57; N.P. Brooks (1984) 264–5; Gneuss (1985) 115, 137, 140; Lapidge (1991a) 68; Dumville (1992a) 25, 58; Dumville (1993g) 122–3, 139; Vaciago (1993) 13 [no. 54]; *ASMMF* II (1994) 19–37 [no. 175; Pulsiano]; Springer (1995) 144; M.P. Brown (1996) 140, 142, 158; R. Gameson (1998a) 237 n. 30; Muir (1998) 15; R. Gameson (1999a) no. 358; Pulsiano (2001a) xxviii; Rushforth (2001) 138–9; K.L. Brown (2004b) 181, 184; R. Gameson (2004); Heslop (2004) 286, 298; Karkov (2006a) 44; Chardonnens (2007b) 509, 550; Shepard (2007) 201; Rushforth (2008a) 30–1; Wieland (2009) 134, 152; R. Gameson (2012a) 40 n. 105, 78 n. 274, 87 n. 316, 88, 91 n. 331; R. Gameson (2012b) 114, 117; Raw (2012) 461 and n. 7; Rushforth (2012) 206 and n. 54, 207 n. 65; Scragg (2012a) nos. 389–91

DEC: Rice (1952) 198; F. Wormald (1952) 66 [no. 26]; E. Temple (1976) no. 66; Deshman (1977) 169–70; Alexander (1978b) no. 16; Brownrigg (1978) 253–4; Ohlgren (1986) no. 171; Deshman (1988); Raw (1990) 213–14; R. Gameson (1991) 73 n. 74, 77; R. Gameson (1992a) 188; Deshman (1995) 117, 119–20, 140, 180, 203–4; R. Gameson (1995a) 111; R. Gameson (1995b) 84–6, 101, 136, 172 *et passim*; McGurk—Rosenthal (1995b) 286 n. 89 [repr. McGurk (1998) no. XV]; R. Gameson (1996a) 217 n.; Gretsch (1999a) 300–3; Dodwell (2000) 106, 122–3, 147; Rushforth (2001) 138; Farr (2003) 126–7; K.L. Brown (2004b) 184–6; Heslop (2004) 286, 292; Karkov (2004) 98; Withers (2007) 64; Inglis (2008) 5–6; R. Gameson (2010) 121; R. Gameson (2012c) 266, 279 and n. 98, 282 and n. 116

FACS: F. Wormald (1934) facing p. 169 [fol. 5r]; A.G. Watson (1979) II, pl. 30 [fol. 182r]; D.M. Wilson (1984) pl. 223 [fol. 133r]; R. Gameson (1992a) pls. XV–XVI [fols. 12r, 53r]; Gibson (1992) pl. 33 (a) [fol. 133r]; *ASMMF* II (1994) no. 175; Deshman (1995) fig. 136 [fol. 133r]; R. Gameson (1995a) pl. 14 (a) [fol. 11r (detail)]; Backhouse (1997) pl. 14 [fol. 133r]; Dodwell (2000) pls. XLIII, XLIV (a), XLIV (b) [fols. 133r (detail), 10r (detail), 9v (detail)]; R. Gameson (2000b) pl. 9 [fol. 133r]; Farr (2003) fig. 6 [fol. 133r]; K.L. Brown (2004b) pls. 2 [fol. 12r], 3 [fols. 133r, 135v, 147r]; Roberts (2005) p. 87 [fol. 133r]; Withers (2007) 281 [fol. 10r]

ED: F. Wormald (1934) 169–81 [liturgical calendar (no. 13)]; Holthausen (1941) [prayers 1–11, 13–23, Latin and OE]; Förster (1942b) 54 [prayer

12, Latin and OE]; Hurst—Fraipont (1955) 419–23 [Bede, Ascension hymn, coll. as Lᵃ]; J.J. Campbell (1963) [prayers 23–39, Latin and OE]; Gneuss (1968) 241–5 [hymns for St Dunstan, coll. as Ar]; Muir (1988) [variants in Arundel 155 of seven prayers in no. **333** coll. as V]; Lapidge (1991a) 148–52 [litany (addition of s. xii)]; Pulsiano (2001a) [Pss. I–L coll. as λ]; Chardonnens (2007b) 390 [Egyptian days in calendar]; Rushforth (2008a) no. 11 [liturgical calendar]

LANG: Gneuss (1968) 171–2, 176–89; Hofstetter (1987) 440–1

ST: Gasquet—Bishop (1908) 28–30, 32–4 *et passim* [liturgical calendar]; Wildhagen (1913); Wilmart (1932) 211–13 [prayers]; Wilmart (1936a) nos. 49, 56, 92 [prayers]; Förster (1942b) [prayers]; Sisam—Sisam (1959) 47–52 [psalter text]; Gjerløw (1961) 20, 134 [prayers]; Southern (1963) 39 [prayers]; Gneuss (1968) 250 [hymnal]; Korhammer (1973) 179–80 [date; division of psalter]; Korhammer (1976) xvi *et passim* [Monastic canticles]; Kotzor (1981) I. 302*–311*; Bestul (1986) 115–16, 123 n. 70, 124 n. 82 [prayers]; Lapidge (1988b) 259 n. 30 [repr. Lapidge (1993a) 217 n. 30] [liturgical calendar]; Heslop (1990) 154, 175–6, 182 [scribe]; Pfaff (1992a) 273–6 [scribe]; Günzel (1993) 198–9, 203–7 [computistica]; Heslop (1995) 54–7, 78–9, 84–5 [liturgical calendar]; Corrêa (1996) 290 n. 18, 294 n. 39 [prayers]; R. Gameson (1998) 237 and n. 30; Pulsiano (1998b) 86 [parallels to no. **407**]; Gretsch (1999a) 290 [scribe]; Thacker (1999) 384 and n. 55 [liturgical calendar]; Crowley (2000) 141 [prayer glosses]; Borst (2001) I.292; N. Orchard (2002) I.204 [liturgical calendar]; N. Orchard (2005) clxii–clxiii

306. 5. London, British Library, Arundel 235

s. xi ex.

Contents: Hugo of Langres, Commentary on the Psalms [Stegmüller no. 3598]; explanation of the Hebrew alphabet; hymn incipit [SK 17048]

MS: Stegmüller no. 3598; R. Gameson (1999a) no. 361; R. Gameson (2012a) 61 and n. 207, 72 n. 248

FACS: R. Gameson (1999a) pls. 6–7 [fols. 31r, 198r]

307. London, British Library, Burney 277, fol. 42

s. xi², SE England

Contents: laws: *Ine** (f)

MS: N.R. Ker (1957) no. 136; R. Gameson (1999a) no. 362; P. Wormald (1999) 165 [table 4.1], 257–8, 265; Grimmer (2007) 103 n. 5; Treharne

(2007b) 19 n. 16; Scragg (2012a) no. 392; P. Wormald (2012) 535 [no. 17]

ED: Liebermann (1903–16) I.88–98 [base MS (= Bu) for *Ine,* prol. — ch. 23]

LANG: Liebermann (1903–16) I.xx

307. 2. London, British Library, Burney 277, fols. 69–72 (with London, BL, Stowe 1061, fol. 125)

s. xi in. or xi¹, Canterbury CC (Exeter?)

Contents: antiphoner (f)

MS: Keynes (1996b) 129, 155 n. 121; Hartzell (2006) no. 127; Wieland (2009) 135; Rankin (2012) 492 and n. 46, 502 and n. 92

FACS: R. Gameson (2012) pl. 22.3 [Stowe 1061, fol. 125r]

307. 4. London, British Library, Cotton Augustus II. 18

704 or 705, S England

Contents: Letter of Wealdhere, bishop of London

MS: *ChLA* III (1963) no. 185; Chaplais (1978) [repr. Chaplais (1981a) no. XIV]; T.J. Brown (1982) 107 [repr. T.J. Brown (1993a) 207]; Bischoff (1986) 58; Dumville (1999) 105–6

FACS: *ChLA* III (1963) no. 185 [face and dorse]; Chaplais (1978) pl. 1 [face]

ED: Haddan—Stubbs (1869–71) III.274–5; Whitelock (1979) no. 164 [translation]

ST: Parkes (1976a) 166 and n. 17 [repr. Parkes (1991) 126 and n. 17]; Chaplais (1978)

307. 6. London, British Library, Cotton Augustus II. 36

1072×1086, CaCC

Contents: survey of lands in Kent

MS: N.R. Ker (1960) 25

307. 8. London, British Library, Cotton Augustus II. 61

s. ix¹, Canterbury

Contents: decree of the synod of Clofesho, A.D. 803

MS: M.P. Brown (1991) no. 8

FACS: Bond—Thompson (1873–83) III.6; M.P. Brown (1991) 11

ED: KCD no. 185; Haddan—Stubbs (1869–71) III.542–4 [repr. from KCD no. 185]; BCS no. 310; Whitelock (1979) no. 210 [translation]

ST: Keynes (1994a) 9; Cubitt (1995) 280

308. London, British Library, Cotton Caligula A. vii, fols. 11–178

s. x², S England

Contents: *Heliand* (in Old Saxon); charm* (s. xi¹)

MS: Priebsch (1925); F. Wormald (1945) 120, 134 [repr. F. Wormald (1984) 59, 72, 175 n. 40]; N.R. Ker (1957) no. 137; Bischoff (1971a) 105 and n. 158; Bischoff (1986) 129, 278; Robinson—Stanley (1991) 24; *ASMMF* I (1994) 1–4 [no. 177; Doane]; Stanley (1994) 122–3; Behaghel (1996) xxx–xxxii [Taeger]; R. Gameson (2012d) 347–8; Scragg (2012a) nos. 414a, 415–16

DEC: F. Wormald (1945) 120, 134 [repr. F. Wormald 1984) 59, 72]; Rice (1952) 179–80; Raw (1976) 148; E. Temple (1976) no. 33; Ohlgren (1986) no. 138; R. Gameson (1995b) 217 n. 152, 225 n. 194; R. Gameson (2012c) 287 and n. 133

FACS: Priebsch (1925) pls. I–III [fols. 7r, 12v, 163r], IV–V [fols. 5r, 15v, 35v (all details)]; E. Temple (1976) ills. 123–4 [fols. 11r, 21v (details)]; Robinson—Stanley (1991) pls. 19.4.1–5 [fols. 176r–178r]; *ASMMF* I (1994) no. 177; Roberts (2005) p. 59 [fol. 11r]

ED: Sievers (1878/1935) [base MS (= C) for *Heliand*]; Storms (1948) no. 8 [OE charm]; Behaghel (1996) [*Heliand* coll. as C]

LANG: Holthausen (1900) 19; Taeger (1979); Taeger (1981a); Taeger (1982); Taeger (1984); Gallée (1993)

ST: Priebsch (1925); Timmer (1948) 16–18; Drögereit (1950); Werlich (1964) 181–5 [on fitts]; Belkin—Meier (1975) [bibliography]; Whitelock (1975) 19–20 and n. 5; J. Campbell (1978) 257–8 and nn. 23–5; Taeger (1981b) [textual criticism]; Schwab (1988) 82–8; R.L. Harris (1992) 65, 73 n. 67 *et passim* [see p. 489]; Gallée (1993) 360–1; Gneuss (1993) 100 n. 26; Gullath (2003) 148–50; R. McKitterick (2012) 331 and nn. 113–14

308. 2. London, British Library, Cotton Caligula A. viii, fols. 121–8

s. xi/xii or xii in., Winchester OM, (prov. Ely)

Contents: *Vita S. Birini* [*BHL* 1361] (f); Wulfstan of Winchester, *Vita S. Æthelwoldi* [*BHL* 2647] (f)

MS: N.R. Ker (1964) 78; A.G. Watson (1987a) 35; Lapidge—Winterbottom (1991b) clxxi–clxxv; Love (1996) lxxix–lxxx; R. Gameson (1999a) nos. 368–9; Lapidge (2004b) 443; Love (2004) xlviii–l

ED: Lapidge—Winterbottom (1991b) 2–68 [Wulfstan, *Vita S. Æthelwoldi*, coll. as C]; Love (1996) 2–46 [*Vita S. Birini* coll. as C]

ST: Lapidge—Winterbottom (1991b) clxxxii–clxxxv [Æthelwold text]; Love (1996) lxxxiii-lxxxviii [Birinus text]

309. London, British Library, Cotton Caligula A. xiv, fols. 1–36 (the 'Cotton Troper')

s. xi³/⁴, prob. Winchester or Worcester, (prov. Worcester)

Contents: troper

MS: Frere (1894b) xxx and n. 1; Husmann (1964) 154–5; N.R. Ker (1964) 35; Hartzell (1975) 29–30; Planchart (1977) I.43–50; Backhouse et al. (1984b) no. 71; Gneuss (1985) 105 [no. C.2]; Teviotdale (1991); Teviotdale (1992a) 312–15; Pfaff (1995a) 42–3 [Teviotdale]; Hartzell (2006) no. 128; R. Gameson (2012a) 60 and n. 205, 70 n. 240, 76 and n. 263; Gullick (2012) 309 and n. 95; Pfaff (2012) 455 and n. 19; Rankin (2012) 500 and n. 81

DEC: Homburger (1912); Rice (1952) 212; Alexander (1970a) 164; E. Temple (1976) no. 97; F. Wormald (1984) 121; Ohlgren (1986) no. 202; Raw (1990) 35, 214; R. Gameson (1991) 85 n. 128; R. Gameson (1995b) 30–2, 74–6, 94–6, 101–2, 113, 141, 156 *et passim*; Heslop (2007) 65–70; R. Gameson (2012c) 272 and n. 71, 288 and n. 137

FACS: Millar (1926) pls. 29 (a)–(b) [fols. 18r, 20v]; Kendrick (1949) pl. XXII [fols. 3v, 20v]; Swarzenski (1954) figs. 152–3 [fols. 30v, 31r]; E. Temple (1976) ills. 293–5 [fols. 22r, 26r, 31r]; Backhouse et al. (1984b) pl. XXI [fol. 22r]; F. Wormald (1984) ill. 120 [fol. 18r]; M.P. Brown (1991) pl. 77 [fol. 20v]; R. Gameson (1991) figs. 23–4 [fols. 3v, 25r]; R. Gameson (1995b) pls. 21 (a)—(b) [fols. 25r, 18r]; Backhouse (1997) pl. 18 [fol. 22r]; Pulsiano—Treharne (1998a) pl. 114 [fol. 33v]; M.P. Brown (2007a) pls. 134–5 [fols. 20v, 22r]; Heslop (2007) figs. 1 [fol. 26r (detail)], 2 [fol. 26v (detail)], 3 (d) [fol. 25r (detail)], 4 (b) [fol. 26r (detail)], 4 (d) [fol. 26v (detail)]; Panayotova (2007) pl. V [fol. 18r]; R. Gameson (2012) pl. 10.11 [fol. 3v]

ED: Frere (1894b) 101–23 [tropes], 124 [list of sequences]; Planchart (1977) II, *passim* [trope repertory as represented in this MS]

ST: Planchart (1977) I.50–5 [relationship between this MS and no. **597**]; Gneuss (1985) 104–5; Teviotdale (1991); Teviotdale (1992a); Teviotdale (1992b); Jacobsson (1993); Corrêa (1996) 288 n.; R. Gameson (1996a) 223; Rankin (1996) 326–7; Kruckenberg (1997) 161–84; Teviotdale (1998) 219–26

310. London, British Library, Cotton Caligula A. xiv, fols. 93–130

s. xi med.

Contents: Ælfric, Lives of St Martin* and St Thomas*; anon., Life of St Mildred*

MS: N.R. Ker (1957) no. 138; A.G. Watson (1978) 309; Rollason (1982) 29; Teviotdale (1991) 12–16, 24–5; Muir (1998) 10; Scragg (1996) 220; Scragg (2012a) nos. 417, 417a

FACS: Wilcox (2006a) fig. 6.1 [fol. 111v]

ED: Skeat (1881–1900) II.242–312 [Ælfric, *Lives of Saints*, no. XXXI (St Martin), coll. as K], II.398–424 [Ælfric, *Lives of Saints*, no. XXXVI (St Thomas), coll. as K]; Swanton (1975) [base MS for anonymous Life of St Mildred]

ST: Scragg (1979) 263; Rollason (1982); Reinsma (1987) 305; J. Hill (1996) 243; Scragg (1996) 220; J. Hill (1997) 409–10, 414–15; Hollis (1998a) 41–2, 44–50, 53–5, 61, 64; Rosser (2000) 140; Biggs et al. (2001) 330–2, 347–50 [SS. Martin, Mildred]; Wilcox (2006a)

311. London, British Library, Cotton Caligula A. xv, fols. 3–117

s. viii² with additions, s. ix¹ and ix/x, NE France, prov. England by s. ix/x

Contents: Jerome, *De uiris inlustribus* [*CPL* 616], *Vita S. Pauli primi eremitae* [*CPL* 617; *BHL* 6596]; Isidore, *Etymologiae* [*CPL* 1186], I.xxi–xxvii; Cyprian, *Ad Quirinum Testimonia* [*CPL* 39], bk. III; Cassiodorus (?), *De computo paschali*; computus texts

MS: Planta (1802) 45–6; *CLA* II (1935) no. 183*; C.W. Jones (1943) 112, 353–5 *et passim* [the 'Canterbury' computus]; McGurk (1961b) 10 [repr. McGurk (1998) no. V]; Bischoff—Nörr (1963) 12 n.; N.R. Ker (1964) 43; Bischoff (1965) 237 n. 30 [repr. Bischoff (1966–81) III.12 n. 30]; Bischoff (1968a) 309; Rella (1977) 165; C.W. Jones (1980) 670; Rella (1980) 111; Baker—Lapidge (1995) xl; Bischoff (1998—) II, no. 2417a; Lapidge (2006) 169, 299, 311, 315, 316; Treharne (2007b) 19 n. 16; Withers (2007) 76; Barker-Benfield (2008) III.1828; Wieland (2009) 130, 153; R. Gameson (2012d) 348 and n. 14

DEC: F. Wormald (1957b) 31, 32, 34 [repr. F. Wormald (1984) 146, 147, 149]; Lawrence (1982) 106, 107; R. Gameson (1995b) 101, 182 n. 148

FACS: Withers (2007) 77 [fol. 122v]

ED: C.W. Jones (1980) 669–72 [*De flexibus digitorum* coll. as C]

ST: Siegmund (1949) 64; C.W. Jones (1965) 265, 280 n. 30; Lambert (1969–72) nos. 260–1; Biggs et al. (2001) 378–81; D. Ganz (2004) 500 and n. 4; Withers (2007) 76–7

London, British Library, Cotton Caligula A. xv, fols. 120–53: see no. **411**

312. London, British Library, Cotton Claudius A. i, fols. 5–36

s. x med., Canterbury CC? glosses s. x^2, (prov. Glastonbury?)

Contents: Fredegaud/Frithegod of Canterbury and Brioude, *Breuiloquium Vitae Wilfridi*, glossed

MS: A. Campbell (1950) vii–ix; N.R. Ker (1957) no. 140; N.R. Ker (1964) 39; Rella (1977) 165; Rella (1980) 111 n. 10; Dumville (1987) 149–50; Lapidge (1988a) 51–3, 58–61 [repr. Lapidge (1993a) 163–9, 174–7]; Dumville (1992b) 158, 181–3; Dumville (1993g) 16, 93, 142; Vaciago (1993) 13–14 [no. 55]; Lapidge (2004a) 135–7, 145; Barker-Benfield (2008) I.609; R. Gameson (2012b) 100; Scragg (2012a) nos. 443–4

FACS: Lapidge (1988a) pls. I–II [fols. 11r, 32v] [repr. Lapidge (1993a) pls. I–II]

ED: Raine (1879–94) I.509–59 [base MS for Frithegod, *Breuiloquium*]; Napier (1900) no. 8 [OE glosses]; A. Campbell (1950) 1–62 [Frithegod, *Breuiloquium*, coll. as C]

ST: Lapidge (1988a) [repr. Lapidge (1993a) 157–84]; Lapidge (1994a) 126–8; Chiesa (2001) 10 n. 29; Lapidge (2004a) 135, 137 n. 10

312. 1. London, British Library, Cotton Claudius A. i, fols. 41-157

s. xi/xii or xi ex. or xii in., West Country?

Contents: Paulinus of Milan, *Vita S. Ambrosii* [*CPL* 169; *BHL* 377]; *Inuentio SS. Geruasii et Protasii* [*BHL* 3514]; *Inuentio S. Nazarii* [*BHL* 6050]; pseudo-Sebastian of Montecassino, *Vita S. Hieronymi* [*CPL* 622; *BHL* 3870]; Venantius Fortunatus, *Vita S. Hilarii* [*CPL*

1038; *BHL* 3885]; Venantius Fortunatus (?), *Epistula ad 'Pascentium papam'*; Hilarius (?), *Epistula*; Hilarius of Arles, *Sermo in depositione S. Honorati* [*BHL* 3975]; pseudo-Jerome, *Liber de ortu B. Mariae et infantia Saluatoris* [*BHL* 5334–7; *CPPM* II, no. 899; *CPL* 633 (*Epist. supp.* xlviii–xlix)]; Paulus Diaconus of Naples, *Vita S. Mariae Aegyptiacae* [*BHL* 5415]; *Vita S. Martialis* [*BHL* 5552]; Leontius of Cyprus, *Vita S. Iohannis Eleemosynarii*, trans. Anastasius Bibliothecarius [*BHL* 4388]; Bede, *Vita S. Cudbercti* (prose) [*CPL* 1379; *BHL* 2019]; Bede, *Historia ecclesiastica* [*CPL* 1375] IV.xxix–xxx

MS: Planta (1802) 188; Colgrave (1940) 30–1; Jane Stevenson (1996a) 40–3; R. Gameson (1999a) no. 371; Magennis (2002) 12–13 and n. 36; Gneuss (2003b) 297–8

ED: Colgrave (1940) 142–307 [Bede, prose *Vita S. Cudbercti*, coll. as Cl]; Jane Stevenson (1996b) 51–98 [Paulus, *Vita S. Mariae Aegyptiacae*, coll. as C]; Magennis (2002) 140–209 [Paulus, *Vita S. Mariae Aegyptiacae*, coll. as C]

ST: Biggs et al. (2001) 321–3 [Magennis]

London, British Library, Cotton Claudius A. iii, fols. 2–7 and 9*: see no. **362**

313. London, British Library, Cotton Claudius A. iii, fols. 9–18 and 87–105

s. xi²/⁴ or xi med., prob. Canterbury CC

Contents: pontifical (including litany and second English Coronation *ordo*) (incomplete)

MS: Liebermann (1903–16) I.xxxii; N.R. Ker (1964) 35; Brückmann (1973) 434–5; T.A.M. Bishop (1971) 20 [no. 22]; D.H. Turner (1971) xxviii–xxxix; Hartzell (1989) 84–5; Lapidge (1991a) 69; Hartzell (2006) no. 130; O'Brien O'Keeffe (2006) 267; Wieland (2009) 124

DEC: Rice (1952) 197–8; D.H. Turner (1971) v, vii–viii; Higgitt (1979) 285–6; Heslop (1984); Ramsay—Sparks (1988) 16, 18; Heslop (1992c) 305 and n. 25

FACS: D.H. Turner et al. (1980) pl. 11 [fol. 87v]

ED: D.H. Turner (1971) 89–113 [base MS for 'Claudius Pontifical II']; Lapidge (1991a) 155–6 [litany]

ST: D.H. Turner et al. (1980) 105; Dumville (1992a) 69, 72, 77–8, 91–3, 124; Davril (1995) 27; Pfaff (1999a) 6

314. London, British Library, Cotton Claudius A. iii, fols. 31–86 and 106–50

s. x/xi, Worcester or York

Contents: metrical inscription (*Thureth*)**; laws: *VI Æthelred*⁺* (s. xi^{1/4}); pontifical (including litany) [incomplete]; benedictional [incomplete]

MS: Liebermann (1903–16) I.xxxii; Dobbie (1942) lxxxviii–xc; K. Sisam (1953a) 279; N.R. Ker (1957) no. 141; T.A.M. Bishop (1971) 14 [no. 16]; N.R. Ker (1971) 321 [repr. N.R. Ker (1985) 15]; D.H. Turner (1971) viii–xxviii; Brückmann (1973) 434–5; A.G. Watson (1979) I, no. 518; Whitelock et al. (1981) I.339; Lapidge (1986a) 270; Lapidge (1991a) 69; Robinson—Stanley (1991) 22; Dumville (1992a) 69, 73 and n. 35, 78–9, 90, 124 and n. 214; C.A. Jones (1999) 126; P. Wormald (1999) 164 [table 4.1], 190–5; Dance (2004) 31 n. 6; C.A. Jones (2004) 334–8, 342, 344–7, 350, 352; A. Orchard (2004) 66 n. 15; P. Wormald (2004) 14; C.A. Jones (2005a) 116–18; C.A. Jones (2005b) 235; N. Orchard (2005) ci–cii, clxxxiii–cxci, 443 *et passim*; O'Brien O'Keeffe (2006) 267; Wieland (2009) 124; A. Orchard (2012) 696 [no. 6]; Scragg (2012a) nos. 307, 450–1; P. Wormald (2012) 534 [no. 5]

DEC: R. Gameson (1991) 68 n. 39; C.A. Jones (2004) 339

FACS: A.G. Watson (1979) II, pls. 29 (a)–(b) [fols. 33v, 35v]; Robinson—Stanley (1991) pl. 10 [fol. 31v]

ED: Liebermann (1903–16) I.246–58, even pages, left-hand column [*VI Atr* (OE) coll. as K], 247–57, odd pages [base MS for *VI Atr* (Latin paraphrase)]; Dobbie (1942) 97 [OE metrical inscription (*Thureth*)]; D.H. Turner (1971) 1–88 [base MS for 'Claudius Pontifical I']; Whitelock et al. (1981) I.362–73 [base MS for *VI Atr* (Latin paraphrase)]; Lapidge (1991a) 153–4 [litany]

ST: Dobbie (1942) lxxxviii; N.R. Ker (1948) 71 n. 3 [repr. N.R. Ker (1985) 55 n. 3]; D.H. Turner et al. (1980) 105; Prescott (1987) 123–4, 139–41; Banting (1989) xx, xxiv *et passim*; Hartzell (1989) 84; Rosenthal (1992) 150; Dumville (1993g) 65 n. 282; O'Brien O'Keeffe (1994) 221; Davril (1995) 27; Corrêa (1996) 302–3; R. Gameson (1996a) 213–14, 238; Pfaff (1999a) 5 n. 10, 6–24; Ronalds—Clunies Ross (2001); N. Orchard (2002) I.87 and n. 200, 90 and n. 206; C.A. Jones (2004) 337–8, 343

315. London, British Library, Cotton Claudius B. iv

s. xi$^{2/4}$, Canterbury StA?, (prov. ibid.)

Contents: Hexateuch* (part trans. Ælfric)

MS: Crawford (1922) 2–3; N.R. Ker (1957) no. 142; F. Wormald (1957b) 30–1, 32 [repr. F. Wormald (1984) 145–7]; N.R. Ker (1964) 43; Morrell (1965) 3–13; Dodwell—Clemoes (1974) 16–42; Backhouse et al. (1984b) no. 157; M.P. Brown (1991) 52–3; Laing (1993) 71; Clemoes (1994b); Noel (1995) 204–5; Withers (1999) 112–18; *ASMMF* VII (2000) 37–43 [no. 182; Doane]; Roberts (2005) 78–81 [no. 17]; Biggs (2007a) 4, 9, 11 [T.N. Hall], 19 [Twomey]; Shepard (2007) 113–14, 122; Withers (2007) 4, 7–11, 18, 44–54, 58–9, 62–4, 78, 81, 83, 105–6, 117, 130–1, 299 n. 24 *et passim*; Barker-Benfield (2008) I.lxi n. 28, 95, 376, 417, 424, 506, II.1380, 1398; Marsden (2008) xlv–l; Graham (2009) 187, 194; Crick (2012) 180 and n. 25; R. Gameson (2012a) 61 n. 213, 75 n. 257; Marsden (2012) 429 and n. 105; Scragg (2012a) nos. 452–3

DEC: Herbert (1911); Dodwell (1950) 82, 91 n. 1; Rice (1952) 206–7; Morrell (1965) 3–13; Dodwell (1971a); Dodwell (1971b) 87, 115–16, 221 n. 47; Raw (1976) 133–48; E. Temple (1976) no. 86; Mellinkoff (1970); Mellinkoff (1973) 155–65; Dodwell—Clemoes (1974) 58–73; Gatch (1975) 3–15; Heimann (1978); Lawrence (1982) 105; Budny (1984); F. Wormald (1984) 106, 119, 145–7, 181 n. 6; Mellinkoff (1986); Ohlgren (1986) no. 191; R. Gameson (1991) 75; Rumble (1994a) 16; R. Gameson (1995a) 122 n.; R. Gameson (1995b) 9, 10 n. 22, 37, 43, 54, 57, 63–4, 69, 109–11, 116, 130, 140–4, 146, 148, 156, 162, 164–5, 169–70 *et passim*; Wieland (1998) 16 n. 17; Budny (1999) 269; Dodwell (2000) 102–5, 111–15, 130–40, 143–5, 147; Binski (2006) 388; Keefer (2007b) 99; Rosenthal (2007) 30; Shepard (2007) 113–14; Withers (2007) 14, 17–19, 21–5, 27–8, 90, 94, 97–8, 102, 104, 129–30, 183–4, 283, 285; Karkov (2009) 246; Broderick (2011) 271–5, 277–80, 283–5; Withers (2011) 247–50, 251–2, 254–7, 265–9; R. Gameson (2012c) 278 and n. 97, 284 and nn. 120–1, 287

FACS: Dodwell—Clemoes (1974) [complete facsimile]; E.M. Thompson (1895) pls. 8 (a)–(b) [fols. not specified]; Millar (1926) pl. 28 [fol. 61v]; Kendrick (1949) pl. XXIV (4) [fol. 61v]; F. Wormald (1952) pls. 19 (a)–(b) [fols. 22v, 36v]; Rickert (1954) pl. 35 [folio not specified]; Swarzenski (1954) figs. 106, 132 [fols. 20r, 139v]; Pächt (1960) pls. 109 (d), 168 (d)–(e) [fols. 4r, 45r, 141r]; Mellinkoff (1973) pls. b, d, e [fols. 107v, 121r, 139v (details)]; Gatch (1975) 3, 8–9 [fols. 14r, 15r];

E. Temple (1976) ills. 265–72 [fols. 2r, 139v, 32r, 36r, 15v, 38r, 110v, 111r (all details)]; Heimann (1978) 3, 8 [fols. 10v, 139v]; Dodwell (1982) figs. 12–13, 33, 35, 38, 46 [fols. 10r, 19r, 27v, 32r, 72v, 76v]; F. Wormald (1984) ills. 123, 177–9 [fols. 15v, 26v, 36v (details)]; Mellinkoff (1986) 53–7 [fols. 78r, 81v, 82v, 123v, 124r]; M.P. Brown (1991) 54 [fols. 63v, 92v, 144r]; Alexander (1992) fig. 64 [fol. 128r]; R. Gameson (1995b) pls. 9 [fol. 2r], 14 [fol. 35v], 29 [fol. 38r]; Backhouse (1997) pl. 17 [fol. 7v]; *ASMMF* VII (2000) no. 182; Dodwell (2000) pls. XXX (b), XXXI, XXXII (a), XXXII (b), XXXIII (a), XXXIII (b), XXXVI (b), XXXVII, XXXVIII (a), XXXVIII (b), XLVI (b), XLVII (a), XLVII (b), XLVIII (a), XLIX (b), L, LI (a), LI (b), LII (a), LII (b), LIII (a), LIV (b), LV [fols. 89r, 121v, 54r, 56r, 49r, 10v, 139v, 42v, 54v, 69r, 35r, 24r, 51v, 33r, 31v, 28r, 35v, 26v, 6r, 55v, 141r, 28r (all details)]; M.P. Brown (2003a) 36 [fol. 144r]; Roberts (2005) colour pl. 2 [fol. 38r], pl. 17 [fol. 38r], p. 81 [fol. 16r]; Rosenthal (2007) 36 [fols. 44v, 47v]; Shepard (2007) figs. 33 [fol. 43v], 34 [fol. 44r (detail)], 37 [fol. 107v (detail)], 41 [fol. 142v (detail)], 42 [fol. 30r (detail)]; Withers (2007) 5 [fol. 19r], 19 [fols. 2v–3r], 20 [28v–29r], 24 [fol. 113v], 27 [fol. 150v], 28 [fol. 148v], 29 [fol. 110v], 30 [fol. 78r], 31 [fol. 7v], 33 [fols. 16v–17r], 34 [fols. 50v–51r], 36 [fol. 38r], 41 [fol. 17v], 42 [fol. 27v], 45 [fols. 41v–42r], 55 [fol. 36r], 56 [fol. 14v], 65 [fol. 26v], 68 [fol. 18v], 75 [fol. 128r], 79 [fol. 142r], 88 [fols. 30v–31r], 91 [fol. 97r], 92 [fol. 102r], 93 [fol. 35v], 95 [fol. 122r], 96 [fols. 125v–126r], 97 [fol. 125v], 98 [fol. 125v], 99 [fol. 27r], 100 [fol. 43v], 101 [fol. 46r], 103 [fol. 34v], 107 [fol. 68v], 108 [fol. 69r], 109 [fols. 69v–70r], 110 [fols. 70v–71r], 111 [fols. 71v–72r], 112 [fols. 72v–73r], 113 [fols. 73v–74r], 114 [fols. 74v–75r], 115 [fols. 75v–76r], 116 [fols. 76v–77r], 122 [fol. 73r], 123 [fol. 112r], 125 [fol. 81r], 126 [fol. 88r], 129 [fol. 73v], 135 [fols. 99v–100r], 151 [fol. 103r], 152 [fol. 103r], 161 [fol. 100v], 164 [fol. 6v], 169 [fols. 38v–39r], 175 [fol. 155v], 185 [fols. 20v–21r], 187 [fol. 21r], 188 [fols. 1v–2r], 197 [fol. 9r], 198 [fols. 9v–10r], 199 [fols. 10v–11r], 200 [fols. 11v–12r], 201 [fol. 12v], 225 [fols. 52v–53r], 235 [fols. 53v–54r], 239 [fol. 54v–55r], 240 [fols. 57v–58r], 241 [fols. 58v–59r], 244 [fols. 59v–60r], 245 [fols. 60v–61r], 246 [fols. 61v–62r], 250 [fols. 62v–63r], 252 [fol. 63v–64r], 253 [fols. 64v–65r], 254 [fols. 65v–66r], 257 [fols. 66v–67r], 258 [fols. 67v–68r], 267 [fol. 139v], 268 [fol. 140r], CD–ROM [fols. 1–156v, front- and backsheet]; Owen-Crocker (2009) figs. 1.4 [fol. 57v], 7.32 [fol. 26r]

ED: Crawford (1922) [base MS (= B) for OE preface to Genesis and OE Genesis — Joshua]; Crawford (1923) 125–8 [base MS for rubrics to illustrations on fols. 4r–v, 5v, 7v, 8v–12v, 14r, 15v, 16v, 17r, 19v, 34v, 40v, 44v, 51r–v, 155v]; A.B. Smith (1985) [glossary to *Hexateuch* coll. as B]; Marsden (2008) 3–189 [OE preface to Genesis and OE Genesis — Joshua coll. as B]

LANG: Wohlfahrt (1885); Brühl (1892); Wilkes (1905); Crawford (1923); A.B. Smith (1985)

ST: E.M. Thompson (1895) 25–6; Burchfield (1953); Swarzenski (1954); Morrell (1965) 3–13; Pope (1967–8) I.85, 143 and nn. 4–5; Dodwell— Clemoes (1974) 13–73; P.S. Baker (1980) 23–8 [Byrhtferth's putative contribution to the translation]; Dodwell (1982); F. Wormald (1984) 123; Reinsma (1987) 293; Raw (1990) 214; Barnhouse (1994); Withers (1994); Marsden (1995) xix, 402–39; Graham (1997b); Withers (1999) 128–9; Barnhouse—Withers (2000); Graham (2000d); Marsden (2000); Rosenthal (2007) 30–1; Withers (2007) 87, 89–90, 94–7, 102, 104 [sources], 174–6 [social impact]; Marsden (2008) lxix–cliii; Doane—Stoneman (2011)

316. London, British Library, Cotton Claudius B. v

s. ix[1], W Germany, prov. England (royal court) by s. x[1], prov. Bath s. x[1]

Contents: Acts of the Council of Constantinople (680)

MS: Thompson—Warner (1881–4) 88; J.A. Robinson (1923) 61–4; N.R. Ker (1964) 7; Rella (1977) 50; Rella (1980) 111; Keynes (1985a) 159–65; Dumville (1987) 175 and n. 159; Bischoff (1998—) II, no. 2418; Karkov (2004) 55; Barker-Benfield (2008) III.1696; R. Gameson (2012d) 349 and n. 17; D. Ganz (2012) 190 n. 14

DEC: Dodwell (1971b) 212 n. 56

FACS: Keynes (1985a) pl. VI [fol. 5r]

ST: Grierson (1940a) 101; Siegmund (1949) 158 and n. 2; Conner (1993) 18; Karkov (2004) 54; R. McKitterick (2012) 330 and n. 107

316. 1. London, British Library, Cotton Claudius B. v, fol. 132v
[miniature pasted on to fol. 132v of no. **316**]

c. 800, Court of Charlemagne

Contents: gospels or gospel lectionary (f)

MS: *CLA* Supplement (1971) no. 1702; McGurk (1961a) no. 21; Bischoff (1965) 55 [repr. Bischoff (1966–81) III.158–9, 161]; Bischoff (1976b) 12 [repr. Bischoff (1966–81) III.177]; Keynes (1985a) 159–60 n. 89; Bischoff (1998—) II, no. 2419; Wieland (2009) 121

DEC: Köhler (1930–60) II.47–8; F. Wormald (1971b) 310–11 and nn. [repr. F. Wormald (1984) 81 and nn.]; Raw (1990) 71, 214

FACS: Köhler (1930–60) *Tafeln* II, pl. 32 (c) [fol. 132v (detail)]

ST: Köhler (1952)

317. London, British Library, Cotton Claudius C. vi, fols. 5–169

s. xi med. (after 1049), Continent, (prov. Canterbury CC?)

Contents: *Notitia Galliarum* [*CPL* 2342]; letters of Popes Leo I and Zosimus; Burchard of Worms, *Decretum*

MS: Z.N. Brooke (1931) 89, 97, 237; A.G. Watson (1969) 19 [repr. A.G. Watson (2004) no. IX]; Kéry (1999) 137

ST: Schanz et al. (1914–20) IV/ii.130 [*Notitia Galliarum*]; R. McKitterick (2012) 330 and n. 109

319. London, British Library, Cotton Cleopatra A. iii

s. x²/⁴ or x med., Canterbury StA

Contents: three glossaries⁺*

MS: Lübke (1890) 396–401; Schlutter (1908); Blomfield (1939); N.R. Ker (1957) no. 143; T.A.M. Bishop (1959–63a) 93; Quinn (1961); Quinn (1966); Pheifer (1974) xxxi–xxxv; P.S. Baker (1980) 29–30; O'Brien O'Keeffe (1985) 67; Voss (1988b); Voss (1989); A.K. Brown (1992) 104–5, 107–8; Dumville (1994a) 137, 139, 142 and n. 48; Rusche (1996); Webster—Brown (1997) 243 [no. 129]; Lapidge (1998) 36–7; Gretsch (1999a) 140–1, 351, 367–8; Lendinara (2001a); Meaney (2004) 495; Barker-Benfield (2008) I.95, 519, II.1381, III.1810, 1814; Wieland (2009) 146; Giliberto (2011) 125 and n. 24

FACS: M.P. Brown (1991) pl. 6 [fol. 77r]

ED: Wright—Wülker (1884) 338–473 [no. 11] [base MS for glossary (art. 1)], 258–83, 475–85 [no. 8 and part of no. 12][base MS for glossary (art. 2)], 485–535 [no. 12][base MS for glossary (art. 3); and see corrections to Wright's text by Sievers (1891) 321–32]; Stryker (1951) [base MS for glossary (art. 1)]; Quinn (1956) 15–92 [base MS for glossaries (arts. 2–3)]; Rusche (1996)

LANG: Jordan (1906) 12; Schabram (1965) 55; Korhammer (1976) 214; Wenisch (1979) 42, 337; Hofstetter (1987) 521; Voss (1988a); Kittlick (1998)

ST: Sievers (1891) 323–32; Lapidge (1998) 36–7 [Aldhelm glosses from glossary (art. 3) quoted by Byrhtferth]; Gretsch (1999a) 102, 140–1, 149–55, 367–8; Pulsiano (2000) 192–3; Lendinara (2001a); Lapidge (2009) 305 [Aldhelm glosses from glossary (art. 3) quoted by Byrhtferth]; Healey (2011) 8; Rusche (2011) 402–14

320. London, British Library, Cotton Cleopatra A. iii*

s. viii², Northumbria? S England (Kent)?, prov. Canterbury StA s. x?

Contents: Augustine, *De consensu Euangelistarum* [*CPL* 273] (f)

MS: *CLA* II (1935) 184*; McGurk (1961b) 11 [no. 25] [repr. McGurk (1998) no. V]; Römer (1972b) 169; Bischoff et al. (1988a) 14 n. 20; Dumville (1992a) 105 and n. 53

321. London, British Library, Cotton Cleopatra A. vi, fols. 2–53

s. x, prob. x med., W England or Wales?

Contents: Donatus, *Ars maior*; a 'parsing grammar' [inc. 'Iustus quae pars']; two grammatical treatises [*BCLL* no. 334]; Iohannes Diaconus (?), *Carmen de Gregorio Magno* [SK 5725]

MS: Bursill-Hall (1981) 115 [no. 100.98 (unreliable)]; Dumville (1987) 157 n. 47; Dumville (1994a) 147 and n. 83; Lapidge (1994b) 116; Law (1995) 202, 276; Wieland (2009) 144; D. Ganz (2012) 195 and n. 42

DEC: F. Wormald (1945) 120–1 [repr. F. Wormald (1984) 59]; Kendrick (1949) 33 n. 1; Rice (1952) 206; E. Temple (1976) no. 27; Brownrigg (1978) 240 n. 4; Ohlgren (1986) no. 115; R. Gameson (1992c) 127 and n. 54, 140 and n. 107, 142 n. 115, 143–4, 147 n. 147

FACS: E. Temple (1976) ill. 96 [fol. 19v]

ST: Law (1982) 87 n. 36 ['Interrogationes' or 'Ars grammatica' on fols. 37v–42v]; *BCLL* (1985) no. 334 ['Ars grammatica']; Gneuss (1990) 12 n. 39 [repr. Scragg (2003) 83 n. 39]; Gneuss (1994) 73 [Greek terms quoted in grammatical treatises]; Knappe (1996) 231 and n. 4; Valtorta (2006) 214 [the fragment of Paulus Diaconus, *Expositio Artis Donati*, on fol. 49]; Lendinara (2007a) 85–6 and n. 105; Mirto (2007) 359 and nn. 44–5

321. 5. London, British Library, Cotton Cleopatra A. vii, fols. 107–47

s. xi ex. or xi/xii

Contents: Helperic, *De computo*; short computus text

MS: Planta (1802) 576; McGurk (1974) 2; R. Gameson (1999a) no. 374

ST: *CSLMA* III (2010) 421–9 [Helperic]

322. London, British Library, Cotton Cleopatra B. xiii, fols. 1–58

s. xi³/⁴, Exeter [one vol. with no. 520?]

Contents: Homilies*; coronation oath*; Ælfric's translations of *Pater noster** and Apostles' Creed*

MS: Bethurum (1957) 7; N.R. Ker (1957) no. 144; N.R. Ker (1964) 82; Pope (1967–8) I.33–4; Collins—Clemoes (1974) 319; Strongman (1977) no. 51; Drage (1978) 359–61; A.G. Watson (1979) I, no. 524; A.G. Watson (1986) 136 [repr. A.G. Watson (2004) no. IV]; Scragg (1992) xxxiii–xxxiv; Conner (1993) 5; Clemoes (1997) 21–4; P. Wormald (1999) 448 n. 118; *ASMMF* VIII (2000) 23–9 [no. 185; Wilcox]; Treharne (2003) 161, 166; Dance (2004) 35 n. 28; Lionarons (2004c) 424; Wilcox (2004b) 392; Clayton (2008) 96–100; Treharne (2009a); Scragg (2012a) nos. 106, 454–63

FACS: A.G. Watson (1979) II, pl. 41 [fol. 10r]; *ASMMF* VIII (2000) no. 185

ED [the order of the following items is that of the manuscript, listed according to the numbering of individual articles in N.R. Ker (1957) 183–4; only the most recent editions are cited]:

art. 1: Napier (1883) 182–90 [base MS (= N) for Hom. XL (*In die iudicii*)]

art. 2: Clemoes (1997) 313–16 [Ælfric, CH I, Hom. XVII (Second Sunday after Easter), coll. as J]

art. 3: Clemoes (1997) 178–89 [Ælfric, CH I, Hom. I (*De initio creaturae*), coll. as J]

art. 4: Bethurum (1957) 246–50 [base MS (= N) for Hom. XVIII (*De dedicatione ecclesie*)]

art. 5: Bethurum (1957) 242–5 [base MS (= N) for Hom. XVII (*Lectio secundum Lucam*)]

art. 6: Luiselli Fadda (1979) 71–99 [base MS for Hom. IV (*In Letania maiore*)]; Bazire—Cross (1982) 16–23 [Hom. 1 (*Feria .II. in Letania maiore*) coll. as J]; Scragg (1992) 315–26 [Vercelli Hom. XIX coll. as P]

art. 7: Stubbs (1874) 355–7 [base MS for *Promissio regis*]; Liebermann (1903–16) I.214–16 [coronation oath only, coll. as Cp]; Clayton (2008) 148–9 [base MS] art. 8: Pope (1967–8) I.357–8 [Ælfric, Suppl. Hom. VIII (Fifth Sunday after Easter), lines 1–19, coll. as J]

art 9: Napier (1883) 130 [last eight lines of Hom. XXVIII ('Her is gyt oþer wel god eaca') coll. as N]

art. 10: as Thorpe (1844–6) II.596, not collated

ST: P.R. Robinson (1978) 238 [repr. P.R. Robinson (1994) 35]; Sauer (1978) 93; Scragg (1979) 255–6; R. Gameson (1996b) 145 nn. 10, 14; Swan (1998) 205–14; Kleist (2007c) 494; A. Orchard (2007) 323 [Bethurum Hom. no. xvii]; Swan (2007a) 404

323. London, British Library, Cotton Cleopatra B. xiii, fols. 59–90

s. xi in. or xi¹, Canterbury StA?, (prov. ibid.)

Contents: B., *Vita S. Dunstani* [*BHL* 2342]; rhymed responsory from an office for St Gregory

MS: Stubbs (1874) xviii–xx, xxxix–xl; N.R. Ker (1964) 43; Dumville (1993g) 147 n. 39; *ASMMF* VIII (2000) 23–9 [no. 185; Wilcox]; Hartzell (2006) no. 131; Treharne (2007b) 17, 20, 24; Barker-Benfield (2008) I.203, III.1746, 1791, 1807; Winterbottom—Lapidge (2012) lxxxiii–lxxxiv

FACS: *ASMMF* VIII (2000) no. 185

ED: Stubbs (1874) 3–52 [B., *Vita S. Dunstani*, coll. as B]; Winterbottom—Lapidge (2012) 2–108 [B., *Vita S. Dunstani*, coll. as D], 147–50 [base MS (= D) for four passages in which rhymed prose replaces verse of B.'s original text]

ST: Stubbs (1874) x–xxx; Whitelock (1979) 897–903 [no. 234 (transla-tion)]; Lapidge (1992e) [repr. Lapidge (1993a) 293–315]; Graham—Watson (1998) 56; Winterbottom (2000); Biggs et al. (2001) 179–81; Treharne (2007a) 262–4; Winterbottom—Lapidge (2012) lxxxv–cxxv; Lapidge (2012a) 693

324. London, British Library, Cotton Cleopatra C. viii, fols. 4–37

s. x/xi, Canterbury CC

Contents: Prudentius, *Psychomachia* [*CPL* 1441]; pseudo-Columbanus (pseudo-Alcuin), *Praecepta uiuendi* [SK 5960] (f)

MS: N.R. Ker (1957) no. 145; T.A.M. Bishop (1959–63b) 421; Backhouse et al. (1984b) no. 45; Vaciago (1993) 14 [no. 56]; Wieland (1997a) 170–1;

K.L. Brown (2004b) 181, 185–6; Petruccione (2008) 234 n. 15; Rankin (2012) 505 n. 112; Scragg (2012a) nos. 464–5

DEC: Rice (1952) 208; F. Wormald (1952) 67 [no. 29]; F. Wormald (1957b) 32 [repr. F. Wormald (1984) 147]; E. Temple (1976) no. 49; Brownrigg (1978) 246 n. 2; Ohlgren (1986) no. 154; Raw (1990) 215; R. Gameson (1992a) 200–6, 211; R. Gameson (1995b) 8, 15, 19 n. 61, 93–4; Wieland (1997a) 169 n. 3, 171, 175–6, 178–83; Wieland (1998) 4, 6–9, 11, 15 n. 6, 17 n. 29, 18 n. 32, 19 n. 48, 20 n. 50; Dodwell (2000) 133; Karkov (2001a) 115 n. 3, 116 n. 7, 124; K.L. Brown (2004b) 187; Heslop (2004) 297 n. 25

FACS: Stettiner (1905) pls. 43–4 [fols. 6v, 19v, 27r, 33v], 45–6 [fols. 31r, 31v, 32r, 33r], 49–50 [fols. 1r, 1v, 2r, 2v, 3v, 4r], 51–2 [fols. 5r, 5v, 7r, 7v, 8r], 51–2 [fols. 5r, 5v, 7r, 7v, 8r], 53–4 [fols. 8v, 9r, 9v, 10r, 10v, 11r], 55–6 [fols. 12v, 13r, 13v, 14r, 14v], 57–8 [fols. 15r, 15v, 16r, 16v, 18r, 18v], 59–60 [fols. 19r, 20r, 20v], 61–2 [fols. 21r, 21v, 22r, 23v, 24r, 24v], 63–4 [fols. 25r, 25v, 26r, 27v, 28r, 28v, 29r]; F. Wormald (1984) ill. 181 [fol. 27r (detail)]; R. Gameson (1992a) pls. 25 (a)–(c) [fols. 5v, 7v, 18r]; Ohlgren (1992) pls. 15.1–15.53 [fols. 4r–5v, 6v–8v, 10r–14r, 15v–19v, 21r–25r, 26v, 27r–29r, 30r–32r, 34r–35r, 36r–36v]; R. Gameson (1995b) pl. 22 [fol. 33r]; Karkov (2001a) pl. II [fol. 7v]; K.L. Brown (2004b) pl. 4 [fol. 4r]; Roberts (2005) frontispiece [fol. 11r]

ST: F.C. Robinson (1973) 457; Korhammer (1980) 38; Wieland (1985) 168–9, 171; Wieland (1987); Heslop (1990) 164, 167; R.I. Page (1992a); *CPPM* II, no. 3216b [*Praecepta uiuendi*]; *CSLMA* II (1999) 76; Wieland (2001); K.L. Brown (2004b) 187–8; Withers (2007) 83

325. London, British Library, Cotton Cleopatra D. i, fols. 1–82

s. xi[1], (prov. Canterbury StA)

Contents: Vitruvius, *De architectura*; Epitaph of Vitalis [SK 13567]

MS: M.R. James (1903) 173, 320, 519; N.R. Ker (1964) 43; Krinsky (1967) 50; T.A.M. Bishop (1971) xi–xii, xviii; L.D. Reynolds (1983) 443; R. Gameson (1995a) 124 n. 102; R. Gameson (1999a) *sub* no. 375; Bodarwé (2000) 113–14; Barker-Benfield (2008) II.938, III.1828; R. Gameson (2012b) 101 and n. 27; R. Gameson (2012d) 361 and n. 68

ED: Rose (1899) [Vitruvius coll. as c]

ST: Ruffel—Soubiran (1960) 132–43; L.D. Reynolds (1983) xxxii n., xxxv n., 441, 443

325. 1. London, British Library, Cotton Cleopatra D. i, fols. 83–128

s. xi^1, Continent?, (prov. Canterbury StA). In England before 1100?

Contents: Vegetius, *Epitome rei militaris*

MS: N.R. Ker (1964) 43; Shrader (1979) 290 [no. 75]; R. Gameson (1995a) 124 n. 102; R. Gameson (1999a) *sub* no. 375

ED: Lang (1885) xxxvii–xxxviii [Vegetius listed as no. 19, but not collated; more recent editions e.g. by A. Önnefors (1995) and M.D. Reeve (2004) do not collate this MS]

ST: Reeve (2000)

326. London, British Library, Cotton Domitian i, fols. 2–55

s. x med., x^2, x/xi, and xi/xii; all parts prob. Canterbury StA, (prov. ibid.)

Contents: eight glosses to lemmata from Isidore, *De differentiis rerum* [*CPL* 1202] (s. x/xi); Bede, *De natura rerum* [*CPL* 1343], ch. ii (s. x^2); Isidore, *De natura rerum* [*CPL* 1188], with world map on fol. 37v (s. x^2); glossary to Abbo, *Bella Parisiacae urbis*, bk. III (s. xi/xii); twenty-one glosses to Priscian, *Institutio de nomine et pronomine et uerbo* [*CPL* 1550] (s. xi/xii); computus tables (incomplete) (s. xi/xii); Remigius, Commentary to Priscian, *Institutio de nomine, pronomine et uerbo* (s. x med.); Bede, *Versus de die iudicii* [*CPL* 1370] (s. x med.); medical recipe* (s. x^2); booklist* (s. x^2 or x/xi)

MS: T.A.M. Bishop (1954–8b) 334–5; N.R. Ker (1957) no. 146; T.A.M. Bishop (1959–63b) 413; T.A.M. Bishop (1971) xiv n. 1; Lapidge (1975a) 76 [repr. Lapidge (1993a) 114]; Lendinara (1990a); Hollis — Wright (1992) 234, 237; Laing (1993) 75; Dumville (1992a) 64; Vaciago (1993) 14 [no. 57]; Lapidge (1994b) 113–14; Lendinara (1996) 623–6, 636, 639; *ASMMF* V (1997) 35–41 [no. 187; Doane]; Lendinara (2007b) 177, 180–1, 205–6 and nn. [no. 28]; Barker-Benfield (2008) I.liii n. 11, 607, II.1396, III.1696, 1714, 1812, 1831, 1922–4; Lapidge (2008a) 132; Graham (2009) 178; Wieland (2009) 145, 151; D. Ganz (2012) 191 n. 18; Scragg (2012a) nos. 466–70

DEC: R. Gameson (1995b) 10 n. 22

FACS: *ASMMF* V (1997) no. 187

ED: Cockayne (1864–6) I.382 [medical recipe]; Napier (1900) nos. 33, 41, 55 [OE glosses]; Hurst — Fraipont (1955) [Bede, *Versus de die iudicii* coll. as β]; Lendinara (1990a) 144–9 [glossary to Abbo and Priscian]; Lapidge (1994b) 114–16 [booklist]

ST: R.S. Cox (1972) 3; Jeudy (1972) 106; *BCLL* (1985) no. 135; Lendinara (1990a); Baker—Lapidge (1995) lii; P. Wormald (1999) 186 n. 100, 187 n. 102; Lendinara (2007b); Teresi (2007c) 351, 364; Lapidge (2008a) 131–7 [MS relationships of Bede, *Versus de die iudicii*]; R. McKitterick (2012) 329

327. London, British Library, Cotton Domitian vii, fols. 15–45 (and added fols.)

c. 840, Lindisfarne or Monkwearmouth-Jarrow?, prov. s. ix ex. Chester-le-Street, prov. s. x ex. Durham; additions from s. ix$^{2/4}$ onwards

Contents: *Liber uitae*; records* (add. s. x ex. and xi med.)

MS: Thompson—Warner (1881–4) 81–4; E. Bishop (1918) 350–1, 355–6; Mynors (1939) no. 13; K. Sisam (1953a) 4; N.R. Ker (1957) no. 147; T.J. Brown (1959) 250 [repr. T.J. Brown (1993a) 245]; N.R. Ker (1964) 73; T.J. Brown (1972) 238 [repr. T.J. Brown (1993a) 115]; E.E. Barker (1977); Piper (1978) 215, 237; A.G. Watson (1979) I, no. 527; D.H. Turner et al. (1980) 107; T.J. Brown (1982a) 110 [repr. T.J. Brown (1993a) 210]; Keynes (1985a) 171 n. 135; Dumville (1987) 158 n. 57; Morrish (1988) 517–18, 522–4, 537; M.P. Brown (1989a) 162; Webster—Backhouse (1991) no. 97; Dumville (1992a) 98, 124; Gullick (1994) 102, 104, 106; I. Wood (1995) 17; M.P. Brown (1996) 166; Keynes (1996a) 56–8; Lapidge (1996c) 416–17; Gullick (1998a) 30 no. 37; Piper (1998a) 161–75; Dumville (1999) 76, 116; R. Gameson (1999a) no. 377; Briggs (2004) 65–8; Gerchow (2004) 57–61; Gullick (2004) 17–19, 24–31, 33, 39–42; Keynes (2004) 152, 161; Moore (2004) 98, 99–100, 101, 106; Piper (2004) 118–19; Rollason et al. (2004); Rollason (2004b) 132–7; Swanson (2004) 233–4, 245–6; Tite (2004) 3–7, 9–10, 14 n. 37; Roberts (2006) 37; R. Gameson (2012a) 90 n. 327; Scragg (2012a) nos. 471–5

FACS: Rollason—Rollason (2007) [complete digitised facsimile]; A.H. Thompson (1923) [complete facsimile]; Thompson—Warner (1881–4) pl. 25 [folio not specified]; A.G. Watson (1979) II, pl. 7 [fol. 21v]; Rollason (1998) pl. 29 [fol. 45r]; M.P. Brown (2003c) fig. 47 [fol. 18r]; Rollason et al. (2004) pls. I–X [fols. 1r, 84v, 3r, 2r, 3v, 9r, 45v, 46r, 15r, 24r, 15v]; Rushforth (2007) fig. 37 [fol. 48v (detail)]

ED: Joseph Stevenson (1841) [base MS for *Liber uitae*]; BCS no. 1254 [record]; Sweet (1885) 153–66 [base MS for *Liber uitae*]; A.J. Robertson (1939) nos. 6, 28 [records]; Gerchow (1988) 304–20 [base MS for *Liber uitae*]; Piper (1998a) 176–85 [names on fol. 45r–v]

LANG: Roberts (2006) 37

ST: Hellwig (1888); R. Müller (1901); Glunz (1933) 265–8; Sawyer (1968) nos. 1659–61; Gerchow (1988) 109–54, 304–20; G. Barrow (2004) 109–16; Briggs (2004) 72–3, 79–93; Gullick (2004) 35–9; Insley (2004) 88–92; Karkov (2004) 71, 87; Moore (2004) 97–107; Piper (2004) 117–25; Rollason et al. (2004); Rollason (2004b) 127–37; Rushforth (2007) 58–9

328. London, British Library, Cotton Domitian viii, fols. 30–70

s. xi/xii, Canterbury CC

Contents: *Anglo-Saxon Chronicle* F*

MS: C. Plummer (1892–9) I.xii–xiii; N.R. Ker (1957) no. 148; Parkes (1976b) 171 [repr. Parkes (1991) 168]; Webber (1995) 158; R. Gameson (1999a) no. 378; P.S. Baker (2000) ix–xxvii; Bredehoft (2001) *ad indicem*; Guimon (2006) 137, 138 and n. 3; Scragg (2012a) no. 78

DEC: R. Gameson (1995a) 142

FACS: Dumville (1995a) [complete facsimile]

ED: C. Plummer (1892–9) [*Anglo-Saxon Chronicle* coll. as F]; P.S. Baker (2000) [base MS (= F) for *Anglo-Saxon Chronicle*]

LANG: A.F. Cameron (1974) 223; P.S. Baker (2000) lxxxii–xcix

ST: Fernquist (1937); Sawyer (1968) no. 90; Horsley—Waterhouse (1984) 224–5; P.S. Baker (2000) xxviii–lxxxi; Keynes (2012) 542, 552 *et passim*

329. London, British Library, Cotton Domitian ix, fols. 2–7

s. x in. or x¹, Canterbury CC

Contents: Aldhelm, *Epistola ad Heahfridum* [*CPL* 1334]

MS: N.R. Ker (1957) no. 149; T.A.M. Bishop (1959–63b) 421; Dumville (1987) 167–8; P.L. Heyworth (1989) 256; Vaciago (1993) 14 [no. 58]; Gwara (1996a) 92–3; Rowley (2004) 13; Lapidge (2012b) 37; Scragg (2012a) no. 476

ED: Napier (1900) no. 13 [OE glosses]; Ehwald (1919) 486–94 [Aldhelm, *Ep. ad Heahfridum*, coll. as C]; Gwara (1996a) 112–34 [Aldhelm, *Ep. ad Heahfridum*, coll. as C]

ST: C.E. Wright (1937); Gwara (1996a) 105–12; Lapidge (2012b) 35–7

329. 5. London, British Library, Cotton Domitian ix, fol. 8

s. viii², possibly England

Contents: alphabets; glossary (f); Dionysius Exiguus, *Epistula de ratione paschae* [*CPL* 2286] (f)

MS: Thompson—Warner (1881–4) 68; *CLA* II (1935) no. 185*; R. Derolez (1954) 3–6, 274; Bischoff (1966–81) II.198, 252, 339; III.143; Zironi (2011) 359

London, British Library, Cotton Domitian ix, fol. 10: see no. **22**

330. London, British Library, Cotton Domitian ix, fol. 11

s. ix ex. (after 883) or x in.. SE England? London, St Paul's?

Contents: extracts from Bede, *Historia ecclesiastica**; runic alphabet (add. s. xi/xii)

MS: Zupitza (1886); T. Miller (1890–8) I.xx–xxi; Hempl (1903–4); C.E. Wright (1936); K. Sisam (1953a) 18–19; R. Derolez (1954) 3–16; N.R. Ker (1957) no. 151; Dumville (1987) 167–8 and nn. 104–5; Graham (1994b) 6–7; R.I. Page (1998) 293; Rowley (2011) 16; Zironi (2011) 359–60; Scragg (2012a) no. 477

FACS: Dumville (1987) pl. II [fol. 11r]

ED: Zupitza (1886); T. Miller (1890–8) [extracts from OE Bede coll. as Z]

ST: Whitelock (1975) 16–17 and 17 n. 1 [repr. Whitelock (1981b) no. II]; Rowley (2011)

330. 5. London, British Library, Cotton Faustina A. v, fols. 99–102

s. xi/xii or xii in.; (prov. Winchester s. xv?)

Contents: pseudo-Jerome (pseudo-Bede), *De quindecim signis ante diem iudicii*; pseudo-Augustine, *De Antichristo quomodo et ubi nasci debeat*

MS: *ASMMF* V (1997) 42–7 [no. 191; Lucas]; R. Gameson (1999a) no. 381

FACS: *ASMMF* V (1997) no. 191

ST: *CPPM* II, no. 411; Rollason (1998) *ad indicem*; Rollason (2000)

331. London, British Library, Cotton Faustina A. x, fols. 3–101

s. xi² or xi³ᐟ⁴; s. xi ex.

Contents: Ælfric, *Grammar*⁺* and *Glossary*⁺*; dialogue on declensions; maxims⁺* (s. xi ex.)

MS: N.R. Ker (1957) no. 154; Robinson—Stanley (1991) 27; Hollis—
Wright (1992) 34; K. Sharpe (1997) 3; R. Gameson (1999a) no. 383;
Menzer (2004) 95, 102, 110–19; R. Gameson (2005a) 92, 101–4;
ASMMF XV (2007) [no. 193; Doane]; Swan (2007b) 36–9; Treharne
(2007b) 19 n. 16; Scragg (2012a) nos. 478–81

FACS: Robinson—Stanley (1991) pl. 32.2 [fol. 100v]; Menzer (2004) 113
[fol. 46v]; *ASMMF* XV (2007) no. 193

ED: Zupitza (1878) 285–6 [proverb and maxims]; Zupitza (1880/2001)
[Ælfric, *Grammar* and *Glossary*, coll. as F]; Dobbie (1942) 109 [max-
ims]; T. Hunt (1991) I.24–6, 110–11 [Anglo-Norman and other glosses
to Ælfric, *Grammar* and *Glossary*]

ST: Zupitza (1880/2001) v–vi; Dobbie (1942) cx–cxi, clxxiii; Gretsch
(1973) 40–2; Gretsch (1974) 126–37 [on OE Rule of St Benedict added
on fols. 102r–148v (s. xii¹)]; Buckalew (1978) 153–64; Kiernan (1994a)
42; Proud (2000) 130; Swan (2000b) 66–7, 76–8, 80–2; Menzer (2004)
109–19

332. London, British Library, Cotton Faustina B. iii, fols. 158–98 (with
London, British Library, Tiberius A. iii, fols. 174–7)

s. xi med., Canterbury CC

Contents: list of Roman emperors (added s. xi/xii or xii¹); *Regularis
concordia*, chs. xiv–xix*; *Regularis concordia*; three formula-letters
announcing the death of a monk, with antiphon and verse

MS: N.R. Ker (1957) no. 155; N.R. Ker (1964) 198; Kornexl (1993)
xcvi–cxvi; M.P. Brown (1996) 160; R. Sharpe et al. (1996) 645–6; C.A.
Jones (1998a) 233, 239–40; R. Gameson (1999a) no. 385; Karkov (2004)
5, 93–9; Boffey—Edwards (2005) nos. 243, 3090; Hartzell (2006)
no. 332; Wieland (2009) 140; Scragg (2012a) nos. 482–3

DEC: R. Gameson (1991) 77 n. 97; R. Gameson (1995a) 142

FACS: Kornexl (1993) pls. II–IV [fols. 186v, 198r, 198v]

ED: Kornexl (1993) 1–147 [*Regularis concordia* coll. as F], 148–9 [base
MS for three formula-letters]

LANG: Kornexl (1993) cxcvii–ccxii

ST: Symons (1953) liii–lv

London, British Library, Cotton Faustina B. vi, fols. 95 and 98–100: see
no. **362**

333. London, British Library, Cotton Galba A. xiv

s. xi²/⁴, Leominster?, prov. Winchester Nun or Shaftesbury? [one vol. with no. 342 (Nero A.ii, fols. 3-13)?]

Contents: prayerbook: computus tables; prayers$^{(*)}$; three hymns [including SK 685, 1013]; apocryphal letter of Christ to Abgar; charm*; seven psalter collects; Mass collects and other liturgical pieces; two litanies; 'Celtic capitella'; processional hymn by Ratpert of St Gallen [SK 1013]; medical recipes*; canticle (*Benedicite*); *Quicumque uult* (Athanasian Creed)

[for references, see also no. 342]

MS: E. Bishop (1918) 384–91; N.R. Ker (1957) no. 157; N.R. Ker (1964) 202; Banks (1965) 207–13; Rella (1977) 82; Lapidge (1981a) 84–5, 86 n. 123 [repr. Lapidge (1993a) 72–3, 74 n. 123]; Lapidge (1986a) 271; Hillaby (1987); Muir (1988) ix–xxxiv; Dumville (1991) 46–7; Lapidge (1991a) 69–70; Dumville (1992a) 57, 102; Hollis—Wright (1992) 230–1, 234, 237 [Ker, arts. ix, xii; Muir App. A]; Vaciago (1993) 14 [no. 59]; *ASMMF* I (1994) 5–14 [no. 197; Doane]; Muir (1998) 12–19; P. Wormald (1999) 186 n. 100; Liuzza (2001) 186 n. 44; Hartzell (2006) no. 135; Rushforth (2008a) 36–8; Crick (2012) 179 and n. 21; R. Gameson (2012b) 110 and n. 59; Raw (2012) 460 and n. 2; Rushforth (2012) 209 and n. 77; Scragg (2012a) nos. 484–91

DEC: Raw (1990) 215

FACS: Muir (1988) pls. I–VIII [fols. 20r, 20v, 21r, 28v, 103r, 103v, 111r, 111v]; *ASMMF* I (1994) no. 197

ED: Banks (1965) 207–13 [base MS for some prayers]; Muir (1988) 27–192 [base MS (= G) for the entire MS]; Lapidge (1991a) 157–71 [litanies]

LANG: Muir (1988) xxi–xxv

ST: Tolhurst (1942) 238–42; Gjerløw (1961) 24–5; Banks (1967–8) 20; Stotz (1972) 36–72 [SK 1013]; Keynes (1978) 243 and n. 90; Frantzen (1983b) 172 n. 62; Meaney (1984) 240–1; Hollis—Wright (1994) 146–7; Kiernan (1994a) 42; Corrêa (1996) 288–90; Keynes (2000) 15 n. 52

334. London, British Library, Cotton Galba A. xviii (with Oxford, Bodleian Library, Rawlinson B. 484, fol. 85 [S.C. 11831]) (the 'Æthelstan Psalter')

s. ix¹, NE France (Liège area or Rheims area?); with additions of s. ix², France and s. x in., England and s. x²/⁴ England; MS in Italy s. ix²? In England from s. ix² or x in., prov. royal court or a Winchester minster

Contents: Psalterium Gallicanum and canticles (s. ix[1]) with additions:
prayers (s. ix[2], France); Ps. CLI; metrical calendar, computus material
(s. x in., England); psalter collects; litany, *Pater noster*, creed and
Sanctus (all in Greek, added s. x[2/4], England)

MS: E. Bishop (1918) 141; J.A. Robinson (1923) 64–5; A.G. Watson
(1963) 208, 212 [repr. A.G. Watson (2004) no. III]; N.R. Ker (1964)
200; Parkes (1976b) 162–3 [repr. Parkes (1991) 159–60]; A.G. Watson
(1979) I, no. 532; Rella (1980) 111; Backhouse et al. (1984b) no. 4;
Lapidge (1984) 343–5 [repr. Lapidge (1993a) 360–2]; Keynes (1985a)
193–6; Lapidge (1986a) 271; McGurk (1986a) 79–80, 84, 86–7, 88–9;
Dumville (1987) 173–8; Gerchow (1988) 219–20 [no. 5]; Dumville
(1992b) 75–7, 88; R. Gameson (1992a) 217; R. Gameson (1992c) 153
n. 175; Dumville (1994a) 143 and n. 53; Bischoff (1998 –) II, no. 2420;
Gretsch (1999a) 275–6, 288, 310–15, 330, 331 n. 212, 336; Gretsch
(2000) 110–14; Pulsiano (2001a) xxviii; Tite (2004) 9 and n. 15; Gretsch
(2005b) 27; Biggs (2007a) 16; Wieland (2009) 117, 152; R. Gameson
(2012a) 76 and n. 263, 77 n. 273; R. Gameson (2012d) 348 and n. 14;
Raw (2012) 460 and n. 2, 464–5; Toswell (2012) 471

DEC: Kendrick (1938) 210; Rice (1952) 178, 182; Köhler–Mütherich
(1971–99) VI/i.17, 19, 31, 46–8, 51, 167–71, VI/ii.49, 51, VII.109, 110;
Pächt–Alexander (1973) no. 19; Deshman (1974) 176; E. Temple
(1976) no. 5; D.M. Wilson (1984) 172; F. Wormald (1984) 54, 76, 115;
Ohlgren (1986) no. 83; Raw (1990) 215–16; Ohlgren (1992) 15–18;
R. Gameson (1995b) 7 n. 8, 31 n. 115, 65, 152–3, 164, 171, 187;
Deshman (1997); Karkov (2004) 62, 87; Karkov (2009) 206, 214, 231–3;
R. Gameson (2012c) 250 and n. 5, 255–6 and n. 16, 257

FACS: Köhler–Mütherich (1971–99) *Tafeln* VI, pl. 113 [fols. 34v–35r,
80r, 121r, 157v (details)]; Pächt–Alexander (1973) pl. II (19)
[Rawlinson leaf, recto]; E. Temple (1976) ills. 14–17 [fols. 9v, 10r, 14r
(details)], 30–3 [Rawlinson leaf, recto; 120v, 2v, 21r]; A.G. Watson
(1979) II, pls. 13 (a)–(b) [fols. 16r, 181r]; Backhouse et al. (1984b) pls.
4 (a)–(b) [fols. 120v–121r; Rawlinson leaf, recto]; D.M. Wilson (1984)
pl. 220 [fol. 2v]; F. Wormald (1984) ills. 86–8 [fols. 2v, 21r, 120v];
R. Gameson (1992a) pl. 26 [fol. 21r]; Ohlgren (1992) pls. 1.1–17 [fols.
2v–3r, 3r–4v, 4v–5v, 5v–6r, 6v–7r, 7v–8r, 8v–9r, 9v–10r, 10v–11r, 11v–
12r, 12v–13r, 13v–14r, 14v–15r, 20v–21r, 34v–35r, 79v–80r, 120v–121r],
1.18 [Rawlinson leaf, recto]; Backhouse (1997) pl. 9 [fols. 120v–121r];
Deshman (1997) pls. IX–XIII [fols. 11v–12r, 2v–3r, 21r; Rawlinson
leaf, recto; 120v]; Karkov (2004) fig. 12 [fol. 120v]; Buzwell (2005)

frontispiece [fol. 21r]; M.P. Brown (2007a) pl. 72 [fol. 2v]; Owen-Crocker (2009) fig. 7.23 [fol. 21r]; M. Wood (2010), figs. 22–3 [fols. 200r, 2v], 24 [Rawlinson leaf, recto], 25 [fols. 120v–121r]

ED: McGurk (1986a) 90–111 [metrical calendar coll. as G]; Lapidge (1991a) 172–3 [Greek litany]; Pulsiano (2001a) [Pss. I–L coll. as µ]

ST: Lapidge (1984) 360–1; Gerchow (1988) 330 [obits]; Lapidge (1991a) 13–25, 70–1; Dumville (1992b) 74–7, 87–8, 92; Lapidge (1992b) 91–3 [repr. Lapidge (1993a) 101–3, 473]; C.D. Wright (1993) 268 n. 193; Bischoff—Lapidge (1994) 168–9; Keynes (1997a) 117–19; Borst (2001) I.162–4 [metrical calendar]; Karkov (2004) 56 n. 12, 62; Huglo (2005) 33; Pfaff (2009) 69–71

336. London, British Library, Cotton Julius A. ii, fols. 10–135

s. xi med.

Contents: Ælfric, Grammar+* and Glossary+*; treatise on Latin verbs

MS: N.R. Ker (1957) no. 158; Bursill-Hall (1981) 115 [no. 149.100]; ASMMF XV (2007) 11–19 [no. 198; Doane]; Wieland (2009) 144; Scragg (2012a) no. 492

FACS: ASMMF XV (2007) no. 198

ED: Zupitza (1880/2001) [Ælfric, Grammar and Glossary, coll. as J]; Wright—Wülker (1884) I.304–37 [base MS for Ælfric, Glossary]

ST: N.R. Ker (1957) no. 159; Korhammer (1976) 165 n. 14; Buckalew (1978) 153–64; Laing (1993) 77; R. Gameson (1999a) no. 388

337. London, British Library, Cotton Julius A. vi

s. xi in.; s. xi¹ or xi med.; additions s. xi ex.; all parts prob. Canterbury CC, (prov. Durham)

Contents: metrical calendar and computus material (s. xi in.); Expositio hymnorum° and Monastic canticles° (s. xi¹ or xi med.); Latin hymn by Peter Damian [AH XLVIII. 52] and Latin poem on the liberal arts [SK 188] (added s. xi ex.)

MS: Joseph Stevenson (1851) xxiii; Mearns (1914) 82; Mynors (1939) no. 21; Grosjean (1943) 92 n. 2; T.A.M. Bishop (1954–8a) 185–7; N.R. Ker (1957) no. 160; N.R. Ker (1964) 72; Gneuss (1968) 91–7; A.G. Watson (1969) 40 [repr. A.G. Watson (2004) no. IX]; Gneuss (1971) 132; Korhammer (1976) 75; Backhouse et al. (1984b) no. 60; Lapidge (1984) 344, 353 [repr. Lapidge (1993a) 361, 370]; Dumville

(1991–5) 145; Dumville (1992a) 20 n. 30, 107; Vaciago (1993) 14–15 [no. 60]; Springer (1995) 145; *ASMMF* IV (1996) 1–13 [no. 199; Pulsiano]; Milfull (1996) 49–51; Bullough (1998a) 123 n. 48; Gretsch (2000) 116; Liuzza (2001) 206 n. 108; Tite (2004) 15 n. 40; Hartzell (2006) no. 136; Graham (2009) 165; Wieland (2009) 135; R. Gameson (2012a) 44; Scragg (2012a) no. 493

DEC: Rice (1952) 218–19; F. Wormald (1952) 68 [no. 30]; Rickert (1954) 46–7; Köhler—Mütherich (1971–99) IV.61; E. Temple (1976) no. 62; Brownrigg (1978) 246 n. 2; D.M. Wilson (1984) 187; Ohlgren (1986) no. 167; R. Gameson (1991) 73 *et passim*; R. Gameson (1995b) 168, 177; E.R. Anderson (1997) 252–3; Niles (1998) 194 n. 84; Dodwell (2000) 151; Karkov (2009) 239–41

FACS: Traill—Mann (1901) 177, 179, 181 [fols. 3r–8v]; J.R. Green (1907) 155, 157, 159 [fols. 3r–8v]; Millar (1926) pl. 24 (c) [fol. 4v]; F. Wormald (1952) pl. 17 (b) [fol. 3v]; D.M. Wilson (1984) pl. 235 [fol. 5v]; M.P. Brown (1991) pl. 74 [fol. 3r]; R. Gameson (1991) fig. 6 [fol. 72v]; Camille (1987) pl. 7 [fol. 3r]; *ASMMF* IV (1996) no. 199; Owen-Crocker (2009) figs. 7.28–9 [fols. 4v, 5v]

ED: Hurst—Fraipont (1955) 419–23 [Bede, Ascension hymn, coll. as L^c]; Gneuss (1968) 265–413 [base MS (= J) for *Expositio hymnorum* and gloss]; Korhammer (1976) 254–350 [Monastic canticles and gloss coll. as J]; McGurk (1986a) 90–111 [metrical calendar coll. as J]; Milfull (1996) 109–472 [*Expositio hymnorum* coll. as J]

LANG: Gneuss (1968) 157–93; Gneuss (1972) 77–8; Korhammer (1976) 151–232; Hofstetter (1987) 101–3, 114–16; Crowley (2000) 143

ST: Hennig (1954); Hohler (1956) 161; Korhammer (1973) 181; A.F. Cameron (1974) 223; Dumville (1976) 27; Korhammer (1976) 75 *et passim*; Korhammer (1980) 42–3; McGurk (1986a) 80, 84–9; Heslop (1990) 153–4; Dumville (1992b) 104–6; Baker—Lapidge (1995) xliii, xlviii [computus]; Gretsch (1999a) 377; Borst (2001) I.169; Teresi (2007c) 352, 365

338. London, British Library, Cotton Julius A. x, fols. 44–175

s. x/xi

Contents: Old English Martyrology* (incomplete)

MS: N.R. Ker (1957) no. 161; Kotzor (1981) I.56*–74*; Roberts (2005) 72–3 [no. 14]; Rauer (2007) 145; Scragg (2012a) nos. 494–7

FACS: Kotzor (1981) I.60*–63* [fols. 44v, 131v, 135v, 170v]; Roberts (2005) pl. 14 [fol. 88r]

ED: Kotzor (1981) vol. II [OE Martyrology coll. as B]

LANG: C. Sisam (1953) 212–16; Kotzor (1981) I.315*–405*; Hofstetter (1987) 409–10

ST: de Gaiffier (1985); Rauer (2003); Lapidge (2005a); Rauer (2007)

339. London, British Library, Cotton Julius E. vii

s. xi in., S England, (prov. Bury St Edmunds)

Contents: Ælfric, Lives of Saints*; four anonymous Lives of Saints* [Euphrosyne, Eustace, Mary of Egypt, Seven Sleepers]; Ælfric (version of Alcuin's) *Interrogationes Sigewulfi in Genesin*, *De falsis diis* (f)

MS: N.R. Ker (1957) no. 162; Pope (1967–8) I.83–5; Torkar (1971); R.M. Thomson (1972) 622–3, 623 n. 27; Collins—Clemoes (1974) 321; Needham (1976) 1, 2, 7 n. 4; Scragg (1979) 257–8; Dumville (1988) 60, 61; Lapidge (1988b) 263 [repr. Lapidge (1993a) 221]; Dumville (1993g) 78–9 and n. 360; J. Hill (1996) 235–59; Scragg (1996) 217–18; Proud (2000) 120–1; Magennis (2002) 16–25; Lapidge (2003a) 580–2; Roberts (2005) 82–4 [no. 18]; Corona (2006) 127–30; Bussières (2007); Upchurch (2007) xi, 52–3; R. Gameson (2012a) 67 n. 232; Scragg (2012a) nos. 498–503

FACS: Roberts (2005) pl. 18 [fol. 203r]; J. Hill (2006b) fig. 2.1 [fol. 4v]

ED [the order of the following items is that of the manuscript, listed according to the numbering of individual articles in N.R. Ker (1957) 207–10; only the most recent editions are cited]:

art. 1: Skeat (1881–1900) I.2–4 [base MS for Ælfric, Latin preface to *Lives of Saints*]

art. 2: Skeat (1881–1900) I.4–6 [base MS for Ælfric, OE preface to *Lives of Saints* addressed to Ealdorman Æthelweard]

art. 3: Skeat (1881–1900) I.8–10 [base MS for *capitula* to Ælfric, *Lives of Saints*]

art. 4: Skeat (1881–1900) I.10–24 [base MS for Ælfric, *Lives of Saints*, no. I (Nativity of our Lord Jesus Christ)]

art. 5: Skeat (1881–1900) I.24–50 [base MS for Ælfric, *Lives of Saints*, no. II (St Eugenia)]

art. 6: Skeat (1881–1900) I.50–90 [base MS for Ælfric, *Lives of Saints*, no. III (St Basil)]; Corona (2006) 152–88 [Ælfric, 'Life of St Basil', coll. as J] art. 7: Skeat (1881–1900) I.90–114 [base MS for Ælfric, *Lives of Saints*, no. IV (SS. Julian and Basilissa)]; Upchurch (2007) 54–70 [base MS for Ælfric, *Lives of Saints*, no. IV (SS. Julian and Basilissa)]

art. 8: Skeat (1881–1900) I.116–46 [base MS for Ælfric, *Lives of Saints*, no. V (St Sebastian)]

art. 9: Skeat (1881–1900) I.148–68 [base MS for Ælfric, *Lives of Saints*, no. VI (St Maur)]

art. 10: Skeat (1881–1900) I.170–86 [base MS for Ælfric, *Lives of Saints*, no. VII, lines 1–295 (St Agnes)]

art. 11: Skeat (1881–1900) I.186–94 [base MS for Ælfric, *Lives of Saints*, no. VII, lines 296–429 (*Alia sententia quam scripsit Terrentianus*: Passio of SS. John and Paul)]

art. 12: Skeat (1881–1900) I.194–208 [base MS for Ælfric, *Lives of Saints*, no. VIII (St Agatha)]

art. 13: Skeat (1881–1900) I.210–18 [base MS for Ælfric, *Lives of Saints*, no. IX (St Lucy)]

art. 14: Skeat (1881–1900) I.218–38 [base MS for Ælfric, *Lives of Saints*, no. X (*Cathedra S. Petri*)]

art. 15: Skeat (1881–1900) I.238–60 [base MS for Ælfric, *Lives of Saints*, no. XI (SS. Forty Soldiers)]

art. 16: Skeat (1881–1900) I.260–82 [base MS for Ælfric, *Lives of Saints*, no. XII (Homily for the Beginning of Lent)]

art. 17: Skeat (1881–1900) I.282–306 [base MS for Ælfric, *Lives of Saints*, no. XIII (*De oratione Moysi*)]

art. 18: Skeat (1881–1900) I.306–18 [base MS for Ælfric, *Lives of Saints*, no. XIV (St George)]

art. 19: Skeat (1881–1900) I.320–6 [base MS for Ælfric, *Lives of Saints*, no. XV, lines 1–103 (St Mark the Evangelist)]

art. 20: Skeat (1881–1900) I.326–36 [base MS for Ælfric, *Lives of Saints*, no. XV, lines 104–226 (*Item alia*)]

art. 21: Skeat (1881–1900) I.336–62 [base MS for Ælfric, *Lives of Saints*, no. XVI (Homily *De memoria sanctorum*)]

art. 22: Skeat (1881–1900) I.364–82 [base MS for Ælfric, *Lives of Saints*, no. XVII (*De auguriis*)]; W. Schipper (1981) [base MS for Homily *De auguriis*]

art. 23: Skeat (1881–1900) I.384–412 [base MS for Ælfric, *Lives of Saints*, no. XVIII (Homily drawn from the Book of Kings)]

art. 24: Skeat (1881–1900) I.414–24 [base MS for Ælfric, *Lives of Saints*, no. XIX, lines 1–154 (St Alban)] art. 25: Skeat (1881–1900) I.424–30 [base MS for Ælfric, *Lives of Saints*, no. XIX, lines 155–258 (*Item alia*)]

art. 26: Skeat (1881–1900) I.432–40 [base MS for Ælfric, *Lives of Saints*, no. XX (St Æthelthryth)]

art. 27: Skeat (1881–1900) I.440–70 [base MS for Ælfric, *Lives of Saints*, no. XXI, lines 1–463 (St Swithun)]; Needham (1976) 60–81 [base MS for Ælfric, 'Life of St Swithun']; Lapidge (2003a) 590–609 [Ælfric, 'Life of St Swithun', coll. as W]

art. 28: Skeat (1881–1900) I.470–2 [base MS for Ælfric, *Lives of Saints*, no. XXI, lines 464–95 (St Macarius)]; Pope (1967–8) II.790–2 [Ælfric, Suppl. Hom. XXIX, lines 4–32, coll. as W]

art. 29: Skeat (1881–1900) I.472–86 [base MS for Ælfric, *Lives of Saints*, no. XXII (St Apollinaris)]

art. 30: Skeat (1881–1900) I.488–540 [base MS for anonymous Life of the Seven Sleepers of Ephesus (Skeat no. XXIII)]; Magennis (1994) 33–57 [base MS for anonymous Life of the Seven Sleepers of Ephesus]

art. 31: Skeat (1881–1900) II.2–52 [base MS for anonymous Life of St Mary of Egypt (Skeat no. XXIIIB)]; Magennis (2002) 58–120 [base MS for anonymous Life of St Mary of Egypt]

art. 32: Skeat (1881–1900) II.54–8 [base MS for Ælfric, *Lives of Saints*, no. XXIV, lines 1–80 (SS. Abdon and Sennes)]

art. 33: Skeat (1881–1900) II.58–66 [base MS for Ælfric, *Lives of Saints*, no. XXIV, lines 81–191 (*Item alia*: Letter of Christ to Abgar)]

art. 34: Skeat (1881–1900) II.66–80 [base MS for Ælfric, *Lives of Saints*, no. XXV, lines 1–204 (Maccabees)]

art. 35: Skeat (1881–1900) II.80–120 [base MS for Ælfric, *Lives of Saints*, no. XXV, lines 205–811 (*Item*: 1 Macc. ii.1–70)]

art. 36: Skeat (1881–1900) II.120–4 [base MS for Ælfric, *Lives of Saints*, no. XXV, lines 812–62 (The three orders of society: *oratores, laboratores, bellatores*)]

art. 37: Skeat (1881–1900) II.124–42 [base MS for Ælfric, *Lives of Saints*, no. XXVI (St Oswald, king and martyr)]; Needham (1976) 27–42 [base MS for 'Life of St Oswald']

art. 38: Skeat (1881–1900) II.144–58 [base MS for Ælfric, *Lives of Saints*, no. XXVII (Exaltation of the Holy Cross)]; Robb (1975) [base MS for Homily on the Exaltation of the Holy Cross]

art. 39: Skeat (1881–1900) II.158–68 [base MS for Ælfric, *Lives of Saints*, no. XXVIII (St Maurice)]

art. 40: Skeat (1881–1900) II.168–90 [base MS for Ælfric, *Lives of Saints*, no. XXIX (St Dionysius)] art. 41: Skeat (1881–1900) II.190–218 [base MS for anonymous 'Life of St Eustace']

art. 42: Skeat (1881–1900) II.218–312 [base MS for Ælfric, *Lives of Saints*, no. XXXI (St Martin)]

Latin note and rhythmical prayer to St Martin (6pp + 6pp) [SK 11194]: Skeat (1881–1900) II.312; Grosjean (1937) 347

art. 43: Skeat (1881–1900) II.314–34 [base MS for Ælfric, *Lives of Saints*, no. XXXII (St Edmund, king and marytr)]; Needham (1976) 43–59 [base MS for 'Life of St Edmund']

art. 44: Skeat (1881–1900) II.334–54 [base MS for anonymous 'Life of St Euphrosyne' (Skeat no. XXXIII)]

art. 45: Skeat (1881–1900) II.356–76 [base MS for Ælfric, *Lives of Saints*, no. XXXIV (St Caecilia)]; Upchurch (2007) 72–84 [base MS for Ælfric, *Lives of Saints*, no. XXXIV (St Caecilia)]

art. 46: Skeat (1881–1900) II.378–98 [base MS for Ælfric, *Lives of Saints*, no. XXXV (SS. Chrysanthus and Daria)]; Upchurch (2007) 86–98 [base MS for Ælfric, *Lives of Saints*, no. XXXV (SS. Chrysanthus and Daria)]

art. 47: Skeat (1881–1900) II.398–424 [base MS for Ælfric, *Lives of Saints*, no. XXXVI (St Thomas the Apostle)]

art. 48: MacLean (1883–4) [base MS for Ælfric, *Interrogationes Sigewulfi*]; Stoneman (1983) [base MS for Ælfric, *Interrogationes Sigewulfi*]

art. 49: Pope (1967–8) II.677–712 [Ælfric, Suppl. Hom. no. XXI (*De falsis diis*), coll. as W]

LANG: Needham (1958) 160–4 [notes on alterations made throughout the MS by a thirteenth–century scribe]; Torkar (1971); Korhammer (1976) 164–5; Gretsch (2003b) 45–67; Upchurch (2007) 26–9

ST: J. Hill (1996) 243; Scragg (1998) 77, 82 n. 9; Rosser (2000) 136, 140 [St Martin]; Biggs et al. (2001) 22–486 *passim*; Lapidge (2003a) 582–5; J. Hill (2006b); Acker (2004) 124 n. 10, 129; Kiernan (2006) 85–9; Wilcox (2006a) 238–41, 252, 256; Bussières (2007) [on Scribe C]; Kleist (2007b) 475–6; Upchurch (2007) 266–7 and n. 5; Alcamesi (2010) 192–3, 200–2

340. London, British Library, Cotton Nero A. i, fols. 3–57

s. xi$^{3/4}$

Contents: Laws*: *I, II Cnut; II* and *III Eadgar; Alfred* and *Ine*, Capitula and Introduction; *Romscot*; '*Judex*' (from Alcuin, *De uirtutibus et uitiis*, ch. xx)

MS: Liebermann (1903–16) I.xxv; K. Sisam (1953a) 279; Bethurum (1957) 6; N.R. Ker (1957) no. 163; Loyn (1971); Gneuss (1977) 209–11; Torkar (1981) 168–85; P. Wormald (1999) 138 n. 82; 165 [table 4.1], 230 n. 268, 224–8; Tite (2004) 9; Hartzell (2006) no. 137; Hough (2006) 114, 123 n. 29; Rumble (2006a) viii; Scragg (2012a) nos. 504–5; P. Wormald (2012) 534 [no. 11]

FACS: Loyn (1971) [complete facsimile]

ED: Liebermann (1903–16) I.278–306, even pages, left-hand column [base MS (= G) for *I Cn.*], 308–70, even pages, left-hand column [base MS (= G) for *II Cn.*], 194–204, even pages, left-hand column [base MS (= G) for *II Eg. and III Eg.*], 16–26, even pages, right-hand column [Capitula to *Alfred and Ine*], 474–6, left-hand column [base MS (= G) for *Romscot*], 26–44, even pages, right-hand column [base MS (= G) for *Alfred and Ine*]; Torkar (1981) 249–55 [base MS (= G) for art. 6 (*Judex*)]

ST: McIntosh (1948); Whitelock (1948) 435–6, 442, 444–5; Torkar (1981); Hough (2006) 121, 132

341. London, British Library, Cotton Nero A. i, fols. 70–177

1003×1023, Worcester or York

Contents: (a version of Wulfstan's 'Handbook'): Wulfstan, *Institutes of Polity**, four Homilies*; Laws*: *I Æthelstan, I Eadmund, III Eadgar, V Æthelred, VIII Æthelred*; *Grið**; texts related to ecclesiastical institutes[(*)]; Wulfstan's Canon Law Collection ('*Excerptiones Pseudo-Egberti*', recension B); Abbo of Saint-Germain-des-Prés, *Serm.* x and xiii (both abbreviated)

MS: Liebermann (1903–16) I.xxv–xxvi; K. Sisam (1953a) 279; Bethurum (1957) 6; N.R. Ker (1957) no. 164; Jost (1959) 10–12; N.R. Ker (1971) 321–4; Loyn (1971); Fowler (1972) xxii–xxvi; Whitelock (1976) 1; Rella (1977) 93, 122; A.G. Watson (1979) I, no. 538; Torkar (1981) 168–85; Backhouse et al. (1984b) no. 159; M.P. Brown (1991) 23; Dumville (1992a) 124; Dumville (1993g) 55, 149 n. 48; Raw (1994) 271; Parkes (1997b) 139 n. 110; C.A. Jones (1998a) 238 nn. 23–4; O'Brien O'Keeffe (1998b) 216, 217 n. 29; P. Wormald (1999) 7 n. 20, 164 [table 4.1], 198–203, 208 n. 178, 212 n. 199, 213–14 [table 4.4], 216 and n. 211, 217–18, 220, 223 n. 240, 292 [table 5.1], 309 n. 206, 458 n. 154; Sauer (2000); Wilcox (2000) 92; Cowen (2004) 397; Dance (2004) 30 n. 4, 31 n. 6; T.N. Hall (2004a) 95, 97, 99, 113; J. Hill (2004) 321; Hollis (2004) 449 n. 18, 456 n. 58; C.A. Jones (2004) 330 n. 23, 331, 351–2; G. Mann (2004) 265 n. 94, 268 n. 100; Meaney (2004) 479 n. 69, 480, 483; A.

Orchard (2004) 66 n. 15, 71; Tite (2004) 9; Wilcox (2004b) 376–7, 379 n. 15, 382–6, 388–91, 393; Ambrose (2005) 114–15; Roberts (2005) 76–7 [no. 16]; Hough (2006) 114; Rumble (2006a) viii; Treharne (2007b) 24; Graham (2009) 187; R. Gameson (2012a) 43 n. 119; R. Gameson (2012b) 110 and n. 61; A. Orchard (2012) 697 [no. 7]; Scragg (2012a) nos. 307, 506–12; P. Wormald (2012) 534 [no. 7]

FACS: Loyn (1971) [complete facsimile]; Cassidy — Ringler (1971) 256 [fol. 110r]; A.G. Watson (1979) II, pls. 28 (a)–(d) [fols. 72r, 103v, 110r, 165v]; Backhouse et al. (1984b) no. 159 [fol. 110r]; M.P. Brown (1991) pl. 21 [fol. 112r (detail)]; Roberts (2005) pl. 16 [fol. 110r]; M.P. Brown (2007a) pl. 96 [fol. 112r]

ED [the order of the following items is that of the manuscript, listed according to the numbering of individual articles in N.R. Ker (1957) 212–14; only the most recent editions are cited]:

art. 1: Jost (1959) 40–50, 52–4, 55–8, 78–80 [either base MS (= G_1) or collated as G_1 for *I Institutes of Polity*, chs. 1–15 (*Be cynge*), 23–30 (*Be cynedom*), 31–9 (*Be cynestole*), 85–93 (*Be eorlum*); then Jost (1959) 84–6 [base MS (= G_2) for *II Institutes of Polity* chs. 102–4 (*Be sacerdan*, first redaction)]; then 109–14 [coll. as G_1 for *I Institutes of Polity* chs. 68–77 (*Be gehadedum munecum*); 122 [coll. as G_1 for *I Institutes of Polity* chs. 78–80 (*Be abbodum*)]; 123–4 [coll. as G_1 for *I Institutes of Polity* chs. 81–3 (*Be munecum*)]; 128 [coll. as G_1 for *I Institutes of Polity* ch. 84 (*Be minecenan*)]; 129 [coll. as G_1 for *I Institutes of Polity* chs. 85–6 (*Be preostum and be nunnan*)]; 130 [coll. as G_1 for *I Institutes of Polity* chs. 87–8 (*Be læwedum mannum*)]; 136 [coll. as G_1 for *I Institutes of Polity* chs. 93–4 (*Be wudewan*)]; 138 [coll. as G_1 for *I Institutes of Polity* chs. 98–9 (*Be circan*)]; 154 [coll. as G_1 for *I Institutes of Polity* chs. 117–18 (*Be eallum cristenum mannum*)]

art. 2: Napier (1883/1967) 65–76 [Hom. X (*Be cristendome*) coll. as I]; Bethurum (1957) 200–10 [Hom. Xc (*Be cristendome*) coll. as I]; A. Orchard (2004) 72, 73–5, 77, 78–80, 83–4, 86–7, 88, 89–90 [parts of Napier Hom. X ptd as I]

art. 3: Napier (1883/1967) 130–4 [Hom. XXVIII (*Be godcundre warnunge*) coll. as I]; Bethurum (1957) 251–4 [base MS (= I) for Hom. XIX (*Be godcundre warnunge*)]

art. 4: Liebermann (1903–16) I.146–8, central column [base MS (= G) for *I As.*]

art. 5: Liebermann (1903–16) I.184 [base MS (= G) for *I Em.*]

art. 6: Liebermann (1903–16) I. 200–4, left-hand column [base MS (= G) for *III Eg.*]

art. 7: Liebermann (1903–16) I.236–46, even pages, left-hand column [base MS (= G) for *V Atr.*]

art. 8: Liebermann (1903–16) I.470–3, left-hand column [base MS (= G) for *Grið*]

art. 9: Liebermann (1903–16) I.263–4 [base MS (= G) for *VIII Atr.*, 1–5]

art. 10: Liebermann (1903–16) I.473 [base MS (= G) for *Nor. grið*]

art. 11: Jost (1959) 59 [*I Institutes of Polity*, chs. 35–7 (*De episcopis*), coll. as G_1]

art. 12: Jost (1959) 67 [*I Institutes of Polity*, chs. 41–2 (*Item. De episcopis*), coll. as G_1]

art. 13: Jost (1959) 210 [Appendix to *Institutes of Polity*, ch. VIII (*Incipit de synodo*) coll. as G_1]

art. 14: Jost (1959) 262–7 [base MS (= G) for 'Exhortation to Bishops']

art. 15: Jost (1959) 84–6 [base MS (=G_2) for *II Institutes of Polity*, chs. 102–4 (*Be sacerdan*)]

art. 16: Jost (1959) 122 [*II Institutes of Polity*, chs. 170–2 (*Be abbodum*) coll. as G_2]

art. 17: Jost (1959) 123–7 [*II Institutes of Polity*, chs. 173–84 (*Be munecum*) coll. as G_2]

art. 18: Jost (1959) 81–6 [*II Institutes of Polity*, chs. 94–104 (*Be gerefan*) coll. as G_2]

art. 19: Jost (1959) 62–6 [*II Institutes of Polity*, chs. 41–57 (*Be þeodwitan*) coll. as G_2]

art. 20: Napier (1883/1967) 156–67 [Hom. XXXIII coll. as I]; Bethurum (1957) 267–75 [Hom. XX coll. as I]; Whitelock (1976) [Wulfstan, *Sermo Lupi*, coll. as I]

art. 21: Napier (1883/1967) 167–9 [Hom. XXXIV coll. as I]; Bethurum (1957) 276–7 [Hom. XXI coll. as I]

art. 22: Liebermann (1903–16) I.236–46, even pages, right-hand column [base MS (= G2) for *V Atr.*]

art. 23: Jost (1959) 39 [*II Institutes of Polity*, chs. 1-3 (*Be hefenlicum cyninge*) coll. as G_3]

art. 24: Jost (1959) 41–5 [base MS (=G_3) for *II Institutes of Polity*, chs. 4–8 (*Be eorðlicum cyninge*)]

art. 25: illegible

art. 26: cf. Jost (1950) 64

art. 27: cf. Napier (1883/1967) 190–1 [Hom. XLI] and Jost (1950) 65 art. 28: cf. Jost (1950) 71

art. 29: cf. Bateson (1895) 717

art. 30: Cross—Brown (1993c) [Abbo of Saint–Germain, *Sermo de reconciliatione post penitentiam* (= the Latin source of Wulfstan, *Hom.* XXXII, ed. Napier), coll. as N]; Cross—Hamer (1999) 66–113 [Wulfstan's Canon Law Collection, Recension A, coll. as Y], 114–72 [base text (= Y) for Wulfstan's Canon Law Collection, Recension B]

LANG: Dance (2004) 34 n. 25; A. Orchard (2004) 69 n. 24, 70 n. 28; Wilcox (2004b) 395 n. 54

ST: Bateson (1895) 712–31; Bethurum (1942); Whitelock (1942) 49; Whitelock (1943) 125; McIntosh (1948); Jost (1959); Whitelock (1965) 219–20; Whitelock (1970) 75, 85 n.; Aronstam (1974); Hohler (1975) 223–4; Whitelock (1976) 1, 3 n. 6, 6, 20, 22, 28–9, 35, 37–45; Cross (1990) 99–100 [missing folios]; Cross—Hamer (1996a); R. Gameson (1996a) 214, 239; Cross (1997) 5 [Recension B of Wulfstan's Handbook]; P. Wormald (2000); P. Wormald (2004) 10 [MS relationship]; Hough (2006) 121, 132 [numerals]

342. London, British Library, Cotton Nero A. ii, fols. 3–13 (with London, British Library, Cotton Galba A. xiv [no. **333**]?)

s. xi$^{2/4}$, Winchester?

Contents: liturgical calendar; *computistica*; poem on King Æthelstan [SK 2143]; two prayers (one to God the Father, one to St Dunstan); Latin poem for St Æthelberht (inc. 'Inclite martir ouans')

MS: N.R. Ker (1957) no. 157; N.R. Ker (1964) 202; Muir (1988) ix–xvi; *ASMMF* I (1994) 15–19 [no. 203; Doane]; Hartzell (2006) no. 135; Chardonnens (2007b) 512, 550; Rushforth (2008a) 36–8 [no. 16]; Rushforth (2012) 209 and n. 77

FACS: *ASMMF* I (1994) no. 203

ED: Stubbs (1874) 440 [prayer to St Dunstan]; F. Wormald (1934) 29–41 [liturgical calendar (no. 3)]; Lapidge (1981a) 83–93, 98 [repr. Lapidge (1993a) 71–81, 86] [poem on King Æthelstan]; Muir (1988) 1–23 [complete contents of MS, numbered 1–8]; Rushforth (2008a) no. 16 [liturgical calendar]; Winterbottom—Lapidge (2012) cxxxvii [prayer to St Dunstan]

ST: Stubbs (1874) lv–lvi; Gasquet—Bishop (1908) 165–76; W.H. Stevenson (1911); J.A. Robinson (1923) 67–8; A.G. Watson (1963) 212 n. 2 [repr. A.G. Watson (2004) no. III]; Kotzor (1981) I.302*–311*;

Lapidge (1981a) 83–93 [repr. Lapidge (1993a) 71–81]; Heslop (1995) 57 n.; Conner (1993) 151; Borst (2001) I.94–5

342. 2. London, British Library, Cotton Nero A. vii, fols. 1–39, 41–112

s. xi/xii, England or Normandy, (prov. prob. Rochester)

Contents: Lanfranc, *Epistolae*; memorandum on the primacy of archbishops of Canterbury; Councils of Winchester (1072) and London (1074×1075); Anselm, *Epistolae* (incomplete)

MS: Clover—Gibson (1979) 15–16; Southern (1990) 398–9, 458–64 [full lists of contents]; R. Gameson (1999a) nos. 389, 391

ED: Clover—Gibson (1979) [*Epistolae* of Lanfranc coll. as N]; Whitelock et al. (1981a) II.591–604 [Council of Winchester (1072) and Memorandum on the primacy of Canterbury coll. as N], 604–5 [base MS for Profession of obedience to Canterbury made by Archbishop Thomas of York], 607–16 [Council of London (1074×1075), coll. as N]

ST: Z.N. Brooke (1931) 59 [Council of London]; C.N.L. Brooke (1967) [Council of London]; R. Sharpe et al. (1996) 489, 507; R. Gameson (1998) 236 n. 25

342. 3. London, British Library, Cotton Nero A. vii, fol. 40

s. xi/xii

Contents: epitaph for Lanfranc; recipe for making red and blue dye (f)

MS: R. Gameson (1999a) no. 390; R. Gameson (2012a) 73 and n. 250

ST: A.G. Watson (1986) 138 [repr. A.G. Watson (2004) no. IV]

342. 6. London, British Library, Cotton Nero C. v, fols. 1–161

s. xi ex. (after 1086), Continent, with additions s. xi ex. in England, prov. Hereford Cathedral

Contents: Marianus Scottus, *Chronicon* [*BCLL* 728]

MS: A.G. Watson (1979) I, no. 540; R. Gameson (1999a) no. 394; Gullick (2001) 104–5; Webber (2012) 222 and n. 57

FACS: A.G. Watson (1979) II, pl. 59 (a)–(b) [fols. 76v, 147r]

ED: Waitz (1844) 495–564 [Marianus Scottus, *Chronicon*, coll. as 'Codex 2'; bk. III only]

ST: Manitius (1911–31) II.388–94; Kenney (1929) no. 443; *BCLL* (1985) no. 728

342. 8. London, British Library, Cotton Nero C. ix, fols. 19–21
(with London, Lambeth Palace Library, 430, flyleaves)

s. xi/xii (prob. in or after 1093), Canterbury CC

Contents: necrology (f; Aug.–Dec.)

MS: N.R. Ker (1964) 36; Gerchow (1988) 269–75 [no. 22]; R. Gameson (1999a) no. 395

ED: Gerchow (1988) 340–2

ST: Boutemy (1935); R. Fleming (1993) 124–6; Keynes (1996a) 60 n. 91

343. London, British Library, Cotton Nero D. iv (the 'Lindisfarne Gospels')

687×689, Lindisfarne, prov. Chester-le-Street s. ix ex., Durham s. x ex., OE gloss s. $x^{3/4}$, prob. before 970

Contents: gospels° (687×689); OE gloss, Latin verses and note, colophon*, s. $x^{3/4}$

MS: Skeat (1871) iii, xi, xxii; J. Wordsworth et al. (1889–1954) I.xiv; *CLA* II (1935) no. 187; Mynors (1939) no. 5; Bischoff (1952) 93; McGurk (1956) 252–3, 257, 260 [repr. McGurk (1998) no. I]; N.R. Ker (1957) no. 165; McGurk (1961a) no. 22; McGurk (1961b) 7, 11 [repr. McGurk (1998) no. V]; McGurk (1962) 29 [repr. McGurk (1998) no. VII]; Bischoff (1962) 328, 332; N.R. Ker (1964) 73, 119; Gamber (1968–88) no. 405; T.J. Brown (1972) 220–35 [repr. T.J. Brown (1993a) 99–113]; Pächt (1973) no. 187; A.G. Watson (1979) I, no. 544; Backhouse (1981); T.J. Brown (1982a) 108 [repr. T.J. Brown (1993a) 208]; Dodwell (1982) 10, 51, 55; G. Henderson (1982) 5, 6, 8, 23, 61–2 n. 86; Bischoff (1986) 33, 119, 123, 262; M.P. Brown (1986) 133; M.P. Brown (1989a) 152–3, 158–9; P.L. Heyworth (1989) 15, 126, 204–5; M.P. Brown (1990) 50–1; M.P. Brown (1991) 64–5; Webster—Backhouse (1991) no. 80; Dumville (1992a) 98; Vaciago (1993) 15 [no. 61]; Blockley (1994); R. Gameson (1994b) 28, 30, 31–2, 35, 37–9, 42, 47–8, 50, 52; McGurk (1994b) 20–1 [repr. McGurk (1998) no. XII]; Netzer (1994) 1, 13, 28, 31, 35–41, 47–50, 52–3, 66, 71, 77–8, 86, 90, 93, 97–100, 110, 115, 208 n. 2, 218 n. 17, 219 nn. 3, 12, 16, 221 n. 12, 222 nn. 27, 31, 35–6, 223 nn. 40–1, 225 n. 45, 227 n. 78, 229 n. 130, 230 n. 157, 236 n. 33, 237 n. 65, 242 n. 4; *ASMMF* III (1995) 1–11 [no. 206; Doane]; J.J. John (1995) 117; McNamara (1995) 89–90; Webster—Brown (1997) 232–3, 235, 238 [nos. 83, 95, 111]; Werner (1997a) 24; Dumville (1999) 45, 62, 64–5,

76–81, 94, 98, 115; Michelli (1999) 355, 357; Netzer (1999) 319–20; Verey (1999) 327; Crowley (2000) 132; Lapidge (2000a) 22; M.P. Brown (2001c) 56 n. 26; R. Gameson (2001d) 10–12 [no. 14]; Stanley (2001) 242–3; M.P. Brown (2002); M.P. Brown (2003a); M.P. Brown (2003b) 131–4; M.P. Brown (2003c); Nees (2003) 333–4; K.L. Brown (2004a) 5; Gullick (2004) 32; Karkov (2004) 60, 69–70; Tite (2004) 9, 15 n. 41; Beall (2005) 191; Dumville (2005) 309; Karkov (2006a) 50, 56; Roberts (2005) 18 [no. 1], 34–7 [no. 5]; Roberts (2006); Keefer (2007b) 87–8; Piper (2007) 87; Barker-Benfield (2008) III.1663; Graham (2009) 163–5; Wieland (2009) 117; M.P. Brown (2011a); M.P. Brown (2012) 132–3, 134, 137, 138–9, 144, 150, 155; R. Gameson (2012a) 17, 18, 25, 37 and n. 89, 42 n. 117, 53 n. 183, 61 and n. 211, 67, 75 and n. 261, 80, 81, 84; R. Gameson (2012b) 107, 114; Gullick (2012) 294 and n. 1; Marsden (2012) 418 and n. 56; Pfaff (2012) 449; Scragg (2012a) no. 316

DEC: Köhler (1930–60) I.76–7, 326–8, 332–4 and III.34; McGurk (1955a) 192–5 [repr. McGurk (1998) no. III]; McGurk (1955b) 106 [repr. McGurk (1998) no. IV]; McGurk (1961a) 11–12 [repr. McGurk (1998) no. VI]; Bischoff (1963b) 288, 296; Dodwell (1971b) 3, 106, 107, 108; Alexander (1975a) 146–7; Nordenfalk (1977) 60–75; Alexander (1978a) no. 9; Alexander (1978b) no. 1; G. Henderson (1982) 12–14, 29, 48–9 n. 21, 53–5 n. 46; D.M. Wilson (1984) 36–40; Ohlgren (1986) no. 9; G. Henderson (1987) 99–122; Backhouse (1989) 165–74; Gilbert (1990) 153–60; R. Gameson (1991) 85 n. 129; McGurk (1993) 243, 246–51 [repr. McGurk (1998) no. XI]; R. Gameson (1994b) 33 n. 42, 34 n. 43, 35 n. 50, 37–9, 47–8, 52; McGurk (1994b) 12 n. 32, 15 n. 46, 18 [repr. McGurk (1998) no. XII]; Deshman (1995) 244; R. Gameson (1999b) 335; Michelli (1999) 345–7, 357; Farr (2003) 117; Nees (2003) 347; K.L. Brown (2004a) 5; Karkov (2004) 60; Pochat (2005) 147; Karkov (2006a) 49, 56; Nees (2006) 91; M.P. Brown (2007a) 89, 105, 108; M.P. Brown (2007c); Keefer (2007b) 107–8; Nees (2007); O'Loughlin (2007) 152; Inglis (2008) 24; Karkov (2009) 206–9, 218–21, 222, 223; M.P. Brown (2011b) 31–2, 35–7, 36, 40, 42; Farr (2011b) 224–5, 226; Nees (2011) 14–16, 21–2, 23, 25, 27; Netzer (2011) 3, 4–5, 11–12; O'Reilly (2011) 197–8; Pulliam (2011) 59, 72–3, 77; Tilghman (2011) 92–4, 106–7; Werner (2011) 307–10; N. Edwards (2012) 245; Netzer (2012) 230, 233–5

FACS: Kendrick et al. (1956–60) [complete facsimile]; M.P. Brown (2002) [complete facsimile]; Dodwell (1982) 40 [fol. 26v]; D.M. Wilson (1984) pls. 30 [fol. 94r], 38 [fol. 25v]; G. Henderson (1987) pls. 137–9 [fols. 2v, 3r, 5v], 140 [fol. 17v], 142 [fol. 11r], 144–8 [fols. 18v, 25v, 26v, 27r, 29r,

93v], 152 [fol. 95r], 155–7 [fols. 131r, 137v, 138v, 139r], 159–61 [fols. 210v, 211r, 259r]; M.P. Brown (1990) 51 [fol. 8r]; M.P. Brown (1991) pls. 51, 55, 65 [fols. 5v, 94r, 94v]; Webster—Backhouse (1991) 112–13 [fols. 3v, 210v]; T.J. Brown (1993a) ill. 28 [fol. 90r]; Netzer (1994) pls. 52, 81–2 [fols. 3v, 137v, 209v]; *ASMMF* III (1995) no. 206; Deshman (1995) fig. 102 [fol. 25v]; M.P. Brown (1996) figs. 31–2 [fols. 25v, 27r]; Backhouse (1997) pl. 1 [fol. 211r]; Nees (2003) figs. 1 (a)–(d) [fol. 259r], 8 [fol. 137v]; M.P. Brown (2003a) 15, 18–21, 23, 25–7, 28, 33, 42 [fols. 2v, 3r, 5r, 8r, 10v, 25v, 26v, 27r, 29r, 93v, 94v, 95r, 137v, 138v, 139v, 209v, 210v, 211r, 259r]; M.P. Brown (2003b) fig. 1 [fol. 8r]; M.P. Brown (2003c) pls. 1, 3–8, 9 (a)–(b), 10–25 [fols. 2v, 3r, 5v, 8r, 10v, 12r, 25r, 25v, 26r, 26v, 27r, 29r, 90r, 91r, 93v, 94r, 94v, 95r, 137r, 137v, 138v, 139r, 209v, 210v, 211r], figs. 45 (a), 53–6, 63–4 [fols. 1r, 137r, 199r, 205v, 253r, 259r, 259v]; K.L. Brown (2004a) pls. 1 [fols. 93v, 95r, 137v, 138v (all details)], 2 [fol. 139r]; Karkov (2004) fig. 6 [fol. 25v]; Roberts (2005) colour pl. 1 [fol. 259r], pl. 5 [fol. 259r], p. 17 [fol. 211r]; M.P. Brown (2007a) pls. 26–30, 80 [fols. 10v, 208r, 26v, 27r, 29r, 259r]; Nees (2007) 45 [fol. 94v]; Inglis (2008) 25 [fol. 29r]; Owen-Crocker (2009) figs. 6.3 [fol. 255r], 7.1 [fol. 29r], 7.11 [fol. 25v], 7.12 [fol. 27r]; R. Gameson (2012) pls. 4.1 [fols. 138v–139r], 4.2 [fol. 259r], 8.1 [fol. 95r]

ED: Skeat (1871, 1874, 1878, 1887) [base MS for Latin text and OE gloss to gospels]; J. Wordsworth et al. (1889–1954) [Latin gospels coll. as Y]; Hurst (1955) ix–xvi [*Capitula euangeliorum* coll. as N]; Boyd (1975) [Aldred's marginalia]; B. Fischer (1988–91) [gospel excerpts coll. as Ny]; Nees (2003) 340–1 [materials added by Aldred]

LANG: Skeat (1871) xxix–xxxii; A. Campbell (1959); Kendrick et al. (1959–60) II, *passim* [indexes of Latin and OE words]; Karl Brunner (1965); Wenisch (1979); Greenfield—Robinson (1980) 333–6 [bibliography]; Hogg (1992); Bullough (1998a) 109; R. Gameson (1999b) 347; Crowley (2000) 133–7

ST: Glunz (1933) 32; Frere (1934) 136; Kunze (1947) 47–9; Kendrick et al. (1956–60) vol. I, *passim*; T.J. Brown (1959) 250 [repr. T.J. Brown (1993a) 245]; T.J. Brown (1959–63) 364 [repr. T.J. Brown (1993a) 20]; McGurk (1963) 172 [repr. McGurk (1998) no. VIII] [on Cassiodoran group]; Morrell (1965) 156–74; T.J. Brown (1972) 221–35, 240–1, 243–5 [repr. T.J. Brown (1993a) 99–113, 117–18, 120–2]; Klauser (1972) xxxii [no. 12]; T.J. Brown (1974) 129–30, 132 [repr. T.J. Brown (1993a) 126–7, 130]; Boyd (1975); T.J. Brown (1975) 270 [repr. T.J. Brown (1993a) 160]; Piper (1978) 214 n. 4, 236–7, 237 n. 71; F.C. Robinson (1980) 24;

Backhouse (1981); T.J. Brown (1982a) 108–9, 111–12 [repr. T.J. Brown (1993a) 207–9, 211–12]; G. Henderson (1982) 10, 35–6 [Greek inscription]; T.J. Brown (1984) 323 [repr. T.J. Brown (1993a) 235]; Horsley — Waterhouse (1984) 217 [Greek 'nomen sacrum']; Lapidge (1994a) 106 [colophon]; *CPL* (1995) no. 1977; B.M. Cox (1995); McGurk (1995a) 256, 259 [repr. McGurk (1998) no. XIII]; McNamara (1995) 100; M.P. Brown (1996) 65, 71–4, 82, 84, 88–9, 94, 96, 103, 115–17, 124–5, 152, 167; Lenker (1997) 102–6, 113, 135–46, 387–9; Marsden (1999) 290; Netzer (1999) 321; Verey (1999) 328, 332; M.P. Brown (2000); R. Gameson (2001b); M.P. Brown (2002) vol. I; M.P. Brown (2003a); M.P. Brown (2003c); Nees (2003); K.L. Brown (2004a) 5–7, 7–10; Beall (2005) 191, 193–4, 197; C. Bishop (2007b) 81; M.P. Brown (2007a) 105; M.P. Brown (2011a); Farr (2011a) 91 and n., 99 n. 49

344. London, British Library, Cotton Nero E. i, vol. I, and vol. II, fols. 1–155

s. xi³/⁴; whole MS Worcester [for vol. II, fols. 166–80 and companion volume, see no. **36**; vol. II, fols. 156–65, are additions of s. xii]

Contents: vol. I, fols. 55–208 and vol. II, fols. 1–155: Office legendary (January–September); Office and mass for St Nicholas; additions (vol. I, fols. 3–54): Byrhtferth, *Vita S. Oswaldi* [*BHL* 6374] (including three acrostic poems by Abbo of Fleury [SK 15822, 10987, 7744]), *Vita S. Ecgwini* [*BHL* 2432]; Lantfred, *Translatio et miracula S. Swithuni* [*BHL* 7944–6]; hymn by Wulfstan of Winchester [SK 1443]

MS: Levison (1919–20) 545–6, 601–2; N.R. Ker (1939–40) 82–3; F. Wormald (1945) 135 [repr. F. Wormald (1984) 75]; Colgrave (1956) 31–2; N.R. Ker (1957) no. 29; N.R. Ker (1960) 49, 53; N.R. Ker (1964) 207; T.A.M. Bishop (1971) 20 n. 1; Zettel (1979); Gneuss (1985) 125 [no. N.1]; Hartzell (1989) 77, 84; Dumville (1992a) 139; Dumville (1993g) 48 n. 210, 68; Gameson (1996a) 219–21, 239; Jackson — Lapidge (1996) [full description of contents]; Love (1996) xviii–xxiii, clxxiv–clxxv; R. Gameson (1999a) no. 397; P. Wormald (1999) 182–5; Pulsiano (2002a) 64; Lapidge (2003a) 239; W. Schipper (2003) 161; Lapidge (2004b) 445; R. Gameson (2005a) 93, 101–4; Corona (2006) 140–1; Biggs (2007a) 25 [T.N. Hall], 43, 45–50, 53–4; T.N. Hall (2007) 247–50; Upchurch (2007) xii, 29, 110–11; Barker-Benfield (2008) III.1665; Lapidge (2009) xciii–xcix

FACS: Ker (1960) pl. 26 [vol. II, fol. 115v]; R. Gameson (1996a) pl. 8 [vol. I, fol. 55v]

ED: Jane Stevenson (1996b) 51–98 [Paulus, *Vita S. Mariae Aegyptiacae*, coll. as N]; Magennis (2002) 139–208 [base MS for Paulus, *Vita S. Mariae Aegyptiacae*]; Pulsiano (2002a) 68–102 [base MS (= N) for *Passio S. Pantaleonis*, together with no. 754. 6]; Lapidge (2003a) 252–332 [Lantfred, *Translatio S. Swithuni*, coll. as N], 783–7 [hymn by Wulfstan coll. as N]; Upchurch (2007) 114–70 [base MS (= N) for *Passio SS. Iuliani et Basilissae*]; Lapidge (2009), 2–203 [base MS (= N) for Byrhtferth, *Vita S. Oswaldi*, including (pp. 92, 166–8) three acrostic poems by Abbo of Fleury: SK 11013, 15822, 10987], 206–303 [base MS (= N) for Byrhtferth, *Vita S. Ecgwini*]

ST: Hohler (1967) [Office of St Nicholas]; Römer (1972b) 169; Lapidge (1979b) [repr. Lapidge (1993a) 293–315]; Kotzor (1981) I.227*, 274*, 277–8*; Zettel (1982); Gwara (1992) [poems by Abbo of Fleury]; Lapidge (1993b) 140–4; Love (1996) xviii–xxiii; Whatley (1996) 19–20; Lapidge—Love (2001) 279–80; Biggs et al. (2001) 11–15 [poems by Abbo of Fleury; Lendinara], 22–486 *passim*; Hartzell (2006) no. 139 [Office of St Nicholas]

344. 5. London, British Library, Cotton Nero E. i, vol. II, fols. 181–4 (with London, British Library, Add. 46204) [part of no. **293** since s. xi?]

s. xi ex., Worcester

Contents: cartulary (f)

MS: N.R. Ker (1948) 67–9 [repr. N.R. Ker (1985) 49–51]; G.R.C. Davis (1958) no. 1069; Sawyer (1968) 49, 52; *Cat. Add. B.M 1946–1950* (1979) 16; Scharer (1982) 287–309; Backhouse et al. (1984b) no. 87(c); Sims-Williams (1990) 182 and n.; Dumville (1992a) 120; Dumville (1993g) 56 and n. 246; R. Gameson (1999a) no. 354; P. Wormald (1999) 184; R. Gameson (2005a) 96, 101–4; Tinti (2009); Hanna—Turville-Petre (2010) 123; Scragg (2012a) no. 367

345. London, British Library, Cotton Nero E. i, vol. II, fols. 185–6

s. x/xi; s. xi[1] or xi med. or xi[2], all prov. Worcester?

Contents: Laws: *IV Eadgar** (s. x/xi); Office lessons (f)

MS: Liebermann (1903–16) I.xxv; N.R. Ker (1957) no. 166; Dumville (1992a) 127 and n. 234; Dumville (1993g) 56 and n. 246; P. Wormald (1999) 164, 182–5; Hough (2006) 115, 122, 136; Rumble (2006a) viii; Scragg (2012a) no. 514; P. Wormald (2012) 533 [no. 3]

ED: Liebermann (1903–16) I.206–14, even pages, left-hand column [base
   MS (= F) for *IV Eg.*]

ST: R. Gameson (1996a) 239; Hough (2006) 122–3, 136

346. London, British Library, Cotton Otho A. i (with Oxford,
Bodleian Library, Arch. Selden B. 26)

s. viii², Mercia or Canterbury?

Contents: decrees of the Council of Clofesho 747 (f); Boniface, *Epist.*
   lxxviii (to Archbishop Cuthbert) (f); charter [Sawyer (1968) no. 92 for
   A.D. 749] (f); Gregory, *Regula pastoralis* [*CPL* 1712], abridged
   [extracts from bks. II–III] (f)

MS: T.S. Smith (1696) 66; *CLA* II (1935) nos. 188*, 229*; N.R. Ker
   (1939–40) 79–80; Sawyer (1968) no. 92; A.G. Watson (1978) 289, 300
   and n. 86, 310 n. 103 [repr. A.G. Watson (2004) no. VII]; Clement
   (1984a) 41; P.L. Heyworth (1989) 64; Keynes (1996b); Lapidge et al.
   (1999) 12 [Keynes]; Schreiber (2003) 7 [and nn.], 23 and n. 6; Rumble
   (2006b) 6; D. Ganz (2012) 188 n. 3

DEC: Pächt—Alexander (1973) 1 [no. 3]

FACS: Keynes (1996b) figs. 2–3 [Arch. Selden B. 26, fol. 34r–v], 4–5
   [Otho A. i, fol. 7r], 6 [facsimile by Wanley from Otho A. i]

ED: Haddan—Stubbs (1869–71) III.362–76 [Council of Clofesho 747;
   base MS, from editions of Spelman, Wilkins and Johnson]; Tangl
   (1916) 161–71 [Boniface, *Epist.* lxxviii]; BCS no. 178 [edition of charter
   (Sawyer no. 92) based on Spelman and Wilkins]

ST: N.P. Brooks (1971) 76 n. 1; A.G. Watson (1978) 299 [repr. A.G.
   Watson (2004) no. VII]; Scharer (1982) 188–95, 293, *et passim* [Sawyer
   no. 92]; Cubitt (1995) 266–7; Keynes (1996b)

347. London, British Library, Cotton Otho A. vi, fols. 1–129

s. x med., SE England

Contents: Boethius (Alfred), *De consolatione Philosophiae**

MS: Sedgefield (1899) xi–xiii; Krapp (1932b) xxxvi–xli; K. Sisam (1953a)
   294–5; N.R. Ker (1957) no. 167; Robinson—Stanley (1991) 20–1;
   Dumville (1994a) 147 and n. 84; Godden (1994a); Kiernan (1994a)
   51–2; Kiernan (1998b); Obst—Schleburg (1998) vii; Szarmach (2001)
   256 n. 2, 258; Bredehoft (2004) 148–9, 152–4, 169; S. Irvine (2005);
   Godden—Irvine (2009) I.18–24

FACS: A.H. Smith (1938) pls. vi–viii [both of fol. 20r]; Robinson –
Stanley (1991) pls. 5.6.11–5.32.2 [all OE verse on fols. 1–129]; Obst –
Schleburg (1998) xiii [fol. 75r]; S. Irvine (2005) pls. V–VI [fols. 15r,
14r]; Godden – Irvine (2009) II, pl. 3 [fol. 108r]

ED: Sedgefield (1899) [base MS (= C) for OE Boethius]; Krapp (1932b)
153–203 [metres of Boethius]; B. Griffiths (1994) [metres of Boethius];
Obst – Schleburg (1998) [base MS (= C) for verse translation of metres
of Boethius]; Godden – Irvine (2009) I.383–541 [base MS for OE
Boethius, partly reconstructed]

LANG: Sedgefield (1899) xxxv–xxxvi, 208–325 [glossary]; Godden –
Irvine (2009) I.152–206, II.524–631 [glossary]

ST: Greenfield – Robinson (1980) 247–8, 314–16 [bibliography]; Kiernan
(1994a) 42, 51–2 [use of ultraviolet photography]; Kiernan (1998b);
Prescott (1998) 268 [note on recovery of MS]; Godden – Irvine (2009)

348. London, British Library, Cotton Otho A. viii (with London,
British Library, Cotton Otho B. x, fol. 66)

s. xi$^{1/4}$; s. xi$^{4/4}$, Canterbury StA?

Contents: Goscelin, *Vita et translatio S. Mildrethae* [*BHL* 5960–1] (s.
xi$^{4/4}$) (f); Bili, Life of St Machutus* [*BHL* 5116a] (s. xi$^{1/4}$) (incomplete,
damaged)

MS: T.S. Smith (1696) 66–7; N.R. Ker (1957) no. 168; Rollason (1982) 20,
107; Yerkes (1982b) 28 [fols. 1–6]; Yerkes (1983b) 30 [fols. 7–34];
Yerkes (1984a) xxvii–xxxii, xlii; Yerkes (1986b); Rollason (1987) 150;
Scragg (1996) 220–1; Prescott (1998) 276–7; R. Gameson (1999a)
no. 398; Crowley (2000) 143–5; Barker-Benfield (2008) III.1748; Scragg
(2012a) no. 515

FACS: Yerkes (1982b) p. 29 [fol. 1r]; Yerkes (1983b) 31 [fol. 20r]

ED: Rollason (1982) 108–43 [Goscelin, *Vita S. Mildrethae*, coll. as G];
Yerkes (1984a) [base MS for OE Life of St Machutus]

LANG: Crowley (2000) 143–5

ST: Scragg (1979) 263; Yerkes (1983a); Yerkes (1987) 89–93; Scragg (1996)
220–1; Whatley (1997) 198–207; Biggs et al. (2001) 308–10, 347–50

349. London, British Library, Cotton Otho A. x (with London, British
Library, Cotton Otho A. xii, fols. 1–7)

s. xi in.

Contents: Æthelweard, *Chronicon* (f)

MS: T.S. Smith (1696) 67; E.E. Barker (1951); N.R. Ker (1957) no. 170; A. Campbell (1962) ix–xii; Prescott (1997) 421, 430; Prescott (1998) 257, 262, 270–3; P. Wormald (1999) 138 n. 82, 258–9; Barker-Benfield (2008) III.1829; Wieland (2009) 142

ED: E.E. Barker (1951) 56–62; A. Campbell (1962) [text from this MS coll. and ptd in italic type]

LANG: A. Campbell (1962) xlv–lx

ST: Gneuss (1976a) 318 [repr. Gneuss (1996a) no. IX]; Keynes (2006) nos. B 56, G 225–8

London, British Library, Cotton Otho A. xii, fols. 1–7: see no. **349**

350. London, British Library, Cotton Otho A. xii, fols. 8–12, 14–16, 18–19

s. xi³/⁴ or xi²

Contents: Osbern, *Vita et translatio S. Ælphegi* [*BHL* 2518–19] (f)

MS: T.S. Smith (1696) 67; N.R. Ker (1957) no. 171; Gneuss (1976a) [repr. Gneuss (1996a) no. IX]; Gneuss (1976b) [repr. Gneuss (1996b) no. IX]; R.I. Page (1993a) 7; Rumble (1994c) 290; Prescott (1997) 392 and n. 16, 430; Prescott (1998) 258–80 and nn.; R. Gameson (1999a) no. 399; P. Wormald (1999) 186 n. 100; Barker-Benfield (2008) III.1684, 1829

ST: Prescott (1998); Biggs et al. (2001) 45–6

NOTE: the first three items of this MS, as seen and described by T.S. Smith (1696) 67, were: (1) Asser, *Vita Ælfredi*; (2) two OE charms; (3) the OE poem 'The Battle of Maldon'. All three were destroyed in 1731. The surviving remnant of the MS, containing Osbern, *Vita et translatio S. Ælphegi*, constituted arts. 4–5 in Smith's catalogue. Arts. 1–5 originally consisted of 86 folios, of which 10 survive.

351. London, British Library, Cotton Otho A. xiii, pt. i (fols. 1–93 [originally fols. 1–150])

s. xi¹ or xi in.

Contents: fragments from a collection of saints' *passiones* and visions: *Passio S. Eustachii* [*BHL* 2760], *Passio S. Marci euangelistae* [*BHL* 5276]; *Passio S. Cassiani* [*BHL* 1626, expanded]; *Passio S. Cornelii* [*BHL* 1958]; *Passio S. Ferreoli* [*BHL* 2912], *Passio S. Saturnini* [*BHL* 7495–6]; *Passio S. Theclae* [*BHL* 8020d]; *Passio SS. Faustae, Euilasii et Eusebii* [*BHL* 2833]; *Vita S. Fursei* [*BHL* 3210]; *Visio Baronti* [*CPL* 1313; *BHL* 997]; *Visio Rothearii*; Heito, *Visio Wettini*

MS: T.S. Smith (1696) 67–8; Levison (1919–20) 602; N.R. Ker (1957) no. 173; Dumville (1992a) 140 and n. 320; Prescott (1998) 277; Gneuss (2003b) 298; Swan (2007b) 33 n. 12

ST: Biggs et al. (2001) 205, 130, 152, 217, 412, 446, 209–10, 219, 101 [T.N. Hall] respectively

352. London, British Library, Cotton Otho A. xviii, fol. 131

s. xi[1]

Contents: Ælfric, Homily on St Laurence* (f)

MS: *Committee of Parliament Report* (1732) 468–8 [no. 7]; Pope (1931); N.R. Ker (1957) no. 174; Clemoes (1997) 59–60 [MS. f[h]]; Scragg (2012a) no. 516

ED: Clemoes (1997) 419–21 [Ælfric, Hom. I. xxix, lines 47–84, coll. as f[h]]

353. London, British Library, Cotton Otho B. ii (with London, British Library, Cotton Otho B. x, fols. 61, 63, 64)

s. x[2] or x/xi, SE England, possibly London

Contents: Gregory (Alfred), *Regula pastoralis** (incomplete)

MS: K. Sisam (1953a) 145; N.R. Ker (1957) no. 175; Carlson (1975–8) I.15–21, 64–5; Horgan (1986) 116–19; R.I. Page (1993a) 102–3; Prescott (1998) 276; Schreiber (2003) 61; Karkov (2004) 101; Scragg (2012a) nos. 517–21

DEC: E. Temple (1976) no. 46; Brownrigg (1978) 257; Ohlgren (1986) no. 151

FACS: Carlson (1975–8) I.199 [fol. 10r], 200 [fol. 28r]

ED: Carlson (1975–8) [base MS for OE *Regula pastoralis*]; Schreiber (2003) [OE *Regula pastoralis* coll. as O]

LANG: Carlson (1975–8) I.37–63; Schreiber (2003) 83–162

ST: Horgan (1973); Horgan (1986) 114–19; R. Gameson (1998) 242 n. 45; Waite (2000) 24–7, 199–226

354. London, British Library, Cotton Otho B. ix

s. ix[2] or ix[4/4], Brittany, prov. English royal court s. x[1], Chester-le-Street prob. 934, Durham s. x ex.

Contents: hymn or prayer (s. x, added in England); gospels (f) (s. ix² or ix⁴/⁴); inscription* and manumissions* (s. x or xi, all lost)

MS: *Committee of Parliament Report* (1732) 471; Mynors (1939) no. 15; N.R. Ker (1957) no. 176; Rella (1977) 50; Piper (1978) 214 n. 4; Rella (1980) 111; Backhouse et al. (1984b) no. 5; Deuffic (1985) 301; Keynes (1985a) 170–9; McGurk (1986b) 45 n. 4, 55 n. 62 [repr. McGurk (1998) no. XIV]; Dumville (1987) 175 and n. 162 [on fol. iv]; A.G. Watson (1987a) 30; Dumville (1992a) 106, 114, 121; Lapidge (1994b) 113; Bischoff (1998 –) II, no. 2422; Prescott (1998) 257; Karkov (2004) 57–8, 69–70; Graham (2009) 194; R. Gameson (2012d) 349 and n. 17; D. Ganz (2012) 190 n. 14; Marsden (2012) 422 and nn. 71–2

DEC: Coatsworth (1989) 300 and n. 78; R. Gameson (1995b) 58, 198 n. 33; Karkov (2004) 4, 56 n. 13, 57, 86, 158, 175; R. Gameson (2012c) 275 and n. 82

FACS: Keynes (1985a) pl. VIII [fol. iv]; Nees (2003) fig. 4 [fol. 7r]

ST: J.A. Robinson (1923) 52–3; Rollason (1989) 413–14, 420–1; C.D. Wright (1993) 268 and n. 193; Bonner (1989b) 390; Kiernan (1994a) 38–9

355. London, British Library, Cotton Otho B. x (except the fols. of nos. **356** sqq. listed below) (with Oxford, Bodleian Library, Rawlinson Q. e. 20 [S.C. 15606])

s. xi¹

Contents: Ælfric, *Hexameron**; Lives of Saints* and Homilies* (most by Ælfric; incomplete, damaged)

MS: *Committee of Parliament Report* (1732) 471–2; Skeat (1881–1900) II.xv–xvii; Crawford (1922) 5–6; R. Derolez (1954) 16–18; N.R. Ker (1957) no. 177; Collins — Clemoes (1974) 322; Godden (1979) lvii–lviii; Scragg (1979) 263; R.M. Thomson (1982b) 16; P.L. Heyworth (1989) 15; Clayton (1994) 41 n. 2, 58–61, 94–5; Scragg (1996) 221; Clemoes (1997) 60–1; Prescott (1998) 227, 276; Withers (1999) 112–18; Kiernan (2002); Magennis (2002) 15–16; Pulsiano (2002b) 167; Lapidge (2003a) 580; Acker (2004) 129; Corona (2006) 130–2; Upchurch (2007) xii, 52; Withers (2007) 62, 229–31, 261–3; Marsden (2008) lvi–lix; Scragg (2012a) nos. 522–5

DEC: Withers (2007) 233

ED [the order of the following items is that of the manuscript, listed according to the numbering of individual articles in N.R. Ker (1957) 225–7; only the most recent editions are cited]:

art. 1: Clemoes (1997) 183–6, 187–8 [parts of Ælfric, CH I, Hom. I (*De initio creaturae*), coll. as fⁱ]

art. 2: Crawford (1921) 61–5 [part of Ælfric, *Exameron*, coll. as E]

art. 3: Skeat (1881–1900) I.50–90 [parts of Ælfric, *Lives of Saints*, no. III (St Basil), coll. as O]; Corona (2006) 152–88 [parts of Ælfric, 'Life of St Basil' (Skeat, no. III), coll. as O]

art. 4: lost

art. 5: Skeat (1881–1900) I.90–114 [parts of Ælfric, *Lives of Saints*, no. IV (SS. Julian and Basilissa), lines 29–91, 219–333, coll. as O]

art. 6: Skeat (1881–1900) I.116–46 [parts of Ælfric, *Lives of Saints*, no. V (St Sebastian), lines 261–85, 469–74, coll. as O]

art. 7: Skeat (1881–1900) I.170–94 [parts of Ælfric, *Lives of Saints*, no. VII, lines 1–100, 187–234 (St Agnes), coll. as O]

art. 8: Skeat (1881–1900) I.186–94 [parts of Ælfric, *Lives of Saints*, no. VII, lines 296–429 (*Alia sententia quam scripsit Terrentianus*: Passio of SS. John and Paul), coll. as O (lines 353–412 only)]

art. 9: Skeat (1881–1900) I.24–50 [parts of Ælfric, *Lives of Saints*, no. II (St Eugenia), lines 117–260, 394–428, coll. as O]

art. 10: Skeat (1881–1900) II.334–54 [parts of anonymous 'Life of St Euphrosyne', lines 1–9, 64–108, 154–99, 241–72, 331–4, coll. as O]

art. 11: as Rypins (1924) 68–76 [parts of anonymous 'Life of St Christopher', not collated]

art. 12: Skeat (1881–1900) II.2–52 [parts of anonymous 'Life of St Mary of Egypt' (Skeat no. XXIIIB), lines 11–91, 318–401, 484–528, coll. as O]

art. 13: Skeat (1881–1900) I.488–540 [parts of anonymous 'Seven Sleepers of Ephesus', lines 17–54, 470–647, 733–818, coll. as O]; Magennis (1994) 58–61 ['Seven Sleepers of Ephesus' coll. as O]

art. 14: lost

art. 15: lost

art. 16: probably all lost

art. 17: lost

art. 18: Napier (1883/1967) 299–306 [Hom. LVIII, not collated]

art. 19: Crawford (1922) 171–204 [parts of Ælfric's translation of OE Genesis, coll. as O]; Marsden (2008) 70–85 [parts of Ælfric's translation of OE Genesis, coll. as O]

art. 20: Skeat (1881–1900) I.440–70 [parts of Ælfric, *Lives of Saints*, no. XXI (St Swithun), not collated]; Needham (1976) 60–81 [Ælfric, 'Life of St Swithun', coll. as O]; Lapidge (2003a) 590–608 [Ælfric, 'Life of St Swithun', coll. as O]

art. 21: Skeat (1881–1900) II.314–34 [part of Ælfric, *Lives of Saints*,
    no. XXXII (St Edmund, king and martyr), lines 1–192, coll. as O];
    Needham (1976) 43–59 [Ælfric, 'Life of St Edmund, king and martyr',
    coll. as O]

art. 22: lost

art. 23: Skeat (1881–1900) I.432–40 [Ælfric, *Lives of Saints*, no. XX
    (St Æthelthryth), lines 61–122, coll. as O]

art. 24: lost

LANG: Fowler (1972) xxii–xxiv; Magennis (1994) 13–19; Magennis
    (2002) 35–43

ST: Lee (1991); J. Hill (1996) 243; Withers (1999) 128–9

356. London, British Library, Cotton Otho B. x, fols. 29–30

s. xi med., (prov. Worcester)

Contents: homilies* (f)

MS: Assmann (1889/1964) xxvii–xxviii [Clemoes]; N.R. Ker (1957)
    no. 178; N.R. Ker (1964) 207; A.F. Cameron (1974) 221; Scragg (1979)
    263; Franzen (1991) 53–4; Laing (1993) 79; R. Gameson (2005a) 93;
    Scragg (2012a) no. 526

ED: Assmann (1889/1964) 114–15 [Ælfric's Summary of the Book of
    Judith, lines 394–445, coll. as O]

London, British Library, Cotton Otho B. x, fol. 51: see **no. 358**

London, British Library, Cotton Otho B. x, fols. 55, 58, 62: see **no. 357**

London, British Library, Cotton Otho B. x, fols. 61, 63, 64: see **no. 353**

London, British Library, Cotton Otho B. x, fol. 66: see **no. 348**

357. London, British Library, Cotton Otho B. xi (with London, British Library, Cotton Otho B. x, fols. 55, 58, 62 + London, British Library, Add. 34652, fol. 2)

s. x med. and xi¹; all parts Winchester, (prov. Southwick, Augustinian
    canons) [other texts lost]

Contents: Bede, *Historia ecclesiastica** (f) (s. x med.); Bede's autobio-
    graphical note [*HE* V. xxiii. 2] (s. xi¹); West Saxon royal genealogy*,
    Anglo-Saxon Chronicle G* (f), Laws*: *Æthelstan II* (f), *Alfred and Ine*
    (f) (all s. xi¹)

MS: Wanley (1705) 219; *Committee of Parliament Report* (1732) 472;
    C. Plummer (1892–9) I.xiii, II.xxviii; Liebermann (1903–16) I.xxxvi;

K. Sisam (1953a) 45, 49, 59, 61–2; N.R. Ker (1957) no. 180; N.R. Ker (1964) 181, 200; Grant (1974); Buckalew (1978) 161; A. Lutz (1981) xxvii–l; Torkar (1981) 39–41, 149–59; P.L. Heyworth (1989) 255, 257; Dumville (1992b) 57, 64–5, 101 n. 217, 125, 128–9; Dumville (1994a) 147–9; P. Wormald (1996); Prescott (1998) 258, 276, 278; P. Wormald (1999) 164, 172–81 and n. 292 *et passim*; Bredehoft (2001) 222; Prescott (2004) 46, 60; Rowley (2004) 13–15, 20–1; Hough (2006) 114, 129–31; Grimmer (2007) 103 n. 5; Graham (2009) 200; Rowley (2011) 20–1; D. Ganz (2012) 189 and n. 12; Scragg (2012a) nos. 527–9; P. Wormald (2012) 533 [no. 2]

FACS: A. Lutz (1981) pls. I [BL, Add. 34652, fol. 2r (detail)], II–III [Otho B. xi, fol. 45r]; Bredehoft (2001) pl. IV [BL, Add. 34652, fol. 2v]; Rowley (2011) pl. 2 [Otho B. xi, fol. 28r]

ED: T. Miller (1890–8) [OE Bede coll. as C]; J.M. Schipper (1897–9) [remaining parts of OE Bede coll. as C: see Miller I.xvi]; Liebermann (1903–16) [Laws; remaining parts pr. as Ot: see Ker, arts. 5–6]; A. Lutz (1981) [base MS. for *Anglo–Saxon Chronicle* G, supplemented from transcript by Nowell and edition by Wheloc]; Bately (1986) 1–50 [variant readings from *Anglo–Saxon Chronicle* G]; Dumville (1986) 21–5 [West Saxon genealogy coll. as Q]

LANG: A. Lutz (1981) cli–cxciii [*Anglo-Saxon Chronicle* G]

ST: Parkes (1976b) 163–71 [repr. Parkes (1991) 160–8]; Torkar (1976); A. Lutz (1977); Meaney (1984) 246–50; Dumville (1986) 5–6; Hollis — Wright (1992) 230–2; O'Brien O'Keeffe (1994) 234, 241; Grant (1996); Waite (2000) 42–5, 321–53; Bredehoft (2001) 6, 27–8; Rowley (2011); Keynes (2012) 542, 552 *et passim*

358. London, British Library, Cotton Otho C. i, vol. I (with London, British Library, Cotton Otho B. x, fol. 51)

s. xi¹ and xi med., prov. Malmesbury?

Contents: gospels* (incomplete) (s. xi¹), bull of Pope Sergius* (s. xi med.)

MS: Skeat (1871) viii–x; Bright (1904–6) I.xviii–xix; N.R. Ker (1957) no. 181; N.R. Ker (1964) 128; Morrell (1965) 184–5; Grünberg (1967) 11–12; R.M. Thomson (1982b) 16; Dumville (1992a) 121; Liuzza (1994–2000) I.xxiii–xxv; *ASMMF* III (1995) 12–15 [no. 218; Liuzza]; Lenker (1997) 16–17; Prescott (1998) 276; Lenker (1999) 141; Scragg (2012a) nos. 530–2

FACS: *ASMMF* III (1995) no. 218

ED: Skeat (1871) [OE gospels of Mark, Luke and John coll. as C]; Bright (1904–6) [OE gospels of Mark, Luke and John coll. as C]; H. Edwards (1986) 16–17 [Bull of Pope Sergius]; Liuzza (1994–2000) I (OE gospels of Mark, Luke and John coll. as C]; Rauer (2006) 271–4 [Bull of Pope Sergius]

LANG: Liuzza (1994–2000) II.121–54

ST: K. Sisam (1953a) 199–200; Metzger (1977) 449; Blockley (1994) 81; Liuzza (1994–2000) vol. II; Lenker (1997) 10–59; Collier (2000) 195, 199; Rauer (2006)

359. London, British Library, Cotton Otho C. i, vol. II

s. xi in. and (from fol. 62 [*Dialogi**]) s. xi med., prob. Worcester, (prov. whole MS Worcester)

Contents: Gregory (Werferth), *Dialogi** (incomplete); three lives from *Verba seniorum** [*CPG* 5570; *BHL* 6527] (= *Vitas patrum*, bk. V), V.37 and 38; Jerome, *Vita S. Malchi* [*CPL* 619; *BHL* 5190]); Letter of Boniface to Eadburg+* (*Epist.* x); Sermon ('Evil tongues')*; three homilies* by Ælfric (s. xi in., SW England?); from fol. 62 [s. xi med.]: Gregory, *Dialogi** [*CPL* 1713], bk. III)

MS: Assmann (1889/1964) xxiv–xxxv [Clemoes]; K. Sisam (1953a) 199–224; N.R. Ker (1957) no. 182; N.R. Ker (1964) 207; Pope (1967–8) I.85–7; A.F. Cameron (1974) 221; McIntyre (1978); Scragg (1979) 258; Laing (1993) 79; *ASMMF* VI (1998) 1–5 [no. 219; Franzen]; Prescott (1998) 276; R. Gameson (2005a) 93, 101–4; Johnson–Rudolf (2010) 5–10; R. Gameson (2012b) 107 and n. 48; Scragg (2012a) nos. 533–8

DEC: Morrell (1965) 184–5

FACS: Yerkes (1984b) 33 [fol. 115r]; Leinbaugh (1986) 109 [fol. 149r]; Robinson–Stanley (1991) pl. 7 [fol. 1r]; *ASMMF* VI (1998) no. 219; Johnson–Rudolf (2010) figs. 4–6 [fol. 113r; fol. 123r (two details)]

ED: Assmann (1889/1964) 195–9 [base MS for OE versions of *Vitas patrum*]; Hecht (1900–7) [OE *Dialogi* coll. as O]; K. Sisam (1953a) 212–24 [base MS for OE Letter of Boniface to Eadburg]; Pope (1967–8) II.641–60 [Ælfric, Suppl. Hom. no. XX (*De populo Israhel*) coll. as X^d]; Yerkes (1979) [list of vocabulary and spelling variants in OE *Dialogi* coll. as O]; Stoneman (1983) [base MS for Ælfric, *De creatore et creatura* (arts. 5–6)]; Tristram (1985) 194–206 [base MS for homily *De sex etatibus mundi* (art. 6)]; Leinbaugh (1986) 108 [base MS for

Ælfric, *De creatore et creatura* (f) (art. 5)]; McDougall—McDougall (1997) [base MS for 'Evil tongues' (art. 4)]

LANG: K. Sisam (1953a) 207–11 [Letter of Boniface to Eadburg]; Yerkes (1979); McDougall—McDougall (1997) 228

ST: Yerkes (1977b) 130–4; Yerkes (1977c); Yerkes (1978b); Yerkes (1984b); Langefeld (1986); Yerkes (1986a); Reinsma (1987) 71–2; Liuzza (1988) 77–80; Franzen (1991) 64–5; P. Jackson (1992) 127–8; R. Gameson (1996a) 214, 218–19, 239; J. Hill (1996) 244; Scragg (1996) 223; Godden (1997) 40–1; Waite (2000) 46–8, 354–68

London, British Library, Cotton Otho C. v: see no. **63**

360. London, British Library, Cotton Otho E. i

s. x/xi, prob. Canterbury StA, prov. Canterbury CC?

Contents: glossary⁺*

MS: *Committee of Parliament Report* (1732) 484; N.R. Ker (1957) no. 184; T.A.M. Bishop (1959–63b) 418, 422; Pheifer (1974) xxxi n. 4; O'Brien O'Keeffe (1985) 65; Wieland (2009) 146; Giliberto (2011) 125 and n. 25; Scragg (2012a) no. 539

FACS: T.A.M. Bishop (1959–63b) pl. XIII (b) [fol. 8r]

ED: Meritt (1961) 445–6 [dry point glosses]; Voss (1996) [base MS for glossary]

ST: Gretsch (1999a) 368; Voss (2005) 301

361. London, British Library, Cotton Otho E. xiii

s. ix/x or x in., Brittany, (prov. Canterbury StA)

Contents: *Liber ex lege Moysi* [*CPL* 1793; *BCLL* 611]; *Collectio canonum Hibernensis* (recension A) [*CPL* 1794; *BCLL* 612]; St Patrick, *Epistola ad episcopos* [*CPL* 1103; *BCLL* 364]; *Canones Wallici* [*CPL* 1880; *BCLL* 995]; *Canones Adamnani* [*CPL* 1792; *BCLL* 609]; Supplement from *Collectio canonum Hibernensis* (recension B) [*BCLL* 613]; Legend of the Seven Sleepers [*BHL* 2316?]

MS: T.S. Smith (1696) 79; Wasserschleben (1885) xxxii–xxxiii; Kenney (1929) nos. 80, 82, 83; Bieler (1963) 14, 21–4; N.R. Ker (1964) 43; Deuffic (1985) 301 [no. 42]; Dumville (1992b) 182 n. 68; Dumville (1994d) 207; Bischoff (1998—) II, no. 2423; Ambrose (2005) 110–11; C.D. Wright (2006) 201, 213–14; Barker-Benfield (2008) I.54, 91 n. c, 755; II.1535, III.1727–8, 1792; Meeder (2009) 182–5

ED: Haddan—Stubbs (1869–71) II.111–14 [*Canones Adamnani* coll. as
C]; Bieler (1963) 136–49 [*Canones Wallici* (A) coll. as O], 176–81
[*Canones Adamnani* coll. as O]; Meeder (2009) 191–218 [*Liber ex lege
Moysi* coll. as O]

LANG: Bieler (1963) 27–47 [Latinity]

ST: Bradshaw (1893); McNeill—Gamer (1938) 445; Frantzen (1985);
Kottje (1987) [*Liber ex lege Moysi*]; Kéry (1999) 73; C.D. Wright
(2006) 205; Meeder (2009) [*Liber ex lege Moysi*]; McKee (2012b) 340
and n. 5

362. London, British Library, Cotton Tiberius A. ii (with London,
British Library, Cotton Claudius A. iii, fols. 2–7 and 9* + Faustina B. vi,
vol. i, fols. 95 and 98–100)

s. ix/x or x in., Lobbes, prov. England (royal court) before 939, prov.
Canterbury CC s. x[1]

Contents: gospels, gospel list; dedication poem praising King Æthelstan
[SK 14294] and prose dedication (929×939); records[(*)] (s. xi[1]—xii in.):
(in Claudius A. iii) Sawyer (1968) no. 914 [Latin and OE], Sawyer
(1968) no. 1090 = Harmer (1952) no. 35; Sawyer (1968) nos. 1229,
1389, 1222, 1047 (all s. xi[1]—xi[2]); spurious letter by Pope Boniface IV
[N.R. Ker (1957) pp. 472–3] and two letters by Pope Sergius (*c.* 1070);
(in Tiberius A. ii, fols. 13v–14r, originally blank leaf) Sawyer (1968)
no. 398 (s. xi ex. or xii in.) [spurious; see N.P. Brooks (1984) 220]; (in
Faustina B. vi) papal letters (s. xii in. [R. Gameson (1999a) no. 386])

MS: Thompson—Warner (1881–4) 35–7; Glunz (1933) 55, 70, 116, 123–4;
N.R. Ker (1957) no. 185; N.R. Ker (1960) 20 and n.; N.R. Ker (1964)
35; Sawyer (1968) no. 398; A.G. Watson (1969) 31 [repr. A.G. Watson
(2004) no. IX]; Rella (1977) 50; Rella (1980) 111; Lapidge (1981a) 93–7
[repr. Lapidge (1993a) 81–5]; Backhouse et al. (1984b) no. 3; Keynes
(1985a) 147–53; McGurk (1986b) 45 n. 4 [repr. McGurk (1998)
no. XIV]; Dumville (1987) 175 and n. 160; Lapidge (1991c) 968 [repr.
Lapidge (1993a) 18]; Dumville (1992a) 121; Dumville (1992b) 181 and
n. 61; Conner (1993) 18, 57, 65, 73; Dumville (1993g) 92; Lenker (1997)
438–42; Bischoff (1998—) II, no. 2424; R. Gameson (1999a) no. 386;
Gretsch (1999a) 337; P. Wormald (1999) 190–5; Rushforth (2001) 138
n. 8, 142; Heslop (2004) 305 n. 41; Karkov (2004) 54; R. Gameson
(2012d) 349 and n. 17, 361 and n. 66; D. Ganz (2012) 190 n. 14; Gullick
(2012) 305 and n. 64; Marsden (2012) 422 and n. 71; Rushforth (2012)
198 n. 3; Scragg (2012a) nos. 445–9

DEC: F. Wormald (1952) 22–3; Schramm—Mütherich (1981) 140, 275; R. Gameson (1995b) 179, 265 n. 197; O'Reilly (2011) 202–3; R. Gameson (2012c) 261 and n. 34

FACS: F. Wormald (1952) pl. 40 (a) [fol. 24v]; Keynes (1985a) pls. II–IV [fols. 24r, 15v, 15r]; Conner (1993) 73 [fol. 15v]; Puhle (2001) II.121–2 [fols. 24r, 24v]

ED: BCS 660 [Sawyer (1968) no. 398 from this MS]; Lapidge (1981a) 95–6 [repr. Lapidge (1993a) 83–4][dedication poem (SK 14294)]; B. Fischer (1988–91) [gospel excerpts coll. as Zv]

ST: Vezin (1968) 285 and n.; D.H. Turner (1971) v and n. 3; M.P. Richards (1988) 66; Noel (1995) 138 and n. 47; Karkov (2004) 61, 83

363. London, British Library, Cotton Tiberius A. iii, fols. 2–173

s. xi med., Canterbury CC

Contents: *Regula S. Benedicti*° [*CPL* 1852]; Ambrosius Autpertus (pseudo-Fulgentius), *Admonitio*°; *Memoriale qualiter*, chs. x–xix°; 'De festiuitatibus anni' (Ansegisus, *Capitularium Collectio* II. 33); *Capitulare monasticum*; *Regularis concordia*°; *Somniale Danielis*°; prognostics° (including two dream *lunaria*); prognostics(*); notes on Adam*, Noah and Old Testament figures*, on the Ages of the World, on Friday fasts*, on the Age of the Virgin*; prayers(*); Handbook for a confessor*; Office for All Saints (Vespers, Lauds); Ælfric, *Colloquium*°; Ælfric, *De temporibus anni** (part); encyclopedic notes* on the dimensions of Noah's Ark, of St Peter's in Rome, of the Temple of Solomon; the names of the thieves hanged with Christ; Life of St Margaret*; Ælfric, *Catholic Homilies* II, Hom. XIV*; Sunday Letter*; the Devil's account of the next world*; homiletic pieces*; examination of a bishop (extract from a pontifical); *Monasterialia indicia* (treatise on monastic sign language)*; lapidary*; excerpt from Isidore, *Synonyma* [*CPL* 1203] (chs. 88–96)*; *Regula S. Benedicti*, ch. iv⁺*; Alcuin, *De uirtutibus et uitiis*, chs. xiv and xxvi*; charm*; Ælfric, Pastoral Letter III*; Office of the Virgin (including litany)

MS: Dewick (1902) xiii–xiv; Förster (1908); Spindler (1934) 1–2; N.R. Ker (1957) no. 186; Morgand (1963) 182–3; Semmler (1963) 506; N.R. Ker (1964) 35; Fowler (1965) 2; L.T. Martin (1981) 39–41; Backhouse et al. (1984) no. 28 [D.H. Turner]; P.L. Heyworth (1989) 256; Lapidge (1991a) 71; Dumville (1992a) 137; Scragg (1992) xxxi–xxxii; Kornexl (1993) cxvii–cxlii [and for descriptions of the MS earlier than Förster

(1908), see pp. cxxi–cxxii]; Vaciago (1993) 15–16 [no. 62]; Mordek (1995) 223–5, 416; R. Gameson (1995a) 111–12 nn. 55–6; Gneuss (1997); Liuzza (2001) 216–18; Bredehoft (2004) 155; Karkov (2004) 84; N.M. Thompson (2004) 60; Wilcox (2004b) 392; Roberts (2005) 91–5 [no. 20]; Biggs (2007a) 15; Chardonnens (2007a) 337; Chardonnens (2007b) 53–7, 512–18, 550–1; Frantzen (2007a) 40–1; M. Heyworth (2007) 218; N.M. Thompson (2007) 117–18; Barker-Benfield (2008) III.1705, 1707, 1829; Scragg (2008a); M. Blake (2009) 9–10; Graham (2009) 166; Scragg (2009b) 78; Wieland (2009) 138, 140; J. Hill (2011) 249 and n. 2; Liuzza (2011) 3–8; Raw (2012) 461 and n. 10, 466; Scragg (2012a) nos. 540–5

DEC: F. Wormald (1935); F. Wormald (1952) 68 [no. 31] *et passim*; Dodwell (1954) 3–5, 37, 120; E. Temple (1976) no. 100; Lawrence (1982) 105; Ohlgren (1986) no. 205; Raw (1990) 216; R. Gameson (1991) 74 n. 79 *et passim*; Kornexl (1993) cxxxviii–cxli; Deshman (1995) 117, 180, 203, 208–9; R. Gameson (1995a) 116 n. 70, 122 n. 96; R. Gameson (1995b) 23, 26, 81 n. 61, 102, 114, 193 n. 4, 196 n. 21, 207; Withers (1997); Gretsch (1999a) 239, 299–300; Karkov (2004) 4, 11, 125, 175; Biggs (2008) 182; R. Gameson (2012c) 276 and n. 87, 291

FACS: Dewick (1902) [fols. 107v–115v]; F. Wormald (1952) pl. 23 [fol. 2v]; Dodwell (1954) pls. 2 (b), 3 (a) [fols. 2v, 117v]; E. Temple (1976) ills. 313–14 [fols. 2v, 117v]; Garmonsway (1978) frontispiece [fol. 60v (detail)]; Sauer (1980a) pl. after p. 16 [fol. 53v]; R. Gameson (1991) fig. 13 [fol. 2v]; Kornexl (1993) pl. I [fol. 20r]; Clayton–Magennis (1994) 111 [fol. 77r]; Deshman (1995) figs. 137–8 [fols. 117v, 2v]; Szarmach (1999) 169–71 [fols. 102r, 102v, 103r]; Karkov (2004) figs. 13, 14 [fols. 2v, 117v]; Roberts (2005) p. 91 [fol. 117v], pl. 20 [fol. 60v], p. 95 [fol. 2v]; Szarmach (2005) pls. 4–6 [fols. 50v, 51r, 51v]; M.P. Brown (2007a) pl. 85 [fol. 2v]; Owen-Crocker (2009) fig. 3.8 [fol. 3r]; Lendinara et al. (2011) pl. IV [fol. 121v]

ED [the order of the following items is that of the manuscript, listed according to the numbering of individual articles in N.R. Ker (1957) 225–7; only the most recent editions are cited (for editions from 1957 to 1996 – listed by Ker article no. – see also Gneuss (1997) 44–6)]:

art. 1: Logemann (1888) [base MS for *Regula S. Benedicti* in Latin and OE]; Hanslik (1977) [*Regula S. Benedicti* coll. as i]; M.C. De Bonis (2011) 296–7 [chs. lxxi–lxxiii]

art. 2: Sauer (1984) 423 [base MS for Latin and OE versions of pseudo-Fulgentius, *Admonitio*] art. 3: Morgand (1963) 229–61 [*Memoriale qualiter*, chs. x–xix, coll. as H]

art. 4: Cross (1992b) ['De festiuitatibus anni' (= Ansegisus, *Capitularium collectio*, II.33); for the text of Ansegisus, see G. Schmitz (1996) 555–6 (this MS not collated)]

art. 5: Semmler (1963) 515–36 [*Capitulare monasticum* coll. as G5]

art. 6: Kornexl (1993) 1–147 [base MS for *Regularis concordia* and OE gloss]

art. 7(a): L.T. Martin (1981) 95–168 [*Somniale Danielis* coll. as T]; Liuzza (2011) 80–122 [base MS (= T) for *Somniale Danielis*]

art. 7(b): Liuzza (2011) 124–46 [base MS (= T) for general *lunarium*]

art. 7(c): Liuzza (2011) 148–52 [base MS (= T) for dream *lunarium*]

art. 7(d): Liuzza (2011) 154–6 [base MS (= T) for yearly weather forecast for the kalends of January]

art. 7(e): Liuzza (2011) 158–62 [base MS (= T) for birth *lunarium*]

art. 7(f): Liuzza (2011) 164–8 [base MS (= T) for medical *lunarium*]

art. 7(g): Liuzza (2011) 170–2 [base MS (= T) for prognostic brontology]

art. 7(h): Liuzza (2011) 174–6 [base MS (= T) for OE dream *lunarium*]

art. 7(i): Liuzza (2011) 178–88 [base MS (= T) for OE alphabetical dreambook]

art. 7(j): Liuzza (2011) 190–2 [base MS (= T) for OE agenda *lunarium*]

art. 7(k): Liuzza (2011) 194 [base MS (= T) for OE medical *lunarium*]

art. 7(l): Liuzza (2011) 196 [base MS (= T) for OE prognostic brontology]

art. 7(m): Liuzza (2011) 198 [base MS (= T) for OE general prognostic for weekdays of the new moon]

art. 7(n): Liuzza (2011) 200 [base MS (= T) for OE note on the growth of the fetus]

art. 7(o): Liuzza (2011) 202–4 [base MS (= T) for OE birth *lunarium*]

art. 7(p): Liuzza (2011) 206 [base MS (= T) for OE yearly forecast for the kalends of January]

art. 7(q): Liuzza (2011) 208–10 [base MS (= T) for OE alphabetical dreambook]

art. 7(r): Liuzza (2011) 212 [base MS (= T) for OE omens in pregnancy]

art. 8(a): [note on Adam, Noah and other OT figures]

art. 8(b): Tristram (1985) 301 [base MS for the Six Ages of the World]

art. 8(c): Napier (1889) 3 [base MS for note on fasting]

art. 8(d): Günzel (1993) 64–5 [base MS for note on the Age of the Virgin]

art. 8(e): Napier (1889) 3 [base MS for penitential note on sins]

art. 9(a): Pulsiano — McGowan (1994) 206–8 [base MS for confessional prayer] art. 9(b): Förster (1908) 46; Förster (1942a) 8–11 [base MS for confessional prayer]

art. 9(c): unprinted Latin prayer (inc. 'Domine Iesu Criste tibi flecto genua mea')

art. 9(d): Pulsiano—McGowan (1994) 209–10 [base MS for confessional prayer]

art. 9(e): Pulsiano—McGowan (1994) 210–12 [base MS for confessional prayer]

art. 9(f): Pulsiano—McGowan (1994) 212–16 [base MS for confessional prayer]

art. 9(g): Szarmach (2005) 168–74 [base MS for excerpts from King Alfred's OE translation of Augustine, *Soliloquia*]

arts. 9(h): Sauer (1980a) 21–3 [base MS for confessional prayer]

art. 9(i): Sauer (1980a) 23–7 [base MS for confessional prayer]

art. 9(j): Fowler (1965) 16 [base MS for *ordo confessionis*]

art. 9(k): Fowler (1965) 17–19 [instructions for confession coll. as N]

art. 9(l): Fowler (1965) 19–20 [instructions for confession coll. as N]

art. 10(a): Lapidge—Winterbottom (1991b) lxxv–lxxvii [base MS for Office for All Saints]

art. 10(b): unprinted Latin prayer (inc. 'Te adoro Deum patrem')

art. 10(c): [Latin and OE Adoration of the Cross]

art. 10(d): Pulsiano (1991a) [Latin and OE charm invoking the Cross]

art. 10(e): [Latin explanation of the four reasons why the Cross is adored; as Günzel (1993) 126–7]

art. 10(f): [Latin prayer addressed to the Cross; as Günzel (1993) 126–7]

art. 10(g): [another Latin prayer addressed to the Cross; as Günzel (1993) 126–7]

art. 11: W.H. Stevenson (1929) 75–99 [base MS for Ælfric, *Colloquium*]; Garmonsway (1978) [base MS for Ælfric, *Colloquium*]

art. 12: Liuzza (2011) 214–18 [base MS for prognostics: bloodletting *lunarium*, prognostic for weekdays]

art. 13: Henel (1942a) [Ælfric, *De temporibus anni*, coll. as A]; M. Blake (2009) [Ælfric, *De temporibus anni*, coll. as A]

art. 14: Dekker (2007) 291–2 nn. 46, 49 [base MS for notes on the dimensions of Noah's Ark, of St Peter's in Rome, of the Temple of Solomon]

art. 15: Clayton—Magennis (1994) 112–47 [base MS for OE Life of St Margaret]

art. 16: Godden (1979) 381–90 [base MS (= X^e) for a redaction of Ælfric, CH II, Hom. XIV (Palm Sunday)]

art. 17: D. Haines (2010) 146–74 [base MS for an OE version of the
  Sunday Letter (Letter F)]
art. 18: F.C. Robinson (1972) 365–8 [base MS for the Devil's Account
  of the Next World]; Scragg (1992) 169–83 [part of Vercelli Hom. IX
  coll. as M]
art. 19(a): Napier (1883/1967) 108–10 [Wulfstan, Hom. XIX, coll. as K];
  Bethurum (1957) 225–32 [Wulfstan, Hom. XIII, coll. as K]
art. 19(b): Napier (1883/1967) 110–11, 112–15, 119–21 [Wulfstan, Hom.
  XX, XXII, XXIV (first para.), coll. as K]
art. 19(c): Napier (1883/1967) 121–2 [Wulfstan, Hom. XXIV (second
  para.), coll. as K]
art. 19(d): Napier (1883/1967) 122 [Wulfstan, Hom. XXIV (third para.),
  coll. as K]
art. 19(e): Napier (1883/1967) 172–5 [base MS (= K) for Wulfstan, Hom.
  XXXVI]
art. 19(f): Napier (1883/1967) 116–18 [Wulfstan, Hom. XXIII, coll. as K]
art. 19(g): Napier (1883/1967) 128–30 [Wulfstan, Hom. XXVII, coll. as K]
art. 19(h): Napier (1883/1967) 274–5 [Wulfstan, Hom. LI, coll. as K]
art. 19(i): Napier (1883/1967) 122–4 [Wulfstan, Hom. XXV, coll. as K]
art. 19(j): Napier (1883/1967) 125–7 [Wulfstan, Hom. XXVI, coll. as K];
  Bethurum (1957) 166–8 [Wulfstan, Hom. VIIa, coll. as K]
art. 19(k): Jost (1959) 85–96 [*To mæssepreostum* coll. as N]
art. 19(l): Jost (1959) 96–102 [another tract *To mæssepreostum* coll. as N]
art. 20: Michael Richter (1973) 118–20 [base MS for *Ordo uel examinatio
  in ordinatione episcopi*]
art. 21(a): Fowler (1965) 19–20 [repeated from art. 9(l), above]
art. 21(b): Fowler (1965) 26 [last para. of confessor's handbook, ch. iv]
art. 21(c): Fowler (1965) 26–7 [*Be dædbetan* i–iii coll. as N]
art. 21(d): Fowler (1965) 27–8 [*Be dædbetan* iv–ix coll. as N]
art. 21(e): Fowler (1965) 28–9 [*Be dædbetan* x–xii coll. as N]
art. 21(f): Fowler (1965) 29–31 [*Be dædbotum* xiii–xvii coll. as N]
art. 21(g): Fowler (1965) 31–2 [*Be dædbetan* xviii–xix coll. as N]
art. 21(h): Spindler (1934) 170 [coll. as N]
art. 21(i): Spindler (1934) 173 [coll. as N]
art. 21(j): Spindler (1934) 174 [coll. as N]
art. 22: Banham (1991) [base MS for *Monasteriales* (sic) *indicia*]
art. 23: Kitson (1978) 31–3 [base MS for OE lapidary]; Giliberto (2007a)
  260–1 [base MS for OE lapidary]
art. 24: Szarmach (1999) 177–81 [OE epitome (called 'Warna') of Isidore,
  Synonyma II.88–96]

art. 25: D'Aronco (1983) 121–8 [base MS (= i) for OE and Latin versions of *Regula S. Benedicti*, ch. iv]

art. 26: Szarmach (1992) 34–9 [base MS for OE version of Alcuin, *De uirtutibus et uitiis*, ch. xiv]

art. 27: Szarmach (1992) 40–2 [base MS for OE version of Alcuin, *De uirtutibus et uitiis*, ch. xxvi]

art. 28: Cockayne (1864–6) III.286 [base MS for charm against theft of livestock]

art. 29: Fehr (1914/1966) 146–221 [Ælfric, Pastoral Letter III, coll. as N]

art. 30: Dewick (1902) cols. 19–48 [base MS for Office of the Virgin]; Lapidge (1991a) 174–7 [litany from the Office of the Virgin]; Milfull (1996) [hymns (nos. 65–6, 90–3, 89, 97) from the Office of the Virgin coll. as T]

LANG: Herbst (1975); D'Aronco (1983) 110–18; Hofstetter (1987) 117–23, 236, 254, 331, 347, 425, 438–9, 442–5; Kornexl (1993) cxcvii–ccxi; Clayton—Magennis (1994) 97–103; Pulsiano—McGowan (1994) 194–8; Gneuss (1997) 37–42; Crowley (2000) 131, 143, 145–8; G.D. De Bonis (2011); Liuzza (2011) 253–77 [glossary]

ST: Hallander (1968); Gretsch (1973) 32–5 *et passim*; F.C. Robinson (1973) 444–5; Gretsch (1974); Hohler (1975) 220 n. 10; Korhammer (1976) 156, 160; Korhammer (1980) 36, 54; Kotzor (1981) I.237*–239*; Sherlock (1989); Clayton (1990) 70–7; Hollis—Wright (1992) 186, 200–2, 257, 259, 270; Clayton—Magennis (1994) 84–92; Gwara (1997d) 239 n. 3; Graham (1998a) 25, 33–4, 54 n. 7, 60 n. 58, 68 n. 149; C.A. Jones (1998a) 233; Treharne (1998) 237–8; Gretsch (1999a) 247; P. Wormald (1999) 136 n. 71, 186 n. 100, 226 n. 253, 345 n. 380, 382 n. 535; Dodwell (2000) 146; J. Hill (2001) 118, 120–5; Liuzza (2001) 216–18 [bibliography]; Szarmach (2002) 300; Karkov (2004) 5, 93–9; Szarmach (2005) 153–63; Lucas (2006) 405, 411, 431; M.C. De Bonis (2007); Dekker (2007) 291–2, 309, 311 n. 121; Di Sciacca (2007b) 116–22; Giliberto (2007a); Giliberto (2007b) 282 n. 122; M. Heyworth (2007) 218–22 [on the 'Late Old English Handbook for the Use of a Confessor']; J. Hill (2007b) 292–4; Swan (2007a) 407; N.M. Thompson (2007) 117–19; Toswell (2007) 212 n. 8; Di Sciacca (2008) 68, 70–1, 109–10, 169–73; Scragg (2008a); Scragg (2008b) 370; Chardonnens (2010) 246–50; Di Sciacca (2010) 339–41; G.D. De Bonis (2011); M.C. De Bonis (2011); Giliberto (2011) 126; Liuzza (2011) 1–77 [prognostics]; Gwara (2012) 527

London, British Library, Cotton Tiberius A. iii, fols. 174–7: see no. **332**

London, British Library, Cotton Tiberius A. iii, fol. 178: see no. **364**

363. 2. London, British Library, Cotton Tiberius A. iii, fol. 179

s. x ex.

Contents: *horologium**; Mass prayer

MS: N.R. Ker (1957) no. 187; Scragg (2012a) no. 546

ED: Cockayne (1864–6) III.218 [*horologium*]

364. London, British Library, Cotton Tiberius A. vi, fols. 1–35 (with London, British Library, Cotton Tiberius A. iii, fol. 178)

s. x$^{3/4}$, prob. 977×979, prob. Abingdon, prov. Canterbury (prob. CC) s. xi^2

Contents: *Anglo-Saxon Chronicle* B*; genealogy of West-Saxon kings*; note on finding a piece of the Cross (s. xi/xii); list of archbishops of Canterbury and popes (s. xi/xii)

MS: C. Plummer (1892–9) I.x–xi; Dickins (1952) 6; N.R. Ker (1957) nos. 188, 409; A.G. Watson (1979) I, no. 549; S. Taylor (1983) xi–xxvii; Dumville (1986) 8–9; A.G. Watson (1986) 137, 149 [repr. A.G. Watson (2004) no. IV]; P.L. Heyworth (1989) 255, 256; Robinson—Stanley (1991) 22–3; Dumville (1993g) 26 n. 84; Laing (1993) 80; Conner (1996) xvi–xvii; Bredehoft (2001) 222; Bredehoft (2004) 156 n. 42, 157, 159–60, 167, 169; C. Bishop (2007b) 103, 106–7; Barker-Benfield (2008) I.95, III.1792; D. Ganz (2012) 190 and n. 13; Scragg (2012a) no. 546a

FACS: Robinson—Stanley (1991) pls. 14.1.3.1–3 [fols. 31r–32r], 14.2.3 [fol. 32v], 14.3.3.1–2 [fol. 33r–v], 14.3.3.2–3 [fols. 33v–34r]; Bredehoft (2001) pl. VI [fol. 12r]

ED: C. Plummer (1892–9) [*Anglo–Saxon Chronicle* (art. 1) coll. as B]; Dickins (1952) 3–5 [base text for genealogy (art. 2)]; S. Taylor (1983) [base MS for *Anglo–Saxon Chronicle* B]; Dumville (1986) 21–5 [genealogy (art. 2)], 28–30 [continuation of the regnal list]; Conner (1996) [*Anglo–Saxon Chronicle* B (art. 1) coll. as B]

LANG: S. Taylor (1983) lxiii–cvi

ST: Rosier (1960b); A.F. Cameron (1973) no. C.10; Torkar (1981) 49–50, 56 n. 4, 67–8, 161; Hart (1982); Graham (1998a) 34, 59 n. 52; Bredehoft (2001) 4; Keynes (2012) 542, 552 *et passim*

365. London, British Library, Cotton Tiberius A. vii, fols. 165–6

s. ix$^{3/4}$, W France; OE gloss added s. xi^1

Contents: Prosper, *Epigrammata ex sententiis S. Augustini*° [*CPL* 526] (f)
and *Versus ad coniugem*° [*CPL* 531; SK 458] (f)

MS: N.R. Ker (1957) no. 189; Rella (1977) 165; Rella (1980) 111; Lapidge
(1982a) 105, 133 n. 48 [repr. Lapidge (1996b) 467 and n. 48]; Bischoff
(1998—) II, no. 2425; Lapidge (2006) 169, 327, 328; R. Gameson
(2012d) 352 and n. 28; Scragg (2012a) no. 547

FACS: Toth (1984) pl. 7 [fol. 165v]

ED: Wright—Wülker (1884) I.248–57; Toth (1984) 23–32

LANG: Jordan (1906) 39; Toth (1984) 14–20; Hofstetter (1987) 445

ST: Toth (1984)

366. London, British Library, Cotton Tiberius A. xiii ('Hemming's Cartulary')

c. 1016 and *c.* 1096, Worcester

Contents: two cartularies (*c.* 1016 and *c.* 1096); homily* (s. xi¹); biographical eulogy of Bishop Wulfstan II+* (s. xi ex.)

MS: N.R. Ker (1948); N.R. Ker (1957) no. 190; G.R.C. Davis (1958)
no. 1068; N.R. Ker (1960) 20; Sawyer (1968) 52–3; N.R. Ker (1971) 324–6
[repr. N.R. Ker (1985) 18–20]; Scragg (1979) 260; A.G. Watson (1979) I,
nos. 550–1; D.H. Turner et al. (1980) 107; Backhouse et al. (1984b)
no. 171; Dumville (1993g) 66–8; Laing (1993) 80; R. Gameson (1999a)
no. 402; Biggs et al. (2001) 458; M.P. Brown (2001b) 284; Gneuss (2003b)
298; J. Barrow (2004) 149 n. 37, 151; Baxter (2004) 162, 164 n. 9, 165–7,
171–3, 176, 191–205; Dance (2004) 31 n. 6; G. Mann (2004) 239–40 and
n. 8; A. Orchard (2004) 66 n. 15; R. Gameson (2005a) 96, 101–4; Foys
(2006) 279–80; Treharne (2007b) 17; M.P. Brown (2012) 146 n. 125;
A. Orchard (2012) 697 [no. 8]; Scragg (2012a) nos. 172, 307, 548–58

FACS: Cross—Morrish Tunberg (1993b) pls. V–VII [fols. 20v, 28r, 116r];
Baxter (2004) 168–70 [fols. 48r, 100r, 70r], 174 [fol. 83r]; Withers (2007)
81 [fol. 2v]

ED: Hearne (1723); Thorpe (1865) 445–7, repr. *PL* CL, cols. 1489–90
[eulogy of Bishop Wulfstan II (OE and Latin)]; Napier (1883/1967)
1–5 [Hom. I coll. as L]; Baxter (2004) 161 [fol. 101v]; Tinti (2009)
492–6 [*Enucleatio libelli* in second cartulary]; and the editions of
charters recorded in Sawyer (1968)

LANG: Fowler (1972) xxi

ST: Scharer (1982) 281–4; J. Barrow (1996) 86–7, 89; Bullough (1996) 3–4; R. Gameson (1996a) 214, 215 n., 239; Mason (1996a) 209–11; Harmsen (2000) 253, 310; Biggs et al. (2001) 485–6; Tinti (2002); Baxter (2004); Tinti (2009); Tinti (2010)

367. London, British Library, Cotton Tiberius A. xiv

s. viii med., Monkwearmouth-Jarrow

Contents: Bede, *Historia ecclesiastica* [*CPL* 1375]

MS: C. Plummer (1896) I.xci–xciii; Arngart (1952) 18 n. 1; Lowe (1960) no. XXXVIII (d); Mynors—Colgrave (1969) xlvi–xlvii; *CLA* Supplement (1971) no. 1703; Lowe (1972b) II.441–9; Rella (1977) 69; Parkes (1982) 12, 27 n. 35, 30 n. 81 [repr. Parkes (1991a) 100 n. 35, 108–9, 116 n. 81]; O'Brien O'Keeffe (1987) 142–3; Webster— Backhouse (1991) no. 92; Parkes (1992) 27–8, 125 nn. 69, 77, 129 n. 17; T.J. Brown (1993b) 199; Saenger (1997) 50; M.P. Brown (2003a) 270 n. 136; Dumville (2007f) 55, 66–7, 73, 93; Lapidge (2008–10) I.lxxxv– lxxxvi; M.P. Brown (2012) 158 n. 173; R. Gameson (2012a) 25 n. 45

FACS: Lowe (1960) pl. XXXVIII (d) [fol. 46v]; Parkes (1982) 14 [fol. 26v (detail)] [repr. Parkes (1991a) pl. 20]; Webster—Backhouse (1991) 128 [fol. 84r]; M.P. Brown (2003a) 256 [fol. 26v]; R. Gameson (2012) pl. 4.4 [fol. 26v]

ED: C. Plummer (1896) [Bede, *Historia ecclesiastica*, coll. as B]; Lapidge (2008–10) [Bede, *Historia ecclesiastica*, coll. as B]

ST: Lapidge (2008b)

368. London, British Library, Cotton Tiberius A. xv, fols. 1–173

s. xi in., prob. Canterbury CC

Contents: Alcuin, a selection of his letters; a collection of letters and poems mainly to tenth-century archbishops of Canterbury [including SK 1384, 4087, 7503, 9863, 10852, 11705, 13764, 15719, 17394]

MS: T.S. Smith (1696) 21; *Committee of Parliament Report* (1732) 451; Stubbs (1874) liii–liv; Dümmler (1895) 9–11; Hohler (1975) 74; C. Brett (1991) 50–5, 57–8, 65–70; Dumville (1993g) 107–8 and n. 125; Lapidge (2003a) 220, 241–2 and nn.; Bullough (2004) 81–101 *et passim*; G. Mann (2004) 252, 255; Vanderputten (2006) 219, 221, 225, 227–32, 235–6; Winterbottom—Lapidge (2012) 151–3

ED: Haddan—Stubbs (1869–71) III.685–6 [letter of Ecgred]; Stubbs (1874) 354–404 [archiepiscopal correspondence]; Dümmler (1895) [Alcuin Letters coll. as A1]; Chase (1975) [twenty–four letters of Alcuin coll. as A$_1$]; C. Brett (1991) 57–8 [letter of Breton pilgrim to K. Æthelstan]; Lapidge (2003a) 220–1 [poem of .L. to Dunstan], 252–4 [letter of Lantfred]; Vanderputten (2006) 237–44 [letters from Wido, Fulrad, Odbert coll. as A]; Winterbottom—Lapidge (2012) 153–61 [base MS for two letters by B.]

ST: Levison (1946) 297–300; Whitelock (1979) nos. 214, 230–1; Chase (1975) 10; Lapidge (1975a) 82, 88–9 [repr. Lapidge (1993a) 120, 126–7]; R.M. Thomson (1982b) 2 n. 8, 7; *BCLL* (1985) no. 902; R.M. Thomson (1987) 129–30, 133, 141, 154–8; Lapidge (1988c) 96–8 [repr. Lapidge (1993a) 190–2]; *CSLMA* II (1999) 171–355 [Alcuin letters]; Bullough (2004); Carley—Petitmengin (2004) 204–8; G. Mann (2004) 242 n. 12, 250, 252, 254 n. 50, 257 n. 65, 266–7; Vanderputten (2006) 219, 234; R. McKitterick (2012) 328

368. 2. London, British Library, Cotton Tiberius A. xv, fol. 174

s. x

Contents: conclusion of gospel of John (XXI.17) [s. x], charter of 1063×1066 [added s. xii]

MS: C. Brett (1991) 51; Dumville (1992a) 121 and n. 185a, 146 n. 366; Dumville (1993f) 96, 98 [no. 13]; R. Gameson (2012d) 365 and n. 89

369. London, British Library, Cotton Tiberius A. xv, fols. 175–80

s. vii/viii, prob. S England, (prov. Malmesbury?)

Contents: Iunillus Africanus, *Instituta regularia diuinae legis* [*CPL* 872] (f)

MS: Thompson—Warner (1881–4) 54–5; *CLA* II (1935) no. 189; Siegmund (1949) 108; R.M. Thomson (1982b) 8–10; R.M. Thomson (1987) 76–98; A.G. Watson (1987a) 48; Bischoff—Lapidge (1994) 248–9; R. Sharpe et al. (1996) 265; Lapidge (2006) 34 and nn.

370. London, British Library, Cotton Tiberius B. i, fols. 3–111

s. xi^1, prov. prob. Abingdon

Contents: Orosius, *Historiae aduersum paganos* [*CPL* 571] in OE translation*

MS: N.R. Ker (1957) no. 191 [art. 1]; Bately (1980) xxv; P.L. Heyworth (1989) 46, 255, 256; *ASMMF* X (2003) 1–6 [no. 227; O'Brien O'Keeffe]; Bately (2006) 40; Treharne (2007b) 19 n. 16; Scragg (2012a) nos. 559–70

DEC: E. Temple (1976) no. 30 (xviii); Ohlgren (1986) no. 135

FACS: *ASMMF* X (2003) no. 227; E. Temple (1976) ill. 116 [fol. 7v]

ED: Bately (1980) [OE Orosius coll. as C]

ST: Buckalew (1978) 159–64; Waite (2000) 38–42, 281–320

370. 2. London, British Library, Cotton Tiberius B. i, fols. 112–64

s. xi med., Abingdon

Contents: OE Metrical Calendar** (mistakenly called *Menologium*); *Maxims II***; *Anglo-Saxon Chronicle* C*

MS: C. Plummer (1892–9) I.xi; N.R. Ker (1957) no. 191 [arts. 2–4]; A.G. Watson (1979) I, no. 552; Backhouse et al. (1984) no. 147; P.L. Heyworth (1989) 46, 255, 256; Robinson—Stanley (1991) 22–4; Dumville (1992a) 130–1 and n. 260; Laing (1993) 80; O'Brien O'Keeffe (1998a); O'Brien O'Keeffe (2001) xx–xxxviii; *ASMMF* X (2003) 1–6 [no. 227; O'Brien O'Keeffe]; Bredehoft (2004) 156 n. 42, 157–60, 163–5, 167–9; Guimon (2006) 137–40, 143, 145; Scragg (2012a) nos. 559–70

DEC: R. Gameson (1991) 71 n. 68; R. Gameson (2012c) 287 and n. 133

FACS: A.G. Watson (1979) II, pls. 39 (a)–(b) [fols. 118v, 158v]; Backhouse et al. (1984) 145 [fol. 151r]; Robinson—Stanley (1991) pls. 14.1.4.1–2 [fol. 141r], 14.2.4 [fol. 142r], 14.3.4.1–2 [fols. 142v–143r], 14.5.1 [fol. 156r], 14.6.1 [fol. 160v], 16.1–6 [fols. 112r–114v], 17.1–2 [fol. 115r]; M.P. Brown (1991) pl. 44 [fol. 140v]; Conner (1996) frontispiece [fol. 143v]; O'Brien O'Keeffe (1998a) pl. 13 [fol. 164r]; O'Brien O'Keeffe (2001) pls. 1–4 [fols. 143r, 143v, 144r, 157v]; Bredehoft (2001) pl. VII [fol. 140r]; *ASMMF* X (2003) no. 227; Owen-Crocker (2009) fig. 2.12 [fol. 141r]

ED: C. Plummer (1892–9) [*Anglo–Saxon Chronicle* coll. as C]; Dobbie (1942) 49–55 [Metrical Calendar], 55–7 [*Maxims II*]; Conner (1996) [so–called 'Abingdon Chronicle' for years 956–1066 coll. as C]; O'Brien O'Keeffe (2001) [base MS for Metrical Calendar, *Maxims II* and *Anglo–Saxon Chronicle* C (arts. 2–4)]

LANG: O'Brien O'Keeffe (2001) xciii–cxii

ST: Bollard (1973); Buckalew (1978) 159–64; F.C. Robinson (1980) 26–9; Lapidge (1991d) 249–50 [OE Metrical Calendar]; Graham (1998a) 34; O'Brien O'Keeffe (1998a); Bredehoft (2001); Keynes (2012) 542, 552 *et passim*

371. London, British Library, Cotton Tiberius B. ii, fols. 2–85

s. xi/xii (prov. Bury St Edmunds)

Contents: Abbo of Fleury, *Passio S. Eadmundi* [*BHL* 2392]; Hermannus Archidiaconus (?), *Miracula S. Eadmundi* [*BHL* 2395] (long version, incomplete)

MS: Arnold (1890–6) I.lxv; N.R. Ker (1957) p. 210; N.R. Ker (1964) 20; Rouse (1966) 484 and n. 33; R.M. Thomson (1972) 626 and n. 49; A.G. Watson (1979) I, no. 553; R. Gameson (1999a) no. 403; R. Gameson (2012a) 61 n. 208, 91 n. 335

FACS: Gransden (1995a) pls. III–IV [fols. 2r, 3r (detail)]

ED: Liebermann (1879) 203–81 [Hermann, *Miracula S. Eadmundi*]; Arnold (1890–6) I.3–25 [Abbo, *Passio S. Eadmundi*], I.26–92 [Hermann, *Miracula S. Eadmundi*]; Winterbottom (1972) 67–87 [base MS for Abbo, *Passio S. Eadmundi*]

ST: Hervey (1907); Winterbottom (1972) 12–13; Gransden (1974) 175; R.M. Thomson (1984) 190 and n. 15; Gransden (1995a) 65–6; Gransden (1995b) 2–6; Biggs et al. (2001) 2–4 [Lendinara]; R. Sharpe (2001) 178

372. London, British Library, Cotton Tiberius B. iv, fols. 3–9, 19–86

s. xi med., xi², W Midlands (Worcester?), (prov. Worcester, previously Canterbury CC?)

Contents: *Anglo-Saxon Chronicle* D*

MS: C. Plummer (1892–9) I.xi–xii; N.R. Ker (1957) no. 192; N.R. Ker (1964) 207; A.G. Watson (1979) I, no. 555; Whitelock (1979) 114–15; Robinson—Stanley (1991) 22–3; Dumville (1993g) 114 n. 18; Laing (1993) 81; Conner (1996) xvii; Cubbin (1996) ix–xvi; Bredehoft (2004) 156 n. 42, 157, 160–3, 165, 167; R. Gameson (2005a) 93; Roberts (2005) 96–8 [no. 21]; Guimon (2006) 137–8, 141–5; C. Bishop (2007b) 100; Treharne (2007b) 17; Graham (2009) 191; Scragg (2012a) nos. 571–580d

DEC: Withers (2011) 265–6

FACS: Robinson—Stanley (1991) pls. 14.1.5.1–3 [fols. 49r–50r], 14.2.5.1–2 [fol. 50r–v], 14.4.1 [fol. 53r], 14.5.2 [fol. 70r], 14.6.2.1–2 [fols. 78v–79r]; Cubbin (1996) frontispiece [fol. 49v]; Bredehoft (2001) pl. VIII [fol. 53r]; Roberts (2005) pl. 21 [fol. 68r]; Owen-Crocker (2009) fig. 6.16 [fol. 20r]

ED: C. Plummer (1892–9) [*Anglo-Saxon Chronicle* coll. as D]; Classen—Harmer (1926) [base MS for *Anglo-Saxon Chronicle* D]; Conner (1996) [*Anglo-Saxon Chronicle* coll. as D]; Cubbin (1996) [base MS for *Anglo-Saxon Chronicle* D]; Bredehoft (2004) 161 [fol. 53r], 162–3 [fol. 53v], 166 [fol. 81r]

LANG: Cubbin (1996) lxxxiv–cliii; Dance (2004) 53 n. 75

ST: R. Gameson (1996a) 239; O'Brien O'Keeffe (1998a) 150; Bredehoft (2004) 164, 168–9; Keynes (2012) 542, 552 *et passim*

London, British Library, Cotton Tiberius B. iv, fol. 87: see no. **521**

373. London, British Library, Cotton Tiberius B. v, fols. 2-73, 77-85

s. xi²/⁴, Canterbury CC? Winchester?, (prov. Battle)

Contents: computus material ('Leofric-Tiberius Computus'); metrical calendar ('of Hampson'); Bede, *De temporibus* ch. xiv; lists of: popes, the seventy-two disciples of Christ (erased), Roman emperors, high priests of Jerusalem, bishops of Jerusalem, Alexandria and Antioch, nineteen lists of bishops of Anglo-Saxon dioceses; royal genealogies of Anglo-Saxon kingdoms⁽*⁾ in sixteen lists; list of the abbots of Glastonbury; Archbishop Sigeric's journey to Rome; Ælfric, *De temporibus anni**; astronomical texts; Cicero, *Aratea* with scholia by Hyginus; excerpts from: Pliny (*Naturalis historia*), Macrobius (*Comm. in Somnium Scipionis*), Martianus Capella (*De nuptiis Philologiae et Mercurii* VI.595–8, VIII.860); map of the world; Priscian, *Periegesis*; *Vita, Miracula, et Translatio S. Nicolai* (in verse: SK 7869); 'Marvels of the East' (*Mirabilia orientis*)⁺*; *Jamnes and Mambres*⁺*

MS: Buescu (1941) 58–60; N.R. Ker (1957) no. 193; Leonardi (1960) 70–1; N.R. Ker (1964) 8, 200; Soubiran (1972) 111–13; Dumville (1976) 26–8; C.W. Jones (1977) 246–7; A.G. Watson (1979) I, no. 556; Munk Olsen (1982—) I.332–3; Rollason (1982) 43; Backhouse et al. (1984b) no. 164; Lapidge (1984) 344, 353 [repr. Lapidge (1993a) 361, 370]; McGurk (1986a) 80, 84–9; P.L. Heyworth (1989) 230; Biggs et al. (1990) 27–9 [T.N. Hall]; Hollis (1992) 117, 120–1; Baker—Lapidge (1995) xlv–xlviii; Webster—Brown (1997) 248 [no. 157]; R. Gameson (1999a) no. 396;

Gretsch (2000) 110, 112, 117; *ASMMF* IX (2001) 65–79 [no. 229; Grade]; Liuzza (2001) 206 n. 108; Simek (2002) 53; Karkov (2004) 66 n. 70, 68; G. Mann (2004) 255; Meaney (2004) 496; Biggs (2007a) 10–11 [T.N. Hall]; Foys (2007) 113–17, 121–6, 140–1, 149–54; Pulsiano (2007) 123; Withers (2007) 37, 280, 286–7, 289; Barker-Benfield (2008) II.1188; M. Blake (2009) 11–12; Wieland (2009) 152, 154, 155; Scragg (2012a) no. 581

DEC: Dodwell (1950) 18 n. 4; Rice (1952) 224–5; Köhler—Mütherich (1971–99) IV.77; E. Temple (1976) no. 87; F. Wormald (1984) 42, 118, 126, 143, 182 n. 14; D.M. Wilson (1984) 187; Ohlgren (1986) no. 192; R. Gameson (1991) 75 n. 82; R. Gameson (1995b) 11, 14, 36, 160, 168, 177 *et passim*; E.R. Anderson (1997) 252–3; Niles (1998) 194 n. 84; Wieland (1998) 16 n. 20; Dodwell (2000) 152–3; Simek (2002) 57; Semple (2003) 241–3; S. Page (2004) 18, 64; Foys (2007) 114–17, 121, 128, 130, 147–9, 151; Keefer (2007b) 99; Withers (2007) 64, 67, 272; Karkov (2009) 242–4

FACS: McGurk et al. (1983) [complete facsimile]; Swarzenski (1954) pl. 61 [fols. 81v, 89v]; E. Temple (1976) ills. 273–6 [fols. 5r, 6v, 85v, 34r]; D.M. Wilson (1984) pls. 236–7 [fols. 5r, 8v]; F. Wormald (1984) ill. 37 [fol. 87v]; M.P. Brown (1991) pl. 31 [fol. 81r]; *ASMMF* IX (2001) no. 229; S. Page (2004) frontispiece [fol. 87v]; Foys (2007) 112 [fol. 56v], 122, 125, 136, 139, 152 [fol. 29r]; Withers (2007) 39 [fol. 82r], 69 [fol. 8r], 70 [fol. 3r], 71 [fol. 6v], 290 [fol. 4v], 291 [fol. 5r]; Owen-Crocker (2009) figs. 5.7 [fol. 34r], 7.31 [fol. 82r]

ED: Stubbs (1874) 391–5 [Archbishop Sigeric's journey]; Buescu (1941) [Cicero, *Aratea*, coll. as C]; Henel (1942a) [Ælfric, *De temporibus anni*, coll. as B]; R.I. Page (1966) 12–17 [lists of bishops]; Soubiran (1972) [Cicero, *Aratea*, coll. as C]; Gibson (1977) [*Wonders of the East*]; McGurk (1986a) ['Metrical Calendar of Hampson' coll. as T]; Ortenberg (1990b) 199–200 [Archbishop Sigeric's journey to Rome]; Viré (1992) [scholia to Cicero, *Aratea*, coll. as C$_2$]; A. Orchard (1995) 175–202 [*Wonders of the East*], 202 [*Jamnes and Mambres*]; M. Blake (2009) 76–103 [Ælfric, *De temporibus anni*, coll. as B]

ST: M.R. James (1901) [*Jamnes and Mambres*]; Förster (1902) [*Jamnes and Mambres*]; J.A. Robinson (1918) 14–16; C.W. Jones (1939) 120; Magoun (1940) [Archbishop Sigeric's journey]; Saxl—Meier (1953) I.119–28 [*Aratea*]; Bodden (1979) 265; Munk Olsen (1982—) I.332–3 [*Aratea*]; Biggs et al. (1990) 27–9 [*Jamnes and Mambres*; T.N. Hall]; Ortenberg (1990b) [Archbishop Sigeric's journey]; Dumville (1992a)

20–38 ['Metrical Calendar of Hampson']; Ortenberg (1992) 327; Baker—Lapidge (1995) xlv–xlviii [Leofric–Tiberius computus]; Biggs—Hall (1996) 70–4 [*Jamnes and Mambres*]; Borst (2001) I.168–9 [metrical calendar]; M. Blake (2009) 19–68

London, British Library, Cotton Tiberius B. v, fols. 74 and 76: see no. **21**

374. London, British Library, Cotton Tiberius B. v, fol. 75

s. viii, prob. Northumbria, prov. Exeter by s. x^1

Contents: gospels (f); records* (s. x^1, x med., xi^1)

MS: *CLA* II (1935) no. 190; N.R. Ker (1957) no. 194; McGurk (1961a) no. 24; N.R. Ker (1964) 82; E.A. Lowe (1964) no. 66; Drage (1978) 362–3; Conner (1993) 5, 14, 20, 25, 29, 50, 165–8, 190; Dumville (1994a) 134–5; R. Gameson (1994b) 40, 43, 48; R. Gameson (1996b) 152; Scragg (2012a) no. 582

FACS: Rose-Troup (1931) pl. 2 [recto]; Conner (1993) 168–70 [recto and verso]

ED: records: KCD no. 1353 [art. a]; Thorpe (1865) [arts. a–c]; Conner (1993) 168–70 [arts. a–c]

ST: Conner (2008) 258–9

375. London, British Library, Cotton Tiberius B. xi (with Kassel, Gesamthochschulbibliothek 4° MS. theol. 131)

890×897, Winchester?

Contents: Gregory (Alfred) *Regula pastoralis** (incomplete [Tiberius MS almost completely destroyed])

MS: Lehmann (1933) 33–5 [Kassel leaf]; N.R. Ker (1957) no. 195; P.L. Heyworth (1971); Horgan (1973); Carlson (1975) 12; A.G. Watson (1979) I, no. 558; Horgan (1986) 111–14, 124; Morrish (1988) 532; P.L. Heyworth (1989) 77, 78; Robinson—Stanley (1991) 21; Prescott (1998) 268, 273; Collier (2000) 202; W. Schipper (2003) 159; Schreiber (2003) 51–2, 64; D. Ganz (2012) 188 n. 4

FACS: N.R. Ker (1956) [complete facsimile]; Robinson—Stanley (1991) pl. 6.1.5 [Tiberius p. 4]

ED: Flasdieck (1938) 208–11 [Kassel leaf]; Carlson (1975) [OE Pastoral Care coll. as C]; Carlson (1978) [OE Pastoral Care coll. as C]; Schreiber (2003) [parts of OE Pastoral Care coll. as Tib/K]

LANG: Horgan (1981); P.P. O'Neill (1997) 153 n. 60; Gretsch (1999a) 319; Gretsch (2000) 98–102, 105; Gretsch (2001) 172; Schreiber (2003) 83–110; Dance (2004) 35–6 and n. 29

ST: Flasdieck (1942); K. Sisam (1953a) 140–7; P.L. Heyworth (1971); Dumville (1987) 163; Prescott (1987) 419–21; R. Gameson (1998) 242 n. 45; Schreiber (2003) 65–79

376. London, British Library, Cotton Tiberius C. i, fols. 43–203

s. xi¹ or xi med., Germany; additions made in England 1070×1100; prov. whole MS Sherborne s. xi², then (prob. from c. 1075) Salisbury

Contents: pontifical (*Pontificale Romano-Germanicum*) [s. xi¹ or xi med., Germany]; pontifical services, three homilies*, prayers*, four homilies; Council of Winchester (1070); penitential articles issued after the Battle of Hastings; litany [added England 1070×1100]

MS: N.R. Ker (1949–50) 182 [repr. N.R. Ker (1985) 207]; N.R. Ker (1957) no. 197; N.R. Ker (1959) 262–70; N.R. Ker (1964) 171; Brückmann (1973) 436; N.R. Ker (1976b) 25, 36, 41, 45, 49 [repr. N.R. Ker (1985) 145, 157, 163, 169, 173]; Lapidge (1983) 17, 21 n. 52 [repr. Lapidge (1993a) 459, 463 n. 52]; Lapidge (1991a) 71–2; Dumville (1992a) 69, 91, 124, 134; Webber (1992) 143–4, 145 n. 17, 159 *et passim*; R. Gameson (1999a) no. 405; *ASMMF* VIII (2000) 30–45 [no. 231; Wilcox]; Crowley (2000) 125; Hamilton (2001) 135 and n. 164, 219; T.N. Hall (2005) 180–3; Schröcker (2005) 343–4, 345–8; Hartzell (2006) no. 140; O'Brien O'Keeffe (2006) 262, 267–8; R. Gameson (2012d) 363 and n. 76; Pfaff (2012) 459 and n. 36; Rushforth (2012) 209 n. 76; Scragg (2012a) nos. 583–5

DEC: Köhler—Mütherich (1971–99) IV.77, 79; Schröcker (2005) 347

FACS: N.R. Ker (1960) pl. 1 (a) [fol. 202r]; N.R. Ker (1985) pl. 20 (b) [fol. 112v]; *ASMMF* VIII (2000) no. 231

ED: N.R. Ker (1959) 272–9 [three OE homilies: address at the dedication of a church (fols. 109v–111r), address to an individual at the beginning of Lent (fols. 200r–202r), address to the congregation at the beginning of Lent (fols. 161v–162v)]; Whitelock et al. (1981a) II.574–6 [Council of Winchester coll. as B], 581–4 [penitential articles issued after the Battle of Hastings, coll. as B]; Tristram (1985) 302 [Age of the World, Ages of Man (fol. 150r)]; Lapidge (1991a) 178–80 [litany]; T.N. Hall (2005) 183–92 [Palm Sunday homily from this MS]; O'Brien O'Keeffe (2006) 259 [oblation formula on fol. 93r–v]

ST: Munk Olsen (1982 —) I.333 [on fols. 2–42]; Baker—Lapidge (1995) lvi [on fols. 2–42]; R. Gameson (1999a) no. 404 [on fols. 2–42]; C.A. Jones (2005a) 114; Schröcker (2005) 344; Pfaff (2009) 351; R. McKitterick (2012) 330 and n. 109

377. London, British Library, Cotton Tiberius C. ii

s. ix$^{2/4}$, S. England, prob. Canterbury (StA?)

Contents: Bede, *Historia ecclesiastica* (with interlinear OE glosses, s. x) [*CPL* 1375]; glossaries^{+*}

MS: Thompson—Warner (1881–4) 78–9; Sweet (1885) 179; C. Plummer (1896) I.xciii–xcviii; *CLA* II (1935) no. 191; Kuhn (1948) 613–14; N.R. Ker (1957) no. 198; K. Sisam (1956); Kuhn (1957); K. Sisam (1957); A. Campbell (1959) 8; McGurk (1962) 28, 31 [repr. McGurk (1998) no. VII]; D.H. Wright (1964) 116; Colgrave—Mynors (1969) xlii; A.G. Watson (1978) 46 and n. 1; T.J. Brown (1980) 13; Lapidge (1981b) 120–1 [repr. Lapidge (1993a) 340–1]; Bischoff (1983b) 293; Morrish (1988) 528–9; P.L. Heyworth (1989) 224, 230, 238; Webster—Backhouse (1991) no. 170 and p. 195 [M.P. Brown]; O'Brien O'Keeffe (1994) 227–8; M.P. Brown (1996) 169–78; Webster—Brown (1997) 217–18, 238–9 [nos. 31, 112]; R. Gameson (1999c) 363; M.P. Brown (2001b); Rowley (2004) 19; Hartzell (2006) no. 141; M.P. Brown (2007a) 91; Dumville (2007f) 58, 73; Barker-Benfield (2008) I.607, III.1810; J.A. Haines (2008) 225; Lapidge (2008–10) I.lxxxvii; Graham (2009) 179; M.P. Brown (2012) 138 and n. 75, 158 n. 173, 165 and n. 223

DEC: Kendrick (1938) 153, 168, 199; Kuhn (1948) 613–14; D.H. Wright (1964) 116; Koehler (1972) 188; Alexander (1978a) no. 33; D.M. Wilson (1984) 94–6; Ohlgren (1986) no. 33; O'Brien O'Keeffe (1987) 143; M.P. Brown (2001c) 51; M.P. Brown (2011b) 37, 41; N. Edwards (2012) 246 n. 14

FACS: Kendrick (1938) pl. LXIX (2) [fol. 5v]; Alexander (1978a) ills. 134, 165 [fols. 60v (detail), 5v (detail)]; D.M. Wilson (1984) pl. 111 [fol. 5v]; M.P. Brown (1986) pl. IV(b) [fol. 94r]; Morrish (1988) pl. 7 [fol. 34v]; T.J. Brown (1993a) ill. 59 [fol. 60v]; M.P. Brown (1996) fig. 17 [fol. 5v]; M.P. Brown (2003a) 7 [fol. 5v]; M.P. Brown (2003c) fig. 51 [fol. 5v]; Lucas (2006) fig. 12.14 [fol. 75r]; J.A. Haines (2008) 226 [fol. 18r]

ED: Sweet (1885) 180–2 [Latin–OE glossaries]; C. Plummer (1896) [Bede, *Historia ecclesiastica*, coll. as C]; Meritt (1945) no. 4 [OE glosses]; Colgrave—Mynors (1969) [Bede, *Historia ecclesiastica*, coll. as c]; Lapidge (2008–10) [Bede, *Historia ecclesiastica*, coll. as C]

LANG: Sweet (1885) 179; Bülbring (1902) 9; Luick (1914–21) 33; Kuhn (1948) 613–19; Vleeskruyer (1953) 52; A. Campbell (1955) 55; A. Campbell (1959) 8

ST: D.H. Wright (1964) 116–17; O'Brien O'Keeffe (1985) 71–2; M.P. Brown (1986) 153–4; O'Brien O'Keeffe (1987) 143; Toon (1991) 85–7; M.P. Brown (1994); O'Brien O'Keeffe (1994) 229–31, 237, 246; M.P. Brown (1996) 17, 20, 22–3, 42, 62, 71, 118, 124–5, 127–8, 135, 169, 171–5, 177–8; R. Gameson (1999b) 363; Lucas (2006) 398–9, 405, 411, 414, 417–18, 431; Lapidge (2008b); Lapidge (2008–10) I.xciv–cxv; Westgard (2010) 210, 214, 217–18

378. London, British Library, Cotton Tiberius C. vi (the 'Tiberius Psalter')

s. xi$^{3/4}$, prob. mid 1060s, Winchester OM?

Contents: computus material ('Winchester Computus' [fragmentary]); picture cycle; notes on the psalter, *Alleluia* and *Gloria*; prayers; *Ordo confessionis* with litany; homily^{+*}; Psalterium Gallicanum° (now incomplete; ends at Ps. CXIIIB. 11) with psalter collects

MS: F. Wormald (1952) 50–3, 68–9 [no. 32]; N.R. Ker (1957) no. 199; F. Wormald (1957b) 31 [repr. F. Wormald (1984) 146]; Sisam—Sisam (1959) 4–5; F. Wormald (1962) [repr. F. Wormald (1984) 130–7]; Morrell (1965) 107–10; T.A.M. Bishop (1971) no. 27; Voigts (1976) 46–7, 58–9; Rella (1977) 57; Backhouse et al. (1984b) no. 66 [D.H. Turner]; Gneuss (1985) 115 [no. H.10]; Lapidge (1991a) 72; Dumville (1993g) 18, 136, 140; R.I. Page (1993a) 102–3; *ASMMF* II (1994) 38–42 [no. 233; Pulsiano]; Keynes (1996a) 115 n. 46; Webster—Brown (1997) 227 [no. 68]; Gneuss (1998) 273, 277; Pulsiano (1998b) 85, 96, 112–13 n. 41; R. Gameson (1999a) no. 406; Gretsch (1999a) 90; Gretsch (2000) 86; Liuzza (2001) 186 n. 29; Pulsiano (2001a) xxiii and nn.; Chardonnens (2007b) 519, 551; Shepard (2007) 254 n. 54; Wieland (2009) 116; R. Gameson (2012a) 70 n. 240, 91 n. 333; Scragg (2012a) no. 586

DEC: F. Wormald (1945) 126 [repr. F. Wormald (1984) 64]; Rice (1952) 219–20; F. Wormald (1952) 68–9 [no. 32]; Dodwell (1954) 5, 18, 23; F. Wormald (1957b) 31–2 [repr. F. Wormald (1984) 146–7]; Steger (1961) 191–3; F. Wormald (1962) [repr. F. Wormald (1984) 130–7]; Alexander

(1970a) 93, 120, 152; Dodwell (1971b) 94; Raw (1976) 138; E. Temple (1976) no. 98; Voigts (1976) 46–7; Deshman (1977) 166–71; C. Page (1977) 305; Brownrigg (1978) 262 and n. 3; G. Henderson (1982) 61 n. 86; D.M. Wilson (1984) 185–7; F. Wormald (1984) 120–2; Ohlgren (1986) no. 203; Voigts (1986) 296 and n. 21; Openshaw (1989); Openshaw (1990); Raw (1990) 216–17; R. Gameson (1991) 65 *et passim*; Heslop (1992a); Openshaw (1993); R. Gameson (1995b) 17, 29–30, 35, 45, 50, 91–6, 137–8, 147–8, 165–6, 171–2, 175–6, 186–9, 190–1, 207–8 *et passim*; M.P. Brown (1996) 114; Deshman (1997) 111–12, 115, 116 n. 34, 133, 136 n. 119; Wieland (1998) 16 n. 16; Brantley (1999) 56 n. 44; Dodwell (2000) 109–11, 140–1, 147–8; Kidd (2000) 45; Shepard (2007) 215; Karkov (2009) 233–5; O'Reilly (2011) 208–9; R. Gameson (2012c) 269 and n. 57, 272 and n. 71, 289 n. 138

FACS: F. Wormald (1952) pls. 30–2 [fols. 13r, 15v, 16r]; F. Wormald (1957b) fig. 11 [fol. 30v]; T.A.M. Bishop (1971) pl. XXIII (c) [fol. 19v]; Voigts (1976) figs. 3–5 [fols. 5v, 71v, 114r]; C. Page (1977) pls. 7–8 [fol. 17r–v]; Dodwell (1982) 28, 173, 184 [fols. 5v, 10v, 71v]; Backhouse et al. (1984b) pl. xx [fol. 14r]; D.M. Wilson (1984) pl. 233 [fol. 13r]; F. Wormald (1984) ills. 124–54 [facsimiles of all the miniatures: fols. 6v, 7v–19r, 30v, 71v, 72r, 114v, 126v]; M.P. Brown (1991) pls. 32, 76 [fols. 6v, 14r]; R. Gameson (1991) figs. 1, 7 [fols. 30v, 60r]; Heslop (1992a) fig. 1 [fol. 6r]; *ASMMF* II (1994) no. 233; R. Gameson (1995b) pls. 13 (b) [fol. 14r], 17 (b) [fol. 16r], 31 [fol. 72r]; Backhouse (1997) pl. 16 [fol. 14r]; Dodwell (2000) pls. XXXV (b), LIII (b) [fols. 11v (detail), 12r (detail)]; Chardonnens (2007b) pl. 5 [fol. 6v]; Shepard (2007) fig. 84 [fol. 6v]; Owen-Crocker (2009) figs. 7.24–5 [fols. 6v, 14r]

ED: Napier (1883/1967) 56–60 [Hom. VIII coll. as O]; Wilmart—Brou (1949) [base MS for psalter collects]; A.P. Campbell (1974) [base MS for Psalterium Gallicanum and OE gloss (fols. 31r–129v)]; Lapidge (1991a) 181 [litany]; Pulsiano (2001a) [Psalms I–L (Latin and OE gloss) coll. as H]; Chardonnens (2007b) 205 ['Sphere of Apuleius']

LANG: A.F. Cameron (1974) 221; Hofstetter (1987) 486–9 [no. 228]; McDougall—McDougall (1997) 221 n. 54; Crowley (2000) 138

ST: Wildhagen (1920); Sisam—Sisam (1959) 59–60; Bierbaumer (1977a); Berghaus (1979) 127–8; Pulsiano (1991c) 81–8; Burnett (1992) 167 [onomastic text]; Baker—Lapidge (1995) xlviii–lii ['Winchester Computus']; Pulsiano (1998b) 86–7; Gretsch (1999a) 26–7, 39, 90, 101, 268, 312–13

378. 5. London, British Library, Cotton Tiberius D. iv

s. xi/xii, N France (or England?), prov. prob. Winchester OM

Contents: forty-two Latin Lives of saints (including a 'Martinellus')

MS: T.S. Smith (1696) 27–8 [full list of contents]; Planta (1802) 39;
Levison (1919–20) 601; Lapidge—Winterbottom (1991b) clxxvii–
clxxix; Love (1996) lxxviii–lxxix; Treharne (1997) 174–7; R. Gameson
(1999a) no. 407; Lapidge (2003a) 612–13, 615–16, 641–2, 644, 747;
Lapidge (2004b) 443

ED: Stubbs (1874) 69–161 [Osbern, *Vita S. Dunstani*, coll. as K];
Lapidge—Winterbottom (1991b) 2–68 [Wulfstan, *Vita S. Æthelwoldi*,
coll. as T]; Love (1996) 2–46 [*Vita S. Birini* coll. as T]; Treharne (1997)
178–97 [base MS for *Vita S. Nicholai*, supplemented by readings from
no. **344**], 198–206 [base MS for *Vita S. Aegidii*]; Lapidge (2003a) 630–8,
648–96 [*Vita* and *Miracula S. Swithuni* coll. as T]

London, British Library, Cotton Tiberius D. iv, fols. 158–66: see no. **759**

379. London, British Library, Cotton Titus A. iv

s. xi med., Winchester? Canterbury StA?

Contents: *Regula S. Benedicti*[+*] [*CPL* 1852]; *Capitulare monasticum*;
Memoriale qualiter; 'De festiuitatibus anni' (Ansegisus, *Capitularium
collectio* II. 33)

MS: Schröer (1885–8/1964) xxiii; Bateson (1894b) 692, 695; N.R. Ker
(1957) no. 200; Morgand (1963) 183; Semmler (1963) 506; T.A.M.
Bishop (1971) 18; Gretsch (1973) 35–7; Hanslik (1977) lxi; Rella (1977)
57; T. Hunt (1991) I.27–8; Dumville (1993g) 8 n., 11 n., 13 n., 23;
Mordek (1995) 225–6; Menzer (2004) 96–7 n. 4; Roberts (2005) 88–90
[no. 19]; N.M. Thompson (2007) 117–18; Barker-Benfield (2008)
III.1705, 1707, 1829; Wieland (2009) 138; *ASMMF* XIX (2010) 65–70
[no. 235; Doane]; Scragg (2012a) nos. 587–9

FACS: Roberts (2005) pl. 19 [fol. 32r]; *ASMMF* XIX (2010) no. 235

ED: Schröer (1885–8/1964) [*Regula S. Benedicti* (OE) coll. as T]; Schröer
(1888/1978) [*Regula S. Benedicti* (Latin) coll. as T]; Morgand (1963)
229–61 [*Memoriale qualiter* coll. as I]; Semmler (1963) 515–35
[*Capitulare monasticum* coll. as G6]; Gretsch (1973) 68–87 [*Regula S.
Benedicti*, chs. v, xxvii–xxx and lviii, coll as j]; Hanslik (1977) [*Regula
S. Benedicti* coll. as j]

ST: Gretsch (1974) 125–51; P. Wormald (1988b) 31 n. 74; Lapidge—
   Winterbottom (1991b) lvii and n. 79; Cross (1992b); Gretsch (1992); T.
   Graham (1998a) 25, 55 n. 9, 60 n. 58; Gretsch (1999a) 116, 214, 226–7,
   247; Gretsch (2003a) 118–20 *et passim*; Jayatilaka (2003) 150–1; Tite
   (2003) 190

379. 3. London, British Library, Cotton Titus C. xv, fol. 1

s. vi/vii, Rome? in England from s. vi/vii?

Contents: Gregory, *Homiliae .xl. in Euangelia* [*CPL* 1711] (f)

MS: *CLA* II (1935) no. 192; Bischoff (1990) 182 n. 10; Babcock (2000);
   Gneuss (2003b) 299; Lapidge (2006) 25, 94 n. 13, 305

FACS: Babcock (2000) pl. 51 [recto]

379. 5. London, British Library, Cotton Titus D. xvi, fols. 2–35

s. xi/xii, St Albans

Contents: Prudentius, *Psychomachia* [*CPL* 1441]; poem on St Laurence
   (inc. 'Reddimus aeternas indulgentissime doctor' [not in SK, SK Suppl.
   or WIC])

MS: R.M. Thomson (1982a) I.91–2; R. Gameson (1999a) no. 411; Lapidge
   (2006) 330

DEC: C.M. Kauffmann (1975) no. 30; R.M. Thomson (1982a) I.91–2

FACS: R.M. Thomson (1982a) II, pls. 26–30 [fols. 1v, 2v, 5v, 16r, 28v]

380. London, British Library, Cotton Titus D. xxvi + xxvii

1023×1031, Winchester NM

Contents: *lunaria*; prognostics; liturgical calendar with necrology; computus
   material ('Winchester Computus'); Ælfric, *De temporibus anni**; alphabet
   with OE sentences*; The Passion according to St John (Euangelium
   Iohannis XVIII–XIX); devotions to the Holy Cross; Offices of the
   Trinity, the Holy Cross, the Virgin; private prayers; directions for private
   devotions*; note in cryptography; notes on the names of the Seven
   Sleepers, on the age of the Virgin*, the Ages of the World, the length of
   Christ's body, on the rainbow; *Somniale Danielis*; medical recipe*; rules
   of confraternity*; collectar; litany; Euangelium Iohannis I.1–14

MS: Birch (1892) 251–83; Dobbie (1942) lxxxiii–lxxxv; Henel (1942a)
   xix–xxi; N.R. Ker (1957) no. 202; D.H. Turner (1960) 360 n. 2; N.R.

Ker (1964) 103; T.A.M. Bishop (1971) xx, 23 [no. 26]; A.G. Watson (1979) I, no. 561; D.H. Turner et al. (1980) 105; Dodwell (1982) 58; Backhouse et al. (1984b) no. 61; Lapidge (1991a) 72–3; Robinson—Stanley (1991) 26; Corrêa (1992) 112–23; Dumville (1992a) 69, 91, 110, 131; Raw (1992) 286, 292; Dumville (1993g) 136; Günzel (1993) 1–6, 6–11, 16–30; M.P. Brown (1996) 140; Keynes (1996a) 111–23; P.P. O'Neill (1997) 162; P. Wormald (1999) 186 n. 100, 187 nn. 101–2, 210 n. 189; M.P. Brown (2001c) 59; R. Gameson (2001d) 4–5, 45; Liuzza (2001) 196, 198–9, 210; Karkov (2004) 60, 121, 127; Keynes (2004) 155; Karkov (2006a) 57; Karkov (2006b) 96, 108, 110–14; Rumble (2006b) 4; Biggs (2007a) 15; Chardonnens (2007b) 519–23, 551–2; Treharne (2007b) 26 n. 39; Rushforth (2008a) 34–5; M. Blake (2009) 14; Wieland (2009) 137; Liuzza (2011) 13–14; R. Gameson (2012a) 50 and n. 156; Raw (2012) 460 and n. 2, 465–6; Scragg (2012a) nos. 222, 590–6

DEC: Rice (1952) 217; F. Wormald (1952) 33–4, 59, 65, 69 [no. 33], 76, 79; Dodwell (1954) 23; E. Temple (1976) no. 77; F. Wormald (1984) 120; Ohlgren (1986) no. 182; Higgitt (1989) 282; Raw (1990) 217; R. Gameson (1991) 68 n. 41; Günzel (1993) 12–15; Deshman (1995) 36, 92, 106–7, 133, 157; Deshman (1997) 110 n. 4; Dodwell (2000) 148 n. 184; R. Gameson (1992a) 208, 212, 216; O'Reilly (1992) 174–5, 178–84; Raw (1992); R. Gameson (1995b) 18, 25, 67–8, 77, 90, 97, 172, 187; Karkov (2004) 60, 129; Karkov (2006b) 97–8, 100, 102–3; Rumble (2006b) 17 and n. 34; M.P. Brown (2007a) 114; Keefer (2007b) 99; Karkov (2009) 229–30; O'Reilly (2011) 211–14, 216; R. Gameson (2012c) 268 and n. 52, 269 and n. 57, 280 and n. 104

FACS: F. Wormald (1952) pls. 16 (a)–(b) [D. xxvii fol. 75v; D. xxvi fol. 19v]; T.A.M. Bishop (1971) pls. 23 (a)–(b) [D. xxvi fols. 67v, 68r]; E. Temple (1976) ills. 243 [D. xxvi fol. 19v], 245–6 [D. xxvii fols. 75v, 65v]; Dodwell (1982) 59 [D. xxvi fol. 19v]; M.P. Brown (1991) pl. 23 [D. xxvii fol. 75v]; Robinson—Stanley (1991) pls. 29.1–3 [D. xxvii fols. 55v–56v]; Raw (1992) pls. 43, 45 [D. xxvii fols. 64v, 75v]; R. Gameson (1992a) pls. 35–6 [D. xxvii fols. 65v, 75v]; Günzel (1993) pls. facing p. 4, between 4–5 [D. xxvii fols. 65v, 75v; D. xxvi fol. 19v]; Deshman (1995) figs. 27, 87 [D. xxvii fol. 75v, D. xxvi fol. 19v]; R. Gameson (1995b) pl. 17 (a) [D. xxvii fol. 65r]; Keynes (1996a) pls. X–XX [D. xxvii fols. 2r–21v]; Backhouse (1997) pl. 15 [D. xxvii fol. 75v]; Noel (2000) pl. 6 [Titus D. xxvii fol. 75v]; Karkov (2006b) figs. 1 [D. xxvii fol. 65v], 2 [D. xxvii fol. 75v], 3 [D. xxvi fol. 19v]; Owen-Crocker (2009) fig. 7.22 [D. xxvii fol. 65v]

ED: Birch (1892) 251–68, 269–93 [base text for D. xxvi (arts. a, b, c, d), D. xxvii (arts. 3, f, i, k etc.)]; F. Wormald (1934) 113–25 [liturgical calendar (no. 9)]; Henel (1942a) [Ælfric, *De temporibus anni*, coll. as D]; Lapidge (1991a) 182–6 [litany]; Günzel (1993) 89–197 [base text for 'Ælfwine's Prayerbook', omitting Ælfric, *De temporibus anni* and gospel of St John]; Chardonnens (2007b) 520–3 [list of edited prognostics]; Rushforth (2008a) no. 14 [liturgical calendar]; M. Blake (2009) 76–103 [Ælfric, *De temporibus anni*, coll. as D]

ST: C.W. Jones (1939) 121; Gjerløw (1961) 23, 140; Gneuss (1968) 112–13; F.C. Robinson (1973) 450 n. 25; Raw (1976) 135–7; Stroud (1979) 230; Kotzor (1981) I.302*–311*; Cross (1982) 79–81; Clayton (1984) 225; Gerchow (1988) 233–44, 332–5; Muir (1988) xxxii; Heslop (1990) 153–4; Hollis (1992) 234, 238; Baker—Lapidge (1995) xlviii–li ['Winchester Computus']; Pfaff (1995a) 45–8, 50–1 [Corrêa]; Corrêa (1996) 296 n. 45; Thacker (1996) 266 n.; Pulsiano (1998b) 88, 99–104; Borst (2001) I.93–4; Knowles et al. rev. C.N.L. Brooke (2001) 81; Liuzza (2001) 219–21; N. Orchard (2002) I.185, 191, 193, 218; R. Gameson (2004a); N. Orchard (2005) clxxviii; Chardonnens (2010) 246–50; Liuzza (2011) 1–77

381. London, British Library, Cotton Vespasian A. i (the 'Vespasian Psalter')

s. viii²⁄⁴, prob. Canterbury StA, with later additions: s. ix, prob. ix med. (OE gloss), s. xi¹ (*Te Deum*°, *Quicumque uult*°, prayers), Canterbury (CC?), (prov. whole MS Canterbury StA)

Contents: introductory texts to the psalms (including SK 10728, 12730); interpretations of *Alleluia*, *Gloria* and Hebrew letters (in Ps. CXVIII); Psalterium Romanum°; excerpts from Cassiodorus, *Expositio psalmorum* [*CPL* 900]; canticles°; three hymns° [SK 15627, 3544, 14234] from the Old Hymnal; *Te Deum*°, *Quicumque uult*° (Athanasian Creed), prayers [added s. xi¹]

MS: Thompson—Warner (1881–4) 8; Wildhagen (1913) 435–41; *CLA* II (1935) no. 193; Kuhn (1943); Weber (1953) xiii; Gneuss (1957); N.R. Ker (1957) no. 203; T.A.M. Bishop (1959–63a) 94; Lowe (1960) 21 [nos. XXVI–XXVII]; N.R. Ker (1964) 43; Bischoff (1966–81) II.252, 333; D.H. Wright (1967) 15–80; Gamber (1968–88) no. 1612; T.A.M. Bishop (1971) 22 [no. 25]; A.G. Watson (1979) I.11; G. Henderson (1982) 14–15, 43–5; Voigts (1988) 84; M.P. Brown (1989a) 155; P.L. Heyworth (1989) 15; Toon (1991) 91; Webster—Backhouse (1991) no. 153 [M.P. Brown]; Dumville (1992a) 1, 99–100, 124; Dumville (1992b) 77–8 and n. 98; Lapidge (1992a) 101 [repr. Lapidge (1993a) 389]; Parkes (1992) 235; Dumville (1993g) 122 n. 57, 130, 139; *ASMMF* II (1994) 43–9 [no. 238; Pulsiano]; Pulsiano (1996); Deshman (1997) 116; Webster — Brown (1997) 226, 241, 243 [nos. 66, 121, 131]; Parkes (1997b) 101 and n. 5; Gneuss (1998) 276; Pulsiano (1998b) 85, 105 n. 1; Gwara (1998) 145 n. 28; Gretsch (1999a) 278, 430; Marsden (1999) 293; Dodwell (2000) 122 n. 96; M.P. Brown (2001c) 48; Rushforth (2001) 139 n. 15; K.L. Brown (2004b) 181–2; M.P. Brown (2004) 291; Gullick (2004) 33 and n. 54; Tite (2004) 15 n. 44; Roberts (2005) 22–6; Emms (2006) 19, 24; Hartzell (2006) no. 142; Karkov (2006a) 44; Hines (2007) 73; Shepard (2007) 201, 243 n. 130; Barker-Benfield (2008) I.93, 442, 454, II.1371, III.1652–3, 1656, 1659, 1689, 1738, 1779, 1780, 1792–3, 1810, 1822; Graham (2009) 160; Wieland (2009) 135; M.P. Brown (2012) 124, 126, 131, 137, 147; R. Gameson (2012a) 17, 28 n. 59, 37 and nn. 88–9, 40 n. 105, 42, 53 n. 183, 56 and n. 191, 80 and n. 283, 81, 84; Marsden (2012) 414 and n. 31; Pfaff (2012) 451; Raw (2012) 461 and n. 8; Scragg (2012a) no. 597; Toswell (2012) 470–1

DEC: Kendrick (1938) 159–62; McGurk (1961a) 14 [repr. McGurk (1998) no. VI]; McGurk (1962) 31 [repr. McGurk (1998) no. VII]; Köhler — Mütherich (1971–99) V.56, VI/i.48, VII.109, 110; Seebass (1974); T.J. Brown (1975) 270 [repr. T.J. Brown (1993a) 160]; Alexander (1978a) no. 29; Alexander (1978b) 8; Brownrigg (1978) 257, 258 and n. 1; G. Henderson (1982) 29, 62 n. 91; Lawrence (1982) 102; D.M. Wilson (1984) 91; Ohlgren (1986) no. 29; G. Henderson (1987) 93; Raw (1990) 217–18; T.J. Brown (1993a) 273 n. 95; R. Gameson (1994b) 29 n. 18, 36, 45 n. 98; McGurk (1994b) 17–18 [repr. McGurk (1998) no. XII]; Netzer (1994) 1, 71, 98, 208 n. 5, 229 n. 129, 240 n. 38; R. Gameson (1995b) 40, 172 n. 103, 187, 197, 226, 233; Noel (1995) 143–4 and n. 84; R. Gameson (1999c) 330–6; Farr (2003) 127; K.L. Brown (2004b) 182; M.P. Brown (2007c); Karkov (2009) 216, 231; M.P. Brown (2011b) 31–2, 34, 42; Farr (2011b) 220, 221–4; Nees (2011) 4, 15, 25; Netzer (2012) 228 and n. 22, 237, 238–9

FACS: D.H. Wright (1967) [complete facsimile]; Kuhn (1943) pl. I [fol. 117v]; Kuhn (1948) pls. I (b) [fol. 53r], II (b) [fol. 43r]; Lowe (1960) pls. XXVI–XXVII [fols. 53r, 141r, 9v]; D.M. Wilson (1984) pl. 112 [fol. 30v]; G. Henderson (1987) 93 [fol. 69v]; Parkes (1992) pl. 43 [fol. 21v]; *ASMMF* II (1994) no. 238; Netzer (1994) pl. 84 [fol. 30v]; Backhouse (1997) pl. 2 [fol. 30v]; R. Gameson (1999b) frontispiece [fols. 30v, 31r (details)], 332 [fol. 21v], 333 [fol. 64v]; K.L. Brown (2004b) p. 1 [fol. 30v]; Roberts (2005) pls. 2 (a) [fol. 93v], 2 (b) [fol. 141v], p. 25 [fol. 30v]; M.P. Brown (2007a) pl. 38 [fols. 30v, 31r]; A. Griffiths (2007) pls. 1–2 [fol. 6r–v]; Pulsiano (2007) 132 [fol. 61r]; Shepard (2007) fig. 76 [fol. 53r (detail)]; Owen-Crocker (2009) figs. 6.1 [fol. 55v], 7.8 [fol. 53r]; R. Gameson (2012) pl. 4.3 [fols. 30v–31r]

ED: Sweet (1885) 188–420 [base text, Latin and OE gloss, for psalter, canticles and hymns]; Weber (1953) [psalter coll. as A]; Kuhn (1965) [base text, Latin and OE gloss, for complete MS]; Milfull (1996) [hymns 2, 15, 31, coll. as A]; Pulsiano (2001a) [Pss. I–L, Latin and OE gloss, coll. as A]

LANG: Sweet (1885) 185–7; Kuhn (1943); Gneuss (1955); I.L. Gordon (1960) 29; A. Campbell in D.H. Wright (1967) 85–90; Bierbaumer (1977a); Wenisch (1979) 65; Bately (1980) 41; Kristensson (1981) 373; Kuhn (1985); Mertens-Fonck (1987); Hofstetter (1987) 456–7; Kitson (1990) 214; Scragg (1994a) 328; Wiesenekker (1994); Treharne (1998) 239; Gretsch (1999a) 318 n.; Crowley (2000) 126; Gretsch (2001) 171; K.L. Brown (2004b) 182; C. Bishop (2007b) 82

ST: Mearns (1914) 51–2, 79, 94; Kuhn (1943); Kuhn (1948); K. Sisam (1953a) 4; K. Sisam (1956); Kuhn (1957); K. Sisam (1957); Sisam— Sisam (1959) 47–52; Gneuss (1968) 16, 17–19, 33–8, 122, 198, 209, 211 n. 11 *et passim*; Lambert (1969–72) nos. 346, 347, 424, 801; G. Watson (1969–77) [bibliography]; Köhler—Mütherich (1971–99) VI/i. 48 and n. 29; Berghaus (1979); Greenfield—Robinson (1980) nos. 189, 5938– 54 [bibliography]; Kuhn (1985); Gerritsen (1989a); Toon (1991) 91; M.P. Brown (1996) 17, 20, 22–3, 71–3 *et passim*; Discenza (1997) 94; Budny (1999) 243, 251–2; Marchesin (1998); R. Gameson (1999c) 332; Gretsch (1999a) 26–7, 33–41, 42–88, 97, 106–7, 182–225, 278, 316–17, 318 n. 177; Gretsch (2000); Pulsiano (2000) 167; Gneuss (2003b) 297; K.L. Brown (2004b) 182; R. Gameson (2004b); A. Griffiths (2007)

382. London, British Library, Cotton Vespasian A. viii, fols. 1–33 (the 'New Minster Charter')

966, Winchester OM, prov. Winchester NM

Contents: Latin distich (inc. 'Sic celso residet': SK Suppl. 15252a); New Minster foundation charter

MS: N.R. Ker (1964) 103; Sawyer (1968) no. 745; T.A.M. Bishop (1971) xxi; A.G. Watson (1979) I, no. 562; Backhouse et al. (1984b) no. 26;

Dumville (1993g) 2, 53, 143, 145; S. Miller (2001) 95–111 [no. 23]; Rumble (2002) 65–73; Karkov (2004) 103; Tite (2004) 11 n. 26; R. Gameson (2012a) 39 and n. 98, 59, 65, 90 n. 330; Rushforth (2012) 200 and n. 15

DEC: Rice (1952) 184; F. Wormald (1963) 23–6 [repr. F. Wormald (1984) 108–10]; E. Temple (1976) no. 16; D.M. Wilson (1984) 174; F. Wormald (1984) 115–16; Ohlgren (1986) no. 94; Deshman (1988) 221–2; Raw (1990) 218; Dumville (1993g) 140; R. Gameson (1995b) 6–7, 8–9, 19, 22, 25, 61, 94–5, 120, 130, 136, 155, 200–2 *et passim*; Karkov (2004) 4, 5, 7, 11, 60, 84, 97, 106, 114, 118, 133, 134, 138, 159, 168, 175; McGurk—Rosenthal (2006) 193; Scott (2007) 23, 25; Inglis (2008) 56; Karkov (2008); Karkov (2009) 214, 237–8; Rosenthal (2011) 238–41; Withers (2011) 264; R. Gameson (2012c) 252–3 and n. 12, 275–6 and n. 85

FACS: *NPS* I, pls. 46–7 [fols. 2v, 11v]; E. Temple (1976) pl. 84 [fol. 2v]; J. Campbell et al. (1991a) pl. 164 [fol. 2v]; Dodwell (1982) 52–3 [fol. 2v]; Backhouse et al. (1984b) pl. 26 [fol. 2v]; D.M. Wilson (1984) pl. 261 [fol. 2v]; F. Wormald (1984) ills. 96–8 [fols. 3v, 4r, 2v]; M.P. Brown (1991) pl. 14 [fol. 2v]; R. Gameson (1991) fig. 15 [fol. 4r]; R. Gameson (1995b) pls. 2 (a)–(b) [fols. 2v, 3r]; Keynes (1996a) pls. I–IV [fols. 2v, 3r, 3v, 4r]; Backhouse (1997) pl. 8 [fol. 2v]; S. Miller (2001) frontispiece [fol. 2v] and pls. I–VIII [fols. 29v, 30r, 30v, 31r, 31v, 32r, 32v, 33r]; Rumble (2002) frontispiece [fol. 2v] and pl. I [fol. 19v]; Karkov (2004) figs. 7–11 [fols. 2v, 3r, 3v, 4r, 30r]; M.P. Brown (2007a) pl. 84 [fol. 2v]; Scott (2007) 22 [fol. 2v]; Inglis (2008) 56 [fol. 6r]; Owen-Crocker (2009) fig. 7.27 [fol. 2v]; R. Gameson (2012) pl. 10.3 [fol. 2v]

ED: BCS no. 1190 [foundation charter coll. as A]; Whitelock et al. (1981a) I.119–33 [no. 31; base text for foundation charter]; S. Miller (2001) no. 23 [foundation charter coll. as A]; Rumble (2002) 70 [distich], 74–97 [foundation charter]

LANG: Lapidge (1975a) 89 and n. 1 [repr. Lapidge (1993a) 127 and n. 1]

ST: T.A.M. Bishop (1954–8b) 333; Finberg (1964) no. 100; E. John (1966) 271–5; Sawyer (1968) no. 746 [fols. 34–43]; Lapidge (1988c) 95–6 [repr. Lapidge (1993a) 189–90]; Lapidge—Winterbottom (1991b) lxxxix–xc; Keynes (1996a) 26–8; Teviotdale (1996) 101 [Latin distich]; Gretsch (1999a) 309–10; Rumble (2002) 65–97; Karkov (2004) 85–93

383. London, British Library, Cotton Vespasian A. xiv, fols. 114–79 ('Letter-book of Archbishop Wulfstan')

1003×1023, Worcester or York

Contents: Alcuin, selected *Epistolae*; various letters, mainly by popes, and to tenth-century Anglo-Saxon bishops; poem addressed to Archbishop Wulfstan [SK 13280]; decrees of the Councils of Chelsea (816) and Hertford (672 = Bede, *Historia ecclesiastica* IV.5); Atto of Vercelli, *De rapinis ecclesiasticarum rerum* [excerpt from *De pressuris ecclesiasticis*]; Archbishop Oda of Canterbury, *Constitutiones* (942×946); *De actiua uita et contemplatiua*

MS: Stubbs (1874) liv–lv; Dümmler (1895) 9–11; Levison (1946) 247; Bethurum (1957) 7–8; N.R. Ker (1957) no. 204; N.R. Ker (1971) 326–7 [repr. N.R. Ker (1985) 20–1]; Whitelock (1976) 28–33; Rella (1977) 71; A.G. Watson (1979) I, no. 564; P.L. Heyworth (1989) 198, 289; C. Brett (1991) 55–6, 65–70; Webster—Backhouse (1991) no. 159 [M.P. Brown]; C.A. Jones (1999) 128 n. 100; P. Wormald (1999) 188 n. 108, 451 n. 125, 462 n. 176; Baxter (2004) 161 n. 1; Bullough (2004) 97–101 *et passim*; Dance (2004) 31 n. 6; J. Hill (2004) 313 n. 11, 321; G. Mann (2004); A. Orchard (2004) 66 n. 15; Vanderputten (2006) 219, 221, 225, 227–32, 235–6; R. Gameson (2012b) 110 n. 61, 111 n. 66; A. Orchard (2012) 697 [no. 9]; Scragg (2012a) no. 597.5

FACS: Loyn (1971) pls. at end [fols. 148v, 171v, 173v]; Cross—Morrish Tunberg (1993b) pls. I–IV [fols. 148v, 149r, 153r, 173v]; G. Mann (2004) figs. 9.1–3 [fols. 171v, 173v, 177v]

ED: Haddan—Stubbs (1869–71) III.579–85 [Council of Chelsea]; Stubbs (1874) 354 [poem addressed to Archbishop Wulfstan], 369–70, 380–1, 383–9, 404–5 [various letters]; Dümmler (1895) 18–481 [Alcuin, *Epistolae*, coll. as A2]; BCS no. 896 [poem addressed to Archbishop Wulfstan]; Bethurum (1957) 374–7 [letters relating to Archbishop Wulfstan], 377–8 [poem addressed to Archbishop Wulfstan]; N.R. Ker (1971) 326–7 [poem addressed to Archbishop Wulfstan]; Chase (1975) [base MS (= A$_2$) for Alcuin, *Epistolae*]; Whitelock et al. (1981a) I.67–74 [base MS for Oda, *Constitutiones*], 441–7 [Letter from the bishops of Britain to the pope]; Cross (1993d) 243–4 [Atto of Vercelli]; G. Mann (2004) 269 [*De actiua uita et contemplatiua*]; Vanderputten (2006) 237–44 [Letters from Wido, Fulrad and Odbert to Canterbury, coll. as B]

ST: Whitelock (1937) 463–4 [repr. Whitelock (1981b), no. VIII]; Bethurum (1942) 929; Whitelock (1942) 30–2, 43 n. 5 [repr. Whitelock (1981b) no. XI]; Levison (1946) 246–8; Bethurum (1949); Cubitt (1995) 308–9 [Council of Chelsea]; R. Gameson (1996a) 213 n., 239; Bullough

(1998b) 24 and n. 71; *CSLMA* II (1999) 172, 178–80, 184, 193, 201, 212–15, 229, 233, 239, 241, 247, 298, 310, 321, 329, 338, 348; Sauer (2000) 341, 372; Bullough (2004); Vanderputten (2006) 219, 234

384. London, British Library, Cotton Vespasian B. vi, fols. 1–103

s. ix$^{2/4}$, Saint-Denis, prov. England by s. xi in.

Contents: Bede, *De temporum ratione* [*CPL* 2320]; lists of Carolingian rulers and Byzantine emperors; tide table; *horologium*

MS: Thompson—Warner (1881–4) II.68, 79; C.W. Jones (1939) 121; C.W. Jones (1943) 146; Laistner—King (1943) 149; N.R. Ker (1957) no. 205; Rella (1977) 25, 77–8, 165; A.G. Watson (1979) I, no. 567; Rella (1980) 112; Santosuosso (1989); Budny (1992) 138; Bischoff (1998—) II, no. 2426; Karkov (2004) 66 nn. 70 and 72, 67 n. 79; Keynes (2004) 151; Hartzell (2006) no. 143; Scragg (2012a) no. 598

FACS: *NPS* I, pls. 166–7 [fols. 39v, 68r]; A.G. Watson (1979) II, pls. 9 (a)–(c) [fols. 24v, 26r, 89r]; Santosuosso (1989) pl. 20 (a) [fol. 26r]; Budny (1992) pl. 8 (g) [fol. 29v (detail)]

ED: Napier (1900) no. 31 [OE glosses to Bede]; C.W. Jones (1943) [Bede, *De temporum ratione*, coll. as L; repr. C.W. Jones (1977) 264–460]

ST: Ziolkowski (2007) 145 and n. 124; R. McKitterick (2012) 328

385. London, British Library, Cotton Vespasian B. vi, fols. 104–9

805×814, Mercia

Contents: 'Metrical Calendar of York' (incomplete); tables of Greek and Roman numerals; chronological note on the death of King Æthelbald of Mercia; Ages of the World; encyclopedic notes: dimensions of Solomon's Temple at Jerusalem, of the Tabernacle, of St Peter's basilica in Rome, of Noah's Ark; numbers of books of the Bible, number of languages of the world, number of bones, veins and teeth in a human body, dimensions of the world, number of verses in the Book of Psalms; excerpts from Eucherius, *Instructiones* [*CPL* 489]: *De mensibus* (on the Hebrew names of the months), *De ponderibus*, *De mensuris*; two additional notes on measurements; verses on the days of the week; the Ages of Man; list of popes from Peter to Leo III, with addenda; names of the seventy-two disciples of Christ; fifteen Anglo-Saxon episcopal lists; Anglian collection of royal genealogies

MS: K. Sisam (1953a) 4–6; K. Sisam (1953b) 289; Dumville (1976) 24–5; A.G. Watson (1979) I, no. 568; Lapidge (1984) 328 [repr. Lapidge (1993a) 345]; Morrish (1988) 517, 522, 537; Webster—Backhouse (1991) no. 29 [Prescott]; M.P. Brown (1996) 170–2; Lapidge (1996c) 430; Webster—Brown (1997) 224 [no. 55]; Karkov (2004) 66 nn. 69 and 72, 67 n. 79; Keynes (2004) 151; Dumville (2005) 310; Keynes (2005b); Dekker (2007) 301–5; M.P. Brown (2012) 164

FACS: Thompson—Warner (1881–4) II, pl. 24 [fol. 104r]; *NPS* I, pl. 165 [fols. 104r, 107r]; A.G. Watson (1979) II, pl. 4 [fol. 106r]

ED: Sweet (1885) 167–71 [Anglian royal genealogies]; M.R. James (1910) [disciples of Christ]; M.R. James (1912) I.428–38 [lists of disciples of Christ, of Anglo–Saxon bishops and kings, coll. with those in no. **56**]; Wilmart (1934) 65–8 [Metrical Calendar of York]; R.I. Page (1966) 3–7 [lists of Anglo–Saxon bishops]; Dumville (1976) 30–1 [Anglian royal genealogies]; Tristram (1985) 300–1 [Ages of the World]; Dekker (2007) 283 [encyclopaedic notes, coll. in footnotes]; Dekker (2010) 170–3 [base MS for Eucherius, excerpts from *Instructiones*, bk. II]

ST: K. Sisam (1953b) [Anglo-Saxon genealogies]; Stenton (1959) [Anglian royal genealogies]; Dumville (1976) [Anglian royal genealogies]; Dumville (1977) 90; Lapidge (1984) 327–32 [repr. Lapidge (1993a) 344–9] [Metrical Calendar of York]; Tristram (1985) 83; *BCLL* (1985) no. 1229; Dolbeau (1992) [Seventy disciples]; Bullough (2003b) 348 [Metrical Calendar of York]; Bullough (2004) 106 n. 264, 208–9 and n. 237, 241–2 and n. 336; Keynes (2005b); Dekker (2007) 256–8, 291, 293, 301–6, 309–10; Dekker (2010) 156–8; Gneuss (2012) 291

386. London, British Library, Cotton Vespasian B. x, fols. 31–124

s. x/xi, prob. Worcester, (prov. ibid.)

Contents: Aethicus Ister, *Cosmographia* [*CPL* 2348]

MS: Wuttke (1853) xxiv; N.R. Ker (1957) no. 206; N.R. Ker (1964) 207; T.A.M. Bishop (1966) xvii; T.A.M. Bishop (1971) xiv; Rella (1977) 83–4; Galloway (1989); Dumville (1993g) 55; Prinz (1993) 63–4; R. Gameson (1996a) 210; Barker-Benfield (2008) II.1104; R. Gameson (2012a) 51 and n. 171; Scragg (2012a) no. 599

DEC: R. Gameson (2012c) 287 and n. 132

FACS: R. Gameson (1996a) pl. 5 [fol. 62v]

ED: Wuttke (1853) 87–8 [OE glosses]

ST: Lambert (1969–72) no. 621; *BCLL* (1985) no. 647; R. Gameson
(1996a) 200 nn. 17–18, 210, 214, 239

387. London, British Library, Cotton Vespasian B. xx

s. xi/xii, Canterbury StA

Contents: *Bulla plumbea* [spurious privilege by Bishop Augustine of
Canterbury (Sawyer (1968) no. 1244)]; Goscelin, *Vitae* and *Miracula S.
Augustini* [of Canterbury] (*Historia minor* and *maior* [*BHL* 777–80]):
Goscelin, *Translatio S. Augustini* [*BHL* 781], *Vita S. Letardi* [*BHL*
4892], *Vita S. Mildrethae* [*BHL* 5960] and *Translatio S. Mildrethae*
[*BHL* 5961], *uitae* of the early archbishops of Canterbury (Laurentius
[*BHL* 4741], Mellitus [*BHL* 5896], Iustus [*BHL* 4601], Honorius [not
in *BHL*], Deusdedit [*BHL* 2153], Theodore [*BHL* 8083]) and of
Abbot Hadrian [*BHL* 3740]; Gregory and Augustine, *Libellus respon-
sionum*; Goscelin (?), *Libellus contra usurpatores S. Mildrethae* [*BHL*
5962]; royal privileges [Sawyer (1968) nos. 1248, 3 and 4: all spurious)]
and papal privileges [listed Levison (1946) 181–2: all dubious] for
St Augustine's Abbey

MS: N.R. Ker (1960) 27, 29, 30; N.R. Ker (1964) 43; Sawyer (1968)
nos. 3, 4, 1244, 1248; Lawrence (1977); Alexander (1978c) 102 n. 39;
Rollason (1982) 20, 105; Rollason (1987) 146–8; A.G. Watson (1987b)
289 [repr. A.G. Watson (2004) no. VIII]; R. Gameson (1995a) 114
n. 64, 144; R. Gameson (1999a) no. 414; T.N. Hall (2004b) 97 n. 17;
Barker-Benfield (2008) I.lxx and n. 42, 64, II.972, 1445, 1446, 1480,
III.1745, 1746, 1749–50, 1793

DEC: F. Wormald (1945) 110 and n. 4 [repr. F. Wormald (1984) 50 and
n. 11]; Rice (1952) 197; Dodwell (1954) 28, 123; Alexander (1978c) 102
n. 39; R. Gameson (1995a) 124 n. 102

FACS: *NPS* I, pl. 85 [fol. 166r]; N.R. Ker (1960) pl. 11 [fols. 174v–175r];
R. Gameson (1995a) pl. 11 [fol. 277r]; F. Gameson (1999) pl. 15.1 [fol.
277r]

ED: Colker (1977) 69–96 [*Libellus contra usurpatores*]; Rollason (1982)
108–43 [base MS for *Vita S. Mildrethae*]; Rollason (1987) 139–210
[base MS for *Translatio S. Mildrethae*]

ST: Hardy (1862–71) I, *passim*; Levison (1946) 181–2, 198–200 and 200
n. 1; Gransden (1974) 64–5, 107 n. 8, 110 n. 30; Yerkes (1983a) 129–30;
F. Barlow (1992) 133–49; Bischoff—Lapidge (1994) 82 n. 2, 140 n. 24;
F. Gameson (1999); R. Sharpe (2001) 152–3

388. London, British Library, Cotton Vespasian D. ii

s. xi/xii, Normandy, in England by 1100?

Contents: penitential texts, incl. *De paenitentia quaedam* and *Canones paenitentiales secundum Hieronymum et Fulbertum* [*CPL* 1896]; Adso of Montier-en-Der, *De Antichristo*; Latin homilies (including two by Wulfstan); Lanfranc, *Collectio Lanfranci* [*Concilia, Decreta pontificum*]; *Narrationes quaedam* [excerpts from Rufinus, *Historia monachorum* (*CPG* 5620) and the *Verba seniorum* (*CPG* 5570; *BHL* 6527)]; *Miracula S. Nicolai et aliorum*; *Ritualia quaedam* (liturgical directions)

MS: Planta (1802) 474; Wasserschleben (1851) 90, 623–4; Napier (1883/1967) 347–8; Bethurum (1957) 7, 281; A.G. Watson (1969) 55 [repr. A.G. Watson (2004) no. IX]; Whitelock (1976) 29 n. 1; Cross (1992) 66 n. 18, 73; R. Gameson (1999a) no. 416; T.N. Hall (2004a) 94, 97; Wieland (2009) 127

ED: Bethurum (1957) 113–15 [Wulfstan, Hom. Ia (*De Antichristo*), coll. as V]

ST: Schulz-Flügel (1990) 95 [Rufinus excerpts]; Cross (1992) [Wulfstan, Latin sermon *De ieiunio quattuor temporum*]; Biggs et al. (2001) 453–5 [Theophilus, *Historia*; Clayton]; T.N. Hall (2004a) 94–5 [Wulfstan Hom. Ia], 97–9 [Wulfstan, Latin sermon *De ieiunio quattuor temporum*]

389. London, British Library, Cotton Vespasian D. vi, fols. 2–77

s. x med. (or x^2), prob. Canterbury StA, (prov. ibid.)

Contents: Prouerbia Salomonis°; glosses on Prouerbia Salomonis; Alcuin, *De uirtutibus et uitiis*°; *Verba seniorum* [*CPG* 5570; *BHL* 6527] (= *Vitas patrum*, bk. V) XVIII. 9 (Life of St Macarius); Kentish Hymn**; note on the Ages of the World*; Kentish Psalm**; *Disticha Catonis* (incomplete); texts from Mass of the Virgin; verse antiphon for St Augustine of Canterbury; Dialogue before the Cross (s. xi/xii); Latin terms of relationship°

MS: Dobbie (1942) lxxviii–lxxxiii; Boas (1952) lxi; T.A.M. Bishop (1954–8b) 327–8; N.R. Ker (1957) no. 207; R.S. Cox (1972) 3; Rella (1977) 96 n. 20; Rella (1980) 111, 131 n. 129; Szarmach (1981b) 137; Torkar (1981) 22–3; Lapidge (1982a) 103 and n. 29 [repr. Lapidge (1996b) 461 and n. 29]; Munk Olsen (1982–) I.70; Carley (1986) 115; Szarmach (1986a) 32; P.L. Heyworth (1989) 13; Keefer (1990b) 70–1;

Robinson—Stanley (1991) 25; P. Jackson (1992) 123–4; Kornexl (1993) xcvi; Dumville (1994a) 140–1, 150 n. 100; Gretsch (1999a) 82; *ASMMF* IV (1996) 14–18 [no. 243; Pulsiano]; Crowley (2000) 141; Szarmach (2002); Kalbhen (2003) 14–31; Hartzell (2006) no. 145; Hines (2007) 72–3; Barker-Benfield (2008) I.lxi n. 28, 417, 424, 425, II.1402

DEC: Kalbhen (2003) 25–6

FACS: Szarmach (1986a) 33 [fol. 62v]; Robinson—Stanley (1991) pls. 21.1–3 [fols. 68v–69v], 22.1–8 [fols. 70r–73v]; *ASMMF* IV (1996) no. 243; Kalbhen (2003) figs. 1–2 [fols. 5v, 20v]

ED: Zupitza (1877) [arts. a, b, f]; Wright—Wülker (1884) I.55–88 [OE glosses to Prouerbia Salomonis and to Alcuin, *De uirtutibus et uitiis*]; Sweet (1887/1978) 172–98 [OE glosses to Prouerbia Salomonis and Alcuin, *De uirtutibus et uitiis*]; Dobbie (1942) 87–94 [Kentish Hymn; Kentish Psalm]; Boas (1952) [*Disticha Catonis* coll. as O]; Kalbhen (2003) 117–61 [OE glosses to Prouerbia Salomonis and to Alcuin, *De uirtutibus et uitiis*; *Ages of the World*]

LANG: A. Campbell (1959) 8; Rosier (1960a) 36; Karl Brunner (1965) 10; Hofstetter (1979) 172–5; Wenisch (1979) 89, 328, 350; Hofstetter (1987) 503; Hofstetter (1988) 503; Crowley (2000) 145; Kalbhen (2003) 163–239; C. Bishop (2007b) 82

ST: I.F. Williams (1905); Taxweiler (1906); Wallach (1955) 181–95; Schüling (1961–3) 322; Calder (1976) 230–1; Brownrigg (1978) 239 n. 2; Cross (1982) 81; Tristram (1985) 31, 44, 85; Liuzza (1988) 75; P. Jackson (1992) 123–7 [Macarius]; Gneuss (1993) 98; Marsden (1994a) 105, 119, 124; Marsden (1995) 48, 308–14, 362; *CSLMA* II (1999) 155; Kalbhen (2003)

390. London, British Library, Cotton Vespasian D. vi, fols. 78–125

s. xi⁴/⁴ (s. xi ex. or later?), Northumbria?, (prov. Yorkshire)

Contents: Stephen of Ripon, *Vita S. Wilfridi* [*CPL* 2151; *BHL* 8889]

MS: Levison (1913) 183; Colgrave (1927) xiii–xiv; P.L. Heyworth (1989) 13; Webster—Backhouse (1991) no. 95; Dumville (1992) 106 and n. 59; *ASMMF* IV (1996) 14–18 [no. 243; Pulsiano]; R. Gameson (1999a) no. 417; Pulsiano (2007) 123; Wieland (2009) 116; R. Gameson (2012b) 107 and n. 49

ED: Levison (1913) 193–263 [Stephen, *Vita S. Wilfridi*, coll. as 'Codex 1']; Colgrave (1927) 2–148 [Stephen, *Vita S. Wilfridi*, coll. as C]

FACS: *ASMMF* IV (1996) no. 243

ST: Lapidge et al. (1999) 428–9 [Lapidge]; R. Sharpe (2001) 633–4; Kalbhen (2003) 85–8; Keynes (2006) B 140

391. London, British Library, Cotton Vespasian D. xii

s. xi med., Canterbury CC

Contents: introductory note (from Isidore *De ecclesiasticis officiis* I.vi and *Etymologiae* VI.xix.17); poem [SK Suppl. 7969a]; hymnal with supplement (s. xi² — xii/xiii); *Expositio hymnorum*°; Monastic canticles; Monastic canticles (with rearranged word-order)°

MS: Mearns (1913) xi; Mearns (1914) 83; N.R. Ker (1957) no. 208; Gneuss (1968) 98–101; Korhammer (1973) 180–1; Hofstetter (1987) 110; Dumville (1992a) 20 n. 30; Springer (1995) 146; *ASMMF* IV (1996) 19–36 [no. 243; Pulsiano]; Milfull (1996) 52–5; Gretsch (1999a) 377; Hartzell (2006) no. 146; Graham (2009) 165; Wieland (2009) 135; Scragg (2012a) nos. 493, 600

DEC: R. Gameson (1991) 74 n. 78

FACS: Gneuss (1968) pls. 3–4 [fols. 44v, 102v]; Korhammer (1976) 252 [fol. 129v]; *ASMMF* IV (1996) no. 243; Roberts (2005) 99 [fol. 11r]

ED: *AH* LI (1908) xvii, xliv, 21–219 [hymns coll. with various sigla, from transcription by H.M. Bannister]; Hurst — Fraipont (1955) 419–23 [Bede's Ascension Hymn coll. as L^d]; Gneuss (1968) 265–413 [*Expositio hymnorum* and OE gloss respectively coll. as Vl and V; base text for some metrical hymns (see p. 259)]; Korhammer (1976) 254–351 [Monastic canticles coll. as Vm; base MS for Monastic canticles in rearranged form and their OE gloss]; Milfull (1996) [hymns coll. as Vm; *Expositio hymnorum* coll. as Vp]

LANG: Gneuss (1968) 157–93; Korhammer (1976) 151–237; Hofstetter (1987) 101–13; Crowley (2000) 143

ST: Gneuss (1968); Korhammer (1973) 180–1; F.C. Robinson (1973) 462, 472; Korhammer (1976); Korhammer (1980) 42–3; Horsley — Waterhouse (1984) 220; Milfull (1996)

392. London, British Library, Cotton Vespasian D. xiv, fols. 170–224

s. ix^{1/4}, N or NE France [Isidore, creeds, hymns], prov. England s. x in. (before 912); additions England s. x¹ (whole MS prov. Canterbury CC?)

Contents: Isidore, *Synonyma de lamentatione animae peccatricis* [*CPL* 1203]; four creeds (attrib. to Ambrose, Gregory the Martyr, Gregory the Great, Jerome *Epist. supp.* xvi [*Libellus fidei: CPL* 633 (p. 220) = *CPL* 731]); hymns [SK 12515 (f), 10768]; additions [s. x¹]: excerpts from Boethius, *De consolatione Philosophiae*: i. metr. 1 and 2, iii. metr. 8, iv. metr. 7; note on dating the *annus praesens*

MS: Thompson—Warner (1884) II.51–2; Förster (1901); Förster (1920); N.R. Ker (1957) no. 210; Bischoff (1965) 238 n. 40 [repr. Bischoff (1966–81) III.13 n. 40]; Bischoff (1968a) 309; Handley (1974); A.G. Watson (1979) I, no. 570; Schmetterer (1981) 3–5; Dumville (1987) 172; Dumville (1992b) 95–6 and nn.; Bischoff (1998—) II, no. 2427; *ASMMF* VIII (2000) 53–64 [no. 245; Wilcox]; Lionarons (2004b) 75 n. 26; N.M. Thompson (2004) 61, 63; Lapidge (2006) 170, 293, 312; Biggs (2007a) 30 [Biggs, Morey], 46, 76, 84 [Biggs, T.N. Hall]; Swan (2007b) 33 n. 12; Di Sciacca (2008) 69–71, 110–11; Elfassi (2009) xxxix and nn.; Wieland (2009) 149; Godden (2011) 70 and n. 11

FACS: Thompson—Warner (1881–4) II, pl. 49 [fol. 219v]; A.G. Watson (1979) II, pl. 14 [fol. 186v]; Dumville (1992b) pl. VIII [fol. 223v]; *ASMMF* VIII (2000) no. 245

ED: Meritt (1961) no. 17 [OE scratched glosses]; R.I. Page (1981) 106, 111–13 [OE scratched glosses]; Elfassi (2009) [Isidore, *Synonyma*, coll. as O]

LANG: Förster (1901)

ST: Förster (1925b) II.8 [creeds]; Bankert et al. (1997) 66 [creeds]; Gneuss (2000) 241–2 and n. 58 [hymns]; Acker (2004) 128 n. 26; Di Sciacca (2008) [Isidore, *Synonyma*, in Anglo-Saxon England]

393. London, British Library, Cotton Vespasian D. xv, fols. 68-101

s. x med.

Contents: confessional prayer and related texts; *Canones Cottoniani* [a version of the *Iudicia Theodori* (*CPL* 1885)]

MS: Planta (1802); Holthausen (1889) 172–3; N.R. Ker (1957) no. 211; Frantzen (1983a) 39 n. 87; Frantzen (1985) 26; Dumville (1992a) 130, 134; Tite (1994) 5; C.A. Jones (2004) 330

ED: Holthausen (1889) 172–3 [OE rubric]; Finsterwalder (1929) 62–74, 271–84 [*Canones Cottoniani*]

ST: Thorpe (1840) [folio ed.] xi, 281, 285, 296, 298–9, 302, 304, 307; Wasserschleben (1851) 181–2; Frantzen (1983a) 27–30; Frantzen (1983b) 132 n. 36, 171 and n. 58; *CPL* (1995) no. 1885; Charles-Edwards (1995); R. McKitterick (2012) 328

394. London, British Library, Cotton Vespasian, D. xv, fols. 102–21

s. x/xi, W. England (Worcester?)

Contents: excerpts from Amalarius, *Liber officialis* (*Retractatio prima*); exegesis and rhyming version of *Pater noster*; duties of a priest

MS: N.R. Ker (1957) lvii; T.A.M. Bishop (1964–8a) 258; Dumville (1993g) 55 n. 242, 149 n. 49; Dumville (1994b) 213–14; T. Graham (1995a) 6 and n. 13

ED: T. Graham (1995a) 14 [Amalarius, *Liber officialis* III.1, on church bells, from fol. 102r–v]

ST: Dumville (1992a) 136 and n. 301; *CSLMA* I (1994) 133 [Amalarius]; C.A. Jones (1998c) 682 and nn. 104, 105; C.A. Jones (2001) 28, 122 and n. 248, 124, 175

395. London, British Library, Cotton Vespasian D. xx, fols. 2–86

s. x med.

Contents: manual of confessional and penitential texts

MS: K. Sisam (1953a) 192 n. 2; A.G. Watson (1969) 40 [repr. A.G. Watson (2004) no. IX]; Frantzen (1983a) 39 and nn.; Frantzen (1983b) 132 and n. 35, 170 and n. 56; Dumville (1992a) 130 and n. 256, 132; Dumville (1994a) 135 n. 13

395. 5. London, British Library, Cotton Vespasian D. xx, fols. 87–93

s. x^1 (*c.* 910 × *c.* 930); addition s. xi^2

Contents: confessional prayer*; charm against toothache [addition s. xi^2]

MS: Planta (1802) 478; N.R. Ker (1957) no. 212; Frantzen (1983a) 39 and nn., 46; Frantzen (1983b) 170 n. 60; Dumville (1994a) 135 and n. 13

ED: Logeman (1889) 97–100 [OE confessional prayer]; Storms (1948) 289–90 [no. 52] [charm]

ST: Logemann (1889) 101–2; Förster (1942a) 27–36; Fowler (1965) 13–14; Frantzen (1983b) 171 n. 60

396. London, British Library, Cotton Vitellius A. vi

s. x med., prob. Canterbury StA

Contents: Gildas, *De excidio Britanniae* [*CPL* 1319; *BCLL* 27] (incomplete)

MS: T.S. Smith (1696) 81; Mommsen (1892–8) III.13–14; M.R. James (1903) lxx n. 1, 293; N.R. Ker (1964) 43; Gransden (1974) 2 n. 4; Winterbottom (1978) 12; Dumville (1993g) 97 n. 74; Dumville (1994a) 140 n. 38; Webster—Brown (1997) 214 [no. 10]; Barker-Benfield (2008) I.91 n. a, II.922; Larpi (2008) 176; Wieland (2009) 143; Larpi (2012) 22–4

FACS: M.P. Brown (1991) pl. 3 [fol. 16v]; M.P. Brown (2007a) pl. 2 [fol. 16v]

ED: Mommsen (1892–8) III.25–85 [Gildas, *De excidio*, coll. as C]

ST: Kenney (1929) no. 23; Gneuss (1968) 115; Winterbottom (1978); *BCLL* (1985) no. 27; Lapidge et al. (1999) 204 [Lapidge]; Larpi (2008); Larpi (2012)

397. London, British Library, Cotton Vitellius A. vii, fols. 1–112

prob. Ramsey after 1030, and Exeter, 1046×1072

Contents: pontifical (including litanies and second English Coronation *ordo*) (now incomplete), with abbreviated versions of two sermons by Abbo of Saint-Germain-des-Prés (nos. x, xiii)

MS: T.S. Smith (1696) 81; Liebermann (1903–16) I.xlii; N.R. Ker (1957) no. 213; N.R. Ker (1964) 154; T.A.M. Bishop (1971) 24 n. 1; Brückmann (1973) 437; Drage (1978) 364–5; A.G. Watson (1979) I, no. 573; Gneuss (1985) 132 [no. R.10]; A.G. Watson (1987a) 36, 57; Lapidge (1991a) 73–4; Dumville (1992a) 69, 79, 88–91, 94; Lapidge (1992a) 114 n. 71 [repr. Lapidge (1993a) 402 n. 71]; Dumville (1993g) 63–5 and nn. 273–81; Lapidge (1996a) 72 and n. 28; Lapidge (1998) 39 n. 12; P. Wormald (1999) 448 n. 118; Treharne (2003) 161; Hartzell (2006) no. 147; O'Brien O'Keeffe (2006) 262 n. 67, 268; Clayton (2008) 100–4; Wieland (2009) 124; Scragg (2012a) no. 601

ED: Liebermann (1903–16) I.412–13 [OE forms of exorcism]; Lapidge (1991a) 187-92 [litanies]; Cross—Brown (1993c) 85–91 [sermons of Abbo coll. as V]; Clayton (2008) 148–9 [*Promissio regis* coll. as J, from now lost part of MS copied in MS Junius 60]

ST: Liebermann (1903–16) I.214 n. 1; Hohler (1975) 224 n. 56, 226 n. 74; Korhammer (1976) 240; Drage (1978); Cowdrey (1981) 56; Conner (1993) 6; R. Gameson (1996b) 145; Thacker (1996) 252 n.; Prescott (1998) 271, 277; Biggs et al. (2001) 21–2 [Cross, A. Brown]; N. Orchard (2002) I.140–1; C.A. Jones (2005a) 114; N. Orchard (2005) ciii n. 180, cxxix *et passim*

398. London, British Library, Cotton Vitellius A. xii, fols. 4–77

s. xi ex., Salisbury

Contents: Egbert, *Dialogus ecclesiasticae institutionis*; Abbo of Fleury, *De differentia circuli et sphaerae* (table: 'De cursu septem planetarum', and pt ii); Hrabanus Maurus, *De computo*; eight short poems, mainly computistical [SK 7632, 6489, 12559, 3727, 12524, 1716, 8931, 12491] and nine short prose texts (as in no. **258**): on the Seven Wonders of the World; on the two Poles of the World; on Egyptian days (*Dies Aegyptiaci*); on the *libri catholici* to be read in the course of the year; on the pronunciation of the letters; Greek and Hebrew alphabets, with interpretations; list of numbers with their corresponding Greek names; on concurrents; on the Six Ages of Man; Isidore, *De natura rerum* [*CPL* 1188] with Isidorian world diagram; Abbo of Fleury, *De duplici signorum ortu uel occasu*; three runic alphabets; liturgical calendar; a second calendar (fols. 72v–77v, added s. xi², continental?)

MS: Planta (1802) 379–80; N.R. Ker (1949–50) 153–6 [repr. N.R. Ker (1985) 177–8 and n.]; R. Derolez (1954) 222–37; N.R. Ker (1976b) 24, 25, 30, 38–9 [repr. N.R. Ker (1985) 144, 145, 150, 159–60]; Stevens (1979) 194; A.G. Watson (1987a) 60; Dumville (1992a) 64–5; Webber (1992) 12, 14, 23, 41, 63, 69, 74, 144–5, 159; R. Gameson (1999a) nos. 419 and 420; Chardonnens (2007b) 524–5, 552; Rushforth (2008a) 53–4

ED: Haddan—Stubbs (1869–71) III.403–13 [Egbert, *Dialogus*, repr. from the edition of Sir James Ware (1664), itself based solely on this MS]; F. Wormald (1934) 85–97 [liturgical calendar (no. 7)]; R. Derolez (1954) 222–37 [runic alphabets]; Stevens (1979) [Hrabanus *De computo* coll. as V]; R.B. Thomson (1985) 120–33 [Abbo, *De differentia circuli et sphaerae*, coll. as G]; Rushforth (2008a) no. 26 [first liturgical calendar]

ST: Van de Vyver (1935) 140–1 [Abbo of Fleury]; Boutemy (1937) [poems]; McNeill—Gamer (1938) 239 [*Dialogus Egberti*]; N.R. Ker (1962–92) IV.813–14 [relationship to no. **258**]; Kotzor (1981)

I.302*–311* [liturgical calendar]; Munk Olsen (1982—) I.336 [SK 12524]; Carley (1986) 112, 117; Conner (1993) 83; Baker—Lapidge (1995) xliv [Abbo of Fleury]; Biggs et al. (2001) 8–9 [Abbo of Fleury; Lendinara]; Borst (2001) I.290–1 [liturgical calendar]; Liuzza (2001) 213, 221 [prognostics]; R. Sharpe (2001) 2–3 [Abbo of Fleury]; N. Orchard (2002) I.54 and n. 102, 176 [liturgical calendar]; Chardonnens (2007a) 338 [prognostics]; Teresi (2007c) 343, 351, 365 [world map]

399. London, British Library, Cotton Vitellius A. xv, fols. 94–209 (the 'Beowulf Manuscript' or 'Nowell Codex')

s. x/xi

Contents: Homily on St Christopher*; 'Marvels of the East' (*Mirabilia orientis*)*; *Letter of Alexander to Aristotle**; *Beowulf***; *Judith*** (incomplete)

MS: Kölbing (1876); Davidson (1890); Förster (1919); Rypins (1921); Hulbert (1928); Hoops (1928–9); Prokosch (1929); Klaeber (1950) xcv–cii; Dobbie (1953) ix–xx; K. Sisam (1953a) 63 n. 1, 65–96; N.R. Ker (1957) no. 216; Taylor—Salus (1968); Korhammer (1976) 165; Scragg (1979) 264; Boyle (1981); Kiernan (1981) 279–89; Fulk (1982); Backhouse et al. (1984b) no. 155 [Backhouse]; Clement (1984b); Kiernan (1984); Conner (1985); Dumville (1988); Gerritsen (1988); P.L. Heyworth (1989) 15, 239; Gerritsen (1991a); Gerritsen (1991b); Kiernan (1991); Robinson—Stanley (1991) 25; Webster—Backhouse (1991) 20–1 [no. 4]; Conner (1994) 315; Kiernan (1994b); Tite (1994) 13–14; Scragg (1996) 222 [St Christopher]; Prescott (1997) 402–3 nn. 93–8; Webster—Brown (1997) 242 [no. 127]; Herren (1998) 102; Lapidge et al. (1999) 62–3 [Scragg]; Lapidge (2000a) 7–9; Pulsiano (2002b) 167; Simek (2002) 53–4; W. Schipper (2003) 161; Meaney (2004) 496; Biggs (2007a) 30 [Biggs, Morey]; Biggs (2007b) 52; C. Bishop (2007b) 78–80, 86–7; Tristram (2007) 203 n. 59; Fulk et al. (2008) xxv–xxxv; A. Orchard (2008) 12–56; Treharne (2009b) 104–6; R. Gameson (2012b) 98; Scragg (2012a) nos. 602–3

DEC: E. Temple (1976) no. 52 [*Wonders of the East*]; Ohlgren (1986) 157; R. Gameson (1995b) 11, 36, 160, 193 n. 2, 224; Wieland (1998) 3; Karkov (2009) 242–3 [cited erroneously as Cotton Vespasian A. xv]; R. Gameson (2012c) 287 and n. 134

FACS [note that we do not list the almost innumerable facsimiles of single folios of the *Beowulf* manuscript]: Malone (1963) [facsimile of entire MS]; Zupitza (1882/1959) [complete facsimile of *Beowulf*]; Malone (1951) [Thorkelin transcripts]; Robinson–Stanley (1991) pls. 20.1–12 [*Judith*]; Kiernan (1999) [digitally enhanced electronic facsimile of entire MS]

ED: [editions of *Beowulf* published before 1972 are listed Greenfield–Robinson (1980) nos. 1632–56; only the most important recent editions (1950–2008) are listed here; for others, see the bibliographies listed under ST, below]; Rypins (1924) [base MS for *Life of St Christopher*, *Wonders of the East*, *Letter of Alexander*]; Klaeber (1950) [base MS for *Beowulf*]; Dobbie (1953) [base MS for *Beowulf*; *Judith*]; A. Orchard (1995) 183–203 [*Wonders of the East* coll. as V], 224–53 [base MS for *Letter of Alexander*]; Griffith (1997) [*Judith*]; Pulsiano (2002b) 171–9 [base MS for *Life of St Christopher*]; Fulk et al. (2008) [*Beowulf*]; Fulk (2010) [base MS for all contents]

LANG: C. Bishop (2007b) 84–5

ST: Wülker (1885) 245–307 [bibliography]; Rypins (1919–20); A.H. Smith (1938); Malone (1941–2); Malone (1949a); Malone (1949b); K. Sisam (1953a) 61–4, 65–96; Nist (1959); Leake (1962) [ME glosses]; Stevick (1968); Fry (1969) [bibliography to 1967]; A.F. Cameron (1974) 221, 225; Greenfield–Robinson (1980) 19–20, 125–97 [bibliography]; Short (1980) [selective bibliography for 1705–1949, exhaustive bibliography for 1950–78]; B. Kelly (1982) and (1983) [review of editions of *Beowulf*]; Kiernan (1986); Gerritsen (1989b); Gunderson (1980); Lucas (1990); Hollis–Wright (1992) 117–21; Hasenfratz (1993) [bibliography]; Kiernan (1994a) 39, 42, 48–51; Biggs (1996) 73; Kiernan (1998a); Lapidge (2000a); McFadden (2001) [*Letter of Alexander*]; Biggs (2007b) [fol. 179]; C. Bishop (2007b) 85–90; J.R. Hall (2012); Scragg (2012b) 556–7

400. London, British Library, Cotton Vitellius A. xviii

s. xi^2, prov. SW England (Wells?)

Contents: computus tables; liturgical calendar; prayers; sacramentary; benedictional; penitential texts; selection of pontifical services

MS: A.G. Watson (1979) I, no. 575; Dumville (1992a) 25, 53–5, 57 n. 108, 61, 65, 67, 90–1 and n. 151, 110; Pfaff et al. (1995) 19–21, 97; Keynes (1997b) 251–3; R. Gameson (1999a) no. 421; N. Orchard (2002) I.94–5 *et passim*; Rushforth (2002) 112; Chardonnens (2007b) 525, 552; Rushforth (2008a) 50–1; Pfaff (2009) 124–6; Pfaff (2012) 457 and n. 26

FACS: A.G. Watson (1979) II, pl. 48 [fol. 100r]

ED: Warren (1883) 303–7 [mass–sets for English saints]; F. Wormald (1934) 99–111 [liturgical calendar (no. 8)]; Gerchow (1988) 231–2, 332 [obits in calendar]; Corrêa (1993) 252 [mass-sets for SS. Patrick, Brigit and Aidan]; Clayton—Magennis (1994) 79 [mass for St Margaret]; Rushforth (2008a) no. 25 [liturgical calendar]

ST: Legg (1891–7) 1444–1628 [cross–refs. to mass-texts in Vitellius A. xviii]; Gasquet—Bishop (1908) 61 n., 73 n., 146, 158–64; J.A. Robinson (1927) 166–71; Henel (1934); Hohler (1975) 70–1, 76–7; Stroud (1979) 231–2; Kotzor (1981) I.302*–311*; Prescott (1987) 133 [Winchester source for benedictional]; Lapidge—Winterbottom (1991b) cxxiii–cxxiv; Corrêa (1993) 245–51; Borst (2001) I.292; C.A. Jones (2005a) 114; N. Orchard (2005) cxxxvii, cxlviii

401. London, British Library, Cotton Vitellius A. xix

s. x$^{2/4}$ or x med., prob. Canterbury StA, prov. prob. ibid. s. x/xi

Contents: Bede, *Vita S. Cudbercti* (prose) [*CPL* 1379; *BHL* 2019], *Vita S. Cudbercti* (verse) [*CPL* 1380; *BHL* 2020]; excerpts from Bede, *Historia ecclesiastica* (IV. xxix–xxx); four Latin poems (SK Suppl. 3716a [*De quattuor clauibus sapientiae*]; SK 15347 [from Iuuencus, *Euang.* I.589–603]; SK Suppl. 7239a; and *De sacro baptismate* [inc. 'Fons sacer est fidei'], not in SK or SK Suppl.); five *Alleluia* verses; note on the Ages of Man (s. x^2)

MS: Jaager (1935) 30; Colgrave (1940) 27, 46; Laistner—King (1943) 88; N.R. Ker (1957) no. 217; T.A.M. Bishop (1959–63a) 93; Sims-Williams (1982) 22; Webster—Backhouse (1991) 129–30 [no. 93; Backhouse]; Dumville (1992a) 105; Lapidge (1992b) 106 n. 63 [repr. Lapidge (1993a) 96 n. 63]; Dumville (1994a) 137, 139; Lapidge (1995c) 130–1, 143 n. 39; Bullough (1998a) 120, 122; *ASMMF* X (2003) 7–12 [no. 252; O'Brien O'Keeffe]; Hartzell (2006) no. 148; Barker-Benfield (2008) I.519, 604, II.1381, III.1696, 1810, 1814; Graham (2009) 173–4; Rankin (2012) 489 and n. 29; Scragg (2012a) no. 604; Tinti (2012) 26–9

DEC: E. Temple (1976) no. 19(ii); Ohlgren (1986) no. 98

FACS: E. Temple (1976) ill. 63 [fol. 9r (detail)]; Bell (2001) 46 [fol. 88r]; *ASMMF* X (2003) no. 252; Owen-Crocker (2009) fig. 6.7 [fol. 32r]; Tinti (2012) figs. 1 [fol. 28v (detail)], 2 [fol. 30v], 3 [fol. 32v (detail)]

ED: Jaager (1935) [Bede, metrical *Vita S. Cudbercti*, coll. as V]; Colgrave (1940) [Bede, prose *Vita S. Cudbercti*, coll. as V]; Meritt (1945) 15 [OE glosses to both Bede's Lives of St Cuthbert]; Sheerin (1977) 178–80 [four Latin poems]; Hartzell (2006) no. 148 [Alleluia verses]

ST: Colgrave (1940) 27, 46; F.C. Robinson (1973) 444 n. 4 [syntactical glosses]; Sheerin (1975a); Sheerin (1977); Korhammer (1980) 28 [syntactical glosses]; Rollason (1989) 419; Sims-Williams (1990) 332–7; Lapidge (1995c) 143–4; Sole (1998) 133; Ziolkowski (2007) 47 n. 25

402. London, British Library, Cotton Vitellius C. iii, fols. 11–85

s. xi^1 or xi med., Canterbury CC?

Contents: Enlarged *Herbarius** (Antonius Musa, *De herba uettonica*; pseudo-Apuleius, *Herbarius*; herbs from pseudo-Dioscorides, *Liber medicinae ex herbis femininis* and *Curae herbarum*); *Medicina de quadrupedibus** (*De taxone liber*; treatise on mulberry tree; Sextus Placitus, *Liber medicinae ex animalibus*); medical recipes$^{(*)}$ (s. xi med. — xi/xii)

MS: M.R. James (1903) xxvi, 509; N.R. Ker (1957) no. 219; N.R. Ker (1964) 36; De Vriend (1972) xi–xviii; Backhouse et al. (1984b) no. 162 [D.H. Turner]; De Vriend (1984) xi–xx; *ASMMF* I (1994) 20–5 [no. 253; Doane]; D'Aronco—Cameron (1998) 14–25; Pulsiano (1998b) 109 n. 23; W. Schipper (2003) 157–8; Roberts (2005) 74–5 [no. 15]; Scragg (2012a) nos. 605–11

DEC: E. Temple (1976) no. 63; Grape–Albers (1977); Ohlgren (1986) no. 168; R. Gameson (1991) 68 *et passim*; R. Gameson (1995b) 14, 17, 121, 159–60, 173, 177, 192 n. 1, 212; D'Aronco—Cameron (1998) 26–43; Wieland (1998) 16 n. 19; S. Page (2004) 22; R. Gameson (2012c) 280 and nn. 105–6, 287 and n. 134

FACS: D'Aronco—Cameron (1998) [complete facsimile]; E. Temple (1976) ills. 186–8 [fols. 56v, 11v, 19r]; De Vriend (1984) frontispiece [fol. 74r]; R. Gameson (1991) fig. 3 [fol. 11v]; *ASMMF* I (1994) no. 253; M. Collins (2000) figs. 49–50 [fols. 30r, 11v], pl. XVII [fol. 19r]; Roberts (2005) pl. 15 [fol. 27r]; M.P. Brown (2007a) pl. 111 [fol. 32v]; R. Gameson (2012) pl. 10.12 [fol. 11v]

ED: Cockayne (1864–6) I.374–8 [Latin and OE medical recipes]; De Vriend (1972) [base MS for *Medicina de quadrupedibus*]; De Vriend (1984) [base MS (= V) for all texts]

LANG: Bierbaumer (1975–9) pt. II [1976]; De Vriend (1984) lxviii–lxxiv

ST: De Vriend (1972); Voigts (1976); Voigts (1977); Brownrigg (1978); Voigts (1978); Greenfield—Robinson (1980) 370–2; Hofstetter (1983);

De Vriend (1984); Hollis—Wright (1992) 234, 238, 311–24, 329–40; M.L. Cameron (1993); D'Aronco—Cameron (1998); D'Aronco (1999); M. Collins (2000) 192–6 *et passim*; Van Arsdall (2002); D'Aronco (2007); D'Aronco (2011) 238 and n. 37

402. 5. London, British Library, Cotton Vitellius C. iii, fols. 86–138

s. ix$^{3/4}$, N France, prov. England before 1100?

Contents: Macrobius, *Saturnalia* (bks. I–II only)

MS: L.D. Reynolds (1983) 235 [P.K. Marshall]; *ASMMF* I (1994) 20–5 [no. 253; Doane]; Bischoff (1998–) II, no. 2428; R. Gameson (2002d) 185–6

FACS: *ASMMF* I (1994) no. 253

ST: Lapidge (2006) 170, 320

403. London, British Library, Cotton Vitellius C. v

s. x/xi, and additions s. xi^1, SW England, (prov. Tavistock?)

Contents: Ælfric, *Catholic Homilies* (First Series, considerably expanded)*

MS: W.M. Temple (1952); K. Sisam (1953a) 184; N.R. Ker (1957) no. 220; N.R. Ker (1964) 188; Pope (1967–8) I.26–32; Collins—Clemoes (1974) 319–20; N.R. Ker (1976a) 123; Godden (1979) lxv–lxvi; Scragg (1979) 261; Dumville (1988) 58; Conner (1993) 36; Clemoes (1997) 18–21; Wilcox (2002) 289–90, 299; Butcher (2003) 13; Acker (2004) 128; *ASMMF* XVII (2008) 21–36 [no. 254; Wilcox]; R. Gameson (2012a) 49 and n. 153, 67 n. 232, 72 n. 246; Scragg (2012a) nos. 612–16

FACS: Pope (1967–8) I, frontispiece [fol. 17v], facing p. 230 [fol. 236v]; Butcher (2003) 14 [fol. 175r]; *ASMMF* XVII (2008) no. 254

ED [the order of the following items is that of the manuscript, listed according to the numbering of individual articles in N.R. Ker (1957) pp. 286–90; only the most recent editions are cited]:

art. 1: Pope (1967–8) I.463–72 [base MS (= H) for Ælfric, Suppl. Hom. XIa (*De sancta trinitate*)]

art. 2: Clemoes (1997) 178–89 [Ælfric, CH I, Hom. I (*De initio creaturae*), coll. as H]

art. 3: Clemoes (1997) 190–7 [Ælfric, CH I, Hom. II (Christmas), coll. as H] art. 4: Pope (1967–8) I.196–216 [base MS (= H) for Ælfric, Suppl. Hom. I (Christmas)]

art. 5: Clemoes (1997) 198–205 [Ælfric, CH I, Hom. III (St Stephen), coll. as H]

art. 6: Clemoes (1997) 206–16 [Ælfric, CH I, Hom. IV (Assumption of St John the Evangelist), coll. as H]

art. 7: as Crawford (1922) 61–8 [part of Ælfric, Letter to Sigeweard on the Old and New Testament, lines 1017–1153, not collated]

art. 8: Clemoes (1997) 217–23 [Ælfric, CH I, Hom. V (Holy Innocents), coll. as H]

art. 9: Clemoes (1997) 224–31 [Ælfric, CH I, Hom. VI (Circumcision of the Lord), coll. as H]

art. 10: Clemoes (1997) 232–40 [Ælfric, CH I, Hom. VII (Epiphany), coll. as H]

art. 11: Clemoes (1997) 241–8 [Ælfric, CH I, Hom. VIII (Third Sunday after Epiphany), coll. as H]

art. 12: Clemoes (1997) 249–57 [Ælfric, CH I, Hom. IX (Purification of B.V.M.), coll. as H]

art. 13: Clemoes (1997) 258–65 [Ælfric, CH I, Hom. X (Quinquagesima Sunday), coll. as H]

art. 14: Clemoes (1997) 266–74 [Ælfric, CH I, Hom. XI (First Sunday in Lent), coll. as H]

art. 15: Godden (1979) 66–71 [Ælfric, CH II, Hom. VIII (Second Sunday in Lent), coll. as H]

art. 16: Pope (1967–8) I.264–80 [Ælfric, Suppl. Hom. IV (Third Sunday in Lent), coll. as H]

art. 17: Clemoes (1997) 275–80 [Ælfric, CH I, Hom. XII (Sunday in Mid–Lent), coll. as H]

art. 18: Clemoes (1997) 281–9 [Ælfric, CH I, Hom. XIII (Annunciation of B.V.M.), coll. as H]

art. 19: Clemoes (1997) 290–8 [Ælfric, CH I, Hom. XIV (Palm Sunday), coll. as H]

art. 20: Clemoes (1997) 299–306 [Ælfric, CH I, Hom. XV (Easter Sunday), coll. as H]

art. 21: Clemoes (1997) 307–12 [Ælfric, CH I, Hom. XVI (First Sunday after Easter), coll. as H]

art. 22: Clemoes (1997) 313–16 [Ælfric, CH I, Hom. XVII (Second Sunday after Easter), coll. as H]

art. 23: Clemoes (1997) 317–24 [Ælfric, CH I, Hom. XVIII (*In Letania maiore*), coll. as H] art. 24: Clemoes (1997) 325–34 [Ælfric, CH I, Hom. XIX (*Feria .III. De dominica oratione*), coll. as H]

art. 25: Clemoes (1997) 335–44 [Ælfric, CH I, Hom. XX (*Feria .IIII. De fide catholica*), coll. as H]

art. 26: Clemoes (1997) 345–53 [Ælfric, CH I, Hom. XXI (Ascension Day), coll. as H]

art. 27: Clemoes (1997) 354–64 [Ælfric, CH I, Hom. XXII (Pentecost), coll. as H]

art. 28: Clemoes (1997) 365–70 [Ælfric, CH I, Hom. XXIII (Second Sunday after Pentecost), coll. as H]

art. 29: Clemoes (1997) 371–8 [Ælfric, CH I, Hom. XXIV (Third Sunday after Pentecost), coll. as H]

art. 30: Godden (1979) 213–20 [Ælfric, CH II, Hom. XXIII (Third Sunday after Pentecost), coll. as H]

art. 31: Pope (1967–8) II.497–507 [Ælfric, Suppl. Hom. XIII (Fifth Sunday after Pentecost), coll. as H]

art. 32: Pope (1967–8) II.515–25 [Ælfric, Suppl. Hom. XIV (Sixth Sunday after Pentecost), coll. as H]

art. 33: Pope (1967–8) II.531–41 [Ælfric, Suppl. Hom. XV (Seventh Sunday after Pentecost), coll. as H]

art. 34: Godden (1979) 230–4 [Ælfric, CH II, Hom. XXV (Eighth Sunday after Pentecost), coll. as H]

art. 35: Godden (1979) 235–40 [Ælfric, CH II, Hom. XXVI (Ninth Sunday after Pentecost), coll. as H]

art. 36: Pope (1967–8) II.547–59 [Ælfric, Suppl. Hom. XVI (Tenth Sunday after Pentecost), coll. as H]

art. 37: Clemoes (1997) 379–87 [Ælfric, CH I, Hom. XXV (St John the Baptist), coll. as H]

arts. 38–9: Clemoes (1997) 388–99 [Ælfric, CH I, Hom. XXVI (SS. Peter and Paul), coll. as H]

arts. 40–1: Clemoes (1997) 400–9 [Ælfric, CH I, Hom. XXVII (St Paul), coll. as H]

art. 42: Clemoes (1997) 410–17 [Ælfric, CH I, Hom. XXVIII (Eleventh Sunday after Pentecost), coll. as H]

art. 43: Clemoes (1997) 418–28 [Ælfric, CH I, Hom. XXIX (St Laurence), coll. as H]

art. 44: Pope (1967–8) II.762–9 [Ælfric, Suppl. Hom. XXVI (Theodosius and Ambrose), coll. as H]

art. 45: Pope (1967–8) II.567–80 [base MS (= H) for Ælfric, Suppl. Hom. XVII (Thirteenth Sunday after Pentecost)]; Butcher (2003) 15–21 [base MS for Ælfric, Hom. for Thirteenth Sunday after Pentecost] art. 46: Pope (1967–8) II.775–9 [base MS (= H) for Ælfric, Suppl. Hom. XXVII (Visions of Departing Souls)]

art. 47: Clemoes (1997) 429–38 [Ælfric, CH I, Hom. XXX (Assumption of B.V.M.), coll. as H]

art. 48: Godden (1979) 255–9 [Ælfric, CH II, Hom. XXIX (Assumption of B.V.M.), coll. as H]

art. 49: Assmann (1889/1964) 13–23 [base MS (= V) for Ælfric, Letter to Sigefyrth]

art. 50: Clemoes (1997) 439–50 [Ælfric, CH I, Hom. XXXI (St Bartholomew), coll. as H]

art. 51: Clemoes (1997) 451–8 [Ælfric, CH I, Hom. XXXII (Decollation of St John the Baptist), coll. as H]

art. 52: Clemoes (1997) 459–64 [Ælfric, CH I, Hom. XXXIII (Seventeenth Sunday after Pentecost), coll. as H]

arts. 53–4: Clemoes (1997) 465–75 [Ælfric, CH I, Hom. XXXIV (Dedication of the Church of St Michael), coll. as H]

art. 55: Clemoes (1997) 476–85 [Ælfric, CH I, Hom. XXXV (Twenty–first Sunday after Pentecost), coll. as H]

arts. 56–7: Clemoes (1997) 486–96 [Ælfric, CH I, Hom. XXXVI (All Saints), coll. as H]

art. 58: Clemoes (1997) 497–506 [Ælfric, CH I, Hom. XXXVII (St Clement), coll. as H]

arts. 59–60: Clemoes (1997) 507–19 [Ælfric, CH I, Hom. XXXVIII (St Andrew), coll. as H]

art. 61: Clemoes (1997) 520–3 [Ælfric, CH I, Hom. XXXIX (First Sunday in Advent), coll. as H]

art. 62: Clemoes (1997) 524–30 [Ælfric, CH I, Hom. XL (Second Sunday in Advent), coll. as H]

art. 63: Pope (1967–8) I.230–42 [base MS (= H) for Ælfric, Suppl. Hom. II (Friday in the First Week of Lent)]

art. 64: Pope (1967–8) I.248–56 [base MS (= H) for Ælfric, Suppl. Hom. III (Friday in the Second Week of Lent)]

art. 65: Pope (1967–8) I.288–300 [Ælfric, Suppl. Hom. V (Friday in the Third Week of Lent), coll. as H]

art. 66: Pope (1967–8) I.311–29 [Ælfric, Suppl. Hom. VI (Friday in the Fourth Week of Lent), coll. as H]

LANG: W.M. Temple (1952); K. Sisam (1953a) 184; Harlow (1959); Clemoes (1994a) 351; Scragg (1994a) 333

ST: W.M. Temple (1952); Clemoes (1959b); A.F. Cameron (1974) 224; Prescott (1998) 268; Scragg (1998) 77 [comparison with no. **50**];

S. Irvine (2000) 46; Butcher (2003); Kleist (2007b) 451 *et passim*; Kleist (2007c) 496; Teresi (2007a) 294 n. 19, 302 n. 42

404. London, British Library, Cotton Vitellius C. viii, fols. 22-5

s. xi¹, WiNM?

Contents: Instruction for prayer⁺*; *Dies Aegyptiaci**; Ælfric, *De temporibus anni** (f); computus notes*

MS: Planta (1802) 424; N.R. Ker (1957) no. 221; Godden (1983); Liuzza (2001) 185, 221–2; *ASMMF* XII (2004) 84–95 [no. 255; Wright—Hollis]; Chardonnens (2007b) 525, 552; M. Blake (2009) 19; Scragg (2012a) nos. 617–18

FACS: *ASMMF* XII (2004) no. 255

ED: Förster (1929) 271–7 [OE *Dies Aegyptiaci*]; N.R. Ker (1957) 292 [Instruction for prayer]; Chardonnens (2007b) 342 [OE *Dies Aegyptiaci*]; M. Blake (2009) 82–96 [part of Ælfric, *De temporibus anni*, coll. as J]

ST: Henel (1934) 40–2, 51–4 [computus notes; this MS not collated]; Hollis—Wright (1992) 260

London, British Library, Cotton Vitellius C. viii, fols. 85–90: see no. **173**

405. London, British Library, Cotton Vitellius C. xii, fols. 114-56

s. xi ex., or s. xii in.? Canterbury StA

Contents: Usuard of Saint-Germain-des-Prés, *Martyrologium*, with obits; confraternity notes

MS: M.R. James (1903) 502, 531; N.R. Ker (1960) 30; N.R. Ker (1964) 43; A.G. Watson (1979) I, no. 577; R. Gameson (1999a) no. 422; Barker-Benfield (2008) I.liv, lvii, lviii, 91 n. c, 407, 408, 460, 461–2, 463, 478, II.940–1, 1397, 1445, 1561, III.1619–22, 1743, 1793, 1795, 1837, 1856–8, 1861

DEC: F. Wormald (1944) 10 [repr. F. Wormald (1984) 161]; F. Wormald (1945) 128 [repr. F. Wormald (1984) 177 and n. 70]; F. Wormald (1952) 55, 61; Boase (1953) 39–40, 87; Dodwell (1954) 27, 62, 123; Rickert (1954) 66; C.M. Kauffmann (1975) no. 18; R. Gameson (1995a) 101–2, 114 n., 144

FACS: F. Wormald (1952) pl. 37 [fol. 139r (detail)]; Boase (1953) pl. 30 (b) [fol. 139r (detail)]; Dodwell (1954) pls. 16 (b) [fol. 121r], 35 (a) [fol. 127r], 35 (b) [fol. 134r (detail)]; Rickert (1954) pl. 46 (c) [fol. 139r];

N.R. Ker (1960) pl. 10 (a) [fol. 134r]; C.M. Kauffmann (1975) pl. 33 [fol. 139r]; A.G. Watson (1979) II, pl. 58 [fol. 120r]; D.H. Turner et al. (1980) pl. 27 [fol. 127r]; R. Gameson (1995a) pl. 8 (a) [fol. 134r (detail)]

ST: Searle (1902); Quentin (1908) 676; D.H. Turner et al. (1980) 105; Heslop (1995) 67 n.; Keynes (1996a) 60 and n. 92 [obits]

406. London, British Library, Cotton Vitellius D. xvii, fols. 4–92

s. xi med.

Contents: Ælfric, originally forty-five items from *Catholic Homilies** and Lives of Saints* (many now lost or fragmentary); anonymous *Passio S. Pantaleonis**

MS: T.S. Smith (1696) 94; Wanley (1705) 206; Pope (1931); N.R. Ker (1957) no. 222; Godden (1979) lviii–lix; Scragg (1979) 264; Scragg (1996) 222; Clemoes (1997) 61–3; Pulsiano (2002a) 63–4; Corona (2006) 132–3; Upchurch (2007) xii, 53; *ASMMF* XIX (2010) 71–90 [no. 256; Doane]; R. Gameson (2012a) 67 n. 232; Scragg (2012a) nos. 619–21a

FACS: *ASMMF* XIX (2010) no. 256

ED [the order of the following items is that of the manuscript, listed according to the numbering of individual articles in N.R. Ker (1957) 293–7; only the most recent editions are cited]:

art. 1: Clemoes (1997) 391–9 [Ælfric, CH I, Hom. XXVI (SS. Peter and Paul), coll as f^k]

art. 2: Godden (1979) 241–7 [Ælfric, CH II, Hom. XXVII (St James), coll. as f^k]

art. 3: lost

arts. 4–5: Godden (1979) 169–73 [Ælfric, CH II, Hom. XVII (SS. Philip and James), coll. as f^k]

art. 6: Clemoes (1997) 439–50 [Ælfric, CH I, Hom. XXXI (St Bartholomew), coll. as f^k]

art. 7: Godden (1979) 280–7 [Ælfric, CH II, Hom. XXXIII (SS. Simon and Jude), coll. as f^k]

art. 8: Skeat (1881–1900) I.320–6 [Ælfric, *Lives of Saints*, no. XV (St Mark), lines 1–103, coll. as V]

art. 9: Skeat (1881–1900) I.326–36 [Ælfric, *Lives of Saints*, no. XV (the Four Evangelists), lines 104–226, coll. as V]

art. 10: Godden (1979) 12–18 [Ælfric, CH II, Hom. II (St Stephen), coll. as f^k]

art. 11: Clemoes (1997) 198–205 [Ælfric, CH I, Hom. III (St Stephen), coll. as f^k]

art. 12: Clemoes (1997) 217–23 [Ælfric, CH I, Hom. V (Holy Innocents), coll. as f^k]

art. 13: Skeat (1881–1900) I.116–46 [Ælfric, *Lives of Saints*, no. V (St Sebastian), coll. as V]

art. 14: Pulsiano (2002a) 69–103 [base MS for anonymous Passio of St Pantaleon]

art. 15: Godden (1979) 272–9 [Ælfric, CH II, Hom. XXXII (St Matthew), coll. as f^k]

art. 16: Godden (1979) 92–109 [Ælfric, CH II, Hom. XI (St Benedict), coll. as f^k]

art. 17: Godden (1979) 288–98 [Ælfric, CH II, Hom. XXXIV (St Martin), coll. as f^k]

art. 18: Godden (1979) 72–80 [Ælfric, CH II, Hom. IX (St Gregory), coll. as f^k]

art. 19: Clemoes (1997) 465–75 [Ælfric, CH I, Hom. XXXIV (Dedication of the Church of St Michael), coll. as f^k]

art. 20: Godden (1979) 174–6 [Ælfric, CH II, Hom. XVIII, lines 1–61 (Discovery of the Holy Cross), coll. as f^k]

art. 21: Godden (1979) 176–9 [Ælfric, CH II, Hom. XVIII, lines 62–156 (SS. Alexander, Eventius and Theodolus), coll. as f^k]

art. 22: Clemoes (1997) 507–19 [Ælfric, CH I, Hom. XXXVIII (St Andrew), coll. as f^k]

art. 23: Clemoes (1997) 418–28 [Ælfric, CH I, Hom. XXIX (St Laurence), coll. as f^k]

art. 24: Clemoes (1997) 496–506 [Ælfric, CH I, Hom. XXXVII (St Clement), coll. as f^k]

art. 25: Skeat (1881–1900) II.356–76 [Ælfric, *Lives of Saints*, no. XXXIV (St Caecilia), coll. as V]

art. 26: Skeat (1881–1900) I.472–86 [Ælfric, *Lives of Saints*, no. XXII (St Apollinaris), coll. as V]

art. 27: lost

art. 28: lost

art. 29: Skeat (1881–1900) II.190–218 [anonymous 'Life of St Eustace' (Skeat, no. XXX) coll. as V]

art. 30: lost

art. 31: Skeat (1881–1900) II.124–42 [Ælfric, *Lives of Saints*, no. XXVI (St Oswald, king and martyr), coll. as V]; Needham (1976) 27–42 [Ælfric, 'Life of St Oswald, king and martyr', coll. as V]

art. 32: lost

art. 33: lost

art. 34: lost

art. 35: Clemoes (1997) 429–38 [Ælfric, CH I, Hom. XXX (Assumption of B.V.M.), coll. as f^k]

art. 36: lost

art. 37: Skeat (1881–1900) II.144–58 [Ælfric, *Lives of Saints*, no. XXVII (Exaltation of the Holy Cross), coll. as V]

art. 38: Assmann (1889/1964) 49–64 [part of Ælfric, Hom. for the Common of a Confessor, mentioned but not collated]

art. 39: Godden (1979) 304–9 [Ælfric, CH II, Hom. XXXVI (Feast for Several Apostles), coll. as f^k]

art. 40: Godden (1979) 318–26 [Ælfric, CH II, Hom. XXXVIII (Feast for a Confessor), coll. as f^k]

art. 41: Godden (1979) 335–45 [Ælfric, CH II, Hom. XL (The Dedication of a Church), coll. as f^k]

art. 42: Skeat (1881–1900) II.314–34 [Ælfric, *Lives of Saints*, no. XXXII (St Edmund, king and martyr), coll. as V]; Needham (1976) 43–59 [Ælfric, 'Life of St Edmund, king and martyr' coll. as V]

art. 43: Skeat (1881–1900) I.50–90 [Ælfric, *Lives of Saints*, no. III (St Basil), coll. as V]; Corona (2006) 152–88 [Ælfric, 'Life of St Basil', coll. as V]

art. 44: Clemoes (1997) 400–9 [Ælfric, CH I, Hom. XXVII (St Paul), coll. as f^k]

art. 45: Skeat (1881–1900) II.66–124 [Ælfric, *Lives of Saints*, no. XXV (Maccabees), coll. as V]

arts. 46–54: all lost

ST: Collins—Clemoes (1974) 322; Söderlind (1995); J. Hill (1996) 243; Prescott (1997) 406, 437; Prescott (1998) 268; Proud (2000) 121, 126, 128; Kleist (2007b) 475–6, 487; Kleist (2007c) 501–2

406. 5. London, British Library, Cotton Vitellius E. xii, fols. 116–60

s. xi^1, Germany, prob. Cologne, prov. York s. xi^2 [fols. 116–52]; s. xi^2 (after 1068), Exeter [fols. 153–60]; prov. whole MS Exeter

Contents: pontifical (*Pontificale Romano-Germanicum*) [fols. 116–52]; additions to the pontifical: benedictions; hymn [SK 5629]; parts of Office of the Dead with sermon; *Laudes regiae* [fols. 153–60]

MS: Brückmann (1973) 437–8; Lapidge (1981–5) 20–3; Lapidge (1983) [repr. Lapidge (1993a) 453–67]; Rankin (1984) 112; Dumville (1992a)

69, 73–4, 90–1, 94 n. 172; Nelson—Pfaff (1995) 89, 96; R. Gameson (1996b) 146, 149; R. Gameson (1999a) no. 423; Hartzell (2006) no. 149; Wieland (2009) 124; R. Gameson (2012d) 363 and n. 76

FACS: Lapidge (1983) figs. 1 [fol. 117v], 2 [fol. 154r] [repr. Lapidge (1993a) figs. VI–VII]

ED: *AH* LI.87 [base MS for processional hymn: SK 5629]; Cowdrey (1981) 70 [amended Lapidge (1983) 15; repr. Lapidge (1993a) 457] [*Laudes regiae*]

ST: Kantorowicz (1946) 171 and n. 62; C.A. Jones (2005a) 114; R. McKitterick (2012) 330 and n. 109

407. London, British Library, Cotton Vitellius E. xviii

s. xi med. or xi$^{3/4}$, Winchester NM, (prov. Winchester OM)

Contents: liturgical calendar; computus material (*) ('Winchester Computus', fragmentary); prognostics* (including *lunaria*); charms*; two veterinary recipes*; prayers; explanations of cryptogrammatic writing^{+*}; Psalterium Gallicanum° with 'argumenta'; Ps. CLI; canticles° (incomplete)

MS: Gasquet—Bishop (1908) 38–9, 41–2, 48–50 *et passim*; Mearns (1914) 96; Wildhagen (1920); N.R. Ker (1957) no. 224; N.R. Ker (1964) 103, 200; T.A.M. Bishop (1971) no. 26; F.C. Robinson (1973) 455 n. 40; Rella (1980) no. 57; Morgan (1981) 431; Dumville (1992a) 22, 25, 50, 52, 57, 110, 125, 129; Hollis—Wright (1992) 234, 238; Bullough (1998a) 221 n. 54; Gneuss (1998) 273, 276; P. Wormald (1999) 186–7 nn. 100–1; *ASMMF* II (1994) 50–6 [no. 258; Pulsiano]; Dodwell (2000) 110 n. 38; Liuzza (2001) 205 n. 106, 222–3; Pulsiano (2001a) xxiii; Biggs (2007a) 16; Chardonnens (2007b) 37–8, 525–8, 552; Rushforth (2008a) 48–9; Liuzza (2011) 14–15; Scragg (2012a) nos. 622–5

DEC: R. Gameson (1991) 81 *et passim*; R. Gameson (1995b) 219 nn. 158 and 159, 220 n. 164; R. Gameson (2012c) 269 and n. 57

FACS: Rosier (1962) pls. I–II [fols. 36v, 128v]; R. Gameson (1991) fig. 18 [fol. 18r]; *ASMMF* II (1994) no. 258; Pulsiano (1998b) pls. 11–12 [fol. 16r-v]; Owen-Crocker (2009) fig. 5.1 [fol. 18r]

ED: Förster (1905) 392–3 [riddle]; Wildhagen (1921) 77–94 [liturgical calendar]; Förster (1929) 262–4 [base MS for *De diebus malis* (art. d)], 266–9 [base MS for entries on blood–letting days (arts. g, i)]; F. Wormald (1934) 156–67 [liturgical calendar (no. 12)]; Storms (1948)

287, 309–11 [charms]; Rosier (1962) [base MS for psalter and canticles]; Gerchow (1988) 231–2, 332 [obits in calendar]; Pulsiano (1991b) [psalter introductions coll. as V]; Pulsiano (1991c) [base MS (= G) for various psalms and gloss]; Pulsiano (1998b); Pulsiano (2001a) [Pss. I–L (Latin and OE gloss) coll. as G]; Liuzza (2005) 44 [base MS for Sphere of Pythagoras]; Chardonnens (2007b) *passim* [prognostics; see 526–8]; Rushforth (2008a) no. 23 [liturgical calendar]

LANG: Bierbaumer (1977a); Hofstetter (1987) 79–81

ST: Lindelöf (1904); Heinzel (1926); K. Sisam (1953a) 55–6, 127; Sisam— Sisam (1959) 48, 58–72; E. Temple (1976) 64, 117; Kotzor (1981) I.302*–311*; Clayton (1984) 225–6 [Marian feasts]; Hollis—Wright (1992) 238, 260; Pulsiano (1993); Pulsiano (1994); Baker—Lapidge (1995) xlviii–lii ['Winchester Computus']; Pfaff (1995a) 64 [Pulsiano]; Corrêa (1996) 292 n. 25, 293 n. 31, 294 n. 39; Keynes (1996a) 67–8, 115 n. 45; Prescott (1998) 268; Pulsiano (1998b); Pulsiano (1998c); Borst (2001) I.289–90; R. Gameson (2001) 47 [no. 35] *et passim*; P.P. O'Neill (2001) 28–30; Keynes (2004) 155–6; Chardonnens (2010) 246–50; Liuzza (2011) 1–77 [prognostics]

408. London, British Library, Egerton 267, fol. 37

s. x ex., prob. Abingdon

Contents: Boethius, *De consolatione Philosophiae* [*CPL* 878] (f) [I, pr. iv], with gloss

MS: T.A.M. Bishop (1971) xii n. 2, 13 [no. 15]; Bolton (1977a) 58; Troncarelli (1987) no. 77; Gibson et al. (1995–2001) I.131 [no. 107]; Wittig (2007) 189; Wieland (2009) 149

ST: Lapidge (2006) 293; Godden (2011) 92

409. London, British Library, Egerton 874

s. ix$^{3/4}$, NE France; additions: s. xi^2; England, (prov. all Canterbury StA).

Contents: Caesarius of Arles, *Expositio in Apocalypsin* [*CPL* 1016]; additions: two Easter hymns [SK 2153, 16087], part of rhymed Office of St Augustine of Canterbury, chant for Gregory the Great, prayers

MS: *Cat. Add. B.M. 1836-40* (1843) 21; Bonner (1957–9); N.R. Ker (1964) 44; Römer (1972b) 170; Bischoff (1998—) II, no. 2436; Hartzell (2006) no. 150; Lapidge (2006) 170, 294; R. Gameson (2012d) 346 n. 9, 350 n. 22

ST: Gneuss (1968) 78

410. London, British Library, Egerton 1046

s. viii, Northumbria

Contents: Old Testament (part): Prouerbia Salomonis (incomplete),
Ecclesiastes, Canticum canticorum, Sapientia, Ecclesiasticus
(incomplete)

MS: *Cat. Add. B.M. 1841–5* (1850) 103; *CLA* II (1935) nos. 194a, 194b;
Quentin et al. (1926–94) XI, p. ix; Marsden (1995) 262–71; Dumville
(1999) 116 n. 9; M.P. Brown (2003a) 187, 258; Wieland (2009) 116; M.P.
Brown (2012) 151, 165 n. 220; Marsden (2012) 420 and n. 68

FACS: Thompson—Warner (1881–4) II, pl. 26 [fol. 22v]; Marsden (1995)
pl. VI [fols. 14v, 17r]

ST: Marsden (1995) 272–306

410. 5. London, British Library, Egerton 3278

s. xi in.

Contents: Bede, *Historia ecclesiastica* (f) [bk. V. xix–xx]

MS: Colgrave—Mynors (1969) xlvii; *Cat. Add. B.M. 1936–45* (1970)
381–2

411. London, British Library, Egerton 3314, fols. 9-72 (with London, British Library, Cotton Caligula A. xv, fols. 120–53)

s. xi ex. (in and after 1073) [Calig. 120–41, Eg. 9–44, Calig. 142–3]; s. xi/
xii [Calig. 144–53]; s. xi/xii [Eg. 45–72]; all parts Canterbury CC (and
StA?)

Contents: Calig. 120–41, Eg. 9–44, Calig. 142–3: computus materials[(*)]
['Canterbury Computus']; prognostics* (including *lunaria*); charms[(*)];
liturgical calendar; Annals of Christ Church, Canterbury[+*] (with later
additions, Calig. 136–9); notes* on Friday fasts, the Ages of the World,
the Age of the Virgin, on Christ, Adam and Noah; pseudo-Damasus
and pseudo-Jerome, Colloquy on celebrating Mass* [cf. *CPL* 633b];
Hermannus Contractus, *Computus*, chs. i–xxv; list of the archbishops
of Canterbury (add. s. xi/xii); extracts from Ælfric, *De temporibus
anni**, chs. vi–viii. Calig. 144–53: Ælfric, *De temporibus anni**, chs.
iv–xi. 4. Eg. 45–72: computus materials

MS: Planta (1802) 45–6; Thompson — Warner (1881–4) 66 [Caligula A.
xv]; M.R. James (1903) 49, 508, 516; Förster (1908); Singer (1917);
Förster (1925–6) 74–6; N.R. Ker (1957) no. 139 [Caligula A. xv,
fols. 120–53]; N.R. Ker (1960) 26–7; N.R. Ker (1964) 35–6; Willetts
(1966); *Cat. Add. B.M. 1936–45* (1970) 400–3; C.W. Jones (1975) xiii;
N.R. Ker (1976a) 124; A.G. Watson (1979) I, no. 517; C.W. Jones
(1980) 670; Backhouse et al. (1984b) no. 65; A.G. Watson (1987a) 124;
A.G. Watson (1987b) 286 [repr. A.G. Watson (2004) no. VIII]; Laing
(1993) 70; Webber (1995) 158; R. Gameson (1999a) no. 370; Pettit
(1999) 43; P. Wormald (1999) 186 n. 100, 187 n. 102; Liuzza (2001)
205, 208 n. 114, 215–16; Schiltz (2004) 121, 132; Chardonnens (2007b)
36–7, 509–12, 550; Barker-Benfield (2008) I.511, II.1122, III.1828;
Rushforth (2008a) 52–3; M. Blake (2009) 14–15; Liuzza (2011)
9–12; Scragg (2012a) nos. 418–29; Webber (2012) 213 and n. 7,
215 n. 15

DEC: Rice (1952) 205; F. Wormald (1952) 67 [no. 27]; Dodwell (1954) 21,
47, 120; Heimann (1966) 40 n. 9; Dodwell — Clemoes (1974) 58; E.
Temple (1976) no. 106; Ohlgren (1986) no. 211; R. Gameson (1990) 40;
R. Gameson (1995a) 116 and n. 69; Kidd (2000) 44–5

FACS: F. Wormald (1952) pls. 34 (a)–(b) [Calig. fols. 122v, 123r (details)];
Dodwell (1954) pls. 12 (a)–(b) [Calig. fols. 123r, 122v]; N.R. Ker (1960)
pl. 8 (a) [Calig. fol. 136r]; Dodwell — Clemoes (1974) pl. V (d) [Calig.
fol. 122v]; E. Temple (1976) ills. 317–18 [Calig. fols. 122v, 123r];
Backhouse et al. (1984b) pl. 65 [Calig. fol. 123r]; Schiltz (2004) 122
[Calig. fols. 123v–124r]; Chardonnens (2007a) pl. 2 [Calig. fol. 125v]

ED: Cockayne (1864–6) III.295 [OE charms]; Napier (1889) 3, 6–7 [notes
on annual fasts, on the Six Ages of the World, on the Virgin, Christ
and Noah, on the proper times for celebrating mass]; Förster (1929)
260 [base MS for art. i], 252–4 [base MS for art. e], 266–9 [base MS for
art. h]; Henel (1934) 42–55 [computus rules]; Henel (1942a) [Ælfric,
De temporibus anni, coll. as E and F]; Storms (1948) nos. 34, 68, 69
[OE charms]; C.W. Jones (1980) 685–9 [*De ratione embolismorum* coll.
as C]; Baker — Lapidge (1995) 429–30 [base MS for notes on epacts];
P.S. Baker (2000) 129–34 [base MS for Easter tables]; Liuzza (2001)
203–4 [art. h]; Rushforth (2008a) no. 26 [liturgical calendar];
Chardonnens (2007b) 234 [art. i], 370 [art. h], 430 [art. q], 450 [art. p],
462–3 [art. a], 487 [art. c], and Latin prognostics (pp. 197–9, 289, 373,
379, 380–1, 384, and 462–3); M. Blake (2009) [Ælfric, *De temporibus
anni*, coll. as E and F]

ST: Singer (1917); C.W. Jones (1939) 120; Tristram (1985) 32 *et passim*;
Hollis—Wright (1992) 152–3, 159, 261; Günzel (1993) 23 n. 21, 63–5;
Baker—Lapidge (1995) xl; Pulsiano (1998b) 87–9, 96, 108 n. 19, 109
n. 22, 112–13 n. 41; Chardonnens (2007a) 337; Liuzza (2011) 1–77
[prognostics]

411. 6. London, British Library, Harley 12, fols. 1–140

s. xi ex., prov. Durham?, (prov. Winchester?)

Contents: Iohannes Diaconus, *Vita S. Gregorii* [*BHL* 3641]

MS: A.G. Watson (1963) 208, 213 [repr. A.G. Watson (2004), no. III];
C.E. Wright (1972) 122, 131; Chaplais (1987); Gullick (1987) 102 n. 6;
R. Gameson (1999a) no. 426; P.R. Robinson (2003) I, no. 127; Hartzell
(2006) no. 151

FACS: A.G. Watson (1963) 210 [fol. 1r] [repr. A.G. Watson (2004)
no. III]

411. 7. London, British Library, Harley 12, fols. 141–3

s. xi ex. or xi/xii, prob. England

Contents: *Vita S. Katherinae* in twelve lessons with responsories

MS: R. Gameson (1999a) no. 427; Hartzell (2006) no. 151

412. London, British Library, Harley 55, fols. 1–4

s. xi[1], prob. York, or Worcester?, (prov. Worcester)

Contents: medical recipes*; laws*: *Eadgar II, III*; record*

MS: Liebermann (1903–16) I.xviii; N.R. Ker (1948) 71 [repr. N.R. Ker
(1985) 55]; N.R. Ker (1957) no. 225; N.R. Ker (1964) 207; Sawyer
(1968) no. 1453 [with refs.]; N.R. Ker (1971) 327 [repr. N.R. Ker
(1985) 21]; C.E. Wright (1972) 372; A.F. Cameron (1974) 221;
Whitelock (1976) 29; A.G. Watson (1979) I, no. 629; Meaney (1984)
240; A.G. Watson (1984) 29; Dumville (1992a) 126, 127; Hollis—
Wright (1992) 230, 232–3; M.L. Cameron (1993) 32; Laing (1993) 87;
R.I. Page (1993a) 48; P. Wormald (1999) 164 table 4.1, 185–90, 253–4,
314 n. 228; W. Schipper (2003) 157; Baxter (2004) 162, 176–9, 182–4,
186–90 [Oswald memorandum]; Dance (2004) 31 n. 6; A. Orchard
(2004) 66 n. 15; Hartzell (2006) no. 152; Hough (2006) 115; Rumble
(2006a) viii; A. Orchard (2012) 697 [no. 10]; Scragg (2012a) nos. 307,
626–9; P. Wormald (2012) 534 [no. 4]

FACS: Loyn (1971) [fols. 3v, 4r, 4v]; A.G. Watson (1979) II, pl. 21 [fol. 3v]; Baxter (2004) fig. 7.5 [fol. 4v]

ED: Cockayne (1864–6) II.280 [medical recipes]; Liebermann (1903–16) I.194–8 [*Eg. II* coll. as A], 200–6 [*Eg. III* coll. as A]; A.J. Robertson (1939) 110–13 [no. 54] [record]

ST: K. Sisam (1953a) 111; Bullough (1996) 17 n. 59; R. Gameson (1996a) 197, 233, 239; Hough (2006) 121, 133

413. London, British Library, Harley 76

s. xi[1], prob. Canterbury CC, prov. s. xi ex. Bury St Edmunds

Contents: gospels, gospel list; documents (s. xi ex.)

MS: Nares et al. (1808–12) I.20; T.A.M. Bishop (1954–8a) 185; N.R. Ker (1960) 20 n. 1; N.R. Ker (1964) 20; T.A.M. Bishop (1971) xiii; R.M. Thomson (1972) 625 and n. 46; C.E. Wright (1972) 372; Backhouse et al. (1984b) no. 58; Dumville (1993g) 33–4 n. 117, 40 n. 165, 78 n. 360, 106 n. 116, 120 n. 52; Lenker (1997) 453; McGurk (2012) 439 and n. 11, 446 [no. 10]

DEC: Kendrick (1949) 103; Rice (1952) 207; E. Temple (1976) no. 75; Brownrigg (1978) 262–3; D.M. Wilson (1984) 176; Ohlgren (1986) no. 180; Raw (1990) 218–19; R. Gameson (1995b) 100, 120, 206; Heslop (2007) 69; R. Gameson (2012c) 272 and n. 70

FACS: T.A.M. Bishop (1954–8a) pl. X (b) [fol. 137r]; E. Temple (1976) ills. 221, 230, 231 [fols. 45r, 8v, 10r]; D.M. Wilson (1984) pl. 263 [fol. 8v]; Ohlgren (1992) pls. 10.1–10.15 [fols. 6r–12v, 45r]; Backhouse (1997) pl. 13 [fol. 9v]; Heslop (2007) fig. 3 (b) [fol. 9v (detail)]

ST: Glunz (1933) 140; Frere (1934) 163; Sawyer (1968) no. 980; Klauser (1972) l; Heslop (1990) 153, 175, 182; Lenker (1997) 442–8; Keefer (2007b) 99

414. London, British Library, Harley 107

s. xi med., SE England

Contents: Ælfric, *Grammar*+* and *Glossary*+*; dialogue on declensions; glossary of names of birds and fishes+*

MS: N.R. Ker (1957) no. 227; C.E. Wright (1972) 373; Buckalew (1982) 25, 28; *ASMMF* XV (2007) 21–4 [no. 261; Doane]; Wieland (2009) 144; Scragg (2012a) nos. 630–2

FACS: *ASMMF* XV (2007) no. 261

ED: Zupitza (1880/2001) [Ælfric, *Grammar* and *Glossary*, coll. as H]; Zupitza (1889) 239

LANG: Korhammer (1976) 163–4, 165 n. 14, 166; Gneuss (1997) 48

ST: A.G. Watson (1966) 58, 304; Hetherington (1975); Buckalew (1978); Bursill-Hall (1981) 336 [dialogue on declensions]; Buckalew (1982) 47 n. 15

415. London, British Library, Harley 110

s. x ex., Canterbury CC

Contents: Prosper, *Epigrammata ex sententiis S. Augustini* [*CPL* 526] and *Versus ad coniugem* [*CPL* 531; SK 458]; Isidore, *Synonyma de lamentatione animae peccatricis* [*CPL* 1203]; all glossed

MS: T.A.M. Bishop (1959–63a) 421–2; N.R. Ker (1957) no. 228; T.A.M. Bishop (1971) xxvi; C.E. Wright (1972) 373; Hetherington (1975) 80 n. 11; Lapidge (1982a) 105 and n. 45 [repr. Lapidge (1996b) 466 and n. 45]; R.I. Page (1982) 150–1; Di Sciacca (2007b) 97 and n. 17, 111–13; Di Sciacca (2008) 68–71; Di Sciacca (2011) 301–2 and nn. 13–14; R. Gameson (2012a) 29 n. 66; Scragg (2012a) nos. 633–4

DEC: F. Wormald (1945) 134 [repr. F. Wormald (1984) 73]; E. Temple (1976) no. 19 (vii); Ohlgren (1986) no. 103

FACS: E. Temple (1976) ill. 69 [fol. 3r (detail)]; Di Sciacca (2007b) pl. 2 (p. 124) [fol. 26v]; Lendinara et al. (2011) pls. VII–VIII [fol. 3r (two details)]

ED: Meritt (1945) nos. 21 [glosses to Isidore], 23 [glosses to Prosper]; Lapidge (1982a) 107 [text and glosses to Prosper, *Epigr.* ii, on fol. 3v] [repr. Lapidge (1996b) 469]

ST: Hetherington (1975) 80 n. 11; Toth (1984); Gretsch (1999a) 216–18; Lapidge (2006) 312, 327, 328; Di Sciacca (2007b) 105–17, 122; Di Sciacca (2008) 110–11, 168–9 *et passim*; Di Sciacca (2011) 302–26 [Latin glosses], 326–30 [OE glosses]

416. London, British Library, Harley 110, fols. 1 and 56

s. xi med., Winchester OM?

Contents: gradual (f)

MS: Hartzell (2006) no. 153; Rankin (2012) 500

FACS: Hiley (1993) pl. 4 [fol. 56r]

417. London, British Library, Harley 208

s. ix[1], Saint-Denis, prov. England s. x/xi, (prov. York)

Contents: Alcuin, a selection of ninety-one of his *Epistolae* and three poems (*Carm.* xlviii, xlv, xl); Dungal, *Epp.* ii–viii; Letter from Charlemagne to Michael Palaeologus; additions (s. x/xi): alphabet; OE verse fragment**; incomplete *Pater noster*

MS: Dümmler (1881) 166; Thompson – Warner (1881–4) II.86; Dümmler (1895) 5–6; N.R. Ker (1957) no. 229; Whitelock (1965) 218–19; C.E. Wright (1972) 374; Whitelock (1976) 32 n. 2; Rella (1980) 98 n. 41, 165; Vezin (1982); Atsma – Vezin (1988) IV.232 n. 118; P.L. Heyworth (1989) 230; Blockley (1994); Bischoff (1998 –) II, no. 2438; Bullough (1998b) 24–5 n. 74; Gerchow (1999) 535 [no. 393]; P. Wormald (1999) 185 n. 95; Gneuss (2003b) 299; Bullough (2004) 75–9 *et passim*; Scragg (2012a) no. 635

FACS: Gerchow (1999) 536 [fols. 7v–8r]

ED: Dümmler (1881) 259–61 [Alcuin, *Carm.* xlvi–xlviii, coll as H]; Dümmler (1895) 18–481 [Alcuin, *Epp.*, coll. as H], 578–83 [base MS for Dungal, *Epistolae* ii–viii]; N.R. Ker (1957) p. 304 (OE verse fragment)

ST: Manitius (1911–31) I.374 [Dungal]; Kenney (1929) no. 346 [Dungal]; F.C. Robinson (1973) 449 [alphabet]; *BCLL* (1985) no. 657 [Dungal]; C. Brett (1991) 56; Webster – Backhouse (1991) no. 129 [Backhouse]; Blockley (1994) 81 [OE verse fragment]; *CSLMA* I (1994) 313–25 [Dungal, *Epp.*]; *CSLMA* II (1999) 56–8 [Alcuin, *Carm.*], 171–335 [Alcuin, *Epp.*]; Bullough (2004); Lapidge (2006) 170; R. McKitterick (2012) 327

418. London, British Library, Harley 213

s. ix[3/3], France, (prov. Winchester OM, by s. xvi York)

Contents: Alcuin, *Expositio in Ecclesiasten* with prologue by Alcuin; Alcuin, *Carm.* lxxvi [SK 8421]; pseudo-Alcuin, 'Vox ecclesie' [anon. comm. on the Canticum canticorum]; two homilies: Augustine, *De disciplina Christiana* [*CPL* 310], and an anonymous Homily (consisting of extracts from Gregory, *Homiliae .xl. in Euangelia* [*CPL* 1711] no. xxxix)

MS: Wanley et al. (1759–63) I.68; Nares et al. (1808–12) I.68; Stegmüller no. 9621; N.R. Ker (1964) 200; C.E. Wright (1972) 356, 366, 375; Bischoff (1998 –) II, no. 2439; T.N. Hall (2001) 135 n. 81; Guglielmetti

(2004) 189; D'Imperio—Guglielmetti (2005) 29; D'Imperio (2008) 23–6; Guglielmetti (2008a) 46–7; Guglielmetti (2008b) 178; Wieland (2009) 125; D. Ganz (2010); R. Gameson (2012d) 350 and n. 19

ED: Dümmler (1881) 297 [SK 8421]; Guglielmetti (2004) 201–32 ['Vox ecclesie' coll. as Lo]

ST: *CSLMA* II (1999) 370; Guglielmetti (2004) 183–97 ['Vox ecclesie']; D'Imperio—Guglielmetti (2005) 27–40 [*Expositio in Ecclesiasten*]; Lapidge (2006) 170; Guglielmetti (2008a) ['Vox ecclesie']

418. 3. London, British Library, Harley 271, fols. 1* and 45*

s. xi² or xi ex.

Contents: missal (f)

MS: A.G. Watson (1969) 58 [repr. A.G. Watson (2004) no. IX]; N. Orchard (1994); Lenker (1997) 492; R. Gameson (1999a) no. 429

FACS: N. Orchard (1994) pl. VIII [fol. 1*v]

ED: N. Orchard (1994) 286–8

418. 6. London, British Library, Harley 491, fols. 1–2

s. xi¹ or xi med., Continent or Durham, prov. Durham

Contents: mass lectionary (f; probably reject leaves)

MS: Mynors (1939) 60 [no. 84]; N.R. Ker (1964) 73; Van Houts (1982) 201–2; A.G. Watson (1987a) 30; Van Houts (1992–5) I.xcviii; Gullick (1994) 104; Gullick (1998a) 27; Gullick (1998b) 119; R. Gameson (1999a) no. 430; Gneuss (2003b) 299–300; Harrison (2004) 71–2

418. 8. London, British Library, Harley 521, fol. 2

s. x/xi, Canterbury StA

Contents: Bede, *De schematibus et tropis* [*CPL* 1567] (f)

MS: Knappe (1996) 242–3; Gneuss (2003b) 300; Berkhout (2006)

FACS: www.u.arizona.edu/~ctb/mss/harley521.jpg

ED: Berkhout (2006)

419. London, British Library, Harley 526, fols. 1–27

s. ix ex., NE France, prov. England by s. x med.

Contents: Bede, *Vita S. Cudbercti* (verse) [*CPL* 1380; *BHL* 2020]

MS: Jaager (1935) 30; Laistner—King (1943) 88; N.R. Ker (1957) no. 230; C.E. Wright (1972) 381; Rella (1977) 166; Rella (1980) 112; Lapidge (1995c) 130, 156; Gullick (1998a) 16, 28; Gretsch (1999a) 357–8; *ASMMF* X (2003) 13–18 [no. 264b; O'Brien O'Keeffe]; R. Gameson (2012d) 350 and n. 21; Scragg (2012a) nos. 636–7

FACS: *ASMMF* X (2003) no. 264b

ED: Jaager (1935) [Bede, *Vita metrica S. Cudbercti*, coll. as H¹]; Meritt (1945) no. 11 [OE glosses]

ST: A.G. Watson (1966) 128 [no. A.246]; F. Barlow (1992) lxxviii–lxxxi [on fols. 38–57]; Lapidge (2006) 170; Lapidge (2008a) 112–20

421. London, British Library, Harley 585

s. xi/xi and xi¹

Contents: enlarged *Herbarius**, part (pseudo-Apuleius, *Herbarius*; herbs from pseudo-Dioscorides, *Liber medicinae ex herbis femininis* and *Curae herbarum*); *Medicina de quadrupedibus** (*De taxone liber*; treatise on mulberry tree; part of Sextus Placitus, *Liber medicinae ex animalibus*); *Lacnunga** (medical recipes, prayers, charms; some in Latin and Irish), including *Lorica* of Laidcenn mac Baith° [*CPL* 1323; *BCLL* 294; SK 15745] and *Dies Aegyptiaci**

MS: Storms (1948) 16–24; Grattan—Singer (1952) 207–9; Beccaria (1956) 249–50 [no. 75]; N.R. Ker (1957) no. 231; De Vriend (1972) xxiii–xxvii; C.E. Wright (1972) 88, 119, 382; A.F. Cameron (1974) 222 and n. 27; P.R. Robinson (1978) 234–5 [repr. P.R. Robinson (1994) 30]; Backhouse et al. (1984b) no. 163 [Backhouse]; De Vriend (1984) xxiii–xxviii; Herren (1987) 3–8, 14; Robinson—Stanley (1991) 24–5; M.L. Cameron (1993) 59; Laing (1993) 89; Pulsiano (1998b) 109 n. 23; *ASMMF* I (1994) 26–36 [no. 265; Doane]; Liuzza (2001) 185, 206; Pettit (2001); Bredehoft (2004) 149–50, 152–5, 169; Menzer (2004) 96 n. 4; Shaw (2006) 98–105; Chardonnens (2007b) 41, 528, 552; R. Gameson (2012a) 18; R. Gameson (2012b) 115 and n. 88; Scragg (2012a) nos. 638–41; Toswell (2012) 469 and n. 7

DEC: F. Wormald (1945) 134, 135 [repr. F. Wormald (1984) 72, 75]; R. Gameson (1995b) 89 n. 104, 230 n. 231

FACS: Grattan—Singer (1952) after p. 94 [fol. 130r]; De Vriend (1972) pl. III [fol. 106v]; De Vriend (1984) pl. III [fol. 66v]; G.H. Brown (1987) fig. 1 [fols. 182v–183r]; T. Hunt (1991) I.47 [fol. 193v]; Robinson—Stanley (1991) pls. 19.5.1–8 [fols. 160r–163v], 19.6.1–2 [fol. 167r],

197.1–3 [fols. 175r–176r], 19.8.1–2 [fols. 180v–181r], 19.9.1–2 [fol. 185r]; *ASMMF* I (1994) no. 265; Doane (1994) figs. 1–3 [fols. 175r, 175v, 176r]

ED: Förster (1929) 271–3 [base MS (= H) for *Dies Aegyptiaci*]; Dobbie (1942) 119–24 [base MS for OE metrical charms]; Storms (1948) 140–2 [OE charms]; Grattan—Singer (1952) 26–205 [base MS for *Lacnunga*]; De Vriend (1972) [*Medicina de quadrupedibus* coll. as H]; De Vriend (1984) 1–233 [*Herbarium* coll. as H], 234–52 [*Medicina de quadrupedibus* coll. as H]; Herren (1987) 76–89 [Laidcenn, *Lorica*, coll. as H]; Doane (1994) 134–45 [charm]; Pettit (2001) vol. I [*Lacnunga*]; Chardonnens (2007b) 342 [*Dies Aegyptiaci*]

LANG: De Vriend (1984) lxviii–lxxiv

ST: Storms (1948) 140–51; Grattan—Singer (1952) 206–11; Meaney (1984) 245, 255–64; De Vriend (1984) 275–85 [textual notes], 286–338 [commentary]; G.H. Brown (1987) 45–52; Hollis—Wright (1992) 219–22, 272–86, 311–24; Pettit (2001) vol. II; Liuzza (2001) 222–3 [bibliography]; Shaw (2006) [charms; *Against a Dwarf*]; Bezzo (2007) 437 n. 14; Chardonnens (2010) 248; C. Lee (2011) 148

422. London, British Library, Harley 603 (the 'Harley Psalter')

s. x/xi or xi[1], Canterbury CC

Contents: Psalterium Romanum [but Ps. C–CV.25 are Gallicanum], incomplete (ends in Ps. CXLIII.11)

MS: T.A.M. Bishop (1959–63a) 94 and n.; T.A.M. Bishop (1959–63b) 420; N.R. Ker (1964) 44; C.E. Wright (1972) 95; Backhouse (1984a); Backhouse et al. (1984b) no. 59; A.G. Watson (1987a) 11 n. 2, 12; Heslop (1990) 154 n. 9, 175; R. Gameson (1992a) 188, 200; Heslop (1992b) 41–2; Dumville (1993g) 122 n. 57, 140; M.P. Brown (1991) 74; Noel (1995); Pulsiano (2001a) xxviii; W. Schipper (2003) 153; R.M. Butler (2004) 204 n. 129; Karkov (2006a) 44; Shepard (2007) 247 n. 105; Withers (2007) 72–6, 78, 83–4, 272; Barker-Benfield (2008) I.92 n. 67, III.1830; Wieland (2009) 116; R. Gameson (2012a) 28, 40 n. 105, 60 n. 203, 61 n. 213, 75; R. Gameson (2012b) 115 and n. 87; R. Gameson (2012d) 351 and n. 25; Rushforth (2012) 204 and n. 49; Toswell (2012) 471, 473

DEC: Rice (1952) 202–3; F. Wormald (1952) 69–70 [no. 34] *et passim*; Dodwell (1954) 1–3 *et passim*; Köhler—Mütherich (1971–99) VI/i.85; C.M. Kauffmann (1975) no. 67 [twelfth-century additions]; E. Temple (1976) no. 64; Brownrigg (1978) 246 n. 2; Duffey (1978); Stanley (1979)

107–8 [fol. 64r]; Hasler (1981); Lawrence (1982) 102, 105; Rabel (1982); Backhouse (1984a); F. Wormald (1984) 117; Ohlgren (1986) no. 169; R. Gameson (1990); Raw (1990) 219; Alexander (1992) 73–4; R. Gameson (1992a) 203–6; R. Gameson (1993); Ohlgren (1993); R. Gameson (1995a) 105, 115 n., 116; R. Gameson (1995b) 12–13, 14, 16–17, 18, 50–3, 59, 64, 67, 69, 103, 112, 139, 163–4, 173, 176–8 *et passim*; Noel (1995) *passim*; Semple (2003); Keefer (2007b) 99; Withers (2007) 74, 76, 84, 287, 369 n. 89; Schichler (2008); Karkov (2009) 205–6, 213; R. Gameson (2010) 121–2; C. Lee (2011) 161–2; R. Gameson (2012c) 263–6, 283–4, 289 n. 138

FACS: F. Wormald (1952) pls. 10 (b) [fol. 4r], 11 (a) [fol. 51v], 12 (a) [fol. 51v], 12 (b) [fol. 21r], 25 (a) [fol. 17v], 25 (b) [fol. 60v] (all details); Dodwell (1954) pls. 1 (a)–(c) [fols. 17r, 70v, 32r]; D.H. Wright (1967) pl. V (o) [fol. 38v]; E. Temple (1976) ills. 200–7 [fols. 2r, 12r, 13v, 15r, 51v, 54v, 66v], 210 [fol. 1r]; Backhouse (1984a), 100–9 [fols. 8r, 25r, 13v, 54v, 65v, 62v, 28r, 2r (detail)]; Backhouse et al. (1984b) pl. XIX [fol. 51v (detail)]; D.M. Wilson (1984) pl. 230 [fol. 15r]; Alexander (1992) fig. 121 [fol. 2r]; R. Gameson (1992a) pls. VII–XIV [fols. 4r, 7r, 14v, 25r, 26r, 55v, 59v, 64v]; Ohlgren (1992) pls. 2.1–2.102 [fols. 1r–73v]; Ohlgren (1993) 36 [fol. 65r]; R. Gameson (1995b) pls. 3 [fol. 7v], 12 [fol 70r], 16 [fol. 71r]; Noel (1995) ills. 1 [fol. 2r], 3 [fol. 65v (detail)], 4 [fol. 51r (detail)], 5 [fol. 32r (detail)], 7 [fol. 22v], 8 [fol. 22v (detail)], 9 [fol. 26r (detail)], 11 [fol. 26r], 13 [fol. 22v (detail)], 14 [fol. 3v (detail)], 16 [fol. 3v], 17 [fol. 8r (detail)], 19 [fol. 8r], 21 [fol. 4v (detail)], 23 [fol. 7v], 25 [fol. 1v (detail)], 26 [fol. 57r (detail)], 28 [fol. 57r], 30 [fol. 54r], 32 [fol. 50r], 33 [fol. 59r (detail)], 35 [fol. 59r], 37 [fol. 70r (detail)], 39 [fol. 67r (detail)], 41 [fol. 72r (detail)], 42 [fol. 70v], 43 [fols. 52v–53r], 44 [fol. 65v (detail)], 45 [fol. 49v (detail)], 46 [fol. 49v], 48 [fol. 28r], 49 [fol. 17r], 50 [fols. 17v–18r], 53 [fol. 51v], 55 [fol. 29r], 57 [fol. 16v], 59 [fol. 12r], 61 [fol. 14v (detail)], 63 [fol. 15v], 66 [fol. 64r], 69 [fol. 4r (detail)], 71 [fol. 59v], 75 [fol. 51v (detail)], 78 [fol. 33r], 83 [fol. 1r]; Backhouse (1997) pl. 12 [fol. 57v]; R. Gameson (2000b) pl. 8 [fol. 2r]; Semple (2003) pls. VI–X [fols. 68v, 73r, 71v, 72r, 67r]; M.P. Brown (2007a) pls. 124–5 [fols. 54v, 55r]; Withers (2007) 73 [fol. 26r], 78 [fol. 28r]; Owen–Crocker (2009) fig. 1.3 [fol. 66v]; R. Gameson (2012) pl. 10.6 [fol. 71r]

ED: Pulsiano (2001a) [Pss. I–L coll. as v]

ST: Sisam—Sisam (1959) 48 n. 1; Köhler—Mütherich (1971–99) VI/i. 85; R. Gameson (2004b); Withers (2007) 72–3, 83–4

423. London, British Library, Harley 647

s. ix²ᐟ⁴ (c. 830), Lotharingia, prov. Fleury?, prov. England (Ramsey?) s. x/
xi, (prov. Canterbury StA)

Contents: prayer; astronomical compilation, including: *De nominibus
stellarum* (add. England s. x/xi); Cicero, *Aratea*, with scholia excerpted
from Hyginus, *Astronomica*; excerpts from Macrobius (*Comm. in
Somnium Scipionis*), Martianus Capella (*De nuptiis Philologiae et
Mercurii*), Pliny (*Naturalis historia*)

MS: Thompson—Warner (1881–4) 69–71; Van de Vyver (1935) 142–3;
C.W. Jones (1939) 122; Saxl—Meier (1953) 149–51; T.A.M. Bishop
(1954–8b) 326; Leonardi (1960) 72–3 [no. 97]; N.R. Ker (1964) 44; C.E.
Wright (1972) 58, 384; Dumville (1976) 27–8; Munk Olsen (1982—)
I.333–4; P.L. Heyworth (1989) 230; Mostert (1989) no. BF 377;
Bischoff (1990) 60, 209; Bischoff (1998—) no. 2440; W. Schipper
(2007b) 40; Barker-Benfield (2008) II.1180–1, 1244, 1381, III.1852,
1918; Wieland (2009) 154

DEC: Dodwell (1971b) 22–3; Köhler—Mütherich (1971–99) IV.73, 74,
77–8, 101–7; F. Wormald (1984) 42; R. Gameson (1995b) 14, 192 n. 1;
Noel (1995) 175–7, 205; E. Morrison (2007) 49

FACS: Thompson—Warner (1881–4) pl. 61 [fols. 11v–12r]; Köhler—
Mütherich (1971–99) *Tafeln* IV, pls. 62 [fols. 19r, 2v], 63 [fols. 3r, 3v],
64 [fol. 4r], 65 [fols. 4v, 5r], 66 [fols. 5v, 6r], 67 [fols. 6r (detail), 7r], 68
[fols. 7v, 8r], 69 [fols. 8v, 9r], 70 [fols. 9v, 10r], 71 [fols. 10v, 11r], 72
[fols. 11v, 12r], 73 [fols. 12v, 13r, 13v], 74 [fol. 21v]; McGurk et al.
(1983) pls. X–XVII [fols. 2v–13v (details)]; F. Wormald (1984) ill. 34
[fol. 10v (detail)]; E. Morrison (2007) 49 [fol. 8v (detail)]

ED: Buescu (1941) [Cicero, *Aratea*, coll. as H]; Soubiran (1972) [Cicero,
Aratea, coll. as H]; Viré (1992) [scholia to Cicero, *Aratea*, coll. as H]

ST: Vogels (1884); G. Kauffmann (1888); Dodwell (1954) 61; McGurk et
al. (1983) 67–78; L.D. Reynolds (1983) 22–4 [M.D. Reeve]; Lapidge
(2006) 170, 297, 308, 320, 325; Mostert (2010) 202–3

423. 3. London, British Library, Harley 648, fol. 207

s. xi, England

Contents: missal (f)

MS: Hartzell (2006) no. 155; Gneuss (2012) 292

423. 9. London, British Library, Harley 652, fols. 1*–4*

s. ix med., prob. N France, (prov. Canterbury StA)

Contents: Alan of Farfa, *Homiliarium* (f)

MS: Cross—Hall (1996d) 53–7 and nn.; Bischoff (1998—) II, no. 2441; T.N. Hall (2004b) 86, 100

ST: Lapidge (2006) 170; Valtorta (2006) 10

424. London, British Library, Harley 652

s. xi/xii, Canterbury StA

Contents: Paulus Diaconus, *Homiliarium* (Easter Saturday to Fourth Sunday after Epiphany); Goscelin (all abridged and in lessons): Translation of St Mildred [*BHL* 5961], *uitae* of Abbot Hadrian [*BHL* 3740] and five early archbishops of Canterbury (Laurentius [*BHL* 4741], Iustus [*BHL* 4601], Honorius [not in *BHL*], Deusdedit [*BHL* 2153], Theodore [*BHL* 8083])

MS: T.A.M. Bishop (1955) 2; T.A.M. Bishop (1959–63a) 95; N.R. Ker (1960) 23 and n. 1, 29, 30; N.R. Ker (1964) 44; Römer (1972b) 172; C.E. Wright (1972) xxx, 384; Rollason (1982) 65; Clayton (1985) 219; M.P. Richards (1988) 104–9 [full description of contents]; R. Gameson (1995a) 102 n. 28, 106 n. 40, 122 n. 95, 144; Heslop (1995) 67 n. 37; Cross—Hall (1996d) 49–52 and nn. [Goscelin's *uitae*]; R. Gameson (1999a) no. 438; T.N. Hall (2004b) 86, 90 and n. 8, 91–5, 98, 100–5; T.N. Hall (2007) 234 n. 20, 241, 242 nn. 51–2, 245, 263; J. Hill (2007a) 93–4; Barker-Benfield (2008) I.lv, lxxxix, 64, 94, 530, 767, II.925, III.1794–5, 1923–4; R. Gameson (2012d) 346 n. 7

DEC: Dodwell (1954) 122; Lawrence (1982) 102; Petzold (1990) 22; R. Gameson (1995a) 126 n. 115, 128 n. 126, 129 n. 129

ST: Rollason (1986); R. Sharpe (2001) 152–3; R. McKitterick (2012) 327

424. 5. London, British Library, Harley 683, fol. 1

s. xi, England?

Contents: Office book [Office for St Martin] (f)

MS: T. Hunt (1991) I.179

425. London, British Library, Harley 863, fols. 8–125

1046×1072, Exeter

Contents: Psalterium Gallicanum, with invitatories and antiphons for Matins and Lauds on ordinary Sundays and ferias; canticles including *Quicumque uult*°; litany; prayers; Offices of a 'sample week' (incomplete); Office of the Dead (incomplete)

MS: Wanley et al. (1759–63) I.462–3; Nares et al. (1808–12) I.462–3; Dewick—Frere (1914–21) I.434, 445–54 [full description of contents]; Mearns (1914) 63; T.A.M. Bishop (1954–8a) 193, 195; N.R. Ker (1957) no. 232; N.R. Ker (1964) 83; C.E. Wright (1972) xv, xxii, 316, 387; Drage (1978) 366–8; A.G. Watson (1979) I, no. 638; Backhouse et al. (1984b) no. 160; Lapidge (1986a) 272; Muir (1988) xxix–xxx; Lapidge (1991a) 74; Dumville (1992a) 90; Dumville (1993g) 63; Lapidge (1994b) 136; R. Gameson (1996b) 145 n. 39; *ASMMF* IV (1996) 37–43 [no. 266; Pulsiano]; Muir (1998) 15; Pulsiano (1998b) 105 n. 1; Pulsiano (2001a) xxix; Treharne (2003) 161; Hartzell (2006) no. 156; Chardonnens (2007b) 528–9, 552; Treharne (2007b) 17; R. Gameson (2012a) 46; Pfaff (2012) 453 and n. 10; Rankin (2012) 503 and n. 100; Scragg (2012a) no. 642

DEC: R. Gameson (1995b) 42 n. 158, 220 n. 164

FACS: Dewick—Frere (1914–21) I, pls. XIII [fol. 108v], XIV [fol. 109r], XV [fol. 109v], XVI [fol. 110r], XVII [fol. 110v], XVIII [fol. 111r]; A.G. Watson (1979) II, pl. 43 [fol. 104r]; *ASMMF* IV (1996) no. 266; Pulsiano (2007) 128 [fol. 54r]

ED: Dewick—Frere (1914–21) I.434–54 [base text for litany and prayers], II.611–13 [base text for invitatories and antiphons in psalter]; Holthausen (1942–3) [*Quicumque uult* with OE gloss]; Muir (1988) 47, 52 [prayers coll. as Q]; Lapidge (1991a) 193–202 [litany]; Pulsiano (2001a) [Pss. I–L coll. as ξ]

ST: E. Bishop (1918) 406–7; Levison (1927) 55–8; Korhammer (1976) 240; Bestul (1977) 168–9; Rankin (1984) 102; R. Gameson (1992c) 130 n. 67; Conner (1993) 6, 201; Corrêa (1996) 288 n. 5, 294 n. 39; Pfaff (1999b) 80–2; Karkov (2001a) 117 n. 10; Pfaff (2009) 134–6

426. London, British Library, Harley 865

s. xi ex., (prov. St Albans)

Contents: Ambrose, *De mysteriis* [*CPL* 155], *De sacramentis* [*CPL* 154]; Eusebius Gallicanus, *Sermo* xvii [*CPL* 966]; Jerome, *Aduersus Iouinianum* [*CPL* 610]; pseudo-Augustine, *Hypomnesticon* [*CPL* 381]

MS: Wanley et al. (1759–63) I.463; Nares et al. (1808–12) I.463; N.R. Ker (1964) 166; Römer (1972b) 172; C.E. Wright (1972) xv, 387; R.M.

Thomson (1982a) I.92–3; Bankert et al. (1997) 15, 46–8; R. Gameson
(1999a) no. 439; Lapidge (2006) 277, 278, 313; Barker-Benfield (2008)
I.539, 550

DEC: F. Wormald (1945) 135 [repr. F. Wormald (1984) 75]

ST: Lambert (1969–72) no. 252

427. London, British Library, Harley 1117

s. x/xi, prob. Canterbury CC

Contents: verses on the Translation of St Edward, king and martyr (inc.
'Omnibus est recolenda dies qua maximus Anglum'; not in SK or SK
Suppl.); Bede, *Vita S. Cudbercti* (prose) [*CPL* 1379; *BHL* 2019];
excerpts from Bede, *Historia ecclesiastica* (IV. xxix–xxx [on
St Cuthbert]; Office of St Cuthbert; Bede, *Vita S. Cudbercti* (verse)
[*CPL* 1380; *BHL* 2020]; poem on Abbot Wigbeorht [inc. 'Iusserat
ecclesiae Wigbeorhtus scribere nabla hoc'; not in SK or SK Suppl.];
Offices of St Benedict and St Guthlac

MS: Jaager (1935) 29; Colgrave (1940) xi, 28; Laistner—King (1943) 88;
Hohler—Hughes (1956) 161; N.R. Ker (1957) no. 234; T.A.M. Bishop
(1959–63b) 415–23; C.E. Wright (1972) 51, 391; F.C. Robinson (1973)
444 n. 4, 459–61; Korhammer (1980) 55; D.H. Turner et al. (1980) 105;
O'Brien O'Keeffe (1985) 65; Dumville (1992a) 109 nn. 80–2; Dumville
(1993g) 108 n. 133, 109 and n. 140; Lapidge (1995c) 130, 142–3 and
n. 36; R. Gameson (1996b) 169 n. 160; Sole (1998); Hartzell (2006)
no. 157; *ASMMF* X (2003) 19–24 [no. 268; O'Brien O'Keeffe]; Barker-
Benfield (2008) I.604, III.1818; Lapidge (2008a) 114; R. Gameson
(2012a) 67 n. 232; Rankin (2012) 490, 504; Scragg (2012a) no. 643

DEC: E. Temple (1976) no. 30(vii); Ohlgren (1986) no. 124; R. Gameson
(1992a) 193, 198

FACS: T.A.M. Bishop (1959–63b) pls. XIII (c), XV [fols. 19r, 45r]; E.
Temple (1976) ills. 108–9 [fol. 45r (two details)]; R. Gameson (1992a)
pl. 21 [fol. 4r]; *ASMMF* X (2003) no. 268

ED: Birch (1881) 66–9 [Office of St Guthlac]; Jaager (1935) 56–133
[Bede, *Vita S. Cudbercti* (verse) coll. as H]; Colgrave (1940) 142–307
[Bede, *Vita S. Cudbercti* (prose) coll. as H]; Meritt (1945) no. 7 [OE
glosses]; Hohler—Hughes (1956) 163–91 [Office for St Cuthbert coll.
as X]; Fell (1971) 17 [verses on the Translation of St Edward]; Lapidge
(1992d) 175 [repr. Lapidge (1996b) 75] [poem on Abbot Wigbeorht];
Sole (1998) 140–3 [rhymed Office of St Cuthbert]

ST: Rankin (1987) 142 [no. 7]; Rollason (1989) 418–19; Andrew Hughes (1993) 257; Rankin (1996) 307 and n. 87, 347 and nn.; Biggs et al. (2001) 187; Hiley (2002); Hiley (2003) 173; Lapidge (2008a) 112–20 [MS transmission of Bede, *Vita S. Cudbercti* (verse)]

428. London, British Library, Harley 2110, fols. 4* and 5*

s. xi¹, (prov. Castle Acre, Norfolk, Cluniac priory?)

Contents: Ælfric, *Catholic Homilies** (f: from CH I, Homilies III-IV)

MS: C.E. Wright (1938); N.R. Ker (1957) no. 235; C.E. Wright (1972) xv, 404; Clemoes (1997) 63; *ASMMF* VIII (2000) 65–8 [no. 269; Wilcox]; R. Gameson (2012a) 29 n. 66; Scragg (2012a) no. 644

FACS: *ASMMF* VIII (2000) no. 269

ED: Clemoes (1997) 204–5 [Ælfric, CH I, Hom. III (f), coll. as f¹], 206–7 [Ælfric, CH I, Hom. IV (f), coll. as f¹]

428. 4. London, British Library, Harley 2506

s. x/xi, Fleury, prov. England s. xi¹

Contents: verse prologue to Hyginus [SK 7896]; Hyginus, *Astronomica*; verse epilogue to Hyginus [SK Suppl. 16255a]; pseudo-Priscian, *Carmen de sideribus* [SK 151]; Abbo of Fleury, *De differentia circuli et sphaerae*; a collection of texts dealing with astronomy: prayer; *De sole et luna*; *De nominibus stellarum*; Cicero, *Aratea* with *Scholia Bernensia*; excerpts from Pliny (*Naturalis historia*), Macrobius (*Comm. in Somnium Scipionis*); *Praeceptum canonis Ptolemaei* [Latin version, incomplete]; Martianus Capella, *De nuptiis Philologiae et Mercurii*, bk. VIII [incomplete]; Remigius of Auxerre, Commentary on Martianus Capella, bk. VIII [incomplete]

MS: Saxl—Meier (1953) 157–60 [full list of contents]; Leonardi (1959) 467 n. 128; Leonardi (1960) 73–5 [no. 98]; Gremont—Donnat (1967) I.775, 776 n. 186, 777 n. 195; T.A.M. Bishop (1971) xii n. 2, 18, 20; Soubiran (1972) 110–11; Munk Olsen (1982 –) I.333; Le Boeuffle (1983) l–li; McGurk et al. (1983) 67–78; Reeve (1983b) 22–4; Reeve (1983d) 187–8; Backhouse et al. (1984b) no. 43; Mostert (1989) no. BF 380; Lapidge (1992a) 111–12 [repr. Lapidge (1993a) 399–400]; Viré (1992) xv, xxxvi–xl; Lapidge—Baker (1997) 8–9 and nn.; Webster—Brown (1997) 247 [no. 153]; Ebersperger (1999) 190; Lapidge (2006) 51–2; Wieland (2009) 154; R. Gameson (2012b) 101 and n. 30

DEC: Homburger (1912) 5; Niver (1939) II.681 n. 66; F. Wormald (1952) 70–1 [no. 35]; Alexander (1970b) 14; Köhler — Mütherich (1971–99) IV.77; E. Temple (1976) no. 42; F. Wormald (1984) 83, 118, 155; Ohlgren (1986) no. 147; R. Gameson (1995b) 192 n. 1, 193 n. 6; R. Gameson (2010) 100–5; R. Gameson (2012c) 281 and n. 109

FACS: F. Wormald (1952) pls. 13 (a)–(b) [fols. 38r, 41r]; E. Temple (1976) ill. 143 [fol. 38v (detail)]; McGurk (1983) pls. X [fols. 36r, 36v], XI [fol. 37v], XII [fols. 38r, 38v, 39r], XIII [fols. 39v, 40r, 40v], XIV [fols. 41r, 41v], XV [fols. 42r, 42v], XVI [fols. 43r, 43v, 44r, 44v], XVII [fol. 44v] (all details); F. Wormald (1984) ill. 121 [fol. 40v (detail)]; Noel (1995) ills. 79 [fols. 42v–43r], 80 [fol. 41r]; Backhouse (1997) pl. 11 [fol. 42r (detail)]; R. Gameson (2010) fig. 8 [fol. 37r]

ED: Vogels (1884) [three texts preceding Cicero, *Aratea*]; Buescu (1941) [Cicero, *Aratea*, coll. as B]; Soubiran (1972) [Cicero, *Aratea*, coll. as B]; Dell'Era (1979) 282–96 [*Scholia Bernensia*]; Le Boeuffle (1983) [Hyginus, *Astronomica*, coll. as U]; R.B. Thomson (1985) 120–33 [Abbo, *De differentia circuli et sphaerae*, coll. as J]; Viré (1992) [Hyginus, *Astronomica*, coll. as L]; Lapidge — Baker (1997) 24–7 [base MS for verse prologue and epilogue to Hyginus]; Pingree (1997) [*Preceptum canonis Ptolemaei*]

ST: Van de Vyver (1935) 141, 143; C.E. Lutz (1962) I.52; G.R. Evans (1979); McGurk et al. (1983) 67–78; Noel (1995) 174–83; Biggs et al. (2001) 8–9, 14–15 [Lendinara]; Lapidge (2006) 51, 297, 308, 320, 321, 325; Mostert (2010) 202–3; Lapidge (2012a) 688

428. 5. London, British Library, Harley 2729

s. xi ex. (1090s), Durham

Contents: Frontinus, *Strategemata*; Eutropius, *Breuiarium historiae Romanae*

MS: Nares et al. (1808–12) I.709; Munk Olsen (1982 —) I.392; Gullick (1998a) 31; R. Gameson (1999a) no. 444

ST: L.D. Reynolds (1983) 160 [Eutropius], 172 [Frontinus]; Lapidge (2006) 302, 303

428. 9. London, British Library, Harley 2892, fols. 1–16

s. xi$^{1/4}$ or xi$^{2/4}$

Contents: pontifical (f): *ordo* for the Blessing of Oils (f)

MS: Woolley (1917) xi–xiii; Pfaff (1999a) 8 n. 13; Hartzell (2006) no. 158

ED: Woolley (1917) xi–xii [collation with no. **429**]

ST: Nelson–Pfaff (1995) 92; Gneuss (2003b) 300

429. London, British Library, Harley 2892, fols. 17–214 (the 'Canterbury Benedictional')

s. xi$^{2/4}$, Canterbury CC (or Winchester, for use at Canterbury?)

Contents: benedictional

MS: C.E. Wright (1972) 418; Brückmann (1973) 440; A.G. Watson (1979) I, no. 709; C.A. Jones (2004) 345 nn. 82, 83; C.A. Jones (2005a) 122–6; C.A. Jones (2005b) 239–41, 253–6, 261–2, 279–83; Hartzell (2006) no. 158; Gullick–Rankin (2009) 279–80

DEC: R. Gameson (1995b) 60 n. 243, 216, 231 n. 233

FACS: Woolley (1917), pls. I–III [fols. 50r, 71v, 126r]; A.G. Watson (1979) II, pl. 34 [fol. 34r]

ED: Woolley (1917) 3–136 [base MS for benedictional]; Moeller (1971–9) [benedictional coll. as 'CANT']; C.A. Jones (2005b) 309–11

ST: Gasquet–Bishop (1908) 76–119 *et passim*; Gneuss (1968) 245; Vezin (1968) 285 n. 13, 288; Prescott (1987) 132–3, 148–55 [full list of benedictions]; Muir (1988) xxxi, 112; Davril (1995) 27; Corrêa (1997) 99–100; Rasmussen (1998) 224–9, 231–54; N. Orchard (2002) I.87, 94, 167, 170–1, 175, 183, 198, 203–4, 223, 226; N. Orchard (2005) cx *et passim*; Pfaff (2009) 92–3, 143

430. London, British Library, Harley 2904 (the 'Ramsey Psalter')

s. x$^{3/3}$ or x ex., Winchester? (for Ramsey?), or Ramsey?

Contents: *Dicta S. Augustini* (inc. 'Quod canticum psalmorum animas decorat' [= Remigius of Auxerre, *In Psalmos praeambula*: PL 131, col. 142]); *Oratio ante psalterium*; Psalterium Gallicanum; Ps. CLI; *Oratio post psalterium*; canticles; litany

MS: Nares et al. (1808–12) I.719; Niver (1939); N.R. Ker (1964) 154; T.A.M. Bishop (1971) 14; C.E. Wright (1972) 280, 418; Rella (1977) 57; Backhouse et al. (1984b) no. 41; Lapidge (1986a) 272; Lapidge (1991a) 74–5; Dumville (1992a) 75–6; Lapidge (1992a) 110–15 [repr. Lapidge (1993a) 398–403]; Dumville (1993g) 59–63 and nn., 65 n. 279, 145 n. 23;

R. Gameson (1995a) 123 n. 101; Pulsiano (2001a) xxix; Biggs (2007a) 16; Karkov (2007a) 145; Barker-Benfield (2008) III.1830; R. Gameson (2012a) 75 and n. 259, 90; R. Gameson (2012b) 101 n. 31, 114

DEC: Homburger (1912) 5; F. Wormald (1944) 129–30 [repr. F. Wormald (1984) 154–5]; F. Wormald (1945) 109–10 [repr. F. Wormald (1984) 48–9]; Rice (1952) 162, 208–10, 217; F. Wormald (1952) 71 [no. 36]; Dodwell (1954) 10; Rickert (1954) 33–5, 54, 58, 64, 200, 223 n. 51; F. Wormald (1957b) 32 [repr. F. Wormald (1984) 147]; Alexander (1970a) 59, 60–3, 67, 70–3, 91; E. Temple (1976) no. 41; Alexander (1978b) no. 15; Brownrigg (1978) 246 n. 2, 247 n. 3; F. Wormald (1984) 117–18; Ohlgren (1986) no. 146; Raw (1990) 219–20; R. Gameson (1992a) 207; R. Gameson (1995b) 24–5, 62 n. 258, 65, 69, 99 n. 159, 100, 122, 127–8, 193–4, 215 n. 144, 219–20; R. Gameson (1996a) 200–4; Karkov (2006b) 102; Karkov (2007a) 145; R. Gameson (2010) 108–10; O'Reilly (2011) 210–12; R. Gameson (2012c) 281 and n. 109, 289 n. 139

FACS: Rice (1952) pls. 73 (a), 74 (a) [fols. 4r (detail), 3v]; F. Wormald (1952) frontispiece, pls. 8–9 [fol. 3v (two details)]; E. Temple (1976) ills. 140–2 [fols. 125r (detail), 4r (detail), 3v]; Backhouse et al. (1984b) pl. IX [fol. 4r]; D.M. Wilson (1984) pl. 221 [fol. 3r]; F. Wormald (1984) ills. 77, 117 [fols. 4r, 3v]; M.P. Brown (1991) pl. 75 [fol. 3v]; R. Gameson (1991) fig. 17 [fol. 4r]; R. Gameson (1992a) pl. V [fol. 3v]; R. Gameson (1996a) pl. 2 [fol. 4r]; M.P. Brown (2007a) pls. 88–90 [fols. 3v, 4r, 125r]; R. Gameson (2010) figs. 9–10 [fols. 3v, 4r]

ED: Lapidge (1991a) 203–9 [litany]; Corrêa (1996) 319 [*Oratio post psalterium*]; Pulsiano (2001a) [Pss. I–L coll. as o]

ST: De Bruyne (1920) 83 [*Oratio ante psalterium*]; Stegmüller (1950) I.448 [*Oratio ante psalterium*]; Sisam—Sisam (1959) 5, 75 n. 2; Gremont—Donnat (1967) 775 n. 184, 776, 777 nn. 191–5; Corrêa (1996) 292–9; Thacker (1996) 253 n. 64; Lapidge (2006) 51 n. 93, 74 with n. 36; Lapidge (2012a) 688

431. London, British Library, Harley 2961 (the 'Leofric Collectar')

s. xi$^{3/4}$, Exeter

Contents: collectar; hymnal; sequences

MS: Warren (1883) xxviii–xxix; Mearns (1913) xi *et passim* [no. E.a]; T.A.M. Bishop (1954–8a) 193–7; N.R. Ker (1957) no. 236; N.R. Ker (1964) 83; Gamber (1968–88) no. 1530; Gneuss (1968) 108–9; C.E. Wright (1972) xxii, 419; Drage (1978) 369–70; A.G. Watson (1979) I, no. 718; Gneuss (1985) 113 [no. G.4]; Dumville (1992a) 90; Lapidge

(1994b) 136; Corrêa (1995) 51–2; Springer (1995) 147; Milfull (1996) 47–9; Treharne (2003) 161; Hartzell (2006) 159; Pfaff (2012) 453 and n. 9; Rankin (2012) 503 and n. 99; Raw (2012) 460

FACS: Dewick—Frere (1914–21) I, pls. I–XII [fols. 2r, 2v, 10r, 10v, 11r, 16r, 31v, 77r, 107r, 218r, 226r, 251r]; A.G. Watson (1979) II, pl. 44 [fol. 36r]; Rankin (1984) pls. XI (a)–(b) [fols. 29r, 29v]

ED: Dewick—Frere (1914–21) I.2–430 [base MS for collectar, hymnal, sequences]; *AH* LI (1908) [hymns collated; various sigla]; Milfull (1996) 109–446 [hymnal coll. as H]

ST: Förster (1933a) 25 n. 78; Gneuss (1968) 239–40; Hohler (1975) 70; Rankin (1984) 102, 109, 111–12; Corrêa (1992) 123–6; Conner (1993) 6, 13 n. 38; Davril (1995) 28; R. Gameson (1996b) 145; Milfull (1996) 13–15; Pfaff (2009) 132–6

432. London, British Library, Harley 2965 (the 'Book of Nunnaminster')

s. viii/ix or ix[1], Mercia or S England?, prov. Winchester Nun

Contents: prayerbook: gospel extracts; prayers; *Lorica* of Laidcenn mac Baith [*CPL* 1323; *BCLL* 294; SK 15745]; two charms; record* (s. ix/x); forms of confession and absolution, prayer (s. x[1])

MS: Thompson—Warner (1881–4) II.61–2; Birch (1889); Kenney (1929) no. 577; *CLA* II (1935) no. 199; K. Sisam (1953a) 269; N.R. Ker (1957) no. 237; Gjerløw (1961) 23, 134; McGurk (1961b) 12 [repr. McGurk (1998) no. V]; N.R. Ker (1964) 202; Sawyer (1968) 55 and no. 1560; C.E. Wright (1972) xxii, 419; Parkes (1976b) 158 n. 3 [repr. Parkes (1991) 155 n. 3]; Alexander (1978a) no. 41; T.J. Brown (1982a) 110 [repr. T.J. Brown (1993a) 210]; Parkes (1983) 131–3 [repr. Parkes (1991) 173–8]; M.P. Brown (1986) 135; M.P. Brown (1986) 135; Dumville (1987) 159, 170 n. 117, 171 n. 129; Herren (1987) 4; Morrish (1988) 518–22, 525–6; Muir (1988) xxxii, 12–19; R. McKitterick (1989a) 316; Webster—Backhouse (1991) no. 164; Dumville (1992a) 96, 101–2, 125; Dumville (1992b) 83–6, 95; *ASMMF* I (1994) 37–43 [no. 271; Doane]; Raw (1997) 145–53; Webster—Brown (1997) 248 [no. 154]; Crowley (2000) 123, 144; Lapidge (2000a) 14–15; M.P. Brown (2001b); M.P. Brown (2012) 158; R. Gameson (2012a) 43 n. 119; Raw (2012) 460 and n. 1, 461 and n. 13, 462–4

DEC: Deshman (1974) 193; Alexander (1978a) no. 41; Ohlgren (1986) no. 41; Raw (1990) 220; M.P. Brown (2001c) 51–8; M.P. Brown (2011b) 37; N. Edwards (2012) 246 n. 14

FACS: Thompson—Warner (1881–4) II, pl. 22 [fol. 16v]; Alexander (1978a) ills. 135, 137–9 [fols. 4v, 11r, 37r, 16v]; Parkes (1983) pls. III (a)–(b) [fols. 41r, 40v (details)] [repr. Parkes (1991) pls. 30 (a)–(b)]; Dumville (1992b) pl. II [fol. 40v (detail)]; T.J. Brown (1993a) ill. 56 [fol. 11r (detail)]; *ASMMF* I (1994) no. 271; M.P. Brown (1996) figs. 10–13 [fols. 16v, 36v–37r, 4v, 40v]; Lapidge (2000a) 15 [fol. 11r (detail)]; M.P. Brown (2001b) fig. 19.1 [fol. 16v]; M.P. Brown (2007a) pls. 48–9 [fols. 16v, 40v]

ED: BCS (1885–99) no. 630 [record]; Birch (1889) 32–3 [record], 39–97 [base MS for prayerbook]; Herren (1987) 76–89 [*Lorica* of Laidcenn coll. as N]

ST: E. Bishop (1918) 192–7; Wilmart (1932) 210–13; Finberg (1964) no. 177 [record]; K. Hughes (1970); *BCLL* (1985) no. 1280; Herren (1987) 3–18 [*Lorica*]; Biggs. et al. (1990) 138–9 [Bestul]; Sims-Williams (1990) 275–327; M.P. Brown (1996) 117–18, 137–42, 154, 168–9, 171–2, 178–9 *et passim*; M.P. Brown (2001c)

432. 5. London, British Library, Harley 3017

s. ix$^{3/4}$, France; prov. Nevers s. x, prov. England s. xi?

Contents: a collection of computistic, scientific and prognostic texts, including *Somniale Danielis*; Sphere of Pythagoras; *lunaria*; Greek alphabets; runic alphabet; excerpts from Bede, *De temporum ratione* [*CPL* 2320], chs. xix, xxxv, xlviii, l, li, lvi

MS: C.W. Jones (1939) 122; C.W. Jones (1943) 152; R. Derolez (1954) 212–17; C.W. Jones (1977) 247; L.T. Martin (1979); Baker—Lapidge (1995) xlii; Bischoff (1998—) II, no. 2466; Liuzza (2001) 223–4; Liuzza (2005) 30, 38; Chardonnens (2007b) 502 and n. 7; Liuzza (2011) 22

FACS: Liuzza (2005) pl. 2 [fol. 58r]

ED: Liuzza (2005) 40–2 [Sphere of Pythagoras coll. as F]

ST: Gneuss (2003b) 300; Liuzza (2005); Chardonnens (2007b) 502 and n. 7; Chardonnens (2010) 236–43; Liuzza (2011) 1–77

433. London, British Library, Harley 3020, fols. 1–34

s. x/xi, Glastonbury or Canterbury StA?, (prov. Glastonbury)

Contents: Bede, *Homiliae in Euangelia* I. 13 [on Benedict Biscop]; Bede, *Historia abbatum* [*CPL* 1378]; anonymous *Vita S. Ceolfridi* [*CPL* 1377; *BHL* 1726]

MS: Nares et al. (1808–12) I.725–6; C. Plummer (1896) I.cxxxiii, cxl; Laistner—King (1943) 112; N.R. Ker (1960) 49; C.E. Wright (1972) 255, 420; Webster—Backhouse (1991) no. 94; Dumville (1992a) 110 n. 92; Carley (1994) 268–76, 279–81; Biggs et al. (2001) 107–8; Hartzell (2006) no. 161; Lapidge (2008a) 75; Wieland (2009) 125

ED: C. Plummer (1896) I.364–87 [Bede, *Historia abbatum*, coll. as H₁], 388–404 [anon. *Vita S. Ceolfridi* coll. as H]

ST: Biggs et al. (2001) 107–8, 133–4; Lapidge (2008a) 74–7 [MS transmission]

433. 1. London, British Library, Harley 3020, fol. 35

s. xi in.

Contents: troper (f)

MS: Carley (1994) 273 and n. 45; Hartzell (2006) no. 161

433. 2. London, British Library, Harley 3020, fols. 36–94

s. x/xi, Canterbury CC, (prov. Glastonbury)

Contents: eight *passiones martyrum*: Pope Callistus I [*BHL* 1523], Pope Stephen I [*BHL* 7845], SS. Abdon and Sennen [*BHL* 6], St Felicity and her seven children [*BHL* 2853], SS. Simplicius, Faustinus and Beatrix [*BHL* 7790], Pope Felix II [*BHL* 2857], St Agapitus [*BHL* 125], Pope Cornelius [*BHL* 1958]; sequence (f) [SK 10021] and responsory (s. xi[1])

MS: Nares et al. (1808–12) I.725–6; T.A.M. Bishop (1959–63b) 421, 423; N.R. Ker (1960) 49; Dumville (1992a) 110 n. 92; Carley (1994) 276–7, 281; Biggs et al. (2001) 108; R.M. Butler (2004) 200; Hartzell (2006) no. 162; T.N. Hall (2007) 257–9; Barker-Benfield (2008) III.1664–5; R. Gameson (2012a) 67 n. 232

ST: Biggs et al. (2001) 127, 434–5, 39–40, 210–11, 427–8, 212, 53, 152 respectively

433. 3. London, British Library, Harley 3020, fols. 95–132

s. x/xi, Winchester?, (prov. Glastonbury)

Contents: riddle; *Passio S. Iulianae* [*BHL* 4522–3]; Eutychianos, *Theophili Actus*, trans. Paulus Diaconus of Naples [*BHL* 8121]

MS: Nares et al. (1808–12) I.725–6; N.R. Ker (1960) 49; Dumville (1992a) 110 n. 92; Carley (1994) 277–9, 281; Biggs et al. (2001) 276–8, 453–5 [M. Clayton]; Lapidge (2006) 341, 342

ED: Meersseman (1963) [*Theophili Actus*]

434. London, British Library, Harley 3080

s. xi ex. or xi/xii, W England

Contents: Augustine, *Confessiones* [*CPL* 251], with *Retractatio* [*CPL* 250] II. vi

MS: N.R. Ker (1960) 8 n. 2; Römer (1972b) 180; C.E. Wright (1972) xxvi, 422; Rella (1977) 80; Webber (1992) 72, 73; R. Gameson (1999a) no. 447; Lapidge (2006) 282, 290

434. 5. London, British Library, Harley 3097

s. xi/xii, (prov. Peterborough)

Contents: Jerome, *Comm. in Danielem* [*CPL* 588]; saints' *uitae*: of St Nicholas (by John the Deacon of Naples) [*BHL* 6104–8], of St Botuulf (by Folcard) [*BHL* 1428], of SS. Tancred, Torhtred and Tova; *Translatio sanctorum* at Thorney; of Guthlac (by Felix; incomplete) [*BHL* 3723; *CPL* 2150]; pseudo-Ambrose, *De dignitate sacerdotali* ('De obseruantia episcoporum') [*CPL* 171a]; Ambrose, *De mysteriis* [*CPL* 155], *De sacramentis* [*CPL* 154], *De utilitate et laude sancti ieiunii* [*CPL* 137]; excerpts from Otloh of St Emmeram, *Vita* and *Miracula S. Nicholai* [*BHL* 6126–7]

MS: Nares et al. (1808–12) I.735; Colgrave (1956) 30–1; N.R. Ker (1964) 151; R. Gameson (1999a) no. 448; Friis-Jensen—Willoughby (2001) 9, 57; Lapidge (2006) 56, 145, 277, 278, 313, 339; Wieland (2009) 130

ED: Birch (1892) 284–6, 286–90 [Lives of SS. Tancred, Torhtred and Tova]; Colgrave (1956) 60–170 [Felix, *Vita S. Guthlaci*, coll. as H]

ST: C. Clark (1979) [SS. Tancred, Torhtred and Tova]; F. Barlow (1992) lii–lvii [Folcard]; Biggs et al. (2001) 119–20, 244–6, 356–60; Lapidge—Love (2001) 234–6 [Folcard]

435. London, British Library, Harley 3271

s. xi¹, Winchester NM?

Contents: grammatical notes⁽*⁾; *Tribal Hidage**; note characterizing the nations (*De proprietatibus gentium*); Ælfric, *Grammar*⁺*; notes on the thirty silver coins of Judas (*De triginta argenteis*)*; and on the dimensions of Noah's Ark*; prognostics (including *lunaria*)⁽*⁾; computistical and medical notes*; note on Solomon's Gold*; Latin parsing grammar ('Beatus quid est'); part of Office for Invention of St Stephen; Latin names of ordinal and cardinal numbers; Abbo of Saint-Germain-des-Prés, *Bella*

Parisiacae urbis, bk. III, prose version with word-for-word translation into OE°; the same bk. III in Latin verse, with interlinear Latin gloss; *Missa pro sacerdote*; glossary material; Ælfric, Homily (*Sermo de septiformi spiritu*)* [Napier (1883/1967) no. VIII] and excerpts from Letter to Sigeweard*; the Ages of the World (*De initio creaturae*)*; sequence incipit [SK 14655, by Notker]

MS: Beccaria (1956) no. 76; N.R. Ker (1957) no. 239; C.E. Wright (1972) 425; Lapidge (1975a) 75 [repr. Lapidge (1993a) 113]; A.G. Watson (1979) I, no. 743; Kotzor (1981) I.3*; Lapidge—Winterbottom (1991b) lxxxvi–lxxxvii; Webster—Backhouse (1991) no. 26; Lendinara (1996) 623, 638 n. 50; Liuzza (2001) 198 n. 88, 224–5; Hartzell (2006) no. 163; *ASMMF* XV (2007) 25–34 [no. 273; Doane]; Chardonnens (2007b) 38–9, 529–31, 552; Chardonnens (2007c); Scragg (2009b) 63; Wieland (2009) 143; Anlezark (2010) 137–9; Lendinara (2011a) 489 and nn. 51–2, 490–1; R. Gameson (2012a) 45–6; Scragg (2012a) nos. 645–56

FACS: Brownbill (1925) pl. before p. 497 [fol. 6v]; Hodgkin (1935) II, pl. 53 [fol. 6v]; A.G. Watson (1979) II, pl. 37 [fols. 128v–129r]; Dumville (1989) 226 [fol. 6v]; Bayless (1993) 84 [fol. 99r]; *ASMMF* XV (2007) no. 273

ED: Zupitza (1880/2001) [Ælfric, *Grammar*, coll. as h]; BCS no. 297 [*Tribal Hidage*]; Napier (1889) 8 [the thirty silver coins]; Mommsen (1892–8) II.389–90 [base MS for *De proprietatibus gentium*]; Winterfeld (1899) 116–21 [Abbo bk. III coll. as A]; W.H. Stevenson (1929) 103–12 [Abbo bk. III in prose, with OE gloss, coll. as H]; Henel (1934) 40, 48–9, 59, 67 [computistical notes]; Henel (1935) 332, 336–7, 339–41, 347 [prognostics and *computistica*]; Stoneman (1983) [*Interrogationes Sigewulfi* coll. as X^n]; Bayless (1993) 85–110 [base MS for Latin grammar ('Beatus quid est')]; Chardonnens (2007b) 284–6 [Dog Days], 344, 372, 376–7, 377–9 [*Dies Aegyptiaci*], 442 [*lunarium* for blood–letting], 473–5 [Regimen]; Dekker (2007) 293 n. 54 [*De Arca Noe*]; Anlezark (2010) 143–4 [*De Arca Noe*], 144–5 [the thirty silver coins], 146–50 [excerpts from Ælfric, Letter to Sigeweard]

LANG: Crowley (2000) 143

ST: Brownbill (1925) [*Tribal Hidage*]; Loyn (1962) 45–6, 306–9 [*Tribal Hidage*]; Bursill–Hall (1981) 118 [no. 149.138]; Tristram (1985) 31, 44, 47; Lendinara (1986) [Abbo of Saint–Germain]; Dumville (1989) 225–30, 286–7; Bayless (1993) 67–82 [Latin grammar ('Beatus quid est')]; Pulsiano (1998b) 88–9, 108 n. 19, 109 n. 20, 110 n. 24; D.W. Porter (2002) 36; Gneuss (2003b) 300; Keynes (2006) B 500 [Tribal Hidage];

Chardonnens (2007a) 322–4 and nn., 329, 339; Chardonnens (2007c); Dekker (2007) 292–3, 308, 311 n. 121; Lendinara (2007b) 183, 189–90; Rauer (2007) 127, 134, 137, 146; Alcamesi (2010) 195–6; Anlezark (2010); Chardonnens (2010) 249; Lendinara (2010) 117–18; Lendinara (2011a) 487 and n. 42 [Abbo]; Liuzza (2011) 1–77 [prognostics]

436. London, British Library, Harley 3376 (with Oxford, Bodleian Library, Lat. misc. a. 3, fol. 49 and Lawrence, University of Kansas, Spencer Research Library, Pryce P2A: 1)

s. x/xi, W England (Worcester?), (prov. prob. Worcester)

Contents: glossary[+][*]

MS: N.R. Ker (1957) no. 240; T.A.M. Bishop (1964–8c) 258; R.L. Collins (1976) no. 5; N.R. Ker (1976a) 124; Franzen (1991) 11, 73–4, 81, 109, 118 n. 41, 136, 138; Dumville (1992a) 136; Lapidge (1992b) 103 [repr. Lapidge (1993a) 93]; Dumville (1993g) 55 n. 242, 149 n. 49; Laing (1993) 96; Gneuss (1994b) 67, 74–8 [repr. Gneuss (1996b), no. IV]; Firchow (2001) 250–3 [description of Pryce P2A]; *ASMMF* VII (2002) 49–53 [no. 274; Doane: Harley 3376], 34–6 [no. 155; Doane: Lawrence leaf], 70–1 [no. 392; Doane: Oxford leaf]; Wieland (2009) 146; R. Gameson (2012a) 17 and n. 14; Scragg (2012a) no. 657

FACS: Firchow (2001) pls. 1, 3 [Lawrence leaf, fol. r and v]; *ASMMF* VII (2002) nos. 155, 274, 392

ED: Wright—Wülker (1884) I.192–247 [only Latin lemmata having OE glosses; corrections by E. Sievers (1891) 319–21, Boll (1904) *passim*, and Napier (1906) 356–7]; Napier (1900) no. 60 [Lawrence leaf]; Oliphant (1966) [unreliable; see reviews by Schabram (1968) and R. Derolez (1970a)]; Firchow (2001) 255, 257 [Lawrence leaf]

LANG: Bülbring (1901) 12; Boll (1904); Luick (1914–21) 31; J.J. Campbell (1955) 71–4; Schabram (1968) 495–500; R. Derolez (1970a); Hofstetter (1987) 523–4; Schabram (1988) 29–34; Herren (1992) 371–9; Laing (1993) 96; Gretsch (1999a) 80–1, 203; Firchow (2001)

ST: N.R. Ker (1957) 312 [literature on sources]; A.F. Cameron (1974) 221; Pheifer (1974) xxxv–xxxvi; Stemmler (1977); Herren (1987) 19–20, 23; Lendinara (1990b); A.K. Brown (1992) 106; Cooke (1993); Springer (1995) 147–8; Cooke (1997a); Cooke (1997b); Stoneman (1997) 115; Firchow (2001); Giliberto (2011) 127 and n. 37

London, British Library, Harley 3405, fol. 4: see no. 277

438. London, British Library, Harley 3826

s. x/xi, prob. Abingdon

Contents: Alcuin, *De orthographia* [redaction I, incomplete]; Bede, *De orthographia* [*CPL* 1566]; Abbo of Saint-Germain-des-Prés, *Bella Parisiacae urbis*, bk. III, glossed; Martianus Capella, *De nuptiis Philologiae et Mercurii*, bk. IV; glossaries, including Greek–Latin list of grammatical and metrical terms, and glosses to Iuvenalis, *Satirae* IV–VIII

MS: Laistner — King (1943) ix, 137; N.R. Ker (1957) no. 241; Leonardi (1960) 78–9; T.A.M. Bishop (1971) 13; C.E. Wright (1972) 435; C.W. Jones (1975) 3–5; Lapidge (1975a) 75 and n. 5, 88 n. 1 [repr. Lapidge (1993a) 113 and n. 5, 126 n. 1]; Gneuss (1994b) [repr. Gneuss (1996b) no. IV]; Jeudy (1996) 254, 272; Lendinara (1996) 632–6, 638 n. 50; Bruni (1997) xxxiv; *ASMMF* XV (2007) 35–40 [no. 276; Doane]; Wieland (2009) 143, 145, 150; Lendinara (2010) 118–20; R. Gameson (2012a) 49; Scragg (2012a) no. 658

FACS: *ASMMF* XV (2007) no. 276

ED: Von Winterfeld (1899) IV/i.112–21 [Abbo, *Bella Parisiacae urbis* bk. III, coll. as H]; C.W. Jones (1975) 2–57 [Bede, *De orthographia*, coll. as H]; Gneuss (1994b) 74–86 [repr. Gneuss (1996b) no. IV] [base MS for Greek–Latin list of grammatical and metrical terms]; Lendinara (1996) 642–55 [base MS for glosses to Iuvenalis, *Satirae*]; Bruni (1997) [Alcuin, *De orthographia*, coll. as H]; Lendinara (1999b) 316–20 [base MS for glosses to Iuvenalis, *Satirae*]

ST: Dionisotti (1982) 130–1, 138; Lendinara (1986) 83 n. 57; Bodden (1988) 218 n. 7, 221 n. 13, 230 n. 49; Lendinara (1996) 632–6; Bruni (1997) xliv–xlvi [relation to no. **69**]; Saenger (1997) 334 n. 19; *CSLMA* II (1999) 143; Lendinara (1999b); D.W. Porter (1999b) 172; D.W. Porter (2002) 36–7 and n. 132; Lapidge (2006) 321; Lendinara (2011a) 487 and n. 42; R. McKitterick (2012) 328

439. London, British Library, Harley 3859

s. xi/xii or xii in., England or France?

Contents: Vegetius, *Epitome rei militaris*; computistical notes; Macrobius, *Saturnalia*; (pseudo?-)Sallust and pseudo-Cicero, *Inuectiuae*; 'Nennius', *Historia Brittonum* ['Harleian Recension']; *Annales Cambriae*; Augustine, *De haeresibus* [*CPL* 314] (f); Solinus, *Collectanea*; *cantus auium*; Aethicus Ister, *Cosmographia* [*CPL* 2348]; Vitruvius, *De architectura*

MS: Wuttke (1853) cxxvi; Krinsky (1967) 52; C.E. Wright (1972) 242,
   436; L.D. Reynolds (1983) 151 n. 8; Dumville et al. (1993) 222; Prinz
   (1993) 64; Webster—Brown (1997) 214–15 [no. 11]; R. Gameson
   (1999a) no. 450

FACS: M.P. Brown (1991) pl. 4 [fol. 187r]; M.P. Brown (2007a) pl. 3
   [fol. 187r]

ED: Faral (1929) III.5–29 (odd pages), 30–44 [*Historia Brittonum* coll.
   as H]; J. Morris (1980) 95–91 [base MS for *Annales Cambriae*, with
   variants from other MSS]

ST: Manitius (1911–31) I.241; Kenney (1929) 154; Lambert (1969–72)
   no. 621; Römer (1972b) 182 [Augustine, *De haeresibus*]; Dumville
   (1972–4); Dumville (1975); L.D. Reynolds (1983a) 350–1 [*Inuectiuae*],
   443 [Vitruvius]; *BCLL* (1985) nos. 127 [*Historia Brittonum*], 135
   [*Annales Cambriae*], 647 [Aethicus Ister]; Bodden (1988) 231; Lapidge
   (2006) 286, 320, 333, 335, 337

439. 3. London, British Library, Harley 3908, fols. 1–100

s. xi/xii or xii in., Canterbury StA

Contents: Goscelin of Canterbury, *Vita S. Mildrethae* [*BHL* 5960];
   Lessons [eight from Goscelin's *Vita S. Mildrethae*, four from Gregory,
   Homiliae .xl. in Euangelia I. xii (abbreviated)] for Nocturns; Mass and
   Office for St Mildred; sequence (inc. 'Christe salus hominum, angelo-
   rum gloria'; not in SK, SK Suppl. or WIC); Goscelin of Canterbury,
   Translatio S. Mildrethae [*BHL* 5961–4]

MS: Hardy (1862–71) I.376–81; N.R. Ker (1960) 30; N.R. Ker (1964) 44;
   Rollason (1982) 106; Rollason (1986) 149–50; R. Sharpe (1990) 510–13;
   Andrew Hughes (1993) 268–70; R. Gameson (1999a) no. 452; Gneuss
   (2003b) 300; Hartzell (2006) no. 164; T.N. Hall (2007) 259

FACS: R. Sharpe (1991) 94 [fol. 48r]

ED: Rollason (1982) 108–43 [Goscelin, *Vita S. Mildrethae*, partly coll.
   as C]; Rollason (1986) 154–210 [Goscelin, *Translatio S. Mildrethae*,
   coll. as C]; Hartzell (2006) 306 [base MS for rhymed Office]

ST: R. Sharpe (1991); N. Orchard (1995b) 91 and n. 24; Biggs et al. (2001)
   347–50; T.N. Hall (2001) 125, 128 and n. 54

439. 6. London, British Library, Harley 5228, fol. 140

s. ix, prob. Wales, (prov. Worcester)

Contents: Gregory, *Regula pastoralis* I. x–xi [*CPL* 1712] (f)

MS: N.R. Ker (1964) 207; Schreiber (2002) 25 and n. 17

ST: Lapidge (2006) 306

439. 9. London, British Library, Harley 5431, fol. 1

s. x/xi, prob. Canterbury, StA

Contents: music book (f)

MS: Hartzell (2006) no. 166

440. London, British Library, Harley 5431, fols. 4–126

s. x/xi or x^2 or x$^{4/4}$, prob. Canterbury StA, (prov. ibid.)

Contents: computus materials; *Regula S. Benedicti* [*CPL* 1852];
  Capitulare monasticum; *Memoriale qualiter*; 'De festiuitatibus anni'
  (Ansegisus, *Capitularium collectio* II. 33, erased)

MS: M.R. James (1903) 246, 517; T.A.M. Bishop (1954–8b) 329; Morgand
  (1963) 182; Semmler (1963) 506; N.R. Ker (1964) 44; T.A.M. Bishop
  (1964–8d) 396 n. 2; T.A.M. Bishop (1971) 18; C.E. Wright (1972) 95,
  239, 457; Gretsch (1973) 25–7; Pächt—Alexander (1973) no. 37;
  Hanslik (1977) lxviii; Rella (1977) 56, 77; D.H. Turner et al. (1980) 104;
  Backhouse et al. (1984b) no. 27 [D.H. Turner]; Ramsay—Sparks (1988)
  24; P. Wormald (1988b) 31 n. 74; Lapidge—Winterbottom (1991b) lvii
  n. 79; Dumville (1993g) 98 n. 78; Mordek (1995) 231–2; N.M.
  Thompson (2007) 117–18; Barker-Benfield (2008) I.lxxxii n. 71, 198,
  246, 315, 316, 413, 641, 653–4, 664–5, 668–9, 718, II.1489, 1610,
  III.1701, 1705, 1706–8, 1723, 1796, 1814, 1829, 1837; Wieland (2009)
  152; R. Gameson (2012a) 29 n. 66, 49 n. 148

DEC: F. Wormald (1945) 120, 134 [repr. F. Wormald (1984) 59 and n. 38,
  72–3]; Kendrick (1949) 31 n., 36 n.; Rice (1952) 206; E. Temple (1976)
  no. 38; Brownrigg (1978) 260; Ohlgren (1986) no. 143; R. Gameson
  (1995b) 122 n. 27

FACS: *NPS* II, pl. 63 [fols. 7r, 75r, 118v]; Kendrick (1949) pl. XXXI (4)
  [fol. 68v (detail)]; E. Temple (1976) ills. 115, 120, 126, 127 [fols. 38v,
  54v, 101r, 16v (all details)]; Backhouse et al. (1984b) 48 [fols. 6v–7r];
  Ramsay—Sparks (1988) 23 [fols. 6v–7r]; M.P. Brown (1991) pl. 70
  [fols. 6v–7r]; M.P. Brown (2007a) pl. 78 [fols. 6v–7r]

ED: Morgand (1963) 229–61 [*Memoriale qualiter* coll. as C]; Semmler
  (1963) 515–35 [*Capitulare monasticum* coll. as G3]; Gretsch (1973)

68–87 [*Regula S. Benedicti*, chs. v, xxvii–xxx, lviii, coll. as h]; Hanslik (1977) [*Regula S. Benedicti* coll as h]

ST: N.R. Ker (1957) p. 263; Meyvaert (1963) 100–1; Morgand (1963) 204–20; Semmler (1963) 512–13; Gretsch (1973) *passim*; Gretsch (1974); Rella (1977) 162; Sauer (1984) 419–21; Cross (1992b); Graham (1998a) 23 n. 9; 25 and nn. 18, 19; 35 and n. 58; Gretsch (1999a) 247; Gretsch (2003a) 116–17, 119

440. 5. London, British Library, Harley 5915, fol. 2

s. xi med.

Contents: Augustine, *In Iohannis epistulam ad Parthos* [*CPL* 279], tractatus V (f)

ST: Lapidge (2006) 289

441. London, British Library, Harley 5915, fols. 8 and 9 (with Bloomington, Indiana University, Lilly Library, Add. 1000)

s. xi¹

Contents: Ælfric, *Grammar*⁺* (f)

MS: Zupitza (1880/2001) vii–viii; N.R. Ker (1957) nos. 242, 384; R.L. Collins (1964); C.E. Wright (1972) xvi, 463; R.L. Collins (1976) 43–4; N.R. Ker (1976a) 125; Gatch (1985) 109; Stoneman (1997) 103–4, 119; *ASMMF* XVI (2008) 1–3 [no. 14; Doane], 69–70 [no. 277; Lucas]; Scragg (2012a) no. 659

FACS: R.L. Collins (1976) pl. 4 [recto of Lilly MS]; *ASMMF* XVI (2008) nos. 14, 277

ED: Zupitza (1880/2001) 201–3 [Bloomington fragment (only) of Ælfric, *Grammar*, coll. as S]

441. 1. London, British Library, Harley 5915, fol. 10 (with Weinheim, Sammlung E. Fischer, s.n. [lost; Ernst Fischer gave his collections, including fragments, to the Universitätsbibliothek, Heidelberg, but this fragment has never been found, and may be in a private collection])

s. viii med., prob. Northumbria [York?]

Contents: Iustinus, *Epitome* of Pompeius Trogus, *Historiae Philippicae* (f)

MS: Brandt (1910); *CLA* IX (1959) no. 1370; T.J. Brown (1975) 286 [repr. T.J. Brown (1993a) 170]; Godman (1982) 125 n.; Munk Olsen (1982—) I.539; L.D. Reynolds (1983) 197–9; Crick (1987) 187–96;

Reynolds—Wilson (1991) 91; Bischoff et al. (1992b) 303; Lapidge (1994b) 109; Lapidge (2006) 41, 130 n. 7; Wieland (2009) 143; Garrison (2012) 649–70 and n. 99

FACS: *CLA* IX (1959) no. 1370 [Weinheim fragment]; Crick (1987) pl. VIII [Harley leaf, verso]

ED: Crick (1987) 195–6 [Iustinus text from Harley leaf]

ST: Lapidge (2006) 130, 318

441. 3. London, British Library, Harley 5915, fol. 12

s. xi ex. (1080s), Canterbury CC

Contents: Augustine, *Contra mendacium* [*CPL* 304] (f), *De cura pro mortuis gerenda* [*CPL* 307] (f)

MS: Gullick (1998c) 175–8, 188–9; R. Gameson (1999a) no. 457

FACS: Gullick (1998c) 176 [fol. 12r (detail)], 177 [fol. 12r]

ST: Lapidge (2006), 283, 284

442. London, British Library, Harley 5915, fol. 13 (with Cambridge, Magdalene College, Pepys 2981 (16))

s. xi in.

Contents: Ælfric, *Catholic Homilies** (f; from CH I, Homilies XX and XXVIII)

MS: N.R. Ker (1957) no. 243; Dumville (1988) 59–61; McKitterick— Whalley (1989) 9; Clemoes (1997) 63–4; Graham (1998a) 57 n. 27; *ASMMF* XVI (2008) 15–16 [no. 66; Lucas], 69–70 [no. 277a; Lucas]; R. Gameson (2012a) 67 n. 232; Scragg (2012a) no. 660

FACS: *ASMMF* XVI (2008) nos. 66, 277a

ED: Clemoes (1997) 339–40 [Ælfric, CH I, Hom. XX (*Feria .IIII. De fide catholica*), coll. as f^m], 413 [Ælfric, CH I, Hom. XXVIII (St Andrew), coll. as f^m]

London, British Library, Harley 5977 no. 59: see no. **524**

442. 3. London, British Library, Harley 5977, no. 62

s. x/xi or xi in.

Contents: gospels (f; Luke VI.23–8)

MS: Gwara (1994c); R. Gameson (1999a) no. 458

442. 4. London, British Library, Harley 5977, no. 64

s. x/xi or xi, Continent? In England before 1100?

Contents: excerpt from Bede, *De arte metrica* [*CPL* 1565] (f)

MS: Gwara (1994c)

443. London, British Library, Harley 7653

s. viii/ix or ix in., Mercia (Worcester?)

Contents: prayerbook (fragmentary: eight prayers, including SK 7891, and litany)

MS: Birch (1889) 114–19 *et passim*; Warren (1895) 87–97; J.A. Robinson (1923) 68; Kenney (1929) 268–9, 718–19 [no. 575]; *CLA* II (1935) no. 104; N.R. Ker (1957) no. 245; Lapidge (1986a) 272; Morrish (1988) 526, 537; Biggs et al. (1990) 139 [Bestul]; Sims-Williams (1990) 256, 275–327; Lapidge (1991a) 75; Webster—Backhouse (1991) no. 162 [M.P. Brown]; Dumville (1992a) 96, 101–2; *ASMMF* I (1994) 49–51 [no. 279; Doane]; M.P. Brown (1996) 153–4 *et passim*; Raw (1997) 145 n. 1; Crowley (2000) 123 n. 2, 144; M.P. Brown (2001b) 282; M.P. Brown (2001c) 51–8; K.L. Brown—R.J.H. Clark (2004b) 181–2; Biggs (2007a) 8; M.P. Brown (2007a) 53; R. Gameson (2012a) 82 n. 297; Raw (2012) 460 and n. 1, 461 and n. 11, 462–4; Scragg (2012a) no. 661

FACS: Webster—Backhouse (1991) 209 [fols. 2v–3r]; *ASMMF* I (1994) no. 279; M.P. Brown (1996) fig. 8 [fols. 2v–3r]; K.L. Brown—R.J.H. Clark (2004b) pl. 1 [fol. 6v]

ED: Warren (1895) 83–97; *AH* LI (1908) 295–6 [metrical prayer (SK 7891) coll. as A]; Lapidge (1991a) 210–11 [litany]

ST: Lambert (1969–72) no. 950 (I); *BCLL* (1985) nos. 1279, 1288; M.P. Brown (1996) 141–2, 151–4, 168–9, 171–2 *et passim*; *CSLMA* II (1999) 480; Pratt (2001) 47 n. 47; K.L. Brown—R.J.H. Clark (2004b) 182–3; Krüger (2007) 75, 345–6

444. London, British Library, Royal 1. A. xviii

s. ix/x or x in., Brittany, prov. England (royal court?), prob. Canterbury StA by 924×939, (prov. ibid.)

Contents: gospels (for use in the Mass)

MS: Thompson—Warner (1881–4) II.37; Warner—Gilson (1921) I.7; Kenney (1929) 656 [no. 504]; N.R. Ker (1964) 44; Rella (1977) 50;

Wormald—Alexander (1977) 10, 13 n. 1; A.G. Watson (1979) I, no. 853; Rella (1980) 112; Deuffic (1985) 302 [no. 48]; Keynes (1985a) 165–70; Dumville (1987) 175 and n. 161; B. Fischer (1988–91) I.18*; O'Reilly (1994) 222–5; Lenker (1997) 115–17, 418, 458–61; Parkes (1997b) 103 and n. 25; Bischoff (1998–) II, no. 2491; Lemoine (2005) 184; Barker-Benfield (2008) I.lv and n. 17, cii n. 103, III.1654 n. 42, 1696, 1734, 1796; R. Gameson (2012d) 349 and n. 17; D. Ganz (2012) 190 n. 14; Marsden (2012) 422 and n. 71

DEC: Cohen—Teviotdale (1999)

FACS: Wormald—Alexander (1977) pl. XXXIV (d) [fol. 162r]; A.G. Watson (1979) II, pl. 17 [fol. 66r]; Keynes (1985a) pl. VII [fol. 3v]

ED: B. Fischer (1988–91) [gospel excerpts coll. as Bc]

ST: Berger (1893) 46–50, 386; J.A. Robinson (1923) 61; Glunz (1933) 63, 90, 111, 112, 119; Frere (1934) 224; Klauser (1972) xxxv [no. 7]; McGurk (1996) [repr. McGurk (1998) no. X]; Lenker (1997) 115–17, 418, 458–61; Cohen—Teviotdale (1999) 69–70 and n. 38; Lapidge (2006) 170

445. London, British Library, Royal 1. B. vii

s. viii[1], prob. Northumbria, prov. S England (royal court?) s. x[1]

Contents: gospels; manumission* (*c.* 925)

MS: Wanley (1705) 181; Thompson—Warner (1881–4) II.19–20; J. Wordsworth et al. (1889–1954) I.xxvi; M.R. James (1903) 532; Warner—Gilson (1921) I.10–11; *CLA* II (1935) no. 213; Bischoff (1952) 93; Kendrick et al. (1956–60) II.33, 43–6 *et passim* [T.J. Brown]; McGurk (1956) 258, 265 [repr. McGurk (1998) no. I]; N.R. Ker (1957) no. 246; McGurk (1961a) no. 28; McGurk (1961b) 12 [repr. McGurk (1998) no. V]; Gamber (1968–88) no. 406; Keynes (1985a) 185–9; Dumville (1987) 171 n. 130; Webster—Backhouse (1991) no. 84; Dumville (1992a) 104, 113, 121; Dumville (1992b) 93–4, 94 n. 192, 157 n. 103; Dumville (1994a) 158; Netzer (1994) 8, 58, 60, 213 n. 62, 218 n. 16, 221 n. 8; O'Sullivan (1994) 81; Lenker (1997) 389; Webster—Brown (1997) 245–6 [no. 143]; Dumville (1999) 96–7; M.P. Brown (2001c) 55; *ASMMF* VII (2002) 54–7 [no. 281; Doane]; K.L. Brown (2004a) 10; Beall (2005) 197; Hartzell (2006) no. 167; M.P. Brown (2007a) 52, 55, 87; Barker-Benfield (2008) III.1830; M.P. Brown (2012) 135, 151; R. Gameson (2012a) 28 n. 59, 42 n. 117, 56 and n. 191; Marsden (2012) 419 and n. 61

DEC: Alexander (1978a) no. 20; Ohlgren (1986) no. 20; R. Gameson (1994b); Tilghman (2011) 98; R. Gameson (2012c) 289 n. 141; Netzer (2012) 225–6 and n. 3, 233

FACS: Alexander (1978a) ills. 70–3 [fols. 15v, 15r, 10v, 84r]; Keynes (1985a) pl. XI [fol. 15v]; M.P. Brown (1991) pls. 45, 53 [fols. 15v, 10v]; R. Gameson (1994b) 25–7 [fols. 55r, 14v, 4v (detail)]; *ASMMF* VII (2002) no. 281; M.P. Brown (2003a) 20 [fol. 10v]; M.P. Brown (2003c) fig. 25 [fol. 15v]; K.L. Brown (2004a) pl. 2 [fols. 9r, 12r]; M.P. Brown (2007a) pls. 34–5 [fols. 10v, 15v]

ED: Harmer (1914) no. 19 [manumission]; Hurst—Fraipont (1955) ix–xvi [*Capitula Euangeliorum* coll. as N; see also *CPL* no. 1977]; B. Fischer (1988–91) [gospel excerpts coll. as Nr]

ST: Morin (1891); Berger (1893) 39, 43, 355, 386; Morin (1893a) 426–35; J.A. Robinson (1923) 66–7; Glunz (1930); Glunz (1933) 31; Frere (1934) 136; Kunze (1947) 48; McGurk (1955a) 192–3 [repr. McGurk (1998) no. III]; Klauser (1972) xxxii; Whitelock (1979) 383, 607 n. 140; Verey et al. (1980) 68–75; Horsley—Waterhouse (1984) 215 n. 31; Conner (1993) 56, 63–5, 66, 68, 70, 72, 75; McGurk (1993) 248–51 [repr. McGurk (1998) no. XI]; McGurk (1994b) 22 [repr. McGurk (1998) no. XII]; M.P. Brown (1996) 130–1 [parallels with no. **28**]; Lenker (1997) 102–6, 389–91 *et passim*; Werner (1997a) 24 n. 6; K.L. Brown—R.J.H. Clark (2004a) 10; Beall (2005) 193–4, 197; Farr (2011a) 99 n. 49, 134; Karkov (2011) 134

446. London, British Library, Royal 1. D. iii

s. xi med., prov. Rochester s. xi ex.

Contents: gospels; *Exultet* [*CPL* 162] (added s. xi ex.)

MS: Warner—Gilson (1921) I.16; N.R. Ker (1964) 161; M.P. Richards (1988) 45, 65 and n. 13; Heslop (1990) 152 n. 3; R. Sharpe et al. (1996) 531; Cohen—Teviotdale (1999) 67 and n. 2, 70 and n. 38; Hartzell (2006) no. 169; R. Gameson (2012a) 44; McGurk (2012) 446 [no. 12]

ST: Berger (1893) 43; Glunz (1933) 63, 112

447. London, British Library, Royal 1. D. ix

s. xi in., Canterbury CC (or Peterborough?), prov. s xi (prob. by 1018) Canterbury CC

Contents: gospels, gospel list; records* (not after 1020): notice of confraternity, writ [Sawyer (1968) no. 985]

MS: J. Wordsworth et al. (1889–1954) I.xxvi; M.R. James (1903) xxv, 515; Warner—Gilson (1921) I.17–18; T.A.M. Bishop (1954–8a) 186; N.R. Ker (1957) no. 247; N.R. Ker (1964) 36; T.A.M. Bishop (1967a) 39, 41; Sawyer (1968) 56 and no. 985; T.A.M. Bishop (1971) xv, 23–4; Backhouse et al. (1984b) no. 52 [D.H. Turner]; McGurk (1986b) 43, 44, 46, 48, 51–4, 56–63 [repr. McGurk (1998) no. XIV]; M.P. Richards (1988) 66–7; Dumville (1992a) 121; Dumville (1993g) 86 n. 4, 113 n. 12, 116–20 and nn., 122 and n. 58, 139–40 and n. 117; McGurk— Rosenthal (1995b) 258–62 [repr. McGurk (1998) no. XV]; Lenker (1997) 451–2; Rushforth (2001) 138 n. 8, 139 n. 12, 142; *ASMMF* VII (2002) 58–61 [no. 282; Doane]; Heslop (2004) 298 n. 27, 305 n. 41; McGurk—Rosenthal (2006) 194 n. 46; Crick (2012) 184 n. 44; R. Gameson (2012a) 44, 73; Gullick (2012) 306 and n. 76; Marsden (2012) 423 and n. 78, 424 and n. 86; McGurk (2012) 446 [no. 13]; Scragg (2012a) nos. 445, 670

DEC: F. Wormald (1945) 132 [repr. F. Wormald (1984) 70]; Rice (1952) 195; E. Temple (1976) no. 70; Brownrigg (1978) 246 n. 2, 249, 264–5; Ohlgren (1986) no. 175; Raw (1990) 220; R. Gameson (1995b) 6 n. 3, 206–7, 215 n. 144, 217 n. 152, 228, 230, 233; McGurk—Rosenthal (1995b) 286 [repr. McGurk (1998) no. XV]; Dodwell (2000) 122 n. 96; McGurk—Rosenthal (2006) 196; R. Gameson (2012c) 283 and n. 118

FACS: Chaplais (1968) pl. II [fol. 44v]; E. Temple (1976) ill. 222 [fol. 111r]; *ASMMF* VII (2002) no. 282

ED: J. Wordsworth et al. (1889-1954) vol. I [Latin gospels coll. as A]; Harmer (1952) no. 26 [writ]; N.R. Ker (1957) 317 [notice of confraternity]

ST: Glunz (1930) 169; Glunz (1933) 140–8 [biblical text]; Frere (1934) 160–3; Harmer (1952) 168–71, 446–8 [writ]; Chaplais (1966) 172 [repr. Ranger (1973) 59]; Klauser (1972) li *et passim*; Heslop (1990) 154, 168 n. 49, 181; Dumville (1992a) 121; Lenker (1997) 442–50, 478; R. Gameson (2004b)

448. London, British Library, Royal 1. E. vi (with Canterbury, Cathedral Library, Add. 16 and Oxford, Bodleian Library, Lat. bib. b. 2(P))

s. ix^1 or ix$^{2/4}$ or ix med., S England, (prov. Canterbury StA)

Contents: Bible (part): gospels (incomplete), Actus Apostolorum (f)

MS: Thompson—Warner (1881–4) II.21; J. Wordsworth et al. (1889–1954) I.xxvi–xxvii; M.R. James (1903) lxv, 516; Warner—Gilson (1921)

I.20; *CLA* II (1935) nos. *214, *244, 262; McGurk (1962) [repr. McGurk (1998) no. VII]; N.R. Ker (1964) 44; *CLA* Supplement (1971) p. 5; Budny (1984); M.P. Brown (1986); B. Fischer (1988–91) I.16*; Morrish (1988) 529, 537; M.P. Brown (1990) 52; Webster—Backhouse (1991) no. 171 [M.P. Brown]; T.J. Brown (1993a) 210, 273 n. 95; Marsden (1995) 42–5, 304, 380 n., 445; M.P. Brown (1996) 93–5, 171–8 *et passim*; Webster—Brown (1997) 240 [no. 118]; Budny (1999) 237–48, 255–60, 264–8, 270–3; R. Gameson (1999c) 363; Marsden (1999) 289, 295–6; M.P. Brown (2003c) 67–8 *et passim*; K.L. Brown—R.J.H. Clark (2004b) 181, 183; Gullick (2004) 33; Emms (2006) 26; Barker-Benfield (2008) I.lxi, lxxxix, xcv, 373, 443, 516, 606, III.1656, 1658, 1730, 1733, 1747, 1801, 1822, 1838; R. Gameson (2008) 56–62; M.P. Brown (2012) 139 and n. 79, 145 n. 113, 156 and n. 166, 159, 160, 163, 165; R. Gameson (2012a) 38 and n. 92, 43 n. 123, 53, 87 n. 311, 90 n. 329; Marsden (2012) 414 and n. 34

DEC: Kendrick (1938) 162; F. Wormald (1945) 112 n. 1 [repr. F. Wormald (1984) 174 n. 15]; Rickert (1955) 19–20, 219 n. 52; Köhler—Mütherich (1971–99) VII.31 n. 31; E. Temple (1976) no. 55; Alexander (1978a) no. 32; Budny (1984); D.M. Wilson (1984) 94–6; F. Wormald (1984) 20, 22, 25; Ohlgren (1986) nos. 32, 160; Raw (1990) 220–1; R. Gameson (1995b) 92, 100 n. 167, 103, 180, 197, 209; K.L. Brown—R.J.H. Clark (2004b) 183–4; McGurk—Rosenthal (2006) 189 n. 21, 196; Karkov (2009) 224; M.P. Brown (2011b) 40, 41–2; Netzer (2012) 240 and n. 86

FACS: Warner—Gilson (1921) IV, pl. 14 [fol. 20v]; E. Temple (1976) ill. 172 [fol. 30v]; Budny (1984) fifty-five pls. from this MS; D.M. Wilson (1984) pls. 103 [fol. 4r (detail)], 114 [fol. 43r]; F. Wormald (1984) ill. 25 [fol. 43r (detail)]; M.P. Brown (1990) 53 [fol. 28v]; T.J. Brown (1993a) ill. 57 [fol. 14r (detail)]; Backhouse (1997) pl. 4 [fol. 5r]; R. Gameson (1999b) pl. VI [fol. 44r], figs. 11.3–5 [fols. 4r, 43r, 28v]; M.P. Brown (2003c) fig. 32 [fol. 34r]; K.L. Brown (2004b) pl. 2 [fols. 4r, 30v, 43r]; McGurk—Rosenthal (2006) fig. 19 [fol. 46r]; M.P. Brown (2007a) pls. 52, 53, 117 [fols. 4r, 43r, 30v]; Withers (2007) 82 [fol. 30v]

ED: B. Fischer (1988–91) [gospels coll. as Er]

ST: Berger (1893) 35, 355, 386–7; Glunz (1933) 29; McGurk (1961a) 13, 16 [repr. McGurk (1998) no. VI]; McGurk (1961b) 12 [repr. McGurk (1998) no. V]; Budny (1984); McGurk (1993) 245 n. 10, 254 n. 35 [repr. McGurk (1998) no. XI]; McGurk (1994b) 2–3 and nn. [repr. McGurk (1998) no. XII]; Withers (2007) 78

449. London, British Library, Royal 1. E. vii + viii

s. x/xi, prov. Canterbury CC

Contents: Bible (pandect)

MS: M.R. James (1903) lxiv, 52; Warner—Gilson (1921) I.20–1; T.A.M. Bishop (1959–63a) 94; N.R. Ker (1964) 36; Dumville (1991–5) 47–8; Dumville (1993g) 109–10, 146 and n. 32; Marsden (1994a); R. Gameson (1995a) 104 n. 31, 111 n., 142; Marsden (1995) 321–78 *et passim*; Webber (1995) 155–6; Parkes (1997b) 111 and n. 62; Pulsiano (2001a) xxix; Biggs (2007a) 58; Shepard (2007) 80 and n. 69, 270; Wieland (2009) 115; R. Gameson (2012a) 20, 33; Marsden (2012) 425 and n. 89; Toswell (2012) 473

DEC: F. Wormald (1952) 71 [no. 37]; Heimann (1966) 53 n. 78; E. Temple (1976) no. 102; Ohlgren (1986) no. 207; Raw (1990) 35, 221; R. Gameson (1995b) 187, 188 n. 175

FACS: E. Temple (1976) ill. 319 [1. E. vii, fol. 1v]; Marsden (1995) pl. VII [1. E. vii, fol. 113r]; Parkes (1997b) pl. 10 [1. E. vii, fol. 4r]

ED: Pulsiano (2001a) [Pss. I–L coll. as π]

ST: Korhammer (1976) 365; N.P. Brooks (1984) 268; M.P. Richards (1988) 63–5, 75–6, 81–3; Biggs et al. (1990) 59 [C.D. Wright]; Marsden (1995) 321–78 *et passim*; Lenker (1997) 101 and n. 30

450. London, British Library, Royal 2. A. xx

s. viii^2 or ix$^{1/4}$, Mercia (Worcester?), OE glosses and note, s. x^1; thirty-three prayers added s. x med. in margins, Worcester

Contents:

s. viii^2 or ix$^{1/4}$: prayerbook: gospel extracts; Pater noster°; Creed°; apocryphal letter of Christ to Abgar; three canticles°; two charms

s. x med.: thirty-three prayers, mainly collects for Mass and Office (including collects and SK 708, 9504); excerpts from Augustine, *Soliloquia* [*CPL* 252] I.1; litany; two creeds (including SK 9568); note on moonrise*; exorcism; two hymns [SK 33 (by Sedulius), 588]

MS: Thompson—Warner (1884) II.60; Kuypers (1902) 200; Mearns (1914) 3; Warner—Gilson (1921) I.33–6; Kenney (1929) 719–20 [no. 576]; *CLA* II (1935) no. *215; N.R. Ker (1957) no. 248; N.R. Ker (1964) 207; Gamber (1968–88) nos. 170, 215; Gneuss (1968) 103–4, 117, 122, 157; T.J. Brown (1980) 13; Morrish (1988) 518–22, 537; Muir (1988) xxx; Biggs et al. (1990) 138 [Bestul]; M.P. Brown (1990) 54 [no. 18]; Sims-Williams (1990) 280–1; M.P. Brown (1991) 40 [no. 39]; Lapidge (1991a) 75; Webster—Backhouse (1991) no. 163 [M.P. Brown]; Dumville (1992a) 70, 101–2; Lapidge (1992b) 102 [repr. Lapidge (1993a) 92]; Dumville (1993g) 76–7, 114 n. 14; *ASMMF* I (1994) 53–8 [no. 283; Doane]; Dumville (1994a) 150 and nn. 98–9; Springer (1995) 148–9; Webster—Brown (1997) 246 [no. 144]; Muir (1998) 12–19; Gretsch (2000) 109; Lapidge (2000a) 15–16; M.P. Brown (2001b); K.L. Brown—R.J.H. Clark (2004b) 181, 183; Crowley (2006) 223–36; Biggs (2007a) 13, 57; M.P. Brown (2012) 158; R. Gameson (2012a) 43 n. 119, 82 n. 297, 86 n. 309; Raw (2012) 460 and n. 1, 461 and n. 12, 462–4

DEC: Alexander (1978a) no. 35; Ohlgren (1986) no. 35; Raw (1990) 221; M.P. Brown (2001c) 51–8; K.L. Brown (2004b) 183; M.P. Brown (2007a) 104; M.P. Brown (2011b) 37

FACS: Thompson—Warner (1881–4) II, pl. 21 [fol. 14v]; L.W. Daly (1982) 97 [fol. 49v]; Morrish (1988) pls. 5–6 [fols. 26r, 39v]; M.P. Brown (1990) 55 [fol. 17r]; M.P. Brown (1991) pl. 39 [fol. 17r]; Dumville (1993g) pl. I [fol. 14v]; *ASMMF* I (1994) no. 283; M.P. Brown (1996) fig. 9 [fols. 16v–17r]; Lapidge (2000a) 16 [fol. 17r]; Crowley (2006) pls. 1–8 [fols. 14v, 14r, 32v, 15r, 40v, 16r, 26v, 38v]; K.L. Brown (2004b) pl. 1 [fols. 4v, 17r]; M.P. Brown (2007a) pl. 47 [fols. 16v–17r]; Owen-Crocker (2009) fig. 2.5 [fol. 17r]

ED: Zupitza (1889) [OE glosses, titles to prayers]; Kuypers (1902) 201–25 [base MS for prayerbook]; *AH* LI (1908) 294–5 [hymn (SK 708 = Warner—Gilson (1921) item 18) coll. as A]; W. Meyer (1917) [hymns]; Hurst—Fraipont (1955) 445–6, 449 [hymns coll. as R]; Muir (1988) [Warner—Gilson (1921) items 18, 22, and 67 coll. as R]; Lapidge (1991a) 212–13 [base MS for litany = Warner—Gilson (1921) item 20]; Corrêa (1996) 311–18 [thirty-three Latin prayers copied in margins of MS]; Crowley (2006) 256–91 [thirty-five Latin prayers copied in margins of MS]

LANG: K. Sisam (1953a) 120; Korhammer (1976) 165; Hofstetter (1987) 507; Crowley (2000); Crowley (2006) 236–41

ST: Birch (1889) 101–13; Warren (1895) 89–102; E. Bishop (1918) 139–51, 192–7; Siegmund (1949) 40 n. 2; Godel (1963) 297–308; Römer (1972b) 185; Gjerløw (1980) I.24–5 [on Ker art. c]; L.W. Daly (1982) 95–7 [Greek palindrome]; Sims-Williams (1982) 23; *BCLL* (1985) no. 1278; Lapidge (1986a) 272–3; Biggs et al. (1990) 138 [Bestul]; Sims-Williams (1990) 274–327, 445; M.P. Brown (1993) 151–4, 157–8, 168–9, 171–2, 175–6 *et passim*; *CPL* (1995) no. 2018; Corrêa (1996) 288–92; R.

Gameson (1996a) 230, 240; Crowley (1997); Raw (1997) 145–53; *CSLMA* II (1999) 106, 480; Pettit (1999) 45; Crowley (2000); M.P. Brown (2001c); Szarmach (2005) 159–60; Crowley (2006); Krüger (2007) 71–2, 346; Cain (2009)

451. London, British Library, Royal 2. B. v (the 'Royal Psalter')

s. x med., prov. Winchester, prov. Canterbury CC s. xi; with additions s. x ex.–xi¹, xi in., xi med. or xi²

Contents: Psalterium Romanum° with commentary; canticles°: s. x med., prov. Winchester, prov. Canterbury CC s. xi. Additions: encyclopedic notes (as in nos. **56** and **90**): on Christ's Incarnation, the Ages of the World (followed here by Bede, *De temporibus*, ch. xvi), the Ages of Man, the numbers of bones, veins and teeth in humans, the Dimensions of the World, the Temple of Solomon, the Tabernacle, St Peter's in Rome, Noah's Ark, the numbers of books in the Old and New Testament, the number of verses in the Psalms, units for measuring distances; thunder prognostics; prayers*; note on Friday fasts*: s. x ex. – xi¹; prayer: s. xi in., Winchester; Office of the Virgin: s. xi med. or xi², Winchester Nun? proverbs⁺*, prayer*: s. xi med.

MS: Dewick (1902) x–xii; Warner—Gilson (1921) I.40–1; N.R. Ker (1957) no. 249; N.R. Ker (1964) 104; Parkes (1976b) 162, 163 n. 4 [repr. Parkes (1991) 159, 160 n. 4]; C.W. Jones (1980) 247; Parkes (1983) 137 n. 50; Hartzell (1989) 86; Dumville (1991–5) 48; Robinson—Stanley (1991) 26; Dumville (1992a) 102 n. 35, 125 n. 221; Dumville (1992b) 63 n. 28; Conner (1993) 63, 65, 70–1, 73, 75–6; Dumville (1993g) 14 and n. 23; *ASMMF* II (1994) 57–64 [no. 284; Pulsiano]; Blockley (1994); Dumville (1994a) 147, 149–50; McDougall—McDougall (1997) 211 n. 8, 221 n. 54; Gneuss (1998) 276; Pulsiano (1998b) 85, 105 n. 1; Gretsch (1999a) 264–8, 430–1; Crowley (2000) 132; Gretsch (2000) 86; Liuzza (2001) 225; Chardonnens (2007b) 46–7, 531–2, 553; P.A. Stokes (2007) [on fol. 198]; Scragg (2008d); Rushforth (2011) 40–2; R. Gameson (2012a) 39 and n. 95; D. Ganz (2012) 193 and n. 32; Raw (2012) 466; Scragg (2012a) nos. 672–82; Toswell (2012) 471, 475

FACS: Dewick (1902) pls. 1–11 [fols. 1r–6r]; Warner—Gilson (1921) IV, pl. 22 {fol. 8r]; Robinson—Stanley (1991) pl. 32.1 [fol. 6r]; *ASMMF* II (1994) no. 284

ED: Logeman (1889) [prayers: Ker arts. c, d, e, f, i; confession and prayers: Ker art. g]; Dewick (1902) cols. 1–18 [base MS for Office of the Virgin]; Roeder (1904) xii–xiii [proverbs], 1–302 [psalter and canticles, in Latin with OE gloss]; Dobbie (1942) 109 [proverbs: Ker art. b]; Sisam—Sisam (1959) [psalter coll. as D]; Hallander (1968) [two confessional prayers: Ker arts. d, e]; Davey (1979) [psalter and commentary]; Arngart (1981) 299 [base MS for proverbs 37 and 39]; Tristram (1985) 301 [Ages of the World]; Chardonnens (2007b) 265 [thunder prognostics]; Dekker (2007) 281–4 [encyclopedic notes]

LANG: Reichenbächer (1934); Gneuss (1972) 79; Bierbaumer (1977a); Hofstetter (1987) 462–4; Gretsch (1999a) 42–131, 135–225; Crowley (2000) 126; Scragg (2008d) 387–92

ST: Wülker (1879); Dewick (1902) 50–4; Wildhagen (1913) 448–53; E. Bishop (1918) 390; Tolhurst (1942) 124; K. Sisam (1953a) 4; Sisam—Sisam (1959) 52–6; Barré (1963); Morrell (1965) 89–92; Gneuss (1968) 112; Bierbaumer (1977a); Pulsiano (1985a); Tristram (1985) 83; P.P. O'Neill (1986) 292–4; Davey (1987); Clayton (1990) 70–7; Keefer (1990a); Ortenberg (1990a); Hollis—Wright (1992) 35; Gretsch (1999a) 261–331 *et passim*; S. Irvine (2000) 43; Dance (2004) 47–8 n. 65; Chardonnens (2007b) 46–7; Dekker (2007); P.A. Stokes (2007) [fol. 198v]; Chardonnens (2010) 247

452. London, British Library, Royal 2. C. iii

s. xi/xii, (prov. Rochester)

Contents: Paulus Diaconus, *Homiliarium* (Septuagesima to Sabbatum Sanctum, Sanctorale, Commune SS.)

MS: Warner—Gilson (1921) I.51; N.R. Ker (1964) 161; Smetana (1978) 87; Clayton (1985) 220; M.P. Richards (1988) 20, 95–103, 108–10, 118 [full list of contents]; R. Sharpe et al. (1996) 490, 504; R. Gameson (1999a) no. 460; J. Hill (2007a) 94

ST: Lambert (1969–72) nos. 217a, 713

453. London, British Library, Royal 2. E. xiii + 2. E. xiv

s. x ex.

Contents: pseudo-Jerome, *Breuiarium in Psalmos* [*CPL* 629; *BCLL* 343] (Pss. I–C only)

MS: Warner—Gilson (1921) I.65; Rushforth (2011) 61–3

ST: Lambert (1969-72) no. 427; Biggs et al. (1990) 98–9 [C.D. Wright]

453. 2. London, British Library, Royal 3. B. i

s. xi/xii, (prov. Rochester)

Contents: Isidore, *Mysticorum expositiones sacramentorum seu Quaestiones in Vetus Testamentum* [*CPL* 1195]; Jerome, *Comm. in epistulas Pauli* (*ad Titum, ad Philemonem*) [*CPL* 591]

MS: Warner—Gilson (1921) I.70; N.R. Ker (1964) 161; M.P. Richards (1988) 18; R. Sharpe et al. (1996) 476–7, 507; R. Gameson (1999a) no. 461; Barker-Benfield (2008) I.504

ST: Lambert (1969–72) no. 219

453. 4. London, British Library, Royal 3. B. xvi

England, s. xi/xii, (prov. Bath)

Contents: Jerome, *Comm. in Hieremiam* [*CPL* 586]

MS: Warner—Gilson (1921) I.74; N.R. Ker (1964) 7 and n. 8; R. Gameson (1999a) no. 462

ST: Lambert (1969–72) no. 211

453. 6. London, British Library, Royal 3. C. iv

s. xi/xii, (prov. Rochester)

Contents: Iob; Gregory, *Moralia in Iob* [*CPL* 1708], bks. I–XVI [companion vol. to no. **469. 3**]

MS: Warner—Gilson (1921) I.74–5; N.R. Ker (1964) 161; M.P. Richards (1988) 29; R. Sharpe et al. (1996) 482, 501; R. Gameson (1999a) no. 463

FACS: R. Gameson (1999a) pl. 18 [fol. 14r]

453. 8. London, British Library, Royal 3. C. x

s. xi/xii, (prov. Rochester)

Contents: Euangelium Iohannis; Augustine, *Tractatus in Euangelium Ioannis* [*CPL* 278]

MS: Warner—Gilson (1921) I.76; N.R. Ker (1964) 161; M.P. Richards (1988) 33; R. Sharpe et al. (1996) 499; R. Gameson (1999a) no. 464

454. London, British Library, Royal 4. A. xiv, fols. 1* and 2*

s. ix ex., Continent (France? Italy s. ix/x?). In England (Worcester?) from s. ix/x?, (prov. Worcester)

Contents: missal (f)

MS: Hartzell (1989) 85–6; Dumville (1992a) 67, 96; *ASMMF* IV (1996) 49 [no. 285; Pulsiano]; Hartzell (1996) 308–15; Bischoff (1998–) II, no. 2492; Wieland (2009) 123; R. Gameson (2012d) 348 and n. 14

FACS: *ASMMF* IV (1996) no. 285; Hartzell (1996) pl. following p. 319 [fol. 1*v]

ED: Hartzell (1996) 315–18

455. London, British Library, Royal 4. A. xiv, fols. 1–106

s. x med., Winchester?, (prov. Worcester)

Contents: Jerome, *Tractatus .lix. in Psalmos* [*CPL* 592] (with interpolations from pseudo-Jerome, *Breuiarium in Psalmos* [*CPL* 629; *BCLL* 343]); excerpts from Origen, *Hom. in Numeros*, trans. Rufinus [*CPG* 1418]; charm** (add. s. xii med.)

MS: Warner—Gilson (1921) I.81–2; Atkins—Ker (1944) 32 [no. 5*]; Colgrave (1956) 26; N.R. Ker (1957) no. 250; N.R. Ker (1964) 104, 207; Parkes (1976b) 163 n. 4 [repr. Parkes (1991) 160 n. 4]; Rella (1977) 161; Parkes (1983) 137 n. 50; Hartzell (1989) 86–7; Dumville (1991–5) 48; Robinson—Stanley (1991) 25; Conner (1993) 57, 63, 67, 70, 73, 75; Dumville (1993g) 14 n. 33; Laing (1993) 100; Dumville (1994a) 148 and n. 87; *ASMMF* IV (1996) 47–50 [no. 285; Pulsiano]; Crick (1997) 70, 74–5; McDougall—McDougall (1997) 210; Gretsch (1999a) 264–7; Swan (2007b) 40; Rushforth (2011) 63–5; R. Gameson (2012a) 59 n. 196; D. Ganz (2012) 193 and n. 32

FACS: Warner—Gilson (1921) IV, pl. 34 [fol. 36r]; Robinson—Stanley (1991) pl. 19.11 [fol. 106v]; *ASMMF* IV (1996) no. 285; R. Gameson (2012) pl. 7a.1 [folio not specified]

ED: Morin (1897a/1958) [base MS (= I) for Jerome, *Tractatus .lix. in Psalmos*]; Dobbie (1942) 128 [OE metrical charm]

ST: Lambert (1969–72) nos. 220, 407; Davey (1987); Biggs et al. (1990) 98–9 [C.D. Wright]; Bammel (1991) 9; R. Gameson (1996a) 232 n. 118, 240; M.P. Brown (2001b) 282

456. London, British Library, Royal 4. A. xiv, fols. 107–8

s. viii/ix or ix in. or ix¹, S England (Winchester?) or Mercia, (prov. Worcester)

Contents: Felix, *Vita S. Guthlaci* [*CPL* 2150; *BHL* 3723] (f)

MS: Warner—Gilson (1921) I.82; *CLA* II (1935) no. 216; Colgrave (1956) 26; N.R. Ker (1957) no. 251; Crick (1987) 187 and n. 38; Webster— Backhouse (1991) no. 172; Dumville (1991–5) 48; Dumville (1992a) 108 n. 75; *ASMMF* IV (1996) 47–50 [no. 285; Pulsiano]; Crick (1997) 70; Biggs et al. (2001) 244–6; W. Schipper (2007b) 34; Wieland (2009) 130; M.P. Brown (2012) 165

FACS: *CLA* II (1935) no. 216 [fol. 107v]; *ASMMF* IV (1996) no. 285; Roberts (2005) p. 21 [fol. 107v]; M.P. Brown (2007a) pl. 55 [fol. 108r]

ED: Colgrave (1956) 60-9 [Felix, *Vita S. Guthlaci*, coll. as R]

456. 2. London, British Library, Royal 5. A. xii, fols. iii–vi

s. xi med. or xi^2, Worcester

Contents: missal (f)

MS: Warner—Gilson (1921) I.99; Hartzell (1989) 47–89; Lenker (1997) 487 and nn.; R. Gameson (2005a) 93, 101–4; Hartzell (2006) no. 173; Rankin (2012) 501 and n. 86

FACS: Hartzell (1989) pls. III [fol. iii r], IV [fol. vi v]

ED: Hartzell (1989) 91–7; Hartzell (2006) 317 [incipits]

ST: Lenker (1997) 118–19, 177, 190

456. 4. London, British Library, Royal 5. B. ii

s. xi/xii, (prov. Bath)

Contents: Augustine, *De pastoribus* [= *Sermo* xlvi], *De ouibus* [= *Sermo* xlvii], *De baptismo contra Donatistas* [*CPL* 332], *De peccatorum meritis et remissione et de baptismo paruulorum* [*CPL* 342], *De unico baptismo contra Petilianum* [*CPL* 336], *De spiritu et littera* [*CPL* 343]

MS: Warner—Gilson (1921) I.101; N.R. Ker (1964) 7 and n. 8; R. Gameson (1999a) no. 475; Webber (2012) 222 and n. 58

ST: Römer (1972b) 188–9

456. 6. London, British Library, Royal 5. B. vi

s. xi/xii, (prov. Rochester)

Contents: Augustine, *In Iohannis Epistulam ad Parthos tractatus .x.* [*CPL* 279]; Quodvultdeus [pseudo-Augustine], *Sermo* iv (*Contra Arianos, Iudaeos et paganos*) [*CPL* 404]; two books of the Bible: Apocalypsis Iohannis, Canticum canticorum

MS: Warner—Gilson (1921) I.102; N.R. Ker (1960) 42 n. 2; N.R. Ker (1964) 162; Römer (1972b) 189; M.P. Richards (1988) 23; R. Sharpe et al. (1996) 471, 493, 500; R. Gameson (1999a) no. 478

456. 8. London, British Library, Royal 5. B. xiv

s. xi/xii or xii[1], Gloucester?, (prov. Bath)

Contents: Augustine, *Confessiones* [*CPL* 251], with *Retractatio* [*CPL* 250] II. vi

MS: Warner—Gilson (1921) I.104; N.R. Ker (1964) 7 and n. 8; Römer (1972b) 190; Webber (1996) 33 and n. 23; R. Gameson (1999a) no. 483

457. London, British Library, Royal 5. B. xv, fols. 57–64

s. xi ex., Canterbury StA

Contents: John Chrysostom, *De muliere Cananaea*, in Latin translation [*CPG* 4529]; Goscelin, *Miracula S. Letardi* [*BHL* 4892; arranged in lessons]

MS: M.R. James (1903) 517; Warner—Gilson (1921) I.104–5; T.A.M. Bishop (1955) 2; N.R. Ker (1964) 44; R. Gameson (1995a) 102 n. 28, 144; R. Gameson (1999a) no. 486

DEC: Lawrence (1982) 102, 104

457. 4. London, British Library, Royal 5. D. i + 5. D. ii

s. xi/xii, (prov. Rochester)

Contents: Augustine, *Enarrationes in psalmos* [*CPL* 283] (Pss. LI–C, CI–CL)

MS: Warner—Gilson (1921) I.110; N.R. Ker (1960) 42 n. 2; N.R. Ker (1964) 162; Römer (1972b) 193–4; M.P. Richards (1988) 23; R. Sharpe et al. (1996) 471, 499; R. Gameson (1999a) nos. 489, 490

457. 6. London, British Library, Royal 5. E. vii, fol. i

s. xi[1]

Contents: gradual (f)

MS: Warner—Gilson (1921) I.114; Hartzell (2006) no. 174; Rankin (2012) 500, 501

ED: Hartzell (2006) 318 [incipits]

457. 8. London, British Library, Royal 5. E. x

s. xi/xii, (prov. Rochester)

Contents: Iulianus Pomerius, *De uita contemplatiua* [*CPL* 998]

MS: Warner—Gilson (1921) I.115; N.R. Ker (1960) 162; M.P. Richards
(1988) 29; R. Sharpe et al. (1996) 483, 508; R. Gameson (1999a) no. 499

458. London, British Library, Royal 5. E. xi

s. x/xi, OE glosses s. xi in., xi med.; all Canterbury CC

Contents: Aldhelm, *De uirginitate* (prose)° [*CPL* 1332]

MS: Ehwald (1919) 223; Warner—Gilson (1921) I.115; N.R. Ker (1957)
no. 252; T.A.M. Bishop (1959–63b) 419–21; Rella (1977) 70;
Korhammer (1980) 26–7; *ASMMF* IV (1996) 51–4 [no. 281; Pulsiano];
Gwara (1996a) 93; Gwara (1996b) 101–5; Gwara (1998) 140 n. 7;
Gretsch (1999a) 136 n. 9, 143; Gwara (2001a) I.170*–177* *et passim*;
R. Gameson (2012a) 23 n. 37, 46–7 and n. 146, 68 and n. 238; Lapidge
(2012b) 27; Rushforth (2012) 206 n. 57; Scragg (2012a) nos. 683–98

DEC: E. Temple (1976) no. 19(ix); Ohlgren (1986) no. 105; R. Gameson
(1992a) 197 n. 44; R. Gameson (1995b) 221–2; Pulsiano (2007) 130

FACS: *ASMMF* IV (1996) no. 286; R. Gameson (2000b) pl. 5 [fol. 9r];
Pulsiano (2007) 132 [fol. 82r]

ED: Napier (1900) nos. 8, 88 [OE glosses]; Ehwald (1919) [Aldhelm,
prose *De uirginitate*, coll. as R⁴]; Meritt (1945) no. 2 [OE scratched
glosses]; Gwara (1996b) [scratched glosses]; Gwara (2001a) [Aldhelm,
prose *De uirginitate* and gloss, all coll. as R4]

ST: F.C. Robinson (1994) 151; R. Gameson (1996a) 220 n. 85; Gwara
(1996a) 108; Gwara (1997a) 567 *et passim*; Gretsch (1999a) 138, 143,
145; Lapidge (2012b) 26–31

459. London, British Library, Royal 5. E. xiii

s. ix ex., N France or Brittany, prov. England by s. x med., (prov.
Worcester)

Contents: pseudo-Jerome, *Liber 'Canon in Hebreica'* [*CPL* 795];
Cyprian, *Ad Quirinum Testimonia* [*CPL* 39]; excerpts from *Collectio
canonum Hibernensis* [*CPL* 1794]; (pseudo-) Bede-Egbert
Poenitentiale ('additiuum' version); penitential texts; excerpt from
Book of Enoch (ch. cvi, abbrev. in Latin); *De uindictis magnis magno-
rum peccatorum*; Gospel of Nicodemus (incomplete)

MS: Thompson—Warner (1881–4) 55; Warner—Gilson (1921) I.116; N.R. Ker (1964) 208; Rella (1977) 166; Rella (1980) 112; Frantzen (1983a) 37–8 and n. 37; Frantzen (1983b) 108 and n. 49, 130 and nn. 26–7; Haggenmüller (1991) 71; Dumville (1993g) 48; C.D. Wright (1993) 270 n. 204; Cross—Hall (1996d) 48–9; Bischoff (1998—) II, no. 2493; Ambrose (2005) 113; Ambrose (2006); C.D. Wright (2006) 214; Biggs (2007a) 9–10, 29–30 [Biggs, Morey], 73–4 [C.D. Wright]

ED: M.R. James (1893) 146–50 [Book of Enoch]; Petitmengin (1993) [*De uindictis magnis magnorum peccatorum*]; Cross (1996b) 138–246 [Gospel of Nicodemus coll. as R]

ST: Siegmund (1949) 36 [Gospel of Nicodemus], 43 [Book of Enoch]; Lambert (1969–72) no. 403 [*'Canon in Hebreica'*]; R.E. Reynolds (1972) 132 [*Collectio canonum Hibernensis*]; Dumville (1973) 331 and n. 204 [Book of Enoch]; H.C. Kim (1973); Frantzen (1983b) 69–77, 107–10 [(pseudo-)Bede–Egbert *Poenitentiale*]; Frantzen (1985) 28 [(pseudo-)Bede–Egbert *Poenitentiale*]; Biggs et al. (1990) 25–7 [Book of Enoch; T.N. Hall], 69-70 [*'Canon in Hebreica'*; C.D. Wright]; Sims-Williams (1990) 260 n. 66 [Book of Enoch]; Haggenmüller (1991) 225 *et passim* [(pseudo-)Bede–Egbert *Poenitentiale*]; *CPPM* II, no. 2406 [*'Canon in Hebreica'*]; Kéry (1999) 75, 78 [*Collectio canonum Hibernensis*]; Lapidge (2006) 170, 299; Biggs (2007a) 9–10 [Book of Enoch]

460. London, British Library, Royal 5. E. xvi

s. xi ex., Salisbury

Contents: pseudo-Augustine, *De unitate S. Trinitatis* [*CPL* 378] (incomplete); excerpts in dialogue form from Isidore, *De differentiis rerum siue Differentiae theologicae uel spiritales* [*CPL* 1202] and *Etymologiae* [*CPL* 1186]; Isidore, *De fide catholica contra Iudaeos* [*CPL* 1198]

MS: Warner—Gilson (1921) I.117–18; N.R. Ker (1949–50) 154 n. 1, 158 n. 7, 168, 174 [repr. N.R. Ker (1985) 176 n. 1, 180 n. 7, 190, 196]; N.R. Ker (1964) 171; N.R. Ker (1976b) 25, 30, 49 [repr. N.R. Ker (1985) 145, 150, 171]; Bodden (1988) 218; Webber (1992) 13, 19 n. 53, 20–1, 145; R. Gameson (1999a) no. 500

461. London, British Library, Royal 5. E. xix

s. xi ex., Salisbury

Contents: Isidore, *Synonyma de lamentatione animae peccatricis* [*CPL* 1203]; two homilies; twelve homilies from the *Homiliarium* of Saint-Père

in Chartres; Alcuin, *Compendium in Canticum canticorum*; anonymous commentary on the Canticum canticorum

MS: Warner—Gilson (1921) I.118; N.R. Ker (1949–50) 154 n. 1, 158 n. 7,
159, 168 [repr. N.R. Ker (1985) 176 n. 1, 180 n. 7, 181, 190]; N.R. Ker
(1964) 171; N.R. Ker (1976b) 25, 26 n. 1, 37, 42, 45, 49 [repr. N.R. Ker
(1985) 145, 146 n. 1, 157, 162, 165, 169]; Cross (1987) 1, 19–41; Webster—
Backhouse (1991) no. 130; Webber (1992) 12–15, 145; R. Gameson
(1999a) nos. 501–3; Bullough (2004) 11 n. 18; Guglielmetti (2004) 33;
Di Sciacca (2007b) 98, 100; Di Sciacca (2008) 68, 70, 110

ED: Guglielmetti (2004) 117–80 [Alcuin, *Compendium in Canticum
canticorum*, coll. as L]

ST: Barré (1962) 18–24 [homilies]; Lambert (1969–72) no. 454 [anon.
commentary on Canticum canticorum]; *CSLMA* II (1999) 117 [Alcuin,
Compendium]; Di Sciacca (2008) 169, 176 [Isidore, *Synonyma*]

462. London, British Library, Royal 5. F. iii

s. ix ex. or ix/x, Mercia (Worcester?), (prov. Worcester)

Contents: Aldhelm, *De uirginitate* (prose) [*CPL* 1332]

MS: Napier (1900) xvi; Ehwald (1919) 218; Warner—Gilson (1921) I.120;
N.R. Ker (1957) no. 253; N.R. Ker (1964) 208; Rella (1977) 59 n. 2, 70;
Dumville (1987) 158 n. 54; Morrish (1988) 535 and n. 76, 537; M.P.
Brown (1990) 60; Lapidge (1991c) 960 n. 23 [repr. Lapidge (1993a) 10
n. 23]; Webster—Backhouse (1991) no. 237; *ASMMF* IV (1996) 55–7
[no. 287; Pulsiano]; M.P. Brown (1996) 180; Gwara (2001a) I.101*–
106* *et passim*; M.P. Brown (2012) 166; R. Gameson (2012a) 59 n. 195;
Lapidge (2012b) 27; Scragg (2012a) nos. 699–703

DEC: F. Wormald (1945) 113–14 and n. 21, 118 [repr. F. Wormald (1984)
52–3, 57, 174 n. 21]; Rice (1952) 177; E. Temple (1976) no. 2; Ohlgren
(1986) no. 80; R. Gameson (1995b) 221 nn. 169 and 173, 222; M.P.
Brown (1996) 177–8; Wieland (1998) 15 n. 10; Keefer (2007b) 97;
Pulsiano (2007) 120

FACS: F. Wormald (1984) ill. 50 [fol. 2v (detail)]; M.P. Brown (1990) 61
[fol. 2v]; *ASMMF* IV (1996) no. 287; M.P. Brown (2007a) pl. 68 [fol.
2v]; Pulsiano (2007) 132 [fol. 32v]

ED: Napier (1900) no. 9 [OE glosses]; Ehwald (1919) [Latin text of
Aldhelm, prose *De uirginitate*, coll. as R¹]; Gwara (2001a) vol. II
[Latin text of Aldhelm, prose *De uirginitate*, with Latin and OE
glosses, all coll. as R1]

ST: Franzen (1991) 76, 136; Gwara (1994b) 109; R. Gameson (1996a) 195–6, 240; Gwara (1997a) 565 *et passim*; Gretsch (1999a) 144; Lapidge (2012b) 26–31

463. London, British Library, Royal 5. F. xiii

s. xi ex., prov. Salisbury

Contents: Ambrose, *Epistulae* [*CPL* 160], *De obitu Theodosii* [*CPL* 159]; pseudo-Ambrose, *De SS. Protasio et Geruasio* [= *Epist.* ii: *CPL* 2195; *BHL* 3514]; Ambrose, *De Nabuthae* [*CPL* 138]

MS: Warner—Gilson (1921) I.124; N.R. Ker (1960) 8 n. 2; Faller—Zelzer (1968–94) IV.348; N.R. Ker (1976b) 44 n. 2 [repr. N.R. Ker (1985) 167 n. 2]; Rella (1977) 160; A.G. Watson (1987a) 61; Webber (1992) 15, 23; Bankert et al. (1997) 14, 30, 50–1; R. Gameson (1999a) no. 507

ED: Faller—Zelzer (1968–94) [Ambrose, *Epistulae*, coll. as L]

463. 5. London, British Library, Royal 5. F. xviii, fols. 29–32

s. xi ex., Salisbury

Contents: pseudo-Methodius, *Apocalypsis uel Reuelationes* in Latin translation [*CPG* 1830]

MS: Warner—Gilson (1921) I.126 [art. 2]; Siegmund (1949) 174; A.G. Watson (1987a) 61; Webber (1992) 13, 20, 22, 24 n. 84, 145–6 and n. 20, 153 n. 55, 159; R. Gameson (1999a) no. 508; Biggs (2007a) 19–20 [Twomey]

ST: Twomey (2007)

464. London, British Library, Royal 6. A. vi

s. x ex., Canterbury CC

Contents: Aldhelm, *Epistola ad Heahfridum* [*CPL* 1334], *De uirginitate* (prose)° [*CPL* 1332]; colophon [SK 16451 and 13375]

MS: Napier (1900) xv; Ehwald (1919) 222; Warner—Gilson (1921) I.129; N.R. Ker (1957) no. 254; T.A.M. Bishop (1959–63b) 415–21; T.A.M. Bishop (1971) no. 9; Pächt—Alexander (1973) no. 37; Goossens (1974) 19; Rella (1977) 70; Korhammer (1980) 27; Gwara (1996a) 90–2 *et passim*; Gretsch (1999a) 143; Gwara (2001a) I.177*–180*; Lapidge (2012b) 27, 37; Scragg (2012a) nos. 704–5

DEC: E. Temple (1976) no. 30 (xi); Ohlgren (1986) no. 128; R. Gameson (1995b) 221 nn. 169 and 172, 222 n. 181; Wieland (1998) 15 n. 10

ED: Napier (1900) nos. 7, 13 [OE glosses to both *Epistola ad Heahfridum* and prose *De uirginitate*]; Ehwald (1919) 228–323 [Aldhelm, prose *De uirginitate*, coll. as R³], 488–94 [Latin text of *Epistola ad Heahfridum* coll. as R]; Gwara (1996a) 112–21 [*Epistola ad Heahfridum* and glosses coll as R3]; Gwara (2001a) vol. II [Aldhelm, prose *De uirginitate* with Latin and OE glosses, coll. as R3]

ST: Lapidge—Herren (1979a) 143–6; Gwara (1994a) 268–9; Gwara (1996a) 104–12; Gwara (1997a) 568 *et passim*; Gretsch (1999a) 170; R. Gameson (2001d) 41–2; Pulsiano (2007) 123; Lapidge (2012b) 26–31, 35–7

464. 9. London, British Library, Royal 6. A. vii, fols. 1 and 162 (flyleaves)

s. xi/xii, Worcester

Contents: responsory; prefatory letter to Gregory, *Homiliae in Hiezechielem* [*CPL* 1710]; two Anglo-Saxon alphabets

MS: Warner—Gilson (1921) I.129; Rankin (1996) 327; R. Gameson (2005a) 96; Hartzell (2006) no. 175

465. London, British Library, Royal 6. A. vii

s. xi in., Worcester

Contents: Iohannes Diaconus, *Vita S. Gregorii* [*BHL* 3641]

MS: Warner—Gilson (1921) I.129; N.R. Ker (1964) 208; T.A.M. Bishop (1971) 20 n. 1; Rella (1977) 84; R. Gameson (2012a) 51–2

DEC: F. Wormald (1945) 134 [repr. F. Wormald (1984) 73]; E. Temple (1976) no. 60; Ohlgren (1986) no. 164

FACS: E. Temple (1976) ill. 257 [fol. 2r (detail)]

ST: Biggs et al. (2001) 243–4

466. London, British Library, Royal 6. B. vii

s. xi ex., (prov. Exeter)

Contents: Aldhelm, *De uirginitate* (prose)° [*CPL* 1332]; list of relics (s. xi/xii)

MS: Napier (1900) xiv; Ehwald (1919) 223; Warner—Gilson (1921) I.136; T.A.M. Bishop (1954–8a) 199; N.R. Ker (1957) no. 255; Drage (1978) 371–3; Conner (1993) 6; R. Gameson (1996b) 155 and n. 85; Martin Richter (1996) xxxvii–xlvi; Gwara (1998) 168; R. Gameson (1999a) no. 516; Gretsch (1999a) 143; Gwara (2001a) I.113*–117*; Lapidge (2012b) 28; Scragg (2012a) no. 706

DEC: R. Gameson (1995b) 221, 222 n. 180

FACS: Warner – Gilson (1921) IV, pl. 46 (a) [fol. 4r]; Goossens (1992) pl. 3 [fols. 13v, 35v, 5r (details)]

ED: Napier (1900) no. 3 [OE glosses]; Ehwald (1919) 228–323 [Aldhelm, prose *De uirginitate*, coll. as R⁵]; Conner (1993) 190–8 [list of Exeter relics, coll. as R]; Martin Richter (1996) [OE glosses]; Gwara (2001a) vol. II [Aldhelm, prose *De uirginitate*, coll. as R5]

LANG: Hofstetter (1987) 454

ST: Förster (1943) 40–59; R. Derolez (1959) 131; Keynes (1985a) 143–6; Goossens (1992); Conner (1993) 26, 171, 173; Gwara (1997a) 566–7 *et passim*; Gwara (1998) 144–6 *et passim*; Lendinara (2001a) 191; Lapidge (2012b) 26–31

467. London, British Library, Royal 6. B. viii, fols. 1–57

s. xi¹–med. [fols. 1–38], s. xi² [fols. 39–57], Canterbury StA

Contents: Isidore, *De fide catholica contra Iudaeos* [*CPL* 1198], bk. I; Alcuin, *Epistolae* ccxxxiv and cxl, *De fide sanctae et indiuiduae Trinitatis, De animae ratione*

MS: Dümmler (1895) 13; Warner – Gilson (1921) I.136–7; R. Gameson (1999a) no. 517

DEC: F. Wormald (1945) 126 [repr. F. Wormald (1984) 64]; E. Temple (1976) no. 54; Ohlgren (1986) no. 159; R. Gameson (1995b) 231

FACS: F. Wormald (1984) pl. 67 [fol. 1v (detail)]; E. Temple (1976) ill. 164 [fol. 1v (detail)]

ED: Dümmler (1895) 222 [Alcuin, *Ep.* cxl, coll. as K], 379–80 [Alcuin, *Ep.* ccxxxiv, coll. as K]

ST: *CSLMA* II (1999) 122, 136, 258, 310; R. Sharpe (2001) 38; Bullough (2004) 80 n. 192, 123

468. London, British Library, Royal 6. B. xii, fol. 38

s. xi²

Contents: pontifical (f)

MS: Warner – Gilson (1921) I.141; Brückmann (1973) 442; R. Gameson (1999a) no. 518; Hartzell (2006) no. 176

469. London, British Library, Royal 6. C. i

s. xi², Canterbury StA, (prov. ibid.)

Contents: Isidore, *Etymologiae* [*CPL* 1186]

MS: M.R. James (1903) 517; Warner—Gilson (1921) I.143; T.A.M. Bishop
(1959–63a) 94 n. 2; N.R. Ker (1964) 44; R. Gameson (1995a) 102 n. 28,
144; R. Gameson (1999a) no. 521; Barker-Benfield (2008) I.cii n. 104, 528

DEC: Lawrence (1982) 102, 103; R. Gameson (1995b) 10 n. 22

FACS: Foys (2007) 116 [fol. 108v]

469. 3. London, British Library, Royal 6. C. vi

s. xi/xii, (prov. Rochester) [companion vol. to no. **453. 6**]

Contents: Gregory, *Moralia in Iob* [*CPL* 1708], bks. XVII–XXXV;
Lanfranc's notes on the *Moralia*

MS: Warner—Gilson (1921) I.145; N.R. Ker (1964) 162; M.P. Richards
(1988) 29; Gibson (1993a) xiii, 442; R. Sharpe et al. (1996) 482, 501;
R. Gameson (1999a) no. 525

469. 5. London, British Library, Royal 6. C. x

s. xi/xii, (prov. Rochester)

Contents: Gregory, *Symbolum fidei* [*CPL* 1714 (p. 558)], *Registrum
epistularum* [*CPL* 1714]

MS: Warner—Gilson (1921) I.146; N.R. Ker (1964) 162; M.P. Richards
(1988) 29; R. Sharpe et al. (1996) 482, 494, 501; R. Gameson (1999a)
no. 527

470. London, British Library, Royal 7. C. iv

s. xi¹, Canterbury CC?, (prov. ibid.); OE gloss s. xi med.

Contents: Defensor of Ligugé, *Liber scintillarum*° [*CPL* 1302]; *Pauca de
uitiis et peccatis*° [extracts from Ecclesiasticus and Isidore, *Sententiae*
(*CPL* 1199)]

MS: Warner—Gilson (1921) I.177; N.R. Ker (1957) no. 256 and p. lxix;
T.A.M. Bishop (1959–63a) 94; T.A.M. Bishop (1959–63b) 415; N.R.
Ker (1964) 37; R. Derolez (1970b); Rella (1977) 96 n. 9, 110 and nn.;
Dumville (1993g) 108–10, 124 n. 67, 146 n. 32 *ASMMF* V (1997) 48–51
[no. 290; Doane]; Lapidge (1998) 37–8; Scragg (2012a) nos. 707–8

DEC: R. Gameson (1995b) 61 n. 253

FACS: Warner—Gilson (1921) IV, pl. 51 [fol. 70v]; *ASMMF* V (1997) no. 290

ED: Rhodes (1889) [Latin text and OE gloss of *Liber scintillarum* and 'Pauca de uitiis et peccatis'] [highly inaccurate]; Getty (1969) [Latin text and OE gloss of *Liber scintillarum* and 'Pauca de uitiis et peccatis']; Verdonck (1974) [OE gloss to *Liber scintillarum* and 'Pauca de uitiis et peccatis']; Cornelius (1995) [OE gloss to 'Pauca de uitiis et peccatis']

LANG: Hofstetter (1987) 433–6

ST: Rochais (1957b) 216; Greenfield—Robinson (1980) 369; Pulsiano (1984); Laing (1993) 101; Cornelius (1995) 40–1; Marsden (1995) 314–20; Bremmer (2008); Healey (2011) 9–10 *et passim*

[471. London, British Library, Royal 7. C. xii, fols. 2 and 3: see now no. **63**]

472. London, British Library, Royal 7. C. xii, fols. 4–218

s. x ex. (prob. 990), SW England, prob. Cerne

Contents: Ælfric, *Catholic Homilies* (First Series)*

MS: Warner—Gilson (1921) I.180–1; K. Sisam (1953a) 171–5; N.R. Ker (1957) no. 257; Eliason—Clemoes (1965) 28–35 [partially repr. M.P. Richards (1994) 345–64]; A.G. Watson (1979) I, no. 877; Backhouse et al. (1984b) no. 158; Dumville (1988) 58; Conner (1993) 58, 62, 71–2, 74, 76; Clemoes (1994a) 345–61; Clemoes (1997) 65–6; Budny (1999) 253; Swan (2000b) 62; W. Schipper (2003) 159; Acker (2004) 128; Roberts (2005) 64–7 [no. 12]; Teresi (2007a) 309; *ASMMF* XVII (2008) 37–51 [no. 29a; Wilcox]; Graham (2009) 166; Scragg (2009b) 61, 70, 81–2; Crick (2012) 181; R. Gameson (2012b) 115 and n. 83; Scragg (2012a) nos. 709–24

FACS: Eliason—Clemoes (1965) [complete facsimile]; Warner—Gilson (1921) IV, pl. 52 [fol. 91r]; M.P. Brown (1991) pl. 20 [fol. 105r]; Roberts (2005) pl. 12 [fol. 105r], p. 67 [fol. 64r]; M.P. Brown (2007a) pl. 97 [fol. 105r]; *ASMMF* XVII (2008) no. 29a; Owen-Crocker (2009) fig. 3.1 [fol. 64r]

ED: Clemoes (1997) 178–530 [base MS (= A) for Ælfric's First Series of *Catholic Homilies* (omitting Ælfric's prefaces)]

LANG: Clemoes (1952); Harlow (1959); Faulkner (1968); Eble (1970); Skulicz (1970); Clemoes (1994a) 362–4; Scragg (2006)

ST: Horsley—Waterhouse (1984) 222; Godden (2000); Scragg (2012b) 558 and n. 18

473. London, British Library, Royal 7. D. xxiv, fols. 82–168

s. x^1 S England (Wessex? Glastonbury?)

Contents: Aldhelm, *De uirginitate* (prose), with gloss (s. x$^{2/3}$–med.), *Epistola ad Heahfridum*

MS: Napier (1900) xv; Ehwald (1919) 222; Warner—Gilson (1921) I.192; N.R. Ker (1957) no. 259; T.A.M. Bishop (1964–8b) 247; Parkes (1976) 163 n. 4 [repr. Parkes (1991) 160 n. 4]; Rella (1977) 70; Parkes (1983) 137 n. 50; Dumville (1987) 174; Webster—Backhouse (1991) no. 59; R. Gameson (1992a) 199; Conner (1993) 55, 63–4; Dumville (1994a) 136 n. 18; Gwara (1996a) 97–8 *et passim*; Gwara (2001a) I.122*–147*; Lapidge (2012b) 27, 37

DEC: F. Wormald (1945) 115 [repr. F. Wormald (1984) 54]; Rice (1952) 178; F. Wormald (1952) 71–2 [no. 38]; E. Temple (1976) no. 4; Brownrigg (1978) 251; Ohlgren (1986) no. 88; Kiff-Hooper (1991); R. Gameson (1995b) 23, 221 nn. 169 and 171, 222

FACS: Warner—Gilson (1921) IV, pl. 54 (a) [fol. 124r]; E. Temple (1976) ills. 11–14 [fols. 138r, 147v, 104v, 86r (all details)]; M.P. Brown (1991) pl. 22 [fols. 85v–86r]; R. Gameson (2012) pl. 7a.2 [folio not specified]

ED: Napier (1900) no. 5 [OE glosses]; Ehwald (1919) 228–323 [Aldhelm, prose *De uirginitate*, coll. as R^2], 488–94 [Aldhelm, *Epistola ad Heahfridum*, coll. as D]; Gwara (1996a) 112–22 [Aldhelm, *Epist. ad Heahfridum* and gloss, coll. as R2]; Gwara (2001a) vol. II [Aldhelm, prose *De uirginitate* with Latin and OE glosses, coll. as R2]

ST: Lapidge (2012b) 26–31, 35–7

474. London, British Library, Royal 8. B. xi

s. x^2, prob. Worcester

Contents: Paschasius Radbertus, *De corpore et sanguine Domini*; unidentified extract

MS: Warner—Gilson (1921) I.223; Paulus (1969) xiii–xiv; T.A.M. Bishop (1971) no. 18; Rella (1977) 162; Dumville (1993g) 54 and n. 238; Hartzell (2006) no. 178; R. Gameson (2012a) 29 n. 66, 40 n. 103; R. Gameson (2012b) 107

FACS: Warner—Gilson (1921) IV, pl. 57 (a) [fol. 4r]

ED: Paulus (1969) [Paschasius, *De corpore et sanguine Domini*, coll. as O]
ST: R. McKitterick (2012) 328

474. 5. London, British Library, Royal 8. B. xiv, fols. 118–44

s. xi[1], France (Saint-Josse, Brittany?); s. xi[2], England; both parts in England (Winchester?) by s. xi ex.

Contents: (all texts are for feasts of St Judoc): Isembard of Fleury, *Vita II S. Iudoci* [*BHL* 4505], *Inuentio S. Iudoci* [incomplete; *BHL* 4506–8], homily on St Iudoc [*BHL* 4509], *Miracula S. Iudoci* [*BHL* 4510]; anon. homily adapted from *BHL* 4509; Lupus of Ferrières, *Sermo* [*BHL* 4510d]; Masses for the Invention and Translation, two hymns [SK 11580, 1319], prayer: all s. xi[1]; metrical *Vita S. Iudoci* [*BHL* 4512; SK 16714]: s. xi[2]

MS: Hardy (1862–71) I.266–8; Warner—Gilson (1921) I.224–5; Levison (1948) 559–61; Lapidge (1989–90) 255–6; Lapidge (1991c) 988 and n. 115 [repr. Lapidge (1993a) 38 and n. 115]; Keynes (1996a) 29 n. 131; Lapidge (2000b) 264–5; Biggs et al. (2001) 275–6; Hartzell (2006) no. 180

ED: Henshaw (1946) [SK 1319 and 11580]; Levison (1948) 561–4 [base MS for Lupus of Ferrières, *Sermo*]; Lapidge (2000b) 272–96 [base MS for metrical *Vita S. Iudoci*]

ST: Levison (1948) 557–66; Lapidge (2000b); Biggs et al. (2001) 275–6

474. 6. London, British Library, Royal 8. B. xiv, fols. 154–6

s. xi ex., Salisbury

Contents: anonymous commentary on the Canticum canticorum (f)

MS: Warner—Gilson (1921) I.224–5; Webber (1992) 13, 146; R. Gameson (1999a) no. 534; T.N. Hall (2007) 259–60

ST: T.N. Hall (2007) 262

475. London, British Library, Royal 8. C. iii

s. x ex., Canterbury StA

Contents: pseudo-Jerome, *Epist. supp.* xxiii [*CPL* 633] (*De diuersis generibus musicorum*, a treatise of Carolingian date); exposition of the Mass (inc. 'Primum in ordine'); Theodulf of Orléans, *De ordine baptismi*; commentary on words of baptismal office; confession of faith (partly from Gennadius, *Liber siue diffinitio ecclesiasticorum dogmatum* [*CPL* 958]); explanation of terms connected with baptism; Alcuin, *De sacramento baptismatis* [= *Epist.* cxxxiv]; exposition of the Mass (inc. 'Dominus uobiscum'); Augustine, *De magistro* [*CPL* 259]

MS: Warner—Gilson (1921) I.229; T.A.M Bishop (1954–8b) 335–6; N.R. Ker (1960) 8 n. 2; Weigel (1961) xv; Daur (1970) 144–5; Rella (1977) 158; Lendinara (1990a) 134; T.N. Hall (2004b) 97 n. 18; C.A. Jones (2004) 329 n. 21; Biggs (2007a) 78 [C.D. Wright]; Barker-Benfield (2008) III.1831

FACS: Warner—Gilson (1921) IV, pls. 57 (b)–(e) [fols. 4r, 35r, 61r, 90r (all details)]; T.A.M. Bishop (1954–8b) pl. XIV (a) [fol. 6r]

ED: Weigel (1961) 3–55 [Augustine, *De magistro*, coll. as T]; Green—Daur (1970) 151–203 [Augustine, *De magistro*, coll. as T]

ST: Lambert (1969–72) no. 323; Römer (1972b) 200; Bullough (1977) 49–50 [repr. Bullough (1991) 19]; Sauer (1978) 5; Dumville (1992a) 135 and n. 190; Dumville (1993g) 151 n. 62; C.D. Wright (1993) 219; C.A. Jones (1998c) 672–3 and nn. 57, 61; *CSLMA* II (1999) 252–3, 527; Nason (2004); R. McKitterick (2012) 329

476. London, British Library, Royal 8. C. vii, fols. 1 and 2

s. xi in.

Contents: Ælfric, Lives of Saints* (f)

MS: Warner—Gilson (1921) I.234–6; N.R. Ker (1957) no. 260; Dumville (1988) 60–1; J. Hill (1996) 243; Wilcox (2006a) 239, 256; Kleist (2007b) 488; Kleist (2007c) 500; Scragg (2012a) no. 725

ED: Herzfeld (1891) [parts of Ælfric, *Lives of Saints*, nos. VII (St Agnes) and VIII (St Agatha), coll. with Skeat (1881–1900)]

477. London, British Library, Royal 8. F. xiv, fols. 3 and 4

s. xi in., prob. Continent, (prov. Bury St Edmunds)

Contents: Vergil, *Aeneid* (f), with scholia

MS: Warner—Gilson (1921) I.270–2; R.M. Thomson (1972) 622–3 and nn. 23, 29; Munk Olsen (1982—) II.733; Williams—Pattie (1982) 137–8

478. London, British Library, Royal 12. C. xxiii

s. x^2 or x/xi, Canterbury CC.

Contents: Iulianus Toletanus, *Prognosticum futuri saeculi* [*CPL* 1258], with glosses; *Enigmata* of Aldhelm, Symposius, Eusebius, Tatwine (all with glosses and scholia); pseudo-Smaragdus, *Opus monitorium*; pseudo-Smaragdus, monitory poems [SK 7810, 10988]; *Versus cuiusdam Scotti de alphabeto* [SK 12594]

MS: Ehwald (1919) 51–2; Warner—Gilson (1921) II.35–6; N.R. Ker (1957) no. 263; T.A.M. Bishop (1959–63b) 421; Hillgarth (1976) xxviii; O'Brien O'Keeffe (1985b) 64–7; Carley (1986) 111, 116–17; Carley (1987) 201–4; A.G. Watson (1987a) 38 and n. 3; Stork (1990) 6–10, 20, 26; Webster—Backhouse (1991) no. 60; Dumville (1993g) 93 n. 45; Biggs (2007a) 29 [C.D. Wright]; Wieland (2009) 150; R. Gameson (2012a) 67 n. 232; Lapidge (2012b) 23; Scragg (2012a) nos. 726–7

DEC: F. Wormald (1945) 135 [repr. F. Wormald (1984) 74]; E. Temple (1976) no. 30 (iii); Brownrigg (1978) 256; Ohlgren (1986) no. 120; R. Gameson (1992a) 196; R. Gameson (1995b) 223

FACS: E. Temple (1976) ill. 113 [fol. 6v (detail)]; R.I. Page (1982) pl. IV [fol. 100v]; Stork (1990) frontispiece [fol. 83r]; M.P. Brown (1991) pl. 34 [fol. 84r]; R. Gameson (1992a) pls. VI, 22 [fols. 1v, 6v]; M.P. Brown (2007a) pl. 72 [fol. 84r]

ED: Strecker (1896) IV/iii.918–24 [monitory poem: *Versus quos Smaragdus…misit* (SK 7810) coll. as L], 924–7 [monitory poem: *Versus … ad Ludouicum Pium* (SK 10988) coll. as L]; Napier (1900) nos. 26 [OE glosses to Aldhelm, *Enigmata*], 42 [OE glosses to Iulianus, *Prognosticum*]; W. Meyer (1907) 55–70 [base MS for pseudo-Smaragdus, *Opus monitorium*]; Ehwald (1919) 75–81, 97–149 [Aldhelm, *Prol.* and *Enigmata*, coll. as B¹]; Glorie (1968) I.165–208 [Tatwine, *Enigmata*, coll. as L], 209–71 [Eusebius, *Enigmata*, coll. as L], 359–540 [Aldhelm, *Prol.* and *Enigmata*, coll. as L], II.611–723 [Symposius, *Enigmata*, coll. as L], 725–41 [*Versus cuiusdam Scotti* coll. as L]; Stork (1990) 83–236 [base MS for Aldhelm, *Prol.* and *Enigmata*, with Latin and OE glosses]; Bergamin (2005) [Symposius, *Enigmata*, coll. as h]

ST: Manitius (1911–31) I.467–8; N.R. Ker (1949–50) 178 [repr. N.R. Ker (1985) 203]; Rädle (1974) 28–39; R.I. Page (1982) 148, 151–4, 160–1, 163–4; Stork (1990); Lapidge (2012b) 23–6

478. 5. London, British Library, Royal 12. D. iv

s. xi/xii, Canterbury CC

Contents: computistical calendar (without saints' feasts); computus tables; Helperic, *De computo*; Bede, *De temporum ratione* [*CPL* 2320], *Epistola ad Wicthedum de paschae celebratione* [*CPL* 2321]

MS: M.R. James (1903) 507; Warner—Gilson (1921) II.38; N.R. Ker (1964) 37; R. Gameson (1995a) 102 n. 27, 121 n. 88; R. Gameson (1999a) no. 544

ST: C.W. Jones (1943) 153, 170 [repr. C.W. Jones (1980) 247, 634]; McGurk (1974); Borst (2001) I.xxii; *CSLMA* III (2010) 421–9 [Helperic]

479. London, British Library, Royal 12. D. xvii ('Bald's Leechbook')

s. x med., Winchester?

Contents: medical handbook ('Bald's Leechbook')*

MS: Warner—Gilson (1921) II.48; Storms (1948) 12–16; Wright—Quirk (1955) 11–30; Beccaria (1956) no. 82; N.R. Ker (1957) no. 264; N.R. Ker (1964) 200; Parkes (1976b) 163 [repr. Parkes (1991) 160]; Bately (1986) xxxiv–xxxv; Robinson—Stanley (1991) 25; Dumville (1992b) 64–5, 136; Conner (1993) 78–80; *ASMMF* I (1994) 60–4 [no. 298; Doane]; Dumville (1994a) 148–9; Liuzza (2001) 186, 206; Bredehoft (2004) 149–51, 169; Hartzell (2006) no. 184; Bezzo (2007) 436–7 and nn. 8–11; C. Bishop (2007b) 108; Chardonnens (2007b) 40–1, 532, 553; D'Aronco (2007) 35 n. 3; R. Gameson (2012a) 39 and n. 95, 59 n. 196, 65 and n. 225; D. Ganz (2012) 189 and n. 12, 193 and n. 33

FACS: Wright—Quirk (1955) [complete facsimile]; Voigts (1979) 13 [fol. 30v]; M.P. Brown (1991) pl. 30 [fol. 52v]; Robinson—Stanley (1991) pls. 19.10.1–2 [fol. 125r]; *ASMMF* I (1994) no. 298; M.P. Brown (2007a) pl. 110 [fol. 52v]

ED: Cockayne (1864–6) vol. II; Leonhardi (1905) 1–112; Olds (1984) [Leechbook III]; Muir (1988) xxix, 150 [Muir no. 70 coll. as L]; Deegan (1991); Bredehoft (2004) 150–1 [fol. 125v]

LANG: Wright—Quirk (1955) 32 [Quirk]

ST: Voigts (1959); A.F. Cameron (1974) 223; Bierbaumer (1975–9) I.vii–x; Meaney (1975); Torkar (1976); Voigts (1979); Greenfield—Robinson (1980) 370–3; M.L. Cameron (1983); M.L. Cameron (1984); Meaney (1984); Meaney (1985) 34; Adams—Deegan (1992); Hankins (1992); Hollis—Wright (1992) 211–18; M.L. Cameron (1993) 35–45 *et passim*; Hollis—Wright (1994) 230–3; M.L. Cameron (1996); P. Wormald (1999) 178 nn. 61–4; Bredehoft (2004) 150; Nokes (2004); N. Orchard (2005) clxxxii; Chardonnens (2010) 247

London, British Library, Royal 12. F. xiv, fols. 1–2, 135: see no. **666**

480. London, British Library, Royal 12. G. xii, fols. 2–9 (with Oxford, All Souls College 38, fols. I–VI and i–vi [flyleaves])

s. xi med.

Contents: Ælfric, *Grammar*⁺* (f)

MS: Zupitza (1880/2001) iv; Warner—Gilson (1921) II.73; N.R. Ker (1957) no. 265; A.G. Watson (1997) 75–6; W. Schipper (2003) 157; *ASMMF* XV (2007) 41–5 [Royal], 51–4 [All Souls] [nos. 299, 335; Doane]; R. Gameson (2012a) 23, 24 and n. 39, 26; Scragg (2012a) nos. 728–9

FACS: Warner—Gilson (1921) IV, pls. 76 (a)–(b) [fols. 2r, 7r]; *ASMMF* XV (2007) nos. 299, 335

ED: Zupitza (1880/2001) [Ælfric, *Grammar*, coll. as A (Royal) and r (All Souls)]

ST: A.G. Watson (1986) 151 [repr. A.G. Watson (2004) no. IV]

481. London, British Library, Royal 13. A. i

s. xi ex.

Contents: pseudo-Callisthenes, *Historia Alexandri* [*Epitome Iulii Valerii*]; *Epistola Alexandri ad Aristotelem*; *Epitaphium Alexandri* [WIC 14648]; Alexander and Dindymus, five letters; *Recapitulatio de Alexandro*

MS: Warner—Gilson (1921) II.74; Boer (1973) xiv; R. Gameson (1999a) no. 547

DEC: Rice (1952) 207; F. Wormald (1952) 72 [no. 39]

ED: Boer (1973) 1–60 [*Epistola Alexandri ad Aristotelem* coll. as Reg.]; A. Orchard (1995) 204–23 [base MS for *Epistola Alexandri ad Aristotelem*]

ST: Cary (1956) 70; Ross (1963) 9, 86 n. 40; B. Hill (1975) 99, 101 [*Epitaphium Alexandri*]

482. London, British Library, Royal 13. A. x, fols. 63–103

s. x² or x/xi

Contents: Bili of Alet, *Vita S. Machuti* [*BHL* 5116a; *BCLL* 825]; poem [not listed in SK; inc. 'Vitales qui cupis doctorum capere fructus']; hymn for St Machutus [SK 1663; *BCLL* 896]; homily for the feast of St Machutus

MS: Warner—Gilson (1921) II.79–80; Yerkes (1984a) xxxiii; Dumville (1993g) 145 n. 26; T.N. Hall (2007) 260–1; Wieland (2009) 130

ED: *AH* XLIII (1903) 222–4 [SK 1663]; Brown—Yerkes (1981) [homily for St Machutus]; Yerkes (1984a) xiv–xv, 2–100 [Bili, *Vita S. Machuti*, coll. as L]

ST: Hardy (1862–71) I.138 [no. 398]; Kenney (1929) no. 205; *BCLL* (1985) nos. 825, 896; Poulin (1990); Biggs et al. (2001) 307–10; *CALMA* II.409 [Lapidge]

483. London, British Library, Royal 13. A. xi

s. xi/xii or xii in., Normandy or NW France rather than England?, not in England by 1100?

Contents: Helperic, *De computo*; *Dies Aegyptiaci*; Bede, *De natura rerum* [*CPL* 1343], *De temporibus* [*CPL* 2318]; Sphere of Pythagoras; Bede, *De temporum ratione* [*CPL* 2320]; treatises and excerpts on astronomical and computistical subjects (including SK 2501); Abbo of Fleury, *De figuratione signorum* [abbrev. from Hyginus], *De differentia circuli et sphaerae*; Dungal, Letter to Charlemagne on eclipses [*Epist.* i]; *Versus Dionisii de annis Domini* [SK 814]; Epiphanius (?), *De mensuris et ponderibus* (in Latin translation) [*CPG* 3746]; Bede, *Epistola ad Wicthedum de paschae celebratione* [*CPL* 2321]; verses on the Seven Liberal Arts [not listed in SK; inc. 'Presedeo cunctis baiulans hoc nobile sceptrum']

MS: Warner—Gilson (1921) II.80–1; C.W. Jones (1943) 153, 165, 171; Laistner—King (1943) 139, 141; C.W. Jones (1975) 177; C.W. Jones (1977) 247; C.W. Jones (1980) 634; Webster—Backhouse (1991) no. 61; R. Gameson (1999a) no. 548; Chardonnens (2007b) 547

FACS: Webster—Backhouse (1991) 77 [fols. 33v–34r]

ED: Dümmler (1895) 570–8 [Dungal, *Epist.* i; this MS not used]; C.W. Jones (1975) 189–234 [Bede, *De natura rerum*, coll. as E]; R.B. Thomson (1985) 113–33 [Abbo, *De differentia circuli et sphaerae*, coll. as L]; Liuzza (2005) 40–2 [Sphere of Pythagoras coll. as R]

ST: Van de Vyver (1935) 140–50 [Abbo, *De figuratione signorum*, *De differentia circuli et sphaerae*]; McGurk (1974) 2–4 [Helperic]; SK 814 [*Versus Dionisii de annis Domini*]; *BCLL* no. 657 [Dungal, *Epist.* i]; Bischoff—Lapidge (1994) 212–13 [Epiphanius, *De mensuris et ponderibus*]; Baker—Lapidge (1995) xliv [Abbo, *De differentia circuli et sphaerae*]; Knappe (1996) 134 n. 1, 196–7 and nn. [verses on the Seven Liberal Arts]; Knappe (1998) 15 n. 44 [verses on the Seven Liberal Arts]; R. Sharpe (2001) 3 [Abbo]; Liuzza (2005) 34, 40–4 [Sphere of Pythagoras]; *CSLMA* III (2010) 421–9 [Helperic]

484. London, British Library, Royal 13. A. xv

s. x med., prob. Worcester

Contents: Felix, *Vita S. Guthlaci* [*CPL* 2150; *BHL* 3723]

MS: Warner—Gilson (1921) II.84; Colgrave (1956) 28–30; N.R. Ker (1957) no. 266; T.A.M. Bishop (1971) xiv n. 1, 16; Rella (1977) 84; Dumville (1993g) 5 n. 16, 53–4 and n. 238, 76 n. 349; R. Gameson (1996a) 198 n. 15, 243; Hartzell (2006) no. 187; Wieland (2009) 130; D. Ganz (2012) 191 n. 18; Scragg (2012a) no. 730

FACS: Warner—Gilson (1921) IV, pls. 77 (a)–(c) [fols. 6v, 24r, 38r]

ED: Birch (1881) 1–64 [base MS for Felix, *Vita S. Guthlaci*, omitting Prologue and list of chapters]; Napier (1900) no. 36 [OE glosses]; Meritt (1945) no. 16 [OE scratched glosses]; Colgrave (1956) 52–4 [OE glosses], 72–170 [Felix, *Vita S. Guthlaci*, coll. as A, scribal alterations coll. as A₂]

ST: F.C. Robinson (1973) 445 n. 5; Carley (1986) 112, 114; Biggs et al. (2001) 245

485. London, British Library, Royal 13. A. xxii

s. xi², Mont Saint-Michel, prov. Canterbury StA?, (prov. Canterbury StA)

Contents: Paulus Diaconus, *Historia Langobardorum* [*CPL* 1179]; excerpts from Frecul of Lisieux, *Historiae* (I.ii.17); poem on the abbey of Saint-Bertin [SK 3639]

MS: Warner—Gilson (1921) II.87–8; N.R. Ker (1964) 45; R. Gameson (1999a) no. 549; Pani (2000) 408; Barker-Benfield (2008) I.lx, cii n. 103, 448, II.924, 940, 946, III.1795

DEC: Dodwell (1954) 55 n. 5; F. Wormald (1952) 72 [no. 40]; Alexander (1970a) 40, 227

ED: Waitz (1878) [Paulus Diaconus, *Historia Langobardorum*, coll. as D*3]

ST: Waitz (1876) 545–6; Chiesa (2000); Chiesa—Stella (2005) 491–5

486. London, British Library, Royal 13. A. xxiii

s. xi², Mont Saint-Michel, prov. Canterbury StA, (prov. ibid.)

Contents: Ado of Vienne, *Chronicon*; lists of Roman emperors, dukes of Normandy, Frankish kings

MS: Warner—Gilson (1921) II.88; N.R. Ker (1964) 45; R. Gameson (1999a) no. 550; Barker-Benfield (2008) I.lx, lxxix, cii n. 103, 448, II.924, 925–6, 940

DEC: Dodwell (1954) 122; Alexander (1970a) 227; R. Gameson (1995a) 110 and n. 54

FACS: Alexander (1970a) pl. 16 (c) [fol. 1v (detail)]

ST: *CSLMA* I (1994) 31–2 [Ado]; *CALMA* I.46 [Ado]

487. London, British Library, Royal 13. C. v

s. x/xi or xi¹, Worcester?, (prov. Gloucester)

Contents: Bede, *Historia ecclesiastica* [*CPL* 1375]

MS: C. Plummer (1896) I.cxiv; Warner—Gilson (1921) II.103; Laistner—King (1943) 98; N.R. Ker (1964) 92; Colgrave—Mynors (1969) li–lii; T.A.M. Bishop (1971) 20 n. 1; Rella (1977) 69, 84; Hartzell (1989) 86; Dumville (1993g) 55–6 n. 245

487. 5. London, British Library, Royal 14. C. viii

s. xi ex.

Contents: Iosephus, *De bello Iudaico*, trans. Hegesippus

MS: Warner—Gilson (1921) II.136; R. Gameson (1999a) no. 555

488. London, British Library, Royal 15. A. v, fols. 30–85

s. xi ex. or xi/xii

Contents: Arator, *Historia apostolica* [*CPL* 1504]; note on recitations of *Historia apostolica* at Rome A.D. 544; poem in praise of Arator's work [SK 17136]; pseudo-Columbanus (pseudo-Alcuin), *Praecepta uiuendi* [SK 5960]

MS: Warner—Gilson (1921) II.142–3; McKinlay (1942) 63; Lapidge (1982a) 117 and 139 n. 106 [repr. Lapidge (1996b) 485 and n. 106]; R. Gameson (1999a) no. 556; Orbán (2006) I.41–2; Wieland (2006)

ED: Orbán (1998–9) and (2000) [base MS for the commentary which here accompanies the text of Arator on fols. 86–147]; Orbán (2006) [Arator, *Historia apostolica*, coll. as Lr]

ST: McKinlay (1960 –); *BCLL* (1985) no. 655 [pseudo-Columbanus]; Wieland (1985) 154–5 and n. 171; *CPPM* II, no. 3216b [*Praecepta uiuendi*]; Orbán (1998–9)

489. London, British Library, Royal 15. A. xvi

s. ix$^{4/4}$ or ix/x, N France or England?, with additions made s. x med. or x$^{3/4}$, England; both parts Canterbury StA by s. x^2, (prov. ibid.)

Contents: Iuvencus, *Euangelia* [*CPL* 1385]; Aldhelm, *Enigmata* [*CPL* 1335]; excerpt from Bede, *De arte metrica* [*CPL* 1565], ch. xxv; *Scholica Graecarum glossarum* (addition s. x med. or x$^{3/4}$)

MS: E.M. Thompson (1881–4) II.74; Huemer (1891) xxvi–xxvii, xxxix; M.R. James (1903) 342; Ehwald (1919) 50; Warner – Gilson (1921) II.146; T.A.M. Bishop (1954–8b) 329; N.R. Ker (1957) no. 267; N.R. Ker (1964) 45; T.A.M. Bishop (1966) xx; Jones – Kendall (1975) 67 [Kendall]; Rella (1977) 165; Rella (1980) 112; Lapidge (1982a) 108 and n. 62, 109 [repr. Lapidge (1996b) 471 and n. 62, 473]; O'Brien O'Keeffe (1985b) 66–8, 70 n. 35; Bodden (1988) 219 n. 10; Alturo (1996) 103–4; Lendinara (1996) 618 n. 9, 619; Parkes (1997b) 102 and n. 6; Bischoff (1998 –) II, no. 2495; Barker-Benfield (2008) I.cii n. 103, 406, 413, II.938, 1378, III.1710; R. Gameson (2012a) 63 and n. 223, 64–5 and n. 224; R. Gameson (2012d) 350 and n. 21; Lapidge (2012b) 22; Scragg (2012a) nos. 731–2

DEC: F. Wormald (1952) 44–5, 72 [no. 41]; E. Temple (1976) no. 85; Brownrigg (1978) 256–7; Ohlgren (1986) no. 190; R. Gameson (1995b) 18

FACS: Warner – Gilson (1921) IV, pl. 88 [fol. 13r]; F. Wormald (1952) pl. 25 (a) [fol. 84r]

ED: Huemer (1891) [Iuvencus, *Euangelia*, coll. as R]; Ehwald (1919) 97–149 [Aldhelm, *Enigmata*, coll. as B]; Laistner (1923) [*Scholica Graecarum glossarum* coll. as R]

ST: Schanz et al. (1914–20) IV/i.112; Lapidge (1982a) 108, 134 n. 62 [repr. Lapidge (1996b) 290 n. 62]; Lendinara (1993); Lapidge (1996c) 420 n. 49; Crick (2011) 7 n. 22; Lapidge (2012b) 23–6; R. McKitterick (2012) 330 and n. 106

490. London, British Library, Royal 15. A. xxxiii

s. ix/x or x in., Rheims, prov. England s. x², (prov. Worcester)

Contents: Remigius of Auxerre, Commentary on Martianus Capella (s. ix/x or x in., Rheims); additions on fols. 1–3, 240r (s. x and xi): liturgical fragments, Tironian fragment; list of animal names (s. x²); medical recipe; note on musical terms; computistical note (by Dunchad?) (s. x¹); zodiacal diagram (s. x)

MS: Warner—Gilson (1921) II.152; Kenney (1929) nos. 377 (i) and (ii); C.E. Lutz (1962) I.55–6; N.R. Ker (1964) 208; Keynes—Lapidge (1983) 214 n.; Dumville (1993g) 48; Bischoff (1998—) II, no. 2496; Hartzell (2006) no. 188; Wieland (2009) 151

FACS: C.E. Lutz (1962) I, frontispiece [fol. 25r]

ED: C.E. Lutz (1962) [base MS for Remigius, Commentary on Martianus Capella]

ST: Esposito (1910); Manitius (1911–31) I.502, 525–6; Esposito (1913b); Laistner (1925); Leonardi (1959) 463 n. 109; Kristeller et al. (1960—) II.373; Glauche (1970) 48; Contreni (1978) 83 n. 17, 113–14; *BCLL* (1985) nos. 720, 1182; Bodden (1988) 219; R. McKitterick (2012) 328

491. London, British Library, Royal 15. B. xix, fols. 1–35

s. x² or x ex., Canterbury CC

Contents: Sedulius, *Carmen paschale* [*CPL* 1447], hymn [*CPL* 1449; SK 1904]; two poems on Sedulius [SK 14842, 14841]

MS: Huemer (1885) 309 n.; Warner—Gilson (1921) II.159–60; C.W. Jones (1943) 147; N.R. Ker (1957) no. 268; T.A.M. Bishop (1959–63b) 421–3; F.C. Robinson (1973) 457–9, 461; Korhammer (1980) 58; Lapidge (1982a) 113, 136 n. 80 [repr. Lapidge (1996b) 479 and n. 80]; R.I. Page (1982) 159–60; Williams—Pattie (1982) 140; Springer (1995) 65; Lendinara (2007a) 83; Scragg (2012a) no. 733

DEC: F. Wormald (1945) 134 [repr. F. Wormald (1984) 73]; E. Temple (1976) no. 19 (iii); Ohlgren (1986) no. 99

FACS: Warner—Gilson (1921) IV, pl. 90 (a) [fol. 29v]

ED: Huemer (1885) 307–10 [two poems on Sedulius coll. as R; but note that Huemer does not collate the *Carmen paschale* and hymn in this MS]; Meritt (1945) no. 29 [OE glosses]

492. London, British Library, Royal 15. B. xix, fols. 36–78

s. ix[4/4], Rheims area, prov. England s. x? or not in England before s. xii or xiii

Contents: Latin devotional poem (f; s. x); Bede, *De temporum ratione* [*CPL* 2320]

MS: Warner–Gilson (1921) II.160; Sanford (1924) 212; C.W. Jones (1977) 247; Rella (1977) 166; Rella (1980) 113; Williams–Pattie (1982) 141; Keynes–Lapidge (1983) 214 n.; Bischoff (1998–) II, no. 2497; Biggs (2007a) 17–18; Lendinara (2007a) 83

FACS: Warner–Gilson (1921) IV, pl. 90(b) [fol. 50r]

ED: C.W. Jones (1943) 175–291 [Bede, *De temporum ratione*, coll. as R]; C.W. Jones (1977) 263–460 [Bede, *De temporum ratione*, coll. as R]

493. London, British Library, Royal 15. B. xix, fols. 79–199

s. x, Rheims; in England not before s. xii or xiii?

Contents: an extensive collection of Latin verse and short prose texts, including individual poems of Ausonius, Martial, etc., as well as: Symposius, *Aenigmata* [*CPL* 1518] (incomplete); Bede, *Versus de die iudicii* [*CPL* 1370]; *Liber monstrorum* [*CPL* 1124]; Persius, *Satirae* and anon. scholia by 'Cornutus'; Sibylline prophecies

MS: Thompson–Warner (1881–4) II.68; Warner–Gilson (1921) II.160–3; Carey (1938) 58; Williams–Pattie (1982) 141; Webber (1992) 165–6 [on fols. 200–5]; Lendinara (1996) 640; Codoñer (2003); Bergamin (2005) cxiv; Alcamesi (2007b) 162–4; Lendinara (2007b) 197; Lapidge (2008a) 132

FACS: Warner–Gilson (1921) IV, pl. 90 (c) [fol. 126v]

ED: Hurst–Fraipont (1955) [Bede, *Versus de die iudicii*, coll. as α]; Clausen (1956) 37–9 [*Vita Persi* coll. as l]; R.P.H. Green (1991) 80, 97, 100, 103 [six poems of Ausonius coll. as b]; A. Orchard (1995) 254–316 [*Liber monstrorum* coll. as Y]; Bergamin (2005) [Symposius, *Aenigmata*, nos. XL–C, coll. as w_a]

ST: Kristeller et al. (1960–) III.215, 217 ['Cornutus' scholia on Persius]; Lambert (1969–72) nos. 0, 990 [Jerome, *Epist.* lii]; Glauche (1970) 53–4 [extracts on satire (by Remigius?)], 65 [*Vita Persi*]; Munk Olsen (1982–) I.336 [Cicero, *Aratea*]; Lapidge (1989) 446 n. 13 [*Voces animantium*]; Knappe (1996) 172–6 ['Diffinitio philosophiae']; Bankert et al. (1997) 62 [SK 11282]; Lendinara (2001b) [Bede, *Versus de die iudicii*]; Pulsiano (2001b) [glosses to Persius]; Lendinara (2003) [*Versus*

Sibyllae]; Alcamesi (2007b) 165–9 [*Versus Sibyllae*]; Chardonnens (2007a) 355 n. 42 [SK 7597]; Lendinara (2007b) 184, 197 [Bede, *Versus de die iudicii*]; Lapidge (2008a) 131–7 [Bede, *Versus de die iudicii*]. Further bibliography on many of the poetic items in this MS may be found in SK under the following numbers: 379; 798; 1226; 1390; 1461; 2423; 2515 [Paulinus of Nola]; 3612 [Ausonius]; 3727; 3736; 4408; 6489; 7221; 8093 [from Ovid, *Amores*]; 8207 [Bede, *Versus de die iudicii*]; 8353 [from Ovid, *Ars amatoria*]; 8495 [*Versus Sibyllae*]; 9914; 10176; 10279; 10363; 10516; 11282 [Ambrose?]; 11864 [Ausonius]; 12164; 12481 [Ausonius]; 12524 [Cicero, *Aratea*]; 12559 [Ausonius]; 12589 [Ausonius]; 12738 [from Martial]; 12755; 13142; 14414; 15031; 15358; 15698; 16600; 16663 [from Ovid, *Ars amatoria*]; 16845

494. London, British Library, Royal 15. B. xxii

s. xi$^{3/4}$ or xi^2

Contents: Ælfric, *Grammar*$^{+*}$

MS: Zupitza (1880/2001) vii; Warner—Gilson (1921) II.164; N.R. Ker (1957) no. 268; R.I. Page (1993a) 10; R. Gameson (1999a) no. 562; *ASMMF* XV (2007) 47–9 [no. 303; Doane]; R. Gameson (2012a) 51 n. 169, 70 and n. 241; Scragg (2012a) no. 734

FACS: Warner—Gilson (1921) IV, pl. 91 [fol. 69r]; *ASMMF* XV (2007) no. 303

ED: Somner (1659) pt. 2, 1–52 [base MS for Ælfric, *Grammar*]; Zupitza (1880/2001) [Ælfric, *Grammar*, coll. as R]

ST: Zupitza (1880/2001) iii–xvi; Buckalew (1978) 164 n. 2; D.W. Porter (2002)

496. London, British Library, Royal 15. C. vii

s. x/xi with additions s. xi^2; Winchester OM

Contents: Lantfred of Winchester, *Translatio et miracula S. Swithuni* [*BHL* 7944–6]; Wulfstan of Winchester, Hymn for St Swithun [SK 1443] and *Narratio metrica de S. Swithuni* [*BHL* 7947] (all s. x/xi); two poems on St Swithun (added s. xi^2)

MS: Warner—Gilson (1921) II.166–7; N.R. Ker (1957) no. 270; A.G. Watson (1963) 209 [repr. A.G. Watson (2004) no. III]; N.R. Ker (1964) 200; Lapidge (1994a) 132–4; Lapidge (2003a) 239–40, 793; Lapidge (2004b) 441, 445; R. Gameson (2012a) 49 and n. 151; Scragg (2012a) no. 735

FACS: Lapidge (2003a) pls. II–IV [fols. 2r, 6r, 52r]

ED: Lapidge (2003a) 252–332 [Lantfred, *Translatio*, coll. as R], 373–550 [base MS. for Wulfstan, *Narratio*], 782, 795 [base MS for two poems on St Swithun], 784–6 [base MS for Hymn for St Swithun (SK 1443)]

ST: Lapidge — Winterbottom (1991b) xx–xxii, xxviii *et passim*; Biggs et al. (2001) 436–8; Lapidge (2003a); Lapidge (2004b) 441–2 [MS relationship]

497. London, British Library, Royal 15. C. x

s. x², Canterbury StA?, (prov. Rochester)

Contents: *Vita Statii*; Statius, *Thebais*

MS: Warner — Gilson (1921) II.168; N.R. Ker (1964) 163; T.A.M. Bishop (1971) xxii, xxv, 4, 18; Munk Olsen (1982 —) II.542–3; Dumville (1993g) 54–5 n. 240, 56–7 n. 250, 76 n. 345; Barker-Benfield (2008) I.331, III.1831; R. Gameson (2012a) 72 n. 245

· ED: Klotz — Klinnert (1902/1973) [Statius, *Thebais*, coll. as r]

ST: M.P. Richards (1988) 2, 39; R. Sharpe et al. (1996) 520

497. 2. London, British Library, Royal 15. C. xi, fols. 113–94

s. xi/xii, Salisbury

Contents: Plautus, *Comoediae* (*Amphitruo, Asinaria, Aulularia, Captiui, Curculio, Casina, Cistellaria, Epidicus*); verse colophon [SK 4783]; Isidore, *Etymologiae* [*CPL* 1186], excerpt from I. xxi

MS: Warner — Gilson (1921) II.168; Tarrant (1983) 304; R.M. Thomson (1986b); A.G. Watson (1987a) 61; Webber (1992) 13, 20–3, 24 n. 84, 41, 63–4, 86, 146, 159; Bertini (1996) 295 n. 23; R. Gameson (1999a) no. 565

ED: Lindsay (1904–5) [Plautus, *Comoediae*, coll. as J]; Webber (1992) 146 n. 22 [verse colophon]

ST: Tarrant (1983) 304–5; Lapidge (2006) 67–8, 311, 325

498. London, British Library, Royal 17. C. xvii, fols. 2, 3 and 163–6

s. x ex. or xi¹

Contents: breviary (f)

MS: Wieland (2009) 134; Rankin (2012) 486–7, 503

498. 0. London, British Library, Sloane 280, fols. 1 and 286

prob. s. x

Contents: *Homiliarium* of Angers (f)

MS: Rudolf (2011) 169–74

FACS: Rudolf (2011) pls. II–III [fols. 1v, 286r]

ST: Étaix (1994); Conti (2007) 372–402; Rudolf (2011); Gneuss (2012)

498. 1. London, British Library, Sloane 475

s. xi ex. or xi/xii, English or Anglo-Norman scribe

Contents: fols. 1–124: medical texts; Remigius Favius (?), *De ponderibus et mensuris* [SK 12104]; pseudo-Hippocrates, Letter; *De cibis*; prognostics

fols. 125–231: Sphere of Pythagoras; Isidore, *Etymologiae* [*CPL* 1186], bk. IV.v; Galen, *Epistola de febribus* (in Latin translation); medical recipes; medical glosses; treatise on urines; gynaecological recipes; *Somniale Danielis* (f); *lunarium*; *Dies Aegyptiaci*; prognostics

MS: Thorndike (1923–58) I.723–6; Beccaria (1956) no. 78; M.L. Cameron (1983) 144; R. Gameson (1999a) nos. 566, 567; Liuzza (2001) 225–7; Biggs (2007a) 15; Chardonnens (2007b) 42–3, 532–4, 553; Banham (2011) 343; Liuzza (2011) 16–19

ED: Liuzza (2005) 44–5 [Sphere of Pythagoras]; Chardonnens (2007b) 211, 246, 380, 499 [prognostics], 328–9 [*Somniale Danielis*], 417–21 [*lunarium*]; Maion (2007) 507–11 [medical recipes]

ST: L.T. Martin (1981) 38–9 [*Somniale Danielis*]; Maion (2007) 504; Chardonnens (2010) 246; Liuzza (2011) 1–77 [prognostics]; D'Aronco (2011) 245 and n. 69

London, British Library, Sloane 1044, fol. 2: see no. **21**

London, British Library, Sloane 1044, fol. 6: see no. **648**

498. 2. London, British Library, Sloane 1044, fol. 16

s. xi

Contents: sacramentary (f)

498. 3. London, British Library, Sloane 1044, fol. 21

s. xi^2 or xi ex.

Contents: missal (f)
MS: R. Gameson (1999a) no. 568

498. 4. London, British Library, Sloane 1086, fol. 45

s. xi^2
Contents: Hrabanus Maurus, *Homiliarium* (f)
MS: R. Gameson (1999a) no. 575

498. 5. London, British Library, Sloane 1086, fol. 109

s. xi^2
Contents: Bible (f., from Numeri)
MS: Marsden (1995) 41, 44, 379, 390–3, 439; Marsden (2012) 426 and
    n. 92
FACS: Marsden (1995) pl. IX (verso)

498. 6. London, British Library, Sloane 1086, fol. 112

s. x/xi or xi in.
Contents: sacramentary (f)

London, British Library, Sloane 1086, fol. 119: see no. **124**

498. 7. London, British Library, Sloane 1122, fols. 9-34

s. xi ex., England (with continental and English scribes)
Contents: anonymous commentary on the Canticum canticorum
MS: Gneuss (2003b) 300 [information from M. Gullick]

498. 8. London, British Library, Sloane 1619, fol. 2

s. x or xi, England?
Contents: computus material (f)

498. 8. 1. London, British Library, Sloane 1621

s. xi med., Bury St Edmunds?, prov. Bury St Edmunds
Contents: medical prayers, *antidota*, recipes; *De urinis* (incomplete)
MS: Rushforth (2002) 58–9; Gneuss (2003b) 300 [information from
    M. Gullick]; Banham (2011) 343, 348–52

498. 9. London, British Library, Sloane 2839

s. xi/xii, England

Contents: medical texts, including a treatise on cauterization; *Epistola per hereseos*; 'Petrocellus' (*Practica Petrocelli*); prognostic texts

MS: Thorndike (1923–58) I.723; Beccaria (1956) no. 81; M.L. Cameron (1983) 143–4 and n. 24; R. Gameson (1999a) no. 578; Chardonnens (2007b) 547; Glaze (2007) 476 and n. 27, 478, 485–9; Maion (2007) 498–506; Banham (2011) 343; D'Aronco (2011) 233–4

DEC: C.M. Kauffmann (1975) no. 12; P.M. Jones (1998) 78–9

ST: Sudhoff (1914) 81; Bonser (1963) 203; Talbot (1965); T. Hunt (1990) 64–5

499. London, British Library, Stowe 2

s. xi med. or xi$^{3/4}$, SW England, prob. Winchester NM

Contents: Psalterium Gallicanum°, with psalter collects; canticles°

MS: Wildhagen (1920); N.R. Ker (1957) no. 271; D.H. Turner (1962) xi; T.A.M. Bishop (1971) xv n. 2; Kimmens (1979) xiii–xix; *ASMMF* II (1994) 65–8 [no. 306; Pulsiano]; Gneuss (1998) 273, 276; Gretsch (1999a) 268; P. Wormald (1999) 209 n. 185; Gretsch (2000) 86; Pulsiano (2001a) xxii–xxiii; R. Gameson (2012a) 70 n. 240, 86 n. 310; Scragg (2012a) nos. 267, 736; Toswell (2012) 472

DEC: F. Wormald (1962) 1, 6 [repr. F. Wormald (1984) 123, 128]; E. Temple (1976) no. 99; Ohlgren (1986) no. 204; R. Gameson (1991) 67; R. Gameson (1995b) 40, 122, 220 n. 164; R. Gameson (2012c) 269 and n. 57

FACS: E. Temple (1976) ill. 296 [fol. 1r]; Kimmens (1979) 2 [fol. 168r]; *ASMMF* II (1994) no. 306

ED: Wilmart—Brou (1949) 112–73 [psalter collects (Hispana Series) coll. as S]; Rosier (1964b) [canticles etc. with OE gloss]; Kimmens (1979) [base MS (= F) for Psalms and canticles, with OE gloss]; Pulsiano (2001a) [Pss. I-L, Latin and OE, coll. as F]

LANG: Bierbaumer (1977a); Kimmens (1979) xxvii–xxx; Schabram (1981); Hofstetter (1987) 67–9

ST: Mearns (1914) 65; Sisam—Sisam (1959) 66–74; Hombergen (1983) [almost useless]; Hofstetter (1987) 69–78; McDougall—McDougall (1997) 221 n. 54; Gretsch (1999a) 26–7, 39, 64, 93, 138

500. London, British Library, Stowe 944, fols. 6–61

A.D. 1031 and additions, Winchester NM

Contents: account of the history of New Minster, Winchester; *Liber uitae* of New Minster; will of King Alfred*; tracts on: the Six Ages of the World*, royal Kentish saints*, 'Resting-places of English saints'*; West Saxon regnal list*; gospel lectionary (incomplete); benedictions; lists of relics; pseudo-Damasus and pseudo-Jerome, Colloquy on celebrating Mass⁺*; *Gloria, Pater noster,* creeds; encyclopedic note on the languages of the world

MS: Birch (1892); T.A.M. Bishop (1954–8a) 191; N.R. Ker (1957) no. 274; N.R. Ker (1964) 104; T.A.M. Bishop (1971) 23; A.G. Watson (1979) I, no. 948; D.H. Turner et al. (1980) 107 n. 66; Backhouse et al. (1984b) no. 62; Gneuss (1985) 141 [no. Y.4]; Gerchow (1988) 155–85; Dumville (1992a) 125; Dumville (1993g) 136 and n. 105, 140; Laing (1993) 107; Keynes (1996a) 124–32; Pulsiano (1998b) 99; Gretsch (1999a) 329; P. Wormald (1999) 170 n. 33, 171 n. 36, 209 n. 188; Gretsch (2000) 117–18; M.P. Brown (2001c) 59; Karkov (2004) 146, 154, 164; Keynes (2004) 156–61; Hartzell (2006) no. 195; Karkov (2006b) 96–7; Rushforth (2007) 20; Withers (2007) 59; Scragg (2012a) nos. 222, 737–44; Webber (2012) 221 and n. 50

DEC: Rice (1952) 203, 217–18; F. Wormald (1952) 72–3 [no. 42]; E. Temple (1976) no. 78; D.M. Wilson (1984) 184–5; F. Wormald (1984) 89, 107, 110, 116, 120; Ohlgren (1986) no. 183; Raw (1990) 221; R. Gameson (1991) 77; Gerchow (1992) 222–30; Deshman (1995) 74–5, 88, 106, 148, 156; R. Gameson (1995b) 22, 25, 73–4, 82–3, 97, 130–1, 139–40, 156, 162, 187–8 *et passim*; Dodwell (2000) 148 n. 184; Townend (2001) 168; Karkov (2004) 4, 5, 7, 10, 60, 118, 121–45, 155, 159, 163, 168, 174–5; Keynes (2004) 157–8; Karkov (2006b) 97; Scott (2007) 23, 25, 28–9; Karkov (2009) 236–7; Pulliam (2011) 71; R. Gameson (2012c) 269 and n. 57, 276 and n. 87, 279, 282

FACS: Keynes (1996a) [complete facsimile]; F. Wormald (1952) pl. 15 [fol. 6r (detail)]; E. Temple (1976) ills. 244, 247–8 [fols. 6r, 6v–7r]; Dodwell (1982) 106 [fols. 6v, 7r], 177 [fol. 6r]; D.M. Wilson (1984) pls. 231–2 [fols. 6r, 7r]; F. Wormald (1984) ill. 114 [fol. 6r]; M.P. Brown (1991) pl. 15 [fol. 6r]; Webster—Backhouse (1991) 265 [fols. 30v–31r]; Deshman (1995) figs. 69, 97 [fols. 6r, 7r]; R. Gameson (1995b) pls. 7 (a)–(b) [fols. 6v, 7r]; Karkov (2004) figs. 17–19 [fols. 6r, 6v, 7r]; M.P. Brown (2007a) pls. 126–7 [fols. 6r, 7r]; Rushforth (2007) 20 [fol. 29r];

Scott (2007) 23 [fol. 6r]; Withers (2007) 57 [fol. 6r]; Owen–Crocker (2009) fig. 7.26 [fol. 6r]

ED: Birch (1892) [entire MS]; Dumville (1986) 7–8, 26–30 [base MS for West Saxon regnal list]; Gerchow (1988) 320–6 [*Liber uitae*]

ST: Sawyer (1968) no. 1507 [will of King Alfred]; Rollason (1982) 28 [royal saints of Kent]; Webster — Backhouse (1991) no. 240; Gerchow (1992) [Cnut's *memoria*]; Laing (1993); Lenker (1997) 116, 466 [gospel lectionary]; Keynes (2004) 160 [on altar]; Conde-Silvestre (2006) 49

London, British Library, Stowe 1061, fol. 125: see no. **307. 2**

501. London, British Library, Loan 11 (the 'Kidderminster Gospels')

c. 1020, Canterbury CC or Peterborough?, (prov. Windsor, St George's Chapel) [owner: Langley Marish Parish Church, Buckinghamshire]

Contents: gospels, gospel list (f)

MS: N.R. Ker (1957) lvii; N.R. Ker (1962–92) III.15–17; N.R. Ker (1964) 203; T.A.M. Bishop (1967a) 39; T.A.M. Bishop (1971) xv, 21; Backhouse et al. (1984b) no. 51 [D.H. Turner]; Dumville (1993g) 116, 139–40; McGurk (2012) 446 [no. 11]

DEC: F. Wormald (1945) 132 [repr. F. Wormald (1984) 70]; E. Temple (1976) no. 71; Ohlgren (1986) no. 176; R. Gameson (1995b) 217 n. 152, 218; R. Gameson (2012c) 283 and n. 118

FACS: A.J.C. (1932), pls. XXXVIII–XXXIX [folios not specified]; E. Temple (1976) ill. 223 [folio not specified]; Backhouse et al. (1984b) 70 [fol. 84r]

ST: Glunz (1933) 140–8; McGurk (1986b) 46–7, 51–2, 54–5 [repr. McGurk (1998) no. XIV]; Heslop (1990) 174 n. 64, 181; Lenker (1997) 442–50, 452 *et passim*

501. 2. London, British Library, Loan 74 (the 'Stonyhurst' or 'Cuthbert Gospel')

s. vii/viii, Monkwearmouth-Jarrow, prov. Lindisfarne, prov. Chester-le-Street, prov. Durham [former owner: The English Province of the Society of Jesus at Stonyhurst College, Whalley, Lancashire. Formerly listed as no. 756]

Contents: Euangelium Iohannis (exc.)

MS: Baldwin Brown (1903–37) VI/i.1–10; *CLA* II (1935) no. 260;
Mynors (1939) no. 2; Mynors—Powell (1956); Lowe (1960) no. VII;
McGurk (1961a) no. 37; R. Powell (1962) 4; T.J. Brown (1969b);
Webster—Backhouse (1991) no. 86; Webster—Brown (1997) 234–5
[no. 93]; Werner (2011); M.P. Brown (2012) 126, 144–5; R. Gameson
(2012b) 117; Gullick (2012) 295–8; Marsden (2012) 417–18 and n. 55

DEC: Netzer (2012) 232 and n. 46; Werner (2011) *passim*

FACS: T.J. Brown (1969b) [complete facsimile]; Mynors—Powell (1956)
pl. XXIII [binding]; Lowe (1960) pls. VII (a) [fols. Iv–1r], VII (b) [fols.
26v–27r], VII (c) [back cover], VII (d) [front cover]; D.M. Wilson (1984)
pl. 20 [binding]; Nixon—Foot (1992) pl. 1 [binding]; T.J. Brown (1993a)
ill. 22 [fols. 28v–29r]; M.P. Brown (2007a) pls. 19–20 [binding; fol. 47r]

ED: J. Wordsworth et al. (1889–1954) [gospel excerpts coll. as S]; B.
Fischer (1988–91) [gospel excerpts coll. as Ns]

ST: McGurk (1956) 252, 264 [repr. McGurk (1998) no. I]; McGurk
(1961a) 13 [repr. McGurk (1998) no. VI]; McGurk (1961b) 12–13 [repr.
McGurk (1998) no. V]; Piper (1978) 236; A.G. Watson (1978) 294;
G. Henderson (1987) 35–6; Nixon—Foot (1992) 1–2 [binding]; T.J.
Brown (1993a) 127, 134, 197–8, 207, 235; McGurk (1994b) 8, 21 [repr.
McGurk (1998) no. XII]; Marsden (1995) 31, 80 n. 23; McGurk—
Rosenthal (1995) 278; Lenker (1997) 412 *et passim*; Farr (2011a) 97

NOTE: the manuscript was sold to the British Library in April 2012,
at which time it was renamed the 'Cuthbert Gospel'.

501. 3. London, British Library, Loan 81

s. vii/viii, Monkwearmouth-Jarrow; prob. from the same book as no. 293
[owner: The National Trust, Kingston Lacy, Dorset]

Contents: Bible (f; from Ecclesiasticus)

MS: Parkes (1982) 3 and n. 7 [repr. Parkes (1991) 95 and n. 7]; Bischoff—
Brown (1985) 351–2; A.G. Watson (1987a) 40 and n. 1; Sims-Williams
(1990) 182 and nn.; Webster—Backhouse (1991) no. 87 (b); Dumville
(1992a) 99–100 and nn., 104, 117; Marsden (1995) xiv, 40, 43–4, 55,
90–3, 123–9; M.P. Brown (1996) 166; Budny (1997) I.614; Marsden
(1998) 79–85; Budny (1999) 249 and n. 32; M.P. Brown (2000) 6 and
n. 27; Beall (2005) 188; M.P. Brown (2012) 142 n. 93

FACS: *The Guardian* 2 Oct. 1982 [detail]

ST: Mason (1996a) 210; Beall (2005) 191

502. London, College of Arms, Arundel 22, fols. 84–5

s. x$^{4/4}$, Winchester OM?

Contents: gospel lectionary (f)

MS: F. Wormald (1969) [repr. F. Wormald (1984) 101–4]; T.A.M. Bishop
(1971) 10; Backhouse et al. (1984b) no. 38; F. Wormald (1984) 89;
Avril—Stirnemann (1987) no. 22; Dumville (1993g) 145; Prescott (2001
[2002]) 24; D. Ganz (2008) 17; Wieland (2009) 122

DEC: E. Temple (1976) no. 26; F. Wormald (1984) 106 and n. 6, 114, 183
n. 5; Ohlgren (1986) no. 114; R. Gameson (1995b) 122 n. 31, 198 n. 31,
202–3; R. Gameson (2012c) 258 and nn. 23 and 25

FACS: E. Temple (1976) colour pl. p. 21 [fol. 84r]; Backhouse et al.
(1984b) colour pl. VII [fol. 84r]; F. Wormald (1984) frontispiece [fol.
84r], ills. 94–5 [fols. 84r, 85v]

ST: Lenker (1997) 115–17, 123, 425 n. 39, 473 and n. 44

503. London, College of Arms, Arundel 30, fols. 5–10 and 208

s. x$^{2/4}$, (prov. Bury St Edmunds)

Contents: [palimpsest, lower script] Vergil, *Aeneid* (f)

MS: Schenkl no. 4513; N.R. Ker (1962–92) I.12; R.M. Thomson (1972)
623 and n. 29; Munk Olsen (1982—) II.733; L.D. Reynolds (1983)
xxxii n. 128; Holtz (1986) 146; Dumville (1994a) 144; Baswell (1995)
286–7; Wieland (2009) 148

504. 3. London, Collection of S.J. Keynes Esq., s.n. (a single leaf; with
two further leaves in Cambridge, MA, Harvard University, Houghton
Library Typ 612 and Tokyo, T. Takamiya, MS 89 [a leaf in a collection
consisting of 29 single leaves])

[three leaves, *olim* Phillipps 29721, were sold by Sotheby's, 21 November
1972, lot 532]

s. x^{1}or x med.

Contents: benedictional (f)

MS: *Catalogue of Manuscripts in the Houghton Library* II.115; Dumville
(1992a) 76 and n. 52, 84–5, 147 n. 370; Dumville (1994a) 147 and n. 82;
Dumville (1994c); Stoneman (1997) 126; Graham—Watson (1998) 37
n. 52

FACS: Sotheby's sale catalogue for 21 Nov. 1972, pl. 3; R. Gameson (2012) pls. 7a.3 (a)–(b) [Harvard, Houghton Library, Typ 612, recto and verso]

504. 4. London, Collection of S.J. Keynes Esq. s.n.

s. xi med., England

Contents: missal (f)

MS: Stoneman (1997) 129; Hartzell (2006) no. 200; Gneuss (2012) 292

FACS: Sotheby's sale catalogue for 23 April 1983, lot 5

504. 8. London, Lambeth Palace Library, 62

s. xi/xii, Préaux, (prov. Canterbury CC)

Contents: Richard of Préaux, *Comm. in Genesim*, pt. i [companion vol. to no. **162. 6**]

MS: M.R. James (1932) 100; R. Gameson (1999a) no. 582; Carley (2002) 58–9; Ganz—Roberts (2007) 50–1

505. London, Lambeth Palace Library, 96, fols. 2–112

s. xi ex.

Contents: Gregory, *Homiliae in Hiezechielem* [*CPL* 1710]

MS: Schenkl no. 4528; M.R. James (1932) 158–9; R. Gameson (1999a) no. 585; Ganz—Roberts (2007) 69–70

506. London, Lambeth Palace Library, 149, fols. 1–139

s. x², prov. s. xi in. SW England, prov. Exeter

Contents: Bede, *Expositio Apocalypseos* [*CPL* 1363]; Augustine, *De adulterinis coniugiis* [*CPL* 302]

MS: Schenkl no. 4547; M.R. James (1932) 237–9; R. Flower (1933) 85–90; Bains (1936) 70; N.R. Ker (1957) no. 275; N.R. Ker (1964) 83; Rella (1977) 88, 158; Drage (1978) 374–6; Dumville (1992a) 83; Conner (1993) 6, 33–7, 210–14 *et passim*; Conner (1994) 304, 310; Dumville (1994d) 210; R. Gameson (1996b) 162, 170–2; Gryson (2001) 50–1; R.M. Butler (2004) 178, 181–3, 185–8, 190–5, 204, 214–15; N.M. Thompson (2004) 60; C. Bishop (2007b) 98; Ganz—Roberts (2007)

36–8; Wieland (2009) 131, 133, 156; R. Gameson (2012a) 59 n. 199; Scragg (2012a) no. 766

FACS: Flower (1933) 86 [fol. 41r]; Conner (1993) pls. VIII–IX [fols. 66r, 138v]; R. Gameson (1996b) pls. V–VI [fols. 59r, 138v]; R.M. Butler (2004) 182 [fol. 183r]; Ganz—Roberts (2007) 37 and back cover [fols. 138r, 138v]; Owen-Crocker (2009) fig. 5.2 [fol. 10r]

ED: Gryson (2001) [Bede, *Expositio Apocalypseos*, coll. as L]

ST: Flower (1933) 85–90; Förster (1933a) 29 and n. 109; Bains (1936) 70; Laistner—King (1943) 28; Römer (1972b) 208–9; N.R. Ker (1976b) 30, 35 [repr. N.R. Ker (1985) 150, 156]; J. Hill (1986); J. Hill (1988); Keynes (1994b) 68–9 and nn.; Lapidge (1994b) 138; R.M. Butler (2004); C. Bishop (2007b) 98–9

507. London, Lambeth Palace Library, 173, fols. 1–156

s. xi/xii, (prov. Lanthony secunda, Gloucs., Augustinian canons?)

Contents: Iosephus, *De bello Iudaico*, trans. Hegesippus

MS: Schenkl no. 4552; M.R. James (1932) 272; Siegmund (1949) 106; R. Gameson (1999a) no. 588; Ganz—Roberts (2007) 48–50

508. London, Lambeth Palace Library, 173, fols. 157–221

s. xi/xii, (prov. Lanthony secunda, Gloucs., Augustinian canons?)

Contents: Ephraem Syrus, *Vita S. Abrahae* [*BHL* 12a, 12b]; James the Deacon, *Vita S. Pelagiae* [*BHL* 6609]; *Vita S. Fursei* [*BHL* 3209]; *Visio Fulradi*; *Visio Baronti* [*CPL* 1313; *BHL* 997]; Heito of Reichenau, *Visio Wettini*; Bede, three otherworld visions (from *Historia ecclesiastica* V.xii-xiv); *Vita S. Eufrasiae* [*BHL* 2718]

MS: Schenkl no. 4552; Levison (1919–20) 609; M.R. James (1932) 272–4; Laistner—King (1943) 107; Siegmund (1949) 106; N.R. Ker (1957) no. 276; Dumville (1992a) 140; R. Gameson (1999a) no. 589; Ganz—Roberts (2007) 48–50; Scragg (2012a) no. 767

FACS: R. Gameson (1999a) pl. 21 [fol. 71v]

ST: Biggs et al. (2001) 40–2 [Ephraem Syrus, *Vita S. Abrahae*], 201 [*Visio Baronti*], 222 [*Vita S. Fursei*], 382–3 [James the Deacon, *Vita S. Pelagiae*]

508. 5. London, Lambeth Palace Library, 173, fols. 223–32

s. xi ex., (prov. Lanthony secunda, Gloucs., Augustinian canons?)

Contents: pseudo-Bede, Homily for All Saints' Day

MS: Schenkl no. 4552; M.R. James (1932) 274; R. Gameson (1999a) no. 590; Ganz—Roberts (2007) 48–50

ST: Cross (1977); M.P. Richards (1988) 100; *CPPM* I, nos. 4046, 6074

509. London, Lambeth Palace Library, 200, fols. 66–113

s. x², Canterbury StA, prov. Barking? (prov. Waltham Abbey, Essex, Augustinian canons)

Contents: Aldhelm, *De uirginitate* (prose) [*CPL* 1332]

MS: Schenkl no. 4558; Ehwald (1919) 216–17; M.R. James (1932) 315–17; T.A.M. Bishop (1954–8b) 331; Backhouse et al. (1984b) no. 30; Gwara (2001) I.101*–108*; Ganz—Roberts (2007) 38–41; Barker-Benfield (2008) II.1104, 1373, 1377, III.1815; Lapidge (2012b) 27

DEC: F. Wormald (1945) 134 [repr. F. Wormald (1984) 73–4, 174 n. 38]; Kendrick (1949) 36–7, 39; F. Wormald (1952) 73 [no. 43]; Dodwell (1971b) 221 n. 45; E. Temple (1976) no. 39; Brownrigg (1978) 246 n. 2; Ohlgren (1986) no. 144; R. Gameson (1995b) 23, 86, 166, 193 n. 3, 221 nn. 169 and 171, 222; R. Gameson (2012c) 252 n. 11

FACS: Kendrick (1949) pls. XXXII–XXXIII [fols. 17v (detail), 69r (detail)]; E. Temple (1976) ills. 131–3 [fols. 80v, 68v, 69r]; Ganz—Roberts (2007) 39–40 [fols. 80v, 68v]; R. Gameson (2012) pl. 10.2 [fol. 68r]

ED: Ehwald (1919) 228–323 [Aldhelm, prose *De uirginitate*, coll. as L]; Gwara (2001) vol. II [Aldhelm, prose *De uirginitate* with accompanying Latin glosses, coll. as L]

ST: Vezin (1968) 287; Whitelock (1975) 30 and n. 6; Gwara (1997a) 565, 597–601; Lapidge (2012b) 26–31

510. London, Lambeth Palace Library, 204

s. xi¹, Canterbury CC?, (prov. Ely)

Contents: Gregory, *Dialogi* [*CPL* 1713]; Ephraem Syrus, *De compunctione cordis* (in Latin translation); Rota poem [SK 11297]

MS: Schenkl no. 4562; M.R. James (1932) 325–7; N.R. Ker (1957) no. 277; N.R. Ker (1964) 78; T.A.M. Bishop (1971) xvi n. 2; Rella (1977) 159; Yerkes (1979) xviii; Ganz—Roberts (2007) 41–3; R. Gameson (2012a) 16 and n. 12; Scragg (2012a) nos. 768–71

DEC: F. Wormald (1945) 134 [repr. F. Wormald (1984) 74]; Kendrick (1949) 36 n. 2; E. Temple (1976) no. 19(x); Ohlgren (1986) no. 106; R. Gameson (1995b) 223

FACS: Ganz—Roberts (2007) 42 [fol. 130r]

LANG: McDougall—McDougall (1997) 214

ST: Siegmund (1949) 69; Yerkes (1976a); Bestul (1981b) 13–14 and n. 50

511. London, Lambeth Palace Library, 218, fols. 131–208

s. x¹ (c. 910 × c. 930), or s. ix ex.?, (prov. Bury St Edmunds)

Contents: Alcuin, *Epistolae* (selection)

MS: Dümmler (1895) 8; M.R. James (1932) 350–2; F. Wormald (1957a) 161–2; R.M. Thomson (1972) 622–3; R. Gameson (1992c) 119, 150 n. 160; R. Gameson (1992d) 202 n. 28; Dumville (1993g) 78 n. 360; D. Ganz (1993) 169–77; Dumville (1994a) 135 and n. 14; Bullough (2004) 68–9 and n.; Ganz—Roberts (2007) 33–6; D. Ganz (2012) 192 and n. 24

FACS: Ganz—Roberts (2007) 35 [fol. 174r]

ED: Dümmler (1895) [Alcuin, *Epistolae*, coll. as L]

ST: *CSLMA* II (1999) 171–355

512. London, Lambeth Palace Library, 237, fols. 146–208

s. ix²/⁴, Arras, prov. England (Glastonbury?) by s. x in.

Contents: Augustine, *Enchiridion* [*CPL* 295]; Sextus (Pythagoraeus), *Sententiae*, trans. Rufinus [*CPG* 1115] (incomplete)

MS: Schenkl no. 4568; M.R. James (1932) 383–4; N.R. Ker (1957) no. 278; H. Chadwick (1959) 4; T.A.M. Bishop (1964–8d) 399; T.A.M. Bishop (1971) 2; Rella (1977) 75, 166; Rella (1980) 113; Bischoff (1998—) II, no. 2501; R. Gameson (2002d) 184; Ganz—Roberts (2007) 30–3; R. Gameson (2012d) 350 and nn. 21–2; Scragg (2012a) no. 772

FACS: T.A.M. Bishop (1964–8d) pl. XXIX (d) [fol. 150r (detail)]; Budny (1992) pl. 8 (e) [fol. 146r (detail)]; R. Gameson (2002d) fig. 2 [fol. 150r]; Ganz—Roberts (2007) 32 [fol. 150r]; R. Gameson (2012) pl. 14.1 [fol. 150r]

ED: H. Chadwick (1959) 9–63 [Rufinus' translation of Sextus, *Sententiae*, coll. as L]

ST: H. Chadwick (1959) 97–181; M. Evans (1969); Römer (1972b) 210–11; R.M. Thomson (1982b) 6–7; Carley (1987) 199 n. 10; Lapidge (2006) 171, 289, 332

513. London, Lambeth Palace Library, 325

s. ix² or ix³/⁴, N. France? (Corbie?), (prov. Durham)

Contents: Ennodius, *Dictiones* [*CPL* 1489], *Epistulae* [*CPL* 1487], *Carmina* [*CPL* 1490]

MS: Schenkl no. 4571; Hartel (1882) iv–v; F. Vogel (1885) xxxviii–xxxix; M.R. James (1932) 426–7; Mynors (1939) no. 17; N.R. Ker (1964) 74; Bischoff (1998—) II, no. 2502; R. Gameson (2002d) 186; Gneuss (2003b) 301; Hartzell (2006) no. 197; Ganz—Roberts (2007) 26; Scragg (2012a) no. 773

FACS: Ganz—Roberts (2007) 27 [fol. 131r]

ED: Hartel (1882) [writings of Ennodius coll. as L]; F. Vogel (1885) [writings of Ennodius coll. as L]

ST: Raine (1838) 31; Rouse—Rouse (1976) 82–3; Piper (1978) 226 n. 33; Piper (1998b) 316 n. 80; Lapidge (2006) 171, 301

514. London, Lambeth Palace Library, 362, fols. 1–12

s. xi² (or xi¹?), Bury St Edmunds?, (prov. Canterbury StA?)

Contents: Abbo of Fleury, *Passio S. Eadmundi* [*BHL* 2392]; hymns for St Edmund [SK 8785, 8793]; mass for St Edmund

MS: Arnold (1890–6) I.lxiv; M.R. James (1932) 489–91; N.R. Ker (1964) 21, 47; Gneuss (1968) 114; R.M. Thomson (1972) 625 n. 39; Gransden (1995a) 63–4; Milfull (1996) 64; Ganz—Roberts (2007) 43; R. Gameson (2012b) 110 and n. 62

FACS: Gransden (1995a) pl. I [fol. 8v (detail)]; Ganz—Roberts (2007) 44 [fol. 7v]

ED: Winterbottom (1972) 90-3 [Abbo, *Passio S. Eadmundi*, coll. as 'Lambeth 362']; Milfull (1996) 458–61 [two hymns for St Edmund]

ST: Hervey (1907) 6–59; Bloor (1933); Winterbottom (1972) 8–9; Lapidge (1994b) 123; Gransden (1995a); Gransden (1998b) 229; Biggs et al. (2001) 2–4 [Lendinara]

515. London, Lambeth Palace Library, 377

s. ix[1] or ix[2/4], Tours, prov. England by s. x med., (prov. Lanthony secunda, Gloucs., Augustinian canons)

Contents: Isidore, *Sententiae* [*CPL* 1199]

MS: Schenkl no. 4592; M.R. James (1932) 519–20; N.R. Ker (1957) no. 279; N.R. Ker (1964) 111 and n. 6; Rella (1977) 166 n. 24; Rella (1980) 113; Bischoff (1998–) II, no. 2503; Cazier (1998) lxx; Lapidge (2006) 171, 312; Ganz–Roberts (2007) 30; R. Gameson (2012d) 350 and n. 21

FACS: Ganz–Roberts (2007) 31 [fol. 39v]

ED: Meritt (1945) no. 20 [OE glosses]; Cazier (1998) [Isidore, *Sententiae*, coll. as Z]

516. London, Lambeth Palace Library, 414, fols. 1–80

s. ix in or ix[1], Saint-Amand, (prov. Canterbury StA); in England by 1100?

Contents: excerpts from Ambrose, Augustine, Cassian, Eucherius, Jerome, etc.; Severus (?), *De septem gradibus ecclesiae*; Victorinus of Pettau, *De fabrica mundi*; On the Seven Wonders of the World and the Seven Wonders of Divine Origin

MS: Schenkl no. 4600; M.R. James (1932) 570–6; N.R. Ker (1964) 45; R.E. Reynolds (1978) 39; Bischoff (1980) 106; Bankert et al. (1997) 32–3; Bischoff (1998–) II, no. 2504; R. Gameson (2002d) 186; Gneuss (2003b) 301; T.N. Hall (2004b) 97 n. 18; Ganz–Roberts (2007) 28; Barker-Benfield (2008) I.58, 59, 60, III.1752, 1772, 1887, 1909; Wieland (2009) 141

ED: Morin (1897b) 100 [*De septem gradibus ecclesiae*]; R.E. Reynolds (1978) 39 [*De septem gradibus ecclesiae*]

ST: Zangemeister (1876) 539; Lambert (1969–72) no. 680 [Jerome, *Epist.* cviii]; Römer (1972b) 212; R.E. Reynolds (1978) 39–41 [*De septem gradibus ecclesiae*]; Obrist (2002) 336; Dekker (2010) 152

517. London, Lambeth Palace Library, 427, fols. 1–202

s. xi[1], SW England (Winchester?), (prov. Lanthony secunda, Gloucs., Augustinian canons)

Content: Psalter prefaces; two *lunaria*; Psalterium Gallicanum°; Ps. CLI; canticles°; form of confession°; prayer°; verse prayer**; litany (later addition)

MS: Schenkl no. 4605; Lindelöf (1909–14) vol. II; Mearns (1914) 63, 79; M.R. James (1932) 588–90; N.R. Ker (1957) no. 280; N.R. Ker (1964) 111; P.P. O'Neill (1991); Robinson—Stanley (1991) 26; P.P. O'Neill (1992); Conner (1993) 241; Pulsiano (1995) 65–6; Gneuss (1998) 277; Pulsiano (1998b) 105 n. 1; Gretsch (2000) 86; Pulsiano (2001a) xxiii–xxiv; Chardonnens (2007b) 48, 534–5, 553; Ganz—Roberts (2007) 45, 48; Rushforth (2011) 42–3; Scragg (2012a) nos. 774–7; Toswell (2012) 471, 477–8

DEC: R. Gameson (1995b) 219 n. 159, 220 n. 164

FACS: Lindelöf (1909–14) I, pl. I [fol. 157v]; Robinson—Stanley (1991) pl. 31.1 [fol. 183v]; Ganz—Roberts (2007) 46 [fol. 17r]; R. Gameson (2012) pl. 21.2 [fol. 181r]

ED: Lindelöf (1909–14) [psalter and canticles with OE gloss]; Förster (1914) 328–9 [prayer; confession]; Dobbie (1942) 94–6 [verse prayer coll. as L]; Lapidge (1991a) 214–18 [litany]; Pulsiano (2001a) [Pss. I–L, Latin and OE gloss, coll. as I]; Chardonnens (2007b) 445, 457 [two *lunaria*]

LANG: Lindelöf (1909–14) I.47–102, and 261–322 [glossary]; Hofstetter (1987) 84–8; Gretsch (1999a) 42–88, 185–225

ST: Sisam—Sisam (1959) 72–4; A.F. Cameron (1974) 220; Stracke (1974); Korhammer (1976) 238–41; Korhammer (1980) 38–9, 54; Rollason (1982) 29–30; Lapidge (1991a) 75–6; P.P. O'Neill (1991); Pulsiano (1991c); P.P. O'Neill (1992); Conner (1993) 241; P.P. O'Neill (1993); Corrêa (1996) 294 n. 39; Pulsiano (1997); T. Graham (1998a) 68 n. 150; Gretsch (1999a) 19, 26–7, 40 *et passim*

518. London, Lambeth Palace Library, 427, fols. 210–11

s. xi², Exeter?, (prov. Lanthony secunda, Gloucs., Augustinian canons)

Contents: Lives of St Mildred* (f) and Kentish royal saints* (f)

MS: N.R. Ker (1957) no. 281; Swanton (1975) 16–17; Korhammer (1976) 241; Rollason (1982) 29–31; R. Gameson (1999a) no. 595; Biggs (2007a) 16; Treharne (2007b) 17; Scragg (2012a) no. 778

ED: Förster (1914) 332–3; Swanton (1975) 24–6 [St Mildred], 26–7 [Kentish royal saints]

LANG: Crowley (2000) 126, 130, 139–40, 142–3, 146–8

ST: Swanton (1975) 15–24; Scragg (1979) 264; Scragg (1996) 222–3; Hollis (1998a) 42–3 and n. 8; Hollis (1998b); Biggs et al. (2001) 347–50, 422–3; Love (2004) xxx–xxxii, lxxxiv, cv–cvi, *et passim*

London, Lambeth Palace Library, 430, flyleaves: see no. **342. 8**

519. London, Lambeth Palace Library, 431, fols. 145–60

s. xi med.—xi³/⁴, Normandy (prov. Lanthony secunda, Gloucs., Augustinian canons)

Contents: Ambrosius Autpertus, *De conflictu uitiorum et uirtutum*

MS: M.R. James (1932) 595–9; N.R. Ker (1964) 111 and n. 9; Bill (1972) 15 [N.R. Ker]; A.G. Watson (1987a) 43; R. Gameson (1999a) no. 596; Ganz—Roberts (2007) 70

ST: Römer (1972b) 212

520. London, Lambeth Palace Library, 489

s. xi³/⁴, Exeter [one vol. with no. 322? Companion vol. to no. 109, pp. 3–98 and 209–24?]

Contents: eight homilies* (six by Ælfric)

MS: M.R. James (1932) 678–81; T.A.M. Bishop (1954–8a) 198; N.R. Ker (1957) no. 283; N.R. Ker (1964) 82 n. 3, 83; Pope (1967–8) I.33–4; R.M. Wilson (1968) 115–16; Drage (1978) 377–8; P.R. Robinson (1978) 238 [repr. P.R. Robinson (1994) 35]; Godden (1979) xlii; Scragg (1979) 255–6; Scragg (1992) xxxiii–xxxiv; Conner (1993) 4, 6, 39, 42, 92; Clemoes (1997) 21–4; *ASMMF* VIII (2000) 79–82 [no. 318; Wilcox]; P.R. Robinson (2003) I, no. 87; Treharne (2003) 161, 166; Millett (2007) 44–5, 48, 50–6, 61; Ganz—Roberts (2007) 60–2; Swan (2007a); Treharne (2007b) 17, 20, 24; Scragg (2012a) nos. 454–63

FACS: *ASMMF* VIII (2000) no. 318; P.R. Robinson (2003) II, pls. 2–3 [fols. 18r, 31r]; Ganz—Roberts (2007) 61 [fol. 25r]

ED [the order of the following items is that of the manuscript, listed according to the numbering of individual articles in N.R. Ker (1957) 344–5; only the most recent editions are cited]:

art. 1: Clemoes (1997) 190–7 [Ælfric, CH I, Hom. II (Christmas), coll. as J]

art. 2: Clemoes (1997) 299–306 [Ælfric, CH I, Hom. XV (Easter), coll. as J] art. 3: Clemoes (1997) 486–96 [Ælfric, CH I, Hom. XXXVI (All Saints), coll. as J]

art. 4: Napier (1883/1967) 291–9 [base MS (= Z) for Hom. LVII (*Sermo ad populum dominicis diebus*)]

art. 5: Clemoes (1997) 325–34 [Ælfric, CH I, Hom. XIX (*Feria .III. De dominica oratione*), with alterations, coll. as J: see Ker (1957) 344]

art. 6: Godden (1979) 335–7, 344–5 [part of Ælfric, CH II, Hom. XL (Dedication of a Church) and materials from other homilies, coll. as J: see Ker (1957) 345]

art. 7: Brotanek (1913) 15–27 [another homily for the Dedication of a Church, coll. without siglum]

art. 8: Ebersperger (1999) 237–62 [Ælfric, Hom. for the Dedication of a Church, coll. as L]

LANG: J. Hall (1920) II.407–13; Ogura (2003)

ST: Napier (1883/1967) 361–2 [Ostheeren]; R.M. Wilson (1968) 116; Lees (1985) 130 and n. 7; J. Hill (1996) 244; Treharne (1998) 242; Ebersperger (1999) 224 and nn.; Millett (2007); Treharne (2007a) 262–4; Scragg (2012b) 559

520. 2. London, Lambeth Palace Library, 1229, fols. 7 and 8

s. x, Ireland (prov. Lanthony secunda, Gloucs., Augustinian canons)

Contents: Commentary on the Euangelium Matthaei [*BCLL* 347] (f)

MS: Bill (1972) 58 [N.R. Ker]; Ganz—Roberts (2007) 22

FACS: Bieler—Carney (1972) pls. I–IV [fols. 7r, 7v, 8r, 8v]; Ganz—Roberts (2007) 23 [fol. 8r]

ED: Bieler—Carney (1972)

ST: Biggs et al. (1990) 104 [C.D. Wright]

520. 3. London, Lambeth Palace Library, 1230, flyleaf (bifolium)

s. xi, Wales?

Contents: passional (f)

MS: Bill (1972) 61 [N.R. Ker]

520. 4. London, Lambeth Palace Library, 1231, flyleaves (one bifolium + one leaf)

s. ix², France; Brittany?

Contents: *Collectio canonum Hibernensis* [*CPL* 1794] (f)

MS: Bill (1972) 61 [N.R. Ker]; Ganz—Roberts (2007) 28

FACS: Ganz—Roberts (2007) 29 [fol. 1v]

520. 5. London, Lambeth Palace Library, 1233 (part of one bifolium)

s. x med.

Contents: Alcuin, *De fide sanctae et indiuiduae Trinitatis* (f)

MS: Bill (1972) 62–3 [N.R. Ker]; Ganz—Roberts (2007) 22, 33

FACS: Ganz—Roberts (2007) 34

521. London, Lambeth Palace Library, 1370 (with London, BL, Cotton Tiberius B. iv, fol. 87) (the 'MacDurnan Gospels')

s. ix², Ireland (prob. Armagh), prov. Canterbury CC by 924×939

Contents: gospels; records* and writs* (s. xi¹)

MS: M.R. James (1932) 843–5; Bieler (1949) 276; McGurk (1956) 250–1, 254, 257–8, 261, 269 [repr. McGurk (1998) no. I]; N.R. Ker (1957) no. 284; G.R.C. Davis (1958) no. 177; N.R. Ker (1964) 37; Sawyer (1968) 58 and nos. 987, 988, 1564; T.J. Brown (1972) 222 [repr. T.J. Brown (1993a) 99, 273 n. 95]; Rella (1977) 50; Dumville (1983b) 53; Keynes (1985a) 153–9; McGurk (1987) 165–8, 173 [repr. McGurk (1998) no. II]; McNamara (1987–8); B. Fischer (1988–91) I.17*; McNamara (1990) 102–11; Dumville (1992a) 121 n. 190; R.I. Page (1993a) 51; C.D. Wright (1993) 268 and nn.; Parkes (1997b) 139 n. 108; P.R. Robinson (2003) I, no. 97; Heslop (2004) 305 n. 41; Ganz—Roberts (2007) 26–8; M.P. Brown (2010); M.P. Brown (2012) 135; R. Gameson (2012d) 349 and n. 17; Marsden (2012) 422 and n. 73; Scragg (2012a) nos. 779–82

DEC: Henry (1967) 102–5; Alexander (1978a) no. 70; Ohlgren (1986) no. 70; R. Gameson (1992a) 140–2

FACS: Alexander (1978a) ills. 321-8 [fols. 2r, 5r, 117r, 172r, 1v, 4v, 115v, 170v], 354 [fol. 70v]; Keynes (1985a) pl. V [fol. 3v]; G. Henderson (1987) 47 [fol. 1v]; P.R. Robinson (2003) II, pl. 1 [fol. 11r]; Ganz—Roberts (2007) 25 [fol. 114r]; N.P. Brooks (2008) 30 [fol. 114r]; M.P. Brown (2010) 30–1 [fols. 4v–5r, 3v–4r, 72r]; Roberts—Webster (2011) pl. I [fol. 1v]

ED: Fischer (1988–91) [gospels coll. as Hy]

ST: J.A. Robinson (1923) 55–9; Kenney (1929) no. 475; *BCLL* (1985) no. 528; Karkov (2004) 54; N.P. Brooks (2008); Farr (2011a) *passim*; McKee (2012b) 342 and n. 13

521. 2. London, Private Collector, s.n.

s. viii², prob. Northumbria

Contents: fragments from Augustine, *Sermo* cclxvA and pseudo-Augustine, *Sermo* clxix

MS: *Sotheby's Western Manuscripts and Miniatures, London, 19 June 2001*, no. 3; A.S.G. Edwards (2002) 234; Gneuss (2003b) 301

London, Private Collector, s.n.: see no. **524**

521. 3. 1. London, Collection of R.A. Linenthal Esq., s.n. [formerly no. **774. 1**]

s. xi¹

Contents: Gregory of Tours, *De uirtutibus S. Martini* [*CPL* 1024; cf. *BHL* 5618d] (f)

MS: Stoneman (1997) 128

521. 3. 2. London, Collection of R.A. Linenthal Esq., s.n.

s. x ex., Canterbury CC

Contents: versary (f)

MS: Hartzell (2006) no. 199; Hornby (2010)

521. 4 and 521. 5. London, The National Record Office (formerly the Public Record Office), **E 31/1 and E 31/2**

1086–7

Contents: Little Domesday Book and Great Domesday Book

MS: Rumble (1985); Gullick (1987); Rumble (1987); R. Gameson (1999a) nos. 598–9; P.R. Robinson (2003) I, nos. 126–7; C.P. Lewis (2007) 132–4 nn. 5–14; Gullick (2012) 304 and n. 59; Webber (2012) 220

FACS:

E 31/1: Williams—Martin (2000) [complete facsimile]; Rumble (1985) pl. 3.3 [fols. 228v–229r]; Gullick (1987) figs. 17 (a)–(d) [fols. 19v, 109r,

338v, 387r, 450r (all details)]; P.R. Robinson (2003) II, pls. 4–6 [fols. 18v, 105r, 118v, 240r, 410r (all details)]

E 31/2: Erskine (1986) [complete facsimile]; Rumble (1985) pls. 3.1, 3.2 [fols. 87v, 299r], 3.4 [fol. 87v (detail)]; Gullick (1987) figs. 8 (a)–(e), 11 (b)–(d), 12–14 [fols. 299r, 87v, 252r, 44v, 63v, 191v, 83v, 332v, 250r, 39v (all details)], 9 [fol. 64v]; P.R. Robinson (2003) II, pl. 7 [fol. 304v (detail)]

ST: Keynes (2006) R230–R305 [bibliography]

521. 7. London, The National Archive, PRO SP 46/125, fol. 302

s. x in.

Contents: Bede, *De temporum ratione* [*CPL* 2320] (f)

MS: Roper (1983); Dumville (1987) 170–1 and nn. 117, 131; Parkes (1991a) 173 n. 8, 185 n.

FACS: Roper (1983) pl. I [fol. 302r]; Parkes (1991a) pl. 28 [fol. 302r]

522. London, Society of Antiquaries, 154*

s. x² (or earlier, if continental), England or Brittany?, prov. England by s. x ex., (prov. Winchester OM)

Contents: sacramentary (f); lists of gospel and epistle pericopes (f); two gospel pericopes

MS: N.R. Ker (1962–92) I.307–8; N.R. Ker (1964) 200; F. Wormald (1976); Lapidge — Winterbottom (1991b) lxiii–lxv; Dumville (1991–5) 48–9; Willetts (2000) 72–3; D. Ganz (2004) 500; Hartzell (2006) no. 202; Rankin (2012) 489 and n. 27, 491

FACS: F. Wormald (1976) pl. XI [fol. 24v]

ST: Pfaff (1995b) 26–8; Lenker (1997) 118, 487–8; P.R. Robinson (2003) I, no. 152; Pfaff (2009) 93

523. London, Wellcome Library for the History and Understanding of Medicine, 46

s. x/xi, with addition, s. xi

Contents: five medical recipes* (f); Latin poem [*CPL* 641; SK 12730] added s. xi (f)

MS: N.R. Ker (1957) p. lxiv and no. 98; N.R. Ker (1962–92) I.393–401; Moorat (1962–73) I.29–30; N.R. Ker (1976a) 124; *ASMMF* IX (2001) 82–3 [no. 320; Doane]; Scragg (2012a) nos. 784–6

FACS: *ASMMF* IX (2001) no. 320

ST: Hollis—Wright (1992) 234–6

523. 5. London, Westminster Abbey Library, 17

s. xi/xii or xii in., England or Continent, (prov. Lincoln, Franciscan convent)

Contents: tract on the virtues; Arator, *Historia apostolica* [*CPL* 1504] (incomplete)

MS: Schenkl III/i (1894) 51; Robinson—James (1909) 74–5; McKinlay (1942) no. 74; N.R. Ker (1964) 118

ST: Bloomfield et al. (1979) nos. 1048, 3011

524. London, Westminster Abbey Library, 36, nos. 17–19 [with London, BL, Add. 62104; London, BL, Harley 5977, no. 59; Lincoln, Cathedral Library, V.5.11 (ptd book), flyleaves; Oxford, BodL, Lat. liturg. e. 38, fols. 7, 8, 13 and 14; and (possibly) London, BL, Add. 79528 + London, Private Collector, s.n.]

s. xi med., Exeter

Contents: missal (f)

MS: N.R. Ker (1954) 28 [no. 285a]; Rella (1977) 81; Rankin (1984) 102, 112; A.G. Watson (1987a) 36 and n. 1; R. Gameson (1996b) 145 and n. 36; Stoneman (1997) 128–9; Gneuss (2003b) 301; Hartzell (2006) no. 203; Wieland (2009) 123; Rankin (2012) 501 and n. 89

FACS: *Sotheby's Western Manuscripts and Miniatures, 8 December 1981, lot 8* [BL, Add. 62104]; Rankin (1984) pl. IX (a) [Oxford, BodL, Lat. liturg. e. 38, fol. 7v (detail)]; De Hamel (1986) pl. 210 [BL, Add. 62104]

ED: Gwara (1994c) 230 [Harley 5977, no. 59]

ST: Hohler (1975) 75 and n. 66

524. 2. London, Westminster Abbey Muniments, 67209

s. xi[1]

Contents: homily* (f)

MS: R.I. Page (1996); Wilcox (2008) 428–9; Scragg (2012a) no. 787

FACS: R.I. Page (1996) pls. IX (a)–(b) [recto and verso]

ED: R.I. Page (1996) 205–7

524. 4. Longleat House (Wiltshire), Marquess of Bath, NMR 10589 (flyleaves)

s. vii/viii, Ireland, prov. Glastonbury

Contents: Isidore, *Etymologiae* [*CPL* 1186] (f)

MS: *CLA* Supplement (1971) no. 1873; Bischoff et al. (1992b) 293; Carley—Dooley (1991)

FACS: Bischoff et al. (1992b) pl. III(b) [backleaf, recto (detail)]

Maidstone, Kent County Archives Office, PRC 49/1 a and b: see no. **211**

Maidstone, Kent County Archives Office, PRC 49/2: see no. **212. 4. 1**

524. 8. Manchester, John Rylands University Library, 109

s. xi ex. or xi/xii, Canterbury CC? (prov. Rochester?)

Contents: Epistulae Pauli, with gloss by Lanfranc

MS: M.R. James (1921) I.193–4; R. Gameson (1999a) no. 604

ST: Gibson (1971) [repr. Gibson (1993a) no. XII]

525. Manchester, John Rylands University Library, Misc. fragm. 11

s. x

Contents: pontifical (f)

MS: Gneuss (1985) 132; Dumville (1992a) 69

525. 5. Nottingham University Library, MI A8, fols. a–d (two bifolia)

s. xi/xii, England

Contents: missal (f)

MS: Hartzell (2006) no. 209

Oxford, Bodleian Library, Arch. Selden, B. 26 (3340), fol. 34: see no. **346**

526. Oxford, Bodleian Library, Ashmole 328 (S.C. 6882 and 7420)

s. xi med., Canterbury CC?

Contents: Byrhtferth, *Enchiridion*+*; homiletic piece [*Ammonitio amici*]*; *Alleluia* verse [prayer to St Dunstan] (s. xi²)

MS: W.H. Black (1845) cols. 218–19; Madan et al. (1895–1953) II/ii.1117, 1135; N.R. Ker (1935); N.R. Ker (1957) no. 288; Lapidge (1980a) 22; Lapidge (1981b) 110 n. 35 [repr. Lapidge (1993a) 330 n. 35];

Baker—Lapidge (1995) cxv–cxxi; Hartzell (2006) no. 239; Scragg (2012a) nos. 803–4

DEC: Pächt—Alexander (1973) no. 49; R. Gameson (1991) 75 n. 82

FACS: Crawford (1929) 16 pls. facing pp. 8, 232 [pp. 7, 9, 85, 91, 94, 117, 146, 152, 163, 168–9, 189, 204, 215, 221, 224–5, 240]; Lapidge (1980a) fig. 12 [p. 168]; Baker—Lapidge (1995) frontispiece [p. 168]

ED: F. Kluge (1885b) [base MS for excerpts from Byrhtferth, *Enchiridion*]; Crawford (1929) [base MS for Byrhtferth, *Enchiridion*]; Baker—Lapidge (1995) 2–240 [base MS for Byrhtferth, *Enchiridion*], 242–8 [base MS for homiletic piece]; Hartzell (2006) no. 239 [*Alleluia* verse]

LANG: P.S. Baker (1980); Hofstetter (1987) 412–15; Baker—Lapidge (1995) xcv–cxv, 430–77 [glossary]

ST: Crawford (1929); Henel (1942b); Jost (1950) 240–3; Hart (1972); Scragg (1979) 261–2 [homiletic piece]; P.S. Baker (1980); P.S. Baker (1981); R. Berry (1982); Hollis—Wright (1992) 149–84; Baker—Lapidge (1995); Knappe (1996) 270–312 *et passim*; Lapidge (2009) xv–xliv

527. Oxford, Bodleian Library, Ashmole 1431 (S.C. 7523)

s. xi/xii, Canterbury StA

Contents: enlarged *Herbarius* (Antonius Musa, *De herba uettonica*; pseudo-Apuleius, *Herbarius*; pseudo-Dioscorides, *Liber medicinae ex herbis femininis*)

MS: W.H. Black (1845) cols. 1165–6; Madan et al. (1895–1953) II/ii.1137; M.R. James (1903) 346, 520; Gunther (1925) xvii, xxvi; N.R. Ker (1957) no. 289; N.R. Ker (1960) 30; R. Gameson (1999a) no. 622; M. Collins (2000) 196 and nn., 228 n. 111; *ASMMF* IX (2001) 84–8 [no. 341; Doane]; Barker-Benfield (2008) I.5 n. 4, 6, II.1204, III.1747, 1801, 1820

DEC: Dodwell (1954) 26, 122; MacKinney (1965) 160; Pächt—Alexander (1973) no. 50; C.M. Kauffmann (1975) no. 10; Ohlgren (1986) no. 221; R. Gameson (1995a) 125 and n. 111, 126 n. 112, 144; R. Gameson (1995b) 14; R. Gameson (2012c) 284 and n. 120

FACS: Gunther (1925) pl. 2 [fols. 31r, 34r (details)]; Pächt—Alexander (1973) pl. VI [fol. 31r (detail)]; C.M. Kauffmann (1975) ills. 22–5 [fols. 31r, 34r, 19r, 20r]; De Hamel (1986) pl. 95 [fol. 20r]; *ASMMF* IX (2001) no. 341

ED: Gough (1974) 273–80 [OE glosses (faulty edition)]; Bierbaumer (1977b) 115–19 [corrects the work of Gough]

ST: Gunther (1925); Howald—Sigerist (1927); Grape-Albers (1977); Riddle (1980) 131; M.L. Cameron (1983) 137, 140; Hofstetter (1983) 359; Yerkes (1983a) 130; Hollis—Wright (1992) 317–24; D'Aronco (2011) 239 and n. 39

528. Oxford, Bodleian Library, Auctarium D. infra 2. 9 (S.C. 2638), fols. 1–110

s. x², Canterbury StA, (prov. Exeter)

Contents: Cassian, *De institutis coenobiorum* [*CPL* 513]; Latin poem [SK 10046] (by Alcuin?)

MS: Petschenig (1888/2004) xvii–xviii; Schenkl no. 792; Madan et al. (1895–1953) II/i.464; T.A.M. Bishop (1954–8b) 327–9; N.R. Ker (1964) 83; T.A.M. Bishop (1971) xxv, 5 [no. 7]; Rella (1977) 85, 162; Drage (1978) 383–5; P.R. Robinson (1978) 233 [repr. P.R. Robinson (1994) 28]; Gneuss (2003b) 301; Wieland (2009) 141; Rushforth (2012) 206 n. 57

FACS: T.A.M. Bishop (1954–8b) pl. XIII [fols. 102r, 41r (details)]; T.A.M. Bishop (1966) pl. C [fol. 84r]; T.A.M. Bishop (1971) pl. V [fol. 67r]

ST: O'Brien O'Keeffe (1985) 67; Carley (1986) 113; *CSLMA* II (1999) 83 [Alcuin poem]; Lake (2003) 41 n. 56

528. 1. Oxford, Bodleian Library, Auctarium D. infra 2. 9 (S.C. 2638), fols. 111–47

s. xi², England?

Contents: Apocalypsis Iohannis, with scholia

MS: Madan et al. (1895-1953) II/i.464–5

529. Oxford, Bodleian Library, Auctarium D. 2. 14 (S.C. 2698)

s. vi ex. or vii in., Italy, prov. England (Lichfield?) s. viii ex., prov. Bury St Edmunds s. xi?

Contents: gospels

MS: J. Wordsworth et al. (1889–1954) I.xiii; Madan et al. (1895–1953) II/i.500–2; Nicholson (1913) xvii–xix; *CLA* II (1935) no. 230; Lowe

(1960) 19; McGurk (1961a) no. 32; T.J. Brown (1980) 9, 13; B. Fischer (1988–91) I.14*; P.L. Heyworth (1989) 69, 144; Dumville (1992a) 102–3, 121, 126; O'Sullivan (1994) 81; R. Gameson (1994b) 44 n. 88; Lapidge (1996c) 428, 441; R. Gameson (1999c) 322–3; Marsden (1999); *ASMMF* VII (2000) 62–6 [no. 339; Doane]; Emms (2006) 20; Hartzell (2006) no. 242; Barker-Benfield (2008) III.1656, 1734–5, 1833; Wieland (2009) 118; R. Gameson (2012a) 53

DEC: Netzer (2012) 226 and n. 5, 236

FACS: Nicholson (1913) pls. I–III [fols. 79r, 149v, 149r]; Lowe (1960) pl. IV [fol. 149v]; R. Gameson (1999c) pl. 13.5 [fol. 80r]; Marsden (1999) pls. 12.3–5 [fols. 7r, 20v, 31r]; *ASMMF* VII (2000) no. 339

ED: J. Wordsworth et al. (1889–1954) [gospels coll. as O]; B. Fischer (1988–91) [gospel excerpts coll. as Jo]

ST: J. Chapman (1908) 191–202; Glunz (1930) 89–114; Glunz (1933) 304–5; T.J. Brown (1972) 223 [repr. T.J. Brown (1993a) 100]; Klauser (1972) 21, 32; *CPL* (1995) no. 1980; Lenker (1997) 102–6, 406–11 *et passim*; Tite (1997a) 263; Dumville (1999) 95; R. Gameson (1999c) 322–3, 348, 354; Verey (1999) 330; D. Ganz (2001b); R. McKitterick (2012) 315

529. 1. Oxford, Bodleian Library, Auctarium D. 2. 14 (S.C. 2698), fol. 173

s. xi^2 or xi ex., prob. Bury St Edmunds

Contents: booklist*; service 'Ad introitum portae'

MS: Madan et al. (1895–1953) II/i.500; A.J. Robertson (1939) 500; N.R. Ker (1957) no. 290; Lapidge (1994b) 146–9; *ASMMF* VII (2000) 62–6 [no. 339; Doane]; Emms (2006) 20; Barker-Benfield (2008) I.lii–liii and n. 10, III.1735; Scragg (2012a) nos. 805–7

FACS: *ASMMF* VII (2000) no. 339

ED: A.J. Robertson (1939) 250, 501 [booklist]; Lapidge (1994b) 146–9 [booklist]

ST: *CLA* II (1935) no. 230 [on the flyleaf (fol. 173)]; Dumville (1992a) 102–3, 121 n. 191; Conner (1993) 6, 15

530. Oxford, Bodleian Library, Auctarium D. 2. 16 (S.C. 2719)

s. x^1, Landévennec (Brittany), prov. N France or Flanders, prov. England s. xi med., prov. Exeter s. xi^2, with additions s. xi$^{3/4}$

Contents: gospels, gospel list (s. x¹); inventory of Leofric's donations to Exeter*, donation inscription*, list of relics* (additions, s. xi³ᐟ⁴)

MS: Madan et al. (1895–1953) II/i.511–12; Nicholson (1913) liii–lvi; Van Dijk (1952) no. 7; N.R. Ker (1957) no. 291; N.R. Ker (1964) 83; Drage (1978) 279–82; *BCLL* (1985) no. 965; Deuffic (1985) no. 65; McGurk (1986b) 45, 52 [repr. McGurk (1998) no. XIV]; McGurk (1987) 165 [repr. McGurk (1998) no. II]; B. Fischer (1988–91) I.18*; R.M. Butler (2004) 174 n. 4; J. Hill (2005a) 85–6; Lemoine (2005) 185, 187–8; Hartzell (2006) no. 243; Scragg (2012a) nos. 808–11

DEC: Schilling (1948); Alexander (1966) 9–10, 13; Pächt—Alexander (1966) nos. 427, 433; Zarnecki et al. (1984) no. 8; R. Gameson (1991) 90 n. 150; Alexander (1992) 77–82; R. Gameson (1995b) 258 n. 155; R. Gameson (1996b) 183 and n. 206; Lemoine (2005) 185; Rushforth (2007) 44

FACS: Nicholson (1913) pl. XXVI [fol. 29r]; Schilling (1948) pls. 7–8 [fols. 72v, 146r]; Alexander (1966) pl. 11 [fol. 146r]; Pächt—Alexander (1966) pl. XXXV [fol. 71v]; Alexander (1992) figs. 123, 126 [fols. 71v, 72v]; Rushforth (2007) 45 [fol. 72v]

ED: Förster (1933a) 11 n. 3 [Leofric's donation inscription coll. as L], 18–30 [inventory of Leofric's donation coll. as B]; A.J. Robertson (1939) 226–30 [base MS for Leofric's donation]; Förster (1943) 63–80 [base MS for list of relics]; Lapidge (1985b) 64–9 [repr. Lapidge (1994b) 134–9] [base MS for list of books in Leofric's donation]; B. Fischer (1988–91) [gospel excerpts coll. as Bm]; Conner (1993) 171–86 [base MS for list of relics]

ST: Nicholson (1913) liii–lvi; Förster (1933a) 10; Glunz (1933) 54, 68; Frere (1934) 198; Förster (1943) 24–5 and n. 2; E. Temple (1976) 78; Sauer (1978) 36; Hartzell (1981) 89 and n. 6; Dumville (1992a) 41, 90, 114, 116, 121; Conner (1993) 6, 11 *et passim*; McGurk (1993) 244 [repr. McGurk (1998) no. XI]; R. Gameson (1996b) 148, 183; Lenker (1997) 430–6 *et passim*; Ebersperger (1999) 149–51; J. Hill (2005a) 85; Lemoine (2005) 187–8, 190

531. Oxford, Bodleian Library, Auctarium D. 2. 19 (S.C. 3946) (the 'Rushworth' or 'MacRegol' Gospels)

s. viii ex. or ix in., Ireland; s. x² N or W England [addition of OE gloss]

Contents: gospels°; poem on the Evangelists [SK 9446; by Iuvencus?]; colophons

MS: J. Wordsworth et al. (1889–1954) I.xiii; Madan et al. (1895–1953) II/ii.792–3; Kenney (1929) no. 472; *CLA* II (1935) no. 231; Bischoff (1952) 11; N.R. Ker (1957) no. 292; McGurk (1961a) no. 33; T.J. Brown (1972) 221 [repr. T.J. Brown (1993a) 98–9]; T. O'Neill (1984) 12–13, 65–6; A.G. Watson (1984) I, no. 43; McGurk (1987) 165, 169, 172–3 [repr. McGurk (1998) no. II]; B. Fischer (1988–91) I.16*; M.P. Brown (1989a) 155; P.L. Heyworth (1989) 53, 69, 126, 191, 197; Dumville (1992a) 112; Blockley (1994); *ASMMF* III (1995) 20–5 [no. 338; Doane]; J.J. John (1995) 118; McGurk (1995a) 259 [repr. McGurk (1998) no. XIII]; McNamara (1995) 105; Breeze (1996a); Netzer (1999) 317; Stanley (2001) 242–3; Graham (2009) 163; Wieland (2009) 117; M.P. Brown (2012) 135, 151; R. Gameson (2012a) 28 n. 59, 67; Scragg (2012a) nos. 812–13

DEC: Köhler (1930–60) I.76; McGurk (1955b) 106 [repr. McGurk (1998) no. IV]; McGurk (1956) 248 [repr. McGurk (1998) no. I]; McGurk (1962) 22 [repr. McGurk (1998) no. VII]; Pächt—Alexander (1973) no. 1269; Alexander (1978a) no. 54; Ohlgren (1986) no. 54; McGurk (1987) 176 [repr. McGurk (1998) no. II]; M.P. Brown (1996) 98; Tilghman (2011) 93, 95–6, 98–9

FACS: Pächt—Alexander (1973) pls. CXIV–CXVI [fols. 1r, 51v, 51r, 127r]; Alexander (1978a) ills. 262–4, 266–9 [fols. 51v, 84v, 126v, 1r, 52r, 85r, 127r]; T. O'Neill (1984) 12 [fol. 169r]; McGurk (1987) pl. 2 [fol. 128v] [repr. McGurk (1998) no. II]; T.J. Brown (1993a) ills. 68–9 [fols. 1v, 2v]; *ASMMF* III (1995) no. 338; Nees (2003) fig. 5 [fol. 169v]; Roberts—Webster (2011) pl. V [fol. 169v]

ED: Skeat (1871–87) [OE gloss; in Appendices, all Latin readings differing from those in no. **343**]; Skeat (1878) 188 [poem on Evangelists]; J. Wordsworth et al. (1889–1954) [Latin gospels coll. as R]; B. Fischer (1988–91) [Latin text of gospel excerpts coll. as Hr]; R. Gameson (2001d) 39–40 [colophons]

LANG: Lindelöf (1901b); Menner (1934); Kuhn (1945); A. Campbell (1959); Karl Brunner (1965); Morrell (1965) 181–2; Greenfield—Robinson (1980) nos. 5849–59; Hofstetter (1987) 482–5; Hogg (1992); Scragg (1994a) 328, 333; *ASMMF* III (1995) 24; Crowley (2000) 130, 133–7, 146–8; C. Bishop (2007b) 82

ST: Cook (1898) 1v; Glunz (1930) 78–86; Förster (1941) 474 n.; McGurk (1956) 254, 263 [repr. McGurk (1998) no. I]; McGurk (1961a) 11 [repr. McGurk (1998) no. VI]; Morrell (1965) 175–82; Greenfield—Robinson (1980) nos. 5849–59; *BCLL* (1985) no. 527; McGurk (1986b) 45 [repr. McGurk (1998) no. XIV]; Ó Cróinín (1989) 197–8; McGurk (1994b)

14, 18 [repr. McGurk (1998) no. XII]; *CPL* (1995) no. 1385 [poem];
McGurk (1995a) 256 [repr. McGurk (1998) no. XIII]; McNamara
(1995) 71, 76, 78–9, 81 *et passim*; *CSLMA* II (1999) 471–2 [poem];
Breeze (1996a); M.P. Brown (1996) 131; Coates (1997); Tite (1997b);
R. Gameson (2001d) 39–40 [colophon of MacRegol]; Nees (2003)
365–6 [colophon of MacRegol]; Farr (2011a) 91, 93; Karkov (2011)
134; McKee (2012b) 343 and n. 18

532. Oxford, Bodleian Library, Auctarium D. 5. 3 (S.C. 27688)

s. ix/x, prob. Brittany, prov. England s. x

Contents: gospels (incomplete)

MS: Madan et al. (1895–1953) V.336; N.R. Ker (1957) no. 293; Hartzell
(1981); Deuffic (1985) no. 66; McGurk (1986b) 45 [repr. McGurk
(1998) no. XIV]; McGurk (1987) 165–6 [repr. McGurk (1998) no. II];
B. Fischer (1988–91) I.18*; Dumville (1992a) 111, 115; Bischoff
(1998—) II, no. 3770; *ASMMF* VII (2000) 62–9 [no. 342; Doane]

DEC: Pächt—Alexander (1966) no. 424

FACS: Pächt—Alexander (1966) pl. XXXV [fol. 44r]; *ASMMF* VII
(2000) no. 342

ED: Meritt (1945) nos. 60–2 [OE glosses]; B. Fischer (1988–91) [gospel
excerpts coll. as Bf]; *ASMMF* VII (2000) 69 [OE glosses, supplement]

533. Oxford, Bodleian Library, Auctarium F. 1. 15 (S.C. 2455), fols. 1–77

s. x², Canterbury StA, prov. Canterbury CC s. x/xi, prov. Exeter s. xi²

Contents: *Vita III Boethii*; *accessus* to *De consolatione Philosophiae*;
Lupus of Ferriéres, *De metris Boethii*; Boethius, *De consolatione
Philosophiae* [*CPL* 878], with commentary by Remigius; donation
inscription+* (s. xi³ᐟ⁴)

MS: Schenkl no. 806; Madan et al. (1895–1953) II/i.373; Nicholson (1913)
lx–lxii; Weinberger (1934) xviii; T.A.M. Bishop (1954–8b) 324, 329;
N.R. Ker (1957) no. 294; T.A.M. Bishop (1959–63b) 413, 415, 418,
421–2; N.R. Ker (1964) 83; T.A.M. Bishop (1971) 7 [no. 9]; R.W. Hunt
(1975) no. 118; Bolton (1977a) 52–3; Rella (1977) 85; Drage (1978)
386–8; Parkes (1992) 293; Gibson et al. (1995–2001) I.178–9; Hartzell
(2006) no. 245; Barker-Benfield (2008) I.lviii, II.1006, III.1815, 1816;
Godden—Irvine (2009) I.xlvi [cited as O]; Wittig (2010) 251 *et passim*;

R. Gameson (2012a) 29 and n. 64; Gullick (2012) 298 and n. 24; Rankin (2012) 505; Scragg (2012a) nos. 106, 814

DEC: Rice (1952) 178; Pächt—Alexander (1973) no. 37; E. Temple (1976) no. 37; Brownrigg (1978) 260–1; F. Wormald (1984) 49–50, 62; Ohlgren (1986) no. 142; R. Gameson (1992a) 191; R. Gameson (1995b) 244 n. 60; R. Gameson (2012c) 261 and n. 33

FACS: Nicholson (1913) pls. XXXII–XXXIII [fols. 5r, 35v]; Rice (1952) pls. 44 (a)–(b) [fols. 5r, 16r (details)]; T.A.M. Bishop (1971) pl. VII [fol. 71r]; E. Temple (1976) ill. 114 [fol. 5r (detail)]; C. Page (1981) 309 [fol. 64v (detail)]; F. Wormald (1984) ill. 68 [fol. 48v]; D.M. Rogers (1991) pl. 25 [fol. 29r]; R. Gameson (1992a) pls. 42 (b), 43 (a) [fols. 5r, 48v]; Parkes (1992) pl. 72 [fol. 18r]

ED: Förster (1933a) 11 n. 3 [donation inscription coll. as B^1]

ST: Pollard (1975) 144–5; Pollard (1976) 55; Bolton (1977a); Bodden (1979) 259, 269; C. Page (1981); Parkes (1992) 293; Conner (1993) 6–7, 13; Lapidge (1994b) 135, 137–8; R. Gameson (1996b) 149; Gwara (1996a) 92–3; Wittig (2007) 191; Ziolkowski (2007) 249–50; Godden (2011) 92; Jayatilaka (2011) 117

534. Oxford, Bodleian Library, Auctarium F. 1. 15 (S.C. 2455), fols. 78–93

s. x^2, Canterbury StA, prov. Canterbury CC by s. x ex.?, prov. Exeter s. xi^2

Contents: donation inscription^{+*} (s. xi$^{3/4}$); Persius, *Satirae*, with gloss

MS: Schenkl no. 806; Madan et al. (1895–1953) II/i.373–4; T.A.M. Bishop (1954–8b) 324, 326, 331, 335; Clausen (1956) 40; N.R. Ker (1957) no. 294; N.R. Ker (1964) 83; R.W. Hunt et al. (1975) no. 118; Drage (1978) 389–90; Clarkson (1996) 164–9; Barker-Benfield (2008) I.lviii, II.1381, 1391–2, III.1815, 1816; Scragg (2012a) no. 815

DEC: Pächt—Alexander (1973) no. 37; E. Temple (1976) no. 37; R. Gameson (1995b) 244 n. 60

ED: Förster (1933a) 11 n. 3 [donation inscription coll. as B^2]

ST: Glauche (1970) 54 n. 91; Pollard (1975) 144–5; Pollard (1976) 55; Kristeller et al. (1960—) III.218 [Persius]; T. Hunt (1991) I.61; Conner (1993) 7; Lapidge (1994b) 135, 139; R. Gameson (1996b) 148; Pulsiano (2001b)

535. Oxford, Bodleian Library, Auctarium F. 2. 14 (S.C. 2657)

s. xi², Sherborne?, (prov. Sherborne)

Contents: Wulfstan of Winchester, *Narratio metrica de S. Swithuno*; *titulus* on a bridge built by St Swithun; poem on St Swithun's miracle of the unbroken eggs; glossary⁺* (s. xii in.); Prudentius, *Dittochaeon* [*CPL* 1444]; Theodulus, *Ecloga* [SK 442]; Avianus, *Fabulae*; Persius, *Satirae*; Phocas, *Ars de nomine et uerbo*; *Ilias latina* [SK 8372]; pseudo-Ovid, *De nuce* [SK 10797]; Serlo of Bayeux, *Contra monachos* [WIC 15005]; two Latin poems [WIC 14029, 2123]; Statius, *Achilleis*; Lactantius, *De aue Phoenice* [*CPL* 90; SK 4500]

MS: Schenkl no. 823; Madan et al. (1895–1953) II/i.475–6; Osternacher (1902) 15; Osternacher (1916) 368; N.R. Ker (1957) no. 295 and pp. 335–6; N.R. Ker (1960) 22 and n.; N.R. Ker (1964) 179; Jeudy (1974a) 123–4; R.W. Hunt et al. (1975) 66–7 [no. 120]; P.R. Robinson (1978) 235 [repr. P.R. Robinson (1994) 30]; R.P.H. Green (1980) 115; Lapidge (1980a) 21; Munk Olsen (1982–) I.417–18; L.D. Reynolds (1983) 192, 285; T. Hunt (1991) I.77–8; Casaretto (1997) cxviii; R. Gameson (1999a) no. 623; Gretsch (1999a) 379–80; Lapidge (2003a) 70, 336 n. 4, 364, 614; Lapidge (2004b) 441; Wieland (2009) 145; Scragg (2012a) nos. 816–19

DEC: Pächt–Alexander (1973) no. 60; R. Gameson (1991) 74 n. 78

FACS: R. Ellis (1903) pl. 12 [fol. 106r]; R.W. Hunt et al. (1975) pl. XX (a) [fol. 11r]; Lapidge (2003a) pl. V [fol. 1v]

ED: Napier (1900) nos. 18B, 45, 52 [glossary; OE glosses to Wulfstan, *Narratio*, and to Phocas]; Osternacher (1902) [*Ecloga Theoduli* coll. as ι]; Lenz (1956) 127–56 [pseudo-Ovid, *De nuce*, coll. as O₁]; Guaglianone (1958) [Avianus, *Fabulae*, coll. as O]; Casaceli (1974) [Phocas, *Ars de nomine*, coll. as I]; R.P.H. Green (1980) 26–35 [base MS (= O) for *Ecloga Theoduli*]; Lapidge (2003a) 372–550 [Wulfstan, *Narratio*, coll. as B], 782 [*titulus* on a bridge coll. as B], 795 [poem on the miracle of the unbroken eggs coll. as B]

ST: R.N. Quirk (1957) 31, 33; R. Derolez (1959) 132; Glauche (1970) 99 n. 86; F.C. Robinson (1973) 453, 457 and n. 46, 459; Sheerin (1975a); Korhammer (1980) 39–40, 57; L.D. Reynolds (1983) 20, 31 n. 19 [Avianus], 192 [*Ilias latina*], 285 [pseudo-Ovid, *De nuce*]; T. Hunt (1991) I.77–8; Lapidge–Winterbottom (1991b) xxi n. 31; Casaretto (1997) [*Ecloga Theoduli*]; R. Gameson (1998) 243 n. 50; Gretsch (1999a) 379–80, 420; Lendinara (2001a) 191; Pulsiano (2001b); Lapidge (2004b) 441–2 [Wulfstan]

536. Oxford, Bodleian Library, Auctarium F. 2. 20 (S.C. 2186)

s. xi ex., prov. Exeter?

Contents: Isidore, *De natura rerum* [*CPL* 1188]; Cicero, *Somnium Scipionis*; Macrobius, *Comm. in Somnium Scipionis*; Sibylline prophecies [SK 8495 (incomplete)]

MS: Schenkl no. 829; Madan et al. (1895–1953) II/i.250; R.W. Hunt et al. (1975) no. 121; R. Gameson (1999a) nos. 624, 625; R. Gameson (2012a) 50 and n. 159

DEC: Pächt—Alexander (1973) no. 62

ST: Saxl—Meier (1953) 291; L.D. Reynolds (1983) 230 [P.K. Marshall]; Teresi (2007b) 133 and n. 6; Alcamesi (2007b); Teresi (2007c) 343, 351, 366

537. Oxford, Bodleian Library, Auctarium F. 3. 6 (S.C. 2666)

s. xi^1, prov. Exeter

Contents: verses on the *passio* of St Romanus [SK 5925]; account of Prudentius; Prudentius, *Praefatio operum* [*CPL* 1437], *Cathemerinon* [*CPL* 1438], *Apotheosis* [*CPL* 1439], *Hamartigenia* [*CPL* 1440], 'Passio S. Romani' from *Peristephanon* X [*CPL* 1443]; *Psychomachia* [*CPL* 1441]; *Contra Symmachum* [*CPL* 1442]; *Dittochaeon* [*CPL* 1444]; *Epilogus* [*CPL* 1445], all with glosses (some OE); two charms*; donation inscription[+*] (s. xi$^{3/4}$)

MS: Schenkl no. 844; Madan et al. (1895–1953) II/i.480–1; Nicholson (1913) lx; N.R. Ker (1957) no. 296; N.R. Ker (1964) 83; M.P. Cunningham (1966) xix; Drage (1978) 391–4; A.G. Watson (1984) I, no. 56; Wieland (1997a) 170; Hartzell (2006) no. 248; Petruccione (2008) 234 n. 15; Wieland (2009) 148; R. Gameson (2012b) 111 n. 64; Rankin (2012) 505; Scragg (2012a) nos. 335, 820–5

FACS: Nicholson (1913) pl. XXXI [fols. 5v–6r]; F. Barlow et al. (1972) pl. VI [fol. iii v]; A.G. Watson (1984) II, pls. 29 (a)–(b) [fols. 93r, 163v]

DEC: Wieland (1998) 4–6, 11–12, 17 nn. 26–7, 19 n. 46; Karkov (2001a) 115 n. 3, 116

ED: Napier (1890) [OE charms]; Napier (1900) no. 46 [OE glosses]; Nicholson (1913) lxi [donation inscription, base MS]; Förster (1933a) 11 [donation inscription coll. as P]; Storms (1948) nos. 77–8 [two charms]; M.P. Cunningham (1966) [Prudentius, *carmina*, coll. as Ox]

ST: Wieland (1985) 168, 171; Wieland (1987); R.I. Page (1992a); Conner (1993) 7, 13; Lapidge (1994b) 138; R. Gameson (1996b) 150 and n. 58;

Wieland (2001) 181–3; Ziolkowski (2007) 263; Petruccione (2008) 248–51

538. Oxford, Bodleian Library, Auctarium F. 4. 32 (S.C. 2176) ('St Dunstan's Classbook')

fols. 1-9: drawing of Christ, with distich by Dunstan [SK 4088], s. x; added: verses by Eugenius of Toledo [SK 13222, lines 1–2], s. x; Eutyches, *Ars de uerbo* (incomplete): s. ix$^{2/4}$ or ix med., Brittany, prov. Wales s. x

fols. 10–18: see no. **538. 5**

fols. 19-36 (the 'Liber Commonei'): 'alphabet of Nemnivus'; computistical material and notes on weights and measures, including extracts from the *Calculus* of Victorius of Aquitaine; Greek alphabet; *De questione apostoli* (commentary on Coloss. II. 14–15); extracts (called *Testimonia*) from Prophetae minores in Greek and Latin; lessons and canticles for the Easter Vigil in Greek and Latin: s. ix^1, Wales

fols. 37–47: Ovid, *Ars amatoria*, bk. I: s. ix/x, Wales

All parts prov. Glastonbury, s. x^2; fols. 1–9 with glosses in Latin and Breton, fols. 19–47 with glosses in Latin and Welsh

MS [descriptions may include no. **538. 5**]: Stubbs (1874) cx–cxi; Bradshaw (1889) 283, 455–8, 483–7; Schenkl no. 869; Madan et al. (1895–1953) II/i.243–5; Lindsay (1912a) no. 2; Mearns (1914) 25; B. Fischer (1952) 144–5; K.H. Jackson (1953) 47, 63; N.R. Ker (1957) no. 297; R.W. Hunt (1961) v–xvii; T.A.M. Bishop (1964–8d) 400; N.R. Ker (1964) 91; R.W. Hunt (1966) no. 35; T.A.M. Bishop (1971) xx, 1, 3; F.C. Robinson (1973) 464, 467 and n. 81; Rella (1977) 73–4; A.G. Watson (1978) 293–4, 310; Bodden (1979); Korhammer (1980) 56; Lapidge (1980a) 20; Backhouse et al. (1984b) no. 31; A.G. Watson (1984) I, no. 59 [fols. 19–36]; Carley (1986) 111, 114; Lapidge (1986c) 93–4; Voigts (1988) 91; P.L. Heyworth (1989) 190, 208, 209, 210; Budny (1992); Parkes (1992) 127 n. 75; Dumville (1993g) 50–1; Lapidge (1994a) 129–31; Parkes (1997b) 103 and n. 24; Bischoff (1998–) II, no. 3774 [fols. 1–9]; Huws (2000) 7; Heslop (2004) 281–2; Rushforth (2007) 32; Shepard (2007) 254 n. 28; Treharne (2007b) 19 n. 16; *ASMMF* XVI (2008) 79–91 [no. 346; Wilcox]; Barker-Benfield (2008) III.1680; Wieland (2009) 148; Charles-Edwards (2012) 400–2 and nn. 64–5; R. Gameson (2012a) 43 n. 122; McKee (2012a) 167 and n. 2, 168–9 and n. 6; Rushforth (2012) 201 and n. 23, 202; Scragg (2012a) nos. 827–8

DEC: F. Wormald (1952) 74 [no. 46]; Dodwell (1954) 54; Pächt—
Alexander (1973) nos. 4 [fols. 37–47], 10 [fols. 19–36], 24 [fols. 1–9]; E.
Temple (1976) no. 11; Deshman (1977) 148–52; Alexander (1978a)
no. 71; F. Wormald (1984) 52, 71, 117; Ohlgren (1986) nos. 71 [fols.
37–47], 89 [fols. 1–9]; R. Gameson (1992a) 211; Deshman (1995) 224–5,
248; R. Gameson (1995b) 26–7, 53, 79–80, 83, 88, 97, 172, 193 n. 3; Raw
(1999) 24, 149, 232–3; Tilghman (2011) 98, 100; N. Edwards (2012) 246
and n. 11; R. Gameson (2012c) 251 and n. 8, 263, 282 and n. 112

FACS: R.W. Hunt (1961) [complete facsimile]; *ASMMF* XVI (2008)
no. 346; and see also the following:

fols. 1–9: *NPS* I, pl. 81 [fol. 8r]; T.A.M. Bishop (1964–8d) pl. XXXIX (e)
[fol. 1v]; Ramsay et al. (1992) pl. I.5 [fols. 1v, 2r (details)]; and the
following facsimiles of **fol. 1r**: Hickes (1703–5) I/i.144 [engraving by
Michael Burghers]; F. Wormald (1952) pl. 1; Pächt—Alexander (1973)
pl. II.24; E. Temple (1976) ill. 41; Deshman (1977) pl. III (a);
Backhouse et al. (1984b) 53; D.M. Wilson (1984) pl. 224; D.M. Rogers
(1991) pl. 23; Ramsay et al. (1992) pl. I.4 (details); M. Irvine (1994) pl.
20; Lockett (2002) pl. IV (a) (details)

fols. 19–36: Lindsay (1912a) pl. III [fol. 22r]; R.W. Hunt (1966) pl. XIII
[fol. 28v]; T.A.M. Bishop (1971) pl. I [fol. 36r (detail)]; D.M. Rogers
(1991) pl. 22 [folio not specified]; Ramsay et al. (1992) pl. I.6–7 [fols.
20r, 27r, 36r (details)]; Rushforth (2007) 32 [fol. 22v]

fols. 37–47: Lindsay (1912a) pl. XI [fol. 40r]; Pächt—Alexander (1973) pl.
I.17 [fol. 37r (detail)]; Alexander (1978a) ill. 333 [fol. 37r]; F. Wormald
(1984) ill. 47 [fol. 37r (detail)]; Ramsay et al. (1992) pl. I.7 [fol. 47r
(detail)]; M. Irvine (1994) pl. 21 [fol. 37r]; Huws (2000) pl. 2 [fol. 37v];
Owen-Crocker (2009) fig. 2.10 [fol. 47r]; R. Gameson (2012) pl. 9.2
[fol. 37r (detail)]

ED: Haddan—Stubbs (1869–71) I.195–7 [Prophetae Minores]; B. Fischer
(1952) 145–54 [repr. B. Fischer (1986) 23–40] [lessons for the Easter
Vigil]; E.J. Kenney (1961) [Ovid, *Ars amatoria*, coll. as O]; Breen (1992)
124–5, 131–40 [*De questione apostoli*; *Testimonia* from Prophetae
minores]; Lapidge (1975a) 108 [repr. Lapidge (1993a) 146] [Dunstan
distich]; Lapidge (1980b) 106 [repr. Lapidge (1993a) 156][distich by
Eugenius]; Winterbottom—Lapidge (2012) 163 [Dunstan distich]

ST: Lindsay (1912a) 7–10 [fols. 19–36]; H. Schneider (1938) 68–70 [lessons
and canticles for Easter vigil]; Siegmund (1949); R. Derolez (1954)
157–9, 340, 343 [alphabet of 'Nemnivus']; Jeudy (1974b) 430 [Eutyches];

R.W. Hunt et al. (1975) no. 117; Gneuss (1978); Lapidge (1980b) [repr. Lapidge (1993a) 151–6]; L.D. Reynolds (1983) xx n. 39, xxx–xxxi and n. 119, 261 and n. 12; *BCLL* (1985) nos. 83 [computus texts], 88 [*De questione apostoli*], 118–19 [lections]; Deuffic (1985) no. 68 [fols. 1–9]; Hexter (1986) 15–41 [fols. 37–47]; Berschin (1988) 20; Bodden (1988) 219, 228–9; Biggs et al. (1990) 108 [*De questione apostoli*; C.D. Wright]; Breen (1992); Budny (1992) 110–14; Dumville (1992a) 118–19 [fols. 19–36]; Dumville (1992b) 71–6 [fols. 37–47]; C.D. Wright (1993) 92; M. Irvine (1994) 407–11; R. Sharpe et al. (1996) 206; R. Gameson (1998) 244 n. 51; McKinley (1998) 56 [fols. 37–47]; Gretsch (1999a) 300 n. 113, 373; Lapidge (2006) 171; Keefer (2007b) 98–9; Charles–Edwards (2012) 390 and n. 7; McKee (2012b) 340 and n. 5, 341 and n. 9

538. 5. Oxford, Bodleian Library, Auctarium F. 4. 32 (S.C. 2176), fols. 10–18

s. xi$^{3/4}$ or xi^2

Contents: homily (for *Inuentio S. Crucis*)*

MS: Madan et al. (1895–1953) II/i.243; N.R. Ker (1957) no. 297; P.R. Robinson (1978) 231, 234 [repr. P.R. Robinson (1994) 26, 30]; Bodden (1987) 5–11; R. Gameson (1999a) no. 627; Swan (1998); Swan (2000b) 64; R.M. Butler (2004) 198; *ASMMF* XVI (2008) 82–3, 85–6 [no. 346; Wilcox]; Scragg (2012a) nos. 829–30

FACS: R.W. Hunt (1961) [complete facsimile]; *NPS* I, pl. 82 [fol. 12r]; Bodden (1987) 6 [fol. 11r]; *ASMMF* XVI (2008) no. 346

ED: Morris (1871) 3–17; Robb (1975); Bodden (1987) 61–103 [base MS for OE homily]

LANG: Bodden (1987) 12–23, 113–26 [glossary]

ST: Robb (1975); Scragg (1979) 257; Bodden (1987); Scragg (1996) 216; *ASMMF* XVI (2008) 82–3 [Wilcox]

539. Oxford, Bodleian Library, Barlow 4 (S.C. 6416)

s. ix$^{3/3}$, prob. NE France, prov. England by s. xi^2, (prov. Worcester)

Contents: homily on the genealogy of Christ (add. s. xi^2); Smaragdus of Saint-Mihiel, *Expositio libri comitis* (s. ix$^{3/3}$)

MS: Schenkl no. 243; Madan (1895–1953) II/ii.1044–5; N.R. Ker (1964) 208; Rädle (1974) 121; J. Hill (1992) 214, 234–5 and nn.; Dumville

(1993g) 49; Bischoff (1998—) II, no. 3782; R. Gameson (1999a)
no. 628; R.M. Thomson (2001) xxii, 58; R. Gameson (2005a) 93, 101–4;
Lapidge (2006) 171; T.N. Hall (2007) 234–6; R. Gameson (2012d) 368
and n. 103

DEC: Pächt—Alexander (1973) no. 40

ST: Lenker (1997) 493; Gneuss (2003b) 301; R. McKitterick (2012) 329
and n. 103

540. Oxford, Bodleian Library, Barlow 25 (S.C. 6463)

s. x, England?

Contents: Iuvencus, *Euangelia* [*CPL* 1385]

MS: Schenkl no. 248; Madan et al. (1895–1953) II/ii.1057; Lapidge (1982a)
134 n. 64 [repr. Lapidge (1996b) 472 n. 64]; R.M. Thomson (1982b) 4
n. 14; Lapidge (2006) 319

541. Oxford, Bodleian Library, Barlow 35 (S.C. 6467)

s. x, Continent, prov. England by s. xi in.

Contents: calendarial rules; prognostics; Alcuin, *Interrogationes Sigewulfi
in Genesin*; *Scholica Graecarum glossarum*; Greek-Latin Glossary;
charm (s. xi in.); pseudo-Cicero, *Synonyma*; glossaries[+*] extracted from
Ælfric's *Grammar* and *Glossary* (s. xi in.)

MS: Schenkl no. 250; Madan et al. (1895–1953) II/ii.1058; N.R. Ker (1957)
no. 298; Rella (1977) 166; Rella (1980) 113; Munk Olsen (1982—) I.345;
Hartzell (2006) 249; *ASMMF* XV (2007) 75–81 [no. 347; Doane];
Chardonnens (2007b) 548; Wieland (2009) 131, 133; Scragg (2012a)
nos. 831–4

DEC: Pächt—Alexander (1973) no. 30

FACS: *ASMMF* XV (2007) no. 347

ED: Liebermann (1894) [Latin—OE glossaries]

ST: Zupitza (1880/2001) ix–x [glossaries]; Laistner (1923) [*Scholica
Graecarum glossarum*]; Laistner (1924) 184 [*Scholica Graecarum glossarum*]; Kenney (1929) no. 401 [*Scholica Graecarum glossarum*]; Lapidge
(1977a) 449 and n. 9; Buckalew (1978) 154–5 [glossaries]; *BCLL* (1985)
no. 1241 [*Scholica Graecarum glossarum*]; Pettit (1999) 33–40, 42–4 [OE
charm]; *CSLMA* II (1999) 486 [Alcuin]; Chardonnens (2010) 235–6

542. Oxford, Bodleian Library, Bodley 49 (S.C. 1946)

s. x med., (prov. Winchester OM)

Contents: Aldhelm, *Carmen de uirginitate* [*CPL* 1333]

MS: Schenkl no. 442; Madan et al. (1895–1953) II/i.127; Ehwald (1919)
344–6; N.R. Ker (1957) no. 299; N.R. Ker (1964) 201; Rella (1977) 70,
161; Dumville (1994a) 137 n. 24; R. Gameson (2012a) 39 and n. 96;
D. Ganz (2012) 193 and n. 34; Lapidge (2012b) 32

DEC: Pächt—Alexander (1973) no. 23; E. Temple (1976) no. 19 (i);
Ohlgren (1986) no. 97; R. Gameson (1995b) 221 n. 168; Wieland (1998)
15 n. 10

FACS: E. Temple (1976) ill. 62 [fol. 67v (detail)]

ED: Napier (1900) nos. 15, 20 [OE glosses]; Ehwald (1919) 350–471
[Aldhelm, *Carmen de uirginitate*, coll. as W]

ST: A.G. Watson (1978) 310 [repr. A.G. Watson (2004) no. VII]; Gretsch
(1999a) 141 n. 21; Lapidge (2012b) 31–5

543. Oxford, Bodleian Library, Bodley 92 (S.C. 1901)

s. xi/xii, prob. Normandy (or England?), (prov. Exeter)

Contents: Ambrose, *De officiis ministrorum* [*CPL* 144]

MS: Schenkl no. 458; Madan et al. (1895–1953) II/i.108; N.R. Ker (1960)
24 n. 3; N.R. Ker (1964) 83; Conner (1993) 7; R. Gameson (1996b) 155
and n. 86; Bankert et al. (1997) 15, 35; R. Gameson (1999a) no. 630

DEC: Pächt—Alexander (1966) no. 462

544. Oxford, Bodleian Library, Bodley 94 (S.C. 1904)

s. xi/xii, (England or) prob. Normandy, (prov. Exeter)

Contents: Ambrose, *De Isaac et anima* [*CPL* 128], *De bono mortis* [*CPL*
129], *De fuga saeculi* [*CPL* 133], *De Iacob et uita beata* [*CPL* 130],
De paradiso [*CPL* 124], *De obitu Valentiniani* [*CPL* 158], *Epistula ad
Vercellensem ecclesiam* [extra collectionem xiv (lxiii)]; Jerome,
Aduersus Iouinianum [*CPL* 610]; Augustine, *Epistulae* ccl, liv, ccix
[*CPL* 262]; Augustine, *Sermones* ccclv, ccclvi [*CPL* 284]

MS: Schenkl no. 460; Madan et al. (1895–1953) II/i.109; N.R. Ker (1960)
24 n. 3; N.R. Ker (1964) 83; Faller—Zelzer (1968–94) IV.349; Conner
(1993) 7; R. Gameson (1996b) 155 and n. 87; Bankert et al. (1997) 15,
22, 26, 27, 29, 51; R. Gameson (1999a) no. 631

DEC: Pächt—Alexander (1966) no. 460

ST: Lambert (1969–72) no. 252; Römer (1972b) 227

545. Oxford, Bodleian Library, Bodley 97 (S.C. 1928)

s. xi in., (prov. Canterbury CC)

Contents: Aldhelm, *De uirginitate* (prose) [*CPL* 1332]

MS: Schenkl no. 462; Madan et al. (1895–1953) II/i.121–2; M.R. James
(1903) 21, 506; Ehwald (1919) 221; N.R. Ker (1957) no. 300; N.R. Ker
(1964) 38, 45; Clarkson (1996) 177–80; Gwara (2001) I.180*–184*;
Barker-Benfield (2008) I.lxxvii–lxxviii, 80, 93, II.1279, 1373, 1376,
III.1800–1; Lapidge (2012b) 27; Scragg (2012a) nos. 835–6

DEC: Pächt—Alexander (1973) no. 39; R. Gameson (1995b) 221 n. 167

ED: Napier (1900) no. 6 [OE glosses]; Ehwald (1919) 226–323 [Aldhelm,
prose *De uirginitate*, coll. as C²]; Gwara (2001) vol. II [Aldhelm, prose
De uirginitate, with OE and Latin glosses, coll. as C2]

ST: Pollard (1975) 148–9; Pollard (1976) 55; Raw (1994) 266; Gwara
(1997a) 568; Gwara (1998) 140 n. 7; Gretsch (1999a) 144; Gwara (2001)
I.140*–147*, 253*–267*, 273*–274*; Lapidge (2012b) 26–31

546. Oxford, Bodleian Library, Bodley 109 (S.C. 1962), fols. 1–60

s. x/xi and xi¹, Canterbury StA

Contents: Bede, *Vita S. Cudbercti* (prose) [*CPL* 1379; *BHL* 2019]
(incomplete) and *Vita S. Cudbercti* (verse) [*CPL* 1380; *BHL* 2020]

MS: Schenkl no. 465; Madan et al. (1895–1953) II/i.134–5; Jaager (1935)
30; Colgrave (1940) xi, 23; Laistner—King (1943) 88; N.R. Ker (1957)
no. 301; Lapidge (1995c) 130, 143; Barker-Benfield (2008) I.604,
III.1816; Lapidge (2008a) 114; Scragg (2012a) no. 837

ED: Jaager (1935) [Bede, *Vita metrica S. Cudbercti*, coll. as O²]; Colgrave
(1940) [Bede, prose *Vita S. Cudbercti*, coll. as O²]

ST: F.C. Robinson (1973) 461, 464 n. 62; Korhammer (1980) 56;
R. Gameson (1999a) no. 632 [on fols. 60v–78r, add. s. xii¹]

547. Oxford, Bodleian Library, Bodley 120 (S.C. 27643), fols. i–iv

s. xi ex.

Contents: sacramentary (f)

MS: Madan et al. (1895–1953) V.318; Van Dijk (1957–60) V.4; R. Gameson (1999a) no. 633

548. Oxford, Bodleian Library, Bodley 126 (S.C. 1990)

s. xi/xii, prob. Winchester OM

Contents: Iulianus Pomerius, *De uita contemplatiua* [*CPL* 998]

MS: Madan et al. (1895–1953) II/i.148; A.G. Watson (1987b) 291 [repr. A.G. Watson (2004) no. VIII]; R. Gameson (1995a) 102 n. 28; R. Gameson (1999a) no. 634; Hartzell (2006) no. 252; Barker-Benfield (2008) III.1833; Webber (2012) 222 n. 61

DEC: Pächt—Alexander (1973) no. 52; R. Gameson (1995a) 124 n. 103, 129 n. 130, 144

FACS: Pächt—Alexander (1973) pl. VI (51) [fol. 1v (detail)]

548. 1. Oxford, Bodleian Library, Bodley 126 (S.C. 1990), fols. ii–iii, 60–1

s. xi med. or xi^2, Winchester OM?

Contents: antiphons and responsories; Office of St Katherine; responsories for the Office of the Dead

MS: Madan et al. (1895–1953) II/i.148–9; R. Gameson (1999a) no. 635; Hartzell (2006) no. 252

549. Oxford, Bodleian Library, Bodley 130 (S.C. 27609)

s. xi ex., prob. Bury St Edmunds, (prov. ibid.)

Contents: enlarged *Herbarius* (Antonius Musa, *De herba uettonica*; pseudo-Apuleius, *Herbarius*; pseudo-Dioscorides, *Liber medicinae ex herbis femininis*); *Curae ex hominibus*; *Medicina de quadrupedibus* (*De taxone liber*; Sextus Placitus, *Liber medicinae ex animalibus*)

MS: Madan et al. (1895–1953) V.302–3; Beccaria (1956) no. 86; N.R. Ker (1957) no. 302; N.R. Ker (1964) 21; De Vriend (1972) xxxv–xxxvi, xlv–liii; R.M. Thomson (1972) 625 and n. 39, 626 and nn. 51–2; R.W. Hunt et al. (1975) no. 122; Hollis—Wright (1992) 325–6, 332–3, 371; *ASMMF* VI (1998) 6–9 [no. 351; Franzen]; R. Gameson (1999a) no. 636; M. Collins (2000) 196–9; Scragg (2012a) no. 838

DEC: Pächt (1950) 29 n. 2; McKinney (1965) 160; Alexander (1970b) 13–14; Gransden (1972) 51; Pächt—Alexander (1973) no. 53; C.M.

Kauffmann (1975) no. 11; Ohlgren (1986) no. 222; R. Gameson (1991) 68; R. Gameson (1995b) 14–15

FACS: Gunther (1925) [complete facsimile]; Alexander (1970b) pls. 35, 36 (a)–(b) [fols. 26r, 91v (detail), 89r (detail)]; Gransden (1972) figs. 9–10 [fols. 26r, 37r]; C.M. Kauffmann (1975) ills. 26–9 [fols. 76r, 93r, 10v, 36v]; Blunt—Raphael (1994) 36 [fol. 58v]; *ASMMF* VI (1998) no. 351; M. Collins (2000) pl. XVIII and fig. 51 [fols. 45r, 26r]

ED: N.R. Ker (1957) 357 [OE plant names]; De Vriend (1972) [selected passages from *Medicina de quadrupedibus*]

ST: Howald—Sigerist (1927) xi; Singer (1927) 39–43; Grattan—Singer (1952) 26; Rouse (1966) 489 n. 52; Riddle (1980) 131; Blunt—Raphael (1994) 37; D'Aronco (2007) 51 n. 67; Lendinara (2007a) 92 n. 135; D'Aronco (2011) 238–9 and nn. 38–9

550. Oxford, Bodleian Library, Bodley 135 (S.C. 1899)

s. xi/xii, (England or) prob. Normandy, (prov. Exeter)

Contents: Augustine, *Contra Faustum Manichaeum* [*CPL* 321]

MS: Madan et al. (1895–1953) II/i.106; N.R. Ker (1960) 24 and n. 3; N.R. Ker (1964) 83; R. Gameson (1996b) 155 and n. 88; R. Gameson (1999a) no. 638

DEC: Pächt—Alexander (1966) no. 456

ST: Römer (1972b) 229

550. 5. Oxford, Bodleian Library, Bodley 137 (S.C. 1903)

s. xi ex., England, prob. Exeter (or Normandy?), (prov. Exeter)

Contents: Ambrose, *De apologia prophetae Dauid* [*CPL* 135], *De Ioseph patriarcha* [*CPL* 131], *De patriarchis* [*CPL* 132], *De paenitentia* [*CPL* 156], *De excessu fratris* [*CPL* 157], *Epistulae* lxiv–lxviii [lxxiv, lxxv, lxviii, lxxx] [*CPL* 160]

MS: Schenkl no. 480; Madan et al. (1895–1953) II/i.109; N.R. Ker (1964) 83; R. Gameson (1996b) 155 and n. 89; R. Gameson (1999a) no. 639; Bankert et al. (1997) 16

ST: Anlezark (2006) 63 n. 6

551. Oxford, Bodleian Library, Bodley 145 (S.C. 1915)

s. xi^2

Contents: Augustine, *Epistulae* [*CPL* 262] cc, ccvii; *De nuptiis et concupiscentia* [*CPL* 350]; *Contra Iulianum* [*CPL* 351]

MS: Schenkl no. 483; Madan et al. (1895–1953) II/i.114; N.R. Ker (1960) xiii–xiv, 12–13; Römer (1972b) 230; Rella (1977) 26; A.G. Watson (1987b) 269, 281 [repr. A.G. Watson (2004) no. VIII]; R. Gameson (1999a) no. 640

FACS: N.R. Ker (1960) pls. 28 (b)–(c) [fols. 104v, 105r (details)]

ST: N.R. Ker (1960) 54–7; Webber (1992) 47

552. Oxford, Bodleian Library, Bodley 147 (S.C. 1918)

s. xi ex., England, prob. Exeter (or Normandy?), (prov. Exeter)

Contents: Eusebius Vercellensis, *De Trinitate* [*CPL* 105]; Vigilius of Thapsus, *Contra Arianos, Sabellianos, Photinianos Dialogus* [*CPL* 807]; Potamius of Lisbon, *Epistula ad Athanasium* [*CPL* 542]; *Epistula Athanasii ad Luciferum* [*CPL* 117]; pseudo-Vigilius of Thapsus, *Solutiones obiectionum Arianorum* [*CPL* 812]; two creeds attributed to Jerome: *De fide catholica apud Bethleem* [*CPL* 554] and *Epist. supp.* [*CPL* 633] xvii (*Explanatio fidei ad Cyrillum*)

MS: Schenkl no. 484; Madan et al. (1895–1953) II/i.116; N.R. Ker (1960) 24 and n. 1; R. Gameson (1996b) 155 and n. 90; R. Gameson (1999a) no. 641

DEC: Dodwell (1954) 115–18; Pächt—Alexander (1966) no. 446

FACS: Boase (1951) pl. 3 [fol. 23v (detail)]

ST: Lambert (1969–72) nos. 315, 317, 511, 512

553. Oxford, Bodleian Library, Bodley 148 (S.C. 1920)

s. xi/xii, England or Normandy, (prov. Exeter)

Contents: Augustine, *De consensu Euangelistarum* [*CPL* 273], with *Retractatio* II. xvi [*CPL* 250]

MS: Schenkl no. 485; Madan et al. (1895–1953) II/i.117; N.R. Ker (1960) 24 and n. 1; R. Gameson (1996b) 155 and n. 91; R. Gameson (1999a) no. 642

DEC: Pächt—Alexander (1966) no. 461

FACS: Gullick (1990) fig. 20 [fol. 104r]

ST: Römer (1972b) 230; Mostert (1989) no. BF 917; Gullick (1990) 83 n. 75

554. Oxford, Bodleian Library, Bodley 155 (S.C. 1974)

s. x/xi or xi in., prov. Barking

Contents: gospels, gospel list; record* (added s. xi/xii, Barking)

MS: Madan et al. (1895–1953) II/i.142; Van Dijk (1952) no. 6; N.R. Ker
(1957) no. 303; Van Dijk (1957–60) I.22; N.R. Ker (1964) 6; Backhouse
et al. (1984b) no. 35 [D.H. Turner]; A.G. Watson (1987b) 291 [repr.
A.G. Watson (2004) no. VIII]; R. Gameson (2012a) 18 n. 20, 68 and
n. 239; R. Gameson (2012b) 99 and n. 18, 115 n. 86; D. Ganz (2012)
194 and n. 41; McGurk (2012) 438 and n. 6, 447 [no. 18]; Scragg
(2012a) no. 839

DEC: Rice (1952) 218; F. Wormald (1952) 75 [no. 47]; Pächt—Alexander
(1973) no. 41; E. Temple (1976) no. 59; Ohlgren (1986) no. 164; Heslop
(1990) 153–4; R. Gameson (1995b) 193 n. 4, 194, 217

FACS: Rice (1952) pl. 70 (b) [fol. 93v]; F. Wormald (1952) pls. 5 (b), 7
[fols. 146v, 93v]; Pächt—Alexander (1973) pl. IV [fol. 93v]; E. Temple
(1976) ills. 177–8 [fols. 93v, 146v]; Backhouse et al. (1984b) 58 [fol. 93v]

ST: Glunz (1933) 68; McGurk (1986b) 44 [repr. McGurk (1998) no. XIV];
Lenker (1997) 430–7

555. Oxford, Bodleian Library, Bodley 163 (S.C. 2016), fols. 1–227, 250–1

s. xi in., (prov. Peterborough); s. xi med. (glossary); s. xi ex. (Caesarius,
Sermo ccxvi); s. xi/xii or xii in. (booklist)

Contents: Bede, *Historia ecclesiastica* [*CPL* 1375]; Ædiluulf, *De abbatibus* [SK 15778]; excerpts from Jerome (*Comm. in Esaiam* V. 14, 22–3)
and Orosius (*Historiae* II. 6, 7–10); *De situ Babylonis*; charm; glos-
sary+* (s. xi med.); Caesarius, *Sermo* ccxvi (f; s. xi ex.); booklist (s. xi/
xii or xii in.)

MS: Schenkl no. 495; Madan et al. (1895–1953) II/i.164–5; C. Plummer
(1896) I.cxviii–cxix; T.A.M. Bishop (1949–53) 441; N.R. Ker (1957)
no. 304; N.R. Ker (1964) 151; Colgrave—Mynors (1969) li; T.A.M.
Bishop (1967a) 41; T.A.M. Bishop (1971) 21; Rella (1977) 69; O'Brien
O'Keeffe (1990) 30–7; Dumville (1993g) 118–19 and nn., 139;
Lendinara (1996) 621–2; Friis-Jensen—Willoughby (2001) 8–9, 77;
ASMMF X (2003) 30–7 [no. 353; O'Brien O'Keeffe]; Biggs (2007a) 20
[Twomey]; Wieland (2009) 142; Scragg (2012a) nos. 840–2

DEC: Pächt—Alexander (1973) no. 71; Brownrigg (1978) 264 and n. 6

FACS: Whitelock (1954) 14, pl. 1 [fol. 1r]; Friis-Jensen—Willoughby (2001) pl. 2 [fol. 251r]; *ASMMF* X (2003) no. 353

ED: C. Plummer (1896) [Bede, *Historia ecclesiastica*, coll. as O₂]; Napier (1900) no. 29 [OE glosses to Bede, *Historia ecclesiastica*]; Dobbie (1937) 38 [Caedmon's Hymn, coll. as Bd]; Storms (1948) 302 [no. 71] [OE charm]; A. Campbell (1967b) [Ædiluulf, *De abbatibus*, coll. as O]; Lapidge (1985b) 76–82 [repr. Lapidge (1994b) 149–57] [booklist]; Lendinara (1988–9) 506–11 [repr. Lendinara (1999a) 347–55] [glossary]; Friis-Jensen—Willoughby (2001) 6–15 [booklist]; Lapidge (2006) 143–7 [booklist]

ST: Hardy (1862–71) nos. 783, 1072; Grierson (1941) 109 n. 3; Lambert (1969–72) no. 990; Dumville (1975) 106 n. [text on fols. 228–49 (s. xii)]; *BCLL* (1985) no. 131 [text on fols. 228–49 (s. xii)]; Lendinara (1988–9) [repr. Lendinara (1999a) 329–55]; R.H.C. Davis (1989) 112–13; Whatley (1996) 20; R. Gameson (1999a) no. 646

555. 5. Oxford, Bodleian Library, Bodley 180 (S.C. 2079)

s. xi/xii

Contents: Boethius (Alfred?), *De consolatione Philosophiae** (OE prose version); prayer*

MS: Madan et al. (1895–1953) II/i.200–1; Sedgefield (1899) xiii–xv; N.R. Ker (1957) no. 305; R. Gameson (1999a) no. 647; Godden—Irvine (2009) I.9–18

FACS: Godden—Irvine (2009) I, frontispiece [fol. 27v]

ED: Sedgefield (1899) 7–149 [OE Boethius coll. as B], 149 [base MS for OE prayer]; Godden—Irvine (2009) II.239–382 [base MS for OE Boethius]

LANG: Sedgefield (1899) 207–325 [glossary (items from this MS marked with asterisk)]; Godden—Irvine (2009) I.152–206, II.520–631 [glossary]

ST: Sedgefield (1899); Waite (2000) 227–58; Godden—Irvine (2009) I.xv–xxxix, 44–72, 140–6; Gneuss (2012) 293

556. Oxford, Bodleian Library, Bodley 193 (S.C. 2100)

s. xi/xii, England or Normandy, (prov. Exeter)

Contents: Gregory (?), *Symbolum fidei* [cf. *CPL* 1714 (p. 558)]; Gregory, *Registrum epistularum* [*CPL* 1714], with supplement

MS: Schenkl no. 503; Madan et al. (1895–1953) II/i.212; N.R. Ker (1960) 24 and n.; Conner (1993) 7; R. Gameson (1996b) 156 and n. 92; R. Gameson (1999a) no. 648

DEC: Pächt—Alexander (1973) no. 67; Alexander (1978c) 101

FACS: Pächt—Alexander (1973) pl. VI [fol. 2r (detail)]

557. Oxford, Bodleian Library, Bodley 218 (S.C. 2054)

s. ix^1, Tours, prov. England by s. x

Contents: Bede, *In Lucae euangelium expositio* [*CPL* 1356]; liturgical fragments from masses (s. x^2)

MS: Schenkl no. 519; Madan et al. (1895–1953) II/i.186; Rand (1929) I, no. 66; Laistner—King (1943) 47; Van Dijk (1957–60) I.210; Rella (1977) 167; Rella (1980) 113; Dumville (1993g) 141 n. 1; Bischoff (1998—) II, no. 3783; Hartzell (2006) no. 254; Lapidge (2006) 171

DEC: Pächt—Alexander (1973) no. 32

FACS: Rand (1929) II, pls. LXXIX [fols. 69r, 114v], LXXX [fol. 166r]

ED: Hurst (1960) 5–425 [Bede, *In Lucae euangelium expositio*, coll. as J]

558. Oxford, Bodleian Library, Bodley 223 (S.C. 2106)

s. xi^2, (prov. Worcester, prov. Windsor, St George's Chapel, before s. xvi?)

Contents: Gregory, *Homiliae in Hiezechielem* [*CPL* 1710]

MS: Schenkl no. 520; Madan et al. (1895–1953) II/i.214–15; N.R. Ker (1960) 8, 22; N.R. Ker (1964) 203, 208; Rella (1977) no. 20; R. Gameson (1999a) no. 650; R. Gameson (2005a) 95, 101–4

559. Oxford, Bodleian Library, Bodley 229 (S.C. 2120)

s. x/xi or xi^1 or xi med., France, prov. Exeter

Contents: Augustine, *Sermones .lxiv. de uerbis Domini*; pseudo-Augustine, *Sermo .i. de uerbis apostoli*; Caesarius of Arles, *Sermones* cliv, clxxiv

MS: Schenkl no. 522; Madan et al. (1895–1953) II/i.219; N.R. Ker (1960) 8 n. 2; Römer (1972b) 234; Pollard (1975) 152; Rella (1977) 87–8, 159; Drage (1978) 395–6; Clarkson (1996) 181–4; R. Gameson (1996b) 151 n. 63; R. Gameson (2012d) 368 and n. 100; Gullick (2012) 299 n. 29

DEC: Pächt—Alexander (1973) no. 46

560. Oxford, Bodleian Library, Bodley 237 (S.C. 1939)

s. xi/xii, (prov. Exeter)

Contents: Florus of Lyon, *Comm. in Epistolas Pauli*

MS: Schenkl no. 526; Madan et al. (1895–1953) II/i.125; N.R. Ker (1960) 24 and n. 3; Römer (1972b) 234; Conner (1993) 8; R. Gameson (1996b) 156; R. Gameson (1999a) no. 651

DEC: Pächt—Alexander (1973) no. 83

561. Oxford, Bodleian Library, Bodley 239 (S.C. 2244)

s. xi/xii or xii in., Normandy? (prov. Exeter)

Contents: Isidore, *Etymologiae* [*CPL* 1186]

MS: Schenkl no. 528; Madan et al. (1895–1953) II/i.276; N.R. Ker (1960) 24 and n. 3; R. Gameson (1996b) 156 and n. 94; R. Gameson (1999a) no. 652

DEC: Pächt—Alexander (1966) no. 465

ST: Knappe (1996) 132–3

563. Oxford, Bodleian Library, Bodley 301 (S.C. 2739)

s. xi/xii, prob. Normandy, (prov. Exeter)

Contents: Augustine, *Tractatus in Euangelium Ioannis* [*CPL* 278]

MS: Schenkl no. 550; Madan et al. (1895–1953) II/i.522; Mynors (1939) 34 n. 1; Pächt (1950b) 99; T.A.M. Bishop (1954–8a) 198; N.R. Ker (1960) 24 and n. 3; Pächt—Alexander (1966) 35; N.R. Ker (1968) 84; Römer (1972b) 236; R. Gameson (1996b) 156 and n. 99; R. Gameson (1999a) no. 658

DEC: F. Wormald (1944) 135 [repr. F. Wormald (1984) 183 n. 17]; Boase (1953) 29; Dodwell (1954) 117 and n. 3, 118; Pächt—Alexander (1966) no. 444; Rollason (1998) pl. 46 [caption]

FACS: Dodwell (1954) pl. 72 (a) [fol. 4r]; Pächt—Alexander (1966) pl. XXXVI [fol. 4r (detail)]

564. Oxford, Bodleian Library, Bodley 310 (S.C. 2121)

s. ix^2 or ix$^{3/4}$, perh. E France, prov. England before 1100 possible

Contents: Gregory, *Moralia in Iob* [*CPL* 1708], bks. XI–XVI

MS: Schenkl no. 554; Madan et al. (1895–1953) II/i.219–20; N.R. Ker (1972b) 77 n. 4; Rella (1977) 167; Biggs (1994); Bischoff (1998 —) II, no. 3784; Lapidge (2006) 171, 306

ST: R. McKitterick (2012) 330 and n. 108

565. Oxford, Bodleian Library, Bodley 311 (S.C. 2122)

s. x^2, N or NW France, in England by s. x/xi, prov. Exeter by s. xi^2?

Contents: *Iudicia Theodori* G ('Canones Gregorii') [cf. *CPL* 1885]; Gregory and Augustine, *Libellus responsionum*; *Poenitentiale Cummeani* [*CPL* 1882]; *Poenitentiale Remense*; excerpts from *Poenitentiale Theodori* [*CPL* 1885]; *Poenitentiale Oxoniense* I [*CPL* 1893b]; pseudo-Jerome, *Epist. supp.* xii [*CPL* 764 (excerpt)]; *Poenitentiale Oxoniense* II [*CPL* 1893g]

MS: Schenkl no. 555; Madan et al. (1895–1953) II/i.220; N.R. Ker (1957) no. 307; Bieler (1963) 13; N.R. Ker (1964) 84; T.A.M. Bishop (1971) xxv, 18; Pollard (1975) 146–7; Rella (1977) 156; Drage (1978) 397–9; Rella (1980) 113–14; Conner (1993) 8, 15, 17, 20; Dumville (1993g) 55 and n. 241; Kottje et al. (1994) xxxviii–xxxix; Clarkson (1996) 169–74; Gameson (1996b) 152 and n. 72; Budny (1997) I.460; R. Gameson (2012a) 29 n. 66; Scragg (2012a) nos. 843–4

ED: Bieler (1963) 108–34 [*Poenitentiale Cummeani* coll. as E]; Asbach (1975) 10–46 [*Poenitentiale Remense* coll. as O]; Kottje et al. (1994) 3–55 and 89-93 [base MS (= O_2) for *Poenitentiale Oxoniense* I], 181–205 [*Poenitentiale Oxoniense* II coll. as O_2]

ST: Lambert (1969–72) no. 312; Römer (1972b) 236; Frantzen (1983a) 37; Frantzen (1983b) 130 and nn. 24–5, 169 n. 52; Frantzen (1985) 23–4, 26, 30–1; Charles-Edwards (1995)

566. Oxford, Bodleian Library, Bodley 314 (S.C. 2129)

s. xi/xii, prob. Exeter, (prov. ibid.)

Contents: Gregory, *Homiliae .xl. in Euangelia* [*CPL* 1711]

MS: Schenkl no. 557; Madan et al. (1895–1953) II/i.224; N.R. Ker (1960) 24, 44, 46 n. 3; N.R. Ker (1964) 84; R.M. Thomson (1986a) 37; Conner (1993) 8; R. Gameson (1996b) 152 and n. 71, 156 and n. 100; R. Gameson (1999a) no. 659; Keefer (2007b) 105

FACS: N.R. Ker (1960) pls. 2–3 [fols. 25v, 26r]

567. Oxford, Bodleian Library, Bodley 314 (S.C. 2129), fols. ii, iii, 98, 99

s. x¹ or x², Brittany, (prov. Exeter)

Contents: sacramentary (f)

MS: Madan et al. (1895–1953) II/i.224; Van Dijk (1957–60) V.18; Gamber (1968–88) no. 622; R. Gameson (1996b) 152; Hartzell (2006) no. 256

ED: Gamber (1962a) 101

567. 5. Oxford, Bodleian Library, Bodley 317 (S.C. 2708)

s. xi/xii, Préaux, (prov. Canterbury)

Contents: Florus of Lyon, *Comm. in Epistolas Pauli* (Ad Corinthios II — Ad Hebraeos)

Companion vol. to no. **165. 5**

MS: Schenkl no. 558; Madan et al. (1895–1953) II/i.506; N.R. Ker (1960) 41 n. 6; N.R. Ker (1964) 38; Römer (1972b) 237; R. Gameson (1999a) no. 660

568. Oxford, Bodleian Library, Bodley 319 (S.C. 2226)

s. x², prob. SW England, (prov. Exeter)

Contents: Isidore, *De fide catholica contra Iudaeos* [*CPL* 1198], II. xxvii with OE gloss

MS: Schenkl no. 559; Madan et al. (1895–1953) II/i.268; N.R. Ker (1957) no. 308; N.R. Ker (1960) 8 and n. 4; N.R. Ker (1964) 84; Pollard (1975) 147–8; N.R. Ker (1976b) 30 [repr. N.R. Ker (1985) 150]; Rella (1977); Drage (1978) 400–1; Conner (1993) 6, 8, 19–20 *et passim*; Clarkson (1996) 174–7; R. Gameson (1996b) 163 and n. 130, 164–79; R.M. Butler (2004) 178, 184, 204–5; C. Bishop (2007b) 98; R. Gameson (2012a) 59 n. 199; Gullick (2012) 300 and n. 38; Scragg (2012a) no. 845

DEC: Pächt—Alexander (1973) no. 27

FACS: Muir (1991b) pls. 5–6 [fols. 26r, 40r]; Conner (1993) pls. X–XI [fols. 27r, 74r]

ED: Napier (1900) no. 40 [OE gloss]

ST: Webber (1992) 68; C. Bishop (2007b) 98–9

569. Oxford, Bodleian Library, Bodley 340 + 342 (S.C. 2404–5)

s. xi in., Canterbury or Rochester; additions of s. xi¹ and xi med., SE England, prob. Rochester, (prov. whole MS, Rochester from s. xi med. or earlier)

Contents: Ælfric, *Catholic Homilies* [both series in the order of the Church year]; eleven anonymous homilies, including five versions of Vercelli Homilies (s. xi in. — s. xi med., Canterbury or Rochester); additions (prob. made at Rochester): account of St Paulinus of York (s. xi med.); Latin prayer and verse, Latin poem [WIC 3311], note in Latin and Old Flemish (s. xi²), hymn for St Mary Magdalene [*AH* XII.174] (s. xi)

MS: Madan et al. (1895–1953) II/i.351–2; N.R. Ker (1933); K. Sisam (1953a) 148–98; N.R. Ker (1957) no. 309; N.R. Ker (1964) 163; Pope (1967–8) I.20; A.F. Cameron (1974) 222–4; P.R. Robinson (1978) 236 [repr. P.R. Robinson (1994) 32]; Godden (1979) xxv–xxviii; Scragg (1979) 237–40; A.G. Watson (1987b) 263, 275–6 n. 12, 294 [repr. A.G. Watson (2004) no. VIII]; R. Sharpe et al. (1996) 490, 511; Clemoes (1997) 7–10; Dronke (2005b) 400–1; *ASMMF* XVII (2008) 53–69 [no. 358; Wilcox]; Scragg (2009b) 68–9, 81; Crick (2012) 181; R. Gameson (2012a) 24 and n. 38, 67 n. 232; Scragg (2012a) nos. 846–51

DEC: Pächt—Alexander (1973) no. 42; E. Temple (1976) no. 30 (xvii); Brownrigg (1978) 260 n. 3; Ohlgren (1986) no. 134; R. Gameson (2012c) 287 and n. 133; Scragg (1996) 212

FACS: D.M. Rogers (1991) pl. 24 [Bodley 340, fol. 169v]; Scragg (1992) pl. IV [Bodley 340, fol. 1r]; *ASMMF* XVII (2008) no. 358; Owen-Crocker (2009) figs. 3.2 [Bodley 340, fol. 1r], 3.3 [Bodley 342, fol. 1r]

ED [the order of the following items is that of the manuscripts, listed according to the numbering of individual articles in N.R. Ker (1957) 361–7; only the most recent editions are cited]:

(Bodley 340)

art. 1: Förster (1932) 107–31 [Vercelli Hom. V (Christmas) coll. as O]; Scragg (1992) 111–21 [Vercelli Hom. V (Christmas) coll. as E]

art. 2: Clemoes (1997) 198–205 [Ælfric, CH I, Hom. III (St Stephen), coll. as D]

art. 3: Clemoes (1997) 206–16 [Ælfric, CH I, Hom. IV (Assumption of St John the Evangelist), coll. as D]

art. 4: Clemoes (1997) 217–23 [Ælfric, CH I, Hom. V (Holy Innocents), coll. as D]

art. 5: Clemoes (1997) 224–31 [Ælfric, CH I, Hom. VI (Circumcision of the Lord), coll. as D]

art. 6: Clemoes (1997) 232–40 [Ælfric, CH I, Hom. VII (Epiphany), coll. as D] art. 7: Förster (1932) 149–59 [Vercelli Hom. VIII (First Sunday after Epiphany) coll. as O]; Scragg (1992) 143–8 [Vercelli Hom. VIII (First Sunday after Epiphany) coll. as E]

art. 8: Förster (1913) 100–16 [Vercelli Hom. IX (Second Sunday after Epiphany) coll. as B]; Szarmach (1981a) 4–7 [Vercelli Hom. IX (Second Sunday after Epiphany) coll. as E]; Scragg (1992) 158–84 [Vercelli Hom. IX (Second Sunday after Epiphany) coll. as E]

art. 9: Clemoes (1997) 241–8 [Ælfric, CH I, Hom. VIII (Third Sunday after Epiphany), coll. as D]

art. 10: Clemoes (1997) 249–57 [Ælfric, CH I, Hom. IX (Purification of B.V.M.), coll. as D]

art. 11: Godden (1979) 72–80 [Ælfric, CH II, Hom. IX (St Gregory), coll. as D]

art. 12: Godden (1979) 81–91 [Ælfric, CH II, Hom. X (St Cuthbert), coll. as D]

art. 13: Godden (1979) 92–109 [Ælfric, CH II, Hom. XI (St Benedict), coll. as D]

art. 14: Clemoes (1997) 281–9 [Ælfric, CH I, Hom. XIII (Annunciation of B.V.M.), coll. as D]

art. 15: Godden (1979) 41–51 [Ælfric, CH II, Hom. V (Septuagesima Sunday), coll. as D]

art. 16: Godden (1979) 52–9 [Ælfric, CH II, Hom. VI (Sexagesima Sunday), coll. as D]

art. 17: Clemoes (1997) 258–65 [Ælfric, CH I, Hom. X (Quinquagesima Sunday), coll. as D]

art. 18: Godden (1979) 60–6 [Ælfric, CH II, Hom. VII (First Sunday in Lent), coll. as D]

art. 19: Förster (1932) 53–71 [Vercelli Hom. III (Second Sunday in Lent) coll. as O]; Scragg (1992) 73–83 [Vercelli Hom. III (Second Sunday in Lent) coll. as E]

art. 20: Assmann (1889/1964) 138–43 [Homily for the Third Sunday in Lent (Hom. XI) coll. as N]

art. 21: as Belfour (1909) 50–9 [Hom. no. VI (Fourth Sunday in Lent), not collated, and specified in Belfour for the Second Sunday in Lent]

art. 22: Assmann (1889/1964) 144–50 [Homily for the Fifth Sunday in Lent (Hom. XII) coll. as N]

art. 23: Ryan (1955) 1–43 [base MS for Homily for Palm Sunday]; Schaefer (1972) 18–33 [Homily for Palm Sunday coll. as C]

art. 24: Assmann (1889/1964) 151–63 [Homily *De cena Domini* (Hom. XIII) coll. as N] art. 25: Förster (1932) 1–43 [Vercelli Hom. I (Good Friday) coll. as O]; Scragg (1992) 7–43 [base MS (= E) for Vercelli Hom. I (Good Friday)]

art. 26: Ryan (1955) 44–100 [base MS for Homily for Holy Saturday]; Schaefer (1972) 83–114 [Homily for Holy Saturday coll. as C]; R. Evans (1981) [base MS for Homily for Holy Saturday]

art. 27: Clemoes (1997) 299–306 [Ælfric, CH I, Hom. XV (Easter Sunday), coll. as D]

art. 28: Clemoes (1997) 307–12 [Ælfric, CH I, Hom. XVI (First Sunday after Easter), coll. as D]

art. 29: Clemoes (1997) 313–16 [Ælfric, CH I, Hom. XVII (Second Sunday after Easter), coll. as D]

art. 30: Godden (1979) 169–73 [Ælfric, CH II, Hom. XVII (SS. Philip and James, apostles), coll. as D]

arts. 31–2: Godden (1979) 174–9 [Ælfric, CH II, Hom. XVIII (Discovery of the Holy Cross), coll. as D]

(Bodley 342)

art. 33: Clemoes (1997) 178–89 [Ælfric, CH I, Hom. I (*De initio creaturae*), coll. as D]

art. 34: Clemoes (1997) 317–24 [Ælfric, CH I, Hom. XVIII (*In Letania maiore*), coll. as D]

art. 35: Godden (1979) 180–9 [Ælfric, CH II, Hom. XIX (*Feria .II. in Letania maiore*), coll. as D]

art. 36: Clemoes (1997) 325–34 [Ælfric, CH I, Hom. XIX (*Feria .III. De dominica oratione*), coll. as D]

art. 37: Godden (1979) 190–8 [Ælfric, CH II, Hom. XX (*Feria .III. in Letania maiore*), coll. as D]

arts. 38–9: Godden (1979) 199–205 [Ælfric, CH II, Hom. XXI (*Alia uisio* from Bede, *HE* V.xii), coll. as D]

art. 40: Clemoes (1997) 335–44 [Ælfric, CH I, Hom. XX (*Feria .IIII. De fide catholica*), coll. as D]

art. 41: Godden (1979) 206–12 [Ælfric, CH II, Hom. XXII (*Feria .IIII. in Letania maiore*), coll. as D]

art. 42: Clemoes (1997) 345–53 [Ælfric, CH I, Hom. XXI (Ascension Day), coll. as D]

art. 43: Clemoes (1997) 354–64 [Ælfric, CH I, Hom. XXII (Pentecost), coll. as D]

art. 44: Clemoes (1997) 365–70 [Ælfric, CH I, Hom. XXIII (Second Sunday after Pentecost), coll. as D] arts. 45–6: Godden (1979) 213–20 [Ælfric, CH II, Hom. XXIII (Third Sunday after Pentecost), coll. as D; and see Pope (1967–8) I.20]

art. 47: Clemoes (1997) 371–8 [Ælfric, CH I, Hom. XXIV (Fourth Sunday after Pentecost), coll. as D]

art. 48: Clemoes (1997) 379–87 [Ælfric, CH I, Hom. XXV (St John the Baptist), coll. as D]

arts. 49–50: Godden (1979) 221–9 [Ælfric, CH II, Hom. XXIV (St Peter), coll. as D]

arts. 51–2: Clemoes (1997) 388–99 [Ælfric, CH I, Hom. XXVI (SS. Peter and Paul), coll. as D]

art. 53: Clemoes (1997) 400–9 [Ælfric, CH I, Hom. XXVII (St Paul), coll. as D]

art. 54: Godden (1979) 230–4 [Ælfric, CH II, Hom. XXV (Eighth Sunday after Pentecost), coll. as D]

art. 55: Godden (1979) 235–40 [Ælfric, CH II, Hom. XXVI (Ninth Sunday after Pentecost), coll. as D]

art. 56: Clemoes (1997) 410–17 [Ælfric, CH I, Hom. XXVIII (Eleventh Sunday after Pentecost), coll. as D]

art. 57: Godden (1979) 241–7 [Ælfric, CH II, Hom. XXVII (St James the Apostle), coll. as D]

art. 58: Godden (1979) 249–54 [Ælfric, CH II, Hom. XXVIII (Twelfth Sunday after Pentecost), coll. as D]

arts. 59–60: Godden (1979) 268–71 [Ælfric, CH II, Hom. XXXI (Sixteenth Sunday after Pentecost), coll. as D]

art. 61: Clemoes (1997) 459–64 [Ælfric, CH I, Hom. XXXIII (Seventeenth Sunday after Pentecost), coll. as D]

art. 62: Clemoes (1997) 476–85 [Ælfric, CH I, Hom. XXXV (Twenty–first Sunday after Pentecost), coll. as D]

art. 63: Godden (1979) 297–8 [Ælfric, CH II, appendix to Hom. XXXIV (St Martin), coll. as D]

art. 64: Godden (1979) 299–303 [Ælfric, CH II, Hom. XXXV (Feast of an Apostle), coll. as D]

art. 65: Godden (1979) 304–9 [Ælfric, CH II, Hom. XXXVI (Feast of Several Apostles), coll. as D]

art. 66: Godden (1979) 310–17 [Ælfric, CH II, Hom. XXXVII (Feast of Holy Martyrs), coll. as D]

art. 67: Godden (1979) 318–26 [Ælfric, CH II, Hom. XXXVIII (Feast of a Confessor), coll. as D]

art. 68: Godden (1979) 327–34 [Ælfric, CH II, Hom. XXXIX (Feast of Holy Virgins), coll. as D] art. 69: Godden (1979) 335–45 [Ælfric, CH II, Hom. XL (Dedication of a Church), coll. as D]

arts. 70–1: Clemoes (1997) 486–96 [Ælfric, CH I, Hom. XXXVI (All Saints), coll. as D]

art. 72: Clemoes (1997) 497–506 [Ælfric, CH I, Hom. XXXVII (St Clement), coll. as D]

art. 73: Clemoes (1997) 520–3 [Ælfric, CH I, Hom. XXXIX (First Sunday in Advent), coll. as D]

art. 74: Clemoes (1997) 524–30 [Ælfric, CH I, Hom. XL (Second Sunday in Advent), coll. as D]

art. 75: Sisam (1953a) 151–2 [base MS for account of St Paulinus of Rochester]

art. 76: Godden (1979) 64–6 [Ælfric, CH II, conclusion to Hom. VII (First Sunday in Lent), coll. as D]

art. 77: Godden (1979) 41–51 [Ælfric, CH II, Hom. V (Septuagesima Sunday), coll. as D (incomplete)]

arts. 78–9: Clemoes (1997) 507–19 [Ælfric, CH I, Hom. XXXVIII (St Andrew), coll. as D]

(additions)

K. Sisam (1953a) 196 [Latin prayer, verse, poem, Latin and Old Flemish note]; Milfull (1996) 471–2 [hymn for St Mary Magdalene]; Dronke (2005b) 400 [Latin prayer, verse, poem, Latin and Old Flemish note]

ST: K. Sisam (1953a) 148–98; Gneuss (1968) 116; Van Loey (1970) 253–4 [Old Flemish on fol. 169v of Bodley 340]; M.P. Richards (1979) 14–17; Wieland (1985) 167; M.P. Richards (1988) 87–9; C.D. Wright (1993) 273–5; Milfull (1996) 65–6; M.P. Richards (2006) 292; Scragg (2012b) 558 and nn. 20–1

569. 4. Oxford, Bodleian Library, Bodley 356 (S.C. 2716), offset of pastedown

s. xi, prob. Bury St Edmunds

Contents: missal (f)

MS: Madan et al. (1895–1953) II/i.510; Van Dijk (1957–60) V.156; Rushforth—Orchard (2005)

FACS: Rushforth—Orchard (2005) fig. 1

570. Oxford, Bodleian Library, Bodley 381 (S.C. 2202)

s. x, England or English scribe on Continent?, prov. Canterbury StA

Contents: Iohannes Diaconus, *Vita S. Gregorii* [*BHL* 3641]

MS: Schenkl no. 570; Madan et al. (1895–1953) II/i.256; T.A.M. Bishop (1949–53) 438; N.R. Ker (1957) no. 311; N.R. Ker (1964) 46; A.G. Watson (1978) 310 [repr. A.G. Watson (2004) no. VII]; Budny (1985) 167–79; Dumville (1994d) 207; Lapidge (1994b) 156; Scragg (2012a) no. 852

ST: R. McKitterick (2012) 328

570. 1. Oxford, Bodleian Library, Bodley 381 (S.C. 2202), fols. i and ii

s. ix$^{3/4}$, prob. NE France (Corbie?), (prov. Canterbury StA)

Contents: gospel list (part)

MS: Madan et al. (1895–1953) II/i.256; Van Dijk (1957–60) V.21; Budny (1985) 170–2; Lenker (1997) 428–9 *et passim*; Bischoff (1998 –) II, no. 3785; Lapidge (2006) 171

571. Oxford, Bodleian Library, Bodley 385 (S.C. 2210)

s. xi/xii, Continent (Low Countries or NE France), (prov. Canterbury CC)

Contents: Jerome, *Comm. in Danielem* [*CPL* 588]; Bede, *De tabernaculo* [*CPL* 1345]; pseudo-Augustine and pseudo-Orosius, *Dialogus quaestionum .lxv.* [*CPL* 373a]

MS: Schenkl no. 574; Madan et al. (1895–1953) II/i.260; Laistner – King (1943) 92; R. Gameson (1995a) 142; R. Gameson (1999a) no. 666

DEC: Dodwell (1954) 120; Pächt – Alexander (1973) no. 57

ST: Lambert (1969–72) no. 215; Römer (1972b) 238

572. Oxford, Bodleian Library, Bodley 386 (S.C. 2211), fols. i and 174

s. x ex or x/xi

Contents: missal (f)

MS: Madan et al. (1895–1953) II/i.260–1; Van Dijk (1957-60) V.163; *Le Graduel Romain* II (1957) 90; Hartzell (2006) no. 258; Wieland (2009) 123

573. Oxford, Bodleian Library, Bodley 391 (S.C. 2222)

s. xi ex., Canterbury StA

Contents: Isidore, *De ortu et obitu patrum* [*CPL* 1191], *Allegoriae quaedam S. Scripturae* [*CPL* 1190]; Jerome, *De uiris inlustribus* [*CPL* 616]; *Decretum Gelasianum de libris recipiendis et non recipiendis* [*CPL* 1676]; Gennadius, *De uiris inlustribus* [*CPL* 957]; Isidore, *De uiris illustribus* [*CPL* 1206]; Augustine, *Retractationes* [*CPL* 250]; Cassiodorus, *Institutiones* [*CPL* 906], bk. I; Isidore, *In libros ueteris ac noui Testamenti prooemia* [*CPL* 1192]

MS: Schenkl no. 577; Madan et al. (1895–1953) II/i.265–6; T.A.M. Bishop (1955) 2; N.R. Ker (1960) 11, 22 and n. 1, 30; N.R. Ker (1964) 46; A.G. Watson (1972–6) 215 [repr. A.G. Watson (2004), no. XIV]; Rella (1977) 23; R. Gameson (1995a) 98 n. 13, 102 n. 28, 106 n. 40, 144; R. Gameson (1999a) no. 668; T.N. Hall (2004b) 97 n. 18

DEC: Dodwell (1954) 122; Pächt—Alexander (1973) no. 51; Alexander (1978c) 102–3; R. Gameson (1995a) 124 n. 103, 132

FACS: Pächt—Alexander (1973) pl. VI [fol. 2r (detail)]

ST: Mynors (1937) xliii, xlvii–xlix; Lambert (1969–72) no. 260; Römer (1972b) 239

574. Oxford, Bodleian Library, Bodley 392 (S.C. 2223)

s. xi ex., Salisbury

Contents: thirty-one homilies by Eusebius Gallicanus [*CPL* 966] and Caesarius of Arles [*CPL* 1008]; Patrick of Dublin, *De tribus habitaculis animae* [*BCLL* 309]

MS: Schenkl no. 578; Madan et al. (1895–1953) II/i.266; Esposito (1932) 264; N.R. Ker (1949–50) 154 n. 1, 158 n. 1, 162 n. 5 [repr. N.R. Ker (1985) 176 n. 1, 180 n. 1, 184 n. 5]; Gwynn (1955) 28–9; N.R. Ker (1964) 171; N.R. Ker (1976b) 25–6, 29, 48 [repr. N.R. Ker (1985) 145 n., 146, 149, 172]; A.G. Watson (1987b) 294 [repr. A.G. Watson (2004) no. VIII]; Webber (1992) 12, 13, 20, 136–7, 146; R. Gameson (1999a) no. 669; R. Gameson (2012a) 52 n. 175

ED: Gwynn (1955) 106–24 [Patrick, *De tribus habitaculis animae*, coll. as A]

ST: Lambert (1969–72) nos. 324, 338; Römer (1972b) 239; *BCLL* (1985) no. 309

575. Oxford, Bodleian Library, Bodley 394 (S.C. 2225), fols. 1–84

s. x², prob. France (or England?), (prov. Exeter)

Contents: Isidore, *De fide catholica contra Iudaeos* [*CPL* 1198]

MS: Schenkl no. 580; Madan et al. (1895–1953) II.i.267–8; A.J. Robertson (1939) 479; N.R. Ker (1964) 84; Drage (1978) 402–3; Conner (1993) 8, 14, 20, 34, 81, 83; Dumville (1994b) 210; Lapidge (1994b) 139; R. Gameson (1996b) 150 and n. 59, 169–70

576. Oxford, Bodleian Library, Bodley 426 (S.C. 2327), fols. 1–118

838×847, Wessex (Winchester or Sherborne?), (prov. Canterbury StA)

Contents: Philippus presbyter, *Comm. in librum Iob* [*CPL* 643]

MS: Madan et al. (1895–1953) II.i.312; M.R. James (1903) 204, 516; *CLA* II (1935) no. 234; N.R. Ker (1964) 46; Chaplais (1965) 57–8 [repr. Ranger (1973) 38 and n. 84]; Sawyer (1968) nos. 298, 1438; De la Mare—Barker-Benfield (1980) 13 [T.J. Brown]; Morrish (1982) 91; N.P. Brooks (1984) 323–5; A.G. Watson (1984) I, no. 88; M.P. Brown (1986) 120 n. 5; A.G. Watson (1987b) 263, 269, 282, 287 [repr. A.G. Watson (2004) no. VIII]; Morrish (1988) 513, 522–4 and n. 45; Conner (1993) 68 and n. 75; M.P. Brown (1996) 171–2; Crick (1997) 65–74; Barker-Benfield (2008) I.lxi n. 28, lxxxix, 222–3, 424, III.1690, 1777, 1810; D. Ganz (2012) 189 and n. 8; M.P. Brown (2012) 164–5

DEC: Pächt—Alexander (1973) no. 6; Alexander (1978a) no. 40; Ohlgren (1986) no. 40

FACS: *CLA* II (1935) no. 234 [fol. 2v (detail)]; Pächt—Alexander (1973) pl. I [fol. 1r (detail)]; Alexander (1978a) ill. 136 [fol. 1v (detail)]; A.G. Watson (1984) II, pl. 7 [fol. 61v]; Morrish (1988) pl. 4 [fol. 61v]; Drogin (1989) pls. 30, 95 [fol. 76r (details)]; M.P. Brown (1996) fig. 21 [fol. 2v (detail)]; Crick (1997) pl. V [fol. 67r]

ST: Lambert (1969–72) no. 413

577. Oxford, Bodleian Library, Bodley 441 (S.C. 2382)

s. xi¹ or xi^{1/4}, SE England?

Contents: gospels*

MS: Skeat (1871) vii–viii; Madan et al. (1895–1953) II/i.340; Bright (1904–6) xvi–xviii [John]; N.R. Ker (1957) no. 312; Morrell (1965) 184; Liuzza (1994–2000) I.xx–xxiii; *ASMMF* III (1995) 26–9 [no. 361;

Liuzza]; Budny (1997) I.578; Lenker (1997) 15–16; Parkes (1997b) 124 and n. 104; Barker-Benfield (2008) III.1735–6, 1833; Graham (2009) 187; R. Gameson (2012a) 45 n. 136; Scragg (2012a) nos. 853–4

FACS: *ASMMF* III (1995) no. 361; Parkes (1997b) pl. 17 [fol. 60r]

ED: Skeat (1871–87) [gospels coll. as B]; Liuzza (1994–2000) [gospels coll. as B]; for other editions, see Liuzza I.xiii–xvi

LANG: Liuzza (1994–2000) II.100–54, 237–369 [glossary]

ST: Grünberg (1967); Greenfield—Robinson (1980) 337–9; Liuzza (1988) 75–80; Liuzza (1994–2000); Lenker (1997)

578. Oxford, Bodleian Library, Bodley 444 (S.C. 2385), fols. 1–27

s. xi ex., Salisbury

Contents: Isidore, *Allegoriae quaedam S. Scripturae* [*CPL* 1190], *In libros ueteris ac noui Testamenti prooemia* [*CPL* 1192], *De ortu et obitu patrum* [*CPL* 1191]

MS: Schenkl no. 596; Madan et al. (1895–1953) II/i.341–2; N.R. Ker (1949–50) 154 n. 1, 158 n. 3 [repr. N.R. Ker (1985) 176 n. 1, 180 n. 3]; N.R. Ker (1976b) 25–6 [repr. N.R. Ker (1985) 145–6]; Webber (1992) 12, 13, 36, 132 n. 71, 146; R. Gameson (1999a) no. 670; R. Gameson (2012a) 68 and n. 238

580. Oxford, Bodleian Library, Bodley 479 (S.C. 2013)

s. xi/xii or xii[1], England or France, (prov. Exeter)

Contents: Bede, *De tabernaculo* [*CPL* 1345]

MS: Schenkl no. 607; Madan et al. (1895–1953) II/i.162; Laistner—King (1943) 72; N.R. Ker (1960) 24 and n. 3; N.R. Ker (1964) 84; Conner (1993) 9; R. Gameson (1996b) 157 and n. 101; R. Gameson (1999a) no. 673

581. Oxford, Bodleian Library, Bodley 516 (S.C. 2570)

s. ix[2], N Italy or, more prob., NE France, prov. Brittany or Wales by s. x, prov. England by s. xi[1], (prov. Salisbury)

Contents: Augustine, *Epist.* cxlvii ('De uidendo Deo'); Ambrose, *Epistula ad Vercellensem ecclesiam* [extra collectionem xiv (lxiii)]; Halitgar of Cambrai, *Poenitentiale*; Cassiodorus, *De anima* [*CPL* 897]; excerpts from Augustine and John Chrysostom

MS: Schenkl no. 614; Goldbacher (1895–1923) V.xxxix; Madan et al. (1895–1953) II/i.430–1; N.R. Ker (1964) 171; Faller—Zelzer (1968–94) IV.349; Rella (1977) 73 and n. 47, 167; Rella (1980) 114; Webber (1992) 77–9; Bischoff (1998—) II, no. 3786; Wieland (2009) 133; R. Gameson (2012d) 351 and n. 27

ED: Goldbacher (1895–1923) III.274–331 [Augustine, *Epist.* cxlvii ('De uidendo Deo') coll. as O]; Faller—Zelzer (1968–94) III.235–95 [Ambrose, *Epistula ad Vercellensem ecclesiam*, coll. as N]

ST: N.R. Ker (1949–50) 157 n. 4, 162 n. 5 [repr. N.R. Ker (1985) 179 n. 4, 184 n. 5]; Siegmund (1949) 99; Römer (1972b) 240; Kottje (1980); Frantzen (1983b) 131; Bankert et al. (1997) 13, 51; *CSLMA* III (2010) 362–6 [Halitgar of Cambrai]; R. McKitterick (2012) 328

581. 1. Oxford, Bodleian Library, Bodley 517 (S.C. 2580)

s. xi/xii, Normandy, or a Norman scribe in England

Contents: William of Jumièges, *Gesta Normannorum ducum* (original redaction; incomplete)

MS: Madan et al. (1895–1953) II/i.435–6; Van Houts (1992–5) I.c–ci; R. Gameson (1999a) no. 674

DEC: Pächt—Alexander (1966) no. 455

ED: Van Houts (1992–5) [William of Jumièges, *Gesta Normannorum Ducum*, coll. as C4]

582. Oxford, Bodleian Library, Bodley 535 (S.C. 2254), fols. 1–38

s. xi$^{3/3}$, Winchester OM? (prov. ibid.)

Contents: Hilduin of Saint-Denis, *Passio S. Dionysii* (verse) [SK Suppl. 12194a]

MS: Schenkl no. 621; Madan et al. (1895–1953) II/i.280–1; N.R. Ker (1960) 23 n. 4; N.R. Ker (1964) 201; Lapidge (1987) 68; M.P. Richards (1988) 70; R. Gameson (1999a) no. 675; Lapidge (2012c) 335

FACS: N.R. Ker (1960) pl. 1(b) [fol. 1r]

ST: Yerkes (1984a) xxxiii–xxxiv; *BCLL* (1985) no. 825 [bibliography]; Lapidge (1987); Biggs et al. (2001) 173–4; *CSLMA* III (2010) 543–4; Lapidge (2012c) 334–7

583. Oxford, Bodleian Library, Bodley 572 (S.C. 2026), fols. 1–50

s. x in or x med., Cornwall [fols. 1–25]; s. x, Cornwall, with additions of s. x/xi and xi med. [fols. 26–40]; s. x, prob. Wales, with additions of s. x/xi and xi/xii [fols. 41–50]; prov. all parts Wales, s. x ex. England (Glastonbury?), s. xi prob. Winchester NM, s. xi ex. Canterbury StA

Contents: [fols. 1–25]: Mass of St Germanus; *Expositio missae* (inc. 'Dominus uobiscum'); Biblical book of Tobias; [fols. 26–40]: Augustine, *Epist.* cxxx ('De orando Deo'); Caesarius of Arles, *Sermo* clxxix; antiphons (s. xi/xii); benedictions (s. x ex.); cryptograms* (s. xi med.), paschal table (s. x/xi); [fols. 41–50]: *De raris fabulis* (scholastic *colloquium* or Latin conversation manual); chants for a burial office (s. x/xi); other chants, sequence (s. xi/xii)

MS: Schenkl no. 630; Madan et al. (1895–1953) II/i.170–3; M.R. James (1903) 204; Lindsay (1912a) 26–32 [no. i]; Nicholson (1913) xxiv–xxviii; N.R. Ker (1957) no. 313; Van Dijk (1957–60) I.201; N.R. Ker (1960) 29 n. 3, 30; Rella (1977) 73; A.G. Watson (1984) I, no. 102; P.L. Heyworth (1989) 191; Dumville (1992a) 116, 130 and n. 257, 135; Dumville (1993g) 97 n. 74, 142 n. 8; Hartzell (2006) no. 259; Gwara (2007) 3; McKee (2012a) 170; Rushforth (2012) 202 and n. 37; Scragg (2012a) no. 855

DEC: Pächt—Alexander (1973) no. 28; M.P. Brown (2011b) 34

FACS: Lindsay (1912a) pls. XIV–XV [fols. 14r, 36r]; Nicholson (1913) pls. XV–XVI [fols. 40v, 49v]; N.R. Ker (1960) pl. 10 (b) [fol. 39v (detail)]; A.G. Watson (1984) II, pl. 17 [fol. 32r]

ED: Haddan—Stubbs (1869–71) I.696–7 [Mass of St Germanus]; W.H. Stevenson (1929) 1–11 [*De raris fabulis*]; Gwara (2002) 123–37 [*De raris fabulis*]

LANG: Lapidge (2010b) 412–18 [*De raris fabulis*]

ST: Nicholson (1913) xxiv–xxviii; K.H. Jackson (1953) 55–6, 255–6, 279; R. Derolez (1954) 165, 168; Römer (1972b) 241; *BCLL* (1985) nos. 85 [*De raris fabulis*], 122 [Mass of St Germanus]; Lapidge (1986c); Marsden (1994b); Marsden (1995) 179–81 *et passim*; Keynes (1996a) 67 n. 12, 114 n. 43; Gwara—Porter (1997c) 19–20; C.A. Jones (1998c) 672; Gwara (2002); Gwara (2007) 5–7; Lapidge (2010b); Charles-Edwards (2012) 390 and n. 7, 402–4; McKee (2012b) 341 and n. 10

583. 3. Oxford, Bodleian Library, Bodley 572 (S.C. 2026), fols. 51-107

s. ix[1], prob. NE France; in England before 1100?

Contents: [penitential collection]: *Poenitentiale Cummeani* [*CPL* 1882] (incomplete); Decrees of the Council of Orange (A.D. 441) [*CPL* 1779b] and other canons; Hormisdas (?), *Epistola per uniuersas prouincias*; pseudo-Jerome, *Inquisitio de poenitentia* [*CPL* 1896]; injunctions concerning penitence; Gregory and Augustine of Canterbury, *Libellus responsionum* (Interrogatio IX et responsio); prologue to *Poenitentiale Egberti* [*CPL* 1887]; Pirmin of Reichenau, *Scarapsus* (*Dicta Pirminii*)

MS: Schenkl no. 630; Madan et al. (1895–1953) II/i.173; Esposito (1929) 248; Mordek (1975) 98–9 n. 3, 416–17; Rella (1977) 126, 156, 167; P.L. Heyworth (1989) 191; Bischoff (1998—) II, no. 3787

ED: Hauswald (2010) [Pirmin, *Scarapsus*]

ST: Lambert (1969–72), no. 611; Römer (1972b) 241; Frantzen (1983a) 34 n. 60; Frantzen (1985) 23–4, 29; Hagenmüller (1991) 86–7, 123; Kéry (1999) 51, 76

584. Oxford, Bodleian Library, Bodley 577 (S.C. 27645)

s. x/xi, Canterbury CC

Contents: Aldhelm, *Carmen de uirginitate* [*CPL* 1333]

MS: Schenkl no. 632; Madan et al. (1895–1953) V.319; Ehwald (1919) 345; N.R. Ker (1957) no. 314; T.A.M. Bishop (1959–63b) 420–1; Rella (1977) 70; R. Gameson (2012a) 68 and n. 238; Lapidge (2012b) 32; Scragg (2012a) no. 858

DEC: F. Wormald (1952) 75 [no. 48]; Pächt—Alexander (1973) no. 33; E. Temple (1976) no. 57; Brownrigg (1978) 246 n. 2; Ohlgren (1986) no. 162; R. Gameson (1995b) 23, 221 nn. 168, 170 and 172

FACS: Pächt—Alexander (1973) pl. III [fol. ii v]; E. Temple (1976) ills. 179–80 [fol. ii r and v]

ED: Napier (1900) nos. 14, 19 [OE glosses]; Ehwald (1919) 350–471 [Aldhelm, *Carmen de uirginitate*, coll. as O]

ST: Lapidge (2012b) 31–5

585. Oxford, Bodleian Library, Bodley 579 (S.C. 2675) (the 'Leofric Missal')

s. ix/x, prob. Canterbury CC (or Arras, Saint-Vaast?), with liturgical additions s. $x^{2/4}$—$x^{4/4}$, prob. Canterbury CC; and additions s. xi med., Exeter; prov. whole MS from s. xi med., or earlier, Exeter

Contents: sacramentary with episcopal benedictions and cues for Mass chants, litanies, pontifical services, coronation *ordo* ('First Anglo-Saxon *Ordo*'), manual services [s. ix/x]; various liturgical additions [s. x$^{2/4}$ — x$^{4/4}$]: liturgical calendar, computus ('Leofric-Tiberius Computus'), *lunaria*; list of relics, masses and other liturgical additions, incipits of gospel and epistle pericopes and of some chants [s. xi med.]; records* and donation inscription^{+*} [s. xi in.—xi ex.]

MS: Warren (1883) xxvi–lxv; Frere (1894–1932) 79 [no. 221]; Madan et al. (1895–1953) II/i.487–9; Nicholson (1913) lvi–lx; T.A.M. Bishop (1954–8a) 193, 196; *Le Graduel romain* II (1957) 87; N.R. Ker (1957) no. 315; Van Dijk (1957–60) I.10; D.H. Turner (1962) vi–vii; N.R. Ker (1964) 84; Gamber (1968–88) no. 950; T.A.M. Bishop (1971) xxiii, 2, 24; Brückmann (1973) 446–8; Hohler (1975) 61, 69–70, 75, 78–80; Rella (1977) 86–7; Drage (1978) 71–144; Higgitt (1979); D.H. Turner et al. (1980) no. 32; A.G. Watson (1984) I, no. 103; Dumville (1987) 176; Gerchow (1988) 253–7; P.L. Heyworth (1989) 196; Dumville (1991) 50; Lapidge (1991a) 76–7; Dumville (1992a) 39–65, 82; Dumville (1993g) 94–6, 99, 102–3, 143–4; Conner (1993) 9, 24–7, 188–91; Dumville (1994a) 144 and n. 62, 148; Lapidge (1994b) 136; Nelson—Pfaff (1995) 93–4; Pfaff (1995a) 100–9 [Keefer]; Pfaff (1995b) 11–14; Bischoff (1998—) II, no. 3788; N. Orchard (2002) I.1–234; R.M. Butler (2004) 173 n. 2, 211; C.A. Jones (2004) 340 n. 62, 341 nn. 65–7, 344 n. 78, 345 n. 82; C.A. Jones (2005a) 110; N. Orchard (2005) xcviii, 445 *et passim*; Hartzell (2006) no. 260 [pp. 400–27]; O'Brien O'Keeffe (2006) 268; Biggs (2007a) 29 [C.D. Wright]; Chardonnens (2007b) 535–6, 553; Shepard (2007) 254 n. 53; Pfaff (2009) 72–7, 136–8, 352–3; Wieland (2009) 121, 123–4, 138; R. Gameson (2012a) 39 and n. 94, 64 and n. 224, 76 and n. 268; R. Gameson (2012d) 348; Pfaff (2012) 452–3 and n. 8; Rankin (2012) 485 and n. 14, 490; Raw (2012) 460; Scragg (2012a) nos. 859–71

DEC: F. Wormald (1945) 132 [repr. F. Wormald (1984) 70]; Rice (1952) 191–2; F. Wormald (1952) 75–6 [no. 49] *et passim*; Pächt—Alexander (1973) nos. 20, 25; Alexander (1975a) 149 and n. 4; E. Temple (1976) no. 17; Deshman (1977); Ohlgren (1986) no. 95; Raw (1990) 233; R. Gameson (1995b) 33 n. 120, 60, 192 n. 1, 197, 198 n. 33, 200 n. 54, 204; Broderick (2011) 283

FACS: Warren (1883) frontispiece [fol. 8v]; Nicholson (1913) pls. XXVIII–XXIX [fols. 111v–112r, 53r, 59v–60r]; T.A.M. Bishop (1971) pl. I (2) [fol. 40v]; Pächt—Alexander (1973) pls. II–III [fols. 154v (detail), 49v]; E. Temple (1976) ills. 53 [fol. 154v (detail)], 54–6 [fols. 49r, 49v, 50r]; Deshman (1977) pls. I (a)–(b), II, V, VI, VIII (b) [fols. 61v, 154v (detail), 49v, 49r, 50v, 50r]; Rankin (1984) pls. IX (b)–(c), X [fols. 22r, 31v (detail), 139v]; A.G. Watson (1984) II, pl. 16 [fol. 55r]; Liuzza (2005) pl. 1 [fol. 50r]

ED: Warren (1883); Legg (1891–7) 1442–1626 [incipits of liturgical forms coll. as Leo]; F. Wormald (1934) 43–55 [liturgical calendar (no. 4)]; Moeller (1971–9) [benedictions coll. as LEOFRIC]; Gerchow (1988) 338 [obits in calendar]; Lapidge (1991a) 225–30 [litanies]; Conner (1993) 192–8 [list of relics], 221–5 [base MS for record of moving the see of Devon to Exeter]; N. Orchard (2002) vol. II [entire MS]; Liuzza (2005) 39–40 [base MS for Sphere of Apuleius]; Chardonnens (2007b) 201, 445 [prognostics]; Rushforth (2008a) no. 7 [liturgical calendar]

ST: Nicholson (1913) lvi–lviii; Gamber (1958) 148; Sawyer (1968) no. 1452; F. Wormald (1971a); Chaplais (1981b); Kotzor (1981) I.302*–311*; Munk Olsen (1982–) I.33; Rankin (1984) 103–12; Prescott (1987) 121; Bullough (1991) 19 and n. 66; Baker—Lapidge (1995) xlv–xlviii; R. Gameson (1996b) 144, 150, 161 n. 126, 169 n. 160; Lenker (1997) 481–6 *et passim*; Sole (1998) 133–4; Borst (2001) I.165–6; Krüger (2007) 261–2, 356; Corrêa (2008) 172 n. 19, 176–7, 185–6; Nelson (2008); Rushforth (2008a) 25–6; Chardonnens (2010) 246–9; Hamilton (2010); Scharer (2011) 42

586. Oxford, Bodleian Library, Bodley 596 (S.C. 2376), fols. 175–214

s. xi ex., Durham, (prov. Canterbury StA)

Contents: Bede, *Vita S. Cudbercti* (prose) [*CPL* 1379; *BHL* 2019] (incomplete), *Vita S. Cudbercti* (verse) [*CPL* 1380; *BHL* 2020] (part); *Historia de S. Cuthberto* [addition of s. xi/xii; incomplete]; Letald of Micy, *Vita S. Iuliani* [*BHL* 4544]; chants for the Office of St Julian

MS: Hardy (1862–71) I.754; Schenkl no. 635; Madan et al. (1895–1953) II/i.335–7; M.R. James (1903) 238, 517; Jaager (1935) 31; Colgrave (1940) 24–5; Laistner—King (1943) 88; Van Dijk (1952) no. 63; Dodwell (1954) 122; Gullick (1994) 97–101; R. Gameson (1995a) 144; Lapidge (1995c) 130; Gullick (1998a) 15, 24; R. Gameson (1999a) no. 680; South (2002) 15–17; Hartzell (2006) no. 261; Barker-Benfield (2008) I.lix, 63, III.1682, 1746, 1747, 1827

DEC: Lawrence (1982) 104

FACS: Gullick (1994) pl. 3 (a) [fol. 175v (detail)]

ED: Jaager (1935) 66–77 [Bede, *Vita metrica S. Cudbercti*, lines 119–252, coll. as O⁴]; Colgrave (1940) 142–306 [Bede, prose *Vita S. Cudbercti*, coll. as O⁴]; South (2002) 48–70 [*Historia de S. Cuthberto* in conflated text, with variants coll. as O]

587. Oxford, Bodleian Library, Bodley 691 (S.C. 2740)

s. xi/xii, England or Normandy, (prov. Exeter)

Contents: Augustine, *De ciuitate Dei* [*CPL* 313] with *Retractatio* II. xliii

MS: Schenkl no. 654; Madan et al. (1895–1953) II/i.522–3; N.R. Ker (1960) 24 and n. 3; N.R. Ker (1964) 84; Römer (1972b) 243; De la Mare (1983) 81, 83–4; Conner (1993) 9, 10; R. Gameson (1996b) 157 and n. 102; R. Gameson (1999a) no. 681; R. Gameson (2001c) 135

DEC: F. Wormald (1945) 135 [repr. F. Wormald (1984) 183 n. 17]; Pächt—Alexander (1966) no. 449

FACS: Pächt—Alexander (1966) pl. XXXVII [fol. 84v (detail)]

589. Oxford, Bodleian Library, Bodley 707 (S.C. 2608)

s. xi ex., prob. Normandy (or England), (prov. Exeter)

Contents: Gregory, *Homiliae in Hiezechielem* [*CPL* 1710]

MS: Schenkl no. 662; Madan et al. (1895–1953) II/i.449; Förster (1933a) 29 n. 106a; N.R. Ker (1960) 24 and n. 3; N.R. Ker (1964) 85; Conner (1993) 9; R. Gameson (1996b) 157 and n. 103; R. Gameson (1999a) no. 683

DEC: Pächt—Alexander (1966) no. 445

590. Oxford, Bodleian Library, Bodley 708 (S.C. 2609)

s. x ex., Canterbury CC, prov. Exeter

Contents: Gregory, *Regula pastoralis* [*CPL* 1712]; donation inscription⁺* [add. s. xi³ᐟ⁴]

MS: Schenkl no. 663; Madan et al. (1895–1953) II/i.449–50; Nicholson (1913) lx; Förster (1933a) 28 and n. 98; N.R. Ker (1957) no. 316; N.R. Ker (1960) 8 n. 2; N.R. Ker (1964) 85; T.A.M. Bishop (1971) xxv, 8; Rella (1977) 85–6, 88, 159; Drage (1978) 405–6; Conner (1993) 9, 13; Dumville (1993g) 103, 107 n. 125; Lapidge (1994b) 137; R. Gameson (1996b) 150 and n. 61; Budny (1998) I.509; Schreiber (2003) 24 and n. 10; Hartzell (2006) no. 262; Scragg (2012a) no. 872

DEC: Pächt—Alexander (1973) no. 35; E. Temple (1976) no. 19 (xi); Ohlgren (1986) no. 107; R. Gameson (1995b) 244 n. 60

FACS: Nicholson (1913) pl. XXX [fol. 110r]; Pächt—Alexander (1973) pl. III [fol. 1r (detail)]; E. Temple (1976) ill. 73 [fol. 1r (detail)]

ST: R. Gameson (1998) 242 n. 45; Schreiber (2003) 23–37

591. Oxford, Bodleian Library, Bodley 717 (S.C. 2631)

s. xi ex., Normandy, prob. Jumièges, (prov. Exeter)

Contents: Jerome, *Comm. in Esaiam* [*CPL* 584]

MS: Schenkl no. 667; Madan et al. (1895–1953) II/i.459; T.A.M. Bishop (1954–8a) 198; N.R. Ker (1960) 24 and n. 3; N.R. Ker (1964) 85; Gullick (1990) 75, 80 n. 51; Conner (1993) 9; R. Gameson (1995a) 107 n. 41, 131 n. 138; R. Gameson (1996b) 157 and n. 104; R. Gameson (1999a) no. 684; Gullick (2005a) 76 n. 35; R. Gameson (2012a) 61 n. 210

DEC: F. Wormald (1945) 135 [repr. F. Wormald (1984) 183 n. 17]; Pächt (1950b); Boase (1953) 29–30, 41, 209; Dodwell (1954) 117; Rickert (1954) 70; Zarnecki et al. (1984) no. 5; R. Gameson (1995b) 232 n. 237

FACS: Boase (1953) pl. 5 (a) [fol. 6v]; Rickert (1954) pl. 56 (a) [fol. vi (verso)]; Pächt—Alexander (1966) pl. XXXVI [fol. 287v]; Alexander (1978c) pl. 19 [fol. 287v (detail)]; De Hamel (1986) pl. 81 [fol. 64r]

ST: Lambert (1969–72) no. 207

592. Oxford, Bodleian Library, Bodley 718 (S.C. 2632)

s. x² or x ex., S England (Canterbury CC? Exeter? Sherborne?), prov. Exeter s. xi²

Contents: a list of chs. i–xx to *Poenitentiale Egberti* [*CPL* 1887], Prologue; First Capitulary of Gerbald of Liège; *Poenitentiale Egberti*, chs. i–xviii; two orders of confession, one with litany; *Quadripartitus* [collection of patristic excerpts and canons], bks. II–IV; excerpts from councils [add. s. xi², xi ex.]; prayer [s. xi/xii]; Letter of Pope Leo IX to Edward the Confessor [s. xi³/⁴]

MS: Haddan—Stubbs (1869–71) III.414; Madan et al. (1895–1953) II/i.459–61; N.R. Ker (1957) 437; Van Dijk (1957–60) III.66; N.R. Ker (1964) 85; Rella (1977) 88; Drage (1978) 407–10; Kerff (1982) 20–4; Frantzen (1983b) 131 and n. 34, 169–70 and nn. 54–5, 172; Hagenmüller (1991) 87–8; Lapidge (1991a) 77; Conner (1993) 37–9 *et passim*; J. Hill (2004) 321; G. Mann (2004) 261 n. 78; Frantzen (2007)

43; R. Gameson (2012a) 67 n. 232; D. Ganz (2012) 194 and n. 39;
A. Orchard (2012) 697 [no. 12]; Rushforth (2012) 203 and n. 42

DEC: F. Wormald (1945) 135 [repr. F. Wormald (1984) 74]; Kendrick
(1949) 17–18, 131; Rice (1952) 178; Pächt—Alexander (1973) no. 36;
E. Temple (1976) no. 30 (xiv); Brownrigg (1978) 246 n. 2; Ohlgren
(1986) no. 131; R. Gameson (1995b) 112 n. 41, 223; R. Gameson
(2012c) 262 n. 38

FACS: Kendrick (1949) pl. XIX (2) [fol. 28v (detail)]; Alexander (1970b)
pl. 12 (a) [fol. 24r (detail)]; Pächt—Alexander (1973) pl. III [fols. 1r, 28v
(details)]; E. Temple (1976) ill. 111 [fol. 1r (detail)]; Ramsay et al. (1992)
pl. 23 [fol. 24v]; Conner (1993) pl. XIV [fol. 28v]; R. Gameson (1996b)
pl. VII [fol. 1r]; R. Gameson (2000b) pl. 3 [fol. 1r]; R. Gameson (2012)
pl. 10.5 [folio not specified]

ED: Haddan—Stubbs (1869–71) III.416–31 [*Poenitentiale Egberti* coll.
as B]; Lapidge (1991a) 231–2 [litany]

ST: Bateson (1894b); Bethurum (1942) 919; Fowler (1972) liv–lviii;
Hohler (1975) 223 n. 47; Mordek (1975) 172 n. 356; Kerff (1982)
passim; Frantzen (1983a) 38–9; Brommer (1984) 10; Frantzen (1985)
29, 37; Hagenmüller (1991) *passim*; Dumville (1992a) 82 and n. 88, 85
n. 111, 90 n. 144, 133 and n. 274; R. Gameson (1996b) 163, 168–9,
176–8; Cross—Hamer (1999) 33, 35, 56, 66, 90–1, 96, 106; Kéry (1999)
167–9; Sauer (2000) 341, 372–3; R. McKitterick (2012) 328

593. Oxford, Bodleian Library, Bodley 739 (S.C. 2736)

s. xi/xii, England, prob. Exeter (Normandy?), (prov. Exeter)

Contents: Ambrose, *De fide* [*CPL* 150]; Gratianus Augustus, *Epistula ad
Ambrosium* [cf. *CPL* 160]; Ambrose, *De Spiritu Sancto* [*CPL* 151],
De incarnationis dominicae sacramento [*CPL* 152]

MS: Schenkl no. 681; Madan et al. (1895–1953) II/i.521; N.R. Ker (1960)
24 and n. 3; N.R. Ker (1964) 85; Conner (1993) 9; R. Gameson (1996b)
157 and n. 105; Bankert et al. (1997) 15, 41, 43, 44; R. Gameson (1999a)
no. 686

DEC: Pächt—Alexander (1966) no. 448

594. Oxford, Bodleian Library, Bodley 756 (S.C. 2526)

s. xi ex., Salisbury

Contents: Ambrosiaster, *Comm. in .xiii. Epistulas Paulinas* [*CPL* 184]

MS: Schenkl no. 689; Madan et al. (1895–1953) II/i.410; N.R. Ker
(1949–50) 154 n., 157 and n., 182 [repr. N.R. Ker (1985) 176 n., 179 and
n., 207]; N.R. Ker (1960) 23 and n. 1; N.R. Ker (1964) 171; N.R. Ker
(1976b) 25, 26 n., 29, 42, 45, 49, 53 [repr. N.R. Ker (1985) 145, 146 n.,
149, 162, 165, 169, 173]; Webber (1992) 12–15, 20, 90 n. 42, 132 n. 71,
134, 147; R. Gameson (1995a) 106 n. 40; Bankert et al. (1997) 69–70;
R. Gameson (1999a) no. 688; R. Gameson (2012a) 52 n. 175

FACS: N.R. Ker (1985) pls. 23 (b), 24 [fols. 1r, 72r (details)]

594. 5. Oxford, Bodleian Library, Bodley 762 (S.C. 2536), fols. 149–226

s. xi ex., (prov. Ely?)

Contents: Gratianus Augustus, *Epistula ad Ambrosium* [cf. *CPL* 160];
Ambrose, *De fide* [*CPL* 150], *De Spiritu Sancto* [*CPL* 151]

MS: Schenkl no. 692; Madan et al. (1895–1953) II/i.415–16; N.R. Ker
(1964) 78; R. Gameson (1999a) no. 689

595. Oxford, Bodleian Library, Bodley 765 (S.C. 2544), fols. 1–9

s. xi ex., Salisbury

Contents: Augustine, *Sermones* [*CPL* 284], cccli, cccxciii

MS: Schenkl no. 693; Madan et al. (1895–1953) II/i.420; N.R. Ker
(1949–50) 154 n. 1, 157 n. 4, 162 n. 5, 175 [repr. N.R. Ker (1985) 176
n. 1, 179 n. 4, 184 n. 5, 197 and 207 (add. note by A.G. Watson)];
Römer (1972b) 244; N.R. Ker (1976b) 25, 29 [repr. N.R. Ker (1985)
145, 149]; Webber (1992) 13, 14, 147

595. 5. Oxford, Bodleian Library, Bodley 765 (S.C. 2544), fols. 10–77

s. xi ex., Salisbury

Contents: Augustine, *De mendacio* [*CPL* 303], *Contra mendacium* [*CPL*
304], *De cura pro mortuis gerenda* [*CPL* 307]; Cyprian, *De dominica
oratione* [*CPL* 43]; Ambrose, *Epistola ad Vercellensem ecclesiam* [extra
collectionem xiv (lxiii)]

MS: Schenkl no. 693; Madan et al. (1895–1953) II/i.420; N.R. Ker
(1949–50) 154 n. 1, 157 n. 4, 162 n. 5, 175 [repr. N.R. Ker (1985) 176
n. 1, 179 n. 4, 184 n. 5, 197 and 207 (add. note by A.G. Watson)];
Faller–Zelzer (1968–94) IV.349; Römer (1972b) 244; N.R. Ker (1976b)
25, 29, 42, 49 [repr. N.R. Ker (1985) 145, 149, 162, 169]; Webber (1992)
12–15, 37 n. 20, 39, 52 n. 31, 132 n. 71, 147; Bankert et al. (1997) 14, 51

FACS: N.R. Ker (1985) pls. 21 (b)–(c) [fols. 18r, 51r (details)], 24 [fol. 18r (detail)]

596. Oxford, Bodleian Library, Bodley 768 (S.C. 2550)

s. xi ex., Salisbury

Contents: Ambrose, *De uirginibus* [*CPL* 145], *De uiduis* [*CPL* 146], *De uirginitate* [*CPL* 147], *Exhortatio uirginitatis* [*CPL* 149]; Nicetas of Remesiana (?), *De lapsu uirginis consecratae* [*CPL* 651]; Ambrose, *De mysteriis* [*CPL* 155], *De sacramentis* [*CPL* 154]

MS: Schenkl no. 494; Madan et al. (1895–1953) II/i.423; N.R. Ker (1949–50) 154 n. 1, 157 and n. 4 [repr. N.R. Ker (1985) 176 n. 1, 179 and n. 4]; N.R. Ker (1976b) 25, 49 [repr. N.R. Ker (1985) 145, 169]; Webber (1992) 12, 15, 21, 51, 58, 132 n. 71, 147; Bankert et al. (1997) 15, 36, 38–40, 46, 48, 65; R. Gameson (1999a) no. 692

DEC: Pächt—Alexander (1973) no. 65; N.R. Ker (1976b) 28, 29 n. [repr. N.R. Ker (1985) 148, 149 n. 2]

ST: Lambert (1969–72) no. 320

597. Oxford, Bodleian Library, Bodley 775 (S.C. 2558)

s. xi med., with additions s. xi$^{3/4}$—xii in., Winchester OM

Contents: troper [*cantatorium*] (including litany), gradual

MS: Frere (1894–1932) no. 200; Frere (1894b) xxvii n. 3; Madan et al. (1895–1953) II/i.425–7; Nicholson (1913) xxix–liii; Van Dijk (1952) no. 20; *Le Graduel Romain* II (1957) 87; Van Dijk (1957–60) I.108; R. Powell (1962) 5; Husmann (1964); N.R. Ker (1964) 201; Holschneider (1968) 24–7; T.A.M. Bishop (1971) xi n. 1, 23; Pollard (1975) 154; Pollard (1976) 55; Planchart (1977) I.34–43; Backhouse et al. (1984b) no. 161; Lapidge (1991a) 78; Dumville (1993g) 136; Teviotdale (1995b) 43–4; Clarkson (1996) 189–93; Lapidge (2004b) 446–7; Hartzell (2006) no. 263; Rankin (2007) 9; Wieland (2009) 122; Gullick (2012) 300 and n. 34, 301 n. 42; Pfaff (2012) 455 and n. 18; Rankin (2012) 499–500

DEC: Pächt—Alexander (1973) no. 48; R. Gameson (1995b) 32 n. 117; R. Gameson (2012c) 288 n. 137

FACS: Frere (1894b) pls. 1–3 [fols. 122r, 122v, 123r]; *NPS* II, pl. 111 [fol. 18v]; Nicholson (1913) pls. XVII–XXV [fols. 18v–19r, 86v–87r, 128v–129r, 176v–177r, 177v–178r, 4v–5r, 159v, 139v–140r, 143v–144r]; Huglo (1987) pl. XIV [fol. 125r]

ED: W.G. Henderson (1874) Appendix [base MS for kyries, sequences]; Frere (1894b) 1–98 [tropes coll. as E]; Lapidge (1991a) 233–4 [litany]; Lapidge—Winterbottom (1991b) cxxvi–cxxx [sequences]; Lapidge (2003a) 90–4, 96–101 [tropes and sequences for feasts of St Swithun]; Hartzell (2006) no. 263 [rubrics and incipits] [NOTE: many tropes and sequences from this MS are ptd or collated at various points in four volumes of *AH*: XXXVII, XL, XLVIII, XLIX]

ST: K. Young (1933) I.xxi, 182–3, 254, 587; Handschin (1936); Holschneider (1968); Planchart (1977); Keynes (1978) 253 n. 89; Lapidge—Winterbottom (1991b) xxx–xxxv, lxxxiii–lxxxiv, clv; Hiley (1995); Lapidge (2003a) 90–4, 96–101, 390 n.; Rankin (2003) 191–202; Huglo (2005) 34–6; Rankin (2005b); Rankin (2007) 55–6 *et passim*

598. Oxford, Bodleian Library, Bodley 783 (S.C. 2610)

s. xi ex. Normandy, (prov. Exeter)

Contents: Gregory, *Regula pastoralis* [*CPL* 1712]

MS: Schenkl no. 698; Madan et al. (1895–1953) II/i.450; N.R. Ker (1960) 24 and n. 3; N.R. Ker (1964) 85; Clement (1984a) 42; Gullick (1990) 75; Conner (1993) 9; R. Gameson (1996b) 157 and n. 106; R. Gameson (1998) 242 n. 45; R. Gameson (1999a) no. 693; R. Gameson (2001c) 136; Schreiber (2003) 24 and n. 15

DEC: Dodwell (1954) 117 n. 3; Pächt—Alexander (1966) no. 442

599. Oxford, Bodleian Library, Bodley 792 (S.C. 2640)

s. xi/xii, England or Normandy, (prov. Exeter)

Contents: Iulianus Toletanus, *Prognosticum futuri saeculi* [*CPL* 1258]; Ambrose, *De uirginibus* [*CPL* 145], *De uiduis* [*CPL* 146], *De uirginitate* [*CPL* 147], *Exhortatio uirginitatis* [*CPL* 149]; Nicetas of Remesiana (?), *De lapsu uirginis consecratae* [*CPL* 651]

MS: Schenkl no. 700; Madan et al. (1895–1953) II/i.465; N.R. Ker (1960) 24 and n. 3; N.R. Ker (1964) 85; Hillgarth (1976) xxx; Conner (1993) 10; R. Gameson (1996b) 157 and n. 107; Bankert et al. (1997) 15, 36, 38–40, 65; R. Gameson (1999a) no. 694

DEC: Pächt—Alexander (1966) no. 469

ST: Lambert (1969–72) no. 320

600. Oxford, Bodleian Library, Bodley 804 (S.C. 2663)

s. xi/xii or xii in., (prov. Exeter)

Contents: Augustine, *Contra mendacium* [*CPL* 304], *De natura et origine animae* [*CPL* 345], bks. I–III

MS: Schenkl no. 706; Madan et al. (1895–1953) II/i.479; N.R. Ker (1960) 24 and n. 3; N.R. Ker (1964) 85; Römer (1972b) 244; Conner (1993) 10; R. Gameson (1996b) 157; R. Gameson (1999a) no. 696

601. Oxford, Bodleian Library, Bodley 808 (S.C. 2667)

s. xi/xii, England or Normandy, (prov. Exeter)

Contents: Jerome, *Liber quaestionum hebraicarum in Genesim* [*CPL* 580]; pseudo-Jerome, *Decem temptationes populi Israel, Hebraicae quaestiones in libros Regum, Hebraicae quaestiones in Paralipomena, Expositio in Canticum Deborae, Expositio in Lamentationes Hieremiae* [*CPL* 630], *Epist. supp.* [*CPL* 633] xxiii (*De diuersis generibus musicorum*, a treatise of Carolingian date)]; Eusebius, *Onomasticon*, trans. Jerome as *De situ et nominibus locorum* [*CPG* 3466]; Jerome, *Liber interpretationis hebraicorum nominum* [*CPL* 581]; Bede, *Nomina regionum atque locorum de Actibus Apostolorum* [*CPL* 1359]

MS: Schenkl no. 707a; Madan et al. (1895–1953) II/i.481–2; N.R. Ker (1960) 24 and n. 3; N.R. Ker (1964) 85; Conner (1993) 10; R. Gameson (1996b) 158; R. Gameson (1999a) no. 697

DEC: Pächt—Alexander (1966) no. 459

ST: Lambert (1969–72) nos. 0 (+add.), 200–2, 409, 411, 412, 460

601. 5. Oxford, Bodleian Library, Bodley 810 (S.C. 2677)

s. xi ex., prob. Normandy, (prov. Exeter)

Contents: *Canones Apostolorum*; Lanfranc, *Collectio Lanfranci* [*Concilia* only]

Companion vol. to no. **258. 3**

MS: Schenkl no. 709; Madan et al. (1895–1953) II/i.489–90; Z.N. Brooke (1931) 231–4; N.R. Ker (1960) 24 and n. 3; N.R. Ker (1964) 85; S. Williams (1971) 82; De La Mare (1983) 86; R. Gameson (1996b) 158 and n. 110; R. Gameson (1999a) no. 698; Kéry (1999) 240–1; Gullick (2001) 110–11

DEC: Pächt—Alexander (1966) no. 467

602. Oxford, Bodleian Library, Bodley 813 (S.C. 2681)

s. xi ex. or xi/xii, England, prob. Exeter (or Normandy?), (prov. Exeter)

Contents: Augustine, *In Ioannis epistulam ad Parthos tractatus .x.* [*CPL* 279]

MS: Schenkl no. 712; Madan et al. (1895–1953) II/i.491; N.R. Ker (1960) 24 and n. 3; N.R. Ker (1964) 85; Römer (1972b) 244; Conner (1993) 10; R. Gameson (1996b) 158 and n. 111; R. Gameson (1999a) no. 699

DEC: Pächt—Alexander (1966) no. 446

603. Oxford, Bodleian Library, Bodley 815 (S.C. 2759)

s. xi ex., (prov. Exeter)

Contents: Augustine, *Confessiones* [*CPL* 251] with *Retractationes* [*CPL* 250] II. vi

MS: Schenkl no. 713; Madan et al. (1895–1953) II/i.530; N.R. Ker (1960) 23 n. 2; N.R. Ker (1964) 85; Römer (1972b) 245; Conner (1993) 10; R. Gameson (1996b) 158 and n. 112; R. Gameson (1999a) no. 700; R. Gameson (2012a) 16 and n. 12

604. Oxford, Bodleian Library, Bodley 819 (S.C. 2699)

s. viii ex. or ix in. (or s. viii[1]?), Northumbria, prob. Monkwearmouth-Jarrow, prov. Chester-le-Street, prov. Durham

Contents: Bede, *Comm. in Parabolas Salomonis* (*In Prouerbia Salomonis*) [*CPL* 1351] (incomplete, with additions s. x^2)

MS: Schenkl no. 715; Madan et al. (1895–1953) II/i.502; *CLA* II (1935) no. 235; Mynors (1939) 21; Laistner—King (1943) 58; Lowe (1958) 185, 187; N.R. Ker (1960) 74; Lowe (1960) 9, 24; Piper (1978) 214 n. 4; De La Mare—Barker-Benfield (1980) 9, 11, 14 [T.J. Brown]; Parkes (1982) 14, 16, 21 [repr. Parkes (1991) 106, 108, 113]; Parkes (1987) 28–31 [repr. Parkes (1991) 14–17]; A.G. Watson (1987b) 263, 296 [repr. A.G. Watson (2004) no. VIII]; Morrish (1988) 513; Parkes (1992) 27–8, 30, 181; Gullick (1998a) 16, 27; Roberts (2006) 31, 34 n. 36; Dumville (2007f) 93; Keefer (2007b) 94; M.P. Brown (2012) 159; R. Gameson (2012a) 37, 42 n. 117, 51, 52

DEC: Pächt—Alexander (1973) no. 8

FACS: Kendrick et al. (1956–60) I, pl. 60 [fols. 11r, 25v]; Schapiro (1958) pl. 22 (a) [fol. 79v]; Lowe (1960) pl. XXXVIII (e) [fol. 79v]; De La

Mare—Barker-Benfield (1980) fig. 2 [fol. 11r]; Bonner et al. (1989a) pl. 33 [fol. 29r]; Parkes (1991) pl. 19 [fol. 16r (detail)]; Parkes (1992) pl. 11 [fol. 16r]

ED: Hurst—Hudson (1983a) 21–163 [Bede, *Comm. in Parabolas Salomonis*, coll. as O]

ST: Kendrick et al. (1956–60) II.32-3 [T.J. Brown]; T.J. Brown (1969a) 23; Boyd (1975) 5 and n. 12; Bonner (1989b) 392

605. Oxford, Bodleian Library, Bodley 827 (S.C. 2718)

s. xi ex., Canterbury CC

Contents: Gratianus Augustus, *Epistula ad Ambrosium* [cf. *CPL* 160 = the preface to Ambrose's *De Spiritu Sancto*]; Ambrose, *De fide* [*CPL* 150], *De Spiritu Sancto* [*CPL* 151], *De incarnationis dominicae sacramento* [*CPL* 152]

MS: Schenkl no. 719; Madan et al. (1895–1953) II/i.511; N.R. Ker (1960) 14–15; N.R. Ker (1964) 38; Pollard (1975) 155; Webber (1995) 158; Clarkson (1996) 195–8; Bankert et al. (1997) 41–6; R. Gameson (1999a) no. 704; Gullick (2012) 303 and n. 50; Webber (2012) 215 n. 15

DEC: Dodwell (1954) 120; Pächt—Alexander (1973) no. 63; R. Gameson (1995a) 108, 121 n. 93

FACS: Pächt—Alexander (1973) pl. VII [fol. i v (detail)]; R. Gameson (1999a) pl. 14 [fol. i v]

ST: Webber (1992) 53; Wegmann—Bankert (1993) 31

606. Oxford, Bodleian Library, Bodley 835 (S.C. 2545)

s. xi ex., Salisbury

Contents: Ambrose, *De Ioseph patriarcha* [*CPL* 131], *De patriarchis* [*CPL* 132], *De paenitentia* [*CPL* 156], *De excessu fratris* [*CPL* 157]

MS: Schenkl no. 723; Madan et al. (1895–1953) II/i.421; N.R. Ker (1949–50) 154 n. 1, 157 and n. 4 [repr. N.R. Ker (1985) 176 n. 1, 179 and n. 4]; N.R. Ker (1964) 171 and nn.; N.R. Ker (1976b) 25, 45 [repr. N.R. Ker (1985) 145, 165]; Webber (1992) 12, 13, 15, 36 n. 19, 58, 132 n. 71, 147; Bankert et al. (1997) 28–9, 48–50; R. Gameson (1999a) no. 705; Gullick (2012) 303 and n. 56

ST: Anlezark (2006) 63 n. 6

607. Oxford, Bodleian Library, Bodley 849 (S.C. 2602)

A.D. 818, W France (Loire region?), prov. SW England s. x, Exeter s. xi

Contents: Bede, *Super Epistulas catholicas expositio* [*CPL* 1362]

MS: Schenkl no. 731; Madan et al. (1895–1953) II/i.447; Förster (1933a)
   29 and n. 110; N.R. Ker (1960) 7; N.R. Ker (1964) 85; Rella (1977) 88,
   167; Drage (1978) 411–12; Rella (1980) 114; A.G. Watson (1984) I,
   no. 116; P.L. Heyworth (1989) 65, 126; Conner (1993) 10, 17, 20;
   Dumville (1994d) 211; Lapidge (1994b) 138; R. Gameson (1996b) 150
   and n. 62; Bischoff (1998–) II, no. 3789; Lapidge (2006) 140, 172

DEC: Pächt–Alexander (1966) no. 413

FACS: Pächt–Alexander (1966) pl. XXXIV [fol. 44v (detail)]; A.G.
   Watson (1984) II, pl. 4 [fol. 86r]

ED: Hurst–Laistner (1983b) 179–342 [Bede, *Super Epistulas catholicas*,
   coll. as O]

608. Oxford, Bodleian Library, Bodley 865 (S.C. 2737), fols. 89–96

s. xi[1], (prov. Exeter)

Contents: Colloquy on the Latin language ('Colloquia Hisperica')

MS: Madan et al. (1895–1953) II/i.521; N.R. Ker (1957) no. 318; N.R.
   Ker (1964) 85; Winterbottom (1968); Drage (1978) 413; Sauer (1978)
   38–9; P.L. Heyworth (1989) 423; Conner (1993) 10; Gwara (1996c)
   21–2

ED: W.H. Stevenson (1929) 12–20 [no. II]; Gwara (1996c) 100–10

ST: *BCLL* (1985) no. 1243 [bibliography]

608. 1. Oxford, Bodleian Library, Bodley 865 (S.C. 2737), fols. 97–112

s. xi[1], (prov. Exeter)

Contents: Theodulf of Orléans, *Capitula* (chs. xxv–xlvi)[+*]

MS: Madan et al. (1895–1953) II/i.521–2; N.R. Ker (1957) no. 318; N.R.
   Ker (1964) 85; Drage (1978) 414–15; Sauer (1978) 38–45; Conner
   (1993) 10; Scragg (2012a) nos. 873–5

FACS: Napier (1916) pl. opp. p. 112 [fol. 107r]; N.R. Ker (1957) pl. III
   [fol. 107v]; Sauer (1978) 517–19 [fols. 105r, 102v, 103r]

ED: Napier (1916) 102–18; Sauer (1978) 339–403

LANG: Sauer (1978) 175–276

ST: Fowler (1972) xxxvi; Sauer (1978); Brommer (1984)

608. 5. Oxford, Bodleian Library, Broxbourne 90.28

[formerly no. 688 in the Collection of Mr A. Ehrman, Clobb Close, Beaulieu, Hants.]

s. xi

Contents: Passion story* (f)

MS: N.R. Ker (1957) no. 112; N.R. Ker (1976a) 124; Liuzza (1998) 16 n. 11; Scragg (2012a) no. 876

[NOTE: although the fragment was reported as missing by both N.R. Ker (1976a) and Liuzza (1998), its presence in the Bodleian Library was confirmed in a letter from B.C. Barker-Benfield to HG dated 27 Oct. 1997]

609. Oxford, Bodleian Library, Digby 39 (S.C. 1640), fols. 50–6

s. xi², (prov. Abingdon)

Contents: excerpt from Bede, *Historia ecclesiastica* III. vii [on St Birinus] and homily and mass prayers for feasts of St Birinus

MS: Hardy (1862–71) I/i.238; Macray (1883) 35–6; Madan et al. (1895–1953) II/i.71; Laistner–King (1943) 106; Van Dijk (1957–60) I.200b; N.R. Ker (1964) 3; A.G. Watson (1978) 284 n. 26, 311 [repr. A.G. Watson (2004) no. VII]; Townsend (1989) 132, 135–6; Love (1996) lxxiv–lxxvi; R. Gameson (1999a) nos. 708–11; T.N. Hall (2007) 261–2; Wieland (2009) 142

ED: Warren (1883) 307 [mass prayers]; Love (1996) 119–22 [homily]

ST: Biggs et al. (2001) 114–15

610. Oxford, Bodleian Library, Digby 53 (S.C. 1654), fol. 69

s. xi/xii, England or France?

Contents: antiphoner (f)

MS: Macray (1883) 54; Madan et al. (1895–1953) II/i.71; Van Dijk (1957–60) VI.53; A.G. Watson (1978) 311 [repr. A.G. Watson (2004) no. VII]; R. Gameson (1999a) no. 712; Hartzell (2006) no. 264

611. Oxford, Bodleian Library, Digby 63 (S.C. 1664)

s. ix^2 (844 or 867×892), Northumbria, prov. Winchester OM by s. x

Contents: computus material ('Canterbury Computus'); liturgical calendar; episcopal letters and writings 'de ratione paschali', including Dionysius Exiguus, *Epistula de ratione paschae* [*CPL* 2286] and excerpts from Bede, *De natura rerum* [*CPL* 1343]

MS: Macray (1883) 64–6; Madan et al. (1895–1953) II/i.71–2 [E.W.B. Nicholson]; Lindsay (1915) 470; Laistner—King (1943) 142; Levison (1946) 6 n. 4; N.R. Ker (1957) no. 319; Van Dijk (1957–60) III.127; N.R. Ker (1964) 201; Jones—Kendall (1975) 178; A.G. Watson (1978) 314 [repr. A.G. Watson (2004) no. VII]; Morrish (1982) 102, 132–3; Dumville (1983a); A.G. Watson (1984) I, no. 419; Morrish (1986) 92–3, 99; Morrish (1988) 531 and n. 60, 534–5; P.L. Heyworth (1989) 65; Dumville (1992a) 25–7 and n. 55, 37 and n. 94, 61, 129 n. 247; Dumville (1992b) 106 n. 238; Stevens (1992) 134 and nn.; Baker—Lapidge (1995) xl; R. Gameson (2001c) 3–4, 21, 25, 36; Dumville (2005) 308–9; Chardonnens (2007b) 536, 553; Rushforth (2008a) 21–2; Wieland (2009) 152

DEC: Pächt—Alexander (1973) no. 16

FACS: Bond—Thompson (1873–83) II, pl. 168 [folio not specified]; Krusch (1926) pls. 1–2 [fols. 9r (detail), 71r (detail)]; Pächt—Alexander (1973) pl. II [fol. 51v (detail)]; A.G. Watson (1984) II, pl. 12 [fol. 26r]; R. Gameson (2001c) pl. 4 [fol. 71r]

ED: F. Wormald (1934) 1–13 [liturgical calendar (no. 1)]; Gerchow (1988) 330 [obits in calendar]; Chardonnens (2007b) 388 [*dies Aegyptiaci* in calendar]; Rushforth (2008a) no. 4 [liturgical calendar]

ST: H.A. Wilson (1896) xxxi–xxxii; Gasquet—Bishop (1908) 151–2, 158–61 *et passim*; Krusch (1926); C.W. Jones (1939) 127; C.W. Jones (1943) 112 *et passim*; Siegmund (1949) 64; C.W. Jones (1977) 248; Stroud (1979) 230–5; C.W. Jones (1980) 680 [*De natiuitate lunae*]; Kotzor (1981) I.302*–311* [no. 1]; *BCLL* (1985) no. 318 [bibliography]; Günzel (1993) 198–200; Baker—Lapidge (1995) xl–xlii ['Canterbury Computus']; Borst (2001) I.40, 92, 161–2, 258; Liuzza (2001) 227; Chardonnens (2007b) 536, 553 *et passim*; Pfaff (2009) 71–2; Chardonnens (2010) 248

612. Oxford, Bodleian Library, Digby 81 (S.C. 1682), fols. 133–40

s. x/xi (988×1006), (prov. Durham)

Contents: Paschal tables; Wandalbert of Prüm, *Horologium* [SK 14026, 8933]; poems related to the calendar [including SK 853, 8931, 1716]

MS: Macray (1883) 87–8; Madan et al. (1895–1953) II/i.72 [E.W.B. Nicholson]; C.W. Jones (1939) 127; Mynors (1939) no. 24; N.R. Ker (1964) 74; A.G. Watson (1984) I, no. 421; Baker—Lapidge (1995) xlvii–xlviii

FACS: A.G. Watson (1984) II, pl. 18 [fol. 138v]

613. Oxford, Bodleian Library, Digby 146 (S.C. 1747), fols. 1–100

s. x ex., prob. Abingdon, (prov. ibid.)

Contents: Aldhelm, *De uirginitate* (prose)° [most OE glosses s. xi med.] [*CPL* 1332]; *Epistola ad Heahfridum*° [*CPL* 1334]

MS: Macray (1883) 143–4; Madan et al. (1895–1953) II/i.74; Napier (1900) xiii; Ehwald (1919) 218–19; N.R. Ker (1957) no. 320; N.R. Ker (1964) 3; Rella (1977) 70; A.G. Watson (1978) 284 n. 26, 311 [repr. A.G. Watson (2004) no. VII]; De La Mare—Barker-Benfield (1980) 20–1 [Lapidge]; Gwara (1994b) 135–7; Gwara (1996a) 98–9; Gwara (1998) 141–3; Gwara (2001a) I.147–56 *et passim*; Meaney (2004) 496; Graham (2009) 168–9; Lapidge (2012b) 27, 37; Scragg (2012a) nos. 877–9

DEC: F. Wormald (1945) 122–3 [repr. F. Wormald (1984) 61]; Kendrick (1949) 36 n. 2; Pächt—Alexander (1973) no. 26; E. Temple (1976) no. 19 (xi); Ohlgren (1986) no. 102; R. Gameson (1995b) 221 n. 169

FACS: F. Wormald (1945) pl. VI (a) [fol. 7r (detail)]; Kendrick (1949) pl. XXXII (1) [fol. 7r (detail)]; Pächt—Alexander (1973) pl. II [fol. 7r (detail)]; E. Temple (1976) ill. 7 [fol. 74 (detail)]; F. Wormald (1984) ill. 66 [fol. 7r (detail)]

ED: Napier (1900) 1–138, 180 [OE glosses to Aldhelm, prose *De uirginitate* and *Epistola ad Heahfridum*]; Ehwald (1919) 228–323 [Aldhelm, prose *De uirginitate*, coll. as O], 486–94 [Aldhelm, *Epistola ad Heahfridum*, coll. as A]; Goossens (1974) [OE glosses to Aldhelm, prose *De uirginitate*, coll. as OEG 1 + number in Napier (1900)]; Gwara (1996a) 112–21 [Aldhelm, *Epistola ad Heahfridum*, coll. as O]; Gwara (2001a) vol. II [Latin text of Aldhelm, prose *De uirginitate*, with Latin and OE glosses, coll. as O]

LANG: Napier (1900) xxvii–xxxi; Goossens (1974) 13–139 *passim*; Hofstetter (1987) 140–1; Hofstetter (1988) 154; Meaney (2004) 496, 498

ST: R. Derolez (1955); R. Derolez (1959) 134; R. Derolez (1960); Fell (1971) xix–xx; P.S. Baker (1980) 28; Korhammer (1980) 36–7; Bodden

(1988) 218, 223, 233–46; Goossens (1992); Gwara (1994a) 268; Gwara (1994b); Gwara (1997a); Gwara (1997b); Gwara (1998); Gretsch (1999a) 132–84, 361 n. 110, 363, 366, 377, 379; Lapidge (2012b) 26–31, 35–7

613. 9. Oxford, Bodleian Library, Digby 174 (S.C. 1775), fol. iii

s. ix, possibly in England before 1100

Contents: Boethius, *De consolatione Philosophiae* [*CPL* 878], with gloss (f); Lupus of Ferrières, *De metris Boetii* (f)

MS: Macray (1883) 186; Madan et al. (1895–1953) II/i.75; N.R. Ker (1964) 46; Gibson et al. (1995–2001) no. 179; Godden (2011) 92

614. Oxford, Bodleian Library, Digby 175 (S.C. 1776)

s. xi/xii, Durham

Contents: Bede, *Vita S. Cudbercti* (prose) [*CPL* 1379; *BHL* 2019] (incomplete) and *Historia ecclesiastica* [*CPL* 1375] IV. xxix–xxx; miracle story from *Capitula de miraculis et translationibus S. Cuthberti* (incomplete); Bede, *Vita S. Cudbercti* (verse) [*CPL* 1380; *BHL* 2020]; *Vita S. Oswaldi* (incomplete; from Bede, *Historia ecclesiastica* III), *Vita S. Aidani* (incomplete; from Bede, *Historia ecclesiastica* III)

MS: Hardy (1862–71) I.299–300; Macray (1883) 187; Madan et al. (1895–1953) II/i.75; Jaager (1935) 30; Colgrave (1940) 22; Laistner—King (1943) 88, 90, 105, 106; A.G. Watson (1978) 311 [repr. A.G. Watson (2004) no. VII]; Gullick (1994) 97–8; Lapidge (1995c) 130, 158 and n. 74; Gullick (1998a) 15, 24; R. Gameson (1999a) no. 714; South (2002) 90 n. 57

DEC: Pächt—Alexander (1973) no. 59

FACS: Gullick (1994) pls. 2 (a)–(b) [fols. 9r, 24r (details)]

ED: Jaager (1935) [Bede, *Vita metrica S. Cudbercti*, coll. as O¹]; Colgrave (1940) 142-306 [Bede, prose *Vita S. Cudbercti*, coll. as O₁]

ST: Biggs et al. (2001) 60–2, 366–8

Oxford, Bodleian Library, Donation f. 458: now Oxford, Bodleian Library, Arch. A. f. 131 [printed book]: see below, no. **857**

615. Oxford, Bodleian Library, Douce 125 (S.C. 21699)

s. x ex. or x/xi, (prov. Winchester OM)

Contents: pseudo-Boethius, *De geometria* [*CPL* 895] bk. I; Euclid in Latin translation, bks. I–IV; *Altercatio duorum geometricorum*

MS: Madan et al. (1895–1953) IV.529 [E.W.B. Nicholson]; N.R. Ker (1964) 201; Folkerts (1970) 175; Bodden (1988) 231; Folkerts (1989) 21; Wieland (2009) 155

DEC: Pächt—Alexander (1973) no. 31

FACS: Pächt—Alexander (1973) pl. III [fol. 23r]

ST: Thorndike—Kibre (1963) 870 [*Altercatio duorum geometricorum*]; Folkerts (1970); Pingree (1981); Folkerts (1982)

616. Oxford, Bodleian Library, Douce 140 (S.C. 21714)

s. vii/viii (before 719), S. England, prov. Glastonbury s. x?

Contents: Primasius of Hadrumentum, *Comm. in Apocalypsin* [*CPL* 873]

MS: Madan et al. (1895–1953) IV.535 [with addenda by E.W.B. Nicholson, IV.717–19 and V.xviii]; Lindsay (1910) 11; Lindsay (1915) 470; *CLA* II (1935) no. 237; T.A.M. Bishop (1964–8d); T.A.M. Bishop (1971) 2; Parkes (1976a) 162–75 [repr. Parkes (1991) 122–35]; Parkes (1976b) 160 n. 3 [repr. Parkes (1991) 157 n. 3]; Rella (1977) 75, 94; De La Mare—Barker-Benfield (1980) 9, 12 [T.J. Brown]; T.J. Brown (1982a) 112 [repr. T.J. Brown (1993a) 213]; A.G. Watson (1984) I, no. 461; Webster—Backhouse (1991) no. 124 [Backhouse]; Budny (1992) 137; Parkes (1992) 125 nn. 61, 72; Lapidge (1994a) 109, 130; Hoffmann (2001); Hussey (2008) 159; M.P. Brown (2012) 157; R. Gameson (2012a) 28 n. 59, 42 n. 117

FACS: Lindsay (1910) pl. IV [fol. 100v]; *CLA* II (1935) no. 237 [fol. 59v (detail)]; T.A.M. Bishop (1964–8d) pl. XXIX (b) [fol. 4v (detail)]; De La Mare—Barker-Benfield (1980) fig. 6 [fol. 77v (part)]; A.G. Watson (1984) II, pls. 2 (a)–(e) [fols. 4r, 40r, 79v, 101v, 115v]; Drogin (1989) pls. 22, 30 [fol. 59v (both details)]; M.P. Brown (1991) pl. 19 [fol. 59v]; Parkes (1991) pls. 24.11–12 [fols. 100v, 7v (details)]; Budny (1992) pl. 8 (a) [fol. 4v (detail)]; M.P. Brown (2007a) pl. 18 [fol. 1r]

ST: Traube (1907) 33, 107; A.C. Clark (1918a) 104–23; Stansbury (1999) 386

617. Oxford, Bodleian Library, Douce 296 (S.C. 21870) (the 'Crowland Psalter')

s. xi$^{2/4}$, prob. Crowland

Contents: liturgical calendar; *computistica*; Psalterium Gallicanum; canticles; litany; prayers; Office of the Trinity

MS: Madan et al. (1895–1953) IV.584 [with addenda by H.M. Bannister and E.W.B. Nicholson]; Van Dijk (1957–60) II.7; N.R. Ker (1964) 56, 79; Backhouse et al. (1984b) no. 68 [D.H. Turner]; A.G. Watson (1984) I, no. 471; Lapidge (1991a) 78; Dumville (1993g) 60 n. 265, 62 nn. 268 and 269, 64 n. 277, 136 n. 6; Pulsiano (2001) xxix; Chardonnens (2007b) 536–7, 553; Rushforth (2007) 78; Rushforth (2008a) 39–40; Rushforth (2008b); Wieland (2009) 116; R. Gameson (2012a) 50 and n. 163, 75, 80 n. 286, 86, 91 n. 331; Rushforth (2012) 209 and n. 75; Scragg (2012a) no. 880

DEC: Rice (1952) 200, 210; Rickert (1954) 52, 226 n. 16; Alexander (1970a) 121 n. 3, 148 n. 3, 150, 169 n. 3; Pächt—Alexander (1973) no. 43; E. Temple (1976) no. 79; F. Wormald (1984) 108, 120, 126; Ohlgren (1986) no. 184; R. Gameson (1995b) 31, 176, 196 n. 21, 204 n. 70, 205 n. 81, 228–9, 230; Rushforth (2007) 35, 49

FACS: Rice (1952) pl. 75 (a) [fol. 40r]; Rickert (1954) pl. 42 [fol. 40r]; Pächt—Alexander (1973) pl. V [fols. 9r, 40r]; E. Temple (1976) ills. 259–60 [fol. 40r–v]; A.G. Watson (1984) II, pl. 21 [fol. 86r]; D.M. Wilson (1984) pl. 222 [fol. 40r]; Rushforth (2007) 19 [fol. 2v], 34 [fol. 9r], 48 [fol. 40r], 78 [fol. 129v]; Rushforth (2008b) pls. I–II [fols. 118r, 130v]

ED: F. Wormald (1934) 253–65 [liturgical calendar (no. 20)]; Gerchow (1988) 331 [obit notes in calendar]; Lapidge (1991a) 235–9 [litany]; Milfull (1996) 109–11 [hymn (SK 10920) in the Office of the Trinity, coll. as O]; Raw (1999) 192–200 [Office of the Trinity]; Pulsiano (2001a) [Pss. I–L coll. as ρ]; Rushforth (2008a) no. 17 [liturgical calendar]

ST: Gasquet—Bishop (1908) 34 n. 1 *et passim*; Sisam—Sisam (1959) 6 n. 2, 48; Gneuss (1968) 113; Gjerløw (1980) I.177–8; Kotzor (1981) I.303*–311*; Keynes (1985b); Gerchow (1988) 228–30; Milfull (1996) 63; Raw (1999); Borst (2001) I.292; N. Orchard (2002) I.141 n. 26; Rushforth (2008b)

618. Oxford, Bodleian Library, e Mus. 6 (S.C. 3567)

s. xi ex. or xii in., Bury St Edmunds, (prov. ibid.)

Contents: Augustine, *Tractatus in Euangelium Ioannis* [*CPL* 278]; Possidius, *Vita S. Augustini* [*CPL* 358; *BHL* 785] (incomplete)

MS: Schenkl no. 300; Madan et al. (1895–1953) II/ii.683–4; T.A.M. Bishop (1949–53) 434; N.R. Ker (1964) 21; Römer (1972b) 247; R.M. Thomson

(1972) 625 n. 39, 627 and n. 57; R. Sharpe et al. (1996) 79; R. Gameson (1999a) no. 717; Biggs et al. (2001) 95–7; Lapidge (2006) 291

619. Oxford, Bodleian Library, e Mus. 7 (S.C. 3568)

s. xi ex. or xii in., Bury St Edmunds?, (prov. ibid.) [companion vol. to no. 620]

Contents: Augustine, *Enarrationes in Psalmos* [*CPL* 283] (Pss. CI–CL)

MS: Schenkl no. 301; Madan et al. (1895–1953) II/ii.684; N.R. Ker (1964) 21; Römer (1972b) 247; R.M. Thomson (1972) 625 n. 39, 627 and n. 57; R. Sharpe et al. (1996) 78; R. Gameson (1999a) no. 718; Lapidge (2006) 288

620. Oxford, Bodleian Library, e Mus. 8 (S.C. 3569)

s. xi ex. or xii in., Bury St Edmunds?, (prov. ibid.) [cf. above, no. 619]

Contents: Augustine, *Enarrationes in Psalmos* [*CPL* 283] (Pss. L–C)

MS: Schenkl no. 302; Madan et al. (1895–1953) II/ii.684; N.R. Ker (1964) 21; Römer (1972b) 247; R.M. Thomson (1972) 625 n. 39, 627 and n. 57; R. Sharpe et al. (1996) 78; R. Gameson (1999a) no. 719; Lapidge (2006) 288

620. 3. Oxford, Bodleian Library, e Mus. 26 (S.C. 3571)

s. xi/xii, (prov. Bury St Edmunds)

Contents: Jerome, *Comm. in Prophetas minores* [*CPL* 589]; *Vita S. Macarii Romani* [*BHL* 5104] (added)

MS: Schenkl no. 305; Madan et al. (1895–1953) II/ii.685; N.R. Ker (1964) 21; Lambert (1969–72) no. 216; N.R. Ker (1979) 203 n. 2 [repr. N.R. Ker (1985) 75 n. 2]; R. Sharpe et al. (1996) 80; R. Gameson (1999a) no. 720

620. 6. Oxford, Bodleian Library, e Mus. 66 (S.C. 3655), offsets of pastedowns

s. vi or vii, prob. N. Italy (or France?), (prov. Canterbury StA)

Contents: Arator, *Historia apostolica* [*CPL* 1504] (f)

MS: Madan et al. (1895–1953) II/ii.721; *CLA* Supplement (1971) no. 1740; McKinlay (1942) 64; N.R. Ker et al. (1944) [repr. Lowe (1972b) I.345–7]; McKinlay (1951) xi; De La Mare—Barker-Benfield (1980) 9, 11–12 [T.J. Brown]; R. Gameson (1999a) no. 721; R.

Gameson (1999c) 323–4; Lapidge (2006) 281; Barker-Benfield (2008) I.lx–lxi, II.1376; Wieland (2009) 149

FACS: N.R. Ker et al. (1944) [two plates]; Lowe (1972b) pls. 59–60; Owen-Crocker (2009) fig. 1.5 [inside front cover board]

ED: McKinlay (1951) [Arator, *Historia apostolica* I.32–63, 85–122, 647–81, 684–724, coll. as B]

621. Oxford, Bodleian Library, Eng. bib. c. 2 (S.C. 31345)

s. xi[1]

Contents: gospels* (f; from John)

MS: Napier (1891); Madan et al. (1895–1953) VI.36; Bright (1904–6) [John] xx–xxi and xxix–xxxix; N.R. Ker (1957) no. 322; Liuzza (1994–2000) I.xxxvi–xxxvii; *ASMMF* III (1995) 30–1 [no. 374; Liuzza]; Lenker (1997) 21, 25–7, 41–2; R. Gameson (2012a) 23–4; R. Gameson (2012b) 115 and n. 84; Scragg (2012a) no. 881

FACS: *ASMMF* III (1995) no. 374

ED: Napier (1891); Liuzza (1994–2000) I.160–2, 169–72 [OE Gospel of John coll. as L]

LANG: Liuzza (1994–2000) II.171–2

ST: Greenfield—Robinson (1980) 337–9; Liuzza (1994–2000); Lenker (1997)

622. Oxford, Bodleian Library, Eng. hist. e. 49 (S.C. 30481)

s. xi[1]

Contents: Orosius, *Historiae aduersum paganos* [*CPL* 571] in OE translation* (f)

MS: Madan et al. (1895–1953) V.816; N.R. Ker (1957) no. 323; Bately (1980) xxvi, xxxiv–xxxv; Carley (1986) 117; Scragg (2012a) no. 889

ED: Bately (1980) 57–9, 66–7 [OE Orosius coll. as B]

LANG: Bately (1980) liii–liv

ST: Bately (1980); Greenfield—Robinson (1980) 321–8; Waite (2000) 38–41, 281–320

Oxford, Bodleian Library, Eng. th. c. 74: see no. **146**

Oxford, Bodleian Library, Fell 1, 3 and 4 (formerly nos. **623–5**) were returned to Salisbury Cathedral Library in 1985: see now nos. **754. 5** and **754. 6** (the former entry no. **624** has been deleted)

626. Oxford, Bodleian Library, Hatton 20 (S.C. 4113)

890×897, S England (Winchester?), prov. Worcester s. ix ex.

Contents: Gregory (Alfred), *Regula pastoralis** [*CPL* 1712]; colophon (s. x)

MS: Madan et al. (1895–1953) II/ii.845–6; N.R. Ker (1941–9) 28 n. 2
[repr. N.R. Ker (1985) 131 n. 2]; Dobbie (1942) cxii–cxiii; N.R. Ker
(1948) 73 [repr. N.R. Ker (1985) 55]; N.R. Ker (1956) 17–26; N.R. Ker
(1957) no. 324; N.R. Ker (1971) 327–8 [repr. N.R. Ker (1985) 21–2];
A.F. Cameron (1974) 221, 228 n. 21; Parkes (1976b) 158 n. 1, 160 [repr.
Parkes (1991) 155 n. 1, 157]; Backhouse et al. (1984b) no. 1; A.G.
Watson (1984) I, no. 517; N.R. Ker (1985) 69 n., 131 n. 3; Keynes
(1985a) 159 n. 85; Dumville (1987) 162–3, 171 and n. 132, 167; Morrish
(1988) 532–3; P.L. Heyworth (1989) 77, 78; Franzen (1991) *passim* [see
Index, p. 226]; Webster—Backhouse (1991) no. 235; Conner (1993)
55–6 *et passim*; Laing (1993) 132; *ASMMF* VI (1998) 10–14 [no. 377;
Franzen]; W. Schipper (2003) 159, 162; Schreiber (2003) 53–5, 75–8;
Dance (2004) 31 n. 6; G. Mann (2004) 245 n. 23; A. Orchard (2004) 66
n. 25; Roberts (2005) 42–4; Roberts (2006) 34 n. 36; Graham (2009)
191; Scragg (2009b) 78, 81–2; Crick (2012) 178; R. Gameson (2012a)
15, 43 n. 123, 53, 62 n. 217, 77; D. Ganz (2012) 188 n. 4; A. Orchard
(2012) 697 [no. 13]; Scragg (2012a) no. 307

DEC: Kendrick (1938) 215; F. Wormald (1945) 113 [repr. F. Wormald
(1984) 52]; Rice (1952) 176; Pächt—Alexander (1973) no. 18; E. Temple
(1976) no. 1; Ohlgren (1986) no. 79; Keefer (2007b) 97; R. Gameson
(2012c) 249 and n. 2, 274 and n. 77, 287 and n. 133

FACS: N.R. Ker (1956) [complete facsimile]; Rice (1952) pl. 42 (a) [fol.
2v (detail)]; Denholm-Young (1954) pl. 4 [fol. 60r (detail)]; Pächt—
Alexander (1973) pl. I [fol. 34v (detail)]; E. Temple (1976) ills. 2–4 [fols.
6v, 93v, 11v (all details)]; Backhouse et al. (1984b) p. 21 [fol. 34v]; A.G.
Watson (1984) II, pl. 13 [fol. 46v]; F. Wormald (1984) ills. 45–6 [fols.
93v, 6v (details)]; Robinson—Stanley (1991) 6.1.4 and 6.2.2.1–2 [fols.
2v, 98r–v]; Webster—Backhouse (1991) p. 260 [fol. 2v]; *ASMMF* VI
(1998) no. 377; Roberts (2005) pl. 6 [fol. 6r]

ED: Sweet (1871) [complete text]; Dobbie (1942) 110–12 [base MS for
Verse preface and Verse epilogue]; Carlson (1975–8) [vocabulary
variants coll. as H]; Schreiber (2003) [coll. as H (partial ed.)]; Dance
(2004) 37, 39–40 [fol. 1r–v]

LANG: A. Campbell (1959) ['CP']; Karl Brunner (1965) ['Cura Past.'];
Horgan (1982); Hofstetter (1987) 305–6; Hogg (1992) ['CP', 'CP(H)'];

Waite (2000) 170–89; Schreiber (2003) 83–135; Dance (2004) 34–5 n. 25, 35–43

ST: K. Sisam (1953a) 140–7; Horgan (1973); S. Kim (1973); Greenfield — Robinson (1980) 250–1, 316–17; Horgan (1986) 110–14; R.I. Page (1992b) 42–3; Waite (2000) 23–7, 199–226

627. Oxford, Bodleian Library, Hatton 23 (S.C. 4115)

s. xi^2, prob. Worcester, (prov. Great Malvern, cell of Westminster)

Contents: Cassian, *Conlationes* [*CPL* 512], chs. i–x; Bede, *In librum beati patris Tobiae allegorica expositio* [*CPL* 1350]

MS: Schenkl no. 334; Madan et al. (1895–1953) II/ii.847; N.R. Ker (1941–9) 28–9 [repr. N.R. Ker (1985) 131 n. 1, 132]; Laistner — King (1943) 81; N.R. Ker (1960) 22 n. 1, 20 n. 4; Pollard (1962) 1 n. 2; N.R. Ker (1964) 209; T.A.M. Bishop (1971) 20 n. 1; Pollard (1975) 152–3; Rella (1977) 96 n. 8; Clarkson (1996) 184–9; R. Gameson (1999a) no. 725; R. Gameson (2005a) 95, 101–4; R. Gameson (2012a) 51 n. 169, 60, 72 n. 248, 76 and n. 266; Gullick (2012) 301 and n. 44, 303 and n. 55

DEC: Pächt — Alexander (1973) no. 55; R. Gameson (2012c) 274 n. 75

FACS: Pollard (1962) pls. I–II [binding (spine)]; Pächt — Alexander (1973) pl. VI [fol. 18v (detail)]; R. Gameson (1999a) pl. 3 [fol. 3v]

ED: Hurst — Hudson (1983a) 1–19 [Bede, *In librum beati patris Tobiae*, coll. as O]

ST: Lake (2003) 41 n. 56

628. Oxford, Bodleian Library, Hatton 30 (S.C. 4076)

940×956, Glastonbury, prov. Worcester, s. x^2

Contents: Caesarius, *Expositio in Apocalypsim* [*CPL* 1016]

MS: Schenkl no. 337; Frere (1894–1932) no. 425; Madan et al. (1895– 1953) II/ii.831; R.W. Hunt (1961) xv; N.R. Ker (1964) 91, 209; T.A.M. Bishop (1971) 20 n. 1; Römer (1972a) 84; Römer (1972b) 265–6; Pollard (1975) 157; Rella (1977) 161; Rella (1980) 110; A.G. Watson (1984) I, no. 519; Hartzell (1989) 87; Budny (1992) 138 [errors rectified in Dumville (1994a)]; R. Gameson (1992d) 206 n. 87; Conner (1993) 57, 63, 70–2, 75; Dumville (1993g) 3 n. 12; Dumville (1994a) 148 and n. 90, 149; Keynes (1994b) 86–7; Clarkson (1996) 202–3; R.M. Butler (2004) 204–7; Barker-Benfield (2008) I.518–19; R. Gameson (2012a) 39 and n. 99, 59 nn. 196, 198; R. Gameson (2012d) 350 n. 22; D. Ganz (2012) 190 n. 13, 193 and n. 31

FACS: A.G. Watson (1984) II, pl. 14 [fol. 46r (detail)]; Budny (1992) pl. 8(b) [fol. 46r (detail)]

Oxford, Bodleian Library, Hatton 30 (S.C. 4076), offsets from pastedowns: see no. **636**

629. Oxford, Bodleian Library, Hatton 42 (S.C. 4117)

s. ix$^{1/3}$, Brittany [fols. 1–142]; s. ix^1, N France? [fols. 142–88]; s. ix med., France [fols. 189–204]; whole MS s. x in. England, prov. Glastonbury?, prov. Canterbury CC s. xi/xi, prov. Worcester by s. xi in.

Contents: fols. 1–142: *Collectio canonum Hibernensis* (recension B) [*CPL* 1794; *BCLL* 613]; *Canones Wallici* [*CPL* 1880; *BCLL* 995]; *Canones Adamnani* [*CPL* 1792; *BCLL* 609]; incipits of Mass texts (added s. xi at Worcester); Gaius, *Institutiones* bk. I; tables of affinity of kinship; notes on weights and measures

fols. 142–88: *Collectio canonum Dionysio–Hadriana*

fols. 189–204: Ansegisus, *Capitularium collectio*, bk. I

MS: Schenkl no. 339; Stubbs (1874) cxii–cxiii; Wasserschleben (1885) xxxiii–xxxiv; Madan et al. (1895–1953) II/ii.848–9; N.R. Ker (1941–9) 28 and n. 1 [repr. N.R. Ker (1985) 131 and n. 1]; N.R. Ker (1948) 73 and n. 3 [repr. N.R. Ker (1985) 55 and n. 3]; T.A.M. Bishop (1959–63b) 415, 421, 423; Bieler (1963) 13; N.R. Ker (1964) 209; T.A.M. Bishop (1971) xxvi; N.R. Ker (1971) 315, 316, 318 n. 4, 328–30 [repr. N.R. Ker (1985) 9, 10, 12 n. 4, 22–4]; Pollard (1975) 143–4; Whitelock (1976) 30–1; Rella (1977) 72–3, 96 n. 9, 127–8, 149–50 nn. 116–19, 156, 168; Lucas (1979a); Rella (1980) 114–15; Deuffic (1985) 307–8; A.G. Watson (1987b) 287 [repr. A.G. Watson (2004) no. VIII]; Budny (1992) 124; Lapidge (1992b) 100 n. 24 [repr. Lapidge (1993a) 90 n. 24]; Barker-Benfield (1993); Dumville (1993e); Dumville (1993g) 3 n. 12, 49; Mordek (1995) 404–6; Clarkson (1996) 163–4; G. Schmitz (1996) 110–13, 229–30; Bischoff (1998–) II, no. 3798; Sauer (2000) 392–3 n. 80; Dance (2004) 31 n. 6, 43 n. 52; Godden (2004) 372; A. Orchard (2004) 66 n. 15; Ambrose (2005) 111–13; Hartzell (2006) no. 266; Lapidge (2006) 172, 303; C.D. Wright (2006) 195, 213; N.M. Thompson (2007) 117–18; *ASMMF* XVI (2008) 93–106 [no. 379; Lucas]; R. Gameson (2012d) 348 and n. 14; A. Orchard (2012) 697 [no. 14]; Scragg (2012a) no. 890

DEC: Pächt—Alexander (1966) nos. 417, 419, 420; Pächt—Alexander (1973) no. 29

FACS: Pächt—Alexander (1966) pl. XXXIV [fol. 142v]; *ASMMF* XVI (2008) no. 379

ED: Wasserschleben (1885) 1–243 [*Collectio canonum Hibernensis* coll. as MS. 8]; Bieler (1963) 136–48, 176–80 [*Canones Wallici* and *Canones Adamnani* coll. as H]; G. Schmitz (1996) 111–12 [Ansegis, *Capitularium collectio* bk. I, coll. as O]

ST: *Collectio canonum Hibernensis*: Wasserschleben (1885); Kenney (1929) 247–50; *BCLL* (1985) no. 613; Cross—Hamer (1999) 33–4; Kéry (1999) 73–4;

Canones Wallici: Wasserschleben (1851) 124; Haddan—Stubbs (1869–71) I.127–37; McNeill—Gamer (1938) 57, 67–8, 373; Bieler (1963) 136–49; *BCLL* (1985) no. 995; Cross—Hamer (1999) 37, 139;

Canones Adamnani: Wasserschleben (1851) 120–3; Haddan—Stubbs (1869–71) II.111–14; Kenney (1929) 245; McNeill—Gamer (1938) 57, 131; Bieler (1963) 176–80; *BCLL* (1985) no. 609;

Collectio canonum Dionysio–Hadriana: Z.N. Brooke (1931) 50 and n. 2; Kéry (1999) 13–20; Cross—Hamer (1999) 23, 36, 154, 158–9;

Ansegisus, *Capitularium collectio*: P. Wormald (1978) 71–3; Cross (1992b); Mordek (1995) 404–6; Cross—Hamer (1999) 23, 36, 154, 158–9; Kéry (1999) 94; C.D. Wright (2006) 207–11 [app. crit.]; Lapidge (2012a) 690–1; McKee (2012b) 340 and n. 5; R. McKitterick (2012) 327

630. Oxford, Bodleian Library, Hatton 43 (S.C. 4106)

s. x/xi [fols. 9–177], s. xi med. [fols. 1–8], Winchester ambit? Glastonbury?, prov. Canterbury CC (at least by s. xii in.)

Contents: Bede, *Historia ecclesiastica* [*CPL* 1375]

MS: Schenkl no. 340; Madan et al. (1895–1953) II/ii.842–3; C. Plummer (1896) I.cxiii; Dobbie (1942) xcvi; Laistner—King (1943) 99; N.R. Ker (1957) no. 326; N.R. Ker (1964) 91; Colgrave—Mynors (1969) xlii–xliii; Rella (1977) 69, 84; Lapidge (2008–10) I.xcii–xciii; Scragg (2012a) no. 891

ED: Dobbie (1942) 106 [Caedmon's Hymn coll. as H]; Lapidge (2008–10) [Bede, *Historia ecclesiastica*, coll. as O; the later corrector and scribe of fols. 1–8 coll. as O²]

ST: Lapidge (2008b)

631. Oxford, Bodleian Library, Hatton 48 (S.C. 4118)

s. vii ex. or viii in. or viii[1], or viii med., S England or Mercia (Worcester? possibly Bath?), prov. Worcester

Contents: *Regula S. Benedicti* [*CPL* 1852]

MS: Madan et al. (1895–1953) II/ii.849–50; Nicholson (1913) xix–xx; Lowe (1929); *CLA* II (1935) no. 240; N.R. Ker (1941–9) [repr. N.R. Ker (1985) 131–3]; N.R. Ker (1957) no. 327; Lowe (1960) 20; D.H. Wright (1961a) 449–50; N.R. Ker (1964) 209; Farmer (1968); Engelbert (1969); Gretsch (1973) 20–2; Pollard (1975) 140–2; Hanslik (1977) xxxviii–xxxix; P.L. Heyworth (1989) 69; Parkes (1992) 125 n. 61; T.J. Brown (1993a) 134, 196; Clarkson (1996) 160–3; *ASMMF* VI (1998) 15–18 [no. 381; Franzen]; R. Gameson (1999c) 360; Barker-Benfield (2008) III.1834; Wieland (2009) 138; M.P. Brown (2012) 146 and n. 121; R. Gameson (2012a) 25, 42 n. 117, 51; Gullick (2012) 301 and n. 44, 303 and n. 56

DEC: Pächt—Alexander (1973) no. 1

FACS: Farmer (1968) [complete facsimile]; Nicholson (1913) pl. IV [fol. 44v]; Lowe (1929) pls. I–V [fols. 1r, 24v, 33r, 44v, 42v, 49v]; Lowe (1960) pl. XX [fol. 24v]; Engelbert (1969) pl. after p. 408 [fol. 72r]; Pächt—Alexander (1973) pl. I [fol. 7v (detail)]; *ASMMF* VI (1998) no. 381; Owen-Crocker (2009) fig. 2.1 [fols. 24v–25r]

ED: Wölfflin (1895) [base text ('pro fundamento ponatur') or variants, coll. as O]; Hanslik (1977) [unreliable; this MS. coll. as O; corrections and variants by original scribe coll. as O°; corrections by later scribes coll. as O², O³, O⁴]

ST: Traube (1910); Meyvaert (1963) 95–100; Bischoff (1966–81) II.333, 337; Gretsch (1973); Gretsch (1974); Parkes (1976a) 166–7 n. 18 [repr. Parkes (1991) 126–7 n. 18]; Sims-Williams (1976) 4–5; P. Wormald (1976) 160–1 n. 39; Lapidge (1986b) 62–4 [repr. Lapidge (1996b) 158–60]; Hartzell (1989) 88 n. 116; Hunter Blair (1990) 200–1; Sims-Williams (1990) 201–5, 208–9; Rankin (1996) 325–6 and fig. 18; Hartzell (2006) no. 267 [art. a]

Oxford, Bodleian Library, Hatton 48 (S.C. 4118), fol. 77: see no. **653**

632. Oxford, Bodleian Library, Hatton 76 (S.C. 4125), fols. 1–67

s. xi[1], Worcester?, (prov. ibid.)

Contents: Gregory (Werferth), *Dialogi**, bks. I–II (revised version; incomplete); pseudo-Basil (trans. Ælfric), *Admonitio** (incomplete)

MS: Madan et al. (1895–1953) II/ii.853–4; Hecht (1900–7) I.ix–x; N.R. Ker (1957) no. 328; N.R. Ker (1964) 209; P.L. Heyworth (1989) 205; Franzen (1991) 65–9 *et passim*; Laing (1993) 133; *ASMMF* VI (1998) 19–25 [no. 382; Franzen]; Menzer (2004) 96 n. 4; Scragg (2012a) nos. 892–4

FACS: *ASMMF* VI (1998) no. 382

ED: H.W. Norman (1849) [*Admonitio*]; Hecht (1900–7) I.1–174, right-hand column [Werferth]; Yerkes (1976b) [corrections to Norman and Hecht]

LANG: Hecht (1900-7) II.134–70; Yerkes (1979); Yerkes (1982a) 9, 11, 85 n. 3; O'Brien O'Keeffe (1985) 72; Hofstetter (1987) 146–9

ST: Hecht (1900–7) vol. II; A.F. Cameron (1974) 221; Yerkes (1977b) 130–5; Yerkes (1977–80); McIntyre (1978); P.S. Baker (1980) 25–6; Greenfield—Robinson (1980) 318–19; Langefeld (1986) 200–4; Reinsma (1987) 153–4 [*Admonitio*]; *CPL* (1995) no. 1155a [*Admonitio*]; Godden (1997) 42–4; Waite (2000) 46–8, 354–68

633. Oxford, Bodleian Library, Hatton 76 (S.C. 4125), fols. 68–139

s. xi med., Worcester? (prov. ibid.)

Contents: Enlarged *Herbarius** (Antonius Musa, *De herba uettonica*; pseudo-Apuleius, *Herbarius*; herbs from pseudo-Dioscorides, *Liber medicinae ex herbis femininis* and *Curae herbarum*); *Medicina de quadrupedibus** (*De taxone liber*; treatise on mulberry tree; Sextus Placitus, *Liber medicinae ex animalibus*); two apocryphal letters from Evax to Tiberius; and a Latin version of the lapidary of Damigeron (add. s. xi/xii)

MS: Madan et al. (1895–1953) II/ii.854; Beccaria (1956) no. 85; N.R. Ker (1957) no. 328; N.R. Ker (1964) 209; De Vriend (1972) xviii–xxiii; De Vriend (1984) xx–xxiii; P.L. Heyworth (1989) 205; Franzen (1991) 65–9 *et passim*; Laing (1993) 133; *ASMMF* VI (1998) 19–25 [no. 382; Franzen]; R. Gameson (1999a) no. 726; W. Schipper (2003) 157; Dance (2004) 41; R. Gameson (2005a) 93, 101–4; Scragg (2012a) nos. 895–6

FACS: De Vriend (1972) pl. II [fol. 125v]; De Vriend (1984) pl. II [fol. 74r]; *ASMMF* VI (1998) no. 382; D'Aronco (1998) pl. IX [fols. 74r, 84v, 124v]

ED: J. Evans (1922) 195–213 [base MS for apocryphal letters and lapidary]; De Vriend (1972) 2–61 [*Medicina de quadrupedibus* coll. as B]; De Vriend (1984) [*Herbarius* and *Medicina de quadrupedibus* coll. as B]

LANG: De Vriend (1984) lxviii–lxxiv; Dance (2004) 41

ST: Thorndike—Kibre (1963) col. 844 [lapidary]; De Vriend (1972); Kitson (1978) 13, 58 [lapidary]; Hofstetter (1983); De Vriend (1984) xxxviii–xliv *et passim*; Hollis—Wright (1992) 311–24, 329–40; M.L. Cameron (1993) 59–64; D'Aronco (1998) 22; M. Collins (2000) 233 n. 193; D'Aronco (2011) 238 and n. 37

635. Oxford, Bodleian Library, Hatton 93 (S.C. 4081)

s. ix^1 or ix$^{1/4}$, Mercia (Lichfield?), (prov. Worcester)

Contents: exposition of the Mass ('Primum in ordine')

MS: Schenkl no. 348; Madan et al. (1895–1953) II/ii.832–3; *CLA* II (1935) no. 241; N.R. Ker (1941–9) 28 and n. 1 [repr. N.R. Ker (1985) 131 and n. 1]; N.R. Ker (1957) no. 329; N.R. Ker (1964) 209; Rella (1977) 59 n. 2; De La Mare—Barker-Benfield (1980) 9, 13 [T.J. Brown]; M.P. Brown (1986) 127; Morrish (1988) 513–14, 522, 524; Webster—Backhouse (1991) no. 166 [M.P. Brown]; Dumville (1992a) 101 and n. 28, 125, 135 and n. 289; T.J. Brown (1993a) 216; Dumville (1993g) 151 n. 62; M.P. Brown (1996) 41–2 *et passim*; C.A. Jones (1998c) 673; C.A. Jones (2004) 330; M.P. Brown (2012) 163; R. Gameson (2012a) 52, 82 n. 297

DEC: Pächt—Alexander (1973) no. 7; M.P. Brown (1986) 135 and n. 67

FACS: Pächt—Alexander (1973) pl. I [fol. 2r (detail)]; Webster—Backhouse (1991) 213 [fol. 2r]; M.P. Brown (1996) figs. 14–15 [fols. 2r, 34r]

ST: *DACL* V (1922) 1014–27 [1020–1]; Wilmart (1936b); Gamber (1968–88) I.349; Sauer (1978) 6; Morrish (1988) 513–14; Dumville (1992a) 116 n. 148; *CSLMA* II (1999) 379–80; C.A. Jones (1998c) 669–74

636. Oxford, Bodleian Library, Hatton 93 (S.C. 4081), fol. 42 (with Oxford, Bodleian Library, Hatton 30, offsets from pastedowns)

s. xi^1 or xi med., (prov. Worcester)

Contents: sacramentary (f)

MS: Warren (1888); Madan et al. (1895–1953) II/ii.832; *CLA* II (1935) no. 241 [stated erroneously to be from a collectar]; N.R. Ker (1957) no. 330; Van Dijk (1957-60) V.6; T.A.M. Bishop (1971) 20 n. 1; Dumville (1992a) 67; R. Gameson (2005a) 93; Hartzell (2006) no. 268; Scragg (2012a) no. 897

637–638. Oxford, Bodleian Library, Hatton 113 (S.C. 5210) + 114 (S.C. 5134)

s. xi² (1064×1083), Worcester

Contents: Hatton 113: Letter to Bishop Wulfstan II; prayers; liturgical calendar with necrology; computus tables; treatise On the Seven Ages of the World⁺*; homilies* (most by Wulfstan or attrib., five by Ælfric); Hatton 114: homilies* (most by Ælfric)

MS: Madan et al. (1895–1953) II/ii.967–8, 983; Atkins (1928); N.R. Ker (1939–40) 83 n. 1; Bethurum (1957) 4–5; N.R. Ker (1957) no. 331; N.R. Ker (1960) 23 n. 1; Pope (1967–8) I.70–7; N.R. Ker (1968) 209; T.A.M. Bishop (1971) 20 n. 1; F.C. Robinson (1973) 450; Pollard (1975) 157; Godden (1979) li–liv; Scragg (1979) 253–5; A.G. Watson (1984) I, no. 520; P.L. Heyworth (1989) 45, 205; Franzen (1991) 30–8 *et passim*; Scragg (1992) xxxii; Laing (1993) 134; Clarkson (1996) 204–6; Lendinara (1996) 637; Clemoes (1997) 41–5; *ASMMF* VI (1998) 26–43 [nos. 384a, 384b; Franzen]; R. Gameson (1999a) nos. 727, 728; W. Schipper (2003) 160; Acker (2004) 121 n. 1, 124 n. 9; J. Barrow (2004) 156; Cowen (2004) 397 n. 2; Godden (2004) 369; T.N. Hall (2004a) 94–5; Lionarons (2004b) 74, 75 n. 26, 80–1, 89; Lionarons (2004c) 424; A. Orchard (2004) 71, 72 n. 42, 73 n. 46, 75 n. 53, 77 n. 56, 81 n. 65, 89 n. 79, 90–1 n. 85; N.M. Thompson (2004) 60, 62 n. 83; Wilcox (2004b) 376–7, 382–91, 393, 395; R. Gameson (2005a) 95, 101–4; Foys (2006) 280; Chardonnens (2007b) 537, 553; Swan (2007b) 36, 40; Treharne (2007a) 262–3; Treharne (2007b) 14 n. 2, 17, 19–21, 23, 25, 26 n. 40; Rushforth (2008a) 46–8; Scragg (2009b) 75; Johnson—Rudolf (2010) 1–3; Crick (2012) 182 and n. 36; R. Gameson (2012a) 18, 43 n. 125, 51 n. 170, 70 and n. 241; Gullick (2012) 300 and n. 34; Scragg (2012a) nos. 87, 172, 898–919

FACS: Atkins (1928) pls. XXXVI–XXXVII [fol. iv v, fol. v r]; A.G. Watson (1984) II, pls. 25 (a) [Hatton 113, fol. viii r], 25 (b) [Hatton 114, fol. 201r]; N.R. Ker (1985) pl. 2 [Hatton 113, fol. 78v]; Franzen (1991) pls. 1 [Hatton 113, fol. 60r], 2 [Hatton 113, fol. 68r], 3 [Hatton 114, fol. 51v], 7 [Hatton 113, fol. 4r (detail)]; *ASMMF* VI (1998) nos. 384a, 384b; R. Gameson (2005a) fig. 1 [fol. 4r]; Johnson—Rudolf (2010) figs. 1–2 [Hatton 114, fols. 27v, 113r (both details)]

ED [the order of the following items is that of the manuscripts, listed according to the numbering of individual articles in N.R. Ker (1957) 391–8; only the most recent editions are cited]:

(Hatton 113)

art. 79: Darlington (1928) 189 [letter to Bishop Wulfstan II]

art. 80: Darlington (1928) 190 [prayers]

art. 81: Dewick—Frere (1921) II.589–601 [liturgical calendar]; F. Wormald (1934) 197–209 [liturgical calendar (no. 16)]; Gerchow (1988) 261–2, 338–9 [obits]; Rushforth (2008a) no. 22 [liturgical calendar]

art. 1: Napier (1883/1967) 1–5 [base MS for Wulfstan, Hom. I (*De initio creature*)]

art. 2: Napier (1883/1967) 311–13 [base MS for Wulfstan, Hom. LXII (*De aetatibus mundi*)]

art. 3: Bethurum (1957) 142–56 [Wulfstan, Hom. VI (*Sermones Lupi episcopi*), coll. as E]

arts. 4–5: Bethurum (1957) 157–65 [Wulfstan, Hom. VII (*De fide catholica*), coll. as E]

art. 6: Bethurum (1957) 175–84 [Wulfstan, Hom. VIIIc (*Sermo de baptismate*), coll. as E]

art. 7: Bethurum (1957) 211–20 [Wulfstan, Hom. XI (*De uisione Isaie prophete*), coll. as E]

art. 8: Bethurum (1957) 185–91 [Wulfstan, Hom. IX (*De septiformi spiritu*), coll. as E]

art. 9: Bethurum (1957) 113–18 [Wulfstan, Hom. Ia–b (*De Antichristo*), coll. as E]

art. 10: Bethurum (1957) 194–210 [Wulfstan, Hom. Xb–c (*De cristianitate*), coll. as E]

art. 11: Bethurum (1957) 134–41 [Wulfstan, Hom. V (*Secundum Marcum*), coll. as E]

art. 12: Bethurum (1957) 119–22 [Wulfstan, Hom. II (*Secundum Matheum*), coll. as E]

art. 13: Bethurum (1957) 123–7 [Wulfstan, Hom. III (*Secundum Lucam*), coll. as E]

art. 14: Bethurum (1957) 128–33 [Wulfstan, Hom. IV (*De temporibus Antichristi*), coll. as E]; Lionarons (2004b) 89–93 [base MS for Wulfstan, *De temporibus Antichristi*]

art. 15: Bethurum (1957) 232–5 [Wulfstan, Hom. XIV (*Sermo in .XL.*), coll. as E]

art. 16: Bethurum (1957) 221–4 [Wulfstan, Hom. XII (*De falsis deis*), coll. as E]

arts. 17–21: Bethurum (1957) 225–32 [Wulfstan, Hom. XIII (*Sermo ad populum*), coll. as E], followed by Napier (1883/1967) 119–24 [base MS for Hom. XXIV–XXV] art. 22: Napier (1883/1967) 134–43 [base MS for Wulfstan, Hom. XXIX (*Her is halwendlic lar*)]

art. 23: Napier (1883/1967) 143–52 [base MS for Wulfstan, Hom. XXX (*Be rihtan cristendome*)]; Scragg (1992) 396–403 [base MS for Wulfstan, *Be rihtan cristendome*]

art. 24: Napier (1883/1967) 152–3 [base MS for Wulfstan, Hom. XXXI]

art. 25: Bethurum (1957) 236–8 [Wulfstan, Hom. XV (*Sermo de cena Domini*), coll. as E]

art. 26: Napier (1883/1967) 177 n. 1 followed by Bethurum (1957) 242–5 [Wulfstan, Hom. XVII (*Lectio secundum Lucam*), coll. as E (part)]

art. 27: Bethurum (1957) 267–75 [Wulfstan, Hom. XX (*Sermo Lupi ad Anglos*), coll. as E]; Whitelock (1976) 47–67 [*Sermo Lupi ad Anglos* coll. as E]

art. 28: Bethurum (1957) 276–7 [Wulfstan, Hom. XXI (*Her is gyt rihtlic warnung*), coll. as E]

art. 29: Napier (1883/1967) 169–72 [base MS for Wulfstan, Hom. XXXV (*Be mistlican gelimpan*)]

art. 30: Bethurum (1957) 242–3 [Wulfstan, Hom. XVII (*Lectio secundum Lucam*), coll. as E (part)]

art. 31: Clemoes (1997) 325–34 [Ælfric, CH I, Hom. XIX (*Feria .III. De dominica oratione*), coll. as T]

art. 32: Pope (1967–8) I.415–47 [Ælfric, Suppl. Hom. XI (*Sermo ad populum in octavis Pentecosten*), coll. as T]

art. 33: Godden (1979) 3–11 [Ælfric, CH II, Hom. I (Christmas), coll. as T]

art. 34: Clemoes (1997) 198–205 [Ælfric, CH I, Hom. III (St Stephen), coll. as T]

art. 35: Clemoes (1997) 206–16 [Ælfric, CH I, Hom. IV (Assumption of St John the Evangelist), coll. as T]

art. 36: Clemoes (1997) 217–23 [Ælfric, CH I, Hom. V (Holy Innocents), coll. as T (the last five lines are in Hatton 114)]

(Hatton 114)

art. 82: Napier (1883/1967) 182–90 [Wulfstan, Hom. XL (*In die iudicii*), coll. as F]; Scragg (1992) 53–65, odd pages [Vercelli Hom. II coll. as O]; Ogawa (2010) 183–6 [base MS]

art. 83: Godden (1979) 127–36 [Ælfric, CH II, Hom. XIII (Fifth Sunday in Lent), coll. as T (extract)] art. 84: Pope (1967–8) II.737–46 [Ælfric, Suppl. Hom. XXIII (SS. Alexander, Eventius and Theodolus), coll. as T]

art. 37: Clemoes (1997) 224–31 [Ælfric, CH I, Hom. VI (Circumcision of the Lord), coll. as T]

art. 38: Clemoes (1997) 232–40 [Ælfric, CH I, Hom. VII (Epiphany), coll. as T]

art. 39: Clemoes (1997) 249–57 [Ælfric, CH I, Hom. IX (Purification of B.V.M.), coll. as T]

art. 40: Clemoes (1997) 281–9 [Ælfric, CH I, Hom. XIII (Annunciation of B.V.M.), coll. as T]

art. 41: Clemoes (1997) 258–65 [Ælfric, CH I, Hom. X (Quinquagesima Sunday), coll. as T]

art. 42: Clemoes (1997) 266–74 [Ælfric, CH I, Hom. XI (First Sunday in Lent), coll. as T]

art. 43: Napier (1883/1967) 282–9 [base MS for Wulfstan (?), Hom. LV]

art. 44: Luiselli Fadda (1977) 43–53 [base MS for Hom. III (Second Sunday in Lent)]

art. 45: Pope (1967–8) I.264–80 [Ælfric, Suppl. Hom. IV (Third Sunday in Lent), coll. as T]

art. 46: Clemoes (1997) 275–80 [Ælfric, CH I, Hom. XII (Sunday in Mid–Lent), coll. as T]

art. 47: as Skeat (1881–1900) no. XIII (*De oratione Moysi* in Mid–Lent), not collated

art. 48: Godden (1979) 137–49 [Ælfric, CH II, Hom. XIV (Palm Sunday), coll. as T]

art. 49: Clemoes (1997) 290–8 [Ælfric, CH I, Hom. XIV (Palm Sunday), coll. as T]

art. 50: Clemoes (1997) 299–306 [Ælfric, CH I, Hom. XV (Easter), coll. as T]

art. 51: Clemoes (1997) 307–12, 533–5 [Ælfric, CH I, Hom. XVI (First Sunday after Easter), with Appendix B.2, coll. as T]

art. 52: Tristram (1970) 430–8; Bazire–Cross (1982) 109–13 [base MS for Hom. 8 (*De Letania maiore*)]

art. 53: Bazire–Cross (1982) 121–3 [base MS for Hom. 9 (Rogationtide)]

art. 54: Luiselli Fadda (1977) 105–21 [base MS for Hom. V (*De letania maiore secunda die*)]; Bazire–Cross (1982) 131–5 [base MS for Hom. 10 (Rogationtide)]

art. 55: Luiselli Fadda (1977) 125–37 [base MS for Hom. VI (*Feria .III. de letania maiore*)]; Bazire–Cross (1982) 140–3 [base MS for Hom. 11 (*Feria .III. de Letania maiore*)] art. 56: Napier (1883/1967) 191–205 [Wulfstan, Hom. XLII (*De tempori-bus Antichristi*), coll. as F]

art. 57: Clemoes (1997) 345–53 [Ælfric, CH I, Hom. XXI (Ascension Day), coll. as T]

art. 58: Clemoes (1997) 354–64 [Ælfric, CH I, Hom. XXII (Pentecost), coll. as T]

art. 59: Godden (1979) 72–80 [Ælfric, CH II, Hom. IX (St Gregory), coll. as T]

arts. 60–1: Godden (1979) 169–73 [Ælfric, CH II, Hom. XVII (SS. Philip and James, apostles), coll. as T]

arts. 62–3: Godden (1979) 174–9 [Ælfric, CH II, Hom. XVIII (Discovery of the Holy Cross), coll. as T]

art. 64: Clemoes (1997) 379–87 [Ælfric, CH I, Hom. XXV (St John the Baptist), coll. as T]

arts. 65–6: Clemoes (1997) 388–99 [Ælfric, CH I, Hom. XXVI (SS. Peter and Paul), coll. as T]

art. 67: Clemoes (1997) 400–9 [Ælfric, CH I, Hom. XXVII (St Paul), coll. as T]

art. 68: Clemoes (1997) 429–38 [Ælfric, CH I, Hom. XXX (Assumption of B.V.M.), coll. as T]

art. 69: Clemoes (1997) 439–50 [Ælfric, CH I, Hom. XXXI (St Bartholomew), coll. as T]

art. 70: as Raith (1933/1964) 3.15, not collated

art. 71: as Raith (1933/1964) 3.16, not collated

art. 72: Assmann (1889/1964) 117–37, left-hand column [base MS (= J) for Homily on Nativity of B.V.M. (= Hom. X)]

art. 73: Clemoes (1997) 465–75 [Ælfric, CH I, Hom. XXXIV (Dedication of the Church of St Michael), coll. as T]

arts. 74–5: Clemoes (1997) 486–96 [Ælfric, CH I, Hom. XXXVI (All Saints), coll. as T]

art. 76: Assmann (1889/1964) 49–64 [Ælfric, Homily for a Confessor (= Hom. IV), coll. as J^1]

art. 77: Ebersperger (1999) 235–62 [*Sermo de dedicatione ecclesie* coll. as H]

art. 78: Wenisch (1993) [base MS for homily on the dedication of a church]

arts. 79–81: see above, beginning of Hatton 113

arts. 82–4: see above, beginning of Hatton 114

art. 85: Förster (1942–3) 168

LANG: Wenisch (1993) 5–9; Dance (2004) 35 n. 26, 57 n. 87; A. Orchard (2004) 69 n. 24, 70 n. 28, 86 n. 72

ST: N.R. Ker (1949) 29 [repr. N.R. Ker (1985) 27]; Van Dijk (1957–60)
III.108; A.F. Cameron (1974) 221–3; Gerchow (1988) 258–65; Baker—
Lapidge (1995) xlviii, lii; Scragg (1996) 216; Borst (2001) I.292; N.
Orchard (2002) I.176–7; Treharne (2007a) 262–4; Lapidge (2009)
lxxxvi, xcvi [liturgical calendar]

639. Oxford, Bodleian Library, Hatton 115 (S.C. 5135), fols. 1–147 (with
Lawrence, Kansas, Kenneth Spencer Research Library, Pryce MS C2: 2)

s. xi$^{3/4}$ or xi^2, (prov. Worcester)

Contents: Ælfric, *Hexameron**; homilies* and sermon notes* (most by
Ælfric); Ælfric, Homily on Book of Judges*, *De duodecim abusiuis
saeculi**, (version of Alcuin's) *Interrogationes Sigewulfi in Genesin**;
prognostics*

MS: Madan et al. (1895–1953) II/ii.968–9; N.R. Ker (1957) no. 332;
Colgrave—Hyde (1962); N.R. Ker (1964) 209; Pope (1967–8) I.53–9;
R.L. Collins (1976) 50–1; N.R. Ker (1976a) 124–5; P.R. Robinson
(1978) 231, 235 [repr. P.R. Robinson (1994) 25, 31]; Godden (1979)
lxvi–lxviii; Scragg (1979) 247–8, 262; Franzen (1991) 38–44 *et passim*;
Scragg (1992) xxxi, xxxvi; Laing (1993) 134; Clemoes (1997) 33–6;
Stoneman (1997) 117; *ASMMF* VI (1998) 44–54 [no. 385; Franzen];
R. Gameson (1999a) no. 729; *ASMMF* VII (2000) 31–3 [no. 154;
Doane]; Godden (2004) 366, 368; W. Schipper (2003) 160; R. Gameson
(2005a) 94, 101–4; Chardonnens (2007b) 50–1, 537–41, 553; Clayton
(2007) 32–8; Swan (2007b) 35–7, 39; Scragg (2009b) 76–7; Liuzza
(2011) 19–20; Scragg (2012a) nos. 920–4

FACS: Pope (1967–8) II, pl. opp. p. 728 [fol. 63r]; R.L. Collins (1976) pl. 7
[Kansas leaf]; Franzen (1991) pls. 8–9 [fols. 5r, 15v]; Scragg (1992) pl. V
[fol. 140r]; *ASMMF* VI (1998) no. 385; *ASMMF* VII (2000) no. 154

ED [the following items are listed according to the numbering of individual articles in N.R. Ker (1957) 399–402; only the most recent
editions are cited.]:

art. 1: Crawford (1921) 33–74 [base MS for Ælfric, *Hexameron*]
art. 2: Clemoes (1997) 325–34 [Ælfric, CH I, Hom. XIX (*Feria .III.
De dominica oratione*), coll. as P]
art. 3: Clemoes (1997) 335–44 [Ælfric, CH I, Hom. XX (*Feria .IIII.
De fide catholica*), coll. as P]
art. 4: Pope (1967–8) II.590–609 [Ælfric, Suppl. Hom. XVIII (*Sermo de
die iudicii*), coll. as P]

art. 5: as Skeat (1881–1900) no. XVII (*De auguriis*), MS not collated

art. 6: Pope (1967–8) II.622–35 [base MS for Ælfric, Suppl. Hom. XIX (*De doctrina apostolica*)]

art. 7: Pope (1967–8) II.752 [base MS for Ælfric, Suppl. Hom. XXIV (*Se þe gelome swerað*]; Godden (1979) 180–9 [Ælfric, CH II, Hom. XIX (*Feria .II. in Letania maiore*), coll. as P]

art. 8: Godden (1979) 190–8 [Ælfric, CH II, Hom. XX (*Feria .III. in Letania maiore*), coll. as P]

arts. 9–10: Godden (1979) 199–205 [Ælfric, CH II, Hom. XXI (*Alia uisio*: Bede, *HE* V.xii), coll. as P]

art. 11: as Skeat (1881–1900) II.120–4 (no. XXV, lines 812–62: *Qui sunt oratores, laboratores, bellatores*), not collated

art. 12: Pope (1967–8) I.325 [Ælfric, Suppl. Hom. VI (*Feria .VI. in quarta ebdomada Quadragesimae*), lines 284–91, coll. as P]

art. 13: as Thorpe (1844–6) II.608, not collated

art. 14: as Napier (1888) 154–5 [*De infantibus non baptizandis*], not collated

art. 15: Clayton (2002) 280–2 [base MS for Ælfric, *Letter to Brother Edward*]

art. 16: Napier (1883/1967) 50–60 [Wulfstan, Hom. VII (*De septiformi spiritu*), lines 10–25 (p. 50), and VIII, coll. as R]

art. 17: Pope (1967–8) II.728–32 [base MS for Ælfric, Suppl. Hom. XXII (*Wyrdwriteras us secgað*)]

art. 18: Scragg (2000) [base MS for OE Exhortation]

art. 19: as Napier (1883/1967) 190 [Wulfstan, Hom. XLI (*Verba Ezechiel*), lines 20–3], not collated

art. 20: as Skeat (1881–1900) I.424–30 (no. XIX, lines 155–258: *Acitofel et Absalon*), not collated

art. 21: Godden (1979) 299–303 [Ælfric, CH II, Hom. XXXV (Feast of an Apostle), coll. as P]

art. 22: Godden (1979) 304–9 [Ælfric, CH II, Hom. XXXVI (Feast of Several Apostles), coll. as P]

art. 23: Godden (1979) 310–17 [Ælfric, CH II, Hom. XXXVII (Holy Martyrs), coll. as P]

art. 24: Godden (1979) 318–26 [Ælfric, CH II, Hom. XXXVIII (Feast of a Confessor) in Hatton 115, with Colgrave—Hyde (1962), coll. as P]

art. 25: Pope (1967–8) II.784 [base MS for Ælfric, Suppl. Hom. XXVIII ('Paulus scripsit ad Thesalonicenses'); Godden (1979) 327–34 [Ælfric, CH II, Hom. XXXIX (Holy Virgins), coll. as P]

art. 26: Godden (1979) 335–45 [Ælfric, CH II, Hom. XL (Dedication of a Church), coll. as P] art. 27: Assmann (1889/1964) 1–12 [base MS (= S¹) for Ælfric's Letter to Wulfgeat]; Pope (1967–8) I.463–72 [Ælfric, Suppl. Hom. XIa (*De sancta trinitate*), partly coll. as P]

art. 28: Clemoes (1997) 184 [Ælfric, CH I, Hom. I (*De initio creaturae*), lines 174–6, coll. as P]

art. 29: Pope (1967–8) II.641–60 [base MS for Ælfric, Suppl. Hom. XX (*De populo Israhel*)]

art. 30: Marsden (2008) 190–200 [Ælfric, Homily on Judges, coll. as H]

art. 31: as Morris (1867–8) 299–304 (*De duodecim abusiuis saeculi*), not collated

art. 32: MacLean (1884) [Ælfric's OE version of Alcuin, *Interrogationes Sigewulfi in Genesin*]

art. 33: as Skeat (1881–1900) I.384–412 (no. XVIII: *Sermo excerptus de libro Regum*), not collated

art. 34: Luiselli Fadda (1977) 191–211 [base MS for Hom. X ('On Penitence')]; Scragg (1992) 159–83, odd pages [base MS (= L) for Vercelli Hom. IX]

art. 35: Chardonnens (2007b) 238–9, 261, 301–4, 424–5, 431–2, 452, 485, 490, 496 [base MS for prognostics]

ST: A.F. Cameron (1974) 222; Treharne (1998) 235–6; Liuzza (2001) 227–9 *et passim*; Acker (2004) 129 n. 30; Alcamesi (2010) 193–4, 200–2; Liuzza (2011) 1–77 [prognostics]

640. Oxford, Bodleian Library, Junius 11 (S.C. 5123) (the 'Caedmon Manuscript' or 'Junius Manuscript')

s. x² and xi¹, both parts S England (Canterbury CC?)

Contents: OE poetry: *Genesis*** (A and B); *Exodus***; *Daniel*** (incomplete) [all s. x²]; *Christ and Satan*** [s. xi¹]

MS: Madan et al. (1895–1953) II/ii.965; Gollancz (1927) xiii–cxix; N.R. Ker (1957) no. 334; N.R. Ker (1964) 38; Lucas (1980); R.M. Thomson (1982b) 16–18; Backhouse et al. (1984b) no. 154; Raw (1984) [repr. M.P. Richards (1994) 251–75]; Parkes (1992) 151 nn. 95, 96; Lockett (2002); A. Orchard (2004) 69 n. 26; Roberts (2005) 68–71 [no. 13]; Biggs (2007a) 9; C. Bishop (2007b) 90–4; Karkov (2007b) 57; Withers (2007) 60, 131, 314 n. 32; Treharne (2009b) 106–8; R. Gameson (2012a) 59 n. 194; Gullick (2012) 294 n. 3; Scragg (2012a) nos. 925–929.5; and see also the studies listed under DEC and ED, below.

DEC: F. Wormald (1945) 120, 134 [repr. F. Wormald (1984) 59, 73]; F. Wormald (1952) 76 [no. 50] *et passim*; F. Wormald (1957b) 31 [repr. F. Wormald (1984) 146]; Dodwell (1971b) 94, 186; Ohlgren (1972a); Ohlgren (1972b); Ohlgren (1972c); Gatch (1975); G. Henderson (1975); Raw (1976); E. Temple (1976) no. 58; Brownrigg (1978) 255, 260 n. 3; Broderick (1983); F. Wormald (1984) 119, 132, 146; Ohlgren (1986) no. 163; Raw (1990) 234; Ohlgren (1992) 10 and nn., 88–99; R. Gameson (1995b) 9, 10 n. 22, 17, 37–8, 39, 43–5, 69, 110, 112, 140–1, 181–2, 194, 205, 224 *et passim*; Finnegan (1998); Karkov (2001b); Lockett (2002); Karkov (2004) 153; Biggs (2007a) 9; C. Bishop (2007b) 90–4; Karkov (2007b) 58–71; Withers (2007) 35, 37, 40, 60, 132, 204, 214, 218, 318 n. 66; Karkov (2009) 246–9; Withers (2011) 252–4, 255–6, 257, 264; R. Gameson (2012c) 284 and n. 120, 287

FACS: Gollancz (1927) [complete facsimile]; Muir (2004) [complete digitized facsimile on CD–ROM]; F. Wormald (1952) pl. 18 [p. 6 (detail)]; Pächt—Alexander (1973) pl. IV [pp. 11, 44, 78 (details)]; E. Temple (1976) ills. 189–96 [pp. 61, 11, 41, 57, 58, 74 (detail), 84, 87]; Backhouse et al. (1984b) 151 [p. 66]; D.M. Wilson (1984) pls. 226–8 [pp. 41, 68, 84]; F. Wormald (1984) pls. 60, 122, 175 [pp. 22, 6, 68 (details)]; Ohlgren (1992) pls. 16.1–51 [pp. 1–3, 6, 7, 9–13, 16, 17, 20, 24, 28, 31, 34, 36, 44–7, 53, 54, 56–63, 66, 68, 70, 73, 74, 76–8, 81, 82, 84, 87, 88, 96]; Lockett (2002) pls. I (a)–(c), II(c), III (a)–(b) [pp. 21, 67, 71, 8 (details), 41, 61]; Roberts (2005) pl. 13 [p. 14], p. 71 [p. 61]; M.P. Brown (2007a) pl. 100 [p. 11]; Karkov (2007b) 72 [p. 3], 73–5 [pp. 9–11], 76 [p. 16], 77 [p. 20], 78 [p. 24], 79 [p. 28], 80 [p. 31], 81 [p. 41], 82–4 [pp. 45–7]; Withers (2007) 38 [p. 41], 205 [p. 51], 206 [p. 53], 207 [p. 54], 208 [p. 56], 209 [p. 57], 210 [p. 58], 211 [p. 59], 212 [p. 62], 213 [p. 63]; Owen-Crocker (2009) figs. 7.33–4 [pp. 16, 47]

ED [note that early editions and partial editions are not recorded]: **complete manuscript**: Wülker (1881–98) vol. II; Krapp (1931); Muir (2004); **Genesis A**: Holthausen (1914); Doane (1978); **Genesis B**: Klaeber (1931); Timmer (1954); Doane (1991); Behagel—Taeger (1996); **Exodus**: Blackburn (1907); Irving (1953/1970); Lucas (1977/1994); Tolkien (1981); **Daniel**: Blackburn (1907); Farrell (1974); **Christ and Satan**: Clubb (1925); Finnegan (1977)

LANG: Menner (1951); C. Bishop (2007b) 91

ST: Gollancz (1927) xiii–cxix; Caie (1979); Lucas (1979b); Greenfield—Robinson (1980) 21–2, 210–11, 222–5, 228–33; Sauer (1980b); J.R. Hall (1986); Stévanovitch (1992); Conde–Silvestre (2006) 49; C. Bishop

(2007b) 77, 92; Withers (2007) 58, 60; Ziolkowski (2007) 207 and nn.; Scragg (2012b) 555–6

640. 1. Oxford, Bodleian Library, Junius 11 (S.C. 5123), offset from pastedown

s. xi

Contents: gospel harmony (f)

MS: Madan et al. (1895–1953) II/ii.965; N.R. Ker (1957) no. 334; Rumble (2006b) 7 n. 36

641. Oxford, Bodleian Library, Junius 27 (S.C. 5139)

s. x^1 (920s?) Winchester?, (prov. Continent by s. xii^2?)

Contents: liturgical calendar (partly metrical); Psalterium Romanum° (incomplete)

MS: Madan et al. (1895–1953) II/ii.971–2; Lindelöf (1901c); Wildhagen (1913) 444–6; Van Dijk (1952) no. 42; N.R. Ker (1957) no. 335; Van Dijk (1957–60) II.5b; N.R. Ker (1964) 201; T.A.M. Bishop (1964–8b) 247; Parkes (1976) 157–64 [repr. Parkes (1991) 154–61]; Parkes (1983) 130, 134–6 [repr. Parkes (1991) 172, 179–81]; Lapidge (1984) 344–5 [repr. Lapidge (1993a) 361–2]; Dumville (1987) 171 and n. 133; Dumville (1992a) 1–38, 50, 65, 140; Dumville (1992b) 72–8, 92–9; Conner (1993) 55 *et passim*; Dumville (1994a) 143 and n. 51; Pfaff (1995a) 62 [Pulsiano]; Pulsiano (2001) xxi and nn.; Rushforth (2008a) 22–3 [no. 5]; R. Gameson (2012a) 39 and n. 96, 77 n. 273; D. Ganz (2012) 189 and n. 11

DEC: F. Wormald (1945) 117–18, 120–1, 122 [repr. F. Wormald (1984) 55–7, 58, 60–1]; Alexander (1970a) 70 n. 1, 72, 129, 161, 193; F. Wormald (1971b) 305, 307, 310 [repr. F. Wormald (1984) 76, 78, 80]; Pächt—Alexander (1973) no. 21; E. Temple (1976) no. 7; Alexander (1978b); Ohlgren (1986) no. 85; Raw (1990) 23, 234; R. Gameson (1992a) 190–1; R. Gameson (1995b) 200, 219, 220 n. 164, 228–30, 233, 254; Farr (2011b) 222; R. Gameson (2012c) 250 and nn. 4 and 6

FACS: *NPS* II, pl. 62 [fols. 52v, 118r, 105r (all details) and 135v]; E. Temple (1976) pl. 1 [fol. 135v], ills. 20–4, 26 [fols. 20r, 27v, 136r, 148v, 71v, 188r (all details)]; D.M. Wilson (1984) pls. 212–15 [fols. 135v, 118r, 148v]; F. Wormald (1984) ills. 56, 57, 81, 82, 83 [fols. 20r, 121v, 118r, 115v, 155v (details)]; Parkes (1991) pl. 27 [fol. 77v]

ED: Brenner (1908) [psalms and OE gloss]; McGurk (1986a) 90–111 [metrical entries in liturgical calendar, coll. as Jun.]; Gerchow (1988) 330 [obits in calendar]; Dumville (1992a) 3–14 [liturgical calendar]; Pulsiano (2001a) [Pss. I–L and OE gloss, coll. as B]; Rushforth (2008a) no. 5 [liturgical calendar]

LANG: Brenner (1908) xv–xxxiii; Sisam—Sisam (1959) 71 n. 2; Gretsch (2000)

ST: Lindelöf (1904); E. Bishop (1918) 254; Heinzel (1926); Hennig (1953); Saxl—Meier (1953) I.220; Sisam—Sisam (1959) 48, 55–6, 63–6; D.H. Wright (1967) 46–8, 77, 84–5 [A. Campbell]; Bierbaumer (1977a); Berghaus (1979); McGurk (1986a); Gerchow (1988) 220; Dumville (1992a) 1–38, 50, 65; Dumville (1992b) 104–6; Wiesenecker (1994); Pulsiano (1996); Gretsch (2000); Gretsch (2001); C. Bishop (2007b) 118

642. Oxford, Bodleian Library, Junius 85 + 86 (S.C. 5196–7)

s. xi med., SE England

Contents: homilies*; charms(*); *Visio S. Pauli**

MS: Madan et al. (1895–1953) II/ii.982–3; N.R. Ker (1957) no. 336; A.F. Cameron (1974) 223; Healey (1978) 3–18; P.R. Robinson (1978) 238 [repr. P.R. Robinson (1994) 34–5]; Godden (1979) lix–lxi; Scragg (1979) 235–6; Scragg (1992) xxvi; Chadbon (1993); Ogawa (1994); Scragg (1996) 211; Biggs (2007a) 80, 82 [C.D. Wright]; Pulsiano (2007) 124; Toswell (2007) 212; *ASMMF* XVII (2008) 113–28 [no. 390; Wilcox]; Barker-Benfield (2008) I.404; R. Gameson (2012a) 18, 43 n. 120; Scragg (2012a) nos. 930–930b

DEC: Pächt—Alexander (1973) no. 47

FACS: *ASMMF* XVII (2008) no. 390

ED [the order of the following items is that of the manuscripts, listed according to Ker's numbering of individual articles (see N.R. Ker (1957) pp. 410–11); only the most recent editions are cited]:

art. 1: Szarmach (1977a) [base MS]; Scragg (1992) 213, lines 271–5 [Vercelli Hom. X (part) coll. as C]

art. 2: Luiselli Fadda (1977) 163–73 [base MS for Hom. VIII ('Dialogue of the Soul and Body')]

art. 3: Storms (1948) [base MS for charms, nos. 45, 49, 41]

art. 4: Healey (1978) 62–73 [base MS for OE version of *Visio S. Pauli*]

art. 5: Godden (1979) 60–1, 63–6 [Ælfric, CH II, Hom. VII (First Sunday in Lent), coll. as f^p] art. 6: Luiselli Fadda (1977) 7–31 [base MS for Hom. I (for Lent)]

art. 7: as Morris (1880) no. IV, not collated [see Cameron (1973) no. B.3.2.14]

art. 8: Szarmach (1981a) 57–62 [Vercelli Hom. XVIII coll. as C]; Scragg (1992) 291–308 [Vercelli Hom. XVIII coll. as C]

ST: Willard (1935a); Willard (1935b); Willard (1949b); Healey (1978); C.D. Wright (1993) 108, 215–18, 244–5, 259, 264–5; Wilcox (2009)

643. Oxford, Bodleian Library, Junius 86 (S.C. 5197), endleaf

prob. s. x^1 or xi med. [leaf lost by 1937]

Contents: Boethius (Alfred), *De consolatione Philosophiae** (f)

MS: Napier (1887); Madan et al. (1895–1953) II/ii.983; Sedgefield (1899) xv–xvi; N.R. Ker (1957) no. 337; Kiernan (2005); Biggs (2007a) 80, 82 [C.D. Wright]; *ASMMF* XVII (2008) 114–15 [no. 390; Wilcox]; Wilcox (2008) 434 and nn. 55, 56; Godden—Irvine (2009) I.34–41; D. Ganz (2012) 188 n. 4

FACS: *ASMMF* XVII (2008) no. 390

644. Oxford, Bodleian Library, Junius 121 (S.C. 5232)

s. xi$^{3/4}$ and additions s. xi^2 and xi ex., Worcester

Contents: (a version of Wulfstan's 'Handbook'): excerpts from canons and penitentials; Council of Winchester (1070); penitential articles issued after the Battle of Hastings; Council of Winchester (1076); Wulfstan, *Institutes of Polity**, 'Canons of Edgar'*, (trans.) *Institutio canonicorum* I.145*; *De ecclesiasticis gradibus**; 'Benedictine Office'* including excerpts from Hrabanus Maurus, *De clericorum institutione* and OE verse paraphrases of *Pater noster***, *Gloria***, Apostles' Creed** and passages from the Psalms; Handbook for a confessor*; penitential* (*Confessionale pseudo-Egberti*); penitential* (*Poenitentiale pseudo-Egberti*); Ælfric, Pastoral Letters I* and III*; homilies* (most by Wulfstan and Ælfric) [companion vol. to nos. **637–638**]

MS: Assmann (1889/1964) xii [Clemoes]; Madan et al. (1895–1953) II/ii.989–90; Liebermann (1903–16) I.xlii; Fehr (1914) xx–xxii; Raith (1933) xiii–xvii; Spindler (1934) 1–2; Dobbie (1942) lxxiv–lxxviii; Bethurum (1957) 5; N.R. Ker (1957) no. 338; Ure (1957) 3–9; Jost (1959) 12–15; Fowler (1965) 2; Pope (1967–8) I.70–7; Fowler (1972) xiii–xiv; McIntyre (1978); Godden (1979) li–liv; P.L. Heyworth (1989)

45; Franzen (1991) 54–8 *et passim*; Clemoes (1997) 41–5; *ASMMF* VI
(1998) 55–67 [no. 391; Franzen]; W. Schipper (2003) 160; Godden
(2004) 369; J. Hill (2004) 321; C.A. Jones (2004) 332 n. 33, 333 n. 37,
352; Meaney (2004) 472 n. 34, 477, 483; A. Orchard (2004) 71; Wilcox
(2004b) 387 n. 30; Ambrose (2005) 114–15; R. Gameson (2005a) 95,
101–4; Scragg (2005) 197–201; Hartzell (2006) no. 269; Biggs (2007a)
31 [Biggs, Morey]; Frantzen (2007) 40–1, 42 n. 10, 53–6, 61–7; M.
Heyworth (2007) 218; Karkov (2007b) 60; Treharne (2007b) 17, 19, 21,
23, 27; Graham (2009) 191; Scragg (2009b) 67, 81; Crick (2012) 184
n. 46; R. Gameson (2012a) 51 n. 170; R. Gameson (2012b) 99 n. 21;
A. Orchard (2012) 697 [no. 15]; Raw (2012) 460; Scragg (2012a)
nos. 87, 172, 898, 902, 908, 916, 931–7

FACS: Fowler (1972) pl. facing p. lxii [fol. 28r (detail)]; Robinson–
Stanley (1991) no. 28.1–21 [fols. 43v–53v]; *ASMMF* VI (1998) no. 391

ED [entries are listed in manuscript order, and using the numbering of
N.R. Ker (1957) 412-16; only the most recent editions are cited]:

(fol. 1r): Hartzell (2006) no. 269a

art. 36: see N.R. Ker (1957) 416

art. 37: Whitelock et al. (1981a) II.575–6 [canons of Council of
Winchester (1070) coll. as C]

art. 38: Whitelock et al. (1981a) II.583–4 [penitential articles issued after
the Battle of Hastings coll. as C]

art. 39: Whitelock et al. (1981a) II.619–20 [base MS for canons of Council
of Winchester (1076)]

arts. 1–4, 6–7, 13–14: Jost (1959) 39–59, 62–116, 118–30, 132–8, 140–64
(even pages) [base MS (= X) for Wulfstan, *II Institutes of Polity*, chs.
i–xxii]

art. 5: Fowler (1972) 3–19, odd pages [base MS (= X) for Wulfstan,
Canons of Edgar]

art. 8: Jost (1959) 217–22 [base MS (= X) for Wulfstan, *II Institutes of
Polity*, ch. xxiii (*Be gehadedum mannum*)]; Whitelock et al. (1981a)
I.423–7 [base MS]

arts. 9–10: Jost (1959) 223–47 [base MS (= X) for Wulfstan, *II Institutes
of Polity*, ch. xxiv (*De ecclesiasticis gradibus*)]

art. 11: Dobbie (1942) 74–86 [OE verse]; Ure (1957) 81–102 [base MS for
OE 'Benedictine Office']

art. 12: Bethurum (1957) 192–3 [base MS for Wulfstan, Hom. Xa (*De
regula canonicorum*)]; Jost (1959) 248–55 [base MS (= X) for Wulfstan,
II Institutes of Polity, ch. xxxiv (*De regula canonicorum*)]

art. 15: Bethurum (1957) 251–4 [Wulfstan, Hom. XIX (*Be godcundre warnunge*), coll. as G]

art. 16: Spindler (1934) 170–94 [base MS (= X) for *Confessionale pseudo–Egberti*]

art. 17: Luiselli Fadda (1977) 35–9 [base MS for Hom. II (for Lent)]

art. 18: Napier (1883/1967) 125–7 [base MS for Wulfstan, Hom. XXVI (*To eallum folce*)]

arts. 19–21 [and art. 2 (from. fol. 23/14)]: Fowler (1965) 19–20, 26–8 [*Be dædbetan* coll. as X]

art. 22: Spindler (1934) 172 (*n–x*) [part of *Confessionale pseudo-Egberti*]

art. 23: Raith (1933/1964) 1–53 [*Poenitentiale pseudo-Egberti* coll. as X]

art. 24: Spindler (1934) 174 [part of *Confessionale pseudo-Egberti*]

art. 25: Raith (1933/1964) 25–6 [part of *Poenitentiale pseudo-Egberti* repeated from art. 23]

art. 26: Fehr (1914/1966) 1–32 [Ælfric, Pastoral Letter I*, coll. as X]; Whitelock et al. (1981a) I.196–226 [Ælfric, Pastoral Letter I*, coll. as X]

art. 27: Fehr (1914/1966) 146–220 [base MS (one of four) for Ælfric, Pastoral Letter III]

art. 28: Assmann (1889/1964) 4–12 [Hom. I (Ælfric's Letter to Wulfgeat) coll. as J]

art. 29: Pope (1967–8) I.378–89 [Ælfric, Suppl. Hom. IX (First Sunday after Ascension Day), coll. as T]

art. 30: Bethurum (1957) 116–18 [Wulfstan, Hom. Ib (*De Antichristo*), coll. as G]

art. 31: Clemoes (1997) 520–3 [Ælfric, CH I, Hom. XXXIX (First Sunday in Advent), coll. as T]

art. 32: Clemoes (1997) 524–30 [Ælfric, CH I, Hom. XL (Second Sunday in Advent), coll. as T]

art. 33: Luiselli Fadda (1972) 998–1010 [base MS for Homily on the Harrowing of Hell]

art. 34: Clemoes (1997) 173–7 [Ælfric, *Praefatio* to CH I, coll. as T] (fol. 155v) Hartzell (2006) no. 269b; see Anselm Hughes (1958–60) no. 2292

art. 35: Godden (1979) 255–9 [Ælfric, CH II, Hom. XXIX (Assumption of B.V.M.), coll. as T]

arts. 36–9: see above (beginning of Junius 121)

LANG: G.K. Anderson (1941)

ST: Bethurum (1942); Sauer (1978) 59–62; Frantzen (1983a) 40–4; Frantzen (1983b) 133–9; Frantzen (1985) 39–40; Houghton (1994); Sauer (2000); Scragg (2012b) 569

645. 5. Oxford, Bodleian Library, Lat. bib. b. 1 (S.C. 30550), fols. 73–4

s. xi[1]

Contents: gospels (or Bible?) (f)

MS: Madan et al. (1895–1953) V.832; T.A.M. Bishop (1967a) 39; Dumville (1993g) 139, 140 n. 119

DEC: R. Gameson (2012c) 283 and n. 118

Oxford, Bodleian Library, Lat. bib. b. 2 (P) (S.C. 2202*): see no. **448**

646. Oxford, Bodleian Library, Lat. bib. c. 8 (P) (S.C. 2570) (with Salisbury, Cathedral Library, 117, fols. 163–4, and Tokyo, Collection of Professor Toshiyuki Takamiya, MS 21)

s. ix[1], Mercia or S England (prov. Salisbury)

Contents: Bible (f; text from Numeri, Deuteronomium)

MS: E.M. Thompson (1880) 23; Schenkl no. 3709; Madan et al. (1895–1953) II/i.430–1; *CLA* II (1935) no. 259; D.H. Wright (1964) 117 [Bischoff]; Morrish (1982) 86–125; Morrish (1988) 527, 538; M.P. Brown (1989b) 41; Sims-Williams (1990) 274–5 and n. 11; Webber (1992) 77, 79 and n. 139; Marsden (1995) 41, 43, 236, 240–9; M.P. Brown (2012) 164 n. 213; Marsden (2012) 415 and n. 36

FACS: Marsden (1995) pls. III–IV [Oxford leaf, verso; Salisbury 117, fol. 164r]

Oxford, Bodleian Library, Lat. bib. d. 1 (P) (S.C. 31089) [formerly listed as no. 647]: see no. **770**

647. 5. Oxford, Bodleian Library, Lat. bib. d. 10

s. xi ex., prob. Normandy, (prov. Exeter)

Contents: gospels (Luke and John only)

MS: De La Mare (1983); A.G. Watson (1987a) 36 and n. 2; Gullick (1990) 74–5; Conner (1993) 10–11; R. Gameson (1996b) 158 and n. 113; R. Gameson (1999a) no. 734; Rushforth (2004–) 120–1 and n. 42

FACS: De La Mare (1983) pls. on pp. 82–4 [fols. 34r, 50r, 34v]

648. Oxford, Bodleian Library, Lat. class. c. 2, fol. 18 (with Cambridge, Corpus Christi College EP-0-6 (ptd bk.), binding fragment; Deene Park Library, Kettering, Northamptonshire, L. 2. 21; London, BL, Sloane 1044, fol. 6; and Oxford, All Souls College 330, nos. 54 and 55)

s. ix$^{2/3}$, W France, prov. England by s. x ex

Contents: Vergil, *Aeneid* (f), *Georgica* (f)

MS: Munk Olsen (1982—) II.752 [no. B.162]; L.D. Reynolds (1983) xxxii
n. 128; Baswell (1995) 286–7; R. Gameson (1996a) 209 and n. 45; A.G.
Watson (1997) 229; Bischoff (1998—) II, no. 3763; Gneuss (2003b)
301–2; D. Ganz (2004) 501; R. Gameson (2012d) 351 and n. 26

649. Oxford, Bodleian Library, Lat. liturg. d. 3 (S.C. 31378), fols. 4-5

s. xi^1, Canterbury CC

Contents: missal (f)

MS: Madan et al. (1895–1953) VI.45 (+ corrigenda); Van Dijk (1957–60)
V.114; *Le Graduel Romain* (1957) II.90; Rankin (2004); Rushforth
(2007) 26; R. Gameson (2012a) 40 n. 105; Rankin (2012) 501 and n. 90

FACS: Rankin (2004) figs. 1–4 [fols. 5v, 4r, 4v, 5r]; Rushforth (2007) 26
[fol. 4r]; R. Gameson (2012) pl. 7b.4 [fol. 4r]

ED: Rankin (2004) 244–52

650. Oxford, Bodleian Library, Lat. liturg. d. 16, fol. 9

s. xi^2, Canterbury StA?

Contents: sacramentary (f)

MS: Madan et al. (1895–1953) II/i.266 [no. 2222 (a leaf removed from
Bodley 391)]; Van Dijk (1957–60) V.265; R. Gameson (1999a) no. 735

Oxford, Bodleian Library, Lat. liturg. e. 38, fols. 7–8, 13–14: see no. **524**

**651. Oxford, Bodleian Library, Lat. liturg. f. 5 (S.C. 29744)
('St Margaret's Gospels')**

s. xi$^{2/4}$ or xi$^{3/4}$, England or Scotland?, prov. Scotland s. xi^2, prov. Durham
s. xi ex.

Contents: gospel lectionary (selection for private devotion); hexameter
poem (s. xi ex. or xi/xii) [*BCLL* 1023]

MS: Madan et al. (1895–1953) V.683–4; Craster (1925); McRoberts (1953)
no. 5; Van Dijk (1957–60) I.70b; N.R. Ker (1964) 74; Backhouse et al.
(1984b) no. 69; A.G. Watson (1984) I, no. 549; A.G. Watson (1987a)
31; Dumville (1991–5) 50–1; R. Gameson (1997); Lenker (1997) 462–3;
Hartzell (2006) no. 277; Rushforth (2007) 12, 25, 27, 33, 51–2, 55, 67,
72–3, 75, 85–6, 99, 103–5; Teviotdale (2010) 87–99; R. Gameson (2012a)
22 and n. 34, 29 n. 65, 45, 70 n. 240, 80 n. 296, 90

DEC: Pächt—Alexander (1973) no. 44; E. Temple (1976) no. 91; Dodwell (1982) 52–3; F. Wormald (1984) 120; Ohlgren (1986) no. 196; R. Gameson (1995b) 91, 98, 100, 155 n. 18, 194–5, 214, 217–18, 252; Karkov (2007c) 57; Rushforth (2007) 28, 39, 41, 43–4, 64, 68, 70; R. Gameson (2012c) 271 and n. 62, 278 and n. 94; McGurk (2012) 440 and n. 21

FACS: Forbes-Leith (1896) [complete facsimile]; Pächt—Alexander (1973) pl. V [fol. 13v]; E. Temple (1976) ills. 277–80 [fols. 3v, 13r, 21r, 30v]; M.P. Brown (2007a) pl. 128 [fol. 21v]; Rushforth (2007) 8–9 [fols. 30v–31r], 12 [fol. 2r], 28 [fol. 21v], 33 [fol. 32v], 36–7 [fols. 13v–14r], 38 [fol. 3v], 40 [fol. 30v], 65 [fol. 13v], 68–9 [fols. 21v–22r], 70–1 [fols. 3v–4r], 73 [fol. 6v]; R. Gameson (2012) pl. 10.10 [fols. 13v–14r]

ED: R. Gameson (1997) 165–6 [the hexameter poem *BCLL* 1023]; Howlett (1999) 117–18 [the hexameter poem *BCLL* 1023]

ST: Dowden (1893–4); Piper (1978) 286 n. 67; *BCLL* (1985) nos. 1023, 1033 [bibliography]; SK Suppl. 2250a; Keynes (2006) R 420–7 [bibliography]

Oxford, Bodleian Library, Lat. misc. a. 3, fol. 49: see no. **436**

651. 5. Oxford, Bodleian Library, Lat. theol. b. 2 (S.C. 30588) fol. 2

s. xi ex. or xi/xii, prob. Canterbury StA

Contents: Augustine, *De Trinitate* [*CPL* 329] (f)

MS: Madan et al. (1895–1953) V.842 [from S.C. 30479 (note by E.W.B. Nicholson)]; N.R. Ker (1960) 29 and n. 4; Barker-Benfield (2008) I.lx, 448, 504, II.924, 926

Oxford, Bodleian Library, Lat. theol. c. 3 [S.C. 31382], fols. 1, 1* and 2: see no. **3**

652. Oxford, Bodleian Library, Lat. theol. c. 4 (S.C. 1926*)

s. x^2, Worcester?

Contents: Sedulius, *Carmen paschale* [*CPL* 1447], with glosses from Remigius (f)

MS: Madan et al. (1895–1953) II/i.121; N.R. Ker (1957) no. 340; T.A.M. Bishop (1971) 19; Rella (1977) 118–19, 162; Rella (1980) 110; Lapidge (1982a) 114 and n. 82, 116 [repr. Lapidge (1996b) 479 and n. 82, 482–3]; Wieland (1985) 155 n. 9, 164–5, 167, 171; Dumville (1993g) 54 and n. 239, 76 n. 349; A. Orchard (1994) 164; Springer (1995) 164;

R. Gameson (1996a) 243; Lapidge (2006) 331; Petruccione (2008) 234
n. 15; Scragg (2012a) no. 938

FACS: T.A.M. Bishop (1971) pl. XIX [fol. 3v]

ST: R. McKitterick (2012) 329

652. 3. Oxford, Bodleian Library, Lat. theol. c. 10, fols. 100–101a

s. xi/xii or xii in.

Contents: Augustine, *Tractatus in Euangelium Ioannis* [*CPL* 278] (f)

MS: R. Gameson (1999a) no. 742

Oxford, Bodleian Library, Lat. theol. d. 24 (S.C. 30591), fols. 1 and 2:
see no. **857**

653. Oxford, Bodleian Library, Lat. theol. d. 33 (with Oxford, Bodleian Library, Hatton 48, fol. 77, and Oxford, St John's College, Ss. 7. 2 (pastedown))

s. xi ex., Worcester, (prov. ibid.).

Contents: Augustine, *Enchiridion* [*CPL* 295] (f)

MS: *CLA* II (1935) no. 240; N.R. Ker (1960) 8; Farmer (1968) 21; T.A.M.
Bishop (1971) 20; Römer (1972b) 2, 252, 266; Rella (1977) 85, 160;
ASMMF VI (1998) 15–18 [no. 381; Franzen]; R. Gameson (1999a)
no. 745; R. Gameson (2005a) 96, 101–4; Lapidge (2006) 289

DEC: Pächt—Alexander (1973) no. 56

FACS: Morison (1972) pl. 120 on p. 195 [fol. 3v (detail)]; Pächt—
Alexander (1973) pl. VII [fol. 1r (detail)]; *ASMMF* VI (1998) no. 381
[Hatton 48, fol. 77]

653. 2. Oxford, Bodleian Library, Lat. theol. d. 34

s. xi/xii, Durham?

Contents: Tertullian, *Apologeticum* [*CPL* 3]; pseudo-Ambrose, *Libellus
de dignitate sacerdotali* [*CPL* 171a]; excerpts from Ambrose, *Expositio
de Psalmo CXVIII* [*CPL* 141]

MS: R. Gameson (1999a) no. 746; Lapidge (2006) 280, 334, 339

654. Oxford, Bodleian Library, Laud gr. 35 (S.C. 1119)

s. vi or vii, Italy (prob. Sardinia), prov. Northumbria s. viii, prov. S
Germany (Abbey of Hornbach) s. viii ex.

Contents: Actus Apostolorum (in Latin and Greek); cypher alphabet (s. ix?); creed, pagan oracle, Invocations to the Virgin, Edict of Flavius Pancratius of Sardinia (all in Greek)

MS: Coxe (1858–85/1973) 518; J. Wordsworth et al. (1889–1954) III/i.ix; Madan et al. (1895–1953) II/i.48; C. Plummer (1896) I.liv and n. 4; Craster (1917–19); Ropes (1923); Ropes (1926) lxxxiv–lxxxviii; Lowe (1928); A.C. Clark (1933) 234–46; *CLA* II (1935) no. 251; Laistner (1935) 257; Laistner (1939) xxxix–xl; Bischoff—Hofmann (1952) 90–1; Bischoff (1966–81) II.323; R.W. Hunt et al. (1966) no. 34; Mango (1973) 688–90; Rella (1977) 13, 31, 37, 40; Knaus (1979) 978; Barbour (1981) 96 [no. 22]; Lapidge (1986b) 51 [repr. Lapidge (1996b) 147]; Berschin (1988) 306 n. 47; Cavallo (1988) 476–8; P.L. Heyworth (1989) 55, 70, 141, 210, 226, 426; Krämer (1989–90) I.368; Gibson (1993b) 22–3 [no. 2]; Bischoff—Lapidge (1994) 170 and nn. 155–6, 241 n. 161; Dumville (1995b) 106; Lapidge (1996c) 411 and n. 11, 443; Radiciotti (1996) 124; Bischoff (1998—) II, no. 3812a; Emms (2006) 20; Lapidge (2006) 26 n. 111, 28 n. 119, 149; Marsden (2012) 415 and n. 40

FACS: Lowe (1928) [repr. Lowe (1972)] pls. 27–30 [fols. 260r, 1r (detail), 2v (detail), 11r (detail), 224v (detail), 226v]; N. Wilson (1972–3) pls. 4, 10 [fols. 219r, 227r]; Barbour (1981) pl. 22 [fol. 70v]

ED: Hearne (1715) [base MS for Greek and Latin texts of Actus Apostolorum]; Tischendorf (1870) 1–226 [base MS for Greek and Latin texts of Actus Apostolorum]; Westcott—Hort (1881) II.92–101 [Greek text of Actus Apostolorum coll. as E_2]; Nestle et al. (1993) [Greek text of Actus Apostolorum coll. as E]

ST: Brock (1995) 53; Harmsen (2000) 234–5, 307 and n. 4; Love (2012) 623 and n. 86

655. Oxford, Bodleian Library, Laud lat. 81 (S.C. 768)

s. xi², N England? Glastonbury?

Contents: Psalterium Gallicanum; canticles; litany; prayers

MS: Coxe (1858–85/1973) 36; Frere (1894–1932) no. 455; Madan et al. (1895–1953) II/i.33; Van Dijk (1957–60) II.10; Sisam—Sisam (1959) 75 n. 2; Cowdrey (1981) 55; Lapidge (1991a) 78–9; Toswell (1995–6) 13–15; R. Gameson (1999a) no. 748; Pulsiano (2001a) xxix; R. Gameson (2012a) 22 and nn. 30, 35, 24 and n. 41; Toswell (2012) 471

DEC: Pächt—Alexander (1973) no. 61; R. Gameson (1991) 71; R. Gameson (1995a) 127 and n. 120

FACS: R. Gameson (1991) fig. 5 [fol. 3r]; Rushforth (2007) 76 [fols. 46r–47v]

ED: Lapidge (1991a) 240–3 [litany]; Pulsiano (2001a) [Pss. I–L coll. as σ]

656. Oxford, Bodleian Library, Laud misc. 482 (S.C. 1054)

s. xi med. or xi², Worcester, (prov. ibid.)

Contents: penitential* (*Poenitentiale pseudo-Egberti*); Canons I–XI of the Synod of Rome (721)*; *Old English Canons of Theodore*; note on Ember Days*; penitential* ('Confessionale pseudo-Egberti'); Handbook for a confessor*; manual offices for the sick and dying(*) (including litany)

MS: Coxe (1858–85/1973) 348–9; Madan et al. (1895–1953) I.45 [E.W.B. Nicholson]; Raith (1933/1964) xvii–xviii; Spindler (1934) 1–4; N.R. Ker (1957) no. 343; Van Dijk (1957–60) III.59; N.R. Ker (1964) 209; Fowler (1972) xxiii; Del Lungo Camiciotti (1990); Franzen (1991) 29 n. 1, 58–9, 74, 79–80, 82; Lapidge (1991a) 79; Dumville (1992a) 131, 133; Laing (1993) 138; R. Gameson (1996a) 241; *ASMMF* VI (1998) 68–72 [no. 398; Franzen]; R. Gameson (2005a) 96, 101–4; V. Thompson (2005) 108; Frantzen (2007) 40–1, 42 n. 10, 51, 53–6, 61–7; M. Heyworth (2007) 218; Treharne (2007b) 17; Fulk—Jurasinski (2012) xiii–xvi; R. Gameson (2012a) 29 n. 66, 33; Scragg (2012a) nos. 939–40

FACS: *ASMMF* VI (1998) no. 398; Fulk—Jurasinski (2012) frontispiece [fol. 22r]

ED: Fehr (1921) 46–64 [manual offices coll. as L (Ker art. 18)]; Raith (1933/1964) 1–69 [base MS (= Y) for 'Poenitentiale pseudo-Egberti' (Ker art. 1)], 71–3 [base MS for Canons of Synod of Rome (Ker art. 4)]; Henel (1934) 61 [base MS for note on Ember Days (Ker art. 6)]; Spindler (1934) 170–94 [*Confessionale pseudo-Egberti* coll. as Y] (Ker arts. 2, 3, 7, 10, 11); Fowler (1965) 19–20, 26–34 [Handbook for a confessor coll. as Y (Ker arts. 8, 12–16)]; Del Lungo Camiciotti (1990) 181–2 [base MS for Directions for a confessor (Ker art. 17)]; Lapidge (1991a) 244–6 [litany from manual offices]; Sauer (1993) 44 [base MS for Directions for a confessor (Ker art. 17)]; Fulk—Jurasinski (2012) 3–14, 17–18 [base MS (= Y) for OE 'Canons of Theodore' = Ker arts. 5 and 7]

LANG: Fulk—Jurasinski (2012) xxviii–xxxv

ST: Raith (1933/1964); P.S. Baker (1980) 23 n. 11; Frantzen (1983a) 40–5; Frantzen (1983b) 133–4; Frantzen (1985) 39–40; Gneuss (1985) 134–5 [repr. Gneuss (1996) no. V]; Sauer (1993); Gittos (2005b) 74–82; Hamilton (2005) 87–9; N. Orchard (2005) cli, clxxix; V. Thompson (2005); Chardonnens (2007b) 130 n. 164; M. Heyworth (2007); Fulk—Jurasinski (2012) xxxvi–lx

657. Oxford, Bodleian Library, Laud misc. 509 (S.C. 942) (with London, BL, Cotton Vespasian D. xxi, fols. 18–40)

s. xi$^{3/4}$ or xi^2

Contents: Hexateuch* (part trans. Ælfric); Ælfric, Homily on Book of Judges*, Letter to Wulfgeat*, *Libellus* to Sigeweard *De Veteri et Nouo Testamento**; OE Life of St Guthlac*; Anglo-Saxon alphabet and first words of *Pater noster* (add. s. xi or xii)

MS: Coxe (1858–85/1973) 368; Madan et al. (1895–1953) II/i.39 [E.W.B. Nicholson]; Crawford (1922) 3–4, 440–1; N.R. Ker (1957) no. 344; Pope (1967–8) I.85; Carley (1997b) 219–20 and nn.; Tite (1997a) 265–6; R. Gameson (1999a) no. 755; *ASMMF* VII (2002) 44–8 [no. 248; Doane], 72–8 [no. 399; Doane]; Godden (2004) 358; Marsden (2005); Treharne (2007b) 19 n. 16; Withers (2007) 8, 62, 131, 156, 229; Marsden (2008) xxxiv–xlv; Graham (2009) 194–5, 197–200; Marsden (2012) 429 and n. 105; Scragg (2012a) nos. 941–943b

DEC: Withers (2007) 124, 187, 264, 327–8 n. 42; Withers (2011) 251, 263

FACS: Graham (2000d) figs. 28–9 [fols. 24r, 58v]; *ASMMF* VII, nos. 248, 399; Owen-Crocker (2009) fig. 6.18 [fol. 24r]

ED: Assmann (1889/1964) 1–12 [Letter to Wulfgeat coll. as L]; Gonser (1909) [base MS for OE Life of St Guthlac]; Crawford (1922) 15–75 [base MS for *Libellus*], 76–8 [base MS for Genesis], 78–400 [Genesis—Joshua coll. as L], 401–13 [base MS for Judges]; Scragg (1992) 383–92 [excerpt from Life of St Guthlac (Vercelli Hom. no. XXIII) coll. as Z]; Marsden (2008) 1–200 [base MS for Genesis—Joshua, Judges; occasional variants coll. as L], 201–30 [base MS for *Libellus*]

ST: Assmann (1889/1964) xi–xvi, 243–6; Roberts (1970) 202–3; A.F. Cameron (1974) 222–3; Dodwell—Clemoes (1974) 42; Roberts (1986); Franzen (1991) 109; Marsden (1994c); Marsden (1995) 402–41; Barnhouse—Withers (2000); Graham (2000d); Marsden (2000); Tite (2004) 9, 11; Marsden (2005); Marsden (2008) ix–clxxix

658. Oxford, Bodleian Library, Laud misc. 546 (S.C. 1380)

s. xi ex. (before 1096), Normandy, prov. Durham, (prov. Finchale)

Contents: Iulianus Toletanus, *Prognosticum futuri saeculi* [*CPL* 1258]

MS: Coxe (1858–85/1973) 395; Madan et al. (1895–1953) I.28; N.R. Ker
    (1960) 23 n. 5; N.R. Ker (1964) 74, 87; Pollard (1975) 154–5; Piper
    (1978) 242; A.G. Watson (1987a) 32; Clarkson (1996) 193–5;
    R. Gameson (1999a) no. 756; Lapidge (2006) 318

DEC: Pächt—Alexander (1973) no. 58

FACS: Piper (1978) pl. 78 [fol. 1r (detail)]

659. Oxford, Bodleian Library, Marshall 19 (S.C. 5265)

s. ix^1, E France? (Soissons?), prov. Malmesbury s. x^2 or x ex., (prov.
    Canterbury StA or CC)

Contents: Jerome, *Liber interpretationis hebraicorum nominum* [*CPL* 581]

MS: Schenkl no. 392; Madan et al. (1895–1953) II/ii.996; N.R. Ker (1964)
    46, 128; Lambert (1969–72) no. 201; R.M. Thomson (1978) 120–1;
    R.M. Thomson (1982b) 7, 16; Bischoff (1998—) II, no. 3870; Lapidge
    (2006) 314; Barker-Benfield (2008) I.xcv, xcvi and nn. 94–5, 5 n. b, 52,
    492, III.1759, 1771, 1804; Gullick (2012) 307 and n. 84

Oxford, Bodleian Library, Rawlinson B. 484 (S.C. 11831), fol. 85: see
    no. **334**

660. Oxford, Bodleian Library, Rawlinson C. 570 (S.C. 12415)

s. x^2, Canterbury StA

Contents: Arator, *Historia apostolica* [*CPL* 1504] (incomplete)

MS: Macray (1862–1900) 308; M.R. James (1903) 364; McKinlay (1942)
    no. 76; McKinlay (1951) xvi; T.A.M. Bishop (1954–8b) 329; T.A.M.
    Bishop (1959–63b) 413, 418; N.R. Ker (1964) 46; T.A.M. Bishop (1966)
    v, viii, xx; Lapidge (1982a) 116, 138 n. 102 [repr. Lapidge (1996b) 485
    and n. 102]; Lapidge (2006) 281; Barker-Benfield (2008) I.lxi n. 29,
    II.1109, 1181

DEC: F. Wormald (1945) 124, 145 [repr. F. Wormald (1984) 62, 74];
    Alexander (1970b) 63 n. 1; Pächt—Alexander (1973) no. 38; E. Temple
    (1976) no. 30 (iv); Ohlgren (1986) no. 121

FACS: F. Wormald (1945) pl. VI (c) [repr. F. Wormald (1984) pl. 69
    [fol. 2r (detail)]; T.A.M. Bishop (1966) App. pl. D [fol. 44r];

Pächt—Alexander (1973) pl. IV [fol. 2r (detail)]; E. Temple (1976) ills. 100, 106 [fols. 44v (detail), 2r (detail)]

ST: McKinlay (1943) 95

661. Oxford, Bodleian Library, Rawlinson C. 697 (S.C. 12541)

s. ix$^{3/4}$, NE France, prov. England by s. x med. (Glastonbury?), (prov. Bury St Edmunds)

Contents: Aldhelm, *Enigmata* [*CPL* 1335]; *Versus cuiusdam Scotti de alphabeto* [SK 12594]; Aldhelm, *Carmen de uirginitate* [*CPL* 1333] with glosses; Prudentius, *Psychomachia* [*CPL* 1441] (*Praefatio operum* [*CPL* 1437] add. s. x, England); acrostic poem [SK 989], add. s. x med., England

MS: Macray (1862–1900) 351–2; Ehwald (1919) 52, 343–4; N.R. Ker (1957) no. 349; T.A.M. Bishop (1964–8d) 399; N.R. Ker (1964) 22; T.A.M. Bishop (1971) 2; R.M. Thomson (1972) 622; Rella (1977) 70–1, 75, 168; Lapidge (1980a) 19–20; Rella (1980) 115; Lapidge (1981a) 72 [repr. Lapidge (1993a) 60]; O'Brien O'Keeffe (1985) 67–8; Dumville (1987) 175 and n. 163; Dumville (1994a) 137 n. 23; Bischoff (1998–) II, no. 3871; R.M. Butler (2004) 198; Lapidge (2006) 172, 330; Barker-Benfield (2008) II.1373, 1374, 1394, III.1855; Wieland (2009) 150; R. Gameson (2012d) 350 and nn. 21–2; Lapidge (2012b) 23, 32; Scragg (2012a) nos. 944–5

FACS: T.A.M. Bishop (1964–8d) pl. XXIX (c) [fol. 36v (detail)]; De La Mare—Barker-Benfield (1980) figs. 10–11 [fols. 17r, 78v (detail)]; Keynes (1985a) pl. I [fol. 78v]

ED: Ehwald (1919) 97–149 [Aldhelm, *Enigmata*, coll. as E], 350–471 [Aldhelm, *Carmen de uirginitate*, coll. as E]; Glorie (1968) 729–40 [*Versus cuiusdam Scotti de alphabeto* coll. as O]; Lapidge (1981a) 72–81 [repr. Lapidge (1993a) 60–71] [acrostic poem]

ST: J.A. Robinson (1923) 69 and n. 2; Keynes—Lapidge (1983) 214 n. 26; O'Brien O'Keeffe—Journet (1983); Keynes (1985a) 144 and n. 13; O'Brien O'Keeffe (1985); Wieland (1987) 215 *et passim*; Stork (1990) 12, 20–2; Gwara (2001) I.135*–140*; Lapidge (2012b) 22–6, 31–5

662. Oxford, Bodleian Library, Rawlinson C. 723 (S.C. 12567)

s. xi ex., Salisbury

Contents: Jerome, *Comm. in Ezechielem* [*CPL* 587]

MS: Macray (1862–1900) 365; N.R. Ker (1949–50) 182 [repr. N.R. Ker (1985) 207]; Lambert (1969–72) no. 213; N.R. Ker (1976) 25, 40 [repr. N.R. Ker (1985) 145, 162, 169]; Webber (1992) 12, 13, 36 n. 19, 38, 132 n. 71, 147; R. Gameson (1999a) no. 758; Lapidge (2006) 314

663. Oxford, Bodleian Library, Rawlinson D. 894, fols. 62 and 63

s. x ex. or x/xi

Contents: antiphoner (f)

MS: Frere (1894–1932) I.141 [no. 426 (b)]; Van Dijk (1957–60) VI.50; Hartzell (2006) no. 286

664. Oxford, Bodleian Library, Rawlinson G. 57 (S.C. 14788) + G. 111 (S.C. 14836]

s. xi ex. or xi/xii

Contents: *Disticha Catonis* (incomplete) with OE glosses and Latin glosses partly from commentary by Remigius; three Latin poems (Ovid, *Amores* III.viii.3–4 [SK 8093], *Ars amatoria* II.279–80 [SK 8353], and WIC 14116); *Ilias latina* [SK 8372], with OE and Latin gloss; two Latin poems [SK 3433 and WIC 5305]; *Cato nouus*; Avianus, *Fabulae*, with fable SK 14414 interpolated; 'Aesopus' (Hexametrical *Romulus*)

MS: Schenkl nos. 29, 55; Madan et al. (1895–1953) III.353, 362; Sanford (1924) 226; N.R. Ker (1957) no. 350; Glauche (1970) 99 n. 86; R.W. Hunt (1975) no. 119; Lapidge (1982a) 103 and nn. 32, 34 [repr. Lapidge (1996b) 462 and nn. 32, 34]; Munk Olsen (1982—) I.73, 418; R.I. Page (1982) 146, 149; Laing (1993) 141; R. Gameson (1999a) no. 759; Lapidge—Mann (2002) 4–5; Lapidge (2006) 129 n. 2, 292, 323, 339; Alcamesi (2007a) 153–4, 163–6; Scragg (2012a) nos. 946–8

ED: Hervieux (1883–9) II.653–713 [Hexametrical *Romulus* (very inaccurately edited)]; Napier (1900) no. 28 [OE glosses to Avianus]; Förster—Napier (1906) 24 [OE glosses to *Disticha Catonis* and *Ilias latina*]; Duff—Duff (1934) 680–734 [Avianus coll. as Rawl.]; Guaglianone (1958) [Avianus coll. as R]; Gaide (1980) [Avianus coll. as R]; Scaffai (1982) [*Ilias latina* coll. as O]; Alcamesi (2007a) 171–8 [Remigian glosses to *Disticha Catonis*]

ST: Manitius (1911–31) III.713–14 [*Cato nouus* in this MS]; R.S. Cox (1972) 3 n. 8; L.D. Reynolds (1983) xxxv, 31 n. 19, 192; T. Hunt (1991) I.67; Lapidge—Mann (2002); Alcamesi (2007a); Gwara (2012) 515

664. 5. Oxford, Bodleian Library, Rawlinson G. 167 (S.C. 14890)

s. viii/ix, Ireland?

Contents: gospels (only Luke and John, both incomplete)

MS: Madan et al. (1895–1953) III.372; Kenney (1929) 648; *CLA* II (1935) no. 256; McGurk (1961a) no. 35; T.J. Brown (1972) 232 [repr. T.J. Brown (1993a) 109–10]; T.J. Brown (1982) 109 [repr. T.J. Brown (1993a) 209]; McGurk (1987) 169 [repr. McGurk (1998) no. II]; B. Fischer (1988–91) I.16*; M.P. Brown (1989a) 160; Bruce-Mitford (1989) 185; M.P. Brown (2003c) 197 n. 100, 257; M.P. Brown (2012) 135, 151; R. Gameson (2012a) 19 n. 25, 41 n. 108, 53 n. 182

DEC: Pächt—Alexander (1973) no. 1268; Alexander (1978a) no. 43; Ohlgren (1986) no. 43; M.P. Brown (2003c) 238, 350, 380; Tilghman (2011) 93, 94

FACS: Pächt—Alexander (1973) pls. CXII–CXIII [fols. 160v, 1r]; Alexander (1978a) ill. 196 [fol. 1r]; T.J. Brown (1993a) ill. 67 [fol. 83v (detail)]; M.P. Brown (2003c) fig. 105 [fol. 1r]

ED: B. Fischer (1988–91) [gospel excerpts coll. as Ho]

ST: *BCLL* (1985) no. 519

Oxford, Bodleian Library, Rawlinson Q. e. 20 (S.C. 15606): see no. **355**

665. Oxford, Bodleian Library, Selden supra 30 (S.C. 3418)

s. viii^1, SE England, prov. Minster in Thanet?, (prov. Canterbury StA)

Contents: Actus Apostolorum; prayers (s. viii or ix^1)

MS: J. Wordsworth et al. (1889–1954) III/ii, pp. vii, xiv; Madan et al. (1895–1953) II/i.626; M.R. James (1903) 210, 516; Nicholson (1913) xx–xxi; *CLA* II (1935) no. 257; Lowe (1960) 21; N.R. Ker (1964) 47; Bischoff (1966–81) I.92, II.392; D.H. Wright (1967) 57 and n. 1; De La Mare—Barker-Benfield (1980) 9, 11, 13–14 [T.J. Brown]; P.R. Robinson (1997b) 83 and nn.; R. Gameson (1999c) 327–30; Hartzell (2006) no. 289; Barker-Benfield (2008) I.lxi n. 28, III.1653, 1730, 1731; R. Gameson (2012a) 28 n. 59, 37 n. 88, 42 n. 117, 45 and n. 138, 53, 62 n. 218; Marsden (2012) 414 and n. 30

DEC: Pächt—Alexander (1973) no. 2; Netzer (2012) 237 and n. 78

FACS: *NPS* II, pl. 56 [pp. 30, 90]; Nicholson (1913) pl. V [p. 102]; Lowe (1960) pl. XXV (a)–(b) [pp. 54, 91]; D.H. Wright (1967) pl. V (l) [p. 39 (detail)]; R. Gameson (1999c) pls. 13.9, 13.10, 13.12 [pp. 1, 41, 102]

Oxford, Bodleian Library, Selden supra 36 (S.C. 3424) fols. 73 and 74: see no. **666**

666. Oxford, Bodleian Library, Selden supra 36* (S.C. 3424*) (with London, British Library, Royal 12. F. xiv, fols. 1–2, 135, and Oxford, Bodleian Library, Selden supra 36, fols. 73–4]

s. xi^1 (xi ex.?), Winchester?

Contents: antiphoner (f)

MS: Madan et al. (1895–1953) II/i.629; Nicholson (1913) xxxi n. 3; Van Dijk (1957–60) VI.51–2; R. Gameson (1999a) no. 546; Hartzell (2006) no. 185; Wieland (2009) 135; Rankin (2012) 502 and nn. 94, 95

FACS: Nicholson (1913) pls. XLV–XLVI [Selden supra 36*, fols. 1r, 1v]

667. Oxford, Bodleian Library, Tanner 3 (S.C. 9823)

s. xi in. or xi$^{2/4}$, (prov. Worcester)

Contents: Gregory, *Dialogi* [*CPL* 1713]; booklist (s. xi ex. or xii in.)

MS: Hackman (1860) 3; N.R. Ker (1960) 8 n. 2; N.R. Ker (1964) 209; T.A.M. Bishop (1971) 20 n. 1; Rella (1977) 160; Yerkes (1979) xviii–xix; Lapidge (2006) 140, 304

DEC: Alexander (1970b) 11; Pächt—Alexander (1973) no. 45; E. Temple (1976) no. 89; Ohlgren (1986) no. 194; R. Gameson (1995b) 205 n. 83, 207

FACS: Alexander (1970b) 11 [fol. 1v]; Pächt—Alexander (1973) pl. V [fol. 1v]; E. Temple (1976) ill. 298 [fol. 1v]

ED: Lapidge (1994b) 139–45 [booklist]; Lapidge (2006) 140–3 [booklist]

ST: H.M. Bannister (1917)

668. Oxford, Bodleian Library, Tanner 10 (S.C. 9830)

s. x in. or xi^1, (prov. Thorney) [fols. 105–14 supplied s. x^2]

Contents: Bede, *Historia ecclesiastica** (incomplete)

MS: Hackman (1860) 11; N.R. Ker (1957) no. 351; N.R. Ker (1964) 189; A.F. Cameron (1974) 222–4; Parkes (1976b) 155, 157–8, 161–3, 165 [repr. Parkes (1991) 149, 154–5, 158–60, 162]; Dumville (1987) 168–9; Bately (1992) 13–26, 33–6; R. Gameson (1992c); Dumville (1994a) 133–5; Bredehoft (2004) 144, 169; Rowley (2004) 13–15, 20, 30–1; Roberts (2005) 56–8 [no. 10]; Rowley (2011) 16–20; D. Ganz (2012)

188 n. 4; R. Gameson (2012a) 59 n. 195, 62 n. 216, 77; R. Gameson (2012b) 110 and n. 62

DEC: Alexander (1970b) 6–7; F. Wormald (1971b) 305, 307, 312 [repr. F. Wormald (1984) 76–8, 82–3]; Pächt—Alexander (1973) no. 22; E. Temple (1976) no. 9; Brownrigg (1978) 251, 261 n.; D.M. Wilson (1984) 157; F. Wormald (1984) 122, 183 n. 14; Ohlgren (1986) no. 87; Bately (1992) 27–32; R. Gameson (1992c); R. Gameson (1995b) 229–30, 231, 254; R. Gameson (2012c) 282 and n. 114, 287 and n. 133

FACS: Bately (1992) [complete facsimile]; Alexander (1970b) pls. 3 (a), 4 (a)–(c) [fols. 115v, 68r, 93r, 38r (all details)]; Pächt—Alexander (1973) pl. II (fol. 54r (detail)); E. Temple (1976) ills. 34–7, 39, 40 [fols. 131r, 43r, 54r, 115r, 42v, 79r (all details)]; D.M. Wilson (1984) pls. 195–6 [fols. 43r, 54r (details)]; F. Wormald (1984) pl. 62 [fol. 93r (detail)]; Roberts (2005) pl. 10 [fol. 54r]; Rowley (2011) pls. 1, 7 [fols. 68r, 1v]

ED: T. Miller (1890–8) [base MS for OE Bede, as far as extant]; J.M. Schipper (1897–9) [OE Bede coll. as T]

LANG: Schabram (1965) 45–8; Hofstetter (1987) 316–18

ST: Whitelock (1962) [repr. Whitelock (1980) no. VIII; repr. Stanley (1990) 227–60]; Whitelock (1974) 277–8; Greenfield—Robinson (1980) 319–21 [bibliography]; Bately (1992); Waite (2000) 42–5, 321–53; Rowley (2004) 21–2; Rowley (2009); Rowley (2011)

Oxford, Bodleian Library, Arch. A. f. 131: see no. **857**

668. 5. Oxford, Bodleian Library, G. 1. 7 Med. + G. 1. 9 Med. (binding fragments)

s. xi in.

Contents: Gregory, *Moralia in Iob* [*CPL* 1708] (f)

MS: Lapidge (2006) 306

668. 7. Oxford, All Souls College 11, fol. 104

s. xi

Contents: gradual (f)

MS: A.G. Watson (1997) 25; Gneuss (2012) 293

Oxford, All Souls College 38, fols. I–VI and i–vi: see no. **480**
Oxford, All Souls College 330, nos. 54 and 55: see no. **648**

668. 9. Oxford, All Souls College SR. 79. g. 8 (printed book)

s. xi

Contents: missal (f)

MS: R.W. Hunt (1971) 103; A.G. Watson (1997) 259; Hartzell (2006) no. 294

669. Oxford, All Souls College, SR. 80. g. 8 (pastedowns from printed book) (with Eton College 220 no. 1 and Oxford, Merton College, 2. f. 10 (printed book), pastedowns)

s. xi ex.

Contents: Origen, *Hom. in Leuiticum*, trans. Rufinus [*CPG* 1416] (f); Gaudentius of Brescia, *Tractatus .xxi.* [*CPL* 215] (f)

MS: N.R. Ker (1954) nos. 1209, 1220, 1688; N.R. Ker (1962–92) II.789 and n. 2; A.G. Watson (1997) 254–5; Wieland (2009) 122

669. 4. Oxford, Balliol College 306, fols. 5–41

s. x, France?, (prov. England)

Contents: Boethius, *De institutione arithmetica* [*CPL* 879]

MS: Coxe (1852) I/ii.100; Mynors (1963) 324–5; Gibson et al. (1995–2001) I.220–1

ST: Biggs et al. (1990) 75–6 [Wittig]

669. 6. Oxford, Brasenose College 18

s. xi? England?

Contents: *Vita Terentii*; Terence, *Comoediae* (*Andria, Eunuchus, Heautontimorumenos, Adelphi, Hecyra, Phormio*)

MS: Coxe (1852) II/iii.6; L.D. Reynolds (1983) xxxvii n. 191; Gneuss (2003b) 302; Lapidge (2006) 334

670. Oxford, Brasenose College, Latham M. 6. 15

s. xi[1]

Contents: Ælfric, Homily (f: from *Catholic Homilies* I, Hom. I)

MS: N.R. Ker (1957) no. 352; Clemoes (1997) 64; *ASMMF* XVI (2008) 107–9 [no. 409; Wilcox]; Scragg (2012a) no. 949

FACS: *ASMMF* XVI (2008) no. 409

ED: Clemoes (1997) 181–2 [Ælfric, CH I, Hom. I (*De initio creaturae*), lines 68–102, coll. as f^q]; Wilcox in *ASMMF* XVI, 108–9 [base MS]

670. 5. Oxford, Christ Church 378, no. 24

s. xi

Contents: unidentified fragment

671. Oxford, Corpus Christi College 74

s. xi²

Contents: *Vitae III-V Boethii*; Atticus of Constantinople (?), *Epistola formata*; Lupus of Ferrières, *De metris Boethii*; Boethius, *De consolatione Philosophiae* [*CPL* 878], with glosses from commentary by Remigius

MS: Coxe (1852) II/iv.27; Weinberger (1934) xviii; Bolton (1977a) 58; Wittig (1983) 187–98; Troncarelli (1987) no. 88; Gibson et al. (1995–2001) I.223–4; Lapidge (1998) 32–3, 41 n. 42; Lapidge (2006) 293; Wittig (2007) 191; Wittig (2010) 251; Godden (2011) 92; R.M. Thomson (2011) 39–40

672. Oxford, Corpus Christi College 197

s. x⁴/⁴, Worcester?, prov. Bury St Edmunds by s. xi med.

Contents: *Regula S. Benedicti*⁺* [*CPL* 1852]; documents relating to Bury St Edmunds, most in OE (s. xi med., s. xi²−xii¹)

MS: Coxe (1852) II/iv.79; N.R. Ker (1957) no. 353; N.R. Ker (1960) 51 n. 3; N.R. Ker (1964) 22; T.A.M. Bishop (1971) xxii; R.M. Thomson (1972) 618, 622 and nn.; Gretsch (1973) 24–5; Hanslik (1977) lx–lxi; Rella (1977) 56; A.G. Watson (1984) I, no. 776; Hartzell (1989) 86; Dumville (1992a) 125; Conner (1993) 58, 62, 76; Dumville (1993g) 19–35, 75–8 *et passim*; Jayatilaka (2003) 151–4, 182–6; Lapidge (2006) 293; Wieland (2009) 138, 156; R.M. Thomson (2011) 98; R. Gameson (2012a) 40 and n. 104, 62 and n. 218; Rushforth (2012) 200 and n. 15; Scragg (2012a) nos. 950–8

FACS: N.R. Ker (1957) pl. II [fol. 89v (lines 4–14)]; A.G. Watson (1984) II, pl. 15 [fol. 51r]; Owen-Crocker (2009) fig. 5.5 [fol. 28v]

ED: Schröer (1885–8/1964) [*Regula S. Benedicti* (Old English) coll. as O]; Schröer (1888/1978) [*Regula S. Benedicti* (Latin) coll. as O]; A.J. Robertson (1939) no. 104 [documents relating to Bury St Edmunds];

Gretsch (1973) [base MS for *Regula S. Benedicti* (Latin), chs. v, xxvii–xxx, lviii]; Hanslik (1977) [*Regula S. Benedicti* (Latin) coll. as x]; Lapidge (1994b) 123–4 [books listed in the documents]

ST: Hervey (1907); Meyvaert (1963) 101–2; Gretsch (1973); Gretsch (1974)

672. 5. Oxford, Corpus Christi College 255A, fols. 1–3

s. x/xi, Winchester OM?

Contents: Paulus Diaconus, *Homiliarium* (f; reject leaves?), containing: dedicatory verses by Paulus Diaconus [SK 15837], *Epistola generalis* by Charlemagne (MGH, Capit. reg. Franc. I.80–1), table of contents, first pericope (f)

MS: Coxe (1952) II/iv.105; Smetana (1978) 87, 96 n. 60; Gneuss (2003b) 302; R.M. Thomson (2011) 133–4

FACS: see: http://image.ox.ac.uk/images/corpus/ms255a/1v.jpg [fol. 1v, here wrongly dated s. ix]

673. Oxford, Corpus Christi College 279B

s. xi in.

Contents: Bede, *Historia ecclesiastica** (incomplete)

MS: Coxe (1852) II/iv.118; Dobbie (1942) xcvi; N.R. Ker (1957) no. 354; Bredehoft (2004) 145–7, 151; Rowley (2004) 13–15, 20, 26; Rowley (2011) 21–3; R.M. Thomson (2011) 141; Scragg (2012a) nos. 959–63

FACS: Robinson—Stanley (1991) no. 2.9 [fol. 112v (detail)]; Rowley (2011) pl. 3 [fol. 31v]

ED: T. Miller (1890–8) [OE Bede coll. as O]; J.M. Schipper (1897–9) [OE Bede coll. as O]; Dobbie (1942) 106 [Caedmon's Hymn from OE Bede coll. as O]

ST: Whitelock (1962); Colgrave—Mynors (1969) p. l [on pt. i of the MS]; Grant (1974) 113 n. 3; Greenfield—Robinson (1980) 319–21 [bibliography]; Waite (2000) 42–6, 321–53; Rowley (2011)

673. 3. Oxford, Corpus Christi College 489 no. 1

s. xi ex. or xi/xii

Contents: Mass prayers (f)

MS: R.M. Thomson (2011) 170

673. 6. Oxford, Exeter College 4

s. xi/xii or xii in., Canterbury?

Contents: Priscian, *Institutiones grammaticae* [*CPL* 1546] (bks. I–XVI)

MS: Coxe (1852) I/iv.2; Gibson (1972) 117; Passalacqua (1978) 208–9
[no. 467]; Alexander—Temple (1985) 4 [no. 8]; R. Gameson (1999a)
no. 771; A.G. Watson (2000) 7–8

FACS: Alexander—Temple (1985) pl. I (8) [fol. 34v]; A.G. Watson (2000)
pl. I (a)–(b) [fols. 24v, 48v]

674. Oxford, Jesus College 37

s. xi ex. or xi/xii, (prov. Priory of St Guthlac, Hereford)

Contents: Iohannes Diaconus, *Vita S. Gregorii* [*BHL* 3641]; four medical
recipes

MS: Coxe (1852) II/vii.14; Hardy (1862–71) I.204–5; N.R. Ker (1936)
47–8; N.R. Ker (1955) 14, 19, 21 [repr. N.R. Ker (1985) 484, 489, 491];
N.R. Ker (1964) 99; R. Gameson (1999a) no. 774

DEC: Alexander—Temple (1985) no. 7

FACS: Alexander—Temple (1985) pl. I [fol. 1r (detail)]

675. Oxford, Jesus College 51, fol. 1

s. xi², (prov. Evesham?)

Contents: antiphoner (f)

MS: Coxe (1852) II/vii.19; Van Dijk (1957–60) VI.36; N.R. Ker (1964) 81;
R. Gameson (1999a) no. 778; Hartzell (2006) no. 301

676. Oxford, Keble College 22

s. xi ex., Salisbury

Contents: excerpts on the Eucharist; Epistulae Pauli, with gloss

MS: N.R. Ker (1976b) 24 *et passim* [repr. N.R. Ker (1985) 144 *et passim*];
Parkes (1978b) 135–40; Parkes (1979) 67–70; A.G. Watson (1987a) 61;
Parkes (1992) 74, 130 n. 36, 139 n. 99, 142 nn. 47 and 51; Webber
(1992) 87–8, 147–8, 200–1 *et passim*; R. Gameson (2012a) 34 n. 79

FACS: N.R. Ker (1976b) pl. V [fol. 6r]; Parkes (1978b) pl. opp. p. 140
[fol. 58r]; N.R. Ker (1985) pl. 22 [fol. 6r]; Webber (1992) pl. 15 [fol. 6r]

ST: Webber (1992) 88–101; Bankert et al. (1997) 69–70

677. Oxford, Lincoln College 92, fols. 165 and 166

s. viii in., Northumbria, prob. Lindisfarne

Contents: gospels (f; Luke VIII.13–50)

MS: Coxe (1852) I/viii.45; *CLA* II (1935) no. 258; Kendrick et al. (1959–60) II/i.89–106 *passim*; McGurk (1961a) no. 36; De La Mare — Barker-Benfield (1980) 9–11 [T.J. Brown]; Verey et al. (1980) 43 and n. 25, 47–8 [T.J. Brown]; B. Fischer (1988–91) I.16*; M.P. Brown (1989a) 160; Netzer (1989) 204 and n. 9; M.P. Brown (2003c) 257 and n. 140; M.P. Brown (2012) 151 and n. 149

FACS: Kendrick et al. (1959–60) pl. 15 (b) [fol. 164v]; De La Mare — Barker-Benfield (1980) fig. 5 [fol. 165r]

ED: B. Fischer (1988–91) [gospel fragment coll. as Ex]

677. 3. Oxford, Magdalen College, lat. 267, fols. 60–1 (with Oslo and London, The Schøyen Collection, 79)

s. xi/xii or xii in., England or Continent

Contents: Gregory, *Moralia in Iob* [*CPL* 1708] (f)

MS: Quaritch Catalogue 1088 (1988) item 17; J. Griffiths (1995) 38; R. Gameson (1999a) no. 789; Lapidge (2006) 306

677. 6. Oxford, Merton College 309, fols. 114–201

s. ix/x, France? in England before 1100?

Contents: Commentary on the *Benedicite*; Cicero, *Topica* (f); two texts derived from Boethius, *De differentiis topicis* [*CPL* 889]: *Communis speculatio de rhetoricae et logicae cognatione* and *Locorum rhetoricorum distinctio*; Boethius, *In Topica Ciceronis* [*CPL* 888]

MS: Coxe (1852) I/iii.122–3; Powicke (1931) nos. 101, 360; Bursill-Hall (1981) 197.10; Munk Olsen (1982–) I.250; Gibson et al. (1995–2001) I.234–6; Lapidge (2006) 172, 293; R.M. Thomson (2009) 238–9

678. Oxford, Merton College, E. 3. 12 (with York, Minster Library, 7. N. 10 (printed book))

s. x/xi

Contents: Boethius, *De consolatione Philosophiae*, with gloss from commentary by Remigius (f)

MS: N.R. Ker (1954/2004) 179 and n. 2; Lapidge (2006) 293; Wittig (2007) 191; R.M. Thomson (2009) 258; Godden (2011) 92

Oxford, Merton College, 2 f. 10 (printed book): see no. **669**

680. Oxford, Oriel College 3

s. x ex., Canterbury CC

Contents: Prudentius, *Praefatio operum* [*CPL* 1437], *Cathemerinon* [*CPL* 1438], *Peristephanon* [*CPL* 1443]; epigrams for the basilica of St Agnes by Constantina [SK 2659] and Damasus [SK 4939]; Prudentius, *Dittochaeon* [*CPL* 1444], *Contra Symmachum* [*CPL* 1442]

MS: Coxe (1852) I/v.1–2; Bergman (1926) xli–xlii; Lavarenne (1943–51) I.xxix; N.R. Ker (1957) no. 358; T.A.M. Bishop (1959–63b) 415–16, 421; Lapidge (2006) 299, 329, 330; R. Gameson (2012a) 61 n. 214; Scragg (2012a) no. 964

DEC: Alexander (1970b) no. 14c; E. Temple (1976) no. 19 (viii); Alexander — Temple (1985) no. 3

FACS: Alexander (1970b) pl. 14 (c) [fol. 6r (detail)]; E. Temple (1976) ills. 71–2 [fols. 70r, 6r (details)]; Alexander — Temple (1985) pl. I [fol. 70r (detail)]

ED: Napier (1900) no. 48 [OE glosses on Prudentius, *Cathemerinon*]; Bergman (1926) [Prudentius, *carmina*, coll. as O]; Lavarenne (1943–51) [Prudentius, *carmina*, coll. as O]

681. Oxford, Oriel College 34, fols. 57–153

s. x, Continent; prov. England prob. s. xi², with additions s. xi/xii or xii in.

Contents: Bede, *Super Epistulas catholicas expositio* [*CPL* 1362] (prologue add. s. xi/xii or xii in.)

MS: Coxe (1852) I/v.12; Laistner — King (1943) 35; N.R. Ker (1957) no. 359; Rella (1977) 168; Rella (1980) 115; Scragg (2012a) no. 965

681. 5. Oxford, Queen's College 202

s. xi/xii, England

Contents: Horace, poetic works, with commentary and glosses: *Carmina, Ars poetica, Epodon liber, Carmen saeculare, Sermones, Epistulae*

MS: Coxe (1852) I/vi.44; R.W. Hunt (1975) 59–60; Munk Olsen (1982 —) I.475

FACS: R.W. Hunt (1975) pl. XVIII (b) [fol. 5v (detail)]

ED: Klingner (1950) [coll. occasionally as Oxon.]

ST: Klingner (1950) xxi; L.D. Reynolds (1983) 184 n. 11 [R.J. Tarrant];
Gneuss (2003b) 302

682. Oxford, Queen's College 320

s. x med., Canterbury?

Contents: poem on *adynata* [SK 14935]; poem by Braulio or by the
Visigothic king Chintila [*CPL* 1534, SK 3763]; Isidore, *Etymologiae*
[*CPL* 1186], bks. I–X

MS: Coxe (1852) I/vi.76; Nettleship (1885) 359–63; Lindsay (1911) I.viii,
xvi; Gneuss (2003) 302; Barker-Benfield (2008) III.1836; R. Gameson
(2012a) 23 and n. 36; D. Ganz (2012) 194 and n. 36

DEC: Brownrigg (1978) 259 n. 6; R. Gameson (1995a) 104; R. Gameson
(1995b) 10 n. 22; R. Gameson (1995b) 148; R. Gameson (1996b) 168
and n. 155

ED: Lindsay (1911) [Isidore, *Etymologiae*, occasionally coll. as Reg.];
Howlett (1997) [poem on *adynata*]

ST: Reydellet (1966) 400 *et passim*; Knappe (1996) 133 nn. 3–4; Gneuss
(2003b) 302

684. Oxford, St John's College, 28

s. x med. and x³/⁴ (or x/xi), prob. Canterbury StA, (prov. Abingdon s.
xii?, prov. prob. Southwick, Augustinian canons, by s. xvi)

Contents:

fols. 1–4, 7, 78–81 (s. x med.): pseudo-Linus, *Martyrium SS. Petri et Pauli*
[*BHL* 6655, 6570];

fols. 5–6, 8–77 (s. x³/⁴ or x/xi): Gregory, *Regula pastoralis* [*CPL* 1712]
with unidentified preface

MS: Coxe (1852) II/vi.9–10; N.R. Ker (1957) no. 361; T.A.M. Bishop
(1966) xix–xx; T.A.M. Bishop (1971) 3, 8; Rella (1977) 158; Backhouse
et al. (1984b) no. 32 [D.H. Turner]; Clement (1984a) 42; Hanna (2002)
45–7; Biggs (2007a) 50–1; Barker-Benfield (2008) I.578, III.1682, 1816;
D. Ganz (2012) 193 and n. 35; Scragg (2012a) no. 966

DEC: F. Wormald (1952) 77 [no. 51] *et passim*; Alexander (1970b) nos. 7,
8; Raw (1976) 137; E. Temple (1976) no. 13; Deshman (1977) 153–4;

Brownrigg (1978) 260 n. 1; Alexander—Temple (1985) nos. 2, 4; Ohlgren (1986) no. 91; R. Gameson (1995b) 193 n. 3; Hanna (2002) 46–7; R. Gameson (2012c) 252 and n. 11

FACS: F. Wormald (1952) pl. 2 [fol. 2r]; Alexander (1970b) pls. 7, 8 [fol. 2r, 81v]; T.A.M. Bishop (1971) pl. 5 [fol. 6v]; E. Temple (1976) ills. 42–3 [fols. 2r, 81v]; D.M. Wilson (1984) pl. 225 [fol. 2r]; Hanna (2002) pl. III [fol. 2r]

ED: Napier (1900) no. 39 [OE glosses]

ST: Clement (1984a); Clement (1985b); Schreiber (2003) 23–37

685. Oxford, St John's College, 89

s. xi/xii, Canterbury CC

Contents: Bede, *Expositio Apocalypseos* [*CPL* 1363]; Caesarius of Arles, *Expositio in Apocalypsim* [*CPL* 1016]

MS: Coxe (1852) II/vi.25; Laistner—King (1943) 29; N.R. Ker (1964) 39; R. Gameson (1995a) 121 n. 88, 142; R. Gameson (1999a) no. 796; Gryson (2001) 62–3; Hanna (2002) 121

686. Oxford, St John's College, 154

s. xi in., (prov. Durham).

Contents: Ælfric, *Grammar*+*, *Glossary*+*; four Latin colloquies (two by Ælfric Bata; Ælfric's *Colloquium* expanded by Bata; redacted version of *De raris fabulis*); Abbo of Saint-Germain-des-Prés, *Bella Parisiacae urbis*, bk. III° (prose version, part, s. xi ex.)

MS: Coxe (1852) II/vi.47; Zupitza (1888/2001) vi–vii; Napier (1900) xxii; W.H. Stevenson (1929) viii–ix; Mynors (1939) no. 20; N.R. Ker (1957) no. 362; N.R. Ker (1964) 75; A.G. Watson (1987a) 32; Gwara (1996c) 20–1; Gwara (1997b); Gwara (1997c) 57–60; Hanna (2002) 221–3; *ASMMF* XV (2007) 83–9 [no. 420; Doane]; Wieland (2009) 144; Lendinara (2011a) 489 and n. 50, 490–1; R. Gameson (2012a) 51 and n. 171; Scragg (2012a) nos. 967–74

FACS: Piper (1978) pl. 60 [fol. 1r (detail)]; *ASMMF* XV (2007) no. 420

ED [entries are listed in manuscript order, and using the numbering of N.R. Ker (1957) 436–7]:

art. 1 (Ælfric, *Grammar and Glossary*): Zupitza (1888/2001) [base MS coll. as O]; Gillingham (1981) [base MS for Ælfric, *Glossary* (only)] art. 2 (first colloquy by Ælfric Bata): W.H. Stevenson (1929) 27–66; Gwara (1991) 39–91; Gwara (1997c) 80–177; Napier (1900) no. 56 [OE glosses 1–72]

art. 3 (second colloquy by Ælfric Bata): W.H. Stevenson (1929) 67–74; Gwara (1991) 92–9; Gwara (1997c) 178–97; Napier (1900) no. 56 [OE glosses 73–338]

art. 4(a) (Ælfric, *Colloquium*, rev. by Ælfric Bata): W.H. Stevenson (1929) 75–101; Garmonsway (1978) 18–49 [Ælfric, *Colloquium*, coll. as J]; Napier (1900) no. 56 [OE glosses 339–435]

art. 4(b) (colloquy by Ælfric Bata): W.H. Stevenson (1929) 21–6; Gwara (1991) 29–38

art. 5 (Abbo, *Bella Parisiacae urbis*, bk. III): W.H. Stevenson (1929) 103–8 [base MS coll. as J]

ST: F.C. Robinson (1973) 455 n. 40; Lapidge (1975a) 98 and n. 4 [repr. Lapidge (1993a) 136 and n. 4]; Buckalew (1978); Garmonsway (1978); Lendinara (1983); Lendinara (1986) 85–6; D.W. Porter (1996b); D.W. Porter (1997)

688. Oxford, St John's College 194

s. ix ex. or x in., prob. Brittany, prov. England s. x med., (prov. Canterbury CC)

Contents: gospels; parts of two poems: SK 1012 (two lines in alphabet of Aethicus Ister) and SK 10046 (two lines of Alcuin in Greek and ornamental script); colophon; three prayers (*Ad pueros tondendos* or *Ad capillaturam*: add. England, s. x)

MS: Coxe (1852) II/vi.66; M.R. James (1903) 527 [App. D]; N.R. Ker (1964) 39; Alexander (1975b) 173; Laing (1993) 150; Bischoff (1998–) II, no. 3876; Hanna (2002) 280–1

DEC: F. Wormald (1952) 77 [no. 52]; Alexander (1970b) 7; E. Temple (1976) no. 12; Brownrigg (1978) 256 n. 2; Alexander–Temple (1985) no. 1; R. Gameson (1995b) 179

FACS: F. Wormald (1952) pl. 40 (b) [fol. 1v]; Alexander (1970b) pl. 5 [fol. 1v]; Alexander (1975b) pl. V (a) [fol. 1v]; E. Temple (1976) ill. 47 [fol. 1v]

ED: B. Fischer (1988–91) [gospel excerpts coll. as Eo]

ST: Glunz (1933) 68; Bischoff (1966–81) III.129; B. Fischer (1988–91) I.16*

Oxford, St John's College, Ss. 7. 2 (ptd bk.), pastedown: see no. **653**

689. Oxford, Trinity College 4

s. x/xi?, Angers or Tours, prov. Canterbury StA prob. s. xi ex.

Contents: excerpts from Gregory of Tours, *De uirtutibus S. Martini*
[*CPL* 1024; cf. *BHL* 5618d]; Augustine, *De gratia et libero arbitrio*
[*CPL* 352], *De agone Christiano* [*CPL* 296]; Gregory of Nazianzus,
Liber apologeticus, trans. Rufinus (= *Oratio* ii) [*CPG* 3010]; Marbod
of Rennes, *Passio S. Mauricii sociorumque eius* [*BHL* 5752]

MS: Coxe (1852) II/v.2; N.R. Ker (1964) 47; Römer (1972b) 309;
R. Gameson (1995a) 109–10 and n. 52; T.N. Hall (2004b) 97 n. 18

ED: Green—Daur (1970) [Augustine, *De gratia et libero arbitrio*, coll.
as C]

ST: Siegmund (1949) 84; Kristeller et al. (1960—) II.131b; Webber (1992)
54 and n. 38; Whatley (1996) 20; Biggs et al. (2001) 338

690. Oxford, Trinity College 28

s. xi (after 1066), Durham? (prov. Winchester OM)

Contents: Bede, *De tabernaculo* [*CPL* 1345]; pseudo-Augustine /
pseudo-Jerome, *De essentia diuinitatis* [= Jerome, *Epist. supp.* xiv: see
CPL 633]; Isidore, *Etymologiae* XVI. xxv-xxvi (*De ponderibus et
mensuris*); Caesarius, *Sermo* c ('De decem plagis et praeceptis') [*CPL*
1008] (add. s. xi/xii)

MS: Coxe (1852) II/v.12; Laistner—King (1943) 73; N.R. Ker (1964) 201;
Chaplais (1987) 73–4; R. Gameson (1999a) no. 799; P.R. Robinson
(2003) I.62; R. Gameson (2012a) 46 n. 144

ST: Lambert (1969–72) no. 314; Römer (1972b) 309; N.R. Ker (1976b) 30
[repr. N.R. Ker (1985) 150]; Webber (1992) 74 and n. 122

691. Oxford, Trinity College 39

s. xi ex., Normandy, (prov. Lanthony secunda, Gloucs., Augustinian canons)

Contents: Gregory, *Moralia in Iob* [*CPL* 1708], bks. I–X

MS: Coxe (1852) II/v.16; N.R. Ker (1964) 111 n. 6, 112; N.R. Ker (1972b)
78; N.R. Ker (1976b) 27 [repr. N.R. Ker (1985) 147 n. 1]; Gameson—
Coates (1988) 35–49; R. Gameson (1999a) no. 800; N.R. Ker (2002) 24;
R. Gameson (2012b) 109 n. 57

FACS: R. Gameson (1999a) pl. 20 [fol. 2r]

692. Oxford, Trinity College 54

s. x med. or x$^{3/4}$

Contents: Augustine, *Enarrationes in psalmos* [*CPL* 283] (pss. L–LXXII only)

MS: Coxe (1852) II/v.21; N.R. Ker (1960) 8 and n. 4; Römer (1972b) 309; Rella (1977) 158; R. Gameson (1992d) 205 n. 68; Dumville (1994a) 150 n. 100; Rushforth (2011) 65–6; R. Gameson (2012a) 23 and n. 36, 59 n. 197

692. 5. Oxford, Trinity College 60

s. xi ex. or xii in.

Contents: pseudo-Clement, *Recognitiones*, trans. Rufinus [*CPG* 1015 (5)]

MS: Coxe (1852) II/v.26; Siegmund (1949) 60; Rehm–Paschke (1965) lxxiv–lxxvi; R. Gameson (1999a) no. 801; Biggs (2007a) 44

ED: Rehm-Paschke (1965) [*Recognitiones* coll. as Θ^x]

693. Oxford, University College 104

s. xi ex., (prov. Battle)

Contents: Iulianus Toletanus, *Prognosticum futuri saeculi* [*CPL* 1258]

MS: Coxe (1852) I/i.31; N.R. Ker (1964) 31; R. Gameson (1999a) no. 803; R. Gameson (2012a) 27 and n. 56

FACS: R. Gameson (1999a) pl. 4 [fols. 27v–28r]

694. Oxford, Wadham College A. 18. 3 [formerly 2 (A. 10. 22)]

s. xi ex.

Contents: gospels

MS: Coxe (1852) II/viii.1; R. Gameson (1999a) no. 806

DEC: Rice (1952) 200, 209; F. Wormald (1952) 78 [no. 53]; Alexander (1970b) 12–13; C.M. Kauffmann (1975) no. 5; Alexander–Temple (1985) no. 6; R. Gameson (2012c) 285 and n. 126

FACS: Rice (1952) pls. 64 (o), 73 (b) [fols. 104v, 3r (detail)]; F. Wormald (1952) pl. 38 [fol. 12v]; Alexander (1970b) pls. 31–4 [fols. 12v, 13r, 104v; details of fols. 3r, 67r]; C.M. Kauffmann (1975) ills. 17–18 [fols. 12v, 104v]

694. 5. Peterborough, Cathedral Library, H. 3. 40 (endleaf from a printed book)

s. ix$^{3/4}$, France, prov. Peterborough? (early in England?)

Contents: Freculf of Lisieux, *Historiae* (f)

MS: Carley (1986–8) 346 [no. 15]; Gneuss (2003b) 302

Redlynch, Major J.R. Abbey [formerly no. 695]: see now no. **212. 2**

696. Ripon, Cathedral Library, MS. frag. 2

s. xi [binding strips detached from XIII.c.39 (ptd bk.); now on deposit at Leeds University Library]

Contents: hymnal (f)

MS: N.R. Ker (1957) no. 372; Gneuss (1968) 103; Milfull (1996) 55–6; *ASMMF* XIV (2007) 131–4 [no. 440; Pulsiano, Doane]; Barker-Benfield (2008) I.551; Wieland (2009) 135; Scragg (2012a) no. 1001

FACS: *ASMMF* XIV (2007) no. 440

ED: N.R. Ker (1957) no. 372 [OE gloss]; Milfull (1996) 55–6 [Latin hymn fragments coll. as Ri]

697. Salisbury, Cathedral Library, 6

s. xi ex., Salisbury

Contents: Augustine, *Confessiones* [*CPL* 251] with *Retractatio* II. vi

MS: E.M. Thompson (1880) 3; Schenkl no. 3605; N.R. Ker (1949–50) 154 n. 1, 170 [repr. N.R. Ker (1985) 176 n. 1, 192]; Römer (1972b) 315; N.R. Ker (1976b) 25, 45 [repr. N.R. Ker (1985) 145, 169]; Webber (1992) 12, 13, 36 n. 19, 37 n. 20, 73, 148; R. Gameson (1999a) no. 823

FACS: R. Gameson (1999a) pl. 10 [fol. 20r]

699. Salisbury, Cathedral Library, 9, fols. 1-60

s. xi ex., Salisbury

Contents: Cyprian, *De dominica oratione* [*CPL* 43], *De bono patientiae* [*CPL* 48], *De opere et eleemosynis* [*CPL* 47], *De mortalitate* [*CPL* 44], *De catholicae ecclesiae unitate* [*CPL* 41]; Gregory of Nazianzus, *De Hieremiae prophetae dictis*, trans. Rufinus (= *Oratio* xvii) [*CPG* 3010]; Caesarius of Arles, *Epistola* ii [*CPL* 1010]; Sisebutus Toletanus (?),

Lamentum poenitentiae [*CPL* 1533]; exegetical dialogues and notes; pseudo-Jerome, *Epist. supp.* xvi [*Libellus fidei*: *CPL* 633 (p. 220) = *CPL* 731]

MS: E.M. Thompson (1880) 4–5; Schenkl no. 3608; N.R. Ker (1949–50) 154 n. 1, 168 [repr. N.R. Ker (1985) 176 n. 1, 190]; N.R. Ker (1964) 172; N.R. Ker (1976b) 25, 29, 47 [repr. N.R. Ker (1985) 145, 149, 171]; Webber (1992) 13, 20, 23–4, 36 n. 19, 59, 148–9, 160–2; R. Gameson (1999a) no. 825; Biggs (2007a) 73–4 [C.D. Wright]; Barker-Benfield (2008) I.521–2, 597

ST: Kristeller et al. (1960—) II.132b [Gregory of Nazianzus, *Oratio* XVII]; Lambert (1969–72) nos. 316, 317; Römer (1972b) 315

700. Salisbury, Cathedral Library, 10

s. xi ex., Salisbury

Contents: Cassian, *Conlationes* [*CPL* 512], chs. i–x, xiv–xv, xxiv, xi

MS: E.M. Thompson (1880) 5; Schenkl no. 3609; N.R. Ker (1949–50) 154 nn. 1 and 4, 171 [repr. N.R. Ker (1985) 176 nn. 1 and 4, 193]; N.R. Ker (1976b) 25, 29 and n. 4, 37, 39, 42, 45 [repr. N.R. Ker (1985) 145, 149 and n. 4, 158, 161, 165, 169]; Webber (1992) 12–14, 17, 20, 84 n. 16, 149, 198; R. Gameson (1999a) no. 826; R. Gameson (2012b) 109 n. 57

FACS: Webber (1992) pl. 5 [fol. 22r]

ST: Lake (2003) 41 n. 56

700. 1. Salisbury, Cathedral Library, 10, flyleaf 1

s. xi in., Continent, (prov. Salisbury)

Contents: Remigius, Commentary on Martianus Capella (f)

MS: E.M. Thompson (1880) 5; Schenkl no. 3609; Webber (1992) 41, 84–5

700. 2. Salisbury, Cathedral Library, 10, flyleaf 2

s. xi in., Continent, (prov. Salisbury)

Contents: *Liber glossarum* (f)

MS: Schenkl no. 3609; Webber (1992) 84–5

701. 5. Salisbury, Cathedral Library, 12, fols. 1–56

s. xi ex., Salisbury

Contents: Smaragdus of Saint-Mihiel, *Diadema monachorum*

MS: E.M. Thompson (1880) 5; Schenkl no. 3611; N.R. Ker (1949–50) 154 n. 1, 162, 166, 173 [repr. N.R. Ker (1985) 176 n. 1, 184, 188, 195]; N.R. Ker (1964) 172; Rädle (1974) 70 n. 178; N.R. Ker (1976b) 25, 28 n. 1, 48 [repr. N.R. Ker (1985) 145, 148 n. 1, 172]; Webber (1992) 13, 20, 22, 24 n. 85, 40, 61, 66, 68, 80, 114 n. 5, 115 n. 8, 149, 162 and nn.; R. Gameson (1999a) no. 828

702. Salisbury, Cathedral Library, 24

s. xi ex., Salisbury

Contents: Jerome, *Comm. in Hieremiam* [*CPL* 586]

MS: E.M. Thompson (1880) 7; Schenkl no. 3622; N.R. Ker (1949–50) 154 n. 1, 170 [repr. N.R. Ker (1985) 176 n. 1, 192]; N.R. Ker (1964) 172; N.R. Ker (1976b) 25, 40 [repr. N.R. Ker (1985) 145, 162]; Webber (1992) 13, 14, 36 n. 19, 38, 58, 133 n. 71, 149; R. Gameson (1999a) no. 829; Lapidge (2006) 314

ST: Lambert (1969–72) no. 211

703. Salisbury, Cathedral Library, 25

s. xi ex., Salisbury

Contents: Jerome, *Comm. in Esaiam* [*CPL* 584]; sequence *Aue praeclara maris stella* [*AH* L.313]

MS: E.M. Thompson (1880) 7; Schenkl no. 3623; N.R. Ker (1949–50) 176 n. 1, 170 [repr. N.R. Ker (1985) 176 n. 1, 192]; N.R. Ker (1964) 172; N.R. Ker (1976b) 25, 28 n. 2, 29 n. 5, 39 and n. 4, 45 [repr. N.R. Ker (1985) 145, 148 n. 2, 149 n. 5, 161 and n. 4, 169]; Webber (1992) 12, 14, 15, 17, 20, 23, 36 n. 19, 38, 58, 133 n. 71, 149; R. Gameson (1999a) no. 830

ST: Lambert (1969–72) no. 207

704. Salisbury, Cathedral Library, 33

s. xi ex., Salisbury [fols. 1–66 are replacement leaves, s. xii²]

Contents: Gregory, *Moralia in Iob* [*CPL* 1708]

MS: E.M. Thompson (1880) 8; Schenkl no. 3631; N.R. Ker (1949–50) 170 [repr. N.R. Ker (1985) 192]; N.R. Ker (1964); N.R. Ker (1976b) 25, 26 n. 2, 29 and n. 4, 31, 37, 40 [repr. N.R. Ker (1985) 145, 146 n. 2, 149 and n. 4, 151, 158, 162]; Webber (1992) 13–15, 17, 19, 20, 38, 59, 149–50 and n. 43; R. Gameson (1999a) no. 831; Lapidge (2006) 306

706. Salisbury, Cathedral Library, 37

s. xi ex., Salisbury

Contents: Bede, *In Lucae euangelium expositio* [*CPL* 1356]

MS: E.M. Thompson (1880) 9; Schenkl no. 3635; N.R. Ker (1949–50) 154
nn., 168 [repr. N.R. Ker (1985) 176 nn., 190]; N.R. Ker (1964); N.R.
Ker (1976b) 25, 28 n. 2, 46 [repr. N.R. Ker (1985) 145, 148 n. 2, 170];
Webber (1992) 12, 15, 20, 38, 133 n. 71, 150; R. Gameson (1999a)
no. 833

706. 5. Salisbury, Cathedral Library, 37, fols. 1–4, 165–6

s. xi, England, prov. Salisbury

Contents: Ambrosiaster, *Quaestiones .cxxvii. Veteris et Noui Testamenti*
[*CPL* 185] (f)

MS: E.M. Thompson (1880) 9; Schenkl no. 3635; N.R. Ker (1949–50) 155
n. 1 [repr. N.R. Ker (1985) 177 n. 1]; N.R. Ker (1976b) 32 and n. 2
[repr. N.R. Ker (1985) 152 and n. 2]; Webber (1992) 60 and n. 56, 76;
Lapidge (2006) 280

707. Salisbury, Cathedral Library, 38

s. x ex., Canterbury (CC or StA?)

Contents: Aldhelm, *Epistola ad Heahfridum* [*CPL* 1334] (incomplete),
De uirginitate (prose)° [*CPL* 1332]

MS: E.M. Thompson (1880) 9; Schenkl no. 3636; Ehwald (1919) 221–2,
487; N.R. Ker (1949–50) 167 [repr. N.R. Ker (1985) 189]; T.A.M.
Bishop (1954–8b) 330, 333; N.R. Ker (1957) no. 378; T.A.M. Bishop
(1959–63b) 412–13, 417–18; N.R. Ker (1964) 173; T.A.M. Bishop
(1971) xxvi; Rella (1977) 70; Webber (1992) 77–8 and nn.; Dumville
(1993g) 149 n. 46; Gwara (1997a) 567; Gwara (2001) I.163*–170*;
Barker-Benfield (2008) II.1373, III.1818; Lapidge (2012b) 28, 37;
Scragg (2012a) nos. 1007–9

DEC: F. Wormald (1945) 134 [repr. F. Wormald (1984) 74]; Kendrick
(1949) 36 n. 2; E. Temple (1976) no. 19 (v); Brownrigg (1978) 260;
Ohlgren (1986) no. 101; R. Gameson (1992a) 193–4 and nn.; R.
Gameson (1995b) 221 nn. 169 and 172, 222, 225

FACS: E. Temple (1976) ills. 65–8 [fols. 46v, 19v, 7v, 37v (all details)];
R. Gameson (1992a) pl. 41 (b) [fol. 46v (detail)]

ED: Logeman (1891) 27–41 [OE glosses]; Napier (1893) [corrections and additions to Logeman (1891)]; Ehwald (1919) 226–323 [Aldhelm, prose *De uirginitate*, coll. as S], 488–94 [Aldhelm, *Epistola ad Heahfridum*, coll. as S]; Gwara (1996a) 112–15 [Aldhelm, *Epistola ad Heahfridum*, coll. as S]; Gwara (2001) vol. II [Aldhelm, prose *De uirginitate*, with Latin and OE glosses, coll. as S]

ST: Napier (1900) xxiii–xxvi; Lendinara (1990a) 134 n. 8; Gwara (1994a) 269; Gwara (1996a) 94–6; Gwara (1997a) *passim*; Gwara (2001) vol. I, *passim*; Lapidge (2012b) 26–31, 35–7

710. Salisbury, Cathedral Library, 63

s. xi ex., Salisbury

Contents: Augustine, *De agone Christiano* [*CPL* 296] with *Retractatio* [*CPL* 250] II. iii; *De disciplina Christiana* [*CPL* 310]; Caesarius of Arles, *Sermo* ccvi [cf. *CPL* 1008]; Theodulf of Orléans, *De processione Spiritus Sancti*; Augustine, *De utilitate credendi* [*CPL* 316], *De gratia Noui Testamenti* [= *Epist.* cxl], *De natura boni* [*CPL* 323] with *Retractatio* II. ix; Quodvultdeus, *Sermo* x (*Aduersus quinque haereses*) [*CPL* 410]

MS: E.M. Thompson (1880) 14–15; Schenkl no. 3656; N.R. Ker (1949–50) 154 n. 1, 171 [repr. N.R. Ker (1985) 176 n. 1, 193]; N.R. Ker (1964) 173; N.R. Ker (1976b) 25 *et passim* [repr. N.R. Ker (1985) 145 *et passim*]; Webber (1992) 12–14, 36 n. 19, 37 n. 20, 54, 150; R. Gameson (1999a) no. 841; Lapidge (2006) 283, 284, 286, 288, 289, 290, 295, 331; R. Gameson (2012b) 109 n. 57

ST: Römer (1972b) 316

711. Salisbury, Cathedral Library, 67

s. xi ex., Salisbury

Contents: Augustine, *Tractatus in Euangelium Ioannis* [*CPL* 278]

MS: E.M. Thompson (1880) 16; Schenkl no. 3660; N.R. Ker (1949–50) 154 nn., 168 [repr. N.R. Ker (1985) 176 nn., 190]; N.R. Ker (1964) 173; N.R. Ker (1976b) 25, 26 n. 2, 31, 40, 46 [repr. N.R. Ker (1985) 145, 146 n. 2, 151, 162, 170]; Webber (1992) 150 and n. 44 *et passim*; R. Gameson (1999a) no. 844; Lapidge (2006) 291

ST: Römer (1972b) 316

712. Salisbury, Cathedral Library, 78

s. xi ex., Salisbury

Contents: *Collectio Lanfranci* [*Concilia, Decreta pontificum*]

MS: E.M. Thompson (1880) 17; Schenkl no. 3670; N.R. Ker (1949–50) 154 n. 1, 168 [repr. N.R. Ker (1985) 176 n. 1, 190]; N.R. Ker (1964) 174; N.R. Ker (1976b) 25, 28 n. 4, 29 n. 2, 30, 44 n. 2, 46 [repr. N.R. Ker (1985) 145, 148 n. 4, 149 n. 2, 150, 167 n. 2, 170]; Webber (1992) 150 *et passim*; R. Gameson (1999a) no. 845

FACS: Webber (1992) pl. 3 [fol. 128r (detail)]

ST: Z.N. Brooke (1931) 231–5; S. Williams (1971) 80; Kéry (1999) 116, 240; Gullick (2001) 110

713. Salisbury, Cathedral Library, 88

s. xi ex., Salisbury

Contents: Jerome, *De uiris inlustribus* [*CPL* 616]; *Decretum Gelasianum de libris recipiendis et non recipiendis* [*CPL* 1676]; Gennadius, *De uiris inlustribus* [*CPL* 957]; Isidore, *De uiris illustribus* [*CPL* 1206]; Augustine, *Retractationes* [*CPL* 250]; Cassiodorus, *Institutiones* [*CPL* 906], bk. I; Isidore, *In libros ueteris et noui Testamenti prooemia* [*CPL* 1192], *De ecclesiasticis officiis* [*CPL* 1207] I.xi–xii, *De ortu et obitu patrum* [*CPL* 1191], *Allegoriae quaedam S. Scripturae* [*CPL* 1190]; grammatical note

MS: E.M. Thompson (1880) 18; Schenkl no. 3680; N.R. Ker (1949–50) 154 nn., 171 [repr. N.R. Ker (1985) 176 nn., 193]; N.R. Ker (1964) 174; N.R. Ker (1976b) 25, 30, 40–1, 46 [repr. N.R. Ker (1985) 145, 150, 162–3, 170]; Rella (1977) 23; Webber (1992) 150–1 *et passim*; Lapidge (2006) 290, 296, 303, 309, 310, 311, 312, 315, 338

ST: Mynors (1937) xv–xvi, xliv; Lambert (1969–72) no. 260; Römer (1972b) 317; Bursill-Hall (1981) 231 [no. 248.1]

714. Salisbury Cathedral, 89

s. xi med., Fécamp, prov. Salisbury

Contents: Gregory of Nazianzus, *Orationes*, trans. Rufinus [*CPG* 3010]; *Laudes regiae* and chants (all add. s. xi ex.)

MS: E.M. Thompson (1880) 18–19; Schenkl no. 3681; N.R. Ker (1949–50) 165 n. 3, 168 [repr. N.R. Ker (1985) 187 n. 3, 190]; N.R. Ker (1964)

174; Webber (1992) 77, 79–80; R. Gameson (1999a) no. 847; Hartzell (2006) no. 324; Lapidge (2006) 307; Gullick—Rankin (2009) 285

ST: C. Wordsworth (1924) [music of the chants]; Siegmund (1949) 85; Cowdrey (1981)

714. 8. Salisbury, Cathedral Library, 94

s. xi ex., written in England?

Contents: Gregory (?), *Symbolum fidei* [*CPL* 1714 (p. 558)]; Gregory, *Registrum epistularum* [*CPL* 1714]

MS: E.M. Thompson (1880) 19; Schenkl no. 3686; N.R. Ker (1949–50) 172, 174 [repr. N.R. Ker (1985) 194, 196]; N.R. Ker (1964) 174; Gneuss (2012) 293–4

715. Salisbury, Cathedral Library, 96

s. x, England?

Contents: Gregory, *Dialogi* [*CPL* 1713] (incomplete)

MS: E.M. Thompson (1880) 19; Schenkl no. 3688; N.R. Ker (1949–50) 168 [repr. N.R. Ker (1985) 190]; N.R. Ker (1960) 49; N.R. Ker (1964) 174; Yerkes (1979) xvii n. 5, xviii; Dumville (1992b) 182 n. 68; Webber (1992) 77, 79; Lapidge (2006) 304

716. Salisbury, Cathedral Library, 101

s. ix ex., W France, prov. Canterbury CC s. x, prov. Salisbury

Contents: Isidore, *Mysticorum expositiones sacramentorum seu Quaestiones in Vetus Testamentum* [*CPL* 1195]; Adalbert of Metz, *Speculum Gregorii* [epitome of the *Moralia*]; Augustine, *In Ioannis epistulam ad Parthos tractatus .x.* [*CPL* 279]

MS: E.M. Thompson (1880) 21; Schenkl no. 3693; N.R. Ker (1949–50) 168 [repr. N.R. Ker (1985) 190]; N.R. Ker (1964) 174; Webber (1992) 23, 76 and nn., 164; Bischoff (1998—) III, no. 5413; Lapidge (2006) 172–3, 290, 312; R. Gameson (2012a) 40 and n. 102; R. Gameson (2012d) 351 and n. 24

ST: Römer (1972b) 318; R. McKitterick (2012) 327

717. Salisbury, Cathedral Library, 106

s. xi ex., Salisbury

Contents: Augustine, *De doctrina Christiana* [*CPL* 263], *De quantitate animae* [*CPL* 257], *Sermo* xxxvii [*CPPM* I, no. 474]; pseudo-Augustine, Easter sermon (part) [*CPPM* I, no. 1363]; Augustine, *De octo Dulcitii quaestionibus* [*CPL* 291], *De libero arbitrio* [*CPL* 260], *De natura boni* [*CPL* 323], *De uera religione* [*CPL* 264], *De disciplina Christiana* [*CPL* 310]

MS: E.M. Thompson (1880) 21; Schenkl no. 3698; N.R. Ker (1949–50) 154 nn., 170, 172, 182 [repr. N.R. Ker (1985) 176 nn., 192, 194, 207]; N.R. Ker (1964) 174; N.R. Ker (1976b) 25 [repr. N.R. Ker (1985) 145 *et passim*]; Webber (1992) 151, 154 n. 60 *et passim*; R. Gameson (1999a) no. 848; Lapidge (2006) 284, 285, 286, 287, 288, 291

ST: Römer (1972b) 318

Salisbury, Cathedral Library, 109, fols. 1–8: see no. **728**

Salisbury, Cathedral Library, 114, fols. 2–5: see no. **728**

720. Salisbury, Cathedral Library, 114, fols. 6–122

s. xi ex., Salisbury

Contents: Augustine, *De Genesi ad litteram* [*CPL* 266]

MS: E.M. Thompson (1880) 22; Schenkl no. 3706; N.R. Ker (1949–50) 155 n. 1, 173 [repr. N.R. Ker (1985) 177 n. 1, 195]; N.R. Ker (1964) 174 and n. 1; N.R. Ker (1976b) 25, 32 and n. 1, 37, 43 [repr. N.R. Ker (1985) 145, 152 and n 1, 158, 166]; A.G. Watson (1987a) 61; Webber (1992) 13, 15, 36 n. 19, 37 n. 20, 38, 151; R. Gameson (1999a) no. 854; Lapidge (2006) 182

ST: Römer (1972b) 318

722. Salisbury, Cathedral Library, 117, fols. 1–162

s. x, Continent?, (prov. Salisbury), in England before 1100?

Contents: Augustine, *De perfectione iustitiae hominis* [*CPL* 347], *De natura et gratia* [*CPL* 344], *Epistulae* ccxiv, ccxv [*CPL* 262], *De gratia et libero arbitrio* [*CPL* 352], *De correptione et gratia* [*CPL* 353], *Epistulae* ccxxv, ccxxvi [*CPL* 262], *De praedestinatione sanctorum* [*CPL* 354], *De dono perseuerantiae* [*CPL* 355]

MS: E.M. Thompson (1880) 23; Schenkl no. 3709; N.R. Ker (1949–50) 168, 175 [repr. N.R. Ker (1985) 190, 197]; N.R. Ker (1964) 175; N.R. Ker (1976b) 33 [repr. N.R. Ker (1985) 153]; Webber (1992) 77, 79;

Lapidge (2006) 284, 285, 286, 287, 289; Barker-Benfield (2008) I.538–9; M.P. Brown (2012) 163, 164

ST: Römer (1972b) 318-19

Salisbury, Cathedral Library, 117, fols. 163–4: see no. **646**

724. Salisbury, Cathedral Library, 119

s. xi ex., Salisbury

Contents: Freculf of Lisieux, *Historiae, pars prior*

MS: E.M. Thompson (1880) 23; Schenkl no. 3711; N.R. Ker (1949–50) 154 n. 1, 168 [repr. N.R. Ker (1985) 176 n. 1, 190]; N.R. Ker (1964) 175; N.R. Ker (1976b) 25, 31–2, 43, 46 [repr. N.R. Ker (1985) 145, 151–2, 166, 170]; Webber (1992) 12, 13, 16 n. 46, 151; R. Gameson (1999a) no. 858; M.I. Allen (2002) I.112*–116*

ED: M.I. Allen (2002) II.17–432 [*pars prior* coll. as S]

ST: *CSLMA* III (2010) 37–42 [Freculf]

725. Salisbury, Cathedral Library, 120

s. xi ex., Salisbury

Contents: Freculf of Lisieux, *Historiae, pars posterior*

MS: E.M. Thompson (1880) 23; Schenkl no. 2712; N.R. Ker (1949–50) 154 n. 1, 168 [repr. N.R. Ker (1985) 176 n. 1, 190]; N.R. Ker (1964) 175; N.R. Ker (1976b) 25, 28 n., 31–2 [repr. N.R. Ker (1985) 145, 148 n., 151–2]; Webber (1992) 13, 14, 151; R. Gameson (1999a) no. 859; M.I. Allen (2002) I.119*–120*

ED: M.I. Allen (2002) II.435–724 [*pars posterior* coll. as I]

ST: *CSLMA* III (2010) 37–42 [Freculf]

728. Salisbury, Cathedral Library, 128, fols. 1-4 (with Salisbury, Cathedral Library, 109, fols. 1–8, and Salisbury, Cathedral Library, 114, fols. 2–5)

s. xi ex., Salisbury

Contents: Augustine, *De Genesi ad litteram* [*CPL* 266] (f)

MS: E.M. Thompson (1880) 22, 24–5; Schenkl no. 3720 [+ 'Nachtrag' III.1 (1894) 76]; N.R. Ker (1949–50) 155 n. 1 [repr. N.R. Ker (1985) 177 n. 1]; N.R. Ker (1976b) 25, 32 n. 1, 43 [repr. N.R. Ker (1985) 145,

152 n. 1, 166]; Webber (1992) 151; R. Gameson (1999a) no. 849;
Lapidge (2006) 285

ST: Römer (1972b) 318 [lists only MS 114, fols. 2–5]

729. Salisbury, Cathedral Library, 128, fols. 5–116

s. xi ex., Salisbury

Contents: Augustine, *De adulterinis coniugiis* [*CPL* 302], *De natura et origine animae* [*CPL* 345]; pseudo-Augustine, *Sermo Ariani cuiusdam* [*CPL* 701], *Contra sermonem Arianorum* (from Syagrius, *Regulae definitionum*) [*CPL* 702]; Augustine, *Contra aduersarium legis et prophetarum* [*CPL* 326]

MS: E.M. Thompson (1880) 24–5; Schenkl no. 3720; N.R. Ker (1949–50) [repr. N.R. Ker (1985) 176 nn., 193]; N.R. Ker (1964) 175; N.R. Ker (1976b) 25, 29, 30 and n. 4, 37–8, 39, 43, 46 [repr. N.R. Ker (1985) 145, 149, 150 and n. 4, 158–9, 161, 166, 170]; Webber (1992) 151 *et passim*; R. Gameson (1999a) no. 862; Lapidge (2006) 282, 283

ST: Römer (1972b) 319; Webber (1992) 68; Gullick (1998c) 188–9

730. Salisbury, Cathedral Library, 129

s. xi ex., Salisbury

Contents: Ambrosiaster, *Quaestiones .cxxvii. Veteris et Noui Testamenti* [*CPL* 185]

MS: E.M. Thompson (1880) 25; Schenkl no. 3721; N.R. Ker (1949–50) 154 n. 4, 171 [repr. N.R. Ker (1985) 176 n. 4, 193]; N.R. Ker (1964) 175; N.R. Ker (1976b) 25, 32 and n. 2, 46 [repr. N.R. Ker (1985) 145, 152 and n. 2, 170]; Webber (1992) 12, 13, 43, 60, 76 and n. 127, 133 n. 71, 152; R. Gameson (1999a) no. 863; Lapidge (2006) 280

ST: Römer (1972b) 319; Bankert et al. (1997) 70–1

733. Salisbury, Cathedral Library, 132

s. xi^2, (prov. Salisbury)

Contents: Gregory, *Homiliae .xl. in Euangelia* [*CPL* 1711], *Oratio de mortalitate* [*CPL* 1714 (p. 557)]

MS: E.M. Thompson (1880) 25; Schenkl no. 3724; N.R. Ker (1949–50) 154 n. 1, 179 [repr. N.R. Ker (1985) 176 n. 1, 204]; N.R. Ker (1964) 175; A.G. Watson (1987a) 61; Webber (1992) 15; R. Gameson (1999a) no. 866; Lapidge (2006) 305

ST: T.N. Hall (2001) 118–20 [*Oratio de mortalitate*]

734. Salisbury, Cathedral Library, 133

s. ix$^{1/4}$, Tours, (prov. Salisbury)

Contents: Alcuin, *Expositio in Ecclesiasten* (incomplete)

MS: E.M. Thompson (1880) 25; Schenkl no. 3725; Lowe (1938) [repr.
Lowe (1972) I.342–4]; N.R. Ker (1949–50) 170 [repr. N.R. Ker (1985)
192]; N.R. Ker (1964) 175; Dumville (1992a) 148 and n. 380; Dumville
(1992b) 182 and n. 68; Webber (1992) 77, 79 and n. 143; Bischoff (1998–)
III, no. 5414; Lapidge (2006) 173; D'Imperio (2008) 23; D. Ganz (2010)

FACS: Lowe (1972) I, pl. 58 [fol. 31v]

ST: *CSLMA* II (1999) 370; D'Imperio (2008) 21–32

735. Salisbury, Cathedral Library, 134

s. x ex., England, (prov. Salisbury)

Contents: Remigius, Commentary on Sedulius, *Carmen paschale* [*CPL*
1447]

MS: E.M. Thompson (1880) 25; Schenkl no. 3726; N.R. Ker (1949–50)
167 n. 1, 171 [repr. N.R. Ker (1985) 189 n. 1, 193]; Lapidge (1982a) 114
and n. 88 [repr. Lapidge (1996b) 480–1 and n. 88]; Jeudy (1991) 497;
Webber (1992) 77, 79 and n. 140, 84 and n. 15; Lapidge (1994b) 143;
Springer (1995) 182; Lapidge (2006) 142; Wieland (2009) 151

736. Salisbury, Cathedral Library, 135

s. xi ex., Salisbury

Contents: *Summa de diuinis officiis*; Isidore, *Mysticorum expositiones
sacramentorum seu Quaestiones in Vetus Testamentum* [*CPL* 1195]
(incomplete)

MS: E.M. Thompson (1880) 25; Schenkl no. 3727; N.R. Ker (1949–50)
154 nn., 173, 178 [repr. N.R. Ker (1985) 176 nn., 195, 203]; N.R. Ker
(1964) 175; N.R. Ker (1976b) 25, 28 n. 2, 37, 46 [repr. N.R. Ker (1985)
145, 148 n. 2, 158, 170]; Webber (1992) 12, 13, 152; R. Gameson
(1999a) nos. 867, 868; Lapidge (2006) 312

ST: N.R. Ker (1962–92) II.835; N.R. Ker (1976b) 34 n. 1 [repr. N.R. Ker
(1985) 154 n. 1]; R.E. Reynolds (1977) 123–4; Webber (1992) 152 and
n. 51; *CSLMA* II (1999) 133–4; C.A. Jones (2010) 64–5 [*Summa de
diuinis officiis*]

738. Salisbury, Cathedral Library, 138

s. xi ex., Salisbury

Contents: Augustine, *Epistulae* cc, ccvii [*CPL* 262], *De nuptiis et concupiscentia* [*CPL* 350], *Contra Iulianum* [*CPL* 351]

MS: E.M. Thompson (1880) 26; Schenkl no. 3730; N.R. Ker (1949–50) 154 n. 1, 168, 173 [repr. N.R. Ker (1985) 176 n. 1, 190, 195]; N.R. Ker (1964) 175; N.R. Ker (1976b) 25, 26 n. 2, 28 n. 2, 30, 32, 37–8, 40, 43 [repr. N.R. Ker (1985) 145, 146 n. 2, 148 n. 2, 150, 152, 158–9, 162, 166]; A.G. Watson (1987a) 61; Webber (1992) 12–15, 20, 24 n. 86, 37 n. 20, 47, 152; R. Gameson (1999a) no. 871; Lapidge (2006) 282, 286, 289

ST: N.R. Ker (1960) 13, 54–7; Lambert (1969–72) no. 216 [flyleaves]; Römer (1972b) 319; Rella (1977) 26

739. Salisbury, Cathedral Library, 140

s. xi ex., Salisbury

Contents: Ambrose, *De fide* [*CPL* 150], *De Spiritu Sancto* [*CPL* 151], *De incarnationis dominicae sacramento* [*CPL* 152]

MS: E.M. Thompson (1880) 26; Schenkl no. 3732; N.R. Ker (1949–50) 154 nn., 172 [repr. N.R. Ker (1985) 176 nn., 194]; N.R. Ker (1964) 175; N.R. Ker (1976b) 25, 29, 38, 46 [repr. N.R. Ker (1985) 145, 149, 159, 170]; Webber (1992) 12–14, 36 n. 19, 39 n. 30, 133 n. 71, 152; R. Gameson (1999a) no. 873; Lapidge (2006) 277, 279

ST: Webber (1992) 53–4 and n. 33; Bankert et al. (1997) 41–4

739. 5. Salisbury, Cathedral Library, 140, fols. 1–2

s. xi ex., Salisbury

Contents: Berengaudus, *Comm. in Apocalypsin* (f)

MS: E.M. Thompson (1880) 26; Schenkl no. 3732; N.R. Ker (1949–50) 182 [repr. N.R. Ker (1985) 207]; N.R. Ker (1976b) 25, 28 n. 2, 43 [repr. N.R. Ker (1985) 145, 148 n. 2, 166]; Webber (1992) 12, 15, 152 n. 52, 153 n. 54; R. Gameson (1999a) no. 874

740. Salisbury, Cathedral Library, 150, fols. 1–151

s. x^2 (prob. 969×987), SW England (Shaftesbury?), OE gloss s. xi/xii, exc. gloss to *Quicumque uult* (s. x^2)

Contents: liturgical calendar; computus material; Psalterium Gallicanum°; Ps. CLI; canticles° (including *Quicumque uult°*); litany (addition of s. xi/xii)

MS: E.M. Thompson (1880) 29; Gasquet—Bishop (1908) 149–50 *et passim*; N.R. Ker (1949–50) 168 [repr. N.R. Ker (1985) 190]; N.R. Ker (1957) no. 379; Sisam—Sisam (1959) 1–7; N.R. Ker (1964) 175; T.A.M. Bishop (1971) 3; Stroud (1979); Backhouse et al. (1984b) no. 29 [D.H. Turner]; A.G. Watson (1987a) 62; Lapidge (1991a) 83–4; Webber (1992) 78 n. 133; Dumville (1993g) 153 n. 71, 156 n. 97; Laing (1993) 152; Pfaff et al. (1995a) 61–84 [Pulsiano]; R. Gameson (1996b) 166 and n. 147; R. Gameson (1999a) no. 875; Pulsiano (2001a) xxiv; Biggs (2007a) 16; Chardonnens (2007b) 544, 554; Rushforth (2007) 63; Rushforth (2008a) 24–5; Wieland (2009) 152; R. Gameson (2012b) 99 and n. 18; D. Ganz (2012) 194 and n. 37; Scragg (2012a) nos. 1010–11

DEC: F. Wormald (1945) 121, 124, 134 [repr. F. Wormald (1984) 59–60 and n. 46, 63, 73]; Rice (1952) 212–13; F. Wormald (1952) 80 [no. 58]; F. Wormald (1971b) 312–13 [repr. F. Wormald (1984) 83]; Raw (1976) 138; E. Temple (1976) no. 18; Ohlgren (1986) no. 96; R. Gameson (1995b) 89 n. 104, 122 n. 27, 200, 219, 229–30; R. Gameson (2012c) 282

FACS: Rice (1952) pl. 78 [fol. 122r]; Sisam—Sisam (1959) at end [fol. 110v]; E. Temple (1976) ills. 57–61 [fols. 122r, 60v (detail), 64v (detail), 3r, 5r]; Backhouse et al. (1984b) 50 [fol. 122r]; F. Wormald (1984) ill. 59 [fol. 54v]; Rushforth (2007) 63 [fol. 60v]

ED: F. Wormald (1934) 15–27 [liturgical calendar (no. 2)]; Sisam—Sisam (1959) 77–308 [Psalms and canticles, Latin and OE gloss]; Lapidge (1991a) 283–7 [litany]; Pulsiano (2001a) [Pss. I–L, Latin text and OE gloss, both coll. as K]; Rushforth (2008a) no. 6 [liturgical calendar]

LANG: Sisam—Sisam (1959) 13–14, 21–39; Hofstetter (1987) 470–3

ST: Lindelöf (1904); Wildhagen (1920); Wildhagen (1921); Henel (1934); Sisam—Sisam (1959) 1–52; F.C. Robinson (1973) 444–5; Bierbaumer (1977a); Kotzor (1981) I.302*–311*; Gerchow (1988) 225, 331; Conner (1993) 53, 58, 62; Günzel (1993) 198–200, 204; Gretsch (1999b) 174–5; Keynes (1999b) 47–8; Borst (2001) I.164–5; N. Orchard (2002) I.54 *et passim*

741. Salisbury, Cathedral Library, 154

s. xi ex., Salisbury

Contents: Amalarius, *Liber officialis* ('Retractatio prima', extensively revised and augmented), with interpolated exposition of the Mass ('Dominus uobiscum')

MS: E.M. Thompson (1880) 30; Schenkl no. 3746; N.R. Ker (1949–50) 154 nn., 173 [repr. N.R. Ker (1985) 176 nn., 195]; N.R. Ker (1964) 175; N.R. Ker (1976b) 25, 29, 30, 34 n. 1, 38, 43 [repr. N.R. Ker (1985) 145, 149, 150, 154 n. 1, 159, 166]; Webber (1992) 12, 13, 133 n., 152–3 and n. 53, 197; R. Gameson (1999a) no. 876; C.A. Jones (2001) 15–17, 268–77

FACS: Webber (1992) pl. 2 [p. 153 (detail)]

ED: C.A. Jones (2001) 181–228 [interpolated passages in Amalarius]

ST: N.R. Ker (1976b) 46–7 [repr. N.R. Ker (1985) 170–1]; Webber (1992) 71 and nn.; C.A. Jones (1998c) 672–3, 677–80, 686–9; C.A. Jones (2001); C.A. Jones (2010) 42–7

742. Salisbury, Cathedral Library, 157, fols. 5–170

s. xi ex., England?, (prov. Normandy s. xiii in.)

Contents: Gregory, *Regula pastoralis* [*CPL* 1712]; chants for the Office of Mary Magdalene; Augustine, *Enchiridion* [*CPL* 295], *Ep.* cxxx (*De orando Deo*) [*CPL* 262]; pseudo-Augustine and pseudo-Orosius, *Dialogus quaestionum .lxv.* [*CPL* 373a]; pseudo-Gregory, *De iuramentis episcoporum*; chants for the Office for the consecration of a church; Isidore, *Allegoriae quaedam S. Scripturae* [*CPL* 1190], *In libros ueteris et noui Testamenti prooemia* [*CPL* 1192], *De ortu et obitu patrum* [*CPL* 1191]

MS: E.M. Thompson (1880) 30–1; Schenkl no. 3749; N.R. Ker (1949–50) 154 n. 1, 155 n. 1, 165 n. 3, 168, 177 [repr. N.R. Ker (1985) 176 n. 1, 177 n. 1, 187 n. 3, 190, 199]; N.R. Ker (1964) 175; N.R. Ker (1976b) 24 n. 4 [repr. N.R. Ker (1985) 144 n. 4]; Rella (1977) 160; Clement (1984a) 42; Webber (1992) 77 n. 133; Schreiber (2003) 24 and n. 14, 32; Hartzell (2006) no. 329; Lapidge (2006) 289, 306, 309, 310, 312

ST: Römer (1972b) 319

743. Salisbury, Cathedral Library, 158, fols. 1–8

s. xi med., France, prov. Salisbury by s. xi ex.

Contents: Helperic, *De computo*

MS: E.M. Thompson (1880) 31; Schenkl no. 3750; N.R. Ker (1949–50) 154 n. 4, 168 [repr. N.R. Ker (1985) 176 n. 4, 190]; N.R. Ker (1964) 175; Webber (1992) 41 and n. 34, 76–7, 133

ST: *CSLMA* III (2010) 421–9 [Helperic]

744. Salisbury, Cathedral Library, 158, fols. 9–83

s. ix² or ix/x, France, prov. Salisbury by s. xi ex.

Contents: computus tables; Bede, *De temporum ratione* [*CPL* 2320]

MS: E.M. Thompson (1880) 31; Schenkl no. 3750; C.W. Jones (1939) 133; C.W. Jones (1943) 156–7; Laistner—King (1943) 150; R.W. Hunt (1947) 63 and n. 2; N.R. Ker (1949–50) 154 n. 4, 190 [repr. N.R. Ker (1985) 176 n. 4, 190]; N.R. Ker (1964) 175; C.W. Jones (1977) 253; Rella (1977) 24; Webber (1992) 41 n. 34, 73–4, 76–7, 133; Bischoff (1998—) III, no. 5415; Lapidge (2006) 173

745. Salisbury, Cathedral Library, 159

s. xi ex., prov. Salisbury

Contents: Origen, *Hom. in Exodum*, trans. Rufinus [*CPG* 1414], *Hom. in Leuiticum*, trans. Rufinus [*CPG* 1416]

MS: E.M. Thompson (1880) 31; Schenkl no. 3751; N.R. Ker (1949–50) 154 nn., 172 [repr. N.R. Ker (1985) 176 nn., 194]; N.R. Ker (1964) 175; N.R. Ker (1976b) 25, 47 [repr. N.R. Ker (1985) 145, 171]; Webber (1992) 12, 21, 36 n. 19, 38, 133 n. 71; R. Gameson (1999a) no. 880; Lapidge (2006) 322

747. 5. Salisbury, Cathedral Library, 162, fols. 1–2, 29–30

s. xi ex., Salisbury

Contents: Berengaudus, *Comm. in Apocalypsin* (f)

MS: E.M. Thompson (1880) 31; Schenkl no. 3754; N.R. Ker (1949–50) 155 n. 1 [repr. N.R. Ker (1985) 177 n. 1]; Webber (1992) 15, 38, 153; R. Gameson (1999a) no. 802

748. Salisbury, Cathedral Library, 164, fols. 64–129

s. xi ex. or xi/xii

Contents: Ivo of Chartres, *Sermones* (incomplete)

MS: E.M. Thompson (1880) 32; Schenkl no. 3756; N.R. Ker (1949–50) 154 n. 1, 173 [repr. N.R. Ker (1985) 176 n. 1, 195]; N.R. Ker (1964) 176; N.R. Ker (1976b) 25, 33 [repr. N.R. Ker (1985) 145, 153]

749. Salisbury, Cathedral Library, 165, fols. 1–87

s. xi ex., Salisbury

Contents: Vigilius of Thapsus (?), *Contra Felicianum Arianum* [*CPL* 808]; pseudo-Methodius, *Apocalypsis uel Reuelationes* in Latin translation [*CPG* 1830]; Bede, *De tabernaculo* [*CPL* 1345]; extract from Isidore, *Etymologiae* [*CPL* 1186] XVI.xxv–xxvi

MS: E.M. Thompson (1880) 32; Schenkl no. 3757; Laistner—King (1943) 73; N.R. Ker (1949–50) 154 nn., 168 [repr. N.R. Ker (1985) 176 nn., 190]; N.R. Ker (1964) 176; N.R. Ker (1976b) 25, 28 n. 2, 30, 43, 44 and n. 1, 47 [repr. N.R. Ker (1985) 145, 148 n. 2, 150, 166, 167 and n. 1, 171]; Webber (1992) 8 n. 3, 12–15, 23, 24 n. 86, 26, 74 n. 121, 133 n. 71, 153–4, 197; R. Gameson (1999a) nos. 885–7; Biggs (2007a) 19–20

FACS: Webber (1992) pl. 1(a) [fol. 23r (detail)]

ST: Sackur (1898) 1–59; Römer (1972b) 319; Prinz (1985) [pseudo-Methodius]; Kortekaas (1988) [pseudo-Methodius]; Laureys—Verhelst (1988) [pseudo-Methodius]; Twomey (2007) [pseudo-Methodius]

749. 5. Salisbury, Cathedral Library, 165, fols. 122–78

s. xi ex., Salisbury

Contents: Alcuin, *De fide sanctae et indiuiduae Trinitatis, De Trinitate ad Fredegisum quaestiones .xxviii., De animae ratione*; Gennadius, *Liber siue diffinitio ecclesiasticorum dogmatum* (second recension) [*CPL* 958a]; *Decretum Gelasianum de libris recipiendis et non recipiendis* [*CPL* 1676]; pseudo-Jerome, *De duodecim scriptoribus*; two Eucharistic miracle stories

MS: E.M. Thompson (1880) 32; Schenkl no. 3757; N.R. Ker (1949–50) 154 nn., 168 [repr. N.R. Ker (1985) 176 nn., 190]; N.R. Ker (1964) 176; N.R. Ker (1976b) 25, 44 n. 1 [repr. N.R. Ker (1985) 145, 167 n. 1]; Webber (1992) 8n., 153–4, 197; R. Gameson (1999a) no. 890; Lapidge (2006) 304, 338

FACS: Webber (1992) pl. 1 (b) [fol. 135r (detail)]

ST: Lambert (1969–72) no. 357; Römer (1972b) 319; Bullough (1998b) 14 and n. 39; *CSLMA* II (1999) 121–5 [*De animae ratione*], 134–9 [*De fide*], 151–5 [*De Trinitate ad Fredegisum*]

750. Salisbury, Cathedral Library, 168

s. xi ex., Salisbury

Contents: Augustine, *De diuersis quaestionibus .lxxxiii.* [*CPL* 289]; *De duodecim abusiuis saeculi* [*CPL* 1106; *BCLL* 339]; Bede, *Versus de die iudicii* [*CPL* 1370]

MS: E.M. Thompson (1880) 33; Schenkl no. 3760; N.R. Ker (1949–50) 154 n. 1, 168 [repr. N.R. Ker (1985) 176 n. 1, 190]; N.R. Ker (1964) 176; N.R. Ker (1976b) 25, 28 n. 4, 32, 44, 48 [repr. N.R. Ker (1985) 145, 148 n. 4, 152, 167, 172]; Webber (1992) 12–15, 21, 36 n. 19, 37 n. 20, 198; R. Gameson (1999a) no. 891; Lapidge (2006) 285, 338; Lendinara (2007b) 206–7; Lapidge (2008a) 132; R. Gameson (2012b) 109 n. 57

FACS: Webber (1992) pl. 4 [fol. 14r]

ST: Römer (1972b) 319–20; *BCLL* (1985) no. 339; Lendinara (2007b) 177, 181 [Bede, *Versus de die iudicii*]; Lapidge (2008a) 131–7 [Bede, *Versus de die iudicii*]

750. 5. Salisbury, Cathedral Library, 169, fols. 1–77

s. xi ex., Salisbury

Contents: Augustine, *Sermones* cccli [*De utilitate agendae paenitentiae*] [*CPL* 284], cccxciii [*De paenitentibus*] [*CPL* 285]; pseudo-Augustine and pseudo-Orosius, *Dialogus quaestionum .lxv.* [*CPL* 373a]; Vigilius of Thapsus (?), *Contra Felicianum Arianum* [*CPL* 808]; Augustine, *De disciplina Christiana* [*CPL* 310]; pseudo-Augustine, *Sermo* xxxvii [*CPPM* I, no. 474]; pseudo-Augustine, *Sermo in die Paschae* [*CPPM* I, no. 1363]; Augustine, *De octo Dulcitii quaestionibus* [*CPL* 291], *Ep.* cxxx (*De orando Deo*) [*CPL* 262]

MS: E.M. Thompson (1880) 33; Schenkl no. 3761; N.R. Ker (1949–50) 154 n. 1, 170 [repr. N.R. Ker (1985) 176 n. 1, 192]; N.R. Ker (1964) 176; N.R. Ker (1976b) 25, 29, 32, 48 [repr. N.R. Ker (1985) 145, 149, 152, 172]; Webber (1992) 154, 168 *et passim*; R. Gameson (1999a) no. 892; Lapidge (2006) 284, 287, 289, 291

ST: Römer (1972b) 320

751. Salisbury, Cathedral Library, 172

s. x², prob. Canterbury

Contents: Augustine, *Enchiridion* [*CPL* 295] (incomplete)

MS: E.M. Thompson (1880) 34; Schenkl no. 3764; N.R. Ker (1949–50) 170 [repr. N.R. Ker (1985) 192]; N.R. Ker (1957) no. 380; T.A.M. Bishop (1959–63b) 412–13; N.R. Ker (1964) 176; T.A.M. Bishop (1971) xxvi; Rella (1977) 159; Webber (1992) 77–8 and n. 135; Lapidge (2006) 289; Barker-Benfield (2008) I.527, III.1818; Scragg (2012a) no. 1012

ST: Römer (1972b) 320

752. Salisbury, Cathedral Library, 173

s x ex., Continent, prov. England, (prov. prob. Salisbury)

Contents: Augustine, *Soliloquia* [*CPL* 252]; Isidore, *Synonyma de lamentatione animae peccatricis* [*CPL* 1203]

MS: E.M. Thompson (1880) 34; Schenkl no. 3765; N.R. Ker (1949–50) 168 [repr. N.R. Ker (1985) 190]; N.R. Ker (1957) no. 381; N.R. Ker (1964) 176; Rella (1977) 168; Rella (1980) 115; Webber (1992) 77, 79 and n. 142; T.N. Hall (2004b) 88, 91–2, 100–5; Hartzell (2006) no. 330; Lapidge (2006) 291, 313; Di Sciacca (2007b) 97; Di Sciacca (2008) 68 and n. 392, 70 and n. 409; Scragg (2012a) nos. 1013–15

ST: Römer (1972b) 320; Di Sciacca (2007b); Di Sciacca (2008) 110, 228 n. 23, 258 n. 160 *et passim*

753. Salisbury, Cathedral Library, 179

s. xi ex., Salisbury

Contents: Paulus Diaconus, *Homiliarium* [Easter to All Saints, Commune SS.]

MS: E.M. Thompson (1880) 35; Schenkl no. 3771; N.R. Ker (1949–50) 154 n. 1, 168 [repr. N.R. Ker (1985) 176 n. 1, 190]; N.R. Ker (1964) 176; N.R. Ker (1976b) 25, 26 n. 2, 27, 28 n. 4, 32, 44 and n. 2 [repr. N.R. Ker (1985) 145, 146 n. 2, 147, 148 n. 4, 152, 167 and n. 2]; Clayton (1985) 220; Gneuss (1985) 124 [no. M.7]; Webber (1992) 12–15, 154, 161 n. 31; R. Gameson (1999a) no. 893; Hartzell (2006) no. 331; Biggs (2007a) 25–6 [Clayton]; T.N. Hall (2007) 243–4; J. Hill (2007a) 94; T.N. Hall (2008a) 33, 55–9; R. Gameson (2012b) 109 n. 57

ST: Römer (1972b) 320; T.N. Hall (2007) 243–4; T.N. Hall (2008a)

754. Salisbury, Cathedral Library, 180

s. ix/x, N France or Brittany, prov. England s. x¹, (prov. Salisbury)

Contents: Psalterium Gallicanum and Hebraicum; Ps. CLI; canticles; litany; prayers

MS: E.M. Thompson (1880) 35; Schenkl no. 3772; N.R. Ker (1949–50) 171 [repr. N.R. Ker (1985) 193]; N.R. Ker (1964) 176; Deuffic (1985) 318; Lapidge (1986a) 276; Lapidge (1991a) 84; Webber (1992) 77, 79; Lapidge (1992b) 100 n. 24 [repr. Lapidge (1993a) 90 n. 24]; Pulsiano (2001a) xxx; Biggs (2007a) 16–17; Wieland (2009) 117; Toswell (2012) 473

ED: Dewick—Frere (1914–21) II.626–33 [litany]; Lapidge (1991a) 288–95 [litany]; Pulsiano (2001a) [Pss. I–L, coll. as χ]

ST: D.H. Wright (1967) 48 [psalter prefaces]; Lambert (1969–72) no. 158; *BCLL* (1985) no. 976; Gneuss (2003b) 303

754. 5. Salisbury, Cathedral Library, 221 [formerly Oxford, Bodleian Library, Fell 4 (returned to Salisbury, August 1985)]

[companion volume to nos. **754. 5** and **215** (?)]

s. xi ex., Salisbury

Contents: Office legendary (January–June)

MS: Schenkl nos. 908, 909; Madan et al. (1895–1953) II/ii.1212 [no. 8689]; N.R. Ker (1949–50) 154 nn., 160, 173, 176–7 [repr. N.R. Ker (1985) 176 nn., 182, 195, 201–2]; Van Dijk (1957–60) II/ii.173; N.R. Ker (1962–92) IV.257–62; N.R. Ker (1964) 172; N.R. Ker (1976b) 25, 26 n. 2, 27, 29 and n. 1, 36–7, 42, 45 [repr. N.R. Ker (1985) 145, 146 n. 2, 147, 149 a nd n. 1, 157–8, 165, 169]; A.G. Watson (1987a) 133; Webber (1992) 12–15, 20, 21, 24, 40 and nn., 70, 154–6 and n. 62 [complete list of contents], 169; R. Gameson (1999a) no. 896; Lapidge (2006) 340, 341; Biggs (2007a) 46–8, 53–4; T.N. Hall (2007) 250; Upchurch (2007) xii, 111

ED: Arnold (1890-6) I.3–25 [base MS for Abbo, *Passio S. Eadmundi*]; Jane Stevenson (1996b) 51–98 [Paulus, *Vita S. Mariae Aegyptiacae*, coll. as S]

ST: Levison (1919–20) 545, 632–3; N.R. Ker (1960) 53; Zettel (1979); Zettel (1982); *BCLL* (1985) no. 1315 [cf. *CSLMA* II (1999) 497–8]; Jackson—Lapidge (1996) 145 n. 16; Love (1996) xviii–xxiii; Whatley (1996) 19, 21, 29 n. 78; Biggs et al. (2001) *passim*; Proud (2002); T.N. Hall (2007) 250

754. 6. Salisbury, Cathedral Library, 222 [formerly Oxford, Bodleian Library, Fell 1 (returned to Salisbury, August 1985)]

s. xi ex., Salisbury

Contents: Office legendary (July–December; now incomplete, ending at 9 Oct.)

MS: Schenkl nos. 908, 909; Madan et al. (1895–1953) II/ii.1212 [no. 8688]; N.R. Ker (1948–55) 173 and n. 1 [repr. N.R. Ker (1985) 127 and n. 1]; N.R. Ker (1949–50) 154 nn., 160, 173, 176–7 [repr. N.R. Ker (1985) 176 nn., 182, 195, 201–2]; Van Dijk (1957–60) II/ii.173; N.R. Ker (1962–92) IV.257–62; N.R. Ker (1964) 172; N.R. Ker (1976b) 25, 26 n. 2, 27, 36, 45 [repr. N.R. Ker (1985) 145, 146 n. 2, 147, 157, 169]; A.G. Watson (1987a) 133; A.G. Watson (1987b) 287 [repr. A.G. Watson (2004) no. VIII]; Webber (1992) 12–15, 18–20, 40 and nn., 70, 154 n., 156–7 [complete list of contents], 169, 170; R. Gameson (1999a) no. 897; Lapidge (2006) 340, 341; Biggs (2007a) 45–6; Barker-Benfield (2008) III.1665

ST: Levison (1919–20) 545, 631–2: N.R. Ker (1960) 53; Zettel (1979); Zettel (1982); Jackson—Lapidge (1996); Love (1996) xviii–xxiii; Magennis (1996) 329 n. 6; Whatley (1996) 19, 21, 29 n. 78; Biggs et al. (2001) *passim*; Proud (2002); Biggs (2007a) 42–3, 45, 49–50, 53, 55–6; T.N. Hall (2007) 250, 262

754. 8. Salisbury, Cathedral Library, Portfolio 4/1

s. xi in., Canterbury CC?, Peterborough?

Contents: gospels (f)

MS: T.A.M. Bishop (1967a) 39; N.R. Ker (2002) 14; Gneuss (2012) 294

755. Shrewsbury, Shropshire Record Office, 1052/1

s. viii², prob. Northumbria

Contents: Jerome, *Comm. in Euangelium Matthaei* [*CPL* 590] (f)

MS: N.R. Ker (1962a) [repr. N.R. Ker (1985) 113–20]; *CLA* Supplement (1971) no. 1760; Sims-Williams (1990) 183 and n. 33; Dumville (1992a) 105; Lapidge (2006) 314

FACS: *CLA* Supplement (1971) no. 1760 [fol. 2r]; N.R. Ker (1985) pl. 16 [fol. 2v]

ED: N.R. Ker (1962a) 11–14 [repr. N.R. Ker (1985) 117–20]; Hurst—Adriaen (1969) [this fragment coll. as S]

ST: Lambert (1969–72) no. 217

755. 5. Shrewsbury, Shrewsbury School, XXI

s. xi/xii, Normandy, (prov. Durham)

Contents: Gregory, *Regula pastoralis* [*CPL* 1712]

MS: N.R. Ker (1962–92) IV.308–10; A.G. Watson (1987a) 33; R. Gameson (1999a) no. 901; Lawrence–Mathers (2003) 266; Schreiber (2003) 24–5 and n. 16; Lapidge (2006) 307

Stonyhurst College, Lancashire, Society of Jesus [formerly no. 756]: see now no. **501. 2**

Stonyhurst College, Lancashire, Society of Jesus, 5. 50 [formerly no. 756. 5]: see now no. **302. 5**

756. 8. Taunton, Somerset County Record Office DD/SAS C/1193/77

s. xi med.

Contents: *Homiliarium* of Angers[+*] (f)

MS: Gneuss (2003b) 303; Gretsch (2004) 147–9; Gneuss (2005a); Gneuss (2008a) 420

FACS: Gretsch (2004) pls. III–IV [pp. 1, 6]

ED: Gretsch (2004) 151–8

ST: Gretsch (2004); Conti (2007) 374 n. 50

757. Ushaw (Co. Durham), St Cuthbert's College, 44

s. viii med., Northumbria

Contents: Office lectionary (f)

MS: Doyle (1992); Pfaff (2012) 451 and n. 3

FACS: Doyle (1992) pls. I–IV [first recto and verso, second recto and verso]

ED: Doyle (1992) 26–7

757. 1. Ushaw (co. Durham), St Cuthbert's College, XX. K. 3. 7

s. xi

Contents: Ælfric, *Grammar*[+*] (f)

[no printed notice; information from A.I. Doyle]

758. Wells, Cathdral Library, 7

s. xi med.

Contents: *Regula S. Benedicti*[+*] [*CPL* 1852] (f)

MS: Schröer (1885–8) xxv–xxvi; N.R. Ker (1957) no. 395; N.R. Ker (1962–92) IV.563–4; Gretsch (1973) 42–3; Rella (1977) 57; Jayatilaka (2003) 157–8, 182–6; Lapidge (2006) 293; Wieland (2009) 138–9; Scragg (2012a) nos. 1037–8

ED: Schröer (1885–8/1964) 78–90, 94–122, 221–2 [base MS for OE text]; Schröer (1888/1978) 102–36 [Latin text of *Regula S. Benedicti* coll. as W]

ST: Schröer (1885–8) xxxvii–xxxviii; Gretsch (1973) 288–303; Gretsch (1974)

759. Winchester, Cathedral Library, 1 (with London, British Library, Cotton Tiberius D. iv, vol. II, fols. 158-66)

s. x/xi or xi in., (prov. Winchester)

Contents: Bede, *Historia ecclesiastica* [*CPL* 1375]; colophon; Ædiluulf, *De abbatibus* [SK and Suppl. 15778]; excerpts from Jerome and Orosius entitled *De situ Babylonis*

MS: Schenkl no. 3806; C. Plummer (1896) I.cix–cxiii [erroneously described as MS 3]; Potter (1935); N.R. Ker (1957) no. 396; N.R. Ker (1962–92) IV.578–9; A. Campbell (1967b) ix–x; Colgrave—Mynors (1969) l–li; Lapidge (1972) 95 n. 2 [repr. Lapidge (1993a) 235 n. 2]; Rella (1977) 69; Dumville (1993g) 119 and nn.; R. Gameson (2012a) 59 n. 194; Scragg (2012a) no. 1039

FACS: Robinson—Stanley (1991) no. 2.21 [fol. 81r (detail)]

ED: C. Plummer (1896) [Bede, *Historia ecclesiastica*, coll. as W]; Dobbie (1942) 105–6 [Cædmon's Hymn coll. as W]; A. Campbell (1967b) [Ædiluulf, *De abbatibus*, coll. as L]; R. Gameson (2001d) 42 [colophon]

ST: T.A.M. Bishop (1971) 21; Lapidge (1990) [repr. Lapidge (1996b) 381–98]; Lapidge—Winterbottom (1991b) clxxvii–clxxix; Love (1996) lxxix; Lapidge et al. (1999) 6; Westgard (2010)

759. 1. Winchester, Cathedral Library, 2

s. xi/xii, prob. Winchester OM

Contents: Augustine, *Tractatus in Euangelium Ioannis* [*CPL* 278];
Possidius, *Vita S. Augustini* [*BHL* 785; *CPL* 358]

MS: Schenkl no. 3798; N.R. Ker (1962–92) IV.579–80; R. Gameson (1999a)
no. 913; Lawrence–Mathers (2003) 272; Gullick (2005a) 32, 75 n. 16

ST: Römer (1972b) 323

759. 3. Winchester, Cathedral Library, 25 [formerly Brockenhurst (Hants.), Parish Church, Parish Register s.n.]

s. ix$^{2/4}$, NE France

Contents: Socrates, Sozomen and Theodoretus, *Historia tripartita*, trans.
Cassiodorus [*CPG* 7502] (f)

MS: Bischoff (1998 —) I, no. 691; R. McKitterick (2004) 280–1 n. 57

759. 4. Winchester, Winchester College, 5

s. xi/xii, prob. Winchester OM

Contents: Paschasius Radbertus, *Comm. in Lamentationes Hieremiae*

MS: N.R. Ker (1962–92) IV.606; R. Gameson (1999a) no. 914; Gullick
(2005a) 32, 75 n. 16

759. 5. Winchester, Winchester College, 40A

s. viii^2, France?

Contents: Basil, *Homiliae super psalmos*, trans. Rufinus [*CPG* 2836] (f)

MS: *CLA* II (1935) no. 261; N.R. Ker (1962–92) IV.628; Lapidge (2006)
292; Rushforth (2011) 59

FACS: *CLA* II (1935) no. 261 [fol. 3v (detail)]

760. Windsor Castle, St George's Chapel, 5

s. xi/xii, (prov. s. xii Canterbury CC)

Contents: Gregory, *Homiliae in Hiezechielem* [*CPL* 1710]; Bede, *Comm.
in Parabolas Salomonis* (*In Prouerbia Salomonis*) [*CPL* 1351]

MS: M.R. James (1903) 32, 507; M.R. James (1933) 76; Laistner — King
(1943) 60; Dodwell (1954) 17; N.R. Ker (1964) 39; R. Gameson (1999a)
no. 915; Lapidge (2006) 305

760. 3. Windsor Castle, Royal Library, Jackson Collection 16

s. ix med. or ix$^{2/4}$, prob. Saint-Amand

Contents: Augustine, *De ciuitate Dei* [*CPL* 313] (f)

MS: Stratford (1981) 82; Stratford (2000) 129–30; Gneuss (2003) 303; Lapidge (2006) 173, 284

FACS: Stratford (1981) pl. 4 [verso]; Stratford (2000) fig. 19 [recto (detail)]

761. Worcester, Cathedral Library, F. 48

s. xi ex., prov. Worcester [fols. 1–48]; s. xi^1, Continent? [fols. 49–104]; and xi med., prob. Worcester [fols. 105–64]; all parts prob. Worcester, prov. Worcester

Contents: fols. 1–48 (s. xi ex., prov. Worcester): Jerome, *Vita S. Pauli primi eremitae* [*CPL* 617; BHL 6596]; Athanasius, *Vita S. Antonii*, trans. Evagrius [*CPG* 2101; *BHL* 609]; Jerome, *Vita S. Hilarionis* [*CPL* 618; *BHL* 3879]

fols. 49–104 (s. xi^1, Continent?): *Historia monachorum*, trans. Rufinus [*CPG* 5620; *CPL* 198p; *BHL* 6524]

fols. 105–64 (s. xi med.): *Verba seniorum* [*CPG* 5570; *BHL* 6527] (171 excerpts)

fol. 164v (text added s. xii^1): *Vita Thais* [*BHL* 8012] (incomplete)

MS: Schenkl no. 4302; Floyer—Hamilton (1906) 22–3; N.R. Ker (1964) 210; T.A.M. Bishop (1971) 17 [cited erroneously as 'F. 148']; N.R. Ker (1949) 30 [repr. N.R. Ker (1985) 29]; McIntyre (1978) 17–18 *et passim*; Schulz–Flügel (1990) 135–6; Dumville (1992a) 140 n. 324; P. Jackson (1992) 122–5; Dumville (1993g) 73–5 and n. 133; R. Gameson (1996a) 210–12, 218 n. 74, 242; R. Gameson (1999a) no. 919; Biggs et al. (2001) 86; R.M. Thomson (2001) 29–30; Gneuss (2003b) 303; R. Gameson (2005a) 96; Lapidge (2006) 281, 316, 337, 339; Wieland (2009) 143

FACS: R. Gameson (1991) fig. 10 [fol. 153r]; R. Gameson (1996a) pls. 6, 9 [fols. 153r, 6r]

ED: Schulz-Flügel (1990) [*Historia monachorum* coll. as W]

ST: Lambert (1969–72) nos. 261, 262; P. Jackson (1992); Biggs et al. (2001) 86, 252, 378–81, 442–4

761. 5. Worcester, Cathedral Library, F. 72, fols. 1 and 2

s. x (decoration added later?), England

Contents: gospels (f: Canon table)

MS: Floyer—Hamilton (1906) 35; R.M. Thomson (2001) 46

FACS: R.M. Thomson (2001) frontispiece [fols. 1v–2r]

762. Worcester, Cathedral Library, F. 91

s. x³/⁴, prob. Worcester, (prov. ibid.)

Contents: Smaragdus of Saint-Mihiel, *Expositio libri comitis*

MS: Schenkl no. 4319; Floyer—Hamilton (1906) 46; N.R. Ker (1964) 211; T.A.M. Bishop (1971) 16; N.R. Ker (1971) 318 n. 4 [repr. N.R. Ker (1985) 12 n. 4]; Rädle (1974) 124 and n. 91; Rella (1977) 162; McIntyre (1978) 209; J. Hill (1991a); J. Hill (1992) 214, 235–7; Dumville (1993g) 49, 54–5; R. Gameson (1996a) 198–200 and n. 15, 242; R.M. Thomson (2001) 58; R. Gameson (2012a) 40 and n. 103

FACS: T.A.M. Bishop (1971) pl. XVI [fol. 96r]; R. Gameson (1996a) pl. 1 [fol. 214r]

ST: Rädle (1974); Hartzell (1989) 85; J. Hill (1992); R. McKitterick (2012) 329

763. Worcester, Cathedral Library, F. 92

[companion vol. to nos. **763. 1** and **763. 2**]

s. xi/xii or xii in., prov. Worcester

Contents: Paulus Diaconus, *Homiliarium* (Advent to Easter)

MS: Schenkl no. 4320; Floyer—Hamilton (1906) 46–7; N.R. Ker (1964) 211; Rella (1977) 117; Clayton (1985) 220; R. Gameson (1999a) no. 921; R.M. Thomson (2001) 58–62; Rittmueller (2002) 333 and n. 2; T.N. Hall (2004b) 88; R. Gameson (2005a) 98; T.N. Hall (2007) 244; J. Hill (2007a) 86, 92; T.N. Hall (2008a) 33 and n. 10

FACS: R. Gameson (2005a) fig. 6 [fol. 36r]

ST: Lambert (1969–72) nos. 218, 990 n. 72; *CPPM* I, no. 4708; T.N. Hall (2007) 244, 249 n. 67, 259

763. 1. Worcester, Cathedral Library, F. 93

s. xi/xii or xii in.

Contents: Paulus Diaconus, *Homiliarium* (Easter to Advent), conflated with the *Homiliarium* of Alan of Farfa (for the same period) [cf. no. **763**]

MS: Schenkl no. 4321; Floyer—Hamilton (1906) 47; N.R. Ker (1964) 211; Clayton (1985) 220; R. Gameson (1999a) no. 922; R.M. Thomson (2001) 62–5; Rittmueller (2002) 333 n. 2; T.N. Hall (2004b) 88, 93, 94 n. 12, 98, 100–5; R. Gameson (2005a) 98; T.N. Hall (2007) 244; J. Hill (2007a) 75, 86–7, 92; Barker-Benfield (2008) III.1838; T.N. Hall (2008a) 33 and n. 10

ST: Römer (1972b) 325–6; *CPPM* I, nos. 1225, 1253, 1689, 1691, 2001, 4758

763. 2. Worcester, Cathedral Library, F. 94

s. xi/xii or xii in.

Contents: Paulus Diaconus, *Homiliarium* (Sanctorale: 3 May to 30 Nov., and Commune SS.) [cf. no. **763**]

MS: Schenkl no. 4322; Floyer—Hamilton (1906) 47; N.R. Ker (1964) 211; Clayton (1985) 220; Whatley (1996) 21; R. Gameson (1999a) no. 923; R.M. Thomson (2001) 65–8; Rittmueller (2002) 333 n. 2; T.N. Hall (2004b) 88; Rittmueller (2004) 119*–121*, 183*–191*; R. Gameson (2005a) 98; T.N. Hall (2007) 244–5; J. Hill (2007a) 91, 92; T.N. Hall (2008a) 33 and n. 10

FACS: R. Gameson (2005a) fig. 7 [fol. 105v]

ED: Rittmueller (2004) 193–9 [Paulus, Hom. lxxxvi, coll. as Wo]

ST: Biggs et al. (1990) 157 [Cross]; *CPPM* I, nos. 174, 5020; Rittmueller (2002) 331, 333–6, 343–54; T.N. Hall (2007) 237 n. 30, 245, 253 n. 88, 255, 257 n. 101; T.N. Hall (2008a) 55–9

764. Worcester, Cathedral Library, F. 173

s. xi med., Winchester OM , prov. Worcester

Contents: missal (part, including litany)

MS: Warren (1885); Delisle (1886) 272; Frere (1894–1932) II, no. 614; Floyer—Hamilton (1906) 98–100; N.R. Ker (1957) no. 397; N.R. Ker (1964) 201; T.A.M. Bishop (1971) xv; Hohler (1975) 73, 224 n. 55; Cowdrey (1981) 56–7; Hartzell (1989) 47 n. 4, 84–9; Lapidge (1991a) 85; Dumville (1992a) 68; Pfaff (1995b) 25–6; R. Gameson (1996a) 243; C.A. Jones (1998b) 86–7 n. 64; R.M. Thomson (2001) 116; Hartzell (2006) no. 362; Keefer (2007b) 105; Swan (2007b) 39; Wieland (2009) 123; Pfaff (2012) 455 and n. 17; Rankin (2012) 488–9, 501; Scragg (2012a) no. 1042

FACS: R. Gameson (2012) pl. 22.2 [fol. 6v]

ED: C.H. Turner (1915–16) 66–8 [prayers for the dying and burial of the dead]; Lapidge (1991a) 300–1 [litany]

764. 1. Worcester, Cathedral Library, F. 173, fol. 1

s. x²

Contents: Psalterium Gallicanum (f) with gloss

MS: Warren (1885) 395; Floyer—Hamilton (1906) 100; Pfaff (1995a) 69 [Pulsiano]; Pulsiano (2001a) xxx; R.M. Thomson (2001) 116; Rushforth (2011) 50–5

FACS: Lendinara et al. (2011) pl. II [fol. 1r]

ED: Pulsiano (2001a) [psalm fragment collated as ω]

765. Worcester, Cathedral Library, Q. 5

s. x ex., Canterbury CC, (prov. Worcester)

Contents: Bede, *De arte metrica* [*CPL* 1565]; inscription [SK 1479]; Bede, *De schematibus et tropis* [*CPL* 1567]; Priscian, *Institutio de nomine, pronomine et uerbo* [*CPL* 1550]; parsing grammar 'Anima quae pars'; grammatical notes; explanations of technical terms and Greek words; two glossarial poems on Greek medical terminology [SK 13822 and 3618; 11969]; Israel the Grammarian, *De arte metrica* [SK 14392]; verses by Alcuin (from *Carm.* lxxx) [SK 11084]; *Pauca de philosophiae partibus*; table of metrical feet; charm[*] (added s. xi med.)

MS: Schenkl no. 4341; Floyer—Hamilton (1906) 105–8; Laistner—King (1943) 135; N.R. Ker (1957) no. 399; T.A.M. Bishop (1959–63b) 414, 421–2; N.R. Ker (1964) 213; Jeudy (1972) 143; Kendall (1975) 60, 72; Pollard (1975) 158–9; McIntyre (1978) 209; Lapidge (1992b) 109 [repr. Lapidge (1993a) 99]; M. Irvine (1994) 404; R. Gameson (1996a) 233 and n. 121; R.M. Thomson (2001) 120–1; Lapidge (2006) 326; R. Gameson (2012b) 117 n. 90; Gullick (2012) 299 and n. 26, 300 and nn. 34 and 37, 308 and n. 94; Scragg (2012a) nos. 1043–4

FACS: M. Wood (2010) fig. 21 [fol. 71v]

ED: Napier (1890) 324 [OE charm]; Napier (1900) no. 30 [two OE glosses to Bede, *De arte metrica*]; Floyer—Hamilton (1906) 105 [inscription SK 1479]; Strecker (1937–9) 500–2 [Israel, *De arte metrica*, coll. as W]; Storms (1948) 276 [OE charm, ptd from copy in BL, Harley 464, including ending lost in Worcester MS]; D. Chapman (2002) [parsing grammar]

ST: Lapidge (1975a) 84, 104 [repr. Lapidge (1993a) 122, 142] [on SK 11969]; Passalacqua (1978) 378 [Priscian, *Institutio*]; Bursill-Hall (1981) 287–8 [Priscian; *grammatica*]; Lapidge (1992b) [repr. Lapidge (1993a) 87–104]; Bayless (1993) 72–4 [parsing grammar]; Knappe (1996) 132 n. 1, 201–3, 242 n. 4 [*Pauca de philosophiae partibus*]; Law (1997) 143, 202, 274 [parsing grammar]; K.-D. Fischer (1998) 13–17 [SK 13822]; *CSLMA* II (1999) 94–5 [Alcuin, *Carm.* lxxx]; D. Chapman (2002) [parsing grammar]; SK Suppl. 14392 [Israel, *De arte metrica*]; M. Wood (2010) 145, 147–9, 152 [Israel the Grammarian]; D'Aronco (2011) 234 and n. 24

765. 1. Worcester, Cathedral Library, Q. 5, fol. 80

s. x in.

Contents: Bible (reject leaf; Isaias LXI.10–11)

MS: R.M. Thomson (2001) 120

766. Worcester, Cathedral Library, Q. 8, fols. 164–71 [with Worcester, Cathedral Library, Add. 7, fols. 1–6]

s. ix/x, France? s. x/xi or xi in. England? (prov. Worcester)

Contents: Statius, *Thebais*, glossed (f)

MS: Schenkl no. 4345; Floyer—Hamilton (1906) 11; N.R. Ker (1962–92) IV.679; T.A.M. Bishop (1971) xviii, xxv, 18; Rella (1977) 88, 163; McIntyre (1978) 209; Dumville (1993g) 54–5 and n. 240; Budny (1997) I.460; R.M. Thomson (2001) 123; Lapidge (2006) 140, 173, 333

FACS: T.A.M. Bishop (1971) pl. XVIII [fol. 167r]

ED: Klotz—Klinnert (1902/1973) [Statius, *Thebais*, coll. as W]

ST: R.D. Williams (1947); R.D. Williams (1948); L.D. Reynolds (1983) xxxii n.

767. Worcester, Cathedral Library, Q. 21

s. x ex., N France or Lotharingia, prov. Worcester by s. xi ex.

Contents: Gregory, *Homiliae .xl. in Euangelia* [*CPL* 1711]

MS: Schenkl no. 4347; Floyer—Hamilton (1906) 119–20; N.R. Ker (1960) 53; N.R. Ker (1964) 213; McIntyre (1978) 42 *et passim*; Dumville (1993g) 49 and n. 216; R. Gameson (1996a) 196 and n. 6, 233; R.M. Thomson (2001) 132; R. Gameson (2012d) 368 and n. 100; Gullick (2012) 299 and n. 25

768. Worcester, Cathedral Library, Q. 28

s. ix^2, France, prov. s. xi (or x^2?) England (Canterbury?), (prov. Worcester)

Contents: Eusebius, *Historia ecclesiastica*, trans. Rufinus [*CPG* 3495]

MS: Schenkl no. 4350; Floyer—Hamilton (1906) 123; H.M. Bannister (1917) 391; Siegmund (1949) 79; N.R. Ker (1964) 213; Dumville (1993g) 49; R. Gameson (1996a) 196 and n., 233; R.M. Thomson (2001) 135; R. Gameson (2012a) 62 n. 216

ST: R. McKitterick (2012) 329

769. Worcester, Cathedral Library, Q. 78 B

s. x in., N France, (prov. Worcester)

Contents: Office lectionary (f)

MS: Floyer—Hamilton (1906) 149; Hartzell (1989) 85; Dumville (1993g) 49; R.M. Thomson (2001) 174

770. Worcester, Cathedral Library, Add. 1 (with Oxford, Bodleian Library, Lat. bib. d. 1 (P) [S.C. 31089])

s. viii ex. or ix in., perh. Canterbury (StA), or Worcester

Contents: gospels (f)

MS: Schenkl no. 4321; Madan et al. (1895–1953) VI.16; Floyer— Hamilton (1906) 47; C.H. Turner (1916) v–ix; *CLA* II (1935) nos. 245 [Oxford MS], 262 [Add. 1]; McGurk (1961a) nos. 34, 38; N.R. Ker (1962–92) IV.678; Bischoff (1966–81) II.336, 338; R. Gameson (1996a) 230 and n. 108; R.M. Thomson (2001) xx and nn., 62; M.P. Brown (2012) 163

FACS: C.H. Turner (1916) pls. 1–6 [Worcester Add. 1, complete]; R.M. Thomson (2001) pl. 10 [folio not specified]

ST: Glunz (1933) 18; Sims-Williams (1990) 181 and n. 25, 210, 280 and n. 32

770. 5. Worcester, Cathedral Library, Add. 2

s. vii, prob. Spain, prov. prob. Worcester s. viii

Contents: Jerome, *Comm. in Euangelium Matthaei* [*CPL* 590] (f)

MS: Schenkl no. 4296; Floyer—Hamilton (1906) 14–15; C.H. Turner (1916) x–xviii; CLA II (1935) no. 263; N.R. Ker (1962a) [repr. N.R.

Ker (1985) 114 and nn.]; N.R. Ker (1962–92) IV.678; Hurst—Adriaen (1969) vi; Bestul (1981b) 9–10 n. 33; Sims-Williams (1990) 183 and n. 33; R.M. Thomson (2001) xx, 20

FACS: C.H. Turner (1916) pls. 7–14 [complete facsimile]; R.M. Thomson (2001) pl. 11 [folio not specified]

ED: Hurst—Adriaen (1969) [Jerome, *Comm. in Euangelium Matthaei*, coll. as W]

771. Worcester, Cathedral Library, Add. 3

s. viii

Contents: Gregory, *Regula pastoralis* [*CPL* 1712] (f)

MS: C.H. Turner (1916) xviii–xxiv; *CLA* II (1935) no. 264; Atkins—Ker (1944) 70; N.R. Ker (1962–92) IV.679; T.J. Brown (1982) 108 [repr. T.J. Brown (1993a) 209]; Clement (1984a) 42; M.P. Brown (1989) 160–1; Sims-Williams (1990) 136 n. 98; R.M. Thomson (2001) xx n. 13, xlvi and n. 265, 110; Schreiber (2003) 23 and n. 2, 27 n. 24; Gullick (2012) 296 n. 12

FACS: C.H. Turner (1916) pls. 15–26 [complete facsimile]; R.M. Thomson (2001) pl. 12 [fol. 1v]

772. Worcester, Cathedral Library, Add. 4

s. viii

Contents: Paterius, *Liber testimoniorum ueteris testamenti quem Paterius ex opusculis S. Gregorii excerpi curauit* [*CPL* 1718] (f; on Gen. XXIV–XXVI, XXXV–XXXVI))

MS: Floyer—Hamilton (1906) 164; C.H. Turner (1916) xxiv–xxvii; *CLA* II (1935) no. 265; Lowe (1960) 23 [no. XXXVI]; N.R. Ker (1962–92) IV.679; Bischoff (1966–81) II.333; Sims-Williams (1990) 183 and n. 33; R.M. Thomson (2001) xx, 116; M.P. Brown (2012) 146 and n. 121; Martello (2012) 29, 121, 128

FACS: C.H. Turner (1916) pls. 27–30 [complete facsimile]; Lowe (1960) pl. XXXVI [fol. 1v]; R.M. Thomson (2001) pl. 13 [fol. 1v]

773. Worcester, Cathedral Library, Add. 5

s. viii^2

Contents: Isidore, *Sententiae* [*CPL* 1199] (f)

MS: *CLA* Supplement (1971) no. 1777; N.R. Ker (1962–92) IV.679; R.M. Thomson (2001) xx and n. 14, 150

Worcester, Cathedral Library, Add. 7, fols. 1–6: see no. **766**

773. 5. Wormsley, nr. Stokenchurch (Bucks.), The Wormsley Library (Collection of the late Sir John Paul Getty), s.n.

s. vii (s. vii[1] or vii med.), Northumbria or Ireland (or Continent?), prov. England s. vii or later

Contents: Eusebius, *Historia ecclesiastica*, trans. Rufinus [*CPG* 3495] (f)

MS: *CLA*, Add. no. 1864; Bischoff—Brown (1985) 348–9; Sotheby sale catalogue *Western Manuscripts and Miniatures* (25 June 1985), lot 50; Breen (1987); Bischoff et al. (1992b) 307; Bammel (1993); Stoneman (1997) 130–1; Dumville (1999) 22–3, 25, 29 and nn.; Lapidge (2006) 302; Fletcher (2007) 2–3 [no. 1]

FACS: Sotheby sale catalogue *Western Manuscripts and Miniatures* (25 June 1985) lot 50, 2 colour plates [complete facsimile]; Bischoff—Brown (1985) pl. XVIII (b) [fols. 1r, 2v]; Breen (1987) pls. 13 [fols. 2r + 9v], 14 [fols. 2v + 9r]; Fletcher (2007) p. 3 [fols. 9v + 2r]

773. 6. York, Minster Library, XVI. Q. 1

s. xi ex. (prov. York)

Contents: Gregory, *Moralia in Iob* [*CPL* 1708], bks. I–X [companion vol. to no. **773. 7**]

MS: N.R. Ker (1962–92) IV.772–3; R. Gameson (1999a) no. 926; Lapidge (2006) 306; R. Gameson (2012a) 26 n. 47

773. 7. York, Minster Library, XVI. Q. 2

s. xi ex. (prov. York)

Contents: Gregory, *Moralia in Iob* [*CPL* 1708], bks. XI–XXII [companion vol. to no. **773. 6**]

MS: N.R. Ker (1962–92) IV.773–4; R. Gameson (1999a) no. 927; Lapidge (2006) 306; R. Gameson (2012a) 50 and n. 160

774. York, Minster Library, Add. 1, fols. 10–161

s. x ex.–xi in., prob. Canterbury CC, prov. York (by 1020–3)

Contents: gospels; additions: records (surveys of archiepiscopal land), three short sermons or tracts*, writ or letter of King Cnut* (all s. xi¹); inventory of liturgical books and church goods* (s. xi med.); prayers* (s. xi¹); list of sureties (s. xi²)

MS: T.A.M. Bishop (1954–8a) 186; N.R. Ker (1957) no. 402; N.R. Ker (1962–92) IV.784–6; N.R. Ker (1964) 216; Whitelock (1965) 216–17 [repr. Whitelock (1981b) no. XV]; T.A.M. Bishop (1971) xvi, 22; N.R. Ker (1971) 330–1 [repr. N.R. Ker (1985) 24–6]; N.R. Ker (1976a) 125; Backhouse et al. (1984b) no. 54; N. Barker et al. (1986); McGurk (1986b) [repr. McGurk (1998) no. XIV]; Heslop (1990) 166–70, 175, 182; Dumville (1991–5) 53–4; R. Gameson (1992a) 200–3 and n. 57, 205, 212–14; Dumville (1993g) 106 n. 116, 108 n. 129, 123, 140; Dance (2004) 31 n. 6; R. Gameson (2004b); Heslop (2004) 279, 286, 304–5; C.A. Jones (2004) 334; Lionarons (2004c) 416 n. 18; G. Mann (2004) 265 nn. 93, 94; Meaney (2004) 481–2; Norton (2004) 214–15, 234; A. Orchard (2004) 66 n. 15; *ASMMF* XIV (2007) 135–49 [no. 494; Doane]; R. Gameson (2012a) 40 n. 105; R. Gameson (2012b) 100 and n. 25, 108 and n. 51, 117 n. 90; Marsden (2012) 423 and n. 77, 425 and n. 87; McGurk (2012) 439, 440, 447 [no. 21]; A. Orchard (2012) 697 [no. 18]; Scragg (2012a) nos. 307, 1045–52; P. Wormald (2012) 534 [no. 6]

DEC: F. Wormald (1944) 129–30 [repr. F. Wormald (1984) 155]; F. Wormald (1952) 41, 75; F. Wormald (1971b) 310 [repr. F. Wormald (1984) 81]; F. Wormald (1973) 240 [repr. and trans. in F. Wormald (1984) 117]; E. Temple (1976) no. 61; Brownrigg (1978) 265–6; Dodwell (1982) 103; Ohlgren (1986) no. 166; R. Gameson (1995b) 91, 98, 116, 178 n. 135, 194, 217–18, 238 n. 18, 239; Heslop (2004) 279, 284, 287, 292, 298, 300–1, 303; R. Gameson (2012c) 282 and n. 116

FACS: N. Barker et al. (1986) [complete facsimile]; *NPS* II, pls. 163–5 [folios not specified]; E. Temple (1976) ills. 181–4 [fols. 22v, 23r, 60v, 85v]; F. Wormald (1984) ill. 111 [fol. 22v]; R. Gameson (1992a) pl. 45 [fol. 61r]; Heslop (2004) 288 [fol. 23v], 289 [fol. 24r], 290 [fol. 23r], 291 [fol. 61r], 293 [fol. 85r], 294 [fol. 60r], 296 [fol. 10r], 299 [fol. 22v], 302 [fol. 114v]; Norton (2004) 216 [fol. 160v], 217 [fol. 161r]; Townend (2004) figs. 7.6, 7.7, 8.2, 8.3, 10.2–10.9 [fols. 156v, 157r, 160r, 161r, 23v, 24r, 23r, 61r, 85r, 60r, 10r, 22v]; *ASMMF* XIV (2007) no. 494

ED: Napier (1883/1967) nos. 59–61 [short sermons or tracts]; Liebermann (1903–16) I.273–5, III.186–9 [writ or letter of King Cnut]; W.H. Stevenson (1912) 10 [prayers], 12 [list of sureties], 15–19 [records]; A.J. Robertson (1939) 164–8 [records], 248 [inventory of liturgical books and ecclesiastical furniture]; Whitelock et al. (1981a) I.435–41 [writ or letter of King Cnut]; Lapidge (1994b) 122–3 [inventory of liturgical books]; Meaney (2004) 482 [fol. 159r]

ST: Napier (1883/1967) 363–5 [Ostheeren]; W.H. Stevenson (1912); Glunz (1933) 134–5; Whitelock (1948) 452 [repr. Whitelock (1981b) no. XII]; N. Barker et al. (1986); McGurk (1986b) [repr. McGurk (1998) no. XIV]; Keynes (1986a); M.P. Brown (1989c); Pfaff (1992a); Lenker (1997) 448 n. 111; Norton (2004) 211–18

774. 1: see now no. **521. 3. 1**

II

Libraries outside the British Isles
(nos. 774. 3–947)

774. 3. Alençon, Bibliothèque municipale, 14, fols. 91–114

s. xi¹, Winchester, prov. Saint-Évroult

Contents: benedictional; two masses *de amico*; *Iudicium Dei*

MS: *Cat. gén. Dép.* (Octavo) II.488–91 [Omont]; Liebermann (1903–16)
I.xix, 401; Delisle (1910); Chibnall (1969–80) I.64 n. 1, 201 n. 1, 202;
Alexander (1970a) 238 n. 1; Dumville (1992a) 95 n. 174; R. Gameson
(2012d) 365 and n. 88

FACS: R. Gameson (2012) pl. 14.3–4 [fols. 114v, 115r]

ED: Liebermann (1903–16) I.417-18 [*Iudicium Dei* coll. as A1]

ST: Hardy (1862–71) I.237, 464, II.515, 582; Delisle (1910) 22–3; Gneuss
(1968) 118, 246–8; Lapidge — Winterbottom (1991b) xxiii, clxxx–clxxxi
et passim; *CSLMA* II (1999) 508; Lapidge (2003a) 365, 783–4

774. 6. Amiens, Bibliothèque municipale, 377, flyleaves

s. x, England?

Contents: sacramentary (f)

MS: *Cat. gén. Dép*. (Octavo) XIX.179 [Coyecque]; Bischoff (1998—) I,
p. 14

775. Antwerp, Plantin-Moretus Museum, M. 16. 2 (47) (with London, British Library, Add. 32246)

s. xi in. and xi¹, prob. Abingdon (or Continent?), with additions at
Abingdon, s. xi¹

Contents: *Excerptiones de Prisciano* (prob. Abingdon, s. xi in.); additions
(made at Abingdon s. xi in. and xi¹): four glossaries (an architectural
glossary; an end-page miscellaneous glossary; an alphabetical glossary
[partly Latin — Old English]; and a class glossary [Latin — Old
English]); Remigius, Commentary on Donatus, *Ars minor*; Ælfric,
Colloquium [incomplete, revised by Ælfric Bata]; Latin poems (on the
virgins Æthelthryth, Ælfgifu and Eadgyth (Edith); on SS. Edward,
Eustace and Kenelm [SK 656a]; in commemoration of Archbishop
Ælfric [SK Suppl. 12418a]; a Latin verse riddle; a Latin verse letter
from Herbert to Abbot Wulfgar of Abingdon [SK Suppl. 15838a]);
an anonymous letter to 'Ælf')

MS: *Cat. Add. B.M. 1882–7* (1889) 96; Förster (1917); Denucé (1927) 45–6;
N.R. Ker (1957) no. 2; N.R. Ker (1964) 2; T.A.M. Bishop (1971) xii n. 2,

xxiv; Pheifer (1974) xxxvii–xxxviii; Garmonsway (1978) 3; D.W. Porter (1999b); D.W. Porter (2002) 3–4, 397; *ASMMF* XIII (2006) 1–10 [no. 4; Bremmer, Dekker]; Lapidge (2006) 62, 293; Wieland (2009) 144; Gneuss (2012) 294; Scragg (2012a) nos. 1, 1a, 2–4

FACS: *ASMMF* XIII (2006) no. 4; Lendinara et al. (2011) pl. III [Add. 32246, fol. 2v]

ED: Dümmler (1884) 351–3 [Latin verse letter from Herbert to Abbot Wulfgar]; Förster (1917) 154–5 [poems SK 656a, 12418a, verse riddle, letter to 'Ælf']; W.H. Stevenson (1929) 75–96 [Ælfric, *Colloquium*, coll. as R_1 and R_2]; Meritt (1945) no. 22 [eight OE glosses to *Excerptiones de Prisciano*]; Kindschi (1955) [alphabetical and class glossaries]; D.W. Porter (2002) [*Excerptiones de Prisciano* coll. as B]; J. Hill (2005b) 339–46 [base MS for Ælfric, *Colloquium*]; D.W. Porter (2011a) [base MS for all four glossaries]; D.W. Porter (2012) 239–45 [base MS for verse letter from Herbert to Wulfgar], 246–7 [anonymous letter to 'Ælf']

LANG: Luick (1914–21) § 703.1; Lapidge (1975a) 99 [repr. Lapidge (1993a) 137]; Hofstetter (1987) 515–17; Dietz (1990)

ST: F. Kluge (1885a) 448–9; Förster (1917); Ladd (1960); Buckalew (1978) 164 n. 2; Lapidge (1988b) 260 [repr. Lapidge (1993a) 218]; A.K. Brown (1992) 105–6; D.W. Porter (1996a); D.W. Porter (1996b); Budny (1997) I.446, 506; Gwara—Porter (1997) 4–7, 44–8, 60–8; Lazzari (1998–9); Lazzari (2003); Schreiber (2003) 109 n. 75; Lazzari (2004); J. Hill (2005b); Lendinara (2010) 124–32; D.W. Porter (2010); D'Aronco (2011) 247 and n. 81; Giliberto (2011) 126 and n. 29; Godden (2011) 92; Healey (2011) 8; Jayatilaka (2011) 117; Lazzari (2011); D.W. Porter (2011b); Rusche (2011) 402–14; D.W. Porter (2012)

776. Antwerp, Plantin-Moretus Museum, M. 16. 8 (190)

s. x/xi, Abingdon

Contents: Boethius, *De consolatione Philosophiae* [*CPL* 878], with commentary by Remigius

MS: Denucé (1927) 147–8; Weinberger (1934) xiv; N.R. Ker (1957) no. 3; N.R. Ker (1964) 2; T.A.M. Bishop (1971) xii n. 2, 13, 18; Bolton (1977a) 39, 41, 55–7; Bieler (1984) xiv; Gibson et al. (1995–2001) II.108–9; Bischoff (1998—) I, p. 24; *ASMMF* XIII (2006) 11–16 [no. 5; Bremmer, Dekker]; Godden—Irvine (2009) I.xlv; R. Gameson (2012a) 45 n. 133; Scragg (2012a) no. 2

FACS: *ASMMF* XIII (2006) no. 5

ED: Weinberger (1934) [Boethius coll. as Antv]; Bolton (1977a) 60–78 [mythological glosses to Boethius coll. as K]; Troncarelli (1981) 156 [text of glosses incompletely preserved in no. **908** supplied from this MS]; Bieler (1984) [Boethius coll. as A]; Moreschini (2000) [Boethius coll. as A]

ST: Wittig (1983) 187, 189–98; Troncarelli (1987) 151; Wittig (2007) 187; Wittig (2010) 249; Godden (2011) 92

776. 2. Antwerp, Plantin-Moretus Museum, M. 16. 15 (194)

s. xi^1, prob. xi$^{2/4}$, Canterbury? or Flanders, written with English and Flemish collaboration? (prov. Bruges, Collégiale de Notre Dame, s. xii in.)

Contents: gospels

MS: Denucé (1927) 152–3; Bischoff (1967) 24 [no. 14]; Derolez—Victor (1997) no. 8; Lenker (1997) 5 n. 7, 114; R. Gameson (2002d) 174 and n. 43; R. Gameson (2012b) 102 and n. 34

777. Arendal, Aust-Agder Arkivet (with Rygnestad, Archives of Ketil Rygnestad, no. 95 and Archives of Knut Rygnestad, no. 99)

s. xi$^{1/3}$, or earlier?

Contents: antiphoner (f)

MS: Gjerløw (1979) 21–3; Rankin (2012) 491 and n. 38

FACS: Gjerløw (1979) pl. 1 [Archives of Ketil Rygnestad, no. 95, verso]

778. Arras, Bibliothèque municipale [Médiathèque], 346 (867)

s. x/xi or xi in., prob. Abingdon, supplemented s. xi med., prob. Exeter, prov. Bath, prov. Saint-Vaast, Arras

Contents: Ambrose, *Exameron* [*CPL* 123]

MS: *Cat. gén. Dép.* (Quarto) IV.345 [Quicherat]; Schenkl (1897) xl–xli; Rella (1977) 163; Bankert et al. (1997) 18–19; R. Gameson (2002d) 177 and n. 59, 186; Lapidge (2006) 138, 279

779. Arras, Bibliothèque municipale [Médiathèque], 764 (739), fols. 1–93

s. ix ex., NE France, prov. England s. x, prov. Bath, prov. Saint-Vaast, Arras

Contents: Hrabanus Maurus, *Comm. in Iudith, Comm. in Hester*

MS: *Cat. gén. Dép.* (Quarto) IV.295 [Quicherat]; Grierson (1940a) 112–13; N.R. Ker (1957) no. 4; Rella (1977) 164; Bischoff (1998—) I, no. 102; R. Gameson (2002d) 166, 181; Lapidge (2006) 139, 167; *ASMMF* XVIII (2012) 23–31 [no. 6; Lucas]; R. Gameson (2012d) 345 and n. 4, 349

FACS: *ASMMF* XVIII (2012) no. 6 [complete facsimile]

ED: N.R. Ker (1957) no. 4 [OE scribbles]

ST: R. McKitterick (2012) 328, 330 and n. 111

780. Arras, Bibliothèque municipale [Médiathèque], 764 (739), fols. 134–81

s. ix/x, Winchester?, prov. Bath by s. xi, prov. Saint-Vaast, Arras

Contents: Isidore, *Allegoriae quaedam S. Scripturae* [*CPL* 1190], *In libros ueteris et noui Testamenti prooemia* [*CPL* 1192], *De ortu et obitu patrum* [*CPL* 1191]

MS: *Cat. gén. Dép.* (Quarto) IV.295 [Quicherat]; Grierson (1940a) 113; *CLA* VI (1953) no. 714; N.R. Ker (1957) no. 5; Bischoff (1966–81) I.183; R. Gameson (2002d) 186; Lapidge (2006) 309, 310, 312; *ASMMF* XVIII (2012) 23–31 [no. 6; Lucas]

FACS: *ASMMF* XVIII (2012) no. 6 [complete facsimile]

ED: N.R. Ker (1957) no. 5 [OE glosses]; Meritt (1961) no. XV [OE glosses]

781. Arras, Bibliothèque municipale [Médiathèque], 1029 (812)

s. x/xi, Canterbury, StA, prov. Bath, prov. Saint-Vaast, Arras

Contents: anonymous *Vita S. Cuthberti* [*BHL* 2019] (incomplete); Felix, *Vita S. Guthlaci* [*BHL* 3723; *CPL* 2150] (incomplete); B., *Vita S. Dunstani* [*BHL* 2342] (incomplete); anonymous *Vita S. Philiberti* [*BHL* 6805]

MS: *Cat. gén. Dép.* (Quarto) IV.322 [Quicherat]; Stubbs (1874) xxvii, xxxviii–xxxix; Levison (1919–20) 575 and n. 2; Colgrave (1940) 17–18; Colgrave (1956) 34–5; Van der Straeten (1971) 52–3; Dumville (1993g) 147 n. 39; McKee (1997) 161–7; R. Gameson (2002d) 177 and n. 58, 187; Lapidge (2006) 138; Wieland (2009) 130; Winterbottom—Lapidge (2012) lxxix–lxxxi; R. Gameson (2012d) 355 n. 42, 364 n. 82

ED: Stubbs (1874) 3–52 [base MS for B., *Vita S. Dunstani*]; Krusch—
Levison (1910) 583–604 [*Vita S. Philiberti* coll. as B1*b*]; Colgrave
(1940) [anonymous *Vita S. Cuthberti* coll. as A]; Colgrave (1956)
[Felix, *Vita S. Guthlaci*, coll. as V]; Winterbottom—Lapidge (2012)
2–108 [B., *Vita S. Dunstani*, coll. as A]

ST: Grierson (1940a); Grierson (1940b); Sims-Williams (1990) 206–7;
Lapidge (1992e) [repr. Lapidge (1993a) 293–315]; Winterbottom
(2000); Biggs et al. (2001) 60, 157–9, 179–81, 244–6, 386–7

[*Note*: the following manuscripts were among the books given by
Sæwold, former abbot of Bath, to the church of Saint–Vaast, Arras (cf.
Lapidge (1985b) 58–64 [repr. Lapidge (1994b) 125–30]), but there is no
proof that they were ever in England: Arras, BM 435 (326), fols. 65–
122; 644 (572); 732 (684); 899 (590); 1068 (276); 1079 (235) fols. 28–80.
See also below, no. **808. 2.**]

782. Avranches, Bibliothèque municipale, 29

s. x/xi, S England, prov. Mont Saint-Michel

Contents: fifty-five homilies on the Epistulae Pauli; two prayers to the
Virgin (s. xi); a 'Martinellus': Sulpicius Severus, *Vita S. Martini* [*CPL*
475; *BHL* 5610] (f); excerpts from Gregory of Tours, *Historia
Francorum* [*CPL* 1023] and *De uirtutibus S. Martini* [*CPL* 1024; cf.
BHL 5618d]; Sulpicius Severus, *Epistula* III [*CPL* 476]

MS: Ravaisson (1841) 115–16; *Cat. gén. Dép.* (Quarto) IV.443–4 [Delisle];
Alexander (1970a) 3 n. 4; Lapidge (2006) 307, 333; Wieland (2009) 125,
143

ED: Ravaisson (1841) 324–31 [base MS for Homilies iv, xiv, xxiii]; Barré
(1963) 199–200 [base MS for prayers to the Virgin]

ST: Lambert (1969–72) no. 700; *CPPM* I, nos. 3925, 3934, 3950

Avranches, Bibliothèque municipale, 48, fols. i and ii + 66, fols. i and ii +
71, fols. A and B: see no. **842**

783. Avranches, Bibliothèque municipale, 81

s. xi², England or NW France?, prov. Mont Saint-Michel

Contents: Augustine, *In Ioannis epistulam ad Parthos tractatus .x.* [*CPL*
279]; pseudo-Eusebius Gallicanus, *Sermo* xii [*CPL* 966]; Alcuin, *De
uirtutibus et uitiis*; Augustine (and pseudo-Augustine), *Serm.* lxviii,
lxxiv, lxxix, lxxxv

MS: *Cat. gén. Dép.* (Quarto) IV.464–5 [Delisle]; Alexander (1970a) 238
  and n. 5; Szarmach (1981b) 135; Jeudy—Riou (1989) 212–14;
  R. Gameson (1999a) no. 6; Lapidge (2006) 289, 290; R. Gameson
  (2012a) 51 n. 169; R. Gameson (2012d) 365 and n. 86

ST: Lambert (1969–72) no. 324; *CPPM* I, no. 4749a; *CSLMA* II (1999) 154

784. Avranches, Bibliothèque municipale, 236

s. x/xi, prov. Mont Saint-Michel by s. xi ex.

Contents: Boethius, *De institutione musica* [*CPL* 880]; excerpts from
  Bede, *De arte metrica* [*CPL* 1565] and *De temporum ratione* [*CPL*
  2320]; conversation phrases in Latin and Greek

MS: *Cat. gén. Dép.* (Quarto) IV.547 [Delisle]; *Cat. gén. Dép.* (Octavo)
  X.115 [Omont]; Samaran—Marichal (1959–85) VII.451; Bischoff
  (1966–81) II.239; Vezin (1968) 286; Alexander (1970a) 3 n. 4, 13 and
  n. 9; Kendall (1975) 65; C.W. Jones (1977) 243; Bischoff (1984b) 248;
  Bower (1988) 211; Lapidge (2006) 294; Wieland (2009) 155

ST: A. White (1981) 197; Biggs et al. (1990) 76–7 [Wittig]

784. 5. Bamberg, Staatsbibliothek, Msc. Ph. 1 (HJ. IV. 6)

s. x, Brittany (or England?), (prov. Bamberg Cathedral)

Contents: Alcuin, *Carm.* lxxvii.1 [SK 9484] and *De dialectica*; anonymous poem [SK 11332]; Porphyrius, *Isagoge*, trans. Boethius; pseudo-
  Apuleius, *Peri hermeneias*; Isidore, *Etymologiae* [*CPL* 1186] II.
  xxix–xxxi; anonymous treatise *De diuisione philosophiae*

MS: Leitschuh—Fischer (1887–1912) I/ii.393–4; Strecker (1914–23) 1128;
  Thomas (1908) xxv; Minio-Paluello (1961) 105 [no. 2088]; Bischoff
  (1966–81) I.273–4, II.257, 267; Minio-Paluello—Dod (1966) xvii;
  Klibansky—Regen (1993) 140; Bischoff (1998—) I, p. 54; Lapidge
  (2006) 311

ED: Dümmler (1881) 298 [Alcuin, *Carm.* lxxvii. 1]; Thomas (1908)
  176–94 [pseudo-Apuleius, *Peri hermeneias*, coll. as B]

ST: *CSLMA* II (1999) 131; *CALMA* II.431

785. Basel, Universitätsbibliothek, F. III. 15b, fols. 1–19

s. viii[1], prob. Northumbria, prov. Fulda

Contents: pseudo-Isidore, *De ordine creaturarum* [*CPL* 1189; *BCLL* 342]

MS: *CLA* VII (1956) no. 844; Díaz y Díaz (1972) 48–9; Gorman (1997) 179 n. 5; Lapidge (2006) 157, 340

ED: Díaz y Díaz (1972) 82–204 [*Liber de ordine creaturarum* coll. as B]

ST: C.D. Wright (1993) 26–7, 250 n. 129

786. Basel, Universitätsbibliothek, F. III. 15f

s. viii[1] or viii med., England, prov. Fulda

Contents: Isidore, *De natura rerum* [*CPL* 1188]

MS: *CLA* VII (1956) no. 848; Fontaine (1960) 163; Bischoff (1966–81) I.183, 185–6; Rella (1977) 18 and n. 66; Parkes (1992) 125 n. 64; Lapidge (2006) 157, 310

ED: Fontaine (1960) 165–337 [Isidore, *De natura rerum*, coll. as A]

787. Basel, Universitätsbibliothek, F. III. 15l

s. viii[1], England, prov. Fulda

Contents: Isidore, *De differentiis rerum* siue *Differentiae theologicae uel spiritales* [*CPL* 1202]; Gennadius, *Liber siue diffinitio ecclesiasticorum dogmatum* [*CPL* 958]

MS: *CLA* VII (1956) no. 849; Bischoff (1966–81) I.183 and n. 74; Rella (1977) 19; Sanz—Adeleida (2006) 130*–131*; Lapidge (2006) 157, 304, 309

788. Basel, Universitätsbibliothek, N. 1. 2, no. 1

s. viii, England

Contents: Psalterium Romanum (f)

MS: *CLA* VII (1956) no. 850; Lowe (1960) no. XXXII; Pulsiano (2001a) xxvii

789. Bergen, Universitetsbiblioteket, 1549. 5

s. xi/xii

Contents: missal (f)

MS: Gjerløw (1970) 83–5, 115; Lenker (1997) 489; R. Gameson (1999a) no. 8

FACS: Gjerløw (1970) pl. 3 [fol. 1v]

790. Berlin, Staatsbibliothek zu Berlin, Preussischer Kulturbesitz, Hamilton 553 (the 'Salaberga Psalter')

s. viii¹, Northumbria, prob. Lindisfarne, (prov. nunnery of Saint-Jean, Laon, *c.* 1120)

Contents: Creed; Psalterium Romanum; canticles (incomplete)

MS: Wildhagen (1913) 427–31; H. Schneider (1938) xi, 76; Weber (1953) xiii; *CLA* VIII (1959), no. 1048; Boese (1966) 270–1; Gamber (1968–88) no. 1613; M.P. Brown (1989a) 160 and n. 49; Parkes (1992) 125 n. 64; Pulsiano (2001a) xxvii; M.P. Brown (2012) 124; Pfaff (2012) 451

DEC: Alexander (1978a) no. 14; Ohlgren (1986) no. 14; Ó Cróinín (1995); Netzer (2012) 28 and n. 24

FACS: *NPS* II, pls. 33 [fol. 27r], 34 (a)–(c) [fols. 2r, 58v, 1r (details)], 35 (a)–(d) [fols. 24r, 48r, 41r, 58v (details)]; Alexander (1978a) ills. 62–5 [fols. 13r, 48r, 2r, 27r]; Ó Cróinín (1994) [complete MS; colour microfiches]

ED: Weber (1953) [Psalterium Romanum coll. as H]; Pulsiano (2001a) [Pss. I–L coll. as β]

ST: Stern (1901); Kenney p. 658; H. Schneider (1938) 75–81

790. 5. Berlin, Staatsbibliothek zu Berlin, Preussischer Kulturbesitz, Lat. fol. 601, fols. 1-67

s. x/xi or xi in.

Contents: Boethius, *De institutione arithmetica* [*CPL* 879]; Latin poem [SK 10046: Alcuin (?), *Carm.* lxv.4]

MS: Quaritch, *Catalogue* 375 (August 1887) no. 38521; Krinsky (1967) 48; Folkerts (1981) 66 [no. 18]; Munk Olsen (1982—) II.829; Guillaumin (1995) lxvi [no. 8]; Gneuss (2003b) 304; Lapidge (2006) 294

791. Berlin, Staatsbibliothek zu Berlin, Preussischer Kulturbesitz, Lat. fol. 877 (with Hauzenstein near Regensburg, Gräflich Walderdorffsche Bibliothek, s.n. [see *Scriptorium* 62 (2008) 73*], and Regensburg, Bischöfliche Zentralbibliothek, Cim 1)

s. viii med., Northumbria, prov. Regensburg s. viii

Contents: liturgical calendar (f), sacramentary (f)

MS: *CLA* VIII (1959) no. 1052; Gamber (1968–88) no. 412; Brandis et al. (1975) 15 [no. 12]; Gamber (1975a) [repr. Gamber (1978) 68–100]; Gamber (1975b) 53–69; Bischoff—Brown (1985) 357; Sotheby's

Western and Oriental Manuscripts, Sale L 072411 [4 Dec. 2007], lot. 44, pp. 60–5; Edwards (2008) 255; Rushforth (2008a) 20; Wieland (2009) 120; Gneuss (2012) 294

FACS: Gamber (1975b) [all fragments]

ED: Siffrin (1930) [Berlin fragment]; Siffrin (1933) [Hauzenstein fragment]; Gamber (1975b) 54–64 [all fragments]

ST: Levison (1946) 146 and n. 5; Bischoff (1974) 172–3, 183–4; Ineichen–Eder (1977) 100–1; Kotzor (1981) I.261*–262*; Bischoff—Lapidge (1994) 164–5 and nn.; Borst (2001) I.xxii; Gretsch (2006) 160 and nn.; Bremmer (2007) 39

791. 3. Berlin, Staatsbibliothek zu Berlin, Preussischer Kulturbesitz, Theol. lat. fol. 355, binding fragments [and other fragments in Berlin, Bonn and Düsseldorf? cf. Barker-Benfield (1991) 54 and n. 48, and Bischoff (1998—) I, no. 458]

s. viii², S England, or Werden, prov. Werden

Contents: saints' Lives (f)

MS: Rose (1893–1905) 307; *CLA* VIII (1959) no. 1068; Barker-Benfield (1991) 49 n. 25, 54 n. 48; Bischoff (1998—) I, nos. 457, 458; Gerchow (1999) 56 [no. 9]; Zechiel-Eckes (2003) 31; Bremmer (2007) 39 and n. 60; Garrison (2012) 646 n. 75

791. 6. Berlin, Staatsbibliothek zu Berlin, Preussischer Kulturbesitz, Fragm. 34

s. viii², prob. England, prov. Werden

Contents: Wigbod [pseudo-Bede], *Quaestionum super Genesin dialogus* (f)

MS: *CLA* VIII (1959) no. 1045; Winter (1986) 11; Barker-Benfield (1991) 53 n. 47; Gerchow (1999) 56 [no. 8]

ST: *CPPM* II, no. 2049

791. 9. Berlin, Staatsbibliothek zu Berlin, Preussischer Kulturbesitz, Grimm 132, 1 (with Budapest, National Széchény Library, Cod. lat. 442, fols. 1–2; Budapest, University Library, Fragm. lat. 1; Munich, Stadtarchiv, Historischer Verein Oberbayern, Hs. 733/16)

s. viii², Fulda?

Contents: Bede, *Vita S. Cudbercti* (verse) [*CPL* 1380; *BHL* 2020] (f)

MS: Lehmann (1938) 4–6; Bartoniek (1940) 397 [no. 442]; Hornung (1960); *CLA* XI (1966) no. 1589; Brandis et al. (1975) 16 [no. 13]; Mezey (1983) 29; R. McKitterick (1986–90) 310–11 and n. 101; Fingernagel (1991) 120–1 [no. 109]; Breslau (1997) 86; Bischoff (1998—) I, no. 347; Gneuss—Lapidge (2003); Lapidge (2006); Lapidge (2008a) 113

FACS: Lehmann (1938) pl. I [Budapest Cod. Lat. 441, fol. 2v]; Brandis et al. (1975) 25 [Berlin Grimm 132,1, fol. 1r]; Mezey (1983) pl. I [Budapest, University Library, Fragm. lat. 1, recto]; Gneuss—Lapidge (2003) pl. I [Munich 733/16, fol. 2v]

ST: Lapidge (1995c); Gneuss—Lapidge (2003); Lapidge (2008a) 112–20

792. Berlin, Staatsbibliothek zu Berlin, Preussischer Kulturbesitz, Grimm 132, 2 + 139, 2

s. viii med., England or Germany?

Contents: Augustine, *Enarrationes in Psalmos* [*CPL* 283] (f); biblical and Leiden-family glosses (f)

MS: *CLA* Supplement (1971) no. 1675; N.R. Ker (1976a) 126 [no. 413]; Lapidge (1986b) 68 [repr. Lapidge (1996b) 164]; Bischoff—Lapidge (1994) 533, 541–3; Aris—Schrimpf (1996) 249–52; Vaciago (1996) 136; Breslau (1997) 86–90; Dietz (2001) 151–5; Lapidge (2006) 288

FACS: Aris—Schrimpf (1996) pls. I–X [complete facsimile]

ED: Bischoff—Lapidge (1994) 543–5 [biblical glosses from Grimm 132, 2]; Aris—Schrimpf (1996) [complete edition of glosses]; Dietz (2001) 156–61 [Grimm 139, 2 complete; OE glosses from Grimm 132, 2]

LANG: Dietz (2001) 163–8

ST: Lapidge (1986b) [repr. Lapidge (1996b) 141–68]; Pheifer (1987) 23–5 and nn.; Bischoff et al. (1988a) 51 n. 10 [Pheifer]; Bischoff—Lapidge (1994) 287, 291–2

793. Berlin, Staatsbibliothek zu Berlin, Preussischer Kulturbesitz, Grimm 139, 1

s. viii[1], Northumbria

Contents: Pelagius, *Expositiones .xiii. Epistularum Pauli* [*CPL* 728] [*ad Philippenses*] (f)

MS: *CLA* Supplement (1971) no. 1676; Breslau (1997) 90; Lapidge (2006) 324

Berlin, Staatsbibliothek zu Berlin, Preussischer Kulturbesitz, Grimm 139, 2: see no. **792**

794. Bern, Burgerbibliothek, 671

s. ix[1], SW England, Cornwall, or Wales; later prov. Great Bedwyn, Wiltshire, s. x[1], prov. France by s. xi/xii

Contents: gospels (s. ix[1]); additions: two acrostic poems addressed (by John the Old Saxon?) to King Alfred [SK 302, 4458] (s. x in.); two records* and two manumissions* (s. x[1] or x med.)

MS: Hagen (1875) 498–9; Lindsay (1912a) 10–16 [no. 3]; McGurk (1956) 250 [repr. McGurk (1998) no. I]; N.R. Ker (1957) no. 6; N.R. Ker (1964) 219; Parkes (1976b) 157 n. 1 [repr. Parkes (1991) 154 n. 1]; Lapidge (1981a) 81 n. 100 [repr. Lapidge (1993a) 69 n. 100]; Parkes (1983) 137 n. 51 [repr. Parkes (1991) 182 n. 51]; Dumville (1987) 170 and n. 121; McGurk (1987) 165 n. 2, 174–5 [repr. McGurk (1998) no. II]; Morrish (1988) 529–31; Dumville (1992b) 79–82, 94, 110 n. 260; Conner (1993) 56, 63, 67, 69–70, 73; Dumville (1993f) 98 [no. 3]; Dumville (1993g) 111 and n. 103, 117 and n. 157, 120, 122; Lapidge (2006) 50 n. 89; *ASMMF* XX (2012) 21–6 [no. 12; McGowan]; Marsden (2012) 412 and n. 19; McKee (2012a) 170

DEC: Homburger (1962) 31

FACS: Lindsay (1912a) pl. V [fol. 74v]; Dumville (1992b) pl. I [fol. 76v]; *ASMMF* XX (2012) no. 12 [complete facsimile]

ED: Meritt (1934) [records and manumissions]; Förster (1941) 791–4 [records], 794–5 [manumissions]; Lapidge (1981a) 82 [repr. Lapidge (1993a) 70] [acrostic poems; for earlier editions see Lapidge (1981a) n. 101]; B. Fischer (1988–91) [gospel excerpts coll. as Hb]

ST: Meritt (1934); Pelteret (1995) xiv, 141 n.; M.P. Brown (1996) 131; Gretsch (1999a) 343–4; R. Sharpe (2001) 288

794. 5. Bern, Burgerbibliothek, 680

s. x ex.

Contents: Augustine, *Enchiridion* [*CPL* 295]

MS: Hagen (1875) 500; Lapidge (2006) 288

795. Bern, Burgerbibliothek, C. 219 (4) (with Leiden, Universiteitsbibliotheek, Voss. lat. Q. 2, fol. 60)

s. ix ex., Wales, or SW England? (prov. Fleury?)

Contents: pseudo-Augustine, *Categoriae decem ex Aristotele decerptae* [*CPL* 362] with glosses; Porphyrius, *Isagoge*, trans. Boethius (f); 'Leiden *Lorica*' [SK 3507]

MS: Hagen (1875) 270–1; Traube (1907) 257–8; Lindsay (1912a) 22–6 [no. 7]; Lindsay (1915) 447 *et passim*; De Meyier (1975) 12; Korhammer (1980) 30; Marenbon (1981) 177–8; Herren (1987) 14–18; Mostert (1989) nos. BF 119, 326

DEC: Homburger (1962) 163–4; N. Edwards (2012) 246 and n. 13

ED: Marenbon (1981) 173–206 [glosses to *Categoriae decem* coll. as B]; Herren (1987) 90–3 [base MS for 'Leiden *Lorica*']; Dronke (1988) 67–9 [base MS for 'Leiden *Lorica*']

ST: Minio-Paluello (1971) *passim* [*Categoriae decem*]; Marenbon (1981) 12–29, 116–38 *et passim* [*Categoriae decem*]; *BCLL* (1985) no. 1239; Dronke (1988) ['Leiden *Lorica*']

796. Besançon, Bibliothèque municipale, 14

s. x ex. (*c.* 980–90), or xi in.?, Winchester NM?, (prov. Abbey of Saint-Claude, Jura, by s. xii ex.)

Contents: gospels

MS: *Cat. gén. Dép.* (Octavo) XXXII. 13–14 [Castan]; T.A.M. Bishop (1971) 10; McGurk (1986b) 43, 46, 54–63 [repr. McGurk (1998) no. XIV]; Heslop (1990) 153, 170–2, 182, 188–91; Dumville (1993g) 145 n. 23; Lenker (1997) 5 n. 7, 114, 425 n. 39; R. Gameson (2012a) 45 and nn. 136–7; R. Gameson (2012b) 108 and n. 51; R. Gameson (2012d) 361 and n. 64; McGurk (2012) 446 [no. 1]

DEC: Homburger (1912) 21 n. 3, 60, 65, 67; Rice (1952) 194; E. Temple (1976) no. 76; Ohlgren (1986) no. 181; Heslop (1990) 171–2; R. Gameson (1995b) 217–18; R. Gameson (2012c) 284 and n. 124

FACS: Homburger (1912) pl. X [fols. 14r, 58v]; E. Temple (1976) ill. 242 [fol. 58v]; Heslop (1990) pls. I (a)–(b) [fols. 18v, 19r (details)], IV (a)–(b) [fols. 10r, 58v (details)]

Bloomington, Indiana University, Lilly Library, Add. 1000: see no. **441**

Bloomington, Indiana University, Lilly Library, Poole 40: see no. **146**

796. 3. Bloomington, Indiana University, Lilly Library, Poole 41

s. x^2 or x ex.

Contents: missal (f)

MS: Faye—Bond (1962) 181 [no. 41]; Stoneman (1997) 118–19; Wieland (2009)

796. 6. Bloomington, Indiana University, Lilly Library, Poole 43

s. xi/xii

Contents: Anso of Lobbes, *Vita S. Ermini* [*BHL* 2614] (f)

MS: Faye—Bond (1962) 181; Stonemann (1997) 119; R. Gameson (1999a) no. 10; Biggs et al. (2001) 193

798. Boulogne-sur-Mer, Bibliothèque municipale, 10

s. x^1 or x med., S England?, (prov. Saint-Vaast, Arras)

Contents: gospels

MS: *Cat. gén. Dép.* (Quarto) IV.577–8 [Michelant]; McGurk (1986b) 43, 45–6, 53 [repr. McGurk (1998) no. XIV]; Dumville (1987) 175 and n. 164; McGurk (1993) 254–5 [repr. McGurk (1998) no. XI]; R. Gameson (2002d) 187; R. Gameson (2009); R. Gameson (2012a) 43 n. 124; R. Gameson (2012b) 115 and n. 85; R. Gameson (2012d) 353 and n. 35, 355 and n. 41; D. Ganz (2012) 192 and n. 27; Marsden (2012) 423 and n. 76; McGurk (2012) 437 and n. 3, 446 [no. 2]

DEC: F. Wormald (1945) 120 and n. 41 [repr. F. Wormald (1984) 59 and n. 41]; Rice (1952) 206; E. Temple (1976) no. 10; Brownrigg (1978) 251; Ohlgren (1986) no. 88; R. Gameson (1995b) 218; Karkov (2006a) 58; R. Gameson (2012c) 250 and n. 4, 283 and n. 117

FACS: E. Temple (1976) ill. 38 [fol. 8r (detail)]; R. Gameson (2012) pl. 10.1 [fol. 8r]

799. Boulogne-sur-Mer, Bibliothèque municipale, 32 (37)

prob. Italy s. vi^1, prov. prob. England s. viii, (prov. Saint-Bertin)

Contents: Ambrose, *De apologia prophetae Dauid* [*CPL* 135], *De Ioseph patriarcha* [*CPL* 131], *De patriarchis* [*CPL* 132], *De paenitentia* [*CPL* 156], *De excessu fratris* [*CPL* 157], *Epistulae* [*CPL* 160] lxiv–lxviii [lxxiv, lxxv, lxxviii, lxxx, lxxxvi]

MS: *Cat. gén. Dép.* (Quarto) IV.592–3 [Michelant]; *CLA* VI (1953)
no. 735; N.R. Ker (1957) lxiii; Faller—Zelzer (1968–94) IV.346;
Bankert et al. (1997) 13, 28–30, 49; R. Gameson (1999c) 323; Lapidge
(2006) 276–9; Wieland (2009) 131, 133; *ASMMF* XVIII (2012) 33–40
[no. 16; Lucas]

FACS: *ASMMF* XVIII (2012) no. 16 [complete facsimile]

ED: Schenkl (1897) 73–122 [*De Ioseph* coll. as B], 125–60 [*De patriarchis*
coll. as B], 299–355 [*De apologia prophetae Dauid* coll. as B]; Faller
(1955) 117–206 [*De paenitentia* coll. as B], 207–325 [*De excessu fratris*
coll. as B]; Meritt (1957) 66 [OE gloss]; Faller—Zelzer (1968–94)
[*Epistulae* lxiv–lxviii coll. as B₁]

ST: Anlezark (2006) 63 n. 6; R. McKitterick (2012) 315 and n. 18

799. 5. Boulogne-sur-Mer, Bibliothèque municipale, 58 (63 and 64)

s. viii¹ or viii², prob. England, (prov. Saint-Bertin)

Contents: Augustine, *Epistulae* [*CPL* 262] clxxxvii and liv (?)

MS: *Cat. gén. Dép.* (Quarto) IV.610–11 [Michelant]; *CLA* VI (1953)
no. 737; T.J. Brown (1984) 319 [repr. T.J. Brown (1993a) 231]; Sims-
Williams (1990) 203–4; T.J. Brown (1993b) 187; Lapidge (2006) 157, 289

800. Boulogne-sur-Mer, Bibliothèque municipale, 63 (70), fols. 1–34

s. xi²′/³, England, (prov. Saint-Bertin)

Contents: excerpts from Iulianus Toletanus, *Prognosticum futuri saeculi*
[*CPL* 1258]; Ælfric, Pastoral Letter 2a; anonymous sermon *In natale
Domini* (by Ælfric?); Gregory, *Regula pastoralis* [*CPL* 1712] I. ix;
excerpts from works of Isidore and Jerome; *De ecclesiasticis gradibus*;
Decretum Gelasianum de libris recipiendis et non recipiendis [*CPL*
1676]; Caesarius, *Sermo* li; *Decalogus Moysi* with exposition; pseudo-
Eusebius Gallicanus, *Sermo* xii [*CPL* 966]

MS: *Cat. gén. Dép.* (Quarto) IV.613 [Michelant]; Assmann (1889/1964)
xxviii–xxix [Clemoes]; Fehr (1914/1966) x–xiv, cxxvii [Clemoes];
Raynes (1957); Clemoes (1960); Hillgarth (1976) xxxiv; Gatch (1977)
131–3; Rella (1977) 107; Lapidge—Winterbottom (1991b) cxlvii–cxlviii;
R. Gameson (2002d) 187; Godden (2004) 371; J. Hill (2004) 323;
Lapidge (2006); R. Gameson (2012d) 350 and n. 21

ED: Fehr (1914/1966) 190–203 [base MS for *Decalogus Moysi*], 222–7
[base MS for Ælfric, Pastoral Letter 2a], 256–8 [base MS for *De*

ecclesiasticis gradibus]; Gatch (1977) 134–46 [base MS for excerpts from Iulianus, *Prognosticum*]; Leinbaugh (1980) [base MS for anonymous sermon *In natale Domini*]; Whitelock et al. (1981a) I.242–55 [base MS for Ælfric, Pastoral Letter 2a]

ST: Grierson (1941) 109 and nn.; Gatch (1966); Lambert (1969–72) no. 324; Gatch (1977) *passim*; Godden (1985) 278–85, 298; *CPPM* I, nos. 1224, 4629, 4749a; *CPPM* II, no. 3003/43; Cross (1996b) 102 n. 40 [pseudo-Eusebius Gallicanus, *Sermo* xii]; C.A. Jones (1998d) 9–16, 41–51; R. Sharpe (2001) 25; Godden (2012) 680 and n. 4

801. Boulogne-sur-Mer, Bibliothèque municipale, 63 (70), fols. 35–86

s. x, France, prov. S England by s. x med., (prov. Saint-Bertin)

Contents: Caesarius, *Expositio in Apocalypsim* [*CPL* 1016]; Augustine, *Epistulae* [*CPL* 262] clxvi, ccv; pseudo-Augustine, *De symbolo*

MS: *Cat. gén. Dép.* (Quarto) IV.613 [Michelant]; Fehr (1914/1966) xiii–xiv; Raynes (1957) 65, 72–3; Rella (1977) 107, 144 n. 16b, 164 n. 2; Rella (1980) 110; Lapidge (2006) 289, 294

802. Boulogne-sur-Mer, Bibliothèque municipale, 74 (82)

s. viii[1], S England or Mercia (Bath?), (prov. Saint-Bertin by s. xii in.)

Contents: Ap(p)onius, *Expositio in Canticum canticorum* [*CPL* 194]) (abridged [as *Expositio breuis* II]); Letter by Burginda

MS: *Cat. gén. Dép.* (Quarto) IV.620 [Michelant]; *CLA* VI (1953) no. 738; Bischoff (1966–81) II.324; T.J. Brown (1975) 263 [repr. T.J. Brown (1993a) 156]; Sims-Williams (1979); De Vregille—Neyrand (1986) xxvii–xxviii; Sims-Williams (1990) 199–221; R. Gameson (2002d) 189; Lapidge (2006) 281; R. Gameson (2012a) 51, 53 n. 182

ED: Sims-Williams (1979) 6, 10 [Letter by Burginda]; De Vregille—Neyrand (1986) 391–463 [base MS for *Expositio Breuis* II]; Sims-Williams (1990) 213 [Letter by Burginda]

803. Boulogne-sur-Mer, Bibliothèque municipale, 82

s. x[1], S England (prov. Saint-Bertin)

Contents: Amalarius, *Liber officialis* ('Retractatio prima')

MS: *Cat. gén. Dép.* (Quarto) IV.624 [Michelant]; Hanssens (1933) 231–2; Hanssens (1948–50) I.129; Parkes (1983) 137 n. 50 [repr. Parkes (1991)

182 n. 50]; Dumville (1987) 170 and n. 122, 175 and n. 165, 176 n. 172; Dumville (1992a) 135; Webber (1992) 71 and n. 111; Dumville (1993d) 8–9; Dumville (1994b) 209; C.A. Jones (2001) 27–32; R. Gameson (2002d) 187; R. Gameson (2012d) 353 and n. 35, 354 and n. 38; D. Ganz (2012) 192 and n. 26

DEC: F. Wormald (1945) 120, 133 [repr. F. Wormald (1984) 59, 72]; Rice (1952) 206; E. Temple (1976) no. 29; Brownrigg (1978) 259 n. 4; Ohlgren (1986) no. 117; R. Gameson (1995b) 3 n. 10, 11 n. 25, 122 n. 27, 230

FACS: E. Temple (1976) ills. 101–2 [fols. 7r, 65r (details)]; F. Wormald (1984) ills. 52, 53 [fols. 1v, 2r (details)]; W. Schipper (2007a) figs. 1 (a) [fol. 45r (detail)], 1 (b) [fol. 114r (detail)]

ED: Hanssens (1948–50) II.59–60, 65–6, 77–81, 89–92, 261–5, 271–5, 277–302, 374–8, 468–73, 486, 509–13, 560–2 [*Liber officialis* ('Retractatio prima') coll. as B]

ST: Lambert (1969–72) nos. 348, 349; Dumville (1993d); *CSLMA* I (1994) 131–5

804. Boulogne-sur-Mer, Bibliothèque municipale, 106 (127), fols. 1–92, 119–71

s. x/xi, Flanders, prov. Bath?, (prov. Saint-Bertin)

Contents: *Vita S. Walarici* [*BHL* 8762]; *Vita S. Philiberti* [*BHL* 6805]; *Vita S. Aichardi* [*BHL* 181]; *Vita S. Bauonis* [*BHL* 1049] (f); Felix, *Vita S. Guthlaci* [*BHL* 3723; *CPL* 2150]; seven homilies (pseudo-Eusebius Gallicanus?)

MS: *Cat. gén. Dép.* (Quarto) IV.637–8 [Michelant]; Krusch—Levison (1910) 561, 575–6; Wilmart (1922–9a) 180; Colgrave (1956) 35–9; Van der Straeten (1971) 129, 137; Sims-Williams (1990) 206–8; Dumville (1992a) 140; R. Gameson (2002d) 187–8; Wieland (2009) 125, 130; R. Gameson (2012a) 60 n. 202

ED: Krusch—Levison (1910) 583–604 [*Vita S. Philiberti* coll. as B1*a*]; Colgrave (1956) 60–170 [Felix, *Vita S. Guthlaci*, coll. as B]

ST: Lambert (1969–72) nos. 324, 338; *CPPM* I, no. 4749a; Biggs et al. (2001) 60, 244, 386–7, 475–6

804. 5. Boulogne-sur-Mer, Bibliothèque municipale, 106 (127), binding strip

s. viii/ix, prob. England (prov. Saint-Bertin)

Contents: Gregory, *Homiliae .xl. in Euangelia* [*CPL* 1711] (f)

MS: Colgrave (1956) 36; *CLA* Supplement (1971) no. 1678; Sims-Williams (1990) 206–8; R. Gameson (2002d) 189; Lapidge (2006) 305; Wieland (2009) 126

805. Boulogne-sur-Mer, Bibliothèque municipale, 189

s. x/xi, Canterbury CC; s. xi in. and xi¹ (addition of OE glosses)

Contents: Sibylline prophecies [SK 8495]; verses excerpted from Optatianus Porphyrius, *Carm.* xxv [SK 1005]; prefatory letter to Fredegaud/Frithegod, *Breuiloquium Vitae Wilfridi* [*BHL* 8891]; collection of drinking verses [SK 4819]; Prudentius, *Praefatio operum*° [*CPL* 1437], *Cathemerinon*° [*CPL* 1438], *Peristephanon*° [*CPL* 1443], *Contra Symmachum*° [*CPL* 1442], *Epilogus*° [*CPL* 1445]

MS: *Cat. gén. Dép.* (Quarto) IV.688 [Michelant]; N.R. Ker (1957) no. 7; T.A.M. Bishop (1959–63b) 415, 420 n. 1, 421; Meritt (1959) ix–x; F.C. Robinson (1973) 443–4, 459; Korhammer (1980) 57; Lapidge (1988a) 57, 62–3 and n. 66 [repr. Lapidge (1993a) 173, 178 and n. 66]; Vaciago (1993) 3 [no. 5]; Gwara (1996a) 92; Biggs et al. (2001) 481–2; Karkov (2001a) 115 n. 3; R. Gameson (2002d) 188; Lapidge (2004a) 144; Lapidge (2006) 321, 329, 330; Alcamesi (2007) 171–3; Graham (2009) 171; *ASMMF* XVIII (2012) 41–55 [no. 17; Lucas]; R. Gameson (2012a) 72 n. 247; R. Gameson (2012d) 355 n. 42; Scragg (2012a) nos. 5–8

DEC: E. Temple (1976) no. 30 (xv); Ohlgren (1986) no. 132

FACS: Meritt (1959) 2 [fol. 4r], 32 [fol. 74r], 62 [fol. 102r], 88 [fol. 120r], 102 [fol. 142r]; *ASMMF* XVIII (2012) no. 17 [complete facsimile]

ED: Holder (1878) 385–6 [poem excerpted from Porphyrius Optatianus, *Carm.* xxv], 386–7 [prefatory letter to Frithegod, *Breuiloquium Vitae Wilfridi*]; Meritt (1959) [OE interlinear glosses to works of Prudentius]

Braunschweig, Stadtbibliothek, Fragm. 70: see no. **856**

805. 5. Brussels, Bibliothèque royale, 444–52 (1103)

s. xi/xii, Canterbury StA

Contents: Augustine, *De perfectione iustitiae hominis* [*CPL* 347], *De natura et gratia* [*CPL* 344], *De gratia et libero arbitrio* [*CPL* 352], *De correptione et gratia* [*CPL* 353]; Prosper, *Pro Augustino responsiones ad capitula obiectionum Gallorum calumniantium* [*CPL* 520]; Hilarius Gallus, *Epistula ad Augustinum de querela Gallorum* [*CPPM* II, no. 1024]; Augustine, *De praedestinatione sanctorum* [*CPL* 354], *De dono perseuerantiae* [*CPL* 355]; pseudo-Augustine, *Hypomnesticon* [*CPL* 381]; Jerome, *Aduersus Iouinianum* [*CPL* 610]

MS: Van den Gheyn et al. (1901–48) II.136–7 [no. 1103]; M.R. James (1903) no. 373; Lambert (1969–72) no. 252; A.G. Watson (1987a) 12; R. Gameson (1999a) no. 11; T.N. Hall (2004b) 97 n. 18; Lapidge (2006) 284–7, 313, 328; Barker-Benfield (2008) I.lix, 74 n. 40, 516, 539, 550, III.1818–19; R. Gameson (2012a) 19 n. 24, 23, 72 n. 244

806. Brussels, Bibliothèque royale, 1650 (1520)

s. xi in., Abingdon; Latin and OE glosses, s. xi[1]

Contents: Aldhelm, *De uirginitate* (prose) [*CPL* 1332], with interlinear and marginal Latin and OE glosses

MS: Van den Gheyn et al. (1901–48) II.410 [no. 1520]; Ehwald (1919) 215–16; N.R. Ker (1957) no. 8; N.R. Ker (1964) 2; F.C. Robinson (1973) 445, 459; Goossens (1975) 5–8; Korhammer (1980) 28; R. Derolez (1992a) 11 n. 2; Gwara (1998) 143–4; Gwara (2001) I.94*–101* *et passim*; *ASMMF* XIII (2006) 17–21 [no. 18; Bremmer, Dekker]; Graham (2009) 168–9; Lapidge (2012b) 27; Scragg (2012a) nos. 2, 3, 9, 10

DEC: R. Gameson (1995b) 221 n. 167

FACS: Van Langenhove (1941) [complete facsimile]; R. Derolez (1992) pl. I [fol. 1v]; *ASMMF* XIII (2006) no. 18; Owen-Crocker (2009) fig. 6.4 [fol. 25r]

ED: Ehwald (1919) 226–323 [Aldhelm, prose *De uirginitate*, coll. as B]; R. Derolez (1956) [glosses in margins]; Goossens (1974) 147–489 [Latin and OE glosses to Aldhelm]; Gwara (2001) vol. II [Aldhelm, prose *De uirginitate* with Latin and OE glosses, coll. as B]

LANG: R. Derolez (1960); Goossens (1974) 53–139 *passim*; Hofstetter (1987) 129–39; Hofstetter (1988) 154; Lendinara (1992) *passim*

ST: Mustanoja (1950); R. Derolez (1959) 130–1; Goossens (1974); P.S. Baker (1980) 28–9; R. Derolez (1986); Goossens (1992); Gwara (1994a); Gwara (1994b) 136–7; Gwara (1996–7); Gwara (1997a); Gwara (1998); Gretsch (1999a) 132–84 *et passim*; Lapidge (2012b) 26–31

807. Brussels, Bibliothèque royale, 1828–30 (185), fols. 36–109

s. xi in., prov. s. xi/xii abbey of Anchin (near Douai)

Contents: *Hermeneumata pseudo-Dositheana* [Version B]; a collection of glossaries, including five Latin—Old English class lists, grammatical and etymological notes, a prayer, a medical recipe, a list of Roman numerals with their names; Jerome, *Liber interpretationis hebraicorum nominum* [*CPL* 581]; Remigius of Auxerre, *Comm. in Martianum Capellam*, bk. IV (incomplete)

MS: Van den Gheyn et al. (1901–48) I.86–7 [no. 185]; N.R. Ker (1957) no. 9; T.A.M. Bishop (1971) xii n. 2; Pheifer (1974) xxxvi–xxxvii; Dionisotti (1984–5); Dionisotti (1988) 27; A.K. Brown (1992) 108–9; Brugnoli—Buonocore (2002) xiii; R. Gameson (2002d) 188; *ASMMF* XIII (2006) 23–31 [no. 19; Bremmer, Dekker]; R. Gameson (2012a) 31 n. 70; R. Gameson (2012d) 355 and n. 42; Scragg (2012a) nos. 11–15

FACS: *ASMMF* XIII (2006) no. 19

ED: Wright—Wülker (1884) 284–303 [Latin—OE glossaries]; Meritt (1945) nos. 67, 68 [OE glosses from Latin glossaries]; Brugnoli—Buonocore (2002) 1–119 [*Hermeneumata pseudo-Dositheana* coll. as HFB]

ST: Bischoff (1966–81) II.261, 266; Lendinara (1992) 217, 220, 228–9; Rusche (2011) 402–14

808. Brussels, Bibliothèque royale, 8558–63 (2498)

fols. 1-79: s. x¹, S England or Mercia; fols. 80–131: s. x med.; fols. 132–53: s. xi¹

Contents: fols. 1-79: Chrodegang, *Regula canonicorum* (enlarged version; incomplete); Augustine, *Soliloquia* [*CPL* 252]; Caesarius, *Sermo* clxxix; fols. 80–131: *Poenitentiale pseudo-Theodori* (incomplete); fols. 132–53: Handbook for a confessor*; *Poenitentiale pseudo-Egberti* in OE, bk. IV*; *Old English Canons of Theodore**

MS: Van den Gheyn et al. (1901–48) IV.10 [no. 2498]; Raith (1933/1964) ix–x; Spindler (1934) 1–4; N.R. Ker (1957) no. 10; Fowler (1965) 1–2; T.A.M. Bishop (1971) 24; Fowler (1972) xv–xvi; Whitelock (1976) 7 n. 1; Rella (1977) 107, 158; Dumville (1987) 175–8; Dumville (1993g) 51–2, 142; Langefeld (2003) 42–4 and nn. 66–75; J. Hill (2004) 321; Meaney (2004) 483 n. 86; Bertram (2005) 175; *ASMMF* XIII (2006) 43–9 [no. 20; Bremmer, Dekker]; Lapidge (2006) 291, 295; Frantzen (2007) 40–1, 51, 63; M. Heyworth (2007) 218–19; Van Rhijn (2009) xlvi–l, liv–lv; Wieland (2009) 141; Fulk—Jurasinski (2012) xvi–xix; R. Gameson (2012a) 44–5 and n. 132; D. Ganz (2012) 191 n. 18; A. Orchard (2012) 696 [no. 1]; Scragg (2012a) nos. 16–17

FACS: *ASMMF* XIII (2006) no. 20; Fulk—Jurasinski (2012) pl. 1 [fol. 153r]

ED: Wasserschleben (1851) 566–622 [records, additions, etc. to text of *Poenitentiale pseudo-Theodori* in CCCC 190 (above, no. **59**) in the Brussels MS]; Raith (1933/1964) 46–69 [*Poenitentiale pseudo-Egberti*, bk. IV, coll. as Bx], 71 [canons from synod of 721, coll. as Bx]; Spindler (1934) 174 [two passages (fols. 145v–146r) of *Confessionale pseudo-Egberti* coll. as Bx]; Meritt (1945) no. 14 [OE glosses to Chrodegang, *Regula canonicorum*]; Fowler (1965) 16–26 [Handbook for a confessor coll. as Bx]; Fowler (1972) 21 [base MS for passage on priests' duties (added s. xii on fol. 140r)]; Langefeld (2003) 162–342 [Chrodegang, *Regula canonicorum* (enlarged version), coll. as B]; Van Rhijn (2009) [*Poenitentiale pseudo-Theodori* coll. as Br]; Fulk–Jurasinski (2012) 3–14, 17–18 [*OE Canons of Theodore* (Texts A, C) coll. as Bx]

LANG: Raith (1933/64) 84–5; Fowler (1972) xvi; Fulk–Jurasinski (2012) xxviii–xxxv

ST: Thorpe (1840) xi; Wasserschleben (1851) 87, 566 n. 1; Frantzen (1983a) 40, 44–5; Frantzen (1983b) 133, 138; Frantzen (1985) 37, 40; Langefeld (1986) 197; Sauer (2000) 340, 372 and n. 75; Fulk–Jurasinski (2012) xxxvi–lx

808. 0. Brussels, Bibliothèque royale, 8654–8672

s. ix$^{1/3}$, prob. NE France (Channel coast?), prov. s. x England? (prov. Saint-Bertin)

Contents: collection of patristic comments on the gospels; collection of creeds; Pelagius, *Libellus fidei ad Innocentium papam* [*CPL* 731]; Gennadius, *Liber siue diffinitio ecclesiasticorum dogmatum* [*CPL* 958]; Bede, *Historia ecclesiastica* [*CPL* 1375] V. xv–xvii; *Admonitio generalis* (of 789), *Duplex capitulare missorum*, and *Capitula incerti anni* [Mordek (1995) nos. 22, 23, 86]; excerpts mainly from *Collectio canonum uetus Gallica* [*CPL* 1784a]; hymn for the coronation of a king [SK 7997]; excerpts from biblical commentaries; Isidore, *Etymologiae* [*CPL* 1186] VII.i–v; pseudo-Bede, *De sex dierum generatione*; Wigbod (pseudo-Bede), *Quaestionum super Genesin dialogus*; Isidore, *De ortu et obitu patrum* [*CPL* 1191]; *Exorcismus* and *Benedictio aquae*; excerpts from writings about computus; excerpts from *ordines* for the Office

MS: Van den Gheyn et al. (1901–48) II.274–5; N.R. Ker (1957) Appendix no. 6; *CLA* X (1963) no. 1542; Bischoff (1966–81) I.248; Mordek (1975) 274–6; Bullough (1983) 47 n. 109; Mordek (1995) 85–90; Bischoff (1998–) I, no. 724; Kéry (1999) 52, 75; D. Ganz (2004) 500; *ASMMF* XIII (2006) 51–61 [no. 21; Bremmer, Dekker]; Gneuss (2008b) 140; Gneuss (2012) 295

FACS: Mordek (1975) pl. IV (a) [fol. 130r (detail)]; *ASMMF* XIII (2006) no. 21

ST: *CSLMA* II (1999) 10

808. 1. Brussels, Bibliothèque royale, 8794–99 (1403), fols. 1–17

s. xi/xii, Rochester

Contents: Ernulf of Beauvais and Rochester, *De incestis coniugibus*; decretals

MS: Van den Gheyn et al. (1901–48) II.329; R. Gameson (1999a) no. 12; R. Sharpe (2001) 113

808. 2. Brussels, Bibliothèque royale, 9850–52 (1221), fols. 4–139, 144–76

s. vii/viii, Soissons, prov. Corbie, s. viii ex.? [fols. 140–3 (Caesarius, *Sermo* xxiii): s. viii ex., Corbie area]. Whole MS prov. Bath?, prov. Saint-Vaast, Arras, by s. xi^2

[cf. note after no. **781**]

Contents: *Verba seniorum* [*CPG* 5570; *BHL* 6527] I–XV. 39 (=*Vitas patrum*, bk. V)]; Caesarius, *Sermones* [*CPL* 1008] (seven *sermones* only); *Decretum Gelasianum de libris recipiendis et non recipiendis* [*CPL* 1676]; anonymous commentary on the gospels; psalter (f): s. ix/x, (prov. Saint-Vaast, Arras, s. xii–xiii?)

MS: Delisle (1884); Van den Gheyn et al. (1901–48) II.224–6; Grierson (1940a) 107–8; *CLA* X (1963) nos. 1547a, 1547b; Batlle (1972) 17; P. Jackson (1992) 123 and n. 21; Lapidge (1994b) 128; Bischoff (1998—) I, no. 737; Lapidge (2006) 138, 295, 337–8; Wieland (2009) 131

808. 3. Brussels, Bibliothèque royale, II. 436

s. viii, England (prov. prob. convent of Münsterbilsen, diocese of Liège)

Contents: gospels (f; Lc XI.10–29)

MS: *CLA* X (1963) no. 1549; B. Fischer (1988–91) I.16*

ED: B. Fischer (1988–91) [gospel fragment coll. as Eu]

808. 4. 1. Brussels, Biblothèque royale, II. 1766, fol. 2

s. viii/ix or ix in. (Insular script)

Contents: unidentified theological text (Gregory, *Moralia in Iob*?) (f)

808. 4. 2. Brussels, Bibliothèque royale, II. 7538

s. viii in., prob. England

Contents: anonymous *Regula monialium* [*CPL* 1861] (f)

MS: Masai (1948); Bischoff (1962) 615 [repr. Bischoff (1966–81) II.339];
   CLA X (1963) no. 1555; Milde (1986) 150

FACS: Masai (1948) pls. 26–7 [recto and verso]

ED: De Bruyne (1923) 128; Masai (1948)

Bückeburg, Niedersächsisches Staatsarchiv, Depot 3/1: see no. **856**

Budapest, National Széchényi Library, Cod. Lat. 442, fols. 1–2: see
   no. **791. 9**

Budapest, University Library, Fragm. lat. 1: see no. **791. 9**

808. 5. Cambrai, Bibliothèque municipale, 470 (441)

s. viii[1] or viii med., prob. English

Contents: Philippus presbyter, *Comm. in librum Iob* [*CPL* 643]

MS: *Cat. gén. Dép.* (Octavo) XVII.174 [Molinier]; Lindsay (1915) 449;
   Lowe (1924) 40 [no. 16]; *CLA* VI (1953) no. 740; Bischoff (1966–81)
   II.339; Parkes (1976a) 166 n. 18 [repr. Parkes (1991) 126 n. 18]; R.
   McKitterick (1989b) 400 and n. 36; Bischoff (1990) 77 n. 174, 199 n. 85;
   T.J. Brown (1993b) 185; Dumville (1995b) 101 and n. 23; Lapidge
   (2006) 157, 325

DEC: E.H. Zimmermann (1916) 145, 307–8

FACS: Chatelain (1901–2) pls. XCIII–XCIV [folios not specified]; *NPS*
   II, pl. 31 [fols. 50r, 23v (detail)]

Cambridge, Mass., Harvard University, Houghton Library, Typ 612: see
   no. **504. 3**

808. 6. Chalons-en-Champagne, Archives de la Marne, Fragm. I. 7

s. x[1]

Contents: Psalterium Romanum (f)

MS: Hourlier-Gandilhon (1956) 62

808. 7. Chicago, Newberry Library, fragm. 15

s. x[2/4]

Contents: Alcuin, *Epist.* cxlix, clv, cxxxvi (f)

MS: Masi (1972) 103; D. Ganz (1993); Bullough (2004) 69 and n. 165

FACS: D. Ganz (1993) pls. VI (a)–(b) [*Epist.* cxlix], VII (a)–(b) [*Epist.* clv, cxxxvi]

ST: *CSLMA* II (1999) 255, 265, 268

808. 9. Christchurch, New Zealand, private collection, s.n.

s. x/xi, Canterbury, prob. CC

Contents: Prudentius, *Contra Symmachum* [*CPL* 1442], with gloss (f)

MS: Maggs, *Catalogue* 973 (London, 1976) 44 [no. 151]; Manion et al. (1989) 138–9 [no. 165]; Stoneman (1997) 127; Lapidge (2006) 329

Città del Vaticano: see under [Rome], Città del Vaticano

809. Coburg, Landesbibliothek, 1

s. ix$^{2/3}$, Metz, prov. England (royal court) *c.* 923×936?, prov. Gandersheim by s. xi in.

Contents: gospel list, gospels

MS: Drögereit (1949) 46–7 and nn.; Hubay (1962a) 9–16; Hubay (1962b); Bullough (1975) 34, 213 n. 45 [repr. Bullough (1991) 287, 295 n. 48]; Keynes (1985a) 189–93; Dumville (1987) 171 and n. 126; B. Fischer (1988–91) I.25*; Dumville (1992b) 94 and n. 193; Dumville (1994a) 158 and n. 138; Lenker (1997) 415–16 *et passim*; Bischoff (1998—) I, no. 930; Lapidge (2006) 169

DEC: Köhler (1930–60) III.106, 163–7; E. Temple (1976) 12; Schramm— Mütherich (1981) 139–40 [no. 63]

FACS: Köhler (1930-60) III, pls. 92 [fols. 10v, 11r], 93 [fols. 11v, 12r, 12v, 13r], 94 [fols. 13v, 14r, 14v, 15r], 95 [fols. 15v, 1v, 18r], 96 [fols. 22r, 58r, 131v, 132r]; Hubay (1962a) pls. 1–2 [fols. 132r, 168r (detail)]; Keynes (1985a) pl. XII [fol. 168r (detail)]

ED: B. Fischer (1988–91) [gospels coll. as Zc]

809. 8. Columbia, University of Missouri Library, Fragmenta manuscripta, F. M. 1

s. x med. or x^2, Brittany?, prov. England by s. x ex.

Contents: Office lectionary (f)

MS: Gatch (1986–90); De Hamel (1987) 203 [no. 69]; Voigts (1988); Dumville (1991–5) 43–4; Marsden (1995) 47; Stoneman (1997) 104–5, 123

FACS: Voigts (1988) pls. VII [recto], VIII [verso]

809. 9. Columbia, University of Missouri Library, Fragmenta manuscripta, F. M. 2

s. ix, prob. Wales, prov. Winchester by s. x in.

Contents: extracts from Bede, *De orthographia* [*CPL* 1566], Priscian, *Institutio de nomine, pronomine et uerbo* [*CPL* 1550] and *Institutiones grammaticae* [*CPL* 1546], and from Audax, *De Scauri et Palladii libris excerpta per interrogationem et responsionem* [Keil, *GL* VII.320–62 (grammatical note attributed to Jerome)]

MS: Gatch (1986–90); Webb (1985) *passim*; Voigts (1988) 83; Parkes (1997a) 1 n. 1; Lapidge (2006) 282, 326; Wieland (2009) 145

810. Columbia, University of Missouri Library, Fragmenta manuscripta, F.M. 3

s. x/xi

Contents: sacramentary (f)

MS: Gatch (1986–90); Stoneman (1997) 105, 123

811. Columbia, University of Missouri Library, Fragmenta manuscripta, F.M. 4

s. x^2

Contents: excerpts from Prophetae minores (f)

MS: Gatch (1986–90); Marsden (1995) 41, 44, 46, 253, 323, 379–86; Stoneman (1997) 105, 123–4; Marsden (2012) 426 and n. 92

FACS: Marsden (1995) pl. VIII [verso]

811. 5. Copenhagen, Kongelige Bibliotek, Acc. 1996 / 12

prob. s. xi[1] [prob. from the same MS as nos. **816. 6** and **830**]

Contents: Ælfric, Homilies* (f; from enlarged First Series of *Catholic Homilies*)

MS: Fausbøll (1995); Clemoes (1997) 59; Abram (2007) 427 and n. 7; Kleist (2007c) 496; Gneuss (2008a) 412–13 and nn.; Scragg (2012a) nos. 299–306

812. Copenhagen, Kongelige Bibliotek, G.K.S. 10 (2°)

s. x ex. or xi in.?, Winchester NM? or Peterborough?, prov. s. xi
Peterborough or Canterbury, (prov.: had left England by s. xii ex.?)

Contents: gospels

MS: Jørgensen (1926) 9–10; T.A.M. Bishop (1954–8b) 333; T.A.M. Bishop
(1967a); T.A.M. Bishop (1971) xv, xxii, 11; Backhouse et al. (1984b)
no. 48 [D.H. Turner]; McGurk (1986b) 43 *et passim* [repr. McGurk
(1998) no. XIV]; Heslop (1990) 191–5 *et passim*; Dumville (1991–5) 44;
Dumville (1993f) 98 [no. 9]; Dumville (1993g) 75 n. 342, 116, 139 n. 5;
Hartzell (2006) no. 74; R. Gameson (2012a) 50 and n. 157, 59 n. 194,
61, 92; R. Gameson (2012b) 108 n. 51; McGurk (2012) 446 [no. 5]

DEC: E. Temple (1976) no. 47; Brownrigg (1978) 255, 265; Ohlgren
(1986) no. 152; G. Henderson (1987) 120; R. Gameson (1995b) 196
n. 21, 198, 204 n. 71, 208; Farr (2003) 117–19; R. Gameson (2012) 283
and n. 118, 284 and n. 124

FACS: T.A.M. Bishop (1967a) fig. 1 [fol. 18v (detail)]; T.A.M. Bishop
(1971) pls. XI (a)–(b) [fols. 9r, 16r (details)]; E. Temple (1976) ills. 151–4
[fols. 2v, 18r, 82v, 17v]; Backhouse et al. (1984b) colour pl. XII [fol. 17v];
G. Henderson (1987) pl. 175 [fol. 17v]; Farr (2003) fig. 1 [fol. 17v]

ST: Glunz (1933) 133, 135

813. Copenhagen, Kongelige Bibliotek, G.K.S. 1588 (4°)

s. xi⁴/⁴, Bury St Edmunds, prov. s. xi ex. Saint-Denis?

Contents: Abbo of Fleury, *Passio S. Eadmundi* [*BHL* 2392]; Office of
St Edmund (incomplete)

MS: Jørgensen (1926) 189; R.M. Thomson (1984); Gransden (1995a)
64–5; Andrew Hughes (1993) 260–1; R. Gameson (1999a) no. 199;
Hartzell (2006) no. 75; Rankin (2012) 504 and n. 106

FACS: Gransden (1995a) pl. II [fol. 20r]

ED: Winterbottom (1972) 91–2 [variant readings from Abbo, *Passio S.
Eadmundi*, coll. as C]; Hartzell (2006) no. 75 [Office of St Edmund]

ST: Gransden (1995a); Biggs et al. (2001) 2–4 [Lendinara]

814. Copenhagen, Kongelige Bibliotek, G.K.S. 1595 (4°)

c. 1002–1023, Worcester (and York?), prov. Denmark (Roskilde) s. xi?

Contents (a version of Wulfstan's 'Handbook'): Amalarius (?), *Eclogae de ordine Romano*; hymn [SK and SK Suppl. 1863]; *Institutio canonicorum* [extracts from the record of the Council of Aachen in 816, with excerpts from works of Isidore and Jerome, and *De ecclesiasticis gradibus*]; anonymous sermon [by someone connected with Wulfstan] *De ieiunio quattuor temporum*; Abbo of Saint-Germain-des-Prés, *Sermones* xiii, vii–x, vi, xi, xii; eight formulary letters about penitence, four by Wulfstan, three by Pope John XVIII and one by Pope Gregory V; Caesarius of Arles, *Sermo* xxxiii (adapted); five sermons by or connected with Wulfstan; Wulfstan, Homily Ia; four more sermons (unidentified); pseudo-Augustine, *Sermo* ccli; sermon on baptism (excerpted from works of Augustine on baptism); ancient continental sermon on vices and the Last Judgement (adapted); excerpts from Scripture [Bethurum, Homily XI, lines 1-87]; exhortation* by Wulfstan; Ælfric, Pastoral Letters 2 and 3; Wulfstan, Homily VIIIa; a passage on chrism; 'De officio missae' (excerpts from Hrabanus Maurus, Theodulf, Isidore and others); various extracts (partly repeating those from the Council of Aachen in 816, listed above)

MS: Fehr (1914/1966) cxxi–cxxii, cxxv–cxxxix [Clemoes]; Jørgensen (1926) 43–6; Bethurum (1942); Whitelock (1942) 47–8 [repr. Whitelock (1981b) no. XI]; Bethurum (1957) 3; N.R. Ker (1957) no. 99; N.R. Ker (1960) 49; Whitelock (1965) 220 [repr. Whitelock (1981b) no. XV]; T.A.M. Bishop (1971) 20 n. 1; N.R. Ker (1971) 319–21 [repr. N.R. Ker (1985) 13–15]; Fowler (1972) lv–lviii; Whitelock (1976) 28; Rella (1977) 84, 107, 122, 136; U. Önnerfors (1985) 25–7; P.L. Heyworth (1989) 45; Dumville (1992a) 135 and n. 297; Cross—Morrish Tunberg (1993b); R.I. Page (1993b) 15–18; Gerritsen (1998); C.A. Jones (1998b) 77–80; C.A. Jones (1998d) 14–16; Sauer (2000); Dance (2004) 31; Godden (2004) 358 n. 21, 359 n. 25, 371; T.N. Hall (2004a) 94–100; J. Hill (2004) 321; C.A. Jones (2004) 327–9, 351–2; G. Mann (2004) 239–40 n. 8, 265 n. 94; A. Orchard (2004) 66 n. 15, 67–70; Hartzell (2006) no. 76; Lapidge (2006) 295; Wieland (2009) 127; R. Gameson (2012a) 27, 49 and n. 152, 58 n. 192; R. Gameson (2012b) 103 and n. 36, 110 and n. 61, 111 n. 66; R. Gameson (2012d) 360 n. 59; Gullick (2012) 295 n. 7; A. Orchard (2012) 696 [no. 4]; Scragg (2012a) no. 307

FACS: Cross—Morrish Tunberg (1993b) [complete facsimile]; N.R. Ker (1971) pl. VII [fol. 66v]; N.R. Ker (1985) 25 [fol. 66v]

ED: Jost (1950) 268–9 [Exhortation* by Wulfstan]; Bethurum (1957) 113–15 [Wulfstan, *Hom.* Ia, coll. as Cop], 169–71 [Wulfstan, *Hom.*

VIIIa, coll. as Cop], 211–14 [Wulfstan, *Hom.* XI, coll. as Cop], 374–6
[Letters about penitence, 1–3, 7, 8, coll. as Cop]; Aronstam (1975)
79–82 [base MS (= C) for letters about penitence]; U. Önnerfors (1985)
63–202 [Abbo of Saint–Germain–des–Prés, *Sermones*, coll. as C];
Dance (2004) 31 [text on fol. 66v], T.N. Hall (2004a) 115–34 [nine
sermons by or connected with Wulfstan], 136–7 [fols. 60v–62r];
A. Orchard (2004) 68 [fol. 66v]

LANG: Dance (2004) 31; A. Orchard (2004) 90

ST: Jost (1950) 268–70; Cross—Hamer (1999) 17–18, 27–8, 31, 38, 40, 60,
72, 141–2, 148

815. Copenhagen, Kongelige Bibliotek, G.K.S. 2034 (4°)

s. x/xi, OE glosses s. xi[1], (prov. Paris, Saint-Victor)

Contents: Bede, *Vita S. Cudbercti* (verse) [*CPL* 1380; *BHL* 2020];
pseudo-Columbanus (pseudo-Alcuin), *Praecepta uiuendi* [SK 5960];
colophon

MS: Jørgensen (1926) 41–2; Jaager (1935) 28–9; N.R. Ker (1957) no. 100;
F.C. Robinson (1973) 453, 459, 461, 464 n. 62; Korhammer (1980);
Dumville (1993f) 98 [no. 10]; Lapidge (1995c) 130, 146–7; R. Gameson
(2002a) 42 [no. 22], 23 and n. 93; Lapidge (2008a) 114; Scragg (2012a)
nos. 308–9

FACS: R. Gameson (2002a) pl. 5 [fol. 22v]

ED: Jaager (1935) [Bede, *Vita metrica S. Cudbercti*, coll. as K]; Meritt
(1945) no. 9 [OE glosses to Bede, *Vita metrica S. Cudbercti*]; Gameson
(2002a) 42 [colophon]

ST: Smit (1971) 233–5 [*Praecepta uiuendi*]; Lapidge (1977b) 871–4;
CPPM II, no. 3216b [*Praecepta uiuendi*]; *CSLMA* II (1999) 75–7;
Lapidge (2008a) 112–20

816. Copenhagen, Kongelige Bibliotek, N.K.S. 167b (4°)

s. x/xi

Contents: *Waldere*** (f)

MS: Dobbie (1942) xix–xx; F. Norman (1949) 1–5; N.R. Ker (1957)
no. 101; Zettersten (1979) 7–11; R. Gameson (2012b) 98; Scragg
(2012a) no. 310

FACS: Zettersten (1979) 14–18 [complete facsimile]

ED: Dobbie (1942) 4; F. Norman (1949) 35–43; Zettersten (1979) 15–21; J. Hill (1983) 23–5, 30–2; Mitchell—Robinson (1998) 208–11; Fulk et al. (2008) 337–9

LANG: F. Norman (1949) 5–7; Zettersten (1979) 11–12

ST: Greenfield—Robinson (1980) 274–7; see also the bibliographies in Dobbie (1942), F. Norman (1949), and Zettersten (1979)

Copenhagen, Rigsarkivet, Middelalderlige Håndskriftfragmenter, 3084 and 3085: see no. **872**

816. 3. Copenhagen, Rigsarkivet, Middelalderlige Håndskriftfragmenter, 3185 and 3186

s. xi

Contents: missal (f)

MS: Hartzell (2006) no. 77

Copenhagen, Rigsarkivet, Middelalderlige Håndskriftfragmenter, 4593: see no. **871**

816. 6. Copenhagen, Rigsarkivet, Aftagne Pergamentfragmenter, 637–64, 669–71, 674–98

s. xi^1

Contents: Ælfric, *Catholic Homilies** (f; from I.xxvi and xxxv–xxxvii) [fifty-six binding strips, prob. from the same MS as nos. **811. 5** and **830**]

MS: Fausbøll (1986) 9–19, 33–8; Clemoes (1997) 58–9; Abram (2007) 427 and n. 7; Kleist (2007c) 496; Scragg (2012a) nos. 299–306

FACS: Fausbøll (1986) [complete facsimile]

ED: Fausbøll (1986) 43–89; Clemoes (1997) [fragments coll. as f^e]

LANG: Fausbøll (1986) 19–27

ST: N.R. Ker (1957) no. 118; Fausbøll (1995)

Damme, Musée van Maerlant [formerly no. 817]: see now no. **848. 8**

818. Darmstadt, Hessische Landes- und Hochschulbibliothek, 4262

s. viii^1, Monkwearmouth-Jarrow

Contents: Bede, *De temporum ratione* [*CPL* 2320] (f)

MS: Bischoff—Brown (1985) 325–6 [= *CLA* no. 1822]; Staub (1986) 1–7; Bischoff (1990) 199 n. 86; Saenger (1997) 334 n. 21; Wallis (1999) lxxxvi and n. 234

FACS: Bischoff—Brown (1985) pl. IV (b) [recto]; Staub (1986) pls. 1–2 [recto and verso]

ED: Staub (1986) 4 and 6

818. 3. Düsseldorf, Universitäts- und Landesbibliothek, A 19 (with Fragm. K 16: Z 1/1, and Tokyo, Collection of Toshiyuki Takamiya MS 45)

s. viii/ix, Werden or England

Contents: Old Testament: Heptateuch (f)

MS: *CLA* Supplement (1971) no. 1685; R. McKitterick (1986–90) 297 and n. 37; Crick (1987) 184 and n. 18; Parkes *apud* Bischoff et al. (1988a) 21 n. 103; M.P. Brown (1989b); Krämer (1989–90) I.827; Barker-Benfield (1991); Bischoff—Brown (1992) 307; Marsden (1995) 42–3; Stoneman (1997) 131; Bischoff (1998—) I, no. 1061; Gerchow (1999) 56 [no. 14] and nn. 42 and 43, 375–6 [no. 84]

FACS: M.P. Brown (1989b) pls. I–II [Takamiya leaf, recto and verso]

818. 5. Düsseldorf, Universitäts- und Landesbibliothek, Fragm. K1: B210 (with San Marino, California, Henry E. Huntington Library RB 99513 (PR 1188F))

s. viii² or viii ex., prob. England, or Werden?

Contents: Isidore, *De ortu et obitu patrum* [*CPL* 1191] (f); *Allegoriae quaedam S. Scripturae* [*CPL* 1190] (f)

MS: *CLA* VIII (1959) no. 1184; Bischoff—Brown (1985) 358; Parkes *apud* Bischoff et al. (1988a) 21 n. 103; Krämer (1989–90) I.827; Stoneman (1997) 130; Gerchow (1999) 56 [no. 7], 373 [no. 78]; Zechiel-Eckes (2003) 23; Lapidge (2006) 309, 310

818. 6. Düsseldorf, Universitäts- und Landesbibliothek, Fragm. K1: B212 (with Werden, Pfarrarchiv Fragm. 1 and New York, Columbia University Library, Plimpton 54)

s. viii, Ireland, prov. England?, prov. Werden

Contents: Laidcenn, *Ecloga de Moralibus in Iob* [*CPL* 1716; *BCLL* 293] (f; xvii.1–174)

MS: Drögereit (1951) 6–7; *CLA* (1959) VIII, no. 1185, and XI (1966) p. 22; Adriaen (1969) vi; Krämer (1989–90) I.827; Barker-Benfield (1991) 53 and n. 41; Gerchow (1999) 55 [no. 1], 372 [no. 74]; Zechiel-Eckes (2003) 24–6; Bremmer (2007) 25 n. 21; Castaldi (2011) 400

ED: Adriaen (1969) 207–12 [Laidcenn, *Ecloga*, coll. as A]

ST: *BCLL* (1985) no. 293; Castaldi (2011) 400–1

818. 7. Düsseldorf, Universitäts- und Landesbibliothek, Fragm. K1: B213 (?with Bonn, Universitätsbibliothek, 366, fols. 34 and 41, palimpsest, lower script)

s. viii/ix, S England or Anglo-Saxon centre in Germany (Werden?)

Contents: Gregory, *Dialogi* [*CPL* 1713] (f)

MS: *CLA* VIII (1959) nos. 1186 [and 1070]; Bischoff (1998–) I, nos. 1068 [and 653]; Gerchow (1999) 56 and n. 44 [no. 15], 381–2 [no. 100]; Zechiel-Eckes (2003) 26; Lapidge (2006) 159; Bremmer (2007) 42, 25 n. 22

819. Düsseldorf, Universitäts- und Landesbibliothek, Fragm. K1: B215, K2: C118, K15:009, K19: Z 8/8, M.Th.u.Sch. 29a (4) (pastedowns)

s. viii med., prob. Northumbria

Contents: John Chrysostom, *De reparatione lapsi* (in Latin translation of Anianus of Celeda?) [*CPG* 4305] (f), *De compunctione cordis* (in Latin translation of Anianus of Celeda) [*CPG* 4308–9] (f); *Passio S. Iusti pueri* [*BHL* 4590] (f); *Pastor Hermas* [*CPG* 1052] (f)

MS: *CLA* VIII (1959) no. 1187; Kotzor (1981) I.271*; Bischoff—Brown (1985) 364; Vezzoni (1987) [K2: C118]; Barker-Benfield (1991) 53 and n. 43; Vezzoni (1994) 42–3 [K2: C118]; Gerchow (1999) 56 [nos. 4 and 18], 372 [no. 76]; Zechiel-Eckes (2002) *passim*; Zechiel-Eckes (2003) 27–8, 30–1, 47, 60, 65–6; Lapidge (2006) 316–17, 341; Biggs (2007a) 65–6 [C.D. Wright]; Bremmer (2007) 41 and n. 62; Love (2007) 74; Garrison (2012) 645 n. 70

FACS: Zechiel-Eckes (2002) pl. following p. 202 [K19: Z 8/8, fol. 2r]; Zechiel-Eckes (2003) pls. 23 [K19: Z 8/8, fol. 2v], 25 [M.Th.u.Sch. 29a (4), back pastedown]

ED: Vezzoni (1987) [transcription of fragments of *Pastor Hermas* in K2: C118]; Vezzoni (1994) 104–16 [K2: C118 (*Pastor Hermas*) coll. as D]

ST: Coens (1951) [*Passio S. Iusti pueri*]; Biggs et al. (2001) 282–3; Love (2007) [John Chrysostom]

820. Düsseldorf, Nordrhein-Westfälisches Hauptstaatsarchiv Z 11/1
(with Düsseldorf, Universitäts- und Landesbibliothek M O41)

s. viii², prob. Northumbria

Contents: Orosius, *Historiae aduersum paganos* [*CPL* 571] (f)

MS: *CLA* Supplement (1971) no. 1687; Oediger (1972) 430; Bischoff — Brown (1985) 366; Parkes *apud* Bischoff et al. (1988a) 22 n. 118; Krämer (1989–90) II.828; Barker-Benfield (1991) 53 and n. 44; Zechiel-Eckes (2002) 203 n. 31; Zechiel-Eckes (2003) 65; Gerchow (1999) 56, 373 [no. 77]; Bullough (2004) 267–8 and n. 46; Lapidge (2006) 323; Wieland (2009) 142; Garrison (2012) 646 n. 72; Jayatilaka (2012) 675 and n. 17

821. Düsseldorf, Universitäts- und Landesbibliothek, Fragm. K15: O17 + K19: Z8/7b (with Gerleve, Stiftsbibliothek, s.n.)

s. viii², prob. Northumbria

Contents: Isidore, *Etymologiae* [*CPL* 1186] (f)

MS: *CLA* VIII (1959) no. 1189 [wtih *CLA* Supplement (1971) p. 6]; Bischoff (1966–81) I.183 and n. 76; Parkes *apud* Bischoff et al. (1988a) 22 n. 118; Barker-Benfield (1991) 53 and n. 45; Gerchow (1999) 56 [no. 6], 374 [no. 79]; Zechiel-Eckes (2003) 48, 59; Lapidge (2006) 311; Garrison (2012) 645 n. 71

822. Düsseldorf, Universitäts- und Landesbibliothek, Fragm. K16: Z 3/1

s. viii¹, Northumbria

Contents: Cassiodorus, *Expositio psalmorum* [*CPL* 900] (breviate version) (f)

MS: *CLA* Supplement (1971) no. 1786; Parkes *apud* Bischoff et al. (1988a) 22 n. 118; *CPPM* II, no. 2121; Knappe (1996) 217–18; Gerchow (1999) 56 [no. 3], 378–9 [no. 91]; Bullough (2004) 256–7 and nn.; Lapidge (2006) 296; Wieland (2009) 131; Rushforth (2011) 59–60; Garrison (2012) 645 n. 69

FACS: Gerchow (1999) 378 [recto]

ST: Halporn (1981); Bailey (1983); Bailey — Handley (1983)

823. El Escorial, Real Biblioteca de San Lorenzo de El Escorial, e. II. 1

s. x/xi or xi in., Continent or England, prov. Horton Abbey, Dorset, s. xi[2]

Contents: Boethius, *De consolatione Philosophiae* [*CPL* 878], with abbreviated version of commentary by Remigius

MS: Antolin (1910–23) II.33–4; N.R. Ker (1957) no. 115; N.R. Ker (1964) 103; T.A.M. Bishop (1971) 18; Bolton (1977a) 57–8; O'Donovan (1988) lxi; Dumville (1993g) 54 n. 240, 55; Budny (1997) I.460; Lapidge (2006) 56 n. 20, 293; Wittig (2007) 189; Ziolkowski (2007) 250; Godden— Irvine (2009) I.xlv; Wittig (2010) 250; R. Gameson (2012a) 29 n. 66; Rankin (2012) 505 n. 111; Scragg (2012a) no. 332

ST: Godden (2011) 92; Jayatilaka (2011) 98, 117

824. Épinal, Bibliothèque municipale, 72 (7), fols. 94–107

s. vii ex. or vii/viii

Contents: glossary[+*] (the 'Épinal-Erfurt Glossary')

MS: *Cat. gén. Dép.* (Quarto) III.429 [Michelant]; *CLA* VI (1953) no. 760; N.R. Ker (1957) no. 114; Pheifer (1974) xxi–xxv; T.J. Brown (1982) I.109 and n. 12 [repr. T.J. Brown (1993a) 210 and n. 12]; Bischoff et al. (1988a) 13–17; A.K. Brown (1992) 106–7 and nn.; Lapidge (2007) 35; Sauer (2008) 439; Wieland (2009) 145, 146; Lapidge (2010a) 130–1; *ASMMF* XVIII (2012) 67–83 [no. 128; Lucas]; Crick (2012) 177 n. 16

FACS: Sweet (1883) [complete facsimile]; Schlutter (1912) [complete facsimile]; Bischoff et al. (1988a) [complete facsimile]; T.J. Brown (1993a) ill. 58 [fol. 96v]; *ASMMF* XVIII (2012) no. 128 [complete facsimile]

ED: Sweet (1885) 36–106 [Latin—Old English entries only]; Sweet (1887/1978) 2–100 [Latin—Old English entries only]; Goetz (1888–1923) V.337–401 [complete glossary]; A.K. Brown (1969) [complete glossary]; Pheifer (1974) 3–58 [Latin—Old English glossary entries only]

LANG: H.M. Chadwick (1899) 188–249; A. Campbell (1959) ['Ep.']; Karl Brunner (1965) ['Ep.']; Pheifer (1974) lvii–xci; Hogg (1992) ['EpGl']

ST: Lindsay (1921b); Pheifer (1974) xl–xli; Pheifer (1987); Bischoff et al. (1988a); Pheifer (1992) 191–205; Pheifer (1994) *passim*; Pheifer (1995) 329–33; Lapidge (2007) 34–48; Sauer (2007); Sauer (2008); Lapidge (2010a) *passim*; Giliberto (2011) 127–8 and n. 40; Rusche (2011) 402–14; R. McKitterick (2012) 325

824. 3. Esztergom, Archiepiscopal Library, s.n.

s. viii², prob. England, possibly Anglo-Saxon centre on the Continent

Contents: Gregory, *Homiliae in Hiezechielem* [*CPL* 1710] (f)

MS: *CLA* XI (1966) no. 1591; Lapidge (2006) 164

824. 5. Évreux, Bibliothèque municipale, 43

s. x, England?, (prov. Lyre, Normandy)

Contents: Proba, preface to *Cento Vergilianus* [SK 14383]; Sedulius, Letter to Macedonius and *Carmen paschale* [*CPL* 1447] with glosses, *Hymni* [*CPL* 1449]

MS: *Cat. gén. Dép.* (Octavo) II.426–7 [Omont]; Nortier (1966) 124, 140; Springer (1995) 49; Bischoff (1998 –) I, p. 254; Lapidge (2006) 327, 331; R. Gameson (2012a) 67 n. 232

825. Florence, Biblioteca Medicea Laurenziana, Amiatino 1 (the 'Codex Amiatinus')

s. vii ex. or viii in. (before 716), Monkwearmouth-Jarrow, prov. Continent s. viii, prov. abbey of Monte Amiato, Italy (by s. ix or x?)

Contents: complete Bible (pandect) with metrical *tituli* [SK and SK Suppl. 2431, 2820]

MS: J. Wordsworth et al. (1889–1954) I.xl; P. Wagner (1912) 66–7; *CLA* III (1938) no. 299; Lowe (1960) 8–13; D.H. Wright (1961a); Bruce-Mitford (1967); Gamber (1968–88) no. 404b; Parkes (1982) 3–6 and n. 4, 20–1 and n. 81 [repr. Parkes (1991) 94–5 and n. 4, 116–17 and n. 81]; Webster—Backhouse (1991) no. 88; Parkes (1992) 179; Marsden (1995) 76–201; Lenker (1997) 392–3; Webster—Brown (1997) 235 [no. 94]; Marsden (1998); Martín Sánchez (2000) 130–2; Magrini (2001); Alidori et al. (2003) 3–58; Chazelle (2003); W. Schipper (2003) 153; Meyvaert (2005); Lapidge (2006) 29, 61; Biggs (2007a) 16; Wieland (2009) 115; Marsden (2011); M.P. Brown (2012) 125–6, 131, 142 and n. 93; R. Gameson (2012a) 37, 46 and n. 140, 51, 53, 82 n. 294, 90 n. 327; R. Gameson (2012b) 108 and n. 54, 114; Gullick (2012) 308 and n. 88; Marsden (2012) 406–7, 412, 416–17

DEC: Köhler (1930–60) III.15, 31, 74; Bruce-Mitford (1967); Alexander (1978a) no. 7; Weitzmann (1977) 24, 126; Ohlgren (1986) no. 7; Merten (1987); Marsden (1995) 102–5, 119–22; G. Henderson (1987); R. Gameson (1995b) 28, 188; Michelli (1999); Chazelle (2003);

Chazelle (2006); Karkov (2009) 209–10; Nees (2011) 14, 15, 16, 22–4, 27; Netzer (2012) 232

FACS: Ricci (2000) [complete facsimile on CD-ROM]; Lowe (1960) pls. VIII–IX [fols. 1v, 989r, 938v, 401r]; D.H. Wright (1961a) pls. I [fol. Iv], II [fols. 195r, 255r, 221r (details)], III [fol. 218r], V (d)–(e) [fols. 276v, 979v (details)]; Bruce-Mitford (1967) pls. I [fol. Iv], II [fol. Vr], IV (1) [fol. 802r (detail)], IV (2) [fol. Vr (detail)], VI [fol. IVv], VII [fol. IIIr (detail)], IX [fol. VIIr], X [fol. 8r], XI [fols. VIr and Ir (details)], XII [fol. VIv], XIII [fol. 796v], XVI [fol. 799r], XX [fol. 86v]; D.M. Wilson (1984) pl. 39 [fol. Vr]; Parkes (1992) pl. 10 [fol. 349v]; Marsden (1995) pl. I [fol. 485r]; Meyvaert (2005) fig. 8 [fol. VIIIr (detail)]; M.P. Brown (2007a) pls. 22–3 [fols. Vr, IIv–IIIr]; Marsden (2011) figs. 11.1–4 [fols. 239r, 438r, 224v, 996v]

ED: Tischendorf (1850) [base MS for complete New Testament]; J. Wordsworth et al. (1889–1954) [base MS for gospels; the remainder of the New Testament coll. as A]; Wordsworth—White (1911) [New Testament coll. as A]; De Sainte-Marie (1954) [Psalterium Hebraicum coll. as A]; B. Fischer (1988–91) [gospel excerpts coll. as Na]; Weber—Gryson et al. (1994) [complete Bible coll. as A]; Martín Sánchez (2000) [*Versus Isidori* coll. as Am]

ST: B. Fischer (1962) [repr. B. Fischer (1985) 9–34]; Klauser (1972) xxxi; Corsano (1987); Hunter Blair (1990) 222–5; R. Gameson (1992b); McGurk (1994b) [repr. McGurk (1998) no. XII]; Netzer (1994) *passim*; Meyvaert (1996); Lenker (1997) *passim*; Marsden (1998); Dumville (1999) 48, 67–9, 81; Farr (1999) 336–44; *CSLMA* II (1999) 87 [Ezra inscription]; M.P. Brown (2003a) *passim*; Gorman (2003); Meyvaert (2005); Meyvaert (2006); Ziolkowski (2007) 190 n. 54; Ferrari (2011) 237

827. Florence, Biblioteca Medicea Laurenziana, Plut. xvii. 20

s. xi$^{2/4}$, Canterbury CC?, prov. Continent s. xi

Contents: gospel lectionary

MS: T.A.M. Bishop (1971) xvi, 22; Heslop (1990) 173–4, 182; Pfaff (1992a) 269; Dumville (1993g) 117–20, 139; Lenker (1997) 467–71; R. Gameson (2004b); Wieland (2009) 122; Teviotdale (2010) 87–99; R. Gameson (2012a) 40 n. 105; R. Gameson (2012d) 363 and n. 79

DEC: F. Wormald (1952) 64–5 [no. 21]; E. Temple (1976) no. 69; Dodwell (1982) 81; Ohlgren (1986) no. 174; Raw (1990) 206; R. Gameson (1992a) 190, 207, 212 n. 108; R. Gameson (2012c) 282 and n. 116

FACS: E. Temple (1976) ill. 232 [fol. 1r]; Dodwell (1982) pl. 15 [fol. 1r]; Dumville (1993g) pl. XII [folio not specified]

ST: Klauser (1972) xcvii [no. 107]; Lenker (1997) *passim*

827. 1. Florence, Biblioteca Medicea Laurenziana, Plut. xlv. 15

s. viii² or viii/ix, Northumbria (York?) or Tours?

Contents: Tiberius Claudius Donatus, *Interpretationes Vergilianae*, bks. I-V

MS: *CLA* III (1938) no. 279a; Lowe (1960) no. XXXIX (b); Hunter Blair (1976) 251–2; T.J. Brown (1982) 115 [repr. T.J. Brown (1993a) 216]; L.D. Reynolds (1983) 157–8 [R.H. Rouse]; Bischoff (1998 —) I, no. 1227

827. 2. Freiburg im Breisgau, Universitätsbibliothek, 702

s. viii¹, Northumbria or Continent (Echternach?)

Contents: gospels (f)

MS: Dold (1935); *CLA* VIII (1959) no. 1195; Lowe (1960) 20; McGurk (1961a) no. 67 and p. 14; D.H. Wright (1961a) 448; Hagenmaier (1980) 200–1; McGurk (1987) 171 [repr. McGurk (1998) no. II]; Netzer (1989) 207–12; Netzer (1994) *passim*; Autenrieth (1995) 179

DEC: Alexander (1978a) no. 25; M.P. Brown (2003a) 316

FACS: Dold (1935) pls. I [fol. 1r], II [fols. 1v, 2r, 2v (details)]; Lowe (1960) pl. XVI [fol. 1r]; Alexander (1978a) ills. 117–18 [fols. 1r, 1v]; Netzer (1989) [fol. 2v]

827. 5. Fulda, Hessische Hochschul- und Landesbibliothek, Aa. 21

s. xi (1051×1064) and Continent 1065×1071, prov. Bavaria *c.* 1071, prov. Weingarten s. xi ex.

Contents: gospels (with omissions)

MS: T.A.M. Bishop (1971) xvi n. 3; Köllner—Jakobi-Mirwald (1976–93) I.51–4 [no. 22]; E. Temple (1976) 110, 112; McGurk (1986b) 44, 46–7, 51–3, 55 [repr. McGurk (1998) no. XIV]; Hausmann (1992); McGurk—Rosenthal (1995b) 289–93 *et passim* [repr. McGurk (1998) no. XV]; McGurk—Rosenthal (2006) 185 and n. 1; R. Gameson (2012d) 362 and n. 74; McGurk (2012) 446 [no. 6]

DEC: R. Gameson (1995b) 54 n. 217; Rosenthal—McGurk (2006);
R. Gameson (2012c) 271 and n. 66

FACS: Köllner—Jakobi-Mirwald (1976–93) II, pls. 177 [fol. 2v], 178 [fol.
3r], 179 [fol. 3v], 180 [fol. 4r], 181 [fol. 35v], 182 [fol. 36r], 183 [fol. 51v],
184 [fol. 52v], 185 [fol. 71v], 186 [fol. 72r], 187 [fol. 4v], 188 [fol. 5r], 189
[fol. 34r], 190 [fol. 50r], 191 [fol. 70r], 192 [fol. 82v], 193 [fol. 64r], 194
[fol. 88r], 195 [fol. 88v], 196 [fol. 89v]

827. 6. Fulda, Hessische Hochschul- und Landesbibliothek, Bonifatianus 1 (the 'Codex Fuldensis')

s. vi[1] (before 546 or 547), S Italy, prov. England s. vii and/or viii[1], prov.
Germany

Contents: Victor of Capua, *Praefatio* to Tatian's *Diatessaron* [*CPL* 953a];
Canon tables; Tatian, *Diatessaron* [*CPG* 1106] in Latin translation,
revised by Victor of Capua; list of Epistle pericopes [*CPL* 1976];
Epistulae Pauli; burial places of the Apostles [*BHL* 651]; Actus
Apostolorum; Epistulae catholicae (with glosses on the Epistula
Iacobi, s. viii); Apocalypsis Iohannis; Damasus, epigram on St Paul
[SK 7486]

MS: J. Wordsworth et al. (1889–1954) I.xii; Lindsay (1910) 10; Lindsay
(1915) 457; McGurk (1955a) [repr. McGurk (1998) no. III]; *CLA* VIII
(1959) no. 1196; R. Powell (1962) 4; Köllner—Jakobi-Mirwald (1976–
93) I.15–18 [no. 1]; Parkes (1976a) [repr. Parkes (1991) 121–42]; T.J.
Brown (1982) 112 [repr. T.J. Brown (1993a) 213]; B. Fischer (1988–91)
I.14*; Hausmann (1992) 3–7; Lapidge (1994a) 108–15; McGurk (1994b)
8, 19 n. 59 [repr. McGurk (1998) no. XII]; M.P. Brown (2003c) 154,
166–7, 171–2, 176, 179–81, 206, 266, 388 n. 66; Aris (2004) 101–4;
Lapidge (2006) 40 and n. 52, 77 n. 50; Hussey (2008) 159; Gullick
(2012) 299 and n. 19

DEC: Köllner—Jakobi-Mirwald (1976–93) I.15 [no. 1]

FACS: Ranke (1860) 2 pls. [illustrating glosses to Epistula Iacobi]; E.M.
Thompson (1912) pl. 91 [folio not specified]; Köllner—Jakobi-Mirwald
(1976–93) II, pls. 1–3 [fols. 5v–6r, 179v–180r, 436v], 921–2 [front and
rear bindings]; Parkes (1991) pls. 23 [fols. 436r, 436v, 435v, 438r (all
details)], 24 [fols. 435v, 436v, 436r (all details)]; M.P. Brown (2003c)
fig. 66 [fols. 5v–6r]; Aris (2004) pp. 101 [fols. 13v, 14r, 450r (detail)], 102
[fols. 5v, 6r], 103 [fols. 435v, 436r], 104 [fols. 434v, 435r, 4v, 5r]

ED: Ranke (1860) 19–29 [glosses to Epistula Iacobi]; Ranke (1868) 1–3 [*Praefatio* by Victor], 5–20 [Canon tables], 21–165 [Tatian, *Diatessaron*, in Latin translation], 165–8 [list of Epistle pericopes], 180–331 [Epistulae Pauli], 332 [burial places of the Apostles], 332–98 [Actus Apostolorum], 399–432 [Epistulae catholicae], 432–62 [Apocalypsis Iohannis], 463–4 [Damasus, poem on St Paul]; J. Wordsworth et al. (1889–1954) [gospels coll. as F]; Ferrua (1942) 82–3 [poem of Damasus]; B. Fischer (1988–91) [gospels coll. as F]; Weber—Gryson (1994) [gospels coll. as F]; Aris—Broszinski (1996) [glosses to Epistula Iacobi]

ST: Ehrismann (1932) 287–8 [Tatian]; R. Derolez (1954) 402; Klauser (1972) xxxi [Epistle list]; *CPL* (1995) no. 1635 [Damasus]; U.B. Schmid (2005) 13–26, 30–44, 48–51, 59–94, 154–65, 223–8 *et passim* [Tatian]; Hussey (2008) 159–60 [glosses]

827. 7. Fulda, Hessische Hochschul- und Landesbibliothek, Bonifatianus 3 (the 'Cadmug Gospels')

s. viii^1 or viii^2, Ireland, prov. S England?, prov. Germany (s. ix ex. Fulda)

Contents: gospels (with some omissions); verses (introducing Mark, Luke and John) from a poem attributed to Iuvencus [SK 9446]; colophon of the scribe Cadmug [*Colophons* 2424]; note on the return of the manuscript to Abbot Huoggi of Fulda (891×899) (s. ix/x)

MS: Lindsay (1910) 4–12; E.H. Zimmermann (1916) 250; McGurk (1956) 250, 252–3 [repr. McGurk (1998) no. I]; *CLA* VIII (1959) no. 1198; McGurk (1961a) no. 68; R. Powell (1962) 4; T.J. Brown (1969b) 13, 45–56; T.J. Brown (1972) 242, 245 [repr. T.J. Brown (1993a) 118, 273 n. 95]; Pollard (1975) 157–8; T.J. Brown (1984) 326 [repr. T.J. Brown (1993a) 239]; Köllner—Jakobi-Mirwald (1976–93) I.21–3 [no. 3]; Spilling (1982) 883–7; McGurk (1987) 165–8 and nn., 173 [repr. McGurk (1998) no. XII]; B. Fischer (1988–91) I.16*; Hausmann (1992) 11–13; T.J. Brown (1993b) 184; Bischoff (1998—) I, no. 1311a [note on return]; Stiegemann—Wemhoff (1999) II.473–5 [A. Schmid and K. Bierbrauer]; Aris (2004) 100; Lapidge (2006) 77 n. 50; R. Gameson (2012a) 22 n. 32

DEC: E.H. Zimmermann (1916) 31, 106, 108, 250; Köllner—Jakobi-Mirwald (1976–93) I.21 [no. 3]; Köhler—Mütherich (1971–99) VII.74; Alexander (1978a) no. 49; Schramm—Mütherich (1981) 138 [no. 59]; Ohlgren (1986) no. 43; Stiegemann—Wemhoff (1999) II.473–5

FACS: Lindsay (1910) pl. III [fol. 54v]; E.H. Zimmermann (1916) *Tafelband* III, pl. 205 (c) [fol. 33v]; Baesecke (1933) pl. 2 [fol. 18v]; Köllner—Jakobi-Mirwald (1976–93) II, pls. 17–20 [fols. 1v–2r, 19v–20r, 33v–34r, 51v–52r]; Alexander (1978a) ill. 228 [fol. 33v]; Hausmann (1992) pl. 2 [fols. 51v–52r]; Stiegemann—Wemhoff (1999) II.474 [fols. 19v–20r]; Aris (2004) 98 [binding], 99 [fols. 65v, 51v, 52r], 100 [fols. 18v, 33r]

ED: B. Fischer (1988–91) [gospels coll. as Hf]

828. Geneva (Cologny-Genève), Bibliotheca Bodmeriana, 2

s. xi^2

Contents: Ælfric, *Catholic Homilies* II.v* (fragment of rewritten version)

MS: N.R. Ker (1957) no. 285; N.R. Ker (1962b); N.R. Ker (1976a) 124; Godden (1979) 348–9; R. Gameson (1999a) no. 300; *ASMMF* XX (2012) 27–8 [no. 112; McGowan]; Scragg (2012a) no. 345

FACS: *ASMMF* XX (2012) no. 112 [complete facsimile]

ED: N.R. Ker (1962b)

829. Geneva (Cologny-Genève), Bibliotheca Bodmeriana, 175 [sold to a private collector in America in 2005]

s. x^2 or xi in., Canterbury?

Contents: Lupus of Ferrières, *De metris Boethii*; Boethius, *De consolatione Philosophiae* [*CPL* 878], with commentary by Remigius; Donatus, *Ars maior* bk. I (excerpt); Latin poems: SK 638; 13123; hymn *Deus piissimum nostra uox canora*, glossed, with two proverbs

MS: Courcelle (1967) 405; Bolton (1977a) 57, 61; Troncarelli (1981) 34, 112, 255–6; Pellegrin (1982) 411–15; De Hamel (1987) 201–2; Bodden (1988) 227 n. 40; Gibson et al. (1995–2001) II.185–6; *Sotheby's Sale L 05240 (5 July 2005)* lot 80; Lapidge (2006) 293, 300; Wittig (2007) 189; Godden—Irvine (2009) I.xlv; Wieland (2009) 144; Wittig (2010) 232 n. 26, 250 *et passim*; Gneuss (2012) 295; Rankin (2012) 505 and n. 109

DEC: F. Wormald (1945) 135 [repr. F. Wormald (1984) 74]; Brownrigg (1978) 259 n. 6

FACS: Pellegrin (1982) pl. 27 [fol. 2r]

ED: Bolton (1977a) 60–78 [mythological glosses to Boethius coll. as K]

ST: Godden (2011) 92; Jayatilaka (2011) 117

829. 2. Gerleve, Westphalia, Abteibibliothek, s.n.

s. viii[1], prob. England, prov. Werden

Contents: Jerome, *Comm. in Epistulas Pauli* [*ad Galatas*] [*CPL* 591]

MS: Bischoff—Brown (1985) 327–8 [= *CLA* Add. no. 1826]; Gerchow (1999) 56 [no. 10]; Lapidge (2006) 314

FACS: Bischoff—Brown (1985) pl. V(c) [recto (detail)]

Gerleve, Westphalia, Abteibibliothek, s.n.: see no. **821**

Göteborg, Friherre August Vilhelm Stiernstedts Samling, no. 3: see no. **936. 1**

Göteborg, Friherre August Vilhelm Stiernstedts Samling, no. 4: see no. **936**

829. 5. Gotha, Forschungs- und Landesbibliothek, Mbr. I. 18

s. viii, Northumbria or Continent (Echternach?), prov. Murbach

Contents: gospels

MS: Nordenfalk (1932); *CLA* VIII (1959) no. 1205; McGurk (1961a) no. 69; B. Fischer (1988–91) I.20*; Hopf (1994) 27; Netzer (1994) 8, 11, 16, 38, 213 nn. 61 and 63, 218 n. 25; McNamara (1995) 91; Bischoff (1998—) II, no. 1417a; R. McKitterick (2000); M.P. Brown (2003a) 168–71

DEC: Alexander (1978a) no. 27; Netzer (2012) 233 and n. 50

FACS: M.P. Brown (2003a) figs. 27, 69 [fols. 126r, 118v]

ED: B. Fischer (1988–91) [gospels coll. as Gu]

829. 6. Gotha, Forschungs- und Landesbibliothek, Mbr. I. 75, fols. 1–22

s. viii ex., S England or possibly Anglo-Saxon centre on the Continent

Contents: Sedulius, *Carmen paschale* [*CPL* 1447] (incomplete); biographical notice of Sedulius; Alcuin (?), three rhythmical poems [SK 684, 301, 1068]

MS: *CLA* VIII (1959) no. 1206; R. McKitterick (1986–90) 295 and n. 26; Hopf (1994) 55–6; Springer (1995) 55; Lapidge (2006) 160 [no. 49]

ED: Huemer (1885) [Sedulius, *Carmen paschale*, coll. as Γ]; Strecker (1914–23) 904–10 [three rhythmical poems]; W. Meyer (1916) [three rhythmical poems]

ST: *CSLMA* II (1999) 104–6

829. 8. Grand Haven, Michigan, The Scriptorium, VK 861

s. x/xi, Canterbury CC?, prov. N France s. xi (doubtful) [a flyleaf]

Contents: three verse riddles [the third of which is listed SK and SK Suppl. 3618]; Eugenius of Toledo (?), *Heptametron de primordio mundi* [SK 12551]; encyclopedic note on the languages of the world; note on loan of books (s. xi/xii)

MS: Quaritch, *Catalogue* 1036 [*Bookhands of the Middle Ages, pt. 1*] (1984) lot 124; Sauer (1989) 61 and n. 1; *Sotheby's Sale LN 7736 (2 Dec. 1997)* lot 13; Stoneman (1997) 129

FACS: Quaritch, *Catalogue* 1036, front cover and pl.; *Sotheby's Sale LN 7736*, p. 17

Haarlem, Stadsbibliotheek, 188 F 53: see no. **141**

830. The Hague, Koninklijke Bibliotheek, 133. D. 22 (21)

s. xi^1 [probably from the same manuscript as nos. **811. 5** and **816. 6**]

Contents: Ælfric, *Catholic Homilies* (f; from I.xxvii–xxix)

MS: N.R. Ker (1957) no. 118; Fausbøll (1986) 9; Clemoes (1997) 56–7; Abram (2007) 427 n. 7; Kleist (2007c) 496; Scragg (2012a) nos. 299–306

830. 5. Hamburg, Staats- und Universitätsbibliothek, cod. theol. 2029 8°, flyleaf

s. viii, prob. England [lost or destroyed?]

Contents: gospels (f)

MS: *CLA* VIII (1959) no. 1213

831. Hannover, Kestner-Museum, W.M. XXIa, 36

c. 1020, Canterbury CC, prov. Germany by s. xi (Hersfeld?, later prov. Lüneburg, abbey of St Michael)

Contents: gospels, gospel list; verse colophon

MS: Stuttmann (1937) 39–47; T.A.M. Bishop (1971) xv, 22; Backhouse et al. (1984b) no. 56; Hoffmann (1986) I.188–9; Heslop (1990) 175–6, 182; Dumville (1993g) 18, 120–4, 127–30, 139–40; Webber (1995) 146 and n. 8; Lenker (1997) 454–6; Härtel (1999) 12–15; R. Gameson (2001d) 45 [no. 29]; R. Gameson (2002b); Heslop (2004) 286, 298; Henke (2005) 65–6; R. Gameson (2008) 49 n. 12, 146; R. Gameson (2012a) 40

n. 105, 45 n. 136; R. Gameson (2012d) 362 and n. 72, 369 and n. 106;
Marsden (2012) 423 and n. 78; McGurk (2012) 446 [no. 7]

DEC: Rice (1952) 194; Alexander (1975a) 148 and n. 8; E. Temple (1976)
no. 67; Ohlgren (1986) no. 172; Raw (1990) 208; R. Gameson (1992a)
189–90; O'Reilly (1992) 178–9, 207, 211–12, 214–16; R. Gameson
(1995b) 83–4, 100, 180, 196 *et passim*; Farr (2003) 125–6; Heslop (2004)
292; Henke (2005) 65–6; Heslop (2007) 69; Karkov (2007c) 56; Karkov
(2009) 221–2; R. Gameson (2010) 121; O'Reilly (2011) 208–9;
R. Gameson (2012c) 267 and n. 51, 272 and n. 70, 282 and n. 116

FACS: T.A.M. Bishop (1971) pl. XXII [fol. 183v]; E. Temple (1976) ills.
224–8 [fols. 9v, 10r, 65v, 147r, 12r, 14r]; R. Gameson (1992a) pls. 38,
47–50 [fols. 147v, 9v, 104, 11r, 14v]; Ohlgren (1992) pls. 8.1–8.21 [fols.
9v–16r, 17v, 65v, 66r, 96v, 97v, 147v, 148r]; Dumville (1993g) pl. XIII
[fol. 18r]; Härtel (1999) pl. IV [fol. 183v]; R. Gameson (2000b) pls.
10–11 [fols. 17v, 18r]; R. Gameson (2002a) pls. V–VII [fols. 183v, 146r,
148r]; Farr (2003) fig. 5 [fol. 147v]; Henke (2005) 65 [fols. 65v–66r], 66
[fols. 13v–14r, 183v–184r]; Karkov (2006a) pl. 8 [fol. 183v]; Owen-
Crocker (2009) figs. 2.11 [fol. 183v], 7.13–18 [fols. 9v, 10r, 17v, 65v, 96v,
147v]; R. Gameson (2012) pl. 10.7 [fol. 147v]

ST: McGurk (1986b) 43–4, 46–9, 52, 54 [repr. McGurk (1998) no. XIV];
Pfaff (1992a); Lapidge (1994a) 104 n. 4; McGurk—Rosenthal (1995b)
258 and n. 30 [repr. McGurk (1998) no. XV]; Heslop (2004) 306–7

831. 2. Hannover, Kestner-Museum, Culemann I. 71/72 (393/394)
(with New Haven, Yale University, Beinecke Library, 441)

s. viii/ix, England or Germany

Contents: Bede, *In Lucae euangelium expositio* [*CPL* 1356] (f; = *CCSL*
120, 149–51)

MS: *CLA* II (1935) no. 220; Mallon et al. (1939) no. 72; Laistner—King
(1943) 46; Hurst (1960) vi; McGurk (1961b) 12 [no. 33] [repr. McGurk
(1998) no. V]; Faye—Bond (1962) 24; Marston (1965); *CLA*
Supplement (1971) pp. 10, 47 and no. **220; Shailor (1984–2004) II.380
[the Beinecke leaf]; Bischoff—Brown (1985) 363; Stoneman (1997) 120;
Bischoff (1998—) I, no. 1499; Härtel (1999) 103

FACS: Mallon et al. (1939) pl. XLVIII (no. 72) [recto of the Beinecke leaf;
the same facsimile as in *CLA* II (1935) no. 220]; *CLA* Supplement
no. **220 [Hannover fol. 72r]

Hauzenstein near Regensburg, Gräflich Walderdorffsche Bibliothek: see no. **791**

831. 4. Herrnstein near Siegburg, Bibliothek der Grafen Nesselrode [formerly at Herten], **192, fols. 1–20**

s. ix^2 or ix/x, prob. S England (or NW Germany?) [destroyed]

Contents: Antonius Musa, *De herba uettonica*; pseudo-Apuleius, *Herbarius*; *De taxone liber*; Sextus Placitus, *Liber medicinae ex animalibus*

MS: Steinmeyer—Sievers (1879–1922) IV.468; Sudhoff (1917); Howald—Sigerist (1927) x–xi; Singer (1927) 39–41; Beccaria (1956) 209–13 [no. 55]; Talbot (1967) 20–1; M.L. Cameron (1983) 149 and n. 47; Hollis—Wright (1992) 321; Kristeller (1993) 475; Bischoff (1998—) I, no. 1524; D'Aronco (1998) 32 n. 44; M. Collins (2000) 228 n. 111, 234 n. 208; Wieland (2009) 155

DEC: C.M. Kauffmann (1975) 58; Grape-Albers (1977) 4

FACS: Sudhoff (1917) fig. 14 [fol. 15r]

Jönköping, Per Brahe gymnasiet, fragm. 5 and 6: see no. **936**

Karlsruhe, Badische Landesbibliothek, Aug. perg. 116 (binding): see no. **831. 7**

831. 6. Karlsruhe, Badische Landesbibliothek, Aug. perg. 221, fols. 54–107

s. viii med., prob. Northumbria (York?)

Contents: Gregory, *Homiliae in Hiezechielem* [*CPL* 1710]; Fastidius (?), *Admonitio* [*CPL* 763]

MS: *CLA* VIII (1959) no. 1095; Bischoff (1998—) I, no. 1712; Lapidge (2006) 158, 305; Wieland (2009) 126

ST: Morin (1934); *BCLL* (1985) no. 1250; *CPPM* I, nos. 157, 707, 1425

831. 7. Karlsruhe, Badische Landesbibliothek, Fragm. Aug. 122 (with Aug. perg. 116 (binding) and Zürich, Staatsarchiv A.G. 19, Nr. XIII, fols. 26–7)

s. viii ex., prob. Northumbria

Contents: Priscian, *Institutio de nomine, pronomine et uerbo* [*CPL* 1550] (f)

MS: *CLA* VII (1956) no. 1009 and VIII (1959) p. 30; Jeudy (1972) 104–5, 143; Passalacqua (1978) 109 [no. 245]; L.D. Reynolds (1983) xxi and n. 46; Passalacqua (1992) xv; Lapidge (2006) 158–9, 326; Garrison (2012) 647 n. 82

ED: Passalacqua (1992) 34–41 [part of Priscian, *Institutio de nomine, pronomine et uerbo*, coll. as P]

831. 8. Karlsruhe, Badische Landesbibliothek, Fragm. Aug. 212

s. x^2 or x/xi, England (or France?)

Contents: Priscian, *Periegesis* [*CPL* 1554; SK 10028] (f)

MS: Lapidge (2006) 327

832. Kassel, Gesamthochschulbibliothek 2° MS.theol. 21

s. viii, Northumbria, prov. Fulda s. ix?

Contents: Jerome, *Comm. in Ecclesiasten* [*CPL* 583]; Ambrose, *De apologia prophetae Dauid* [*CPL* 135]; Jerome, *Altercatio Luciferiani et Orthodoxi* [*CPL* 608] (incomplete), *Epistula* lvii [*CPL* 620]

MS: Hilberg (1910–18) I.503; Lindsay (1915) 451; Baesecke (1933) 20–1, 87–8, 90, 98–9, 110; Christ (1933) 30, 277–8; *CLA* VIII (1959) no. 1134; Bischoff (1966–81) II.287; Crick (1987) 187; Wiedemann (1994) 26–7; Canellis (2000) 2* and n. 5; Lapidge (2006) 159, 276, 313, 315; Wieland (2009) 131

FACS: Baesecke (1933) pl. 14 [fol. 44r]

ED: Canellis (2000) [Jerome, *Altercatio Luciferiani et Orthodoxi*, coll. as K]

ST: Lambert (1969–72) nos. 0, 205, 250; Godman (1982) 122 [note on line 1541]; Bankert et al. (1997) 30

833. Kassel, Gesamthochschulbibliothek 2° MS.theol. 32

s. viii, S England, prov. Germany, prob. Fulda, s. viii/ix

Contents: Gregory, *Regula pastoralis* [*CPL* 1712]

MS: Baesecke (1933) 20–1, 88; *CLA* VIII (1959) no. 1138; Clement (1984a) 40; Wiedemann (1994) 39; Bischoff (1998—) I, no. 1808a; Schreiber (2003) 23 and n. 5, 27, 30; Lapidge (2006) 159, 306

DEC: Alexander (1978a) 65

FACS: Baesecke (1933) pl. 15 [fol. 23r]

834. Kassel, Gesamthochschulbibliothek 2° MS.theol. 65

s. vi, Italy, prov. England s. viii, prov. Fulda s. viii?, (prov. ibid.)

Contents: Iosephus, *De bello Iudaico*, trans. Hegesippus

MS: Lowe (1924) 41 [no. 19]; Lehmann (1925) 15; Ussani—Mras (1932–60) II.xv–xvi; Siegmund (1949) 106 and n. 3; N.R. Ker (1957) no. 121; Blatt (1958) 98; *CLA* VIII (1959) no. 1139; Meritt (1961) no. XIV; Hofmann (1963) 50–2; Vaciago (1993) 12 [no. 48]; Wiedemann (1994) 96; Lapidge (2006) 40, 317; Wieland (2009) 143

ED: Ussani—Mras (1932–60) I.20–417 [Iosephus, *De bello Iudaico*, trans. Hegesippus, coll. as C]

ST: Schanz et al. (1914–20) I.109–11

Kassel, Gesamthochschulbibliothek 2° MS.theol. 265: see no. **849**

834. 5. Kassel, Gesamthochschulbibliothek 2° MS.theol. 267 [formerly Anhang 18]

s. viii², probably England, possibly an Anglo-Saxon centre on the Continent

Contents: Cassian, *Conlationes* [*CPL* 512]

MS: *CLA* VIII (1959) no. 1143; Wiedemann (1994) 272; Lake (2003) 29 n. 8; Lapidge (2006) 159; Bremmer (2007a) 44 and n. 65

835. Kassel, Gesamthochschulbibliothek 4° MS.theol. 2

s. viii², Southumbria (Kent?), prov. Fulda prob. s. ix

Contents: Bede, *Historia ecclesiastica* [*CPL* 1375], bks. IV and V

MS: *CLA* VIII (1959) no. 1140; Colgrave—Mynors (1969) xlii; Van Els (1972) 3–39 [with bibliography of earlier notices, p. 3 n. 1]; O'Brien O'Keeffe (1987) 143; Dumville (2007f) 57–8, 78, 98 and n. 172; Lapidge (2008–10) I.lxxxvii–lxxxix; R. Gameson (2012a) 25 n. 45; Gullick (2012) 296 n. 12, 307 and n. 83

FACS: Van Els (1972) pls. (unnumbered) on pp. 267–72 [fols. 21r, and 5v, 15r, 24r, 31r (all details)]

ED: Lapidge (2008–10) II.158–484 [Bede, *Historia ecclesiastica*, bks. IV and V, coll. as K]

LANG: Van Els (1972) 59–235, 238–41

ST: Van Els (1972) xxvii–xxx, 40–58, 235–8; Lapidge (2008b)

Kassel, Gesamthochschulbibliothek 4° MS.theol. 131: see no. **375**

836. Köln (Cologne), Dombibliothek, 213

s. viii in., Northumbria, prov. Köln by s. viii ex.

Contents: canon collection (*Collectio Sanblasiana*)

MS: Maassen (1870) 504–12; L.W. Jones (1929) 57; N.R. Ker (1957)
no. 98; *CLA* VIII (1959) no. 1163 and Supplement (1971) p. 62;
Hofmann (1963) 42; Bischoff (1966–81) III.75; T.J. Brown (1982) 111
[repr. T.J. Brown (1993a) 212]; R. McKitterick (1985) 111–15; Lapidge
(1986b) 66 and nn. [repr. Lapidge (1996b) 162 and nn.]; Webster—
Backhouse (1991) nos. 126, 127; Bischoff—Lapidge (1994) 153–4 and
nn. 89–90; Plotzek (1998) 110–16 [no. 18]; Kéry (1999) 30; *ASMMF* IX
(2001) 37–52 [no. 149; Doane]; Bullough (2004) 231 and n. 309, 232,
350; M.P. Brown (2012) 135; R. Gameson (2012a) 51 n. 168

DEC: Alexander (1978a) no. 13; Ohlgren (1986) no. 13; G. Henderson
(1987) 88–90, 96; M.P. Brown (2003a) 238; Farr (2011b) 225

FACS: G. Henderson (1987) pls. 128–9 [fols. 4v, 36v (details)]; Bischoff
(1990) pl. 7 [fol. 19v]; T.J. Brown (1993a) ill. 38 [fol. 2v (detail)];
Plotzek (1998) 111 [fol. 1r], 112 [fols. 2v, 4v], 113 [fols. 11r, 36r];
ASMMF IX (2001) no. 149

ST: Lambert (1969–72) no. 628; Lapidge (1986b) 64–6 [repr. Lapidge
(1996b) 160–2]; M. Brett (1995) 122–5

836. 5. Köln (Cologne), Historisches Archiv der Stadt, GB Kasten B, nos. 24, 123, 124 [from the same MS as no. 856. 3?]

s. viii med., prob. Northumbria

Contents: Sacramentarium Gelasianum (f)

MS: H.M. Bannister (1910–11b); Frank (1954) 83–8; Gamber (1958) 63;
CLA VIII (1959) no. 1165; Stiegemann—Wemhoff (1999) I.487
[Freise]; Spiegel (2007) 9–10

FACS: Stiegemann—Wemhoff (1999) II, pl. on p. 487 [one bifolium
(unspecified)]

ST: *CPL* (1995) no. 1918h

Lawrence, University of Kansas, Kenneth Spencer Research Library,
Pryce C2: 1: see no. **117**

Lawrence, University of Kansas, Kenneth Spencer Research Library,
Pryce C2: 2: see no. **639**

Lawrence, University of Kansas, Kenneth Spencer Research Library, Pryce P2A: 1: see no. **436**

837. Le Havre, Bibliothèque municipale, 330

s. xi$^{3/4}$ or xi^2 (or xi^1?), Winchester NM, (prov. Saint-Wandrille before s. xviii?)

Contents: missal (incomplete)

MS: *Cat. gén. Dép.* (Octavo) II.331–2 [Baillard]; Leroquais (1924) I.190–2; *Le Graduel romain* (1957) II.54; D.H. Turner (1962) v–xiii; N.R. Ker (1964) 200; Gamber (1968–88) no. 1489; T.A.M. Bishop (1971) xv; Dumville (1992a) 67; Dumville (1993f) 89, 98 [no. 11]; Lenker (1997) 478–81 *et passim*; R. Gameson (1999a) no. 326; Hartzell (2006) no. 102; Pfaff (2009) 110–11; Wieland (2009) 123; R. Gameson (2012a) 47–8 and n. 147; R. Gameson (2012d) 365 and n. 88; Pfaff (2012) 455 and n. 20; Rankin (2012) 501

FACS: D.H. Turner (1962) frontispiece [fol. 62r]

ED: D.H. Turner (1962)

ST: D.H. Turner (1962) xiii–xxvii; N. Orchard (1995c) 4 and n. 13; N. Orchard (2002) I.170–2, 175, 197, 202, 233

838. Leiden, Universiteitsbibliotheek, Voss. Lat. F. 4, fols. 4–33

s. viii$^{1/3}$, Northumbria

Contents: Pliny, *Naturalis historia*, bks. II–VI (incomplete)

MS: *CLA* X (1963) no. 1578; Mayhoff (1967) vi; De Meyier (1973) 7–8; T.J. Brown (1975) 275 [repr. T.J. Brown (1993a) 163]; T.J. Brown (1982a) 109 [repr. T.J. Brown (1993a) 210]; Munk Olsen (1982–) II.248; L.D. Reynolds (1983) xxi, 309–11, 315; Reynolds–Wilson (1991) 91; Bischoff (1998–) II, no. 2183; Lapidge (2006) 130, 325; Reeve (2007) 141 n. 82; Garrison (2012) 650 and nn. 104–5; Reeve (2012) 246

DEC: Alexander (1978a) no. 18; Ohlgren (1986) no. 18

FACS: Reynolds–Wilson (1991) pl. XII [fol. 20v]; T.J. Brown (1993a) ills. 54 (a)–(b) [fols. 30r, 20v (details)]

ED: Mayhoff (1967) 128–522 [Pliny, *Naturalis historia*, coll. as A]

ST: Reeve (2007); Reeve (2012)

Leiden, Universiteitsbibliotheek, Voss. Lat. Q. 2, fol. 60: see no. **795**

839. Leiden, Universiteitsbibliotheek, Scaliger 69

s. x^2, Canterbury, StA, prov. Glastonbury?

Contents: Aethicus Ister, *Cosmographia* [*CPL* 2348]

MS: Wuttke (1853) cxxvi; T.A.M. Bishop (1959–63b) 412; N.R. Ker (1964) 42; T.A.M. Bishop (1966) xvii; Rella (1977) 83; Galloway (1989); Dumville (1993f) 98 [no. 12]; Prinz (1993) 60; Herren (2011) ciii; R. Gameson (2012a) 29 n. 66; Rushforth (2012) 204 and n. 45

DEC: E. Temple (1976) no. 30 (v); Ohlgren (1986) no. 122; R. Gameson (2012c) 287 and n. 132

FACS: T.A.M. Bishop (1966) [complete facsimile]

ED: Prinz (1993) [Aethicus Ister, *Cosmographia*, coll. as S]; Herren (2011) [Aethicus Ister, *Cosmographia*, coll. as S]

ST: Lambert (1969–72) no. 621; *BCLL* (1985) no. 647; Jayatilaka (2011) 114 and n. 64

840. Leipzig, Universitätsbibliothek, Rep. I. 58a + II. 35a

s. viii^1, Northumbria?

Contents: gospels (f)

MS: *CLA* VIII (1959) no. 1229 and Supplement (1971) p. 11; B. Fischer (1988–91) I.16*

DEC: Micheli (1939) 47; Alexander (1978a) no. 15; Ohlgren (1986) no. 15

FACS: Micheli (1939) pl. 11 [Rep. I. 58a]

ED: B. Fischer (1988–91) [gospel fragment in Rep. II. 35a coll. as El]

840. 5. St Petersburg, Russian National Library, F. v. I. 3, fols. 1–38

s. viii^2, prob. Northumbria, (prov. Corbie)

Contents: Iob, with interlinear gloss drawn from Philippus presbyter, *Comm. in librum Iob* [*CPL* 643] and from Gregory, *Moralia in Iob* [*CPL* 1708]

MS: Staerk (1910) I.34–5; Lindsay (1915) 16 *et passim*; Lowe (1960) 23; *CLA* XI (1966) no. 1599; Bernadskaya et al. (1983) no. 17; D. Ganz (1990) 129–30; Dobiaš-Roždestvenskaya—Bakhtine (1991) 32–6; Kilpiö—Kahlas-Tarkka (2001) 35–7

FACS: Staerk (1910) II, pl. XXVIII [fol. 38r]; Kilpiö—Kahlas-Tarkka (2001) pl. 9 [fol. 9r]

840. 6. St Petersburg, Russian National Library, F. v. I. 3, fols. 39–108

s. viii², prob. Northumbria, (prov. Corbie)

Contents: Jerome, *Comm. in Esaiam* [*CPL* 584] (abbreviated; incomplete)

MS: Staerk (1910) I.34–5; Bischoff (1966–81) II.333; *CLA* XI (1966) no. 1600; Bernadskaya et al. (1983) no. 18; Dobiaš-Roždestvenskaya—Bakhtine (1991) 32–6; *CPPM* II, no. 2336a; Kilpiö—Kahlas-Tarkka (2001) 36–7

ST: Lambert (1969–72) nos. 207, 414

841. St Petersburg, Russian National Library, F. v. I. 8

s. viii ex. or ix in., Northumbria? S England (Kent)?, (prov. Saint-Maur-les-Fossés)

Contents: gospels

MS: Staerk (1910) I.25–6; McGurk (1961a) no. 126; *CLA* XI (1966) no. 1605; T.J. Brown (1972) 234–5 [repr. T.J. Brown (1993a) 112]; Bernadskaya et al. (1983) no. 23; B. Fischer (1988–91) I.16*; Dobiaš-Roždestvenskaya—Bakhtine (1991) no. 26; Parkes (1992) 125 n. 64; Dumville (1993f) 99 [no. 48]; R. Gameson (1994b) 28, 32–3, 35; Kockelkorn (2000); Kilpiö—Kahlas-Tarkka (2001) 41–4; M.P. Brown (2003a) 55 *et passim*; Wieland (2009) 117; M.P. Brown (2012) 135, 151

DEC: E.H. Zimmermann (1916) 35, 143–4, 304–5; Micheli (1939) 28–30 *et passim*; Alexander (1978a) no. 39; Bierbrauer (1979) 70 n. 244; D.M. Wilson (1984) 88; M.P. Brown (1986) 134–6; Ohlgren (1986) no. 39; M.P. Brown (1989a) 155, 161; R. Gameson (1995b) 40, 220; Bruno (2001); Netzer (2012) 233 and n. 50

FACS: E.H. Zimmermann (1916) *Tafelband* IV, pls. 321–6 [fols. 12r, 12v, 13v and 16r, 18r, 177r and 1r, 78r and 119r], 329 (a) [fol. 108r]; D.M. Wilson (1984) pl. 110 [fol. 18r]; Kilpiö—Kahlas-Tarkka (2001) pls. 11–12 [fols. 1r, 13r]; M.P. Brown (2003a) figs. 26 [fol. 18r], 68 [fol. 16r]

ED: B. Fischer (1988-91) [gospels coll. as Ec]

ST: McGurk (1993) 248–51 [repr. McGurk (1998) no. XI]; Lenker (1997) 106 n. 39, 140–1

842. St Petersburg, Russian National Library, O. v. I. 1, fols. 1 and 2

(with Avranches, Bibliothèque municipale, 48 fols. i and ii, 66 fols. i and ii, and 71, fols. A and B)

s. viii¹, Northumbria, (prov. Mont Saint-Michel)

Contents: gospels (f)

MS: *Cat. gén. Dép.* (Quarto) IV.452 [Delisle]; Staerk (1910) I.27–8; *CLA*
VI (1953) no. 730; Lowe (1960) 22; McGurk (1961a) no. 49 and p. 13;
Bernadskaya et al. (1983) no. 3; B. Fischer (1988–91) I.16* ['Ek'; not
collated]; Dobiaš-Roždestvenskaya—Bakhtine (1991) no. 25; Dumville
(1993f) 99 [no. 49]; McGurk (1994b) 5, 12 [repr. McGurk (1998)
no. XII]; R. Gameson (1999c) 347–9; Kilpiö—Kahlas-Tarkka (2001)
31–2; Marsden (2012) 414 and n. 33

FACS: Staerk (1910) I, pl. VII [fol. 1v], II, pl. XXV [fol. 1r]; Lowe (1960)
pls. XXIX (a) [Avranches 66, fol. i v], XXIX (b) [St Petersburg, fol. 2r];
R. Gameson (1999c) pl. 13.24 [Avranches, flyleaf]

842. 5. St Petersburg, Russian National Library, O. v. I. 45

[returned to Poland before 1928, but lost or destroyed (in Kraków or
Warsaw)]

s. xi/xii, England

Contents: psalter (incomplete); canticles; colophon*

MS: R. Gameson (1999a) after no. 820 [the reference to the manuscript in
Warsaw is mistaken]; Gneuss (2008a) 418–19 [with edition of colophon]

843. St Petersburg, Russian National Library, O. v. XIV. 1

s. x med., prob. Canterbury CC, (prov. Corbie)

Contents: Fredegaud/Frithegod of Canterbury and Brioude,
Breuiloquium Vitae Wilfridi [*BHL* 8891; SK 8137] (incomplete; lines
1–1218 only)

[originally formed one volume with St Petersburg, Russian National
Library, O. v. XVI. 1 and Paris, BNF, lat. 14088, fols. 99–119]

MS: Staerk (1918) I.222; Bernadskaya et al. (1983) no. 82; Lapidge (1988a)
53–61 [repr. Lapidge (1993a) 169–77, with supplementary note, p. 481];
Dumville (1993g) 92–4, 142; Lapidge (1994a) 126; Kilpiö—Kahlas-
Tarkka (2001) 37–8; Lapidge (2004a) 135, 137; R. Gameson (2012b)
100 n. 24

FACS: Staerk (1910) II, pl. LXX [fol. 107r]; Lapidge (1988a) pls. III–IV
[fols. 99v, 117r] [repr. Lapidge (1993a) pls. III–IV]; Kilpiö—Kahlas-
Tarkka (2001) pl. 18 [fols. 8v, 9r]

ED: A. Campbell (1950) [Fredegaud/Frithegod, *Breuiloquium* lines
1–1218, coll. as L]

LANG: Lapidge (1975a) 78–81 [repr. Lapidge (1993a) 116–19]

ST: Manitius (1911–31) II.501; Lapidge (1988a) [repr. Lapidge (1993a) 157–81]; Biggs et al. (2001) 481–2; Lapidge (2004a)

844. St Petersburg, Russian National Library, O. v. XVI. 1, fols. 1–16

s. x in. or x¹, England; with additions made s. xi (on Continent?); (prov. Corbie)

Contents: Priscian, *Institutio de nomine, pronomine et uerbo* [*CPL* 1550]; *Passio SS. Dionysii, Rustici et Eleutherii* [f; *BHL* 2171]; maxim*; on Gregory the Great (f): all s. x in. or x¹; additions (s. xi): hymn (inc. 'Iubilemus Deo nostro / fratres dilectissimi / uoto uoci consonante'); two prayers; three sequences [WIC 20298, SK 9879 and 17050]

MS: N.R. Ker (1976a) 127; Bernadskaya et al. (1983) no. 83; Jeudy (1984) 147–8; Dumville (1987) 175, 177; Lapidge (1988a) 55 [repr. Lapidge (1993a) 171]; Hollis—Wright (1992) 36; Passalacqua (1992) xvi; Blockley (1994) 83; Kilpiö—Kahlas-Tarkka (2001) 56–7; Lapidge (2006) 326, 341

ED: N.R. Ker (1976a) 127 [OE maxim]

ST: Biggs et al. (2001) 171–2

845. St Petersburg, Russian National Library, Q. v. I. 15

s. viii², SW England, prov. Corbie s. viii

Contents: Isidore, *In libros ueteris et noui Testamenti prooemia* [*CPL* 1192], *De ortu et obitu patrum* [*CPL* 1191]; Jerome, *Epist.* liii [*CPL* 620]; Isidore, *De ecclesiasticis officiis* [*CPL* 1207]; solutions to Aldhelm's *Enigmata*; Isidore, *De differentiis rerum* siue *Differentiae theologicae uel spiritales* [*CPL* 1202], bk. II; *Quicumque uult*; Boniface (?), acrostic poem [SK 8331]; Isidore, *Synonyma de lamentatione animae peccatricis* [*CPL* 1203] bks. I–II. 33 [part of *Synonyma* continued at Corbie]; poems on the zodiac and the winds [SK 1037, 13113; added at Corbie, s. ix]; Aldhelm, *Enigmata* [*CPL* 1335]

MS: Staerk (1910) I.225–8; Lindsay (1915) *passim*; Ehwald (1919) 43–4; Dobiaš-Roždestvenskaya (1934) 37, 132–4; Bischoff (1966–81) I.183–6; *CLA* XI (1966) no. 1618; Parkes (1976a) 162–5, 167, 170–2 [repr. Parkes (1991) 122–5, 127, 129, 131–5]; Spilling (1978) 49 and n. 5; Bernadskaya et al. (1983) no. 29; R. McKitterick (1986–90) 304; R. McKitterick (1989b) 413; D. Ganz (1990) 20, 42, 70, 130; Dobiaš-Roždestvenskaya—Bakhtine (1991) 63–8 [no. 28]; Lapidge (1994a) 110–15; Crick (1997) 69

n. 31; Bischoff (1998 –) II, no. 2317g; Kilpiö – Kahlas-Tarkka (2001) 39–40; Gneuss (2003b) 304; Andrés Sanz (2006) 129*–130*; Lapidge (2006) 40, 309, 310, 312, 313, 315; Di Sciacca (2008) 69–74 *et passim*; Hussey (2008) 151–2, 158–60; Elfassi (2009) xxxvii and nn.; Wieland (2009) 150; Lapidge (2012b) 21

FACS: Burn (1909), pls. XVIII-XIX [fols. 63r, 63v]; Staerk (1910) II, pl. LXXIII [fol. 2r]; Dobiaš-Roždestvenskaya (1934) pls. 1, 49; Parkes (1991) pl. 24 [fol. 63r (detail)]; Lapidge (1994a) pl. I [fol. 63r]; Kilpiö – Kahlas-Tarkka (2001) pl. 10 [fol. 21v]

ED: Ehwald (1919) 97–149 [Aldhelm, *Enigmata*, coll. as A]; Lawson (1989) [Isidore, *De ecclesiasticis officiis*, coll. as C]; Lapidge (1994a) 111–12 [acrostic poem]; Elfassi (2009) [Isidore, *Synonyma*, coll as L]; Andrés Sanz (2006) [Isidore, *Differentiae*, bk. II, coll. as C]

ST: Lambert (1969–72) no. 53; Lapidge (2012b) 19–26 [transmission of Aldhelm, *Enigmata*]

846. St Petersburg, Russian National Library, Q. v. I. 18 (the 'Leningrad Bede')

s. viii², Monkwearmouth-Jarrow

Contents: Bede, *Historia ecclesiastica* [*CPL* 1375]

MS: Staerk (1910) I.52-3; Dobiache-Rojdestvensky (1928); O.S. Anderson (1941); N.R. Ker (1957) no. 122; Lowe (1958) [repr. Lowe (1972b) II.441–9]; Lowe (1960) 23; Meyvaert (1961); D.H. Wright (1961b); Bévenot (1962); *CLA* XI (1966) no. 1621; Okasha (1968); Colgrave – Mynors (1969) xliv; T.J. Brown (1972) 235, 241, 243 [repr. T.J. Brown (1993a) 113, 118, 120]; T.J. Brown (1975) 261, 286 [repr. T.J. Brown (1993a) 155, 170–1]; P.R. Robinson (1978) 233 [repr. (1994) 27–8]; T.J. Brown (1982) 115, 118 [repr. T.J. Brown (1993a) 216, 220]; Parkes (1982) 5–12 [repr. Parkes (1991) 97–106]; Bernadskaya et al. (1983) no. 31; Crick (1987) 187–8; O'Brien O'Keeffe (1987); Parkes (1992) 27, 69; T.J. Brown (1993b) 199–200; Lapidge (1994a) 116–19; O'Brien O'Keeffe (1994); Kilpiö – Kahlas-Tarkka (2001) 29–31; W. Schipper (2003) 153–6; Lapidge et al. (2005) I.56–7; Roberts (2005) 18; Dumville (2007f) 79–84 *et passim*; Lapidge (2008–10) I.lxxxix–xc; G.H. Brown (2009); M.P. Brown (2012) 133 and n. 50, 158 n. 173; R. Gameson (2012a) 25, 51

DEC: Schapiro (1958); Alexander (1978a) no. 19; Ohlgren (1986) no. 19; Higgitt (1989) 274–5; M.P. Brown (2003a) 76, 234; Karkov (2009) 216; Rosenthal (2011) 223

FACS: Arngart (1952) [complete facsimile]; Staerk (1910) I, pl. XIV
[fol. 123v], II, pl. I [fol. 26v]; E.H. Zimmermann (1916) *Tafelband* IV,
pl. 332 (a) [fol. 26v]; Lowe (1960) pl. XXXVIII (a) [fol. 23v (detail)];
Alexander (1978a) ills. 83–4 [fols. 3r, 26v (details)]; Parkes (1982) pls. 1,
3 [fols. 107r, 37v (details)]; D.M. Wilson (1984) pls. 54–5 [fols. 3v, 26v
(details)]; Bonner et al. (1989a) pl. 21 [fol. 26v (detail)]; Parkes (1991)
pls. 16, 18 [fols. 107r, 37v (details)]; Robinson—Stanley (1991) pl. 2.3
[fol. 107r]; Lapidge (1994a) pl. II [fol. 86v]; Voronova—Sterligov
(1996) 282 [fol. 3v], 283 [fol. 26v]; Kilpiö—Kahlas-Tarkka (2001) pls.
7–8 [fols. 26v, 107r]; W. Schipper (2003) fig. 1 [fol. 107r]; Roberts
(2005) pl. 1 [fol. 107r]; Dumville (2007f) 68 [fol. 159r]

ED: Colgrave—Mynors (1969) [base MS ('m-text') for Bede, *Historia
ecclesiastica*]; Lapidge et al. (2005) [Bede, *Historia ecclesiastica*, coll.
as L]; Lapidge (2008–10) [Bede, *Historia ecclesiastica*, coll. as L]

ST: P.Z. Thompson (1984) 495; Crépin in Lapidge et al. (2005) I.7–90;
Lapidge (2008a) 78–112; Lapidge (2008b); Lapidge (2008–10) I.xv–
clxxii, cxxv–cxxxvii [bibliography]; R. McKitterick (2012) 333

847. St Petersburg, Russian National Library, Q. v. XIV. 1

s. viii[1], Northumbria (Lindisfarne?), (prov. Corbie)

Contents: flyleaf with pen trials (school verse) [s. viii], Paulinus of Nola,
Carmina natalitia [*CPL* 203], nos. xv, xvi, xviii, xxviii, xxvii, xvii

MS: Hartel (1894) xxix–xxx; Staerk (1910) I.222–3; *CLA* XI (1966)
no. 1622; T.J. Brown (1982) 111–12 [repr. T.J. Brown (1993a) 212];
Bernadskaya et al. (1983) no. 36; O'Brien O'Keeffe (1987) 144;
Brown—Mackay (1988) 16–20; M.P. Brown (1989a) 162; D. Ganz
(1990) 41, 130; Parkes (1992) 28; Bischoff (1998—) II, no. 2333a;
Kilpiö—Kahlas-Tarkka (2001) 45–6; Lapidge (2006) 37 and nn., 324;
M.P. Brown (2012) 159

DEC: De Mérindol (1976) II.1082–5; Alexander (1978a) no. 42; Ohlgren
(1986) no. 42

FACS: Staerk (1910) II, pl. 71 [fol. 2r]; Alexander (1978a) ill. 179 [fol. 1r];
T.J. Brown (1993a) ills. 52 (a)–(b) [fols. 8v, 1r (details)]; Kilpiö—
Kahlas-Tarkka (2001) pls. 13–14 [fols. 1r, 2r]; Story (2003) 262 [fol. 1r]

ED: Hartel (1894) 51–118, 262–305 [Paulinus, *Carmina*, coll. as G]

ST: Bischoff (1966–81) I.78; Mackay (1976) 77 and nn. 3–4; Lapidge
(2006) 135, 146, 183, 221–2, 231, 242; Love (2012) 614 and n. 42

847. 5. Leuven, Katholieke Universiteit, Centrale Bibliotheek, s.n.

s. x med.

Contents: Psalterium Gallicanum (f; Pss. XXIV. 8–11, XXV. 1–2)

[NOTE: no printed notice; according to N.R. Ker (letter to HG dated 26 May 1980) the script is Anglo-Saxon Square minuscule of mid-tenth-century date]

848. Louvain-la-Neuve, Centre Général de Documentation, Université Catholique de Louvain, Fragmenta H. Omont 3

recto: eleven medical recipes* (f): s. ix ex. or x in.

verso: pen trials (?): writing in continental Half uncial, s. vii/viii, unidentified text; line from an antiphon; beginning of an OE prayer, s. xi in.; part of an alphabet, s. xii

MS: N.R. Ker (1976a) 128; Schaumann—Cameron (1977); M.L. Cameron (1983) 168–70; Meaney (1984) 243–5; Dumville (1987) 156 n. 46; Dumville (1995b) 106 and n. 46; Hollis—Wright (1992) 233–4; *ASMMF* XIII (2006) 114–15 [no. 322; Bremmer, Dekker]; Bezzo (2007) 435–7, 441–2

FACS: Schaumann—Cameron (1977) after p. 296 [recto and verso]; *ASMMF* XIII (2006) no. 322

ED: Schaumann—Cameron (1977) 291–3, 297; Pollington (2000) 74–6

Lund, Universitetsbiblioteket, Fragm. membr. lat. 1: see no. **936**

848. 4. Luzern (Lucerne), Staatsarchiv, Fragm. PA 1034/21007

s. viii^2, Northumbria

Contents: Isidore, *Sententiae* [*CPL* 1199] (f)

MS: Bischoff et al. (1992b) 294 [= *CLA* no. 1874]; Lapidge (2006) 312; Di Sciacca (2008) 215 n. 212

848. 6. Maaseik, Église Sainte-Catherine, Trésor, s.n., fols. 1–6

s. viii^1, Northumbria or Echternach, prov. abbey of Aldeneik

Contents: gospels (f: canon tables)

MS: E.H. Zimmermann (1916) 66, 128, 142–3, 303–4; McGurk (1961a) no. 44; *CLA* X (1963) no. 1559; Netzer (1989) 207–12; McGurk (1993)

254 [repr. McGurk (1998) no. XI]; A. Derolez (1994); McNamara (1995) 91; M.P. Brown (2003a) 180

DEC: T.J. Brown (1972) 235, 246 [repr. T.J. Brown (1993a) 112–13, 273 n. 95]; Alexander (1978a) no. 22; Bonner et al. (1989a) 282, 298; M.P. Brown (2003a) 301

FACS: E.H. Zimmermann (1916) *Tafelband* IV, pls. 318 [fols. 0r and 2r], 319 [fols. 3r and 1r], 320 (a)–(g) [canon tables (details); folios not specified]; Alexander (1978a) ills. 87 [fol. 1r], 88–9 [fols. 3r–v], 90–1 [fols. 5r, 5v], 92–3 [fols. 2r, 2v], 94–5 [fols. 4r, 4v], 96–7 [fols. 6r, 6v]; Bonner et al. (1989a) pl. 30 [fol. 3v]

ST: Coppens et al. (1994)

848. 7. Maaseik, Église Sainte-Catherine, Trésor, s.n., fols. 7–100, 100a–132

s. viii[1], Northumbria or Echternach, prov. abbey of Aldeneik

Contents: gospels; incomplete set of canon tables (s. ix)

MS: McGurk (1961a) no. 44; McGurk (1961b) 7 [repr. McGurk (1998) no. V]; McGurk (1963) 170 [repr. McGurk (1998) no. VIII]; *CLA* X (1963) no. 1558; B. Fischer (1988–91) I.20*; Netzer (1989) 207–12; A. Derolez (1994); McNamara (1995) 91

DEC: Alexander (1978a) no. 22; D.M. Wilson (1984) 131; Ohlgren (1986) no. 22; Netzer (2012) 236

FACS: Alexander (1978a) ills. 98–9 [fols. 7r, 7v], 100–1 [fols. 8r, 8v], 102–3 [fols. 9r, 9v], 104–5 [fols. 10r, 10v], 106–7 [fols. 11r, 11v]; D.M. Wilson (1984) pl. 155 [fol. 1r]

ED: B. Fischer (1988–91) [gospels coll. as Gm]

ST: Netzer (1987); Coppens et al. (1994)

848. 8. Malibu, now Los Angeles, California, J. Paul Getty Museum, 9

[formerly listed as no. 817]

s. x/xi or xi in., Canterbury?

Contents: gospels (f)

MS: Boutemy (1966); Dumville (1993f) 98 [no. 14]; Dumville (1993g) 58 n. 259; Lenker (1997) 116–17, 463–4; Stoneman (1997) 129–30; Cohen—Teviotdale (1999)

DEC: Alexander (1975a) 150–3; E. Temple (1976) no. 53; Ohlgren (1986) no. 158; Higgitt (1989) 283; Raw (1990) 225; R. Gameson (1995b) 35 n. 130; Cohen—Teviotdale (1999); McGurk (2012) 440 and n. 21

FACS: Boutemy (1966) pls. 7 (b), 8–10 [folios not specified]; Alexander (1975a) pls. IV (d) [fol. 2v], VIII [fol. 1v]; E. Temple (1976) ills. 173–6 [fols. ii r, iv r, i r, ii v]; Cohen—Teviotdale (1999) pls. 16–19 [fols. 1r, 1v, 2r, 2v, 8v]

849. Marburg, Hessisches Staatsarchiv, Hr 2, 17 [with Kassel, Gesamthochschulbibliothek 2° Ms. theol. 265]

s. viii ex., England

Contents: Jerome, *Comm. in Danielem* [*CPL* 588] (f)

MS: *CLA* VIII (1959) no. 1145; Auerbach (1977); Bischoff—Brown (1985) 357–8; Wiedemann (1994) 271; Lapidge (2006) 313

849. 3. Marburg, Hessisches Staatsarchiv, Hr 2, 18 [formerly Oberkaufungen, Archiv des Ritterschaftlichen Stifts Kaufungen, s.n.]

s. viii med., S England

Contents: Boniface, *Ars grammatica* [*CPL* 1564b] (f)

MS: Eckhardt (1969) 280–5; *CLA* Supplement (1971) no. 1803; Parkes (1976a) 162, 164–5 [repr. Parkes (1991) 122, 124–5, 142 n.]; Gebauer—Löfstedt (1980) vi; Parkes (1982) 30 n. 79 [repr. Parkes (1991) 46 n. 79]; Bischoff (1990) 93; Lapidge (2006) 40

FACS: Eckhardt (1969) pl. 99 [fols. 6v, 3r]

ED: Eckhardt (1969) 286–97 [complete transcription]; Gebauer—Löfstedt (1980) 58–9, 69–71 [parts of Boniface, *Ars grammatica*, coll. as K]

ST: Law (1982) 77–80 *et passim*; Law (1997) 106–7, 169–97

849. 6. Marburg, Hessisches Staatsarchiv, 319 Pfarrei Spangenberg Hr Nr. 1

[formerly listed as no. 935]

s. viii¹, SW England, prov. s. viii prob. Fulda

Contents: Servius, *Comm. in Aeneida* [= 'Servius auctus'] (f)

MS: *CLA* Supplement (1971) no. 1806; T.J. Brown (1976) 287 [repr. T.J. Brown (1993a) 171]; N.R. Ker (1976a) 130 [no. 421]; Parkes (1976a) 162, 164–5 [repr. Parkes (1991) 122, 124–5]; T.J. Brown (1982a) 112 [repr. T.J. Brown (1993a) 213]; Parkes (1982) 30 n. 79 [repr. Parkes (1991) 116 n. 79]; L.D. Reynolds (1983) 385 and n. 3 [Marshall]; R.M. Thomson (1987) 106; Sims-Williams (1990) 235 and n. 79; Marshall

(2000); *ASMMF* IX (2001) 94–6 [no. 467; Doane]; Gneuss (2003b) 304; Lapidge (2006) 40, 130, 332

FACS: Marshall (2000) pls. I–II [fols. 1r, 1v]; *ASMMF* IX (2001) no. 467

ED: Marshall (2000) 196–207

ST: Parkes (1997a) 11 and n. 51

850. Miskolc, Lévay József Library, s.n.

s. viii, S England

Contents: Aldhelm, *Enigmata* (f) and *Epistola ad Acircium* (f)

MS: Mady (1965); *CLA* Supplement (1971) no. 1792; O'Brien O'Keeffe (1985) 66; Bischoff et al. (1992b) 307; Wieland (2009) 150; Lapidge (2012b) 19–20

851. Montecassino, Archivio della Badia, BB. 437

s. xi med. (*c.* 1065?) England, prov. Bavaria *c.* 1071, prov. Italy *c.* 1089

Contents: gospels

MS: Inguanez (1915–41) III.46; T.A.M. Bishop (1971) xvi and n. 3; McGurk (1986b) 44, 46–7, 51–4 [repr. McGurk (1998) no. XIV]; McGurk—Rosenthal (1995) 293–6 *et passim* [repr. McGurk (1998) no. XV]; McGurk—Rosenthal (2006) 185 and n. 1; Stiegmann— Wemhoff (2006) II.302–3; V. Brown (2007) 104, 111, 121; R. Gameson (2012d) 363 and n. 78; McGurk (2012) 439, 447 [no. 14]

DEC: E. Temple (1976) no. 95; F. Wormald (1984b) 120; Ohlgren (1986) no. 200; Ohlgren (1992) 8, 72–3; R. Gameson (1995b) 59, 100 n. 164, 178 n. 135, 194, 195 n. 14, 197, 208 n. 106, 209 n. 118, 252–3; Rosenthal—McGurk (2006); R. Gameson (2012c) 272 and n. 68

FACS: E. Temple (1976) ills. 287–8 [pp. 126, 127]; R. Gameson (1991) figs. 4, 8 [fols. 102v, 3r]; Ohlgren (1992) pls. 13.1–13.8 [pp. 2, 3, 102, 103, 126, 127, 166, 167]

ST: Gneuss (2003b) 304; R. Gameson (2012c) 271–2 and nn.

Mortain, Collégiale Saint-Évroult, s.n.: see no. **930**

851. 6. München (Munich), Bayerische Staatsbibliothek, clm 14096, fols. 1–99

s. viii/ix, Wales or Cornwall or Brittany, (prov. Regensburg, St Emmeram)

Contents: Isidore, *In libros ueteris et noui Testamenti prooemia* [*CPL* 1192], *De ortu et obitu patrum* [*CPL* 1191], *Allegoriae quaedam S. Scripturae* [*CPL* 1190]; *Testimonia diuinae Scripturae* [*CPL* 385: *florilegium* from the Bible and the Fathers; by Eligius of Noyon?]

MS: Halm et al. (1868–81) IV/ii.128; Bischoff (1966–81) I.186–7, II.119, III.40; Bischoff (1974) I.229; Rella (1977) 20; Bischoff (1980) II.119; Bischoff (1984b) 106; Lehner (1987) 44–8; Bischoff (1998 —) II, no. 3131; C.D. Wright (2006) 195, 197–9

ED: Lehner (1987) 53–127 [base MS for *Testimonia diuinae Scripturae*]

ST: Biggs et al. (1990) 115 [C.D. Wright]; C.D. Wright (1993) 66 and n. 90

852. München (Munich), Bayerische Staatsbibliothek, clm 29336 (1

[formerly clm 29031b]

s. x ex. or xi in., (prov. Germany s. xv)

Contents: Prudentius, *Psychomachia* [*CPL* 1441] with glosses (f)

MS: N.R. Ker (1957) no. 286; Wieland (1987) 216, 221–2, 225; Biggs et al. (1990) 153–4 [Wieland]; Dumville (1993f) 98 [no. 15]; Hauke (1994) 315; Sauer (2005) 38 [Ebersperger]; Scragg (2012a) no. 798

DEC: Stettiner (1895) 20; F. Wormald (1952) 73 [no. 44]; E. Temple (1976) no. 50; Ohlgren (1986) no. 155; Wieland (1997a) 170–1, 178–9

FACS: Stettiner (1905) pls. 47–8 [recto and verso]; E. Temple (1976) ill. 165 [verso]; Sauer (2005) pl. 3 [verso]

853. München (Munich), Bayerische Staatsbibliothek, clm 29270 (9

[formerly clm 29155d]

s. viii in., Northumbria?

Contents: gospels (f)

MS: *CLA* IX (1959) no. 1335; Hauke (1994) 91; Sauer (2005) 36 [Ebersperger]

FACS: Sauer (2005) pl. 2 [recto]

854. München (Munich), Bayerische Staatsbibliothek, clm 29270 (2

[formerly clm 29155e]

s. vii ex.

Contents: gospels (f)

MS: *CLA* IX (1959) no. 1336; Lowe (1960) 20; D.H. Wright (1967) 56–7; B. Fischer (1988–91) I.32*; Hauke (1994) 88; Sauer (2005) 34 [Ebersperger]

FACS: Lowe (1960) pl. XIX [verso]; Sauer (2005) pl. 1 [verso]

ED: B. Fischer (1988–91) [gospel fragment coll. as Yo]

855. 5. München (Munich), Hauptstaatsarchiv, Raritäten-Selekt 108

s. viii², Northumbria or Continent?, prov. Tegernsee or Ilmmünster s. ix [lost]

Contents: liturgical calendar [*CPL* 2036] (f)

MS: Bauerreiss (1933); F. Wormald (1934) v and n. 4; Levison (1946) 146–7 n. 5; *CLA* IX (1959) no. 1236; Grosjean (1961); Gamber (1968–88) no. 413; Bischoff (1974) 167; Gamber (1975b) 49–52; C.W. Jones (1980) 565; Gerchow (1988) 213–15, 329; N. Orchard (2002) I.53; Gretsch (2006); Rushforth (2008a) 20–1; Wieland (2009) 156

ED: Bauerreiss (1933) 178–9; Grosjean (1961) 322; Gamber (1975b) 50–2; Rushforth (2008a) no. 3

ST: Borst (2001) I.xxii

München (Munich), Stadtarchiv, Historischer Verein Oberbayern Hs. 733/16: see no. **791. 9**

856. Münster in Westfalen, Staatsarchiv, MSC I. 243, fols. 1–2, 11–12
(with Bückeburg, Niedersächsisches Staatsarchiv, Depot 3/1)

s.viii²/⁴, Northumbria, prov. Fulda

Contents: Bede, *De temporum ratione* [*CPL* 2320] (f); Dionysius Exiguus, *Cyclus paschalis magnus* [*CPL* 2284], with Northumbrian annals

MS: *CLA* IX (1959) no. 1233 and Supplement (1971) p. 4; Lowe (1960) 20; Petersohn (1966a); Petersohn (1966b); C.W. Jones (1977) no. 37; Parkes (1982) 4 and n. 15 [repr. Parkes (1991) 96 and n. 15]; Bischoff et al. (1992b) 303; Wallis (1997) lxxxvi; Gerchow (1999) 56 [no. 24]; Story (2005) 61–6 *et passim*

FACS: Lowe (1960) pls. XVIII (a)–(c) [Münster, fols. 1v, 1r, 12v]; Petersohn (1966b) pls. XVII (a) [Bückeburg Depot 3/1, recto], XVII (b) [Münster fol. 12v], XVII (c) [Münster fol. 1v], XVIII (a) [Bückeburg Depot 3/1, verso]; Story (2005) pl. I (a) [Münster, fol. 12v]

ST: Drögereit (1951) 26–7 [fols. 3–10]; *CLA* IX (1959) no. 1234 [on fols. 3–10]; Barker-Benfield (1991) 57–8 and n. 70; Bischoff (1998 –) II, no. 3546a

856. 1. Münster in Westfalen, Universitäts- und Landesbibliothek, Fragmentenkapsel 1, no. 2

s. viii²

Contents: Gregory, *Dialogi* [*CPL* 1713] (f)

MS: Bischoff – Brown (1985) 339 [= *CLA* no. 1847]; Lapidge (2006) 304

FACS: Bischoff – Brown (1985) pl. XII (c) [fol. 4r]

856. 2. Münster in Westfalen, Universitäts- und Landesbibliothek, Fragmentenkapsel 1, no. 3

s. viii², Northumbria, prov. Werden

Contents: Bede, *Historia ecclesiastica* [*CPL* 1375] (f; bk. IV.viii–ix)

MS: Bischoff – Brown (1985) 340 [= *CLA* no. 1848]; Bischoff (1990) 19 n. 73; Freise (1993) 35–40; Gerchow (1999) 56 [no. 11], 372 [no. 75]; Stiegemann – Wemhoff (1999) II.489–90 [Freise]; Lapidge (2006) 166; Dumville (2007f) 57, 98 and n. 172; Story (2009) 178 n. 43; Wieland (2009) 142; Westgard (2010) 223; Garrison (2012) 646 n. 74

FACS: Bischoff – Brown (1985) pl. XIII (a) [verso (detail)]; Gerchow (1999) pl. 373 [recto]; Stiegemann – Wemhoff (1999) pl. I on p. 489 [recto]

ED: Dumville (2007f) 101–4 [base MS for Bede, *Historia ecclesiastica*, IV.viii–ix]

856. 3. Münster in Westfalen, Universitäts- und Landesbibliothek, Fragmentensammlung IV. 8 [from the same MS as no. **836. 5**?]

s. viii¹, Northumbria (prov. Werden)

Contents: sacramentary [Gelasianum mixtum] (f)

MS: Gamber (1968–88) suppl. p. 50 [no. 235]; Bischoff et al. (1992b) 298 [= *CLA* no. 1880]; Gerchow (1999) 55 [no. 2], 375 [no. 82]; Stiegemann – Wemhoff (1999) II.485–7 [Freise]; Wieland (2009) 120; Garrison (2012) 645 n. 69

FACS: Bischoff et al. (1992b) pl. V (b) [fol. 2r (detail)]; Gerchow (1999) pl. on p. 375 [fols. 1v, 2r]; Stiegemann – Wemhoff (1999) II, pls. on p. 486 [fols. 1v, 2r]

New Haven, Yale University, Beinecke Library, 320: see no. **157**

857. New Haven, Yale University, Beinecke Library, 401 + 401A (with Cambridge, University Library, Add. 3330 + London, British Library, Add. 50483K and 71687 + Oslo and London, the Schøyen Collection, 197 + Oxford, Bodleian Library, Arch. A. f. 131 (ptd bk.) and Lat. theol. d. 24, fols. 1 and 2 (S.C. 30591) + Philadelphia, Free Library, John Frederic Lewis Collection, ET 121)

s. ix in. (or viii ex.?), OE glosses added s. x^2

Contents: Aldhelm, *De uirginitate*° (prose) [*CPL* 1332] (f)

MS: Madan et al. (1895–1953) V.843 [S.C. 30591]; Ehwald (1919) 214; Lowe (1927) 191–2; N.R. Ker (1957) no. 12; Morston (1970); R.L. Collins (1976) 29–31; N.R. Ker (1976a) 122; Rella (1977) 59 n. 2, 69–70; Cahn—Marrow (1978) 178–9 [no. 3; F.C. Robinson]; Euw—Plotzek (1979–85) III.66–9; Shailor (1984–2004) II.280–4; Clemoes (1985) no. 37; Morrish (1988) 527 and n. 50, 537; Gwara (1994b) 112–18, 121–5; Rusche (1994) 195–203; J. Griffiths (1995) 39–40; Stoneman (1997) 101, 111, 118, 124, 132; *Cat. Add. B.M., 1956–1965* (2000) I.317; Gwara (2001) I.85*–94* *et passim*; Gneuss (2008a) 421; Ringrose (2009) 90–1; Wieland (2009) 150; Lapidge (2012b) 28; Scragg (2012a) nos. 225–6

FACS: R.L. Collins (1976) pls. 1–2 [New Haven 401, fol. 7r; Philadelphia leaf, recto]; *Sotheby's The History of Script: Sixty Important Manuscript Leaves from the Schøyen Collection, London 10 July 2012* (London, 2012) lot 26 [facsimile of one page of the Schøyen Collection, 197]

ED: Napier (1900) nos. 11 [OE glosses from New Haven 401], 12 [OE glosses from Cambridge UL leaves]; Ehwald (1919) 226–323 [Aldhelm, prose *De uirginitate*, from New Haven 401 and Cambridge UL, coll. as P]; Meritt (1952) [OE glosses from Schøyen leaves]; Meritt (1961) 441 [scratched glosses in New Haven 401]; R.L. Collins (1976) 323 [OE glosses from Philadelphia leaves]; Rusche (1994) 204–13 [scratched glosses in New Haven 401]; Gwara (2001) vol. II [Aldhelm, *De uirginitate*, Latin text with OE glosses from all fragments listed above, coll. as A]

LANG: Napier (1900) xxxii; Rusche (1994) 198 n. 18

ST: <http://www.schoyencollection.com/natregscr.html>; *Sotheby's The History of Script: Sixty Important Manuscript Leaves from the Schøyen Collection, London 10 July 2012* (London, 2012) lot 26; Lapidge (2012b) 26–31

[NOTE: the Schøyen leaf (no. 197) was sold as lot 26 at Sotheby's sale (10 July 2012) to an unknown buyer]

New Haven, Yale University, Beinecke Library, 401A: see no. **857**

New Haven, Yale University, Beinecke Library, 441: see no. **831. 2**

858. New Haven, Yale University, Beinecke Library, 516

s. viii¹, Monkwearmouth-Jarrow

Contents: Gregory, *Moralia in Iob* [*CPL* 1708] (f)

MS: C.E. Lutz (1973) [repr. C.E. Lutz (1975) 20–3]; Cahn—Marrow (1978) 177 [no. 1; F.C. Robinson]; Parkes (1982) 4 and n. 10 [repr. Parkes (1991) 95 and n. 10]; Bischoff—Brown (1985) 340–1 [= *CLA* no. 1849]; Stoneman (1997) 125–6

FACS: C.E. Lutz (1975) frontispiece [verso]; Bischoff—Brown (1985) pl. XIII (b) [verso (detail)]

ST: Love (2012) 613–14 and n. 39

859. New Haven, Yale University, Beinecke Library, 578

s. x/xi or xi¹, SE England?, (prov. prob. SW England, Tewkesbury?)

Contents: gospels* (f)

MS: N.R. Ker (1957) no. 1 and p. lxiv; R.L. Collins (1976) 36–7; N.R. Ker (1976a) 121; Cahn—Marrow (1978) 182 [no. 7; F.C. Robinson]; Liuzza (1988); Liuzza (1994–2000) I.xli–xlii; Budny (1997) I.578; Lenker (1997) 19–21 *et passim*; Stoneman (1997) 126–7; Scragg (2012a) nos. 799, 799.1

FACS: R.L. Collins (1976) pl. 3 [verso (detail)]

ED: Liuzza (1994–2000) I.64–5 [OE gospels coll. as Y]

LANG: Liuzza (1994–2000) II.173; Lenker (1997) 20–1

ST: Abel (1962) 372–90; Lenker (1997) 195–9, 203–5, 246–50, 286–90

New Haven, Yale University, Beinecke Library, Osborn fa 26: see no. **146**

860. New York, Pierpont Morgan Library, M 708

s. xi med. (*c.* 1065?), England, prov. Bavaria *c.* 1071, prov. Weingarten s. xi ex.

Contents: gospels

MS: Lehmann (1918) 399; Harrsen (1930); De Ricci—Wilson (1935–40)
II.1485; Bond—Faye (1962) 354; N.R. Ker (1964) 189 [rejected];
T.A.M. Bishop (1971) xvi–xvii and n. 3; McGurk (1986b) 44, 46–7, 53,
54 [repr. McGurk (1998) no. XIV]; Krämer (1989–90) II.807; Lapidge
(1994b) 97; McGurk—Rosenthal (1995) 296–9 *et passim* [repr. McGurk
(1998) no. XV]; Stoneman (1997) 112–13; R. Gameson (2012a) 33, 80
and n. 286; R. Gameson (2012d) 362 and n. 74; Gullick (2012) 295 n. 7,
307 and n. 77; McGurk (2012) 447 [no. 15]

DEC: E. Temple (1976) no. 94 [with references to further literature (since
1835) and to numerous plates]; F. Wormald (1984b) 120–1; Ohlgren
(1986) no. 199; Raw (1990) 320; O'Reilly (1992) 169 n. 13; R. Gameson
(1995b) 16, 21, 59, 70 n. 10, 100, 103 n. 184, 128, 155 n. 18, 179–80,
194–5; Rosenthal—McGurk (2006); Karkov (2007c) 57; R. Gameson
(2012c) 271 and n. 64, 272 and n. 69

FACS: E. Temple (1976) ill. 286 [fol. 2v]; R. Gameson (1991) fig. 14 [fol.
43r]; Ohlgren (1992) pls. 12.1–9 [binding and fols. 2v, 3r, 26v, 27r, 42v,
43r, 66v, 67r]; R. Gameson (1995b) pl. 4 [jewelled front cover];
McGurk—Rosenthal (1995) [repr. McGurk (1998)] pls. V–VI [fols.
46v, 9r]; McGurk—Rosenthal (2006) figs. 3 [fol. 2v], 4 [fol. 3r], 6 [fol.
26v], 8 [fol. 42v], 10 [fol. 66v]

ST: McGurk—Rosenthal (2006) 185–99

861. New York, Pierpont Morgan Library, M 709

s. xi med. (*c*. 1065?), England, prov. Bavaria *c*. 1071, prov. Weingarten
s. xi ex.

Contents: gospels

MS: Lehmann (1918) 399; Harrsen (1930); De Ricci—Wilson (1935–40)
II.1485–6; Bond—Faye (1962) 354; T.A.M. Bishop (1971) xvi–xvii and
n. 3; McGurk (1986b) 44, 46–7, 51–3, 55, 56–63 [repr. McGurk (1998)
no. XIV]; M.P. Richards (1988) 66–7; Krämer (1989–90) II.807; Lapidge
(1994b) 97; McGurk—Rosenthal (1995) 299–303 *et passim* [repr.
McGurk (1998) no. XV]; Stoneman (1997) 112–13; R. Gameson (2012a)
32, 80 and n. 286; R. Gameson (2012d) 362 and n. 74; Gullick (2012)
307 and n. 77; McGurk (2012) 447 [no. 16]

DEC: F. Wormald (1944) 130–1, 132 [repr. F. Wormald (1984) 156–7,
162–4, 166]; F. Wormald (1962) 7 [repr. F. Wormald (1984) 133]; E.
Temple (1976) nos. 93–4; D.M. Wilson (1984) 174; F. Wormald (1984b)
120–1; Ohlgren (1986) no. 198; Raw (1990) 231; O'Reilly (1992) 170–4,

182–4; Raw (1992) 297–300; R. Gameson (1995b) 21, 25–6, 59, 100, 103 n. 184, 129, 157, 172, 190, 195–6, 207–9, 217–18, 230, 251–2; Karkov (2006b) 102; Rosenthal (2007) 21–5, 28–9; Rushforth (2007) 80; Scott (2007) 28–9; Karkov (2009) 249–50; O'Reilly (2011) 214–18; Pulliam (2011) 71, 75; R. Gameson (2012c) 271 and nn. 64–5, 272 and n. 68, 290 and n. 144

FACS: F. Wormald (1944) pl. 2 [fol. 1v]; E. Temple (1976) ills. 285, 289 [fols. 2v, 1v]; D.M. Wilson (1984) pl. 262 [fol. 48v]; F. Wormald (1984) ill. 184 [fol. 1v]; R. Gameson (1991) fig. 21 [fol. 1v]; Ohlgren (1992) pls. 11.1–10 [binding and fols. 1v, 2v, 3r, 48v, 49r, 77v, 78r, 122v, 123r]; Ramsay et al. (1992) pls. 31–2 [fols. 2v, 1v]; Raw (1992) pl. 46 [fol. 1v]; McGurk—Rosenthal (1995) [repr. McGurk (1998) no. XV] pls. III–IV [fols. 42v, 49r]; McGurk—Rosenthal (2006) figs. 1 [fol. 2v], 2 [fol. 3r], 5 [fol. 48v], 7 [fol. 77v], 9 [fol. 122v]; McGowan (2007) 205–7; Rosenthal (2007) 33 [fol. 1v]; Rushforth (2007) 50 [front board], 80 [fol. 1v]; Scott (2007) 28 [fol. 1v (detail)]; Withers (2007) 150 [fol. 122v]; Owen-Crocker (2009) fig. 7.35 [fol. 1v]; R. Gameson (2012) pls. 10.9 [fol. 1v], 18.2 [fol. 2v], 18.5 [fol. 11v]

ST: McGurk—Rosenthal (2006) 186–99; Rosenthal (2007) 23–4, 30–1

862. New York, Pierpont Morgan Library, M 776 (the 'Blickling Psalter')

s. viii med., prov. S England?, OE and Latin glosses s. ix (Wessex) and x², (prov. Lincoln)

Contents: Psalterium Romanum (incomplete), with glosses in OE and Latin

MS: Morris (1874–80/1967) II.251–2 [E. Brock]; Wildhagen (1913) 432–5; De Ricci—Wilson (1935–40) II.1502, 2320; Weber (1953) xiii; N.R. Ker (1957) no. 287; Salmon (1959) 49 *et passim*; *CLA* XI (1966) no. 1661; D.H. Wright (1967) 61 n. 3, 63–4, 68; R.L. Collins (1976) no. 10; Gamber (1968–88) no. 1613; T.J. Brown (1974) 259 [repr. T.J. Brown (1993a) 153]; T.J. Brown (1982) 108 [repr. T.J. Brown (1993a) 209]; T.J. Brown (1993b) 197; Crick (1997) 68–75; Stoneman (1997) 113–14; R. Gameson (1999c) 359–60; Pulsiano (2001a) xxv–xxvi; Hartzell (2006) no. 206; Biggs (2007a) 16; Pulsiano (2007) 120; Rushforth (2011) 42; M.P. Brown (2012) 124, 134; Pfaff (2012) 451; Scragg (2012a) no. 801; Toswell (2012) 472, 476–7

DEC: Alexander (1978a) no. 31; Ohlgren (1986) no. 31; Netzer (2012) 228 and n. 23

FACS: *NPS* I, pls. 231–2 [folios not specified]; E.H. Zimmermann (1916) *Tafelband* III, pl. 251 [fol. 27r]; R.L. Collins (1976) pl. 11 [fol. 40r]; T.J. Brown (1993a) ill. 40 [fol. 27r (detail)]; Crick (1997) pls. VII–VIII [fols. 6r (detail), 64v]; Pulsiano (2007) 128 [fol. 60v], 129 [fols. 40v, 41r, 51r, 78v], 130 [fol. 40r]; R. Gameson (2012) pl. 21.1 [fol. 51v]

ED: E. Brock in Morris (1874–80/1967) 251–63 [all OE glosses]; Sweet (1885) 122–3 [OE glosses of s. ix]; Weber (1953) [Latin psalms coll. as N]; Pulsiano (1982) [all Latin and OE glosses]; Pulsiano (2001a) xxxvii–xxxviii [OE glosses of s. ix], 1–739 [Pss. I–L coll as M; OE glosses coll. as M* and M²]

ST: R.L. Collins (1963); Pulsiano (1982); Pulsiano (1983); Pulsiano (1985a)

863. New York, Pierpont Morgan Library, M 826

s. viii ex., Northumbria, prov. Bath? and (s. xi²) Saint-Vaast, Arras?

Contents: Bede, *Historia ecclesiastica* [*CPL* 1375] (f; bk. IV.xxix–xxx)

MS: Lowe (1926); Grierson (1940a) 110 n. 22; Bond—Faye (1962) 361–2; *CLA* XI (1966) no. 1662; Colgrave—Mynors (1969) xlv–xlvi; Lapidge (1994b) 129; Stoneman (1997) 114–15; Dumville (2007f) 57, 78–9; Wieland (2009) 142 [erroneously cited as Yale University, Beinecke Library, M 826]; R. Gameson (2012a) 25 n. 45

ED: Dumville (2007f) 105–8 [base MS for Bede, *Historia ecclesiastica*, IV.xxix–xxx]

863. 5. New York, Pierpont Morgan Library, M 827 (the 'Anhalt Morgan Gospels')

s. x², NE France, prov. England s. x/xi or xi¹? (prov. Nienburg, Germany, s. xii)

Contents: gospels

MS: Swarzenski (1949); Bond—Faye (1962) 362; Krämer (1989–90) II.605; Stoneman (1997) 115; R. Gameson (2012b) 101 n. 31

DEC: F. Wormald (1962) 7 [repr. F. Wormald (1984) 129]; Dodwell (1971b) 82, 83; E. Temple (1976) no. 45; F. Wormald (1984b) 118; Ohlgren (1986) no. 150; Raw (1990) 231; McGurk—Rosenthal (2006) 195; R. Gameson (2010) 110, 114–15; R. Gameson (2012c) 281 and n. 109

FACS: Swarzenski (1949) figs. 1 [binding], 4–7 [folios not specified], 12 [folio not specified], 13 [fol. 67r], 14 [folio not specified], 15 [fol. 1v], 16 [folio not specified], 17 [fols. 18v–19r], 18–23 [folios not specified]; E. Temple (1976) ill. 146 [fol. 98v]; R. Gameson (2010) figs. 11–13 [fols. 17v, 19r, 66v]

864. New York, Pierpont Morgan Library, M 869 (the 'Arenberg Gospels')

s. x ex., prob. Canterbury CC, (prov. Köln, St Severin, by s. xii, or s. xi?)

Contents: gospels

MS: T.A.M. Bishop (1954–8b) 333; Bond—Faye (1962) 366; Voelkle (1974) no. 6; Deshman (1976) 392; Backhouse et al. (1984b) no. 47; McGurk (1986b) 43, 45, 48, 50, 56–63 [repr. McGurk (1998) no. XIV]; Krämer (1989–90) II.452; Dumville (1993f) 98 [no. 16]; Dumville (1993g) 106–7 and nn. 117 and 118, 124 n. 67; Stoneman (1997) 115–16; R. Gameson (2012a) 49 n. 148, 60, 73, 75; R. Gameson (2012d) 362 and n. 73; Marsden (2012) 423 and n. 77; McGurk (2012) 439, 447 [no. 17]

DEC: F. Wormald (1952) 80 [no. 59]; Rosenthal (1974); E. Temple (1976) no. 56; Brownrigg (1978) 246 n. 2, 252–3, 265; F. Wormald (1984b) 119; Rosenthal (1985); Ohlgren (1986) no. 161; Heslop (1990) 153 and n. 7, 165, 169–70 and n. 53, 170 and n. 55, 182; Raw (1990) 84–5, 111–28; R. Gameson (1992a) 190, 200–3 and n. 56, 208–9, 211, 213 n. 109, 214, 216; Ohlgren (1992) 4–5, 56–9; O'Reilly (1992) 169–70, 179; Rosenthal (1992) 162 n. 90; McGurk (1993) 255 and n. 37 [repr. McGurk (1998) no. XI]; R. Gameson (1995b) 17–18, 45, 50, 71, 73, 98, 100, 127, 178, 180, 182, 194; Karkov (2006a) 56; McGurk—Rosenthal (2006) 192 n. 36; Rosenthal (2011) 229, 230, 232–3, 234–8, 241, 245, 246; R. Gameson (2012c) 262 and n. 35, 263 and n. 40, 290 and n. 144, 291

FACS: E. Temple (1976) ills. 167–71 [fols. 11v, 13v, 17v, 83v, 9v]; Backhouse et al. (1984b) colour pl. XI [fol. 126v]; F. Wormald (1984) ill. 115 [fol. 11v]; Ohlgren (1992) pls. 6.1–17 [fols. 9v–13v, 17v, 18r, 57v, 58r, 83v, 84r, 126v, 127r]; Ramsay et al. (1992) pls. 30, 46 [fols. 126v, 83v]; R. Gameson (1995b) pl. 19 [fol. 57v]; R. Gameson (2000b) pls. 6–7 [fols. 17v, 18r]; R. Gameson (2012) pl. 18.1 [fol. 51v]

ST: Heslop (2004) 305–6; Farr (2011a) 95 n. 38

865. New York, Pierpont Morgan Library, M 926, fols. 1–41

s. xi/xii, Continent, (prov. St Albans), in England by 1100?

Contents: Leontius of Cyprus, *Vita S. Iohannis Eleemosynarii*, trans. Anastasius Bibliothecarius [*BHL* 4388]

MS: Hartzell (1975) 20–1, 46 n. 112; R.M. Thomson (1982a) I.115–16; Stoneman (1997) 121–2; R. Gameson (1999a) no. 608

ST: Biggs et al. (2001) 269–70

865. 1. New York, Pierpont Morgan Library, M 926, fols. 42–52

s. xi³/⁴, St Albans

Contents: three hymns to St Alban: 'Ecclesiae prosapies' [*AH* XI.67–8], 'Sollempnis dies remeat' [unptd], and 'Ecce uotiua recoluntur festa' [*AH* XI.68–9]); rhymed Office and mass of St Alban

MS: Hartzell (1975) 21, 23–38; R.M. Thomson (1982a) I.115–16; Andrew Hughes (1993) 252–3; R. Gameson (1999a) no. 609; Hartzell (2006) no. 207(a)

FACS: Hartzell (1975) pls. I–II [fols. 42v, 44r]

ED: Hartzell (1975) 49–57 [hymns; rhymed Office]

865. 2. New York, Pierpont Morgan Library, M 926, fols. 53–68

s. xi³/⁴, (prov. St Albans)

Contents: hymn to St Dunstan [SK 7449]; Adelard, *Lectiones in depositione S. Dunstani* [*BHL* 2343]

MS: Hartzell (1975) 21, 42–4; R.M. Thomson (1982a) I.115–16; R. Gameson (1999a) no. 610; Winterbottom—Lapidge (2012) cxxxiii–cxxxiv

ED: Hartzell (1975) 57 [hymn to St Dunstan]; Winterbottom—Lapidge (2012) 111–45 [Adelard, *Lectiones*, coll. as P]

ST: Biggs et al. (2001) 181–2

865. 3. New York, Pierpont Morgan Library, M 926, fols. 70–3

s. xi/xii, (prov. St Albans)

Contents: anonymous *Vita S. Alexii* [*BHL* 286]

MS; Hartzell (1975) 22, 44–7; R.M. Thomson (1982a) I.115–16; R. Gameson (1999a) no. 611; T.N. Hall (2007) 261

865. 4. New York, Pierpont Morgan Library, M 926, fols. 74–8

s. xi$^{3/4}$, (prov. St Albans)

Contents: rhymed Office of St Birinus (incomplete); Odo of Cluny, Sermon for the feast of St Benedict; fragment of an unidentified sermon (excerpted from Augustine, *De ordine* [*CPL* 255])

MS: Hartzell (1975) 22, 38–42; R.M. Thomson (1982a) I.115–16; Andrew Hughes (1993) 254–5; Love (1996) lxiv–lxvi; R. Gameson (1999a) 22; Hartzell (2006) no. 207(b)–(c)

ED: Hartzell (1975) 58–9 [base MS for rhymed Office of St Birinus]

ST: Biggs et al. (2001) 67–9

865. 5. New York, Pierpont Morgan Library, G 30

s. vii ex., prob. Northumbria

Contents: Gregory, *Moralia in Iob* [*CPL* 1708] (f)

MS: Bond—Faye (1962) 396; *CLA* XI (1966) no. 1664; Bischoff (1966–81) II.339; J. Plummer (1968) no. 4; Adriaen (1979–85) I.xxiii; Milde (1986) 149 [no. 1]; Ryskamp (1989) 69 [G.T. Clark]; Stoneman (1997) 116

FACS: Milde (1986) 163–4 [recto and verso]

866. New York, Pierpont Morgan Library, G 63

s. xi^2

Contents: Hexateuch* (f: from Exodus)

MS: Crawford (1922/1969) 456–7 [N.R. Ker]; J. Plummer (1968) no. 11; R.L. Collins (1976) no. 11; N.R. Ker (1976a) 128; Stoneman (1997) 120; R. Gameson (1999a) no. 605; Marsden (2008) lxi–lxiii; Scragg (2012a) no. 800

FACS: Crawford (1922/1969) 461 [fol. 3v (detail)]; R.L. Collins (1976) pl. 12 [fol. 1r]

ED: N.R. Ker in Crawford (1922/1969) 458–60 [text of OE Exodus from the two complete leaves]; Marsden (2008) [text of OE Exodus coll. as P]

866. 5. New York, Public Library, 115 (the 'Harkness Gospels')

s. ix$^{3/3}$, Landévennec (Brittany), prov. SW England s. x med., (prov. s. xviii Italy)

Contents: gospels, gospel list

MS: Morey (1929); Morey et al. (1931); De Ricci—Wilson (1935–40)
II.1333; Hartzell (1981); Deuffic (1985) 303 [no. 53]; McGurk (1986b)
45 n. 3, 48 and n. 27 [repr. McGurk (1998) no. XIV]; McGurk (1987)
165 n. 2, 189 n. 54 [repr. McGurk (1998) no. II]; B. Fischer (1988–91)
I.18*; Dumville (1993f) 98 [no. 17]; McGurk (1993) 254 [repr. McGurk
(1998) no. XI]; Lenker (1997) 430–5, 437 *et passim*; Bischoff (1998—)
II, no. 3625; Sole (1998) 135–6; Cohen—Teviotdale (1999) 70; Lemoine
(2005) 183, 187–8; Hartzell (2006) no. 208; Rankin (2012) 489 and n. 30

FACS: Morey (1929) pls. 1–10 [folios not specified]; Morey et al. (1931)
pls. 1–5, 7, 11–16, 22–52; Hartzell (1981) pls. on pp. 87–8, 91, 94–5
[fols. 13v, 48r, 76r, 46v, 47v, 108v]; Cohen—Teviotdale (1999) pl. 24
[fol. 21v]

ED: B. Fischer (1988–91) [gospels coll. as Bl]

ST: *BCLL* (1985) no. 962 [bibliography]; Lemoine (2005) 186–8, 190

867. Orléans, Médiathèque, 127 (105)

s. x³/⁴, Winchcombe? or s. x⁴/⁴, Ramsey?, prov. Fleury s. xi in.

Contents: sacramentary (including litany)

MS: Delisle (1886) 211–18; *Cat. gén. Dép.* (Octavo) XII.51 [Cuissard];
Fehr (1921) 30; Gougaud (1923) 24–5; J.A. Robinson (1923) 97–8 n. 2;
Leroquais (1924) I.89–91; Samaran—Marichal (1959–84) VII.219;
Gremont—Donnat (1967); T.A.M. Bishop (1971) 12; Hohler (1975) 61,
65–6 and n. 23; C.E. Lutz (1977) 41; Vezin (1977) 109–10; Hartzell
(1989) 80 and n. 87; Mostert (1989) no. BF 538; Lapidge (1991a) 76;
Lapidge (1992a) 103–6, 115 [repr. Lapidge (1993a) 391–4, 417];
Dumville (1993g) 58 n. 259, 60 n. 265; Davril (1995) 1–26; Corrêa
(1996) 296–9, 308–10; Saenger (1997) 208 and n. 38; R. Gameson
(1996a) 204–5 and n. 33; J. Barrow (2004) 154; Keats-Rohan (2004)
174; C.A. Jones (2005a) 110; N. Orchard (2005) lxi–lxii, lxx–xcii;
Stevinson—Stevinson (2008); R. Gameson (2012a) 66 and n. 227, 87
n. 311, 88 n. 320; R. Gameson (2012d) 358 and n. 52; Pfaff (2012) 454

DEC: E. Temple (1976) no. 31; Ohlgren (1986) no. 136; R. Gameson
(1995b) 33 n. 120; Roger—Bosc (2008) 406, 417–18, 420, 422, 426

FACS: E. Temple (1976) ill. 139 [p. 8 (detail)]; Davril (1995) pls. I-IV
[pp. 7, 8, 177, 178]; Bosc-Lauby —Notter (2004) p. 145 [p. 8]; Roger—
Bosc (2008) 435 [p. 8 (detail)]

ED: Legg (1891-7) III.1447–1628 [mass prayers coll. as Whc]; Lapidge (1991a) 219–24 [litany]; Davril (1995) [complete MS]

ST: Lapidge (2012a) 692

868. Orléans, Médiathèque, 342 (290), pp. 1–68

[palimpsest, lower script]

s. viii

Contents: unidentified text

MS: *CLA* VI (1953) no. 820; Lowe (1964) no. 108; Mostert (1989) no. BF 859; Biggs et al. (2001) 357

869. Orléans, Médiathèque, 342 (290)

s. x/xi, England or Fleury?, (prov. Fleury)

Contents: six Lives of saints: *Vita S. Nicholai* [*BHL* 6104-8], *Vita S. Alexii* [*BHL* 286], *Vita S. Athanasii* [*BHL* 730], *Inuentio S. Crucis* [*BHL* 4171], *Miraculum S. Anastasii Persae* [*BHL* 412], *Passio S. Theclae* [*BHL* 8024g]; six sermons [including *CPL* 404, 920, 844 no. 4, 245]; pseudo-Jerome, *Epistulae supposititiae* [CPL 633] xlviii–xlix

MS: *Cat. gén. Dép.* (Octavo) XII.186–7 [Cuissard]; Van der Straeten (1982) 72; Mostert (1989) nos. BF 858–61; Dumville (1993f) 98 [no. 18]; R. Gameson (1995a) 100 n. 21; Whatley (1996) 20; Biggs et al. (2001) 67, 90–1, 263, 356–7, 360, 447; Di Sciacca (2010) 319, 321 n. 73; R. Gameson (2012a) 19 n. 27

ST: Lambert (1969–72) nos. 348–9 [pseudo-Jerome]

870. Oslo, Riksarkivet, Lat. fragm. 201 (with Oslo, Nasjonalbiblioteket, Lat. fragm. 9)

s. $x^{1/4}$

Contents: mass lectionary (f)

MS: Gjerløw (1957) 109–17; Gjerløw (1979) 265–6; Dumville (1991–5) 49; Dumville (1994a) 134 and n. 9; Lenker (1997) 115, 131, 457–8

DEC: R. Gameson (1995b) 243 n. 55

FACS: Gjerløw (1957) figs. 1–3 [Nasjonalbiblioteket, Lat. fragm. 9, verso; Riksarkivet, Lat. fragm. 201, recto and verso]; Gjerløw (1979) pl. 2 [Nasjonalbiblioteket, Lat. fragm. 9, verso]

ED: Gjerløw (1957) 112–13

870. 2. Oslo, Riksarkivet, Lat. fragm. 202, 1–2

s. xi¹, England? Scandinavia?

Contents: missal (f)

MS: Gjerløw (1974) 77–81; Hartzell (2006) no. 230

FACS: Gjerløw (1974) pl. 2 [fol. 1v]

870. 3. Oslo, Riksarkivet, Lat. fragm. 203, 1–5 and 205, 3–4, and 210, 4

s. xi/xii, England? Scandinavia?

Contents: missal (f)

MS: Hartzell (2006) no. 231; Gullick—Rankin (2009) 285

871. Oslo, Riksarkivet, Lat. fragm. 204a, 1–4 and 9–10 (with Copenhagen, Rigsarkivet, M. H. 4593)

s. xi med., England? Scandinavia?

Contents: missal (f)

MS: Gjerløw (1974) 81–2, 124; Dumville (1992a) 68; Lenker (1997) 489–90 *et passim*; Hartzell (2006) no. 232

DEC: R. Gameson (1995b) 243 n. 55

FACS: Gjerløw (1974) pl. 3 [fols. 3r, 3v (details)]

Oslo, Riksarkivet, Lat. fragm. 204b, 5–6 and 205, 1–2: see no. **936**

871. 5. Oslo, Riksarkivet, Lat. fragm. 206, 1 and 209, 1-4, and 239, 6-7

s. x/xi, England? Scandinavia?

Contents: missal (f)

MS: Dumville (1992a) 68; Hartzell (2006) no. 229; Corrêa (2008); Rankin (2012) 501 n. 84

872. Oslo, Riksarkivet, Lat. fragm. 207, 1-4, and 208, 1-8 and 210, 1-3 (with Copenhagen, Rigsarkivet, M.H. 3084 and 3085)

s. x/xi, possibly Winchester?

Contents: missal (f)

MS: Gjerløw (1961) 29–67; T.A.M. Bishop (1971) xxii n. 1; Gjerløw (1980) I.16; Dumville (1992a) 68, 81; Lenker (1997) 490–1 *et passim*; Hartzell (2006) no. 228; Rankin (2007) 22; Wieland (2009) 123; Rankin (2012) 501 n. 84

DEC: R. Gameson (1995b) 243 n. 55

FACS: Gjerløw (1961) pp. 52–3 [Lat. fragm. 207, 1–2 recto; Lat. fragm. 208, 7 recto]

ED: Gjerløw (1961) 54–67

Oslo, Riksarkivet, Lat. fragm. 208: see no. **872**

Oslo, Riksarkivet, Lat. fragm. 209, 1–4: see no. **871. 5**

Oslo, Riksarkivet, Lat. fragm. 210: see no. **872**

872. 5. Oslo, Riksarkivet, Lat. fragm. 211, 1–2

s. xi, England? Scandinavia?

Contents: mass lectionary (f)

MS: Gjerløw (1957) 117–22; Dumville (1991–5) 49; Lenker (1997) 115, 177, 190, 458

FACS: Gjerløw (1957) figs. 4–5 [Lat. fragm. 211, 1–2 recto]

ED: Gjerløw (1957) 119–20

872. 8. Oslo, Riksarkivet, Lat. fragm. 214, 2–3

s. xi^2

Contents: gradual (f)

MS: Hartzell (2006) no. 222

873. Oslo, Riksarkivet, Lat. fragm. 223, 1–2

s. xi ex., England? Scandinavia?

Contents: antiphoner (f)

MS: Gjerløw (1979) 24–5; R. Gameson (1999a) no. 614; Hartzell (2006) no. 214

873. 3. Oslo, Riksarkivet, Lat. fragm. 224, 1–4

s. xi^2

Contents: antiphoner (f)

MS: Gjerløw (1979) 25–6; Hartzell (2006) no. 213

873. 5. Oslo, Riksarkivet, Lat. fragm. 225, 1 and 2

s. xi/xii, England, or uncertain origin?

Contents: antiphoner (f)

MS: Gjerløw (1979) 26–7; R. Gameson (1999a) no. 615; Hartzell (2006) no. 212

FACS: Gjerløw (1979) pl. 5 [verso]

874. Oslo, Riksarkivet, Lat. fragm. 226, 1 and 2

s. xi$^{2/4}$

Contents: antiphoner (f)

MS: Gjerløw (1979) 23–4; R. Gameson (1999a) no. 616; Hartzell (2006) no. 211

DEC: R. Gameson (1995b) 243 n. 55

FACS: Gjerløw (1979) pl. 4 [recto]

874. 3. Oslo, Riksarkivet, Lat. fragm. 226, 3–9, and Box (45), XXXV, s.n., 1

s. xi, England? Scandinavia?

Contents: gradual (f)

MS: Hartzell (2006) no. 221; Gullick—Rankin (2009) 285

874. 6. Oslo, Riksarkivet, Lat. fragm. 227, 1–23

s. xi^1

Contents: missal (f)

MS: Gjerløw (1979) 219 n. 1; Dumville (1992a) 68; Rankin (2012) 501 n. 84

875. Oslo, Riksarkivet, Lat. fragm. 228, 1–21, and 4A 13611

s. xi med. or xi$^{3/4}$, Winchester, NM?

Contents: missal (f)

MS: Gjerløw (1974) 75–7, 123–4; Dumville (1992a) 68; Lenker (1997) 491 *et passim*; R. Gameson (1999a) no. 617; Hartzell (2006) no. 234; Rankin (2007) 22 and n. 10; Rankin (2012) 501 n. 84

DEC: R. Gameson (1995b) 243 n. 55

FACS: Gjerløw (1974) pl. 1 [fol. 7v]

875. 1. 1. Oslo, Riksarkivet, Lat. fragm. 230, 1

s. xi, England? Scandinavia?

Contents: missal (f)

MS: Gjerløw (1970) 76–9

FACS: Gjerløw (1970) pl. 1 [verso]

ED: Gjerløw (1970) 77–8

Oslo, Riksarkivet, Lat. fragm. 239, 6–7: see no. **871. 5**

875. 1. 2. Oslo, Riksarkivet, Lat. fragm. 274, 1

s. xi[1]

Contents: missal (f)

875. 1. 3. Oslo, Riksarkivet, Dipl. perg. 1589

s. xi med.

Contents: antiphoner (f)

Oslo, Nasjonalbiblioteket, Lat. fragm. 9: see no. **870**

875. 4. Oslo and London, The Schøyen Collection, MS 76

s. xi/xii, England or Continent

Contents: Bede, *De tabernaculo* [*CPL* 1345]

MS: *Quaritch Catalogue 1088* (1988) no. 4; J. Griffiths (1995) 38; R. Gameson (1999a) no. 619; http://www.schoyencollection.com/carolingian.html

FACS: http://www.schoyencollection.com/carolingian.html

Oslo and London, The Schøyen Collection, MS 79: see no. **677. 3**

Oslo and London, The Schøyen Collection, MS 197: see no. **857**

875. 5. Oslo and London, The Schøyen Collection, MS 674

s. xi med., Exeter?

Contents: missal (f; incl. Mass for Friday before Palm Sunday)

MS: *Sotheby's Sale (19 June 1990)*, lot 10; Lenker (1997) 315 [no. 100]; Stoneman (1997) 133; *Sotheby's The History of Script: Sixty Important Manuscript Leaves from the Schøyen Collection. London 10 July 2012* (London, 2012) lot 39

FACS: *Sotheby's Sale (19 June 1990)*, lot 10 [prob. verso of fragment]; *Sotheby's The History of Script: Sixty Important Manuscript Leaves from the Schøyen Collection. London 10 July 2012* (London, 2012) lot 39 [facsimile of one side of leaf fragment]

[NOTE: this fragment was sold as lot 39 at Sotheby's sale (10 July 2012) to Mr Gifford Combs of California]

875. 6. Oslo and London, The Schøyen Collection, MS 1542

s. xi[1]

Contents: missal (f)

MS: *Sotheby's Sale (17 December 1991)* lot 4; Stoneman (1997) 133; http://www.schoyencollection.com/carolingian.html

FACS: http://www.schoyencollection.com/carolingian.html

875. 7. Oslo and London, The Schøyen Collection, MS 2366

s. xi med.

Contents: Augustine, *Enchiridion* [CPL 295] (f)

MS: http://www.schoyencollection.com/carolingian.html; *Sotheby's The History of Script: Sixty Important Manuscript Leaves from the Schøyen Collection. London 10 July 2012* (London, 2012) lot 40

FACS: http://www.schoyencollection.com/carolingian.html; *Sotheby's The History of Script* (2012) [facsimile of part of one page]; *Sotheby's The History of Script: Sixty Important Manuscript Leaves from the Schøyen Collection. London 10 July 2012* (London, 2012) lot 40

[NOTE: this fragment was sold as lot 40 at Sotheby's sale (10 July 2012) to Mr Gifford Combs of California]

875. 8. Östersund, Landsarkivet, Oviken LI: 1

s. xi[2], England (prov. Norway?)

Contents: missal (f)

MS: Gneuss (2012) 296 [information from M. Gullick]

875. 9. Paris, Bibliothèque de l'Arsenal, 236

s. xi/xii, English and continental scribes

Contents: Ambrose, *De uirginibus* [CPL 145], *De uiduis* [CPL 146], *De mysteriis* [CPL 155], *De sacramentis* [CPL 154]; Nicetas of Remesiana

(?), *De lapsu uirginis consecratae* [*CPL* 651], *Epistula ad uirginem lapsam* [*CPL* 652]

MS: H. Martin (1885–96) I.146; R. Gameson (1999a) no. 808; Gneuss (2012) 302 [information from M. Gullick]

Paris, Bibliothèque de l'Arsenal, 903, fols. 1–52: see no. **903**
Paris, Bibliothèque de l'Arsenal, 933: see under no. **902. 9**

876. Paris, Bibliothèque nationale de France, anglais 67

s. xi[1]

Contents: Ælfric, *Grammar*+* (f)

MS: Delisle (1868–81) II.318; P. Meyer (1873) 598; Zupitza (1880/2001) xii; Förster (1927) 131; Dubois (1943) 370–2; N.R. Ker (1957) no. 363; Ebersperger (1999) 18–20; *ASMMF* XV (2007) 91–2 [no. 421; Doane]; Scragg (2012a) no. 978

FACS: Dubois (1943) pl. 4 [fol. 1r]; *ASMMF* XV (2007) no. 421

ED: Zupitza (1880/2001) 193–202 [Ælfric, *Grammar*, coll. as P]; Dubois (1943) 370–1 [prints text on fol. 1r]; Ebersperger (1999) 19 [corrections to Zupitza's collation]

876. 5. Paris, Bibliothèque nationale de France, français 2452, fols. 75–84

s. ix[1], Wales or SW England

Contents: Psalterium Hebraicum (f)

MS: *Catalogue des manuscrits français* (1868–95) I.420; Delisle (1876) I.81; B. Fischer (1971) 110; McNamara (1973) 202, 231–2, 263; Ebersperger (1999) 20–2

DEC: Avril—Stirnemann (1987) no. 12

FACS: Avril—Stirnemann (1987) pl. III (12) [fol. 84v]

877. Paris, Bibliothèque nationale de France, lat. 272

s. x[2] or x ex. or x/xi, Winchester? (prov. prob. Normandy — Fécamp, s xi or later)

Contents: gospel list, gospels

MS: Lauer et al. (1939—) I.100; Vezin (1968) 287, 290–1; T.A.M. Bishop (1971) 10; McGurk (1986b) 43, 46–8, 53–5 [repr. McGurk (1998) no. XIV]; Heslop (1990) 152 n. 3, 173 and n. 62, 182; Dumville (1993f) 99 [no. 20]; Dumville (1993g) 145; Lenker (1997) 425–8 *et passim*; Ebersperger (1999) 23–7; R. Gameson (2003) 154–5; R. Gameson

(2012a) 45 n. 136, 70 n. 240; R. Gameson (2012d) 358 and n. 53; McGurk (2012) 447 [no. 19]

DEC: Alexander (1970a) 235, 237; Avril—Stirnemann (1987) no. 22; R. Gameson (2012c) 258 n. 24

FACS: R. Gameson (2012) pl. 18.4 [fol. 96r]

ST: Frere (1934) 135–6; Klauser (1972) lx, no. 286

878. Paris, Bibliothèque nationale de France, lat. 281 + 298 (the 'Codex Bigotianus')

s. viii ex., S England, perhaps Canterbury (or Mercia?), (prov. Fécamp s. xi or later)

Contents: gospels

MS: Delisle (1868–81) II.364, III.214–15, IV.vii; J. Wordsworth et al. (1889–1954) xi; Kenney (1929) 653–4; Lauer et al. (1939–) I.103, 107; Mallon et al. (1939) no. 45; *CLA* V (1950) no. 526; Lowe (1960) xxx–xxxi; McGurk (1961a) no. 58; Nortier (1966) 6, 19, 26; M.P. Brown (1986) 126; B. Fischer (1988–91) I.16*; Bischoff (1990) 59–60; Webster—Backhouse (1991) no. 155 [M.P. Brown]; Dumville (1993f) 89 and n. 32, 99 [no. 21]; R. Gameson (1994b) 28; McGurk (1994b) 6 [repr. McGurk (1998) no. XII]; Ebersperger (1999) 27–32; R. Gameson (1999c) 349–55; M.P. Brown (2003a) 196 n. 59; M.P. Brown (2012) 134, 146 and n. 121; R. Gameson (2012a) 28 n. 59, 37 n. 88, 52, 53 n. 183; Marsden (2012) 414 and n. 33

DEC: Brøndsted (1924) 99–100, 108–9, 111–13, 123–4; Micheli (1939) 50–1, 193; Alexander (1978a) no. 34; Ohlgren (1986) no. 34; Avril—Stirnemann (1987) no. 7; M.P. Brown (2003a) 234 and n. 84

FACS: Delisle (1868–81) IV, pls. X (1), X (2) [lat. 281, fols. 5r, 114r]; Micheli (1939) pl. 73 [lat. 281, fol. 137r]; Lowe (1960) pls. XXX (a) [lat. 281, fol. 5r], XXX (b) [lat. 281, fol. 4v], XXXI [lat. 281, fol. 137r]; Alexander (1978a) ills. 166–8 [lat. 281, fol. 137r (detail), lat. 281, fol. 86r (detail), lat. 298, fol. 2r (detail)]; Webster—Backhouse (1991) 201 [lat. 281, fol. 137r (detail)]; R. Gameson (1999c) pls. 13.25 [lat. 281, fol. 4v], 13.26 [fol. 136r], 13.27 [fol. 137r]

ED: J. Wordsworth et al. (1889–1954) [gospels coll. as B]; B. Fischer (1988–91) [gospels coll. as Eb]

ST: B. Fischer (1952) [repr. B. Fischer (1986)]

879. Paris, Bibliothèque nationale de France, lat. 943

s. x$^{3/4}$ [after 959], prob. Canterbury CC, with additions s. x/xi—xi¹, Sherborne; prov. whole MS Sherborne by s. x/xi, France s. xi²

Contents: Letter (spurious?) from Pope John XII to Dunstan; pontifical (including litanies and second English Coronation *ordo*); benedictional; prologue to *Poenitentiale Egberti* [*CPL* 1887]; First Capitulary of Gerbald of Liège; forms of absolution. Additions (s. x/xi—xi¹): list of bishops of Sherborne; letter to Bishop Wulfsige III of Sherborne; two homilies for the Dedication of a church* (one by Ælfric); rules of confraternity* and formula-letter announcing the death of a monk; part of Mass of the Dead; two penitential letters; writ by Bishop Æthelric of Sherborne*

MS: Delisle (1868–81) I.320, III.268–70; Liebermann (1903–16) I.xxxvii; Brotanek (1913) 33–49; Wildhagen (1913) 456–7; Förster (1927) 116; Leroquais (1937) II.6–10; Lauer et al. (1939—) I.335–6; N.R. Ker (1957) no. 364; Samaran—Marichal et al. (1959–84) II.43 [d'Alverny]; T.A.M. Bishop (1964–8b) 246 n. 1; N.R. Ker (1964) 179; Vezin (1965) 86; Vezin (1968) 287; T.A.M. Bishop (1971) xxii; Korhammer (1973) 174; Rella (1977) 106–7; Backhouse et al. (1984b) no. 34; Prescott (1987) 126–8; Haggenmüller (1991) 87, 152, 289; Lapidge (1991a) 79–80; Dumville (1992a) 69, 72, 82–5, 90–4, 125; Rosenthal (1992); Scragg (1992) xxxiv, 330 and n. 3; Conner (1993) 19–20 *et passim*; Dumville (1993f) 89, 92, 95–6, 99 [no. 22]; Dumville (1993g) 100, 148; Dumville (1994c) 293–4; Nelson—Pfaff (1995) 89–90; R. Gameson (1996b) 163, 173–5; Rasmussen (1998) 258–317; Ebersperger (1999) 32–44; C.A. Jones (2004) 341 n. 67, 343 n. 73, 344 nn. 77–80; C.A. Jones (2005a) 111, 128; C.A. Jones (2005b) 234; Keynes (2005a) 62–3 and nn. 64–72; N. Orchard (2005) xcviii–xcix, cxxix, 444 *et passim*; Stockdale (2005) 169; Hartzell (2006) no. 310; O'Brien O'Keeffe (2006) 268–9; Pulsiano (2007) 124–5; Wieland (2009) 124; Winterbottom—Lapidge (2012) xxxviii and n. 121, xl, lx, clviii n. 560, 84 n. 247, 139 n. 92; R. Gameson (2012a) 40, 67 n. 232; R. Gameson (2012b) 114; D. Ganz (2012) 190 n. 13, 194 and nn. 38–9; Pfaff (2012) 458 and n. 32; Rankin (2012) 490; Rushforth (2012) 203 and n. 42; Scragg (2012a) nos. 979–83

DEC: F. Wormald (1945) 135 [repr. F. Wormald (1984) 74]; Rice (1952) 162, 197, 209, 212–13; F. Wormald (1952) 78 [no. 54]; Dodwell (1954) 8; E. Temple (1976) no. 35; Brownrigg (1978) 246 n. 2, 252; Rosenthal (1981); F. Wormald (1984) 107; F. Wormald (1984b) 117; Ohlgren

(1986) no. 140; Avril—Stirnemann (1987) no. 16; Raw (1990) 92, 111–28, 235; R. Gameson (1992a) 189 n. 9 *et passim*; R. Gameson (1995a) 140 n. 171; R. Gameson (1995b) 22–3, 127, 153, 156–7, 194, 223 n. 183; C.A. Jones (2005a) 111; R. Gameson (2012c) 262 and n. 37, 280

FACS: *NPS* I, pls. 111–12 [fols. 10r, 156r]; Rice (1952) pls. 42 (d) [fol. 10r], 64 (b) [fol. 4v]; F. Wormald (1952) pls. 4 (a), 4 (b), 5 (a) [fols. 5v, 6r, 6v]; Dodwell (1954) pl. 5 (a) [fol. 4v]; E. Temple (1976) ills. 134–8 [fols. 4r, 5v, 6r, 6v, 10r]; D.M. Wilson (1984) pl. 234 [fol. 4v]; F. Wormald (1984) ill. 113 [fol. 5v]; Huglo (1987) pl. XVI [fol. 10v]; Ramsay et al. (1992) pls. IV, 1–3 [fols. 4v, 5v, 6r, 6v]; Eales—Sharpe (1995) pl. 6 (b) [fol. 6v]; Rasmussen (1998) pls. 9–10 [fols. 10r, 108r]; Keynes (2005a) figs. 5–6 [fols. 1v, 2r]

ED: Stubbs (1874) cxiii [list of bishops of Sherborne], 406–8 [letter to Bishop Wulfsige], 408–9 [two penitential letters]; Liebermann (1903–16) I.401–9 [*Iudicium Dei* coll. as Ps]; Brotanek (1913) 15–27 [base MS for anon. Homily for the Dedication of a church], 27–8 [rules of confraternity], 38 [list of bishops of Sherborne]; Harmer (1952) no. 63 [writ by Æthelric]; Moeller (1971–9) [benedictions coll. as *Paris 943*]; Whitelock et al. (1981a) I.88–92 [letter from Pope John XII to Dunstan], 226–8 [letter to Bishop Wulfsige], 230–1 [first penitential letter]; Brommer (1984) 16–21 [Gerbald, First Capitulary, coll. as P$_3$]; H. Zimmermann (1984–5) I.271–4 [letter from Pope John XII to Dunstan]; O'Donovan (1988) no. 13 [writ by Æthelric]; Lapidge (1991a) 247–9 [litanies for Dedication of a church]; Conn (1993) [pontifical and benedictional]; Ebersperger (1999) 237–62 [base MS for Ælfric, Homily for Dedication of a church]; Rumble (2002) 233–7 [Letter from Pope John XII]

LANG: Schabram (1965) 99–100; Wenisch (1979) 22, 45, 327; Hofstetter (1987) 219

ST: H.A. Wilson (1903); Woolley (1917) 139–65; D.H. Turner (1971) xvi–xxxix; Scragg (1979) 256; Frantzen (1983b) 131; N.P. Brooks (1984) 244, 248, 267, 274, 281, 378 n. 153; Vollrath (1985) 338–46; Prescott (1987) 141–7; Gardner (1988) 65–7; Sole (1998) 134–5; Cross—Hamer (1999) 35; N. Orchard (2002) I.108 n. 252, 238; Heslop (2004) 282 n. 5; C.D. Wright (2009) 182–4 [Letter from Pope John XII]; Hamilton (2010) 426

880. Paris, Bibliothèque nationale de France, lat. 987

s. x$^{2/3}$, Winchester OM [fols. 1–84]; s. xi$^{2/4}$ or xi$^{3/4}$, Canterbury CC [fols. 85–111]; (prov. France before late s. xvi?)

Contents: benedictional; Sanctorale et Commune sanctorum added on fols. 85–111

MS: Delisle (1886) 215–17; Warner—Wilson (1910) xi, xxiv, lviii; Lauer et al. (1939—) I.351–2; Gjerløw (1961) 35, 46; N.R. Ker (1964) 39, 154, 201, 390; Vezin (1968) 287–90; T.A.M. Bishop (1971) 10; D.H. Turner (1971) xvi–xx; Rella (1977) 57, 79; Vezin (1977) 111; Backhouse et al. (1984b) no. 39 [D.H. Turner]; Prescott (1987) 120–3, 129–30, 133; Mostert (1989) nos. BF1012, BF1013; Heslop (1990) 153, 170–1, 173, 182; Dumville (1992a) 28, 69, 80, 84–5, 90, 92–3; Dumville (1993f) 89, 99 [no. 23]; Dumville (1993g) 53, 139, 145; Nelson—Pfaff (1995) 90–1; Corrêa (1999) 99; Ebersperger (1999) 44–51; R. Gameson (2012a) 39 and n. 98, 59, 65, 88 n. 320; R. Gameson (2012d) 357 n. 51

DEC: Rice (1952) 194; Dodwell (1954) 21–2, 121; F. Wormald (1959) 9–10 [repr. F. Wormald (1984) 87–9]; F. Wormald (1969) 44 [repr. F. Wormald (1984) 102]; Alexander (1970a) 238 n. 6; E. Temple (1976) no. 25; F. Wormald (1984) 87, 89; D.M. Wilson (1984) 169; Ohlgren (1986) no. 113; Avril—Stirnemann (1987) nos. 17, 24, 29, 188; R. Gameson (1995b) 182, 195, 198 n. 36, 201 n. 55, 202–3, 205 n. 86, 212; R. Gameson (2012c) 258–9 and nn. 23 and 27

FACS: *NPS* I, pls. 83–4 [folios not specified]; Dodwell (1954) pl. 12 (c) [fol. 111r]; E. Temple (1976) ills. 92–3 [fols. 41r, 43r]; Backhouse et al. (1984b) p. 61 [fol. 41r]; Dumville (1993g) pl. XIV [fol. 89r]; Bosc-Lauby—Notter (2004) p. 146 [fol. 84r]; Owen-Crocker (2009) fig. 2.9 [fol. 7r]

ED: Moeller (1971–9) [benedictional coll. as *Paris 987*]

ST: Woolley (1917) xix–xxv, 139–65; Corrêa (1997) 99–109

881. Paris, Bibliothèque nationale de France, lat. 1751

s. xi^2 or xi ex., Canterbury StA?

Contents: Ambrose, *De uirginibus* [*CPL* 145], *De uiduis* [*CPL* 146], *De uirginitate* [*CPL* 147], *Exhortatio uirginitatis* [*CPL* 149]; Nicetas of Remesiana (?), *De lapsu uirginis consecratae* [*CPL* 651]; Ambrose, *De mysteriis* [*CPL* 155], *De sacramentis* [*CPL* 154]; pseudo-Jerome, *Epistula supp.* [*CPL* 633] xxxviii ('Homilia de corpore et sanguine Christi')

MS: Lauer et al. (1939—) II.156; Quynn (1939); Cazzaniga (1948) vii; Cazzaniga (1954) vii; Faller (1955) xiv; Vezin (1968) 286, 295–6; Rella (1977) 160; Webber (1992) 51 nn. 25–6; Ebersperger (1999) 52–5; R. Gameson (1999a) no. 809; Lapidge (2006) 278, 279, 280

ED: Faller (1933) [Ambrose, *De uirginibus*, partly coll. as P]; Cazzaniga (1948) [Ambrose, *De uirginibus*, coll. as *Paris*]; Cazzaniga (1954) [Ambrose, *De uirginitate*, coll. as b]

ST: Lambert (1969–72) nos. 320, 338; Bankert et al. (1997) 14, 36–40, 46–8, 65

881. 7. Paris, Bibliothèque nationale de France, lat. 2621, fols. 84–92

s. xi/xii, England or Normandy

Contents: Hermannus Archidiaconus (?), *Miracula S. Eadmundi* [*BHL* 2395]

MS: Liebermann (1879) 230; Lauer et al. (1939–) II.550; Gransden (1995b) 6–7

ED: Martène–Durand (1724–33) VI.821–34 [base MS for excerpts from Hermannus, *Miracula S. Eadmundi*]

882. Paris, Bibliothèque nationale de France, lat. 2825, fols. 57–81

s. ix/x, NE France, prov. England by s. x med.

Contents: Bede, *Vita S. Cudbercti* (verse) [*CPL* 1380; *BHL* 2020], with Latin and OE glosses (s. x); grammatical notes; encyclopedic notes (cf. nos. **56, 90** and **451**): on the Ages of the World, the Ages of Man, the numbers of bones, veins and teeth in the human body, Dimensions of the world, the Temple of Solomon, Noah's Ark, the numbers of books in the Old and New Testament, the number of verses in the psalms, units for measuring distances

MS: Jaager (1935) 26–7; Lauer et al. (1939–) III.118–20; N.R. Ker (1957) no. 365; Vezin (1968) 286; F.C. Robinson (1973) 453, 459, 461, 464 n. 62; Korhammer (1980) 58; Dumville (1993f) 88, 99 [no. 24]; Lapidge (1995c) 130–1, 136–7, 156–7; Ebersperger (1999) 55–8; Karkov (2004) 66 n. 70; Lapidge (2006) 172; Dekker (2007) 279 n. 1, 305–9; Graham (2009) 171; Scragg (2012a) no. 984

DEC: Avril–Stirnemann (1987) no. 23

ED: Jaager (1935) [Bede, *Vita metrica S. Cudbercti*, coll. as P]; Jaager (1936) [OE glosses to Bede, *Vita metrica S. Cudbercti*]; Meritt (1945) no. 10 [OE glosses to Bede, *Vita metrica S. Cudbercti*]; Dekker (2007) 281–4 nn. [notes on the Ages of the world, etc.]

ST: Whatley (1996) 20; Alcamesi (2010) 195 n. 113; Chardonnens (2010) 234; Dekker (2010) 164 n. 82

883. Paris, Bibliothèque nationale de France, lat. 4210

s. x/xi, ?England, ?NE France, prov. Fécamp

Contents: Smaragdus of Saint-Mihiel, *Expositio in Regulam S. Benedicti*

MS: Nortier (1966) 237; T.A.M. Bishop (1971) 2; Spannagel—Engelbert
(1974) xviii, li–liii; Rella (1977) 76, 161; Branch (1979) 163, 172;
Dumville (1993f) 89, 99 [no. 25]; Dumville (1993g) 8 n. 4; Ebersperger
(1999) 198; R. Gameson (2003) 159; Wieland (2009) 140

ED: Spannagel—Engelbert (1974) [Smaragdus, *Expositio*, coll. as P^1]

ST: R.M. Butler (2004) 202

884. Paris, Bibliothèque nationale de France, lat. 4839

s. x/xi, England

Contents: Priscian, *Periegesis* [*CPL* 1554; SK 10028]; Nemesianus,
Cynegetica [SK 17029]; Q. Serenus Sammonicus, *Liber medicinalis* [SK
11975]

MS: Delisle (1868–81) I.361–4; Baehrens (1879–83) III.106, 175; Van de
Woestijne (1937) 20–1; Van de Woestijne (1953) 25–7; Volpilhac (1975)
89–90; Passalacqua (1978) 384; Munk Olsen (1982—) II.107–8, 480;
L.D. Reynolds (1983) xxxii and nn. 132, 133, 246 and n. 2, 384; Deuffic
(1985) 309 [no. 78]; Ebersperger (1999) 198–9; Lapidge (2006) 321, 327,
332; Wieland (2009) 156

ED: Baehrens (1879–83) III.107–58 [Sammonicus, *Liber medicinalis*, coll.
as d], 190–202 [Nemesianus, *Cynegetica*, coll. as B]; Van de Woestijne
(1937) [Nemesianus, *Cynegetica*, coll. as B]; Van de Woestijne (1953)
[Priscian, *Periegesis*, coll. as R]; Volpilhac (1975) [Nemesianus,
Cynegetica, coll. as B]

ST: Manitius (1911–31) I.347 [Nemesianus]

885. Paris, Bibliothèque nationale de France, lat. 4871, fols. 161–8

s. viii/ix, Northumbria?

Contents: Isidore, *Etymologiae* [*CPL* 1186] (f)

MS: Delisle (1868–81) I.457–8, 519; II.440; Omont (1930); *CLA* V (1950)
no. 559; Ebersperger (1999) 59–61

885. 3. Paris, Bibliothèque nationale de France, lat. 5362, fols. 1–84

s. xi ex., England (or Normandy?), (prov. Fécamp)

Contents: Bede, *Vita S. Cudbercti* (prose) [*CPL* 1379; *BHL* 2019];
excerpts from Bede, *Historia ecclesiastica* [concerning Lives of SS.
Cuthbert, Oswald, Birinus, and Æthelthryth]; excerpt from the
Historia de S. Cuthberto [ch. xxxiii]; Abbo of Fleury, *Passio S.
Eadmundi* [*BHL* 2392]; epitome of Lantfred, *Translatio et miracula S.
Swithuni* [*BHL* 7948]; Ælfric, *Vita S. Æthelwoldi* [*BHL* 2646]

MS: Hardy (1862–71) I.526; Delisle (1877) 48; *Catalogus codicum
hagiographicorum … Bibliotheca Nationali Parisiensi* (1889–93)
II.354–66; Colgrave (1940) 35; Lapidge—Winterbottom (1991b)
cxlvii–cxlix, clxxx, 70; R. Sharpe (2001) 25; Lapidge (2003a) 555–7; J.
Hill (2004) 323 n. 45; Kleist (2009) 381–2 and n. 40; Wieland (2009)
128, 142

FACS: Lapidge (2003a) pl. VI [fol. 70v]

ED: *Catalogus codicum hagiographicorum … Bibliotheca Nationali
Parisiensi* (1889–93) II.356 [*Historia de S. Cuthberto*, ch. xxxiii, from
this MS]; Colgrave (1940) 142–306 [Bede, *Vita S. Cudbercti* (prose),
coll. as P_1]; Lapidge—Winterbottom (1991b) 71–80 [Ælfric, *Vita S.
Æthelwoldi*, from this MS]; Lapidge (2003a) 564–72 [epitome of
Lantfred, *Translatio et miracula S. Swithuni*, from this MS]

ST: Winterbottom (1972) 10; Love (1996) lxx–lxxi; Corrêa (1997) 80
n. 10; Biggs et al. (2001) 2 [Lendinara], 367, 438; South (2002) 117

885. 5. Paris, Bibliothèque nationale de France, lat. 5574, fols. 1–39

s. ix/x or $x^{1/4}$, (prov. France, s. xii)

Contents: *Passio S. Christophori* [*BHL* 1769]; *Inuentio S. Crucis* [*BHL*
4169 (incomplete)]; *Exaltatio S. Crucis* [partly as *BHL* 4178]; *Passio S.
Margaretae* [*BHL* 5303], *Passio S. Iulianae* [*BHL* 4522 (incomplete)]

MS: *Catalogus codicum hagiographicorum … Bibliotheca Nationali
Parisiensi* (1889–93) II.482–3; Dumville (1991–5) 49; Dumville (1992a)
140; Clayton—Magennis (1994) 8, 41, 95–6; Dumville (1994a) 134;
Ebersperger (1999) 61–5; Biggs (2002) 328–30; D. Ganz (2004) 501 and
n. 8; Lapidge (2006) 341

DEC: Avril—Stirnemann (1987) no. 12 *bis*

FACS: Avril—Stirnemann (1987) pl. III [fol. 18r]

ED: Clayton—Magennis (1994) 192–223 [*Passio S. Margaretae* from this
MS, with lacuna supplied from no. **930. 5**]

ST: Geith (1965) 57; Biggs et al. (2001) 138–9, 259, 262, 264–5 [Biggs,
Whatley], 276–8, 318–19 [Magennis]

885. 6. Paris, Bibliothèque nationale de France, lat. 5575, fols. 1–41

s. x^2

Contents: *Passio et inuentio S. Quintini* [*BHL* 7005–7]; *Inuentio altera S. Quintini* [*BHL* 7014]; *Miracula S. Quintini* [*BHL* 7017–18]

MS: *Catalogus codicum hagiographicorum ... Bibliotheca Nationali Parisiensi* (1889–93) II.483–5; Ebersperger (1999) 65–6; Biggs et al. (2001) 399–401; Lapidge (2006) 341

886. Paris, Bibliothèque nationale de France, lat. 6401

s. x/xi, England or Fleury?, prov. Fleury s. xi

Contents: Radulf of Liège and Ragimbold of Cologne, Letters on geometry (s. xi); Boethius, *De consolatione Philosophiae* [*CPL* 878], *De institutione arithmetica* [*CPL* 879]; *Oratio animae poenitentis* [incomplete]; *Epitaphium Gauzlini* (s. xi) [SK 12423]

MS: Delisle (1868–81) II.364; Weinberger (1934) xviii; E.J. Daly (1950) 216; Courcelle (1967) 91; Vezin (1977) 110 and n. 5; Troncarelli (1981) 4, 37, 46, 56; A. White (1981) 174 and n. 67; Backhouse et al. (1984b) no. 44; Mostert (1989) no. BF 1083; Biggs et al. (1990) 75–6 [Wittig]; Dumville (1993g) 58, 140; Guillaumin (1995) lxxviii; Ebersperger (1999) 190–1; Oosthout—Schilling (1999) ix; Hartzell (2006) no. 311; Lapidge (2006) 293, 294; Wieland (2009) 155; R. Gameson (2012d) 357 and n. 49

DEC: F. Wormald (1971b) 311–13 [repr. F. Wormald (1984) 82–3]; Raw (1976) 138 and n. 2, 143; E. Temple (1976) no. 32; Deshman (1977) 160–1; Brownrigg (1978) 256, 258 n. 2; F. Wormald (1984) 116–17; Ohlgren (1986) no. 137; Avril—Stirnemann (1987) no. 19; Raw (1990) 175 n. 79, 235–6; R. Gameson (1995b) 197, 205 n. 84, 228 n. 214; Cohen—Teviotdale (1999) 65 n. 11

FACS: F. Wormald (1971b) pls. III (d), V (c), VI [fols. 5v, 159r (details), 158v]; E. Temple (1976) ills. 94–5 [fols. 158v, 159r (detail)]; Deshman (1977) pl. V (d) [fol. 5v (detail)]; Troncarelli (1981) pl. opp. p. 19 [fol. 5v]; Backhouse et al. (1984b) p. 64 [fol. 158v]; F. Wormald (1984) ills. 84, 109 [fols. 159r (detail), 158v]; Avril—Stirnemann (1987) colour pl. B [fol. 158v]; Bosc-Lauby—Notter (2004) p. 201 [fols. 5v, 158v]

ED: Tannery—Clerval (1901) [base MS for Radulf of Liège and Ragimbold of Cologne, Letters on geometry]; Bautier—Labory (1969) 188 [Epitaphium Gauzlini from this MS]

ST: Tannery—Clerval (1901) 491–3; Manitius (1911–31) II.778–81; Bodden (1986) 58–9; Bodden (1988) 227 and n. 40; Saenger (1997) 197 and n. 31

887. Paris, Bibliothèque nationale de France, lat. 6401A

s. x ex. or x/xi, Canterbury CC, prov. France (Saint-Vaast, Arras?) s. xi (or later?)

Contents: Boethius, *De consolatione Philosophiae* [*CPL* 878], with glosses and commentary by Remigius [redaction BN]

MS: Delisle (1868–81) II.354; Weinberger (1932) xviii–xix; Courcelle (1939) 123; E.J. Daly (1950) 216; T.A.M. Bishop (1959–63b) 416, 421–2; Courcelle (1967) 406; Vezin (1968) 286 and n. 14; T.A.M. Bishop (1971) xxv; Bolton (1977a) 40, 52; Rella (1977) 77, 163; Troncarelli (1981) 4, 5, 36, 46, 56; Wittig (1983) 188; Dumville (1993f) 92, 96 [no. 26]; Dumville (1993g) 93 n. 49, 132 n. 91; Ebersperger (1999) 67–71; R. Gameson (2002d) 188; Lapidge (2006) 293; Wittig (2007) 191; Godden—Irvine (2009) I.xlvi; Wittig (2010) 251; R. Gameson (2012d) 355 and n. 40

DEC: F. Wormald (1963); E. Temple (1976) no. 30 (viii); Brownrigg (1978) 253, 261 n. 2; Ohlgren (1986) no. 125; Avril—Stirnemann (1987) no. 21; R. Gameson (1992a) 191 n. 22, 195 and n. 36, 198–9; R. Gameson (1995b) 225 n. 195; R. Gameson (2012c) 261 and n. 33

FACS: F. Wormald (1963) pls. 1, 2, 5 [fols. 1r, 57v, 79r (details)]; E. Temple (1976) ill. 119 [fol. 57v (detail)]; F. Wormald (1984) ill. 70 [fol. 57v (detail)]; Avril—Stirnemann (1987) pl. V (21) [fol. 15r]; R. Gameson (1992a) pl. 42 (b) [fol. 57v (detail)]; Dumville (1993g) pl. XI [fol. 10v (detail)]

ED: Bolton (1977a) 60–78 [mythological glosses to Boethius coll. as BN]

ST: Minnis (1981) 356–9; N.P. Brooks (1984) 268; Bodden (1986) 57–9; Bodden (1988) 222, 227; M. Irvine (1994) 389–90; Godden (2011) 92; Jayatilaka (2011) 117

888. Paris, Bibliothèque nationale de France, lat. 7299, fols. 3–12, 12 bis–71

fols. 3–12: s. x ex., prob. Ramsey [liturgical calendar and computus material]

fols. 12bis–71: s. x, Fleury, prov. temporarily Ramsey [Helperic, *De computo* and computus texts; Macrobius, *Comm. in Somnium Scipionis*] both parts prov. Fleury s. xi

Contents: liturgical calendar; computus materials [incl. SK 10525, 11148, 14982] (s. x ex.) [fols. 3–12]; Helperic, *De computo* and computus texts; Macrobius, *Comm. in Somnium Scipionis* [fols. 12bis–71]

MS: Delisle (1868–81) II.365; M.–T. Vernet (1960) 21–3; McGurk (1974) 1, 3, 4 n. 5; Barker-Benfield (1976) 150, 152–5; Vezin (1977) 110–11 and n. 7; Lapidge (1984) 356 n. 117 [repr. Lapidge (1993a) 373 n. 117]; Lapidge (1986a) 266; Lapidge (1988b) 259 n. 30 [repr. Lapidge (1993a) 217 n. 30]; Mostert (1989) no. BF 1099; Lapidge (1992a) 107–8, 116, 129 [repr. Lapidge (1993a) 395–6, 404, 417]; Dumville (1993g) 59; Günzel (1993) 198–9; Ebersperger (1999) 71–6, 189; Lapidge (2006) 51; Rushforth (2008a) 27; R. Gameson (2012d) 356 and n. 48; Gneuss (2012) 302

ED: Rushforth (2008a) no. 8 [liturgical calendar]

ST: SK Suppl. 10525, 11148; Lapidge (2012a) 687–8

889. Paris, Bibliothèque nationale de France, lat. 7585

s. ix$^{2/4}$ or ix^2, NE France, in England (prob. Canterbury StA) by s. x^2

Contents: Isidore, *Etymologiae* [*CPL* 1186] with glosses (s. ix$^{2/4}$ or ix^2 France, and x^2 England); passages on the Trinity: excerpt from pseudo-Augustine, *Serm.* ccxlv, the creed *Quicumque uult*, and excerpts from Isidore, *Etymologiae* bk. VII (all s. x^2, England); excerpt from Ælfric, *De falsis diis** (s. xi^1)

MS: Förster (1927) 130–1; Dubois (1943) 362–6; N.R. Ker (1957) no. 366; Díaz y Díaz (1959) 41–3; Pope (1967–8) I.87–8, II.676; Vezin (1968) 286 and n. 14; T.A.M. Bishop (1971) xxx, 4; Rella (1977) 99 n. 72, 168; Rella (1980) 115; Dumville (1993f) 92, 99 [no. 27]; Dumville (1993g) 102; Bischoff (1998 —) III, no. 4486; Ebersperger (1999) 76–83; Lapidge (2006) 172, 311; Rumble (2006b) 10 n. 58; Scragg (2012a) nos. 985–6

DEC: E. Temple (1976) no. 30 (ii); Ohlgren (1986) no. 119; Avril—Stirnemann (1987) no. 15; R. Gameson (1992a) 194–5

FACS: T.A.M. Bishop (1971) pls. IV (a)–(b) [fols. 44r, 76v (details)]; E. Temple (1976) ill. 104 [fol. 164r (detail)]; Avril—Stirnemann (1987) pl. IV (15) [fol. 210r]

ED: Meritt (1961) 448 [OE glosses to Isidore, *Etymologiae*]; Pope (1967–8) II.682–5 [excerpts from Ælfric, *De falsis diis*, coll. as X^k]

889. 5. Paris, Bibliothèque nationale de France, lat. 8085, fols. 2–82

s. ix²/³ or ix med., France, prob. Loire region, prov. England prob. by s. x/xi

Contents: Prudentius, *Cathemerinon* [*CPL* 1438], *Peristephanon* [*CPL* 1443], *Apotheosis* [*CPL* 1439], *Hamartigenia* [*CPL* 1440], *Psychomachia* [*CPL* 1441], *Contra Symmachum* [*CPL* 1442], *Dittochaeon* [*CPL* 1444]

MS: M.P. Cunningham (1966) xvi; Bischoff (1998 —) III, no. 4525; Ebersperger (1999) 200; Lapidge (2006) 172, 328, 329, 330, 331; Wieland (2009) 148; R. Gameson (2012d) 345 and nn. 5–6

DEC: Stettiner (1895) 38–42; Woodruff (1930) 10, 23–30; Degenhart (1950) 142, 151; *Les manuscrits à peintures* (1954) no. 100

FACS: Stettiner (1895) pls. 75, 77, 79, 80, 83, 84, 86, 88, 90, 92, 94, 96, 98, 100, 103, 108 [folios not specified]; Woodruff (1930) ills. 26, 52, 63–4, 67, 74, 103, 124 [folios not specified]; Degenhart (1950) pls. 92–4, 102; Stiegemann — Wemhoff (1999) III ['Beiträge'], pl. 3 [fol. 61v]

ED: M.P. Cunningham (1966) [Prudentius, *carmina*, coll. as F]

ST: Schanz et al. (1914–20) IV/i.258

890. Paris, Bibliothèque nationale de France, lat. 8092

s. xi²/⁴, England, prov. France (s. xi²?)

Contents: Sedulius, Letter I to Macedonius, *Carmen paschale* [*CPL* 1447] with glosses (some in OE), *Hymni* [*CPL* 1449; SK 1904, 33]; poems in honour of Sedulius [SK 14842, 14841]; two Latin poems [SK 15583, SK Suppl. 16506a]; pseudo-Columbanus (pseudo-Alcuin), *Praecepta uiuendi* [SK 5960]; Bede, *Versus de die iudicii* [*CPL* 1370] with glosses; Latin poem [SK Suppl. 1418a]; Arator, *Historia apostolica* [*CPL* 1504] with glosses (incomplete)

MS: McKinlay (1942) 14–15; Laistner — King (1943) 128; McKinlay (1951) xii; Whitbread (1967) 163; Vezin (1968) 294–5 and n. 43; Lapidge (1982a) 114, 117, 120–1, 136–8 [repr. Lapidge (1996b) 480, 485, 489–90, 516]; Lapidge (1982b); P.P. O'Neill (1989); M. Irvine (1994) 400; Springer (1995) 7, 28, 78–9; Ebersperger (1999) 83–8; Lapidge (2006) 281, 331, 332; Lendinara (2007b) 177, 180, 182, 184, 204 and n. 121; Wieland (2009) 151; R. Gameson (2012b) 98 and n. 15; Scragg (2012a) no. 987

DEC: Pulsiano (2007) 120

FACS: McKinlay (1942) pl. IV [fol. 50r (detail)]; Vezin (1968) pl. facing p. 292 [fol. 36v]; Pulsiano (2007) 132 [fol. 84r]

ED: McKinlay (1951) [Arator, *Historia apostolica*, coll. as Γ]; Lapidge (1982b) 3–4 [Latin poems SK 14483, SK Suppl. 16506a, 1418a], 9–17 [OE glosses to Sedulius], P.P. O'Neill (1989) [further OE glosses to Sedulius]

ST: *CPPM* II, no. 3216b [*Praecepta uiuendi*]; *CSLMA* II (1999) 76; Lendinara (2007b)

890. 5. Paris, Bibliothèque nationale de France, lat. 8431, fols. 21–48

948×958, Canterbury CC, prov. France (s. x²?)

Contents: Fredegaud/Frithegod of Canterbury and Brioude, prefatory *Epistola*, *Breuiloquium Vitae Wilfridi* [SK 8137], with commentary

MS: A. Campbell (1950) vii–x; Lapidge (1988a) 55–61, 64 [repr. Lapidge (1993a) 171–7]; Dumville (1993g) 93; Ebersperger (1999) 88–92; Lapidge (2004a) 135–7, 145

FACS: Lapidge (1988a) pl. V [fol. 35r]; Lapidge (1993a) 167 [fol. 35r]

ED: A. Campbell (1950) 1–62 [Fredegaud/Frithegod, prefatory *Epistola* and *Breuiloquium*, coll. as P]

ST: Lapidge (1988a) [repr. Lapidge (1993a) 157–81, with add. notes on p. 481]; Biggs et al. (2001) 481–2; Lapidge (2004a)

891. Paris, Bibliothèque nationale de France, lat. 8824

s. xi med., Canterbury? (prov. France by s. xiv)

Contents: Psalms I-L: Psalterium Romanum and OE prose translation (prob. by King Alfred), both preceded by *argumenta* and Latin 'Christian' *tituli*; Psalms LI–CL: Psalterium Romanum and OE metrical version, both preceded by Latin 'Christian' *tituli*; canticles; litany; eight prayers; colophon

MS: Delisle (1868–81) I.57–8, 65, 420, III.170–3; Wildhagen (1913) 466–72; Förster (1927) 129–30; Krapp (1932b) vii–xxvi; Lauer et al. (1939—) VIII.4–5; Leroquais (1940–1) II.76–8; N.R. Ker (1957) no. 367; Colgrave (1958) 11–20; Samaran—Marichal (1959–85) III.727; Sisam—Sisam (1959) 8, 11, 48, 60 n. 1, 75; Vezin (1968) 286, 291–2; Lapidge (1991a) 43–4, 80; Toswell (1991); Dumville (1992a) 53, 57, 132; Dumville (1993f) 88, 90, 99 [no. 28]; Dumville (1993g) 12, 60–1, 64;

Toswell (1996); Ebersperger (1999) 92–103; Emms (1999); P.P. O'Neill (2001) 1–22; W. Schipper (2003) 157; R. Gameson (2012a) 22 n. 30, 24 n. 41, 29 n. 66, 30–1; Marsden (2012) 429 and n. 103; Scragg (2012a) no. 988; Toswell (2012) 471

DEC: F. Wormald (1952) 78–9 [no. 55]; F. Wormald (1962) 3 [repr. F. Wormald (1984) 125, 172 n. 23]; Köhler—Mütherich (1971–99) VI/i.85; E. Temple (1976) no. 83; Ohlgren (1986) no. 188; Avril—Stirnemann (1987) no. 25; Ohlgren (1992) 3–4, 50–2; R. Gameson (1995b) 17, 31 n. 114, 49, 62 n. 257, 112, 220; R. Gameson (2012c) 278 and n. 97, 284 and n. 124

FACS: Colgrave (1958) [complete facsimile]; NPS II, pls. 123–4 [fols. 2r, 2v, 3r, 5r, 6r (details)]; E. Temple (1976) ills. 208–9 [fol. 3v (details)]; Avril—Stirnemann (1987) pl. VI (25) [fol. 1r (detail)]; Ohlgren (1992) pls. 4.1–11 [fols. 1r, 1v, 2r, 2v, 3r, 3v, 4r, 5r, 6r (all details)]; Owen-Crocker (2009) fig. 1.1 [fols. 1v–2r]

ED: Krapp (1932b) 3–150 [base MS for OE metrical psalms LI–CL]; Lapidge (1991a) 250–3 [litany]; R. Gameson (2001d) 46 [colophon]; P.P. O'Neill (2001) 100–63 [base MS for OE prose psalms I–L and *argumenta*]; Pulsiano (2001a) [Latin Pss. I–L coll. as ç]

LANG: Schabram (1965) 48–51, 124–6; Wenisch (1979) 68, 89, 327–8; Bately (1982); Hofstetter (1987) 296–7, 536–9; Ebersperger (1999) 97; P.P. O'Neill (2001) 55–71; C. Bishop (2007b) 77

ST: Krapp (1932b); Bromwich (1950); Colgrave (1958); P.P. O'Neill (1981); P.P. O'Neill (2001)

892. Paris, Bibliothèque nationale de France, lat. 9377, fol. 3

s. viii[1], Northumbria?, prov. France (s. viii?)

Contents: Epistulae Pauli [ad Corinthios II] (f)

MS: CLA VI (1953) p. xvii; CLA Supplement (1971) no. 1746; R. McKitterick (1989b) 416 and n. 125; McGurk (1994b) 10 [repr. McGurk (1998) no. XII]; Ebersperger (1999) 103–5; Marsden (2012) 420 and n. 69

893. Paris, Bibliothèque nationale de France, lat. 9389 (the 'Echternach Gospels')

s. vii/viii, Northumbria, prob. Lindisfarne (Ireland? Echternach?), prov. Echternach

Contents: gospels; explanations of Hebrew names in lists following each gospel [the same lists occur in nos. **63, 213, 214, 220, 907**]; colophon

MS: Delisle (1868–81) III.231, IV.viii; Kenney (1929) no. 460; *CLA* V (1950) no. 578; Kendrick et al. (1959–60) II, *passim*; Samaran—Marichal (1959–85) III.728; McGurk (1961a) no. 59; Bischoff (1966–81) II.323, 328, 332; T.J. Brown (1972) 222, 225 *et passim* [repr. T.J. Brown (1993a) 100, 103 *et passim*]; Ó Cróinín (1982); Ó Cróinín (1984); B. Fischer (1988–91) I.20*; R. McKitterick (1989b) 423–7; Netzer (1989); Bischoff (1990) 9, 91, 200–1; McNamara (1990) *passim*; Webster—Backhouse (1991) no. 82; Netzer (1994) *passim*; McNamara (1995) 75 *et passim*; Dumville (1999) 93–8; Ebersperger (1999) 105–14; Verey (1999) 327, 329–30, 333–4; M.P. Brown (2000) 20; M.P. Brown (2003a) *passim*; M.P. Brown (2004) 291; Gullick (2004) 32 and n. 50; Nees (2006) 91 n. 41; Keefer (2007b) 87; Wieland (2009) 117; M.P. Brown (2012) 136, 149, 159; R. Gameson (2012a) 19 and n. 23, 80, 84; R. Gameson (2012b) 114; Marsden (2012) 418–19 and n. 60

DEC: E.H. Zimmermann (1916) 122–7 *et passim*; Köhler (1930–60) I.326–8, 331, 333; Werckmeister (1967) 7–97; Koehler (1972) *passim*; Nordenfalk (1977) *passim*; Alexander (1978a) no. 11; Ohlgren (1986) no. 11; Avril—Stirnemann (1987) no. 7; G. Henderson (1987) 57–99; Nees (2011) 14, 15; Netzer (2011) 3; Pulliam (2011) 70; Werner (2011) 293; N. Edwards (2012) 245; Netzer (2012) 230

FACS: E.H. Zimmermann (1916) *Tafelband* IV, pls. 255 (a) [fol. 18v], 255 (b) [fol. 176v], 256 (a) [fol. 75v], 256 (b) [fol. 115v], 257 [fol. 177r], 258 (a)–(c) [fols. 20r, 19r, 116r]; Kendrick et al. (1959–60) I, pls. 3 [fol. 1r], 5 [fol. 111v], 7 [fols. 20r, 177r], 9 [fol. 18v], 12 [fols. 10r–75v *passim* (details)], 13 [fols. 110v–175r *passim* (details)], 14 [fols. 116r, 222v], 19 (d) [fol. 18v], 26 (e)–(h) [folios unspecified (details)], 33 (d) [fol. 11v], 50 (c) [fol. 177r (detail)]; Alexander (1978a) ills. 48 [fol. 177r], 51–6 [fols. 19r, 20r, 116r, 18v, 115v, 75v], 59 [fol. 176v]; G. Henderson (1987) pls. 97–102 [fols. 116r, 76r, 1r, 20r, 19r, 18v], 105 [fol. 75v], 108 [fol. 176v], 110 [fol. 115v]; Bonner et al. (1989a) pls. 16, 18 [fols. 19r, 1v, 116r (details)]; M.P. Brown (2003a) pls. 29 [fol. 177r], 30 [fols. 18v, 20r, 19r, 75v]; M.P. Brown (2007a) pl. 13 [fol. 75v]

ED: J. Wordsworth et al. (1889–1954) [gospels coll. as EP]; B. Fischer (1988–91) [gospels coll. as Ge]; McGurk (1994a) [repr. McGurk (1998) no. IX] [explanations of Hebrew names coll. as Ge]; R. Gameson (2001d) 33–4 [colophon]

ST: Szerwiniack (1994) 193–4

893. 5. Paris, Bibliothèque nationale de France, lat. 9488, fols. 3–4

s. viii, prob. Northumbria (or Echternach?)

Contents: sacramentary ('Gelasianum mixtum') (f)

MS: H.M. Bannister (1908) 398–406; Gamber (1958) 63; *CLA* V (1950)
no. 581; Gamber (1968–88) no. 803; Huglo (1990) 145; Mayr–Harting
(1991) 180 and n. 33; Ferrari (1994) 12; Netzer (1994) 7, 10, 38–9, 113,
115, 212 n. 38; *CPL* (1995) no. 1905*l*; Pfaff (1995a) 9; Hen (1997) 55–6,
62; Ebersperger (1999) 171–2; Ferrari (1999) 125 n. 14; Stiegemann—
Wemhoff (1999) II.485; Pfaff (2009) 42–3

DEC: Avril—Stirnemann (1987) no. 6

FACS: Avril—Stirnemann (1987) pl. II (6) [fol. 4r (detail)]

ED: H.M. Bannister (1908) 402–6; Moeller (1992–2004) [coll. as *Paris²*]

893. 8. Paris, Bibliothèque nationale de France, lat. 9555, fol. 1

[palimpsest, lower script] s. viii, prob. England (or Echternach?)

Contents: unidentified patristic fragment

MS: Degering (1921) 74 [no. 28]; *CLA* Supplement (1971) no. 1747;
Lowe (1972) II.506; Schroeder (1977) 362; R. McKitterick (1989b) 428;
Ebersperger (1999) 183

894. Paris, Bibliothèque nationale de France, lat. 9561

s. viii[1] or viii med., S England, (prov. Saint-Bertin by s. xiv or xv)

Contents: pseudo-Isidore, *De ordine creaturarum* [*CPL* 1189; *BCLL*
342]; colophon; Gregory, *Regula pastoralis* [*CPL* 1712] (with *c.* 100
OE scratched glosses, s. x); a second colophon

MS: Lindsay (1915) 473; Wilmart (1922–9b); *CLA* V (1950) no. 590; N.R.
Ker (1957) no. 369 and p. lxiv; Samaran—Marichal et al. (1959–84)
III.729; Lowe (1960) 23; Bischoff (1966–81) II.332–3; Díaz y Díaz
(1972) 47-8; Lowe (1972) I.287; Clement (1984a) 39; R. McKitterick
(1989b) 419 n. 148; Iudic et al. (1991) I.91 n. 6, 109–10, 112; Dumville
(1993f) 90, 99 [no. 29]; Ebersperger (1999) 115–18; R. Gameson
(1999c) 360–1; Lapidge (2006) 306, 340; R. Gameson (2012b) 112 n. 68

DEC: Avril—Stirnemann (1987) no. 5

FACS: Lowe (1960) no. XXXV [fol. 18r]; Avril—Stirnemann (1987) pl. I
(5) [fol. 37v]; R. Gameson (1999c) pl. 13.30 [fol. 50r]; R. Gameson
(2001c) pl. 3 (a) [fol. 81v]

ED: Meritt (1957) 65–6 [90 OE glosses to Gregory, *Regula pastoralis*]; Díaz y Díaz (1972) 82–205 [*De ordine creaturarum* coll. as P]; S. Morrison (1987) [10 further OE glosses to *Regula pastoralis*]; Judic et al. (1992) [Gregory, *Regula pastoralis*, coll. as B]; R. Gameson (2001d) no. 5 [second colophon]

LANG: Wenisch (1979) 43, 112, 114, 327; Hofstetter (1987) 508

ST: Díaz y Díaz (1953); Schreiber (2003) 23–33

895. Paris, Bibliothèque nationale de France, lat. 10062, fols. 162–3

s. xi in., Canterbury CC, (prov. Saint-Évroult)

Contents: liturgical calendar (f)

MS: Delisle (1868–81) II.405; T.A.M. Bishop (1959–63b) 415, 420–1; Samaran—Marichal et al. (1959–84) III.151; N.R. Ker (1964) 39; Nortier (1966) 103, 106–7, 109, 119; Vezin (1968) 295 and n. 47; N.P. Brooks (1984) 269; Dumville (1993f) 88–9, 92, 96, 99 [no. 30]; Dumville (1993g) 109 and n. 130, 115 n. 23, 124 n. 67; Heslop (1995) 69, 79; Ebersperger (1999) 118–28; N. Orchard (2002) I.171–2; R. Gameson (2003) 155; Rushforth (2008a) 29–30; R. Gameson (2012d) 365 and n. 88

ED: Ebersperger (1999) 123–7 [liturgical calendar]; Rushforth (2008a) no. 10 [liturgical calendar]

896. Paris, Bibliothèque nationale de France, lat. 10575 (the 'Egbert Pontifical')

s. med or x² or x/xi, prov. Évreux s. xi

Contents: prologue to *Poenitentiale Egberti* [*CPL* 1887]; First Capitulary of Gerbald of Liège; pontifical (including litanies and First English Coronation *ordo*); benedictional; charter boundaries, partly erased [Sawyer (1968) no. 1602]; pontifical texts (added at Évreux, s. xi)

MS: Delisle (1868–81) II.285; Liebermann (1903–16) I.xxxvii; Cabrol (1920–1); Förster (1927) 113–16; Leroquais (1940–1) I.xxv, II.160–4; N.R. Ker (1957) no. 370; Gamber (1968–88) no. 1570; Prescott (1987) 128–9, 141–7; Banting (1989) ix–xxxvii; Dumville (1991–5) 51; Lapidge (1991a) 80–1; Dumville (1992a) 69, 85–6, 125; Dumville (1993f) 89, 95, 99 [no. 31]; Dumville (1994a) 150 n. 100; R. Gameson (1996b) 166–7 and n. 146; Ebersperger (1999) 128–35; R. Gameson (2003) 155; C.A. Jones (2004) 327–8, 337, 339, 340 nn. 62–3, 341 nn. 65–6, 343, 344 nn. 77–80, 345 n. 82, 346 n. 85, 351–2; C.A. Jones (2005a) 115, 117–18, 120;

N. Orchard (2005) c, 444 *et passim*; Hartzell (2006) no. 312; O'Brien O'Keeffe (2006) 269; Wieland (2009) 124; R. Gameson (2012a) 50; D. Ganz (2012) 194; Rankin (2012) 491 and n. 39, 494–5; Scragg (2012a) nos. 989–91

DEC: Alexander (1970a) 237; Avril—Stirnemann (1987) no. 13; Pulsiano (2007) 120

FACS: Avril—Stirnemann (1987) pl. III (13) [fol. 92v (detail)]; Huglo (1987) [fols. 53v, 41v]; Banting (1989) pl. 1 [fol. 10v]; Pulsiano (2007) 132 [fol. 1r]

ED: Martène (1763) I.92, 275; II.31–6, 188–9, 199, 214–15, 246–50, 285, 294 [excerpts, including most of the pontifical and part of the benedictional]; Greenwell (1853) [pontifical and benedictional]; Liebermann (1903–16) I.217 [*Promissio regis* from Coronation *ordo*, coll. as P]; N.R. Ker (1957) no. 370c [charter bounds from Sawyer no. 1602]; Moeller (1971–9) [fourteen benedictions and collects, all coll. as *Egbert*]; Banting (1989) 3–153 [complete MS]; Lapidge (1991a) 254–8 [two litanies for Dedication of a church]

ST: Schramm (1934) 152–68, 209–20; Gjerløw (1961) 20, 22, 41; D.H. Turner (1971) xvi–xxviii, xxxvi; Hohler (1975) 72, 223–4 [*Poenitentiale Egberti* and Gerbald]; Frantzen (1983a) 52–3; Frantzen (1985) 29 [*Poenitentiale Egberti*]; Nelson (1986b) [Coronation *ordo*]; Haggenmüller (1991) 95–6, 152, 289 [*Poenitentiale Egberti*]; Conner (1993) 43 and nn.; Rasmussen (1998) 189–94 *et passim*; Cross—Hamer (1999) 35 [Gerbald, Capitulary]; N. Orchard (2002) I.68, 84, 91, 99–100, 104, 151; Keynes (2006) nos. B 470–6 and M 65–74 [coronation *ordines*]; Clayton (2008) 108; Karkov (2011) 42–3

897. Paris, Bibliothèque nationale de France, lat. 10837, fols. 34–41 and 44

s. viii in., England? Echternach? prov. Echternach

Contents: liturgical calendar; Easter tables

MS: Delisle (1868–81) II.361–2, III.229–30; H.M. Bannister (1908) 406–11; Gasquet—Bishop (1908) 146 and n. 2; H.A. Wilson (1918) ix–xxiii; Kenney (1929) no. 69; Levison (1946) 65 and n. 1 *et passim*; *CLA* V (1950) no. 606a; Samaran—Marichal et al. (1959–84) II.639–40; Bischoff (1966–81) I.92; Gamber (1968–88) no. 414; Rella (1977) 13; Schroeder (1979) 380–3; Ó Cróinín (1984); M.P. Brown (1986) 124;

Gerchow (1988) 199–212, 328–9; R. McKitterick (1989b) 423, 426–7; Netzer (1989) 206; Ó Cróinín (1989) 192, 195–6; Webster—Backhouse (1991) no. 123; Bischoff—Lapidge (1994) 162–6; Lapidge (1994a) 105 n. 10; Netzer (1994) *passim*; *CPL* (1995) no. 2037; Hohler (1995) 227–8, 230; Hen (1997) 52, 54 and nn.; Ebersperger (1999) 185–6; Rushforth (2008a) 18–19; Wieland (2009)

DEC: Alexander (1978a) 52; Avril—Stirnemann (1987) no. 3; Nees (2011) 21

FACS: *NPS* I, pl. 183 (a)–(b) [fols. 8r, 42v]; H.A. Wilson (1918) pls. I–XII [fols. 34v–40r]; Avril—Stirnemann (1987) pl. I (3) [fols. 34v, 37r]

ED: H.A. Wilson (1918) [liturgical calendar]; Rushforth (2008a) no. 1 [liturgical calendar]

ST: Borst (2001) I.xxii, xlii

898. Paris, Bibliothèque nationale de France, lat. 10861

s. ix$^{1/4}$ or ix^1, S England (Canterbury CC?), or an English scribe abroad, prov. France s. x or xi (prov. Beauvais s. xii or xiii)

Contents: nineteen *passiones sanctorum* [*BHL* 6815, 4057, 1495, 7543, 8631, 2038–9, 1970, 3514, 3236, 2895, 2578, 1836, 7539, 2708, 156, 108, 134, 4522, 2696 respectively]; five *dicta* or riddles, two ascribed to Alcuin and Gregory the Great (add. s. x or xi)

MS: Delisle (1868–81) II.293, 339; *Catalogus codicum hagiographicorum … Bibliotheca Nationali Parisiensi* (1889–93) II.605–6; Philippart (1977) 30, 34–5, 38–9, 40–2, 87; Cross (1982) 53; M.P. Brown (1986); Morrish (1986) 94–5; Morrish (1988) 528–9, 538; Biggs et al. (1990) 61 [C.D. Wright]; Dumville (1992a) 140; Dumville (1993f) 89, 99 [no. 32]; M.P. Brown (1996) 42–3 *et passim*; Love (1996) xiv–xv; Whatley (1996) 15, 20, 29 n. 79; Ebersperger (1999) 135–41; R. Gameson (1999c) 363; Lapidge (2003b) 151–5, 169 n. 33; Biggs (2007a) 45–6, 53–4; M.P. Brown (2007a) 78; M.P. Brown (2012) 165; R. Gameson (2012a) 38 and n. 92

DEC: Alexander (1978a) no. 67; M.P. Brown (1986) 135–7; Ohlgren (1986) no. 67; Avril—Stirnemann (1987) no. 11

FACS: M.P. Brown (1986) pls. I, IV (a) [fols. 2r, 75v]; M.P. Brown (1996) pl. 16 [fol. 2r]; M.P. Brown (2007a) pl. 56 [fol. 2r]

ED: Lapidge (2003b) 156–65 [base MS for *Passio S. Iulianae* (*BHL* 4522)]

ST: Biggs et al. (2001) 51, 55 *et passim*

898. 5. Paris, Bibliothèque nationale de France, lat. 13089, fols. 49–76

s. viii med. or viii^2, Northumbria (Monkwearmouth-Jarrow?)

Contents: Gregory, *Regula pastoralis* [*CPL* 1712], III.9–29

MS: Delisle (1868–81) II.411; *CLA* V (1950) no. 651; Clement (1984a) 39; Mews (1997); Ebersperger (1999) 141–3; Schreiber (2003) 23, 32–3 and n. 45; Lapidge (2006) 156, 306

899. Paris, Bibliothèque nationale de France, lat. 14380, fols. 1–65

s. x ex., Canterbury CC, (prov. Paris, Saint-Victor, Augustinian canons)

Contents: Boethius, *De consolatione Philosophiae* [*CPL* 878], with *accessus* and commentary by Remigius

MS: Weinberger (1934) xix; Courcelle (1939) 123, 130; Courcelle (1967) 406, 410; Vezin (1968) 286 n. 14; T.A.M. Bishop (1971) xiii, xxvi; Bolton (1977a) 54, 59; Rella (1977) 77, 163; Troncarelli (1981) 4, 5, 36, 46, 56; Wittig (1983) 188; Bodden (1984) 268; N.P. Brooks (1984) 268; Bodden (1988) 227 n. 40; Dumville (1993f) 99 [no. 33]; Ebersperger (1999) 144–6; Lapidge (2006) 293; Wittig (2007) 192; Godden—Irvine (2009) xlvi; Wittig (2010) 251; Rankin (2012) 505 n. 111; R. Gameson (2012d) 346

FACS: Troncarelli (1981) pl. 12 [fol. 10v]

ST: Godden (2011) 92; Jayatilaka (2011) 117

900. Paris, Bibliothèque nationale de France, lat. 14782

s. xi^2 or xi ex., Exeter, (prov. Paris, Saint-Victor)

Contents: gospels

MS: Alexander (1966); De la Mare (1982–5); McGurk (1986b) 45 n. 4 [repr. McGurk (1998) no. XIV]; A.G. Watson (1987a) 36; Conner (1993) 11; Dumville (1993f) 92, 99 [no. 34]; McGurk (1993) 244 [repr. McGurk (1998) no. XI]; R. Gameson (1996b) 158 and n. 114, 160; Ebersperger (1999) 147–52; R. Gameson (1999a) no. 813; R. Gameson (2012a) 45 nn. 136–7, 50 and n. 158, 91 n. 332, 92

DEC: C.M. Kauffmann (1975) no. 2; Ohlgren (1986) no. 213; Avril—Stirnemann (1987) no. 26; Alexander (1992) 77–82; R. Gameson (1995b) 196, 205 n. 82, 209 nn. 105 and 107, 230, 258 n. 155; R. Gameson (2012c) 273 and n. 73, 286 and n. 129

FACS: Alexander (1966) pls. 6, 7, 8, 12, 15, 16, 18, 20 [fols. 16v, 52v, 108v, 74v, 132r, 75r, 9r, 10v, 11r (all details)]; C.M. Kauffmann (1975) ills. 3–6 [fols. 16v, 52v, 74v, 108v]; Avril—Stirnemann (1987) pls. C [fols. 52v–53r], VI (26) [fol. 9r]

900. 5. Paris, Bibliothèque nationale de France, lat. 17177, fols. 5–12
(with Rome, Biblioteca Apostolica Vaticana, lat. 340, flyleaf)

s. viii¹ or viii/ix, S England or Mercia, or continental centre with Anglo-Saxon connections (prov. Corbie)

Contents: Theodore of Mopsuestia, *Comm. in Epistulas Pauli minores* in Latin translation [*CPG* 3845] (f)

MS: *CLA* I (1934) no. 4; Laistner (1947) 22; Siegmund (1949) 132; *CLA* V (1950) p. 42 [no. **4]; Farmer (1968) 13 and n. 6; Sims-Williams (1979) 3, 17 and nn. 17, 19; D. Ganz (1990) 128; Sims-Williams (1990) 202 and n. 116; Bischoff—Lapidge (1994) 248 n. 23; Bischoff (1998—) III, no. 4989; Lapidge (2006) 156

901. Paris, Bibliothèque nationale de France, lat. 17814

s. x ex., prob. Canterbury CC

Contents: Boethius, *De consolatione Philosophiae* [*CPL* 878], with *accessus* and commentary by Remigius

MS: Weinberger (1934) xx; Courcelle (1939) 122; Courcelle (1967) 405; Vezin (1968) 286 n. 14; T.A.M. Bishop (1971) xiii n. 2, xxvi; Bolton (1977a) 39, 48, 54; Rella (1977) 77, 163; Troncarelli (1981) 4, 5, 36, 46, 56; Wittig (1983) 188; Bodden (1988) 227 n. 40; Dumville (1993f) 99 [no. 35]; Ebersperger (1999) 152–6; Godden (2005) 336, 339; Lapidge (2006) 293; Wittig (2007) 192; Godden—Irvine (2009) I.xlvi; Wittig (2010) 252; R. Gameson (2012a) 61 and n. 213, 67 n. 232

DEC: F. Wormald (1971b) 310 n. 1 [repr. F. Wormald (1984) 80–1 and n. 20]; E. Temple (1976) no. 30 (xii); Ohlgren (1986) no. 129; Avril—Stirnemann (1987) no. 30

FACS: E. Temple (1976) ill. 110 [fol. 46r (detail)]; Avril—Stirnemann (1987) pl. IV (30) [fols. 78r, 106r (details)]

ED: Bolton (1977a) 60–78 [mythological glosses to Boethius coll. as R]

ST: Godden (2011) 92; Jayatilaka (2011) 117

902. Paris, Bibliothèque nationale de France, nouv. acq. lat. 586, fols. 16–131

s. x² or xi¹ (prov. France by s. xii)

Contents: *Excerptiones de Prisciano* [fols. 1–15 supplied s. xii] with scholia; excerpt from Bede, *De temporum ratione* [*CPL* 2320], ch. iv; glossary of tree names

MS: N.R. Ker (1957) no. 371; Vezin (1968) 286, 292–3; Ebersperger (1999) 156–9; D.W. Porter (1999a) 89–90; D.W. Porter (2002) 3, 6–9; Wieland (2009) 144, 154; R. Gameson (2012a) 17 and n. 14, 51 n. 169; Scragg (2012a) no. 992

DEC: Avril—Stirnemann (1987) no. 14

FACS: Vezin (1968) pl. opp. p. 285 [fol. 61r]

ED: N.R. Ker (1957) no. 371 [OE glosses to *Excerptiones de Prisciano*]; D.W. Porter (1999a) 103 [Old French scratched glosses to *Excerptiones de Prisciano*]; D.W. Porter (2002) 44–324 [base MS for *Excerptiones de Prisciano*], 361–78 [scholia to *Excerptiones de Prisciano* coll. as P], 395–6 [glossary of tree names]

ST: M. Irvine (1994) 539 n. 29; D.W. Porter (1999a); D.W. Porter (2002) 1–39; Gneuss (2005b)

902. 9. Paris, Bibliothèque Sainte-Geneviève, 2409 (with Paris, Bibliothèque de L'Arsenal 933, fols. 128–334)

s. x/xi Canterbury, prob. StA

Contents: Flodoard of Rheims, *De triumphis Christi* [with gloss in MS Arsenal, fols. 166–334]

MS: Muzurelle (1969) 109–12; Jacobsen (1978) 88 n. 2; Lapidge (1982a) 108, 134–5 n. 65 [repr. Lapidge (1996b) 472 n. 65]; Ebersperger (2003); C.A. Jones (2007) 48 n. 163

FACS: Ebersperger (2003) pls. 1–3 [Sainte-Geneviève 2409, fols. 20v, 15r, and Arsenal 933, fol. 185r (all details)]

ED: PL 135, 491–886 [base MS (= G) for Flodoard, *De triumphis Christi*]

ST: Manitius (1911–31) II.165; C.A. Jones (2007); *CSLMA* III (2010) 15–17

903. Paris, Bibliothèque Sainte-Geneviève 2410 (with Paris, Bibliothèque de l'Arsenal 903, fols. 1–52)

s. x ex. – xi in., Canterbury, prob. StA

Contents: Iuvencus, *Euangelia* [*CPL* 1385]; commentary on the gospel of Matthew (incomplete; related to *BCLL* 341); Greek litany and *Sanctus*;

Eugenius of Toledo (?), *Heptametron de primordio mundi* [SK 12551]; Israel the Grammarian, *De arte metrica* [SK 14392]; *Rubisca* [*BCLL* 314; SK 11608]; metrical versions of *Pater noster* and creed [SK 10905; 15347 (from Iuvencus, *Euangelia* I.589–603)]; Greek numbers in Latin letters; poem *De quattuor clauibus sapientiae* [SK Suppl. 3716a]; two distichs from Ovid (*Amores* iii.8.3–4 [SK 8093] and *Ars amatoria* ii.279–80 [SK 8353]); verses by Alcuin (from *Carm.* lxxx. 1 [SK 11084]); Sedulius, Letter I to Macedonius, *Carmen paschale* [*CPL* 1447] (glossed), *Hymnus* I [*CPL* 1449; SK 33]; poems on Sedulius [SK 14842, 14841]; excerpt from Aldhelm, *Epistola ad Acircium* [*CPL* 1335]; Odo of Cluny, *Occupatio* (bks. I and II are glossed)

MS: Lapidge (1982a) 108 and n. 65, 114 and n. 85, 116 n. 93 [repr. Lapidge (1996b) 472 and n. 65, 480 and n. 85, 483 n. 93]; N.P. Brooks (1984) 268; Herren (1987) 18–21; Lapidge (1992b) 105–8 [repr. Lapidge (1993a) 95–8]; Dumville (1993f) 99 [no. 36]; Springer (1995) 7, 10, 23, 91–2; Lapidge (1996c) 419 n. 45; Ebersperger (1999) 160–7; Ebersperger (2003) 177–83; Lapidge (2006) 129 n. 2, 319, 323, 331, 332; C.A. Jones (2007) 10 n. 35, 48 n. 163; Gneuss (2008a) 416; Wieland (2009) 133, 148; Lapidge (2012b) 20; Scragg (2012a) no. 992.5

DEC: E. Temple (1976) no. 30 (xvi); Ohlgren (1986) no. 133; Ebersperger (1999) 166-7

FACS: E. Temple (1976) ill. 122 [Sainte-Geneviève 2410, fol. 126r (detail)]

ED: Swoboda (1900) [base MS for Odo, *Occupatio*]; Strecker et al. (1937–9) 501–2 [Israel, *De arte metrica*, coll. as G]; Herren (1987) 94–102 [*Rubisca*, variants and glosses coll. as P]

ST: Manitius (1911–31) II.27; Bischoff (1966–81) II.263; *BCLL* (1985) nos. 314, 723; Sims-Williams (1990) 334; Lapidge (1991a) 14–15; Bayless—Lapidge (1998) 209; *CSLMA* II (1999) 94–5

Philadelphia, Free Library, John Frederic Lewis Collection, ET 121: see no. **857**

904. Prague, Národni Knihovna České Republiky, Roudnice MS. VI. Fe. 50 (now kept in the Lobkowica Collections, Nelahozeves)

s. viii[1], Northumbria

Contents: gospels (f)

MS: *CLA* X (1963) no. 1567; Lenker (1997) 134 n. 3

905. Princeton, N.J., Princeton University Library, W.H. Scheide Collection, 71

s. x/xi

Contents: Homilies* (the 'Blickling Homilies', including homilies for the following saints: Andrew, John the Baptist, Martin, Michael, Mildred, Peter and Paul)

MS: N.R. Ker (1957) no. 382; Willard (1960); R.L. Collins (1976); J.V. Fleming (1976); Scragg (1985); Scragg (1992) xxv–xxvi; Conner (1993) 59, 62 *et passim*; Stoneman (1997) 99–100, 114; R.J. Kelly (2003) xxix–xlv, 196–8; Rumble (2006b) 4 n. 18; N.M. Thompson (2007) 97–8, 101–3; Toswell (2007) 215, 219, 220–5; *ASMMF* XVII (2008) 129–42 [no. 439; Wilcox]; Scragg (2012a) nos. 993–9

DEC: Rosenthal (2011) 234; Withers (2011) 262–5

FACS: Willard (1960) [complete facsimile]; R.J. Kelly (2003) pl. facing p. 1 [fol. 127r]; *ASMMF* XVII (2008) no. 439; Princeton University Library, Original Collections [on-line colour facsimile]

ED: Morris (1874–80) [base MS for 'Blickling Homilies']; Dawson (1969) [base MS for 'Blickling Homilies']; Scragg (1992) 196–8 [Blickling Homily IX coll. as B], 291–307 [Blickling Homily XVII coll. as B]; R.J. Kelly (2003) [base MS for 'Blickling Homilies']

LANG: A.K. Hardy (1899); Menner (1949); Wenisch (1979); Hofstetter (1987) 168–70; Toswell (2007) 218

ST: Willard (1936); Willard (1949a); Willard (1949b); Greenfield—Robinson (1980) 357–8; Swan (2006)

Regensburg, Bischöfliche Zentralbibliothek, Cim. 1: see no. **791**

906. Rheims, Bibliothèque municipale, 9

s. xi med., prov. 1062×1065 Saint-Remi, Rheims

Contents: gospels

MS: *Cat. gén. Dép.* (Octavo) XXXVIII.14–15 [Loriquet]; Boutemy (1948) 125–6; Hinkle (1970); De Lemps—Laslier (1978) no. 16; McGurk (1986b) 44, 46–7 [repr. McGurk (1998) no. XIV]; Dumville (1993g) 6 n. 20, 128 n. 85; Cohen—Teviotdale (1999) 70 n. 38; R. Gameson (2012a) 43 and n. 127, 70 n. 240; R. Gameson (2012d) 360 and n. 63; Marsden (2012) 424 and n. 80; McGurk (2012) 447 [no. 20]

DEC: E. Temple (1976) no. 105; Ohlgren (1986) no. 210; Raw (1990) 58, 241; R. Gameson (1995b) 41, 208 nn. 106 and 107, 218, 263; Karkov (2009) 217–18; R. Gameson (2012c) 271 and n. 63

FACS: Hinkle (1970) 23, fig. 1 [fol. 134v]; E. Temple (1976) ill. 299 [fol. 88r]; De Lemps—Laslier (1978) two pls. [fols. not specified]; R. Gameson (1991) fig. 20 [fol. 60r]; Owen-Crocker (2009) fig. 7.10 [fol. 23r]

906. 5. Rheims, Bibliothèque municipale, 1097

s. x² and xi/xii, (prov. France s. xii)

Contents: Priscian, *Partitiones .xii. uersuum Aeneidos principalium* [*CPL* 1551] (s. x²); Anglo-Saxon regnal list (s. xi/xii)

MS: *Cat. gén. Dép.* (Octavo) XXXIX.290–1 [Demaison]; Glück (1967) 63; Jeudy (1971) 124 n.; De Lemps—Laslier (1978) no. 15; Passalacqua (1978) no. 572; Gneuss (1988) 201–3 [repr. Gneuss (1996a) no. VII]; Lapidge (2006) 66

FACS: De Lemps—Laslier (1978) two pls. [fols. not specified]; Gneuss (1988) pl. 8 [fol. 82r]

ED: Glück (1967) 10*–12* [glosses by Remigius to first two folios of Priscian, *Partitiones*]; Gneuss (1988) 203–9 [regnal list]

ST: Lapidge (2006) 327

907. [Rome], Città del Vaticano, Biblioteca Apostolica Vaticana, Barberini lat. 570 (the 'Barberini Gospels')

s. viii² or viii ex., Mercia or Northumbria? S England?

Contents: gospels; explanations of Hebrew names in lists following Matthew and John; colophon

MS: *CLA* I (1934) no. 63; McGurk (1961a) no. 137; T.J. Brown (1972) 234 [repr. T.J. Brown (1993a) 112]; M.P. Brown (1986) 134 n. 64; B. Fischer (1988–91) I.16*; Webster—Backhouse (1991) no. 160; Dumville (1993f) 99 [no. 37]; McGurk (1994b) 21 [repr. McGurk (1998) no. XII]; M.P. Brown (1996) 120–5, 167–78 *et passim*; R. Gameson (1999c) 361–2; Stiegemann—Wemhoff (1999) II.446–7 [Bierbrauer, Schmidt]; C. Porter (2002) 61–2; M.P. Brown (2003a) 242, 265, 347 *et passim*; M.P. Brown (2007b) 90–3, 96–8, 100, 115; M.P. Brown (2012) 138 and n. 73, 143, 151, 154–5; R. Gameson (2012a) 37 and n. 89, 42 n. 117, 53 n. 183, 67, 88, 89 and n. 323; R. Gameson (2012b) 111 n. 67; Gullick (2012) 308 and n. 93

DEC: E.H. Zimmermann (1916) 25, 34, 128, 140–2, 300–2; F. Wormald (1945) 112, 114, 118–19 [repr. F. Wormald (1984) 50, 52–3, 56–7]; Henry (1965) 60–4 *et passim*; F. Wormald (1971b) 305, 307–8 [repr. F. Wormald (1984) 76–9]; Henry (1974) 163 *et passim*; Alexander (1978a) no. 36; D.M. Wilson (1984) 157; Ohlgren (1986) no. 36; G. Henderson (1987) 132, 137, 165; G. Henderson (2001); Nees (2006) 90; M.P. Brown (2007b) 89–91, 93, 97, 101–2, 104–11, 113–15; M.P. Brown (2011b) 40; Rosenthal (2011) 226; Netzer (2011) 3; N. Edwards (2012) 246 n. 14; Netzer (2012) 230

FACS: *NPS* II, pls. 58 [fol. 41r], 59 [fol. 125r], 60 (a)–(d) [fols. 1r, 11v, 18r, 51r]; E.H. Zimmermann (1916) *Tafelband* IV, pls. 313 [fols. 11v, 50v], 314 [fols. 79v, 124v], 315 [fols. 80r, 18r], 316 [fols. 125r, 51r], 317 [fols. 1r, 12r]; Alexander (1978a) ills. 169–78 [fols. 12r, 18r, 80r, 125r, 1r, 50v, 51r, 79v, 124v, 11v]; D.M. Wilson (1984) pl. 194 [fol. 7r (detail)]; F. Wormald (1984) ills. 44, 49 [fols. 125r, 12r (detail)]; G. Henderson (1987) pl. 198 [fol. 1r]; Webster—Backhouse (1991) 206–7 [fols. 124v, 125r]; M.P Brown (1996) pls. 36–40 [fols. 1r, 124v, 125r, 51r, 51v]; Stiegemann—Wemhoff (1999) II.447–9 [fols. 1r, 79v, 80r], III ('Beiträge') frontispiece [fol. 80r (detail)]; M.P. Brown (2003a) figs. 99 (a), 106, 132 [fols. 80r, 51r, 1r]; M.P. Brown (2007a) pls. 44–5 [fols. 11v, 51r]; M.P. Brown (2007b) 92 [fol. 125r], 94 [fol. 11v], 103 [fol. 18r], 105 [fol. 7r], 112 [fol. 51r]; Minnis—Roberts (2007) pls. 1–2 [fols. 1r, 80r]

ED: B. Fischer (1988–91) [gospel excerpts coll. as Ev]; McGurk (1994a) [repr. McGurk (1998) no. IX] [explanations of Hebrew names]; R. Gameson (2001d) 35 [no. 7] [colophon]

ST: Szerwiniack (1994) 193–4; M.P. Brown (2007b)

[Rome], Città del Vaticano, Biblioteca Apostolica Vaticana, Vat. lat. 304, flyleaf: see no. **900. 5**

907. 5. [Rome], Città del Vaticano, Biblioteca Apostolica Vaticana, Vat. lat. 3228

s. x^2, England?

Contents: Cicero, *Orationes Philippicae*

MS: L.D. Reynolds (1983) 75 and n. 122 [M.D. Reeve, R.H. Rouse]

ED: A.C. Clark (1918b) [Cicero, *Orationes Philippicae*, coll. as s]; Fedeli (1982) [Cicero, *Orationes Philippicae*, coll. as s]

ST: Lapidge (2006) 297

908. [Rome], Città del Vaticano, Biblioteca Apostolica Vaticana, Vat. lat. 3363

s. ix¹, Loire region (Orléans? Fleury?), prov. Wales or Cornwall or SW England s. ix ex., prov. England (Glastonbury?) by s. x med.

Contents: Boethius, *De consolatione Philosophiae* [*CPL* 878], with commentary (s. ix ex.) and annotations (s. x med.); glossary to Prudentius, *Psychomachia*

MS: Weinberger (1934) xxi; Courcelle (1939) 45–6, 121; Courcelle (1967) 121, 269–70, 405–6; Troncarelli (1973) 371–2, 377–8; Bolton (1977a) 35–7, 40; Rella (1977) 47–8 and nn., 76–7, 163, 168; Rella (1980) 115–16 [no. 34]; Parkes (1981) [repr. Parkes (1991) 259–62]; Troncarelli (1981) 137–51; Wittig (1983) 161 n. 20, 170 n. 37, 172 n. 41, 189–98; Dumville (1987) 176–7 and nn. 171, 176; Voigts (1988) 91 and n. 36; Mostert (1989) no. BF 1313; Budny (1992) 138; Parkes (1992) 291; Dumville (1993g) 3 n. 9, 51, 97; Parkes (1997a) 1 n. 2; Bischoff (1998–) III, no. 6877; Godden (2005); Hartzell (2006) no. 313; Wittig (2007) 193; Godden–Irvine (2009) I.xlvi; Wieland (2009) 149; Papahagi (2010) 24–7 and nn.; Wittig (2010) 252; D. Ganz (2012) 188 n. 3; Rankin (2012) 505 n. 111; R. Gameson (2012d) 347 and n. 11

FACS: Troncarelli (1981) pls. XI [fol. 9r], XIII–XVI [fols. 144v, 4r, 2v, 3r]; Parkes (1991) pls. 51–2 [fols. iii, x]; Parkes (1992) pl. 71 [fol. xi]; Ramsay et al. (1992) pl. 8 (d) [fol. iii (detail)]; Papahagi (2010) p. 167 [fol. 46r (detail)], pl. X [fol. 46r]

ED: Weinberger (1934) [Boethius, *De consolatione Philosophiae*, coll. as V]; Troncarelli (1981) 153–96 [commentary to Boethius, *De consolatione Philosophiae*]; Bieler (1984) [Boethius, *De consolatione Philosophiae*, coll. as V]; Parkes (1997a) 21–2 [base MS for *De consolatione Philosophiae* iii met. 12, lines 14–44]; Moreschini (2000) [Boethius, *De consolatione Philosophiae*, coll. as V]

ST: Bolton (1977b); Troncarelli (1981) 144–51; *BCLL* (1985) no. 1240; Godden (2005); Sims-Williams (2005); Godden (2011) 70, 71 n. 15, 76–80, 92; Jayatilaka (2011) 98, 117; Jayatilaka (2012) 673 and nn. 12–13

909. [Rome], Città del Vaticano, Biblioteca Apostolica Vaticana, Pal. lat. 68, fols. 1-46

s. viii, Northumbria, prov. Lorsch or Mainz by s. ix?

Contents: exegetical catena on the Psalms (Pss. XXXIX–CLI only); colophon

MS: Stevenson—De Rossi (1886) 12; Lindsay (1910) 67–70; Kenney (1929) no. 465; *CLA* I (1934) no. 78; Bischoff (1954b) no. 6A [repr. Bischoff (1966–81) I.238]; N.R. Ker (1957) no. 388; K. Hughes (1971) 59; McNamara (1973) 218–19, 281–4; McNamara (1979); Bischoff (1989a) 86 n. 98, 116–17; Biggs et al. (1990) 96 [C.D. Wright]; Bischoff (1990) 199 n. 83; T.J. Brown (1993a) 159, 239; Biggs (2007a) 24 [T.N. Hall]; Rushforth (2011) 57–8; R. Gameson (2012a) 37, 42 n. 117, 53 n. 182; R. Gameson (2012b) 112 n. 68

FACS: Lindsay (1910) pl. XII [fol. 46r (detail)]; R. Gameson (2001c) pl. 3 (b) [fol. 46r]

ED: Napier (1900) no. 78 [OE glosses]; Kenney (1929) 637 [lists editions by W. Stokes of Old Irish glosses]; McNamara (1986) [catena on the Psalms]; R. Gameson (2001d) 35 [no. 6] [colophon]

ST: *BCLL* (1985) no. 1261 [bibliography]; P.P. O'Neill (2002)

910. [Rome], Città del Vaticano, Biblioteca Apostolica Vaticana, Pal. lat. 235, fols. 4-29

s. viii in., Northumbria (Lindisfarne? Monkwearmouth-Jarrow?), prov. s. viii Germany (Lorsch? Fulda?)

Contents: Paulinus of Nola, *Carmina natalitia* [*CPL* 203] xv, xvi, xviii, xxviii, xxvii, xvii

MS: Stevenson—De Rossi (1886) 57–8; Hartel (1894) xxx–xxxi; *CLA* I (1934) no. 87; T.J. Brown (1982a) 111, 113, 114 [repr. T.J. Brown (1993a) 212, 214–15]; T.J. Brown (1984) 314, 320 [repr. T.J. Brown (1993a) 224, 232]; O'Brien-O'Keeffe (1987) 144; Brown—Mackay (1988); Bischoff (1989a) 86 n. 98, 120–1; Webster—Backhouse (1991) no. 85 [M.P. Brown]; M.P. Brown (1989a) 162; T.J. Brown (1993b) 191, 200; M.P. Brown (2003a) 262, 402; Häse (2002) 298–300; Story (2003) 263–5; Lapidge (2006) 37 n. 32, 324; Biggs (2007a) 15, 75; Dumville (2007f) 74; M.P. Brown (2012) 159

FACS: Brown—Mackay (1988) [complete facsimile]; M.P. Brown (1989a) pl. 6 [fol. 4r]; T.J. Brown (1993a) ill. 51 [fol. 8r (detail)]; M.P. Brown (2003a) fig. 108 [fol. 8r]

ED: Hartel (1894) [Paulinus, *carmina*, coll. as R]

ST: Mackay (1976); *BCLL* (1985) no. 713; Love (2012) 614

911. [Rome], Città del Vaticano, Biblioteca Apostolica Vaticana, Pal. lat. 259

s. viii/ix, England? or Anglo-Saxon centre on the Continent?

Contents: Gregory, *Homiliae in Hiezechielem* [*CPL* 1710] II. 2 (incomplete)—II. 10

MS: Stevenson—De Rossi (1886) 67; *CLA* I (1934) no. 90; Bischoff—Hofmann (1952) 8, 73; Bischoff (1966–81) I.78; Crick (1987) 186; Bischoff (1990) 94 n. 90; Bischoff (1998—) III, no. 6510a; T.N. Hall (2001) 131 and n. 62; Lapidge (2006) 79, 155, 305; Wieland (2009) 126; R. Gameson (2012a) 42, 51, 53 n. 182

911. 5. [Rome], Città del Vaticano, Biblioteca Apostolica Vaticana, Pal. lat. 554, fols. 5–13

s. viii/ix, England or Continent (Lorsch?), prov. s. ix¹ Lorsch

Contents: *Poenitentiale Egberti* [*CPL* 1887], Prologue and chs. i–xiii; *Edictio Bonifatii*

MS: H.J. Schmitz (1883) 566, 573; Stevenson—De Rossi (1886) 177; *CLA* I (1934) no. 95; McNeill—Gamer (1938) 55 n. 14, 67, 435–6, 449; Frantzen (1983a) 26, 30 n. 37; Frantzen (1983b) 70 n. 36, 72–3 and nn. 47–8; Bischoff (1989a) 57–8, 86 n. 98, 92 n. 42, 124–5; Haggenmüller (1991) 108–9, 149 *et passim*; Bischoff (1998—) III, no. 6538; Lapidge (2006) 155

ED: H.J. Schmitz (1898) 660–73 [*Poenitentiale Egberti* coll. as α]

912. [Rome], Città del Vaticano, Biblioteca Apostolica Vaticana, Reg. lat. 12

s. xi²/⁴, prob. Canterbury CC, prov. Bury St Edmunds, (prov. Jouarre s. xii)

Contents: liturgical calendar; computus material; Psalterium Gallicanum; Ps. CLI; canticles; litany; prayers (*orationes post psalterium*)

MS: Ehrensberger (1897) 34–6; Wilmart (1930) 198–200; Wilmart (1937–45) I.30–5; N.R. Ker (1964) 22; Salmon (1968–72) I.23 [no. 40]; R.M. Thomson (1972) 622–3 and n. 25, 643 n. 167; Lapidge (1991a) 84–5; Dumville (1993f) 99 [no. 38]; Dumville (1993g) 33–4 and nn., 37, 41–3, 47–8, 60–2, 64 n. 277, 78 n. 360; Noel (1995) 150–69 *et passim*; Pulsiano

(2001a) xxx; Rushforth (2002); Rushforth—Orchard (2005) 568 and nn.; Biggs (2007a) 16–17; Chardonnens (2007b) 544, 554; Rushforth (2008a) 40–1; R. Gameson (2012b) 95 and n. 3; Rushforth (2012) 209 and n. 75; Toswell (2012) 471

DEC: F. Wormald (1945) 109 n. 9, 125, 132 [repr. F. Wormald (1984) 64, 71, 173 n. 9]; F. Wormald (1952) 47–9, 79 [no. 56]; Dodwell (1954) 10, 27, 74, 79; R.M. Harris (1960); F. Wormald (1962) 1, 7, 8, 13 [repr. F. Wormald (1984) 123, 129, 131, 135]; Heimann (1966); Dodwell (1971b) 80, 220 n. 36; F. Wormald (1971b) 312 and n. 2 [repr. F. Wormald (1984) 83 and n. 26]; Raw (1976) 137–8 and nn.; E. Temple (1976) no. 84; Brownrigg (1978) 248 n. 2, 250 n. 1; D.M. Wilson (1984) 190; F. Wormald (1984) 106; F. Wormald (1984b) 120; Ohlgren (1986) no. 189; Raw (1990) 249–50; R. Gameson (1992a) 205, 211–13; R. Gameson (1995b) 17, 38–40, 42, 49–50, 53, 65–7, 84, 100–2, 108, 114–15, 119–21, 139, 162, 164 *et passim*; Keefer (2007b) 99; Pulsiano (2007) 119; Karkov (2009) 235; R. Gameson (2012c) 269 and n. 58, 284 and n. 124, 289 n. 138

FACS: *NPS* II, pls. 166–8 [fols. 35r, 65v, 73v, 109v (all details)]; F. Wormald (1952) pls. 26–8 [fols. 66v, 72r, 90v, 74r, 37v, 108r (all details)]; Dodwell (1954) pl. 59 (c) [fol. 92r]; M.W. Evans (1969) pl. 21 [fol. 87v]; E. Temple (1976) ills. 262–4 [fols. 62r, 36r, 73v]; D.M. Wilson (1984) pl. 238 [fol. 90v (detail)]; R. Gameson (1991) fig. 16 [fol. 88v]; Ohlgren (1992) pls. 3.1–49 [fols. 21r, 21v, 22r, 22v, 24r, 25r, 27v, 28r, 29r, 30r, 35r, 36r, 37v, 40r, 54r, 62r, 62v, 63v, 66v, 68v, 69v, 70v, 71v, 72r, 73v, 74r, 78v, 80r, 81r, 83v, 87v, 88r, 88v, 90v, 92r, 93r, 95r, 98r, 103r, 107v, 108r, 109r, 109v, 117r, 118r, 120v, 168v, 169r]; Ramsay et al. (1992) pls. 15–16 [fols. 73v, 103r]; R. Gameson (1995b) pls. 15 (a)–(b) [fols. 78v, 35r]; Noel (1995) ills. 65 [fol. 36r], 70 [fol. 25r], 72 [fol. 120v], 73 [fol. 109r], 74 [fol. 107v], 76 [fol. 68v]

ED: Wilmart (1930) [prayers]; F. Wormald (1934) 239–51 [liturgical calendar (no. 19)]; Lapidge (1991a) 296–9 [litany]; Corrêa (1996) 319–20 [*Orationes post psalterium*]; Pulsiano (2001a) [Pss. I–L coll. as ʋ]; Chardonnens (2007b) 289, 391 [prognostics in liturgical calendar]; Rushforth (2008a) no. 18 [liturgical calendar]

ST: Gasquet—Bishop (1908) 60 n. 1, 147 n. 1; Wilmart (1930); Kotzor (1981) I.303*–311*; Thacker (1992) 242 n. 142; Keynes (1994b) 56 n. 65; Gransden (1995b) 36–9; Borst (2001) I.292; Rushforth (2005); Chardonnens (2007a) 320 n. 8; Pfaff (2009) 195–6

912. 5. [Rome], Città del Vaticano, Biblioteca Apostolica Vaticana, Reg. lat. 40, fols. i, ii

s. xi ex., Canterbury?

Contents: psalter (f) and prayer [*Oratio Gregorii papae*] (f)

MS: Wilmart (1930) 209; Wilmart (1937–45) I.95–6

913. [Rome], Città del Vaticano, Biblioteca Apostolica Vaticana, Reg. lat. 204

s. xi in., Canterbury StA (CC?), (prov. Bonneval by s. xiv)

Contents: Office of St Cuthbert (f); Bede, *Vita S. Cudbercti* (verse) [*CPL* 1380; *BHL* 2020], with glosses; note on the Six Ages of Man

MS: H.M. Bannister (1913) no. 291; Jaager (1935) 29, 33; Wilmart (1937–45) I.482–3; N.R. Ker (1957) no. 389; T.A.M. Bishop (1959–63b) 413, 417; T.A.M. Bishop (1966) xx; Sims-Williams (1990) 337; Dumville (1992a) 109 n. 81; Dumville (1993f) 99 [no. 39]; Lapidge (1995c) 130, 143 and n. 37; Sole (1998) 124–8; Hartzell (2006) no. 314; Rankin (2012) 490–1; Scragg (2012a) no. 1025

FACS: H.M. Bannister (1913) pl. 62 (a) [fol. 1r]

ED: Napier (1900) no. 32 [OE glosses to Bede, *Vita metrica S. Cudbercti*]; Jaager (1935) [Bede, *Vita metrica S. Cudbercti*, coll. as R]; Hohler—Hughes (1956) 161, 185–6 [Office fragment coll. as Y]; Sole (1998) 143–4 [Office fragment coll. as Y]

914. [Rome], Città del Vaticano, Biblioteca Apostolica Vaticana, Reg. lat. 338, fols. 64–126

s. x^2 or x/xi, N France or Germany?, prov. England s. xi^1?

Contents: 'Metrical Calendar of York' (incomplete); Amalarius (?), *Eclogae de ordine Romano*; Caesarius, *Sermo* x ('De decem plagis et praeceptis') [*CPL* 1008]; *horologium*; seven alphabets [two Hebrew, one Greek, one 'Chaldaean', one 'Egyptian', one runic, one of obscure origin]; two pontifical *ordines* [*Ad clericum faciendum*; *Confirmatio*]; benedictional; *Benedictio nuptiarum*; pseudo-Jerome, *Breuiarium in Psalmos* [*CPL* 629; *BCLL* 343]; hymnal (incomplete); additions (s. xi^1): charm against fever*; note on blood-letting*; prayer *Pro iter agentibus*

MS: Ehrensberger (1897) 564–6; H.M. Bannister (1913) I.11, 75; Wilmart (1937–45) II.258–63; R. Derolez (1954) 237–48 *et passim*; N.R. Ker

(1957) no. 390; D.H. Turner (1960) 362; Gneuss (1968) 44 and n. 13; Salmon (1968–72) I.51 [no. 98]; Moeller (1971–9) III.101; Lapidge (1984) 335–6 and nn. [repr. Lapidge (1993a) 352–3 and nn.]; Dumville (1992a) 69, 86, 136–7; Dumville (1993f) 99 [no. 40]; Corrêa (1996) 303–5 and n. 75; Lapidge (2006) 295; Wieland (2009) 125, 135; Rushforth (2011) 59; Scragg (2012a) nos. 1026–7

FACS: H.M. Bannister (1913) pl. 4 (a) [fol. 114r]

ED: W. Stokes (1891) 144 [charm against fever*; note on blood–letting*]; *AH* LI (1908) [hymns coll. under various sigla]; Hanssens (1948–50) III.229–65 [Amalarius, *Eclogae de ordine Romano*, coll. as R2]; R. Derolez (1954) 242–7 [runic alphabet]; N.R. Ker (1957) no. 390 [charm against fever*; note on blood-letting*]

ST: Biggs et al. (1990) 98–9 [C.D. Wright]; Mordek (1995) 822–3 [on fols. 1–63]; Rasmussen (1998) 413–14; C.A. Jones (2004) 328

915. [Rome], Città del Vaticano, Biblioteca Apostolica Vaticana, Reg. lat. 489, fols. 61-124

s. xi¹ or earlier, Canterbury CC

Contents: a 'Martinellus': Sulpicius Severus, *Vita S. Martini* [*CPL* 475; *BHL* 5610], *Epistulae* [*CPL* 476], *Dialogi* [*CPL* 477]; Gregory of Tours, extracts from *Historia Francorum* [*CPL* 1023], *De uirtutibus S. Martini* [*CPL* 1024; cf. *BHL* 5618d], and *Vita S. Bricii* [BHL 1452, from *Historia Francorum* II. 1]

MS: Wilmart (1937–45) II.682–5; T.A.M. Bishop (1971) xvi n. 2, xxv–xxvi; Dumville (1993g) 9 n. 4, 98 n. 79, 99; Lapidge (2006) 307, 333, 334; Wieland (2009) 143; R. Gameson (2012a) 72 n. 247

916. [Rome], Città del Vaticano, Biblioteca Apostolica Vaticana, Reg. lat. 497, fol. 71

s. xi, (prov. Trier, s. xii?)

Contents: Orosius, *Historiae aduersum paganos* [*CPL* 571] in OE translation* (f); poem (inc. 'Treberis urbs multis bellorum compta triumphis') added s. xii

MS: Ehrensberger (1897) 100–1; Wilmart (1937–45) II.713; N.R. Ker (1957) no. 391; Bately (1964); Bately (1980) xxvi, xxxv; Luiselli Fadda (1980) 7–22; Szarmach (1981c); R. Gameson (2012d) 362 and n. 71; Scragg (2012a) no. 1028

FACS: Szarmach (1981c) 35 [fol. 71v]

ED: Bately (1964) [base MS for fragment of OE Orosius]; Bately (1980) 109 [OE Orosius coll. as V]; Luiselli Fadda (1980) 10 [poem added on fol. 71v]

LANG: Bately (1980) liv

917. [Rome], Città del Vaticano, Biblioteca Apostolica Vaticana, Reg. lat. 946, fols. 72–6

s. xi^1, (prov. Normandy, prob. Avranches, in or before s. xii)

Contents: legal decree (X Æthelred*), prob. from a service-book

MS: Liebermann (1903–16) I.xlii, 269 n.; N.R. Ker (1957) no. 392; Dumville (1993f) 99 [no. 41]; R. Gameson (2003) 158–9; R. Gameson (2012d) 365 n. 89; Scragg (2012a) nos. 1029–30; P. Wormald (2012) 535 [no. 16]

ED: Liebermann (1903–16) I.269–70 (left-hand column) [base MS (= Vr) for X Atr]

ST: Whitelock (1976) 24 [repr. Whitelock (1981b) no. XIV]

918. [Rome], Città del Vaticano, Biblioteca Apostolica Vaticana, Reg. lat. 1283, fol. 114

s. x^2 and xi^1

Contents: grammatical note; excerpts from Augustine (s. x^2); excerpts from Ælfric, *De temporibus anni** [chs. iv. 31–3 and i. 19–21] (s. xi^1)

MS: Henel (1942a) xxix; N.R. Ker (1957) no. 393; T.A.M. Bishop (1971) xii–xiii n. 2; Mostert (1989) sub no. BF 1488; M. Blake (2009) 18; Scragg (2012a) no. 1031

ED: Steinmeyer (1880) 192 [Ælfric, *De temporibus anni*; see corrections by N.R. Ker (1957) no. 393]; Henel (1942a) [Ælfric, *De temporibus anni*, coll. as H]; M. Blake (2009) 99–100 [variants to Ælfric, *De temporibus anni*, recorded as H]

919. [Rome], Città del Vaticano, Biblioteca Apostolica Vaticana, Reg. lat. 1671

s. x^2 or x/xi or xi$^{1/4}$, Worcester

Contents: Vergil, *Bucolica*, *Georgica* and *Aeneid*, all with glosses (s. xi) derived partly from Servius, and (*Georgica*, *Aeneid*) with *argumenta* by pseudo-Ovid; excerpts from pseudo-Vergil, *Culex*, and Ovid, *Metamorphoses* (xiii. 100); five Latin poems [SK 12542, 10279 and 16845 (pseudo-Vergil), 7221, 638]

MS: T.A.M. Bishop (1964–8b) 249 n. 1; T.A.M. Bishop (1971) xviii, 17; Pellegrin et al. (1975–91) II/i.352–4; Hunter Blair (1976) 252 and nn.; Rella (1977) 84, 162; Munk Olsen (1982–) II.782; Lapidge (1982a) 101 and nn. 16, 18 [repr. Lapidge (1996b) 458–9 and nn. 16, 18; 516]; Dumville (1993f) 99 [no. 42]; Dumville (1993g) 69–75; Baswell (1995) 287; Bullough (1996) 20 n. 7; R. Gameson (1996a) 205–10 and nn.; Lapidge (2006) 323, 336; Wieland (2009) 148; R. Gameson (2012a) 29 and n. 61, 67 n. 232, 72 n. 245

DEC: E. Temple (1976) no. 30 (ix); Ohlgren (1986) no. 126; R. Gameson (1996a) 208-9

FACS: T.A.M. Bishop (1971) pl. XVII [fol. 90r]; Dumville (1993g) pls. VI–VII [fols. 2r, 216v (details)]; R. Gameson (1996a) pls. 3–4 [fols. 1r, 90r]

ST: L.D. Reynolds (1983) xxxii n., 128; Baswell (1995) 287, 324 n. 59, 326 n. 76; Ziolkowski (2007) 45 n. 16, 274, 286

919. 2. Rouen, Bibliothèque municipale, 24 (A. 41)

s. x, England?; prov. Saint-Évroul

Contents: *psalterium duplex* (Gallicanum and Hebraicum), glossed

MS: *Cat. gén. Dép.* (Octavo) I.7 [Omont]; Kenney no. 489; Nortier (1957) 223; Chibnall (1969–80) II.42 n. 1

919. 3. Rouen, Bibliothèque municipale, 26 (A. 292)

s. ix[1] or ix med., N France; additions made in England, s. x; whole MS prov. England s. x? prov. Jumièges s. xi?

Contents: Old Testament books (Prouerbia Salomonis, Ecclesiastes, Canticum canticorum); commentary on the Canticum canticorum (excerpted from Alcuin's commentary on the same text); Alcuin, *Carm.* lxxviii [SK 7355]; proverbs; poem [WIC 4803]; Sapientia (OT book); Augustine, *Enchiridion* [*CPL* 295]; Isidore, *Etymologiae* [*CPL* 1186] XI. i–ii; tract on the Office; tract on the temperaments; Gregory and Augustine of Canterbury, *Libellus responsionum* [Responsio IX]; exposition of the Mass (inc. 'Primum in ordine'); computistical, astronomical and other scientific treatises, including excerpt from

Isidore, *De natura rerum* [*CPL* 1188] and a tract on the winds; *Ordo Romanus* XIII A; Mass prayers; Office antiphons and responsories. Later additions to MS: drawing on fol. 48 (added in England, s. x?); verses from Hrabanus Maurus, *De laudibus S. Crucis* (s. x²); and poem [WIC 4803, added s. xi/xii]

MS: *Cat. gén. Dép.* (Octavo) I.8–10 [Omont]; Hesbert (1954b); Corbin (1955) 914; Cordoliani (1955); Samaran—Marichal et al. (1959–85) VII.261; Gamber (1968–88) no. 1305; Avril (1975b) no. 5; Hartzell (1980); Raw (1990) 243–4; *CPL* (1995) no. 1934a; Bischoff (1998—) III, no. 5367; R. Gameson (2003) 138 and nn., 156 [no. 14]; Hartzell (2006) no. 315; Lapidge (2006) 172, 289, 311; W. Schipper (2009) 284–5 and nn.; Wieland (2009) 131, 133, 134, 151; R. Gameson (2012a) 63 and n. 223; R. Gameson (2012d) 365 and n. 87

DEC: Dodwell (1954) 8–9; Hartzell (1982); Ohlgren (1986) no. 226; Raw (1990) 83 n. 58, 111–12, 119, 124, 243–4

FACS: Dodwell (1954) pl. 5 (b) [fol. 48r]; Hartzell (1982) 84 [fol. 48r]; Raw (1990) pl. V (b) [fol. 48r]

ST: *CPPM* II, no. 2371b [comm. on Canticum canticorum]; *CSLMA* II (1999) 24, 117, 379; R. Gameson (2012d) 344 and n. 2

919. 6. Rouen, Bibliothèque municipale, 32 (A. 21)

s. xi ex., Abingdon (prov. Jumièges s. xii)

Contents: colophon; gospels (incomplete)

MS: *Cat. gén. Dép.* (Octavo) I.12 [Omont]; Hesbert (1955b) 902; Nortier–Marchand (1955) 602–3; Ortenberg (1992) 273; R. Gameson (1999a) no. 818; R. Gameson (2003) 159; Hartzell (2006) no. 316; R. Gameson (2012d) 365 and n. 90; Webber (2012) 220 and n. 46

DEC: R. Gameson (2012c) 273 and n. 74

FACS: R. Gameson (2003) pl. 11 [fol. 64r (detail)]

920. Rouen, Bibliothèque municipale, 231 (A. 44)

s. xi ex., prob. Canterbury StA (prov. Jumièges)

Contents: Psalterium Gallicanum (incomplete); canticles; litany; prayers; hymnal; Monastic canticles

MS: *Cat. gén. Dép.* (Octavo) I.45–6 [Omont]; Leroquais (1940–1) II.194–7; Nortier–Marchand (1955) 602; Samaran—Marichal et al.

(1959–85) VII.273; Nortier (1966) 146 n. 29, 165; Gneuss (1968) 82
n. 18; Avril (1975b) no. 85; A.G. Watson (1987a) 13; Lapidge (1991a)
81; Dumville (1993f) 99 [no. 44]; R. Gameson (1995a) 126–7, 129
n. 130, 144; Heslop (1995) 64, 84–5; Springer (1995) 181; Saenger
(1997) 210 and n. 56; R. Gameson (1999a) no. 819; Pulsiano (2001a)
xxx; Toswell (2012) 474 and n. 35

FACS: R. Gameson (1995a) pls. 10 (a)–(b) [fols. 149r, 198r]

ED: Gjerløw (1961) 132–7 [prayers]; Lapidge (1991a) 265–9 [litany];
Pulsiano (2001a) [Pss. IX.8 — L, coll. as ψ]

ST: Mearns (1913) xv *et passim*; Gjerløw (1961) 20, 22 *et passim*;
Korhammer (1976) xvi, 9, 25, 52–3, 119–21, 147

921. Rouen, Bibliothèque municipale, 274 (Y. 6) (the 'Sacramentary of Robert of Jumièges')

1014×1023, prov. (and origin?) Canterbury CC, prov. Jumièges s xi med.

Contents: liturgical calendar; computus material; sacramentary (including litany)

MS: *Cat. gén. Dép.* (Octavo) I.53 [Omont]; Warren (1883) 275–93; H.A.
Wilson (1896) xix–lxx; Fehr (1921) 27–8; Leroquais (1924) I.99; Atkins
(1928); Tolhurst (1933); Förster (1943) 39; Hesbert (1955c) 722,
729–31, 733; Hohler (1955); Nortier–Marchand (1955) 602; Tolhurst
(1955); N.R. Ker (1957) no. 377; N.R. Ker (1964) 104; T.A.M. Bishop
(1967a) 39–41; T.A.M. Bishop (1971) xv; Hohler (1975) 74 and nn.;
Grant (1979) 33–40; Backhouse et al. (1984b) no. 50 [D.H. Turner];
Gerchow (1988) 224, 331; Heslop (1990) 155, 182; Dumville (1991–5)
52; Lapidge (1991a) 82; Dumville (1992a) 25–6, 37–8 *et passim*; Lapidge
(1992a) 105–6 and nn. [repr. Lapidge (1993a) 393–4 and nn.]; Dumville
(1993g) 116–18 and nn., 139; N. Orchard (1995c) 4 n. 12; Pfaff (1995)
15–19; Saenger (1997) 210 and nn.; N. Orchard (2002) I.61 *et passim*;
R. Gameson (2003) 133, 157–8; C.A. Jones (2004) 345 n. 82; Hartzell
(2006) no. 317; O'Brien O'Keeffe (2006) 269; Chardonnens (2007b)
544, 554; Rushforth (2008a) 31–2; Wieland (2009) 121; *ASMMF* XVIII
(2012) 117–25 [no. 445; Lucas]; R. Gameson (2012a) 34 n. 78, 43 and
n. 126, 49–50, 70 n. 240, 80 n. 284; R. Gameson (2012d) 358 and n. 53;
Pfaff (2012) 457 and n. 25; Raw (2012) 460; Scragg (2012a) no. 1002;
Winterbottom — Lapidge (2012) cxxxix–cxli

DEC: Alexander (1970a) 114 *et passim*; Dodwell (1971b) 86, 221 n. 74;
Alexander (1975a) 149–50; E. Temple (1976) no. 72 [with extensive

bibliography]; D.M. Wilson (1984) 174; Ohlgren (1986) no. 177; Raw (1990) 244–5 *et passim*; R. Gameson (1995b) 16, 30, 32–5, 59, 110, 114, 116, 148, 159, 163, 166, 177, 189, 196, 206, 210 *et passim*; McGurk— Rosenthal (2006) 196 n. 55; Rushforth (2007) 44, 46; Karkov (2009) 224; Withers (2011) 260, 262; R. Gameson (2012c) 270 and n. 59, 283 and n. 118

FACS: H.A. Wilson (1896) pls. I–XV [fols. 32v, 33r, 36v, 37r, 71r, 71v, 72r, 72v, 81v, 84v, 132v, 164v, 158v, 207r, 228r]; Leroquais (1924) IV, pls. XX–XXIII [fols. 71v, 72r, 81v, 158v]; Rice (1952) pls. 53–5 [fols. 37r, 71v, 72r, 84v, 81v, 72v]; E. Temple (1976) ills. 237–40 [fols. 36v, 72r, 81v, 164r]; Backhouse et al. (1984b) pl. XIV [fol. 32v]; D.M. Wilson (1984) pl. 265 [fol. 72r]; Raw (1990) pl. XV [fol. 71v]; R. Gameson (2003) pls. 3, 15 [fols. 25v, 114r]; Rushforth (2007) 46 [fol. 72r]; *ASMMF* XVIII (2012) no. 445 [complete facsimile]

ED: H.A. Wilson (1896) [complete MS]; Muir (1988) xxix *et passim* [five prayers coll. as J]; Lapidge (1991a) 270–2 [litany from service for Visitation of the Sick and Dying]; Rushforth (2008a) no. 12 [liturgical calendar]; Winterbottom—Lapidge (2012) cxl [mass-set for St Dunstan]

ST: Gasquet—Bishop (1908) 160–1 *et passim*; Henel (1934); Dubois (1955); Bullough (1977) 50 n. 61b; Kotzor (1981) I.302*–311*; Baker— Lapidge (1995) xlviii; Heslop (1995) 56, 59 n., 79; Borst (2001) I.166–7; N. Orchard (2005) lxii *et passim*; Pfaff (2009) 88–91

922. Rouen, Bibliothèque municipale, 368 (A. 27) (the 'Lanalet Pontifical')

s. xi in. or xi¹, SW England (St Germans?), prov. Crediton by 1027×1046 (or Wells before 1014?), (prov. Jumièges)

Contents: pontifical (including litanies) and benedictional, including Prologue to *Poenitentiale Egberti* [*CPL* 1887], Gerbald of Liège, First Capitulary, and First English Coronation *ordo*

MS: *Cat. gén. Dép.* (Octavo) I.69–70 [Omont]; Liebermann (1903–16) I.xxxviii; Leroquais (1937) II.287; Doble (1937); Stéphan (1955); N.R. Ker (1957) no. 374; Gamber (1968–88) no. 1565; D.H. Turner (1971) xxxiii–xxxix; Prescott (1987) 128 and nn., 141–7; Dumville (1991) 51–2; Haggenmüller (1991) 98; Lapidge (1991a) 82–3; Dumville (1992a) 69, 86–7, 91–2 and nn., 117 and nn.; Conner (1993) 43–4; Dumville (1993f) 99 [no. 43]; Dumville (1993g) 60–1, 145 n. 23; Nelson—Pfaff (1995) 93; Saenger (1997) 201 and n. 57; N. Orchard (2002) I.76; R. Gameson (2003)

155–6; C.A. Jones (2004) 343 n. 73, 344 nn. 78–80; C.A. Jones (2005a)
113, 232; N. Orchard (2005) ciii, clxxxiii–cxci; Hartzell (2006) no. 318;
O'Brien O'Keeffe (2006) 269–70; *ASMMF* XVIII (2012) 85–96 [no. 442;
Lucas]; Rankin (2012) 491–2 and n. 40; Scragg (2012a) nos. 1003–5

DEC: F. Wormald (1952) 79–80 [no. 57]; E. Temple (1976) no. 90;
Ohlgren (1986) no. 195; Raw (1990) 127 and n. 97, 243; R. Gameson
(1995b) 35 n. 128, 184

FACS: Doble (1937) pl. I [fol. 2r]; Leroquais (1937) pls. I–II [fols. 1v, 2v];
Rice (1952) pl. 70 (a) [fol. 2v]; E. Temple (1976) ill. 256 [fol. 1v];
Dumville (1993g) pl. V [fol. 183v (detail)]; *ASMMF* XVIII (2012)
no. 442 [complete facsimile]

ED: Doble (1937) [complete MS]; Moeller (1971–9) [benedictions coll. as
LAN]; Lapidge (1991a) 273–9 [three litanies: two from Dedication of
a Church, one from Visitation of the Sick and Dying]

ST: Fehr (1921) 28–30; Hesbert (1955b) 902, 906; Rella (1977) 107; *BCLL*
(1985) no. 1285; Nelson (1986b); Rasmussen (1998) 173–87, 189–95,
211–16, 218–24; Cross—Hamer (1999) 35; Pfaff (1999a) 6, 12–14, 16;
Pfaff (2009) 74 n. 34

923. Rouen, Bibliothèque municipale, 369 (Y. 7) (the 'Benedictional of Archbishop Robert')

s. x$^{4/4}$ (s. xi$^{2/4}$?) Winchester NM (for Selsey?), (prov. Rouen cathedral
from s. xii^1)

Contents: benedictional; pontifical (including litanies and Second English
Coronation *ordo*)

MS: *Cat. gén. Dép.* (Octavo) I.70 [Omont]; Liebermann (1903–16) I.xxxix;
H.A. Wilson (1903); Leroquais (1937) II.300–5; Samaran—Marichal
et al. (1959–85) VII.578; D.H. Turner (1971) xvi–xxviii *et passim*;
Backhouse et al. (1984b) no. 40 [D.H. Turner]; Prescott (1987) 124–6,
141–7; Dumville (1991) 53; Lapidge (1991a) 83; Dumville (1992a) 69,
87–9 and nn., 91 and n. 160; Dumville (1993f) 99 [no. 46]; Dumville
(1993g) 65 n. 281; Nelson—Pfaff (1995) 94; N. Orchard (2002) I.70–1,
265 *et passim*; R. Gameson (2003) 158; C.A. Jones (2004) 340 nn. 62–3,
341 n. 64, 344 nn. 77–80; C.A. Jones (2005a) 113, 232; N. Orchard
(2005) c–ci, cxxix–cxxxvi, clxviii; Hartzell (2006) no. 319; O'Brien
O'Keeffe (2006) 270; Biggs (2007a) 34 [Clayton]; R. Gameson (2012a)
41 n. 107, 60 n. 202, 90 n. 330; R. Gameson (2012b) 109 and n. 50;
R. Gameson (2012d) 358 and n. 53; Rushforth (2012) 205 and n. 51

DEC: F. Wormald (1945) 131–2 [repr. F. Wormald (1984) 70, 173 n. 9];
F. Wormald (1959) 9, 15 [repr. F. Wormald (1984) 87, 96]; Alexander
(1970a) 132, 152, 169, 237; Dodwell (1971b) 86, 145, 221 n. 74; E.
Temple (1976) no. 24; D.M. Wilson (1984) 169; F. Wormald (1984b)
116; Ohlgren (1986) no. 112; Raw (1990) 94, 133, 152, 156, 245;
R. Gameson (1995b) 30–2, 47–8, 143–4, 148, 158, 187, 196, 205, 209;
Karkov (2009) 224; R. Gameson (2012c) 258–9 and nn. 23, 28–9 and 31

FACS: H.A. Wilson (1903) pls. I–VI [fols. 29v, 30r, 67v, 95r, 187v, 191v];
Leroquais (1937) pls. III–VI [fols. 21v, 22r, 29v, 54v]; E. Temple (1976)
ills. 87, 89 [fols. 54r, 21v]; Backhouse et al. (1984b) pl. VIII [fol. 21v];
F. Wormald (1984) ill. 108 [fol. 54v]; Huglo (1987) pl. XV [fol. 97r];
R. Gameson (1995b) pl. 11 (b) [fol. 54v]

ED: H.A. Wilson (1903) [complete MS]; Lapidge (1991a) 280-2 [two
litanies from Dedication of a Church]

ST: Rella (1977) 57, 107; O'Brien O'Keeffe (1982); Conner (1993);
Rasmussen (1998) 173–85, 187–210, 217–29, 265–70, 274–80, 286–306;
Pfaff (1999a)

924. Rouen, Bibliothèque municipale, 506 (A. 337)

s. x ex., prob. Canterbury CC, prov. Jumièges by s. xi[2] or xii

Contents: Gregory, *Dialogi* [*CPL* 1713] (part)

MS: *Cat. gén. Dép.* (Octavo) I.111 [Omont]; T.A.M. Bishop (1971) xxvi;
Avril (1975b) no. 6; Yerkes (1976a); Rella (1977) 159; Yerkes (1979)
xvii–xviii; R. Gameson (2003) 138–40 and nn., 156; Lapidge (2006) 304;
R. Gameson (2012d) 365 and n. 86

DEC: Alexander (1970a) 141, 236 n. 4; Brownrigg (1978) 259 n. 6, 260
n. 3; Ohlgren (1986) no. 227; R. Gameson (1992a) 191 n. 21, 193 n. 30,
200 n. 54, 207 n. 84; R. Gameson (1995b) 228

FACS: R. Gameson (2003) fig. 6 [fol. 55r], pl. 2 [fol. 51r]

925. Rouen, Bibliothèque municipale, 1382 (U. 109), fols. 173–98

s. xi[1] or xi med., (prov. Jumièges s. xii)

Contents: (a version of Wulfstan's 'Handbook'): *Ordo Romanus* XIII A;
Institutio beati Amalarii (excerpts from *Liber officialis*); sermon *De
ieiunio quattuor temporum*; *De ecclesiastica consuetudine* (including
excerpts from Amalarius, *Liber officialis* and the *Regularis concordia*);
Wulfstan's 'Canon Law Collection' ('Excerptiones pseudo-Egberti',

recension A); excerpts from the *Admonitio generalis* (789) and from the *Institutio canonicorum* (of the Aachen Council of 816); prologue to the *Poenitentiale Egberti* [*CPL* 1887]; First Capitulary of Gerbald of Liège

MS: *Cat. gén. Dép.* (Octavo) I.354–6 [Omont]; Aronstam (1974); Haggenmüller (1991) 98; Cross (1992); Mordek (1995) 643–4; Springer (1995) 181–2; Cross—Hamer (1997); C.A. Jones (1998a) 235 and n. 8, 237–9; Cross—Hamer (1999) *passim*; Sauer (2000) 342, 373 and n. 76 *et passim*; R. Gameson (2003) 157; T.N. Hall (2004a) 97; J. Hill (2004) 321; C.A. Jones (2004) 330 n. 22, 347, 351–2; A. Orchard (2004) 66 n. 15; Ambrose (2005) 114; Wieland (2009) 140; A. Orchard (2012) 697 [no. 17]

ED: C.A. Jones (1998a) 257–71 [two texts from Wulfstan's 'Handbook' coll. as R]; Cross—Hamer (1999) 66–113 [Wulfstan's 'Canon Law Collection' (recension A), coll. as R (complete MS section)]

ST: Fehr (1914/1966) xcvii–cx

925. 5. Rouen, Bibliothèque municipale, 1384 (U. 26), fols. 1–4

s. x$^{4/4}$, England or Jumièges (English scribes)?, prov. Jumièges s. xi^2

Contents: pseudo-Alcuin, *Vita prima S. Iudoci* [*BHL* 4504]

MS: *Cat. gén. Dép.* (Octavo) I. 358–60 [Omont]; Le Bourdellès (1993) 910–15; Lapidge (2000b) 260 and n. 16; Biggs et al. (2001) 274–5; R. Gameson (2003) 156; Upchurch (2007) xii, 110

ED: Le Bourdellès (1993) 916–28 [*Vita prima S. Iudoci* coll. as R]; Upchurch (2007) 114–71 [*Vita prima S. Iudoci* coll. as R]

ST: *BCLL* (1985) no. 1315; Le Bourdellès (1995); *CSLMA* II (1999) 497–8; Lapidge (2000b) 259–64

926. Rouen, Bibliothèque municipale, 1385 (U. 107), fols. 20–7

s. x/xi, Winchester or Worcester?, (prov. Jumièges)

Contents: *Memoriale qualiter* (incomplete); 'Acta praeliminaria' of Council of Aachen (816); Office from Holy Thursday to Holy Saturday

MS: *Cat. gén. Dép.* (Octavo) I.360–2 [Omont]; Delisle (1903); Hesbert (1954a) 38–40; Morgand (1955); Morgand (1963) 191–2; Semmler (1963) 434; T.A.M. Bishop (1971) xxv, 18; Gretsch (1973) 27; Lapidge— Winterbottom (1991b) lvii and nn.; Dumville (1993f) 99 [no. 45]; Dumville (1993g) 8 n. 4, 55; Mordek (1995) 642–3; R. Gameson (2003)

157; Gretsch (2003) 118; Lapidge (2003a) 238 n. 134; Wieland (2009) 140; *ASMMF* XVIII (2012) 107–16 [no. 444; Lucas]; Scragg (2012a) no. 1006

FACS: *ASMMF* XVIII (2012) no. 444 [complete facsimile]

ED: Morgand (1963) 229–61 [*Memoriale qualiter* coll. as G]; Semmler (1963) 435–6 [base MS for 'Acta praeliminaria' of Council of Aachen]

927. Rouen, Bibliothèque municipale, 1385 (U. 107), fols. 28–85

s. x ex., Winchester OM, (prov. Jumièges)

Contents: Wulfstan of Winchester, Hymn to St Swithun [SK 1530]; Lantfred, *Translatio et miracula S. Swithuni* [*BHL* 7944–6]; Wulfstan of Winchester, Hymns to SS. Birinus [SK 474], Swithun [SK 1443 (Rouen redaction)], Æthelwold [SK 591]; Latin metrical version of *Hymnus trium puerorum*, preceded by a Prohemium [SK 11045: 'O sator omniparens, es qui per secula clemens']

MS: *Cat. gén. Dép.* (Octavo) I.360–2 [Omont]; Delisle (1903); N.R. Ker (1957) no. 376; Lapidge—Winterbottom (1991b) xxviii–xxix and nn., lvii and nn.; R. Gameson (2003) 157; Lapidge (2003a) 238–9, 787, 790; Hartzell (2006) no. 320; *ASMMF* XVIII (2012) 107–16 [no. 444; Lucas]; R. Gameson (2012a) 66 n. 229; R. Gameson (2012d) 365 and n. 86; Scragg (2012a) no. 1006

FACS: Lapidge (2003a) pl. I [fol. 82v]; *ASMMF* XVIII (2012) no. 444 [complete facsimile]

ED: *AH* XLVIII (1905) 9–18 [four hymns from this MS]; Lapidge (2003a) 252–333 [Lantfred, *Translatio et miracula S. Swithuni*, coll. as J], 787–91 [base MS for Wulfstan, two hymns to St Swithun: SK 1443 (Rouen redaction) and SK 1530]

ST: Lapidge—Winterbottom (1991b) xiii–xxxix, ci–cxii; Biggs et al. (2001) 436-8; Lapidge (2003a)

Rygnestad (Norway), Archives of Ketil Rygnestad, no. 95, and of Knut Rygnestad, no. 99 [private archives]: see no. 777

928. St Gallen, Stadtbibliothek, Vadianische Sammlung, 337

995×1004, Canterbury StA, prov. Fleury s. x/xi, ?prov. La Réole s. xi in.

Contents: Wulfric, abbot of St Augustine's, Canterbury, letter to Abbo of Fleury; B., *Vita S. Dunstani* [*BHL* 2342]

MS: Scherrer (1864) 94–5; Stubbs (1874) xxvii–xxviii; Mostert (1989) no. BF 1292; Dumville (1993g) 84 n. 388, 147 n. 39; McKee (1997) 127–9; Biggs et al. (2001) 179–82; R. Sharpe (2001) 66, 824; R. Gameson (2012a) 40, 50 and n. 161, 60, 65; R. Gameson (2012d) 357 and n. 50; Winterbottom—Lapidge (2012) lxxxi–lxxxii, lxxxiv–lxxxvii

FACS: Bosc-Lauby—Notter (2004) p. 144 [fol. 1r]

ED: Winterbottom—Lapidge (2012) 2–108 [base MS (= C) for B., *Vita S. Dunstani*], 162 [base MS for Wulfric, letter to Abbo]

ST: Stubbs (1874); Lapidge (1992e) [repr. Lapidge (1993a) 293–315]; Winterbottom (2000); Lapidge (2012a) 693 and n. 34; Winterbottom—Lapidge (2012)

929. St Gallen, Stiftsbibliothek, 1394, pp. 95–8

s. viii in., Northumbria, or Ireland?

Contents: sacramentary (f)

MS: Scherrer (1875) 459; Warren (1881) 179; Kenney (1929) no. 557 (ii); *CLA* VII (1956) no. 979; Gamber (1958) 33; Gamber (1968–88) no. 115; T.J. Brown (1982) 109 [repr. T.J. Brown (1993a) 209]; Pfaff (1995) 9; Mersiowsky (2007) 81 n. 54, 92

FACS: T.J. Brown (1993a) ill. 65 [p. 98 (detail)]

ED: Forbes (1864) xlviii [entire fragment]; Warren (1881) 179–80 [base MS for litany from fragment]; MacCarthy (1886) 233–7 [entire fragment]

ST: *BCLL* (1985) no. 797; *CPL* (1995) no. 1927

930. Mortain, Collégiale Saint-Évroult, s.n. (formerly Saint-Lô, Archives de la Manche, 1)

s. xi$^{3/4}$ or xi^2, (prov. Saint-Évroult, prob. s. xi ex.)

Contents: gospels

MS: *Cat. gén. Dép.* (Octavo) X.267 [Boulay]; Dumville (1993f) 99 [no. 47]; R. Gameson (1999a) no. 820; R. Gameson (2003) 136–7, 154, 158; Biggs (2007a) 29–31 [Biggs, Morey], 31–2 [T.N. Hall]; R. Gameson (2012a) 70 n. 240; R. Gameson (2012d) 365 and n. 89; Gneuss (2012) 296–7

DEC: Dodwell (1954) 14–15; Alexander (1970a) 238; Ohlgren (1986) no. 225; R. Gameson (1995b) 208 n. 105

FACS: Dodwell (1954) pls. 6 (b) [fol. 42v], 6 (d) [fol. 5r]; E. Temple (1976) ill. 25 [fol. 5r]; R. Gameson (2003) fig. 5 [fol. 80r]

930. 5. Saint-Omer, Bibliothèque municipale, 202

s. ix², NE France, prov. England (Exeter?) by s. xi med., (prov. Saint-Bertin)

Contents: Gospel of Nicodemus; *Passio S. Margaretae* [*BHL* 5303]; *Vindicta Saluatoris*; thirty-five Homilies from Paulus Diaconus, *Homiliarium*

MS: *Cat. gén. Dép.* (Quarto) III.107 [Michelant]; Izydorczyk (1993) 167–8 [no. 334]; Clayton—Magennis (1994) 8 and n. 3, 192; Cross—Crick (1996e); Bischoff (1998—) III, no. 5403; Lapidge (2006) 172, 341; Biggs (2007a) 30 [Biggs, Morey]; Wieland (2009) 126

FACS: Cross (1996b) pls. I–IV [fols. 2r, 86r, 103r, 117v]

ED: Clayton—Magennis (1994) 204, 214, 216 [gaps in text of Paris MS of *Passio S. Margaretae* supplied from this MS]; Cross (1996b) 138–246 [base MS for Gospel of Nicodemus], 248–92 [base MS for *Vindicta Saluatoris*]

ST: H.C. Kim (1973); Cross (1996b); Biggs et al. (2001) 318–20 [Magennis]; Thornbury (2011) 300–4

931. Saint-Omer, Bibliothèque municipale, 257, fols. 1–7

s. viii¹, Northumbria

Contents: gospels (f)

MS: *Cat. gén. Dép.* (Quarto) III.130 [Michelant]; *CLA* VI (1953) no. 826; McGurk (1961a) no. 65; T.J. Brown (1982) 109 [repr. T.J. Brown (1993a) 210]; R. Gameson (2012a) 53 n. 183

932. Saint-Omer, Bibliothèque municipale, 279, fols. 1–2

s. viii, England? (prov. Saint-Bertin)

Contents: Isidore, *De differentiis uerborum* [*CPL* 1187] (f: II. 36–7, 39–40)

MS: *Cat. gén. Dép.* (Quarto) III. 140 [Michelant]; Lindsay (1915) 486; *CLA* VI (1953) no. 827; Andrés Sanz (2006) 152*; Lapidge (2006) 309

933. St Paul in Carinthia, Stiftsbibliothek, 2¹ (25. 2. 16)

s. viii¹, prov. *c.* 800 Murbach

Contents: Pompeius, *Comm. artis Donati* [extracts]; poem [SK 3536; add. s. viii²/³]; *Anonymi ad Cuimnanum Expossitio Latinitatis* [*CPL* 1561c]; Sergius, *Explanationes in Donatum*, bk. II

MS: *CLA* X (1963) nos. 1451, 1452, 1453; Schindel (1975) 242–5; Law (1982) 17 n. 28, 87–90 *et passim*; Bischoff—Löfstedt (1992a) vii–ix [Bischoff]; Bischoff (1998—) III, no. 5933c; Lapidge (2006) 326, 332; Wieland (2009) 144

ED: Schindel (1975) 258–79 [base MS for Sergius, *Explanationes in Donatum*, bk. II]; Bischoff—Löfstedt (1992a) ix [poem SK 3536], 1–160 [base MS (= L) for *Anonymi ad Cuimnanum Expossitio*]; M. Irvine (1994) 297–8 [excerpt from *Anonymi ad Cuimnanum Expossitio*]

LANG: Bischoff—Löfstedt (1992a) xxiv–xxxviii [Löfstedt]

ST: Bischoff (1966–81) I.97, 273–88; Holtz (1971); Holtz (1977) 524; Holtz (1981) 267–71, 284–94, 311–12, 476–8; *BCLL* (1985) no. 331; M. Irvine (1986) 17–24; M. Irvine (1994) 280–7, 297–8 *et passim*; Knappe (1996) 232–3 and nn.; Law (1997) 34 *et passim*

933. 5. St Paul in Carinthia, Stiftsbibliothek, 979 (29. 4. 9), fol. 4

s. viii/ix

Contents: sacramentary (f)

MS: *CLA* X (1963) no. 1459; Gamber (1968–88) no. 237; Gamber (1969) 332–9; Gamber (1970); Gamber (1975b) 77–8

ED: Gamber (1969) 332–9; Gamber (1975b) 78–9

St Petersburg, Russian National Library: see above, nos. **840. 5–847**

934. San Marino (California), Henry E. Huntington Library, HM 62

s. xi², Canterbury CC?, prov. Rochester

Contents: Bible

MS: De Ricci—Wilson (1935–40) I.48; N.R. Ker (1964) 164; McGurk (1986b) 54 n. 60 [repr. McGurk (1998a) no. XIV]; M.P. Richards (1988) 26, 62–84; Dutschke (1989) I.124–30; Marsden (1994a) 103 n. 14; R. Gameson (1995a) 104 n. 31; Marsden (1995a) 42 n. 211, 324 n. 17; R. Sharpe et al. (1996) 477, 494, 503; Stonemann (1997) 101–2, 112; R. Gameson (1999a) nos. 899–900; Marsden (2012) 426 and n. 93

ST: Glunz (1933)

San Marino (California), Henry E. Huntington Library, RB 99513 (PR 1188F): see no. **818. 5**

Sondershausen, Schlossmuseum, Lat. liturg. IX. 1: see no. **141**

Spangenberg, Pfarrbibliothek: see no. **849. 3**

[Stockholm, Riksarkivet: the shelfmarks of the fragments in Stockholm are those now assigned in the catalogue 'Medeltida Pergament Omslag', completed in 2004, and available to readers on a database at the Riksarkivet.]

936. Stockholm, Riksarkivet, Fr. 25906, 25908-11, 25913-20 (with Göteborg, Universitetsbiblioteket, Friherre August Vilhelm Stiernstedts Samling no. 4 (Fr. 25922) + Jönköping, Per Brahe gymnasiet, Fragm. 5-6 [Fr. 25907, 25905] + Växjö, Smålands Museum, Fragm. L 1505/15 [Fr. 25912] + Lund, Universitetsbiblioteket, Fragm. membr. lat. 1 + Oslo, Riksarkivet, Lat. fragm. 204, 5–6 and 205, 1–2)

s. xi^1, England? Scandinavia?

Contents: missal (f)

MS: T. Schmid (1944); T. Schmid (1963) 187; Lapidge—Winterbottom (1991b) lxvii and n. 111; Dumville (1992a) 68, 88 and nn.; Brunius (2000) 159; Lapidge (2003a) 58, 78–9 and n. 15; Gullick (2005a) 32 and n. 11, 69 and n. 91; Hartzell (2006) no. 340; Rankin (2007) 22 and n. 11; Gullick— Rankin (2009) 285; Toy (2009) 170; R. Gameson (2012d) 360 and n. 61

DEC: R. Gameson (1995b) 243 n. 55

936. 1. Stockholm, Riksarkivet, Fr. 26449–26451 (with Göteborg, Universitetsbiblioteket, Friherre August Vilhelm Stierstedts Samling no. 3 (Fr. 25921))

s. xi$^{2/4}$

Contents: missal (f)

MS: Gullick (2005a) 32, 68 and n. 87, 74 n. 10; Hartzell (2006) no. 342; R. Gameson (2012d) 360 and n. 61; Rankin (2012) 501 n. 84

FACS: Abukhanfusa (2004) pl. 18 [Fr. 26449, fol. 1r]; Gullick (2005a) pl. 1 [Fr. 26449, fol. 1r]

936. 2. Stockholm, Riksarkivet, Fr. 194 and 195

s. xi ex.; written in Normandy, probably came to Scandinavia via England

Contents: Augustine, conclusion of *Serm.* clvi and beginning of *Serm.* ccxciv [i.e. extracts from the Augustinian collection *Sermones .lxiv. de uerbis Domini*] (f)

MS: R. Gameson (1999a) no. 904; Gullick (2005a) 57–8, 69, 76 nn. 35–8; Lapidge (2006) 291

FACS: Gullick (2005a) pl. 19 [Fr. 194]

936. 4. Stockholm, Riksarkivet, Fr. 2070 and 2071

s. xi, England? Scandinavia?

Contents: missal (f)

MS: Gullick (2005a) 32, 68, 74 n. 11; Björkvall (2002) 160; Hartzell (2005) 83–90, 97 n. 1; Toy (2005) 103; Hartzell (2006) no. 346; Gullick—Rankin (2009) 285; Toy (2009) 17, 109; R. Gameson (2012d) 360 and n. 61

FACS: Björkvall (2002) 167 [fol. 3v]; Abukhanfusa (2004) pl. 19 [Fr. 2070, fols. 3v and 4r]; Hartzell (2005) pl. 48 [Fr. 2070 fols. 3v and 4r]

936. 5. Stockholm, Riksarkivet, Fr. 2427

s. xi $^{2/4}$

Contents: missal (f)

MS: Gullick (2005a) 32, 68; Hartzell (2006) no. 354; R. Gameson (2012d) 360 and n. 61; Rankin (2012) 501 n. 84

936. 6. 1. Stockholm, Riksarkivet, Fr. 2497

s. xi, England? Scandinavia?

Contents: missal (f)

MS: Gullick (2005a) 32, 68; Hartzell (2006) no. 3; Gullick—Rankin (2009) 285

936. 6. 2. Stockholm, Riksarkivet, Fr. 2688

s. xi/xii, Winchester?

Contents: missal (f)

MS: Gullick (2005a) 32, 56, 68, 75 n. 16; Hartzell (2005) 92–7 and nn.

FACS: Gullick (2005a) pl. 2; Hartzell (2005) pl. 50

936. 7. Stockholm, Riksarkivet, Fr. 11511

s. xi^2

Contents: missal or manual (f)

MS: there is no printed notice, but a description is available in the Databas över Medeltida Pergamentsamslag of the Riksarkivet in Stockholm

936. 8. Stockholm, Riksarkivet, NoFr. 3

s. xi ex.

Contents: missal (f)

936. 9. Stockholm, Kungliga Biblioteket, A. 128

s. xi$^{3/4}$

Contents: gradual (f)

MS: P. Wagner (1925) 205–8; R. Gameson (1999a) no. 903; Hartzell (2005) 90–2; Hartzell (2006) no. 335

FACS: P. Wagner (1925) pl. on p. 209 [fol. 1r]; Hartzell (2005) pl. 49 [fol. 1r]

ST: P. Wagner (1925)

937. Stockholm, Kungliga Biblioteket, A. 135 (the 'Codex Aureus')

s. viii med., Kent (Minster-in-Thanet or Canterbury?), prov. Canterbury CC

Contents: gospels; donation inscription* (added s. ix med.)

MS: N.R. Ker (1957) no. 385; Lowe (1960) 22; McGurk (1961a) no. 111; N.R. Ker (1964) 39; *CLA* XI (1966) no. 1642; D.H. Wright (1967) 57–8, 79; T.J. Brown (1972) 234, 239 [repr. T.J. Brown (1993a) 112, 117, 273 n. 95]; T.J. Brown (1974) 133 [repr. T.J. Brown (1993a) 134]; T.J. Brown (1975) 270 [repr. T.J. Brown (1993a) 160]; N.P. Brooks (1984) 151, 201–2; B. Fischer (1988–91) I.16*; Webster—Backhouse (1991) no. 154; T.J. Brown (1993b) 195, 198; Dumville (1993f) 99 [no. 50]; Webster—Brown (1997) 232 [no. 81]; R. Gameson (1999c) 336–46; R. Gameson (2001c); Eberlein (2003) 388; Gerchow (2004) 52 n. 20; Gullick (2004) 33; Roberts (2005) 28–30; Emms (2006) 24; Wieland (2009) 117; M.P. Brown (2012) 139, 147–8; Crick (2012) 178 n. 17; R. Gameson (2012a) 18, 25, 37 and n. 88, 38 and n. 91, 42, 51, 53, 67, 73, 76, 77 and n. 271, 87 n. 311, 88, 89, 90; R. Gameson (2012b) 113 and n. 75, 114; Gullick (2012) 308 and n. 89; Marsden (2012) 414 and n. 32; Pfaff (2012) 449

DEC: E.H. Zimmermann (1916) 128, 131–5, 139, 286–9; Köhler (1930–60) I.76–8, 326–8, 331–4; Nordenfalk (1951); F. Wormald (1954) 10–11 [rev. and repr. F. Wormald (1984c) 20–2]; D.H. Wright (1967) 63, 68; Koehler (1972) 16, 22, 24, 78–88, 104, 112–13, 184; Nordenfalk (1977) 17, 96–106; Alexander (1978a) no. 30; Dodwell (1982) 9, 55, 100, 158; D.M. Wilson (1984) 91, 94; De Hamel (1986) 20–1; Ohlgren (1986) no. 30; R. Gameson (1995b) 197; M.P. Brown (1996) 92–3 *et passim*; M.P. Brown (2003a) 234, 277, 289, 316, 335, 380; Karkov (2009) 210–11; M.P. Brown (2011b) 34; Nees (2011) 14, 15; Netzer (2011) 3; Netzer (2012) 237, 239–40

FACS: R. Gameson (2001c) and (2002a) [complete facsimile]; F. Wormald (1954) pl. XV [fols. 9v, 150v]; D.H. Wright (1967) pl. V (p) [fol. 1r (detail)]; Nordenfalk (1977) pls. 33–8 [fols. 16r, 5r, 6v, 9v, 150r, 11v]; Alexander (1978a) ills. 147 [fol. 150v], 152–9 [fols. 11r, 9v, 5r, 6v, 151r, 97r, 16r, 161r]; D.M. Wilson (1984) pls. 101–2 [fols. 8v, 9v], 114 [fol. 11r]; Webster—Backhouse (1991) 199 [fols. 150r, 11r], 200 [fol. 9v]; T.J. Brown (1993a) ill. 43 [fol. 161r]; R. Gameson (1999c) pl. 13.15 [fol. 9v], 13.16 [fol. 22r], 13.17 [fol. 63r], 13.18 [fol. 150r], 13.21 [fol. 6r]; Roberts (2005) pl. 3 [fol. 11r]; M.P. Brown (2007a) pls. 40–2 [fols. 9v, 11r, 16r]; Owen-Crocker (2009) figs. 7.2 [fol. 150v], 7.3 [fol. 16r], 7.4 [fol. 11r]; R. Gameson (2012) pls. 8.2–3 [fols. 9v, 11r]

ED: J. Wordsworth et al. (1889–1954) [gospels coll. as aur]; Harmer (1914) 12–13 [donation inscription]; B. Fischer (1988–91) [gospel excerpts coll. as Ea]

LANG: A. Campbell (1959) 8 and n. 2

ST: Kuhn (1948) 592–8; K. Sisam (1956) 7–8, 115–16; Kuhn (1957) 364–6; K. Sisam (1957); Whitelock (1979) 539–40; Breeze (1996b); Campos Villanova (1996); Keynes (1996a) 55 and n. 49; Lenker (1997) 134 n. 3

937. 1. Stockholm, Kungliga Biblioteket, Isl. perg. 8°, no. 8 (pastedowns)

s. xi med.

Contents: missal (sacramentary?) (f)

MS: Gjerløw (1980) I.9–17; Hartzell (2006) no. 336; Rankin (2012) 501 n. 84

FACS: Gjerløw (1980) II, pls. 1–3 [fols. 1v, 2r, 2v]

ED: Gjerløw (1980) I.10–14

937. 3. Stuttgart, Württembergische Landesbibliothek, Theol. et philos. Q. 628

s. vii/viii, England (Northumbria) or Continent?

Contents: Gregory, *Dialogi* [*CPL* 1713]

MS: *CLA* IX (1959) no. 1356; Bischoff (1966–81) II.339; Bischoff (1998—) III, no. 6062a; Lapidge (2006) 304

937. 5. Tokyo, Collection of Professor Toshiyuki Takamiya, 55

s. xi/xii, Canterbury CC [from a companion volume to nos. **170-1**]

Contents: Augustine, *Enarrationes in Psalmos* [*CPL* 283] (f)

MS: A.G. Watson (1987a) 11; Takamiya (1989); R. Gameson (1995a) 132 n. 143; Gullick (1998c) 175, 181; R. Gameson (1999a) no. 905; Lapidge (2006) 288; Takamiya (2010) 431

Tokyo, Collection of Professor Toshiyuki Takamiya, 89 (formerly in the leaf collection in Takamiya 45): see no. **504. 3**

Tokyo, Collection of Professor Toshiyuki Takamiya, 90 (formerly in the leaf collection in Takamiya 45): see no. **818. 3**

938. Urbana (Illinois), University of Illinois Library, 128

s. x med., prob. Worcester, (prov. Malmesbury)

Contents: sylloge of Latin inscriptions (Bishop Milred's Collection: sixteen poems and inscriptions [SK 2799, 3476, 4455, 5374, 5868, 6618, 6873, 7122, 7704, 8406, 9405, 9993, 13209, 15514, 15611, 17321]) (f)

MS: Wallach (1975); Lapidge (1975b) [repr. Lapidge (1996b) 357–79, with addenda at pp. 510–12]; Schaller (1977) [rev. and repr. Schaller (1995) 184–96, 423–4]; Sheerin (1977); Sims-Williams (1982) [repr. Sims-Williams (1995) no. IX]; R.M. Thomson (1982b) 14 and nn. 78–9; Sims-Williams (1983) [repr. Sims-Williams (1995) no. X]; Dumville (1987) 149 and n. 6; A.G. Watson (1987a) 48; Sims-Williams (1990) 339–59; Dumville (1994a) 148 and n. 91, 149 and n. 95; Stoneman (1997) 117; Carley—Petitmengin (2004) 209

FACS: H.P. Kraus, *Catalogue 88: Fifty Mediaeval and Renaissance Manuscripts* (New York, 1958) 8–10, 124 [three pages]; Wallach (1975) [fol. 2v]

939. Utrecht, Universiteitsbibliotheek, 32 (Script. eccl. 484), fols. 1–91 (the 'Utrecht Psalter')

s. ix¹ (*c.* 816 × *c.* 840), Hautvillers or Rheims, prov. Canterbury CC by s. x ex. or xi in.

Contents: Psalterium Gallicanum; canticles

MS: Birch (1876); N.R. Ker (1964) 39; Engelbregt (1965); Köhler—Mütherich (1971–99) VI/i. 38–9, 85–7; Van der Horst—Engelbregt (1982–4); Keynes—Lapidge (1983) 214; N.P. Brooks (1984) 262–4; F. Wormald (1984a); Dumville (1993g) 105–6 and n. 116, 140; Chazelle (1997); Prescott (1997) 431 and n. 334; Tite (1997a) 271–2; Bischoff (1998—) III, no. 6322; Gullick (2004) 32 and n. 49; Tite (2004) 9, 11 n. 26; Lapidge (2006) 49 n. 87, 173; Shepard (2007) 247 n. 105; Withers (2007) 72–4; Wieland (2009) 117; M.P. Brown (2012) 141, 147 and n. 128; R. Gameson (2012a) 90 n. 327; R. Gameson (2012d) 351 and n. 25, 352, 369 and n. 106; Rushforth (2012) 204 and n. 49; Toswell (2012) 473, 480

DEC: De Wald (1933); D. Panofsky (1943); Rice (1952) 201–3; F. Wormald (1952) 29–35, 69–70; Dodwell (1954) 27 *et passim*; F. Wormald (1957b) 31, 32 [repr. F. Wormald (1984) 146, 147]; Tselos (1959); Dodwell (1971b) 22, 30–3, 41, 115; Köhler—Mütherich (1971–99) IV.29, VI/i.14, 35–9, 51, 85–135, VII.108, 110; Raw (1976) 143, 146; E. Temple (1976) no. 64; Deshman (1977) 156–8; Dufrenne (1978); Raw (1990) 249 *et passim*; G. Henderson (1994) 263–5, 266, 268, 270–3; R. Gameson (1995b) 10, 12–13, 14, 16–19, 35, 38, 48–53, 59, 64–5, 66–7, 171 *et passim*; Van der Horst et al. (1996); Dodwell (2000) 117–20, 150–1; Noel (2000); Koslin (2006) 422; McGurk—Rosenthal (2006) 192 n. 36; McIlwain Nishimura (2006) 163; Shepard (2007) 132, 149, 249 n. 18; Withers (2007) 162–3; Schichler (2008); Karkov (2009) 206, 231; O'Reilly (2011) 202, 212, 213; Rosenthal (2011) 235–6; Withers (2011) 247, 257, 260–1; R. Gameson (2012c) 261 and n. 34, 263; Netzer (2012) 232 and n. 46

FACS: De Wald (1933) [complete facsimile]; Van der Horst—Engelbregt (1982–4) [complete facsimile]; Rice (1952) pl. 65 (a) [folio not specified]; F. Wormald (1952) pl. 10 (a) [folio not specified]; Köhler—Mütherich (1971–99) *Tafelband* VI, pls. 21 [fol. 1v], 22 [fols. 2r, 2v (details)], 23 [fols. 3r, 3v, 4r (details)], 24 [fols. 4v, 5r, 6r (details)], 25 [fols. 6v, 7r (details)], 26 [fols. 7v, 8r (details)], 27 [fols. 8v, 9r, 10v (details)], 28 [fols. 11r, 11v, 12r (details)], 29 [fols. 13r, 13v, 14r (details)], 30 [fols. 14v, 15r, 15v (details)], 31 [fols. 16r, 16v, 17r (details)],

32 [fols. 18r, 18v, 19r (details)], 33 [fols. 19v, 20v, 21r (details)], 34
[fols. 22r, 22v (details)], 35 [fols. 23r, 24r, 24v (details)], 36 [fol. 25r], 37
[fols. 26r, 26v, 27r (details)], 38 [fols. 27v, 28r, 28v (details)], 39 [fols.
29r, 30r (details)], 40 [fol. 30v], 41 [fols. 31r, 31v, 32r (details)], 42 [fols.
32v, 33r, 34r (details)], 43 [fol. 34v], 44 [fols. 35r, 35v, 36r (details)], 45
[fols. 36v, 37r, 37v (details)], 46 [fols. 38v, 39v, 40r (details)], 47 [fols.
40v, 41v, 42r (details)], 48 [fols. 43r, 43v, 44r (details)], 49 [fols. 45r, 46v
(details)], 50 [fols. 47r, 48r (details)], 51 [fol. 48v], 52 [fols. 49r, 49v
(details)], 53 [fols. 50r, 50v (details)], 54 [fols. 51r, 51v (details)], 55
[fols. 53r, 53v (details)], 56 [fols. 54r, 54v (details)], 57 [fols. 55r, 55v,
56r (details)], 58 [fols. 56v, 57r (details)], 59 [fol. 57v], 60 [fols. 58r, 59r,
59v (details)]; 61 [fols. 60v, 61v, 62v (details)]; 62 [fols. 64v, 65r, 65v
(details)], 64 [fol. 66r], 65 [fol. 67r], 66 [fol. 67v], 67 [fols. 68v, 71v
(details)], 68 [fol. 72r], 69 [fol. 72v], 70 [fol. 73r], 71 [fol. 73v], 72 [fols.
74r, 74v (details)], 73 [fols. 75r, 75v (details)], 74 [fols. 76r, 77r (details)], 75 [fols. 77v, 78r, 78v (details)], 76 [fols. 79r, 79v (details)], 77
[fols. 80r, 80v, 81v (details)], 78 [fols. 81v, 82r, 82v (details)], 79 [fol.
83r], 80 [fols. 83v, 84r, 84v (details)], 81 [fols. 85r, 85v, 86r (details)], 82
[fols. 87v, 88r, 88v (details)], 83 [fols. 89r, 89v (details)], 84 [fol. 90r],
85 [fols. 90v, 91v (details)]; D.M. Wilson (1984) pl. 229 [fol. 15r]; F.
Wormald (1984) pls. 32–3 [fols. 13r, 66r], 35–7 [fols. 32v, 67r, 58r
(details)]; Noel (1995) ills. 2 [fol. 2r], 6 [fol. 22v], 12 [fol. 22v (detail)],
15 [fol. 3v], 18 [fol. 8r], 20 [fol. 4v (detail)], 22 [fol. 7v], 24 [fol. 1v
(detail)], 27 [fol. 65r], 29 [fol. 62v], 31 [fol. 58r], 34 [fol. 67r], 36 [fol.
77r (detail)], 38 [fol. 74r (detail)], 40 [fol. 79r (detail)], 47 [fol. 28r], 51
[fol. 18r], 52 [fol. 59v], 54 [fol. 30v], 56 [fol. 16v], 58 [fol. 12r], 60
[fol. 14v], 62 [fol. 15v], 67 [fol. 71v], 68 [fol. 4r], 77 [fol. 34v]; Chazelle
(1997) pls. 1, 2, 3, 5, 7, 8, 11, 13, 14, 16 [fols. 90v, 88r, 65v, 29r, 67r, 1r,
28v, 57r, 14r (all details)]; Noel (2000) pls. 3–5 [fols. 85v, 64r, 12r];
Withers (2007) 163 [fol. 45r]

ED: Quentin et al. (1926–94) vol. X [Psalms coll. as U]; Pulsiano (2001a)
[Pss. I–L coll. as ψ]

ST: Dufrenne (1964); Dodwell (1990); R. McKitterick (1990a) 310–12;
Gibson et al. (1992); Noel (1995) *passim*

940. Utrecht, Universiteitsbibliotheek, 32 (Script. eccl. 484), fols. 94–105

s. viii in., Monkwearmouth-Jarrow

Contents: gospels (f)

MS: Lowe (1952) [repr. Lowe (1972) II.385–8]; Lowe (1960) 19; McGurk
(1961a) no. 81; D.H. Wright (1961a) 443–4, 455; *CLA* X (1963)
no. 1587; Bischoff (1966–81) II.257, 323, 330; B. Fischer (1988–91)
I.15*; McGurk (1994b) 5 and n. 15 [repr. McGurk (1998) no. XII];
Gullick (2004) 32 and n. 49; Tite (2004) 9, 11 n. 26; Emms (2006) 23–5
and n. 29; M.P. Brown (2012) 134 n. 53, 143 n. 102; R. Gameson
(2012a) 37 and n. 86; R. Gameson (2012b) 114

DEC: Alexander (1978a) no. 8; Ohlgren (1986) no. 8

FACS: Van der Horst—Engelbregt (1982–4) [complete facsimile]; Lowe
(1960) pls. XI [fol. 101v], XII (a)–(d) [fols. 102r, 95v, 96r, 99v (all
details)]; D.H. Wright (1961a) pls. IV [fols. 105r, 94r, 95v (all details)],
V (a) [fol. 97v (detail)]

ED: J. Wordsworth et al. (1889–1954) [gospels coll. as U]; B. Fischer
(1988–91) [gospel excerpts coll. as Nu]

940. 5. Valenciennes, Bibliothèque municipale, 195 (187)

s. ix in., S. England?, prov. s. ix/x Saint-Amand

Contents: Alcuin, *De fide sanctae et indiuiduae Trinitatis* (with dedicatory preface, *Ep.* cclvii), *De Trinitate ad Fredegisum quaestiones .xxviii.*
(with dedicatory preface, *Ep.* cclxxxix), *De animae ratione* (with
dedicatory preface, *Ep.* cccix, and including poems SK 13293, 16078,
9692)

MS: *Cat. gén. Dép.* (Octavo) XXV.273–4; Bischoff (1998—) III, no. 6366a

ST: *CSLMA* II (1999) 123, 137, 152

Vatican City: see under [Rome], Città del Vaticano

Växjö, Smålands Museet, Fragm. L 1505/15: see no. **936**

941. Vercelli, Biblioteca Capitolare, CXVII (the 'Vercelli Book')

s. x², SE England (Canterbury StA? Rochester?)

Contents: Homilies*, including part of the OE Life of St Guthlac; OE
poetry: *Andreas***; Cynewulf, *Fates of the Apostles***; *Soul and Body
I***; *Homiletic Verse Fragment***; *Dream of the Rood***; Cynewulf,
*Elene***

MS: Förster (1913a) 21–32, 35–86; Förster (1913b) 7–70; Krapp (1932a)
xi–xxxv; K. Sisam (1953a) 109–18; N.R. Ker (1957) no. 394; Scragg
(1971); C. Sisam (1976); Szarmach (1977b); Szarmach (1979); M.

Martin (1978); Scragg (1979) 225–33, 267–77; Szarmach (1981a)
xix–xxi; Scragg (1992) xxiii–xxv, lxxiv–lxxix; Scragg (1994a); Scragg
(1996) 209–10; W. Schipper (2003) 161; C. Bishop (2007b) 94–7;
Toswell (2007) 218; Treharne (2007a) 253–5, 257–61, 264; Zacher
(2007) 175–7; Treharne (2009b) 101–4; R. Gameson (2012d) 363 and
n. 77; Gullick (2012) 294 n. 3; Scragg (2009b) 62, 80–1; Scragg (2012a)
nos. 1032–5

DEC: F. Wormald (1945) 120 n. 1, 134 [repr. F. Wormald (1984) 58–9,
73]; E. Temple (1976) no. 28; Brownrigg (1978) 240 nn. 5 and 6, 243
n. 3; Ohlgren (1986) no. 116; R. Gameson (1995b) 88, 94; Werner
(2011) 292

FACS: Förster (1913b) [complete facsimile]; C. Sisam (1976) [complete
facsimile]; Wülker (1894) [poetry only]; E. Temple (1976) ills. 97–9
[fols. 112r, 49r, 49v (all details)]; Scragg (1992) pl. I [fol. 80v]; Owen-
Crocker (2009) fig. 4.3 [fol. 104v]

ED (poetry) [the following items are listed according to Ker's numbering
of individual entries (see N.R. Ker (1957) 461–3); only the most recent
editions are listed]:

art. 6. *Andreas*: Krapp (1932a) 1–51; K.R. Brooks (1961) 1–55

art. 7. Cynewulf, *Fates of the Apostles*: Krapp (1932a) 51–4; K.R. Brooks
(1961) 56–60

art. 21. *Soul and Body*: Krapp (1932a) 54–9

art. 22. *Homiletic Verse Fragment*: Krapp (1932a) 59–60

art. 23. *Dream of the Rood*: Krapp (1932a) 61–5; Dickins—Ross (1954);
Cassidy—Ringler (1971) 309–17; Swanton (1987); Pope (2001) 9–15;
Mitchell—Robinson (2007) 270–5

art. 28. Cynewulf, *Elene*: Krapp (1932a) 66–102; Gradon (1977)

ED (prose) [the following items are listed according to Ker's numbering
of individual entries (see N.R. Ker (1957) 461–3); only the most recent
editions are listed]:

art. 1. *Vercelli Homily* I (Friday before Easter): Förster (1932) 1–43;
Scragg (1992) 6–43

art. 2. *Vercelli Homily* II (eschatological homily; no occasion specified):
Förster (1913a) 87–95; Förster (1932) 44–53; Scragg (1992) 52–65

art. 3. *Vercelli Homily* III (Second Sunday in Lent): Förster (1932) 53–71;
Scragg (1992) 73–83

art. 4. *Vercelli Homily* IV (eschatological homily; no occasion specified): Förster (1932) 72–107; Scragg (1992) 90–104

art. 5. *Vercelli Homily* V (for 'Midwinter' [i.e. Christmas Day]): Förster (1932) 107–31; Scragg (1992) 111–21

art. 8. *Vercelli Homily* VI (Christmas Day): Förster (1913a) 96–100; Förster (1932) 131–7; Scragg (1992) 128–31

art. 9. *Vercelli Homily* VII (exhortation to toil and temperance; no occasion specified): Förster (1932) 137–49; Scragg (1992) 134–7

art. 10. *Vercelli Homily* VIII (eschatological homily; no occasion specified): Förster (1932) 149–59; Scragg (1992) 143–8

art. 11. *Vercelli Homily* IX (eschatological homily; no occasion specified): Förster (1913a) 100–16; Szarmach (1981a) 4–7; Scragg (1992) 158–84; C.D. Wright (1993) 276–90

art. 12. *Vercelli Homily* X (eschatological homily; no occasion specified): Szarmach (1981a) 11–16; Scragg (1992) 196–213

art. 13. *Vercelli Homily* XI (homily for the first Rogation Day): Willard (1949a); Szarmach (1981a) 19–21; Scragg (1992) 221–5

art. 14. *Vercelli Homily* XII (homily for the second Rogation Day): Szarmach (1981a) 23–4; Scragg (1992) 228–30

art. 15. *Vercelli Homily* XIII (homily for the third Rogation Day): Szarmach (1981a) 27–8; Scragg (1992) 234–6

art. 16. *Vercelli Homily* XIV (homily for any occasion): Szarmach (1981a) 29–32; Scragg (1992) 239–46

art. 17. *Vercelli Homily* XV (another eschatological homily *de die iudicii*): Förster (1913a) 116–28; Szarmach (1981a) 35–8; Scragg (1992) 253–61

art. 18. *Vercelli Homily* XVI (homily for Epiphany): Szarmach (1981a) 43–6; Scragg (1992) 267–74

art. 19. *Vercelli Homily* XVII (homily for the Purification of the Virgin): Szarmach (1981a) 51–3; Scragg (1992) 281–6

art. 20. *Vercelli Homily* XVIII (homily for St Martin): Szarmach (1981a) 57–62; Scragg (1992) 291–308 [with gaps supplied from nos. **642** and **905**]

art. 24. *Vercelli Homily* XIX (homily for Rogationtide?): Luiselli Fadda (1977) 71–99 [no. IV, coll. as V]; Szarmach (1981a) 69–72; Bazire—Cross (1982) 16–23 [no. 1, coll. as V]; Scragg (1992) 315–26

art. 25. *Vercelli Homily* XX (homily for Rogationtide?): Szarmach (1981a) 77–80; Bazire—Cross (1982) 31–8 [no. 2, coll. as V]; Scragg (1992) 332–43 art. 26. *Vercelli Homily* XXI (homily for Rogationtide?): Szarmach (1981a) 83–8; Scragg (1992) 351–62

art. 27. *Vercelli Homily* XXII (homily on spiritual contemplation): Förster (1913a) 137–48; Szarmach (1981a) 91–4; Scragg (1992) 368–78

art. 29. *Vercelli Homily* XXIII (excerpt from the Life of St Guthlac): Gonser (1909); Szarmach (1981a) 97–9; Scragg (1992) 383–92

[and note two unpublished editions of *Vercelli Homilies*: Willard (1925), *Vercelli Homilies* I, IV, V, VII, VIII, XI, XII; and Peterson (1951), *Vercelli Homilies* XII, XIV, XVI–XXI]

LANG: Förster (1913a) 32–5, 148–79; K.R. Brooks (1961) xxxi–xxxix; Scragg (1970); C. Sisam (1976) 32–6; Gradon (1977) 9–15; Hofstetter (1987) 172–82; Scragg (1992) xliii–lxxiv; C. Bishop (2007b) 95; Scragg (2009a)

ST: Erickson (1972); Pollard (1975) 158; Greenfield—Robinson (1980) 22; Fell (1981); Whitbread (1983); Roberts (1986); C.D. Wright (1993) 215–91; Biggs et al. (2001) 246; Treharne (2007a) 260–4; Zacher (2007); Di Sciacca (2008) 77–104; Scragg (2008b); Remley (2009) [comprehensive bibliography of studies on the Vercelli MS and its contents]; Zacher (2009); Zacher—Orchard (2009); Scragg (2012b) 554–5

941. 5. Vienna, Österreichische Nationalbibliothek, series nova 3644

s. viii, England, presumably N England, or possibly an Anglo-Saxon centre on the Continent

Contents: Eusebius, *Historia ecclesiastica*, trans. Rufinus [*CPG* 3495] (f)

MS: Unterkircher (1954–5) 237, 251–5; *CLA* X (1963) no. 1515; Mazal—Unterkircher (1963–75) III.233

FACS: Unterkircher (1954–5) pl. IV [recto]

942. Warsaw, Biblioteka Narodowa, I. 3311 [formerly St Petersburg, Imperial Library, O. v. I. 10]

s. x/xi

Contents: two collections of gospel pericopes (both incomplete)

MS: Staerk (1910) I.235; E. Temple (1976) no. 92; Lenker (1997) 471–3 *et passim*; R. Gameson (1999a) no. 912 [erroneously listed with contents and shelfmark of no. **842. 5**]; Mews (2002) 112 [no. 69]

DEC: F. Wormald (1952) 65 [no. 23]; E. Temple (1976) no. 92; Brownrigg (1978) 255–6; Heslop (2004) 307 n. 47; Keefer (2007b) 97

FACS: Staerk (1910) II, pl. LXXVII [fol. 83v]; E. Temple (1976) pls. 281–4 [fols. 83v, 69r, 15r, 55r], ills. 51–5, 59 [fols. 28r, 84r, 2r, 1r, 11r, 13r]

[943]: see now no. 842. 5.

943. 2. Washington, DC, Folger Shakespeare Library, ptd bk (binding)

s. xi

Contents: unidentified text* (f)

MS: Clement (1989); Stoneman (1997) 132; Scragg (2012a) no. 1036

FACS: Clement (1989)

943. 4. Weimar, Landesbibliothek, Fol. 414a

s. viii², prob. England

Contents: Isidore, *De natura rerum* [*CPL* 1188] (f)

MS: *CLA* IX (1959) no. 1369; Bischoff (1966–81) I.185 and n. 91; Lapidge (2006) 310

Weinheim, olim Sammlung E. Fischer, s.n.: lost? see no. 176
Weinheim, olim Sammlung E. Fischer, s.n.: lost? see no. 441. 1

943. 6. Wrisbergholzen (near Alfeld/Leine), Archiv der Grafen von Goertz-Wrisberg, Hs. 3

s. ix^{1/3}, England or Anglo-Saxon centre in Germany

Contents: Jerome, *Tractatus .lix. in Psalmos* [*CPL* 592] (f)

MS: Drögereit (1953) [repr. Drögereit (1978) I.147–60]; Bischoff (1998—) I, no. 1501; Lapidge (2006) 316; Rushforth (2011) 58

FACS: Drögereit (1953) pl. opp. p. 10

ED: Drögereit (1953) 12–15 [repr. Drögereit (1978) I.157–60] [complete fragment]

943. 8. Wrocław (Breslau), Biblioteka Uniwersytecka, Akc. 1955/2 and 1969/430

s. viii¹ or viii med., Northumbria

Contents: Gregory, *Dialogi* [*CPL* 1713] (f)

MS: Bischoff (1966–81) II.339; *CLA* XI (1966) no. 1595; *CLA* Supplement (1971) p. 31; Yerkes (1975); Yerkes (1977d); Yerkes (1979) xix; Milde (1986); Mews (1997) 306; Lapidge (2006) 304

FACS: Milde (1986) pls. on pp. 153–65 [complete MS]

944. Würzburg, Universitätsbibliothek, M. p. th. q. 2

s. v, Italy, prov. England s. vii, Worcester diocese *c.* 700, prov. Würzburg s. viii

Contents: Jerome, *Comm. in Ecclesiasten* [*CPL* 583]; *ex-libris* of Cuthswith*

MS: Bischoff—Hofmann (1952) 88–9 *et passim*; N.R. Ker (1957) no. 401; *CLA* IX (1959) nos. 1430a, 1430b; Lowe (1960) 17–18; Bischoff (1966–81) I.78, II.323, 329, 333, 338; Lowe (1972) I.243 *et passim*; T.J. Brown (1975) 259 [repr. T.J. Brown (1993a) 154]; Sims-Williams (1976); Rella (1977) 31–2; Knaus (1979) 949, 975, 985; Thurn (1984) 86–7; Thurn (1988) 46–7; Bischoff (1990) 200 and nn. 87, 89; Sims-Williams (1990) 190–6; Parkes (1991) 12; Parkes (1997b) 101 and n. 3; Thurn et al. (2005) 12; Emms (2006) 20; Lapidge (2006) 56 n. 21, 163, 314; Cain (2009) 187–9; M.P. Brown (2012) 146 and n. 120; Crick (2012) 177 and n. 15

FACS: Chroust (1899–1906) I pt. 5, pls. 2 [fols. 4v, 5r], 3 [fols. 63v, 64r]; Bischoff (1952) pl. 13 [fol. 1r]; Lowe (1960) pls. I (a) [fol. 12v], I (b) [fol. 1r]; Lambert (1969–72) Ia, frontispiece [fol. 3v]; Thurn (1988) pl. 4 [fol. 1r]; Owen-Crocker (2009) fig. 1.6 [fol. 1r]

ED: Adriaen (1959) [base MS (= W) for Jerome, *Comm. in Ecclesiasten*]; Thurn (1989) [corrections to Adriaen's collations]

ST: Hofmann (1952); Bischoff (1966–81) I.78; Lambert (1969–72) no. 205

944. 3. Würzburg, Universitätsbibliothek, M. p. th. q. 24

s. viii², England (or Anglo-Saxon centre in Germany?), prov. Würzburg

Contents: Isidore, *Mysticorum expositiones sacramentorum seu Quaestiones in Vetus Testamentum* [*CPL* 1195] (incomplete)

MS: Bischoff—Hofmann (1952) 6, 97 *et passim*; *CLA* IX (1959) no. 1433; Díaz y Díaz (1959) no. 121; Spilling (1978) 50; Knaus (1979) 975, 983; Thurn (1984) 100; Krämer (1989–90) II.856; Lapidge (2006) 163, 312

944. 5. Würzburg, Universitätsbibliothek, M. p. th. f. 43

s. viii med., England (or Anglo-Saxon centre on the Continent?) [both parts, which were bound together at an early date]

Contents: fols. 1–17, 41–53: Augustine, *Enarrationes in psalmos* [*CPL* 283], Pss. LXXXIV, LXXXV, CXIX, XC; fols. 18–40: Gregory, *Homiliae in Hiezechielem* [*CPL* 1710] I. 8 and 9

MS: Lowe (1928) 9 [repr. Lowe (1972) I.244]; Bischoff—Hofmann (1952) 9, 96–7, 144, 147; *CLA* IX (1959) nos. 1410 and 1411; Spilling (1978) 50; Thurn (1984) 31–2; Thurn (1988) 49; Lapidge (2006) 162, 288, 305; Wieland (2009) 126, 131

944. 8. Würzburg, Universitätsbibliothek, M. p. th. f. 62

s. viii med., England or Anglo-Saxon scribe in Italy (Rome), prov. Würzburg s. viii

Contents: liturgical calendar of Rome; epistle list; gospel list

MS: Frere (1934) 74; Bischoff—Hofmann (1952) 96 *et passim*; *CLA* IX (1959) no. 1417; Gamber (1968–88) nos. 1000, 1001; Thurn (1968); Klauser (1972) 3–4; Spilling (1978) 50 and n. 15; Knaus (1979) 950–1, 975; Thurn (1984) 45–6; Thurn (1988) 45–6; *CPL* (1995) nos. 1982, 1985; Lenker (1997) 413–14 *et passim*

FACS: Thurn (1968) [complete facsimile]; Thurn (1988) p. 2 [fol. 2v]

ED: Morin (1910) 47–72 [epistle list]; Morin (1911) 297–317 [gospel list]; Klauser (1972) 13–46 [gospel list coll. as W]

ST: Beissel (1907) 145–59; Gamber (1958) 86 n. 6; Thurn (1968) 18–22; Rusch (1970); Chavasse (1981); C. Vogel (1986) 339–40; Martimort (1992) 31–2

945. Würzburg, Universitätsbibliothek, M. p. th. f. 68 ('Burghardsevangeliar')

s. vi, Italy with additions s. vii/viii, prob. Northumbria, and s. viii, Continent (Luxeuil?); prov. entire MS Würzburg

Contents: gospels; with later additions: prologues and chapter–lists on fols. 10–21 and pericope notes in the gospel margins (s. vii/viii); canon tables on fols. 1r–9v (s. viii)

MS: Frere (1934) 221–4; Bischoff—Hofmann (1952) 93–4 *et passim*; *CLA* IX (1959) nos. 1423a, 1423b; T.J. Brown in Kendrick et al. (1959–60) II.34–5; Lowe (1960) 17–18; McGurk (1961) no. 80 and pp. 8 n. 3, 13;

D.H. Wright (1961a) 446–8, 455–6; B. Fischer (1965) 198–9; Bischoff (1966–81) II.323, 329–30, 338; Gamber (1968–88) no. 407; Klauser (1972) xxxv [no. 37], xxxvi [no. 11]; Knaus (1979) 975; Parkes (1982) 4 and n. 11, 21 n. 87 [repr. Parkes (1991) 95 and n. 11, 118 n. 87]; Thurn (1984) 54–6; B. Fischer (1988–91) I.14*; Thurn (1988) 45; Sims-Williams (1990) 290 and n. 74; Parkes (1991) 12–14; *CPL* (1995) no. 1979; Parkes (1997b) 101 and n. 4; Lenker (1997) 394–6 *et passim*; Bischoff (1998—) III, no. 7500a; Dumville (1999) 70 and n. 64, 96 n. 175; Meyvaert (2005) 1132; Wieland (2009) 118; M.P. Brown (2012) 144 n. 105

DEC: E.H. Zimmermann (1916) 146, 177 *et passim*; Netzer (2012) 232 and n. 46

FACS: Chroust (1899–1906) I pt. 6, pl. 2 [fols. 95r, 138r]; E.H. Zimmermann (1916) *Tafelband* I, pls. 1 (a) [fol. 92r], 71 [fols. 3r, 2v, 6v], 72 [fols. 2r, 4r]; Lowe (1960) pls. III–IV [fols. 144r, 149v]; D.H. Wright (1961a) pls. VI (a)–(e) [details from fols. 11v, 13r, 16r, and fols. 6v, 7r, 7v, 8r]

ED: Morin (1893b) [pericope notes]; B. Fischer (1988–91) [gospel excerpts coll. as Jw]

ST: Beissel (1907) 119–27, 171–6, 181–92; Morin (1911); Kunze (1947) 49–50; McGurk (1955a) 192–3 [repr. McGurk (1998) no. III]; Gamber (1962b); C. Vogel (1986) 337; Martimort (1992) 24; McGurk (1993) 248–51 [repr. McGurk (1998) no. XI]; Bischoff—Lapidge (1994) 155–60

946. Würzburg, Universitätsbibliothek, M. p. th. f. 79

s. viii¹, S England or Mercia, prov. Germany, Rhine-Main area (Mainz?) s. viii ex., then Würzburg

Contents: Isidore, *Synonyma de lamentatione animae peccatricis* [*CPL* 1203] (incomplete)

MS: Bischoff—Hofmann (1952) 6–9, 95–6 *et passim*; N.R. Ker (1957) no. 400; *CLA* IX (1959) no. 1426; Lowe (1960) 22; Bischoff (1966–81) I.183, II.333; Rella (1977) 19; Knaus (1979) 950, 975; Thurn (1984) 66; R. McKitterick (1986–90) 291; Thurn (1988) 49–50; Krämer (1989–90) II.855; Sims-Williams (1990) 202–3; T.J. Brown (1993b) 196; Bischoff (1998—) III, no. 7506a; Bergmann—Stricker (2005) IV.1880–2; Hussey (2005) 88–93; Lapidge (2006) 162–3, 313; Di Sciacca (2008) 69–72, 162 *et passim*; Hussey (2008) 151–8; Elfassi (2009) xliii–xliv

FACS: Baesecke (1933) pl. 37 [fol. 26r]; Lowe (1960) pl. XXXIII [fol. 1r]; Thurn (1988) pl. 10 [fol. 1v]

ED: Elfassi (2009) [Isidore, *Synonyma*, coll. as W]

LANG: Hussey (2008) 157

ST: Baesecke (1933) 22, 88, 108; Hofmann (1963) 29, 32, 47, 57–65; Bergmann (1973) no. 994; Moulin-Fankhänel (2001) 364; Hussey (2008)

946. 5. Würzburg, Universitätsbibliothek, M. p. th. f. 149a

s. viii^2, Mercia? or Anglo-Saxon centre on the Continent; prov. Würzburg

Contents: Gregory, *Moralia in Iob* [*CPL* 1708], bks. XXXII–XXXV

MS: Bischoff—Hofmann (1952) 67–8, 98 *et passim*; *CLA* IX (1959) no. 1427; Lowe (1960) 25; N.R. Ker (1972b) 81 n. 20; Knaus (1979) 975; Thurn (1984) 75–6; McKitterick (1986–90) 296 and n. 33; Thurn (1988) 50; Krämer (1989–90) II.856; Bischoff (1998—) III, no. 7515a; Lapidge (2006) 163, 306

FACS: Lowe (1960) pl. XL (a) [fol. 46r]; Thurn (1988) pl. 11 [fol. 15r]

ST: Hofmann (1963) 67–8; Moulin-Fankhänel (2001) 364; Bergmann et al. (2005) no. 997

947. Zürich, Zentralbibliothek, Z. XIV. 30, no. 11

s. viii med.

Contents: Eucherius, *Formulae spiritalis intelligentiae* [*CPL* 488] (f)

MS: *CLA* Supplement (1971) no. 1778; Lapidge (2006) 301; Dekker (2010) 152, 168

ST: Dekker (2010) 152

III

Untraced

For lost or untraced manuscripts or fragments, see nos. **30. 3, 176, 441. 1, 643, 830. 5, 831. 4, 842. 5, 855. 5,** and Ker (1957) nos. 403—12.

Bibliography

[A.J.C.] (1932), 'The Kederminster Gospels', *British Museum Quarterly* 6: 93 [and pls.].

Abel, A.H. (1962), 'Ælfric and the West-Saxon Gospels' (unpubl. PhD dissertation, University of Pennsylvania, PA).

Abram, C. (2007), 'Anglo-Saxon Homilies in their Scandinavian Context', in Kleist (2007a), 425–44.

Abukhanfusa, K. (2004), *Mutilated Books. Wondrous Leaves from Swedish Bibliographical History* (Stockholm).

Acker, P. (2004), 'Three Tables of Contents, One Old English Homiliary, in Cambridge, Corpus Christi College, MS 178', in Lionarons (2004a), 121–37.

Adams, J.N. and M. Deegan (1992), 'Bald's Leechbook and the *Physica Plinii*', *ASE* 21: 87–114.

Adriaen, M., ed. (1958), *Magni Aurelii Cassiodori Expositio psalmorum*, 2 vols., CCSL 97–8 (Turnhout).

– ed. (1959), 'S. Hieronymi Presbyteri Commentarius in Ecclesiasten', in CCSL 72 (Turnhout), 246–361.

– ed. (1969), *Egloga quam scripsit Lathcen Filius Baith de Moralibus Iob quas Gregorius fecit*, CCSL 145 (Turnhout).

– ed. (1979–85), *S. Gregorii Magni Moralia in Iob*, 3 vols., CCSL 143, 143A, 143B (Turnhout).

Aird, W.M. (1994), 'An Absent Friend: The Career of Bishop William of St Calais', in Rollason et al. (1994), 283–97.

Alcamesi, F. (2007a), 'Remigius's Commentary to the *Disticha Catonis* in Anglo-Saxon Manuscripts', in Lendinara et al. (2007), 143–85.

– (2007b), 'The *Sibylline Acrostic* in Anglo-Saxon Manuscripts: The Augustinian Translation and the Other Versions', in Bremmer—Dekker (2007), 147–73.

– (2010), 'Ælfric's *Quaestiones Sigewulfi in Genesin*: an Educational Dialogue', in Bremmer—Dekker (2010), 175–202.

– (2011), 'The Old English Entries in the First Corpus Glossary (CCCC 144, ff. 1r–3v)', in Lendinara et al. (2011) 508–40.

Alcoy i Pedrós, R. (2005), 'Les illustrations recyclées du *psautier anglo-catalan* de Paris: du douzième siècle anglais à l'italianisme pictural de Ferrer Bassa', in Dekeyzer—Van der Stock (2005a), 81–92.

Alexander, J.J.G. (1966), 'A Little-Known Gospel Book of the later Eleventh Century from Exeter', *Burlington Magazine* 108: 6–16.

– (1970a), *Norman Illumination at Mont St Michel 966–1100* (Oxford).

– (1970b), *Anglo-Saxon Illumination in Oxford Libraries* (Oxford).

– (1975a), 'Some Aesthetic Principles in the Use of Colour in Anglo-Saxon Art', *ASE* 4: 145–54.

– (1975b), 'The Benedictional of St Æthelwold and Anglo-Saxon Illumination of the Reform Period', in Parsons (1975), 169–83, 241–5.

– and M.T. Gibson, eds. (1976), *Medieval Learning and Literature: Essays Presented to Richard William Hunt* (Oxford).

– (1978a), *A Survey of Manuscripts Illuminated in the British Isles*, I: *Insular Manuscripts: 6th to the 9th Century* (London).

– (1978b), *Initialen aus grossen Handschriften* (Munich).

– (1978c), 'Scribes as Artists: The Arabesque Initial in Twelfth-Century English Manuscripts', in Parkes—Watson (1978), 87–116.

– and E. Temple (1985), *Illuminated Manuscripts in Oxford College Libraries, the University Archives and the Taylorian Institution* (Oxford).

– (1992), *Medieval Illuminators and their Methods of Work* (New Haven, CT).

Alidori, L. et al., eds. (2003), *Bibbie miniate della Biblioteca Medicea Laurenziana di Firenze* (Florence).

Allen, M.I., ed. (2002), *Frechulfi Lexoviensis Episcopi Opera Omnia*, 2 vols., CCCM 169–169A.

Allen, T.P. (1968), 'A Critical Edition of the Old English Gospel of Nicodemus' (unpubl. PhD dissertation, Rice University, TX).

Alton, E.H. and P. Meyer, eds. (1951), *Evangeliorum Quattuor Codex Cenannensis*, 3 vols. (Olten and Lausanne).

Alturo, J. (1996), 'I glossari latini altomedievali della Catalogna con alcune notizie sui settimani', in Hamesse (1996), 101–20.

Álvarez-López, F.J. (2007a), 'Changing Scripts: A Case Study of the Use of Different Scripts in the Bilingual Text of Cambridge, Corpus Christi College, 178, Part B', *Quaestio Insularis* 8: 19–35.

– (2007b), 'DCL, B. IV. 24: A Palaeographical and Codicological Study of a Durham's *Cantor's Book*', in Moskowich-Spiegel—Crespo-García (2007), 209–26.

Ambrose, S. (2005), 'The *Collectio Canonum Hibernensis* and the Literature of the Anglo-Saxon Benedictine Reform', *Viator* 36: 107–18.

– (2006), 'The Codicology and Palaeography of London, BL, Royal 5. E. xiii and its Abridgement of the *Collectio Canonum Hibernensis*', *Codices Manuscripti* 54–5: 1–26.

Amos, A.C. (1980), *Linguistic Means of Determining the Dates of Old English Literary Texts* (Cambridge, MA).

Anderson, E.R. (1997), 'The Seasons of the Year in Old English', *ASE* 26: 231–63.

Anderson, G.K. (1941), 'Notes on the Language of Ælfric's English Pastoral Letters in Corpus Christi College 190 and Bodleian Junius 121', *JEGP* 40: 5–13.

Anderson, O.S. (1941), *Old English Material in the Leningrad MS. of Bede's Ecclesiastical History* (Lund).

Andrés Sanz, M.A., ed. (2006), *Isidori Hispalensis episcopi Liber Differentiarum (II)*, CCSL 111A (Turnhout).

Andrieu, M., ed. (1931–61), *Les 'Ordines Romani' du haut moyen âge*, 5 vols. (Louvain).

Ångstrøm, M. (1937), *Studies in Old English MSS: With Special Reference to the Delabialisation of y to i* (Uppsala).

Anlezark, D. (2006), 'Reading "The Story of Joseph" in MS Cambridge, Corpus Christi College 201', in Magennis – Wilcox (2006), 61–94.

– ed. (2009), *The Old English Dialogues of Solomon and Saturn*, AST 7 (Cambridge).

– (2010), 'Understanding Numbers in London, British Library, Harley 3271', *ASE* 38: 137–55.

Antolin, G. (1910–23), *Catálogo de los Códices Latinos de la Real Biblioteca del Escorial*, 5 vols. (Madrid).

Antropoff, R. von (1965), *Die Entwicklung der Kenelm-Legende* (Bonn).

Aris, M.-A. and G. Schrimpf (1996), 'Aus fuldischen Handschriften. Die Fragmente 132.2 und 139.2 im Nachlass der Brüder Grimm', *Archiv für mittelrheinische Kirchengeschichte* 48: 241–83.

– and H. Broszinski, eds. (1996), *Die Glossen zum Jakobusbrief aus dem Victor-Codex (Bonifatianus 1 in der Hessischen Landesbibliothek zu Fulda)* (Fulda).

– (2004), '"Der Trost der Bücher". Bonifatius und seine Bibliothek', in *Bonifatius. Vom angelsächsischen Missionar zum Apostel der Deutschen*, ed. M. Imhof and K. Stasch (Petersberg, 2004), 95–110.

Arngart, O.S. (1943–4), 'The Calendar of St Willibrord: A Little Used Source of Old English Personal Names', *SN* 16: 128–34.

– ed. (1952), *The Leningrad Bede: an 8th Century Manuscript of the Venerable Bede's 'Historia Ecclesiastica Gentis Anglorum' in the Public Library, Leningrad*, EEMF 2 (Copenhagen).

– (1956), 'The Durham Proverbs: An Eleventh-Century Collection of Anglo-Saxon Proverbs Edited from Durham Cathedral M.S. B. III. 32', *Lunds Universitets Årsskrift* 52.2: 1–24.

- (1973), 'On the Dating of Early Bede Manuscripts', *SN* 45: 47–52.
- (1977), 'Further Notes on the Durham Proverbs', *ES* 58: 101–4.
- (1981), 'The Durham Proverbs', *Speculum* 56: 288–300.

Arnold, T., ed. (1890–6), *Memorials of St Edmund's Abbey*, 3 vols., RS 96 (London).

Arnott, R., ed. (2002), *The Archaeology of Medicine: Papers given at a Session of the Annual Conference of the Theoretical Archaeology Group held at the University of Birmingham on 20 December 1998*, BAR, Internat. Ser. 1046 (Oxford)

Aronstam, R.A. (1974), 'The Latin Canonical Tradition in Late Anglo-Saxon England: The Excerptiones Egberti' (unpubl. PhD dissertation, Columbia University, NY).
- (1975), 'Penitential Pilgrimages to Rome in the Early Middle Ages', *Archivum Historiae Pontificiae* 13: 65–83.

Asbach, F.B. (1975), 'Das *Poenitentiale Remense* und der sogennante *Excarpsus Cummeani*. Überlieferung, Quellen und Entwicklung zweier kontinentaler Bussbücher aus der 1. Hälfte des 8. Jahrhunderts' (Dr phil dissertation, University of Regensburg).

Assmann, B., ed. (1889/1964), *Angelsächsische Homilien und Heiligenleben*, Bibliothek der angelsächsischen Prosa 3 [repr. with supplementary introduction by P. Clemoes, Darmstadt, 1964] (Kassel).

Atkins, I. (1928), 'An Investigation of Two Anglo-Saxon Calendars (Missal of Jumièges and St Wulfstan's Homiliary)', *Archaeologia* 78: 219–54.
- and N.R. Ker (1944), *Catalogus Librorum Manuscriptorum Bibliothecae Wigorniensis made in 1622–1623 by Patrick Young, Librarian to King James I* (Cambridge).

Atsma, H. and J. Vezin (1988), 'Le dossier suspect des possessions de Saint-Denis en Angleterre révisité (VIIIᵉ–IXᵉ siècle)', in Setz (1988–90) IV. 221–36.

Atwood, E.B. and A.A. Hill, eds. (1969), *Studies in Language, Literature and Culture of the Middle Ages and Later: In Honour of Rudolph Willard* (Austin, TX).

Auerbach, I. (1977), 'Ein Fragment des Daniel-Kommentars von Hieronymus im Staatsarchiv Marburg', *Archiv für Diplomatik* 23: 55–103.

Autenrieth, J., and F. Brunhölzl, eds. (1971), *Festschrift Bernhard Bischoff zu seinem 65. Geburtstag, dargebracht von Freunden, Kollegen und Schülern* (Stuttgart).
- (1995), 'Bücher im Übergang von der Spätantike zum Mittelalter', *Scriptorium* 49: 169–89.

Avril, F. and J. Hoffeld, eds. (1975a), *The Year 1200: a Symposium / Metropolitan Museum of Art* (New York).

– (1975b), *Bibliothèque municipale de Rouen. Manuscrits normands XI–XII siècles: février-mars 1975, Musée des Beaux-Arts* (Rouen) [exhibition catalogue].

– and P.D. Stirnemann (1987), *Manuscrits enluminés d'origine insulaire, VIIe–XXe siècle* (Paris).

Aylmer, G. and J. Tiller, eds. (2000), *Hereford Cathedral: a History* (London).

Babcock, R.G. (2000), 'A Papyrus Codex of Gregory the Great's *Forty Homilies on the Gospels* (London, Cotton Titus C. xv)', *Scriptorium* 54: 280–9.

Backhouse, J. (1981), *The Lindisfarne Gospels* (Oxford).

– (1984a), 'The Making of the Harley Psalter', *BLJ* 10: 97–113.

– et al., eds. (1984b), *The Golden Age of Anglo-Saxon Art, 966–1066* (London).

– (1989), 'Birds, Beasts and Initials in Lindisfarne's Gospel Books', in Bonner et al. (1989a), 165–74.

– (1997), *The Illuminated Page* (London).

Baehrens, E., ed. (1879–83), *Poetae Latini Minores*, 5 vols. (Leipzig).

Baesecke, G. (1933), *Der Vocabularius Sti. Galli in der angelsächsischen Mission* (Halle).

Bailey, R.N. (1978), *The Durham Cassiodorus*, The Jarrow Lecture (Jarrow).

– and R. Handley (1983), 'Early English Manuscripts of Cassiodorus' *Expositio Psalmorum*', *Classical Philology* 78: 51–5.

– (1983), 'Bede's Text of Cassiodorus' Commentary on the Psalms', *JTS* n.s. 34: 189–93.

Bains, D. (1936), *A Supplement to Notae Latinae (Abbreviations in Latin MSS of 850 to 1050 A. D.)*, with a Foreword by W.M. Lindsay (Cambridge).

Baker, M. (1978), 'Medieval Illustrations of Bede's *Life of St Cuthbert*', *JWCI* n.s. 41: 16–49 [with an appendix by D.H. Farmer].

Baker, P.S. (1980), 'The Old English Canon of Byrhtferth of Ramsey', *Speculum* 55: 22–37.

– (1981), 'Byrhtferth's *Enchiridion* and the Computus in Oxford, St John's College 17', *ASE* 10: 123–42.

– and M. Lapidge, eds. (1995), *Byrhtferth's Enchiridion*, EETS s.s. 15 (Oxford).

– and N. Howe, eds. (1998), *Words and Works: Studies in Medieval English Language and Literature in Honour of Fred C. Robinson* (Toronto).

– ed. (2000), *The Anglo-Saxon Chronicle: a Collaborative Edition, vol. VIII: MS F: A Semi-diplomatic Edition with Introduction and Indices* (Cambridge).

Baldwin Brown, G. (1903–37), *The Arts in Early England*, 6 vols. (London).

Bammel, C.H. (1991), 'Insular Manuscripts of Origen in the Carolingian Empire', in Jondorf–Dumville (1991), 5–16.

– (1993), 'Das neue Rufinfragment in irischer Schrift und die Überlieferung der Rufin'schen Übersetzung der Kirchengeschichte Eusebs', in *Philologia Sacra*.

Biblische und patristische Studien für Hermann J. Frede und Walter Thiele zu ihrem siebzigsten Geburtstag, ed. R. Gryson, 2 vols. (Freiburg, 1993), 483–513.

Bammesberger, A. (2001), 'Sprachgeschichtliche Probleme der frühen altenglischen Glossen: sechs Einzelbeispiele', in Bergmann (2001), 137–46.

Banham, D., ed. (1991), *Monasteriales* [sic] *Indicia: The Anglo-Saxon Monastic Sign Language* (Pinner).

– (2002), 'Investigating the Anglo-Saxon *materia medica*: Archaeobotany, Manuscript Art, Latin and Old English', in Arnott (2002), 95–9.

– (2011), 'England Joins the Medical Mainstream: New Texts in Eleventh-Century Manuscripts', in Sauer et al. (2011), 341–52.

Bankert, D.A. et al. (1997), *Ambrose in Anglo-Saxon England with pseudo-Ambrose and Ambrosiaster*, OEN Subsidia 25 (Kalamazoo).

Banks, R.A. (1965), 'Some Anglo-Saxon Prayers from British Museum MS Cotton Galba A. xiv', *N&Q* 210: 207–13.

– (1967-8), 'A Study of the Old English Versions of the Lord's Prayer, the Creeds, the Gloria, and Some Prayers Found in the British Museum MS. Cotton Galba A. xiv, together with a New Examination of the Place of Liturgy in the Literature of Anglo-Saxon Magic and Medicine' (unpubl. PhD dissertation, University of London).

Bannister, A.T. (1927), *A Descriptive Catalogue of the Manuscripts in the Hereford Cathedral Library* (Hereford).

Bannister, H.M. (1908), 'Liturgical Fragments', *JTS* 9: 398–427.

– (1910–11a), 'Irish Psalters', *JTS* 12: 278–82.

– (1910–11b), 'Fragments of an Anglo-Saxon Sacramentary', *JTS* 12: 451–5.

– ed. (1913), *Monumenti vaticani di Paleografia musicale latina*, Codices e Vaticanis selecti phototypice expressi 12 (Leipzig).

– (1917), 'Bishop Roger of Worcester and the Church of Keynsham, with a List of Vestments and Books possibly belonging to Worcester', *EHR* 32: 387–93.

Banting, H.M.J., ed. (1989), *Two Anglo-Saxon Pontificals. The Egbert and Sidney Sussex Pontificals*, HBS 104 (London).

Barbour, R. (1981), *Manuscripts of the Greek Bible. An Introduction to Greek Palaeography* (Oxford).

Barker, E.E. (1951), 'The Cottonian Fragments of Æthelweard's Chronicle', *Bulletin of the Institute of Historical Research* 24: 46–62.

– (1977), 'Two Lost Documents of King Æthelstan', *ASE* 6: 137–43.

Barker, K., D.A. Hinton and A. Hunt, eds. (2005), *St Wulfsige and Sherborne. Essays to Celebrate the Millennium of the Benedictine Abbey, 998–1998* (Oxford).

Barker, N. et al., eds. (1986), *The York Gospels: a Facsimile*. With introductory essays by J.J.G. Alexander, P. McGurk, S. Keynes and B. Barr (London).

Barker-Benfield, B.C. (1976), 'A Ninth-Century Manuscript from Fleury: *Cato de senectute cum Macrobio*', in Alexander — Gibson (1976), 145–65.
- (1991), 'The Werden "Heptateuch"', *ASE* 20: 43–64.
- (1993), 'Not St Dunstan's Book', *N&Q* 238: 431–3.
- ed. (2008), *St Augustine's Abbey, Canterbury*, Corpus of British Medieval Library Catalogues 13, 3 vols. (London, 2008).
Barlow, C.W., ed. (1950), *Martini Bracarensis Opera Omnia* (New Haven, CT).
Barlow, F. et al. (1972), *Leofric of Exeter* (Exeter).
- ed. (1992), *The Life of King Edward who rests at Westminster*, 2nd ed. (Oxford).
Barney, S., ed. (1991), *Annotation and its Texts* (New York).
Barnhouse, R.A. (1994), 'Text and Image in the Illustrated Old English Hexateuch' (unpubl. PhD dissertation, University of North Carolina).
- and B.C. Withers, eds. (2000), *The Old English Hexateuch. Aspects and Approaches* (Kalamazoo, MI).
Barré, H. (1962), *Les homéliaires carolingiens de l'école d'Auxerre: Authenticité, inventaire, tablaux comparatifs, initia*, Studi e testi 225 (Vatican City).
- (1963), *Prières anciennes de l'Occident à la mère du Sauveur, des origines à S. Anselme* (Paris).
Barrow, G. (2004), 'Scots in the Durham *Liber Vitae*', in Rollason (2004a), 109–16.
Barrow, J. (1996), 'The Community of Worcester, 961–c. 1100', in Brooks — Cubitt (1996), 84–99.
- (2004), 'Wulfstan and Worcester: Bishop and Clergy in the Early Eleventh Century', in Townend (2004), 141–60.
- and N.P. Brooks, eds. (2005), *St Wulfstan and his World* (Aldershot).
- and A. Wareham, eds. (2008), *Myth, Rulership, Church and Charters: Essays in Honour of Nicholas Brooks* (Aldershot).
Bartoniek, E. (1940), *Codices Manu Scripti Latini*, I. *Codices Latini Medii Aevi*, Catalogi Bibliothecae Musaei Nationalis Hungarici 12 (Budapest).
Bassett, S., ed. (1989), *The Origins of Anglo-Saxon Kingdoms* (London).
Baswell, C. (1995), *Virgil in Medieval England. Figuring the 'Aeneid' from the Twelfth Century to Chaucer*, Cambridge Studies in Medieval Literature 24 (Cambridge).
Bately, J.[M.], and D.J. Ross (1961), 'A Checklist of Manuscripts of Orosius, *Historiarum adversum paganos libri septem*', *Scriptorium* 15: 329–34.
- (1964), 'Notes and News. The Vatican Fragment of the Old English Orosius', *ES* 45: 224–30.
- ed. (1980), *The Old English Orosius*, EETS s.s. 6 (London).
- (1982), 'Lexical Evidence for the Authorship of the Prose Psalms in the Paris Psalter', *ASE* 10: 69–95.

– ed. (1986), *The Anglo-Saxon Chronicle: a Collaborative Edition, vol. III: MS A: a Semi-diplomatic Edition with Introduction and Indices* (Cambridge).
– ed. (1992), *The Tanner Bede: The Old English Version of Bede's Historia Ecclesiastica, Oxford Bodleian Library Tanner 10 together with the Medieval Binding Leaves, Oxford Bodleian Library Tanner 10* and the Domitian Extracts, London British Library Cotton Domitian A.IX fol. 11*, EEMF 24 (Copenhagen).
– (1993), *Anonymous Old English Homilies. A Preliminary Bibliography of Source Studies* (Binghamton, NY).
– (2006), 'The Language of Ohthere's Report to King Alfred: Some Problems and Some Puzzles for Historians and Linguists', in Keynes–Smyth (2006), 39–53.
Bateson, M. (1894a), 'The Supposed Latin Penitential of Egbert and the Missing Work of Halitgar of Cambrai', *EHR* 9: 320–6.
– (1894b), 'Rules for Monks and Secular Canons after the Revival under King Edgar', *EHR* 9: 690–708.
– (1895), 'A Worcester Cathedral Book of Ecclesiastical Collections Made *c.* 1000 A.D.', *EHR* 10: 712–31.
Batlle, C.M. (1972), *Die Adhortationes Sanctorum Patrum (Verba Seniorum) im lateinischen Mittelalter*, Beiträge zur Geschichte des alten Mönchtums und des Benediktinerordens 31 (Münster i. W.).
Battiscombe, C.F., ed. (1956), *The Relics of St Cuthbert* (Oxford).
Bauerreiss, R. (1933), 'Ein angelsächsisches Kalenderfragment des bayrischen Hauptstaatsarchivs in München', *Studien und Mitteilungen zur Geschichte des Benediktinerordens und seiner Zweige* 51: 177–82.
Baumstark, A. (1927), 'Ein altgelasianisches Sakramentarbruchstück insularer Herkunft', *Jahrbuch für Liturgiewissenschaft* 7: 130–6.
Bautier, R.-H. and G. Labory, eds. (1969), *André de Fleury: Vie de Gauzlin, abbé de Fleury*, Sources d'histoire médiévale 2 (Paris).
Baxter, S., C. Karkov, J.L. Nelson and D. Pelteret, eds. (2009), *Early Medieval Studies in Memory of Patrick Wormald* (Farnham).
– (2004), 'Archbishop Wulfstan and the Administration of God's Property', in Townend (2004), 161–207.
Bayless, M. (1993), '*Beatus quid est* and the Study of Grammar in Late Anglo-Saxon England', *Historiographia Linguistica* 20: 67–110.
– and M. Lapidge, eds. (1998), *Collectanea Pseudo-Bedae*, Scriptores Latini Hiberniae 14 (Dublin).
Bazire, J. and J.E. Cross, eds. (1982), *Eleven Old English Rogationtide Homilies*, Toronto OE Series 7 (Toronto).

Beadle, R., ed. (1995), *New Science out of Old Books: Studies in Manuscripts and Early Printed Books in Honour of A.I. Doyle* (Aldershot).

Beall, B.A. (2005), 'Entry Point to the *Scriptorium* Bede Knew at Wearmouth and Jarrow: The Canon Tables of the *Codex Amiatinus*', in Lebecq et al. (2005), 187–97.

Beccaria, A. (1956), *I codici di medicina del periodo presalernitano* (Rome).

Becker, W. (1976), 'The Latin Manuscript Sources of the Old English Translation of the Sermon *Remedia Peccatorum*', *MÆ* 45: 145–52.

Beeson, C. (1913), *Isidor-Studien* (Munich).

Behaghel, O., ed. (1996), *Heliand und Genesis*, 10th ed. rev. by B. Taeger (Tübingen).

Behrends, F., ed. (1976), *The Letters and Poems of Fulbert of Chartres* (Oxford).

Beissel, S. (1907), *Entstehung der Perikopen des römischen Messbuches* (Freiburg im Breisgau).

Belfour, A.O., ed. (1909), *Twelfth-Century Homilies in MS. Bodley 343*, EETS o.s. 137 (Oxford).

Belkin, J. and J. Meier (1975), *Bibliographie zu Otfrid von Weissenburg und zur altsächsischen Bibeldichtung (Heliand und Genesis)* (Berlin).

Bell, N. (2001), *Music in Medieval Manuscripts* (London).

[Benedictines of Stanbrook] (1897), *Gregorian Music: An Outline of Musical Palaeography Illustrated by Facsimiles of Ancient Manuscripts* (London).

Benedikz, B.S. (1986), *Lichfield Cathedral Library: A Catalogue of the Cathedral Library Manuscripts*, 3rd ed. (Birmingham).

Bennett, A., 'Devotional Literacy of a Noblewoman in a Book of Hours of *ca.* 1300 in Cambrai', in Dekeyzer—Van der Stock (2005a), 149–58.

Bergamin, M., ed. (2005), *Aenigmata Symposii. La fondazione dell'enigmistica come genere poetico*, Per Verba 22 (Florence).

Berger, S. (1893), *Histoire de la Vulgate pendant les premiers siècles du moyen âge* (Paris).

Berghaus, F. (1979), *Die Verwandtschaftsverhältnisse der altenglischen Interlinearversionen des Psalters und der Cantica*, Palaestra 272 (Göttingen).

Bergman, J. ed. (1926), *Aurelii Prudentii Clementis Carmina*, CSEL 61 (Vienna).

Bergmann, R. (1973), *Verzeichnis der althochdeutschen und altsächsischen Glossenhandschriften. Mit Bibliographie der Glosseneditionen, der Handschriftenbeschreibungen und der Dialektbestimmungen* (Berlin).

– (1996), 'Latin-Old High German Glosses and Glossaries: A Catalogue of Manuscripts', in Hamesse (1996), 547–614.

– et al., eds. (2001), *Mittelalterliche volkssprachige Glossen*, Germanistische Bibliothek 13 (Heidelberg).

- ed. (2003), *Volkssprachig-lateinische Mischtexte*, Germanistische Bibliothek 17 (Heidelberg).
- and S. Stricker (2005), *Katalog der althochdeutschen und altsächsischen Glossenhandschriften*, 6 vols. (Berlin).
Berkhout, C.T. and M.McC. Gatch, eds. (1982), *Anglo-Saxon Scholarship: The First Three Centuries* (Boston, MA).
- (2006), 'An Early Insular Fragment of Bede's *De schematibus et tropis*', *N&Q* 251: 10–12.
Bernadskaya, E.V., T.P. Voronova and S.O. Vialova (1983), *Latinskiye rukopisi V–XII vekov Gosudarstvennoy Publichnoy Biblioteki im. M.E. Saltykova-Schedrina* [Latin Manuscripts of the V–XII Centuries of the Saltykov-Schedrin Library] (Leningrad).
Berry, M. (1988), 'What the Saxon Monks Sang: Music in Winchester in the late Tenth Century', in Yorke (1988), 149–60.
Berry, R. (1982), '"Ealle þing [*recte* þing] wundorlice gesceapen": The Structure of the *Computus* in Byrhtferth's Manual', *Revue de l'Université d'Ottawa* 52: 130–41.
Berschin, W. (1988), *Greek Letters and the Latin Middle Ages*, trans. J.C. Frakes, with revisions and additions by the author (Washington) [German original: *Griechisch-lateinisches Mittelalter. Von Hieronymus zu Nikolaus von Kues* (Bern, 1980)]
- (2000), 'Diptychonformat', *Philobiblon* 44: 231–40.
Bertini, F. (1996), 'Osberno di Gloucester', in Hamesse (1996), 283–97.
Bertram, J., ed. (2005), *The Chrodegang Rules: The Rules for the Common Life of the Secular Clergy from the Eighth and Ninth Centuries. Critical Texts with Translations and Commentary* (Aldershot).
Best, R.I. (1926–8), 'An Early Monastic Grant in the Book of Durrow', *Ériu* 10: 135–42.
Bestul, T.H. (1977), 'A Note on the Contents of the Anselm Manuscript, Bodleian Library, Laud Misc. 508', *Manuscripta* 21: 167–70.
- (1979), 'The Book of Cerne and the English Devotional Tradition', *Manuscripta* 23: 3–4.
- (1981a), 'British Library MS Arundel 60 and the Anselmian Apocrypha', *Scriptorium* 35: 271–5.
- (1981b), 'Ephraim the Syrian and Old English Poetry', *Anglia* 99: 1–24.
- (1984), 'The Collection of Private Prayers in the *Portiforium* of Wulfstan of Worcester and the *Orationes sive Meditationes* of Anselm of Canterbury: A Study in the Anglo-Norman Devotional Tradition', in Foreville (1984), 355–64.
- (1986), 'Continental Sources of Anglo-Saxon Devotional Writing', in Szarmach (1986c), 103–26.

– (1990), 'Liturgy', in Biggs (1990), 135–40.

Bethell, D.L. (1969), 'English Black Monks and Episcopal Elections in the 1120s', *EHR* 84: 671–98.

Bethurum, D. (1942), 'Archbishop Wulfstan's Commonplace Book', *PMLA* 57: 916–29.

– (1949), 'A Letter of Protest from the English Bishops to the Pope', in Kirby–Woolf (1949), 97–104.

– ed. (1957), *The Homilies of Wulfstan* (Oxford).

Bévenot, M. (1961), *The Tradition of Manuscripts: A Study in the Transmission of St Cyprian's Treatises* (Oxford).

– (1962), 'Towards Dating the Leningrad Bede', *Scriptorium* 16: 365–9.

– (1980), 'The Oldest Surviving Manuscript of St Cyprian now in the British Library', *JTS* n.s. 31: 368–77.

Bezzo, L. (2007), 'Parallel Remedies: Old English *Paralisin þæt is lyftadl*', in Lendinara et al. (2007) 435–45.

Bicchieri, M. (2001), 'Non-Destructive Analysis of the *Bibbia Amiatina* by XRF, PIXE-α and Raman', *Quinio* 3: 169–79.

Biddle, M., ed. (1976a), *Winchester in the Early Middle Ages: An Edition and Discussion of the Winton Domesday*, Winchester Studies 1 (Oxford).

– (1976b), 'The Corrections in the Winton Domesday', in Biddle (1976a), 522–6.

Bieler, L. (1949), 'Insular Palaeography: Present State and Problems', *Scriptorium* 3: 267–94.

– ed. (1963), *The Irish Penitentials*, Scriptores Latini Hiberniae 5 (Dublin).

– and J. Carney, eds. (1972), 'The Lambeth Commentary', *Ériu* 23: 1–55.

– ed. (1984), *Boethius: Consolatio Philosophiae*, CCSL 94 (Turnhout).

Bierbaumer, P. (1975–9), *Der botanische Wortschatz des Altenglischen*, 3 vols. (Frankfurt a. M.).

– (1977a), 'On the Interrelationships of the Old English Psalter-Glosses', *Arbeiten aus Anglistik und Amerikanistik* 2: 123–48.

– (1977b), 'Zu J. V. Goughs Ausgabe einiger altenglischer Glossen', *Anglia* 95: 115–21.

Bierbrauer, K. (1979), *Die Ornamentik frühkarolingischer Handschriften aus Bayern*, Bayerische Akademie der Wissenschaften, phil.-hist. Klasse, Abhandlungen N.F. 84 (Munich).

Biggs, F.M. et al., eds. (1990), *Sources of Anglo-Saxon Literary Culture: a Trial Version* (Binghamton, NY).

– (1994), 'Part III of the *Moralia* in MS. Bodley 310: A New College Manuscript', *BLR* 15: 13–19.

– (1996), 'Ælfric as Historian: His Use of Alcuin's *Laudationes* and Sulpicius's *Dialogues* in his Two Lives of Martin', in Szarmach (1996), 289–315.

- and T.N. Hall (1996), 'Traditions Concerning Jamnes and Mambres in Anglo-Saxon England', *ASE* 25: 69–89.
- et al., eds. (2001), *Sources of Anglo-Saxon Literary Culture*, I. *Abbo of Fleury, Abbo of Saint-Germain-des-Prés, and Acta Sanctorum*, Sources of Anglo-Saxon Literary Culture 1 (Kalamazoo, MI) [note that citations from this volume are by E.G. Whatley unless otherwise specified].
- (2002), 'Comments on the Codicology of Two Paris Manuscripts (BN lat. 13408 and 5574)', in T.N. Hall (2002), 326–30.
- (2007a), *Sources of Anglo-Saxon Literary Culture. The Apocrypha*, Instrumenta Anglistica Mediaevalia 1 (Kalamazoo, MI).
- (2007b), 'Folio 179 of the *Beowulf* Manuscript', in C.D. Wright et al. (2007), 52–9.
- (2008), 'A Picture of Paul in a Parker Manuscript', in Blanton—Scheck (2008) 169–89.
Bill, E.G.W. (1972), *A Catalogue of Manuscripts in Lambeth Palace Library, MSS 1222–1860* (with a supplement to M. R. James' *Descriptive Catalogue of the Manuscripts in the Library of Lambeth Palace* by N.R. Ker) (Oxford).
Binski, P. and W. Noel, eds. (2001), *New Offerings, Ancient Treasures: Studies in Medieval Art for George Henderson* (Stroud).
- and S. Panayotova, eds. (2005), *The Cambridge Illuminations. Ten Centuries of Book Production in the Medieval West* (London).
- (2006), 'John the Smith's Grave', in L'Engle—Guest (2006), 387–93.
- and P. Zutshi (2011), *Western Illuminated Manuscripts: A Catalogue of the Collection in Cambridge University Library* (Cambridge).
Birch, W. de G. (1876), *The History, Art and Palaeography of the Manuscript styled the Utrecht Psalter* (London).
- (1881), *Memorials of Saint Guthlac of Crowland* (Wisbech).
- ed. (1889), *An Ancient Manuscript of the Eighth or Ninth Century: formerly belonging to St. Mary's Abbey, or Nunnaminster, Winchester*, Hampshire Record Society 2 (London).
- (1892), *Liber Vitae: Register and Martyrology of New Minster and Hyde Abbey*, Hampshire Record Society 5 (London and Winchester).
Bischoff, B. (1951), 'Ars Sacra', *Scriptorium* 5: 306–8.
- and J. Hofmann (1952), *Libri Sancti Kyliani. Die Würzburger Schreibschule und die Dombibliothek im VIII. und IX. Jahrhundert*, Quellen und Forschungen zur Geschichte des Bistums und Hochstifts Würzburg 6 (Würzburg).
- (1954a), *Übersicht über die nichtdiplomatischen Geheimschriften des Mittelalters* (Graz).
- (1954b), 'Wendepunkte in der Geschichte der lateinischen Exegese im Frühmittelalter', *Sacris Erudiri* 6: 191–281 [repr. Bischoff (1966–81) I.205–73].

- (1957), 'Paläographie', in Stammler (1957), 379–451.
- (1962), Review of E.A. Lowe, *English Uncial*, in *Gnomon* 34: 605–15 [repr. Bischoff (1966–81) II.328–39].
- and D. Nörr (1963), *Eine unbekannte Konstitution Kaiser Julians (c. Iuliani de postulando)*, Bayerische Akademie der Wissenschaften, phil.-hist. Klasse, Abhandlungen, N. F. 58 (Munich).
- (1965), 'Panorama der Handschriftenüberlieferung aus der Zeit Karls des Grossen', in *Karl der Grosse. Lebenswerk und Nachleben*, II. *Das geistige Leben*, ed. B. Bischoff (Düsseldorf, 1965), 233–54 [repr. Bischoff (1966–81) III.5–38].
- (1966–81), *Mittelalterliche Studien. Ausgewählte Aufsätze zur Schriftkunde und Literaturgeschichte*, 3 vols. (Stuttgart).
- ed. (1967) [with members of the Zentralinstitut für Kunstgeschichte], *Mittelalterliche Schatzverzeichnisse 1: Von der Zeit Karls des Grossen bis zur Mitte des 13. Jahrhunderts*, Veröffentlichungen des Zentralinstituts für Kunstgeschichte in München 4 (Munich).
- (1968a), 'Frühkarolingische Handschriften und ihre Heimat', *Scriptorium* 22: 306–14.
- (1968b), 'Die Handschrift. Paläographische Untersuchungen', in [Württembergische Landesbibliothek Stuttgart], *Der Stuttgarter Bilderpsalter, Bibl. Fol. 23, Württembergische Landesbibliothek Stuttgart 2: Untersuchungen* (Stuttgart), 15–30.
- (1974), *Die südostdeutschen Schreibschulen und Bibliotheken in der Karolingerzeit*, I: *Die bayerischen Diözesen*, 3rd rev. ed. (Wiesbaden).
- (1976a), Review of *Chartae Latinae Antiquiores 3–5* ed. A. Bruckner and R. Marichal, *HZ* 223: 689–96.
- (1976b), 'Die Hofbibliothek unter Ludwig dem Frommen', in Alexander—Gibson (1976), 3–22 [repr. Bischoff (1966–81) III.170–86].
- (1980), *Die südostdeutschen Schreibschulen und Bibliotheken der Karolingerzeit*, II: *Die vorwiegend österreichischen Diözesen* (Wiesbaden).
- (1981), 'Die ältesten Handschriften der *Regula Benedicti* in Bayern', *Studien und Mitteilungen zur Geschichte des Benediktinerordens* 92: 7–16.
- (1983a), 'Manoscritti nonantulani dispersi dell'epoca carolingia', *La Bibliofilia* 85: 99–124.
- (1983b), Review of *A Survey of Manuscripts Illuminated in the British Isles. vol. I: Insular Manuscripts: 6th to the 9th Century*, ed. J.J.G. Alexander, *MLJ* 18: 292–3.
- (1984a), 'Italienische Handschriften des 9. bis 11. Jahrhunderts in frühmit- telalterlichen Bibliotheken ausserhalb Italiens', in Questa—Raffaelli (1984), 169–94.

– (1984b), *Anecdota novissima. Texte des vierten bis sechzehnten Jahrhunderts*, Quellen und Untersuchungen zur lateinischen Philologie des Mittelalters 7 (Stuttgart).

– and V. Brown (1985), 'Addenda to *Codices Latini Antiquiores* (I)', *MS* 47: 317–66.

– (1986), *Paläographie des römischen Altertums und des abendländischen Mittelalters*, 2nd ed. (Berlin).

– et al., eds. (1988a), *The Épinal, Erfurt, Werden, and Corpus Glossaries: Épinal, Bibliothèque Municipale 72 (2), Erfurt, Wissenschaftliche Bibliothek Amplonianus 2° 42, Düsseldorf Universitätsbibliothek Fragm. K 19, Munich Bayerische Staatsbibliothek Cgm. 187 III, Cambridge Corpus Christi College 144*, EEMF 22 (Copenhagen).

– (1988b), Review of Francis Wormald, *Collected Writings I: Studies in Medieval Art from the Sixth to the Twelfth Centuries*, ed. J.J.G. Alexander, T.J. Brown, and J. Gibbs, *Peritia* 6/7: 321–2.

– (1989a), *Die Abtei Lorsch im Spiegel ihrer Handschriften*, 2nd ed. (Lorsch).

– et al. (1989b), *Aratea. Kommentar zum Aratus des Germanicus. Ms. Voss. Lat. Q. 79, Bibliotheek der Rijksuniversiteit Leiden* (Luzern).

– (1990), *Latin Palaeography: Antiquity and the Middle Ages*, trans. D. Ó Cróinín and D. Ganz (Cambridge).

– (1991), 'Die Schrift des Quedlinburger Evangeliars', in Mütherich–Dachs (1991), 29–-34.

– and B. Löfstedt, eds. (1992a), *Anonymus ad Cuimnanum Expossitio Latinitatis*, CCSL 133D (Turnhout).

– et al. (1992b), 'Addenda to *Codices Latini Antiquiores* (II)', *MS* 54: 286–307.

– and M. Lapidge (1994), *Biblical Commentaries from the Canterbury School of Theodore and Hadrian*, CSASE 10 (Cambridge).

– (1998–), *Katalog der festländischen Handschriften des 9. Jahrhunderts (mit Ausnahme der wisigotischen)*, ed. B. Ebersperger (Wiesbaden).

Bishop, C., ed. (2007a), *Text and Transmission in Medieval Europe* (Cambridge).

– (2007b), 'The "Lost" Literature of England: Text and Transmission in Tenth-Century Wessex', in Bishop (2007a), 76–126.

Bishop, E. (1918), *Liturgica Historica: Papers on the Liturgy and Religious Life of the Western Church* (Oxford).

Bishop, T.A.M. (1949–53), 'Notes on Cambridge Manuscripts, Part I', *TCBS* 1: 432–41.

– (1954), 'A Fragment in Northumbrian Uncial', *Scriptorium* 8: 111–13.

– (1954–8a), 'Notes on Cambridge Manuscripts, Parts II and III', *TCBS* 2: 185–99.

– (1954–8b), 'Notes on Cambridge Manuscripts, Part IV: MSS connected with St Augustine's Canterbury', *TCBS* 2: 323–36.

- (1955), 'Canterbury Scribe's Work', *The Durham Philobiblon* 2.1: 1–3.
- (1959–63a), 'Notes on Cambridge Manuscripts, Part V: MSS connected with St Augustine's Canterbury, continued', *TCBS* 3: 93–5.
- (1959–63b), 'Notes on Cambridge Manuscripts, Part VI', *TCBS* 3: 412–23.
- (1964–8a), 'Notes on Cambridge Manuscripts, Part VII: Pelagius in Trinity College, B.10.5', *TCBS* 4: 70–7.
- (1964–8b), 'An Early Example of the Square Minuscule', *TCBS* 4: 246–52.
- (1964–8c), 'The Corpus Martianus Capella', *TCBS* 4: 257–75.
- (1964–8d), 'An Early Example of Insular-Caroline', *TCBS* 4: 396–400.
- ed. (1966), *Aethici Istrici Cosmographia Vergilio Salisburgensi Rectius Adscripta: Codex Leidensis Scaligeranus 69* (Amsterdam) [facsimile].
- (1967a), 'The Copenhagen Gospel Book', *Nordisk Tidskrift för Bok- och Biblioteksvåsen* 54: 33–41.
- (1967b), 'Lincoln Cathedral 182', *Lincolnshire History and Archaeology* 2: 73–6.
- (1971) *English Caroline Minuscule* (Oxford).
- (1990), 'The Scribes of the Corbie *a-b*', in Godman—Collins (1990), 523–36.
Bjorklund, N.B. (2004), 'Parker's Purposes Behind the Manuscripts: Matthew Parker in the Context of his Early Career and Sixteenth-Century Church Reform', in Lionarons (2004a), 217–41.
Björkvall, G. (2002), 'The Remnants of Medieval Book Culture in Sweden: A Current Cataloguing Project of Fragments at the National Archives in Stockholm', in Perani—Ruini (2002), 157–68.
Black, W.H. (1845), *A Descriptive, Analytical and Critical Catalogue of the Manuscripts Bequeathed unto the University of Oxford by Elias Ashmole Esq.* (Oxford).
Blackburn, F.A., ed. (1907), *Exodus and Daniel: Two Old English Poems preserved in MS. Junius 11* (Boston).
Blake, E.O., ed. (1962), *Liber Eliensis*, Camden Third Series 92 (London).
Blake, M., ed. (2009), *Ælfric's De Temporibus Anni*, AST 6 (Cambridge).
Blake, N.F., ed. (1990), *The Phoenix*, rev. ed. (Exeter).
Blanton, V. and H. Scheck, eds. (2008), *Intertexts: Studies in Anglo-Saxon Culture presented to Paul E. Szarmach*, MRTS 334 (Tempe, AZ).
Blatt, F., ed. (1958), *The Latin Josephus, Introduction and Text; The Antiquities, Books I–V*, Acta Jutlandica 30 (Copenhagen).
Bleskina, O. et al. (2001), 'Descriptions of the NLR Manuscripts', in Kilpiö—Kahlas-Tarkka (2001), 25–92.
Bliss, A.J. (1971), 'Some Unnoticed Lines of OE Verse', *N&Q* 216: 404.
- and A.J. Frantzen (1976), 'The Integrity of *Resignation*', *RES* n.s. 27: 385–402.
Blockley, M. (1994), 'Further Addenda and Corrigenda to N. Ker's *Catalogue*', rev. ed. in Richards (1994), 79–86. [orig. publ. *N&Q* 227: 1–3].

Blomfield, J. (1939), 'The Source of the Cleopatra Glosses' (unpubl. PhD dissertation, University of Oxford, 1939).

Bloomfield, M.W. et al. (1979), *Incipits of Latin Works on the Virtues and Vices, 1100–1500 A. D.*, Mediaeval Academy of America Publications 88 (Cambridge, MA).

Bloor, W.A. (1933), 'The Proper of the Mass for the Feast of St Edmund', *The Douai Magazine* 7 no. 4: 226–8.

Blume, C., ed. (1908), *Der Cursus S. Benedicti Nursini und die liturgischen Hymnen des 6. – 9. Jahrhunderts in ihrer Beziehung zu den Sonntags- und Ferialhymnen unseres Breviers: eine hymnologisch-liturgische Studie auf Grund handschriftlichen Quellenmaterials*, Hymnologische Beiträge 3 (Leipzig).

Blunt, W. and S. Raphael (1994), *The Illustrated Herbal*, 2nd ed. (London).

Boas, M., ed. (1952), *Disticha Catonis* (Amsterdam).

Boase, T.S.R. (1951), *English Romanesque Illumination*, Bodleian Picture Book 1 (Oxford).

– (1953), *English Art: 1100–1216* (Oxford).

Bock, N. et al., eds. (2002), *Art, cérémonial et liturgie au moyen âge* (Rome).

Bodarwé, K. (2000), 'Schriftlichkeit und Bildung im ottonischen Essen', in *Herrschaft, Bildung und Gebet: Gründung und Anfänge des Frauenstifts Essen*, ed. G. Berghaus, T. Schilp and M. Schlagheck (Essen, 2000), 101–17.

Bodden, M.C. (1979), 'Detailed Description of Oxford Bodleian Manuscript Auctarium F. 4.32, along with a Close Study of its Second Gathering: An 11th-century Old English Homily on the Finding of the True Cross' (unpubl. PhD dissertation, University of Toronto).

– (1986), 'The Preservation and Transmission of Greek in Early England', in Szarmach (1986c), 53–63.

– ed. (1987), *The Old English 'Finding of the True Cross'* (Cambridge).

– (1988), 'Evidence for Knowledge of Greek in Anglo-Saxon England', *ASE* 17: 217–46.

Boer, W.W., ed. (1973), *Epistola Alexandri ad Aristotelem*, Beiträge zur klassischen Philologie 50 (Meisenheim am Glan).

Boese, H. (1966), *Die lateinischen Handschriften der Sammlung Hamilton zu Berlin* (Wiesbaden).

Boffey, J. and A.S.G. Edwards (2005), *A New Index of Middle English Verse* (London).

Bohara, A.M. (1985), 'More than Words Can Reckon: The Rhetoric of Afterlife Descriptions in Anglo-Saxon Poetry and Prose' (unpubl. PhD dissertation, University of Pennsylvania, PA).

Böhmer, H., ed. (1921), *Texte und Forschungen zur englischen Kulturgeschichte. Festgabe für Felix Liebermann zum 20. Juli 1921* (Halle).

Boll, P. (1904), *Die Sprache der altenglischen Glossen im MS. Harley 3376*, Bonner Beiträge zur Anglistik 15 (Bonn).

Bollard, J.K. (1973), 'The Cotton Maxims', *Neophilologus* 57: 179–87.

Bolton, D.K. (1977a), 'The Study of the Consolation of Philosophy in Anglo-Saxon England', *AHDLMA* 44: 33–78.

– (1977b), 'Remigian Commentaries on the *Consolation of Philosophy* and their Sources', *Traditio* 33: 381–94.

Bond, E.A. and E.M. Thompson (1873–83), *The Palaeographical Society: Facsimiles of Manuscripts and Inscriptions. First Series*, 3 vols. (London).

Bonner, G. (1957–9), 'A Misidentified Manuscript', *British Museum Quarterly* 21: 12–13.

– ed. (1976), *Famulus Christi: Essays in Commemoration of the Thirteenth Centenary of the Birth of the Venerable Bede* (London).

– D. Rollason and C. Stancliffe, eds. (1989a), *St Cuthbert, his Cult and his Community to AD 1200* (Woodbridge).

– (1989b), 'St Cuthbert at Chester-le-Street', in Bonner et al. (1989a), 387–95.

Bonser, W. (1963), *The Medical Background of Anglo-Saxon England* (London).

Boone, G.M., ed. (1995), *Essays in Medieval Music in Honor of David G. Hughes* (Cambridge).

Borg, A. and A. Martindale, eds. (1981), *The Vanishing Past. Studies of Medieval Art, Liturgy and Metrology presented to Christopher Hohler*, BAR Internat. Ser. 111 (Oxford).

Borland, C.R. (1916), *A Descriptive Catalogue of the Western Manuscripts in Edinburgh University Library* (Edinburgh).

Bornstein, G. and T. Tinkle, eds. (1998), *The Iconic Page in Manuscript, Print, and Digital Culture* (Ann Arbor, MI).

Borst, A. (2001), *Der karolingische Reichskalender und seine Überlieferung bis ins 12. Jahrhundert*, 3 vols., MGH, Libri memoriales 2 (Hannover).

Bosc-Lauby, A. and A. Notter, eds. (2004), *Lumières de l'an mil en Orléannais: autour du Millénaire d'Abbon de Fleury* (Turnhout).

Bosworth J. and G. Waring, eds. (1865), *The Gothic and Anglo-Saxon Gospels in Parallel Columns with the Versions of Wycliffe and Tyndale by Joseph Bosworth Assisted by George Waring* (London).

Bouet, P. and M. Dosdat, eds. (2005), *Manuscrits et enluminures dans le monde normand (X^e – XVe siècles)*, 2nd ed. (Caen).

Bourque, E. (1949–52), *Étude sur les sacramentaires romains*, 2 vols. (Quebec and Vatican City).

Boutemy, A. (1935), 'Two Obituaries of Christ Church, Canterbury', *EHR* 50: 292–9.

– (1937), 'Notice sur le recueil poétique du ms. Cotton Vitellius A. xii du British Museum', *Latomus* 1: 278–323.
– (1938), 'Le recueil poétique du manuscrit Additional 24199 du British Museum', *Latomus* 2: 30–52.
– (1948), 'Notes de voyages sur quelques manuscrits de l'ancien archdiocèse de Reims', *Scriptorium* 2: 123–9.
– (1966), 'Les feuillets de Damme', *Scriptorium* 20: 60–5.
– (1994–5), 'Le type de l'évangeliste et la lettre ornée dans les évangiles rémois du IXe siècle', *Bulletin de la Société Nationale des Antiquaires de France*, 25–8.
Bower, C.M. (1988), 'Boethius' *De institutione musica*: A Handlist of Manuscripts', *Scriptorium* 42: 205–51.
Boyd, W.J.P. (1975), *Aldred's Marginalia: Explanatory Comments in the Lindisfarne Gospels*, Exeter Medieval Texts and Studies 4 (Exeter).
Boyle, L.E. (1981), 'The Nowell Codex and the Poem of Beowulf', in Chase (1981), 23–32.
Boynton, S. (1999), 'Eleventh Century Continental Hymnaries Containing Latin Glosses', *Scriptorium* 53: 200–51.
Bradley, D.R. (1984), 'Iam dulcis amica uenito', *MLJ* 19: 104–15.
– (1985), 'Carmina Cantabrigiensia 23: Vestiunt silve tenera ramorum', *MÆ* 54: 259–65.
Bradshaw, H. (1889), *The Collected Papers of Henry Bradshaw* (Cambridge).
– (1893), *The Early Collection of Canons known as the Hibernensis: Two Unfinished Papers* (Cambridge).
Bräm, A. (2002), 'Bilder der Liturgie in liturgischen Handschriften bis in ottonische Zeit', in Bock (2002), 141–68.
Branch, B. (1979), 'Inventories of the Library of Fécamp from the 11th and 12th Centuries', *Manuscripta* 23: 159–72.
Brandis, T. et al. (1975), *Zimelien. Abendländische Handschriften des Mittelalters aus den Sammlungen der Stiftung Preussischer Kulturbesitz* (Wiesbaden).
Brandt, S. (1910), 'Über ein Fragment einer Handschrift des Justinus aus der Sammlung E. Fischer in Weinheim', *Neue Heidelberger Jahrbücher* 16: 109–14.
Brantley, J. (1999), 'The Iconography of the Utrecht Psalter and the Old English Descent into Hell', *ASE* 28: 43–63.
Brasington, B.C. and K.G. Cushing, eds. (2008), *Bishops, Texts and the Use of Canon Law around 1100. Essays in Honour of Martin Brett* (Aldershot).
Brechter, S. (1938), 'Versus Simplicii Casinensis abbatis', *RB* 50: 89–135.
Bredehoft, T.A. (2001), *Textual Histories: Readings in the Anglo-Saxon Chronicle* (Toronto).
– (2004), 'The Boundaries between Verse and Prose in Old English Literature', in Lionarons (2004a), 139–72.

- (2006), 'Filling the Margins of CCCC 41: Textual Space and a Developing Archive', *RES* n.s. 57: 721–32.
Breen, A. (1987), 'A New Irish Fragment of the "Continuatio" to Rufinus-Eusebius, *Historia ecclesiastica*', *Scriptorium* 41: 185–204.
- (1992), 'The Liturgical Materials in MS Oxford, Bodleian Library, Auct. F. 4. 32', *Archiv für Liturgiewissenschaft* 34: 121–53.
Breeze, A. (1996a), 'The Provenance of the Rushworth Mercian Gloss', *N&Q* 241: 394–5.
- (1996b), 'The Stockholm Golden Gospels in Seventeenth-Century Spain', *N&Q* 241: 395–7.
Bremmer, R.H., ed. (1998), *Franciscus Junius and His Circle* (Amsterdam).
- et al., eds. (2001), *Rome and the North: The Early Reception of Gregory the Great in Germanic Europe*, Mediaevalia Groningana 4 (Paris).
- (2007), 'The Anglo-Saxon Continental Mission and the Transfer of Encyclopaedic Knowledge', in Bremmer—Dekker (2007), 19–50.
- and K. Dekker, eds. (2007), *Foundations of Learning: The Transfer of Knowledge in the Early Middle Ages* (Leuven).
- (2008), 'The Reception of Defensor's *Liber Scintillarum* in Anglo-Saxon England', in Lendinara (2008), 75–89.
- and K. Dekker, eds. (2010), *Practice in Learning: The Transfer of Encyclopaedic Knowledge in the Early Middle Ages* (Leuven).
Breslau, R. (1997), *Der Nachlass der Brüder Grimm: Katalog*, 2 vols. (Wiesbaden).
Bressie, R., 'Libraries of the British Isles in the Anglo-Saxon Period', in J.W. Thompson (1957), 102–25.
Brett, C. (1991), 'A Breton Pilgrim in England in the Reign of King Æthelstan', in Jondorf—Dumville (1991), 43–70.
Brett, M. (1992), 'The *Collectio Lanfranci* and its Competitors', in *Intellectual Life in the Middle Ages: Essays presented to Margaret Gibson*, eds. L. Smith and B. Ward (1992), 157–74.
- (1995), 'Theodore and the Latin Canon Law', in Lapidge (1995a), 120–40.
Breul, K. (1915), *The Cambridge Songs: A Goliard's Song Book of the XIth Century Edited from the Unique Manuscript in the University Library* (Cambridge).
Briggs, E. (2004), 'Nothing but Names: the Original Core of the Durham *Liber Vitae*', in Rollason et al. (2004), 63–85.
Bright, J.W., ed. (1904–6), *The Gospels in West-Saxon*, 4 vols. (London).
British Library Catalogue of Illuminated Manuscripts (2004—) [on-line catalogue].
Brock, S. (1995), 'The Syriac Background', in Lapidge (1995a), 30–53.

Broderick, H.R. (1983), 'Observations on the Method of Illustration in MS Junius 11 and the Relationship of the Drawings to the Text', *Scriptorium* 37: 161–77.

– (2011), 'The Veil of Moses as Exegetical Image in the Illustrated Old English Hexateuch (London, BL, Cotton Ms. Claudius B. iv)', in Hourihane (2011), 271–86.

Brommer, P., ed. (1984), MGH, *Capitula episcoporum* I (Hannover).

Bromwich, J. (1950), 'Who was the Translator of the Prose Portion of the Paris Psalter', in C. Fox and B. Dickins, eds., *The Early Cultures of North-West Europe: H.M. Chadwick Memorial Studies* (Cambridge, 1950), 289–303.

Brøndsted, J. (1924), *Early English Ornament. The Sources, Development and Relation to Foreign Styles of Pre-Norman Ornamental Art in England* (Copenhagen).

Brooke, C.N.L. (1967), 'Archbishop Lanfranc, the English Bishops and the Council of London of 1075', *Studia Gratiani* 12 [= *Collectanea Stephan Kuttner* 2], 40–59.

Brooke, Z.N. (1931), *The English Church and the Papacy from the Conquest to the Reign of John* (Cambridge [repr. 1952]).

Brooks, K.R., ed. (1961), *Andreas and the Fates of the Apostles* (Oxford).

Brooks, N.P. (1971), 'The Development of Military Obligations in Eighth- and Ninth-Century England', in Clemoes—Hughes (1971), 69–84.

– ed. (1982), *Latin and the Vernacular Languages in Early Medieval Britain* (Leicester).

– (1984), *The Early History of the Church of Canterbury: Christ Church from 597 to 1066* (Leicester).

– and C. Cubitt, eds. (1996), *St Oswald of Worcester: Life and Influence* (London).

– (2008), 'An Early Boundary of the Dioceses of Canterbury and Rochester', in *A Commodity of Good Names: Essays in Honour of Margaret Gelling*, eds. O.J. Padel and D.N. Parsons (Donington, 2008), 28–43.

Brotanek, R. (1913), *Texte und Untersuchungen zur altenglischen Literatur und Kirchengeschichte* (Halle).

Brown, A.K., ed. (1969), 'The Epinal Glossary. Edition with Critical Commentary', 2 vols. (unpubl. PhD dissertation, Stanford University, CA).

– (1992), 'Toward Unifying the Corpus of Old English Glossaries', in Derolez (1992), 97–114.

Brown, D. (1982), *The Lichfield Gospels* (London).

Brown, G.H. (1987), 'Solving the "Solve" Riddle in B.L. MS Harley 585', *Viator* 18: 45–52.

- (2009), 'The St Petersburg Bede: Sankt-Peterburg, Publichnaja Biblioteka, MS. lat. Q. V. I. 18', in *Anglo-Saxons and the North. Essays reflecting the Theme of the 10th Meeting of the International Society of Anglo-Saxonists in Helsinki, August 2001*, ed. M. Kilpiö, L. Kahlas-Tarkka, J. Roberts and O. Timofeeva (Tempe, AZ, 2009), 121–9.
- and L.E. Voigts, eds. (2010), *The Study of Medieval Manuscripts of England: Festschrift in Honor of Richard W. Pfaff*, MRTS 384 (Tempe, AZ, 2010).
- Brown, L.E.G. (1904), 'Two Pages of an Anglo-Saxon Service Book', *Transactions of the Bristol and Gloucestershire Archaeological Society* 27: 207–8.
- Brown, K.L. and R.J.H. Clark (2004a), 'The Lindisfarne Gospels and two other 8th century Anglo-Saxon/Insular Manuscripts: Pigment Identification by Raman Microscopy', *Journal of Raman Spectroscopy* 35: 4–12.
- and R.J.H. Clark (2004b), 'Analysis of Key Anglo-Saxon Manuscripts (8–11th centuries) in the British Library: Pigment Identification by Raman Microscopy', *Journal of Raman Spectroscopy* 35: 181–9.
- Brown, M.P. (1986), 'Paris, B. N., lat. 10861 and the Scriptorium of Christ Church, Canterbury', *ASE* 15: 119–37.
- (1989a), 'The Lindisfarne Scriptorium from the Late Seventh to the Early Ninth Century', in Bonner et al. (1989a), 151–64.
- (1989b), 'A New Fragment of a Ninth-Century English Bible', *ASE* 18: 33–43.
- (1989c), Review of N. Barker (1986), *The Book Collector* 38: 551–5.
- (1990), *A Guide to Western Historical Scripts from Antiquity to 1600* (London).
- (1991), *Anglo-Saxon Manuscripts* (London).
- (1993), 'Cambridge University Library, Manuscript Ll. I. 10. The Book of Cerne' (unpubl. PhD dissertation, University of London).
- (1994), 'Echoes: The Book of Kells and Southern English Manuscript Production', in O'Mahony (1994), 333–43.
- (1996), *The Book of Cerne. Prayer, Patronage and Power in Ninth-Century England* (London).
- (1997), '*Explicit*: The Book of Cerne and the Culmination of the Insular Tradition', *OEN* 30.3: A 34.
- (2000), *In the Beginning was the Word: Books and Faith in the Age of Bede*, Jarrow Lecture (Jarrow on Tyne).
- and C.A. Farr, eds. (2001a), *Mercia: An Anglo-Saxon Kingdom in Europe* (London).
- (2001b), 'Mercian Manuscripts? The Tiberius Group and Its Historical Context', in Brown—Farr (2001a), 278–91.
- (2001c), 'Female Book-Ownership and Production in Anglo-Saxon England: The Evidence of the Ninth-Century Prayerbooks', in Kay—Sylvester (2001), 45–67.

- (2002), *Das Buch von Lindisfarne: Cotton MS Nero D. iv der British Library London*, 3 vols. (Lucerne) [facsimile].
- (2003a), *Painted Labyrinth: The World of the Lindisfarne Gospels* (London).
- (2003b), 'House Style in the Scriptorium: Scribal Reality and Scholarly Myth', in Karkov—Brown (2003), 131–50.
- (2003c), *The Lindisfarne Gospels. Society, Spirituality and the Scribe* (London) [includes CD-ROM].
- (2004), 'Fifty Years of Insular Palaeography, 1953–2003: An Outline of Some Landmarks and Issues', *Archiv für Diplomatik* 50: 277–325.
- (2007a), *Manuscripts from the Anglo-Saxon Age* (London).
- (2007b), 'The Barberini Gospels: Context and Intertextual Relationship', in Minnis—Roberts (2007), 89–116.
- (2007c), 'An Early Outbreak of "Influenza"? Aspects of Influence, Medieval and Modern', in Lowden—Bovey (2007), 1–10.
- (2007d), 'The Lichfield Angel and the Manuscript Context: Lichfield as a Centre of Insular Art', *Journal of the British Archaeological Association* 160: 8–19.
- (2008), 'The Lichfield/Llandeilo Gospels Reinterpreted', in Kennedy—Meecham-Jones (2008), 57–70.
- (2010), 'The MacDurnan Gospels', in *Lambeth Palace Library. Treasures from the Collections of the Archbishops of Canterbury*, eds. R. Palmer and M.P. Brown (London, 2010), 28–31.
- (2011a), *The Lindisfarne Gospels and the Early Medieval World* (London).
- (2011b), 'Southumbrian Book Culture: The Interface between Insular and Anglo-Saxon', in Hourihane (2011), 31–42.
- (2012), 'Writing in the Insular World', in R. Gameson (2012), 121–66.
- Brown, P.R. and C.R. Crampton, eds. (1986), *Modes of Interpretation in Old English Literature. Essays in Honour of Stanley B. Greenfield* (Toronto).
- Brown, R. and D. Yerkes (1981), 'A Sermon on the Birthday of St Machutus', *AB* 99: 160–4.
- Brown, T.J. (1959), 'The St Ninian's Isle Silver Hoard: the Inscriptions', *Antiquity* 33: 250–5 [repr. T.J. Brown (1993a), 245–51].
- (1959-63), 'Latin Palaeography since Traube: Inaugural Address in the Chair of Palaeography, London', *TCBS* 3: 361–81 [repr. T.J. Brown (1993a), 17–37, 263–8].
- ed. (1969a), *The Durham Ritual: A Southern English Collectar of the Tenth Century with Northumbrian Additions. Durham Cathedral Library A.IV.19*, EEMF 16 (Copenhagen).
- ed. (1969b), *The Stonyhurst Gospel of St John*, Roxburghe Club (Oxford) [facsimile].

– (1972), 'Northumbria and the Book of Kells', *ASE* 1: 219–46 [repr. T.J. Brown (1993a), 97–124, 270–6].

– (1974), 'The Distribution and Significance of Membrane Prepared in the Insular Manner', in Glénisson (1974), 127–35 [repr. T.J. Brown (1993a), 125–39, 276].

– (1975), 'An Historical Introduction to the Use of Classical Latin Authors in the British Isles from the 5th to the 11th Century', *Settimane* 22: 237–99 [repr. T.J. Brown (1993a), 144–77, 276–84].

– (1976), 'The Manuscript and the Handwriting', in Biddle (1976a), 520–2.

– (1980), 'Late Antique and early Anglo-Saxon Books', in De La Mare—Barker-Benfield (1980), 9–14.

– (1982), 'The Irish Element in the Insular System of Scripts to circa AD 850', in Löwe (1982) 101–19 [repr. T.J. Brown (1993a), 201–20, 284–7].

– (1984), 'The Oldest Irish Manuscripts and their Late Antique Background', in Ní Chatháin—Richter (1984), 311–27 [repr. T.J. Brown (1993a), 221–41, 287].

– and T.W. Mackay (1988), *Codex Vaticanus Palatinus latinus 235. An Early Insular Manuscript of Paulinus of Nola*, Armarium codicum insignium 4 (Turnhout) [facsimile].

– (1989), 'Palaeography: An Overview', in Loyn (1989) 57–9, 162–4, 217–19 [repr. T.J. Brown (1993a), 51–9, 268].

– (1993a), *A Palaeographer's View. The Selected Writings of Julian Brown*, ed. J. Bately et al. (London).

– (1993b), 'Tradition, Imitation and Invention in Insular Handwriting of the Seventh and Eighth Centuries', unpubl. Chambers Memorial Lecture, London 1978–79, in T.J. Brown (1993a), 179–200, 284.

Brown, V. (2007), 'Palimpsested Texts in Beneventan Script: A Handlist with some Identifications', in Declerq (2007), 99–145.

Brownbill, J. (1925), 'The Tribal Hidage', *EHR* 40: 497–503.

Browne, A.C. (1988), 'Bishop William of St. Carilef's Book Donations to Durham Cathedral Priory', *Scriptorium* 42: 140–55.

Brownrigg, L.L. (1978), 'Manuscripts containing English Decoration 871–1066, Catalogued and Illustrated: A Review', *ASE* 7: 239–66.

– ed. (1990), *Medieval Book Production: Assessing the Evidence* (Los Altos Hills, CA).

– and M.M. Smith, eds. (2000), *Interpreting and Collecting Fragments of Medieval Books* (Los Altos Hills, CA, and London).

Bruce-Mitford, R. (1967), *The Art of the Codex Amiatinus*, Jarrow Lecture (1967) [also publ. in *Journal of the British Archaeological Association*, 3rd ser. 32 (1969) 1–25].

– (1989), 'The Durham-Echternach Calligrapher', in Bonner et al. (1989a), 175–88.

Brückmann, J. (1973), 'Latin Manuscript Pontificals and Benedictionals in England and Wales', *Traditio* 29: 391–458.

Brugnoli, G. and M. Buonocore, eds. (2002), *Hermeneumata Vaticana (Cod. Vat. Lat. 6925)*, Studi e Testi 410 (Rome).

Brühl, C. (1892), *Die Flexion des Verbums in Ælfrics Heptateuch und Buch Hiob* (Dr. phil. dissertation, University of Marburg).

Brunhölzl, F. (1975), *Geschichte der lateinischen Literatur des Mittelalters*, I: *Von Cassiodor bis zum Ausklang der karolingischen Erneuerung* (Munich).

Bruni, S., ed. (1997), *Alcuino. De Orthographia* (Florence).

Brunius, J. (2000), 'Medieval Manuscript Fragments in Sweden: A Catalogue Project', in Brownrigg—Smith (2000), 157–66.

– ed. (2005), *Medieval Book Fragments in Sweden. An International Seminar in Stockholm, 13–16 November 2003* (Stockholm).

Brunner, I.A., ed. (1965), 'The Anglo-Saxon Translation of the Distichs of Cato', (unpubl. PhD dissertation, Columbia University, NY).

Brunner, Karl (1960–2), *Die Englische Sprache. Ihre geschichtliche Entwicklung*, 2 vols., 2nd rev. ed. (Tübingen).

– (1965), *Altenglische Grammatik: Nach der angelsächsischen Grammatik von Eduard Sievers*, 3rd rev. ed. (Tübingen).

Brunner, K. and G. Jaritz, eds. (2003), *Text als Realie. Internationaler Kongress, Krems an der Donau, 3. bis 6. Oktober 2000* (Vienna).

Bruno, V.A. (2001), 'The St Petersburg Gospels and the Sources of Southumbrian Art', in Redknap (2001), 179–90.

Buchholz, R. (1890), *Die Fragmente der 'Rede der Seele an den Leichnam' in zwei Handschriften zu Worcester und Oxford*, Erlanger Beiträge zur Englischen Philologie 6 (Erlangen).

Buckalew, R.E. (1978), 'Leland's Transcript of Ælfric's Glossary', *ASE* 7: 149–64.

– (1982), 'Nowell, Lambarde, and Leland: The Significance of Laurence Nowell's Transcript of Ælfric's Grammar and Glossary', in Berkhout—Gatch (1982), 19–50.

Budny, M. (1984), 'British Library Manuscript Royal 1 E.vi: The Anatomy of an Anglo-Saxon Bible Fragment' (unpubl. PhD dissertation, University of London).

– (1991) '*Canterbury at Corpus*: An Exhibition of Manuscripts from St Augustine's Abbey, Canterbury, to Mark the Enthronement of the 103rd Archbishop in April 1991, Selected, with Texts and Photographs by M. Budny', The Parker Library, Corpus Christi College Cambridge (Cambridge).

– (1992), '"St Dunstan's Classbook" and its Frontispiece: Dunstan's Portrait and Autograph', in Ramsay et al. (1992), 103–43.

- (1993), 'Worcester Manuscripts at Corpus Christi College, Cambridge: a Report on Recent Research', *OEN* 26.3: 22–36.
- and T. Graham (1993), 'Dunstan as Hagiographical Subject or Osbern as Author? The Scribal Portrait in an Early Copy of Osbern's *Vita Sancti Dunstani*', *Gesta* 32: 83–96.
- (1997), *Insular, Anglo-Saxon and Early Anglo-Norman Manuscript Art at Corpus Christi College, Cambridge: an Illustrated Catalogue*, 2 vols. (Kalamazoo, MI).
- (1999), 'The Biblia Gregoriana', in R. Gameson (1999b), 237–85.
Buescu, V., ed. (1941), *Cicéron. Les Aratea* (Paris; repr. Hildesheim, 1966).
Bülbring, K.D. (1902), *Altenglisches Elementarbuch, Teil 1* (Heidelberg).
Bullough, D.A. (1972), 'The Educational Tradition in England from Alfred to Ælfric: Teaching *utriusque linguae*', *Settimane* 19: 453–94 [repr. in Bullough, *Carolingian Renewal: Sources and Heritage* (Manchester, 1991), 297–334].
- (1975), 'The Continental Background of the Reform', in Parsons (1975), 20–36, 210–14.
- (1977), 'Roman Books and Carolingian *Renovatio*', *Studies in Church History* 14: 23–50.
- (1983), 'Alcuin and the Kingdom of Heaven: Liturgy, Theology, and the Carolingian Age', in *Carolingian Essays*, ed. U.-R. Blumenthal (Washington, DC), 1–69.
- (1991), *Carolingian Renewal: Sources and Heritage* (Manchester).
- (1996), 'St Oswald: Monk, Bishop and Archbishop', in Brooks—Cubitt (1996), 1–22.
- (1998a), 'A Neglected Early-Ninth-Century Manuscript of the Lindisfarne *Vita S. Cuthberti*', *ASE* 27: 105–37.
- (1998b), 'Alcuin's Cultural Influence: The Evidence of the Manuscripts', in Houwen—MacDonald (1998), 1–26.
- (2003a), 'Charlemagne's Court Library Revisited', *Early Medieval Europe* 12: 339–63.
- (2003b), 'York, Bede's Calendar and a pre-Bedan English Martyrology', *AB* 121: 329–55.
- (2004), *Alcuin: Achievement and Reputation (being Part of the Ford Lectures delivered in Oxford in Hilary Term 1980)*, Education and Society in the Middle Ages and Renaissance 16 (Leiden).
Bunte, B., ed. (1875), *Hygini Astronomica ex codicibus a se primum collatis: Accedunt prolegomena, commentarius, excerpta ex codicibus, index, epimetron* (Leipzig).
Burchfield, R. (1953), 'A Source of Scribal Error in Early Middle English Manuscripts' *MÆ* 22: 10–17.

Burlin, R.B. and E.B. Irving, eds. (1974), *Old English Studies in Honour of John C. Pope* (Toronto, and Buffalo, NY).

Burn, A.E., ed. (1909), *Facsimiles of the Creeds from Early Manuscripts*, HBS 36 (London).

Burnell, S. and E. James (1999), 'The Archaeology of Conversion on the Continent in the Sixth and Seventh Centuries: Some Observations and Comparisons with Anglo-Saxon England', in R. Gameson (1999b), 83–107.

Burnett, C. (1992), 'The Prognostications of the Eadwine Psalter', in M. Gibson (1992), 165–7.

Bursill-Hall, G.L. (1981), *A Census of Medieval Latin Grammatical Manuscripts*, Grammatica Speculativa 4 (Stuttgart).

Burton, P. (2000), *The Old Latin Gospels: A Study of Their Texts and Language* (Oxford).

Busch, W., ed. (1978), *Kunst als Bedeutungsträger. Gedenkschrift für Günter Bandmann* (Berlin).

Bussières, M. (2007), 'The Controversy about Scribe C in British Library, Cotton MSS, Julius E. vii', *LSE* 38: 53–72.

Butcher, C.A. (2003), 'Recovering Unique Ælfrician Texts Using the Fiber Optic Light Cord: Pope XVII in London, BL Cotton Vitellius C. v', *OEN* 36.3: 13–22.

Butler, R.M. (2004), 'Glastonbury and the Early History of the Exeter Book', in Lionarons (2004a), 173–216.

Buzwell, G. (2005), *Saints in Medieval Manuscripts* (London).

Bzdyl, D.G. (1977), 'The Sources of Ælfric's Prayers in Cambridge University Library MS Gg.3.28', *N&Q* 222: 98–102.

Cahn, W. and J. Marrow (1978), 'Medieval and Renaissance Manuscripts at Yale: A Selection', *Yale University Library Gazette* 52: 173–284.

Caie, G.D. (1979), *Bibliography of Junius XI MS with an Appendix on Caedmon's Hymn*, Anglica et Americana 6 (Copenhagen).

– ed. (2000), *The Old English Poem 'Judgement Day II'*, AST 2 (Cambridge).

Cain, C. (2009), 'Sacred Words, Anglo-Saxon Piety, and the Origins of the *Epistola Salvatoris* in London, British Library, Royal 2. A. XX', *JEGP* 108: 168–89.

Calder, D.G. and M.J.B. Allen, eds. (1976), *Sources and Analogues of Old English Poetry*, I: *The Major Latin Texts in Translation* (Cambridge).

Caldini Montanari, R. (2002), *Tradizione medievale ed edizione critica del 'Somnium Scipionis'* (Florence).

Caldwell, J. (1998), 'Winchester Troper', *Die Musik in Geschichte und Gegenwart. Allgemeine Enzyklopädie der Musik. Sachteil*, 2nd ed. (Kassel) IX, 2047–8.

Callison, T. C. (1973), 'An Edition of Previously Unpublished Anglo-Saxon Homilies in MSS CCCC 302 and Cotton Faustina A. ix' (unpubl. PhD dissertation, University of Wisconsin).

Cameron, A.F. (1973), 'A List of Old English Texts', in Frank—Cameron (1973), 25–306.

– (1974), 'Middle English in Old English Manuscripts', in Rowland (1974), 218–29.

Cameron, M.L. (1983), 'The Sources of Medical Knowledge in Anglo-Saxon England', *ASE* 11: 135–55.

– (1984), 'Bald's Leechbook: Its Sources and their Use in its Compilation', *ASE* 12: 153–82.

– (1993), *Anglo-Saxon Medicine*, CSASE 7 (Cambridge).

– (1996), 'Bald's *Leechbook* and Cultural Interactions in Anglo-Saxon England', *ASE* 19: 5–12.

Camille, M. (1987), 'Labouring for the Lord: The Ploughman and the Social Order in the Luttrell Psalter', *Art History* 10: 423–54.

Campbell, A., ed. (1950), *Frithegodi Monachi Breviloquium Vitae Beati Wilfredi et Wulfstani Cantoris Narratio Metrica De Sancto Swithuno* (Zurich).

– ed. (1953), *The Tollemache Orosius: British Museum Additional Manuscript 47967*, EEMF 3 (Copenhagen).

– (1955), Review of *The Life of St. Chad: An Old English Homily edited with Introduction, Notes, Illustrative Texts and Glossary*, by R. Vleeskruyer, *MÆ* 24: 52–6.

– (1959), *Old English Grammar* (Oxford).

– ed. (1962), *The Chronicle of Æthelweard* (London).

– (1967a), 'The Glosses', in D.H. Wright (1967), 81–92.

– ed. (1967b), *Æthelwulf De Abbatibus* (Oxford).

– and S. Keynes, eds. (1998), *Encomium Emmae Reginae* (Cambridge).

Campbell, A.P., ed. (1974), *The Tiberius Psalter: Edited from British Museum MS Cotton Tiberius C. vi* (Ottawa).

Campbell, J.J. (1955), 'The Harley Glossary and "Saxon Patois"', *PQ* 34: 71–4.

– ed. (1959), *The Advent Lyrics of the Exeter Book* (Princeton).

– (1963), 'Prayers from MS Arundel 155', *Anglia* 81: 82–117.

Campbell, J. (1978), 'England, France, Flanders and Germany: Some Comparisons and Corrections', in D. Hill (1978), 255–70.

– E. John and P. Wormald, eds. (1991a), *The Anglo-Saxons* (London).

– (1991b), 'The First Christian Kings', in Campbell et al. (1991a), 45–69.

Campos Villanova, X. (1996), 'The Busy Ups and Downs of an Anglo-Saxon *Codex Aureus* in the Spain of the Habsburgs', *SELIM* 6: 42–8.

Canellis, A., ed. (2000), *S. Hieronymi Presbyteri Opera* III. 4: *Altercatio Luciferiani et Orthodoxi*, CCSL 79 B (Turnhout).

Carey, F.M. (1938), 'The Scriptorium of Reims during the Archbishopric of Hincmar (845–882 A.D.)', in *Classical and Mediaeval Studies in Honor of Edward Kennard Rand, presented upon the Completion of his Fortieth Year of Teaching*, ed. L.W. Jones (New York), 41–60.

Carley, J.P. (1986), 'John Leland and the Contents of English Pre-Dissolution Libraries: Glastonbury Abbey', *Scriptorium* 40: 107–20.

– (1986-8), 'John Leland and the Contents of English Pre-Dissolution Libraries: Lincolnshire', *TCBS* 9: 330–57.

– (1987), 'Two Pre-Conquest Manuscripts from Glastonbury Abbey', *ASE* 16: 197–212.

– and A. Dooley (1991), 'An Early Irish Fragment of Isidore of Seville's *Etymologiae*', in L. Abrams and J.P. Carley, eds., *The Archaeology and History of Glastonbury Abbey: Essays in Honour of the Ninetieth Birthday of C.A. Ralegh Radford* (Woodbridge, 1991), 135–61.

– (1994), 'More Pre-Conquest Manuscripts from Glastonbury Abbey', *ASE* 23: 265–81.

– and C.G.C. Tite, eds. (1997a), *Books and Collectors 1200–1700: Essays presented to Andrew Watson* (London).

– (1997b), 'The Royal Library as a Source for Sir Robert Cotton's Collection: A Preliminary List of Acquisitions', in C.J. Wright (1997), 208–29 [repr. from *BLJ* 18 (1992) 52–73].

– (2002), '"A great gatherer of books": Archbishop Bancroft's Library at Lambeth (1610) and its Sources', *Lambeth Palace Library Annual Review* 2001 (n.d. [2002]), 51–64.

– and P. Petitmengin (2004), 'Pre-Conquest Manuscripts from Malmesbury Abbey and John Leland's Letter to Beatus Rhenanus concerning a Lost Copy of Tertullian's Works', *ASE* 33: 195–223.

Carlson, I., ed. (1975), *The Pastoral Care: Edited from British Museum Ms. Cotton Otho B.ii, Part I: Ff.1-25va/4*, Stockholm Studies in English. Acta Universitatis Stockholmiensis 34 (Stockholm).

– ed. (1978), *The Pastoral Care: Edited from British Museum MS Cotton Otho B.ii, Part II: Ff. 25va/4-end*, completed by L.-G. Hallander et al., Stockholm Studies in English. Acta Universitatis Stockholmiensis 48 (Stockholm).

Caro, G. (1898), 'Die Varianten der Durhamer HS. und des Tiberius-Fragments der ae. Prosa-Version der Benediktinerregel und ihr Verhältnis zu den übrigen HSS.', *EStn* 24: 161–76.

Caron, W.J.H. (1963), 'Het Taalspel van de *Probatio Pennae*', *Tijdschrift voor Nederlandse Taal- en Letterkunde* 79: 253–70.

Cary, G. (1956), *The Medieval Alexander* (Cambridge).

Casaceli, F., ed. (1974), *Foca: Ars de nomine et verbo* (Naples).

Casaretto, F.M., ed. (1997), *Teodulo: Ecloga. Il canto della verità e della menzogna* (Florence).

Cassidy, B. and R. Muir Wright, eds. (2000), *Studies in the Illustration of the Psalter* (Stamford).

Cassidy, F.G. and R. Ringler, eds. (1971), *Bright's Old English Grammar and Reader*, 3rd ed. (New York).

Castaldi, L. (2010), 'La trasmissione e rielaborazione dell'esegesi patristica nella letteratura ibernica delle origini', *Settimane* 57: 393–428.

Catalogue des manuscrits français. Ancien fonds, ed. Bibliothèque Nationale, Départment des manuscrits, 5 vols. (Paris, 1868–1902).

Catalogue of Manuscripts in the Houghton Library, Harvard University, 8 vols. (Alexandria, VA, 1986–7).

Catalogue of the Stowe Manuscripts in the British Museum, 2 vols. (London, 1895–6).

Catalogus codicum hagiographicorum latinorum antiquiorum saeculo XVI qui asservantur in Bibliotheca Nationali Parisiensi, ed. Bollandists, Subsidia Hagiographica 2, 4 vols. (Brussels, 1889–93).

Cavadini, J.C., ed. (1996), *Gregory the Great: A Symposium* (Notre Dame).

Cavallo, G. (1988), 'Le tipologie della cultura nel reflesso delle testimonianze scritte', *Settimane* 34: 467–516.

Cazier, P., ed. (1998), *Isidorus Hispalensis: Sententiae*, CCSL 111 (Turnhout).

Cazzaniga, E., ed. (1948), *S. Ambrosii Mediolanensis episcopi De Virginibus libri tres* (Turin).

– ed. (1954), *S. Ambrosii Mediolanensis episcopi De Virginitate liber unus* (Turin).

Chadbon, J.N. (1993), 'Oxford, Bodleian Library, MSS Junius 85 and 86: An Edition of a Witness to the Old English Homiletic Tradition' (unpubl. PhD dissertation, University of Leeds).

Chadwick, H., ed. (1959), *The Sentences of Sextus. A Contribution to the History of Early Christian Ethics* (Cambridge).

Chadwick, H.M. (1899), 'Studies in Old English', *Transactions of the Cambridge Philological Society* 4: 85–265.

Chamberlin, J., ed. (1982), *The Rule of St Benedict: The Abingdon Copy*, Toronto Medieval Latin Texts 13 (Toronto).

Chambers, R.W., ed. (1912), *Widsith: A Study in Old English Heroic Legend* (Cambridge).

– et al., eds. (1933), *The Exeter Book of Old English Poetry* (London) [facsimile].

Chaplais, P. (1965), 'The Origin and Authenticity of the Royal Anglo-Saxon Diploma', *Journal of the Society of Archivists* 3.2: 48–61 [repr. in Ranger (1973) 28–42].

– (1966), 'The Anglo-Saxon Chancery: From the Diploma to the Writ', *Journal of the Society of Archivists* 3.4: 160–76 [repr. in Ranger (1973) 43–62].

– (1968), 'Some Early Anglo-Saxon Diplomas on Single Sheets: Originals or Copies?', *Journal of the Society of Archivists* 3.7: 315–36 [repr. in Ranger (1973) 63–87].

– (1978), 'The Letter from Bishop Wealdhere of London to Archbishop Brihtwold of Canterbury: The Earliest Original "Letter Close" Extant in the West', in Parkes–Watson (1978) 3–21 [repr. with Addendum in Chaplais (1981a) no. XIV].

– ed. (1981a), *Essays in Medieval Diplomacy and Administration* (London).

– (1981b), 'The Authenticity of the Royal Anglo-Saxon Diplomas of Exeter', in Chaplais (1981a), no. XV [orig. publ. *Bull. of the Inst. of Hist. Research* 39, 1–34].

– (1987), 'William of Saint-Calais and the Domesday Survey', in Holt (1987), 65–77.

Chapman, D. (2002), '*Anima quae pars*: A Tenth-Century Parsing Grammar', *JMLat* 12: 181–204.

Chapman, J. (1908), *Notes on the Early History of the Vulgate Gospels* (Oxford).

Chardonnens, L.S. (2007a), 'Context, Language, Date and Origin of Anglo-Saxon Prognostics', in Bremmer–Dekker (2007), 317–40.

– ed. (2007b), *Anglo-Saxon Prognostics, 900–1100: Study and Texts* (Leiden).

– (2007c), 'London, British Library, Harley 3271: The Composition and Structure of an Eleventh-Century Anglo-Saxon Miscellany', in Lendinara et al. (2007), 3–34.

– (2010), 'Appropriating Prognostics in late Anglo-Saxon England: A Preliminary Source Study', in Bremmer–Dekker (2010), 203–55.

Charles-Edwards, G., and H. McKee (2008), 'Lost Voices from Anglo-Saxon Lichfield', *ASE* 37: 79–89.

Charles-Edwards, T. (1995), 'The Penitential of Theodore and the *Iudicia Theodori*', in Lapidge (1995a), 141–74.

– (2012), 'The Use of the Book in Wales, *c.* 400–1100', in R. Gameson (2012), 389–405.

Chase, C., ed. (1975), *Two Alcuin Letter-Books*, Toronto Medieval Latin Texts 5 (Toronto).

– ed. (1981), *The Dating of Beowulf*, Toronto OE Series 6 (Toronto).

Chatelain, E. (1901–2), *Uncialis scriptura codicum Latinorum nouis exemplis illustrata* (Paris).

Chavasse, A. (1981), 'L'Épistolier romain du codex de Wurtzbourg', *RB* 91: 280–331.

Chazelle, C. (1997), 'Archbishops Ebo and Hincmar of Reims and the Utrecht Psalter', *Speculum* 72: 1054–77.

– (2003), 'Ceolfrid's Gift to St Peter: The First Quire of the Codex Amiatinus and the Evidence of its Roman Destination', *EME* 12: 129–58.

– (2006), 'Christ and the Vision of God: The Biblical Diagrams of the Codex Amiatinus', in *The Mind's Eye: Art and Theological Argument in the Middle Ages*, ed. J.F. Hamburger and A.-M. Bouché (Princeton, NJ, 2006), 84–111.

– and F. Lifshitz, eds. (2007), *Paradigms and Methods in Early Medieval Studies* (Basingstoke).

Chedzey, J. (2003), 'Manuscript Production in Medieval Winchester', *Reading Medieval Studies* 29: 1–18.

Chibnall, M., ed. (1969–80), *The Ecclesiastical History of Orderic Vitalis*, 6 vols. (Oxford).

Chiesa, P. and L. Pinelli, eds. (1994), *Gli autografi medievali. Problemi paleografici e filologici* (Spoleto).

– (2000), 'Caratteristiche della trasmissione dell' "Historia Langobardorum"', in *Paolo Diacono e il Friuli altomedievale* (Spoleto, 2000), 45–66.

– (2001), 'Varianti d'autore nell'alto medioevo: fra filologia e critica letteraria', *Filologia mediolatina* 8: 1–23.

– and L. Castaldi, eds. (2004), *La trasmissione dei testi latini del medioevo: Te.Tra* I (Florence).

– and L. Castaldi, eds. (2005), *La trasmissione dei testi latini del medioevo: Te.Tra* II (Florence).

– and F. Stella (2005), 'Paulus Diaconus', in Chiesa–Castaldi (2005), 482–506.

– and L. Castaldi, eds. (2008), *La trasmissione dei testi latini del medioevo: Te.Tra* III (Florence).

– and L. Castaldi, eds. (2012), *La trasmissione dei testi latini del medioevo: Te.Tra* IV (Florence).

Christ, K. (1933), *Die Bibliothek des Klosters Fulda im 16. Jahrhundert: Die Handschriften-Verzeichnisse*, Beihefte zum Zentralblatt für Bibliothekswesen 64 (Leipzig).

Chroust, A. (1899–1906), *Monumenta palaeographica: Denkmäler der Schreibkunst des Mittelalters, Series I*, 3 vols. in 24 parts [Lieferungen] (Munich and Leipzig).

Cichoń, K. (2002), 'Tablice kanonów: symbolika dekoracji architektonicznej', *Acta Universitatis Lodziensis, Folia Historica* 74: 87–108.

Cilluffe, G. (1981), *Il Salomone e Saturno in prosa del MS CCCC 422*, Quaderni di filologia germanica 2 (Palermo).

Clark, A.C. (1918a), *The Descent of Manuscripts* (Oxford).

– ed. (1918b), *M. Tulli Ciceronis Orationes* (Oxford).

– ed. (1933), *The Acts of the Apostles* (Oxford).

Clark, C., ed. (1970), *The Peterborough Chronicle, 1070–1154*, 2nd ed. (Oxford).

- (1979), 'Note on a *Life* of Three Thorney Saints', *Proceedings of the Cambridge Antiquarian Society* 69: 45–52.
- (1984), 'British Library Additional MS 40,000 ff. 1v–12r', *ANS* 7: 50–65 [with a codicological appendix by E.M.C. van Houts, 'The Genesis of British Library Additional MS 40,000 ff. 1–12', ibid. 66–8].
- (1987), 'A Witness to Post-Conquest English Cultural Patterns: The *Liber Vitae* of Thorney Abbey', in Simon-Vandenbergen (1987), 73–85.
Clark, J.G., ed. (2007), *The Culture of Medieval English Monasticism*, Studies in the History of Medieval Religion 30 (Woodbridge).
Clarkson, C. (1996), 'Further Studies in Anglo-Saxon and Norman Bookbinding: Board Attachment Methods Re-examined', in *Roger Powell. The Compleat Binder*, ed. J.L. Sharpe, Bibliologia 14 (Turnhout, 1996), 154–214.
Classen, E. and F.E. Harmer, eds. (1926), *An Anglo-Saxon Chronicle from British Museum, Cotton MS., Tiberius B. IV* (Manchester).
Classen, P. (1980), 'Anonymus, normannischer', *LMA* I. 673–4.
Clausen, W.V., ed. (1959), *A. Persi Flacci et D. Iuni Iuvenalis Saturae* (Oxford).
Clayton, M. (1984), 'Feasts of the Virgin in the Liturgy of the Anglo-Saxon Church', *ASE* 13: 209–33.
- (1985), 'Homiliaries and Preaching in Anglo-Saxon England', *Peritia* 4: 207–42.
- (1986), '*Assumptio Mariae*: An Eleventh-Century Latin Poem from Abingdon', *AB* 104: 419–26.
- (1990), *The Cult of the Virgin Mary in Anglo-Saxon England*, CSASE 2 (Cambridge).
- and H. Magennis, eds. (1994), *The Old English Lives of St Margaret*, CSASE 9 (Cambridge).
- (2002), 'An Edition of Ælfric's *Letter to Brother Edward*', in Treharne—Rosser (2002), 263–83.
- (2005), 'Ælfric's *De auguriis* and Cambridge, Corpus Christi College 178', in O'Brien O'Keeffe—Orchard (2005) II, 376–94.
- (2007), 'Letter to Brother Edward', *OEN* 40.3: 31–46.
- (2008), 'The Old English *Promissio regis*', *ASE* 37: 91–150.
Clement, R.W. (1984a), 'A Handlist of Manuscripts containing Gregory's *Regula Pastoralis*', *Manuscripta* 28: 33–44.
- (1984b), 'Codicological Considerations in the *Beowulf* Manuscript', *Proceedings of the Illinois Medieval Association* 1: 13–27.
- (1985a), 'King Alfred and the Latin Manuscripts of Gregory's *Regula Pastoralis*', *Journal of the Rocky Mountain Medieval and Renaissance Association* 6: 1–13.
- (1985b), 'Two Contemporary Gregorian Editions of Pope Gregory the Great's *Regula pastoralis* in Troyes MS 504', *Scriptorium* 39: 89–97.

– (1986), 'The Production of the *Pastoral Care*: King Alfred and his Helpers', in Szarmach (1986b), 129–52.

– (1989), 'An Anglo-Saxon Fragment at the Folger Shakespeare Library', *OEN* 22.2: 56–7.

Clemoes, P. (1952), *Liturgical Influence on Punctuation in Late Old English and Early Middle English Manuscripts*, Department of Anglo-Saxon Occasional Papers 1 (Cambridge).

– ed. (1959a), *The Anglo-Saxons: Studies in Some Aspects of their History and Culture Presented to Bruce Dickins* (London).

– (1959b), 'The Chronology of Ælfric's Works', in Clemoes (1959a), 212–47.

– (1960), 'The Old English Benedictine Office, Corpus Christi College, Cambridge, MS 190, and the Relations between Ælfric and Wulfstan: A Reconsideration', *Anglia* 78: 265–83.

– and K. Hughes, eds. (1971), *England before the Conquest: Studies in Primary Sources Presented to Dorothy Whitelock* (Cambridge).

– (1974), 'The Composition of the Old English Text', in Dodwell–Clemoes (1974), 42–53.

– (1980), *The Chronology of Ælfric's Works*, OEN Subsidia 5 (Binghampton, NY, 1980) [repr. of Clemoes (1959b)].

– (1985), *Manuscripts from Anglo-Saxon England. An Exhibition in the University Library Cambridge to Mark the Conference of the International Society of Anglo-Saxonists, August 1985* [privately printed].

– (1994a), 'History of the Manuscript' and 'Punctuation', rev. ed. in Richards (1994), 345–64 [orig. publ. in Eliason (1965), 28–35 and 24–5].

– (1994b), 'The Production of an Illustrated Version', in Richards (1994), 365–73 [orig. publ. in Dodwell–Clemoes (1974), 54–8].

– ed. (1997), *Ælfric's Catholic Homilies. The First Series. Text*, EETS s.s. 17 (Oxford).

Clover, H. and M. Gibson, eds. (1979), *The Letters of Lanfranc, Archbishop of Canterbury* (Oxford).

Clubb, M.D., ed. (1925), *Christ and Satan: An Old English Poem* (New Haven, CT).

Coates, R. (1997), 'The Scriptorium of the Mercian Rushworth Gloss: A Bilingual Perspective', *N&Q* 242: 453–8.

Coatsworth, E. (1989), 'The Pectoral Cross and Portable Altar from the Tomb of St Cuthbert', in Bonner et al. (1989a), 287–301.

– (2006), 'Inscriptions on Textiles Associated with Anglo-Saxon England', in Rumble (2006a), 71–95.

Cochiarelli, J.J. (1986), 'The Old English Version of the Enlarged Rule of St Chrodegang' (unpubl. PhD dissertation, Fordham University, NY).

Cochrane, L.E. (2007), '"The Wine in the Vines and the Foliage in the Roots": Representations of David in the Durham Cassiodorus', *Studies in Iconography* 28: 23–50.

Cockayne, T.O., ed. (1864–6), *Leechdoms, Wortcunning, and Starcraft of Early England*, 3 vols., RS 35 (London).

Codoñer, C. (1996), 'Isidore de Séville: Différences et Vocabulaires', in Hamesse (1996), 57–77.

– (2003), 'Un manoscrito escolar del siglo IX: Royal 15. B. XIX', *International Journal on Manuscripts and Text Transmission* 1: 229–45.

Coens, M. (1956), 'Aux origines de la céphalophorie. Un fragment retrouvé d'une ancienne passion de S. Just', *AB* 74: 86–114.

Cohen, A.S. and E.C. Teviotdale (1999), 'The Getty Anglo-Saxon Leaves and New Testament Illustration around the Year 1000', *Scriptorium* 53: 63–81.

Colgrave, B., ed. (1927), *The Life of Bishop Wilfrid* (Cambridge).

– ed. (1940), *Two Lives of Saint Cuthbert* (Cambridge).

– ed. (1956), *Felix's Life of Saint Guthlac* (Cambridge).

– ed. (1958), *The Paris Psalter: MS Bibliothèque Nationale Fonds Latin 8824*, EEMF 8 (Copenhagen).

– and A. Hyde (1962), 'Two Recently Discovered Leaves from Old English Manuscripts', *Speculum* 37: 60–78.

– and R.A.B. Mynors, eds. (1969), *Bede's Ecclesiastical History of the English People* (Oxford).

Colker, M.L. (1965), 'Texts of Jocelyn of Canterbury which Relate to the History of Barking Abbey', *Studia monastica* 7: 383–460.

– (1977), 'A Hagiographic Polemic', *MS* 34: 60–108.

– (1991), *Trinity College Library Dublin: Descriptive Catalogue of the Medieval and Renaissance Latin Manuscripts*, 2 vols. (Aldershot).

Collier, W. (2000), 'The Tremulous Hand and Gregory's *Pastoral Care*', in Swan—Treharne (2000a), 195–208.

Collins, M. (2000), *Medieval Herbals. The Illustrative Tradition* (London).

– and S. Raphael (2003), *A Medieval Herbal. A Facsimile of British Library Egerton MS 747* (London).

Collins, R.L. (1960), 'An Ælfric Manuscript Fragment', *Times Literary Supplement* (2 Sept. 1960): 561.

– (1963), 'A Re-examination of the Old English Glosses in the Blickling Psalter', *Anglia* 81: 124–8.

– (1964), 'Two Fragments of Ælfric's Grammar: The Kinship of Ker 384 and Ker 242', *AnM* 5: 5–12.

– and P. Clemoes (1974), 'The Common Origin of Ælfric Fragments at New Haven, Oxford, Cambridge, and Bloomington', in Burlin—Irving (1974), 285–326.

– (1976), *Anglo-Saxon Vernacular Manuscripts in America* (New York).

Committee of Parliament Report on the Cottonian Library (1732): see under *Report*

Conde-Silvestre, J.C. and M. Salvador (2006), 'Old English Studies in Spain: Past, Present and ... Future?', *OEN* 40.1: 38–58.

Condello, E. and G. de Gregorio, eds. (1995), *Scribi e colofoni. Le sottoscrizioni di copisti dalle origini all'avvento della stampa* (Spoleto).

Conn, M.A. (1993), 'The Dunstan and Brodie (Anderson) Pontificals: An Edition and Study' (unpubl. PhD dissertation, Univ. of Notre Dame).

Conner, P.W. (1985), 'The Section Numbers in the *Beowulf* Manuscript', *ANQ* 24: 33–8.

– (1993), *Anglo-Saxon Exeter: A Tenth-Century Cultural History*, Studies in Anglo-Saxon History 4 (Woodbridge).

– (1994), 'The Structure of the Exeter Book Codex (Exeter, Cathedral Library MS 3501)', in Richards (1994), 301–16 [orig. publ. *Scriptorium* 40: 233–42].

– ed. (1996), *The Anglo-Saxon Chronicle: A Collaborative Edition*, X: *The Abingdon Chronicle: A.D. 956–1066 (MS. C, with reference to BDE)* (Cambridge).

– (2008), 'Parish Guilds and the Production of Old English Literature in the Public Sphere', in Blanton—Scheck (2008), 255–71.

Conrad-O'Briain, H., A.M. D'Arcy, and V.J. Scattergood, eds. (1999), *Text and Gloss: Studies in Insular Learning and Literature presented to Joseph Donovan Pheifer* (Dublin).

Conso, D., ed. (1994), *Mélanges François Kerlouégan*, Annales littéraires de l'Université de Besançon 515 (Paris).

Constantinescu, R. (1974), 'Alcuin et les *Libelli precum* de l'époque carolingienne', *Revue d'histoire de la spiritualité* 50: 17–56.

Conti, A. (2007), 'The Circulation of the Old English Homily in the Twelfth Century: New Evidence from Oxford, Bodleian Library, MS Bodley 343', in Kleist (2007a), 365–402.

Contreni, J.J. (1975), 'Martin Scottus (819–875) and the *Scholica Graecarum glossarum*', *Manuscripta* 19: 70.

– (1978), *The Cathedral School of Laon from 850 to 930: Its Manuscripts and Masters*, Münchener Beiträge zur Mediävistik und Renaissance-Forschung 29 (Munich).

Conservation. An Exhibition of Problems and Materials. The Parker Library, Corpus Christi College, Cambridge (Cambridge, 1985–6).

Cook, A.S. (1898), *Biblical Quotations in Old English Prose Writers* (London).

Cooke, J. (1993), 'The Harley Manuscript 3376: A Study in Anglo-Saxon Glossography' (unpubl. PhD dissertation, Cambridge Univ.).

– (1997a), 'Worcester Books and Scholars and the Making of the Harley Glossary (British Library MS Harley 3376)', *Anglia* 115: 441–68.

– (1997b), 'Problems of Method in Early English Lexicography: The Case of the Harley Glossary', *NM* 98: 241–51.

Coppens, C., A. Derolez, and H. Heymans, eds. (1994), *Codex Eyckensis: An Insular Gospel Book from the Abbey of Aldeneik* (Maaseik).

Corbin, S. (1955), 'Valeur et sens de la notation alphabétique à Jumièges et en Normandie', in *Jumièges* (1955) II, 913–24.

Cordoliani, A. (1955), 'Le plus ancien manuscrit de comput ecclésiastique du fonds de Jumièges', in *Jumièges* (1955) II, 691–702.

Cornelius, R., ed. (1995), 'Die altenglische Interlinearversion zu *De vitiis et peccatis* in der Hs. British Library Royal 7. C. iv' (Dr Phil dissertation, University of Göttingen; published Frankfurt a. M.).

Corona, G. (2002), 'Saint Basil in Anglo-Saxon England', *N&Q* 247: 316–20.

– (2006), *Ælfric's Life of Saint Basil the Great: Background and Context*, AST 5 (Cambridge).

Corrêa, A., ed. (1992), *The Durham Collectar*, HBS 107 (Woodbridge).

– (1993), 'A Mass for St Patrick in an Anglo-Saxon Sacramentary', in Dumville—Abrams (1993a), 245–52.

– (1995), 'Daily Office Books: Collectars and Breviaries', in Pfaff (1995a), 45–60.

– (1996), 'The Liturgical Manuscripts of Oswald's Houses', in Brooks—Cubitt (1996), 285–324.

– (1997), 'St Austroberta of Pavilly in the Anglo-Saxon Liturgy', *AB* 115: 77–112.

– (2008), 'A Mass for St Birinus in an Anglo-Saxon Missal from the Scandinavian Mission-Field', in Barrow—Wareham (2008), 167–88.

Corsano, K. (1987), 'The First Quire of the Codex Amiatinus and the *Institutiones* of Cassiodorus', *Speculum* 41: 3–34.

Courcelle, P. (1939), 'Étude critique sur les commentaires de la Consolation de Boèce', *AHDMLA* 12: 50–140.

– (1967), *La Consolation de Philosophie dans la tradition littéraire. Antecédents et posterité de Boèce* (Paris).

Cowdrey, H.E.J. (1981), 'The Anglo-Norman *Laudes regiae*', *Viator* 12: 37–78.

– (2003), *Lanfranc: Scholar, Monk and Archbishop* (Oxford).

Cowen, A. (2004), '*Byrstas* and *bysmeras*: The Wounds of Sin in the *Sermo Lupi ad Anglos*', in Townend (2004), 397–412.

Cox, B.M. (1995), 'The Book as Relic: The Lindisfarne Gospels and the Politics of Sainthood' (unpubl. PhD dissertation, Stanford University, CA).

Cox, H.L. and V.F. Vanacker, eds. (1986), *Wortes Anst, Verbi Gratia: Donum Natalicium Gilbert A. R. de Smet* (Leuven).

Cox, R.S., ed. (1965), 'The Old English Dicts of Cato and Others' (unpubl. PhD dissertation, Indiana Univ.).

– ed. (1972), 'The Old English Dicts of Cato', *Anglia* 90: 1–42.

Coxe, H.O. (1852), *Catalogus codicum manuscriptorum qui in collegis aulisque Oxoniensibus hodie adservantur* (Oxford).

– (1858–85/1973), *Catalogi codicum manuscriptorum Bibliothecae Bodleianae* [Quarto Catalogues] II. *Laudian Manuscripts*, repr. with corrections and additions, and an historical introduction by R.W. Hunt (Oxford, 1973).

Cramp, R. (1989), 'The Artistic Influence of Lindisfarne within Northumbria', in Bonner et al. (1989a), 213–28.

Craster, H.H.E. (1917–19), 'The Laudian Acts', *The Bodleian Quarterly Record* 2: 288–90.

– (1925), 'St Margaret's Gospel-Book', *The Bodleian Quarterly Record* 4: 202–3.

Crawford, S.J., ed. (1921/1968), *Exameron Anglice or The Old English Hexameron*, Bibliothek der angelsächsischen Prosa 10 (Hamburg, 1921; repr. Darmrstadt, 1968).

– ed. (1922/1969), *The Old English Version of the Heptateuch, Ælfric's Treatise on the Old and New Testament and his Preface to Genesis edited from all existing MSS and Fragments, with the Text of Two Additional Manuscripts transcribed by N.R. Ker* (1969), EETS o.s. 160 (London).

– (1923), 'The Late Old English Notes of MS (British Museum) Cotton Claudius B. iv', *Anglia* 47: 124–35.

– (1928), 'The Worcester Marks and Glosses of the Old English Manuscripts in the Bodleian, together with the Worcester Version of the Nicene Creed', *Anglia* 52: 1–25.

Crick, J. (1987), 'An Anglo-Saxon Fragment of Justinus's *Epitome*', *ASE* 16: 181–96.

– (1997), 'The Case for a West Saxon Minuscule', *ASE* 26: 63–78.

– (2011), 'Script and Sense of the Past in Anglo-Saxon England', in Roberts– Webster (2011), 1–29.

– (2012), 'English Vernacular Script', in R. Gameson (2012), 174–86.

Crivellucci, A., ed. (1914), *Pauli Diaconi Historia Romana* (Rome).

Cross, J.E. (1977), '"Legimus in ecclesiasticis historiis" — A Sermon for All Saints, and its Use in Old English Prose', *Traditio* 33: 105–21.

– (1982), 'Saints' Lives in Old English: Latin Manuscripts and Vernacular Accounts: The *Old English Martyrology*', *Peritia* 1: 38–62.

– and T.D. Hill, eds. (1982), *The Prose Solomon and Saturn and Adrian and Ritheus, edited from the British Library Manuscripts with Commentary*, McMaster Old English Studies and Texts 1 (Toronto).

– (1987), *Cambridge Pembroke College MS 25: A Carolingian Sermonary used by Anglo-Saxon Preachers*, KCLMS 1 (London).

– and A. Brown (1989), 'Literary Impetus for Wulfstan's *Sermo Lupi*', *LSE* 20: 271–91.

- (1990), 'Missing Folios in Cotton MS Nero A. i', *BLJ* 16: 99–100.
- (1991), 'Wulfstan's *De Antichristo* in a Twelfth-Century Worcester Manuscript', *ASE* 20: 203–20.
- (1992a), 'A Newly Identified Manuscript of Wulfstan's "Commonplace Book", Rouen, Bibliothèque Municipale, MS 1382 (U. 109), fols. 173r–198v', *JMLat* 2: 63–83.
- (1992b), '*De festiuitatibus anni* and Ansegisus *Capitularum* [sic] *Collectio* (827) in Anglo-Saxon Manuscripts', *Liverpool Classical Monthly* 17. 8: 119–20
- and T.N. Hall (1993a), 'The Fragments of Homiliaries in Canterbury Cathedral Library MS Add. 127/1 and in Kent, County Archives Office, Maidstone, MS PRC 49/2', *Scriptorium* 47: 186–92.
- and J. Morrish Tunberg, eds. (1993b), *The Copenhagen Wulfstan Collection, Copenhagen Kongelige Bibliotek, Gl. Kgl. Sam. 1595*, EEMF 25 (Copenhagen).
- and A. Brown (1993c), 'Wulfstan and Abbo of Saint-Germain des Prés', *Mediaevalia* 15: 71–91.
- (1993d), 'Atto of Vercelli, *De pressuris ecclesiasticis*, Archbishop Wulfstan, and Wulfstan's "Commonplace Book"', *Traditio* 48: 237–46.
- and A. Hamer (1996a), 'Source-Identification and Manuscript Recovery: The British Library Wulfstan MS Cotton Nero A. i', *Scriptorium* 50: 132–6.
- ed. (1996b), *Two Old English Apocrypha and their Manuscript Source: The Gospel of Nicodemus and the Avenging of the Saviour*, CSASE 19 (Cambridge) [ch. 2 is by J.E. Cross and J.C. Crick].
- (1996c), 'Saint-Omer 202 as the Manuscript Source for the Old English Texts', in Cross (1996b), 82–104.
- and T.N. Hall (1996d), 'Fragments of Alanus of Farfa's Roman Homiliary and Abridgments of Saints' Lives by Goscelin in London, British Library, Harley 652', in *Bright is the Ring of Words. Festschrift für Horst Weinstock zum 65. Geburtstag*, ed. C. Pollner, H. Rohlfing and F.-R. Hausmann (Bonn, 1996), 49–61.
- and J. Crick (1996e), 'The Manuscript: Saint-Omer, Bibliothèque municipale, 202', in Cross (1996b), 10–35.
- and A. Hamer (1997), 'Ælfric's *Letters* and the *Excerptiones Ecgberhti*', in Roberts—Nelson (1997), 5–13.
- and A. Hamer, eds. (1999), *Wulfstan's Canon Law Collection*, AST 1 (Cambridge).
Crowley, J. (1997), 'Greek Interlinear Glosses from the Beginnings of the Monastic Reform in Worcester: British Library, Royal 2.A.xx', *Sacris Erudiri* 37: 133-9.
- (2000), 'Anglicized Word Order in the Old English Continuous Interlinear Glosses in London, British Library, Royal 2.A.xx', *ASE* 29: 123–52.

- (2006), 'Latin Prayers added into the Margins of the Prayerbook British Library, Royal 2. A. xx at the Beginnings of the Monastic Reform in Worcester', *Sacris Erudiri* 45: 223–303.

Cubbin, G.P., ed. (1996), *The Anglo-Saxon Chronicle: A Collaborative Edition, vol. VI: MS D: A Semi-Diplomatic Edition with Introduction and Indices* (Cambridge).

Cubitt, C. (1995), *Anglo-Saxon Church Councils, c. 650–c. 850* (London).

Cucina, C. (2008), *Il 'Seafarer'. La 'navigatio' cristiana di un poeta anglosassone* (Rome).

Cunningham, I.C. (1973), 'Latin Classical Manuscripts in the National Library of Scotland', *Scriptorium* 27: 64–90.

Cunningham, M.P., ed. (1966), *Aurelii Prudentii Clementis Carmina*, CCSL 126 (Turnhout).

Curtius, E.R. (1948), *Europäische Literatur und lateinisches Mittelalter* (Bern).

Cyrus, V.J., ed. (1968), 'The Tollemach Orosius: Text with Spacing Notation Edited for Computer Analysis' (unpublished PhD dissertation, Univ. of Washington).

Daly, E.J. (1950), 'An Early Ninth Century Manuscript of Boethius', *Scriptorium* 4: 205–19.

Daly, L.W. (1982), 'A Greek Palindrome in Eighth-Century England', *American Journal of Philology* 103: 95–7.

Dance, R. (2004), 'Sound, Fury, and Signifiers; or Wulfstan's Language', in Townend (2004), 29–61.

Darlington, R.R., ed. (1928), *The Vita Wulfstani of William of Malmesbury*, Camden Society 3rd ser. 40 (London).

D'Aronco, M.A. (1983), 'Il IV capitolo della *Regula Sancti Benedicti* del ms. Londra, B.M., Cotton Tiberius A. iii', in *feor and neah. Scritti di filologia germanica in memoria di Augusto Scaffidi Abbate*, ed. P. Lendinara and L. Melazzo (Palermo, 1983), 105–28.

- ed. (1988–9), *Studi sulla cultura germanica dei secoli IV–XII in onore di Giulia Mazzuoli Porru* [= *Romanobarbarica* 10] (Rome).
- and M.L. Cameron, eds. (1998), *The Old English Illustrated Pharmacopoeia: British Library Cotton Vitellius C.III*, EEMF 27 (Copenhagen).
- (1999), 'Herbals', in Lapidge et al. (1999), 233–4.
- (2007), 'The Transmission of Medical Knowledge in Anglo-Saxon England: The Voices of Manuscripts', in Lendinara et al. (2007) 35–58.
- (2011), 'Anglo-Saxon Medical and Botanical Texts, Glosses and Glossaries after the Norman Conquest: Continuations and Beginnings, an Overview', in Lendinara et al. (2011), 229–48.

Davey, W.J. (1979), 'An Edition of the *Regius Psalter* and its Latin Commentary' (unpubl. PhD dissertation, Ottawa Univ.).

– (1987), 'The Commentary of the Regius Psalter: Its Main Source and Influence on the Old English Gloss', *MS* 49: 335–51.

Davidson, C. (1890), 'Differences between the Scribes of *Beowulf*', *MLN* 5: 43–5 [with reply by C.F. McClumpha, *MLN* 5: 123; rejoinder by C. Davidson, *MLN* 5: 189–90].

Davis, G.R.C. (1958), *Medieval Cartularies of Great Britain: A Short Catalogue* (London).

Davis, N. and C. L. Wrenn (1962), *English and Medieval Studies presented to J. R. R. Tolkien on the Occasion of his Seventieth Birthday* (London).

– (1969), 'Another Fragment of Richard Coeur de Lyon', *N&Q* 16: 447–52.

Davis, R.H.C. (1989), 'Bede after Bede', in Harper-Bill (1989), 103–16.

Davril, A., ed. (1995), *The Winchcombe Sacramentary (Orléans, Bibliothèque Municipale 127 [105])*, HBS 109 (Woodbridge).

Dawson, R. MacG. (1969), 'An Edition of the Blickling Homilies' (unpubl. DPhil dissertation, Oxford Univ.).

De Bonis, G.D. (2011), 'Glossing the Adjectives in the Interlinear Gloss to the *Regularis concordia* in London, British Library, Cotton Tiberius A. iii', in Lendinara et al. (2011), 443–73.

De Bonis, M.C. (2007), 'Learning Latin through the *Regula Sancti Benedicti*: The Interlinear Glosses in London, British Library, Cotton Tiberius A. iii', in Lendinara et al. (2007), 187–216.

– (2011), 'The Interlinear Glosses to the *Regula S. Benedicti* in London, British Library, Cotton Tiberius A. iii: A Specimen of a New Edition', in Lendinara et al. (2011), 269–97.

DeBrún, P. and M. Herbert (1986), *Catalogue of Irish Manuscripts in Cambridge Libraries* (Cambridge).

De Bruyne, D. (1923), 'Un feuillet oncial d'une règle de moniales', *RB* 35: 126–8.

Declerq, G. (2007), *Early Medieval Palimpsests*, Bibliologia 26 (Turnhout).

Deegan, M. (1991), 'A Critical Edition of MS B.L. Royal 12.D.xvii: Bald's "Leechbook"' (unpubl. PhD dissertation, Manchester Univ.).

Degenhart, B. (1950), 'Autonome Zeichnungen bei mittelalterlichen Künstlern', *Münchener Jahrbücher der Bildenden Kunst*, 3rd ser. 1: 93–158.

Degering, H. (1921), 'Handschriften aus Echternach und Orval in Paris', in *Aufsätze Fritz Milkau gewidmet*, ed. G. Leyh (Leipzig, 1921), 48–85.

De Hamel, C. (1986), *A History of Illuminated Manuscripts* (Oxford).

– (1987), 'Medieval and Renaissance Manuscripts from the Library of Sir Sydney Cockerell (1867–1962)', *BLJ* 13: 187–210.

– (2004), 'Phillipps Fragments in Tokyo', in Matsuda (2004), 19–44.

Dekeyzer, B. and J. Van der Stock, eds. (2005a), *Manuscripts in Transition: Recycling Manuscripts, Text and Images. Proceedings of the International*

Congress held in Brussels (5–9 November 2002), Corpus of Illuminated Manuscripts 15 (Paris).

– (2005b), 'From Word to Image: The Illustrations of "Religious" Manuscripts throughout the Middle Ages', in Dekeyzer–Van der Stock (2005a), 7–22.

Dekker, K. (2007), 'Anglo-Saxon Encyclopaedic Notes: Tradition and Function', in Bremmer–Dekker (2007), 279–315.

– (2010), 'Eucherius of Lyons in Anglo-Saxon England: The Continental Connections', in Bremmer–Dekker (2010), 147–73.

De La Mare, A.C. and B.C. Barker-Benfield, eds. (1980), *Manuscripts at Oxford: An Exhibition in Memory of Richard William Hunt (1908–1979), Keeper of Western Manuscripts at the Bodleian Library Oxford, 1945–1975, on Themes Selected and Described by some of his Friends* (Oxford).

– (1982–5), 'A Probable Addition to the Bodleian's Holdings of Exeter Cathedral Manuscripts', *BLR* 11: 79–88.

De Lemps, M. and R. Laslier (1978), *Trésors de la Bibliothèque Municipale de Reims* (Reims).

Delen, K.M. et al. (2002), 'The *Paenitentiale Cantabrigiense*: A Witness of the Carolingian Contribution to the Tenth-Century Reforms in England', *Sacris Erudiri* 41: 341–73.

Delisle, L. (1868–81), *Le cabinet des manuscrits de la Bibliothèque Nationale*, 3 vols. (Paris).

– (1876), *Inventaire général et méthodique des manuscrits français de la Bibliothèque Nationale* (Paris).

– (1877), *Bibliotheca Bigotiana Manuscripta* (Paris).

– (1884), 'Notice d'un manuscrit mérovingien de la Bibliothèque royale de Belgique, no. 9850–9852', *Notices et extraits des manuscrits de la Bibliothèque Nationale* 31: 33–47.

– (1886), 'Mémoire sur d'anciens sacramentaires', *Mémoires de l'Académie des inscriptions et belles-lettres* 32: 57–423.

– (1903), 'Vers et écriture d'Ordéric Vital', *Journal des Savants* n.s. 1: 429–35.

– (1910), 'Notes sur les manuscrits autographes d'Orderic Vital', in *Matériaux pour l'édition de Guillaume de Jumièges*, ed. J. Lair (Paris, 1910), 1–46.

Del Lungo Camiciotti, G. (1990), 'Un brano confessionale in inglese antico, Laud misc. 482, ff. 46r–47r', *Aevum* 64: 175–82.

Dell'Era, A. (1979), 'Una rielaborazione dell'Arato latino', *SM* 3rd ser. 20: 269–301.

De Mérindol, C. (1976), *La production des livres peints à l'abbaye de Corbie au XIIe siècle. Étude historique et archéologique*, 3 vols. (Paris).

De Meyier, K.A. (1973), *Codices Vossiani Latini, Pars I: Codices in Folio*, Bibliotheca Universitatis Leydensis Codices manuscripti 13 (Leiden).

– (1975), *Codices Vossiani Latini, Pars II: Codices in Quarto*, Bibliotheca Universitatis Leydensis Codices manuscripti 14 (Leiden).

Denholm-Young, N. (1964), *Handwriting in England and Wales*, 2nd ed. (Cardiff).

Dennery, É., ed. (1968), *Humanisme actif. Mélanges d'art et de littérature offerts à Julien Cain*, 2 vols. (Paris).

Dennison, L., ed. (2001), *The Legacy of M.R. James. Papers from the 1995 Cambridge Symposium* (Donington).

Denucé, J. (1927), *Musaeum Plantin-Moretus: Catalogue des manuscrits* (Antwerp).

Derolez, A. (1994), 'The Manuscript and its History', in Coppens et al. (1994), 17–34.

– and B. Victor, eds. (1997), *Corpus Catalogorum Belgii: The Medieval Booklists of the Southern Low Countries*, 1. *Provincie West-Vlaanderen*, 2nd ed. (Brussels).

Derolez, R. (1954), *Runica manuscripta* (Bruges).

– (1955), 'De Oudengelse Aldhelmglossen in HS. 1650 van de Koninklijke Bibliotheek te Brussel', *Handelingen IX der Zuidnederlandse Maatschappij voor Taal- en Letterkunde en Geschiedenis*: 37–50.

– (1956), 'Aldhelmus Glossatus 2: Zu den Brüsseler Aldhelmglossen', *Anglia* 74: 153–80.

– (1959), 'Aldhelmus Glossatus 3', *ES* 40: 129–34.

– (1960), 'Aldhelmus Glossatus 4: Some *Hapax Legomena* among the Old English Aldhelm Glosses', *Studia Germanica Gandensia* 2: 81–95.

– (1970a), Review of *The Harley Latin-Old English Glossary* by R. T. Oliphant, *ES* 51: 149–51.

– (1970b), 'Some Notes on the *Liber scintillarum* and its Old English Gloss', in *Philological Essays. Studies in Old and Middle English Literature in Honour of Herbert Dean Meritt*, ed. J.L. Rosier (The Hague, 1970), 142–51.

– (1972), 'A New Psalter Fragment with O.E. Glosses', *ES* 53: 401–8.

– (1986), 'Aldhelm im Schulzimmer: einige Bemerkungen zu einer Brüsseler Aldhelmhandschrift', in Cox—Vanacker (1986), 117–27.

– ed. (1992), *Anglo-Saxon Glossography: Papers read at the International Conference (1. International Colloquium on Anglo-Saxon Glossography) held in the Koninklijke Academie voor Wetenschappen, Letteren en Schone Kunsten van België, Brussels, 8 and 9 September 1986* (Brussels).

– (1992a), 'Anglo-Saxon Glossography: A Brief Introduction', in Derolez (1992), 9–43.

De Sainte-Marie, H., ed. (1954), *Sancti Hieronymi Psalterium iuxta Hebraeos*, Collectanea Biblica Latina 11 (Rome).

Deshman, R. (1974), 'Anglo-Saxon Art after Alfred', *Art Bulletin* 56: 176–200.

– (1976), '*Christus rex et magi reges*: Kingship and Christology in Ottonian and Anglo-Saxon Art', *FMS* 10: 367–405.

– (1977), 'The Leofric Missal and Tenth-Century English Art', *ASE* 6: 145–73.

– (1988), '*Benedictus Monarcha et Monachus*. Early Medieval Ruler Theology and the Anglo-Saxon Reform', *FMS* 22: 204–40.

– (1995), *The Benedictional of Æthelwold*, Studies in Manuscript Illumination 9 (Princeton, NJ).

– (1997), 'The Galba Psalter: Pictures, Texts and Context in an Early Medieval Prayerbook', *ASE* 26: 109–38.

Deuffic, J.-L. (1986), 'La production manuscrite des scriptoria bretons (VIIIe–XIe siècles)', in *Landévennec et le monachisme breton dans le haut moyen âge* (Bannalec), 289–321.

De Vregille, B. and L. Neyrand, eds. (1986), *Apponii in Canticum Canticorum Expositio*, CCSL 19 (Turnhout).

De Vriend, H.J., ed. (1972), *The Old English Medicina de Quadrupedibus* (Tilburg).

– ed. (1984), *The Old English Herbarium and Medicina de Quadrupedibus*, EETS o.s. 286 (London).

De Wald, E.T. (1933), *The Illustrations of the Utrecht Psalter* (Princeton, NJ).

Dewick, E.S. (1902), *Facsimiles of Horae de beata Maria virgine from English MSS of the Eleventh Century*, HBS 21 (London).

– and W.H. Frere, eds. (1914–21), *The Leofric Collectar compared with the Collectar of St Wulfstan*, 2 vols., HBS 45, 56 (London).

Díaz y Díaz, M.C. (1953), 'Isidoriana I. Sobre el *Liber de ordine creaturarum*', *Sacris erudiri* 5: 147–66.

– (1959), *Index scriptorum latinorum medii aevi hispanorum* (Madrid).

– ed. (1961), *Isidoriana. Estudios sobre San Isidoro de Sevilla en el XIV centenario de su nacimiento* (Léon).

– ed. (1972), *Liber de ordine creaturarum: un anónimo irlandés del siglo VII* (Santiago de Compostela).

Dickins, B. (1952), *The Genealogical Preface to the Anglo-Saxon Chronicle*, Department of Anglo-Saxon Occasional Papers 2 (Cambridge).

– and A.S.C. Ross, eds. (1954), *The Dream of the Rood*, rev. ed. (London).

Dietrich, F. (1854a), *Indices lectionum et publicarum et privatarum quae in Academia Marburgensi per semestre hibernum inde a d. XXIII m. Oct. MDCCCLIV usque ad d. XV m. Martii a. MDCCCLV habendae proponuntur* (Marburg).

– (1854b), 'Anglosaxonica', in Dietrich (1854a) [without pagination].

Dietz, K. (1968), 'Die Ae. Psalterglossen der Hs. Cambridge, Pembroke College 312', *Anglia* 86: 273–9.

- (1990), 'Die südaltenglische Sonorisierung anlautender Spiranten', *Anglia* 108: 292–313.
- (2001), 'Die frühaltenglischen Glossen der Handschrift, Staatsbibliothek zu Berlin – Preussischer Kulturbesitz, Grimm-Nachlass 132,2 + 139,2', in Bergmann (2001), 147–70.

D'Imperio, F.S. and R. Guglielmetti (2005), 'Alcuinus Eboracensis ep.', in Chiesa—Castaldi (2005), 22–70.
- (2008), 'Le fonti nella "recensio" dei commentari biblici carolingi: Alcuino lettore di Girolamo', *Filologia mediolatina* 15: 18–43.

Dionisotti, A.C. (1982), 'On Bede, Grammars and Greek', *RB* 92: 111–41.
- (1984–5), 'From Stephanus to Du Cange', *Revue d'histoire des textes* 14–15: 305–12.
- (1988), 'Greek Grammars and Dictionaries in Carolingian Europe', in Herren (1988), 1–56.
- (1996), 'On the Nature and Transmission of Latin Glossaries', in Hamesse (1996), 205–52.

Di Sciacca, C. (2007a), 'An Unpublished *ubi sunt* Piece in Wulfstan's "Commonplace Book": Cambridge, Corpus Christi College 190, pp. 94–96', in Lendinara et al. (2007), 217–50.
- (2007b), 'The Manuscript Tradition, Presentation, and Glossing of Isidore's *Synonyma* in Anglo-Saxon England: The Case of CCCC 448, Harley 110, and Cotton Tiberius A. iii', in Bremmer—Dekker (2007), 95–124.
- (2008), *Finding the Right Words: Isidore's Synonyma in Anglo-Saxon England* (Toronto).
- (2010), 'Teaching the Devil's Tricks: Anchorites' *Exempla* in Anglo-Saxon England', in Bremmer—Dekker (2010), 311–45.
- (2011), 'Glossing in late Anglo-Saxon England: A Sample Study of the Glosses in Cambridge, Corpus Christi College 448 and London, British Library, Harley 110', in Lendinara et al. (2011), 299–336.

Doane, A.N., ed. (1978), *Genesis A* (Madison, WI).
- ed. (1991), *The Saxon Genesis: An Edition of the West Saxon Genesis B and the Old Saxon Vatican Genesis* (Madison, WI).
- (1994), 'Editing Old English Oral/Written Texts: Problems of Method (with an Illustrative Edition of Charm 4, *Wið færsticce*)', in Scragg—Szarmach (1994b), 125–45.
- and K. Wolf, eds. (2006), *Beatus Vir. Studies in Early English and Norse Manuscripts in Memory of Phillip Pulsiano* (Tempe, AZ).
- and W.P. Stoneman (2011), *Purloined Letters: Twelfth-Century Reception of the Anglo-Saxon Illustrated Hexateuch (British Library, Cotton Claudius B. iv)* (Tempe, AZ).

Dobbie, E. van Kirk, ed. (1942), *The Anglo-Saxon Minor Poems*, The Anglo-Saxon Poetic Records 6 (London).

– ed. (1953), *Beowulf and Judith*, The Anglo-Saxon Poetic Records 4 (London).

Dobiaš-Roždestvenskaya [Dobiache-Rojdestvensky], O.A. (1928), 'Un manuscrit de Bède à Leningrad', *Speculum* 3: 304–10.

– (1934), *Histoire de l'atelier graphique de Corbie de 651 à 830, reflétée dans les manuscrits de Leningrad* (Leningrad).

– and W.W. Bakhtine (1991), *Les anciens manuscrits latins de la Bibliothèque publique Saltykov-Ščedrin de Leningrad, VIIIe–début IXe siècle*, trans. X. Grichina (Paris).

Doble, G.H., ed. (1937), *Pontificale Lanalatense*, HBS 74 (London).

Dobszay, L., ed. (1998), *Cantus Planus. Papers Read at the 7th Meeting. Sopron, Hungary, 1995* (Budapest).

Dodwell, C.R. (1954), *The Canterbury School of Illumination, 1066–1200* (Cambridge).

– (1971a), 'L'originalité iconographique de plusieurs illustrations Anglo-Saxonnes de l'ancien testament', *Cahiers de civilisation médiévale* 14: 319–28.

– (1971b), *Painting in Europe: 800–1200* (Harmondsworth).

– and P. Clemoes, eds. (1974), *The Old English Illustrated Hexateuch: British Museum, Cotton Claudius B. iv*, EEMF 18 (Copenhagen).

– (1982), *Anglo-Saxon Art: A New Perspective*, Manchester Studies in the History of Art 3 (Manchester).

– (1990), 'The Final Copy of the Utrecht Psalter and its Relationship with the Utrecht and Eadwine Psalters (Paris, B. N. Lat. 8846, ca. 1170–1190)', *Scriptorium* 44: 21–53.

– (2000), *Anglo-Saxon Gestures and the Roman Stage*, CSASE 28 (Cambridge).

Dolbeau, F. (1988), 'Du nouveau sur un sermonnaire de Cambridge', *Scriptorium* 42: 131–9.

– (1992), 'Listes latines d'apôtres et de disciples, traduites du grec', *Apocrypha* 3: 259–79.

Dold, A. (1935), 'Eine kostbare Handschriftenreliquie', *Zentralblatt für Bibliothekswesen* 52: 125–35.

Dooley, A. (2007), 'Re-Drawing the Bounds: Marginal Illustrations and Interpretative Strategies in the Book of Kells', in Keefer—Bremmer (2007a), 9–24.

Dornier, A., ed. (1977), *Mercian Studies* (Leicester).

Douglas, D.C., ed. (1944), *The Domesday Monachorum of Christ Church, Canterbury* (London).

Dowden, J. (1893–4), 'Notes on the MS. Liturg. f. 5 ('Queen Margaret's Gospel-book') in the Bodleian Library', *Proceedings of the Society of Antiquaries of Scotland* 28: 244–53.

Doyle, A.I. (1988), 'The Printed Books of the Last Monks of Durham', *The Library*, 6th ser., 10: 203–19.

– (1992), 'A Fragment of an Eighth Century Northumbrian Office Book', in Korhammer (1992), 11–27.

Drage, E.M. (1978), 'Bishop Leofric and the Exeter Cathedral Chapter, 1050–1072: A Reassessment of the Manuscript Evidence' (unpubl. PhD dissertation, Oxford Univ.).

Drögereit, R. (1949), 'Sachsen und Angelsachsen', *Niedersächsisches Jahrbuch für Landesgeschichte* 21: 1–62.

– (1950), *Werden und der Heliand: Studien zur Kulturgeschichte der Abtei Werden und der Herkunft des Heliand* (Essen).

– (1951), 'Die Heimat des Heliand', *Jahrbuch der Gesellschaft für niedersächsische Kirchengeschichte* 49: 1–18.

Drogin, M. (1989), *Medieval Calligraphy. Its History and Technique*, rev. ed. (New York).

Dronke, P. (1981), 'Arbor caritatis', in *Medieval Studies for J.A.W. Bennett*, ed. P.L. Heyworth (Oxford, 1981), 207–53.

– M. Lapidge and P. Stotz (1982), 'Die unveröffentlichten Gedichte der Cambridger Liederhandschrift (CUL Gg. 5. 35)', *MLJ* 17: 54–95.

– (1988), 'Towards the Interpretation of the Leiden Love-Spell', *CMCS* 16: 61–75.

– (2005a), 'Arbor eterna: A Ninth-Century Welsh Latin Sequence', in *Britannia Latina. Latin in the Culture of Great Britain from the Middle Ages to the Twentieth Century*, ed. C. Burnett and N. Mann (London and Turin, 2005), 14–26.

– (2005b), 'Latin and Vernacular Love-Lyrics: Rochester and St Augustine's, Canterbury', *RB* 115: 400–10.

Dubois, M.M. (1943), *Ælfric. Sermonnaire, docteur et grammarien* (Paris).

– (1955), 'Les rubriques en vieil anglais du missel de Robert de Jumièges', in *Jumièges* (1955) I, 305–8.

Duchesne, L. (1890), 'La vie de Saint-Malo: étude critique', *Revue celtique* 11: 1–22.

Duckett, E.S. (1951), *Alcuin, Friend of Charlemagne* (New York).

Duff, J.W. and A.M. Duff, eds. (1934), *Minor Latin Poets*, The Loeb Classical Library 284 (London and Cambridge, MA).

Duffey, J.E. (1978), 'The Inventive Group of Illustrations in the Harley Psalter (British Museum MS. Harley 603)' (unpubl. PhD dissertation, University of California at Berkeley).

Dufour, A. and G. Labory, eds. (2008), *Abbon, un abbé de l'an mil*, Bibliothèque d'histoire culturelle du moyen âge 6 (Turnhout).

Dufrenne, S. (1964), 'Les copies anglaises du Psautier d'Utrecht', *Scriptorium* 18: 185–99.

– (1978), *Les illustrations du Psautier d'Utrecht: Sources et apport carolingien* (Paris).

Dümmler, E., ed. (1881), MGH, PLAC 1 (Berlin).

– (1884), 'Lateinische Gedichte des neunten bis elften Jahrhunderts', *Neues Archiv der Gesellschaft für deutsche Geschichtskunde* 10: 331–57.

– ed. (1895), MGH, Epist. IV [= Epistolae Karolini Aevi II] (Berlin).

Dumville, D.N. (1972), 'Liturgical Drama and Panegyric Responsory from the Eighth Century? A Re-Examination of the Origin and Contents of the Ninth-Century Section of the Book of Cerne', *JTS* n.s. 23: 374–406.

– (1972–4), 'Some Aspects of the Chronology of the *Historia Brittonum*', *Bulletin of the Board of Celtic Studies* 25: 439–45.

– (1973), 'Biblical Apocrypha and the Early Irish: A Preliminary Investigation', *PRIA* 73C: 299–338.

– (1975), 'The *Liber Floridus* of Lambert of Saint-Omer and the *Historia Brittonum*', *BBCS* 26: 103–22.

– (1976), 'The Anglian Collection of Royal Genealogies and Regnal Lists', *ASE* 5: 23–50.

– (1977), 'Kingship, Genealogies and Regnal Lists', in *Early Medieval Kingship. Six Lectures delivered in the University of Leeds, 1977*, ed. P.H. Sawyer and I.N. Wood (Leeds, 1977), 72–104.

– (1983a), 'Motes and Beams: Two Insular Computistical Manuscripts', *Peritia* 2: 248–56.

– (1983b), 'Some Aspects of Annalistic Writing at Canterbury in the Eleventh and early Twelfth Centuries', *Peritia* 2: 23–57.

– and M. Lapidge, eds. (1984), *The Anglo-Saxon Chronicle: A Collaborative Edition, vol. 17. The Annals of St Neots with Vita Prima Sancti Neoti* (Cambridge).

– (1986), 'The West Saxon Genealogical Regnal List: Manuscripts and Texts', *Anglia* 104: 1–32.

– (1987), 'English Square Minuscule Script: The Background and Earliest Phases', *ASE* 16: 147–79.

– (1988), '*Beowulf* Come Lately. Some Notes on the Palaeography of the Nowell Codex', *ASNSL* 225: 49–63 [repr. Dumville (1993c), no. VII].

– (1989), 'The Tribal Hidage: An Introduction to its Texts and their History', in Bassett (1989), 225–30, 286–7.

– (1991–5), 'On the Dating of Some Late Anglo-Saxon Liturgical Manuscripts', *TCBS* 10: 40–57.

– (1992a), *Liturgy and the Ecclesiastical History of Late Anglo-Saxon England: Four Studies* (Woodbridge).

– (1992b), *Wessex and England from Alfred to Edgar: Six Essays on Political, Cultural, and Ecclesiastical Revival*, Studies in Anglo-Saxon History 3 (Woodbridge).

– et al., eds. (1993a), *St Patrick, A.D. 493–1993* (Woodbridge).
– (1993b), 'St Patrick in an Anglo-Saxon Martyrology', in Dumville et al. (1993a), 243–4.
– (1993c), *Britons and Anglo-Saxons in the Early Middle Ages* (Aldershot).
– (1993d), 'The English Element in Tenth-Century Breton Book-Production', in Dumville (1993c), no. XIV.
– (1993e), 'Wulfric cild', *N&Q* 238: 5–9.
– (1993f), 'Anglo-Saxon Books: Treasure in Norman Hands?', *ANS* 16: 83–99.
– (1993g), *English Caroline Script and Monastic History: Studies in Benedictinism, A.D. 950–1030*, Studies in Anglo-Saxon History 6 (Woodbridge).
– (1993h), 'St Patrick at his "First Synod"', in Dumville et al. (1993a), 175–8.
– (1994a), 'English Square Minuscule Script: The Mid-Century Phases', *ASE* 23: 133–64.
– (1994b), 'Breton and English Manuscripts of Amalarius's *Liber Officialis*', in Conso (1994), 205–14.
– (1994c), 'John Bale, Owner of St Dunstan's Benedictional', in *N&Q* 239: 291–5.
– (1994d), 'English Libraries before 1066: Use and Abuse of the Manuscript Evidence', in Richards (1994), 169–219 [rev. version of article originally ptd in M.W. Herren, ed., *Insular Latin Studies* (Toronto, 1981), 153–78].
– ed. (1995a), *The Anglo-Saxon Chronicle. A Collaborative Edition*, I. *Facsimile of MS. F: The Domitian Bilingual* (Cambridge).
– (1995b), 'The Importation of Mediterranean Manuscripts into Theodore's England', in Lapidge (1995a) 96–119.
– (1997), *Three Men in a Boat: Scribe, Language and Culture in the Church of Viking-Age Europe* (Cambridge).
– (1999), *A Palaeographer's Review: the Insular System of Scripts in the Early Middle Ages* (Osaka).
– (2005), 'English Script in the Second Half of the Ninth Century', in O'Brien O'Keeffe – Orchard (2005) I, 305–25.
– (2007a), *Celtic Essays, 2001–2007*, vol. I (Aberdeen).
– (2007b), *Celtic Essays, 2001–2007*, vol. II (Aberdeen).
– (2007c), *The Palaeography of the 'Book of Deer'*, I. *The Original Manuscript and the Liturgical Additions*, Aberdeen Studies in Palaeography and Codicology 1 (Aberdeen).
– (2007d), 'The Corpus of Gaelic Manuscripts of the Eleventh and Twelfth Centuries' in Dumville (2007b), 83–91.
– (2007e), *Anglo-Saxon Essays, 2001–2007*, Studies on Anglo-Saxon Culture 1 (Aberdeen).
– (2007f), 'The Two Earliest Manuscripts of Bede's *Ecclesiastical History*?', *Anglo-Saxon* [Aberdeen] 1: 55–108.

Duncan, E. (2004), *The Southampton Psalter. A Palaeographical and Codicological Exploration* (Cambridge).

Dunning, T.P. and A.J. Bliss, eds. (1969), *The Wanderer* (London).

Dutschke, C.W. (1989), *Guide to Medieval and Renaissance Manuscripts in the Huntington Library*, 2 vols. (San Marino, CA).

Eales, R. and R. Sharpe, eds. (1995), *Canterbury and the Norman Conquest: Churches, Saints and Scholars, 1066–1109* (London).

Earle, J., ed. (1861), *Gloucester Fragments*, 2 parts (London).

Eberlein, J.K. (2003), 'Der Wert illustrierter Bücher im Mittelalter', in Brunner—Jaritz (2003), 387–94.

Ebersperger, B. (1999), *Die angelsächsischen Handschriften in den Pariser Bibliotheken, mit einer Edition von Ælfrics Kirchweihhomilie aus der Handschrift Paris, BN, lat. 943* (Heidelberg).

– (2003), 'BSG MS 2409 + Arsenal, MS 933, ff. 128–334: an Anglo-Saxon Manuscript from Canterbury?', in Kornexl—Lenker (2003), 177–93.

Eble, C.C. (1970), 'Noun Inflection in Royal 7 C. XII, Ælfric's First Series of Catholic Homilies' (unpubl. PhD dissertation, University of North Carolina at Chapel Hill, NC).

Les Échanges culturels au moyen âge: XXXIIe Congrès de la SHMES (Université du Littoral Côte d'Opale, juin 2001), Séries histoire ancienne et médiévale 70 (Paris, 2002).

Eckhardt, W.A. (1969), 'Das Kaufunger Fragment der Bonifatius-Grammatik', *Scriptorium* 23: 280–97.

Edwards, A.S.G. and J. Griffiths (2000), 'The Tollemache Collection of Medieval Manuscripts', *The Book Collector* 49: 349–64.

– (2002), 'Manuscripts at Auction: January 2001 to December 2001', *English Manuscript Studies 1100–1700* 10: 231–6.

– (2004), 'The Bradfer-Lawrence Collection of Medieval Western Manuscripts', *Book Collector* 53: 64–9.

– (2008), 'Manuscripts at Auction: January 2006 to December 2007', *English Manuscript Studies 1100–1700* 14: 251–8.

Edwards, H. (1986), 'Two Documents from Aldhelm's Malmesbury', *Bulletin of the Institute of Historical Research* 69: 1–19.

Edwards, N. (2012), 'The Decoration of the earliest Welsh Manuscripts', in R. Gameson (2012), 244–8.

Ehrensberger, H. (1897), *Libri liturgici Bibliothecae Apostolicae Vaticanae Manu Scripti* (Freiburg im Breisgau).

Ehrisman, G. (1932), *Geschichte der deutschen Literatur bis zum Ausgang des Mittelalters. Erster Teil: Die althochdeutsche Literatur* (Munich).

Ehwald, R., ed. (1919), *Aldhelmi Opera*, MGH, AA 15 (Berlin).

Eizenhöfer, L. (1970), 'Zu dem angelsächsischen Sakramentarfragment von St Paul in Kärnten (Stiftsbibl. Cod. 979 fol. 4)', *RB* 80: 291–3.

Elbern, V.H. (1955), 'Die Dreifaltigkeitsminiatur im Book of Durrow', *Wallraf-Richartz Jahrbuch* 17: 7–42.

Elfassi, J., ed. (2009), *Isidori Hispalensis Episcopi Synonyma*, CCSL 111B (Turnhout).

Eliason, N. and P. Clemoes, eds. (1965), *Ælfric's First Series of Catholic Homilies, British Museum Royal 7 C.XII, fols. 4–218*, EEMF 13 (Copenhagen).

Ellis, M. (1998), 'A Missing Bifolium and other Textual Problems in CCCC MS 12 of the Old English Pastoral Care', *Anglia* 116: 498–507.

Ellis, P.B. and R. Ellsworth (1994), *The Book of Deer* (London).

Ellis, R. (1903), *Specimens of Latin Palaeography from Manuscripts in the Bodleian Library* (Oxford).

– ed. (1907), *Appendix Vergiliana sive Carmina minora Vergilio adtributa* (Oxford).

Elstob, E., ed. (1709), *An English Saxon Homily of the Birth-Day of St Gregory* (London).

Emms, R. (1999a), 'The Early History of Saint Augustine's Abbey', in R. Gameson (1999b), 410–29.

– (1999b), 'The Scribe of the Paris Psalter', *ASE* 28: 179–83.

– (2006), 'Books and Writing in Seventh-Century Kent', in Rumble (2006a), 18–27.

Engelbert, P. (1969), 'Paläographische Bemerkungen zur Faksimileausgabe der ältesten Handschrift der *Regula Benedicti* (Oxford, Bodl. Libr. Hatton 48)', *RB* 79: 399–413.

Engelbregt, J.H.A. (1965), *Het Utrechts Psalterium* (Utrecht).

Erickson, J.L. (1972), 'The Readings of Folios 77 and 86 of the Vercelli Codex', *Manuscripta* 16: 14–23.

Erskine, R.W.H., ed. (1986), *Great Domesday*, 6 boxes (London) [facsimile].

– ed. (1987), *Domesday Book Studies* (London).

Escudier, D., 'La notation musicale de Saint-Vaast d'Arras: Étude d'une particularité graphique', in Huglo (1987), 107–20.

Esposito, M. (1910), 'Note on a Ninth-Century Commentary on Martianus Capella', *Zeitschrift für celtische Philologie* 7: 499–507.

– (1910–11), 'Analecta Varia, Part II', *Hermathena* 16: 86–90.

– (1913a), 'La vie de sainte Vulfhilde par Goscelin de Cantorbéry', *AB* 32: 10–26.

– (1913b), 'Irish Commentaries on Martianus Capella', *Zeitschrift für celtische Philologie* 9: 159–63.

– (1929), 'Notes on Latin Learning and Literature in Mediaeval Ireland, I', *Hermathena* 20: 225–60 [repr. in Esposito (1988) no. IV].

– (1932), 'Notes on Latin Learning and Literature in Mediaeval Ireland, II', *Hermathena* 22: 253–71 [repr. in Esposito (1988) no. V].

– (1988), *Latin Learning in Mediaeval Ireland*, ed. M. Lapidge (Aldershot).

Étaix, R. (1994), 'L'homiliaire carolingien d'Angers', *RB* 104: 148–90.

– (1996), 'Repertoire des manuscrits des homélies sur l'Evangile de saint Grégoire le Grand', *Sacris Erudiri* 36: 107–45.

– ed. (1999), *Gregorius Magnus: Homiliae in Evangelia*, CCSL 141 (Turnhout).

Euw, A. von, and J.M. Plotzek (1979–85), *Die Handschriften der Sammlung Ludwig*, 4 vols. (Cologne).

Evans, G.R. (1979), 'Schools and Scholars: The Study of the Abacus in English Schools *c.* 980–*c.* 1150', *EHR* 94: 71–89.

Evans, J. (1922), *Magical Jewels of the Middle Ages and the Renaissance particularly in England* (Oxford).

– and M. S. Serjeantson, eds. (1933), *English Mediaeval Lapidaries*, EETS o.s. 190 (Oxford).

Evans, M., ed. (1969), *Augustinus: Enchiridion ad Laurentium de fide et spe et caritate*, CCSL 46: 49–114.

Evans, M.W. (1969), *Medieval Drawings* (New York).

Evans, R. (1981), 'An Anonymous Old English Homily for Holy Saturday', *LSE* n.s. 12: 129–53.

Eward, S.M. (1972), *A Catalogue of Gloucester Cathedral Library* (Gloucester).

Faller, O., ed. (1933), *Sancti Ambrosii De virginibus*, Florilegium Patristicum 31 (Bonn).

– ed. (1955), *Sancti Ambrosii Opera: Pars Septima*, CSEL 73 (Vienna).

– and M. Zelzer, eds. (1968–94), *Sancti Ambrosii Opera. Pars Decima*: *Epistulae et Acta*, 4 vols., CSEL 82 (Vienna).

Faraci, D., ed. (1990), *Il Bestiario medioinglese (MS. Arundel 292 della British Library)* (Rome).

Faral, E., ed. (1929), *La légende arthurienne*, 3 vols. (Paris).

Faris, M.J., ed. (1976), *The Bishop's Synod ('The First Synod of St Patrick'). A Symposium with Text, Translation and Commentary* (Liverpool).

Farmer, D.H., ed. (1968), *The Rule of St Benedict: Oxford, Bodleian Library, Hatton 48*, EEMF 15 (Copenhagen).

Farr, C.A. (1997), *The Book of Kells, its Function and Audience* (London).

– (1999), 'The Shape of Learning at Wearmouth-Jarrow: the Diagram Pages in the *Codex Amiatinus*', in Hawkes — Mills (1999), 336–44.

– (2003), 'Style in Late Anglo-Saxon England: Questions of Learning and Intention', in Karkov—Brown (2003), 115–30.

– (2007), '*Bis per chorum hinc et inde*: The "Virgin and Child with Angels" in the Book of Kells', in Minnis—Roberts (2007), 117–34.

- (2011a), 'Irish Pocket Gospels in Anglo-Saxon England', in Roberts—Webster (2011), 87–100.
- (2011b), '*Vox Ecclesiae*: Performance and Insular Manuscript Art', in Hourihane (2011), 219–28.

Farrell, R.T., ed. (1974), *Daniel and Azarias* (London).

Faulkner, D.R. (1968), 'The Phonology of British Museum Manuscript Royal 7 C.xii, folios 25v–45v and 91–218' (unpubl. PhD dissertation, University of North Carolina at Chapel Hill, NC).

Fausbøll, E. (1986), *Fifty-Six Ælfric Fragments. The Newly-Found Copenhagen Fragments of Ælfric's 'Catholic Homilies'. With Facsimiles*, Publications of the Department of English, University of Copenhagen 14 (Copenhagen).
- (1995), 'More Ælfric Fragments', *ES* 76: 302–6.

Faye, C.U. and W.H. Bond (1962), *Supplement to the Census of Medieval and Renaissance Manuscripts in the United States and Canada* (New York).

Fedeli, P., ed. (1982), *M. Tulli Ciceronis Scripta quae manserunt omnia, 28: In M. Antonium Orationes Philippicae XIV* (Leipzig).

Fehr, B., ed. (1914/1966), *Die Hirtenbriefe Ælfrics in altenglischer und lateinischer Fassung*, Bibliothek der angelsächsischen Prosa 9 [repr. with supplementary introduction by P. Clemoes, Darmstadt, 1966] (Hamburg).
- (1921), 'Altenglische Ritualtexte für Krankenbesuch, heilige Ölung und Begräbnis', in Förster—Wildhagen (1921a), 20–67.

Fell, C.E., ed. (1971), *Edward King and Martyr* (Leeds).
- (1981), 'Richard Cleasby's Notes on the Vercelli Codex', *LSE* 12: 13–42.

Fellows-Jensen, G. and P. Springborg, eds. (2005), *Care and Conservation of Manuscripts 8. Proceedings of the Eighth International Seminar held at the University of Copenhagen, 16th–17th October 2003* (Copenhagen).

Fenlon, I., ed. (1982), *Cambridge Music Manuscripts* (Cambridge).

Fernquist, C.H. (1937), *Study on the Old English Version of the Anglo-Saxon Chronicle in Cott. Domitian A. viii*, Studier i Modern Språkvetenskap 13: 39–103.

Ferrabino, A., ed. (1957), *Atti del X Congresso internazionale di scienze storiche, Roma 4–11 settembre 1955* (Rome).

Ferrari, M.C. (1994), *Sancti Willibrordi venerantes memoriam. Echternacher Schreiber und Schriftsteller von den Angelsachsen bis Iohann Bertels* (Luxembourg).
- (1999), 'Schulfragmente. Text und Glosse im mittelalterlichen Echternach', in *Die Abtei Echternach 698-1998*, ed. M.C. Ferrari, J. Schroeder and H. Trauffler (Luxembourg, 1999), 123–64.
- (2011), '*Manu hominibus praedicare*. Cassiodors Vivarium im Zeitalter des Übergangs', in *Bibliotheken im Altertum*, ed. E. Blumenthal and W. Schmitz,

Wolfenbütteler Schriften zur Geschichte des Buchwesens 45 (Wiesbaden, 2011), 223–49.

Ferrua, A., ed. (1942), *Epigrammata Damasiana*, Sussidi allo studio delle antichità cristiane 2 (Rome).

Finberg, H.P.R. (1961), *The Early Charters of the West Midlands* (Leicester).

– (1964), *The Early Charters of Wessex* (Leicester).

Fingernagel, A. (1991), *Die illuminierten lateinischen Handschriften deutscher Provenienz der Staatsbibliothek Preussischer Kulturbesitz Berlin, 8.–12. Jahrhundert*, 2 vols. (Wiesbaden).

Finlayson, C.P., ed. (1962), *Celtic Psalter: Edinburgh University Library MS. 56*, Umbrae Codicum Occidentalium 7 (Amsterdam).

Finnegan, R.E., ed. (1977), *Christ and Satan: A Critical Edition* (Waterloo, Ontario).

– (1998), 'The Man in "Nowhere": A Previously Undiscovered Drawing in Bodleian MS Junius 11', *ES* 79: 23–32.

Finsterwalder, P.W. (1929), *Untersuchungen zu den Bussbüchern des 7., 8. und 9. Jahrhunderts. 1: Die Canones Theodori Cantuariensis und ihre Überlieferungsformen* (Weimar).

Firchow, E.S. (2001), 'Harley 3376 und das Glossarfragment Pryce MS P 2 A:1 in der Spencer Bibliothek der Kansas Universität in Lawrence, Kansas: Das Beispiel eines lateinischen Glossars mit nennenswerten altenglischen Elementen', in Bergmann (2001), 243–60.

Fischer, B. (1952), 'Die Lesungen der römischen Ostervigil unter Gregor dem Grossen', in *Colligere Fragmenta. Festschrift Alban Dold zu 70. Geburtstag*, ed. B. Fischer and V. Fiala (Beuron, 1952), 144–59 [repr. Fischer, *Beiträge zur Geschichte der lateinischen Bibeltexte* (Freiburg im Breisgau, 1986), 18–50].

– (1962), 'Codex Amiatinus und Cassiodor', *Biblische Zeitschrift* n.s. 6: 57–79 [repr. in Fischer, *Lateinische Bibelhandschriften im frühen Mittelalter*, Vetus latina: Aus der Geschichte der lateinischen Bibel 11 (Freiburg im Br., 1985), 19–34].

– (1965), 'Bibeltext und Bibelreform unter Karl dem Grossen', in *Karl der Grosse*, II. *Das geistige Leben*, ed. B. Bischoff (Düsseldorf), 156–216.

– (1971), 'Bedae de titulis psalmorum liber', in Autenrieth—Brunhölzl (1971), 90–110.

– (1988–91), *Die lateinischen Evangelien bis zum 10. Jahrhundert*, 4 vols., Vetus Latina: Aus der Geschichte der lateinischen Bibel 13, 15, 17, 18 (Freiburg im Breisgau).

Fischer, K.-D. (1998), 'Beiträge zu den pseudo-soranischen *Quaestiones medicinales*', in *Text and Tradition: Studies in Ancient Medicine and its Transmission presented to Jutta Kolesch*, ed. K.-D. Fischer, D. Nickel and P. Potter (Leiden, 1998), 1–54.

Fisiak, J., ed. (1988), *Historical Dialectology: Regional and Social* (Berlin).

Flasdieck, H.M. (1938), 'Das Kasseler Bruchstück der *Cura pastoralis*', *Anglia* 62: 193–233.

– (1942), 'Weiteres zum Kasseler Bruchstück der *Cura pastoralis*', *Anglia* 66: 56–8.

Fleming, J.V. (1976), 'The Old English Manuscripts in the Scheide Library', *Princeton University Library Chronicle* 37: 126–38.

Fleming, R. (1993), 'Christchurch's Sisters and Brothers: An Edition and Discussion of Canterbury Obituary Lists', in *The Culture of Christendom. Essays in Medieval History in Commemoration of D.L.T. Bethell*, ed. M.A. Meyer (London, 1993), 115–53.

Fletcher, H.G., ed. (2007), *The Wormsley Library. A Personal Selection by Sir Paul Getty KBE*, 2nd ed. (London and New York).

Flower, R. (1933), 'The Script of the Exeter Book', in Chambers (1933), 83–92.

– and H. Smith, eds. (1941), *The Parker Chronicle and Laws: A Facsimile*, EETS o.s. 208 (London).

Floyer, J.K. and S.G. Hamilton (1906), *Catalogue of Manuscripts preserved in the Chapter Library of Worcester Cathedral* (Worcester).

Folkerts, M., ed. (1970), *'Boethius' Geometrie II. Ein mathematisches Lehrbuch des Mittelalters* (Wiesbaden).

– (1981), 'Mittelalterliche mathematische Handschriften in westlichen Sprachen in der Berliner Staatsbibliothek. Ein vorläufiges Verzeichnis', in *Mathematical Perspectives. Essays on Mathematics and its Historical Development*, ed. J.W. Dauben (New York, 1981), 53–94.

– (1982), 'Die Altercatio in der Geometrie I des pseudo-Boethius: Ein Beitrag zur Geometrie im mittelalterlichen Quadrivium', in *Fachprosa-Studien. Beiträge zur mittelalterlichen Wissenschafts- und Geistesgeschichte* (Berlin, 1982).

– (1989), *Euclid in Medieval Europe* (Winnipeg).

– and R. Lorch, eds. (2000a), *'Sic itur ad astra'. Studien zur Geschichte der Mathematik und Naturwissenschaften* (Wiesbaden).

– (2000b), 'Frühe westliche Benennungen der indisch-arabischen Ziffern und ihr Vorkommen', in Folkerts—Lorch (2000a), 216–33.

Fontaine, J., ed. (1960), *Isidore de Séville. Traité de la nature* (Bordeaux).

– et al., eds. (1992), *Ambroise de Milan: Hymnes* (Paris).

Forbes, A.P., ed. (1864), *Liber Ecclesie Beati Terrenani de Arbuthnott* (Burntisland).

Forde, H. (1986), *Domesday Preserved* (London).

Foreville, R., ed. (1984), *Les Mutations socio-culturelles au tournant des XIe–XIIe siècles: Etudes anselmiennes (IVe session)*, Spicilegium Beccense 2 (Paris).

Forsey, G.F. (1928), 'Byrhtferth's Preface', *Speculum* 3: 505–22.

Forshall, J. (1834–40), *Catalogue of Manuscripts in the British Museum*. New Series (London) [catalogue of Arundel and Burney MSS].

Förster, M. (1901), 'Two Notes on Old English Dialogue Literature: (a) A Fragment of an Old English Elucidarium, (b) Middle English Echoes', in W.P. Ker (1901), 86–106.

– (1902), 'Das lateinisch-ae. Fragment der Apocryphe von Jamnes und Mambres', *ASNSL* 108: 15–28.

– (1905), 'Ein altenglisches Prosa-Rätsel', *ASNSL* 115: 392–3.

– and A.S. Napier (1906), 'Englische Cato- und Ilias-Glossen des 12. Jahrhunderts', *ASNSL* 117: 17–28.

– (1907–8), 'Adams Erschaffung und Namengebung. Ein lateinisches Fragment des sogenannten slawischen Henoch', *Archiv für Religionswissenschaften* 11: 477–529.

– (1908), 'Beiträge zur mittelalterlichen Volkskunde III', *ASNSL* 121: 30–46.

– (1913a), 'Der Vercelli-Codex CXVII nebst Abdruck einiger altenglischer Homilien der Handschrift', in Holthausen–Spies (1913), 20–179.

– ed. (1913b), *Il codice Vercellese con omelie e poesie in lingua anglosassone* (Rome) [facsimile].

– (1914), 'Die ae. Beigaben des Lambeth-Psalters', *ASNSL* 132: 328–35.

– (1917), 'Die altenglische Glossenhandschrift Plantinus 32 (Antwerpen) und Additional 32246 (London)', *Anglia* 41: 94–161.

– (1919), *Die Beowulf-Handschrift*, Berichte über die Verhandlungen der sächsischen Akademie der Wissenschaften zu Leipzig, phil.-hist. Klasse 71 (Leipzig).

– (1920), 'Der Inhalt der altenglischen Handschrift Vespasianus D. xiv', *EStn* 54: 46–68.

– and K. Wildhagen, eds. (1921a), *Texte und Forschungen zur englischen Kulturgeschichte. Festgabe für Felix Liebermann zum 20. Juli 1921* (Halle).

– (1921b), 'Keltisches Wortgut im Englischen: Eine sprachliche Untersuchung', in Förster–Wildhagen (1921a), 119–242.

– (1925a), 'Die Weltzeitalter bei den Angelsachsen', in Sievers (1925), 183–203.

– (1925b), 'Die spätaltenglische Übersetzung der pseudo-Anselmschen Marienpredigt', in *Anglica. Untersuchungen zur englischen Philologie, Alois Brandl zum siebzigsten Geburtstag überreicht*, 2 vols., Palaestra 147–8 (Leipzig, 1925), 8–69.

– (1927), 'Die altenglischen Texte der Pariser Nationalbibliothek', *EStn* 62: 113–31.

– (1929), 'Die altenglischen Verzeichnisse von Glücks- und Unglückstagen', in Malone (1929), 258–77.

– (1930), 'Die Freilassungsurkunden des Bodmin-Evangeliars', in *A Grammatical Miscellany offered to Otto Jespersen on his Seventieth Birthday*, ed. N. Bøgholm, A. Brusendorff and C.A. Bodelsen (Copenhagen), 77–99.

- (1932), *Die Vercelli-Homilien: 1.-8. Homilie*, Bibliothek der angelsächsischen Prosa 12 (Hamburg).
- (1933a), 'The Donations of Leofric to Exeter', in Chambers (1933), 10–32.
- (1933b), 'The Preliminary Matter of the Exeter Book', in Chambers (1933), 44–54.
- (1933c), 'Lokalisierung und Datierung der altenglischen Version der Chrodegang-Regel', *Sitzungsberichte der Bayerischen Akademie der Wissenschaften, phil.-hist. Abt.*, Schlussheft 7–8 (Munich, 1933).
- (1941), *Der Flussname Themse und seine Sippe. Studien zur Anglisierung keltischer Eigennamen und zur Lautchronologie des Altbritischen*, Sitzungsberichte der Bayerischen Akademie der Wissenschaften, phil.-hist. Abteilung 1 (Munich).
- (1942a), 'Zur Liturgik der angelsächsischen Kirche', *Anglia* 66: 1–51.
- (1942b), 'Zu den ae. Texten aus MS Arundel 155', *Anglia* 66: 52–5.
- (1942–3), 'Die altenglischen Bekenntnisformeln', *EStn* 75: 159–69.
- (1943), *Zur Geschichte des Reliquienkultus in Altengland*, Sitzungsberichte der Bayerischen Akademie der Wissenschaften, phil.-hist. Abteilung, Heft 8 (Munich).
- Forsyth, K., ed. (2008), *Studies on the Book of Deer* (Dublin).
- *La Fortuna di Virgilio. Convegno internazionale sulla fortuna di Virgilio, Napoli 24–26 ottobre 1983* (Naples, 1986).
- Fowler, R.G. (1963), '"Archbishop Wulfstan's Commonplace Book" and the Canons of Edgar', *MÆ* 32: 1–10.
- (1965), 'A Late Old English Handbook for the Use of a Confessor', *Anglia* 83: 1–34.
- ed. (1972), *Wulfstan's Canons of Edgar*, EETS o.s. 266 (London).
- Fox, M. (2012), 'Ælfric's *Interrogationes Sigewulfi*', in *Old English Literature and the Old Testament*, ed. M. Fox and M. Sharma (Toronto, 2012), 25–63.
- Fox, P., ed. (1990), *The Book of Kells. MS 58, Trinity College Library Dublin*, 2 vols. (Lucerne) [facsimile and commentary].
- Foys, M.K. (2006), 'An Unfinished *mappa mundi* from Late Eleventh-Century Worcester', *ASE* 35: 271–84.
- (2007), *Virtually Anglo-Saxon. Old Media, New Media, and Early Medieval Studies in the Late Age of Print* (Gainesville, FL).
- Frank, H. (1954), 'Die Briefe des hl. Bonifatius und das von ihm benutzte Sakramentar', in *Sankt Bonifatius. Gedenkgabe zum zwölfhundertsten Todestag* (Fulda), 58–88.
- Frank, R., and A. Cameron, eds. (1973), *A Plan for the Dictionary of Old English*, Toronto OE Series 2 (Toronto).
- (1998), 'When Lexicography Met the Exeter Book', in Baker—Howe (1998), 207–21.

Frantzen, A.J. (1983a), 'The Tradition of Penitentials in Anglo-Saxon England', *ASE* 11: 23–56.

– (1983b), *The Literature of Penance in Anglo-Saxon England* (New Brunswick, NJ).

– (1985), revised ed. of C. Vogel, *Les 'Libri Paenitentiales'* (I, III.ii), Typologie des sources du moyen âge occidental 27 (Turnhout) [separately printed].

– (2007), 'Sin and Sense: Editing and Translating Anglo-Saxon Handbooks of Penance', in Healey — Kiernan (2007), 40–71.

Franzen, C.R. (1991), *The Tremulous Hand of Worcester: A Study of Old English in the Thirteenth Century* (Oxford).

– (2001a), 'On the Attribution of Copied Glosses in CCCC MS 41 to the Tremulous Hand of Worcester', *N&Q* 246: 373–4.

– (2001b), 'The Cerne "Trembling" Hand and the Tremulous Hand of Worcester', *N&Q* 246: 374–5.

Frede, H.J. (1961), *Pelagius, der irische Paulustext, Sedulius Scottus*, Vetus Latina 3 (Freiburg im Breisgau).

– (1964), *Altlateinische Paulus-Handschriften*, Vetus Latina 4 (Freiburg im Breisgau).

Freise, E. (1993), 'Vom vorchristlichen Mimigernaford zu "honestum monasterium" Liudgers', in *Geschichte der Stadt Münster* I, ed. F.-J. Jakobi (Münster, 1993), 1–51.

Frere, W.H. (1894–1932), *Bibliotheca Musico-Liturgica: A Descriptive Handlist of the Musical and Latin-Liturgical MSS of the Middle Ages Preserved in the Libraries of Great Britain and Ireland*, 2 vols. (London).

– ed. (1894b), *The Winchester Troper from Mss of the Xth and XIth Centuries with other Documents illustrating the History of Tropes in England and France*, HBS 8 (London).

– (1923), *Pars antiphonarii. A Reproduction in Facsimile of a Manuscript of the Eleventh Century in the Chapter Library of Durham (MS. B. III. 11)* (London).

– (1934), *Studies in Early Roman Liturgy*, II: *The Roman Gospel-Lectionary* (Oxford).

Friend, A.M. (1939), 'The Canon Tables of the Book of Kells', in *Studies in Memory of Arthur Kingsley Porter*, ed. W.R.W. Koehler, 2 vols. (Cambridge, MA) II, 611–41.

Friis-Jensen, K. and J.M.W. Willoughby, eds. (2001), *Peterborough Abbey*, Corpus of British Medieval Library Catalogues 8 (London).

Fry, D.K. (1969), *Beowulf and the Fight at Finnsburh: A Bibliography* (Charlottesville, VA).

Fryde, E.B. et al., eds. (1986), *Handbook of British Chronology*, 3rd ed. (London).

Fuchs, R. (2005), 'Old Restorations and Repairs in Manuscripts', in Fellows-Jensen — Springborg (2005), 224–41.

Fulk, R.D. (1982), 'Dating of Beowulf to the Viking Age', *PQ* 61: 341–59.
- R.E. Bjork and J.D. Niles, eds. (2008), *Klaeber's Beowulf*, 4th ed. (Toronto).
- ed. (2010), *The Beowulf Manuscript: Complete Texts and The Fight at Finnsburg* (Cambridge, MA, and London).
- and S. Jurasinski, eds. (2012), *The Old English Canons of Theodore*, EETS ss 25 (Oxford).
Gaide, F., ed. (1980), *Avianus: Fables* (Paris).
Gaiffier, B. de (1985), 'Le martyrologe en vieil anglais du IXe siècle', *AB* 103: 163–6.
Galbraith, V.H. (1974), *Domesday Book. Its Place in Administrative History* (Oxford).
Gallagher, S. et al. (2003), *Western Plainchant in the First Millennium* (Aldershot).
Gallée, J.H. (1993), *Altsächsische Grammatik*, 3rd ed. mit Berichtigungen und Literaturnachträgen von Heinrich Tiefenbach (Tübingen).
Galloway, A. (1989), 'On the Medieval and Post-Medieval Collation of St Dunstan's *Aethicus*', *Scriptorium* 43: 106–11.
Gamber, K. (1958), *Sakramentartypen: Versuch einer Gruppierung der Handschriften und Fragmente bis zur Jahrtausendwende* (Beuron).
- (1962a), *Das Sakramentar von Jena* (Beuron).
- (1962b), 'Die kampanische Lektionsordnung', *Sacris Erudiri* 13: 326–52.
- (1968–88), *Codices Liturgici Latini Antiquiores*, 3 vols. (Fribourg).
- (1969), 'Das altkampanische Sakramentar. Neue Fragmente in angelsächsischer Überlieferung', *RB* 79: 329–42 [and cf. Eizenhöfer (1970)].
- (1975a), 'Das Regensburger Fragment eines Bonifatius-Sakramentars. Ein neuer Zeuge des vorgregorianischen Messkanons', *RB* 85 (1975) 266–302.
- (1975b), *Das Bonifatius-Sakramentar und weitere frühe Liturgiebücher aus Regensburg* (Regensburg).
- (1978), *Sakramentarstudien und andere Arbeiten zur frühen Liturgiegeschichte* (Regensburg).
Gameson, F. (1999), 'Goscelin's Life of Augustine of Canterbury', in R. Gameson (1999b), 391–410.
Gameson, R. and A. Coates (1988), *The Old Library, Trinity College, Oxford* (Oxford).
- (1990), 'The Anglo-Saxon Artists of the Harley 603 Psalter', *Journal of the British Archaeological Association* 143: 29–48.
- (1991), 'English Manuscript Art in the Mid-Eleventh Century: The Decorative Tradition', *AntJ* 71: 64–122.
- (1992a), 'Manuscript Art at Christ Church Canterbury, in the Generation after St Dunstan', in Ramsay (1992), 187–221.
- (1992b), 'The Cost of the Codex Amiatinus', *N&Q* 237: 2–9.

- (1992c), 'The Decoration of the Tanner Bede', *ASE* 21: 115–59.
- (1992d), 'The Fabric of the Tanner Bede', *BLR* 14: 176–206.
- (1993), 'The Romanesque Artist of the Harley 603 Psalter', *English Manuscript Studies 1100–1700*, 4: 24–61.
- ed. (1994a), *The Early Medieval Bible. Its Production, Decoration and Use* (Cambridge).
- (1994b), 'The Royal 1.B.vii Gospels and English Book Production in the Seventh and Eighth Centuries', in R. Gameson (1994a), 24–52.
- (1995a), 'English Manuscript Art in the Late Eleventh Century: Canterbury and its Context', in Eales—Sharpe (1995), 95–144.
- (1995b), *The Role of Art in the late Anglo-Saxon Church* (Oxford).
- (1996a), 'Book Production and Decoration at Worcester in the Tenth and Eleventh Centuries', in Brooks—Cubitt (1996), 194–243.
- (1996b), 'The Origin of the Exeter Book of Old English Poetry', *ASE* 25: 135–85.
- (1997), 'The Gospels of Margaret of Scotland and the Liturgy of an Eleventh-Century Queen', in *Women and the Book: Assessing the Visual Evidence*, ed. L. Smith and J.H.M. Taylor (London, 1997), 149–71.
- (1998), 'English Book Collections in the Late Eleventh and Early Twelfth Century: Symeon's Durham and its Context', in Rollason (1998), 230–53.
- (1999a), *The Manuscripts of Early Norman England (c. 1066–1130)* (Oxford).
- ed. (1999b), *St Augustine and the Conversion of England* (Stroud).
- (1999c), 'The Earliest Books of Christian Kent', in R. Gameson (1999b), 313–74.
- (2000a), 'The Hereford Gospels', in Aylmer—Tiller (2000), 536–43.
- (2000b), 'Books, Culture and the Church in Canterbury around the Millennium', in *Vikings, Monks and the Millennium: Canterbury in about 1000 A.D.*, ed. R. Eales and R. Gameson (Canterbury), 15–39.
- and H. Leyser, eds. (2001a), *Belief and Culture in the Middle Ages: Studies presented to Henry Mayr-Harting* (Oxford).
- (2001b), 'Why Did Eadfrith Write the Lindisfarne Gospels?', in Gameson—Leyser (2001a), 45–58.
- ed. (2001c), *The Codex Aureus: An Eighth-Century Gospel Book. Stockholm, Kungliga Bibliotek, A.135, part I*, EEMF 28 (Copenhagen).
- (2001d), *The Scribe Speaks? Colophons in Early English Manuscripts*, H.M. Chadwick Memorial Lectures 12 (Cambridge).
- ed. (2002a), *The Codex Aureus: An Eighth-Century Gospel Book. Stockholm, Kungliga Bibliotek, A.135, part II*, EEMF 29 (Copenhagen).
- (2002b), 'The Colophon of the Eadwig Gospels', *ASE* 31: 201–22.
- (2002c), 'The Insular Gospel Book at Hereford Cathedral', *Scriptorium* 56: 48–79.

– (2002d), 'L'Angleterre et le Flandre aux Xe et XIe siècles: le témoignage des manuscrits', in *Société des historiens médiévistes de l'enseignement supérieur public* (2002), 165–206.
– (2003), 'La Normandie et l'Angleterre au XIe siècle: le témoignage des manuscrits', in *La Normandie et l'Angleterre au moyen âge*, ed. P. Bouet and V. Gazeau (Caen, 2003), 129–59.
– (2004a), 'Aelsinus', in *ODNB* I.393.
– (2004b), 'Eadwig [Eadui] Basan (fl. c. 1020)', in *ODNB* XVII.542–3.
– (2005a), 'St Wulfstan, the Library of Worcester and the Spirituality of the Medieval Book', in Barrow—Brooks (2005), 59–104.
– (2005b), 'A Scribe's Confession and the Making of the Anchin Hrabanus (Douai, Bibliothéque Municipale, MS. 340)', in Dekeyzer—Van der Stock (2005a), 65–79.
– ed. (2007), *Treasures of Durham University Library* (London).
– (2008), *The Earliest Books of Canterbury Cathedral. Manuscripts and Fragments* (London).
– (2009), 'The Last Chi-Rho in the West: From Insular to Anglo-Saxon in the Boulogne 10 Gospels', in *Form and Order in the Anglo-Saxon World*, ed. H. Hamerow and L. Webster (Oxford, 2009), 89–107.
– (2010), 'An Itinerant English Master around the Millennium', in Rollason et al. (2010), 87–134.
– ed. (2012), *The History of the Book in Britain*, I. *c. 400–1100* (Cambridge).
– (2012a), 'The Material Fabric of Early British Books', in R. Gameson (2012), 13–93.
– (2012b), 'Anglo-Saxon Scribes and Scriptoria', in R. Gameson (2012), 94–120.
– (2012c), 'Book Decoration in England, *c.* 871–*c.* 1100', in R. Gameson (2012), 249–93.
– (2012d), 'The Circulation of Books between England and the Continent, *c.* 871–*c.* 1100', in R. Gameson (2012), 344–72.
Gansweidt, B. (1995), Review of *Through a Gloss Darkly. Aldhelm's Riddles*, by N.P. Stork, *MLJ* 29: 136–7.
Ganz, D. (1990), *Corbie in the Carolingian Renaissance*, Beihefte der Francia 20 (Sigmaringen).
– (1993), 'An Anglo-Saxon Fragment of Alcuin's Letters in the Newberry Library, Chicago', *ASE* 22: 167–77.
– (2001a), 'Carolingian Manuscripts with Substantial Glosses in Tironian Notes', in Bergmann (2001), 101–8.
– (2001b), 'The Annotations in Oxford, Bodleian Library, Auct. D. II. 14', in Gameson—Leyser (2001a), 35–44.
– (2002), 'Roman Manuscripts in Francia and Anglo-Saxon England', *Settimane* 49: 607–49.

- (2004), Review of H. Gneuss, *Handlist of Anglo-Saxon Manuscripts*, *Anglia* 122: 498–502.
- and J. Roberts, with R. Palmer, eds. (2007), *Lambeth Palace Library and its Anglo-Saxon Manuscripts. Exhibition mounted for the Biennial Conference of the International Society of Anglo-Saxonists, 3rd August 2007* (London).
- (2008), 'Three Scribes in Search of a Centre', in Kresten—Lackner (2008), 13–17.
- (2010), 'Handschriften der Werke Alkuins aus dem 9. Jahrhundert', in *Alkuin von York und die geistige Grundlegung Europas. Akten der Tagung vom 30. September bis zum 2. Oktober 2004 in der Stiftsbibliothek St Gallen*, ed. E. Tremp and K. Schmuki (St Gallen, 2010), 185–94.
- (2012), 'Square Minuscule', in R. Gameson (2012), 188–96.
Ganz, P., ed. (1986), *The Role of the Book in Medieval Culture*, 2 vols. (Turnhout).
Garmonsway, G.N., ed. (1978), *Ælfric's Colloquy*, rev. ed. (Exeter).
Garrison, M. (2012), 'The Library of Alcuin's York', in R. Gameson (2012), 633–64.
Garrod, H.W. (1904), 'The S. John's College (Cambridge) MS of *The Thebaid*', *The Classical Review* 18: 38–42.
- ed. (1906), *P. Papini Stati Thebais et Achilleis* (Oxford).
Gasparri, F. (1966), 'Le scriptorium de Corbie à la fin du VIIIe siècle et le problème de l'écriture *a-b*', *Scriptorium* 20: 265–72.
Gasquet, F.A. and E. Bishop (1908), *The Bosworth Psalter* (London).
Gatch, M.McC. (1966), 'MS Boulogne-sur-Mer 63 and Ælfric's First Series of *Catholic Homilies*', *JEGP* 65: 482–90.
- (1975), 'Noah's Raven in Genesis A and the Illustrated Old English Hexateuch', *Gesta* 14/2: 3–15.
- (1977), *Preaching and Theology in Anglo-Saxon England: Ælfric and Wulfstan* (Toronto).
- (1985), 'John Bagford as a Collector and Disseminator of Manuscript Fragments', *The Library* 6th ser. 7: 95–114.
- (1986–90), 'Fragmenta Manuscripta and Varia at Missouri and Cambridge', *TCBS* 9: 434–75.
- (1992), 'Piety and Liturgy in the Old English *Vision of Leofric*', in Korhammer (1992), 159–79.
Gatti, E.A. (2007), 'Building the Body of the Church: A Bishop's Blessing in the Benedictional of Engilmar of Parenzo', in Ott—Trumbore Jones (2007), 92–121.
Gebauer, G.J. and B. Löfstedt, eds. (1980), *Bonifatii (Vynfreth) Ars grammatica, accedit Ars metrica*, CCSL 133B (Turnhout).
Geddes, J. (1998), 'The Art of the Book of Deer', *Proceedings of the Society of Antiquaries of Scotland* 128: 537–49.

Geith, K.-E. (1965), *Priester Arnolts Legende von der Heiligen Juliana. Untersuchungen zur lateinischen Juliana-Legende und zum Text des deutschen Gedichtes* (Freiburg).

George, J.-A. (2001), '*Hwalas ðec herigað*: Creation, Closure and the *Hapax Legomena* of the OE *Daniel*', in Kay—Sylvester (2001), 105–16.

Gerchow, J. (1988), *Die Gedenküberlieferung der Angelsachsen. Mit einem Katalog der* libri vitae *und Nekrologien*, Arbeiten zur Frühmittelalterforschung 20 (Berlin).

– (1992), 'Prayers for King Cnut', in Hicks (1992), 219–39.

– ed. (1999), *Das Jahrtausend der Mönche: Kloster Welt Werden, 799–1803* (Essen) [exhibition catalogue].

– (2004), 'The Origins of the Durham *Liber Vitae*', in Rollason et al. (2004), 45–61.

Gerritsen, J. (1988), 'British Library MS Cotton Vitellius A.xv: A Supplementary Description', *ES* 69: 293–302.

– (1989a), 'Correction and Erasure in the *Vespasian Psalter* Gloss', *ES* 70: 477–83.

– (1989b), 'Have with You to Lexington! The *Beowulf* Manuscript and *Beowulf*', in Lachlan Mackenzie (1989), 15–34.

– (1991a), 'A Reply to Dr Kiernan's "Footnote"', *ES* 72: 497–500.

– (1991b), 'The Thorkelin Transcripts of *Beowulf*: a Codicological Description, with Notes on their Genesis and History', *The Library* 6th ser. 13: 1–22.

– (1998), 'The Copenhagen Wulfstan Manuscript: A Codicological Study', *ES* 79: 501–11.

Le Geste et les gestes au moyen âge, Sénéfiance 41 (Aix-en-Provence, 1998).

Getty, S.S., ed. (1969), 'An Edition, with Commentary, of the Latin/Anglo-Saxon Liber Scintillarum' (unpubl. PhD dissertation, Univ. of Pennsylvania).

Gibb, P.A. (1977), 'Wonders of the East: a Critical Edition and Commentary' (unpubl. PhD dissertation, Duke University, NC).

Gibson, M.[T.] (1971), 'Lanfranc's Commentary on the Pauline Epistles', *JTS* n.s. 22: 86–112 [repr. Gibson (1993a) no. XII].

– (1972), 'Priscian, *Institutiones Grammaticae*: a Handlist of Manuscripts', *Scriptorium* 26: 105–24.

– (1978), *Lanfranc of Bec* (Oxford).

– ed. (1981), *Boethius: His Life, Thought and Influence* (Oxford).

– (1982), 'Latin Commentaries on Logic before 1200', *Bulletin de philosophie médiévale* 24: 54–64.

– M. Lapidge and C. Page (1983), 'Neumed Boethian *metra* from Canterbury: A Newly Recovered Leaf of Cambridge, University Library, Gg. 5. 35 (the "Cambridge Songs" Manuscript)', *ASE* 12: 141–52.

– ed. (1992), *The Eadwine Psalter – Text, Image, and Monastic Culture in Twelfth-Century Canterbury*, Publications of the Modern Humanities Research Association 14 (London).

- (1993a), *'Artes' and Bible in the Medieval West* (Aldershot).
- (1993b), *The Bible in the Latin West* (Notre Dame, IN).
- L. Smith and M. Passalacqua, eds. (1995–2001), *Codices Boethiani: a Conspectus of Manuscripts of the Works of Boethius*, 3 vols. (London).
Gieschen, L. (1887), *Die charakteristischen Unterschiede der einzelnen Schreiber im Hatton MS der Cura Pastoralis* (Dr Phil Diss. Greifswald).
Gilbert, J.E.P. (1990), 'The Lindisfarne Gospels – How Many Artists?', *DUJ* 82: 153–60.
Giles, P.M. (1972–6a), 'A Handlist of the Bradfer-Lawrence Manuscripts Deposited on Loan at the Fitzwilliam Museum', *TCBS* 6: 86–99.
- (1972–6b), 'A Handlist of the Additional Manuscripts in the Fitzwilliam Museum, part VI', *TCBS* 6: 243–51.
Giliberto, C. (2007a), 'Stone Lore in Miscellany Manuscripts: The Old English Lapidary', in Bremmer—Dekker (2007), 253–78.
- (2007b), 'An Unpublished *De lapidibus* in its Manuscript Tradition, with Particular Regard to the Anglo-Saxon Area', in Lendinara et al. (2007), 251–83.
- (2011), 'Precious Stones in Anglo-Saxon Glosses', in Lendinara et al. (2011), 119–51.
Gillingham, R.G. (1981), 'An Edition of Abbot Ælfric's Old English-Latin Glossary with Commentary' (unpubl. PhD dissertation, Ohio State University).
Gittos, H., and M. Bradford Bedingfield, eds. (2005a), *The Liturgy of the Late Anglo-Saxon Church*, HBS Subsidia 5 (London).
- (2005b), 'Is There Any Evidence for the Liturgy of Parish Churches in Late Anglo-Saxon England? The Red Book of Darley and the Status of Old English', in Tinti (2005), 63–82.
Gjerløw, L. (1957), 'Fragments of a Lectionary in Anglo-Saxon Script found in Oslo', *Nordisk Tidskrift för Bok- och Biblioteksväsen* 44: 109–22.
- (1961), *Adoratio crucis: the Regularis Concordia and the Decreta Lanfranci; Manuscript Studies in the Early Medieval Church of Norway* (Oslo).
- (1970), 'Missaler brukt in Bjørgvin bispedømme fra misionstiden til Nidarosordinariet', in *Bjørgvin bispestol. Byen og bispedømmet*, ed. P. Juvkam (Bergen, 1970), 73–115.
- (1974), 'Missaler brukt i Oslo bispedømme fra misjonstiden til Nidarosordinariet', in *Oslo bispedømme 900 år. Historiske Studier*, ed. F. Birkeli, A.O. Johnsen and E. Molland (Oslo, 1974), 73–129.
- ed. (1979), *Antiphonarium Nidrosiensis Ecclesiae*, Libri Liturgici Provinciae Nidrosiensis Medii Aevi 3 (Oslo).
- (1980), *Liturgica Islandica*, 2 vols., Bibliotheca Arnamagnæana 35–6 (Copenhagen).

Glauche, G. (1970), *Schullektüre im Mittelalter: Entstehung und Wandlungen des Lektürekanons bis 1200 nach den Quellen dargestellt*, Münchener Beiträge zur Mediävistik und Renaissance-Forschung 5 (Munich).

Glaze, F.E. (2007), 'Master-Student Medical Dialogues: The Evidence of London, British Library, Sloane 2839', in Lendinara et al. (2007), 467–94.

Glénisson, J., ed. (1974), *La paléographie hébraïque médiévale* (Paris).

Glorie, F., ed. (1968), *Variae Collectiones Aenigmatum Merovingicae Aetatis*, 2 vols., CCSL 133–133A (Turnhout).

Glück, M. (1967), *Priscians Partitiones und ihre Stellung in der spätantiken Schule*, Spudasmata 12 (Hildesheim).

Glunz, H.H. (1930), *Britannien und Bibeltext. Der Vulgatatext der Evangelien in seinem Verhältnis zur irisch-angelsächsischen Kultur des Frühmittelalters*, Kölner Anglistische Arbeiten 12 (Leipzig).

– (1933), *History of the Vulgate in England from Alcuin to Roger Bacon: Being an Inquiry into the Text of some English Manuscripts of the Vulgate Gospels* (Cambridge).

Gneuss, H. (1957), 'Zur Geschichte des MS Vespasian A.I', *Anglia* 75: 125–33 [repr. Gneuss (1996a), no. VII].

– (1968), *Hymnar und Hymnen im englischen Mittelalter. Studien zur Überlieferung, Glossierung und Übersetzung lateinischer Hymnen in England*, Buchreihe der Anglia 12 (Tübingen).

– (1971), Review of J.D.A. Ogilvy, *Books known to the English: 597–1066*, in *Anglia* 89: 129–34.

– (1972), 'The Origin of Standard Old English and Æthelwold's School at Winchester', *ASE* 1: 63–83 [repr. Gneuss (1996b), no. I].

– (1976a), 'Die Handschrift Cotton Otho A. XII', *Anglia* 94: 289–318 [repr. Gneuss (1996a), no. IX].

– (1976b), 'Die *Battle of Maldon* als historisches und literarisches Zeugnis', in Bayrische Akademie der Wissenschaften, phil.-hist. Klasse, Sitzungsberichte, Jahrgang 1976, Heft 5 (Munich), 3–68 [repr. Gneuss (1996b), no. IX].

– (1977), Review of *The Durham Ritual*, ed. T.J. Brown, *Anglia* 95: 207–13.

– (1978), 'Dunstan und Hrabanus Maurus: Zur Hs. Bodleian Auctarium F.4.32', *Anglia* 96: 136–48 [repr. Gneuss (1996a), no. VIII].

– (1985), 'Liturgical Books in Anglo-Saxon England and their Old English Terminology', in Lapidge—Gneuss (1985a), 91–141 [repr. Gneuss (1996a), no. V].

– (1988), 'Eine angelsächsische Königsliste', in Krämer—Bernhard (1988), 201–9 [repr. Gneuss (1996a) no. VII].

– (1990), 'The Study of Language in Anglo-Saxon England', *BJRL* 72: 3–32 [repr. with 'Postscript' (pp. 102–5) in Scragg (2003) 75–102].

- (1992), '*Anglicae Linguae Interpretatio*: Language Contact, Lexical Borrowing and Glossing in Anglo-Saxon England', *PBA* 82: 107–48.
- (1993), 'Der älteste Katalog der angelsächsischen Handschriften und seine Nachfolger', in Grinda—Wetzel (1993), 91–106 [repr. Gneuss (1996a), no. X].
- (1994), 'A Grammarian's Greek-Latin Glossary in Anglo-Saxon England', in Godden et al. (1994b), 60–86 [repr. Gneuss (1996b), no. IV].
- (1996a), *Books and Libraries in Early England* (Aldershot).
- (1996b), *Language and History in Early England* (Aldershot).
- (1997), 'Origin and Provenance of Anglo-Saxon Manuscripts: The Case of Cotton Tiberius A. iii', in Robinson—Zim (1997a), 13–48.
- (1998), 'A Newly-Found Fragment of an Anglo-Saxon Psalter', *ASE* 27: 273–87.
- (2000), 'Zur Geschichte des Hymnars', *MLJ* 35,2: 227–47.
- (2000–3), 'Humfrey Wanley Borrows Books in Cambridge', *TCBS* 12: 145–60.
- and M. Lapidge (2003a), 'The Earliest Manuscript of Bede's Metrical *Vita S. Cudbercti*', *ASE* 32: 43–54.
- (2003b), 'Addenda and Corrigenda to the *Handlist of Anglo-Saxon Manuscripts*', *ASE* 32: 293–305.
- (2005a), 'The Homiliary of the Taunton Fragments', *N&Q* 250: 440–2.
- (2005b), 'The First Edition of the Source of Ælfric's *Grammar*', *Anglia* 123: 246–59.
- (2008a), 'More Old English from Manuscripts', in Blanton—Scheck (2008), 411–21.
- (2008b), Review of *ASMMF* vols. IX–XIII, *Anglia* 126: 134–41.
- (2012), 'Second Addenda and Corrigenda to the *Handlist of Anglo-Saxon Manuscripts*', *ASE* 40: 287–300.
Godden, M., ed. (1979), *Ælfric's Catholic Homilies: The Second Series, Text*, EETS s.s. 5 (London).
- (1983), 'Ælfric's *De temporibus anni*', in McGurk et al. (1983), 59–64.
- (1994a), 'Editing Old English and the Problem of Alfred's *Boethius*', in Scragg—Szarmach (1994b), 163–76.
- D. Gray and T. Hoad, eds. (1994b), *From Anglo-Saxon to Early Middle English. Studies presented to E.G. Stanley* (Oxford).
- (1996), 'Experiments in Genre: The Saints' Lives in Ælfric's *Catholic Homilies*', in Szarmach (1996), 261–87.
- (1997), 'Wærferth and King Alfred: The Fate of the Old English *Dialogues*', in Roberts—Nelson (1997), 35–51.
- (2000), *Ælfric's Catholic Homilies: Introduction, Commentary and Glossary*, EETS s.s.18 (London).
- (2004), 'The Relations of Wulfstan and Ælfric: Reassessment', in Townend (2004), 353–74.

- (2005), 'Alfred, Asser and Boethius', in O'Brien O'Keeffe—Orchard (2005) I, 326–48.
- and S. Irvine, eds. (2009), *The Old English Boethius. An Edition of the Old English Version of Boethius's De Consolatione Philosophiae*, 2 vols. (Oxford).
- (2011), 'Glosses to the *Consolation of Philosophy* in late Anglo-Saxon England: Their Origins and their Uses', in Lendinara et al. (2011), 67–92.
- (2012), 'Ælfric's Library', in R. Gameson (2012), 679–84.

Godel, W. (1963), 'Irisches Beten im frühen Mittelalter', *Zeitschrift für katholische Theologie* 85: 261–321, 390–439.

Goetz, G., ed. (1888–1923), *Corpus Glossariorum Latinorum*, 7 vols. (Leipzig).

Godman, P., ed. (1982), *Alcuin: The Bishops, Kings and Saints of York* (Oxford).

Goldbacher, A., ed. (1895–1923), *Augustinus: Epistulae*, 4 vols. in 5, CSEL 34, 44, 57, 58 (Vienna).

Gollancz, I., ed. (1927), *The Cædmon Manuscript of Anglo-Saxon Biblical Poetry. Junius XI in the Bodleian Library* (Oxford).

Gonser, P. (1909), *Das angelsächsische Prosa-Leben des hl. Guthlac*, Anglistische Forschungen 27 (Heidelberg).

Goodyear, F.R.D., ed. (1965), *Incerti auctoris Aetna* (Cambridge).

Goolden, P., ed. (1958), *The Old English Apollonius of Tyre*, Oxford English Monographs 6 (London).

Goossens, L., ed. (1974), *The Old English Glosses of MS Brussels, Royal Library, 1650 (Aldhelm's De Laudibus Virginitatis)*, Verhandelingen van de Koninklijke Academie voor Wetenschappen, Letteren en Schone Kunsten van België, Klasse der Letteren 74 (Brussels).
- (1992), 'Latin and Old English Aldhelm Glosses: A Direct Link in the Abingdon Group', in Derolez (1992), 139–49.

Gordon, I.L., ed. (1997), *The Seafarer*, rev. ed. with bibliography by M. Clayton (Exeter).

Gorman, M. (1997), 'A Critique of Bischoff's Theory of Irish Exegesis. The Commentary on Genesis in Munich Clm. 6302 (Wendepunkte 2)', *JMLat* 7: 178–233.
- (2003), 'The Codex Amiatinus: A Guide to the Legends and Bibliography', *SM* 44: 863–910.

Gougaud, L. (1923), 'Les relations de l'abbaye de Fleury-sur-Loire avec la Bretagne armoricaine et les îles Britanniques (Xe et XIe siècles)', *Mémoires de la Société d'histoire et d'archéologie de Bretagne* 4: 3–30.

Gough, J.V. (1974), 'Some Old English Glosses', *Anglia* 92: 273–90.

Govern, D.S. (1983), 'Unnoticed Punctuation in the Exeter Book', *MÆ* 52: 90–9.

Gradon, P.O.E., ed. (1977), *Cynewulf's Elene*, rev. ed. (Exeter).

Le Graduel Romain: Édition critique par les Moines de Solesmes, II: *Les Sources* (Paris, 1957).

Graham, T. (1993), 'The Old English Liturgical Directions in Corpus Christi College, Cambridge, MS 422', *Anglia* 111: 439–46.

– (1991–5a), 'A Parkerian Transcript of the List of Bishop Leofric's Procurements for Exeter Cathedral: Matthew Parker, the Exeter Book, and Cambridge University Library MS Ii. 2. 11', *TCBS* 10: 421–55.

– (1991–5b), 'Matthew Parker and the Conservation of Manuscripts: The Case of CUL MS Ii. 2. 4', *TCBS* 10: 630–41.

– (1994), 'Robert Talbot's "Old Saxonice Bede"', *Cambridge Bibliographical Society Newsletter* (Summer 1994): 6–7.

– (1995), 'The Old English Prefatory Texts in the Corpus Canterbury Pontifical', *Anglia* 113: 1–15.

– (1996), 'A Runic Entry in an Anglo-Saxon Manuscript from Abingdon and the Scandinavian Career of Abbot Rodulf (1051–2)', *Nottingham Medieval Studies* 40: 16–24.

– (1997a), 'Abraham Wheelock's Use of CCCC MS 41 (Old English Bede) and the Borrowing of Manuscripts from the Library of Corpus Christi College', *Cambridge Bibliographical Society Newsletter* (Summer 1997): 10–16.

– (1997b), 'Early Modern Study of the Old English Hexateuch: Robert Talbot and William L'Isle', *OEN* 30.3: A–39.

– (1998a), 'Cambridge, Corpus Christi College 57 and its Anglo-Saxon Users', in Pulsiano—Treharne (1998a), 21–70.

– and A.G. Watson (1998b), *The Recovery of the Past in Early Elizabethan England. Documents by John Bale and John Joscelyn from the Circle of Matthew Parker* (Cambridge, 1998).

– (2000a), 'The Corpus Sedulius: An Anglo-Saxon Classbook', *OEN* 33.3: A–10.

– ed. (2000b), *The Recovery of Old English. Anglo-Saxon Studies in the Sixteenth and Seventeenth Centuries* (Kalamazoo, MI).

– (2000c), 'John Joscelyn, Pioneer of Old English Lexicography', in Graham (2000b), 83–140.

– (2000d), 'Early Modern Users of Claudius B. iv: Robert Talbot and William L'Isle', in Barnhouse—Withers (2000), 271–316.

– (2009), 'Glosses and Notes in Anglo-Saxon Manuscripts', in Owen-Crocker (2009), 159–203.

Gransden, A. (1972), 'Realistic Observation in Twelfth-Century England', *Speculum* 47: 29–51.

– (1974), *Historical Writing in England, I: c. 550 to c. 1307* (London).

– (1995a), 'Abbo of Fleury's *Passio Sancti Eadmundi*', *RB* 105: 20–78.

– (1995b), 'The Composition and Authorship of the *De miraculis Sancti Eadmundi* Attributed to "Hermann the Archdeacon"', *JMLat* 5: 1–52.

– ed. (1998a), *Bury St Edmunds. Medieval Art, Architecture, Archaeology and Economy*, The British Archaeological Association Transactions 20 (London).

- (1998b), 'Some Manuscripts in Cambridge from Bury St Edmunds Abbey: Exhibition Catalogue', in Gransden (1998a), 228–85.
Grant, R.J.S. (1974), 'Laurence Nowell's Transcript of BM Cotton Otho B. xi', *ASE* 3: 111–24.
- ed. (1979), *Cambridge Corpus Christi College 41: The Loricas and the Missal* (Amsterdam).
- ed. (1982), *Three Homilies from Cambridge, Corpus Christi College 41. The Assumption, St Michael and the Passion* (Ottawa).
- (1989), *The B-Text of the Old English Bede: A Linguistic Commentary* (Amsterdam).
- (1996), *Laurence Nowell, William Lambarde and the Laws of the Anglo-Saxons* (Amsterdam).
Grape-Albers, H. (1977), *Spätantike Bilder aus der Welt des Arztes. Medizinische Bilderhandschriften der Spätantike und ihre mittelalterliche Überlieferung* (Wiesbaden).
Grattan, J.H.G. and C. Singer (1952), *Anglo-Saxon Magic and Medicine. Illustrated specially from the Semi-Pagan Text 'Lacnunga'* (London).
Green, J.R. (1907), *A Short History of the English People*, I (London).
Green, R.P.H., ed. (1980), *Seven Versions of Pastoral* (Reading).
- ed. (1991), *The Works of Ausonius* (Oxford).
Green, W.M. and K.-D. Daur, eds. (1970), *Augustinus: Contra academicos, De beata vita, De ordine, De magistro, De libero arbitrio*, CCSL 29 (Turnhout).
Greenfield, S.B. and F. C. Robinson (1980), *A Bibliography of Publications on Old English Literature to the End of 1972* (Toronto).
Greenwell, W., ed. (1853), *The Pontifical of Egbert, Archbishop of York, A.D. 732–766*, Surtees Society 27 (Durham).
Gremont, D. and L. Donnat (1967), 'Fleury, le Mont Saint-Michel et l'Angleterre à la fin du Xe et au début du XIe siècle. A propos du manuscrit d'Orléans 127 (105)', in *Millénaire monastique du Mont Saint-Michel*, ed. J. Laporte, 5 vols. (Paris) I, 751–93.
Gretsch, M. (1973), *Die Regula Sancti Benedicti in England und ihre altenglische Übersetzung*, TUEPh 2 (Munich).
- (1974), 'Æthelwold's Translation of the *Regula Sancti Benedicti* and its Latin Exemplar', *ASE* 3: 125–51.
- (1999a), *The Intellectual Foundations of the English Benedictine Reform*, CSASE 25 (Cambridge).
- (1999b), 'Elizabeth Elstob: A Scholar's Fight for Anglo-Saxon Studies', *Anglia* 117: 163–200, 481–524.
- (2000), 'The Junius Psalter Gloss: Its Historical and Cultural Context', *ASE* 29: 85–122.

- (2001), 'Die sprachliche und kulturelle Bedeutung der altenglischen Glossierung des Junius-Psalters', in Bergmann (2001), 171–4.
- (2003a), 'Cambridge, Corpus Christi College 57: A Witness to the Early Stages of the Benedictine Reform in England?', *ASE* 32: 111–45.
- (2003b), 'In Search of Standard Old English', in Kornexl—Lenker (2003), 33–67.
- (2004), 'The Taunton Fragment: A New Text from Anglo-Saxon England', *ASE* 33: 145–93.
- and H. Gneuss (2005), 'Anglo-Saxon Glosses to a Theodorean Poem?', in O'Brien O'Keeffe—Orchard (2005) I, 9–46.
- (2006), 'Æthelthryth of Ely in a Lost Calendar from Munich', *ASE* 35: 159–77.
Grierson, P. (1940a), 'Les livres de l'Abbé Seiwold de Bath', *RB* 52: 96–116.
- (1940b), 'La bibliothèque de Saint-Vaast d'Arras', *RB* 52: 117–40.
- (1940c), 'Grimbald of St Bertin's', *EHR* 55: 529–61.
- (1941), 'The Relations Between England and Flanders before the Norman Conquest', *TRHS* 4th ser. 23: 71–112.
Griffith, M., ed. (1997), *Judith* (Exeter).
Griffiths, A. (2007), 'The Canterbury Psalter's Alphabet Glosses: Eclectic but Incompetent?', in Bremmer—Dekker (2007), 213–51.
Griffiths, B., ed. (1994), *Alfred's Metres of Boethius*, rev. ed. (Pinner).
Griffiths, J. (1995), 'Manuscripts in the Schøyen Collection copied or owned in the British Isles before 1700', *English Manuscript Studies 1100–1700* 5: 36–42.
Grimmer, M. (2007), 'Britons in Early Wessex: The Evidence of the Law Code of Ine', in Higham (2007), 102–14.
Grinda, K.R. and C.-D. Wetzel, eds. (1993), *Anglo-Saxonica: Beiträge zur Vor- und Frühgeschichte der englischen Sprache und zur altenglischen Literatur. Festschrift für Hans Schabram zum 65. Geburtstag* (Munich).
Grosjean, P. (1937), 'Gloria postuma S. Martini Turonensis apud Scottos et Britannos', *AB* 55: 300–48.
- (1943), 'Notes d'hagiographie celtique [nos. 1–4]', *AB* 61: 91–107.
- (1961), 'Un fragment d'obituaire anglo-saxon du VIIIe siècle conservé à Munich', *AB* 79: 320–45.
Gruber, K.W. (1904), *Die Hauptquellen des Corpus-, Epinaler und Erfurter Glossares* (Erlangen).
Grünberg, M. (1967), *The West-Saxon Gospels: A Study of the Gospel of St Matthew with Text of the Four Gospels* (Amsterdam).
Gryson, R., ed. (2001), *Bedae presbyteri Expositio Apocalypseos*, CCSL 121A (Turnhout).
Guaglianone, A., ed. (1958), *Aviani Fabulae* (Turin).
Guenther Discenza, N. (1997), 'Power, Skill, and Virtue in the Old English *Boethius*', *ASE* 26: 81–108.

– (2000), 'Alfred the Great: A Bibliography with Special Reference to Literature', in Szarmach (2000), 463–502.

Guglielmetti, R.E., ed. (2004), *Alcuino: Commento al Cantico dei cantici, con i commenti anonimi 'Vox ecclesie' e 'Vox antique ecclesie'* (Florence).

– (2008a), 'Il commento "Vox ecclesie" al Cantico dei cantici: Il contributo delle fonti al riconoscimento della versione originale', *Filologia mediolatina* 15: 45–65.

– (2008b), 'Tradizione manoscritta e fortuna del commento al Cantico di Giusto d'Urgell', in *Il Cantico dei cantici nel medioevo*, ed. R.E. Guglielmetti (Florence, 2008), 155–87.

Guillaumin, J.-Y., ed. (1995), *Boèce: Institution arithmétique* (Paris).

Guimon, T.V. (2006), 'The Writing of Annals in Eleventh-Century England: Palaeography and Textual History', in Rumble (2006a), 137–45.

Gullath, B. (2003), 'Deutsche Philologie / Literaturwissenschaft', in *Lebendiges Büchererbe. Säkularisation, Mediatisierung und die Bayerische Staatsbibliothek*, ed. C. Jahn and D. Kudorfer (Munich, 2003), 142–55.

Gullick, M. (1987), 'The Great and Little Domesday Manuscripts', in Erskine (1987), 93–112.

– (1990), 'The Scribe of the Carilef Bible: A New Look at some Late-Eleventh-Century Durham Cathedral Manuscripts', in Brownrigg (1990), 61–83.

– D. Marner and A. Piper (1993), *Anglo-Norman Durham 1093–1193: A Catalogue for an Exhibition of Manuscripts in the Treasury, Durham Cathedral* (Durham).

– (1994), 'The Durham Cantor's Book (Durham, Dean and Chapter Library, MS B. IV. 24)', in Rollason et al. (1994), 93–109.

– (1996–9a), 'The Origin and Date of Cambridge, Corpus Christi College MS 163', *TCBS* 11: 89–91.

– (1996–9b), 'The Origin and Importance of Cambridge, Trinity College R. 5. 27', *TCBS* 11: 239–62.

– (1998a), 'The Hand of Symeon of Durham: Further Observations on the Durham Martyrology Scribe', in Rollason (1998), 14–31.

– (1998b), 'The Two Earliest Manuscripts of the *Libellus de exordio*', in Rollason (1998), 106–19.

– (1998c), 'The Scribal Work of Eadmer of Canterbury to 1109', *Archaeologia Cantiana* 118: 173–90.

– (1998d), 'Professional Scribes in Eleventh- and Twelfth-Century England', *English Manuscript Studies 1100–1700* 7: 1–24.

– (2000), 'A Scribe at Work: Fragments as Witnesses to Changes in Style', in Brownrigg–Smith (2000), 205–10.

– (2001), 'The English-Owned Manuscripts of the *Collectio Lanfranci*', in Dennison (2001), 99–117.

- and R.W. Pfaff (2001), 'The Dublin Pontifical (TCD 98 [B. 3. 6]): St Anselm's?', *Scriptorium* 55: 284–94 [and pls. 58–60].
- (2004), 'The Make-Up of the *Liber Vitae*: The Codicology of the Manuscript', in Rollason et al. (2004a), 17–42.
- (2005a), 'Preliminary Observations on Romanesque Manuscript Fragments of English, Norman and Swedish Origin in the Riksarkivet (Stockholm)', in Brunius (2005), 31–82.
- (2005b), 'Manuscrits et copistes normands en Angleterre (XIe–XIIe siècles)', in Bouet—Dosdat (2005), 83–99.
- (2008), 'Lanfranc and the Oldest Manuscript of the *Collectio Lanfranci*', in Brasington—Cushing (2008), 79–89.
- and S. Rankin (2009), Review of Hartzell (2006), *Early Music History* 28: 262–85.
- (2010), 'A Christ Church Scribe of the Eleventh Century', in *The Medieval Book. Glosses from Friends and Colleagues of Christopher de Hamel*, ed. J.H. Marrow, R.A. Linenthal and W. Noel (Houston, TX, 2010), 2–10.
- (2012), 'Bookbindings', in R. Gameson (2012), 294–309.
Gunderson, L.L. (1980), *Alexander's Epistle to Aristotle about India* (Meisenheim am Glan).
Gunther, R.T., ed. (1925), *The Herbal of Apuleius Barbarus: From the Early 12th-Century Manuscript formerly in the Abbey of Bury St Edmunds* (Oxford).
Günzel, B., ed. (1993), *Ælfwine's Prayerbook*, HBS 108 (London).
Guy, J.A. (1972–6), 'A Lost Manuscript of Solinus: Five Fragments from Bury St Edmunds in the Library of Clare College, Cambridge', *TCBS* 6: 65–6.
Gwara, S. (1992), 'Three Acrostic Poems by Abbo of Fleury', *JMLat* 2: 203–35.
- (1993), 'Literary Culture in Late Anglo-Saxon England and the Old English and Latin Glosses to Aldhelm's *Prosa de Virginitate*' (unpubl. PhD dissertation, Toronto Univ.).
- (1994a), 'Unpublished Old English Inked Glosses from Manuscripts of Aldhelm's *Prosa de Virginitate*', *NM* 95: 267–71.
- (1994b), 'Manuscripts of Aldhelm's *Prosa de virginitate* and the Rise of Hermeneutic Literacy in Tenth-Century England', *SM* 35: 101–59.
- (1994c), 'Newly Identified Eleventh-Century Fragments in a Bagford Album, now London, British Library, MS Harley 5977', *Manuscripta* 38: 228–36.
- (1996–7), 'Canterbury Affiliations', *Romanobarbarica* 14: 359–74.
- (1996a), 'A Record of Anglo-Saxon Pedagogy: Aldhelm's *Epistola ad Heahfridum* and its Gloss', *JMLat* 6: 84–134.
- (1996b), 'Drypoint Glossing in a Twelfth-Century Manuscript of Aldhelm's Prose Treatise on Virginity', *Traditio* 51: 99–145.
- ed. (1996c), *Latin Colloquies from Pre-Conquest Britain*, Toronto Medieval Latin Texts 22 (Toronto).

- (1997a), 'Glosses to Aldhelm's *Prosa de virginitate* and Glossaries from the Anglo-Saxon Golden Age, ca. 670–800', *SM* 38: 561–645.
- (1997b), 'Further Old-English Scratched Glosses and Merographs from Corpus Christi College, Cambridge MS 326 (Aldhelm's *Prosa de Virginitate*)', *ES* 78: 201–36.
- ed. (1997c), *Anglo-Saxon Conversations: The Colloquies of Ælfric Bata*, with an introduction by D. W. Porter (Woodbridge).
- (1997d), 'Ælfric Bata's Manuscripts', *Revue d'histoire des textes* 27: 239–55.
- (1998), 'The Transmission of the "Digby" Corpus of Bilingual Glosses to Aldhelm's *Prosa de virginitate*', *ASE* 27: 139–68.
- ed. (2001), *Aldhelmi Malmesbiriensis Prosa de virginitate*, 2 vols., CCSL 124–124A (Turnhout).
- (2002), 'The *Hermeneumata pseudodositheana*, Latin Oral Fluency, and the Social Function of the Cambro-Latin Dialogues called *De raris fabulis*', in *Latin Grammar and Rhetoric, from Classical Theory to Medieval Practice*, ed. C.D. Lanham (London and New York, 2002), 109–38.
- (2007), 'A Possible Arthurian Epitome in a Tenth-Century Manuscript from Cornwall', *Arthuriana* 17.2: 3–9.
- (2012), 'Anglo-Saxon Schoolbooks', in R. Gameson (2012), 507–24.
- Gwynn, A. (1954), 'Some Notes on the History of the Book of Kells', *Irish Historical Studies* 9: 131–61.
- ed. (1955), *The Writings of Bishop Patrick, 1074–1084*, Scriptores Latini Hiberniae 1 (Dublin).
- Hackman, A. (1860), *Catalogi codicum manuscriptorum Bibliothecae Bodleianae, IV. Codices viri admodum reverendi Thomae Tanner complectens* (Oxford).
- Haddan, A.W. and W. Stubbs, eds. (1869–71), *Councils and Ecclesiastical Documents Relating to Great Britain and Ireland*, 3 vols. (Oxford).
- Hadgraft, N. and K. Swift, eds. (1994), *Conservation and Preservation in Small Libraries* (Cambridge).
- Hagen, H. (1875), *Catalogus codicum Bernensium (Bibliotheca Bongarsiana)* (Bern).
- Hagenmaier, W. (1980), *Die lateinischen mittelalterlichen Handschriften der Universitätsbibliothek Freiburg im Breisgau (ab Hs. 231)*, Kataloge der Universitätsbibliothek Freiburg i. B., 1: Die Handschriften der Universitätsbibliothek, Teil 3 (Wiesbaden).
- Haggenmüller, R. (1991), *Die Überlieferung der Beda und Egbert zugeschriebenen Bussbücher*, Europäische Hochschulschriften: Reihe 3, Geschichte und ihre Hilfswissenschaften 461 (Frankfurt am Main).
- Haines, D. (2010), *Sunday Observance and The Sunday Letter in Anglo-Saxon England*, AST 8 (Cambridge).
- Haines, J.A. (2008), 'A Musical Fragment from Anglo-Saxon England', *Early Music* 36: 219–29.

Hale, W.C. (1978), 'An Edition and Codicological Study of Corpus Christi College Cambridge MS 214' (unpubl. PhD dissertation, University of Pennsylvania).

Hall, J., ed. (1920), *Selections from Early Middle English 1130–1250*, 2 vols. (Oxford).

Hall, J.R. (1975), 'Some Liturgical Notes on Ælfric's Letter to the Monks of Eynsham', *Downside Review* 93: 297–303.

– (1986), 'On the Bibliographic Unity of the Bodleian MS Junius 11', *ANQ* 24: 104–7.

– (2012), 'Supplementary Evidence and the Manuscript Text of *Beowulf*: A Survey of Sources', in *English Past and Present. Selected Papers from the IAUPE Malta Conference in 2010*, ed. W. Viereck (Frankfurt am Main, 2012), 9–24.

Hall, T.N. and M.W. Twomey (1990), 'Old Testament Apocrypha', in Biggs et al. (1990), 23–34.

– (1996), 'The *Euangelium Nichodemi* and *Vindicta Salvatoris* in Anglo-Saxon England', in Cross (1996b), 36–81.

– (2001), 'The Early English Manuscripts of Gregory the Great's *Homilies on the Gospel* and *Homilies on Ezechiel*: A Preliminary Survey', in Bremmer (2001), 115–36.

– T.D. Hill and C.D. Wright, eds. (2002), *Via Crucis: Essays on Early Medieval Sources and Ideas in Memory of J.E. Cross*, Medieval European Studies 1 (Morgantown, VA).

– (2002), 'The Earliest Anglo-Latin Text of the *Trinubium Annae* (*BHL* 505zl)', in Hall et al. (2002), 104–37.

– (2004a), 'Wulfstan's Latin Sermons', in Townend (2004), 93–139.

– (2004b), 'The Bibliography of Anglo-Saxon Sermon Manuscripts', in Wilcox (2004a), 85–105.

– (2005), 'A Palm Sunday Sermon from Eleventh-Century Salisbury', in O'Brien O'Keeffe—Orchard (2005) II, 180–96.

– (2006), 'Latin Sermons and Lay Preaching: Four Latin Sermons from Post-Reform Canterbury', in Magennis—Wilcox (2006), 132–70.

– (2007), 'Latin Sermons for Saints in Early English Homiliaries and Legendaries', in Kleist (2007a), 227–63.

– and D. Scragg, eds. (2008), *Anglo-Saxon Books and their Readers. Essays in Celebration of Helmut Gneuss's 'Handlist of Anglo-Saxon Manuscripts'* (Kalamazoo, MI).

– (2008a), 'The Development of the Common of Saints in the Early English Versions of Paul the Deacon's Homiliary', in Hall—Scragg (2008), 31–67.

Hallam, E. and D. Bates, eds. (2001), *Domesday Book* (Stroud).

Hallander, L.-G. (1968), 'Two Old English Confessional Prayers', *Stockholm Studies in Modern Philology* n.s. 3: 87–110.

Halm, K. et al. (1868-81), *Catalogus Codicum Latinorum Bibliothecae Regiae Monacensis*, 7 vols. (Munich).

Halporn, J.W. (1974), 'A New Fragment of Durham Cathedral Library MS. B. II. 30', *Classical Philology* 69: 124–5.

– (1981), 'The Manuscripts of Cassiodorus' *Expositio psalmorum*', *Traditio* 37: 388–96.

– (1985), 'Further on Early English Manuscripts of Cassiodorus's *Expositio Psalmorum*', *Classical Philology* 80: 46–50.

– (1987), 'The Modern Editions of Cassiodorus' Psalm Commentary', *Texte und Untersuchungen der altchristlichen Literatur* 133: 239–47.

Hamesse, J., ed. (1996), *Les manuscrits des lexiques et glossaires de l'antiquité tardive à la fin du moyen âge* (Louvain-la-Neuve).

Hamilton, S. (2001), *The Practice of Penance, 900–1050* (Woodbridge).

– (2005), 'Remedies for "Great Transgressions": Penance and Excommunication in late Anglo-Saxon England', in Tinti (2005), 83–105.

– (2010), 'The Early Pontificals: The Anglo-Saxon Evidence reconsidered from Continental Perspective', in Rollason et al. (2010), 411–28.

Handley, R. (1974), 'British Museum MS Cotton Vespasian D. xiv', *N&Q* 219: 243–50.

Handschin, J. (1936), 'The Two Winchester Tropers', *JTS* 37: 34–45, 156–72.

Haney, K. (2002), *The St. Albans Psalter. An Anglo-Norman Song of Faith*, Studies in the Humanities 60 (New York).

Hankins, F.R. (1992), 'Bald's "Leechbook" Reconsidered' (unpubl. PhD dissertation, University of North Carolina).

Hanley, T. (1979), 'Selected Rogationtide Homilies' (unpubl. PhD dissertation, University of Ottawa).

Hanna, R. (2002), *A Descriptive Catalogue of the Western Medieval Manuscripts of St John's College, Oxford, using Material Collected by the late Jeremy Griffiths* (Oxford).

– and T. Turville-Petre, eds. (2010), *The Wollaton Manuscripts. Texts, Owners and Readers* (York).

Hanslik, R., ed. (1977), *Benedicti Regula*, 2nd ed., CSEL 75 (Vienna).

Hanssens, J.M. (1933–5), 'Le texte du "Liber officialis" d'Amalaire', *Ephemerides Liturgicae* 47 (1933), 48 (1934), 49 (1935) [nine individual articles].

– ed. (1948–50), *Amalarii episcopi Opera liturgica omnia*, 3 vols., Studi e testi 138–40 (Vatican City).

Harbison, P. (2011), 'An Irish Stroke of European Genius: Irish High Crosses and the Emperor Charles the Bald', in Hourihane (2011), 133–48.

Hardwick, C. (1854), 'A Litany used by Members of the English Church in the Tenth Century', *Journal of Classical and Sacred Philology* 1: 266–70.

– and H.R. Luard (1856–67), *A Catalogue of the Manuscripts preserved in the Library of the University of Cambridge*, 5 vols. and index (Cambridge).

Hardy, A.K. (1899), *Die Sprache der Blickling Homilies* (diss. Leipzig).

Hardy, T.D. (1862–71), *Descriptive Catalogue of Materials relating to the History of Great Britain and Ireland*, 3 vols. in 4, RS 26 (London).

Harlow, C.G. (1959), 'Punctuation in some Manuscripts of Ælfric', *RES* n.s. 10: 1–19.

Harmer, F.E., ed. (1914), *Select English Historical Documents of the Ninth and Tenth Centuries* (Cambridge).

– ed. (1952), *Anglo-Saxon Writs* (Manchester).

Harmsen, T. (2000), *Antiquarianism in the Augustan Age: Thomas Hearne 1678–1735* (Oxford).

Harper-Bill, C. et al., eds. (1989), *Studies in Medieval History presented to R. Allen Brown* (Woodbridge).

Harris, R.L., ed. (1992), *A Chorus of Grammars: The Correspondence of George Hickes and his Collaborators on the Thesaurus Linguarum Septentrionalium*, Publications of the Dictionary of Old English 4 (Toronto).

Harris, R.M. (1960), 'The Marginal Drawings of the Bury St Edmunds Psalter (Rome, Vatican Library, MS Reg. lat. 12)' (unpublished PhD dissertation, Princeton University).

Harrison, J. (2004), 'The Mortuary Roll of Turgot of Durham (d. 1115)', *Scriptorium* 58: 67–83.

Harrsen, M. (1930), 'The Countess Judith of Flanders and the Library of Weingarten Abbey', *Papers of the Bibliographical Society of America* 24: 1–13.

Hart, C. (1966), *The Early Charters of Eastern England* (Leicester).

– (1972), 'Byrhtferth and his Manual', *MÆ* 41: 95–109.

– (1982), 'The B Text of the *Anglo-Saxon Chronicle*', *Journal of Medieval History* 8: 241–99.

Härtel, H. (1999), *Handschriften des Kestner-Museums zu Hannover* (Wiesbaden).

Hartel, W., ed. (1882), *Magni Felicis Ennodii Opera Omnia*, CSEL 6 (Vienna).

– ed. (1894), *Sancti Pontii Meropii Paulini Nolani Carmina*, CSEL 30 (Vienna; 2nd ed. rev. M. Kamptner, Vienna, 1999).

Hartung, A.E., ed. (1972), *A Manual of the Writings in Middle English 1050–1500, based upon A Manual of Writings in Middle English: 1050–1400 by J. E. Wells*, III. *Dialogues, Debates and Catechisms; Thomas Hoccleve, Malory and Caxton* (New Haven, CT).

Hartzell, K.D. (1975), 'A St Albans Miscellany in New York', *MLJ* 10: 20–61.

– (1980), 'An English Antiphoner of the Ninth Century', *RB* 90: 234–48.

– (1981), 'The Early Provenance of the Harkness Gospels', *Bulletin of Research in the Humanities* 84: 85–97.

- (1982), 'Some New English Drawings of the Tenth Century', in *The Early Middle Ages*, ed. W.H. Snyder, Acta 6 (Binghamton, NY, 1982), 83–93.
- (1989), 'An Eleventh-Century English Missal Fragment in the British Library', *ASE* 18: 45–97.
- (1996), 'An Early Missal Fragment in the British Library', *RB* 106: 308–18.
- (2005), 'Some Early English Liturgical Fragments in Sweden', in Brunius (2005), 83–98.
- (2006), *Catalogue of Manuscripts Written or Owned in England up to 1200 Containing Music* (Woodbridge)

Harvey, A. (1991), 'The Cambridge Juvencus Glosses – Evidence of Hiberno-Welsh Interaction?' in Sture Ureland—Broderick (1991), 181–98.

Häse, A. (2002), *Mittellateinische Bücherverzeichnisse aus Kloster Lorsch: Einleitung, Edition und Kommentar*, Beiträge zum Buch- und Bibliothekswesen 42 (Wiesbaden).

Hasenfratz, R.J. (1993), *Beowulf Scholarship. An Annotated Bibliography 1979–1990* (New York).

Hasler, R. (1981), 'Zu zwei Darstellungen aus der ältesten Kopie des Utrecht-Psalters (British Library, Codex Harleianus 603)', *Zeitschrift für Kunstgeschichte* 44: 317–39.

Haug, A., C. März and L. Welker, eds. (2004), *Der lateinische Hymnus im Mittelalter. Überlieferung—Ästhetik—Ausstrahlung*, Monumenta Monodica Medii Aevi, Subsidia 4 (Kassel).

Hauke, H. (1994), *Katalog der lateinischen Fragmente der Bayerischen Staatsbibliothek München*, I: *Clm 29202–29311*, Catalogus codicum manuscriptorum Bibliothecae Monacensis 4.12/1 (Wiesbaden).

Hausmann, R. (1992), *Die theologischen Handschriften der Hessischen Landesbibliothek Fulda bis zum Jahr 1600. Codices Bonifatiani 1-3, Aa 1-145a*, Die Handschriften der Hessischen Landesbibliothek Fulda, I (Wiesbaden).

Hauswald, E., ed. (2010), *Pirmin: Scarapsus*, MGH Quellen zur Geistesgeschichte des Mittelalters 25 (Hannover).

Hawkes, J. and S. Mills, eds. (1999), *Northumbria's Golden Age* (Stroud).

Healey, A. di Paolo, ed. (1978), *The Old English Vision of St Paul*, Speculum Anniversary Monographs 2 (Cambridge, MA).

- and K. Kiernan, eds. (2007), *Making Sense: Constructing Meaning in Early English*, Publications of the Dictionary of Old English 7 (Toronto).
- (2011), 'Late Anglo-Saxon Glossography: The Lexicographic View', in Lendinara *et al.* (2011), 1–18.

Hearne, T., ed. (1715), *Acta apostolorum Graeco-Latine, litteris majusculis e codice Laudiano* (Oxford).

- ed. (1723), *Hemingi Chartularium Ecclesiae Wigorniensis*, 2 vols. (Oxford).

Hecht, H., ed. (1900–7), *Bischof Wærferths von Worcester Übersetzung der Dialoge Gregors des Grossen*, 2 vols. (Hamburg).

Heimann, A. (1966), 'Three Illustrations from the Bury St Edmund's Psalter and their Prototypes', *JWCI* 29: 39–59.

– (1975), 'The Last Copy of the Utrecht Psalter', in Avril—Hoffeld (1975), 313–38.

– (1978), 'Moses-Darstellungen', in Busch (1978), 1–17.

Heinzel, O. (1926), *Kritische Entstehungsgeschichte des ags. Interlinear-Psalters*, Palaestra 151 (Leipzig).

Hellwig, H. (1888), *Untersuchungen über die Namen des nordhumbrischen Liber Vitae*, I (Berlin).

Hempl, G. (1903–4), 'Hickes's Additions to the Runic Poem', *MP* 1: 134–41.

Hen, Y. (1997), 'The Liturgy of St Willibrord', *ASE* 26: 41–62.

– (2007), 'Liturgical Palimpsests from the Early Middle Ages', in Declerq (2007), 37–54.

Henderson, G. (1975), 'The Programme of the Illuminations in Bodleian MS Junius XI', in Robertson—Henderson (1975), 113–45.

– (1982), *Losses and Lacunae in Early Insular Art*, University of York Monograph Series 3 (York).

– (1987), *From Durrow to Kells. The Insular Gospel-Books 650–800* (London).

– (1994), 'Emulation and Invention in Carolingian Art', in R. McKitterick (1994), 248–3.

– (2001), 'The Barberini Gospels (Rome, Vatican, Biblioteca Apostolica Barberini Lat. 570) as a Paradigm of Insular Art', in Redknap (2001), 157–68.

Henderson, I. (2008), 'Understanding the Figurative Style and Decorative Programme of the Book of Deer', in Forsyth (2008), 32–66.

Henderson, W.G., ed. (1874), *Missale ad usum insignis ecclesiae Eboracensis*, Surtees Society 59–60 (London).

Henel, H. (1934), *Studien zum altenglischen Computus*, Beiträge zur englischen Philologie 26 (Leipzig).

– (1935), 'Altenglischer Mönchsaberglaube', *EStn* 69: 329–49.

– ed. (1942a), *Ælfric's De temporibus anni*, EETS o.s. 213 (London).

– (1942b), 'Notes on Byrhtferth's *Manual*', *JEGP* 41: 427–43.

Henke, T. (2005), *Fromme Bilderwelten: mittelalterliche Textilien und Handschriften im Kestner-Museum* (Hannover).

Henkel, N. (1988), *Deutsche Übersetzungen lateinischer Schultexte. Ihre Verbreitung und Funktion im Mittelalter und in der frühen Neuzeit*, Münchener Texte und Untersuchungen zur deutschen Literatur des Mittelalters 90 (Munich and Zurich).

Hennig, J. (1954), 'Studies in the Literary Tradition of the *Martyrologium Poeticum*', *Proceedings of the Royal Irish Academy* 56 C: 197–226 [repr. in

Hennig, *Medieval Ireland, Saints and Martyrologies. Selected Studies*, ed. M. Richter (Northampton, 1989), no. VI].

Henry, F. (1960), 'Remarks on the Decoration of Three Irish Psalters', *PRIA* 61 C: 23–40.

– (1963), 'The Lindisfarne Gospels', *Antiquity* 37: 100–10.

– (1965), *Irish Art in the Early Christian Period (to A.D. 800)* (London).

– (1967), *Irish Art during the Viking Invasions, 800–1020 A.D.* (London).

– (1974), *The Book of Kells* (London).

Henshaw, M. (1946), 'Two Hymns for St Jodocus', *Speculum* 21: 325–6.

Herbert, J.A. (1911), *Illuminated Manuscripts* (London).

Herbst, L., ed. (1975), *Die altenglische Margaretenlegende in der Hs. Cotton Tiberius A.iii* (Dr Phil dissertation, University of Göttingen).

Herren, M.W., ed. (1987), *The Hisperica Famina*, II: *Related Poems*, Studies and Texts 85 (Toronto).

– ed. (1988), *The Sacred Nectar of the Greeks: The Study of Greek in the West in the Early Middle Ages*, KCLMS 2 (London).

– (1992), 'Hiberno-Latin Lexical Sources of Harley 3376: A Latin-Old English Glossary', in Korhammer (1992), 371–9.

– ed. (1993), *Iohannis Scotti Eriugenae Carmina*, Scriptores Latini Hiberniae 12 (Dublin).

– (1998), 'The Transmission and Reception of Graeco-Roman Mythology in Anglo-Saxon England, 670–800', *ASE* 27: 87–103.

– et al., eds. (2002), *Latin Culture in the Eleventh Century: Proceedings of the Third International Conference on Medieval Latin Studies, Cambridge, September 9–12, 1998*, 2 vols., Publications of the Journal of Medieval Latin 5 (Turnhout).

– ed. (2011), *The Cosmography of Aethicus Ister. Edition, Translation and Commentary*, Publications of the Journal of Medieval Latin 8 (Turnhout).

Hervey, F. (1907), *Corolla Sancti Eadmundi: The Garland of Saint Edmund, King and Martyr* (London).

– ed. (1929), *The History of King Eadmund the Martyr and the Early Years of his Abbey* (London).

Hervieux, L., ed. (1883–9), *Les fabulistes latins*, 5 vols. (Paris).

Herzfeld, G. (1891), 'Bruchstücke von Ælfric's Lives of Saints', *EStn* 16: 151–2

Hesbert, R.-J. (1954a), 'Un curieux antiphonaire palimpseste de l'Office: Rouen, A. 292 (IXe s.)', *RB* 64: 28–45.

– (1954b), *Les manuscrits musicaux de Jumièges*, Monumenta musicae sacrae 2 (Mâcon).

– (1955a), 'Les manuscrits liturgiques de Jumièges', in *Jumièges* (1955) II, 855–72.

– (1955b), 'Les manuscrits musicaux de Jumièges', in *Jumièges* (1955) II, 901–12.

- (1955c), 'Les manuscrits enluminés de l'ancien fonds de Jumièges', in *Jumièges* (1955) II, 721–36.
- (1963–79), *Corpus Antiphonalium Officii*, 6 vols., Rerum Ecclesiasticarum Documenta, Ser. maior 7–12 (Rome).

Heslop, T.A. (1990), 'The Production of *de luxe* Manuscripts and the Patronage of King Cnut and Queen Emma', *ASE* 19: 151–95.
- (1992a), 'A Dated "Late Anglo-Saxon" Illuminated Psalter', *AntJ* 72: 171–4.
- (1992b), 'Decoration and Illustration', in M. Gibson (1992), 25–61.
- (1992c), 'Twelfth-Century Forgeries as Evidence for Earlier Seals: The Case of St Dunstan', in Ramsay et al. (1992), 299–310.
- (1995), 'The Canterbury Calendars and the Norman Conquest', in Eales—Sharpe (1995), 53–86.
- (2004), 'Art and the Man: Archbishop Wulfstan and the York Gospelbook', in Townend (2004), 279–308.
- (2007), 'Manuscript Illumination at Worcester *c.* 1055–1065: The Origins of the Pembroke Lectionary and the Caligula Troper', in Panayotova (2007), 65–71.

Hessels, J.H., ed. (1890), *An Eighth-Century Latin—Anglo-Saxon Glossary preserved in the Library of Corpus Christi College, Cambridge (MS No. 144)* (Cambridge).

Hetherington, M.S. (1975), 'Sir Simonds D'Ewes and Method in Old English Lexicography', *Texas Studies in Literature and Language* 17: 75–92.

Hexter, R.J. (1986), *Ovid and Medieval Schooling. Studies in Medieval School Commentaries on Ovid's 'Ars amatoria'* (Munich).

Heyworth, M. (2007), 'The "Late Old English Handbook for the Use of a Confessor": Authorship and Connections', *N&Q* 252: 218–21.

Heyworth, P.L. (1971), 'Alfred's *Pastoral Care*: MS Cotton Tiberius B. xi', *N&Q* 216: 3–4.
- ed. (1989), *Letters of Humfrey Wanley, Palaeographer, Anglo-Saxonist, Librarian, 1672–1726* (Oxford).

Hickes, G., ed. (1689), 'Catalogus Veterum Librorum Septentrionalium', *Institutiones Grammaticae Anglo-Saxonicae et Moeso-Gothicae* (Oxford).
- (1703–5), *Linguarum vett. Septentrionalium Thesaurus: Grammatico-Criticus et Archaeologicus*, 2 vols. (Oxford).

Hicks, C., ed. (1992), *England in the Eleventh Century: Proceedings of the 1990 Harlaxton Symposium* (Stamford).

Higgitt, J. (1979), 'Glastonbury, Dunstan, Monasticism and Manuscripts', *Art History* 2: 275–90.
- (1989), 'The Iconography of St Peter in Anglo-Saxon England, and St Cuthbert's Coffin', in Bonner et al. (1989a), 267–85.

Higgs, J.W.Y. (1965), *English Rural Life in the Middle Ages*, Bodleian Picture Book 14 (Oxford).

Higham, N., ed. (2007), *Britons in Anglo-Saxon England*, Publications of the Manchester Centre for Anglo-Saxon Studies 7 (Woodbridge).

Hilberg, I., ed. (1910–18), *Sancti Eusebii Hieronymi Epistulae*, 3 vols., CSEL 54–6 (Vienna).

Hiley, D. (1986), 'Thurstan of Caen and Plainchant at Glastonbury: Musical Reflections on the Norman Conquest', *PBA* 72: 57–90.

– (1993), *Western Plainchant* (Oxford).

– (1995), 'The Repertory of Sequences at Winchester', in Boone (1995), 153–93.

– (1998), 'The English Benedictine Version of the *Historia Sancti Gregorii* and the Date of the "Winchester Troper"', in Dobszay (1998), 287–303.

– (2002), *Chants in Honour of St Cuthbert of Lindisfarne*, Plainsong and Medieval Music Society, Occasional Series 4 (London).

– (2003), 'Style and Structure in Early Offices of the Sanctorale', in Gallagher et al. (2003), 157–79.

Hilka, A. and O. Schumann, eds. (1930–70), *Carmina Burana*, 2 vols. (Heidelberg).

Hill, B. (1975), '*Epitaphia Alexandri* in English Medieval Manuscripts', *LSE* 8: 96–104.

Hill, D., ed. (1978), *Ethelred the Unready: Papers from the Millenary Conference*, BAR Brit. Ser. 59 (Oxford).

– (1981), *An Atlas of Anglo-Saxon England* (Oxford).

– and A.R. Rumble, eds. (1996), *The Defence of Wessex: The Burghal Hidage and Anglo-Saxon Fortifications* (Manchester).

Hill, J., ed. (1983), *Old English Minor Heroic Poems* (Durham).

– (1986), 'The Exeter Book and Lambeth Palace Library MS 149: A Reconsideration', *ANQ* 24: 112–16.

– (1988), 'The Exeter Book and Lambeth Palace Library MS 149: The Monasterium of Sancta Maria', *ANQ* n. s. 1: 4–9.

– (1991a), 'Missing Leaves from Worcester Cathedral Library Manuscript F. 91', *N&Q* 236: 1–2.

– (1991b), 'The *Regularis Concordia* and its Latin and Old English Reflexes', *RB* 101: 199–315.

– (1992), 'Ælfric and Smaragdus', *ASE* 21: 203–37.

– (1996), 'The Dissemination of Ælfric's Lives of Saints: A Preliminary Survey', in Szarmach (1996), 235–59.

– (1997), 'The Preservation and Transmission of Ælfric's Saints' Lives: Reader-Reception and Reader-Response in the Early Middle Ages', in Szarmach–Rosenthal (1997), 405–30.

- (2001), 'Lexical Choices for Holy Week: Studies in Old English Ecclesiastical Vocabulary', in Kay—Sylvester (2001), 117–27.
- (2004), 'Archbishop Wulfstan: Reformer?', in Townend (2004), 309–24.
- (2005a), 'Leofric of Exeter and the Practical Politics of Book Collecting', in Kelly—Thompson (2005), 77–98.
- (2005b), 'Ælfric's *Colloquy*: The Antwerp-London Version', in O'Brien O'Keeffe—Orchard (2005) II, 331–48.
- (2006a), 'Making Women Visible: An Adaptation of the *Regularis Concordia* in Cambridge, Corpus Christi College MS. 201', in Karkov—Howe (2006), 153–67.
- (2006b), 'Identifying "Texts" in Cotton Julius E. vii: Medieval and Modern Perspectives', in Doane—Wolf (2006), 27–40.
- (2007a), 'Ælfric's Manuscript of Paul the Deacon's Homiliary: A Provisional Analysis', in Kleist (2007a), 67–92.
- (2007b), 'Ælfric's Grammatical Triad', in Lendinara et al. (2007), 285–307.
- (2011), 'The *Regularis concordia* Glossed and Translated', in Lendinara et al. (2011), 249–67.
Hillaby, J. (1987), 'Early Christian and pre-Conquest Leominster', *Transactions of the Woolhope Naturalists' Field Club* 45: 557–685.
Hillgarth, J.N. (1957), 'El *prognosticum futuri saeculi* de san Julián de Toledo', *Analecta Sacra Tarraconensia* 30: 5–61.
- ed. (1976), *Iulianus Toletanus: Opera*, CCSL 115 (Turnhout).
Hines, J. (2007), 'The Writing of English in Kent: Contexts and Influences from the Sixth to the Ninth Century', *NOWELE: North-Western European Language Evolution* 50–1: 63–92.
Hinkle, W.M. (1970), 'The Gift of an Anglo-Saxon Gospel Book to the Abbey of Saint-Remi, Reims', *Journal of the British Archaeological Association* 3rd ser. 33: 21–35.
Hodgkin, R. H. (1935), *A History of the Anglo-Saxons*, 2 vols. (Oxford).
Hoffmann, H. (1986), *Buchkunst und Königtum im ottonischen und frühsalischen Reich*, MGH, Schriften 30, 2 vols. (Stuttgart).
- (2001), 'Autographa des früheren Mittelalters', *DAEM* 57: 1–62.
Hofmann, J. (1952), 'Das "ex-libris" der Äbtissin Cuthsuuitha', in *Heiliges Franken: Festchronik zum Jahr der Frankenapostel 1952*, ed. T. Krämer (Würzburg, 1952), 5–6.
- (1963), 'Altenglische und althochdeutsche Glossen aus Würzburg und im weiteren angelsächsischen Missionsgebiet', *BGDSL* (Halle) 85: 27–131.
Hofstetter, W. (1979), 'Der Erstbeleg von altenglisch *Pryte/Pryde*', *Anglia* 97: 172–5.

- (1983), 'Zur lateinischen Quelle des altenglischen pseudo-Dioskurides', *Anglia* 101: 315–60.
- (1987), *Winchester und der spätaltenglische Sprachgebrauch: Untersuchungen zur geographischen und zeitlichen Verbreitung altenglischer Synonyme*, TUEPh 14 (Munich).
- (1988), 'Winchester and the Standardization of Old English Vocabulary', *ASE* 17: 139–62.

Hogg, R.M. (1992), *A Grammar of Old English*, I. *Phonology* (Oxford).

Hohler, C.E. (1955), 'Les Saints insulaires dans le missel de l'Archevêque Robert', in *Jumièges* (1955) I, 293–303.
- and A. Hughes (1956), 'The Durham Services in Honour of St Cuthbert', in Battiscombe (1956), 155–91.
- (1967), 'The Proper Office of St Nicholas and Related Matters', *MÆ* 36: 40–8.
- (1972), 'The Red Book of Darley', *Nordisk Kollokvium for Latinsk Liturgiforskning* 2: 39–47.
- (1975), 'Some Service Books of the Later Saxon Church', in Parsons (1975), 60–83, 217–27.
- (1980), Review of R.J.S. Grant, *Cambridge, Corpus Christi College 41: The Loricas and the Missal*, in *MÆ* 49: 275–8.
- (1995), 'Theodore and the Liturgy', in Lapidge (1995a), 222–35.

Holder, A. (1878), 'Die Bouloneser angelsächsischen Glossen zu Prudentius', *Germania* 23: 385–403.

Hollis, S. and M. Wright (1992), *Old English Prose of Secular Learning*, Annotated Bibliographies of Old and Middle English Literature 4 (Cambridge).
- and M. Wright (1994), 'The Remedies in British Library, MS Cotton Galba A. xiv, fols. 139 and 136ʳ', *N&Q* 239: 146–7.
- (1998a), 'The Minster-in-Thanet Foundation Story', *ASE* 27: 41–64.
- (1998b), 'The Old English "Ritual of the Admission of Mildrith" (London, Lambeth Palace, 427, fol. 210)', *JEGP* 97: 311–21.
- (2004), '"The Protection of God and the King": Wulfstan's Legislation on Widows', in Townend (2004), 443–60.

Holschneider, A. (1968), *Die Organa von Winchester. Studien zum ältesten Repertoire polyphoner Musik* (Hildesheim).

Holt, J.C., ed. (1987), *Domesday Studies. Papers read at the Novocentenary Conference of the Royal Historical Society and the Institute of British Geographers, Winchester, 1986* (Woodbridge).

Holthausen, F. (1889), 'Anglo-Saxonica', *Anglia* 11: 171–4.
- (1900), *Altsächsisches Elementarbuch* (Heidelberg).
- and H. Spies, eds. (1913), *Festschrift für Lorenz Morsbach*, Studien zur Englischen Philologie 50 (Halle).

– ed. (1914), *Die ältere Genesis* (Heidelberg).

– (1941), 'Altenglische Interlinearversionen lateinischer Gebete und Beichten', *Anglia* 65: 230–54.

– (1942–3), 'Eine altenglische Interlinearversion des athanasianischen Glaubensbekenntnisses', *EStn* 75: 6–8.

Holtz, L. (1971), 'Tradition et diffusion de l'oeuvre grammaticale de Pompée, commentateur de Donat', *Revue de philologie, litérature et d'histoire ancienne* 45: 48–83.

– (1977), 'A l'école de Donat, de saint Augustin à Bède', *Latomus* 36: 522–38.

– (1981), *Donat et la tradition de l'enseignement grammatical: Etude sur l'Ars Donati et sa diffusion (IVe–IXe siècle) et édition critique* (Paris).

– (1986), 'Les manuscrits carolingiens de Virgile (Xe et XIe siècles)', in *La Fortuna di Virgilio* (1986), 125–49.

Homberben, J. (1983), 'Some Remarks on the Spelman Psalter', *Amsterdamer Beiträge zur älteren Germanistik* 19: 105–37.

Homburger, O.S. (1912), *Die Anfänge der Malschule von Winchester im X. Jahrhundert*, Studien über christliche Denkmäler 13 (Leipzig).

– (1962), *Die illustrierten Handschriften der Burgerbibliothek Bern: Die vor-karolingischen und karolingischen Handschriften* (Bern).

Honegger, T., ed. (2004), *Riddles, Knights and Cross-dressing Saints. Essays on Medieval English Language and Literature*, Sammlung / Collections / Variations 5 (Bern).

Hoops, J. (1928–9), 'Die Foliierung der *Beowulf*-Handschrift. Fr. Klaeber zum 65. Geburtstag', *EStn* 63: 1–11.

Hopf, C. (1994), *Die abendländischen Handschriften der Forschungs- und Landesbibliothek Gotha. Bestandsverzeichnis*, I. *Grossformatige Pergamenthandschriften* (Gotha).

Hopkin-James, L.J., ed. (1934), *The Celtic Gospels: Their Story and their Text* (Oxford).

Horgan, D.M. (1973), 'The Relationship between the Old English Manuscripts of King Alfred's Translation of Gregory's *Pastoral Care*', *Anglia* 91: 153–69.

– (1981), 'The Lexical and Syntactic Variants Shared by Two of the Later Manuscripts of King Alfred's Translation of Gregory's *Cura pastoralis*', *ASE* 9: 213–21.

– (1982), 'The Distribution of West Saxon Dialect Criteria in the Extant Manuscripts of the *Pastoral Care*', *SN* 54: 217–35.

– (1986), 'The Old English Pastoral Care: The Scribal Contribution', in Szarmach (1986b), 108–27.

Hörmann, W. and J. Hemmerle, eds. (1960), *Bayerns Kirche im Mittelalter. Handschriften und Urkunden aus Bayrischem Staatsbesitz* (Munich).

Hornby, E. (2010), 'Interaction between Brittany and Christ Church, Canterbury in the Tenth Century: The Linenthal Leaf', in *Essays in the History of English Music in Honour of John Caldwell: Sources, Style, Performance, Historiography*, ed. E. Hornby and D. Maw (Woodbridge, 2010), 47–65.

Hornung, H. (1960), 'Ein Fragment der metrischen St. Cuthbert Vita im Nachlass der Brüder Grimm', *Scriptorium* 14: 344–6.

Horsley, G.H.R. and E.R. Waterhouse (1984), 'The Greek 'Nomen Sacrum' XP in Some Latin and Old English Manuscripts', *Scriptorium* 38: 211–30.

Hough, C. (2001), 'Palaeographical Evidence for the Compilation of *Textus Roffensis*', *Scriptorium* 55: 57–79.

– (2006), 'Numbers in Manuscripts of Anglo-Saxon Law', in Rumble (2006a), 114–36.

Houghton, J.W. (1994), 'The Old English Benedictine Office and its Audience', *ABR* 45: 431–45.

Houlier, J. and R. Gandilhon (1956), 'Inventaire sommaire de fragments de manuscrits et d'imprimés conservés aux Archives de la Marne (sous-série 3 J)', *Mémoires de la Société d'agriculture, commerce, sciences et arts du Départment de la Marne*, 2nd ser. 30: 57–130.

Hourihane, C., ed. (2011), *Insular & Anglo-Saxon Art and Thought in the early Medieval Period*, The Index of Christian Art Occasional Papers 13 (Princeton, NJ).

Houwen, L.A.J.R. and A.A. MacDonald, eds. (1998), *Alcuin of York. Scholar at the Carolingian Court. Proceedings of the Third Germania Latina Conference held at the University of Groningen, May 1995* (Groningen).

Howald, E. and H. Sigerist, eds. (1927), *Antonii Musae de Herba Vettonica Liber, Pseudoapulei Herbarius, etc.*, Corpus Medicorum Latinorum 4 (Stuttgart).

Howlett, D.R. (1997), 'Miscouplings in Couplets', *Bulletin du Cange: Archivum Latinitatis Medii Aevi* 55: 271–6.

– (1999), '*Medius* as "Middle" and "Mean"', *Peritia* 13: 93–126.

– (2007), 'Two Cambro-Latin Sequences from the Welsh Church', *Bulletin du Cange: Archivum Latinitatis Medii Aevi* 65: 236–45.

Hubay, I. (1962a), *Die Handschriften der Landesbibliothek Coburg* (Coburg).

– (1962b), 'Zur Lebensgeschichte des Gandersheimer Evangeliars', *Jahrbuch der Coburger Landesstiftung* (1962), 3–8.

Huber-Rebenich and C. Hirschler, eds. (2004), *Bestandskatalog zur Sammlung Handschriften- und Inkunabelfragmente des Schlossmuseums Sondershausen* (Sondershausen).

Huemer, J., ed. (1885), *Sedulii Opera Omnia*, CSEL 10 (Vienna).

– ed. (1891), *Gai Vetti Aquilini Iuvenci Evangeliorum libri quattuor*, CSEL 24 (Vienna).

Hughes, Andrew (1993), 'British Rhymed Offices: A Catalogue and Commentary', in Rankin—Hiley (1993), 239–84.

Hughes, Anselm, ed. (1958–60), *The Portiforium of Saint Wulstan*, 2 vols., HBS 89–90 (London).

– ed. (1963), *The Bec Missal*, HBS 94 (London).

– (1972), *The Music of Aldwyn's House at Jarrow and the Early Twelfth-Century Music at Durham Priory*, Jarrow Lecture 1972.

Hughes, H.D. (1925), *A History of Durham Cathedral Library* (Durham).

Hughes, K. (1970), 'Some Aspects of Irish Influence on Early English Private Prayer', *Studia Celtica* 5: 48–61.

– (1971), 'Evidence for Contacts between the Churches of the Irish and the English from the Synod of Whitby to the Viking Age', in Clemoes—Hughes (1971), 49–67.

– (1980), *Celtic Britain in the Early Middle Ages: Studies in Scottish and Welsh Sources*, ed. D.N. Dumville (Woodbridge).

Huglo, M. (1971), *Les tonaires: inventaire, analyse, comparison* (Paris).

– ed. (1987), *Musicologie médiévale: Notations et séquences* (Paris).

– (1990), 'Les Fragments d'Echternach (Paris, Bibliotheque Nationale, MS Lat. 9488)', in Kiesel—Schroeder (1990), 144–9.

– (2005), *Les anciens répertoires de plain-chant* (Aldershot).

Huisman, G.C. (1984), 'Notes on the Manuscript Tradition of Dudo of Saint-Quentin's *Gesta Normannorum*', *ANS* 6: 107–21.

Hulbert, J.A. (1928), 'The Accuracy of the B-Scribe of *Beowulf*', *PMLA* 43: 1196–9.

Hulme, W.H., ed. (1903–4), 'The Old English Gospel of Nicodemus', *MP* 1: 579–614.

Hunt, R.W. (1947), Review of C.W. Jones (1943), *MÆ* 16: 62–4.

– et al., eds. (1948), *Studies in Medieval History presented to Frederick Maurice Powicke* (Oxford).

– ed. (1961), *Saint Dunstan's Classbook from Glastonbury: Codex Biblioth. Bodleianae Oxon. Auct. F. 4. 32*, Umbrae Codicum Occidentalium 4 (Amsterdam).

– ed. (1966), *Greek Manuscripts in the Bodleian Library. An Exhibition held in Connection with the XIIIth International Congress of Byzantine Studies* (Oxford).

– (1971), 'Pastedowns from All Souls Books', in H.H.E. Craster, *The History of All Souls College Library*, ed. E.F. Jacob (London, 1971), 102–11.

– (1975), *The Survival of Ancient Literature* (Oxford).

– (1979), 'Manuscript Evidence for Knowledge of the Poems of Venantius Fortunatus in Late Anglo-Saxon England', *ASE* 8: 279–95.

Hunt, T. (1990), *Popular Medicine in Thirteenth-Century England* (Cambridge).

- (1991), *Teaching and Learning Latin in Thirteenth-Century England*, 3 vols. (Cambridge).

Hunter Blair, P., ed. (1959), *The Moore Bede: An 8th Century Manuscript of the Venerable Bede's 'Historia Ecclesiastica Gentis Anglorum'*, Cambridge University Library MS Kk. 5. 16, EEMF 9 (Copenhagen).

- (1976), 'From Bede to Alcuin', in Bonner (1976), 239–60.

- (1990), *The World of Bede*, 2nd ed. with Preface and Bibliography by M. Lapidge (Cambridge).

Hurst, D. and J. Fraipont, eds. (1955), *Bedae Venerabilis Opera homiletica, Opera rhythmica*, CCSL 122 (Turnout).

- ed. (1960), *Bedae Venerabilis In Lucae Evangelium expositio, In Marci Evangelium expositio*, CCSL 120 (Turnhout).

- ed. (1962), *Bedae Venerabilis In primam partem Samuhelis libri IIII, In Regum librum XXX Quaestiones*, CCSL 119 (Turnhout).

- ed. (1969), *Bedae Venerabilis De Tabernaculo, De Templo Salomonis, In Ezram et Neemiam*, CCSL 119A (Turnhout).

- and M. Adriaen, eds. (1969), *Hieronymus: Commentariorum in Matheum Libri IV*, CCSL 77 (Turnhout).

- and J.E. Hudson, eds. (1983a), *Bedae Venerabilis In Tobiam, In Proverbia Salomonis, In Cantica Canticorum, In Canticum Habacuc*, CCSL 119B (Turnhout).

- and M.L.W. Laistner, eds. (1983b), *Bedae Venerabilis Expositio Actuum Apostolorum, Retractatio in Actus Apostolorum, Nomina regionum atque locorum de Actibus Apostolorum, In Epistolas VII Catholicas*, CCSL 121 (Turnhout).

Husmann, H. (1964), *Tropen- und Sequenzenhandschriften*, Répertoire international des sources musicales, ser. B, 5 (Munich).

Hussey, M.T. (2005), 'Ascetics and Aesthetics: The Anglo-Saxon Manuscripts of Isidore of Seville's *Synonyma*' (unpublished PhD dissertation, University of Wisconsin-Madison).

- (2008), '*Transmarinis litteris*: Southumbria and the Transmission of Isidore's *Synonyma*', *JEGP* 107: 141–68.

Huws, D. (2000), *Medieval Welsh Manuscripts* (Cardiff).

Ineichen-Eder, C.E., ed. (1977), *Bistümer Passau und Regensburg*, MBKDS IV/i (Munich).

Inglis, E. (2008), *Faces of Power and Piety* (Los Angeles).

Inguanez, D.M. (1915–41), *Codicum Casinensium Manuscriptorum Catalogus*, 3 vols. (Montecassino).

Insley, J. (2004), 'The Scandinavian Personal Names in the later Part of the Durham *Liber Vitae*', in Rollason et al. (2004a), 87–96.

Irvine, M. (1986) 'Bede the Grammarian and the Scope of Grammatical Studies in Eighth-Century Northumbria', *ASE* 15: 15–44.

– (1994), *The Making of Textual Culture: 'Grammatica' and Literary Theory, 350–1100*, Cambridge Studies in Medieval Literature 19 (Cambridge).

Irvine, S. (1990), 'Bones of Contention: The Context of Ælfric's Homily on St Vincent', *ASE* 19: 117–32.

– ed. (1993), *Old English Homilies from MS Bodley 343*, EETS o.s. 302 (Oxford).

– (2000), 'The Compilation and Use of Manuscripts containing Old English in the Twelfth Century', in Swan–Treharne (2000a), 41–61.

– ed. (2004), *The Anglo Saxon Chronicle. A Collaborative Edition*, VII: *MS. E* (Cambridge).

– (2005), 'Fragments of Boethius: The Reconstruction of the Cotton Manuscript of the Alfredian Text', *ASE* 34: 169–81.

Irving, E.B., ed. (1953/1970), *The Old English Exodus*, with 'Errata' and 'Supplement to the Bibliography' (Hamden, CT).

Izydorczyk, Z. (1993), *Manuscripts of the Evangelium Nicodemi: A Census* (Toronto).

Jaager, W., ed. (1935), *Bedas metrische Vita Sancti Cuthberti*, Palaestra 198 (Leipzig).

– (1936), 'Angelsächsische Glossen zur Vita Cuthberti', *BGDSL* 60: 380–3.

Jackson, B.D. (1975), *Augustine: De Dialectica, trans. with Introduction and Notes, from the Text newly edited by Jan Pinborg* (Dordrecht and Boston).

Jackson, K.H. (1953), *Language and History in Early Britain* (Edinburgh).

– (1972), *The Gaelic Notes in the Book of Deer* (Cambridge).

Jackson, P. (1992), 'The *Vitas Patrum* in Eleventh-Century Worcester', in Hicks (1992), 119–34.

– and M. Lapidge (1996), 'The Contents of the Cotton-Corpus Legendary', in Szarmach (1996), 131–46.

Jacobsen, P.C. (1978), *Flodoard von Reims. Sein Leben und seine Dichtung 'De triumphis Christi'*, Mittellateinische Studien und Texte 10 (Leiden).

Jacobsson, R. (1993), 'Unica in the Cotton Caligula Troper', in Rankin–Hiley (1993), 11–45.

James, M.R. (1893), *Apocrypha Anecdota* [First Series] (Cambridge).

– (1895), *A Descriptive Catalogue of the Manuscripts in the Library of Jesus College, Cambridge* (Cambridge).

– (1897), *A Descriptive Catalogue of the Manuscripts in the Library of Sidney Sussex College, Cambridge* (Cambridge).

– (1899), *A Descriptive Catalogue of the Manuscripts in the Library of Peterhouse* (Cambridge).

– (1900–4), *The Western Manuscripts in the Library of Trinity College, Cambridge: A Descriptive Catalogue*, 4 vols. (Cambridge).

- (1901), 'A Fragment of the "Penitence of Jannes and Jambres"', *JTS* 2: 572–7.
- (1903), *The Ancient Libraries of Canterbury and Dover: The Catalogues of the Libraries of Christ Church Priory and St Augustine's Abbey at Canterbury and of St Martin's Priory at Dover* (Cambridge).
- (1905a), *A Descriptive Catalogue of the Western Manuscripts in the Library of Clare College, Cambridge* (Cambridge).
- (1905b), *A Descriptive Catalogue of the Manuscripts in the Library of Pembroke College, Cambridge* (Cambridge).
- (1907), *A Descriptive Catalogue of the Manuscripts in the Library of Trinity Hall, Cambridge* (Cambridge).
- (1907–8), *A Descriptive Catalogue of the Manuscripts in the Library of Gonville and Caius College, Cambridge*, 2 vols. (Cambridge).
- (1910), 'An Ancient List of the Seventy Disciples', *JTS* 11: 459–62.
- (1912), *A Descriptive Catalogue of the Manuscripts in the Library of Corpus Christi College, Cambridge*, 2 vols. (Cambridge).
- (1913), *A Descriptive Catalogue of the Manuscripts in the Library of St John's College, Cambridge* (Cambridge).
- (1921), *A Descriptive Catalogue of the Latin Manuscripts in the John Rylands Library at Manchester*, 2 vols. (Manchester).
- (1923), *Bibliotheca Pepysiana*, III. *Mediaeval Manuscripts* (London).
- and C. Jenkins (1930–2), *A Descriptive Catalogue of the Manuscripts in the Library of Lambeth Palace* (Cambridge), with supplemental vols. by E.G.W. Bill: *A Catalogue of Manuscripts in Lambeth Palace Library, MSS 1222-1860* (Oxford, 1972); *MSS 1907-2340* (Oxford, 1976); *MSS 2341-2750* (Oxford, 1983).
- (1932), *A Catalogue of the Medieval Manuscript in the University Library, Aberdeen* (Cambridge).
- (1933), 'The Manuscripts of St. George's Chapel, Windsor', *The Library*, 4th ser. 13: 55–76.
- (1935), 'The Manuscripts of Bede', in A.H. Thompson (1935), 230–6.
James, P. (1996), 'The Lichfield Gospels: The Question of Provenance', *Parergon* 13.2: 51–61.
Jan, L. and K. Mayhoff, eds. (1892–1909), *Plinii naturalis historiae libri XXXVII* (Leipzig).
Jayatilaka, R. (1996), 'The *Regula Sancti Benedicti* in Late Anglo-Saxon England: The Manuscripts and their Readers' (unpubl. PhD dissertation, University of Oxford).
- (2003), 'The Old English Benedictine Rule: Writing for Women and Men', *ASE* 32: 147–87.
- (2011), '*Descriptio Terrae*: Geographical Glosses on Boethius's *Consolation of Philosophy*', in Lendinara et al. (2011), 93–117.

– (2012), 'King Alfred and his Circle', in R. Gameson (2012), 670–8.

Jeffery, C.D. (1980), 'The Latin Texts Underlying the Old English *Gregory's Dialogues* and *Pastoral Care*', *N&Q* 225: 483–8.

Jenkins, D. and M.E. Owen (1983), 'The Welsh Marginalia in the Lichfield Gospels, Part I', *CMCS* 5: 37–66.

– and M.E. Owen (1984), 'The Welsh Marginalia in the Lichfield Gospels, Part II: The Surrexit Memorandum', *CMCS* 7: 91–120.

Jenner, H. (1923), 'The Bodmin Gospels', *Journal of the Royal Institution of Cornwall* 21/2: 113–45.

– (1924), 'The Manumissions in the Bodmin Gospels', *Journal of the Royal Institution of Cornwall* 21/3: 235–60.

Jeudy, C. (1971), 'La tradition manuscrite des *Partitiones* de Priscien et la version longue du commentaire de Remi d'Auxerre', *Revue d'histoire des textes* 1: 123–43.

– (1972), 'L'*Institutio de nomine, pronomine et verbo* de Priscien: Manuscrits et commentaires médiévaux', *Revue d'histoire des textes* 2: 73–144.

– (1974a), 'L'*Ars de nomine et verbo* de Phocas: Manuscrits et commentaires médiévaux', *Viator* 5: 61–156.

– (1974b), 'Les manuscrits de l'*Ars de verbo* d'Eutychès et le commentaire de Remi d'Auxerre', in *Études de la civilisation médiévale (IXe–XIIe siècles). Mélanges offerts à Edmond-René Labande* (Poitiers, 1974), 421–36.

– (1984), 'Nouveau complément à un catalogue récent des manuscrits de Priscien', *Scriptorium* 38: 140–50.

– and Y.-F. Riou (1989–), *Les manuscrits classiques latins des Bibliothèques publiques de France* (Paris).

– (1991), 'Remigii Autissiodorensis Opera (Clavis)', in *L'école carolingienne d'Auxerre. De Murethach à Remi, 830–908*, ed. D. Iogna-Prat, C. Jeudy and G. Lobrichon (Paris, 1991), 457–500.

– (1996), 'Glossaires juvénaliens du Haut Moyen Âge', in Hamesse (1996), 253–82.

John, E. (1966), *Orbis Britanniae and Other Studies* (Leicester).

John, J.J. (1995), 'The Named (and Namable) Scribes in *Codices Latini Antiquiores*', in Condello–de Gregorio (1995), 107–21.

Johnson, D.F. (1997), 'Winchester Revisited: Æthelwold, Lucifer, and the Date and Provenance of MS Junius 11', *OEN* 30.3: A50–A51.

– and W. Rudolf (2010), 'More Notes by Coleman', *MÆ* 79: 1–13.

Jolly, K.L. (2007), 'On the Margins of Orthodoxy: Devotional Formulas and Protective Prayers in Cambridge, Corpus Christi College MS 41', in Keefer–Bremmer (2007a), 135–83.

– (2012), *The Community of St Cuthbert in the late Tenth Century: The Chester-le-Street Additions to Durham, Cathedral Library, A. IV. 19* (Columbus, OH).

Jondorf, G. and D.N. Dumville, eds. (1991), *France and the British Isles in the Middle Ages and Renaissance. Essays by Members of Girton College, Cambridge, in Memory of Ruth Morgan* (Woodbridge).

Jones, C.A. (1998a), 'Two Composite Texts from Archbishop Wulfstan's "Commonplace Book": The *De ecclesiastica consuetudine* and the *Institutio beati Amalarii de ecclesiasticis officiis*', *ASE* 27: 233–71.

– ed. (1998b), *Ælfric's Letter to the Monks of Eynsham*, CSASE 24 (Cambridge).

– (1998c), 'The Book of the Liturgy in Anglo-Saxon England', *Speculum* 73: 659–702.

– (1998d), '*Meatim sed et rustica*: Ælfric of Eynsham as a Medieval Latin Author', *JMLat* 8: 1–57.

– (1999), 'A Liturgical Miscellany in Cambridge, Corpus Christi College 190', *Traditio* 54: 103–40.

– ed. (2001), *A Lost Work by Amalarius of Metz: Interpolations in Salisbury, Cathedral Library, MS 154*, HBS Subsidia 2 (London).

– (2004), 'Wulfstan's Liturgical Interests', in Townend (2004), 325–52.

– (2005a), 'The Chrism Mass in later Anglo-Saxon England', in Gittos – Bedingfield (2005a), 105–42.

– (2005b), 'The Origins of the "Sarum" Chrism Mass at Eleventh-century Christ Church, Canterbury', *MS* 67: 219–316.

– (2007), 'Monastic Identity and Sodomitic Danger in the *Occupatio* by Odo of Cluny', *Speculum* 82: 1–53.

– (2010), 'A Lost Treatise of Amalarius: New Evidence from the Twelfth Century', in *The Study of Medieval Manuscripts of England: Festschrift in Honor of Richard W. Pfaff*, ed. G.H. Brown and L.E. Voigts (Tempe, AZ, and Turnhout, 2010), 41–67.

Jones, C.W. (1939), *Bedae Pseudepigrapha: Scientific Writings falsely attributed to Bede* (Ithaca, NY).

– ed. (1943), *Bedae Opera de temporibus* (Cambridge, MA).

– and C.B. Kendall, eds. (1975), *Bedae Venerabilis De orthographia, De arte metrica et schematibus et tropis, De natura rerum*, CCSL 123A (Turnhout).

– (1976), 'Bede's Place in Medieval Schools', in Bonner (1976), 261–85.

– ed. (1977), *Bedae Venerabilis De temporum ratione liber*, CCSL 123B (Turnhout).

– ed. (1980), *Bedae Venerabilis Magnus circulus seu Tabula paschalis, Kalendarium sive martyrologium, De temporibus liber, Epistolae (ad Pleguinam, ad Helmwaldum, ad Wicthedum)*, CCSL 123C (Turnhout).

Jones, L.W. (1929), 'Cologne MS. 106: A Book of Hildebald', *Speculum* 4: 27–61.

Jones, P.M. (1998), *Medieval Medicine in Illuminated Manuscripts* (London).

Jordan, R. (1906), *Eigentümlichkeiten des anglischen Wortschatzes: Eine wort-geographische Untersuchung mit etymologischen Anmerkungen*, Anglistische Forschungen 17 (Heidelberg).

Jørgensen, E. (1926), *Catalogus Codicum Latinorum Medii Aevi Bibliothecae Regiae Hafniensis* (Copenhagen).

– (1933), 'Bidrag til ældre nordisk Kirke- og Literaturhistorie', *Nordisk Tidskrift för Bok- och Biblioteksväsen* 20: 186–8.

Jost, K. (1913), 'Zu den Handschriften der *Cura Pastoralis*', *Anglia* 37: 63–8.

– (1950), *Wulfstanstudien*, Schweizer Anglistische Arbeiten / Swiss Studies in English 23 (Bern).

– ed. (1959), *Die 'Institutes of Polity, Civil and Ecclesiastical'. Ein Werk Erzbischof Wulfstans von York*, Schweizer Anglistische Arbeiten / Swiss Studies in English 47 (Bern).

Judge, C.B. (1934), 'Anglo-Saxonica in Hereford Cathedral Library', *Harvard Studies and Notes in Philology and Literature* 16: 89–96.

Judic, B., F. Rommel and C. Morel, eds. (1992), *Grégoire le Grand: Règle pastorale*, 2 vols., SChr 381–2 (Paris).

Jumièges. Congrès scientifique du XIIIe centenaire, 2 vols. (Rouen, 1955).

Junius, F. (2000), *Caedmonis monachi Paraphrasis Geneseos ac praecipuarum Sacrae paginae Historiarum, abhinc annos MLXX*, ed. P.J. Lucas, Early Studies in Germanic Philology 3 (Amsterdam).

Kalbhen, U. (2003), *Kentische Glossen und kentischer Dialekt im Altenglischen*, TUEPh 28 (Frankfurt am Main).

Kantorowicz, E.H. (1946), *Laudes regiae* (Berkeley, CA).

Karkov, C.E. (2001a), 'Broken Bodies and Singing Tongues: Gender and Voice in the Cambridge, Corpus Christi College 23 *Psychomachia*', *ASE* 30: 115–36.

– (2001b), *Text and Picture in Anglo-Saxon England. Narrative Strategies in the Junius 11 Manuscript*, CSASE 31 (Cambridge).

– and G.H. Brown, eds. (2003), *Anglo-Saxon Styles* (Albany, NY).

– (2004), *The Ruler Portraits of Anglo-Saxon England* (Woodbridge).

– and N. Howe, eds. (2006), *Conversion and Colonization in Anglo-Saxon England*, MRTS 318 (Tempe, AZ).

– (2006a), 'Writing and Having Written: Word and Image in the Eadwig Gospels', in Rumble (2006a), 44–61.

– (2006b), 'Text as Image in Ælfwine's Prayerbook', in Magennis—Wilcox (2006), 95–114.

– (2007a), 'Text and Image in the Red Book of Darley', in Minnis—Roberts (2007), 135–48.

- (2007b), 'Margins and Marginalization: Representations of Eve in Oxford, Bodleian Library, MS Junius 11', in Keefer—Bremmer (2007a), 57–84.
- (2007c), 'Evangelist Portraits and Book Production in Late Anglo-Saxon England', in Panayotova (2007), 55–9.
- (2008), 'The Frontispiece to the New Minster Charter and the King's Two Bodies', in Scragg (2008c), 224–41.
- (2009), 'Manuscript Art', in Owen-Crocker (2009), 205–51.
- (2011), 'Tracing the Anglo-Saxons in the Epistles of Paul: The Case of Würzburg, Universitätsbibliothek, M. p. th. f. 69', in Roberts—Webster (2011), 133–44.

Kauffmann, C.M. (1975), *A Survey of Manuscripts in the British Isles*, III: *Romanesque Manuscripts, 1066–1190* (London).
- (2003), *Biblical Imagery in Medieval England, 700–1550* (London).
Kauffmann, G. (1888), *De Hygini memoria scholiis in Ciceronis Aratum Harleianis servata* (Berlin).
Kay, C.J. and L.M. Sylvester, eds. (2001), *Lexis and Texts in Early English* (Amsterdam).
Keats-Rohan, K.S.B. (2004), 'Testimonies of the Living Dead: The Martyrology-Necrology and Necrology in the Chapter Book of Mont Saint-Michel (Avranches, Bibliothèque municipale, MS 214)', in Rollason (2004a), 165–89.
Keefer, S.L. (1990a), 'The *ex-libris* of the Regius Psalter', *ANQ* 3: 155–9.
- and D.R. Burrows (1990b), 'Hebrew and the *Hebraicum* in late Anglo-Saxon England', *ASE* 19: 67–80.
- (1996), 'Margin as Archive: The Liturgical Marginalia of a Manuscript of the Old English Bede', *Traditio* 51: 147–77.
- (1997), 'Another Pre-Conquest Inscription in Durham Cathedral Library MS A. II. 17', *Durham Archaeological Journal* 13: 65.
- (1998), 'Looking at the Glosses in London, British Library Additional 57337 (The Anderson Pontifical)', *Anglia* 116: 215–22.
- and R. H. Bremmer, eds. (2007a), *Signs on the Edge. Space, Text and Margin in Medieval Manuscripts* (Paris).
- (2007b), 'Use of Manuscript Space for Design, Text and Image in Liturgical Books owned by the Community of St Cuthbert', in Keefer—Bremmer (2007a), 85–115.
Kelly, B. (1982), 'The Formative Stages of *Beowulf* Textual Scholarship: Part I', *ASE* 11: 247–74.
- (1983), 'The Formative Stages of *Beowulf* Textual Scholarship: Part II', *ASE* 12: 239–75.
Kelly, R.J., ed. (2003), *The Blickling Homilies* (London).
Kelly, S. and J.J. Thompson, eds. (2005), *Imagining the Book*, Medieval Texts and Cultures of Northern Europe 7 (Turnhout).

Kelly, S.E., ed. (1995), *Charters of St Augustine's Abbey, Canterbury, and Minster-in-Thanet*, Anglo-Saxon Charters 4 (Oxford).
– ed. (1998), *Charters of Selsey*, Anglo-Saxon Charters 6 (Oxford).
Kendall, C.B., ed. (1975), '[Bedae] De arte metrica et De schematibus et tropis', in Jones–Kendall (1975), 59–171.
– trans. (1991), *Beda: Libri II De Arte Metrica et de Schematibus et Tropis: The Art of Poetry and Rhetoric*, Bibliotheca Germanica, Ser. nova, 2 (Saarbrücken).
– and P.S. Wells, eds. (1992), *Voyage to the Other World. The Legacy of Sutton Hoo*, Medieval Studies at Minnesota 5 (Minneapolis, MN).
Kendrick, T.D. (1938), *Anglo-Saxon Art to AD 900* (London).
– (1949), *Late Saxon and Viking Art* (London).
– et al., eds. (1956–60), *Evangeliorum Quattuor Codex Lindisfarnensis*, 2 vols. (Olten and Lausanne).
Kennedy, E.D. (1989), *A Manual of the Writings in Middle English*, VIII. *Chronicles and Other Historical Writing* (New Haven, CT).
Kennedy, R. and S. Meecham-Jones, eds. (2008), *Authority and Subjugation in Writing of Medieval Wales* (New York).
Kenney, E.J., ed. (1961), *P. Ovidi Nasonis Amores, Medicamina faciei femineae, Ars amatoria, Remedia amoris* (Oxford).
Kenyon, F.G. (1900), *Facsimiles of Biblical Manuscripts in the British Museum* (London).
Ker, N.R. (1932), 'The Scribes of the Trinity Homilies', *MÆ* 1: 138–40.
– (1933), 'A Study of the Additions and Alterations in MSS Bodley 340 and 342' (unpubl. PhD dissertation, Oxford Univ.).
– (1935), 'Two Notes on MS. Ashmole 328 (*Byrhtferth's Manual*)', *MÆ* 4: 16–19.
– (1936), 'The Medieval Pressmarks of St. Guthlac's Priory (Hereford) and Roche Abbey, Yorks.', *MÆ* 5: 47–8.
– (1937), 'The Date of the "Tremulous" Worcester Hand', *LSE* 6: 28–9 [repr. N.R. Ker (1985), 67–9].
– (1939–40), 'Membra Disiecta, Second Series', *British Museum Quarterly* 14: 79–86.
– (1941–9), 'The Provenance of the Oldest Manuscript of the Rule of St. Benedict', *BLR* 2: 28–9 [repr. N.R. Ker (1985) 131–3].
– (1942–3), 'The Migration of Manuscripts from the English Medieval Libraries', *The Library*, 4th ser. 23: 1–11 [repr. N.R. Ker (1985) 459–70].
– (1943), 'Aldred the Scribe', *Essays and Studies* 28: 7–12 [repr. N.R. Ker (1985) 3–8].
– E.A. Lowe and A.P. McKinlay (1944), 'A New Fragment of Arator in the Bodleian', *Speculum* 19: 351–9 [repr. Lowe (1972b) I.345–7].
– (1948), 'Hemming's Cartulary: A Description of the Two Worcester Cartularies in Cotton Tiberius A. xiii', in R.W. Hunt (1948), 49–75 [repr. N.R. Ker (1985) 31–59].

- (1948–55), 'A Palimpsest in the National Library of Scotland [Advocates MSS 18. 6. 12, 18. 7. 7, 18. 7. 8]: Early Fragments of Augustine *De Trinitate*, the *Passio S. Laurentii*, and other Texts', *Edinburgh Bibliographical Society Transactions* 3: 169–78 [repr. N.R. Ker (1985) 121–30].
- (1949), 'Old English Notes Signed "Coleman"', *MÆ* 18: 29–31 [repr. N.R. Ker (1985), 27–30].
- (1949–50), 'Salisbury Cathedral Manuscripts and Patrick Young's Catalogue', *Wiltshire Archaeological and Natural History Magazine* 53: 153–83 [repr. N.R. Ker (1985), 175–208].
- (1949–53), 'Medieval Manuscripts from Norwich Cathedral Priory', *TCBS* 1: 11–21 [repr. N.R. Ker (1985) 243–72].
- (1954), *Fragments of Medieval Manuscripts used as Pastedowns in Oxford Bindings, with a Survey of Oxford Binding, c. 1515–1620*, Oxford Bibliographical Society Publications n.s. 5 (Oxford; repr. with addenda, 2004).
- (1955), 'Sir John Prise', *The Library* 5th ser. 10: 1–24 [repr. N.R. Ker (1985) 471–96].
- ed. (1956), *The Pastoral Care: King Alfred's Translation of St Gregory's Regula Pastoralis. MS Hatton 20 in the Bodleian Library at Oxford, MS Cotton Tiberius B.XI in the British Museum, MS Anhang 19 in the Landesbibliothek at Kassel*, EEMF 6 (Copenhagen).
- (1957), *Catalogue of Manuscripts containing Anglo-Saxon* (Oxford).
- (1959), 'Three Old English Texts in a Salisbury Pontifical, Cotton Tiberius C. i', in Clemoes (1959a) 262–79.
- (1960), *English Manuscripts in the Century after the Norman Conquest* (Oxford).
- (1962a), 'Fragments of Jerome's Commentary on St. Matthew', *Medievalia et Humanistica* 14: 7–14 [repr. N.R. Ker (1985), 113–20].
- (1962b), 'The Bodmer Fragment of Ælfric's Homily for Septuagesima Sunday', in Davis–Wrenn (1962), 77–83.
- (1962–92), *Medieval Manuscripts in British Libraries*, 4 vols. [vol. IV ed. with A.J. Piper] (Oxford) [and see N.R. Ker (2002)].
- (1964), *Medieval Libraries of Great Britain: A List of Surviving Books*, 2nd ed. (London).
- (1971), 'The Handwriting of Archbishop Wulfstan', in Clemoes–Hughes (1971), 315–31 [repr. N.R. Ker (1985) 9–26].
- (1972a), 'A Catalogue of the Medieval Literary Manuscripts', in Eward (1972), 1–6.
- (1972b), 'The English Manuscripts of the *Moralia* of Gregory the Great', in *Kunsthistorische Forschungen Otto Pächt zu seinem 70. Geburtstag*, ed. A. Rosenauer and G. Weber (Salzburg), 77–89.

- (1976a), 'A Supplement to *Catalogue of Manuscripts Containing Anglo-Saxon*', *ASE* 5: 121–31.
- (1976b), 'The Beginnings of Salisbury Cathedral Library', in Alexander—Gibson (1976), 23–49 [repr. N.R. Ker (1985) 143–73].
- (1979), 'Copying and Exemplar: Two Manuscripts of Jerome on Habakkuk', in *Miscellanea Codicologica F. Masai Dicata*, ed. P. Cockshaw, M. Garand and P. Jodogne (Ghent, 1979), 203–10 [repr. N.R. Ker (1985) 75–86].
- (1985), *Books, Collectors and Libraries: Studies in the Medieval Heritage*, ed. A.G. Watson (London).
- (2002), *Medieval Manuscripts in British Libraries*, V. *Indexes and Addenda*, ed. A. Watson and I. Cunningham (Oxford) [and see N.R. Ker (1962–92)].
- Ker, W.P. et al., eds. (1901), *An English Miscellany Presented to Dr. Furnivall in Honour of his Seventy-Fifth Birthday* (New York).
- Kerff, F. (1982), *Der Quadripartitus. Ein Handbuch der karolingischen Kirchenreform: Überlieferung, Quellen und Rezeption* (Sigmaringen).
- Kéry, L. (1999), *Canonical Collections of the Early Middle Ages (ca. 400–1140). A Bibliographical Guide to the Manuscripts and Literature* (Washington, DC).
- Keynes, S.D. (1978), 'The Declining Reputation of King Æthelred the Unready', in D. Hill (1978), 227–54.
- (1980), *The Diplomas of King Æthelred 'the Unready' 978–1016: A Study in their Use as Historical Evidence* (Cambridge).
- and M. Lapidge, trans. (1983), *Alfred the Great: Asser's 'Life of King Alfred' and other Contemporary Sources* (Harmondsworth).
- (1985a), 'King Æthelstan's Books', in Lapidge—Gneuss (1985a), 143–201.
- (1985b), 'The Crowland Psalter and the Sons of King Edmund Ironside', *BLR* 11: 359–70.
- (1986a), 'The Additions in Old English', in Barker et al. (1986), 81–99.
- (1986b), 'Episcopal Succession in Anglo-Saxon England', in Fryde et al. (1986), 209–24.
- ed. (1991), *Facsimiles of Anglo-Saxon Charters*, Anglo-Saxon Charters, Supplementary Volume 1 (Oxford).
- (1992), *Anglo-Saxon Manuscripts and other Items of Related Interest in the Library of Trinity College, Cambridge*, OEN Subsidia 18 (Binghamton, NY).
- (1994a), *The Councils of Clofesho*, Univ. of Leicester Vaughan Paper 38 (Leicester).
- (1994b), 'Cnut's Earls', in Rumble (1994b), 43–88.
- ed. (1996a), *The Liber Vitae of the New Minster and Hyde Abbey Winchester: British Library Stowe 944, together with Leaves from British Library Cotton Vespasian A.VIII and British Library Cotton Titus D.XXVII*, EEMF 26 (Copenhagen).

- (1996b), 'The Reconstruction of a Burnt Cottonian Manuscript: The Case of Cotton MS. Otho A. i', *BLJ* 22: 113–60.
- (1997a), 'Anglo-Saxon Entries in the *Liber Vitae* of Brescia', in Roberts — Nelson (1997), 99–119.
- (1997b), 'Giso, Bishop of Wells (1061–88)', *Anglo-Norman Studies* 19: 203–71.
- (1999a), 'Episcopal Lists', in Lapidge et al. (1999), 172–4.
- (1999b), 'King Alfred the Great and Shaftesbury Abbey', in *Studies in the Early History of Shaftesbury Abbey*, ed. L. Keen (Dorchester, 1999), 17–72.
- (2000), 'Diocese and Cathedral before 1056', in Aylmer — Tiller (2000), 3–20.
- (2003), 'Ely Abbey 672–1109', in Meadows — Ramsay (2003), 3–58.
- (2004), 'The *Liber Vitae* of the New Minster, Winchester', in Rollason et al. (2004), 149–63.
- (2005a), 'Wulfsige, Monk of Glastonbury, Abbot of Westminster (c.990–3), and Bishop of Sherborne (c.993–1002)', in Barker et al. (2005), 53–94.
- (2005b), 'Between Bede and the *Chronicle*: London, BL, Cotton Vespasian B. vi, fols. 104–9', in O'Brien O'Keeffe — Orchard (2005) I, 47–67.
- (2006), *Anglo-Saxon England. A Bibliographical Handbook for Students of Anglo-Saxon History*, 7th ed. (Cambridge).
- and A. Smyth, eds. (2006), *Anglo-Saxons: Studies Presented to Cyril Roy Hart* (Dublin).
- (2007), 'An Abbot, an Archbishop, and the Viking Raids of 1006–7 and 1009–12', *ASE* 36: 151–220.
- (2012), 'Manuscripts of the *Anglo-Saxon Chronicle*', in R. Gameson (2012), 537–52.

Kidd, P. (2000), 'A Re-Examination of the Date of an Eleventh-Century Psalter from Winchester (British Library, MS Arundel 60)', in Cassidy — Muir Wright (2000), 42–53.

Kiernan, K.S. (1981), 'The Eleventh-Century Origin of *Beowulf* and the *Beowulf* Manuscript', in Chase (1981), 9–22.
- (1984), 'The State of the *Beowulf* Manuscript, 1882–1983', *ASE* 13: 23–42.
- (1986), 'Madden, Thorkelin, and MS Vitellius/Vespasian A.xv', *The Library* 6th ser. 8: 127–32.
- (1990), 'Old English Manuscripts: The Scribal Deconstruction of "Early Northumbrian"', *ANQ* 3: 48–55.
- (1991), 'A Long Footnote for J. Gerritsen's "Supplementary" Description of BL Cotton MS Vitellius A.xv', *ES* 72: 489–96.
- (1994a), 'Old Manuscripts / New Technologies', in Richards (1994), 37–54.
- (1994b), 'The Eleventh-Century Origin of *Beowulf* and the *Beowulf* Manuscript', in Richards (1994), 277–300 [orig. publ. in Chase (1981), 9–21].
- (1996), *Beowulf and the Beowulf Manuscript*, rev. ed. (Ann Arbor, MI).

- (1998a), 'The Conybeare-Madden Collation of Thorkelin's *Beowulf*', in Pulsiano—Treharne (1998a), 117–36.
- (1998b), 'Alfred the Great's Burnt *Boethius*', in Bornstein—Tinkle (1998), 7–32.
- ed. (1999), *Electronic Beowulf* (London); 3rd ed. (London and Chicago, 2011) [2 CD-ROM].
- et al. (2002), 'The Reappearance of St. Basil the Great in British Library MS Otho B. x', *The Computer and the Humanities* 36: 7–26.
- (2005), 'The Source of the Napier Fragment of Alfred's Boethius', *Digital Medievalist* 1.1 (Spring 2005).
- (2006), 'Odd Couples in Ælfric's *Julian and Basilissa* in British Library, Cotton MS. Otho B. x', in Doane—Wolf (2006), 85–106.

Kiesel, G. and J. Schroeder, eds. (1990), *Willibrord: Apostel der Niederlande, Gründer der Abtei Echternach*, 2nd ed. (Luxembourg).

Kiff-Hooper, J. (1991), 'Class-Books or Works of Art? Some Observations on the Tenth-Century Manuscripts of Aldhelm's *De laude virginitatis*', in *Church and Chronicle in the Middle Ages*, ed. I. Wood and G. Load (London), 15–20.

Kilpiö, M. and L. Kahlas-Tarkka, eds. (2001), *Ex Insula Lux: Manuscripts and Hagiographical Material Connected with Medieval England* (Helsinki).

Kim, H.C., ed. (1973), *The Gospel of Nicodemus. Gesta Salvatoris*, Toronto Medieval Latin Texts 2 (Toronto).

Kim, S. (1973), 'A Collation of the Old English MS Hatton 20 of King Alfred's *Pastoral Care*', *NM* 74: 425–42.

Kimmens, A.C., ed. (1979), *The Stowe Psalter*, Toronto OE Series 1 (Toronto).

Kindschi, L. (1955), 'The Latin-Old English Glossaries in Plantin-Moretus MS 32 and British Museum Additional 32246' (unpubl. PhD dissertation, Stanford University, CA).

Kirby, T.A. and H.B. Woolf, eds. (1949), *Philologica: The Malone Anniversary Studies* (Baltimore).

Kiss, A. et al., eds. (2002), *The Iconography of the Fantastic. Eastern and Western Traditions of European Iconography 2*, Papers in English and American Studies X/ Studia Poetica 11 (Szeged).

Kitson, P. (1978), 'Lapidary Traditions in Anglo-Saxon England: Part I, the Background; the Old English Lapidary', *ASE* 7: 9–60.

- (1983), 'Lapidary Traditions in Anglo-Saxon England: Part II, Bede's *Explanatio Apocalypsis* and Related Works', *ASE* 12: 73–123.
- (1990), 'On Old English Nouns of more than one Gender', *ES* 71: 185–221.

Kittlick, W. (1998), *Die Glossen der Hs. British Library, Cotton Cleopatra A.III: Phonologie, Morphologie, Wortgeographie* (Frankfurt am Main).

Kitzinger, E. (2002), *Studies in Late Antique, Byzantine and Medieval Western Art*, 2 vols. (London).

Klaeber, F., ed. (1931), *The Later Genesis and other Old English and Old Saxon Texts relating to the Fall of Man*, 2nd ed. with supplement (Heidelberg).

‒ ed. (1950), *Beowulf and the Fight at Finnsburg*, 3rd ed. with 1st and 2nd supplements (Boston, MA).

‒ ed. (2008): see under Fulk, R.D. et al.

Klauser, T. (1972), *Das römische Capitulare Evangeliorum. Texte und Untersuchungen zu seiner ältesten Geschichte*, I: *Typen*, 2nd ed., Liturgiewissenschaftliche Quellen und Forschungen 28 (Münster).

Kleist, A.J., ed. (2007a), *The Old English Homily. Precedent, Practice and Appropriation* (Turnhout).

‒ (2007b), 'Anglo-Saxon Homiliaries in Tudor and Stuart England', in Kleist (2007a), 445–92.

‒ (2007c), 'Appendix: Anglo-Saxon Homiliaries as Designated by Ker', in Kleist (2007a), 493–506.

‒ (2009), 'Assembling Ælfric: Reconstructing the Rationale behind Eleventh- and Twelfth-Century Compilations', in Magennis‒Swan (2009), 369–98.

Klibansky, R. and F. Regen (1993), *Die Handschriften der philosophischen Werke des Apuleius. Ein Beitrag zur Überlieferungsgeschichte* (Göttingen).

Klinck, A.L. (1992), *The Old English Elegies. A Critical Edition and Genre Study* (Montreal).

Klingner, F., ed. (1950), *Q. Horati Flacci Opera*, 2nd ed. (Leipzig).

Klotz, A., rev. T.C. Klinnert, eds. (1902/1973), *P. Papini Stati Thebais* (Leipzig).

Kluge, F. (1885a), 'Angelsächsische Glossen', *Anglia* 8: 448–52.

‒ (1885b), 'Angelsächsische Excerpte aus Byrhtferths Handboc oder Enchiridion', *Anglia* 8: 298–337.

‒ (1885c), 'Zu altenglischen Dichtungen, 2. Nochmals der *Seefahrer*; 3. Zum *Phönix*', *EStn* 8: 472–9.

‒ (1897), *Angelsächsisches Lesebuch*, 2nd ed. (Halle).

‒ (1901), 'Geschichte der englischen Sprache', in Paul (1891–1905), vol. I, 2nd rev. ed. (1901), 926–1151.

Knappe, G. (1996), *Traditionen der klassischen Rhetorik im angelsächsischen England*, Anglistische Forschungen 236 (Heidelberg).

‒ (1998), 'Classical Rhetoric in Anglo-Saxon England', *ASE* 27: 5–29.

‒ ed. (2005), *Englische Sprachwissenschaft und Mediävistik: Standpunkte – Perspektiven – Neue Wege*, University of Bamberg Studies in English Linguistics 48 (Frankfurt am Main).

Knaus, H. (1979), *Das Bistum Würzburg*, MBKDS IV/ii (Munich), 869–1020.

Knowles, D., ed. (1951), *The Monastic Constitutions of Lanfranc* (Edinburgh).

‒ (1963), *The Monastic Order in England: A History of its Development from the Times of St Dunstan to the Fourth Lateran Council, 940–1216*, 2nd ed. (Cambridge).

– et al., eds. (2001), *The Heads of Religious Houses, England and Wales, 940–1216*, 2nd ed. (Cambridge).

– ed., rev. C.N.L. Brooke (2002), *The Monastic Constitutions of Lanfranc* (Oxford).

Kockelkorn, R. (2000), *Evangeliorum quattuor codex Petropolitanus (Lat. F. v. I N 8): Das hiberno-sächsische Evangeliar in der Russischen Nationalbibliothek von Sankt Petersburg* (Luxembourg).

Köhler, W., ed. (1930–60), *Die karolingischen Miniaturen*, Denkmäler der Deutschen Kunst I–III, 3 vols. of *Text* and *Tafeln* (Berlin).

– (1952), 'An Illustrated Evangelistary of the Ada School and its Model', *JWCI* 15: 48–66.

– and F. Mütherich, eds. (1971–99), *Die karolingischen Miniaturen*, Denkmäler der Deutschen Kunst IV–VII, 4 vols. in 6 of *Text* and *Tafeln* (Berlin).

– (1972), *Buchmalerei des frühen Mittelalters. Fragmente und Entwürfe aus dem Nachlass*, ed. E. Kitzinger and F. Mütherich (Munich).

Kölbing, E. (1876), 'Zur Béowulf-Handschrift', *ASNSL* 56: 91–118.

Köllner, H. and C. Jakobi-Mirwald (1976–93), *Die illuminierten Handschriften der Hessischen Landesbibliothek Fulda* (Stuttgart).

Kooper, E., ed. (2002), *The Medieval Chronicle*, II: *Proceedings of the 2nd International Conference on the Medieval Chronicle, Driebergen/Utrecht, 16–21 July 1999* (Amsterdam).

Korhammer, M. (1973), 'The Origin of the Bosworth Psalter', *ASE* 2: 173–87.

– ed. (1976), *Die monastischen Cantica im Mittelalter und ihre altenglischen Interlinearversionen: Studien und Textausgabe*, TUEPh 6 (Munich).

– (1980), 'Mittelalterliche Konstruktionshilfen und altenglische Wortstellung', *Scriptorium* 34: 18–58.

– ed. (1992), *Words, Texts and Manuscripts: Studies in Anglo-Saxon Culture presented to Helmut Gneuss on the Occasion of his Sixty-Fifth Birthday* (Cambridge).

Kornexl, L., ed. (1993), *Die Regularis Concordia und ihre altenglische Interlinearversion*, TUEPh 17 (Munich).

– and U. Lenker, eds. (2003), *Bookmarks from the Past. Studies in Early English Language and Literature in Honour of Helmut Gneuss*, TUEPh 30 (Frankfurt am Main).

Kortekaas, G.A.A. (1988), 'The Transmission of the Text of Pseudo-Methodius in cod. Paris. lat. 13348', *Revue d'histoire des textes* 18: 63–79.

Koslin, D. (2006), 'Under the Influence: Copying the 'Revelaciones' of St. Birgitta of Sweden', in L'Engle — Guest (2006), 415–27.

Kottje, R. (1980), *Die Bussbücher Halitgars von Cambrai und des Hrabanus Maurus* (Berlin).

– (1987),'Der *Liber ex lege Moysis*', in *Irland und die Christenheit*, ed. P. Ní Chatháin and M. Richter (Stuttgart, 1987), 59–69.

– L. Körntgen and U. Spengler-Reffgen, eds. (1994), *Paenitentialia Minora Franciae et Italiae saeculi VIII–IX*, CCSL 156 (Turnhout).

Kotzor, G. (1974), 'St Patrick in the Old English Martyrology: On a Lost Leaf of MS CCCC 196', *N&Q* 219: 86–7.

– ed. (1981), *Das altenglische Martyrologium*, Bayerische Akademie der Wissenschaften, phil.-hist. Klasse, Abhandlungen, N.F., vol. 88, pts. 1–2 (Munich).

Krämer, S. and M. Bernhard, eds. (1988), *Scire Litteras: Forschungen zum mittelalterlichen Geistesleben*, Bayerische Akademie der Wissenschaften, phil.-hist. Klasse, Abhandlungen, N.F., vol. 99 (Munich).

– (1989–90), *Handschriftenerbe des deutschen Mittelalters*, 3 vols., MBKDS Ergänzungsband 1 (Munich).

Krapp, G.P., ed. (1931), *The Junius Manuscript*, ASPR 1 (New York).

– ed. (1932a), *The Vercelli Book*, ASPR 2 (New York).

– ed. (1932b), *The Paris Psalter and the Meters of Boethius*, ASPR 5 (New York).

– and E.V.K. Dobbie, eds. (1936), *The Exeter Book*, ASPR 3 (New York).

Kresten, O. and F. Lackner, eds. (2008), *Régionalisme et internationalisme: Problèmes de paléographie et de codicologie du moyen âge. Actes du XVe Colloque du Comité international de paléographie latine (Vienne, 13–17 Septembre 2005)*, Veröffentlichungen der Kommission für Schrift- und Buchwesen des Mittelalters IV/v (Vienna).

Krinsky, C.H. (1967), 'Seventy-Eight Vitruvius Manuscripts', *JWCI* 30: 36–70.

Kristeller, P.O., F.E. Cranz, et al., eds. (1960–), *Catalogus Translationum et Commentariorum: Medieval and Renaissance Latin Translations and Commentaries* (Washington; in progress).

– (1993), *Latin Manuscript Books before 1600: A List of the Printed Catalogues and Unpublished Inventories of Extant Collections*, 4th ed. rev. S. Krämer, MGH Hilfsmittel 13 (Munich), with *Ergänzungsband 2006* by S. Krämer and B.C. Arensmann, MGH Hilfsmittel 23 (Hannover, 2007).

Kristensson, G. (1981), 'The Origins of "Ancrene Wisse"', *SN* 53: 371–6.

Krohn, F., ed. (1912), *Vitruvii De architectura libri decem* (Leipzig).

Kruckenberg, L. (1997), 'The Sequence from 1050 to 1150: A Study of a Genre in Change' (unpubl. PhD dissertation, University of Iowa).

Krüger, A. (2007), *Litanei-Handschriften der Karolingerzeit*, MGH Hilfsmittel 24 (Hannover).

Krusch, B. and W. Levison, eds. (1910), *Passiones vitaeque sanctorum aevi Merovingici et antiquiorum aliquot*, MGH, SS rer. Meroving. 5 (Hannover).

– and W. Levison, eds. (1913), *Passiones vitaeque sanctorum aevi Merovingici et antiquiorum aliquot*, MGH, SS rer. Meroving. 6 (Hannover).

– and W. Levison, eds. (1919–20), *Passiones vitaeque sanctorum aevi Merovingici et antiquiorum aliquot*, MGH, SS rer. Meroving. 7 (Hannover).

Kuhn, S. M. (1939), 'The Dialect of the Corpus Glossary', *PMLA* 54: 1–19.

– (1943), 'The *Vespasian Psalter* and the Old English Charter Hands', *Speculum* 18: 458–83.

– (1945), 'E and Æ in Farman's Mercian Glosses', *PMLA* 60: 631–69.

– (1948), 'From Canterbury to Lichfield', *Speculum* 23: 591–629.

– (1957), 'Some Early Mercian Manuscripts', *RES* n.s. 8: 355–74.

– ed. (1965), *The Vespasian Psalter* (Ann Arbor, MI).

– (1985), 'On the Originality of the *Vespasian Psalter* Gloss', *ES* 66: 1–6.

Kunze, G. (1947), *Die gottesdienstliche Schriftlesung. Teil I: Stand und Aufgaben der Perikopenforschung* (Göttingen).

Kuypers, A.B., ed. (1902), *The Prayer Book of Aedeluald the Bishop, Commonly Called the Book of Cerne* (Cambridge).

Lachlan Mackenzie, J., ed. (1989), *In Other Words: Transcultural Studies in Philology, Translation and Lexicography Presented to Hans Heinrich Meier on the Occasion of his Sixty-fifth Birthday* (Dordrecht).

Ladd, C.A. (1960), 'The "Rubens" Manuscript and Archbishop Ælfric's Vocabulary', *RES* n.s. 11: 353–64.

Laing, M. (1993), *Catalogue of Sources for a Linguistic Atlas of Early Medieval English* (Cambridge).

– and A. McIntosh (1995), 'Cambridge Trinity College, MS 335: Its Texts and their Transmission', in Beadle (1995), 14–52.

Laistner, M.L.W., ed. (1923), 'Notes on Greek from the Lectures of a Ninth-Century Monastic Teacher', *BJRL* 7: 421–56.

– (1924), 'The Revival of Greek in Western Europe in the Carolingian Age', *History* n.s. 9: 177–87.

– (1925), 'Martianus and his Commentators', *BJRL* 9: 130.

– (1935), 'The Library of the Venerable Bede', in A.H. Thompson (1935), 237–66.

– ed. (1939), *Bedae Venerabilis Expositio Actuum Apostolorum et Retractatio*, Mediaeval Academy of America Publications 35 (Cambridge, MA) [repr. CCSL 121 (1983) 1–163].

– and H.H. King (1943), *A Handlist of Bede Manuscripts* (Ithaca, NY).

– (1947), 'Antiochene Exegesis in Western Europe during the Middle Ages', *Harvard Theological Review* 40: 19–31.

Lake, S. (2003), 'Knowledge of the Writings of John Cassian in early Anglo-Saxon England', *ASE* 32: 27–41.

Lambert, B., ed. (1969–72), *Bibliotheca Hieronymiana Manuscripta. La tradition manuscrite des oeuvres de Saint Jérôme*. Instrumenta Patristica 4, 7 vols. (Steenbrugge).

Lang, C., ed. (1885), *Flavi Vegeti Renati Epitoma Rei Militaris*, 2nd ed. (Leipzig).

Langefeld, B. (1986), 'A Third Old English Translation of Part of Gregory's *Dialogues*, this Time Embedded in the Rule of Chrodegang', *ASE* 15: 197–204.

– ed. (2003), *The Old English Version of the Enlarged Rule of Chrodegang; Edited together with the Latin Text and an English Translation*, TUEPh 26 (Frankfurt am Main).

Lapidge, M. (1972), 'Three Latin Poems from Æthelwold's School at Winchester', *ASE* 1: 85–137 [repr. Lapidge (1993a), 225–77].

– (1975a), 'The Hermeneutic Style in Tenth-Century Anglo-Latin Literature', *ASE* 4: 67–111 [repr. Lapidge (1993a), 105–49].

– (1975b), 'Some Remnants of Bede's Lost *Liber epigrammatum*', *EHR* 90: 798–820 [repr. Lapidge (1996b), 357–79].

– (1977a), 'L'influence stylistique de la poésie de Jean Scot', in Roques (1977), 441–52.

– (1977b), 'The Authorship of the Adonic Verses *Ad Fidolium* attributed to Columbanus', *SM* 3rd ser. 18: 815–80.

– and M. Herren, trans. (1979a), *Aldhelm: The Prose Works* (Cambridge).

– (1979b), 'Byrhtferth and the *Vita S. Ecgwini*', *MS* 41: 331–53 [repr. Lapidge (1993a), 293–315].

– (1980a), 'The Revival of Latin Learning in Late Anglo-Saxon England', in De La Mare—Barker-Benfield (1980), 18–22.

– (1980b), 'St Dunstan's Latin Poetry', *Anglia* 98: 101–6 [repr. Lapidge (1993a), 151–6].

– (1981a), 'Some Latin Poems as Evidence for the Reign of Æthelstan', *ASE* 9: 61–98 [repr. Lapidge (1993a), 49–86].

– (1981b), 'Byrhtferth of Ramsey and the Early Sections of the *Historia Regum* attributed to Symeon of Durham', *ASE* 10: 97–122 [repr. Lapidge (1993a), 317–42].

– (1981–5), 'The Origin of CCCC 163', *TCBS* 8: 18–28.

– (1982a), 'The Study of Latin Texts in Late Anglo-Saxon England: The Evidence of Latin Glosses', in N.P. Brooks (1982) 99–140 [repr. Lapidge (1996b) 455–98].

– (1982b), 'Some Old English Sedulius Glosses from BN lat. 8092', *Anglia* 100: 1–17.

– (1983), 'Ealdred of York and MS Cotton Vitellius E.xii', *Yorkshire Archaeological Journal* 55: 11–25 [repr. Lapidge (1993a), 453–67].

– (1984), 'A Tenth-Century Metrical Calendar from Ramsey', *RB* 94: 326–69 [repr. Lapidge (1993a), 343–86].

– and D. Dumville, eds. (1984), *Gildas: New Approaches* (Woodbridge).

– and H. Gneuss, eds. (1985a), *Learning and Literature in Anglo-Saxon England. Studies presented to Peter Clemoes on the Occasion of his Sixty-Fifth Birthday* (Cambridge).

- (1985b), 'Surviving Booklists from Anglo-Saxon England', in Lapidge—
  Gneuss (1985a), 33–89 [repr. Lapidge (1994b)].
- (1986a), 'Litanies of the Saints in Anglo-Saxon Manuscripts: A Preliminary
  List', *Scriptorium* 40: 264–77.
- (1986b), 'The School of Theodore and Hadrian', *ASE* 15: 45–72 [repr. Lapidge
  (1996b) 141–68].
- (1986c), 'Latin Learning in Dark Age Wales: Some Prolegomena', in
  Proceedings of the Seventh International Congress of Celtic Studies, ed. D.E.
  Evans, J.G. Griffith and E.M. Jope (Oxford), 91–107.
- (1987), 'The Lost *Passio metrica S. Dionysii* by Hilduin of Saint-Denis', *MLJ*
  22: 56–79.
- (1988a), 'A Frankish Scholar in Tenth-Century England: Frithegod of
  Canterbury / Fredegaud of Brioude', *ASE* 17: 45–65 [repr. Lapidge (1993a),
  157–81].
- (1988b), 'Æthelwold and the *Vita S. Eustachii*', in Krämer—Bernhard (1988),
  255–65 [repr. Lapidge (1993a), 213–23].
- (1988c), 'Æthelwold as Scholar and Teacher', in Yorke (1988) 89–117 [repr.
  Lapidge (1993a) 183–211].
- (1988–9), 'An Isidorian Epitome from Early Anglo-Saxon England',
  Romanobarbarica 10: 443–83 [repr. Lapidge (1996b), 183–223]
- (1989–90), 'Tenth-Century Anglo-Latin Verse Hagiography', *MLJ* 24–25:
  249–60.
- (1990), 'Aediluulf and the School of York', in Lehner (1990), 161–78 [repr.
  Lapidge (1996b), 381–98].
- ed. (1991a), *Anglo-Saxon Litanies of the Saints*, HBS 106 (London).
- and M. Winterbottom, eds. (1991b), *Wulfstan of Winchester: The Life of
  St Æthelwold* (Oxford, 1991).
- (1991c), 'Schools, Learning and Literature in Tenth-Century England',
  Settimane 38: 951–98 [repr. Lapidge (1993a) 1–48].
- (1991d), 'The Saintly Life in Anglo-Saxon England', in *The Cambridge
  Companion to Old English Literature*, ed. M. Godden and M. Lapidge
  (Cambridge, 1991), 243–63.
- (1992a), 'Abbot Germanus, Winchcombe, Ramsey and the Cambridge Psalter',
  in Korhammer (1992), 99–130 [repr. Lapidge (1993a) 387–417].
- (1992b), 'Israel the Grammarian in Anglo-Saxon England', in Westra (1992),
  97–114 [repr. Lapidge (1993a) 87–104].
- (1992c), 'Old English Glossography: The Latin Context', in Derolez (1992),
  45–57 [repr. Lapidge (1996b), 169–81].
- (1992d), 'Artistic and Literary Patronage in Anglo-Saxon England', *Settimane*
  39: 137–91 [repr. Lapidge (1996b) 37–91].

- (1992e), 'B. and the *Vita S. Dunstani*', in Ramsay et al. (1992), 247–59 [repr. Lapidge (1993a) 293–315].
- (1993a), *Anglo-Latin Literature 900–1066* (London).
- (1993b), 'The Edition, Emendation and Reconstruction of Anglo-Saxon Texts', in *The Politics of Editing Medieval Texts*, ed. R. Frank (New York, 1993), 131–57.
- (1994a), 'Autographs of Insular Latin Authors of the Early Middle Ages', in Chiesa—Pinelli (1994), 103–36.
- (1994b), 'Surviving Booklists from Anglo-Saxon England', rev. ed. in Richards (1994), 87–169 [orig. publ. in Lapidge—Gneuss (1985a) 33–89].
- ed. (1995a), *Archbishop Theodore: Commemorative Studies on his Life and Influence*, CSASE 11 (Cambridge).
- (1995b), 'Theodore and Anglo-Latin Octosyllabic Verse', in Lapidge (1995a), 260–80 [repr. Lapidge (1996b) 225–45].
- (1995c), 'Prolegomena to an Edition of Bede's Metrical *Vita Sancti Cuthberti*', *Filologia Mediolatina* 2: 127–63.
- (1996a), 'Byrhtferth and Oswald', in Brooks—Cubitt (1996), 64–83.
- (1996b), *Anglo-Latin Literature 600–899* (London).
- (1996c), 'Latin Learning in Ninth-Century England', in Lapidge (1996b), 409–54.
- and P.S. Baker (1997), 'More Acrostic Verse by Abbo of Fleury', *JMLat* 7: 1–27.
- (1998), 'Byrhtferth at Work', in Baker—Howe (1998), 25–44.
- J. Blair, S. Keynes and D. Scragg, eds. (1999), *The Blackwell Encyclopaedia of Anglo-Saxon England* (Oxford).
- (2000a), 'The Archetype of *Beowulf*', *ASE* 29: 5–41.
- (2000b), 'A Metrical *Vita S. Iudoci* from Tenth-Century Winchester', *JMLat* 10: 255–306.
- and R.C. Love (2001), 'The Latin Hagiography of England and Wales (600–1550)', in G. Philippart (2001), 203–325.
- and J. Mann (2002), 'Reconstructing the Anglo-Latin Aesop: The Literary Tradition of the *Hexametrical Romulus*', in Herren et al. (2002) I, 1–33.
- (2003a), *The Cult of St Swithun*, Winchester Studies 4.ii (Oxford).
- (2003b), 'Cynewulf and the *Passio S. Iulianae*', in *Unlocking the Wordhord. Anglo-Saxon Studies in Memory of Edward B. Irving*, ed. M.C. Amodio and K. O'Brien O'Keeffe (Toronto, 2003), 147–71.
- (2004a), 'Frithegodus Cantuariensis diac.', in Chiesa—Castaldi (2004), 134–45.
- (2004b), 'Wulfstanus Wintoniensis Mon.', in Chiesa—Castaldi (2004), 439–47.
- (2005a), 'Acca of Hexham and the Origin of the *Old English Martyrology*', *AB* 123: 29–78.
- A. Crépin, P. Monat and P. Robin, eds. (2005b), *Bède le Vénérable, Histoire ecclésiastique du peuple anglais*, 3 vols., SChr 489–91 (Paris).

- (2006), *The Anglo-Saxon Library* (Oxford).
- (2007), 'The Career of Aldhelm', *ASE* 36: 15–69.
- (2008a), 'Beda Venerabilis', in Chiesa—Castaldi (2008), 44–137.
- (2008b), 'The Latin Exemplar of the Old English *Bede*', in Lendinara (2008), 235–46.
- ed. (2008–10), *Beda: Storia degli Inglesi*, 2 vols. (Milan).
- ed. (2009), *Byrhtferth of Ramsey: The Lives of St Oswald and St Ecgwine* (Oxford).
- (2010a), 'Aldhelm and the "Épinal-Erfurt Glossary"', in *Aldhelm and Sherborne: Essays to Celebrate the Founding of the Bishopric*, ed. K. Barker and N. Brooks (Oxford, 2010), 129–63.
- (2010b), 'Colloquial Latin in the Insular Latin Scholastic *colloquia*', in *Colloquial and Literary Latin*, ed. E. Dickey and A. Chahoud (Cambridge), 406–18.
- (2012a), 'The Library of Byrhtferth', in R. Gameson (2012), 685–91.
- (2012b), 'Aldhelmus Malmesberiensis Abb. et Scireburnensis ep.', in Chiesa—Castaldi (2012), 14–38.
- (2012c), 'Hilduinus Sancti Dionysii Parisiensis Abb.', in Chiesa—Castaldi (2012), 315–48.
Larpi, L. (2008), 'Gildas Sapiens', in Chiesa—Castaldi (2008), 175–86.
- (2012), *Prolegomena to a New Edition of Gildas Sapiens 'De excidio Britanniae'* (Florence).
Lauer, P. et al. (1939—), *Bibliothèque Nationale. Catalogue géneral des manuscrits latins* (Paris [in progress]).
Laurent, C. and H. Davis, eds. (1994), *Irlande et Bretagne, vingt siècles d'histoire; actes du colloque de Rennes, 29–31 mars 1993* (Rennes).
Laureys, M. and D. Verhelst (1988), 'Pseudo-Methodius, Revelationes: Textgeschichte und kritische Edition. Ein Leuven-Groninger Forschungsprojekt', in *The Use and Abuse of Eschatology in the Middle Ages*, ed. W. Verbeke, D. Verhelst and A. Welkenhuysen, Mediaevalia Lovaniensia, Studia 15 (Leuven, 1988), 112–36.
Lavarenne, M., ed. (1943–51), *Prudence*, 4 vols. (Paris).
Law, V. (1982), *The Insular Latin Grammarians* (Woodbridge).
- (1997), *Grammar and Grammarians in the Early Middle Ages* (London).
Lawrence, A. (1977), 'The Canterbury Manuscripts of 1060–90' (unpublished MA thesis, University of London).
- (1982), 'Manuscripts of Early Anglo-Norman Canterbury', in *Medieval Art and Architecture of Canterbury before 1220*, British Archaeological Conference Transactions 5: 101–11.
- (1994), 'The Artistic Influence of Durham Manuscripts', in Rollason et al. (1994), 451–69.

Lawrence-Mathers, A. (2003), *Manuscripts in Northumbria in the Eleventh and Twelfth Centuries* (Woodbridge).

Lawson, C.M., ed. (1989), *S. Isidori Episcopi Hispalensis De ecclesiasticis officiis*, CCSL 113 (Turnhout).

Lazzari, L. (1998–9), 'Il lessico medico anglosassone: descrizione e classificazione delle glosse sul f. 4 del MS London, B.L. Ad. 32246', *Quaderni della Sezione di glottologia e linguistica* [U. of Chieti] 10–11: 159–93.

– (2003), 'Il glossario latino-inglese antico nel manoscritto di Anversa e Londra ed il "Glossario" di Ælfric: dipendenza diretta o derivazione comune?', *Linguistica e filologia* 16: 159–90.

– (2004), 'I *portenta* dalle *Etymologiae* di Isidoro al glossario latino-inglese antico di Anversa e Londra', in *Fabelwesen, mostri e portenti nell'immaginario occidentale: Medioevo germanico e altro* (Alessandria, 2004), 199–236.

– (2011), 'Learning Tools and Learned Lexicographers: The Antwerp-London and the Junius 71 Latin – Old English Glossaries', in Lendinara et al. (2011), 179–207.

Leake, J.A. (1962), 'Middle English Glosses in the *Beowulf*-Codex', *MLQ* 23: 229–32.

Lebecq, S., M. Perrin and O. Szerwiniack, eds. (2005), *Bède le Vénérable entre tradition et postérité / The Venerable Bede. Tradition and Posterity,* Histoire de l'Europe du nord-Ouest 34 (Lille).

Le Boeuffle, A., ed. (1983), *Hygin, L'Astronomie* (Paris).

Le Bourdellès, H. (1993), 'Vie de S. Josse avec commentaire historique et spiri-tuel', *SM* 3rd ser. 34: 861–958.

– (1995), 'Les Bretons à Montreuil-sur-Mer vers 920. Leur création culturelle', *Bulletin de la Société nationale des antiquaires de France* (1995), 44–52.

Lee, C. (2011), 'Body Talks: Disease and Disability in Anglo-Saxon England', in Roberts—Webster (2011), 145–64.

Lee, S.D. (1991), 'Two Fragments from Cotton MS Otho B. x', *BLJ* 17: 83–7.

– (2000), 'Oxford, Bodleian Library, MS Laud Misc. 381: William L'Isle, Ælfric, and the *Ancrene Wisse*', in Graham (2000b), 207–42.

Lees, C.A. (1983), 'The "Sunday Letter" and the "Sunday Lists"', *ASE* 14: 129–51.

– ed. (1986), 'Theme and Echo in an Anonymous Old English Homily for Easter', *Traditio* 42: 115–42.

– ed. (1988), 'The Blickling Palm Sunday Homily and its Revised Version', *LSE* 19: 1–30.

Lega-Weekes, E. (1916–17), 'An Ancient Liturgical MS Discovered in Exeter Cathedral Library', *Devon and Cornwall Notes and Queries* 9: 33–5.

Legg, J.W., ed. (1891–7), *Missale ad usum Ecclesie Westmonasteriensis*, 3 vols., HBS 1, 5, and 12 (London).

– ed. (1900), *Three Coronation Orders*, HBS 19 (London).

Lehmann, P. (1917), 'Cassiodorstudien [Teil 4]', *Philologus* 74: 351–83.

– (1918), *Die Bistümer Konstanz und Chur*, MBKDS 1 (Munich).

– (1925), *Fuldaer Studien*, Sitzungsberichte der Bayerischen Akademie der Wissenschaften, phil.-hist. Klasse, Jahrgang 1925, Abteilung 3 (Munich).

– (1933), *Mitteilungen aus Handschriften* IV, Sitzungsberichte der Bayerischen Akademie der Wissenschaften, phil.-hist. Klasse, Jahrgang 1933, Abteilung 9 (Munich).

– (1938), *Mitteilungen aus Handschriften* V, Sitzungsberichte der Bayerischen Akademie der Wissenschaften, phil.-hist. Klasse, Jahrgang 1938, Abteilung 4 (Munich).

Lehner, A., ed. (1987), *Florilegia: Florilegium Frisingensis (Clm 6433), Testimonia divinae scripturae (et patrum)*, CCSL 108D (Turnhout).

– and W. Berschin, eds. (1990), *Lateinische Kultur im VIII. Jahrhundert. Traube-Gedenkschrift* (St. Ottilien).

Leinbaugh, T. (1980), 'The Liturgical Homilies in Ælfric's *Lives of Saints*' (unpubl. PhD dissertation, Harvard Univ.).

– (1986), 'A Damaged Passage in Ælfric's *De Creatore et Creatura*: Methods of Recovery', *Anglia* 104: 104–14.

Leitschuh, F. and H. Fischer (1887–1912), *Katalog der Handschriften der Königlichen Bibliothek zu Bamberg*, 3 vols. (Leipzig).

Lemoine, L. and B. Merdrignac, eds. (2004a), *Corona Monastica. Mélanges offerts au père Marc Simon*, Britannica Monastica 8 (Rennes).

– (2004b): 'Autour du scriptorium de Landévennec', in Lemoine – Merdrignac (2004a), 183–96.

Lendinara, P. (1983), 'Il Colloquio di Ælfric e il colloquio di Ælfric Bata', in *feor and neah. Scritti di filologia germanica in memoria di Augusto Scaffidi Abbate*, ed. P. Lendinara and L. Melazzo (Palermo, 1983), 173–249.

– (1986), 'The Third Book of the *Bella Parisiacae Urbis* by Abbo of Saint-Germain-des-Prés and its Old English Gloss', *ASE* 15: 73–91.

– (1988–9), 'Il glossario del MS Oxford, Bodleian Library, Bodley 163', in D'Aronco (1988-89), 485–516.

– (1990), 'The Abbo Glossary in London, British Library, Cotton Domitian i', *ASE* 19: 133–49.

– (1992), 'Glosses and Glossaries: The Glossator's Choice', in Derolez (1992), 207–43.

– (1993), 'An Old English Gloss to the *Scholica Graecarum Glossarum*', *ANQ* n.s. 6: 175–80.

– (1996), 'L'attività glossatoria del periodo anglosassone', in Hamesse (1996), 615–55.

– (1999a), *Anglo-Saxon Glosses and Glossaries* (Aldershot).

- (1999b), 'Glossarial Activity in the Anglo-Saxon Period (with an Edition of the Glossary to Juvenal, *Satires* IV–VIII in London, British Library, Harley 3826)', in Lendinara (1999a), 289–328 [English translation of Lendinara (1996)]
- (2001a), 'The Glossaries in London, BL, Cotton Cleopatra A.iii', in Bergmann (2001), 189–216.
- (2001b), 'Alcuino e il *De die iudicii*', *Pan* 18–19: 303–24.
- (2003), 'The *Versus Sibyllae de die iudicii* in Anglo-Saxon England', in Powell—Scragg (2003), 85–101.
- (2005), 'Contextualized Lexicography', in O'Brien O'Keeffe—Orchard (2005) II, 108–31.
- L. Lazzari and M.A. d'Aronco, eds. (2007), *Form and Content of Instruction in Anglo-Saxon England in the Light of Contemporary Manuscript Evidence* (Turnhout).
- (2007a), 'Instructional Manuscripts in England: The Tenth- and Eleventh-Century Codices and the early Norman Ones', in Lendinara et al. (2007), 59–113.
- (2007b), 'The *Versus de die iudicii*: Its Circulation and Use as a School Text in late Anglo-Saxon England', in Bremmer—Dekker (2007), 175–212.
- ed. (2008), *... un tuo serto di fiori in man recando. Scritti in onore di Maria Amalia D'Aronco* II (Udine).
- (2010), 'A Storehouse of Learned Vocabulary: The Abbo Glossaries in Anglo-Saxon England', in Bremmer—Dekker (2010), 101–32.
- L. Lazzari and C. Di Sciacca, eds. (2011), *Rethinking and Recontextualizing Glosses. New Perspectives in the Study of Late Anglo-Saxon Glossography* (Porto).
- (2011a), 'Glossing Abbo in Latin and the Vernacular', in Lendinara et al. (2011), 475–508.

L'Engle, S. and G.B. Guest, eds. (2006), *Tributes to Jonathan J.G. Alexander: The Making and Meaning of Illuminated Medieval & Renaissance Manuscripts, Art & Architecture* (Turnhout).

Lenker, U. (1997), *Die westsächsische Evangelienversion und die Perikopenordnungen im angelsächsischen England*, TUEPh 20 (Munich).
- (1999), 'The *West Saxon Gospels* and the Gospel Lectionary in Anglo-Saxon England: Manuscript Evidence and Liturgical Practice', *ASE* 28: 141–78.

Lenz, F.W., ed. (1956), *P. Ovidii Nasonis Halieutica, Fragmenta, Nux*, 2nd ed. (Turin).

Leonardi, C. (1959), 'I codici di Marziano Capella (I)', *Aevum* 33: 443–89.
- (1960), 'I codici di Marziano Capella (II)', *Aevum* 34: 1–99, 411–542.

Leonhardi, G. (1905), *Kleinere angelsächsische Denkmäler*, Bibliothek der angelsächsischen Prosa 6 (Hamburg).

Leroquais, V. (1924), *Les sacramentaires et les missels manuscrits des bibliothèques publiques de France*, 4 vols. (Paris).

– (1937), *Les pontificaux manuscrits des bibliothèques publiques de France*, 3 vols. (Paris).

– (1940–1), *Les psautiers manuscrits latins des bibliothèques publiques de France*, 3 vols. (Mâcon).

Les manuscrits à peintures en France du VIIe au XIIe siècle, 2nd ed. (Paris, 1943) [exhibition catalogue].

Leslie, R.F., ed. (1985), *The Wanderer*, 2nd ed. (Exeter).

– ed. (1988), *Three Old English Elegies*, rev. ed. (Exeter).

Lester, G.A. (1973), 'A Possible Early Occurrence of Moses with Horns in the Benedictional of St Æthelwold', *Scriptorium* 27: 30–3.

Levison, W., ed. (1913), 'Vita Wilfridi I episcopi Eboracensis', in Krusch– Levison (1913), 193–263.

– (1919–20), 'Conspectus codicum hagiographicorum', in Krusch–Levison (1919–20), 529–706.

– (1927), 'Das Werden der Ursula-Legende', *Bonner Jahrbücher* 132: 1–164.

– (1946), *England and the Continent in the Eighth Century* (Oxford).

– (1948), *Aus rheinischer und fränkischer Frühzeit. Ausgewählte Aufsätze von Wilhelm Levison* (Düsseldorf).

Lewis, C.P. (2007), 'Welsh Territories and Welsh Identities in Late Anglo-Saxon England', in Higham (2007), 130–43.

Lewis, S. (1980), 'Sacred Calligraphy: The Chi-Rho Page in the Book of Kells', *Traditio* 36: 139–59.

Liebermann, F. (1879), *Ungedruckte anglo-normannische Geschichtsquellen* (Strassburg).

– (1894), 'Aus Ælfrics Grammatik und Glossar', *ASNSL* 92: 413–15.

– (1889), *Die Heiligen Englands* (Hannover).

– (1900), 'Matrosenstellung aus Landgütern der Kirche London, um 1000', *ASNSL* 104: 17–24.

– (1901), 'Lanfranc and the Anti-Pope', *EHR* 16: 328–32.

– ed. (1903–16), *Die Gesetze der Angelsachsen*, 3 vols. (Halle).

Lindelöf, U. (1890), *Die Sprache des Rituals von Durham: Ein Beitrag zur altenglischen Grammatik* (Helsingfors).

– (1901a), 'Wörterbuch zur Interlinearglosse des *Rituale Ecclesiae Dunelmensis*', *Bonner Beiträge zur Anglistik* 9: 105–220.

– (1901b), 'Die südnorthumbrische Mundart des 10. Jahrhunderts: Die Sprache der sog. Glosse Rushworth²', *Bonner Beiträge zur Anglistik* 10 (Bonn).

– (1901c), *Die Handschrift Junius 27 der Bodleiana Bibliotheca*, Mémoires de la Société neophilologique à Helsingfors 3 (Helsingfors [Helsinki]).

- (1904), *Studien zu altenglischen Psalterglossen*, Bonner Beiträge zur Anglistik 13 (Bonn).
- ed. (1909), 'Die altenglischen Glossen im Bosworth-Psalter (Brit. Mus. MS. Addit. 37517)', *Mémoires de la Société néophilologique de Helsingfors* 5: 139–231.
- ed. (1909–14), *Der Lambeth-Psalter*, 2 vols., Acta Societatis Scientiarum Fennicae 35.1 and 43.3 (Helsingfors [Helsinki]).
- ed. (1927), *Rituale Ecclesiae Dunelmensis. The Durham Collectar*, Publications of the Surtees Society 140 (Durham).
Lindsay, W.M., ed. (1904–5), *T. Macci Plauti Comoediae*, 2 vols. (Oxford).
- (1910), *Early Irish Minuscule Script*, St Andrews University Publications 6 (Oxford).
- ed. (1911), *Isidori Hispalensis Episcopi Etymologiarum sive Originum libri XX* (Oxford).
- (1912a), *Early Welsh Script*, St. Andrews University Publications 10 (Oxford).
- (1912b), 'The Abbreviation Symbols of *ergo*, *igitur*', *Zentralblatt für Bibliothekswesen* 29.2: 56–64.
- (1915), *Notae Latinae: An Account of Abbreviations in Latin Manuscripts of the Early Minuscule Period (c. 700–850)* (Cambridge).
- (1917), 'The St Gall Glossary', *American Journal of Philology* 38: 349–69.
- ed. (1921a), *The Corpus Glossary* (Cambridge).
- (1921b), *The Corpus, Épinal, Erfurt and Leyden Glossaries*, Publications of the Philological Society 8 (Oxford).
Lionarons, J.T., ed. (2004a), *Old English Literature in its Manuscript Context* (Morgantown, WV).
- (2004b), 'Textual Appropriation and Scribal (Re)Performance in a Composite Homily: The Case for a New Edition of Wulfstan's *De Temporibus Antichristi*', in Lionarons (2004a), 67–94.
- (2004c), 'Napier Homily L: Wulfstan's Eschatology at the Close of his Career', in Townend (2004), 413–28.
Liuzza, R.M. (1988), 'The Yale Fragments of the West Saxon Gospels', *ASE* 17: 67–82.
- ed. (1994–2000), *The Old English Version of the Gospels*, 2 vols., EETS o.s. 304, 314 (Oxford).
- (1998), 'Who Read the Gospels in Old English?', in Baker—Howe (1998), 3–24.
- (2000), 'Scribal Habit: The Evidence of the Old English Gospels', in Swan—Treharne (2000a), 143–65.
- (2001), 'Anglo-Saxon Prognostics in Context: A Survey and Handlist of Manuscripts', *ASE* 30: 181–230.

- (2005), 'The Sphere of Life and Death: Time, Medicine, and the Visual Imagination', in O'Brien O'Keeffe—Orchard (2005) II, 28–52.
- ed. (2011), *Anglo-Saxon Prognostics. An Edition and Translation of Texts from London, British Library, MS Cotton Tiberius A. iii*, AST 8 (Cambridge).

Lockett, L. (2002), 'An Integrated Re-Examination of the Dating of Oxford, Bodleian Library, Junius 11', *ASE* 31: 141–73.

Löfstedt, B. (1981), 'Miscellanea grammatica', *Rivista di cultura classica e medioevale* 23: 159–64.

Logeman, H., ed. (1888), *The Rule of S. Benet: Latin and Anglo-Saxon Interlinear Version*, EETS o.s. 90 (London).
- (1889), 'Anglo-Saxonica Minora', *Anglia* 11: 97–120.
- (1890), 'Junius's Transcript of Old English Texts', *Academy* 38 [no. 960]: 274.
- (1891), 'New Aldhelm Glosses', *Anglia* 13: 26–41.

Love, R.C., ed. (1996), *Three Eleventh-Century Anglo-Latin Saints' Lives* (Oxford).
- ed. (2004), *Goscelin of Saint-Bertin: The Hagiography of the Female Saints of Ely* (Oxford).
- (2005), 'Frithegod of Canterbury's Maundy Thursday Hymn', *ASE* 34: 219–36.
- (2007), 'Bede and John Chrysostom', *JMLat* 17: 72–86.
- (2012), 'The Library of the Venerable Bede', in R. Gameson (2012), 606–32.

Lowden, J. and A. Bovey, eds. (2007), *Under The Influence: The Concept of Influence and the Study of Illuminated Manuscripts* (Turnhout).

Lowe, E.A. (1924), 'A Hand-List of Half-Uncial Manuscripts', in *Miscellanea Francesco Ehrle. Scritti di storia e paleografia ... in occasione dell'ottantesimo natalizio dell' e.mo Cardinale Francesco Ehrle*, 6 vols., Studi e testi 37–42 (Rome) IV, 34–61.
- (1926), 'A New Manuscript Fragment of Bede's *Ecclesiastical History*', *EHR* 41: 244–6.
- (1927), 'Membra disiecta', *RB* 34: 191–2.
- (1928), 'An Eighth-Century List of Books in a Bodleian Manuscript from Würzburg and its Probable Relation to the Laudian Acts', *Speculum* 3: 3–15 [repr. Lowe (1972) I, 239–50].
- (1929), *Regula S. Benedicti. Specimina selecta e codice antiquissimo Oxoniensi* (Oxford).
- (1938), 'A Manuscript of Alcuin in the Script of Tours', in *Classical and Mediaeval Studies in Honor of Edward Kennard Rand*, ed. L.W. Jones (New York, 1938), 191–3 [repr. in Lowe (1972) I, 342–4].
- (1952), 'The Uncial Gospel Leaves attached to the Utrecht Psalter', *Art Bulletin* 34: 357–8 [repr. Lowe (1972) II, 385–8].

- (1958a), 'A Key to Bede's Scriptorium: Some Observations on the Leningrad Manuscript of the *Historia ecclesiastica gentis Anglorum*', *Scriptorium* 12: 182–90 [repr. Lowe (1972) II, 441–9].
- (1958b), 'An Autograph of the Venerable Bede?', *RB* 68: 200–2.
- (1960), *English Uncial* (Oxford).
- (1964), 'Codices rescripti: A List of the Oldest Palimpsests with Stray Observations on their Origin', *Mélanges Eugène Tisserant* V pt. ii, Studi e Testi 235 (Vatican City), 67–113.
- (1972), *Palaeographical Papers*, ed. L. Bieler, 2 vols. (Oxford).
Löwe, H., ed. (1982), *Die Iren und Europa im früheren Mittelalter* (Stuttgart).
Loyn, H.R. (1962), *Anglo-Saxon England and the Norman Conquest* (London; 2nd ed., London, 1991).
- ed. (1971), *A Wulfstan Manuscript, Containing Institutes, Laws and Homilies: British Museum, Cotton Nero A.i*, EEMF 17 (Copenhagen).
Lübke, H. (1890), 'Über verwandtschaftliche Beziehungen einiger altenglischer Glossare', *ASNSL* 44: 383–410.
Lucas, P.J. (1972), 'On the Blank Daniel-Cycle in MS Junius 11', *JWCI* 42: 207–13.
- ed. (1977), *Exodus* (Exeter; rev. ed. 1994).
- (1979a), 'MS. Hatton 42: Another Manuscript containing Old English', *N&Q* 224: 8.
- (1979b), 'On the Incomplete Ending of *Daniel* and the Addition of *Christ and Satan* to MS Junius 11', *Anglia* 97: 46–59.
- (1980), 'MS Junius 11 and Malmesbury', *Scriptorium* 34: 197–220, 35: 3–22.
- (1990), 'The Place of Judith in the Beowulf-Manuscript', *RES* n.s. 41: 463–78.
- (1995), 'The *Metrical Epilogue* to the Alfredian *Pastoral Care*: A Postscript from Junius', *ASE* 24: 43–50.
- (2006), 'Abraham Wheelock and the Presentation of Anglo-Saxon: From Manuscript to Print', in Doane—Wolf (2006), 383–439.
Luce, A.A., G.O. Simms, P. Meyer and L. Bieler, eds. (1960), *Evangeliorum quattuor Codex Durmachensis*, 2 vols. (Olten and Lausanne).
Luick, K. (1914–21), *Historische Grammatik der englischen Sprache*, I (Stuttgart).
Luiselli Fadda, A. M. (1972), '*De descensu Christi ad inferos*: una inedita omelia anglosassone', *SM* 13: 989–1011.
- ed. (1977), *Nuove omelie anglosassoni della rinascenza benedettina* (Florence).
- (1980), 'Il frammento Vaticano Reg. Lat. 497, f. 71, Dell' Orosio anglosassone', in *Filologia Germanica* 23: 7–22.
Lutz, A. (1977), 'Zur Rekonstruktion der Version G der Angelsächsischen Chronik', *Anglia* 95: 1–19.
- ed. (1981), *Die Version G der Angelsächsischen Chronik: Rekonstruktion und Edition*, TUEPh 11 (Munich).

– (1982), 'Das Studium der angelsächsischen Chronik im 16. Jahrhundert: Nowell und Joscelyn', *Anglia* 100: 301–56.

– (2000), 'The Study of the Anglo-Saxon Chronicle in the Seventeenth Century and the Establishment of Old English Studies in the Universities', in Graham (2000b), 1–82.

Lutz, C.E., ed. (1962), *Remigii Autissiodorensis Commentum in Martianum Capellam*, 2 vols. (Leiden).

– (1971), 'Martianus Capella', in Kristeller et al. (1960–) II, 367–81.

– (1973), 'A Manuscript Fragment from Bede's Monastery', *Yale University Library Gazette* 48: 135–8.

– (1975), *Essays on Manuscripts and Rare Books* (Hamden, CT).

– (1977), *Schoolmasters of the Tenth Century* (Hamden, CT).

Maassen, F. (1870), *Geschichte der Quellen und der Literatur des canonischen Rechts im Abendlande, I. Die Rechtssammlungen bis zur Mitte des 9. Jahrhunderts* (Graz).

MacCarthy, B. (1886), 'On the Stowe Missal', *Transactions of the Royal Irish Academy* 27: 135–268.

MacGregor Dawson, R. (1969), 'An Edition of Blickling Homilies' (unpubl. PhD dissertation, Oxford Univ.).

Mackay, T.W. (1976), 'Bede's Hagiographical Method: His Knowledge and Use of Paulinus of Nola', in Bonner (1976), 77–92.

MacKinney, L. (1965), *Medical Illustrations in Medieval Manuscripts* (Berkeley, CA).

MacLean, G.E. (1883–4), 'Ælfric's Anglo-Saxon Version of *Alcuini Interrogationes Sigewulfi in Genesin*', *Anglia* 6: 425–73, 7: 1–59.

MacLean, D. (1999), 'Northumbrian Vine-Scroll Ornament and the *Book of Kells*', in Hawkes–Mills (1999), 178–90.

Macray, G.D. (1862–1900), *Catalogi codicum manuscriptorum Bibliothecae Bodleianae, V: Viri munificentissimi Ricardi Rawlinson codicum classes A-D ... complectens* (Oxford).

– (1883), *Catalogi codicum manuscriptorum Bibliothecae Bodleianae, IX: Codices a Kenelm Digby anno 1634 donatos complectens* (London).

Madan, F. et al. (1895–1953), *A Summary Catalogue of Western Manuscripts in the Bodleian Library at Oxford*, 7 vols. in 8 (Oxford).

Mady, Z. (1965), 'An VIIIth Century Aldhelm Fragment in Hungary', *Acta Antiqua Academiae Scientiarum Hungaricae* 13: 441–53.

Magennis, H., ed. (1994), *The Anonymous Old English Legend of the Seven Sleepers* (Durham).

– (1996), 'Ælfric and the Legend of the Seven Sleepers', in Szarmach (1996), 317–31.

– ed. (2002), *The Old English Life of St Mary of Egypt: An Edition of the Old English Text with Modern English Parallel-Text Translation* (Exeter).

– and J. Wilcox, eds. (2006), *The Power of Words. Anglo-Saxon Studies presented to Donald G. Scragg on his Seventieth Birthday* (Morgantown, WV).

– and M. Swan, eds. (2009), *A Companion to Ælfric* (Leiden).

Magoun, F.P. (1940), 'An English Pilgrim-Diary of the Year 990', *MS* 2: 231–52.

– (1949), 'King Alfred's Letter on Educational Policy according to the Cambridge Manuscripts', *MS* 11: 113–22.

Magrini, S. (2001), '"Per difetto del legatore …": Storia delle rilegature della Bibbia Amiatina in Laurenziana', *Quinio* 3: 137–67.

Maion, D. (2007), 'The Fortune of the so-called *Practica Petrocelli Salernitani* in England: New Evidence and Some Considerations', in Lendinara et al. (2007), 495–512.

Makothakat, J.M. (1972), 'The Bosworth Psalter: A Critical Edition' (unpubl. PhD dissertation, University of Ottawa).

Mallon, J. et al. (1939), *L'écriture latine* (Paris).

Malmberg, L., ed. (1982), *Resignation*, rev. ed. (Durham).

Malone, K., ed. (1929), *Studies in Philology: A Miscellany in Honor of Frederick Klaeber* (Minneapolis, MN).

– (1941–2), 'Thorkelin's Transcripts of *Beowulf*', *SN* 14: 25–30.

– (1949), 'Readings from the Thorkelin Transcripts of *Beowulf*', *PMLA* 64: 1190–218.

– ed. (1951), *Beowulf. The Thorkelin Transcripts of Beowulf in Facsimile*, EEMF 1 (Copenhagen).

– ed. (1962), *Widsith*, 2nd ed. (Copenhagen).

– ed. (1963), *The Nowell Codex: British Museum Cotton Vitellius A.xv, Second MS*, EEMF 12 (Copenhagen).

– ed. (1977), *Deor*, rev. ed. (Exeter).

Mango, C. (1973), 'La culture grecque et l'Occident au VIIIe siècle', *Settimane* 20: 683–721.

Manion, M.M., V.F. Vines and C. De Hamel (1989), *Medieval and Renaissance Manuscripts in New Zealand Collections* (Melbourne).

– and B.J. Muir, eds. (1991), *Medieval Texts and Images from the Middle Ages* (Sydney).

– and B.J. Muir, eds. (1998), *The Art of the Book. Its Place in Medieval Worship* (Exeter).

Manitius, M. (1911–31), *Geschichte der lateinischen Literatur des Mittelalters*, 3 vols. (Munich).

Mann, G. (2004), 'The Development of Wulfstan's Alcuin Manuscript', in Townend (2004), 235–78.

Mann, V.B. (1974–5), 'Architectural Conventions on the Bayeux Tapestry', *Marsyas* 17: 59–65.

Marchesin, I. (1998), 'Le corps musical dans les miniatures psalmiques carolin-giennes et romanes', in *Centre universitaire d'études et de recherches médié-vales* (1998), 401–27.

Marenbon, J. (1981), *From the Circle of Alcuin to the School of Auxerre. Logic, Theology and Philosophy in the Early Middle Ages* (Cambridge).

Markey, D. (1992), 'The Anglo-Norman Version', in M. Gibson (1992), 139–56.

Marner, D. (2002), 'The Sword of the Spirit. The Word of God and the Book of Deer', *Society for Medieval Archaeology* 46: 1–28.

Marsden, R. (1991), 'Ælfric as Translator: The Old English Prose Genesis', *Anglia* 109: 319–58.

– (1994a), 'The Old Testament in Late Anglo-Saxon England: Preliminary Observations on the Textual Evidence', in R. Gameson (1994a), 101–24.

– (1994b), 'The Survival of Ceolfrith's Tobit in a Tenth-Century Insular Manuscript', *JTS* n.s. 45: 1–23.

– (1994c), 'Old Latin Interventions in the Old English *Heptateuch*', *ASE* 23: 229–64.

– (1995), *The Text of the Old Testament in Anglo-Saxon England*, CSASE 15 (Cambridge).

– (1998), '*Manus Bedae*: Bede's Contribution to Ceolfrith's Bibles', *ASE* 27: 65–85.

– (1999), 'The Gospels of St Augustine', in R. Gameson (1999b), 285–313.

– (2000), 'Translation by Committee? The "Anonymous" Text of the Old English Hexateuch', in Barnhouse—Withers (2000), 41–89.

– (2005), 'Latin in the Ascendant: The Interlinear Gloss of Oxford, Bodleian Library, Laud Misc. 509', in O'Brien O'Keeffe—Orchard (2005) II, 132–52.

– ed. (2008), *The Old English Heptateuch and Ælfric's Libellus de Veteri Testamento et Novo*, I. *Introduction and Text*, EETS o.s. 330 (Oxford).

– (2011), 'Amiatinus in Italy: The Afterlife of an Anglo-Saxon Book', in Sauer et al. (2011), 217–43.

– (2012), 'The Biblical Manuscripts of Anglo-Saxon England', in R. Gameson (2012), 406–35.

Marshall, P.K. (2000), 'The Spangenberg Bifolium of Servius: The Manuscript and the Text', *Rivista di filologia* 128: 190–209.

Marston, T.E. (1965), 'A Collection of Early Manuscript Leaves', *Yale University Library Gazette* 40: 9.

Martello, F. (2012), *All'ombra di Gregorio Magno: il notaio Paterio e il 'Liber testimoniorum'* (Rome).

Martène, E. and U. Durand, eds. (1724–33), *Veterum scriptorum et monumento-rum amplissima collectio*, 9 vols. (Paris).

– ed. (1763), *De antiquis ecclesiae ritibus*, 2nd ed., 4 vols. (Antwerp).

Martimort, A.G. (1992), *Les lectures liturgiques et leurs livres*, Typologie des sources du moyen âge occidental 64 (Turnhout).

Martin, H. (1885–96), *Catalogue des manuscrits de la Bibliothèque de l'Arsenal*, 7 vols. (Paris).

Martin, L.T. (1979), 'The Earliest Versions of the Latin *Somniale Danielis*', *Manuscripta* 23: 131–41.

– ed. (1981), *Somniale Danielis. An Edition of a Medieval Latin Dream Interpretation Handbook* (Frankfurt am Main).

Martin, M. (1978), 'A Note on Marginalia in "The Vercelli Book"', *N&Q* 223: 485–6.

Martín Sánchez, J.M., ed. (2000), *Isidori Hispalensis Versus*, CCSL 113A (Turnhout).

Masai, F. (1948), 'Fragment en onciale d'une règle monastique inconnue démarquant celle de S. Benoît', *Scriptorium* 2: 215–20.

Masi, M. (1972), 'Newberry MSS Fragments, s. vii–xv', *MS* 34: 99–112.

Mason, E. (1996a), *St Wulfstan of Worcester, c. 1008–1095* (Oxford).

– (1996b), 'St Oswald and St Wulfstan', in Brooks–Cubitt (1996), 269–84.

Matsuda, T. et al., eds. (2004), *The Medieval Book and a Modern Collector. Essays in Honour of Toshiyuki Takamiya* (Cambridge).

Mayhoff, K., ed. (1967), *C. Plinii Secundi Naturalis Historiae Libri XXXVII (post Ludovici Iani obitum recognovit)*, I. *Libri I–VI* (Stuttgart).

Mayor, J.E.B. and Lumby, J.R., eds. (1881), *Venerabilis Bedae Historiae ecclesiasticae gentis Anglorum libri III–IV*, rev. ed. (Cambridge).

Mayr-Harting, H. (1991), *The Coming of Christianity to Anglo-Saxon England*, 3rd ed. (London).

Mazal, O. and F. Unterkircher (1963–75), *Katalog der abendländischen Handschriften der Österreichischen Nationalbibliothek, 'Series Nova'*, 4 vols. (Vienna).

McBain, A. (1994–5), 'The Book of Deer', *Transactions of the Gaelic Society of Inverness* 11: 137–66.

McCulloh, J., ed. (1979), *Hrabanus Maurus: Martyrologium*, CCCM 44 (Turnhout).

McDougall, D. and I. McDougall (1997), '"Evil Tongues": A Previously Unedited Old English Sermon', *ASE* 26: 209–29.

McFadden, B. (2001), 'The Social Context of Narrative Disruption in *The Letter of Alexander to Aristotle*', *ASE* 30: 91–114.

McGovern, D.S. (1983), 'Unnoticed Punctuation in the Exeter Book', *MÆ* 52: 90–9.

McGowan, J.P. (2007), 'On the "Red" Blickling Psalter Glosses', *N&Q* 252: 205–7.

McGurk, P. (1955a), 'The Canon Tables in the Book of Lindisfarne and in the Codex Fuldensis of St. Victor of Capua', *JTS* n.s. 6: 192–8 [repr. McGurk (1998) no. III].

– (1955b), 'Two Notes on the Book of Kells and its Relation to Other Insular Gospel Books', *Scriptorium* 9: 105–7 [repr. McGurk (1998) no. IV].

– (1956), 'The Irish Pocket Gospel Book', *Sacris Erudiri* 8: 249–69 [repr. McGurk (1998) no. I].

– (1961a), *Latin Gospel Books from AD 400 to AD 800* (Paris) [Introduction repr. McGurk (1998) no.VI].

– (1961b), 'Citation Marks in early Latin Manuscripts', *Scriptorium* 15: 3–13 [repr. McGurk (1998) no. V].

– (1962), 'An Anglo-Saxon Bible Fragment of the Late Eighth Century, Royal 1.E VI', *JWCI* 25: 18–34 [repr. McGurk (1998) no. VII].

– (1963), 'The Ghent Livinus Gospels and the Scriptorium of St. Amand', *Sacris Erudiri* 14: 164–205 [repr. McGurk (1998) no. VIII].

– (1973), '*Germanici Caesaris Aratea cum Scholiis*: A New Illustrated Witness from Wales', *NLWJ* 18: 197–216.

– (1974), '*Computus Helperici*: Its Transmission in England in the Eleventh and Twelfth Centuries', *MÆ* 43: 1–5.

– et al., eds. (1983), *An Eleventh-Century Anglo-Saxon Illustrated Miscellany: British Library, Cotton Tiberius B.v, pt. 1, together with Leaves from British Library, Cotton Nero D.ii*, EEMF 21 (Copenhagen).

– (1986a), 'The Metrical Calendar of Hampson: A New Edition', *AB* 104: 79–125.

– (1986b), 'Text from *The York Gospels*', in Barker et al. (1986), 43–65 [repr. McGurk (1998) no. XIV].

– (1987), 'The Gospel Book in Celtic Lands before A.D. 850: Contents and Arrangement', in Ní Chatháin—Richter (1987), 165–89 [repr. McGurk (1998) no. II].

– (1993), 'The Disposition of Numbers in Latin Eusebian Canon Tables' in *Philologica sacra. Biblische und patristische Studien für Hermann J. Frede und Walter Thiele zu ihrem siebzigsten Geburtstag*, ed. R. Gryson, Aus der Geschichte der lateinischen Bibel 24 (Freiburg im Breisgau), 242–58 [repr. McGurk (1998) no. XI].

– (1994a), 'An Edition of the Abbreviated and Selective Set of Hebrew Names Found in the Book of Kells', in O'Mahoney (1994), 102–32 [repr. McGurk (1998) no. IX].

– (1994b), 'The Oldest Manuscripts of the Latin Bible', in R. Gameson (1994a), 1–23 [repr. McGurk (1998) no. XII].

– (1995a), 'Theodore's Bible: The Gospels', in Lapidge (1995a), 255–9 [repr. McGurk (1998) no. XIII].

- and J. Rosenthal (1995b), 'The Anglo-Saxon Gospelbooks of Judith, Countess of Flanders: Their Text, Make-Up and Function', *ASE* 24: 251–308 [repr. McGurk (1998) no. XV].
- (1996), 'Des recueils d'interprétations de noms hébreux', *Scriptorium* 50: 117–22 [repr. McGurk (1998) no. X].
- (1998), *Gospel Books and Early Latin Manuscripts* (Aldershot).
- (2001), 'The Canon Tables of the Book of Kells', in Binski—Noel (2001), 40–60.
- and J. Rosenthal (2006), 'Author, Symbol and Word: The Inspired Evangelists in Judith of Flanders's Anglo-Saxon Gospel Books', in L'Engle—Guest (2006), 185–202.
- (2012), 'Anglo-Saxon Gospel-books, c. 900–1066', in R. Gameson (2012), 436–48.
McHugh, G. (1983), 'Corpus Christi College Cambridge 279. A Partial Edition and Study' (unpubl. MA dissertation, University College, Dublin).
McIlwain Nishimura, M. (2006), 'The Grey Gospels: A Frankish Curiosity in Cape Town', in L'Engle—Guest (2006), 159–70.
McIntosh, A. (1948), 'Wulfstan's Prose', *PBA* 34: 109–42.
McIntyre, E. (1978), 'Early Twelfth-Century Worcester Cathedral Priory, with Special Reference to the Manuscripts Written there' (unpubl. PhD dissertation, Oxford Univ.).
McKee, H. (1997), 'St Augustine's Abbey, Canterbury: Book-Production in the Tenth and Eleventh Centuries' (unpubl. PhD dissertation, Cambridge Univ.).
- (2000a), 'Scribes and Glosses from Dark Age Wales: The Cambridge Juvencus Manuscript', *CMCS* 39: 1–22.
- ed. (2000b), *The Cambridge Juvencus Manuscript Glossed in Latin, Old Welsh and Old Irish: Text and Commentary* (Aberystwyth).
- ed. (2000c), *Juvencus: Codex Cantabrigiensis – A Ninth-Century Manuscript Glossed in Welsh, Irish and Latin* (Aberystwyth) [facsimile edition].
- (2012a), 'Script in Wales, Scotland and Cornwall', in R. Gameson (2012), 167–73.
- (2012b), 'The Circulation of Books between England and the Celtic Realms', in R. Gameson (2012), 338–43.
McKinlay, A.P. (1942), *Arator: The Codices* (Cambridge, MA).
- (1943), 'Studies in Arator II: the Classification of the Manuscripts of Arator', *Harvard Studies in Classical Philology* 54: 93–115.
- ed. (1951), *Aratoris subdiaconi De actibus apostolorum*, CSEL 72 (Vienna).
- (1960—), 'Arator', in Kristeller et al. (1960—) I, 241–7.
McKinley, K.L. (1998), 'Manuscripts of Ovid in England, 1100–1500', *English Manuscript Studies 1100–1700* 7: 41–85.

McKitterick, D.J. (1986), *Cambridge University Library, A History: The Eighteenth and Nineteenth Centuries* (Cambridge).

McKitterick, R. (1977), *The Frankish Church and the Carolingian Reforms, 789–895*, Royal Historical Society Studies in History 2 (London).

– (1985), 'Knowledge of Canon Law in the Frankish Kingdoms before 789: The Manuscript Evidence', *JTS* n.s. 36: 97–117.

– (1986–90), 'Anglo-Saxon Missionaries in Germany: Reflections on the Manuscript Evidence', *TCBS* 9: 291–329.

– (1989a), *The Carolingians and the Written Word* (Cambridge).

– (1989b), 'The Diffusion of Insular Culture in Neustria between 650 and 850: The Implications of the Manuscript Evidence', in *La Neustrie. Les payes au nord de la Loire de 650 à 850. Colloque historique international*, ed. H. Atsma (Sigmaringen, 1989), 395–431.

– and J.I. Whalley (1989), *Catalogue of the Pepys Library at Magdalene College, Cambridge, IV. Music, Maps and Calligraphy* (Cambridge).

– ed. (1990), *The Uses of Literacy in Early Medieval Europe* (Cambridge).

– (1990a), 'Text and Image in the Carolingian World', in McKitterick (1990), 297–318.

– and R. Beadle (1992), *Catalogue of the Pepys Library at Magdalene College, Cambridge, V. Manuscripts, Part i: Medieval* (Cambridge).

– ed. (1994a), *Carolingian Culture: Emulation and Innovation* (Cambridge).

– (1994b), 'Script and Book Production', in McKitterick (1994a), 221–47.

– (2000), 'Le scriptorium d'Echternach aux huitième et neuvième siècles', in *L'Évangelisation des régions entre Meuse et Moselle et la fondation de l'abbaye d'Echternach (Ve-IXe siècle)*, ed. M. Polfer (Luxembourg, 2000), 501–22.

– (2004), *History and Memory in the Carolingian World* (Cambridge).

– (2005), 'The Coming of Christianity: Pagans and Missionaries', in Binski–Panayotova (2005), 39–74.

– (2012), 'Exchanges between the British Isles and the Continent, *c.* 450–*c.*900', in R. Gameson (2012), 313–37.

McLachlan, L. (1929), 'St Wulfstan's Prayerbook', *JTS* 30: 174–7.

McNamara, M. (1973), 'Psalter Text and Psalter Study in the Early Irish Church (A.D. 600–1200)', *PRIA* 73C: 201–98.

– (1975), *The Apocrypha in the Irish Church* (Dublin).

– (1979), 'Ireland and Northumbria as Illustrated by a Vatican Manuscript', *Thought* 54: 274–90.

– (1986), *Glossa in Psalmos: The Hiberno-Latin Gloss on the Psalms of Codex Palatinus 68 (Psalms 39:11–151:17)*, Studi e Testi 310 (Vatican City).

– (1987–8), 'The Echternach and MacDurnan Gospels: Some Common Readings and their Significance', *Peritia* 6–7: 217–22.

– (1990), *Studies on Texts of Early Irish Latin Gospels (AD 600–1200)*, Instrumenta Patristica 20 (Steenbrugge).
– (1995), 'The Celtic-Irish Mixed Gospel Text: Some Recent Contributions and Centennial Reflections', *Filologia Mediolatina* 2: 69–108.
– (2002), 'Irish Homilies A.D. 600–1100', in T.N. Hall et al. (2002), 235–84.
McNeill, J.T. and H.M. Gamer (1938), *Medieval Handbooks of Penance. A Translation of the Principal 'Libri poenitentiales' and Selections from Related Documents* (New York).
McRoberts, D. (1953), *Catalogue of Scottish Medieval Liturgical Books and Fragments* (Glasgow).
Meadows, P. and N. Ramsay, eds. (2003), *A History of Ely Cathedral* (Woodbridge).
Meaney, A.L. (1975), 'King Alfred and his Secretariat', *Parergon* 11: 16–24.
– (1984), 'Variant Versions of Old English Medical Remedies and the Compilation of Bald's Leechbook', *ASE* 13: 235–68.
– (1985), 'London, BL Add. MS 43703', *OEN* 19.1: 34–5.
– (2004), '*And we forbeodað eornostlice ælcne hæðenscipe*: Wulfstan and Late Anglo-Saxon and Norse "Heathenism"', in Townend (2004), 461–500.
Mearns, J. (1913), *Early Latin Hymnaries: An Index of Hymns and Hymnaries before 1100, with an Appendix from Later Sources* (Cambridge).
– (1914), *The Canticles of the Christian Church, Eastern and Western, in Early and Medieval Times* (Cambridge).
Meeder, S. (2004–7), 'Defining Doctrine in the Carolingian Period: The Contents and Context of Cambridge, Pembroke College, MS 108', *TCBS* 13: 133–51.
– (2009), 'The *Liber ex lege Moysi*: Notes and Text', *JMLat* 19: 173–218.
Meehan, B. (1986), *Treasures of the Library: Trinity College Dublin* (Dublin).
– (1994a), *The Book of Kells* (London).
– (1994b), 'Durham Twelfth-Century Manuscripts in Cistercian Houses', in Rollason et al. (1994), 439–49.
– (1996), *The Book of Durrow: A Medieval Masterpiece at Trinity College, Dublin* (Dublin).
– (1998a), 'The Book of Kells and the Corbie Psalter', in *A Miracle of Learning: Studies in Manuscripts and Irish Learning. Essays in Honour of William O'Sullivan*, ed. T.C. Barnard, D. Ó Cróinín and K. Simms (Aldershot), 29–39.
– (1998b), 'Notes on the Preliminary Texts and Continuations to Symeon of Durham's *Libellus de exordio*', in Rollason (1998), 128–39.
– (2000), 'The Book of Kells and the Corbie Psalter (with a Note on Harley 2788)', in Cassidy – Muir Wright (2000), 12–23.
Meersseman, G.G. (1963), *Kritische Glossen op de Griekse Theophilus-Legende (7 eeuw) en haar latijnse Vertaling (9 eeuw)* (Brussels).

Mellinkoff, R. (1970), *The Horned Moses in Medieval Art and Thought*, California Studies in the History of Art 14 (Berkeley, CA).

– (1973), 'The Round, Cap-Shaped Hats Depicted on Jews in BM Cotton Claudius B. iv' *ASE* 2: 155–65.

– (1986), 'Serpent Imagery in the Illustrated Old English Hexateuch', in Brown–Crampton (1986), 51–64.

Menner, R.J. (1934), 'Farman Vindicatus: The Linguistic Value of *Rushworth I*', *Anglia* 58: 1–27.

– ed. (1941), *The Poetical Dialogues of Solomon and Saturn* (New York).

– (1949), 'The Anglian Vocabulary of the Blickling Homilies', in Kirby–Woolf (1949), 56–64.

– (1951), 'The Date and Dialect of Genesis A, 852–2936', *Anglia* 70: 285–94.

Menzer, M. (2004), 'Multilingual Glosses, Bilingual Text: English, French and Latin in Three Manuscripts of Ælfric's Grammar', in Lionarons (2004a), 95–119.

Meritt, H.D. (1934), 'Old English Entries in a Manuscript at Bern', *JEGP* 33: 343–51.

– (1945), *Old English Glosses (A Collection)* (London and New York).

– (1952), 'Old English Aldhelm Glosses', *MLN* 67: 553–4.

– (1957), 'Old English Glosses to Gregory, Ambrose and Prudentius', *JEGP* 56: 65–8.

– ed. (1959), *The Old English Prudentius Glosses at Boulogne-sur-Mer*, Stanford Studies in Language and Literature 16 (Stanford, CA).

– (1961), 'Old English Glosses, Mostly Dry Point', *JEGP* 60: 441–50.

Mersiowsky, M. (2007), 'Preserved by Destruction. Carolingian Original Letters and Clm 6333', in Declerq (2007), 73–98.

Merten, J. (1987), 'Die Esra-Miniatur des Codex Amiatinus: zu Autorenbild und Schreibgerät', *Trierer Zeitschrift* 50: 301–19.

Mertens-Fonck, P. (1987), 'Spelling Variation in the *Vespasian Psalter* Gloss', in Simon-Vandenbergen (1987), 351–61.

Metzenthin, E.C. (1922), 'Die Heimat der Adressaten des Heliand', *JEGP* 21: 191–228.

Metzger, B.M. (1977), *The Early Versions of the New Testament: Their Origin, Transmission and Limitations* (Oxford).

Mews, C. (2002), 'Manuscripts in Polish Libraries Copied before 1200 and the Expansion of Latin Christendom in the Eleventh and Twelfth Centuries', *Scriptorium* 56: 80–118.

Meyer, C., M. Huglo and N.C. Phillips (1992), *The Theory of Music*, IV. *Manuscripts from the Carolingian Era up to c. 1500 in Great Britain and the United States of America. Descriptive Catalogue*, Répertoire international des sources musicales B. III. 4 (Munich).

- (2003), *The Theory of Music*, VI. *Manuscripts from the Carolingian Era up to c. 1500. Addenda, Corrigenda. Descriptive Catalogue*, Répertoire international des sources musicales B. III. 6 (Munich).

Meyer, P. (1873), untitled article in *The Academy* (8 Nov. 1873), 59.

Meyer, W. (1907), 'Smaragds Mahnbüchlein für einen Karolinger', *Nachrichten von der königlichen Gesellschaft der Wissenschaften zu Göttingen*, phil.-hist. Klasse (1907), 39–70.

- (1916), 'Drei Gothaer Rhythmen aus dem Kreise des Alkuins', *Nachrichten von der königlichen Gesellschaft der Wissenschaften zu Göttingen*, phil.-hist. Klasse (1916), 645–82.

- (1917), 'Poetische Nachlese aus dem sogenannten Book of Cerne in Cambridge und aus dem Londoner Codex Regius 2.A.XX', *Nachrichten von der königlichen Gesellschaft der Wissenschaften zu Göttingen*, phil.-hist. Klasse (1917), 597–625.

Meyvaert, P. (1961), 'The Bede "Signature" in the Leningrad Colophon', *RB* 71: 274–86.

- (1963), 'Towards a History of the Textual Transmission of the *Regula S. Benedicti*', *Scriptorium* 17: 83–110.

- (1989), 'The Book of Kells and Iona', *Art Bulletin* 71: 6–19.

- (1996), 'Bede, Cassiodorus and the Codex Amiatinus', *Speculum* 71: 827–83.

- (2005), 'The Date of Bede's *In Ezram* and his Image of Ezra in the Codex Amiatinus', *Speculum* 80: 1087–1133.

- (2006), 'Dissension in Bede's Community shown by a Quire of Codex Amiatinus', *RB* 116: 295–308.

Mezey, L. (1983), *Fragmenta Codicum in Bibliothecis Hungariae*, I. 1. *Fragmenta Latina Codicum in Bibliotheca Universitatis Budapestinensis* (Wiesbaden).

Micheli, G.L. (1939), *L'enluminure du haut moyen âge et les influences irlandaises* (Brussels).

Michelli, P. (1999), 'What's in the Cupboard? Ezra and Matthew Reconsidered', in Hawkes—Mills (1999), 345–58.

Milani, C. (1984), 'Note sul *Corpus Glossary*', *Quaderni di lingue e letterature* 9: 185–319.

Milde, W. (1986), 'Paläographische Bemerkungen zu den Breslauer Unzialfragmenten der Dialoge Gregors des Grossen', in *Probleme der Bearbeitung mittelalterlicher Handschriften*, ed. H. Härtel, W. Milde, J. Piroźyński and M. Zwiercan, Wolfenbütteler Forschungen 30 (Wiesbaden, 1986), 145–65.

Milfull, I.B., ed. (1996), *The Hymns of the Anglo-Saxon Church: A Study and Edition of the 'Durham Hymnal'*, CSASE 17 (Cambridge).

- (2004), 'Spuren kontinentaler Einflüsse in spätangelsächsischen Hymnaren', in Haug et al. (2004), 173–98.

Millar, E.G. (1926), *English Illuminated Manuscripts from the Xth to the XIIIth Century* (Paris).

Miller, S., ed. (2001), *Charters of the New Minster, Winchester*, Anglo-Saxon Charters 9 (Oxford).

Miller, T., ed. (1890–8), *The Old English Version of Bede's Ecclesiastical History of the English People*, 2 vols. in 4 parts, EETS o.s. 95–6, 110–11 (London).

Millett, B. (2007), 'The Pastoral Context of the Trinity and Lambeth Homilies', in Scase (2007), 43–64.

Minio-Paluello, L., ed. (1961), *Aristoteles Latinus: Codices. Supplementa Altera* (Bruges).

– and B.G. Dod, eds. (1966), *Porphyrii Isagoge. Translatio Boethii et Anonimi fragmentum vulgo vocatum 'Liber sex principiorum', accedunt Isagoges fragmenta M. Victorino interprete et specimina translationum recentiorum Categoriarum*, Aristoteles Latinus I.6–7 (Bruges and Paris).

– (1971), 'Nuovi impulsi allo studio della logica: la seconda fase della riscoperta di Aristotele e di Boezio', *Settimane* 19: 743–66.

Minnis, A. (1981), 'Aspects of the Medieval French and English Traditions of the *De consolatione Philosophiae*', in Gibson (1981), 312–61.

– and J. Roberts, eds. (2007), *Text, Image, Interpretation. Studies in Anglo-Saxon Literature and its Insular Context in Honour of Éamonn Ó Carragáin*, Studies in the Middle Ages 18 (Turnhout).

Mirto, I.M. (2007), 'Of the Choice and Use of the Word *beatus* in the *Beatus quid est*: Notes by a Non-Philologist', in Lendinara et al. (2007), 349–61.

Mitchell, B. and F.C. Robinson, eds. (1998), *Beowulf. An Edition with Relevant Shorter Texts* (Oxford).

– and F.C. Robinson, eds. (2007), *A Guide to Old English*, 7th ed. (Oxford).

Mittler, F., ed. (1986), *Bibliotheca Palatina. Katalog zur Ausstellung vom 8. Juli bis 2. November 1986, Heiliggeistkirche Heidelberg*, 2 vols. (Heidelberg).

Moeller, E.E., ed. (1971–9), *Corpus benedictionum pontificalium*, 4 vols., CCSL 162–162C (Turnhout).

– et al., eds. (1992–2004), *Corpus orationum*, 14 vols., CCSL 160–160M (Turnhout).

Mohlberg, L.C., ed. (1960), *Liber sacramentorum Romanae aecclesiae ordinis anni circuli (Sacramentarium Gelasianum)* (Rome).

Mommsen, T., ed. (1892–8), *Chronica minora*, 3 vols., MGH, AA 9, 11, 13 (Berlin).

Moorat, S.A.J. (1962–73), *Catalogue of Western Manuscripts on Medicine and Science in the Wellcome Historical Medical Library*, 2 vols. (London).

Moore, J.S. (2004), 'Anglo-Norman Names recorded in the Durham *Liber Vitae*', in Rollason et al. (2004), 97–107.

Mordek, H. (1975), *Kirchenrecht und Reform im Frankenreich. Die 'Collectio Vetus Gallica', die älteste systematische Kanonessammlung des fränkischen Gallien* (Berlin and New York).

– (1995), *Bibliotheca capitularium regum Francorum manuscripta. Überlieferung und Traditionszusammenhang der fränkischen Herrschererlasse*, MGH, Hilfsmittel 15 (Munich).

Moreschini, C., ed. (2000), *Boethius: De consolatione Philosophiae, Opuscula theologica* (Munich).

Morey, C.R. (1929), 'The Landevennec Gospels. A Breton Illuminated Manuscript of the Ninth Century', *Bulletin of the New York Public Library* 33: 643–53 [and 10 pls.].

– E.K. Rand and C.H. Kraeling (1931), *The Gospel Book of Landevennec (The Harkness Gospels) in the New York Public Library* (Cambridge, MA).

Morgan, N. (1981), 'Notes on the Post-Conquest Calendar, Litany and Martyrology of the Cathedral Priory of Winchester with a Consideration of Winchester Diocese Calendars of the Pre-Sarum Period', in Borg—Martindale (1981), 133–71.

– (1982), *A Survey of Manuscripts Illuminated in the British Isles*, IV: *Early Gothic Manuscripts*, 2 vols. (London).

– and S. Panayotova (2009), *A Catalogue of Western Book Illumination in the Fitzwilliam Museum and the Cambridge Colleges*, 2 vols. (London and Turnhout).

Morgand, C.L. (1955), 'Le Memoriale Monachorum', in *Jumièges* (1955) II, 765–74.

Morgand, D.C., ed. (1963), 'Memoriale qualiter', CCM I, 177–261.

Morin, G. (1891), 'La liturgie de Naples au temps de Saint Grégoire d'après deux évangeliaires du septième siècle', *RB* 8: 481–93, 529–37.

– (1893a), *Monumenta ecclesiasticae antiquitatis*, Anecdota Maredsolana 1 (Maredsous).

– (1893b), 'Les notes liturgiques de l'Évangeliaire de Burchard', *RB* 10: 113–26.

– ed. (1897a/1958), *Sancti Hieronymi presbyteri Tractatus siue Homiliae in psalmos*, Anecdota Maredsolana 3.ii (Oxford; repr. CCSL 78 [Turnhout, 1958]).

– (1897b), 'Notes d'ancienne littérature chrétienne: Le "Responsum sancti Severi" sur les sept dégres de la hiérarchie ecclésiastique', *RB* 14: 100–1.

– (1910), 'Le plus ancien *comes* ou lectionnaire de l'église romane', *RB* 27: 41–74.

– (1911), 'Liturgie et basiliques de Rome au milieu du VIIe siècle d'après les listes d'évangiles de Würzburg', *RB* 28: 296–330.

– (1934), 'Fastidius ad Fatalem', *RB* 46: 3–17.

– ed. (1953), *Caesarii Arelatensis Opera*, 2 vols., CCSL 103–4 (Turnhout).

Morison, S. (1972), *Politics and Script. The Lyell Lectures 1957*, ed. and completed by N. Barker (Oxford).

Morrell, M.C. (1965), *A Manual of Old English Biblical Materials* (Knoxville, TN).

Morris, J., ed. (1980), *Nennius: British History and the Welsh Annals* (London).

Morris, R., ed. (1867–8), *Old English Homilies and Homiletic Treatises of the Twelfth and Thirteenth Centuries*, 2 vols., EETS o.s. 29, 34 (London).

– ed. (1871), *Legends of the Holy Rood*, EETS o.s. 46 (London).

– ed. (1872), *Old English Homilies of the Twelfth Century: With Three Thirteenth-Century Hymns*, EETS o.s. 53 (London).

– ed. (1874–80), *The Blickling Homilies*, EETS o.s. 58, 63 and 73 (London; 3 vols. repr. as 1, 1966).

– ed. (1887), *Specimens of Early English. Introduction, Notes and Glossarial Index. Part I: From 'Old English Homilies' to 'King Horn' A. D. 1150–A. D. 1300*, 2nd ed. (Oxford).

Morrish, J. (1982), 'An Examination of Literacy and Learning in the Ninth Century' (unpubl. PhD dissertation, Oxford Univ.).

– (1986), 'King Alfred's Letter as a Source on Learning in England in the Ninth Century', in Szarmach (1986b), 87–107.

– (1988), 'Dated and Datable Manuscripts Copied in England during the Ninth Century: A Preliminary List', *MS* 50: 512–38.

Morrison, E. (2007), *Beasts: Factual and Fantastic* (Los Angeles).

Morrison, S. (1987), 'On Some Noticed and Unnoticed Old English Scratched Glosses', *ES* 68: 209–13.

Morston, T. (1970), 'The Earliest Manuscript of St Aldhelm's *De laude virginitatis*', *Yale University Library Gazette* 44: 204–6.

Mortensen, L.B. (1999–2000), 'The Diffusion of Roman Histories in the Middle Ages. A List of Orosius, Eutropius, Paulus Diaconus and Landolfus Sagax Manuscripts', *Filologia Mediolatina* 6–7: 101–200.

Moskowich-Spiegel, I. and B. Crespo-García, eds. (2007), *Bells Chiming from the Past. Cultural and Linguistic Studies on Early English*, Costerus New Series 174 (Amsterdam and New York).

Mostert, M. (1989), *The Library of Fleury* (Hilversum).

– (2010), 'Relations between Fleury and England', in Rollason et al. (2010), 185–208.

Moulin-Fankhänel, C. (2001), 'Glossieren an einem Ort. Zur althochdeutschen Glossenüberlieferung der ehemaligen Dombibliothek Würzburg', in Bergmann et al. (2001), 353–79.

Muir, B.J., ed. (1981), 'An Edition of British Library Manuscripts Cotton Galba A.xiv and Cotton Nero A.ii (ff. 3r–13v)' (unpubl. PhD dissertation, University of Toronto).

– ed. (1988), *A Pre-Conquest English Prayer-Book: BL MSS Cotton Galba A.xiv and Nero A.ii (ff. 3–13)*, HBS 103 (London).

- (1989), 'A Preliminary Report on a New Edition of the Exeter Book', *Scriptorium* 43: 273–88.
- (1991a), 'Editing the Exeter Book: A Progress Report', in Manion—Muir (1991), 149–76.
- (1991b), 'Watching the Exeter Book Scribe Copy Old English and Latin Texts', *Manuscripta* 35: 3–22.
- (1998), 'The Early Insular Prayer Book Tradition and the Development of the Book of Hours', in Manion—Muir (1998), 9–19.
- ed. (2000), *The Exeter Anthology of Old English Poetry. An Edition of Exeter, Dean and Chapter, MS 3501*, 2nd ed., 2 vols. (Exeter).
- ed. (2004), *A Digital Facsimile of Oxford, Bodleian Library, MS. Junius 11*, Bodleian Digital Texts 1 (Oxford) [CD-ROM].
- ed. (2006), *The Exeter DVD. The Exeter Anthology of Old English Poetry* (Exeter) [CD-ROM].

Müller, R. (1901), *Untersuchungen über die Namen des nordhumbrischen Liber Vitae*, Palaestra 9 (Berlin).

Munk Olsen, B. (1979), 'Les classiques latins dans les florilèges médiévaux antérieurs au XIIIe siècle (I)', *Revue d'histoire des textes* 9: 47–121.
- (1980), 'Les classiques latins dans les florilèges médiévaux antérieurs au XIIIe siècle (II)', *Revue d'histoire des textes* 10: 115–64.
- (1982—), *L'Étude des auteurs classiques latins aux XIe et XIIe siècles*, 4 vols. in 5 pts. (Paris [in progress]).

Murray, J.A.H. (1900), *The Evolution of English Lexicography*, The Romanes Lecture 1900 (Oxford).

Mustanoja, T.F. (1950), 'Notes on Some Old English Glosses in Aldhelm's *De Laudibus Virginitatis*', *NM* 51: 49–61.

Mütherich, F. and K. Dachs, eds. (1991), *Das Samuhel-Evangeliar aus dem Quedlinburger Dom*, Bayerische Staatsbibliothek: Ausstellungskataloge 53 (Munich).

Mutzenbecher, A., ed. (1984), *Augustinus: Retractationum Libri II*, CCSL 57 (Turnhout).

Muzerelle, D. (1969), 'Flodoard, *De triumphis Christi apud Italiam*: Etude des sources, édition des livres I–IV et XII', École Nationale des Chartes, Positions des thèses (Paris).

Mynors, R.A.B., ed. (1937), *Cassiodori Senatoris Institutiones* (Oxford).
- (1939), *Durham Cathedral Manuscripts to the End of the Twelfth Century* (Oxford).
- and R. Powell (1956), 'The Stonyhurst Gospels', in Battiscombe (1956), 356–74.
- (1963), *Catalogue of the Manuscripts of Balliol College* (Oxford).

– and R.M. Thomson (1993), *Catalogue of the Manuscripts of Hereford Cathedral Library* (Cambridge).

Napier, A.S., ed. (1883/1967), *Wulfstan. Sammlung der ihm zugeschriebenen Homilien nebst Untersuchungen über ihre Echtheit*, mit einem bibliographischen Anhang von K. Ostheeren, 2nd ed. (Dublin und Zürich, 1967).

– (1887), 'Bruchstück einer altenglischen Boethiushandschrift', *ZfdA* 31: 52–4.

– (1888), 'Ein altenglisches Leben des Heiligen Chad', *Anglia* 10: 131–56.

– (1889), 'Altenglische Kleinigkeiten', *Anglia* 11: 1–10.

– (1890), 'Altenglische Miscellen', *ASNSL* 84: 323–7.

– (1891), 'Bruchstücke einer altenglischen Evangelienhandschrift', *ASNSL* 87: 255–61.

– (1893), 'Collation der altenglischen Aldhelmglossen des Codex 38 der Kathedralbibliothek zu Salisbury', *Anglia* 15: 204–9.

– (1894), *History of the Holy Rood-Tree: A Twelfth Century Version of the Cross-Legend, with Notes on the Orthography of the Ormulum (with a Facsimile) and a Middle English Compassio Mariae*, EETS o.s. 103 (London).

– ed. (1900), *Old English Glosses: Chiefly Unpublished*, Anecdota Oxoniensia 4 (Oxford).

– (1900–7), 'An Old English Vision of Leofric, Earl of Mercia', *Transactions of the Philological Society*: 180–8.

– (1901), 'Contributions to Old English Literature: I. An Old English Homily on the Observance of Sunday', *An English Miscellany: Presented to Dr Furnivall in Honour of his Seventy-Fifth Birthday* (Oxford), 355–62.

– (1903), 'The Rule of Chrodegang in Old English', *MLN* 18: 241.

– (1906), *Contributions to Old English Lexicography* (Hertford).

– ed. (1916), *The Old English Version of the Enlarged Rule of Chrodegang together with the Latin Original. An Old English Version of the Capitula of Theodulf together with the Latin Original. An Interlinear Old English Rendering of the Epitome of Benedict of Aniane*, EETS o.s. 150 (1916).

Nares, R. et al. (1808–12), *A Catalogue of the Harleian Manuscripts in the British Museum*, 4 vols. (London).

Nason, C.M. (2004), 'The Mass Commentary *Dominus vobiscum*, its Textual Transmission and the Question of Authorship', *RB* 114: 75–91.

Needham, G.I. (1958), 'Additions and Alterations in Cotton MS Julius E. vii', *RES* n.s. 9: 160–4.

– ed. (1976), *Ælfric: Lives of Three English Saints*, rev. ed. (Exeter).

Nees, L. (2003), 'Reading Aldred's Colophon for the Lindisfarne Gospels', *Speculum* 78: 333–77.

– (2006), 'The Jonathan Gospels (Biblioteca Apostolica Vaticana, Cod. Pal.lat. 46)', in L'Engle—Guest (2006), 85–98.

– (2007), 'Ethnic and Primitive Paradigms in the Study of Early Medieval Art',
   in Chazelle—Lifshitz (2007), 41–60.
– (2011), 'Recent Trends in Dating Works of Insular Art', in Hourihane (2011),
   14–30.
Nelson, J.L. (1986a), *Politics and Ritual in Early Medieval Europe* (London).
– (1986b), 'The Earliest Surviving Royal *Ordo*: Some Liturgical and Historical
   Aspects', in Nelson (1986a), 341–60 [orig publ. in Tierney—Linehan (1980),
   29–48].
– and R.W. Pfaff (1995), 'Pontificals and Benedictionals', in Pfaff (1995a), 87–98.
– (2008), 'The First Use of the Second Anglo-Saxon Ordo', in Barrow—
   Wareham (2008), 117–26.
Nestle, E., K Aland and B. Aland, eds. (1993), *Novum Testamentum Graece et
   Latine* 27th ed. (Stuttgart).
Nettleship, H. (1885), 'Four Oxford Manuscripts of the *Origines* of Isidore',
   in his *Lectures and Essays on Subjects connected with Latin Literature and
   Scholarship* (Oxford), 359–63.
Netzer, N. (1987), 'The Trier Gospels (Trier Domschatz MS 61): Text, Construction,
   Script and Illustration' (unpubl. PhD dissertation, Harvard Univ.).
– (1989), 'Willibrord's Scriptorium at Echternach and its Relationship to Ireland
   and Lindisfarne', in Bonner et al. (1989a), 203–12.
– (1994), *Cultural Interplay in the Eighth Century. The Trier Gospels and the
   Making of a Scriptorium at Echternach*, Cambridge Studies in Palaeography
   and Codicology 3 (Cambridge).
– (1999), 'The *Book of Durrow*: the Northumbrian Connection', in Hawkes—
   Mills (1999), 315–26.
– (2011), 'New Finds Versus the Beginning of the Narrative in Insular Gospel
   Books', in Hourihane (2011), 3–13.
– (2012), 'The Design and Decoration of Insular Gospel-Books and other
   Liturgical Manuscripts, c. 600–c. 900', in R. Gameson (2012), 225–43.
Neuman de Vegvar, C. (1992), 'A Paean for a Queen: The Frontispiece to the
   Encomium Emmae Reginae', *OEN* 26.1: 57–8.
Neville, J. (2002), 'Making Their Own Sweet Time: The Scribes of *Anglo-Saxon
   Chronicle A*', in Kooper (2002), 166–77.
Ní Chatháin, P. and M. Richter, eds. (1984), *Irland und Europa* (Stuttgart).
– and M. Richter, eds. (1987a), *Ireland and Christendom: The Bible and the
   Missions* (Stuttgart).
– (1987b), 'Notes on the Würzburg Glosses', in Ní Chatháin—Richter (1987a),
   190–9.
– and M. Richter, eds. (2002), *Ireland and Europe in the Early Middle Ages:
   Texts and Transmission* (Stuttgart).

Nicholson, E.W.B. (1913), *Introduction to the Study of Some of the Oldest Latin Musical Manuscripts in the Bodleian Library*, Early Bodleian Music 3 (Oxford).

Niles, J.D., ed. (1980), *Old English Literature in Context: Ten Essays* (Cambridge).

– (1998), 'Exeter Book Riddle 74 and the Play of the Text', *ASE* 27: 169–207.

Nineham, R. (1964–8), 'K. Pellens' Edition of the Tracts of the Norman Anonymous', *TCBS* 4: 302–9.

Nist, J.A. (1959), *The Structure and Texture of Beowulf* (Sao Paolo).

Niver, C. (1939), 'The Psalter in British Museum, Harley 2904', in *Medieval Studies in Memory of Kingsley Porter*, ed. W.R.W. Koehler, 2 vols. (Cambridge, MA) II, 667–87.

Nixon, H.M. (1976), ' The Binding of the Winton Domesday', in Biddle (1976a), 526–40.

– and M.M. Foot (1992), *The History of Decorated Bookbinding in England* (Oxford).

Noel, W. (1993), 'The Making of BL Harley MSS 2506 and 603' (unpubl. PhD dissertation, Cambridge Univ.).

– (1995), *The Harley Psalter*, Cambridge Studies in Palaeography and Codicology 4 (Cambridge).

Nokes, R.S. (2004), 'The Several Compilers of Bald's Leechbook', *ASE* 33: 51–76.

Nordenfalk, C. (1932), 'On the Age of the Earliest Echternach Manuscripts', *Acta Archaeologica* 3: 57–62.

– (1947), 'Before the Book of Durrow', *Acta Archaeologica* 18: 141–74.

– (1951), 'A Note on the Stockholm *Codex Aureus*', *Nordisk Tidskrift för Bok- och Biblioteksväsen* 38: 145–55.

– (1977), *Celtic and Anglo-Saxon Painting: Book Illustration in the British Isles 600–800* (New York).

– (1978), Review of *An Early Breton Gospel Book. A Ninth Century Manuscript from the Collection of H.L. Bradfer-Lawrence (1887–1965)*, by F. Wormald, ed. by J.J.G. Alexander (printed for the members of The Roxburghe Club, Cambridge, 1977), *Burlington Magazine* 120: 243–4.

– (2000), 'Medieval Charades and the Visual Syntax of the Utrecht Psalter', in Cassidy—Muir Wright (2000), 34–41.

Norman, F., ed. (1949), *Waldere* (London).

Norman, H.W. (1849), *The Anglo-Saxon Version of the Hexameron of St Basil, or Be Godes Six Daga Weorcum: And the Saxon Remains of St Basil's Admonitio ad Filium Spiritualem*, 2nd ed. (London).

Nortier, G. (1957), 'Les bibliothèques médiévales des abbayes bénédictines de Normandie', *Revue Mabillon* 47: 219–44.

- (1966), *Les bibliothèques médiévales des abbayes bénédictines de Normandie* (Caen).
Nortier-Marchand, G. (1955), 'La bibliothèque de Jumièges au moyen âge', in *Jumièges* (1955) II, 599–614.
Norton, C. (1998), 'History, Wisdom and Illumination', in Rollason (1998), 61–105.
- (2004), 'York Minster in the Time of Wulfstan', in Townend (2004), 207–34.
Oates, J.C.T. (1982), 'Notes on the Later History of the Oldest Manuscript of Welsh Poetry: The Cambridge Juvencus', *CMCS* 3: 81–7.
- (1986), *Cambridge University Library: A History from the Beginnings to the Copyright Act of Queen Anne* (Cambridge).
O'Brien O'Keeffe, K. (1982), 'Six Hexameral Blessings: A Curiosity in the Benedictional of Archbishop Robert', *Medievalia et Humanistica* n.s. 11: 99–109.
- and A.R.P Journet (1983), 'Numerical Taxonomy and the Analysis of Manuscript Relationships', *Manuscripta* 27: 131–45.
- (1985), 'The Text of Aldhelm's *Enigma* no. c in Oxford, Bodleian Library, Rawlinson C. 697 and Exeter Riddle 40', *ASE* 14: 61–73.
- (1987), 'Graphic Cues for Presentation of Verse in the Earliest English Manuscripts of the *Historia Ecclesiastica*', *Manuscripta* 31: 139–46.
- (1990), *Visible Song. Transitional Literacy in Old English Verse*, CSASE 4 (Cambridge).
- (1994), 'Orality and the Developing Text of Caedmon's Hymn', in Richards (1994), 221–50 [orig. publ. *Speculum* 62 (1987), 1–20].
- (1998a), 'Reading the C-Text: The After-Lives of London, British Library, Cotton Tiberius B. i', in Pulsiano—Treharne (1998a), 137–60.
- (1998b), 'Body and Law in Late Anglo-Saxon England', *ASE* 27: 209–32.
- ed. (2001), *The Anglo-Saxon Chronicle: A Collaborative Edition*, V: *MS C* (Cambridge).
- and A. Orchard, eds. (2005), *Latin Learning and English Lore. Studies in Anglo-Saxon Literature for Michael Lapidge*, 2 vols. (Toronto).
- (2006), 'Goscelin and the Consecration of Eve', *ASE* 35: 251–70.
O'Brien, S.M. (1985), 'An Edition of Seven Homilies from Lambeth Palace Library MS 487' (unpubl. PhD dissertation, Oxford Univ.).
Obrist, B. (2000), 'The Astronomical Sundial in St Willibrord's Calendar and its Early Medieval Context', *AHDLMA* 67: 71–118.
- (2002), 'Les manuscrits du *De cursu stellarum* de Grégoire de Tours et le manuscrit Laon, Bibliothèque municipale 422', *Scriptorium* 56: 335–45.
Obst, W. and F. Schleburg, eds. (1998), *Lieder aus König Alfreds Trostbuch: Die Stabreimverse der altenglischen Boethius-Übertragung* (Heidelberg).

Ó Carragáin, É. (2001), 'Cynewulf's Epilogue to *Elene* and the Tastes of the Vercelli Compiler: A Paradigm of Meditative Reading', in Kay—Sylvester (2001), 187–201.

Ó Cróinín, D. (1982), 'Pride and Prejudice', *Peritia* 1: 352–62.

– (1984), 'Rath Melsigi, Willibrord and the Earliest Echternach Manuscripts', *Peritia* 3: 17–49.

– (1989), 'Is the Augsburg Gospel Codex a Northumbrian Manuscript?', in Bonner et al. (1989a), 189–202.

– ed. (1994), *Psalterium Salabergae. Staatsbibliothek zu Berlin – Preussischer Kulturbesitz – MS. Hamilton 553*, Codices Illuminati Medii Aevi 30 (Munich) [facsimile].

– (1995), 'The Salaberga Psalter', in *From the Isles of the North. Early Medieval Art in Ireland and Britain. Proceedings of the Third International Conference on Insular Art held at the Ulster Museum, Belfast, 7–11 April 1994*, ed. C. Bourke (Belfast, 1995), 127–35.

– (2001), 'The Earliest Old Irish Glosses', in Bergmann (2001), 7–32.

O'Donnell, D.P. (2001), 'Junius's Knowledge of the Old English Poem *Durham*', *ASE* 30: 231–45.

– (2002), 'The Accuracy of the *St Petersburg Bede*', *N&Q* 247: 4–6.

O'Donovan, M.A., ed. (1988), *Charters of Sherborne*, Anglo-Saxon Charters 3 (Oxford).

Oediger, F.W. (1972), *Das Hauptstaatsarchiv Düsseldorf und seine Bestände*, 5. *Archive des nichtstaatlichen Bereichs: Handschriften* (Siegburg).

Oess, G., ed. (1910), *Der altenglische Arundel-Psalter. Eine Interlinearversion in der Handschrift Arundel 60 des Britischen Museums*, Anglistische Forschungen 30 (Heidelberg).

Ogawa, H. (1994), 'The Retoucher in MSS Junius 85 and 86', *N&Q* 239: 6–10.

– (2010), *Language and Style in Old English Composite Homilies*, MRTS 36 (Tempe, AZ).

Ogura, M. et al., eds. (2003), *A Concordance to Select Homilies in MS Lambeth Palace 487 and MS Trinity College Cambridge B. 14. 52* (Tokyo).

Ohlgren, T.H. (1972a), 'Five New Drawings in the MS Junius 11: Their Iconography and Thematic Significance', *Speculum* 47: 227–33.

– (1972b), 'The Illustrations of the *Caedmonian Genesis*', *Medievalia et Humanistica* 3: 199–212.

– (1972c), 'Visual Language in the Old English *Caedmonian Genesis*', *Visible Language* 6: 253–76.

– (1975), 'Some New Light on the Old English *Caedmonian Genesis*', *Studies in Iconography* 1: 38–73.

– (1986), *Insular and Anglo-Saxon Illuminated Manuscripts: An Iconographic Catalogue c. AD 625 to 1100* (New York).

- (1991), *Anglo-Saxon Art: Texts and Contexts*, OEN Subsidia 17.
- (1992), *Anglo-Saxon Textual Illustration. Photographs of Sixteen Manuscripts with Descriptions and Index* (Kalamazoo, MI).
- (1993), 'Martial Iconography in the Harley Psalter: Dubbing or Drubbing?', *OEN* 26.3: 36–8.
Okasha, E. (1968), 'The Leningrad Bede', *Scriptorium* 22: 35–7.
- (2006), 'Script-Mixing in Anglo-Saxon Inscriptions', in Rumble (2006a), 62–70.
Oldfather, W.A. (1943), *Studies in the Text Tradition of St. Jerome's Vitae Patrum* (Urbana, IL).
Olds, B.M. (1984), 'The Anglo-Saxon Leechbook III: A Critical Edition and Translation' (unpubl. PhD dissertation, University of Denver, CO).
Oliphant, R.T., ed. (1966), *The Harley Latin—Old English Glossary edited from British Museum MS Harley 3376* (The Hague).
O'Loughlin, T. (1999), 'The Eusebian Apparatus in Some Vulgate Gospel Books', *Peritia* 13: 1–92.
- (2007), 'Division Systems for the Gospels: The Case of the Stowe St John (Dublin, RIA, D. II. 3)', *Scriptorium* 61: 150–64.
- (2009), 'The Biblical Text of the Book of Deer (C.U.L. Ii. 6. 32): Evidence for the Remains of a Division System from its Manuscript Ancestry', *Scriptorium* 63: 30–57.
Olson, L. (1989), *Early Monasteries in Cornwall*, Studies in Celtic History 11 (Woodbridge).
O'Mahony, F., ed. (1994), *The Book of Kells. Proceedings of a Conference at Trinity College Dublin, 6–9 September 1992* (Aldershot).
O'Meara, J.J. and B. Naumann, eds. (1976), *Latin Script and Letters A.D. 400–900. Festschrift presented to Ludwig Bieler on the Occasion of his 70th Birthday* (Leiden).
Omont, H. (1930), 'Fragment d'un manuscrit anglo-saxon des Étymologies d'Isidore de Seville', *Bibliothèque de l'École des Chartes* 91: 405.
O'Neill, P.P. (1981), 'The Old English Introductions to the Prose Psalms of the Paris Psalter: Sources, Structure and Composition', *Studies in Philology* 78: 20–38.
- (1986), 'A Lost Old-English Charter Rubric: The Evidence from the Regius Psalter', *N&Q* 231: 292–4.
- (1989), 'Further Old English Glosses on Sedulius in BN lat. 8092', *Anglia* 107: 415.
- (1991), 'Latin Learning at Winchester in the Early Eleventh Century: The Evidence of the Lambeth Psalter', *ASE* 20: 143–66.
- (1992), 'Syntactical Glosses in the Lambeth Psalter and the Reading of Old English Interlinear Translation as Sentences', *Scriptorium* 46: 250–6.

- (1993), 'Further Old English Glosses and Corrections in the Lambeth Psalter', *Anglia* 111: 82–93.
- (1997), 'On the Date, Provenance and Relationship of the "Solomon and Saturn" Dialogues', *ASE* 26: 139–68.
- ed. (2001), *King Alfred's Old English Prose Translation of the First Fifty Psalms* (Cambridge, MA).
- (2002), 'Irish Transmission of Late Antique Learning: The Case of Theodore of Mopsuestia's Commentary on the Psalms', in Ní Chatháin—Richter (2002), 68–77.
- ed. (2012), *Psalterium Suthantoniense*, CCCM 240 (Turnhout).
O'Neill, T. (1984), *The Irish Hand: Scribes and their Manuscripts from the Earliest Times to the Seventeenth Century, with an Exemplar of Irish Scripts* (Mountrath).
Önnerfors, U., ed. (1985), *Abbo von Saint-Germain-des-Prés: 22 Predigten. Kritische Ausgabe und Kommentar*, Lateinische Sprache und Literatur des Mittelalters 16 (Frankfurt am Main).
Oosthout, H. and J. Schilling, eds. (1999), *Anicii Manlii Severini Boethii De Arithmetica*, CCSL 94A (Turnhout).
Openshaw, K.M.J. (1989), 'The Battle Between Christ and Satan in the Tiberius Psalter', *JWCI* 52: 14–33.
- (1990), 'Images, Texts and Contexts: the Iconography of the Tiberius Psalter, London, British Library, Cotton MS Tiberius C. vi' (unpubl. PhD dissertation, University of Toronto).
- (1993), 'Weapons in the Daily Battle: Images of the Conquest of Evil in the Early Medieval Psalter', *The Art Bulletin* 75: 17–38.
Orbán, A.P. (1998–9) and (2000), 'Ein anonymer Aratorkommentar in Hs. London, Royal MS. 15. A. V', *Sacris Erudiri* 38: 317–51, and 40: 131–239.
- ed. (2006), *Aratoris subdiaconi Historia apostolica*, 2 vols., CCSL 130–130A (Turnhout).
Orchard, A. (1994), *The Poetic Art of Aldhelm*, CSASE 8 (Cambridge).
- (1995), *Pride and Prodigies. Studies in the Monsters of the Beowulf-Manuscript* (Cambridge).
- (2003), *A Critical Companion to Beowulf* (Cambridge).
- (2004), 'Re-editing Wulfstan: Where's the Point?', in Townend (2004), 63–91.
- (2007), 'Wulfstan as Reader, Writer, and Rewriter', in Kleist (2007a), 311–41.
- (2012), 'The Library of Wulfstan of York', in R. Gameson (2012), 694–700.
Orchard, N. (1994), 'An Eleventh-Century Anglo-Saxon Missal Fragment', *ASE* 23: 283–9.
- (1995a), 'A Note on the Masses for St Cuthbert', *RB* 105: 79–98.

- (1995b), 'The Bosworth Psalter and St Augustine's Missal', in Eales—Sharpe (1995), 87–94.
- (1995c), 'An Anglo-Saxon Mass for St. Willibrord and its Later Liturgical Uses', *ASE* 24: 1–10.
- ed. (2002), *The Leofric Missal*, 2 vols., HBS 113–14 (London).
- ed. (2005), *The Sacramentary of Ratoldus (Paris, Bibliothèque nationale de France, lat. 12052)*, HBS 116 (London).

O'Reilly, J. (1992), 'St John as a Figure of the Contemplative Life: Text and Image in the Art of the Anglo-Saxon Benedictine Reform', in Ramsay et al. (1992), 165–87.
- (1994), 'The Book of Kells and Two Breton Gospel Books', in Laurent—Davis (1994), 217–34.
- (2011), 'St John the Evangelist: Between Two Worlds', in Hourihane (2011), 189–218.

Ortenberg, V. (1990a), 'An Unknown Late Anglo-Saxon Text about Old St Peter's in Rome', *AntJ* 70: 115–17.
- (1990b), 'Archbishop Sigeric's Journey to Rome in 990', *ASE* 19: 197–246.
- (1992), *The English Church and the Continent in the Tenth and Eleventh Centuries: Cultural, Spiritual and Artistic Exchanges* (Oxford).

Orton, P. (2001), 'To be a Pilgrim: The Old English *Seafarer* and its Irish Affinities', in Kay—Sylvester (2001), 213–23.

Oshitari, K. et al., eds. (1988), *Philologica Anglica: Essays Presented to Prof. Y. Terasawa on the Occasion of his 60th Birthday* (Tokyo).

Osternacher, J., ed. (1902), *Theoduli ecloga* (Irfahr).
- (1916), 'Die Ueberlieferung der Ecloga Theoduli', *Neues Archiv der Gesellschaft für ältere deutsche Geschichtskunde* 40: 331–76.

O'Sullivan, W. (1958–9), 'The Donor of the Book of Kells', *Irish Historical Studies* 11: 5–7.
- (1994), 'The Lindisfarne Scriptorium: For and Against', *Peritia* 8: 80–94.

Ott, J.S. and A. Trumbore Jones, eds. (2007), *The Bishop Reformed* (Aldershot).

Owen-Crocker, G.R., ed. (2009), *Working with Anglo-Saxon Manuscripts* (Exeter).

Pächt, O. (1950a), 'Early Italian Nature Studies and the Early Calendar Landscape', *JWCI* 13: 13–47.
- (1950b), 'Hugo Pictor', *BLR* 3: 96–103.
- et al. (1960), *The St Albans Psalter (Albani Psalter)*, Studies of the Warburg and Courtauld Institutes 25 (London).
- and J.J.G. Alexander (1966), *Illuminated Manuscripts in the Bodleian Library Oxford*, I. *German, Dutch, Flemish, French and Spanish Schools* (Oxford).
- and J.J.G. Alexander (1973), *Illuminated Manuscripts in the Bodleian Library Oxford*, III: *British, Irish and Icelandic Schools. With Addenda to vols. I and II* (Oxford).

Page, C. (1977), 'Biblical Instruments in Medieval Manuscript Illustration', *Early Music* 5: 299–309.

– (1981), 'The Boethian Metrum "Bella bis quinis": A New Song from Saxon Canterbury', in M. Gibson (1981), 306–11.

Page, R.I. (1965a), 'Anglo-Saxon Episcopal Lists, Parts I and II', *Nottingham Medieval Studies* 9: 71–95.

– (1965b), 'A Note on the Text of Manuscript Cambridge, Corpus Christi College 422', *MÆ* 34: 36–9.

– (1966), 'Anglo-Saxon Episcopal Lists, Part III', *Nottingham Medieval Studies* 10: 2–24.

– (1972–6), 'Anglo-Saxon Texts in Early Modern Transcripts', *TCBS* 6: 69–85.

– (1973), *An Introduction to English Runes* (London; 2nd rev. ed., Woodbridge, 1999).

– (1974), 'The Lost Leaf of MS. CCCC 196', *N&Q* 219: 472–3.

– (1975), 'More Aldhelm Glosses from Corpus Christi College Cambridge 326', *ES* 56: 481–90.

– (1978), 'Old English Liturgical Rubrics in Corpus Christi College, Cambridge, MS 422', *Anglia* 96: 148–58.

– (1979), 'More Old English Scratched Glosses', *Anglia* 97: 27–45.

– (1981), 'New Work on Old English Scratched Glosses', in Tilling (1981), 105–15.

– (1981–5), 'Matthew Parker's Copy of *Prosper his Meditation with his Wife*', *TCBS* 8: 342–9.

– (1982), 'The Study of Latin Texts in Late Anglo-Saxon England [2]: The Evidence of English Glosses', in Brooks (1982), 141–65.

– (1989), 'Roman and Runic on St Cuthbert's Coffin', in Bonner et al. (1989a), 257–65.

– (1992a), 'On the Feasibility of a Corpus of Anglo-Saxon Glosses: The View from the Library', in Derolez (1992), 77–97.

– (1992b), 'The Sixeenth-Century Reception of Alfred the Great's Letter to his Bishops', *Anglia* 110: 36–64.

– (1993a), *Matthew Parker and his Books: Sandars Lectures in Bibliography Delivered on 14, 16, 18 May 1990 at the University of Cambridge* (Kalamazoo, MI).

– (1993b), 'Runes in Two Anglo-Saxon Manuscripts', *Nytt om Runer* 8: 15–19.

– et al. (1995), 'Two Fragments of an Old English Manuscript in the Library of Cambridge, Corpus Christi College', *Speculum* 70: 502–29.

– (1996), 'An Old English Fragment from Westminster Abbey', *ASE* 25: 201–7.

– (1998), 'Two Runic Notes', *ASE* 27: 289–94.

– (2001), 'Recent Work on Old English Glosses: The Case of Boethius', in Bergmann (2001), 217–42.

Page, S. (2004), *Magic in Medieval Manuscripts* (Toronto).

Palmer, R., First Earl of Selborne (1892), *Ancient Facts and Fictions Concerning Churches and Tithes*, 2nd ed. (London).

Panayotova, S., ed. (2007), *The Cambridge Illuminations: The Conference Papers* (London and Turnhout).

Pani, L. (2000), 'Aspetti della tradizione manoscritta dell' "Historia Langobardorum"', in *Paolo Diacono. Uno scrittore fra tradizione longobarda e rinnovamento carolingio*, ed. P. Chiesa (Udine, 2000), 367–412.

Panofsky, D. (1943), 'The Textual Basis of the Utrecht Psalter Illustrations', *Art Bulletin* 25: 50–8.

Papahagi, A. (2010), *Boethiana mediaevalia. A Collection of Studies on the Early Medieval Fortune of Boethius' Consolation of Philosophy* (Bucharest).

Parkes, M.B. (1976a), 'The Handwriting of St Boniface: A Reassessment of the Problems', *BDGSL* 98: 161–79 [repr. Parkes (1991), 121–42].

- (1976b), 'The Palaeography of the Parker Manuscript of the Chronicle, Laws and Sedulius, and Historiography at Winchester in the Late Ninth and Tenth Centuries', *ASE* 5: 149–71 [repr. Parkes (1991), 143–69].

- and A.G. Watson, eds. (1978a), *Medieval Scribes, Manuscripts and Libraries. Essays Presented to N.R. Ker* (London).

- (1978b), 'Punctuation, or Pause and Effect', in *Medieval Eloquence. Studies in the Theory and Practice of Medieval Rhetoric*, ed. J.J. Murphy (Berkeley, CA, 1978), 127–40.

- (1979), *The Medieval Manuscripts of Keble College, Oxford: A Descriptive Catalogue* (London).

- (1981), 'A Note on MS Vatican, Bibl. Apost., lat. 3363', in M. Gibson (1981), 425–7 [repr. Parkes (1991), 260–2].

- (1982), 'The Scriptorium of Wearmouth-Jarrow', *Jarrow Lecture* (1982) [repr. Parkes (1991), 93–120].

- (1983), 'A Fragment of an Early-Tenth-Century Anglo-Saxon Manuscript and its Significance', *ASE* 12: 129–40 [repr. Parkes (1991), 171–85].

- (1987), 'The Contribution of Insular Scribes of the Seventh and Eighth Centuries to the "Grammar of Legibility"', in *Grafia e interpunzione del latino nel medioevo*, ed. A. Maierù (Rome), 15–29 [repr. Parkes (1991) 1–18].

- (1991), *Scribes, Scripts and Readers. Studies in the Communication, Presentation and Dissemination of Medieval Texts* (London).

- (1992), *Pause and Effect: An Introduction to the History of Punctuation in the West* (Aldershot).

- (1997a), '*Rædan, areccan, smeagan*: How the Anglo-Saxons Read', *ASE* 26: 1–22.

- (1997b), 'Archaizing Hands in English Manuscripts', in Carley—Tite (1997), 101–41.

Parsons, D., ed. (1975), *Tenth-Century Studies: Essays in Commemoration of the Millennium of the Council of Winchester and Regularis Concordia* (London).

Passalacqua, M. (1978), *I codici di Prisciano*, Sussidi Eruditi 29 (Rome).

– ed. (1992), *Prisciani Caesariensis Institutio de nomine et pronomine et uerbo*, Testi grammaticali latini 2 (Urbino).

Paul, H., ed. (1891–3), *Grundriss der germanischen Philologie*, 2 vols. in 3 (Strassburg; 2nd ed., 3 vols., Strassburg, 1900–9).

Paulus, B., ed. (1969), *Paschasius Radbertus: De corpore et sanguine Domini, Epistola ad Fredugardum*, CCCM 16 (Turnhout).

Pellegrin, E., ed. (1975–91), *Les manuscrits classiques latins de la Bibliothèque Vaticane: Catalogue*, 3 vols. (Paris).

– (1982), *Manuscrits latins de la Bodmeriana* (Cologny-Genève).

Pellens, K. (1964–8), 'The Tracts of the Norman Anonymous: C.C.C.C. M.S. 415', *TCBS* 4: 155–65.

– ed. (1966), *Die Texte des Normannischen Anonymus. Unter Konsultation der Teilausgaben von H. Böhmer, H. Scherrinsky und G. H. Williams neu aus der Handschrift 415 des Corpus Christi College, Cambridge*, Veröffentlichungen des Instituts für Europäische Geschichte Mainz 42: Abteilung für abendländische Religionsgeschichte (Wiesbaden).

– (1973), *Das Kirchengedenken des Normannischen Anonymus*, Veröffentlichungen des Instituts für Europäische Geschichte Mainz 69 (Wiesbaden, 1973).

– (1977), *Der Codex 415 des Corpus Christi College Cambridge: Facsimile-Ausgabe der Text-Überlieferung des Normannischen Anonymus*, Veröffentlichungen des Instituts für Europäische Geschichte Mainz 82 (Wiesbaden, 1977).

Pelteret, D.A.E. (1990), *Catalogue of English Post-Conquest Vernacular Documents* (Woodbridge).

– (1995), *Slavery in Early Medieval England: From the Reign of Alfred until the Twelfth Century* (Woodbridge).

– ed. (2000), *Anglo-Saxon History: Basic Readings* (New York).

Perani, M. and C. Ruini, eds. (2002), *'Fragmenta ne pereant'. Recupero e studio dei frammenti di manoscritti medievali e rinascimentali riutilizzati in legature* (Ravenna).

Perry, B.E., ed. (1965), *Babrius and Phaedrus*, The Loeb Classical Library 436 (London).

Petersohn, J. (1966a), 'Die Bückeburger Fragmente von Bedas *De temporum ratione*', *DAEM* 22: 587–97.

– (1966b), 'Neue Bedafragmente in Northumbrischer Unziale saec. VIII', *Scriptorium* 20: 215–47.

Peterson, W. (1951), 'The Unpublished Homilies of the Old English Vercelli Book' (unpubl. PhD dissertation, University of New York).

Petitmengin, P. (1993), 'La compilation "De uindictis magnis magnorum peccatorum": Exemples d'anthropophagie tirés des sièges de Jérusalem et de Samarie', in *Philologia Sacra. Biblische und patristische Studien für Hermann J. Frede und Walter Thiele zu ihrem siebzigsten Geburtstag*, ed. R. Gryson, 2 vols. (Freiburg), 622–38.

Petrucci, A. (1971), 'L'onciale romana', *SM* 3rd ser. 12: 75–134.

Pertuccione, J.F. (2008), 'The *Q:*, *Quaere Hoc*, and *Ad Quid* Glosses: Observations on their Purpose and Distribution', *Scriptorium* 62: 231–51.

Petschenig, M., ed. (1888/2004), *Iohannis Cassiani de Institutis Coenobiorum*, CSEL 17 (Vienna 1888; 2nd ed. with Supplement by G. Krenz, 2004).

Pettit, E. (1999), 'Anglo-Saxon Charms in Oxford, Bodleian Library MS Barlow 35', *Nottingham Medieval Studies* 43: 33–46.

– ed. (2001), *Anglo-Saxon Remedies, Charms and Prayers from British Library MS Harley 585: The Lacnunga*, 2 vols. (Lewiston, NY).

Petzold, A. (1990), 'Colour Notes in English Romanesque Manuscripts', *BLJ* 16: 16–25.

Pfaff, R.W. (1992a), 'Eadui Basan: *Scriptorum Princeps*?', in Hicks (1992), 267–83.

– (1992b), 'The *Tituli*, Collects, Canticles, and Creeds', in M. Gibson (1992), 88–107.

– (1994), 'N.R. Ker and the Study of English Medieval Manuscripts', in Richards (1994), 55–78.

– ed. (1995a), *The Liturgical Books of Anglo-Saxon England*, OEN Subsidia 23 (Kalamazoo, MI).

– (1995b), 'Massbooks: Sacramentaries and Missals' in Pfaff (1995a), 7–34.

– (1999a), 'The Anglo-Saxon Bishop and his Book', *BJRL* 81: 3–24.

– (1999b), 'The "Sample Week" in the Medieval Latin Divine Office', in Swanson (1999), 78–88.

– (2001), 'M.R. James and the Liturgical Manuscripts of Cambridge', in Dennison (2001), 174–93.

– (2009), *The Liturgy in Medieval England. A History* (Cambridge).

– (2012), 'Liturgical Books', in R. Gameson (2012), 449–59.

Pheifer, J.D., ed. (1974), *Old English Glosses in the Épinal-Erfurt Glossary* (Oxford).

– (1987), 'Early Anglo-Saxon Glossaries and the School of Canterbury', *ASE* 16: 17–44.

– (1992), 'The Relationship of the Second Erfurt Glossary to the Épinal-Erfurt and Corpus Glossaries', in Derolez (1992), 189–205.

– (1994), 'How not to edit Glossaries', in Scragg – Szarmach (1994b), 263–309.

– (1995), 'The Canterbury Bible Glosses: Facts and Problems', in Lapidge (1995a), 281–333.

Philippart, G. (1977), *Les légendiers latins et autres manuscrits hagiographiques* (Turnhout).

– ed. (2001), *Hagiographies* III (Turnhout).

Pickwoad, N. (1994), 'The Conservation of Cambridge, Corpus Christi College MS. 197B', in Hadgraft—Swift (1994), 114–22.

Pingree, D. (1981), 'Boethius' Geometry and Astronomy', in Gibson (1981), 155–61.

– ed. (1997), *Preceptum canonis Ptolemaei* (Louvain).

Piper, A.J. (1978), 'The Libraries of the Monks of Durham', in Parkes—Watson (1978), 213–49.

– (1994), 'The Durham Cantor's Book (Durham, Dean and Chapter Library, MS B. IV. 24)', in Rollason (1994), 79–92.

– (1998a), 'The Early Lists and Obits of the Durham Monks', in Rollason (1998), 161–200.

– (1998b), 'The Historical Interests of the Monks of Durham', in Rollason (1998), 301–32.

– (2004), 'The Names of the Durham Monks', in Rollason (2004a), 117–25.

– (2007), 'The Monks of Durham and the Study of Scripture', in J.G. Clark (2007), 86–103.

Planchart, A.E. (1977), *The Repertory of Tropes at Winchester*, 2 vols. (Princeton, NJ).

Planta, J. (1802), *A Catalogue of the Manuscripts in the Cottonian Library, Deposited in the British Museum* (London; repr. New York, 1974).

Plotzek, J.M. (1998), *Glaube und Wissen im Mittelalter* [Ausstellung, Erzbischöfliches Diözesanmuseum Köln, 7. August bis 15. November 1998] (Munich).

Plummer, C., ed. (1892–9), *Two of the Saxon Chronicles Parallel with Supplementary Extracts from the Others*, 2 vols. (Oxford).

– ed. (1896), *Venerabilis Baedae Opera Historica*, 2 vols. (Oxford).

Plummer, J. (1968), *The Glazier Collection of Illuminated Manuscripts* (New York).

Pochat, G. (2005), 'Virtuelle Raumvorstellung und frühmittelalterliche Ikonik', in Vavra (2005), 135–48.

Polara, G. (1971), *Ricerche sulla tradizione manoscritta di Publilio Optaziano Porfirio* (Salerno).

– ed. (1973), *Publilii Optatiani Porfyrii Carmina*, 2 vols. (Torino).

Pollard, G. (1962), 'The Construction of English Twelfth-Century Bookbindings', *The Library*, 5th ser. 17: 1–22.

- (1975), 'Some Anglo-Saxon Bookbindings', *Book Collector* 24: 130–59.
- (1976), 'Describing Medieval Bookbindings', in Alexander—Gibson (1976), 50–65.

Pollington, S. (2000), *Leechcraft: Early English Charms, Plant Lore and Healing* (Hockwold-cum-Wilton).

Pope, J.C. (1931), 'The Manuscripts of Ælfric's Catholic Homilies' (unpubl. PhD dissertation, Yale University).
- ed. (1967–8), *Homilies of Ælfric*, 2 vols., EETS o.s. 259–60 (Oxford).
- (1969), 'The Lacuna in the Text of Cynewulf's Ascension (Christ II, 556b)', in Atwood—Hill (1969), 210–19.
- (1974), 'An Unsuspected Lacuna in the Exeter Book', *Speculum* 49: 615–22.
- (1978), 'Palaeography and Poetry: Some Solved and Some Unsolved Problems of the Exeter Book', in Parkes—Watson (1978), 25–68.
- (1981), 'The Text of a Damaged Passage in the Exeter Book: Advent (Christ I) 18–32', *ASE* 9: 137–56.
- ed. (2001), *Eight Old English Poems*, 3rd ed. rev. R.D. Fulk (Indianapolis).

Poppe, E. and B. Ross, eds. (1996), *The Legend of Mary of Egypt* (Blackrock).

Porter, C. (2002), 'The Identification of Purple in Manuscripts', *Dyes in History and Archaeology* 21: 59–64.

Porter, D.W. (1996a), 'A Double Solution to the Latin Riddle in MS. Antwerp, Plantin-Moretus Museum M. 16. 2', *ANQ* 9.1: 3–9.
- (1996b), 'Ælfric's *Colloquy* and Ælfric Bata', *Neophilologus* 80: 639–60.
- (1997), 'Anglo-Saxon Colloquies: Ælfric, Ælfric Bata and *De raris fabulis retractata*', *Neophilologus* 81: 467–80.
- (1999a), 'The Earliest Texts with English and French', *ASE* 28: 87–110.
- (1999b), 'On the Antwerp-London Glossaries', *JEGP* 98: 170–92.
- ed. (2002), *Excerptiones de Prisciano: The Source for Ælfric's Latin-Old English Grammar*, AST 4 (Cambridge).
- (2010), 'The Antwerp-London Glossary and Ælfric's Glossary', *N&Q* 255: 305–10.
- ed. (2011a), *The Antwerp-London Glossaries. The Latin and Latin-Old English Vocabularies from Antwerp, Museum Plantin-Moretus 16. 2 – London, British Library Add. 32246, I: Texts and Indexes* (Toronto).
- (2011b), 'The Antwerp-London Glossaries and the First English School Text', in Lendinara et al. (2011), 153–77.
- (2012), 'The Anglo-Latin Elegy of Herbert and Wulfgar', *ASE* 40: 225–47.

Potter, S. (1935), 'The Winchester Bede', *Wessex* 3.2: 39–49.

Poulin, J.-C. (1990), 'Les dossiers de S. Magloire de Dol et de S. Malo d'Alet (province de Bretagne)', *Francia* 17: 159–209.

Powell, K. and D. Scragg, eds. (2003), *Apocryphal Texts and Traditions in Anglo-Saxon England* (Cambridge).
– (2008), 'Viking Invasions and Marginal Annotations in Cambridge, Corpus Christi College 162', *ASE* 37: 151–71.
Powell, R. (1956), 'The Book of Kells. The Book of Durrow. Comments on the Vellum, the Make-up, and Other Aspects', *Scriptorium* 10: 3–21.
– (1962), 'The Construction of English Twelfth-Century Bindings', *The Library* 5th ser. 17: 1–22.
– (1965), 'The Lichfield St. Chad's Gospels: Repair and Rebinding, 1961–2', *The Library* 5th ser. 20: 259–76.
Powicke, F.M. (1931), *The Medieval Books of Merton College* (Oxford).
Pratt, D. (2001), 'The Illnesses of King Alfred the Great', *ASE* 30: 39–90.
Prescott, A. (1987), 'The Structure of English Pre-Conquest Benedictionals', *BLJ* 13: 118–59.
– (1988), 'The Text of the Benedictional of St. Æthelwold', in Yorke (1988), 119–47.
– (1997), '"Their Present Miserable State of Cremation": The Restoration of the Cotton Library', in C.J. Wright (1997), 391–454.
– (1998), 'The Ghost of Asser', in Pulsiano – Treharne (1998a), 255–93.
– ed. (2001), *The Benedictional of Saint Æthelwold, a Masterpiece of Anglo-Saxon Art: A Facsimile*, 2 vols. (London).
– (2004), 'Robin Flower and Laurence Nowell', in Wilcox (2004a), 41–61.
Priebsch, R. (1925), *The Heliand Manuscript Cotton Caligula A .vii in the British Museum: A Study* (Oxford).
Prinz, O. (1985), 'Eine frühe abendländische Aktualisierung der lateinischen Übersetzung des Pseudo-Methodius', *DAEM* 41: 1–23.
– ed. (1993), *Die Kosmographie des Aethicus*, MGH, Hilfsmittel 14 (Munich).
Prokosch, E. (1929), 'Two Types of Scribal Errors in the *Beowulf* MS', in Malone (1929), 196–207.
Proud, J. (2000), 'Old English Prose Saints' Lives in the Twelfth Century: The Evidence of the Extant Manuscripts', in Swan – Treharne (2000a), 117–31.
– (2002), 'The Cotton-Corpus Legendary into the Twelfth-Century: Notes on Salisbury Cathedral Library MSS 221 and 222', in Treharne – Rosser (2002), 341–52.
Puhle, M., ed. (2001), *Otto der Grosse. Magdeburg und Europa*, 2 vols. [exhibition catalogue] (Mainz).
Pulliam, H. (2011), 'Looking to Byzantium: Light, Color, and Cloth in Insular Art', in Hourihane (2011), 59–78.
Pulsiano, P. (1982), 'Materials for an Edition of the Blickling Psalter' (unpubl. PhD dissertation, State University of New York at Stony Brook).

– (1983), 'A New Look at the Anglo-Saxon Glosses in the Blickling Psalter', *Manuscripta* 27: 32–7.
– (1984), 'A New Anglo-Saxon Gloss in the *Liber scintillarum*', *N&Q* 229: 152–3.
– (1985a), 'The Latin and Old English Glosses in the Blickling and Regius Psalters', *Traditio* 41: 79–115.
– (1985b), 'Hortatory Purpose in the OE *Visio Leofrici*', *MÆ* 54: 109–16.
– (1991a), 'British Library, Cotton Tiberius A.iii, fol. 59rv: An Unrecorded Charm in the Form of an Address to the Cross', *ANQ* n.s. 4: 3–5.
– (1991b), 'The Old English Introductions in the *Vitellius Psalter*', *SN* 63: 13–35.
– (1991c), 'Old English Glossed Psalters: Editions Versus Manuscripts', *Manuscripta* 35: 75–95.
– (1993), 'New Old English Glosses in the Vitellius Psalter', *ANQ* n.s. 6: 180–2.
– (1994), 'New Old English Glosses in the Vitellius Psalter (II)', *ANQ* n.s. 7: 3–6.
– and J. McGowan (1994), 'Four Unedited Prayers in London, British Library, Cotton Tiberius A. iii', *MS* 56: 189–216.
– (1995), 'Psalters', in Pfaff (1995a), 61–85.
– (1996), 'The Originality of the Old English Gloss of the *Vespasian Psalter* and its Relation to the Gloss of the *Junius Psalter*', *ASE* 25: 37–62.
– (1997), 'A Middle English Gloss in the Lambeth Psalter', *ANQ* n.s. 10: 2–9.
– and E. Treharne, eds. (1998a), *Anglo-Saxon Manuscripts and their Heritage* (Aldershot).
– (1998b), 'The Prefatory Matter of London, British Library, Cotton Vitellius E. xviii', in Pulsiano—Treharne (1998a), 85–116.
– (1998c), 'Abbot Ælfwine and the Date of the Vitellius Psalter', *ANQ* n.s. 11.2: 3–12.
– (2000), 'The Old English Gloss of the *Eadwine Psalter*', in Swan—Treharne (2000a), 166–94.
– ed. (2001a), *Old English Glossed Psalters: Psalms 1–50* (Toronto).
– (2001b), 'Persius's *Satires* in Anglo-Saxon England', *JMLat* 11: 142–55.
– ed. (2002a), 'The Old English *Life of St Pantaleon*', in Hall—Hill (2002), 61–103.
– ed. (2002b), 'The Passion of St Christopher', in Treharne—Rosser (2002), 167–99.
– (2007), 'Jaunts, Jottings and Jetsam in Anglo-Saxon Manuscripts', in Keefer—Bremmer (2007a), 119–33.
Quadri, R. (1966), *I Collectanea di Eirico di Auxerre* (Fribourg).

Quentin, H. (1908), *Les martyrologes historiques du moyen âge. Étude sur la formation du martyrologe romain* (Paris).

– et al., eds. (1926–94), *Biblia Sacra iuxta latinam uulgatam uersionem ad codicum fidem, cura et studio monachorum Abbatiae pontificiae Sancti Hieronymi in Urbe O.S.B. edita*, 18 vols. (Rome).

Questa, C. and R. Raffaelli, eds. (1984), *Atti del Convegno internazionale — il libro e il testo, Urbino 20–23 settembre 1982* (Urbino).

Quiggin, E.C. (1911), 'A Fragment of an Old Welsh Computus', *Zeitschrift für keltische Philologie* 8: 407–10.

Quinn, J.J. (1956), 'The Minor Latin-Old English Glossaries in MS Cotton Cleopatra A. iii' (unpubl. PhD dissertation, Stanford Univ.).

– (1961), 'Ghost Words, Obscure Lemmata, and Doubtful Glosses in a Latin-Old English Glossary', *PQ* 40: 313–18.

– (1966), 'Some Puzzling Lemmata and Glosses in MS Cotton Cleopatra A. iii', *PQ* 45: 434–7.

Quirk, R.N. (1957), 'Winchester Cathedral in the Tenth Century', *Archaeological Journal* 114: 28–68.

Quynn, D.M. (1939), 'The Provenance of MS. Lat. 1751 of the Bibliothèque Nationale', *Speculum* 14: 490–1.

Rabel, C. (1982), 'Autour d'une copie anglo-saxonne du Psautier d'Utrecht', *Bulletin monumental* 140: 347–8.

Radiciotti, P. (1996), 'Aspetti di storia della scrittura greco-latina in relazione ai glossari tra l'Antichità ed il Medioevo', in Hamesse (1996), 121–6.

Rädle, F. (1974), *Studien zu Smaragd von Saint-Mihiel*, Medium Aevum: Philologische Studien 29 (Munich).

Raine, J., ed. (1838), *Catalogi Veteres Librorum Ecclesiae Cathedralis Dunelm.*, Surtees Society 7 (London).

Raine, J., ed. (1879–94), *The Historians of the Church of York and its Archbishops*, 3 vols., RS 71 (London).

Raios, D.K. (1983), *Recherches sur le Carmen de ponderibus et mensuris* (Ioannina).

Raith, J., ed. (1933/1964), *Die altenglische Version des Halitgar'schen Bussbuches (sog. Poenitentiale Pseudo-Ecgberti)*, Bibliothek der angelsächsischen Prosa 13 (Hamburg; repr. with a new preface, Darmstadt, 1964).

Rambaran-Olm, M.R. (2007), 'Two Remarks Concerning Folio 121 of the Exeter Book', *N&Q* 252: 207–8.

Ramsay, N. and M. Sparks (1988), *The Image of St Dunstan* (Canterbury).

– et al., eds. (1992), *St Dunstan, his Life, Times and Cult* (Woodbridge).

Ramsay, R.L. (1912), 'Theodore of Mopsuestia and St Columban on the Psalms', *Zeitschrift für celtische Philologie* 8: 452–97.

Rand, E.K. (1929), *Studies in the Script of Tours, I. A Survey of the Manuscripts of Tours*, 2 vols. (Cambridge, MA).

Ranger, F., ed. (1973), *Prisca Munimenta. Studies in Archival and Administrative History presented to Dr A.E.J. Hollaender* (London).

Ranke, E., ed. (1860), *Specimen Codicis Novi Testamenti Fuldensis* (Marburg).

– ed. (1868), *Codex Fuldensis. Novum Testamentum latine ex manuscripto Victoris Capuani* (Marburg).

Rankin, S. (1984), 'From Memory to Record: Musical Notations in Manuscripts from Exeter', *ASE* 13: 97–112.

– (1985), 'The Liturgical Background of the Old English Advent Lyrics: A Reappraisal', in Lapidge–Gneuss (1985), 317–40.

– (1987), 'Neumatic Notations in Anglo-Saxon England', in Huglo (1987), 129–40.

– and D. Hiley, eds. (1993), *Music in the Medieval English Liturgy* (Oxford).

– (1996), 'Some Reflections on Liturgical Music at Late Anglo-Saxon Worcester', in Brooks–Cubitt (1996), 325–48.

– (2003), 'St Swithun in Medieval Liturgical Music', in Lapidge (2003), 191–213.

– (2004), 'An Early Eleventh-Century Missal Fragment copied by Eadwig Basan: Bodleian Library, MS. Lat. liturg. d. 3, fols. 4–5', *BLR* 18: 220–52.

– (2005a), 'Music at Wulfstan's Cathedral', in Barrow–Brooks (2005), 219–29.

– (2005b), 'Making the Liturgy: Winchester Scribes and their Books', in Gittos–Bedingfield (2005a), 29–52.

– ed. (2007), *The Winchester Troper: Facsimile, Edition and Introduction*, Early English Church Music 50 (London).

– (2012), 'Music Books', in R. Gameson (2012), 482–506.

Rasmussen, N.K. (1998), *Les pontificaux du haut moyen âge. Genèse du livre de l'évêque*, ed. M. Haverals, Spicilegium sacrum Lovaniense, Études et documents 49 (Louvain).

Rauer, C. (2003), 'The Sources of the *Old English Martyrology*', *ASE* 32: 89–109.

– (2006), 'Pope Sergius I's Privilege for Malmesbury', in *LSE* 37: 261–81.

– (2007), 'Usage of the Old English Martyrology', in Bremmer–Dekker (2007), 125–46.

Ravaisson, F. (1841), *Rapports au Ministre de l'instruction publique sur les bibliothèques des Départements de l'Ouest, suivis de pièces inédites* (Paris).

Raw, B.C. (1961), 'A Latin-English Word-List in MS Arundel 60', *EGS* 7: 37–42.

– (1976), 'The Probable Derivation of Most of the Illustrations in Junius 11 from an Illustrated Old Saxon Genesis', *ASE* 5: 133–48.

– (1984), 'The Construction of Oxford, Bodleian Library, Junius 11', *ASE* 13: 187–207 [repr. in Richards (1994), 251–75].

– (1990), *Anglo-Saxon Crucifixion Iconography and the Art of the Monastic Revival*, CSASE 1 (Cambridge).

- (1992), 'What do We Mean by the Source of a Picture?', in Hicks (1992), 285–300.
- (1997), 'Alfredian Piety: The Book of Nunnaminster', in Roberts—Nelson (1997), 145–53.
- (1999), 'The Office of the Trinity in the Crowland Psalter (Oxford, Bodleian Library, Douce 296)', *ASE* 28: 185–200.
- (2012), 'Anglo-Saxon Prayerbooks', in R. Gameson (2012), 460–7.

Raynes, E.M. (1957), 'MS Boulogne-sur-Mer 63 and Ælfric', *MÆ* 26: 65–73.

Redknap, M., ed. (2001), *Pattern and Purpose in Insular Art. Proceedings of the Fourth International Conference on Insular Art held at the National Museum & Gallery, Cardiff, 3–6 September 1998* (Oxford).

Reeve, M.D. (1983a), 'Agrimensores', in L.D. Reynolds (1983), 1–6.
- (1983b), 'Aratea', in L.D. Reynolds (1983), 18–24.
- (1983c), 'Avianus', in L.D. Reynolds (1983), 29–32.
- (1983d), 'Hyginus', in L.D. Reynolds (1983) 187–90.
- (2000), 'The Transmission of Vegetius's *Epitoma rei militaris*', *Aevum* 74: 242–354.
- (2007), 'The Editing of Pliny's Natural History', *Revue d'histoire des textes* n.s. 2: 107–79.
- (2012), 'Excerpts from Pliny's Natural History', in *Ways of Approaching Knowledge in Late Antiquity and the Early Middle Ages: Schools and Scholarship*, ed. P.F. Farmhouse and D. Paniagua (Nordhausen), 245–63.

Rehm, B. and F. Paschke (1965), *Die Pseudoklementinen*, II. *Rekognitionen in Rufins Übersetzung*, Die griechischen christlichen Schriftsteller der ersten drei Jahrhunderte 51 (Berlin).

Reichenbächer, E. (1934), *Glossar zum altenglischen Regius-Psalter* (Diss. Jena, Teildruck).

Reinsma, L.M. (1987), *Ælfric: An Annotated Bibliography* (New York).

Rella, F.A. (1977), 'Some Aspects of the Indirect Transmission of Christian Latin Sources for Anglo-Saxon Prose from the Reign of Alfred to the Norman Conquest' (unpubl. BLitt thesis, Oxford Univ.).
- (1980), 'Continental Manuscripts Acquired for English Centers in the Tenth and Early Eleventh Centuries: A Preliminary Checklist', *Anglia* 98: 107–16.

Remley, P.G. (2009), 'The Vercelli Book and its Texts: A Guide to Scholarship', in Zacher—Orchard (2009), 318–415.

Report from the Committee [of the House of Commons] appointed to view the Cottonian Library… (London, 1732) [repr. in Thomas Smith, *Catalogue of the Manuscripts in the Cottonian Library*, ed. C.G.C. Tite (Cambridge, 1984) *ad finem*].

Reydellet, M. (1966), 'La diffusion des *Origines* d'Isidore de Seville au haut moyen âge', *Ecole française de Rome: Mélanges d'archéologie et d'histoire* 78: 383–437.

Reynolds, L.D., ed. (1983), *Texts and Transmission: A Survey of the Latin Classics* (Oxford).

- (1983a), 'Appendix Sallustiana', in L.D. Reynolds (1983), 349–52.

- ed. (1991), *C. Sallusti Crispi Catilina, Iugurtha, Historiarum fragmenta selecta, Appendix Sallustiana* (Oxford).

- and N.G. Wilson (1991), *Scribes and Scholars. A Guide to the Transmission of Greek and Latin Literature*, 3rd ed. (Oxford).

Reynolds, R.E. (1972), 'The *De Officiis VII Graduum*: Its Origins and Early Medieval Development', *MS* 34: 113–51.

- (1977), 'Marginalia in a Tenth-Century Text on Ecclesiastical Offices', in *Law, Church and Society. Essays in Honor of Stephan Kuttner*, ed. K. Pennington and R. Somerville (Philadelphia, 1977), 115–29.

- (1978), *The Ordinals of Christ from their Origins to the Twelfth Century* (Berlin and New York).

Rhodes, E.W., ed. (1889), *Defensor's Liber Scintillarum*, EETS o.s. 93 (London).

Ricci, L.G.G., ed. (2000), *La Bibbia Amiatina / The Codex Amiatinus. Riproduzione integrale su CD-ROM del manoscritto / Complete Reproduction on CD-ROM of the Manuscript Firenze, Biblioteca Medicea Laurenziana, Amiatino 1* (Florence).

Rice, D.T. (1952), *English Art: 871–1100*, The Oxford History of English Art 2 (Oxford).

Richards, M. (1973), 'The Lichfield Gospels', *NLWJ* 18: 135–46.

Richards, M.P. (1973), 'On the Date and Provenance of MS Cotton Vespasian D.xiv ff. 4–169', *Manuscripta* 17: 31–5.

- (1979), 'Innovations in Ælfrician Homiletic Manuscripts at Rochester', *AnM* 19: 13–26.

- (1986), 'The Manuscript Contexts of the Old English Laws: Tradition and Innovation', in Szarmach (1986b), 171–92.

- (1988), *Texts and their Traditions in the Medieval Library of Rochester Cathedral Priory*, Transactions of the American Philosophical Society 78.3 (Philadelphia, PA).

- ed. (1994), *Anglo-Saxon Manuscripts: Basic Readings*, Basic Readings in Anglo-Saxon England 2 (New York).

- (2000), 'Fragmentary Versions of Genesis in Old English Prose: Context and Function', in Barnhouse—Withers (2000), 145–63.

- (2006), 'The Rochester Cathedral Library: A Review of Scholarship 1987–2005, including Annotations to the 1996 Edition of the Catalogues in *CBMLC*, vol. 4', *LSE* 37: 283–320.

Richter, Martin, ed. (1996), *Die altenglischen Glossen zu Aldhelms 'De laudibus virginitatis' in der Handschrift BL, Royal 6 B.vii*, TUEPh 19 (Munich).

Richter, Michael (1973), *Canterbury Professions*, Canterbury and York Society 67 (Torquay).

Rickert, M. (1954), *Painting in Britain: The Middle Ages*, 2nd ed. (Baltimore).

Riddle, J.M. (1980), 'Dioscorides', in Kristeller et al. (1960—) IV (1980), 1–143.

Ridyard, S. (1988), *The Royal Saints of Anglo-Saxon England* (Cambridge).

Rigg, A.G. and G.R. Wieland (1975), 'A Canterbury Classbook of the mid-eleventh Century (the 'Cambridge Songs' Manuscript)', *ASE* 4: 113–30.

Ringrose, J. (2009), *Summary Catalogue of the Additional Medieval Manuscripts in Cambridge University Library acquired before 1940* (Woodbridge).

Rittmueller, J. (2002), 'Links between a Twelfth-Century Worcester (F. 94) Homily and the Eighth-Century Hiberno-Latin Commentary *Liber questionum in evangeliis*', in T.N. Hall et al. (2002), 331–54.

– ed. (2004), *Liber questionum in euangeliis*, CCSL 108F (Turnhout).

Robb, A.P. (1975), 'The History of the Holy Rood-Tree: Four Anglo-Saxon Homilies' (unpubl. PhD dissertation, University of Illinois at Urbana-Champaign, IL).

Roberts, J. (1970), 'An Inventory of Early Guthlac Materials', *MS* 32: 193–233.

– ed. (1979), *The Guthlac Poems of the Exeter Book* (Oxford).

– (1986), 'The Old English Prose Translation of Felix's *Vita Sancti Guthlaci*', in Szarmach (1986b), 363–79.

– and J. Nelson, eds. (1997), *Alfred the Wise: Studies in Honour of Janet Bately on the Occasion of her Sixty-Fifth Birthday* (Cambridge).

– and J. Nelson, eds. (2000), *Essays on Anglo-Saxon and Related Themes in Memory of Lynne Grundy*, KCLMS 17 (London).

– (2005), *Guide to Scripts Used in English Writings up to 1500* (London).

– (2006), 'Aldred Signs Off from Glossing the Lindisfarne Gospels', in Rumble (2006a), 28–43.

– and L. Webster, eds. (2011), *Anglo-Saxon Traces*, MRTS 405 (Tempe, AZ).

Robertson, A.J., ed. (1939), *Anglo-Saxon Charters* (Cambridge; rev. ed., 1956).

Robertson, G. and G. Henderson, eds. (1975), *Studies in Memory of David Talbot Rice* (Edinburgh).

Robertson, S.F.H. (1905), 'On a Fragment of an Anglo-Saxon Benedictional in Exeter Cathedral Library', *Transactions of the St Paul's Ecclesiological Society* 5: 221–9.

Robinson, F.C. (1967), 'Old English Research in Progress: 1966–67', *NM* 68: 193–208.

– (1972), 'The Devil's Account of the Next World: An Anecdote from Old English Homiletic Literature', *NM* 73: 362–71.

– (1973), 'Syntactical Glosses in Latin Manuscripts of Anglo-Saxon Provenance', *Speculum* 48: 443–75.

- (1980), 'Old English Literature in its Most Immediate Context', in Niles (1980), 11–29.
- (1989), "'The Rewards of Piety'": Two Old English Poems in Their Manuscript Context', in *Hermeneutics and Medieval Culture*, ed. P.J. Gallacher and H. Damico (Albany, NY, 1989), 193–200.
- and E.G. Stanley, eds. (1991), *Old English Verse Texts from Many Sources: A Comprehensive Collection*, EEMF 23 (Copenhagen).
- (1994), *The Editing of Old English* (Oxford).
Robinson, J.A. and M.R. James (1909), *The Manuscripts of Westminster Abbey* (Cambridge).
- (1918), *The Saxon Bishops of Wells: A Historical Study in the Tenth Century* (London).
- (1923), *The Times of St Dunstan* (Oxford).
- (1927), 'Medieval Calendars of Somerset', in *Muchelney Memoranda from a Breviary of the Abbey in the Possession of J. Meade Faulkner*, ed. B. Schofield, Somerset Record Society 42 (1927), 143–87.
Robinson, P.R. (1978), 'Self-Contained Units in Composite Manuscripts of the Anglo-Saxon Period', *ASE* 7: 231–8 [repr. in Richards (1994), 25–35].
- (1988), *Catalogue of Dated and Datable Manuscripts c. 737–1600 in Cambridge Libraries*, 2 vols. (Cambridge).
- (1989), 'Hereford Gospels', *LMA* IV, 2151–2.
- and R. Zim, eds. (1997a), *Of the Making of Books. Medieval Manuscripts, their Scribes and Readers. Essays presented to M.B. Parkes* (Aldershot).
- (1997b), 'A Twelfth-Century *Scriptrix* from Nunnaminster', in Robinson— Zim (1997a), 73–93.
- (2003), *Catalogue of Dated and Datable Manuscripts c. 888–1600 in London Libraries*, 2 vols. (London).
Rochais, H. (1950), 'Bibliographie. Les manuscrits du *Liber scintillarum*', *Scriptorium* 4: 294–309.
- (1953), 'Contribution à l'histoire des florilèges ascétiques du haut moyen âge latin: Le *Liber Scintillarum*', *RB* 63: 246–91.
- (1957), 'Defensoriana: Archéologie du "Liber scintillarum"', *Sacris Eruditi* 9: 199–264.
Roesdahl, E., J. Graham-Campbell, P. Connor and K. Pearson, eds. (1981), *The Vikings in England* (York).
Roger, P. and A. Bosc (2008), 'Étude sur les couleurs employées dans des manuscrits datés du VIIIe au XII siècle provenant de l'Abbaye de Fleury', in Dufour—Labory (2008), 415–36.
Rogers, D.M. (1991), *The Bodleian Library and its Treasures 1320–1700* (Henley-on-Thames).

Rogers, H. (1981), 'The Oldest West-Saxon Text?', *RES* n.s. 32: 257–66.

Rohr, G.W. (1912), *Die Sprache der altenglischen Prosabearbeitungen der Benediktinerregel* (Dr.phil. dissertation, Bonn).

Rollason, D.W. (1982), *The Mildrith Legend: A Study in Early Medieval Hagiography in England* (Leicester).

– (1986), 'Goscelin of Canterbury's Account of the Translation and Miracles of St Mildreth (BHL 5961/4): An Edition with Notes', *MS* 48: 139–210.

– (1989), 'St Cuthbert and Wessex: The Evidence of CCCC MS 183', in Bonner et al. (1989a), 413–24.

– et al., eds. (1994), *Anglo-Norman Durham: 1093–1193* (Woodbridge).

– ed. (1998), *Symeon of Durham, Historian of Durham and the North* (Stamford).

– ed. (2000), *Symeon of Durham, Libellus de exordio atque procursu istius hoc est Dunelmensis ecclesiae* (Oxford).

– A.J. Piper, M. Harvey and L. Rollason, eds. (2004a), *The Durham Liber Vitae and its Context* (Woodbridge).

– (2004b), 'The Late Medieval Non-Monastic Entries in the Durham *Liber Vitae*', in Rollason (2004a) 127–39.

– and L. Rollason, eds. (2007), *The Durham Liber Vitae. British Library MS. Cotton Domitian A. VII. Edition and Digital Facsimile with Introduction, Codicological, Prosopographical and Linguistic Commentary and Indexes*, 3 vols. (London) [with CD-ROM].

– C. Leyser and H. Williams, eds. (2010), *England and the Continent in the Tenth Century. Studies in Honour of Wilhelm Levison (1876–1947)* (Turnhout).

Römer, F. (1972a), *Die handschriftliche Überlieferung der Werke des heiligen Augustinus*, II/1: *Grossbritannien und Irland: Werkverzeichnis*, Österreichische Akademie der Wissenschaften, phil.-hist. Klasse, Sitzungsberichte 276 (Vienna).

– (1972b), *Die handschriftliche Überlieferung der Werke des heiligen Augustinus*, II/2: *Grossbritannien und Irland: Verzeichnis nach Bibliotheken*, Österreichische Akademie der Wissenschaften, phil.-hist. Klasse, Sitzungsberichte 281 (Vienna).

Ronalds, C. and M. Clunies Ross (2001), '*Thureth*: A Neglected Old English Poem and its History in Anglo-Saxon Scholarship', *N&Q* 48: 358–70.

Roper, M. (1983), 'A Fragment of Bede's *De temporum ratione* in the Public Record Office', *ASE* 12: 125–8.

Ropes, J.H. (1923), 'The Greek Text of Codex Laudianus', *Harvard Theological Review* 16: 175–86.

– (1926), *The Text of Acts* (London, 1926).

Roques, R., ed. (1977), *Jean Scot Érigène et l'histoire de la philosophie*, Colloques Internationaux du Centre National de la Recherche Scientifique 561 (Paris).

Rose, V. (1893–1905), *Verzeichniss der lateinischen Handschriften* 1–2.3. *Handschriftenverzeichnisse der Königlichen Bibliothek zu Berlin* 12–13.3 (Berlin).

– ed. (1899), *Vitruvii De architectura libri decem* (Leipzig).

Rose-Troup, F. (1931), 'The Ancient Monastery of St Mary and St Peter at Exeter', *Transactions of the Devonshire Association* 63: 179–220.

Rosenthal, J. (1974), 'The Historiated Canon Tables of the Arenberg Gospels' (unpubl. PhD dissertation, Columbia University, NY).

– (1981), 'Three Drawings in an Anglo-Saxon Pontifical: Anthropomorphic Trinity or Threefold Christ?', *The Art Bulletin* 63: 547–62.

– (1985), 'The Unique Architectural Settings of the Arenberg Evangelists', in *Studien zur mittelalterlichen Kunst, 800–1250. Festschrift für Florentine Mütherich zum 70. Geburtstag*, ed. K. Bierbrauer, P.K. Klein and W. Sauerländer (Munich, 1985), 145–56.

– (1992), 'The Pontifical of St Dunstan', in Ramsay et al. (1992), 143–63.

– and P. McGurk (2006), 'Author, Symbol and Word: The Inspired Evangelists in Judith of Flanders's Anglo-Saxon Gospel Books', in L'Engle – Guest (2006), 185-202.

– (2007), 'An Unprecedented Image of Love and Devotion: The Crucifixion in Judith of Flanders's Gospel Book', in Smith – Krinsky (2007), 21–36.

– (2011), 'The Image in the Arenberg Gospels of Christ Beginning to be "What He Was Not"', in Hourihane (2011), 229–46.

Rosier, J.L. (1960a), 'The Sources of John Joscelyn's Old-English–Latin Dictionary', *Anglia* 78: 28–39.

– (1960b), 'Old English Glosses to an Epistle of Boniface', *JEGP* 59: 710–13.

– ed. (1962), *The Vitellius Psalter. Ed. from Brit. Museum MS Cotton Vitellius E. XVIII*, Cornell Studies in English 42 (Ithaca, NY).

– (1964a), 'Contributions to Old English Lexicography: Some Boethius Glosses', *ASNSL* 200: 197–8.

– ed. (1964b), 'The Stowe Canticles', *Anglia* 82: 397–432.

Ross, D.J.A. (1963), *Alexander Historiatus. A Guide to Medieval Illustrated Alexander Literature* (London).

Rosser, S. (2000), 'Old English Prose Saints' Lives in the Twelfth Century: The *Life of Martin* in Bodley 343', in Swan – Treharne (2000a), 132–42.

Rouse, R.H. (1966), 'Bostonus Buriensis and the Author of the *Catalogus Scriptorum Ecclesiae*', *Speculum* 41: 471–99.

– and M.A. Rouse (1976), 'The *Florilegium Angelicum*: Its Origin, Content and Influence', in Alexander – Gibson (1976), 66–114.

Rowland, B., ed. (1974), *Chaucer and Middle English Studies in Honour of Rossell Hope Robbins* (London).

Rowley, S.M. (2004), 'Nostalgia and the Rhetoric of Lack: The Missing Exemplar for Corpus Christi College, Cambridge, Manuscript 41', in Lionarons (2004a), 11–36.

– (2009), 'The Fourteenth-Century Glosses and Annotations in Oxford, Bodleian Library, MS Tanner 10', *Manuscripta* 53: 49–86.

– (2011), *The Old English Version of Bede's Historia Ecclesiastica* (Cambridge).

Rud, T. (1825), *Codicum Manuscriptorum Ecclesiae Cathedralis Dunelmensis Catalogus Classicus*, ed. with an appendix by J. Raine (Durham).

Rudolf, W. (2011), 'The Homiliary of Angers in Tenth-Century England', *ASE* 39: 163–92.

Ruffel, P. and J. Soubiran (1960), 'Recherches sur la tradition manuscrite de Vitruve', *Pallas* 9.2: 113–44.

Ruh, K. et al., eds. (1978 –), *Die deutsche Literatur des Mittelalters: Verfasserlexikon*, 2nd ed. (Berlin).

Rule, M., ed. (1896), *The Missal of St. Augustine's Abbey Canterbury with Excerpts from the Antiphonary and Lectionary of the Same Monastery* (Cambridge).

Rumble, A.R. (1985), 'The Palaeography of the Domesday Manuscripts', in *Domesday Book: A Reassessment*, ed. P.H. Sawyer (London), 28–49.

– (1987), 'The Domesday Manuscripts: Scribes and Scriptoria', in Holt (1987), 79–99.

– (1994a), 'Using Anglo-Saxon Manuscripts', in Richards (1994), 3–24.

– ed. (1994b), *The Reign of Cnut: King of England, Denmark and Norway* (London).

– (1994c), 'Textual Appendix: Translatio Sancti Ælfegi Cantuariensis Archiepiscopi et Martiris (BHL 2519): Osbern's Account of the Translation of St Ælfheah's Relics from London to Canterbury, 8–11 June 1023' [with a translation by R. Morris and A.R. Rumble], in Rumble (1994b), 283–315.

– ed. (2002), *The Anglo-Saxon Minsters of Winchester*, III: *Property and Piety in Early Medieval Winchester. Documents relating to the Topography of the Anglo-Saxon and Norman City and its Minsters*, Winchester Studies 4.iii (Oxford).

– ed. (2006a), *Writing and Texts in Anglo-Saxon England* (Cambridge).

– (2006b), 'The Study of Anglo-Saxon Manuscripts, Collections and Scribes: in the Footsteps of Wanley and Ker', in Rumble (2006a), 1–17.

Rusch, W.G. (1970), 'A Possible Explanation of the Calendar in the Würzburg Lectionary', *JTS* n.s. 21: 105–11.

Rusche, P.G. (1994), 'Dry-Point Glosses to Aldhelm's *De laudibus virginitatis* in Beinecke 401', *ASE* 23: 195–213.

- (1996), 'The Cleopatra Glossaries: An Edition with Commentary on the Glosses and their Sources' (unpubl. PhD dissertation, Yale Univ.).
- (2002), 'St Augustine's Abbey and the Tradition of Penance in early Tenth-Century England', *Anglia* 120: 159–83.
- (2011), 'The Translation of Plant Names in the *Old English Herbarium* and the Durham Glossary', in Lendinara et al. (2011), 395–414.

Rushforth, R. (2001), 'The Prodigal Fragment: Cambridge, Gonville and Caius College 734/782a', *ASE* 30: 137–44.
- (2002), 'The Eleventh- and Early Twelfth-Century Manuscripts of Bury St Edmunds Abbey' (unpubl. PhD dissertation, Cambridge Univ.).
- (2004–7), 'The Barrow Knight, the Bristol Bibliographer and a lost Old English Prayer', *TCBS* 13: 112–31.
- and N. Orchard (2005), 'A Lost Eleventh-Century Missal from Bury St Edmunds Abbey', *BLR* 18: 565–76.
- (2007), *St Margaret's Gospel-Book. The Favourite Book of an Eleventh-Century Queen of Scots* (Oxford).
- ed. (2008a), *Saints in English Kalendars before A.D. 1100*, HBS 117 (London).
- (2008b), 'The Crowland Psalter and Gundrada de Warenne', *BLR* 21: 156–68.
- (2008 –), 'The Script and Text of the Achadeus Psalter Gloss: Re-using Continental Materials in Eleventh-Century England', *TCBS* 14: 89–112.
- (2009), 'Two Fragmentary Anglo-Saxon Manuscripts at St John's College, Cambridge', *Scriptorium* 63: 73–8.
- (2011), 'Annotated Psalters and Psalm Study in Late Anglo-Saxon England: The Manuscript Evidence', in Lendinara et al. (2011), 39–66.
- (2012), 'English Caroline Minuscule', in R. Gameson (2012), 197–210.

Russel, J.C. (1947), 'The Tribal Hidage', *Traditio* 5: 193–209.

Ryan, M., ed. (1987), *Ireland and Insular Art, A.D. 500–1200* (Dublin).

Ryan, W.M. (1955), 'Four Unpublished Old English Homilies' (unpubl. PhD dissertation, University of Texas at Austin).

Rydén, T. (2001), *Det anglosaxiska Köpenhamnsevangeliariet: det Kongelige Bibliotek Gl. Kongl. Saml. 10 2°*, Skrifter utgivna av Vetenskapssocieteten i Lund 91 (Lund).

Rypins, S.I. (1921), 'A Contribution to the Study of the *Beowulf* Codex', *PMLA* 36: 167–85.
- ed. (1924), *Three Old English Texts in MS Cotton Vitellius A.xv*, EETS o.s. 161 (London).
- (1932), 'The *Beowulf* Codex', *Colophon* 10: 9–12 [orig. publ. *MP* 17: 541–7].

Ryskamp, C., ed. (1989), *Twenty-First Report to the Fellows of the Pierpont Morgan Library* (New York).

Sackur, E. (1898), *Sibyllinische Texte und Forschungen. Pseudo-Methodius, Adso und die Tiburtinische Sibylle* (Halle).

Saenger, P. (1997), *Space Between Words: The Origins of Silent Reading* (Stanford, CA).

Salmon, P. (1959), *Les 'Tituli Psalmorum' des manuscrits latins*, Collectanea Biblica Latina 12 (Rome).

– (1968–72), *Les Manuscrits liturgiques latins de la Bibliothèque Vaticane*, 5 vols., Studi e Testi 251, 253, 260, 267, 270 (Vatican City).

– (1976) 'Livrets de prières de l'époque carolingienne', *RB* 86: 218–34.

Samaran, C., R. Marichal, et al., eds. (1959–85), *Catalogue des manuscrits en écriture latine portant des indications de date, de lieu ou de copiste*, 7 vols. (Paris).

Sanford, E.M. (1924), 'The Use of Classical Latin Authors in the *Libri Manuales*', *Transactions and Proceedings of the American Philological Association* 55: 190–248.

Sansterre, J.-M. (2006), '*Omnes qui coram hac imagine genua flexerint*: La vénération d'images de saints et de la Vièrge d'après les textes écrits en Angleterre du milieu du XIe aux premières décennies du XIIIe siècle', *Cahiers de civilisation médiévale* 49: 257–94.

Santini, C., ed. (1979), *Eutropii Breviarium ab urbe condita* (Leipzig).

Santosuosso, I.C. (1989), 'Music in Bede's *De temporum ratione*: An 11th-Century Addition to MS London, British Library, Cotton Vespasian B. vi', *Scriptorium* 43: 255–9.

Sato, S. (1997a), *Back to the Manuscripts. Papers from the Symposium 'The Integrated Approach to Manuscript Studies: A New Horizon' held at the Eighth General Meeting of the Japan Society for Medieval English Studies, Tokyo, December 1992* (Tokyo).

– (1997b) 'Back to the Manuscripts: Some Problems in the Physical Description of the Parker Chronicle', in Sato (1997a), 69–104.

Sauer, H., ed. (1978), *Theodulfi Capitula in England*, TUEPh 8 (Munich).

– ed. (1980a), 'Zwei spätaltenglische Beichtermahnungen aus HS Cotton Tiberius A.iii', *Anglia* 98: 1–33.

– (1980b), Review of '*Exodus*', ed. P.J. Lucas, *BGDSL* 102: 139–43.

– (1983), 'Die 72 Völker und Sprachen der Welt: Ein mittelalterlicher Topos in der englischen Literatur', *Anglia* 101: 29–48.

– (1984), 'Die Ermahnung des Pseudo-Fulgentius zur Benediktregel und ihre altenglische Glossierung', *Anglia* 102: 419–25.

– (1989), 'Die 72 Völker und Sprachen der Welt: Einige Ergänzungen', *Anglia* 107: 61–4.

– ed. (1993), 'Altenglische Beichtermahnungen aus den Handschriften CCCC 320 und Laud. Misc. 482. Edition und Kommentar', in Grinda—Wetzel (1993), 21–51.

– (1996), 'Theodulf', in *LMA* VIII, 647–8.

– (2000), 'The Transmission and Structure of Archbishop Wulfstan's "Commonplace Book"', in Szarmach (2000), 339–93 [orig. publ. in German, *DAEM* 36, 341–84].

- et al. (2005), *Angelsächsisches Erbe in München – Anglo-Saxon Heritage in Munich. Anglo-Saxon Manuscripts, Scribes and Authors from the Collections of the Bavarian State Library in Munich* (Frankfurt a. M.).
- (2007), 'Old English Words for People in the Épinal-Erfurt Glossary', in *Beowulf and Beyond*, ed. H. Sauer and R. Bauer (Frankfurt, 2007), 119–81.
- (2008), 'Language and Culture: How Anglo-Saxon Glossators adapted Latin Words and their World', *JMLat* 18: 437–68.
- J. Story and G. Waxenberger, eds. (2011), *Anglo-Saxon England and the Continent*, MRTS 394 (Tempe, AZ).
Savage, H.E. (1915), 'The Story of St. Chad's Gospels', *Transactions of the Birmingham Archaeological Society*, 41: 5–21.
Sawyer, P.H., ed. (1957), *Textus Roffensis: Rochester Cathedral Library Manuscript A. 3. 5*, Pt. I, EEMF 7 (Copenhagen).
- ed. (1962), *Textus Roffensis: Rochester Cathedral Library Manuscript A. 3. 5*, Pt. II, EEMF 11 (Copenhagen).
- (1968), *Anglo-Saxon Charters: An Annotated List and Bibliography* (London).
Saxl, F. and H. Meier (1953), *Catalogue of Astrological and Mythological Manuscripts of the Latin Middle Ages*, III. *Manuscripts in English Libraries*, ed. H. Bober (London).
Scaffai, M., ed. (1982), *Baebii Italici Ilias Latina* (Bologna).
Scase, W., ed. (2007), *Essays in Manuscript Geography: Vernacular Manuscripts of the English West Midlands from the Conquest to the Sixteenth Century*, Medieval Texts and Cultures of Northern Europe 10 (Turnhout).
Schabram, H. (1965), *Superbia. Studien zum altenglischen Wortschatz, Teil I: Die dialektale und zeitliche Verbreitung des Wortguts* (Munich).
- (1968), Review of *The Harley Latin-Old English Glossary,* ed. from the British Museum MS Harley 3376 by R. T. Oliphant, *Anglia* 86: 495–500.
- (1981), Review of *The Stowe Psalter*, ed. A.C. Kimmens, *Anglia* 99: 492–6.
- (1988), 'The Latin and Old English Glosses to "electrum" in the Harley Glossary', in Oshitari (1988), 29–34.
Schaefer, K.G. (1972), *An Edition of Five Old English Homilies for Palm Sunday, Holy Saturday and Easter Sunday* (New York).
Schaller, D. (1977), 'Bemerkungen zur Inschriften-Sylloge von Urbana', *MLJ* 12: 9–21.
- (1995), *Studien zur lateinischen Dichtung des Frühmittelalters* (Stuttgart).
Schanz, M., C. Hosius and G. Krüger (1914–20), *Geschichte der römischen Literatur bis zum Gesetzgebungswerk des Kaisers Justinian*, IV: *Die römische Literatur von Constantin bis zum Gesetzgebungswerk Justinians*, 2 vols. (Munich).
Schapiro, M. (1958), 'The Decoration of the Leningrad Manuscript of Bede', *Scriptorium* 12: 191–207.

Scharer, A. (1982), *Die angelsächsische Königsurkunde im 7. und 8. Jahrhundert* (Vienna).

– (1999), 'The Gregorian Tradition in Early England', in R. Gameson (1999b), 187–202.

– (2011), 'Objects of Royal Representation in England and on the Continent', in Roberts—Webster (2011), 31–45.

Schaumann, B. and A. Cameron (1977), 'A Newly-Found Leaf of Old English from Louvain', *Anglia* 95: 289–312.

Schenkl, C., ed. (1897), *Sancti Ambrosii Opera: Pars Altera*, CSEL 32.ii (Vienna).

Scherrer, G. (1864), *Verzeichniss der Manuscripte und Incunabeln der Vadianischen Bibliothek in St Gallen* (St Gallen).

– (1875), *Verzeichniss der Handschriften der Stiftsbibliothek von St Gallen* (Halle).

Schichler, R.L. (2008), 'Ending on a Giant Theme: The Utrecht and Harley Psalters, and the Pointed-Helmet Coinage of Cnut', in Blanton—Scheck (2008), 241–54.

Schieffer, R. (1971), 'Zur lateinischen Überlieferung von Kaiser Justinians ΟΜΟΛΟΓΙΑ ΤΗΣ ΟΡΘΗΣ ΠΙΣΤΕΩΣ (*Edictus de recta fide*)', *Kleronomia* 3: 285–301.

– (1972), 'Nochmals zur Überlieferung von Justinians ΟΜΟΛΟΓΙΑ ΤΗΣ ΟΡΘΗΣ ΠΙΣΤΕΩΣ', *Kleronomia* 4: 267–84.

Schilling, R. (1948), 'Two Unknown Flemish Miniatures of the Eleventh Century', *Burlington Magazine* 90: 312–17.

Schiltz, G. (2004), 'Der Canterburyspruch oder "Wie finden dänische Runen und englische Komputistik zusammen?". Ein Beitrag zur historischen Textlinguistik', in Honegger (2004), 115–38.

Schindel, U. (1975), *Die lateinischen Figurenlehren des 5.–7. Jahrhunderts und Donats Vergilkommentar (mit zwei Editionen)*, Abhandlungen der Akademie der Wissenschaften in Göttingen, phil.-hist. Klasse, Dritte Folge, Nr. 91 (Göttingen).

Schipper, J.M., ed. (1897–9), *König Alfreds Übersetzung von Bedas Kirchengeschichte*, Bibliothek der angelsächsischen Prosa 4 (Leipzig).

Schipper, W. (1981), 'Ælfric's *De Auguriis*: A Critical Edition with Introduction and Commentary' (unpubl. PhD dissertation, Queens University, Ontario).

– (1981–5), 'A Composite Old English Homiliary from Ely: Cambridge, University Library MS Ii. 1. 33', *TCBS* 8: 285–98.

– (1987), 'A Worksheet of the Worcester "Tremulous" Glossator', *Anglia* 105: 28–49.

– (1994), 'Dry-Point Compilation Notes in the Benedictional of St Æthelwold', *BLJ* 20: 17–34.

– (2003), 'Style and Layout of Anglo-Saxon Manuscripts', in Karkov—Brown (2003), 151–68.

- (2004), 'Digitizing (Nearly) Unreadable Fragments of Cyprian's "Epistolary"', in *The Book Unbound: Editing and Reading Medieval Manuscripts and Texts*, ed. S. Echard and S. Partridge (Toronto, 2004), 159–68.
- (2007a), 'The Origin of the Trinity College Rabanus (B. 16. 3)', in Panayotova (2007), 45–53.
- (2007b), 'Textual Varieties in Manuscript Margins', in Keefer—Bremmer (2007a), 25–54.
- (2009), 'Hrabanus Maurus in Anglo-Saxon England: *In honorem sanctae crucis*', in Baxter et al. (2009), 283–98.

Schlutter, O.B. (1908), 'Gildas, *Libellus Querulus de Excidio Britannorum* as a Source of Glosses in the Cottoniensis (Cleopatra A. III = WW. 338–473) and in the Corpus Glossary', *American Journal of Philology* 29: 432–48.
- (1909), 'Randglossen aus dem Brüsseler Cod. no. 8558-63', *Anglia* 32: 508–14.
- ed. (1912), *Das Epinaler und Erfurter Glossar. Teil I: Faksimile und Transliteration des Epinaler Glossars: Text*, Bibliothek der angelsächsischen Prosa 8 (Hamburg).

Schmetterer, V. (1981), *Drei altenglische religiöse Texte aus der Handschrift Cotton Vespasianus D. xiv*, Dissertationen der Universität Wien 150 (Vienna).

Schmid, H., ed. (1981), *Musica et scolica enchiriadis una cum aliquibus tractatulis adjunctis* (Munich).

Schmid, T. (1944), 'Smärre Liturgiska Bidrag, VIII: Om Sankt Swithunusmässen i Sverige', *Nordisk Tidskrift för Bok- och Biblioteksväsen* 31: 25–34.
- (1963), 'Problemata', *Fornvännen* 58: 174–90.

Schmid, U.B. (2005), *'Unum ex quatuor'. Eine Geschichte der lateinischen Tatianüberlieferung*, Aus der Geschichte der lateinischen Bibel 37 (Beuron).

Schmitt, L.E., ed. (1970), *Kurzer Grundriss der germanischen Philologie bis 1500*, I (Berlin).

Schmitz, G., ed. (1996), *Die Kapitulariensammlung des Ansegis (Collectio capitularium Ansegisi)*, MGH, Capitularia regum Francorum 1 (Hannover).

Schmitz, H.J. (1883), *Die Bussbücher und die Bussdisziplin der Kirche* (Mainz).
- (1898), *Die Bussbücher und das kanonische Bussverfahren* (Düsseldorf).

Schneider, H. (1938), *Die altlateinischen biblischen Cantica* (Beuron).

Schneider, J. (2003), 'Latein und Althochdeutsch in der Cambridger Liedersammlung: *De Heinrico, Clericus et nonna*', in Bergmann (2003), 297–314.

Schøyen Collection: see 'The Schøyen Collection'

Schramm, P.E. (1934), 'Die Krönung bei den Westfranken und Angelsachsen von 878 bis um 1000', *Zeitschrift der Savigny-Stiftung für Rechtsgeschichte* 54 [*Kanonistische Abteilung* 23]: 117–242 [repr. and rev. in Schramm, *Kaiser, Könige und Päpste. Gesammelte Aufsätze zur Geschichte des Mittelalters*, 5 vols. (Stuttgart, 1968–71), II/ii.140–248].

– and F. Mütherich (1981), *Denkmale der deutschen Könige und Kaiser*, I. *Ein Beitrag zur Herrschergeschichte von Karl dem Grossen bis Friedrich II, 768–1250*, 2nd ed. (Munich).

Schreiber, C. (2003), *King Alfred's Old English Translation of Pope Gregory The Great's* Regula Pastoralis *and its Cultural Context: A Study and Partial Edition According to All Surviving Manuscripts, Based on Cambridge, Corpus Christi College 12*, TUEPh 25 (Frankfurt am Main).

Schröcker, A. (2005), 'MS Cotton Tiberius C. i and the Question of (Public) Penance in late Anglo-Saxon England', in Knappe (2005), 337–50.

Schroeder, J. (1977), *Bibliothek und Schule der Abtei Echternach um die Jahrtausendwende*, Publications de la section historique de l'Institut Grand-Ducal de Luxembourg 91 (Luxembourg, 1977), 201–378.

– (1979), 'Zu den Beziehungen zwischen Echternach und England/Irland im Frühmittelalter', *Hémecht* 31: 363–89.

Schröer, A., ed. (1885–8/1964), *Die angelsächsischen Prosabearbeitungen der Benediktinerregel*, Bibliothek der angelsächsischen Prosa 2 (Kassel) [2nd ed., with appendix by H. Gneuss (Darmstadt, 1964)].

– ed. (1888/1978), *Die Winteney-Version der Regula S. Benedicti* (Halle) [repr. with appendix by M. Gretsch (Tübingen, 1978)].

Schuler, S. (1999), *Vitruv im Mittelalter: Die Rezeption von 'De architectura' von der Antike bis in die frühe Neuzeit*, Pictura et Poesis 12 (Cologne).

Schüling, H. (1961–3), 'Die Handbibliothek des Bonifatius', *Archiv für Geschichte des Buchwesens* 4: 285–348.

Schullian, D.M. (1935), 'The Excerpts of Heiric *Ex libris Valerii Maximi Memorabilium Dictorum vel Factorum*', *Memoirs of the American Academy in Rome* 12: 155–84.

– (1981), 'A Revised List of Manuscripts of Valerius Maximus', in *Miscellanea Augusto Campana*, Medioevo e umanesimo 44–5 (Padua), 695–728.

Schulz-Flügel, E., ed. (1990), *Historia monachorum sive De vita sanctorum patrum: Tyrannius Rufinus*, Patristische Texte und Studien 34 (Berlin).

Schwab, U., ed. (1967), *Waldere. Testo e commento* (Messina).

– (1988), *Einige Beziehungen zwischen altsächsischer und angelsächsischer Dichtung* (Spoleto).

Scott, M. (2009), *Medieval Dress and Fashion* (London).

Scragg, D.G. (1969–70), 'The Language of the Vercelli Homilies' (unpubl. PhD dissertation, Manchester Univ.).

– (1971), 'Accent Marks in the Old English Vercelli Book', *NM* 72: 699–710.

– (1979), 'The Corpus of Vernacular Homilies and Prose Saints' Lives before Ælfric', *ASE* 8: 223–77.

- (1985), 'The Homilies of the Blickling Manuscript', in Lapidge—Gneuss (1985a), 299–316.
- ed. (1992), *The Vercelli Homilies and Related Texts*, EETS o.s. 300 (Oxford).
- (1994a), 'The Compilation of the Vercelli Book', in Richards (1994), 317–43 [rev. from *ASE* 2 (1973), 189–207].
- and P.E. Szarmach, eds. (1994b), *The Editing of Old English. Papers from the 1990 Manchester Conference* (Cambridge).
- (1996), 'The Corpus of Anonymous Lives and their Manuscript Context', in Szarmach (1996), 209–34.
- (1998), 'Cambridge, Corpus Christi College 162', in Pulsiano—Treharne (1998a), 71–84.
- (2000), 'An Unpublished Vernacular Exhortation from Post-Conquest England and its Manuscript Context', in Roberts—Nelson (2000), 511–24.
- ed. (2003), *Textual and Material Culture in Anglo-Saxon England. Thomas Northcote Toller and the Toller Memorial Lectures* (Cambridge).
- (2005), 'A Late Old English Harrowing of Hell Homily from Worcester and Blickling Homily VII', in O'Brien O'Keeffe—Orchard (2005) II, 197–211.
- (2006), 'Ælfric's Scribes', *LSE* 37: 179–89.
- (2008a), 'Cotton Tiberius A. iii Scribe 3 and Canterbury Libraries', in Hall—Scragg (2008), 22–30.
- (2008b), 'The Vercelli Homilies and Kent', in Blanton—Scheck (2008), 369–80.
- ed. (2008c), *Edgar, King of the English 959–975: New Interpretations*, Publications of the Manchester Centre for Anglo-Saxon Studies 8 (Woodbridge).
- (2008d), 'London, British Library, Royal 2. B. V, Christ Church, Canterbury, and the English Language in the Eleventh Century', in Lendinara (2008), 381–93.
- (2009a), 'Studies in the Language of Copyists of the Vercelli Homilies', in Zacher—Orchard (2009), 41–61.
- (2009b), 'Manuscript Sources of Old English Prose', in Owen-Crocker (2009), 61–87.
- (2012a), *A Conspectus of Scribal Hands writing English, 960–1100* (Cambridge).
- (2012b), 'Old English Homiliaries and Poetic Manuscripts', in R. Gameson (2012), 553–61.
Scrase, D. (2005), *Treasures of the Fitzwilliam Museum* (London).
Scrivener, F.H.A. (1887), *Codex S. Ceaddae Latinus. Evangelia SS. Matthaei, Marci Lucae ad cap. III. 9 complectens, circa septimum vel octavum saeculum scriptus, in ecclesia cathedrali Lichfieldiensi servatus* (Cambridge).
Searle, W.G. (1902), 'Lists of the Deans, Priors and Monks of Christ Church, Canterbury', *Cambridge Antiquarian Society Publications, Octavo Series* 34: 153–95.

Sedgefield, W.J. (1899), *King Alfred's Old English Versions of Boethius 'De Consolatione Philosophiae'* (Oxford).

Seebass, T. (1974), *Musikdarstellungen und Psalterillustration im frühen Mittelalter*, 2 vols. (Tübingen).

Selig K.L. and R. Somerville, eds. (1987), *Florilegium Columbianum: Essays in Honor of Paul Oskar Kristeller* (New York).

Semmler, J., ed. (1963), 'Synodi I. Aquisgranensis acta praeliminaria (816)' and 'Regula Sancti Benedicti abbatis Anianensis sive Collectio capitularis', CCM I, 433-6, 501–35.

Semple, S. (2003), 'Illustrations of Damnation in Anglo-Saxon Manuscripts', *ASE* 32: 231–45.

Setz, W., ed. (1988–90), *Fälschungen im Mittelalter, Internationaler Kongress der Monumenta Germaniae Historica, München 16.–19. September 1986*, 5 vols. (Hannover).

Shailor, B.A. et al. (1984–2004), *Catalogue of Medieval and Renaissance Manuscripts in the Beinecke Rare Book and Manuscript Library, Yale University*, 4 vols. (Binghamton, NY).

Shannon, A. (1964), *A Descriptive Syntax of the Parker Manuscript of the Anglo-Saxon Chronicle from 734 to 891* (The Hague).

Sharpe, K. (1997), 'Introduction: Rewriting Sir Robert Cotton', in C.J. Wright (1997), 1–39.

Sharpe, R. (1984), 'Gildas as a Father of the Church', in Lapidge—Dumvielle (1984), 193–205.

– (1990), 'Goscelin's St Augustine and St Mildreth: Hagiography and Liturgy in Context', *JTS* n.s. 41: 502–16.

– (1991), 'Words and Music by Goscelin of Canterbury', *Early Music* 19: 94–7.

– et al., eds. (1996), *English Benedictine Libraries. The Shorter Catalogues*, Corpus of British Medieval Library Catalogues 4 (London).

– (1998), 'Symeon, Hildebert, and the Errors of Origen', in Rollason (1998), 282–300.

– (2001), *A Handlist of the Latin Writers of Great Britain and Ireland before 1540*, 2nd ed. (Turnhout).

– and T. Webber (2009), 'Four Early Booklets of Anselm's Works from Salisbury Cathedral: MS Cambridge, Trinity College, B. 1. 37', *Scriptorium* 63: 58–71.

Shaw, P. (2006), 'The Manuscript Texts of *Against a Dwarf*', in Rumble (2006a), 96–113.

Sheerin, D.J. (1975a), 'John Leland at Work: Bodl. MS Auct. F. 2.14 and British Library. MS Cotton Vitellius A. xix', *Manuscripta* 19: 83 [abstract of unpublished paper].

- (1975b), 'Some Observations on the Date of Lanfranc's *Decreta*', *Studia Monastica* 17: 13–28.
- (1977), 'John Leland and Milred of Worcester', *Manuscripta* 21: 172–80.

Shepard, D.M. (2007), *Introducing the Lambeth Bible: A Study of Texts and Imagery* (Turnhout).

Sheppard, J. M. (2005), 'The Census of Western Medieval Bookbinding Structures to 1500 in British Libraries, Stage 1: Cambridge. A Final Report – and a Glimpse at some "Treasures"', in Fellows-Jensen—Springborg (2005), 175–89.

Sherlock, D. (1989), 'Anglo-Saxon Monastic Sign Language at Christ Church, Canterbury', *Archaeologia Cantiana* 107: 1–27.

Shippey, T.A., ed. (1976), *Poems of Wisdom and Learning in Old English* (Cambridge).

Short, D.D. (1980), *Beowulf Scholarship: An Annotated Bibliography* (New York).

Shrader, C.R. (1979), 'A Handlist of Extant Manuscripts Containing the *De re militari* of Flavius Vegetius Renatus', *Scriptorium* 33: 280–305.

Siegmund, A. (1949), *Die Überlieferung der griechischen christlichen Literatur in der lateinischen Kirche bis zum 12. Jahrhundert* (Munich-Pasing).

Sievers, E., ed. (1878/1935), *Heliand* (Halle) [2nd ed., 'vermehrt um das Prager Fragment des Heliand und die vaticanischen Fragmente von Heliand und Genesis' (Halle, 1935)].
- (1891), 'Zu den angelsächsischen Glossen', *Anglia* 13: 309–32.
- et al., eds. (1925), *Neusprachliche Studien. Festgabe Karl Luick zu seinem sechzigsten Geburtstage* (Marburg).

Siffrin, P. (1930), 'Zwei Blätter eines Sakramentars in irischer Schrift des 8. Jh. aus Regensburg', *Jahrbuch für Liturgiewissenschaft* 10: 1–39.
- (1933), 'Das Walderdorffer Kalenderfragment saec. VIII und die Berliner Blätter eines Sakramentars aus Regensburg', *Ephemerides Liturgicae* 47: 201–24.

Silagi, G., ed. (1982), *Paläographie 1981. Colloquium des Comité international de paléographie, München, 15.–18. September 1981* (Munich).

Simek, R. (2002), 'The Earthrim-dwellers' Favourite Abode: Crosscurrents Between Literary and Iconographic Traditions on Monstrous Races in Medieval European Manuscripts', in Kiss et al. (2002), 49–60.

Simmons, F.T., ed. (1879), *The Lay Folks Mass Book or the Manner of Hearing Mass with Rubrics and Devotions for the People*, EETS o.s. 71 (London).

Simon-Vandenbergen, A.M., ed. (1987), *Studies in Honour of René Derolez* (Ghent).

Simpson, H. (1994), 'Ireland, Tours and Brittany: The Case of Cambridge, Corpus Christi College, MS. 279', in Laurent—Davis (1994), 108–23.

Sims-Williams, P. (1976), 'Cuthswith, Seventh-Century Abbess of Inkberrow, near Worcester, and the Würzburg Manuscript of Jerome on Ecclesiastes', *ASE* 5: 1–21.

‒ (1979), 'An Unpublished Seventh- or Eighth-Century Anglo-Latin Letter in Boulogne-sur-Mer MS 74 (82)', *MÆ* 48: 1–22.

‒ (1982), 'Milred of Worcester's Collection of Latin Epigrams and its Continental Counterparts', *ASE* 10: 21–38.

‒ (1983), 'William of Malmesbury and *La silloge epigrafica di Cambridge*', *Archivum Historiae Pontificiae* 21: 9–33.

‒ (1990), *Religion and Literature in Western England, 600–800*, CSASE 3 (Cambridge).

‒ (1995), *Britain and Early Christian Europe* (Aldershot).

‒ (2005), 'A New Brittonic Gloss on Boethius: *ud rocashaas*', *CMCS* 50: 77–86.

Singer, C. (1917), 'A Review of the Medical Literature of the Dark Ages, with a New Text of About 1100', *Proceedings of the Royal Society of Medicine* 10: 107–60.

‒ (1927), 'The Herbal in Antiquity', *Journal of Hellenic Studies* 47: 1–52.

Sisam, C. (1951), 'The Scribal Tradition of the Lambeth Homilies', *RES* n.s. 2: 105–13.

‒ (1953), 'An Early Fragment of the Old English *Martyrology*', *RES* n.s. 4: 209–20.

‒ and K. Sisam, eds. (1959), *The Salisbury Psalter*, EETS o.s. 242 (London).

‒ ed. (1976), *The Vercelli Book: A Late Tenth-Century Manuscript containing Prose and Verse, Vercelli Biblioteca Capitolare CXVII*, EEMF 19 (Copenhagen).

Sisam, K. (1944), Review of *The Poetical Dialogues of Solomon and Saturn*, ed. R.J. Menner, *MÆ* 13: 28–36.

‒ (1953a), *Studies in the History of Old English Literature* (Oxford).

‒ (1953b), 'Anglo-Saxon Royal Genealogies', *PBA* 39: 287–348.

‒ (1956), 'Canterbury, Lichfield, and the *Vespasian Psalter*', *RES* n.s. 7: 1–10, 113–31.

‒ (1957), 'Mr. Sisam writes' in Kuhn (1957), 370–.

Skeat, W.W. (1871), *The Gospel According to Saint Mark in Anglo-Saxon and Northumbrian Versions* (Cambridge).

‒ (1874), *The Gospel According to Saint Luke in Anglo-Saxon and Northumbrian Versions* (Cambridge).

‒ (1878), *The Gospel According to Saint John in Anglo-Saxon and Northumbrian Versions* (Cambridge).

‒ ed. (1881–1900), *Ælfric's Lives of Saints*, EETS o.s. 76, 82, 94, 114 (Oxford) [repr. in 2 vols., 1967].

‒ (1887), *The Gospel According to Saint Matthew in Anglo-Saxon, Northumbrian and Old Mercian Versions* (Cambridge).

‒ (1902), Report on 'An Anglo-Saxon Fragment found in the Binding of a Book in the Library of Queens' College, Cambridge', *Athenaeum* (20 Dec.): 831–2.

Skulicz, M.V. (1970), 'A Descriptive Syntax of Aelfric's First Series of Catholic Homilies, MS Royal 7 C XII' (unpubl. PhD dissertation, University of North Carolina at Chapel Hill, NC).

Smetana, C.L. (1978), 'Paul the Deacon's Patristic Anthology', in Szarmach—Huppé (1978), 75–97.

Smit, J.W. (1971), *Studies on the Language and Style of Columba the Younger (Columbanus)* (Amsterdam).

Smith, A.B., ed. (1985), *The Anonymous Parts of the Old English Hexateuch: A Latin-Old English / Old English-Latin Glossary* (Cambridge).

Smith, A.H., ed. (1935), *The Parker Chronicle, 832–900* (London).

– (1938), 'The Photography of MSS', *London Medieval Studies* 1: 179–207.

Smith, K.A. and C.H. Krinsky, eds. (2007), *Studies in Illuminated Manuscripts. Tributes to Lucy Freeman Sandler* (Turnhout).

Smith, L. (2001), *Masters of the Sacred Page: Manuscripts of Theology in the Latin West to 1274*, The Medieval Book 2 (Notre Dame, IN).

Smith, T.S. (1696), *Catalogus Librorum Manuscriptorum Bibliothecae Cottonianae: cui praemittuntur Roberti Cottoni Vita et Bibliothecae Cottonianae Historia et Synopsis* (Oxford), repr. as *Catalogue of the Manuscripts in the Cottonian Library (Catalogus Librorum Manuscriptorum Bibliothecae Cottonianae)*, repr. from Sir Robert Harley's copy, together with documents relating to the fire of 1731, by C.G.C. Tite (Cambridge, 1984).

Smyth, M.W. (1905), 'The Numbers in the Manuscript of the OE *Judith*', *MLN* 20: 197–9.

Söderlind, J. (1995), 'The Old English Homiliary British Library Cotton Vitellius D. xvii', *SN* 67: 3–10.

Solari, R. (1974), 'Studi sulle glosse di Lindisfarne al Vangelo di San Luca (rivisione dell' edizione dello Skeat)', *Rendiconti dell'Istituto lombardo, classe di lettere e scienze morali e storiche* 108: 551–74.

Sole, L.M. (1998), 'Some Anglo-Saxon Cuthbert Liturgica: The Manuscript Evidence', *RB* 108: 104–44.

Somner, W. (1659), *Dictionarium Saxonico-Latino-Anglicum* (London) [repr. as English Linguistics 1500–1800, no. 247 (Menston, 1970)].

Sotheby's Sale Catalogue (London, 1972) [for 21 Nov. 1972].

Sotheby's The History of Script. Sixty Important Manuscript Leaves from the Schøyen Collection (London, 2012) [for 10 July 2012].

Soubiran, J., ed. (1972), *Cicéron, Aratea, Fragments poétiques* (Paris).

South, T.J., ed. (2002), *Historia de Sancto Cuthberto: A History of Saint Cuthbert and a Record of His Patrimony*, AST 3 (Cambridge).

Southern, R.W. (1963), *Saint Anselm and His Biographer: A Study of Monastic Life and Thought, 1059–c.1130* (Cambridge).

– (1990), *Saint Anselm. A Portrait in a Landscape* (Cambridge).

Spannagel, A., and P. Engelbert, eds. (1974), *Smaragdi Abbatis Expositio in Regulam S. Benedicti*, CCM 8 (Siegburg).

Sparks, H.D.F. (1954), 'A Celtic Text of the Latin Apocalypse preserved in Two Durham Manuscripts of Bede's Commentary on the Apocalypse', *JTS* n.s. 5: 227–31.

Spencer, H.L. (1982), 'Vernacular and Latin Versions of a Sermon for Lent: "A Lost Penitential Homily Found"', *MS* 44: 271–305.

Spiegel, F. (2007), 'The *tabernacula* of Gregory the Great and the Conversion of the Anglo-Saxons', *ASE* 36: 1–13.

Spilling, H. (1978), 'Angelsächsische Schrift in Fulda', in *Von der Klosterbibliothek zur Landesbibliothek. Beiträge zum zweihundertjährigen Bestehen der Hessischen Landesbibliothek Fulda*, ed. A. Brall (Stuttgart, 1978), 47–98.

– (1982), 'Irische Handschriftenüberlieferung in Fulda, Mainz und Würzburg', in Löwe (1982), 867–902.

Spindler, R., ed. (1934), *Das altenglische Bussbuch (sog. Confessionale Pseudo-Egberti). Ein Beitrag zu den kirchlichen Gesetzen der Angelsachsen* (Leipzig).

Springer, C.P.E. (1995), *The Manuscripts of Sedulius: A Provisional Handlist* (Philadelphia, PA).

Sprockel, C. (1965), *The Language of the Parker Chronicle*, I. *Phonology and Accidence* (The Hague).

Squires, A. (1971), 'Collation of the Anglo-Saxon Gloss to the Durham Ritual', *N&Q* 216: 362–6.

– (1973), 'Some Curious Abbreviations in the Durham Ritual', *N&Q* 218: 403–9.

Staerk, A. (1910), *Les manuscrits latins du Ve au XIIIe siècle conservés à la Bibliothèque Impériale de Saint-Pétersbourg*, 2 vols. (St Petersburg).

Stammler, W., ed. (1957), *Deutsche Philologie im Aufriss*, 2nd ed. (Berlin).

Stanley, E.G. (1979), '*Geweorþa*: "Once Held in High Esteem"', in *J.R.R. Tolkien, Scholar and Storyteller. Essays in Memoriam*, ed. M. Salu and R.T. Farrell (Ithaca, NY), 99–119.

– ed. (1990), *British Academy Papers on Anglo-Saxon England* (Oxford).

– (1994), *In the Foreground: Beowulf* (Cambridge).

– (1998), 'The Sources of Junius's Learning as Revealed in the Junius Manuscripts in the Bodleian Library', in Bremmer (1998), 159–77.

– (2001), 'Linguistic Self-Awareness at Various Times in the History of English from Old English Onwards', in Kay—Sylvester (2001), 237–53.

Stansbury, M. (1999), 'Source-Marks in Bede's Biblical Commentaries', in Hawkes—Mills (1999), 383–9.

Staub, K.H. (1983), 'Ein Beda-Fragment des 8. Jahrhunderts in der hessischen Landes- und Hochschulbibliothek Darmstadt', *Bibliothek und Wissenschaft* 17: 1–7.

Steffens, F. (1909), *Lateinische Paläographie: 125 Tafeln in Lichtdruck mit gegen-überstehender Transkription*, 2nd enlarged ed., 3 vols. (Trier).

Steger, H. (1961), *David rex et propheta: König David als vorbildliche Verkörperung des Herrschers und Dichters im Mittelalter, nach Bilddarstellungen des achten bis zwölften Jahrhunderts*, Erlanger Beiträge zur Sprach- und Kunstwissenschaft 6 (Nürnberg).

Stein, W.A. (1980), 'The Lichfield Gospels' (unpubl. PhD dissertation, University of California at Berkeley, CA).

Steiner, R. (2007), 'Lenten Antiphons *in evangelio*', in *Studies in Medieval Chant and Liturgy in Honour of David Hiley*, ed. T. Bailey and L. Dobszay (Budapest and Ottawa, 2007), 385–412.

Steinmeyer, E. and E. Sievers, eds. (1879–1922), *Die althochdeutschen Glossen*, 5 vols. (Berlin).

– (1880), 'Angelsächsisches aus Rom', *ZfdA* 24: 191–3.

Stemmler, T. (1977), 'Über die Schwierigkeit, englische Lyrik des Mittelalters zu edieren', *Mannheimer Berichte aus Forschung und Lehre an der Universität Mannheim* 15: 409–13.

Stenton, F.M. (1955), *The Latin Charters of the Anglo-Saxon Period* (Oxford).

– (1959), 'The East Anglian Kings of the Seventh Century', in Clemoes (1959a), 43–52.

Stéphan, J. (1955), 'Tavistock et Jumièges: nouvel examen du "Pontificale Lanalatense"', in *Jumièges* (1955) I, 309–16.

Stern, L.C. (1901), Review of J.A. Bruun, *An Enquiry in the Art of the Illuminated Manuscripts of the Middle Ages, I. Celtic Illuminated Manuscripts* (Stockholm, 1897), in *Zeitschrift für celtische Philologie* 3: 444–6.

Stettiner, R. (1895), *Die illustrierten Prudentiushandschriften* (Berlin).

– (1905), *Die illustrierten Prudentiushandschriften: Tafelband* (Berlin).

Stévanovitch, C., ed. (1992), *La Genèse du manuscrit Junius XI de la Bodléienne*, 2 vols. (Paris).

Stevens, W., ed. (1979), *Rabani Mogontiacensis episcopi de computo*, CCCM 44 (Turnhout), 163–321.

– (1992), 'Sidereal Time in Anglo-Saxon England', in Kendall—Wells (1992), 125–52.

Stevenson, H. and G.B. De Rossi (1886), *Bibliothecae Apostolicae Vaticanae Codices Manuscripti Recensiti iubente Leone XIII Pont. Max.: Codices Palatini Latini* (Rome).

Stevenson, Jane (1996a), 'The Holy Sinner: The Life of Mary of Egypt', in Poppe—Ross (1996), 19–50.

– ed. (1996b), '*Vita Sanctae Mariae Egiptiace*', in Poppe—Ross (1996), 51–98.

Stevenson, Joseph, ed. (1841), *Liber Vitae Ecclesiae Dunelmensis*, Publ. of the Surtees Society 13 (Durham).

– (1851), *The Latin Hymns of the Anglo-Saxon Church, with Interlinear Anglo-Saxon Gloss; Derived Chiefly from Manuscripts of the Eleventh Century, Preserved in the Library of the Dean and Chapter of Durham*, Publ. of the Surtees Society 23 (Durham).

Stevenson, W.H. (1912), 'Yorkshire Surveys and other Eleventh-Century Documents in the York Gospels', *EHR* 27: 1–25.

– ed. (1929), *Early Scholastic Colloquies*, with introduction by W.M. Lindsay, Anecdota Oxoniensia 4 (Oxford).

Stevick, R.D. (1968), *Suprasegmentals, Meter, and the Manuscript of 'Beowulf'*, Janua Linguarum, Series Practica 71 (The Hague).

Stevinson, J. and J. Stevinson (2008), *Winchcombe Abbey's Thousand Year Old Book: The Winchcombe Sacramentary c. 970 A.D.* (Winchcombe).

Stewart, H.F. (1917), 'A Commentary by Remigius of Auxerre on the *De consolatione Philosophiae* of Boethius', *JTS* 17: 22–42.

Stiegemann, C. and M. Wemhoff, eds. (1999), *799. Kunst und Kultur der Karolingerzeit. Karl der Grosse und Papst Leo III. in Paderborn*, 3 vols. [exhibition catalogue] (Mainz).

– and M. Wemhoff, eds. (2006), *Canossa 1077. Erschütterung der Welt. Geschichte, Kunst und Kultur am Aufgang der Romanik*, 2 vols. (Munich).

Stilwell, R.S. (1947), 'A Glossary for the Vercelli Prose Homilies' (unpubl. PhD dissertation, University of Texas at Austin, TX).

Stirnemann, P. (1992), 'Paris, BN, MS lat. 8846 and the Eadwine Psalter', in M. Gibson (1992), 186–92.

Stockdale, R. (2005), 'Benedictine Books, Writers and Libraries, some Surviving Manuscripts from Sherborne and South-West England', in Barker et al. (2005), 164–76.

Stokes, P.A. (2007), 'The Regius Psalter, Folio 198v: A Reexamination', *N&Q* 254: 208–11.

Stokes, W. (1860), 'Cambrica', *Transactions of the Philological Society*: 204–49.

– (1872), *Old-Welsh Glosses on Martianus Capella* (Simla).

– (1873), 'The Old-Welsh Glosses on Martianus Capella, with Some Notes on the Juvencus Glosses', *Beiträge zur vergleichenden Sprachforschung* 7: 385–416.

– (1891), 'Glosses from Turin and Rome', *Beiträge zur Kunde der indogermanischen Sprachen* 17: 144–5.

– and J. Strachan, eds. (1901–3), *Thesaurus Palaeohibernicus*, 2 vols. (Cambridge).

Stoneman, W.P. (1983), 'A Critical Edition of Ælfric's Translation of Alcuin's *Interrogationes Sigwulfi presbiteri* and of the Related Texts' (unpubl. PhD dissertation, University of Toronto).

– (1987), 'Another Old English Note Signed "Coleman"', *MÆ* 56: 78–82.

- (1997), 'Writ in Ancient Character and of no Further Use: Anglo-Saxon Manuscripts in American Collections', in Szarmach—Rosenthal (1997), 99–138.

Stoppacci, P., ed. (2012—), *Cassiodoro, Expositio Psalmorum. Tradizione mano-scritta, fortuna, edizione critica* (Florence).

Stork, N.P. (1990), *Through a Gloss Darkly: Aldhelm's Riddles in the British Library MS Royal 12 C. XXIII*, Studies and Texts 98 (Toronto).

- (1992), 'Revising Napier: New Light on some Old English Glosses', in Derolez (1992), 153–65.

Storms, G., ed. (1948), *Anglo-Saxon Magic* (The Hague).

Story, J.E. (1993), 'The Archaeology of Early Medieval Manuscripts: Durham Cathedral Library MS A. II. 16: An Eighth-Century Northumbrian Gospel Book', *Durham Archaeological Journal* 9: 19–26.

- (1998), 'Symeon as Annalist', in Rollason (1998), 202–13.

- (2003), *Carolingian Connections: Anglo-Saxon England and Carolingian Francia, c. 750–870* (Aldershot).

- (2005), 'The Frankish Annals of Lindisfarne and Kent', *ASE* 34: 59–108.

- (2009), 'After Bede: Continuing the *Ecclesiastical History*', in *Early Medieval Studies in Memory of Patrick Wormald*, ed. S. Baxter et al. (Farnham, 2009), 165–84.

Stotz, P. (1972), *Ardua spes mundi: Studien zu lateinischen Gedichten aus Sankt Gallen*, Geist und Werk der Zeiten 32 (Bern).

Stracke, J.R. (1974), 'Eight Lambeth Psalter-Glosses', *PQ* 53: 121–8.

Stratford, J. (1981), *Catalogue of the Jackson Collection of Fragments in the Royal Library, Windsor Castle* (London).

- (2000), 'Manuscript Fragments at Windsor Castle and the Entente Cordiale', in Brownrigg—Smith (2000), 114–37.

Strecker, K., ed. (1914–23), MGH, PLAC 4/ii–iii (Berlin).

- ed. (1926), *Die Cambridger Lieder*, MGH, Scriptores rerum Germanicarum in usum scholarum 40 (Berlin).

- et al., eds. (1937–9), MGH, PLAC 5 (Berlin).

Strongman, S. (1977–80), 'John Parker's Manuscripts: An Edition of the Lists in Lambeth Palace MS 737', *TCBS* 7: 1–27

Stroud, D.I. (1979), 'The Provenance of the Salisbury Psalter', *The Library*, 6th ser. 1: 225–35.

Stryker, W.G. (1951), 'The Latin-Old English Glossary in MS Cotton Cleopatra A III' (unpubl. PhD dissertation, Stanford Univ.).

Stuart, J., ed. (1869), *The Book of Deer* (Edinburgh).

Stubbs, W., ed. (1874), *Memorials of St Dunstan*, RS 63 (London).

Sture Ureland, P. and G. Broderick, eds. (1991), *Language Contact in the British Isles. Proceedings of the Eighth International Symposium on Language Contact in Europe, Douglas, Isle of Man, 1988* (Tübingen).

Stuttmann, F. (1937), *Der Reliquienschatz der Goldenen Tafel des St Michaelisklosters in Lüneburg* (Berlin).

Sudhoff, K. (1914), *Beiträge zur Geschichte der Chirurgie im Mittelalter*, I (Leipzig).

– (1917), 'Codex medicus Hertensis (Nr. 192)', *Archiv für Geschichte der Medizin* 10: 265–313.

Swan, M. (1998), 'Memorialised Readings: Manuscript Evidence for Old English Homily Composition', in Pulsiano—Treharne (1998a), 205–18.

– and E.M. Treharne, eds. (2000a), *Rewriting Old English in the Twelfth Century*, CSASE 30 (Cambridge)

– (2000b), 'Ælfric's Catholic Homilies in the Twelfth Century', in Swan—Treharne (2000a), 62–82.

– (2006), 'Cambridge, Corpus Christi College 198 and the Blickling Manuscript', *LSE* 37: 89–100.

– (2007a), 'Preaching Past the Conquest: Lambeth Palace 489 and Cotton Vespasian A. xxii', in Kleist (2007a), 403–23.

– (2007b), 'Mobile Libraries: Old English Manuscript Production in Worcester and the West Midlands, 1090–1215', in Scase (2007), 29–42.

Swanson, R.N., ed. (1999), *Continuity and Change in Christian Worship*, Studies in Church History 35 (Woodbridge).

– (2004), 'Books of Brotherhood: Registering Fraternity and Confraternity in Late Medieval England', in Rollason (2004a), 233–46.

Swanton, M. (1975), 'A Fragmentary Life of St Mildred and other Kentish Royal Saints', *Archaeologia Cantiana* 91: 15–27.

– ed. (1987), *The Dream of the Rood*, rev. ed. (Exeter).

Swarzenski, H. (1949), 'The Anhalt-Morgan Gospels', *Art Bulletin* 31: 77–83.

– (1954), *Monuments of Romanesque Art: The Art of Church Treasures in North-Western Europe* (Chicago).

Sweet, H., ed. (1871), *King Alfred's West-Saxon Version of Gregory's Pastoral Care*, 2 vols., EETS o.s. 45, 50 (London).

– ed. (1883), *The Épinal Glossary: Latin and Old-English of the Eighth Century*, EETS o.s. 79 B (London).

– ed. (1885), *The Oldest English Texts*, EETS o.s. 83 (London).

– (1887/1978), *A Second Anglo-Saxon Reader*, 2nd ed., rev. by T. F. Hoad (Oxford).

Swoboda, A., ed. (1900), *Odonis abbatis Cluniacensis Occupatio* (Leipzig).

Symons, T., ed. (1953), *Regularis Concordia Anglicae Nationis Monachorum Sanctimonialiumque; The Monastic Agreement of the Monks and Nuns of the English Nation* (London).

– and S. Spath, eds. (1984), 'Regularis Concordia Anglicae Nationis', CCM VII/3, 61–147.

Szarmach, P.E. (1977a), 'MS Junius 85 f. 2r and Napier 49', *ELN* 14: 241–6.

- (1977b), 'The Scribe of the Old English Vercelli Book', *Manuscripta* 21: 24.
- and B.F. Huppé, eds. (1978), *The Old English Homily and its Backgrounds* (Albany, NY).
- (1979), 'The Scribe of the Vercelli Book', *SN* 51: 179–88.
- ed. (1981a), *Vercelli Homilies ix–xxiii*, Toronto OE Series 5 (Toronto).
- (1981b), 'A Preliminary Handlist of Manuscripts Containing Alcuin's *Liber de Virtutibus et Vitiis*', *Manuscripta* 25: 131–40.
- (1981c), 'Vatican Library, MS. Reg. Lat. 497 fol. 71v', *OEN* 15: 34–5.
- (1986a), 'British Library, Cotton Vespasian D. vi, fol. 62v', *OEN* 20: 32–3.
- ed. (1986b), *Studies in Earlier Old English Prose: Sixteen Original Contributions* (Albany, NY).
- ed. (1986c), *Sources of Anglo-Saxon Culture* (Kalamazoo, MI).
- (1992), 'Cotton Tiberius A. iii, Arts. 26 and 27', in Korhammer (1992), 29–42.
- ed. (1996), *Holy Men and Holy Women: Old English Prose Saints' Lives and their Contexts* (Albany, NY).
- and J.T. Rosenthal, eds. (1997), *The Preservation and Transmission of Anglo-Saxon Culture – Selected Papers from the 1991 Meeting of the International Society of Anglo-Saxonists* (Kalamazoo, MI).
- (1999), 'A Return to Cotton Tiberius A. iii, art. 24, and Isidore's *Synonyma*', in Conrad-O'Briain et al. (1999), 166–81.
- ed. (2000), *Old English Prose: Basic Readings*, Basic Readings in Anglo-Saxon England 5 (New York).
- (2001), 'The *Timaeus* in Old English', in Kay—Sylvester (2001), 255–67.
- (2002), 'Pembroke College 25, arts. 93-95', in Hall—Hill (2002), 295–325.
- (2005), 'Alfred's *Soliloquies* in London, BL, Cotton Tiberius A. iii (art. 9g, fols. 50v–51v)', in O'Brien O'Keeffe—Orchard (2005) II, 153–79.
- (2006), 'Vercelli Homily XIV and the Homiliary of Paul the Deacon', *LSE* 37: 75–87.
Szerwiniack, O. (1994), 'Des recueils d'interprétations de noms Hébreux chez les Irlandais et le Wisigoth Théodulf', *Scriptorium* 48: 187–258.
Taeger, B. (1979), (1981a), (1982), (1984), 'Das Straubinger Heliand-Fragment. Philologische Untersuchungen', *BGDSL* 101: 181–228; 103: 402–24; 104: 10–43; 106: 364–89.
- (1981b), 'Heliand', in Ruh et al. (1978—) III, 958–79.
Takamiya, T. (1989), 'Fragments of *Augustinus super psalmos*, possibly copied by Eadmer', *Reports of the Institute of Linguistic and Cultural Studies, Keio University* 21: 175–89.
- (2010), 'A Handlist of Western Medieval Manuscripts in the Takamiya Collection', in *The Medieval Book. Glosses from Friends and Colleagues of Christopher De Hamel*, ed. J.H. Marrow, R. Linenthal and W. Noel ('t Goy-Houten), 421–40.

Talbot, C.H. (1965), 'Some Notes on Anglo-Saxon Medicine', *Medical History* 9: 156–68.

– (1967), *Medicine in Medieval England* (London).

Tangl, M., ed. (1916), *Die Briefe des heiligen Bonifatius und Lullus*, MGH, Epistolae selectae 1 (Berlin).

Tannery, P. and J.-A. Clerval (1901), 'Une correspondence d'écolatres du XIe siècle', *Notices et extraits des manuscrits de la Bibliothèque nationale et autres bibliothèques* 36.2: 487–543.

Tarrant, R.J. (1983), 'Plautus', in L.D. Reynolds (1983), 302–7.

Taxweiler, R. (1906), *Angelsächsische Urkundenbücher von kentischem Lokalcharakter* (Berlin).

Taylor, P.B. and P.H. Salus (1968), 'The Compilation of Cotton Vitellius A. xv', *NM* 69: 199–204.

Taylor, S., ed. (1983), *The Anglo-Saxon Chronicle: A Collaborative Edition, 4: MS B* (Cambridge).

Temple, E. (1976), *A Survey of Manuscripts Illuminated in the British Isles*, II: *Anglo-Saxon Manuscripts 900–1066* (London).

Temple, W.M. (1952), 'An Edition of the Old English Homilies contained in B. M. MS Cotton Vitellius C. v' (unpubl. PhD dissertation, University of Edinburgh).

Teresi, L. (2000), 'Mnemonic Transmission of Old English Texts in the post-Conquest Period', in Swan—Treharne (2000a), 98–116.

– (2002), '*Be Heofonwarum 7 be Helwarum*: A Complete Edition', in Treharne—Rosser (2002), 211–44.

– (2007a), 'Ælfric's or Not? The Making of a *Temporale* Collection in late Anglo-Saxon England', in Kleist (2007a), 284–310.

– (2007b), 'The Drawing on the Margin of Cambridge, Corpus Christi College 206, f. 38r: An Intertextual Exemplification to Clarify the Text?', in Lendinara et al. (2007), 131–40.

– (2007c), 'Anglo-Saxon and Early Anglo-Norman *Mappaemundi*', in Bremmer—Dekker (2007), 341–67 [and pls. 1–10].

– (2011), 'Making Sense of Apparent Chaos: Recontextualising the so-called "Note on the Names of the Winds"', in Lendinara et al. (2011), 415–42.

Teviotdale, E.C. (1991), 'The Cotton Troper (London, British Library, Cotton MS Caligula A. xiv, ff. 1–36): A Study of an Illustrated English Troper of the Eleventh Century' (unpubl. PhD dissertation, University of North Carolina at Chapel Hill, NC).

– (1992a), 'The Making of the Cotton Troper', in Hicks (1992), 301–16.

– (1992b), 'Some Thoughts on the Place of Origin of the Cotton Troper' in *Cantus Planus. Papers read at the Fourth Meeting of the Cantus Planus*

Study Group of the International Musicological Society, Pécs, Hungary, 3–8 September 1990, ed. L. Dobszay (Budapest, 1992), 407–12.

–   (1995a), 'The "Hereford Troper" and Hereford', in *Medieval Art, Architecture and Archaeology at Hereford*, ed. D. Whitehead (Leeds, 1995), 75–81.

–   (1995b), 'Tropers', in Pfaff (1995a), 39–44.

–   (1996), 'Latin Verse Inscriptions in Anglo-Saxon Art', *Gesta* 35: 99–110.

–   (1998), 'An Episode in the Medieval Afterlife of the Caligula Troper', in Pulsiano–Treharne (1998a), 219–26.

–   (2010), 'Pembroke College 302: Abbreviated Gospel Book or Gospel Lectionary?', in Brown–Voigts (2010), 69–99.

Thacker, A. (1988), 'Æthelwold and Abingdon', in Yorke (1988), 43–64.

–   (1992), 'Cults at Canterbury: Relics and Reform under Dunstan and his Successors', in Ramsay et al. (1992), 221–45.

–   (1996), 'Saint-Making and Relic Collecting by Oswald and his Communities', in Brooks–Cubitt (1996), 244–68.

–   (1999), 'In Gregory's Shadow? The Pre-Conquest Cult of St Augustine', in R. Gameson (1999b), 374–91.

'The Schøyen Collection': http://www.nb.no/baser/schoyen/4/4.4/ [and note that numerical references to individual manuscripts in the collection are to be understood as supplementary to the web address given here].

Thiel, M. (1969), *Grundlagen und Gestalt der Hebräischkenntnisse des frühen Mittelalters* (Spoleto).

Thomas, P., ed. (1908), *Apuleius III. De philosophia libri* (Leipzig).

Thompson, A.H., ed. (1923), *Liber Vitae Ecclesiae Dunelmensis*, Publications of the Surtees Society 136 (Durham) [facsimile].

–   and U. Lindelöf, eds. (1927), *Rituale Ecclesiae Dunelmensis*, Surtees Society 140 (Durham).

–   ed. (1935), *Bede: His Life, Times, and Writings. Essays in Commemoration of the Twelfth Centenary of his Death* (Oxford).

Thompson, E.M. (1880), 'Catalogue of Manuscripts in the Cathedral Library of Salisbury', in [anon.], *Catalogue of the Library of the Cathedral Church of Salisbury* (London), 3–44.

–   and G.F. Warner (1881–4), *Catalogue of Ancient Manuscripts in the British Museum, Part II: Latin* (London).

–   (1895), *English Illuminated Manuscripts* (London).

–   (1912), *An Introduction to Greek and Latin Palaeography* (Oxford).

Thompson, J.W. (1957), *The Medieval Library*, 2nd ed. with supplement by B. Boyer (New York).

Thompson, N.M. (2004), 'Anglo-Saxon Orthodoxy', in Lionarons (2004a), 37–66.

- (2007), 'The Carolingian *De festivitatibus* and the Blickling Book', in Kleist (2007a), 97–119.

Thompson, P.Z. (1984), 'Biography of a Library: The Western European Manuscript Collection of Peter P. Dubrovskii in Leningrad', *The Journal of Library History* 19: 477–503.

Thompson, V. (2005), 'The Pastoral Contract in late Anglo-Saxon England: Priest and Parishioner in Oxford, Bodleian Library, MS Laud Miscellaneous 482', in Tinti (2005), 106–20.

Thomson, R. (2000), 'Newly Discovered Fragments of Music at Worcester Cathedral: A Preliminary Account', in Brownrigg—Smith (2000), 89–97.

Thomson, R.B. (1985), 'Two Astronomical Tractates of Abbo of Fleury', in *The Light of Nature. Essays in the History and Philosophy of Science presented to A.C. Crombie*, ed. J.D. North and J.J. Roche (Dordrecht), 114–33.

Thomson, R.L. (1981), 'Ælfric's Latin Vocabulary', *LSE* 12: 155–61.

Thomson, R.M. (1972), 'The Library of Bury St Edmunds Abbey in the Eleventh and Twelfth Centuries', *Speculum* 47: 617–45.

- (1975), 'The Reading of William of Malmesbury', *RB* 85: 362–94.
- (1978), 'The "scriptorium" of William of Malmesbury', in Parkes—Watson (1978), 117–45.
- (1982a), *Manuscripts from St. Albans Abbey, 1066–1235*, 2 vols. (Woodbridge).
- (1982b), 'Identifiable Books from the Pre-Conquest Library of Malmesbury Abbey', *ASE* 10: 1–19.
- (1984), 'The Music for the Office of St Edmund King and Martyr', *Music and Letters* 65: 189–93.
- (1986a), 'The Norman Conquest and English Libraries', in P. Ganz (1986) I, 27–40.
- (1986b), 'British Library Royal 15. C. XI: a Manuscript of Plautus' Plays from Salisbury Cathedral (c. 1100)', *Scriptorium* 40: 82–7.
- (1987), *William of Malmesbury* (Woodbridge) [rev. ed. 2003].
- (1989), *Catalogue of the Manuscripts of Lincoln Cathedral Chapter Library* (Woodbridge).
- (2001), *A Descriptive Catalogue of the Medieval Manuscripts in Worcester Cathedral Library* (Woodbridge).
- (2009), *A Descriptive Catalogue of the Medieval Manuscripts of Merton College, Oxford, with a Description of the Greek Manuscripts by N.G. Wilson* (Cambridge).
- (2011), *A Descriptive Catalogue of the Medieval Manuscripts of Corpus Christi College, Oxford* (Cambridge).

Thorn, F. and C. Thorn (2001), 'The Writing of Great Domesday Book', in Hallam—Bates (2001), 37–72.

Thornbury, E.V. (2011), 'Building with the Rubble of the Past: The Translator of the Old English *Gospel of Nicodemus* and his Flawed Source', in Roberts—Webster (2011), 297–318.

Thorndike, L. (1923–58), *A History of Magic and Experimental Science during the First Thirteen Centuries of our Era*, 8 vols. (New York).

— and P. Kibre (1963), *A Catalogue of Incipits of Mediaeval Scientific Writings in Latin*, rev. ed. (Cambridge, MA).

Thorpe, B. (1840), *Ancient Laws and Institutes of England* (London).

— (1842), *Ða Halgan Godspel on Englisc: The Anglo-Saxon Version of the Holy Gospels* (London).

— ed. (1844–6), *The Homilies of the Anglo-Saxon Church. The First Part, containing the Sermones Catholici, or Homilies of Ælfric*, 2 vols. (London).

— (1865), *Diplomatarium Anglicum Ævi Saxonici* (London).

Thulin, C. (1911), *Zur Überlieferungsgeschichte des Corpus agrimensorum. Exzerpten-Handschriften und Kompendien* (Göteborg).

Thurn, H., ed. (1968), *Comes Romanus Wirziburgensis. Faksimileausgabe des Codex M. p. th. f. 62 der Universitätsbibliothek Würzburg* (Graz).

— (1984), *Die Handschriften der Universitätsbibliothek Würzburg*, III. 1: *Die Pergamenthandschriften der ehemaligen Dombibliothek* (Wiesbaden).

— (1988), [descriptions of MSS in] *Die Bibliothek des Würzburger Domstifts: 742–1803* [exhibition catalogue] (Würzburg).

— (1989), 'Zum Text des Hieronymus-Kommentars zum Kohelet', *Biblische Zeitschrift* 33: 234–44.

— K. Morvay, H.-G. Schmidt and P.G. Schmidt, *Die datierten Handschriften der Universitätsbibliothek Würzburg*, Datierte Handschriften in Bibliotheken der Bundesrepublik Deutschland 5 (Stuttgart).

Tibbetts, S. (2003), '*Praescriptiones*, Student Scribes and the Carolingian Scriptorium', in *La collaboration dans la production de l'écrit médiéval, Actes du XIIIe colloque du Comité international de paléographie latine (Weingarten, 22–25 septembre 2000)*, ed. H. Spilling (Paris, 2003), 25–38.

Tierney, B. and P. Linehan, eds. (1980), *Authority and Power: Studies in Medieval Law and Government presented to Walter Ullmann* (Cambridge).

Tilghman, B.C. (2011), 'Writing in Tongues: Mixed Scripts and Style in Insular Art', in Hourihane (2011), 93–108.

Tilling, P.M., ed. (1981), *Studies in English Language and Early Literature in Honour of Paul Christopherson* (Ulster).

Timmer, B., ed. (1948), *The Later Genesis* (Oxford).

Tinti, F. (2002), 'From Episcopal Conception to Monastic Compilation: Hemming's Cartulary in Context', *EME* 11: 233–61.

- ed. (2005), *Pastoral Care in late Anglo-Saxon England*, Anglo-Saxon Studies 6 (Cambridge).
- (2009), '*Si litterali memorie commendaretur*: Memory and Cartularies in Eleventh-Century Worcester', in Baxter et al. (2009), 475–97.
- (2010), *Sustaining Belief. The Church of Worcester from c. 870 to c. 1100* (Farnham).
- (2012), 'Personal Names in the Composition and Transmission of Bede's Prose *Vita S. Cuthberti*', *ASE* 40: 15–42.
Tischendorf, C., ed. (1850), *Novum Testamentum latine interprete Hieronymo ex celeberrimo codice Amiatino omnium et antiquissimo et praestantissimo* (Leipzig).
- ed. (1870), *Monumenta Sacra Inedita: Codex Actuum Laudianus* (Leipzig).
Tite, C.G.C. (1980), 'The Early Catalogues of the Cottonian Library', *BLJ* 6: 144–57.
- ed. (1984), *Catalogue of the Manuscripts in the Cottonian Library, 1696. Reprinted from Sir Robert Harley's Copy. Together with Documents relating to the Fire of 1731* (Cambridge).
- (1994), *The Manuscript Library of Sir Robert Cotton* (London).
- (1997a), '"Lost or Stolen or Strayed": A Survey of Manuscripts Formerly in the Cotton Library', in C.J. Wright (1997), 262–306 [repr. from *BLJ* 18 (1992) 107–47].
- (1997b), 'Sir Robert Cotton, Sir Thomas Tempest and an Anglo-Saxon Gospel Book: A Cottonian Paper in the Harleian Library', in Carley — Tite (1997), 429–39.
- (2003), *The Early Records of Sir Robert Cotton's Library: Formation, Cataloguing, Use* (London).
- (2004), 'The Durham *Liber Vitae* and Sir Robert Cotton', in Rollason et al. (2004), 3–15.
Todd, H.J., ed. (1812), *A Catalogue of the Archiepiscopal Manuscripts in the Library at Lambeth Palace, with an Account of the Archiepiscopal Registers and other Records there Preserved* (London, 1812; repr. London, 1965, Oxford, 1972).
Tolhurst, J.B.L. (1933), 'An Examination of Two Anglo-Saxon Manuscripts of the Winchester School: The Missal of Robert of Jumièges and the Benedictional of St. Æthelwold', *Archaeologia* 83: 27–44.
- (1942), *Introduction to the English Monastic Breviaries: Monastic Breviary of Hyde Abbey, Winchester* VI, HBS 80 (London).
- (1955), 'Le Missel de Robert de Jumièges, sacramentaire d'Ely', in *Jumièges* (1955) I, 287–93.

Tolkien, J.R.R. [ed.] (1981), *The Old English Exodus*, ed. J. Turville-Petre (Oxford).

Toneatto, L. (1994), *Codices artis mensoriae: i manoscritti degli antichi opuscoli latini d'agrimensura (V-XIX sec.)*, 3 vols. (Spoleto).

Toon, T.E. (1991), 'Dry-Point Annotations in Early English Manuscripts', in Barney (1991), 74–93.

Torkar, R. (1971), 'Zu den Vorlagen der ae. Handschrift Cotton Julius E. vii.', *NM* 72: 711–15.

– (1976), 'Zu den altenglischen Medizinaltexten in Otho B. xi und Royal 12 D. XVII, mit einer Edition der Unica (Ker, No. 180 art. 11a-d)', *Anglia* 94: 319–38.

– ed. (1981), *Eine altenglische Übersetzung von Alcuin's 'De Virtutibus et Vitiis', Kap. 20 (Liebermanns Judex): Untersuchungen und Textausgabe mit Anhang: die Gesetze II und V Æthelstan nach Otho B.xi und Add. 43703*, TUEPh 7 (Munich).

– (1986), 'Cotton Vitellius A. xv (part I) and the *Legend of St Thomas*', *ES* 67: 290–303.

Toswell, M.J. (1991), 'Studies in the *Paris Psalter*, Metrical Version' (unpubl. PhD dissertation, Oxford Univ.).

– (1995-6), 'The Late Anglo-Saxon Psalter: Ancestor of the Book of Hours?', *Florilegium* 14: 1–24.

– (1996), 'The Format of Bibliothèque Nationale MS lat. 8824: The Paris Psalter', *N&Q* 241: 130–3.

– (2007), 'The Codicology of Anglo-Saxon Homiletic Manuscripts, especially the Blickling Homilies', in Kleist (2007a), 209–26.

– (2012), 'Psalters', in R. Gameson (2012), 468–81.

Toth, K. (1984), 'Altenglische Interlinearglossen zu Prospers *Epigrammata* und *Versus ad coniugem*', *Anglia* 102: 1–36.

Townend, M. (2001), 'Contextualizing the *Knútsdrápur*: Skaldic Praise-Poetry at the Court of Cnut', *ASE* 30: 145–79.

– ed. (2004), *Wulfstan, Archbishop of York*, The Proceedings of the Second Alcuin Conference (Turnhout).

Townsend, D. (1989), 'An Eleventh-Century Life of Birinus of Wessex', *AB* 107: 129–59.

Toy, J. (2005), 'The Fragments Reveal New Evidence of the Cult of English Saints in Sweden', in Brunius (2005), 99–108.

– (2009), *English Saints in the Medieval Liturgies of Scandinavian Churches*, HBS Subsidia 6 (London).

Traherne, J.B. (1973), 'Amalarius *Be Becnum*: A Fragment of the *Liber Officialis* in Old English', *Anglia* 91: 475–8.

Traill, H.D. and J.S. Mann (1901), *Social England: A Record of the Progress of the People in Religion, Laws, Learning, Arts, Industry, Commerce, Science, Literature and Manners, from the Earliest to the Present Day*, I (London).

Traube, L., ed. (1886–96), MGH, PLAC 3 (Berlin).

– (1907), *Nomina sacra* (Munich).

– (1909–20), *Vorlesungen und Abhandlungen*, ed. F. Boll, 3 vols. (Munich).

– (1910), *Textgeschichte der Regula S. Benedicti*, ed. H. Plenkers, Abhandlungen der königlich bayerischen Akademie der Wissenschaften, phil.-hist. Klasse 25, 2nd ed. (Munich).

Traxel, O.M. (2004), *Language Change, Writing and Textual Interference in Post-Conquest Old English Manuscripts. The Evidence of Cambridge, University Library, Ii. 1. 33*, TUEPh 32 (Frankfurt am Main).

Treharne, E.M. (1992), 'Corpus Christi College, Cambridge, 303 and the Lives of Saints Margaret, Giles and Nicholas' (unpubl. PhD dissertation, Manchester Univ.).

– ed. (1997), *The OE Life of St Nicholas with the OE Life of St Giles* (Leeds).

– (1998) , 'The Dates and Origins of Three Twelfth-Century Old English Manuscripts', in Pulsiano—Treharne (1998a), 227–54.

– (2000a) , 'Introduction', in Swan—Treharne (2000a), 1–10.

– (2000b), 'The Production and Script of Manuscripts containing English Religious Texts in the first half of the Twelfth Century', in Swan—Treharne (2000a), 11–40.

– and S. Rosser, eds. (2002), *Early Medieval English Texts and Interpretations: Studies presented to Donald G. Scragg*, MRTS 252 (Tempe, AZ).

– (2003), 'Producing a Library in Late Anglo-Saxon England: Exeter, 1050–1072', *RES* n.s. 54: 155–72.

– (2007a), 'The Form and Function of the Vercelli Book', in Minnis—Roberts (2007), 253–66.

– (2007b), 'Bishops and their Texts in the Later Eleventh Century: Worcester and Exeter', in Scase (2007), 13–28.

– (2009a), 'The Bishop's Book: Leofric's Homiliary and Eleventh-Century Exeter', in Baxter et al. (2009), 521–37.

– (2009b), 'Manuscript Sources of Old English Poetry', in Owen-Crocker (2009), 89–111.

Tristram, H.L.C. (1970), *Vier altenglische Predigten aus der heterodoxen Tradition, mit Kommentar, Übersetzung und Glossar sowie drei weiteren Texten im Anhang* (Diss. Freiburg im Breisgau).

– (1985), *Sex aetates mundi: die Weltzeitalter bei den Angelsachsen und den Iren. Untersuchungen und Texte*, Anglistische Forschungen 165 (Heidelberg).

– (2007), 'Why don't the English speak Welsh?', in Higham (2007), 192–214.

Troncarelli, F. (1973), 'Per una ricerca sui commenti altomedievali al *De consolatione di Boezio'*, in *Miscellanea in memoria di Giorgio Cencetti* (Turin, 1973), 363–80.

– (1981), *Tradizioni perdute: la 'Consolatio philosophiae' nell'alto medioevo* (Padua).

– (1987), *Boethiana aetas. Modelli grafici et fortuna manoscritta della 'De consolatione Philosophiae'* (Alessandria).

Tselos, D. (1959), 'English Manuscript Illustration and the Utrecht Psalter', *Art Bulletin* 41: 137–49.

– (1960), *The Sources of the Utrecht Psalter Miniatures*, 2nd ed. (Minneapolis, MN).

Tupper, F. (1895), 'Anglo-Saxon Dæg-Mæl', *PMLA* 10: 111–241.

– (1904-5), 'Riddles of the Bede Tradition', *MP* 2: 561–72.

Turner, A.J. and B.J. Muir, eds. (2006), *Eadmer of Canterbury: Lives and Miracles of Saints Oda, Dunstan and Oswald* (Oxford).

Turner, C.H. (1909), 'Iter Dunelmense: Durham Bible MSS, with the Text of a Leaf lately in the Possession of Canon Greenwell of Durham, now in the British Museum', *JTS* 10: 529–44.

– (1915–16), 'The Churches at Winchester in the Early Eleventh Century', *JTS* 17: 65–8.

– (1916), *Early Worcester MSS. Fragments of Four Books and a Charter of the Eighth Century Belonging to Worcester Cathedral* (Oxford).

– (1917–18), 'The Earliest List of Durham MSS', *JTS* 19: 121–32.

– (1931), *The Oldest Manuscript of the Vulgate Gospels* (Oxford).

Turner, D.H. (1960), 'The Prayer-Book of Archbishop Arnulph II of Milan', *RB* 70: 360–92.

– ed. (1962), *The Missal of the New Minster, Winchester*, HBS 93 (London).

– , ed. (1971), *The Claudius Pontificals from Cotton MS Claudius A.III in the British Museum*, HBS 97 (London).

– et al. (1980), *The Benedictines in Britain* (London) [exhibition catalogue].

Twomey, M.W. (2007), 'The *Revelations* of pseudo-Methodius and Scriptural Study at Salisbury in the Eleventh Century', in Biggs—Hall (2007), 370–86.

Unterkircher, F. (1954–5), 'Drei Fragmente mit irischer und angelsächsischer Schrift in der ÖNB', *Libri* 5: 237–55.

Upchurch, R.K. (2007a), 'Homiletic Contexts for Ælfric's Hagiography: The Legend of Saints Cecilia and Valerian', in Kleist (2007a), 265–84.

– (2007b), *Ælfric's Lives of the Virgin Spouses* (Exeter).

Ure, J.M., ed. (1957), *The Benedictine Office. An Old English Text* (Edinburgh).

Ussani, V. and K. Mras, eds. (1932–60), *Hegesippi qui dicitur Historiae libri V*, 2 vols., CSEL 66 (Vienna).

Utley, F.L. (1972), 'Dialogues, Debates, and Catechisms', in Hartung (1972), 669–745, 829–902.

Vaciago, P. (1993), 'Old English Glosses to Latin Texts: a Bibliographical Handlist', *Medioevo e Rinascimento* 7: 1–67.

– (1996), 'Towards a Corpus of Carolingian Biblical Glossaries: A Research in Progress Report', in Hamesse (1996), 127–44.

Valtorta, B. (2006), *Clavis Scriptorum Latinorum Medii Aevi: Auctores Italiae (700–1000)* (Florence).

Van Arsdall, A. (2002), *Medieval Herbal Remedies. The Old English Herbarium and Anglo-Saxon Medicine* (London).

Van de Vyver, A. (1935), 'Les œuvres inédites d'Abbon de Fleury', *RB* 47: 125–69.

Van de Woestijne, P., ed. (1937), *Cynegétiques de Némésien: édition critique* (Antwerp).

– ed. (1953), *Périégèse de Priscien: édition critique* (Bruges, 1953).

Van den Gheyn, J. et al. (1901–48), *Catalogue des manuscrits de la Bibliothèque royale de Belgique*, 13 vols. (Brussels).

Van der Horst, K. and J.H.A. Engelbregt, eds. (1984), *Utrecht Psalter: Vollständige Faksimile-Ausgabe der Handschrift 32 aus den Besitz der Bibliotheek der Rijksuniversiteit te Utrecht*, 2 vols. (Graz).

– (1990), *Illuminated and Decorated Medieval Manuscripts in the University Library, Utrecht: an Illustrated Catalogue* (Cambridge).

– W. Noel and W.C.M. Wüstefeld, eds. (1996), *The Utrecht Psalter: Picturing the Psalms of David* (London).

Vanderputten, S. (2006), 'Canterbury and Flanders in the Late Tenth Century', *ASE* 35: 219–44.

Van der Straeten, J. (1971), *Les manuscrits hagiographiques d'Arras et de Boulogne-sur-Mer*, Subsidia Hagiographica 50 (Brussels).

– (1981), *Les manuscrits hagiographiques d'Orléans, Tours et Angers*, Subsidia Hagiographica 64 (Brussels).

Van Dijk, S.J.P. (1952), *Latin Liturgical Manuscripts and Printed Books. Guide to an Exhibition held during 1952* (Oxford).

– (1957–60), 'Handlist of the Latin Liturgical Manuscripts in the Bodleian Library Oxford', 6 vols. [typescript deposited in the Bodleian Library] (Oxford).

– and J. Hazelden Walker (1960), *The Origins of the Modern Roman Liturgy: The Liturgy of the Papal Court and the Franciscan Order in the Thirteenth Century* (London).

Van Els, T.J.M. (1972), *The Kassel Manuscript of Bede's 'Historia Ecclesiastica Gentis Anglorum' and its Old English Material* (Assen).

Van Houts, E.M.C. (1982), *Gesta Normannorum Ducum. Een studie over de handschriften, de tekst, het geschiedwerk en het genre* (Groningen).

– ed. (1992–5), *The Gesta Normannorum Ducum of William of Jumièges, Orderic Vitalis and Robert of Torigni*, 2 vols. (Oxford).

Van Langenhove, G. (1941), *Aldhelm's De laudibus virginitatis with Latin and Old English Glosses. Manuscript 1650 of the Royal Library in Brussels. With an Introductory Chapter*, Rijksuniversiteit Gent: Werken uitgegeven door de Faculteit van de Wijsbegeerte en Letteren. Extra serie: Facsimiles 2 (Bruges).

Van Loey, A. (1970), 'Altniederländisch und Mittelniederländisch', in Schmitt (1970), 253–87.

Van Rhijn, C., ed. (2009), *Paenitentialia Franciae, Italiae et Hispaniae saeculi VIII–XI*, III. *Paenitentiale Pseudo-Theodori*, CCSL 156B (Turnhout).

Vaughan, R. and J. Fines (1959–63), 'A Handlist of Manuscripts in the Library of Corpus Christi College, not described by M.R. James', *TCBS* 3: 113–23.

Vavra, E. (2005), *Virtuelle Räume: Raumwahrnehmung und Raumvorstellung im Mittelalter. Akten des 10. Symposiums des Mediävistenverbandes, Krems, 24.–26. März 2003* (Berlin).

Verdonck, J., ed. (1974), 'The Old English Glosses of MS. London B.M. Royal 7. C. iv (Defensor's *Liber scintillarum* with an Appendix *De vitiis et peccatis*)' (unpubl. PhD dissertation, University of Ghent).

Verey, C.D. (1969), 'A Collation of the Gospel Texts contained in Durham Cathedral MSS. A. II. 10, A. II. 16 and A. II. 17' (unpubl. MA dissertation, Durham Univ.).

– et al., eds. (1980), *The Durham Gospels: Together with Fragments of a Gospel Book in Uncial. Durham, Cathedral Library, MS A.II.17*, EEMF 20 (Copenhagen).

– (1989), 'The Gospel Texts at Lindisfarne at the Time of St Cuthbert', in Bonner et al. (1989a), 143–50.

– (1999), 'Lindisfarne or Rath Maelsigi? The Evidence of the Text', in Hawkes–Mills (1999), 327–35.

Vernet, A. (1948), 'Notice et Extraits d'un Manuscrit d'Édimbourg. Adv. MSS. 18. 6. 12, 18. 7. 8, 18. 7. 7', *Bibliothèque de l'École des Chartes* 107: 33–51.

Vernet, M.-T. (1960), 'Notes de Dom André Wilmart sur quelques manuscrits latins anciens de la Bibliothèque Nationale de Paris (fin)', *Bulletin d'information de l'Institut de recherche et d'histoire des textes* 8: 7–46.

Vezin, J. (1965), 'Les manuscrits datés de l'ancien fonds latin de la Bibliothèque Nationale de Paris', *Scriptorium* 19: 83–9.

– (1968), 'Manuscrits des dixième et onzième siècles copiés en Angleterre en minuscule caroline et conservés à la Bibliothèque Nationale de Paris', in Dennery (1968) II, 283–96.

– (1973), 'La répartition du travail dans les "scriptoria" carolingiens', *Journal des savants*: 212–27.

- (1977), 'Leofnoth. Un scribe anglais à Saint-Benoît-sur-Loire', *Codices Manuscripti* 3: 109–20.
- (1981), 'Les manuscrits copiés à Saint-Denis en France pendant l'époque carolingienne', *Paris et Ile-de-France: Mémoires publiés par la fédération des sociétés historiques et archéologiques de Paris et de l'Ile-de-France* 32: 273–87.
- (1982), 'Observations sur l'origine des manuscrits légués par Dungal à Bobbio', in Silagi (1982), 125–44.
- (1986), 'Les relations entre Saint-Denis et d'autres scriptoria', in P. Ganz (1986) I, 17–39.
Vezzoni, A. (1987), 'Un testimone testuale inedito della versione Palatina del Pastore di Erma', *Studi classici ed orientali* 37: 241–65.
- ed. (1994), *Il Pastore di Erma: Versione Palatina* (Florence).
Vickrey, J.F., ed. (1960), *Genesis B: A New Analysis and Edition* (Ann Arbor, MI).
Viré, G., ed. (1992), *Hyginus de Astronomia* (Stuttgart and Leipzig).
Vitz, E.B. (2006), 'Liturgical Versus Biblical Citation in Medieval Vernacular Literature', in L'Engle—Guest (2006), 443–50.
Vleeskruyer, R., ed. (1953), *The Life of St Chad: An Old English Homily* (Amsterdam).
Voelkle, W. (1974), *Mediaeval and Renaissance Manuscripts: Major Acquisitions of the Pierpont Morgan Library, 1924–1974* (New York).
Vogel, C. and R. Elze, eds. (1963–72), *Le Pontifical romano-germanique du dix-ième siècle*, 3 vols., Studi e testi 226–7, 269 (Vatican City).
- (1986), *Medieval Liturgy. An Introduction to the Sources*, trans. and rev. W. Storey and N. Rasmussen (Washington, DC).
Vogel, F., ed. (1885), *Magni Felicis Ennodi Opera*, MGH, AA 7 (Berlin).
Vogels, J. (1884), 'Scholia in Ciceronis Aratea aliaque ad astronomiam pertinentia e cod. Mus. Brit. Harl. 647, pars I', *Wissenschaftliche Beilage zum Programm des Gymnasiums zu Crefeld* (1884), 9–13.
Voigts, L.E. (1959), 'Anglo-Saxon Plant Remedies', *Isis* 70: 250–68.
- (1976), 'A New Look at a Manuscript Containing the Old English Translation of the *Herbarium Apulei*', *Manuscripta* 20: 40–60.
- (1977), 'One Anglo-Saxon View of the Classical Gods', *Studies in Iconography* 3: 3–16.
- (1978), 'British Library, Cotton Vitellius C. iii, f. 82', *OEN* 12.1: 12–13.
- (1979), 'British Library, Royal 12 D.XVII, f. 30v', *OEN* 13.1: 12–13.
- (1986), 'The Latin Verse and Middle English Prose Texts on the Sphere of Life and Death in Harley 3719', *Chaucer Review* 21: 291–305.
- (1988), 'A Fragment of an Anglo-Saxon Liturgical Manuscript at the University of Missouri', *ASE* 17: 83–92.
Vollrath, H. (1985), *Die Synoden Englands bis 1066* (Paderborn).

Volpilhac, P., ed. (1975), *Oeuvres de Némésien* (Paris).

Voronova, T. and A. Sterligov, eds. (1996), *Western Illuminated Manuscripts in the St Petersburg Public Library* (Bournemouth and St Petersburg).

Voss, M. (1988a), 'Old English Glossaries and Dialectology', in Fisiak (1988), 601–8.

– (1988b), 'Strykers Edition des alphabetischen Cleopatraglossars: Corrigenda und Addenda', *Arbeiten aus Anglistik und Amerikanistik* 13: 123–38.

– (1989), 'Quinns Edition der kleineren Cleopatraglossare: Corrigenda und Addenda', *Arbeiten aus Anglistik und Amerikanistik* 14: 127–39.

– (1996), 'Altenglische Glossen aus MS British Library, Cotton Otho E. i', *Arbeiten aus Anglistik und Amerikanistik* 21: 179–203.

– (2005), Review of D.W. Porter (2002) in *Speculum* 80: 300–2.

Wagner, M. (1945), *Rufinus the Translator* (Washington, DC).

Wagner, P. (1912), *Neumenkunde: Paläographie des gregorianischen Gesangs*, 2nd rev. ed. (Fribourg).

– (1925), 'Eine musikalische Reliquie des Kgl. Bibliothek in Stockholm', *Nordisk Tidskrift för Bok- och Biblioteksväsen* 12: 205–22.

Waite, G. (2000), *Old English Prose Translations of King Alfred's Reign*, Annotated Bibliographies of Old and Middle English Literature 6 (Cambridge).

Waitz, G., ed. (1844), 'Mariani Scoti Chronicon', MGH, SS 5 (1844), 481–564.

– (1876), 'Über die handschriftliche Überlieferung und die Sprache der Historia Langobardorum des Paulus', *Neues Archiv der Gesellschaft für ältere deutsche Geschichtskunde* 1: 535–66.

– ed. (1878), *Scriptores rerum Langobardicarum et Italicarum saec. VI–IX*, MGH, Scriptores rerum Langobardicarum et Italicarum (Berlin).

Wallace-Hadrill, J.M. (1950), 'The Franks and the English in the Ninth Century: Some Common Historical Interests', *History* 35: 202–18.

Wallach, L. (1955), 'Alcuin on Virtues and Vices: A Manual for a Carolingan Soldier', *Harvard Theological Review* 48: 175–95.

– (1975), 'The Urbana Anglo-Saxon Sylloge of Latin Inscriptions', in *Poetry and Poetics from Ancient Greece to the Renaissance: Studies in Honor of James Hutton*, ed. G.M. Kirkwood (Ithaca, NY, 1975), 134–51.

Wallis, F. (1999), *Bede: The Reckoning of Time*, Translated Texts for Historians 29 (Liverpool).

Wanley, H. (1705), *Librorum Veterum Septentrionalium, qui in Angliae Bibliothecis extant…Catalogus Historico-Criticus* (Oxford).

– (1759–63), *A Catalogue of the Harleian Collection of Manuscripts…Preserved in the British Museum*, 2 vols. (London).

Ward, A.W. and A.R. Waller, eds. (1907), *The Cambridge History of English Literature*, I: *From the Beginnings to the Cycles of Romance* (Cambridge).

Warner, G.F. and J.P. Gilson (1921), *Catalogue of Western Manuscripts in the Old Royal and King's Collections*, 4 vols. (London).

– and H.A. Wilson, eds. (1910), *The Benedictional of St. Æthelwold*, Roxburghe Club 156 (Oxford).

Warren, F.E. (1881), *The Liturgy and Ritual of the Celtic Church* (Oxford).

– ed. (1883), *The Leofric Missal* (Oxford).

– (1885), 'An Anglo-Saxon Missal at Worcester', *The Academy* (12 December 1885), 394–5.

– (1888), 'Hatton MS. 93', *The Academy* (13 Oct. 1888), 242.

– ed. (1895), *The Antiphonary of Bangor. An Early Irish Manuscript in the Ambrosian Library of Milan, Part II*, HBS 10 (London).

Wasserschleben, F.W.H. (1851), *Die Bussordnungen der abendländischen Kirche* (Halle).

– (1885), *Die irische Kanonensammlung*, 2nd ed. (Leipzig).

Watson, A.G. (1963), 'A Sixtenth-Century Collector: Thomas Dackomb, 1496–c.1572', *The Library* 5th ser. 18: 204–17 [repr. A.G. Watson (2004) no. III].

– (1965), 'Christopher and William Carye, Collectors of Monastic Manuscripts, and "John Carye"', *The Library* 5th ser. 20: 135–42.

– (1966), *The Library of Sir Simonds D'Ewes* (London).

– (1969), *The Manuscripts of Henry Savile of Banke* (London) [repr. A.G. Watson (2004) no. IX].

– (1972–6), 'A St Augustine's Abbey, Canterbury, Manuscript Reconstructed: Harley 625; Digby 178, fols. 1–14, 88–115; Cotton Tiberius B. ix, fols. 1–4, 225–35', *TCBS* 6: 211–17 [repr. A.G. Watson (2004) no. XIV].

– (1978), 'Thomas Allen of Oxford and his Manuscripts', in Parkes – Watson (1978), 279–314 [repr. A.G. Watson (2004) no. VII].

– (1979), *Catalogue of Dated and Datable Manuscripts c. 700–1600 in the Department of Manuscripts, The British Library* (London).

– (1981), 'An Early Thirteenth-Century Low Countries Booklist', *BLJ* 7: 39–46 [repr. A.G. Watson (2004) no. XI].

– (1984), *Catalogue of Dated and Datable Manuscripts c. 435–1600 in Oxford Libraries*, 2 vols. (Oxford).

– (1986), 'John Twyne of Canterbury (d. 1581) as a Collector of Medieval Manuscripts: A Preliminary Investigation', *The Library* 6th ser. 8: 133–51 [repr. A.G. Watson (2004) no. IV]

– (1987a), *Medieval Libraries of Great Britain: A List of Surviving Books; Supplement to the Second Edition* (London).

– (1987b), 'The Manuscript Collection of Sir Walter Cope (d. 1614)', *BLR* 12: 262–97 [repr. A.G. Watson (2004) no. VIII].

- (1997), *A Descriptive Catalogue of the Medieval Manuscripts of All Souls College* (Oxford).
- (2000), *A Descriptive Catalogue of the Medieval Manuscripts of Exeter College, Oxford* (Oxford).
- (2004), *Medieval Manuscripts in Post-Medieval England* (Aldershot).
Watson, G., ed. (1969–77), *The New Cambridge Bibliography of English Literature*, 5 vols. (Cambridge).
Webb, N.H. (1985), 'Early Medieval Welsh Book-Production' (unpubl. PhD dissertation, London Univ.).
Webber, T. (1989), 'Salisbury and Exon Domesday: Some Observations Concerning the Origin of Exeter Cathedral MS 3500', *English Manuscript Studies* 1: 1–18.
- (1992), *Scribes and Scholars at Salisbury Cathedral ca. 1075–1125* (Oxford).
- (1995), 'Script and Manuscript Production at Christ Church Canterbury after the Norman Conquest', in Eales—Sharpe (1995): 145–58.
- (1996), 'The Diffusion of Augustine's Confessions in England during the Eleventh and Twelfth Centuries', in *The Cloister and the World: Essays in Medieval History in Honour of Barbara Harvey*, ed. J. Blair and B. Golding (Oxford), 29–45.
- (1997), 'The Patristic Content of English Book Collections in the Eleventh Century: Towards a Continental Perspective', in Robinson—Zim (1997), 191–205.
- (1998), 'The Provision of Books for Bury St Edmunds Abbey in the Eleventh and Twelfth Centuries', in Gransden (1998a), 186–93.
- and A.G. Watson, eds. (1998), *The Libraries of the Augustinian Canons*, Corpus of British Medieval Library Catalogues 6 (London).
- (2006), 'The Books of Leicester Abbey', in *Leicester Abbey. Medieval History, Archaeology and Manuscript Studies*, ed. J. Story, J. Bourne and R. Buckley (Leicester, 2006), 127–46.
- (2012), 'The Norman Conquest and Handwriting in England to 1100', in R. Gameson (2012), 211–24.
Weber, R., ed. (1953), *Le Psautier romain et les autres anciens psautiers latins*, Collectanea Biblica Latina 10 (Rome).
- R. Gryson et al., eds. (1994), *Biblia sacra iuxta vulgatam versionem*, 4th ed. (Stuttgart).
Webster, L. and J. Backhouse, eds. (1991), *The Making of England: Anglo-Saxon Art and Culture AD 600–900* (London).
- and M.P. Brown, eds. (1997), *The Transformation of the Roman World* (London).
Wegmann, J. and D. Bankert (1993), 'Ambrose in the Sources of Anglo-Saxon Literary Culture', *OEN* 27.1: 30–4.

Weigel, G., ed. (1961), *Augustinus: De magistro liber unus*, CSEL 77 (Vienna).

Weinberger, W., ed. (1934), *Anicii Manlii Severini Boethii Philosophiae consolationis libri quinque*, CSEL 67 (Vienna).

Weitzmann, K. (1977), *Late Antique and Early Christian Book Illumination* (New York).

Welch, M. (1983), *Early Anglo-Saxon Sussex*, BAR British Series 112 (Oxford).

Wellek, R. (1941), *The Rise of English Literary History* (Chapel Hill, NC).

Wellhausen, A., ed. (2003), *Die lateinische Übersetzung der Historia Lausiaca des Palladius*, Patristische Texte und Studien 51 (Berlin).

Wells, D.M., ed. (1969), *A Critical Edition of the Old English Genesis A with a Translation* (Ann Arbor, MI).

Wenisch, F. (1979), *Spezifisch anglisches Wortgut in den nordhumbrischen Interlinearglossierungen des Lukasevangeliums*, Anglistische Forschungen 132 (Heidelberg).

– (1992), '*Nu bidde we eow for Godes lufon*: a Hitherto Unpublished Old English Homiletic Text in CCCC 162', in Korhammer (1992), 43–52.

– (1993), 'The Anonymous Old English Homily for the Dedication of a Church in MS Hatton 114: An Annotated Edition', in Grinda—Wetzel (1993), 1–19.

Werlich, E. (1964), *Der westgermanische Skop: Der Aufbau seiner Dichtung und sein Vortrag* (Dr Phil Diss. Münster).

Werner, M. (1969), 'The Four Evangelist Symbols Page in the Book of Durrow', *Gesta* 8: 3–17.

– (1972), 'The *Madonna and Child* Miniature in the Book of Kells', *The Art Bulletin* 54: 1–23, 129–39.

– (1990), 'The Cross-Carpet Page in the Book of Durrow: The Cult of the True Cross, Adomnan, and Iona', *The Art Bulletin* 72: 174–223.

– (1997a), 'The Book of Durrow and the Question of Programme', *ASE* 26: 23–39.

– (1997b), 'Three Works on the Book of Kells', *Peritia* 11: 250–326.

– (2011), 'The Binding of the Stonyhurst Gospel of St John and St John', in Hourihane (2011), 287–314.

Westcott, B.F. and F.J.A. Hort, eds. (1881), *The New Testament in the Original Greek*, 2 vols. (Cambridge).

Westgard, J.A. (2010), 'The Wilfridian Annals in Winchester, Cathedral Library, MS 1, and Durham, Cathedral Library, MS B. II. 35', in Brown—Voigts (2010), 209–23.

Westlake, J.S. (1907), 'From Alfred to the Conquest', in Ward—Waller (1907), 108–48.

Westra, H.J., ed. (1992), *From Athens to Chartres: Neoplatonism and Medieval Thought. Studies in Honour of Edouard Jeauneau* (Leiden).

Westwood, J.O. (1843–5), 'Anglo-Saxon Books of Moses, & c.', *Palaeographia Sacra Pictoria: Being a Series of Illustrations of the Ancient Versions of the Bible, copied from Illuminated Manuscripts, Executed between the Fourth and Sixteenth Centuries* (London).

– (1868), *Fac-similes of the Miniatures and Ornaments of Anglo-Saxon and Irish Manuscripts* (London).

Whatley, E.G. (1996), 'An Introduction to the Study of Old English Prose Hagiography: Sources and Resources', in Szarmach (1996), 3–34.

– (1997), 'Lost in Translation: Omission of Episodes in some Old English Prose', *ASE* 26: 187–208.

Wheeler, H. (1977), 'Aspects of Mercian Art: The Book of Cerne', in Dornier (1977), 235–44.

Whitbread, L. (1959), 'MS C.C.C.C. 201: A Note on its Character and Provenance', *PQ* 38: 106–12.

– (1968), 'After Bede: The Influence and Dissemination of his Doomsday Verses', *ASNSL* 204: 250–66.

– (1983), 'A Scribal Jotting from Medieval English', *N&Q* 228: 198–9.

White, A. (1981), 'Boethius in the Medieval Quadrivium', in Gibson (1981), 162–205.

White, C.L. (1898), *Ælfric: A New Study of his Life and Writings*, Yale Studies in English 2 (New Haven, CT; 2nd ed. with supplementary bibliography by M.R. Godden, Hamden, CT, 1974).

Whitelock, D. (1937), 'A Note on the Career of Wulfstan the Homilist', *EHR* 52: 460–6 [repr. in Whitelock (1981b) no. VIII].

– (1940), 'Scandinavian Personal Names in the *Liber Vitae* of Thorney Abbey', *Saga-Book of the Viking Society for Northern Research* 12: 127–53 [repr. Whitelock (1981b), no. XVII].

– (1942), 'Archbishop Wulfstan, Homilist and Statesman', *TRHS* 4th ser. 24: 42–60 [repr. Whitelock (1981b), no. XI].

– (1943), 'Two Notes on Ælfric and Wulfstan', *MLR* 38: 122–6 [repr. Whitelock (1981b), no. X].

– (1948), 'Wulfstan and the Laws of Cnut', *EHR* 63: 433–52 [repr. Whitelock (1981b), no. XII].

– ed. (1954), *The Peterborough Chronicle: The Bodleian Manuscript Laud Misc. 636*, EEMF 4 (Copenhagen).

– (1962), 'The Old English Bede', *PBA* 48: 57–90 [repr. Whitelock (1980) no. VIII, and also in Stanley (1990) 227–60].

– (1965), 'Wulfstan at York', in Bessinger—Creed (1965), 214–31 [repr. Whitelock (1981b), no. XV].

– (1969), 'Fact and Fiction in the Legend of St Edmund', *Proceedings of the Suffolk Institute of Archaeology* 31: 217–33.

- (1970), 'Wulfstan's Authorship of Cnut's Laws', *EHR* 85: 72–85 [repr. Whitelock (1981b), no. XIII].
- (1974), 'The List of Chapter-Headings in the Old English Bede', in Burlin— Irving (1974), 263–84.
- (1975), 'Some Anglo-Saxon Bishops of London', *The Chambers Memorial Lecture, delivered 4 May 1974* (London, 1975), 3–34 [repr. Whitelock (1981b), no. II].
- (1976), *Wulfstan: Sermo Lupi ad Anglos*, Exeter Medieval English Texts, 3rd ed., repr. with additional bibliography (Exeter).
- ed. and trans. (1979), *English Historical Documents, I: c. 500–1042*, 2nd ed. (London).
- (1980), *From Bede to Alfred* (London).
- M. Brett and C.N.L. Brooke, eds. (1981a), *Councils & Synods with other Documents relating to the English Church, 871–1204*, 2 vols. (Oxford).
- (1981b), *History, Law, and Literature in 10th–11th Century England* (London).
Wiedemann, K. (1994), *Die Handschriften der Gesamthochschulbibliothek und Murhardsche Bibliothek der Stadt Kassel, I. 1. Manuscripta theologica. Die Handschriften in Folio* (Wiesbaden).
Wieland, G.R. (1982), *The Canterbury Hymnal: Edited from British Library MS Additional 37517*, Toronto Medieval Latin Texts 12 (Toronto).
- (1983), *The Latin Glosses on Arator and Prudentius in Cambridge Universiity Library, MS Gg. 5. 35* (Toronto).
- (1985), 'The Glossed Manuscript: Classbook or Library Book?', *ASE* 14: 153–73.
- (1987), 'The Anglo-Saxon Manuscripts of Prudentius's *Psychomachia*', *ASE* 16: 213–31.
- (1997a), 'The Origin and Development of the Anglo-Saxon *Psychomachia* Illustrations', *ASE* 26: 169–86.
- (1997b), 'The Prudentius Manuscript CCCC 223', *Manuscripta* 38: 211–27.
- (1998), 'Gloss and Illustration: Two Means to the Same End?', in Pulsiano— Treharne (1998a), 1–20.
- (2001), 'The Relationship of Latin to Old English Glosses in the *Psychomachia* of Cotton Cleopatra C. viii', in Bergmann (2001), 175–88.
- (2006a), 'British Library MS Royal 15. A. v: One Manuscript or Three?', in Doane—Wolf (2006), 3–25.
- et al., eds. (2006), *Insignis Sophiae Arcator: Essays in Honour of Michael W. Herren on his 65th Birthday* (Turnhout).
- (2009), 'A Survey of Latin Manuscripts', in Owen-Crocker (2009), 113–57.
Wiesenekker, E. (1994), 'The Vespasian and Junius Psalters Compared: Glossing or Translation?', *Amsterdamer Beiträge zur älteren Germanistik* 40: 21–39.

Wilcox, J. (1988), 'The Compilation of Old English Homilies in MSS. Cambridge, Corpus Christi College, 419–421' (unpubl. PhD dissertation, Cambridge Univ.).

– (2000), 'Wulfstan and the Twelfth Century', in Swan–Treharne (2000a), 83–97.

– (2002), 'The Transmission of Ælfric's *Letter to Sigefryth* and the Mutilation of London, British Library, Cotton Vespasian D. XIV', in Treharne–Rosser (2002), 285–300.

– (2004a), *Old English Scholarship and Bibliography. Essays in Honor of Carl T. Berkhout*, OEN Subsidia 32 (Kalamazoo).

– (2004b), 'Wulfstan's *Sermo Lupi ad Anglos* as Political Performance: 16 February 1014 and Beyond', in Townend (2004), 375–96.

– (2006a), 'The Audience of Ælfric's *Lives of Saints* and the Face of Cotton Caligula A. xiv, fols. 93–130', in Doane–Wolf (2006), 229–63.

– (2006b), 'Rewriting Ælfric: An Alternative Ending of a Rogationtide Homily', *LSE* 37: 229–39.

– (2008), 'New Old English Texts: The Expanding Corpus of Old English', in Blanton–Scheck (2008), 423–36.

– (2009), 'The Use of Ælfric's Homilies: MSS Oxford, Bodleian Library, Junius 85 and 86 in the Field', in Magennis–Swan (2009), 345–68.

Wildhagen, K., ed. (1910), *Der Cambridger Psalter. Zum ersten Male herausgegeben mit besonderer Berücksichtigung des lateinischen Textes*, Bibliothek der angelsächsischen Prosa 7 (Hamburg).

– (1913), 'Studien zum Psalterium Romanum in England und zu seinen Glossierungen (in geschichtlicher Entwicklung)', in Holthausen–Spies (1913), 419–72.

– (1920), 'Das Psalterium Gallicanum in England und seine altenglischen Glossierungen', *EStn* 54: 35–45.

– (1921), 'Das Kalendarium der Handschrift Vitellius E. xviii', in Böhmer (1921), 68–118.

Wilkes, J. (1905), *Lautlehre zu Ælfrics Heptateuch und Buch Hiob* (Dr. phil. dissertation, Universität Bonn).

Willard, R. (1925), 'The Vercelli Homilies: An Edition of Homilies I, IV, V, VII, VIII, XI and XII' (unpubl. PhD dissertation, Yale Univ.)

– (1935a), 'The Address of the Soul to the Body', *PMLA* 50: 957–83.

– ed. (1935b), *Two Apocrypha in Old English Homilies*, Beiträge zur Englischen Philologie 30 (Leipzig).

– (1936), 'On Blickling Homily XIII: The Assumption of the Virgin', *RES* 12: 1–17.

– (1949a), 'Vercelli Homily XI and its Sources', *Speculum* 24: 76–87.

- (1949b), 'The Blickling-Junius Tithing Homily and Caesarius of Arles', in Kirby—Woolf (1949), 65–78.
- (1950), 'The Punctuation and Capitalization of Ælfric's Homily for the First Sunday in Lent', *Texas Studies in English* 29: 1–32.
- ed. (1960), *The Blickling Homilies: The John H. Scheide Library, Titusville, Pennsylvania*, EEMF 10 (Copenhagen).
Willetts, P.J. (1966), 'A Reconstructed Astronomical Manuscript from Christ Church Library Canterbury', *British Museum Quarterly* 30: 22–30.
- (2000), *Catalogue of Manuscripts in the Society of Antiquaries of London* (Woodbridge).
Williams, A. and G.H. Martin, eds. (2000), *Little Domesday Book*, 6 vols. (London) [facsimile].
Williams, I. (1926–7), 'The Computus Fragment', *BBCS* 3: 245–72.
Williams, I.F. (1905), *A Grammatical Investigation of the Old Kentish Glosses* (Bonn).
Williams, R.D. (1947), 'The Worcester Fragments of Statius' *Thebaid*', *Classical Review* 61: 88–90.
- (1948), 'Two Manuscripts of Statius' *Thebaid*', *Classical Quarterly* 42: 105–12.
- and T.S. Pattie (1982), *Virgil. His Poetry through the Ages* (London).
Williams, S. (1971), *Codices Pseudo-Isidoriani: A Palaeographico-Historical Study*, Monumenta Iuris Canonici: Series C: Subsidia 3 (New York).
Williamson, C., ed. (1977), *The Old English Riddles of the Exeter Book* (Chapel Hill, NC).
Williman, D. (1996–9), 'Some Additional Provenances of Cambridge Latin Manuscripts', *TCBS* 11: 427–48.
Wilmart, A. (1922), 'Le recueil latin des apophtegmes', *RB* 34: 185–98.
- (1922–9a), 'Les livres de l'abbé Odbert', *Bulletin historique de la Société des antiquaires de la Morinie* 14: 169–88.
- (1922–9b), 'Un ancien manuscrit de Saint-Bertin en lettres onciales', *Bulletin historique de la Société des antiquaires de la Morinie* 14: 353–60.
- (1930), 'The Prayers of the Bury Psalter', *Downside Review* 48: 198–216.
- (1932), *Auteurs spirituels et textes dévots du moyen âge latin: études d'histoire littéraire* (Paris).
- (1934), 'Un témoin anglo-saxon du calendrier métrique d'York', *RB* 46: 41–69.
- (1936a), 'Le Manuel de prières de Saint Jean Gualbert', *RB* 48: 258–97.
- (1936b), 'Un traité sur la Messe copié en Angleterre vers l'an 800', *Ephemerides liturgicae* 50: 133–9.
- (1937–45), *Codices Bibliothecae Apostolicae Vaticanae manuscripti recensiti iussu Pii XI Pontificis Maximi: Codices Reginenses Latini*, 2 vols. (Rome).

– and L. Brou, eds. (1949), *The Psalter Collects*, HBS 83 (London).

Wilson, D.M. (1984), *Anglo-Saxon Art from the Seventh Century to the Norman Conquest* (London).

– (2001), 'Lindisfarne Gospels', *Reallexikon der germanischen Altertumskunde*, 2nd ed. XVIII, 466–8.

Wilson, H.A., ed. (1896), *The Missal of Robert of Jumièges*, HBS 11 (London).

– ed. (1903), *The Benedictional of Archbishop Robert*, HBS 24 (London).

– ed. (1910), *The Pontifical of Magdalen College, with an Appendix of Extracts from other English MSS of the Twelfth Century*, HBS 39 (London).

– ed. (1918), *The Calendar of St Willibrord. From MS. Paris. lat. 10837. A Facsimile with Transcription, Introduction and Notes*, HBS 55 (London).

Wilson, N. (1972–3), *Medieval Greek Bookhands. Examples Selected from Greek Manuscripts in Oxford Libraries*, 2 vols., Mediaeval Academy of America Publications 81 (Cambridge, MA).

Wilson, R.M. (1968), *Early Middle English Literature* , 3rd rev. ed. (London).

Winter, U. (1986), 'Die Fragmentensammlung der Deutschen Staatsbibliothek. Katalog der Fragmente des 4.–10. Jahrhunderts', *Studien zum Buch- und Bibliothekswesen* 4: 7–24.

Winterbottom, M. (1968), 'On the *Hisperica Famina*', *Celtica* 8: 126–39.

– ed. (1972), *Three Lives of English Saints* (Toronto).

– (2000), 'The Earliest Life of St Dunstan', *Scripta Classica Israelica* 19: 163–79.

– and M. Lapidge, eds. (2012), *The Early Lives of St Dunstan* (Oxford).

Winterfeld, P. von, ed. (1899), MGH, PLAC 4/i (Berlin).

Withers, B.C. (1994), 'Present Patterns, Past Tense: Text and Illustration in London, British Library, Cotton MS. Claudius B. iv' (unpubl. PhD dissertation, University of Chicago).

– (1997), 'Interaction of Word and Image in Anglo-Saxon Art, II: Scrolls and Codex in the Frontispiece to the *Regularis Concordia*', *OEN* 31.1: 36–40.

– (1999), 'Unfulfilled Promise: The Rubrics of the Old English Prose Genesis', *ASE* 28: 111–39.

– (2001), 'Interaction of Word and Image in Anglo-Saxon Art, IV: Literal Illustration and Spiritual Vision in the Bury Psalter', *OEN* 33.1: 35–8.

– (2007), *The Illustrated Old English Hexateuch, Cotton MS. Claudius B. iv* (London) [with CD-ROM].

Wittig, J.S. (1983), 'King Alfred's *Boethius* and its Latin Sources: A Reconsideration', *ASE* 11: 157–98.

– (2007), 'The Remigian Glosses on Boethius's *Consolatio Philosophiae* in Context', in Wright et al. (2007), 168–200.

– (2010), 'The Old English Boethius, the Latin Commentaries, and Bede', in Brown — Voigts (2010), 225–52.

– (2011), 'Satan's Mandorla: Translation, Transformation, and Interpretation in Late Anglo-Saxon England', in Hourihane (2011), 247–70.

Wohlfahrt, T. (1885), *Die Syntax des Verbums in Ælfrics Übersetzung des Heptateuch und des Buches Hiob* (Dr. phil. diss., Universität Leipzig).

Wölfflin, E., ed. (1895), *Benedicti Regula Monachorum* (Leipzig).

Wood, I. (1995), 'The Most Holy Abbot Ceolfrid', Jarrow Lecture 1995 (Jarrow).

Wood, M. (2010), 'A Carolingian Scholar in the Court of King Æthelstan', in Rollason et al. (2010), 135–62.

Woodruff, H. (1930), *The Illustrated Manuscripts of Prudentius* (Cambridge, MA).

Wooldridge, H.E. (1897), *Early English Harmony from the 10th to the 15th Century*, I (London).

Woolf, R., ed. (1993), *Cynewulf's Juliana*, rev. ed. (Exeter).

Woolley, R.M., ed. (1917), *The Canterbury Benedictional*, HBS 51 (London).

– (1927), *Catalogue of the Manuscripts of Lincoln Cathedral Chapter Library* (London).

Wordsworth, C. (1885), *The Pontifical Offices of David de Bernham* (Edinburgh).

– (1924), 'The Library and the Use of Sarum', in J.M.J. Fletcher, *Notes on the Cathedral Church of St Mary the Blessed Virgin of Salisbury*, with preface by the Bishop of Salisbury [G.H. Bourne] (Salisbury, 1924), 106–37.

Wordsworth, J. et al., eds. (1889–1954), *Novum Testamentum Latine*, 4 vols. (Oxford).

– and H.J. White, eds. (1911), *Novum Testamentum Latine. Editio Minor* (Oxford).

Wormald, F., ed. (1934), *English Kalendars before A.D. 1100*, HBS 72 (London).

– (1935), 'Two Anglo-Saxon Miniatures Compared', *The British Museum Quarterly* 9: 113–15.

– (1944), 'The Survival of Anglo-Saxon Illumination after the Norman Conquest', *PBA* 30: 127–45 [repr. F. Wormald (1984), 153–68].

– (1945), 'Decorated Initials in English Manuscripts from A.D. 900 to 1100', *Archaeologia* 91: 107–35 [repr. F. Wormald (1984), 47–75].

– (1946), 'The English Saints in the Litany in Arundel MS 60', *AB* 64: 72–86.

– (1952), *English Drawings of the Tenth and Eleventh Centuries* (London).

– (1954), *The Miniatures in the Gospels of St Augustine* (Cambridge).

– (1957a), 'The Insular Script in the Late Tenth-Century English-Latin Manuscripts', in Ferrabino (1957), 160–5.

– (1957b), 'The Bayeux Tapestry: Style and Design', in *The Bayeux Tapestry*, ed. F. Stenton (London, 1957), 25–36 [repr. F. Wormald (1984), 138–52].

– (1959), *The Benedictional of St Ethelwold* (London).

– (1962), 'An Eleventh-Century Psalter with Pictures, British Museum, Cotton MS Tiberius C. vi', *The Walpole Society* 38: 1–13 [repr. F. Wormald (1984), 123–37].

- (1969), 'A Fragment of a Tenth-Century English Gospel Lectionary', in *Calligraphy and Palaeography. Essays presented to Alfred Fairbank*, ed. A.S. Osley (London), 43–6 [repr. F. Wormald (1984), 101–4].
- (1971a), 'The Liturgical Calendar of Glastonbury Abbey', in Autenrieth (1971), 325–45.
- (1971b), 'The "Winchester School" before St Æthelwold', in Clemoes—Hughes (1971), 305–15 [repr. F. Wormald (1984), 76–84].
- (1976), 'Fragments of a Tenth-Century Sacramentary from the Binding of the Winton Domesday' in Biddle (1976a), 541–9.
- and J.J.G. Alexander (1977), *An Early Breton Gospel Book. A Ninth Century Manuscript from the Collection of H. L. Bradfer-Lawrence (1887–1965)*, Roxburghe Club (Cambridge).
- and P.M. Giles (1982), *A Descriptive Catalogue of the Additional Illuminated Manuscripts in the Fitzwilliam Museum acquired between 1895 and 1979*, 2 vols. (Cambridge).
- (1984), *Collected Writings*, I: *Studies in Medieval Art from the Sixth to the Twelfth Centuries*, ed. J.J.G. Alexander, T.J. Brown and J. Gibbs (London).
- (1984a) 'The Utrecht Psalter', in F. Wormald (1984), 36–46 [orig. publ. for the Members of the Utrecht Institute of Art History (Utrecht, 1953)].
- (1984b), 'Anglo-Saxon Painting', in F. Wormald (1984), 111–22 [orig. publ. in French: 'L'Angleterre', in Grodecki et al., *Le siècle de l'an mil* (Paris, 1973), 227–54].
- (1984c), 'The Miniatures in the Gospels of St. Augustine, Corpus Christi College, Cambridge, MS 286', in F. Wormald (1984), 13–35 [expanded version of F. Wormald (1954)].
Wormald, P. (1976), 'Bede and Benedict Biscop', in Bonner (1976), 141–69.
- (1978), 'Æthelred the Lawmaker', in D. Hill (1978), 47–80.
- (1988a), 'A Handlist of Anglo-Saxon Lawsuits', *ASE* 17: 247–81.
- (1988b), 'Æthelwold and his Continental Counterparts: Contact, Comparison, Contrast', in Yorke (1988), 13–42.
- (1996), 'BL Cotton MS. Otho B. xi: A Supplementary Note', in Hill—Rumble (1996), 59–68.
- (1999), *The Making of English Law: King Alfred to the Twelfth Century* (Oxford).
- (2000), 'Archbishop Wulfstan and the Holiness of Society', in Pelteret (2000), 191–224.
- (2004), 'Archbishop Wulfstan: Eleventh-Century State-Builder', in Townend (2004), 9–28.
- (2012), 'Law Books', in R. Gameson (2012), 525–36.
Woudhuysen, P., et al. (1982), *Treasures of the Fitzwilliam Museum* (Cambridge).

Wright, C.D. (1990), 'Hiberno-Latin and Irish-Influenced Biblical Commentaries, Florilegia, and Homily Collections', in Biggs (1990), 87–123.

– (1993), *The Irish Tradition in Old English Literature*, CSASE 6 (Cambridge).

– (2002), 'The Old English "Macarius" Soul-and-Body Homily, Vercelli Homily IV, and Ephraem the Syrian's *De paenitentia*', in *Via Crucis: Studies in Medieval Sources and Ideas in Memory of J.E. Cross*, ed. T.D. Hill, T.N. Hall and C.D. Wright (Morgantown, WV, 2002), 210–34.

– (2006), 'The *Prouerbia Grecorum*, the Norman Anonymous, and the Early Medieval Ideology of Kingship: Some New Manuscript Evidence', in Wieland et al. (2006), 193–215.

– (2007), 'Old English Homilies and Latin Sources', in Kleist (2007a), 15–66.

– F.M. Biggs and T.N. Hall, eds. (2007), *Source of Wisdom: Old English and Early Medieval Latin Studies in Honour of Thomas D. Hill* (Toronto).

– (2008), 'Why the Left Hand is Longer (or Shorter) than the Right: Some Irish Analogues for an Etiological Legend in the Homiliary of St. Père de Chartres', in Blanton—Scheck (2008), 161–8.

– (2009), 'Vercelli Homily XV and *The Apocalypse of Thomas*', in Zacher—Orchard (2009), 150–84.

Wright, C.E. (1936), 'A Postscript to "Late Old English Rune-Names"', *MÆ* 5: 149–51.

– (1937), 'Robert Talbot and Domitian A. ix', *MÆ* 6: 170–1.

– (1938), 'Two Ælfric Fragments', *MÆ* 7: 50–5.

– (1949–53), 'The Dispersal of the Monastic Libraries and the Beginnings of Anglo-Saxon Studies', *TCBS* 1: 208–37.

– and R. Quirk, eds. (1955), *Bald's Leechbook: British Museum Royal MS 12 D. XVII*, EEMF 5 (Copenhagen).

– (1972), *Fontes Harleiani: A Study of the Sources of the Harleian Collection of Manuscripts Preserved in the Department of Manuscripts in the British Museum* (London).

Wright, C.J., ed. (1997), *Sir Robert Cotton as Collector: Essays on an Early Stuart Courtier and his Legacy* (London).

Wright, D.F. (1972), 'The Manuscripts of St Augustine's *Tractatus in Evangelium Iohannis*: A Preliminary Survey and Check-List', *Recherches augustiniennes* 8: 55–143.

Wright, D.H. (1961a), 'Some Notes on English Uncial', *Traditio* 17: 441–56.

– (1961b), 'The Date of the Leningrad Bede', *RB* 71: 265–73.

– (1964), Review of P. Hunter Blair, *The Moore Bede* [EEMF 9], in *Anglia* 82: 110–17.

– ed. (1967), *The Vespasian Psalter: British Museum, Cotton Vespasian A.I*, EEMF 14 (Copenhagen) [with a contribution by A. Campbell].

Wright, T. and R.P. Wülker, eds. (1884), *Anglo-Saxon and Old English Vocabularies*, 2nd ed., 2 vols. (London).

Wülker, R.P. (1879), 'Aus englischen Bibliotheken', *Anglia* 2: 354–94.

– ed. (1881-98), *Bibliothek der angelsächsischen Poesie*, 3 vols. (Kassel).

– (1882), 'Über das Vercellibuch', *Anglia* 5: 451–65.

– (1885), *Grundriss zur Geschichte der angelsächsischen Litteratur. Mit einer Übersicht der angelsächsischen Sprachwissenschaft* (Leipzig).

– (1894), *Codex Vercellensis. Die angelsächsische Handschrift zu Vercelli in getreuer Nachbildung* (Leipzig) [facsimile].

Wuttke, H. (1853), *Die Kosmographie des Istriers Aithicos im lateinischen Auszuge des Hieronymus* (Leipzig).

Wynn, J.B. (1962), 'An Edition of the Anglo-Saxon Corpus Glosses' (unpubl. PhD dissertation, Oxford Univ.).

Yerkes, D. (1975), 'Two Early Manuscripts of Gregory's Dialogues', *Manuscripta* 19: 171–3.

– (1976a), 'The Place of Composition of the Opening of Napier Homily I', *Neophilologus* 60: 452–4.

– (1976b), 'A New Collation of MS. Hatton 76, part A', *Anglia* 94: 163–5.

– (1977a), 'A New Collation of the Cambridge Manuscript of the Old English Translation of Gregory's Dialogues', *Mediaevalia* 3: 165–72.

– (1977b), 'The Text of the Canterbury Fragment of Werferth's Translation of Gregory's Dialogues and its Relation to the other Manuscripts', *ASE* 6: 121–42.

– (1977c), 'An Elementary Way to Illuminate Details of Textual History', *Manuscripta* 21: 38–41.

– (1977d), 'An Unnoticed Omission in the Modern Critical Editions of Gregory's "Dialogues"', *RB* 87: 178–9.

– (1977-80), 'The Medieval Provenance of CCCC 322', *TCBS* 7: 245–7.

– (1978), 'A Neglected Transcript of the Cotton Manuscript of Wærferth's Old English Translation of Gregory's *Dialogues*', *NM* 79: 21–2.

– (1979), *Two Versions of Werferth's Translation of Gregory's Dialogues: An Old English Thesaurus*, Toronto OE Series 4 (Toronto).

– (1982a), *Syntax and Style in Old English: A Comparison of the Two Versions of Werferth's Translation of Gregory's Dialogues*, MRTS 5 (Binghampton, NY).

– (1982b), 'British Library, Cotton Otho A. viii, fols. 1–6', *OEN* 16.1: 28–9.

– (1983a), 'Earliest Fragments of Goscelin's Writings on St Mildred', *RB* 93: 128–31.

– (1983b), 'British Library, Cotton Otho A. viii, fols. 7–34', *OEN* 17.1: 30–1.

– ed. (1984a), *The Old English Life of Machutus*, Toronto OE Series 9 (Toronto).

- (1984b), 'British Library, Cotton Otho C. i., vol. II, fol. 115r', *OEN* 18.1: 32–3.
- (1986a), 'The Translation of Gregory's Dialogues and its Revision: Textual History, Provenance, Authorship', in Szarmach (1986b), 335–43.
- (1986b), 'The Provenance of the Unique Copy of the Old English Translation of Bili, *Vita Sancti Machuti*', *Manuscripta* 30: 108–11.
- (1987), 'The Foliation of the Old English Life of Machutus', in Selig—Somerville (1987), 89–93.

Yorke, B., ed. (1988), *Bishop Æthelwold: His Career and Influence* (Woodbridge).

Young, J. and H. Aitken (1908), *A Catalogue of the Manuscripts in the Library of the Hunterian Museum in the University of Glasgow* (Glasgow).

Young, K. (1933), *The Drama of the Medieval Church*, 2 vols. (Oxford).

Youngs, S.G. (1995), 'A New Edition of "Instructions for Christians": C.U.L. MS Ii.1.33' (unpubl. PhD dissertation, University of Wisconsin at Madison, WI).

Zacher, S. (2007), 'Re-Reading the Style and Rhetoric of the Vercelli Homilies', in Kleist (2007a), 173–207.

- (2009), *Preaching the Converted: The Style and Rhetoric of the Vercelli Book Homilies* (Toronto).
- and A. Orchard, eds. (2009), *New Readings in the Vercelli Book* (Toronto).

Zangemeister, K. (1876), 'Bericht über die im Auftrage der Kirchenväter-Commission unternommene Durchforschung der Bibliotheken Englands', *Sitzungsberichte der kaiserlichen Akademie der Wissenschaften in Wien, phil.-hist. Klasse* 84: 485–584.

Zarnecki, G. et al., eds. (1984), *English Romanesque Art 1066–1200*, Arts Council Exhibition Catalogue (London).

Zechiel-Eckes, K. (2002), 'Vom *armarium* in York in den Düsseldorfer Tresor. Zur Rekonstruktion einer Liudger-Handschrift aus dem mittleren 8. Jahrhundert', *DAEM* 58: 193–203.

- (2003), *Katalog der frühmittelalterlichen Fragmente der Universitäts- und Landesbibliothek Düsseldorf. Vom beginnenden achten bis zum ausgehenden neunten Jahrhundert* (Wiesbaden).

Zettel, P.H. (1979), 'Ælfric's Hagiographic Sources and the Latin Legendary preserved in B.L. MS. Cotton Nero E. i + CCCC MS. 9 and Other Manuscripts' (unpubl. PhD dissertation, Oxford Univ.).

- (1982), 'Saints' Lives in Old English: Latin Manuscripts and Vernacular Accounts: Ælfric', *Peritia* 1: 17–37.

Zettersten, A., ed. (1979), *Waldere* (Manchester).

Zimmermann, E.H. (1916), *Vorkarolingische Miniaturen*, 1 vol. of text and 4 vols. of plates [*Tafeln*] (Berlin).

Zimmermann, H., ed. (1984–5), *Papsturkunden 896–1046*, 2 vols., Österreichische Akademie der Wissenschaften, phil.-hist. Klasse, Denkschriften 174, 177 (Vienna).

Ziolkowski, J.M., ed. (1994), *The Cambridge Songs (Carmina Cantabrigiensia)* (New York; repr. as MRTS 192 (Tempe, AZ, 1998)).

– (2000), 'Nota Bene: Why the Classics Were Neumed in the Middle Ages', *JMLat* 10: 74–114.

– (2007), *Nota Bene. Reading Classics and Writing Melodies in the Early Middle Ages*, Publications of the Journal of Medieval Latin 7 (Turnhout).

Zironi, A. (2011), 'Marginal Alphabets in the Carolingian Age: Philological and Codicological Considerations', in Lendinara et al. (2011), 353–70.

Zupitza, J. (1876), 'Englisches aus Prudentiushandschriften', *ZfdA* 20: 36–45.

– (1877), 'Kentische Glossen des neunten Jahrhunderts', *ZfdA* 21: 1–59.

– (1878), 'Lateinisch-englische Sprüche', *Anglia* 1: 285–6.

– ed. (1880/2001), *Ælfrics Grammatik und Glossar: Text und Varianten*, 3rd ed., with a new introduction by H. Gneuss (Hildesheim).

– ed. (1882/1959), *Beowulf. Reproduced in Facsimile from the Unique Manuscript*, 2nd ed. containing a new reproduction of the manuscript, with an introductory note by N. Davis, EETS o.s. 245 (London, 1959).

– (1886), 'Drei alte Excerpta aus Ælfreds Beda', *ZfdA* 30: 185–6.

– (1889), 'Altenglische Glossen', *ZfdA* 33: 237–42.

Index of authors and texts

All references are to the serial numbers of the preceding *Bibliographical Handlist*.

The following symbols and abbreviations have been used:

*   text in Old English prose
**   text in Old English alliterative verse
(*)   text partly in Old English
+*   text in Latin and Old English prose, or Latin—Old English glossary
°   Latin text with continuous Old English gloss, or with substantial sections or a fairly large number of words, glossed in Old English
e   excerpts or parts of a text
f   incomplete text or fragment
(?)   authorship doubtful

Where appropriate, references to *BCLL, BHL, CPG, CPL, CPPM*, SK, SK Suppl. and WIC have been added in order to facilitate identification.

Hugo of Langres, Commentary on the Psalms: 306.5
human body, encyclopedic note on number of bones, veins and teeth: 56, 90, 385, 451, 882
Husband's Message**: 257
Hwætberht: *see* Eusebius
Hyginus, *Astronomica*: 1.5, 186, 373e, 423e, 428.4, 483e
Hyginus Gromaticus, *De limitibus*: 185
hymnals: 104, 244°, 291, 306, 381°e, 391, 431, 696f, 914f, 920; *see also Expositio hymnorum, Indicium regulae*
hymns (Office hymns not included in hymnals): 7, 12, 28, 51, 56, 59, 155.5e, 196, 306.5e, 333, 354 (?), 392, 406.5, 409, 450, 474.5, 482, 514, 569, 808.0, 814, 829, 844, 865.1, 865.2
Hymnus trium puerorum (Latin verse): 927

Ilias latina [SK 8372]: 535, 664°
Immaculate Conception, note on: *see under* Virgin Mary, Immaculate Conception, Latin Homily on
Indicium regulae [on use of hymns]: 29
Institutio canonicorum: *see under* capitularies and related texts
Instruction for Prayer⁺*: 404
Inuolutio sphaerae (extract from Aratus, *Phainomena*, in Latin): 186
Iohannes Diaconus
   Carmen de Gregorio Magno [SK 5725] (?): 321
   Vita S. Gregorii [BHL 3641]: 411.6, 465, 570, 674
   Vita S. Nicholai [BHL 6104–5]: 267, 434.5
Iohannes Scottus Eriugena, *Carmina*: 70e
Iosephus (in Latin)
   Antiquitates Iudaicae: 225.5
   De bello Iudaico, trans. Hegesippus: 225.5, 487.5, 507, 834
Irish charms: 421
Irish glosses: 7, 81, 148
Isembard of Fleury
   Inuentio S. Iudoci [BHL 4506–8]: 474.5
   Miracula S. Iudoci [BHL 4510]: 474.5
   Vita II S. Iudoci [BHL 4505]: 474.5
Isidore of Seville
   Allegoriae quaedam S. Scripturae [CPL 1190]: 263, 573, 578, 713, 742, 780, 818.5f, 851.6
   De differentiis rerum siue *Differentiae theologicae uel spiritales* [CPL 1202]: 460e, 787, 845e
   De differentiis uerborum [CPL 1187]: 188.8e, 932f

Martin of Braga, *Formula honestae uitae* [*CPL* 1080]: 112
Martyrologium: *see* Usuard of Saint-Germain-des-Prés
Martyrology, OE*: 39f, 62, 282f, 298f, 338f
'Marvels of the East' (*Mirabilia orientis*): 373⁺*; 399*
Mass texts (not in missals or sacramentaries)
    Mass chants: 106, 433.2, 526, 585
    Mass collects: 333
    Mass lectionaries: 120.6f, 224f, 418.6f, 870f, 872.5f; *see also* gospel lectionaries; gospel lists and pericope notes; gospel and epistle lists
    Masses and Mass prayers: 104, 111, 223, 291, 306, 363.2, 435, 557f, 585, 629, 673.3f, 774.3, 919.3
    Masses: Of the Dead: 879e; Of the Holy Trinity: 291; Of the Virgin: 389e
    Masses for saints (not in missals): Alban: 865.1; Birinus: 609; Cuthbert: 56, 155; Dunstan: 94; Edmund: 514; Germanus: 583; Iudoc: 474.5; Mildred: 439.3; Nicholas: 344
    see also missals; sacramentaries; graduals; tropers; *and also* expositions of the Mass
mathematics: *see* arithmetic; geometry
*Maxims I***: 257
*Maxims II***: 370.2
maxims, proverbs, sentences and apophthegms: 93, 182*, 244⁺*, 331⁺*, 451⁺*, 844*, 898, 903, 919.3
measures: *see* weights and measures
Medicina de quadrupedibus: 402*, 421*, 549, 633*
medicine
    medical texts: 12, 145, 222.3, 498.1, 498.8.1, 498.9
    medical handbook (Bald's Leechbook)*: 479
    medical recipes (Latin): 12, 70, 98, 490, 498.1, 674, 807; *see also* veterinary recipes
    medical recipes (OE)*: 39, 326, 333, 380, 402, 412, 421 [*Lacnunga*], 435, 523f, 848f
    Liber Aurelii de acutis passionibus: 145
    Liber Esculapii de chronicis passionibus: 145
    'Petrocellus' (*Practica Petrocelli*): 12e, 498.9
    poems on Greek medical terminology [SK 3618, 11969, 13822]: 12, 765
    tract on the temperaments: 919.3
    treatise on cauterization: 498.9
    treatises on urines: 498.1, 498.8.1f
    see also Galen; pseudo-Hippocrates; Serenus Sammonicus; Soranus; *and* charms; human body; and the collections of medical texts in nos. 402, 421, 527, 549, 633, 831.4

Note: All or most of the texts of Apostles' Creed (*Credo in Deum patrem
omnipotentem*), Athanasian Creed (*Quicumque vult*), *Gloria*, *Pater noster*, and
Te Deum occur at the end of the collection of the canticles for the Office in the
following psalter MSS: 4, 77, 104, 106, 291, 304, 306, 334, 407, 425, 430, 451, 499,
517, 617, 655, 740, 754, 891, 912, 920, 939.
  These texts are not individually listed in the 'Contents' sections of the
manuscripts.

Toronto Anglo-Saxon Series

Lightning Source UK Ltd.
Milton Keynes UK
UKHW012208080719
345806UK00006B/230/P